shakespearean criticism

"Thou art a Monument without a tomb,
And art alive still while thy Book doth
live
And we have wits to read and praise to
give."

*Ben Jonson, from the preface
to the First Folio, 1623.*

Mr. WILLIAM

SHAKESPEARES

COMEDIES, HISTORIES, & TRAGEDIES.

Publiſhed according to the True Originall Copies.

LONDON

Printed by Iſaac Iaggard, and Ed. Blount. 1623.

Frontispiece to the First Folio (1623). By permission of the Folger Shakespeare Library.

ISSN 0883-9123

Volume 63

Shakespearean Criticism

Excerpts from the Criticism of
William Shakespeare's Plays and Poetry,
from the First Published Appraisals
to Current Evaluations

Michelle Lee
Editor

GALE GROUP
THOMSON LEARNING
Detroit • New York • San Diego • San Francisco
Boston • New Haven, Conn. • Waterville, Maine
London • Munich

Janet Witalec, Lynn M. Zott, *Managing Editors, Literature Product*
Kathy D. Darrow, Ellen McGeagh, *Product Liaisons*
Michelle Lee, *Editor*
Mark W. Scott, *Publisher, Literature Product*

Jessica Menzo, Madeline S. Harris, *Associate Editors*
Jenny Cromie, *Technical Training Specialist*
Deborah J. Morad, Joyce Nakamura, Kathleen Lopez Nolan, *Managing Editors, Literature Content*
Susan M. Trosky, *Director, Literature Content*

Maria L. Franklin, *Permissions Manager*
Kim Davis, Debra Freitas, *Permissions Associates*

Victoria B. Cariappa, *Research Manager*
Sarah Genik, *Project Coordinator*
Tamara C. Nott, Ron Morelli, Tracie A. Richardson, *Research Associates*
Michelle Campbell, *Administrative Specialist*

Dorothy Maki, *Manufacturing Manager*
Stacy L. Melson, *Buyer*

Mary Beth Trimper, *Composition and Prepress Manager*
Carolyn Roney, *Composition Specialist*

Randy Bassett, *Imaging Supervisor*
Robert Duncan, Dan Newell, Luke Rademacher, *Imaging Specialists*
Pamela A. Reed, *Imaging Coordinator*
Kelly A. Quin, *Editor, Imaging and Multimedia Content*
Michael Logusz, *Graphic Artist*

Library of Congress Catalog Card Number 86-645085
ISBN 0-7876-5238-5
ISSN 0883-9123
Printed in the United States of America

10 9 8 7 6 5 4 3 2 1

Contents

Preface vii

Acknowledgments ix

List of Plays and Poems Covered in *SC* xi

Literary Criticism Series Advisory Board xv

All's Well That Ends Well 1
Introduction 1
Overviews and General Studies 1
Character Studies 21
Gender Issues 41
Marriage 84
Further Reading 111

Henry VI, Parts 1, 2, and 3 113
Introduction 113
Overviews and General Studies 114
Character Studies 124
Henry VI as Comedy 144
Playing with History 158
Unity and Design 185
Further Reading 217

Julius Caesar 219
Introduction 219
Overviews and General Studies 219
Dramaturgy and Metadrama 225
Philosophy and Theology 252
Rhetoric and Meaning 278
The Roman Hero: Interpreting Character 295
Further Reading 333

The Two Gentlemen of Verona 335
Introduction 335
Overviews and General Studies 336
Love and Courtesy 341
Patriarchy 357
Staging and Production 361
Further Reading 376

Cumulative Character Index 377

Cumulative Topic Index 389

Cumulative Topic Index, by Play 411

Preface

Shakespearean Criticism (*SC*) provides students, educators, theatergoers, and other interested readers with valuable insight into Shakespeare's drama and poetry. A multiplicity of viewpoints documenting the critical reaction of scholars and commentators from the seventeenth century to the present day derives from hundreds of periodicals and books excerpted for the series. Students and teachers at all levels of study will benefit from *SC,* whether they seek information for class discussions and written assignments, new perspectives on traditional issues, or the most noteworthy of analyses of Shakespeare's artistry.

Scope of the Series

Volumes 1 through 10 of the series present a unique historical overview of the critical response to each Shakespearean work, representing a broad range of interpretations.

Volumes 11 through 26 recount the performance history of Shakespeare's plays on the stage and screen through eyewitness reviews and retrospective evaluations of individual productions, comparisons of major interpretations, and discussions of staging issues.

Volumes 27 through 56 in the series focus on criticism published after 1960, with a view to providing the reader with the most significant modern critical approaches. Each volume is ordered around a theme that is central to the study of Shakespeare, such as politics, religion, or sexuality. The topic entry that introduces each volume is comprised of general essays that discuss this theme with reference to all of Shakespeare's works. Following the topic entry are several entries devoted to individual works.
Beginning with volume 57 in the series, *SC* provides a works-based approach; each of the four entries contained in a regular volume focuses on a specific Shakespearean play or poem. The entries will include the most recent criticism available on the works, as well as earlier criticism not previously included in *SC*. Select volumes contain topic entries comprised of essays that analyze various topics, or themes, found in Shakespeare's works. Past topic entries have covered such subjects as Honor, Jealousy, War and Warfare, and Elizabethan Politics.

Until volume 48, published in October 1999, *SC* compiled an annual volume of the most noteworthy essays published on Shakespeare during the previous year. The essays, reprinted in their entirety, were recommended to Gale by an international panel of distinguished scholars.

Organization of the Book

An *SC* entry consists of the following elements:

- The **Introduction** contains background information that introduces the reader to the work or topic that is the subject of the entry and outlines modern interpretations of individual Shakespearean topic, plays, and poems.
- Reprinted **Criticism** for each entry consists of essays arranged chronologically under a variety of subheadings to facilitate the study of different aspects of the play, poem, or topic. This provides an overview of the major areas of concern in the analysis of Shakespeare's works, as well as a useful perspective on changes in critical evaluation over recent decades. The critic's name and the date of composition or publication of the critical work are given at the beginning of each piece of criticism. Unsigned criticism is preceded by the title of the source in which it appeared. Footnotes are reprinted at the end of each essay or excerpt. In the case of excerpted criticism, only those footnotes that pertain to the excerpted texts are included.
- A complete **Bibliographical Citation** of the original essay or book precedes each piece of criticism.

- Critical essays are prefaced by **Explanatory Notes** as an aid to students using *SC*. The explanatory notes summarize the criticism that follows.

- Each volume includes such **Illustrations** as reproductions of images from the Shakespearean period, paintings and sketches of eighteenth- and nineteenth-century performers, photographs of modern productions, and stills from film adaptations.

- An annotated bibliography of **Further Reading** appears at the end of each entry and suggests resources for additional study. In some cases, significant essays for which the editors could not obtain reprint rights are included here.

Indexes

A **Cumulative Character Index** identifies the principal characters of discussion in the criticism of each play and non-dramatic poem.

A **Cumulative Topic Index** identifies the principal topics in the criticism and stage history of each work. The topics are arranged alphabetically, by topic.

A **Cumulative Topic Index, by Play identifies the principal topics in the criticism and stage history of each work. The topics are arranged alphabetically, by play.**

Citing *Shakespearean Criticism*

When writing papers, students who quote directly from any volume in the Literary Criticism Series may use the following general format to footnote reprinted criticism. The first example pertains to material drawn from periodicals, the second to material reprinted from books.

> Tetsuya Motohashi. "Body Politic and Political Body in *Coriolanus,*" in *Forum for Modern Language Studies* XXX, no. 2 (April 1994): 97-112; reprinted in *Shakespearean Criticism,* vol. 50, ed. Kathy D. Darrow (Farmington Hills, Mich.: The Gale Group, 2000), 119-128.
>
> Mary Hamer. "Authority and Violence," in *William Shakespeare: Julius Caesar* (Northcote House, 1998), 12-20; reprinted in *Shakespearean Criticism,* vol. 50, ed. Kathy D. Darrow (Farmington Hills, Mich.: The Gale Group, 2000), 230-34.

Suggestions are Welcome

Readers who wish to suggest new features, topics, or authors to appear in future volumes, or who have other suggestions or comments are cordially invited to call, write, or fax the Managing Editor:

Managing Editor, Literary Criticism Series
The Gale Group
27500 Drake Road
Farmington Hills, MI 48331-3535
1-800-347-4253 (GALE)
Fax: 248-699-8054

Acknowledgments

The editors wish to thank the copyright holders of the excerpted criticism included in this volume and the permissions managers of many book and magazine publishing companies for assisting us in securing reproduction rights. We are also grateful to the staffs of the Detroit Public Library, the Library of Congress, the University of Detroit Mercy Library, Wayne State University Purdy/Kresge Library Complex, and the University of Michigan Libraries for making their resources available to us. Following is a list of the copyright holders who have granted us permission to reproduce material in this volume of *SC*. Every effort has been made to trace copyright, but if omissions have been made, please let us know.

COPYRIGHTED EXCERPTS IN *SC*, VOLUME 63, WERE REPRODUCED FROM THE FOLLOWING PERIODICALS:

English Literary Renaissance, v. 5, Spring, 1975; v. 18, Winter, 1988; v. 24, Spring, 1994; v. 26, Spring, 1996; v. 28, Winter, 1998. Copyright © 1975, 1988, 1994, 1996, 1998 by *English Literary Renaissance.* All reproduced by permission.—***English Studies,*** v. 80, April, 1999. Copyright © 1999, Swets & Zeitlinger. Reproduced by permission.—***Huntington Library Quarterly,*** v. 26, February, 1963. Reproduced with the permission from the Henry E. Huntington Library.—***Literature and Psychology,*** v. 1, 1974; v. 32, 1986. Copyright © Editor 1974, 1986. Both reproduced by permission of *Literature and Psychology: a Psychoanalytic and Cultural Criticism.*—***Midwest Quarterly,*** v. 21, Summer, 1980. Copyright © 1980 by *The Midwest Quarterly,* Pittsburgh State University. Reproduced by permission.—***Modern Language Quarterly,*** v. 32, March, 1971. Reproduced by permission.—***Pacific Coast Philology,*** v. 9, April, 1974. Reproduced by permission.—***Philological Quarterly,*** v. 66, Winter, 1987 for "The Making of Virgins and Mothers: Sexual Signs, Substitute Scenes, and Doubled Presences in *All's Well That Ends Well,*" by Barbara Hodgdon. Copyright © 1987 by The University of Iowa. Reproduced by permission of the author.—***Renaissance Papers,*** 1978. Reproduced by permission.—***Renaissance Quarterly,*** v. 42, Spring, 1989. Reproduced by permission.—***Shakespeare-Jahrbuch,*** v. 120, 1984. Reproduced by permission.—***Shakespeare Quarterly,*** v. 24, Autumn, 1973; v. 25, Summer, 1974; v. 49, Summer, 1998. Copyright © The Folger Shakespeare Library, 1973, 1974, 1998. All reproduced by permission.—***Shakespeare Studies,*** v. 15, 1982; v. 18, 1986. Copyright © 1982, 1986 by Associated University Presses, Inc. All rights reserved. Both reproduced by permission.—***Shakespeare Survey,*** v. 40, 1988 for "The Speculative Eye: Problematic Self-Knowledge in *Julius Caesar*" by William O. Scott. Reproduced by permission of Cambridge University Press and the author.—***Shakespeare Yearbook,*** v. 1, Spring, 1990. Reproduced by permission.—***Studies in English Literature, 1500-1900,*** v. 28, Spring, 1988. Copyright © The Johns Hopkins University Press. Reproduced by permission.—***Studies in the Literary Imagination,*** v. 5, April, 1972. Reproduced by permission.—***Thalia,*** v. 1, Autumn, 1978. Copyright © 1978 by Jacqueline Tavernier-Courbin. Reproduced by permission.—***Theatre Journal,*** v. 42, May, 1990. Copyright © 1990, University and College Theatre Association of the American Theatre Association. Reproduced by permission of The Johns Hopkins University Press.

COPYRIGHTED EXCERPTS IN *SC*, VOLUME 63, WERE REPRODUCED FROM THE FOLLOWING BOOKS:

Bathory, Dennis. From "'With Himself at War': Shakespeare's Roman Hero and the Republican Tradition," in ***Shakespeare's Political Pageant: Essays in Literature and Politics.*** Edited by Joseph Alulis and Vickie Sullivan. Rowman & Littlefield, 1996. Copyright © 1996 by Rowman & Littlefield. All rights reserved. Reproduced by permission.—Blits, Jan H. From "Politics and the Ethics of Intention: Brutus' Glorious Failure," in ***The End of the Ancient Republic: Essays on 'Julius Caesar.'*** Carolina Academic Press, 1982. Copyright © 1982 by Carolina Academic Press. All rights reserved. Reproduced by permission.—Bradbrook, Muriel C. From "Love and Courtesy in *The Two Gentlemen of Verona,*" in ***Shakespeare in His Context: the Constellated Globe, The Collected Papers of Muriel Bradbrook, Volume IV.*** Harvester Wheatsheaf, 1989. Copyright © 1989 by Harvester Wheatsheaf. All rights reserved. Reproduced by permission.—Bulman, James C. From "Ironic Heroism in *Julius Caesar*: A Repudiation of the Past," in ***Modern Critical Interpretations: William Shakespeare's Julius Caesar.*** Edited by Harold Bloom. Chelsea House Publishers, 1988. Copyright © 1988 by Chelsea House Publishers. All rights reserved. Reproduced by permission.—Burckhardt, Sigurd. From "'I Am But Shadow of Myself': Ceremony and Design in *1 Henry VI,*" in ***Shakespearean Meanings.*** Princeton University Press, 1968. Copyright © 1968 by Princeton University Press. All rights reserved. Reproduced by permission.—Carlisle, Carol L. and Patty S. Derrick. From "*The Two Gentlemen of Verona* on Stage: Protean Problems and Protean Solutions," in ***Shakespeare's Sweet Thunder: Essays on the Early Comedies.*** Edited by Michael J. Collins. University of Delaware Press, 1997. Copyright © 1997 by University of Delaware Press. All rights reserved. Reproduced by permission.—Cartelli, Thomas. From "Jack Cade in the Garden: Class Consciousness and Class Conflict in *2 Henry VI,*" in ***Enclosure Acts: Sexuality, Property, and***

Culture in Early Modern England. Edited by Richard Burt and John Michael Archer. Cornell University Press, 1994. Copyright © 1994 by Cornell University Press. All rights reserved. Reproduced by permission.—Felheim, Marvin and Philip Traci. From "*The Two Gentlemen of Verona,*" in ***Realism in Shakespeare's Romantic Comedies: "O Heavenly Mingle."*** University Press of America, 1980. Copyright © 1980 by University Press of America. All rights reserved. Reproduced by permission.—Hall, Jonathan. From "Patriarchy Rescued in *The Two Gentlemen of Verona,*" in ***Anxious Pleasures: Shakespearean Comedy and the Nation-State.*** Fairleigh Dickinson University Press, 1995. Copyright © 1995 by Fairleigh Dickinson University Press. All rights reserved. Reproduced by permission.—Howe, James. From "The Cause of Suffering and the Birth of Compassion in *Julius Caesar,*" in ***A Buddhist's Shakespeare: Affirming Self-Deconstructions.*** Associated University Presses, 1994. Copyright © 1994 by Associated University Presses. All rights reserved. Reproduced by permission.—Mack, Maynard. From "The Modernity of *Julius Caesar,*" in ***Everybody's Shakespeare: Reflections Chiefly on the Tragedies.*** University of Nebraska Press, 1993. Copyright © 1993 by University of Nebraska Press. All rights reserved. Reproduced by permission.—Maquerlot, Jean-Pierre. From "*Julius Caesar* and 'Dramatic Coquetry'," in ***Shakespeare and the Mannerist Tradition: A Reading of Five Problem Plays.*** Cambridge University Press, 1995. Copyright © 1995 by Cambridge University Press. All rights reserved. Reproduced by permission of the publisher and the author.—McCandless, David. From "*All's Well That Ends Well,*" in ***Gender and Performance in Shakespeare's Problem Comedies.*** Indiana University Press, 1997. Copyright © 1997 by Indiana University Press. All rights reserved. Reproduced by permission.—Nevo, Ruth. From "Motive and Meaning in *All's Well That Ends Well,*" in ***"Fanned and Winnowed Opinions": Shakespearean Essays Presented to Harold Jenkins.*** Edited by John W. Mahon and Thomas A. Pendleton. Methuen, 1987. Copyright © 1987 by Methuen. All rights reserved. Reproduced by permission of the author.—Pearlman, E. From "The First, Second and Third Parts of *King Henry the Sixth,*" in ***William Shakespeare: The History Plays.*** Twayne Publishers, 1992. Copyright © 1992 by Twayne Publishers. All rights reserved. Reproduced by permission of The Gale Group.—Walch, Günter. From "The Historical Subject as Roman Actor and Agent of History: Interrogative Dramatic Structure in *Julius Caesar,*" in ***Shakespearean Illuminations: Essays in Honor of Marvin Rosenberg.*** Edited by Jay L. Halio and Hugh Richmond. Associated University Presses, 1998. Copyright © 1998 by Associated University Presses. All rights reserved. Reproduced by permission.

PHOTOGRAPHS APPEARING IN *SC*, VOLUME 63, WERE RECEIVED FROM THE FOLLOWING SOURCES:

Christie, Robert as Caesar, and members of the Festival Company in Act I, scene ii of William Shakespeare's *Julius Caesar,* photograph. The Stratford Festival. Reproduced by permission.—Engraving of a scene from William Shakespeare's *2 Henry VI,* above engraving are statues, left to right, of Cardinal Beaufort, Queen Margaret, Henry VI, Humphrey, and Richard, photograph. Special Collections Library, University of Michigan. Reproduced by permission.—Engraving of a scene from William Shakespeare's *3 Henry VI,* photograph. Special Collections Library, University of Michigan. Reproduced by permission.—Engraving of Act II, scene v, The Tower of London, from William Shakespeare's *1 Henry VI,* photograph. Special Collections Library, University of Michigan. Reproduced by permission.—Heldt, Sharon, Emma Richler, Lucy Peacock, Hazel Desbarats, Sally Cahill, and Kim Scarcella in Act III, scene viii of William Shakespeare's *All's Well That Ends Well,* photograph by Michael Cooper. The Stratford Festival. Reproduced by permission.—Holm, Sarah-Jane and Alison Reid, in a scene from a 1993 Royal Shakespeare Company production of *The Two Gentlemen of Verona,* photograph. Copyright © Robbie Jack/Corbis. Reproduced by permission.—Holman, Clare, and Barry Lynch in a scene from a 1992 Royal Shakespeare Company production of *The Two Gentlemen of Verona,* photograph by Robbie Jack. Copyright © Robbie Jack/Corbis. Reproduced by permission.—Hutt, William as Brutus, and members of the Festival Company in Act III, scene ii of William Shakespeare's *Julius Caesar,* photograph. The Stratford Festival. Reproduced by permission.—Macready, William as Cassius and Edward Loomis Davenport as Brutus, in Act IV, scene iii of William Shakespeare's *Julius Caesar,* engraving by Hollis from an original painting by Reid, the latter from a daguerreotype by John Mayall, published by John Tallis and Company, London, between 1860-1880. The Library of Congress.—Marston, Henry as Marc Antony in Act II, scene ii of William Shakespeare's *Julius Caesar,* engraving by John Tallis & Company from a daguerreotype by Paine of Islington, London, 1870-1890. The Library of Congress.—Moore, Richard and Irish wolfhound Wolly in a 1991 Royal Shakespeare Company production of *The Two Gentlemen of Verona,* photograph. Copyright © Robbie Jack/Corbis. Reproduced by permission.—Mrs. Ternan as Countess Rousillon and Mr. Lewis Ball as a Clown in William Shakespeare's *All's Well That Ends Well,* engraving. Copyright © Historical Picture Archive/Corbis. Reproduced by permission.—Pettle, Jordan, Graham Abbey, David W. Smith, Steve Ross, Rory Feore, David Kirby, and Mark Harapiak in Act IV, scene i of William Shakespeare's *The Two Gentleman of Verona,* photograph by Cylla von Tiedmann. The Stratford Festival. Reproduced by permission.—Reid, Fiona, Joseph Shaw, John Novak, Cheryl Swarts, Seana McKenna, and Lee J. Campbell in Act II, scene iii of William Shakespeare's *All's Well That Ends Well,* photograph by Robert C. Ragsdale. The Stratford Festival. Reproduced by permission.—Roux, Jean-Louis as Burgundy, Martha Henry as Joan la Pucelle, and members of the Festival Company as French soldiers in Act III, scene iii of William Shakespeare's *Henry VI,* photograph by Peter Smith. The Stratford Festival. Reproduced by permission.—Wright, Susan, Allan Gray, Richard Curnock, Antoni Cimoino, Kim Scarcella, Michel La Fleche, Robert Smith, Keith Thomas, Emma Richler, Tony Martin, and David Brown in Act I, scene i of William Shakespeare's *All's Well That Ends Well,* photograph by Michael Cooper. The Stratford Festival. Reproduced by permission.

List of Plays and Poems Covered in *SC*

Vol. 1
The Comedy of Errors
Hamlet
Henry IV, Parts 1 and 2
Timon of Athens
Twelfth Night

Vol. 2
Henry VIII
King Lear
Love's Labour's Lost
Measure for Measure
Pericles

Vol. 3
Henry VI, Parts 1, 2, and 3
Macbeth
A Midsummer Night's Dream
Troilus and Cressida

Vol. 4
Cymbeline
The Merchant of Venice
Othello
Titus Andronicus

Vol. 5
As You Like It
Henry V
The Merry Wives of Windsor
Romeo and Juliet

Vol. 6
Antony and Cleopatra
Richard II
The Two Gentlemen of Verona

Vol. 7
All's Well That Ends Well
Julius Caesar
The Winter's Tale

Vol. 8
Much Ado about Nothing
Richard III
The Tempest

Vol. 9
Coriolanus
King John
The Taming of the Shrew
The Two Noble Kinsmen

Vol. 10
The Phoenix and Turtle
The Rape of Lucrece
Sonnets
Venus and Adonis

Vol. 11
King Lear
Othello
Romeo and Juliet

Vol. 12
The Merchant of Venice
A Midsummer Night's Dream
The Taming of the Shrew
The Two Gentlemen of Verona

Vol. 13
1989 Yearbook

Vol. 14
Henry IV, Parts 1 and 2
Henry V
Richard III

Vol. 15
Cymbeline
Pericles
The Tempest
The Winter's Tale

Vol. 16
1990 Yearbook

Vol. 17
Antony and Cleopatra
Coriolanus
Julius Caesar
Titus Andronicus

Vol. 18
The Merry Wives of Windsor
Much Ado about Nothing
Troilus and Cressida

Vol. 19
1991 Yearbook

Vol. 20
Macbeth
Timon of Athens

Vol. 21
Hamlet

Vol. 22
1992 Yearbook

Vol. 23
As You Like It
Love's Labour's Lost
Measure for Measure

Vol. 24
Henry VI, Parts 1, 2, and 3
Henry VIII
King John
Richard II

Vol. 25
1993 Yearbook

Vol. 26
All's Well That Ends Well
The Comedy of Errors
Twelfth Night

Vol. 27
Shakespeare and Classical Civilization
Antony and Cleopatra
Timon of Athens
Titus Andronicus
Troilus and Cressida

Vol. 28
1994 Yearbook

Vol. 29
Magic and the Supernatural
Macbeth
A Midsummer Night's Dream
The Tempest

Vol. 30
Politics
Coriolanus
Henry V
Julius Caesar

Vol. 31
Shakespeare's Representation of Women
Much Ado about Nothing
King Lear
The Taming of the Shrew

Vol. 32
1995 Yearbook

Vol. 33
Sexuality in Shakespeare
Measure for Measure
The Rape of Lucrece
Romeo and Juliet
Venus and Adonis

Vol. 34
Appearance versus Reality
The Comedy of Errors
Twelfth Night
As You Like It

Vol. 35
Madness
Hamlet
Othello

Vol. 36
Fathers and Daughters
Cymbeline
Pericles
The Winter's Tale

Vol. 37
1996 Yearbook

Vol. 38
Desire
All's Well That Ends Well
Love's Labour's Lost
The Merry Wives of Windsor
The Phoenix and Turtle

Vol. 39
Kingship
Henry IV Parts 1 and 2
Henry VI Parts 1, 2, and 3
Richard II
Richard III

Vol. 40
Gender Identity
The Merchant of Venice
Sonnets
The Two Gentlemen of Verona

Vol. 41
Authorship Controversy
Henry VIII
King John
The Two Noble Kinsmen

Vol. 42
1997 Yearbook

Vol. 43
Violence
The Rape of Lucrece
Titus Andronicus
Troilus and Cressida

Vol. 44
Psychoanalytic Criticism
Hamlet
Macbeth

Vol. 45
Dreams
A Midsummer Night's Dream
The Tempest
The Winter's Tale

Vol. 46
Clowns and Fools
As You Like It
King Lear
Twelfth Night

Vol. 47
Deception
Antony and Cleopatra
Cymbeline
The Merry Wives of Windsor

Vol. 48
1998 Yearbook

Vol. 49
Law and Justice
Henry IV, 1 and 2
Henry V
Measure for Measure

Vol. 50
Social Class
Coriolanus
Julius Caesar
The Two Noble Kinsmen

Vol. 51
Love and Romance
Pericles
The Phoenix and Turtle
Romeo and Juliet
Sonnets
Venus and Adonis

Vol. 52
Morality
Richard II
Richard III
Timon of Athens

Vol. 53
Race
Othello
The Merchant of Venice

Vol. 54
Beginnings and Endings
The Comedy of Errors
Love's Labour's Lost
The Two Gentlemen of Verona

Vol. 55
Feminist Criticism
All's Well That Ends Well
Much Ado about Nothing
The Taming of the Shrew

Vol. 56
Historical Revision
Henry VI, Parts 1, 2 and 3
Henry VIII
King John

Vol. 57
As You Like It
Henry IV, Parts 1 and 2
Macbeth
The Winter's Tale

Vol. 58
Antony and Cleopatra
A Midsummer Night's Dream
Richard II
The Two Noble Kinsmen

Vol. 59
Hamlet
The Merry Wives of Windsor
The Rape of Lucrece
Troilus and Cressida

Vol. 60
Topics Volume
Death
Homosexuality
Myth
Succession

Vol. 61
Cymbeline
Henry VIII
King Lear
The Tempest

Vol. 62
Richard III
Sonnets
Titus Andronicus
Twelfth Night

Future Volumes

Vol. 63
All's Well That Ends Well
Henry VI, Parts 1, 2, and 3
Julius Caesar
The Two Gentlemen of Verona

Vol. 64
Coriolanus
Love's Labour's Lost
The Phoenix and Turtle
The Taming of the Shrew

Vol. 65
Romeo and Juliet
Measure for Measure
Time

Literary Criticism Series Advisory Board

The members of the Gale Group Literary Criticism Series Advisory Board—reference librarians and subject specialists from public, academic, and school library systems—represent a cross-section of our customer base and offer a variety of informed perspectives on both the presentation and content of our literature criticism products. Advisory board members assess and define such quality issues as the relevance, currency, and usefulness of the author coverage, critical content, and literary topics included in our series; evaluate the layout, presentation, and general quality of our printed volumes; provide feedback on the criteria used for selecting authors and topics covered in our series; provide suggestions for potential enhancements to our series; identify any gaps in our coverage of authors or literary topics, recommending authors or topics for inclusion; analyze the appropriateness of our content and presentation for various user audiences, such as high school students, undergraduates, graduate students, librarians, and educators; and offer feedback on any proposed changes/ enhancements to our series. We wish to thank the following advisors for their advice throughout the year.

All's Well That Ends Well

For further information on the critical and stage history of *All's Well That Ends Well,* see *SC,* Volumes 7, 26, 38, and 55.

INTRODUCTION

Scholars believe that Shakespeare wrote *All's Well That Ends Well* between 1602 and 1605, though some commentators propose an even earlier composition date. The play is based on a story from Giovanni Boccaccio's *Decameron* (1353), which deals with a common folktale motif—the achievement of an impossible task. Critics have long considered *All's Well* to be a "problem play" because of its questionable plot elements, unlikable characters, and unsatisfactory ending. In the late twentieth century, however, scholars began to view the play as a bridge between Shakespeare's earlier festive comedies and his later tragedies; many adherents of this view now praise *All's Well* as a compelling dramatic experiment on Shakespeare's part. While earlier critics focused on such themes as social rank, virtue, and intergenerational strife, commentators from the nineteenth century onward have emphasized Helena's dynamic role in the dramatic action, the relationship between the sexes, and the interplay between romance and realism in the comedy.

Twentieth-century critics have demonstrated a continuing interest in Shakespeare's sophisticated characterization in *All's Well.* For example, Anthony Brennan (1980) discusses Helena in relation to the concept of time implicit in the play, noting that she alone of all the younger characters has a strong connection with the older generation. According to Brennan, this bond enables her to challenge the constraints of time and to accomplish her aim of winning Bertram as her husband. Susan Snyder (1988) focuses on the overt aggressiveness of Helena's quest to win Bertram. Snyder points out how this aggressiveness reveals an undercurrent of sexuality in the play, particularly through indirect and suppressed speech. The critic contends that ultimately the play illustrates the difficulties of being an assertive woman in a patriarchal setting. Some of the minor characters in *All's Well* also have attracted critical attention. Christopher Roark (1988), for example, probes the characterization of Lavatch as an indicator of the play's unresolved themes. According to Roark, Lavatch represents a "wise fool" who fails to serve his master because he is incapable of providing counsel, just as the play itself ultimately holds out no answers to the moral questions it poses.

Closely associated with critical analyses of the problematic relationship between Helena and Bertram are discussions of gender issues. Carolyn Asp (1986) maintains that Helena challenges the notion of "woman-as-subject-of-desire" and surmounts "attitudes and theories of female deprivation and inferiority." Asp then focuses on the reversal of power—inspired by Helena's desire—that allows Helena to succeed in her plans to win Bertram. Critic Barbara Hodgdon (1987) examines the gender theme on a structural level, revealing how Shakespeare's use of the various instances of doubling and substitution—most notably in the bed-trick scene—help to bring about the marital compromises that conclude the action of the play. David McCandless (1997) also emphasizes the bed-trick as a motif that Shakespeare used to exploit assumptions about gender. In addition, McCandless traces the evolution of gender roles, particularly those of Helena and Bertram, throughout the course of the play.

Connected to the gender issues in *All's Well* is the theme of betrothal and marriage. Many twentieth-century scholars have turned to Shakespeare's historical milieu in an effort to understand the playwright's complex treatment of matrimony in the play. Margaret Loftus Ranald (1963) studies historical documents, such as Elizabethan matrimonial contracts, in order to demonstrate how Shakespeare both criticized the matrimonial practices of his time and made use of them to explain the actions of Helena and Bertram to his audience. Like Ranald, Peggy Muñoz Simonds (1989) examines both the classical precedents as well as Renaissance matrimonial texts to illuminate how Shakespeare's audience might have reacted to the characters of Bertram and Helena. In a similar context, Susan Bassnett-McGuire (1984) discusses marriage in terms of the social issues of Shakespeare's day, examining the nature of the marriage contract itself and, more broadly, the role of the individual in relation to the state. Taking a different approach, W. Speed Hill (1975) explores the marriage of Helena and Bertram in the context of their familial situations, pointing out that their union "symbolizes on both parts an acceptance of their own faulty parental experiences." According to Hill, it is only when Bertram comes to terms with his past that he is finally freed to assume his proper role within the comic plot of *All's Well.*

OVERVIEWS AND GENERAL STUDIES

Alexander Leggatt (essay date 1971)

SOURCE: "*All's Well That Ends Well*: The Testing of Romance," in *Modern Language Quarterly,* Vol. 32, No. 1, March, 1971, pp. 21-41.

[*In the following essay, Leggatt explores the tension between elements of romance and elements of realism in* All's Well That Ends Well, *noting that this tension is never resolved and therefore lends an experimental quality to the play.*]

It has been commonly observed that romance and realism are in conflict in *All's Well That Ends Well.*[1] But, to a surprising extent, critics have been content to state the fact and then drop it, while they pursue issues relating to the play's ideas, its characterization, its source material, or what have you. Perhaps this is because we are so much in the habit of searching Shakespeare's plays for abstract ideas or for characterization which is psychologically explicable. The idea that the play's form may in itself be the controlling factor, the key to understanding, has not received the attention it merits. But these other lines of investigation inevitably become involved with the peculiar tensions of the play, and much debate has ensued. The play has been denounced and defended to the point where, if one sets oneself the task of reading a range of criticism on it, one rises with a feeling of having spent the day in a police court.

Much of the debate centers on the characters. Is Bertram a cad or a promising young fellow who simply needs to grow up? Is Helena a ministering angel or a vulture? Debates like this do not spring out of nothing, and the play provides enough evidence both ways to keep the controversy burning merrily for some time to come. My concern here is not to bring in a verdict of guilty or not guilty on Shakespeare and his characters, but to discover how the trouble started in the first place. I propose to do this by examining the characters, not as "real people" or as vehicles for certain ideas, but as creations springing from, and inextricably wedded to, the peculiar dramatic mode of the play. Or perhaps I should say *modes.* For Shakespeare is doing something rather unusual here: he is bringing two kinds of dramatic convention together, not in harmony (as in some of the earlier comedies), but in a positive and deliberate conflict. There is nothing here of the easy confidence with which Shakespeare moves from Rosalind's cool, satiric examination of love and marriage to the final masque of Hymen, and makes both acceptable. Here, the values of romance are tested in a world of down-to-earth and often unpleasant realism. The various tests which take place during the play reflect its essential nature: it is a play about testing, and a play which in itself is a test. Nor is the test in any way rigged; the tension between the two dramatic modes is genuine and intense, and the outcome is by no means certain.

In *As You Like It,* realism could work well enough with romance, since the former was represented by the easygoing animality of Touchstone and the only half-serious cynicism of Jaques. But in *All's Well,* as in *Troilus and Cressida,* the realities of life are harsher and much more hostile to romance. The King suffers, not from a genteel complaint like consumption, but from a fistula.[2] Parolles, condemning his brother officers, does not restrict himself to the usual charges of cowardice, but says of Dumaine: "in his sleep he does little harm, save to his bedclothes about him; but they know his conditions and lay him in straw" (IV.iii.246-49).[3] The dangers of pox are recalled by Bertram's velvet patch, which might hide an honorable scar or a syphilitic chancre (IV.v.90-97). The clown Lavatch is not just a joker, but a "foul-mouth'd and calumnious knave" (I.iii.54-55), almost a Thersites. It is in a world like this—a world of fistulas, venereal disease, and bedwetting—that Helena tries to win a husband by the romantic device of passing a test.

Of course, not everyone in the play talks like Parolles and Lavatch. The older aristocrats are aware of living in a fallen world, and they are rather weary of it; yet they are also aware that there are higher potentials in life than those that are being achieved at present. Being old, they look to the past for their ideals. There is, for example, the memory of Helena's father, whose skill very nearly lifted him above mortality. Shakespeare places his depiction of man's possible capabilities in a realistic context, and therefore keeps it this side of magic—but only just:

> Countess: This young gentlewoman had a father—O that "had," how sad a passage 'tis!—whose skill was almost as great as his honesty; had it stretch'd so far, would have made nature immortal, and death should have play for lack of work. . . .
> Lafew: He was excellent indeed, madam . . . he was skilful enough to have liv'd still, if knowledge could be set up against mortality.
>
> (I.i.16-29)

The King says of Bertram's father,

> Such a man
> Might be a copy to these younger times;
> Which, followed well, would demonstrate them now
> But goers backward.
>
> (I.ii.45-48)

The play opens with four of the leading characters in mourning for the Count, and his shadow lies over the first few scenes, which are full of reminiscence, giving a sense of past greatness and present decay. The decay is reflected symbolically in the King's sickness, which robs the court of the powerful central personality it needs, and makes virtue the property only of those who have survived from former days.[4] The King casts a critical eye over the young courtiers who surround him; compared with Bertram's father, they seem frivolous and lacking in honor (I.ii.31-35). They are restless for action in the field, but the King, though willing to give them a chance, does not seem confident about their conduct. On bidding them farewell, he urges them to honor, but adds a very down-to-earth warning: "Those girls of Italy, take heed of them" (II.i.19). In Bertram's case in particular, the King's doubts are justified; and we see nothing in the later military scenes to indicate that any of the young lords has attained the old-fashioned honor of warfare.

Into this world of decay, in which memory alone seems noble, Shakespeare introduces Helena. Of all the sympathetic characters in the first part, she alone has forgotten the past and is launching with romantic aspirations into the future:

I think not on my father,
And these great tears grace his remembrance more
Than those I shed for him. What was he like?
I have forgot him; my imagination
Carries no favour in't but Bertram's.

(I.i.77-81)

As in the earlier comedies, romantic love leads to the idealization of the beloved. The King recalls human perfection in a dead friend; Helena sees it in a living man, on whom her future hopes are pinned. Her imagination gives Bertram a splendor that the actual man as we see him later does not seem to deserve. Her devotion to him is like the devotion of a worshiper to a god; the vocabulary of her love is religious:

'Twas pretty, though a plague,
To see him every hour; to sit and draw
His arched brows, his hawking eye, his curls,
In our heart's table—heart too capable
Of every line and trick of his sweet favour.
But now he's gone, and my idolatrous fancy
Must sanctify his relics.

(I.i.90-96)

Thus, Indian-like,
Religious in mine error, I adore
The sun that looks upon his worshipper
But knows of him no more

(I.iii.199-202)

At this point in the play, we have not seen enough of Bertram to doubt seriously Helena's view of him. We may agree with G. Wilson Knight that "Helena's love sees Bertram as he potentially is, that core and inmost music of his personality which no faults can disturb . . . and this outspaces the moral judgement, which, though present, is surpassed. . . ."[5] Moral judgment is not so easily surpassed later, when we see more of him; but Helena's view of the *potential* Bertram sustains her all the way through, and for the moment we can share it.

Courtly and military honor seem now to be things of the past; if there is an ideal to cling to in this world, it looks as though it must be an ideal of love, for Helena's imagination offers the play's only living impulse toward perfection. One of the signs of this is the way her love unites youth and age. The King and his young courtiers remain aloof from each other; he doubts their capacity for honor, and they get no inspiration from him. But Helena enlists the sympathy of the Countess, who recalls her own youthful love and justifies the conduct of love as following the demands of nature:

this thorn
Doth to our rose of youth rightly belong;
Our blood to us, this to our blood is born:
It is the show and seal of nature's truth,
Where love's strong passion is impress'd in youth.

(I.iii.124-28)

This is recognized even at court, for Helena enlists the sympathy of the King and Lafew, who seem more enthusiastic about her than about the more courtly members of the younger generation. And there is another reason for confidence in Helena. She is not merely an idealist, out of touch with everything except her dream of romantic perfection. She can also hold her own in a down-to-earth battle of wits, as we see when she tangles with Parolles on the question of virginity. She appears to embrace the two aspects of the play's vision, and thus seems capable of bringing the play, in the end, to a satisfactory resolution, as Rosalind, a heroine with a similar double awareness, does in *As You Like It.*[6]

For the moment, however, her capacity to descend to market-place realities is kept in reserve. Her first project to win Bertram operates on the romantic, folk-tale level. She will win him as Bassanio wins Portia, by fulfilling a task, a task with a certain aura of magic—the curing of the King. Taken realistically, her skill as a physician would be an irrelevant claim on Bertram's love—and it is to this realistic level that we will later descend. But, for the moment, the logic of romance holds the two purposes together. Moreover, Shakespeare does what he did not do even in the riddle of Portia's caskets; he skirts the edge of the supernatural. The success of Helena's project depends on its working on a level higher than that of natural reality. We see a hint of this when the scheme is first mentioned. The Countess, though not unsympathetic, withholds actual encouragement until Helena mentions the magic properties of the cure:

There's something in't
More than my father's skill, which was the great'st
Of his profession, that his good receipt
Shall for my legacy be sanctified
By th'luckiest stars in heaven; and would your honour
But give me leave to try success, I'd venture
The well-lost life of mine on his grace's cure
By such a day, an hour.
COUNTESS: Dost thou believe't?
HELENA: Ay, madam, knowingly.
COUNTESS: Why, Helen, thou shalt have my leave and love. . . .

(I.iii.237-46)

The offer of Helena's death as the price of failure takes us more firmly on to the folk-tale level. The offer of sacrifice and the hint of magic are what really win the Countess over; in Helena she recognizes something more than mortal, and her acceptance of it is something like an act of faith. Just as realism, in this play, is pushed to one extreme and becomes sordid, so romance is pushed to the other, and becomes spiritual.

In the scene in which Helena persuades the King to let her undertake the cure, we have the high-water mark of romance in the play. The style, and especially the use of rhyme, is important, as Knight has remarked: "Observe the gnomic, formal, incantatory quality of the rhymes, functioning, as in Helena's first recognition of her own magical powers . . . as the language of inspiration: she seems to be mesmerizing the King."[7] The scene certainly seems to work on these terms in the theater.[8] We are being lifted out of ordinary reality, and the rhyme, by making the speeches stylized, contributes powerfully to this effect. It is interesting to note that the King is the first to use rhyme. His first couplet sounds final and dismissive, as though he is trying to bring the argument to a close; and Helena takes it in this spirit, retiring discouraged. But as she is about to go, the King resumes the debate, still in couplets. It is as though, at the bottom of his mind, he does not really want her to leave and is trying to keep her with him by continuing the argument. She seems to sense this, for she responds, in couplets, to the point he has raised, and continues in this vein until she has won him over. In a sense, the King himself has made the first overture; and this is important. What will cure him is not so much the power of the medicine as his own willingness to believe in it. As Paulina says before the statue of Hermione comes to life, "It is required / You do awake your faith." When Helena invokes God, Heaven, and Grace, the King responds:

> Methinks in thee some blessed spirit doth speak
> His powerful sound within an organ weak;
> And what impossibility would slay
> In common sense, sense saves another way.
>
> (II.i.174-77)

The King's cure is not so much a medical achievement as an act of faith and grace; this is why we feel that he is really cured before he leaves the stage, and the "Flourish" which sounds at the end of the scene (unusual for an exit involving only two people) underlines the sense of triumph. We may contrast this with the doubts and qualifications of the play's ending, in which Bertram seems less capable of faith and asks for proof before he will submit to Helena.

For the moment, however, Helena's victory seems complete. Her magic makes itself felt even at the lower levels of reality. The stylized, incantatory verse of the interview with the King is its natural literary medium, but the wonder of it also affects the down-to-earth Lafew, who describes Helena's power in a more racy, comic way:

> I have seen a medicine
> That's able to breathe life into a stone,
> Quicken a rock, and make you dance canary
> With sprightly fire and motion; whose simple touch
> Is powerful to araise King Pippen, nay,
> To give great Charlemain a pen in's hand
> And write to her a love-line.
>
> (II.i.71-77)

And, in his reaction to the cure, he states in prose what the King and Helena have said in verse:

> They say miracles are past; and we have our philosophical persons to make modern and familiar, things supernatural and causeless. Hence is it that we make trifles of terrors, ensconcing ourselves into seeming knowledge when we should submit ourselves to an unknown fear.
>
> (II.iii.1-6)

Lafew, a chatty old courtier with an earthy sense of humor, is there partly to provide a dramatic balance to the stylized "incantation" scene;[9] but he also shows that the values of romance, centered on Helena, are now beginning to penetrate the world at large. The tired court that we saw at the beginning of the play is starting to wake up, for it now has something to believe in. And, most important, it *wants* to believe. Helena's magic has worked, because the King was receptive to it. Everything seems set, in fact, for a straightforward comic finale—the successful invasion of the ordinary world by the values of romance, and the final dance in which the couples, their difficulties overcome, join hands. Shakespeare creates something like the ending of one of his more conventional comedies—in the middle of Act II.

This brings us to the crucial scene of Bertram's refusal, which needs to be studied in some detail. Helena's entrance with the King after the cure seems designed to give a sense of triumph appropriate to the finale of a comedy; Lafew's exclamation, "Why, he's able to lead her a coranto" (II.iii.42-43), suggests that this may be precisely what he is doing; and a coranto is a very lively dance. The surprise of Parolles, which Lafew seems to share, that the woman before them is Helena may indicate that Helena, for the first time in the play, is splendidly dressed, so that she is for a moment unrecognizable. She now speaks in a manner recalling Portia when Bassanio has made his choice; she formally and triumphantly renounces maidenhood and embraces marriage, of which she now seems certain:

> Now, Dian, from thy altar do I fly,
> And to imperial Love, that god most high
> Do my sighs stream.
>
> (II.iii.74-76)

The sequence in which she passes among the lords, addressing them in formal rhymed couplets, suggests a dance, with the changing of partners; it has, in fact, been staged this way.[10] Lafew's grumbling prose comments about the young men do not break the air of romance; rather, they maintain his role as a realistic spokesman who believes in the romantic values represented by Helena—and help to emphasize, by contrast, the formality of the other speeches. The romantic vision of the play seems to be proceeding to its consummation—and then Bertram, speaking in *un*rhymed verse, breaks the formal pattern by rejecting Helena's choice:

> BERTRAM: My wife, my liege! I shall beseech your highness,
> In such a business give me leave to use

The help of mine own eyes.
KING: Know'st thou not, Bertram,
What she has done for me?
BERTRAM: Yes, my good lord,
But never hope to know why I should marry her.

(II.iii.106-10)

We come back to earth with a bump. It is as though Portia had said to Bassanio, "You may be good at riddles, but who ever said this was a sound basis for marriage?" The logic of romance requires Bertram's acceptance, but the logic of daylight reality suggests that personal compatibility is necessary in marriage; and Bertram does not want to marry Helena.[11]

Romance has passed its first test in the fallen world—the curing of the King—but only because Helena has picked two receptive people, the King and Lafew, both of whom are capable of faith and of a response to the romantic. But such a response is beyond Bertram. When we get to know more of him, we see that Shakespeare has drawn a realistic portrait of a shallow, immature young man whose values are crass and earthbound, and whose two most important actions in the play—the refusal of Helena and the assault on Diana—spring, the first from snobbery, and the second from sensuality. Such a figure clearly does not fit the patterns of romance; his motivations are only too realistic. His refusal to accept Helena is the critical moment of the play, for it shows a direct clash between the values of romance and the values of reality. Helena has established a claim on Bertram, but not a realistic one. For the rest of the play, her task will be to win Bertram on his own terms.

The use of rhyme in this scene is as interesting as that in the King-Helena scene, though it has been less frequently remarked on. As before, it is associated with the romantic values centered on Helena. Bertram's first refusal, in blank verse with run-on lines, makes a deliberate, jarring contrast with the formal couplets of the "choice" scene. In reply, the King's lecture to Bertram on Helena's natural virtue, which should overcome rank, swells appropriately into rhyme. Bertram's second refusal breaks the rhyme again, and the rest of the scene is in blank verse, as the King, his appeal to higher values having failed, simply bullies Bertram into submission.

The romantic finale has been shattered; and the impression made by the scenes that follow is deliberately loose, scattered, and anticlimactic. There is no dramatic showdown between Helena and Bertram; he uses Parolles as an intermediary to tell her that he has been called away. When they do meet, they hardly know what to say to one another. She is formal and polite; he is clearly uncomfortable:

HELENA: Sir, I can nothing say
But that I am your most obedient servant.
BERTRAM: Come, come; no more of that.
HELENA: And ever shall
With true observance seek to eke out that
Wherein toward me my homely stars have fail'd
To equal my great fortune.
BERTRAM: Let that go.
My haste is very great. Farewell. Hie home.

(II.v.71-77)

There is a striking sense of the actual in this scene of embarrassment. We are back in the world of reality, and very cold reality at that. For this, Bertram is largely responsible. He is quite brutal about Helena behind her back, referring to her as "my clog" (II.v.53). He has a coldly prosaic explanation for his apparently temporary parting from her:

Prepar'd I was not
For such a business; therefore am I found
So much unsettled.

(II.v.61-63)

Helena has been an enchantress; she is now a practical problem, a nuisance, a clog. The magic of the King's cure has evaporated completely.

Bertram's response to the wedding is that of a child to whom brutal adults have done something dreadful: "O my Parolles, they have married me!" (II.iii.268). This shows us what Helena's problem now is. It is a problem on a realistic level, involving human wills and personalities rather than behavior imposed by the conventions of romance. Helena must win the acceptance—and, if possible, the love—of a recalcitrant husband who is not really ready for marriage. The problem is stated, however, in folk-tale terms. Helena once more has a task to perform: "When thou canst get the ring upon my finger, which never shall come off, and show me a child begotten of thy body that I am father to, then call me husband . . ." (III.ii.56-58).[12] This looks like a kind of artistic compromise; the folk-tale task is a symbolic way of achieving the personal adjustment that reality requires. Bertram's refusal to consummate his marriage is a symbolic rejection of it.[13] By getting him to sleep with her, Helena will achieve—again, symbolically—the personal acceptance necessary for marriage.[14] However, the compromise is an uneasy one, for Bertram himself does not see the test on the folk-tale level, but regards it as simply an elaborate way of saying that he is not going to accept Helena as his wife. Having stated the conditions, he adds: "then call me husband; but in such a 'then' I write a 'never'" (III.ii.58-59). On the naturalistic level, the achievement of the task is nearly as irrelevant to the achieving of marriage as is the curing of the King. It *represents* the personal adjustment which was the important factor missing from Helena's first task, but whether Bertram is really prepared to take symbolism for reality is still dubious. And, as we will see, it is the problem of Bertram's conversion that provides most difficulty at the end of the play.

The dramatic treatment of Helena at this point reflects the change in the nature of the task before her; winning Bertram is now seen as more of a practical problem than it was before; it cannot be done by magic alone. The enchantress-heroine has been rebuffed and told, in effect, that she has gained her husband by means that are not really valid. In asking Bertram for a kiss, she says that she "like a timorous thief, most fain would steal / What law does vouch mine own" (II.v.81-82). She seems disturbed by what she has done; she recognizes that the law provides an external sanction for her marriage, but that until the internal sanction—the consent of her husband—is provided, she is no better than a thief if she tries to claim his love, for that love is not rightly hers:

> Ambitious love hath so in me offended
> That barefoot plod I the cold ground upon,
> With sainted vow my faults to have amended.
>
> (III.iv.5-7)

The religious vocabulary of love now expresses penance; she has offended the object of her worship. Helena the enchantress has failed, and must withdraw to make room for a new Helena, in whom the practical side will be uppermost.[15] The old Helena is seen from a greater distance; she comes to us at second hand in the letter (written in rhymed verse, a sad reminder of her earlier triumph) which is read aloud by the Countess's steward. As she disappears, she becomes more and more idealized by the other characters. The Countess, adopting the religious vocabulary that has been associated with Helena's love, describes her as a saint interceding for Bertram:

> What angel shall
> Bless this unworthy husband? He cannot thrive,
> Unless her prayers, whom heaven delights to hear
> And loves to grant, reprieve him from the wrath
> Of greatest justice.
>
> (III.iv.25-29)

This idealization of the absent Helena continues to the end of the play. She becomes, like Bertram's father, a distant memory of perfection, in a world which once more seems fallen and imperfect.

Realism is now firmly re-established as the dominant mode of the play. The magic which temporarily transformed the court of France is gone, and the next movement takes place in a harsh daylight that flatters nobody. The war for which Bertram has left his wife is treated critically.[16] We are immediately suspicious when the Duke of Florence's explanation of the war elicits the comment from the First Lord,

> Holy seems the quarrel
> Upon your Grace's part; black and fearful
> On the opposer.
>
> (III.i.4-6)

Our suspicions will be strengthened if we remember that the King had refused to take sides on the matter, allowing his men to choose either party (I.ii.1-15). And there is nothing particularly glorious, or even satisfactory, about the actual fighting. The battle in which the drum was lost seems to have been mismanaged and confused; owing to a mix-up in the orders, the Florentine cavalry, of which Bertram is the general, has attacked its own infantry (III.vi.45-47).[17] There is not even a decisive impression of victory or defeat; all Bertram can say about the battle is, "Well, we cannot greatly condemn our success . . ." (III.vi.52). We never even hear who wins the war, if anybody does; all we know is that a peace has been arranged (IV.iii.38). There is no honor or glory in this war; it is a shambles, frustrating to the participants, and finally, for all we know, indecisive.

Just as there is no glamour in war, there is no romance in relations between the sexes. The idealism of Helena's love poetry in the first part of the play has now given way to a matter-of-fact view of sex. The warnings of Mariana, the widow's neighbor, when she advises Diana to guard her chastity, take us to the crass, prosy side of sex, the world of back-alley seductions (III.v.18-21). It is on this level that Bertram—as Parolles describes him, "a foolish idle boy, but for all that very ruttish" (IV.iii.207)—now operates. The sophistry he uses in attempting to seduce Diana recalls the arguments of Parolles himself in the "virginity" dialogue: "And now you should be as your mother was / When your sweet self was got" (IV.ii.9-10). This rather reduces him to Parolles' level; the attack on virginity masquerades as a defense of fertility. Like all seducers, Bertram is really thinking of the moment of pleasure and does not plan to be around nine months later.

In this cynical, disordered, and very real world of war and sex, the ideal values have not been quite forgotten. They are not so close to us as the romantic passion of Helena, or even the recent memory of Bertram's father; they seem to belong to a vaguer, more distant past. But they are there, and they are seen specifically in opposition to Bertram, who has immersed himself in the cynical world of the present. In his attempted seduction of Diana, he is betraying the nobility of his ancestry, symbolized by the ring, a priceless heirloom that he is willing to surrender for a moment of cheap pleasure:

> a ring the county wears
> That downward hath succeeded in his house
> From son to son some four or five descents
> Since the first father wore it. This ring he holds
> In most rich choice; yet, in his idle fire,
> To buy his will it would not seem too dear,
> Howe'er repented after.
>
> (III.vii.22-28)

He is asking a similar sacrifice of Diana, whose honor is, like the ring, a priceless treasure that should not be lightly thrown away. When he shows himself reluctant to give her the ring, her response has a formal quality, given not in this case by rhyme, but by the repetition of Bertram's own words (a repetition that also underlines his hypocrisy in standing by his own honor and asking her to part with hers):

> Bertram: It is an honour 'longing to our house,
> Bequeathed down from many ancestors,
> Which were the greatest obloquy i'th'world
> In me to lose.

DIANA: Mine honour's such a ring;
My chastity's the jewel of our house,
Bequeathed down from many ancestors,
Which were the greatest obloquy i'th'world
In me to lose.

(IV.ii. 42-49)

Diana herself, by the way, provides an interesting echo from the earlier part of the play. Diana was the goddess of Helena's prayers before her marriage (I.iii.110,[18] 207; II.iii.74). Now, instead of a goddess, we have the ideal of chastity embodied in an ordinary woman. The ideal is the same, but its expression is more suited to the realistic world we now inhabit.

A similar transformation has now taken place in Helena herself. The romantic Helena has, as we have seen, retreated into the distance, and the new Helena appears more subdued. Her first entrance (III.v) is very quiet and low-key. She comes now not to a court, but to the house of a widow in reduced circumstances who takes in lodgers. She comes, however, bringing the old values with her. There is a repetition of the feeling we had in the first part of the play that she represents a power higher than her own. There is a drop in levels, however. She came to the King bearing the power of heaven; she comes now to the widow, assured of the power of the King:

That you may well perceive I have not wrong'd you
One of the greatest in the Christian world
Shall be my surety; for whose throne 'tis needful,
Ere I can perfect mine intents, to kneel.

(IV.iv.1-4)

The power of heaven is here too, though it is working at a more mundane level than it did when she was curing the King:

Doubt not but heaven
Hath brought me up to be your daughter's dower,
As it hath fated her to be my motive
And helper to a husband.

(IV.iv.18-21)

Helena is still an agent for the values of romance, but she is working more in terms of the market place than she did before: "After, / To marry her I'll add three thousand crowns / To what is pass'd already" (III.vii.34-36). This new practicality fits the more practical nature of the task she has now in hand.

That task is regarded with a certain amount of uneasiness by the characters involved—and it seems to me that their uneasiness is justified, and reflects a deep tension in the play. Helena is winning what the law claims rightly belongs to her, and her sleeping with Bertram is entirely legal. There is, all the same, something distasteful about it. She is at once deceiving him and gratifying his lust, and the widow is not sure at first that what she is being asked to do is not ordinary pandering (III.vii.4-7). One speech in which Helena justifies her purposes is couched in riddling terms which, while they reflect the folk-tale nature of the task, also reveal its moral ambiguity:

Why then tonight
Let us assay our plot; which, if it speed,
Is wicked meaning in a lawful deed,
And lawful meaning in a lawful act,
Where both not sin, and yet a sinful fact.
But let's about it.

(III.vii. 43-48)

The last line offers a clue to the spirit in which Helena is now operating. Although she may contemplate for a moment the moral ambiguities of what she is doing, her chief concern is to get the job done. The practical side is dominant. This is reflected in the expression that gives the play its title: "All's well that ends well; still the fine's the crown. / Whate'er the course, the end is the renown" (IV.iv.35-36). In other words, Helena asks us not to think too closely about the device by which she gains her husband, but to accept that the end justifies the means. If romance conquers, we should not be too concerned at the stooping involved.

In a purely romantic context, such considerations would not worry us; but Shakespeare has placed us in a real world in which there is not much to stop us from looking at the bed-trick literally. And if we look at it literally, it becomes, for all its legality, a bit sordid. The play's title, which at first seemed an expression of confidence, now looks more like an embarrassed apology. Helena's speeches seem to me to reflect Shakespeare's own uneasiness with the bed-trick, an uneasiness that is branded on the whole play by its title. Other Shakespearean comedy titles suggest that the playwright was impatient with the business of naming his play; this is the only one that suggests he was nervous about his material. And the fact that the bed-trick is a conventional act, symbolic of—but not literally representing—a psychological adjustment in Bertram, creates more problems, as I have suggested. Will Bertram's repentance be purely conventional and arbitrary, stemming entirely from the symbolic consummation of the marriage? Or will the playwright try to show that a real psychological adjustment is taking place, preparing the ground, so that when Helena fulfills the task, Bertram will be able—both symbolically and literally—to accept her? The latter course might have been more satisfactory, and Shakespeare seems to have been tempted by it. But he does not, evidently, have full confidence in it.

The Countess asks the King to excuse Bertram's conduct, which she attributes to his immaturity, with the implication that he will behave more worthily once he has grown up a bit:

'Tis past, my liege,
And I beseech your majesty to make it
Natural rebellion done i'th' blade of youth,
When oil and fire, too strong for reason's force,
O'erbears it and burns on.

(V.iii.4-8)

Something of the sort seems to be suggested by a passage at the beginning of the "drum" scene, in which the Second Lord describes Bertram's reaction to a letter from his mother, presumably telling him of Helena's death: "there is something in't that stings his nature, for on the reading it he chang'd almost into another man" (IV.iii.2-4). We have our doubts about this change, however, when we realize that he is still determined to consummate his affair with Diana. And when Bertram actually appears, any suggestion that he is softened by his wife's death is dispelled:

> I have tonight dispatch'd sixteen businesses a month's length apiece. By an abstract of success: I have congied with the duke, done my adieu with his nearest, buried a wife, mourn'd for her, writ to my lady mother I am returning, entertain'd my convoy, and between these main parcels of dispatch effected many nicer deeds; the last was the greatest, but that I have not ended yet.
>
> (IV.iii.82-89)

He explains the latter point with a sardonic echo of his argument against virginity: "I mean, the business is not ended, as fearing to hear of it hereafter" (IV.iii.93-94). The curt, businesslike tone of his farewell to Helena still clings to him. Her death and his "mourning" for her are simply incidents in a busy evening, no more important than anything else that happened, and the "greatest" business is still the seduction of Diana. Nor does the unmasking of Parolles do much to change him; he has one illusion less, but his behavior is not appreciably different.[19] When, on being forgiven by the King, Bertram expresses a sense of shame at his past conduct—"My high-repented blames / Dear sovereign, pardon to me" (V.iii.36-37)—we can be forgiven for wondering if the place and the company, rather than his own feelings, call forth these words. If Shakespeare meant to show that Bertram has repented and is ready for Helena even before she appears, he has not carried out his purpose with any great conviction.[20] It looks as though Bertram's acceptance of Helena will have to depend on romantic convention.

To confirm this, the quality of folk tale and romance, present only in a fitful way since Bertram's refusal, returns with a rush in the final scene. The "dead" Helena is idealized in preparation for her triumphant return. Lafew says of Bertram:

> He lost a wife
> Whose beauty did astonish the survey
> Of richest eyes; whose words all ears took captive;
> Whose dear perfection hearts that scorn'd to serve
> Humbly call'd mistress.
>
> (V.iii.15-19)

The power of romance is set against Bertram; his accuser Diana speaks in highly formal, patterned verse, with an appeal to absolute values of faith and duty:

> If you shall marry
> You give away this hand and that is mine,
> You give away heaven's vows and those are mine,
> You give away myself which is known mine;
> For I by vow am so embodied yours
> That she which marries you must marry me—
> Either both or none.
>
> (V.iii.168-74)

Helena's entrance to claim her husband is prepared by Diana's rhymed-verse riddles, which take us to the folk-tale level:

> He knows himself my bed he hath defil'd;
> And at that time he got his wife with child.
> Dead though she be she feels her young one kick.
> So there's my riddle: one that's dead is quick,
> And now behold the meaning.
>
> (V.iii.294-98)

Once again, romance is set in definite opposition to Bertram; accused in this formal incantatory style, he defends himself in a sordid way: "She's impudent, my lord, / And was a common gamester to the camp" (V.iii.186-87). His unpleasant behavior in this scene makes us feel that some kind of magic conversion will indeed be necessary for a satisfactory ending. Something of the sort seems to happen, in fact, when Helena enters, seemingly risen from the dead:

> KING: Is there no exorcist
> Beguiles the truer office of mine eyes?
> Is't real that I see?
> HELENA: No, my good lord;
> 'Tis but the shadow of a wife you see;
> The name and not the thing.
> BERTRAM: Both, both. O pardon!
>
> (V.iii.298-302)

Shakespeare seems, at this point, to have decided on a romantic, conventionalized ending, with the magical appearance of Helena producing a change in Bertram and a reconciliation between the two. It is not magic alone, however. Shakespeare reiterates, through Helena's first words, a point made in the curing of the King. Magic is not sufficient in itself unless confirmed by human will. The King, like the spectators by Hermione's statue, was required to awake his faith. Helena's magical return from the dead will not be meaningful unless Bertram really accepts her as a wife. His first reaction seems to give us the confirmation of love that Helena requires. It looks like a fairy-tale ending.

But the impulse in Shakespeare's imagination that produced the element of realism in the play has not been stilled. The miraculous conversion would be acceptable in a purely romantic context; but this play does not provide such a context. There is a hint of doubt, a slight qualification, in Bertram's next words: "If she, my liege, can make me know this clearly / I'll love her dearly, ever, ever dearly" (V.iii.309-10).[21] And the suggestion that the happy ending is not complete, but depends on certain conditions, is taken up in the King's closing speech: "All yet seems well, and if it end so meet, / The bitter past, more welcome is the sweet" (V.iii.327-28). The happy ending is not seriously in doubt; but it is not completely confirmed, either.[22] According to H. B. Charlton, "the play hardly generates the imaginative conviction that the good [Helena] secures must necessarily come out of the circumstances presented."[23] It is not that we cannot accept the Elizabethan convention of quick repentances;[24] the experienced reader of Elizabethan plays soon learns to do with very little in the way of repentance speeches. We could have been satisfied if Shakespeare had merely cut the offending couplet and left Bertram with "Both, both. O pardon!" The problem is rather that the penitent himself is not co-operating; his repentance still depends on certain conditions. The ending is an honest reflection of the tensions created by the play as a whole. Bertram is a realistic character being acted on by a romantic convention whose power is not fully established. We are still not entirely sure that the solving of a riddle can make one person love another.

In other Shakespearean comedies which contain this tension between romance and realism, some kind of resolution is generally achieved. *As You Like It,* after all its satiric joking about love and marriage, ends with a masque of Hymen. *The Tempest,* after the masque of Prospero, with its vision of an ideal order, returns us to the ordinary, unpredictable world.[25] *Love's Labour's Lost* fuses romance and reality in that the lovers, while brought to regard love as a serious business, not just a springtime game, express this new awareness in a series of highly romantic vows. But in *All's Well That Ends Well* the pull between these two magnetic centers in the playwright's imagination remains unresolved. Romance sets out to impose its values on an intractable world of reality; it suffers one serious rebuff, and while victory may be in sight at the end, we never see it achieved.

I stated at the beginning that my purpose was not to attack or defend *All's Well That Ends Well,* but to try to examine the tensions which give it its peculiar quality. Yet it is difficult to be quite neutral about this play, and any explanation of its peculiarities other than bad taste or incompetence is bound to be a defense of some sort. One may or may not *like* the play, but I think it deserves to be recognized as an important dramatic experiment, conducted with unusual courage and honesty. In the earlier plays, the attacks on romance were softened by the fact that they were only half-serious, and that, as Rosalind put it, "the whippers are in love too." Bertram is an antiromantic character of a different order, however, one who resists love's magic not just with his mind, but with his whole nature. And yet the play is not a simple send-up of romance either; its values are established, especially in the early scenes, as serious and important. When Bertram refuses to play the game, we can see his point, but we feel a definite shock as well. Helena, as a miracle worker, has charm and power; and it is embarrassing to watch her cheating and tricking her way to a husband. The testing of romance is a painful business, and to feel disturbed by the play is, I think, a truer response than to try to explain its tensions away, for tension and uncertainty are its very life. It is the work, not of a confident artist, but of a courageous one, who is willing to ask awkward questions about the assumptions behind his own art.

Notes

1. G. K. Hunter, in his introduction to the Arden Edition of *All's Well That Ends Well* (London, 1962), p. xxxiii, notes that "the play juxtaposes extreme romantic conventions with down-to-earth and critical realism." E. M. W. Tillyard, *Shakespeare's Problem Plays* (Toronto, 1950), p. 2, says "there is something radically schizophrenic" about this play and *Measure for Measure.* According to Clifford Leech, "The Theme of Ambition in *All's Well That Ends Well,*" *ELH,* 21 (1954), 19, "the esemplastic power does not seem to have been fully at work."

2. As Hunter's note on this passage points out, the term "fistula" in Shakespeare's day did not necessarily mean an abscess external to the rectum, but could apply to a burrowing abscess in any part of the body. This removes some of the unpleasantness, but it is still a nasty and embarrassing complaint to have.

3. Quotations from *All's Well That Ends Well* are from Hunter's edition, cited in note 1.

4. M. C. Bradbrook, "Virtue is the True Nobility: A Study of the Structure of *All's Well That Ends Well,*" *RES,* 26 (1950), 289-301, points out that a court could be a center of nobility or of corruption, and that the King's illness left his courtiers exposed to the dangers of the place.

5. *The Sovereign Flower* (London, 1958), p. 139.

6. Hunter, in his introduction, p. xxxvii, puts it another way: "The magic of Helena is clearly associated with this elder age, but she herself must make her way in the new world of social mobility and opportunism. . . ."

7. *The Sovereign Flower,* p. 152.

8. See M. St. Clare Byrne's account of Tyrone Guthrie's 1959 production at Stratford-upon-Avon, in "The Shakespeare Season at The Old Vic, 1958-59 and Stratford-upon-Avon, 1959," *SQ,* 10 (1959), 545-67, especially p. 563.

9. Dramatic balance is also provided by the prose comedy of the Countess and the Clown (II.ii), which is interposed between the "incantation" scene and the scene in which the King appears, cured, dancing with Helena.

10. See M. St. Clare Byrne, "The Shakespeare Season," pp. 565-66. For Robert Grams Hunter, *Shakespeare and the Comedy of Forgiveness* (New York and London, 1965), pp. 116-17, the scene suggests a children's party game in which one of the guests

refuses to be "it." Hunter stresses the formal quality of the scene, as does Knight (*The Sovereign Flower,* p. 146).

11. As a ward of the court, Bertram is legally in the King's power; but that does not mean that his personal wishes are regarded by Shakespeare as irrelevant. Helena herself accepts Bertram's refusal and in effect asks the King to withdraw his power of enforcing Bertram's choice (II.iii.147-48).

12. For the folk-tale analogues to this task, see William Witherle Lawrence, *Shakespeare's Problem Comedies,* 2nd ed. (New York, 1960), pp. 41-45.

13. This point is developed by S. Nagarajan, "The Structure of *All's Well That Ends Well,*" *EIC,* 10 (1960), 24-31, especially p. 25.

14. John F. Adams, "*All's Well That Ends Well*: The Paradox of Procreation," *SQ,* 12 (1961), 268, points out the sexual pun in the test of the ring, and compares Lavatch's bawdy remark about "Tib's rush" (ring) and "Tom's forefinger" (II.ii.21-22).

15. This effect is analyzed by Harold S. Wilson, "Dramatic Emphasis in *All's Well That Ends Well,*" *HLQ,* 13 (1950), 217-40, especially p. 226.

16. Leech reminds us that this play was written not long after *Troilus and Cressida* ("The Theme of Ambition," p. 22).

17. Josephine Waters Bennett, "New Techniques of Comedy in *All's Well That Ends Well,*" *SQ,* 18 (1967), 351, speaks of "Bertram's success as a soldier" as a sign of his growing maturity. But she bases this on the gossip of the women, and there is a satiric contrast between this and what we hear in the camp, from the soldiers.

18. This reference to Diana is conjectural interpolation by Theobald, but a very convincing one.

19. The view that the unmasking of Parolles is the turning point in Bertram's development has been attacked by several critics; see, for example, Bertrand Evans, *Shakespeare's Comedies* (Oxford, 1960), pp. 160-61.

20. There is a rather confusing passage (V.iii.42-67) in which the King and Bertram discuss a woman whom Bertram loved at first, then scorned, and loved again after he had lost her. The King's words at the beginning of the exchange identify the woman as Lafew's daughter Maudlin. But the passage ends, with no indication that the subject has changed, "Be this sweet Helen's knell, and now forget her" (V.iii.67). One might say, "textual corruption," and thus cut one Gordian knot only to tie another. But sense can be made of the passage as it stands; Bertram's speech describing the course of his feelings (V.iii.44-55) seems to refer to Maudlin. The King's response, describing how we love too late those we have lost (V.iii.55-67), is couched in more general terms, and it may be that his reflections, though they begin with Maudlin, lead him to think of Helena and to apply the same thoughts to her. This is consistent with my view that Bertram has not really repented his treatment of his wife; and the idea that the passage is corrupt leaves us in the dark, or at the most extends into the final scene Shakespeare's earlier indecision over Bertram's response to the letter.

21. For obvious reasons, this couplet has bothered those who would prefer a purely romantic ending. M. St. Clare Byrne's account of this moment in the Guthrie production indicates that the reconciliation was satisfying because the stage picture of a contrite Bertram and a forgiving Helena allowed the words to pass unnoticed ("The Shakespeare Season," pp. 557-58). But the words are there, and we cannot wish them away.

22. The "conditional" nature of the ending is discussed by John Russell Brown, *Shakespeare and His Comedies,* 2nd ed. (London, 1962), p. 192; and Clifford Leech, "Shakespeare and the Idea of the Future," *UTQ* 35 (1966), 225.

23. *Shakespearian Comedy* (1938; rpt. New York, 1961), p. 264.

24. Robert G. Hunter argues that the repentance fails to communicate to us because Shakespeare is depending on a convention which he counts on his audience to accept (*Shakespeare and the Comedy of Forgiveness,* pp. 130-31). I would argue that the problem is not the failure of the repentance to communicate, but the fact that the repentance is incomplete in itself.

25. See Leech, "Shakespeare and the Idea of the Future," pp. 226-28.

Ruth Nevo (essay date 1987)

SOURCE: "Motive and Meaning in *All's Well That Ends Well,*" in *"Fanned and Winnowed Opinions": Shakespearean Essays Presented to Harold Jenkins,* edited by John W. Mahon and Thomas A. Pendleton, Methuen, 1987, pp. 26-51.

[*In the following essay, Nevo asserts that* All's Well That Ends Well *should not be classified as a problem play since its structure resembles that of Shakespeare's earlier maturation comedies.*]

All's Well That Ends Well has been classified among the problem comedies, perhaps mainly because Bertram has failed to captivate; he has been found even more devoid of charm than Angelo in *Measure for Measure,* the companion 'problem' comedy. Bertram is, as my students invariably inform me, a creep. And in this they have the critics on their side: that he is 'a thoroughly disagreeable, peevish and vicious person' (Lawrence, 61) seems to be the consensus. One is hard put to it, indeed, to think of a fictional character less popular than the young Count of Rossillion. Yet Helena has come in for her share of criticism too. She is forward, obstinate, manipulative, opportunistic. She does not heal the king out of patriotic fervour but because she has an eye for the main chance. And so on. To rebellious, feminist Katherine Mansfield,

> Helena is a terrifying female. Her virtue, her persistence, her pegging away after the odious Bertram (and disguised as a pilgrim—so typical!) and then telling the whole story to that good widow-woman! And that tame fish Diana. As to lying in Diana's bed and enjoying the embraces meant for Diana—well, I know nothing more sickening. It would take a respectable woman to do such a thing. The worst of it is I can so well imagine . . . acting in precisely that way, and giving Diana a present afterwards. . . . But to forgive such a woman! Yet Bertram would. There's an espece of mothers-boyisme in him which makes him stupid enough for anything.
>
> (*Journal,* 274)

Critics who, on the other hand, fall in love with Helena—Coleridge, it will be recalled, found her 'Shakespeare's loveliest character' (Raysor, II, 113)—attempt desperately, for her sake, to exculpate Bertram of at least the worst of his lies and infidelities. Those who scold her for being a shameless hussy forcing herself (twice!) upon an unwilling partner feel that a thoroughly unattractive couple, evidently conceived by Shakespeare 'in a time of illness or mental disturbance' (Nicoll, 116) get, in each other, no more than they deserve.

On the face of it, and considered in terms of the modular properties it shares with the festive comedies and their New Comedy paradigms, *All's Well* would not seem to be in line for presenting a problem at all. It possesses, conspicuously, many of the features of its distinguished predecessors. It has a resourceful heroine, an autocratic father-figure to be eluded or outwitted, true love which doesn't run smooth, a comic device involving mistaken identities which through its deception reveals a truth, a wonderful fop who is resoundingly exposed, and a fool whose ribaldries provide a low-life counterpoint to the concerns of his betters. And there is a final match-making which puts the recalcitrant young man firmly in his place in the scheme of things by making an honest father of him. To make of it a problem because its male protagonist is a callow youth and its female protagonist determinedly in pursuit of her man (which of the comic heroines, save Beatrice, is not?) is surely nonsense as criticism, reducing our expectation of a Shakespearean play to the level of a tabloid magazine.

Yet generic uneasiness, a sense of generic impropriety, remains. The paradigm ground-plan outlines as many problems as it sets out to skirt. For the play seems to break as many rules as it keeps. It starts, not with young men and women in search of a mate but with the death of a father, two fathers indeed, and with mourning. A foster-father is at once provided, but instead of constituting the obstacle to a match desired by the young he positively forces a marriage upon his resistant foster-son. Instead of the canonical *senex* of the Terentian New Comedy formula, whose law or writ or interference with young lovers must be overcome or evaded, we have a blocking son. This too is a clash between a father, or father-figure, and a son, but upside down, as it were. Similarly topsy-turvy, the young woman, enterprising and triumphant trickster-heroine of the earlier comedies, is a victim-bride (like her single precursor, Hero) who must be done to death before resolutions can be found, and she plays the role of therapeutic, even thaumaturgic, quasi-daughter to the King which becomes canonical for daughters only in the later romances.

Then again, though it looks like a courtship comedy, it is one which is constrained to get along without courtship, since the young man takes flight to the Italian wars, and the young woman follows him to Italy, but not, as previous comedies might have led one to anticipate, in page disguise. One has only to imagine Helena in pursuit of her Bertram in page disguise, with the opportunities thus offered for masked witty courtship, for a playful battle of the sexes in which a balance, for both sexes, between pursuit and defence, winning and losing, is articulated, to see that this device might well have transformed *All's Well* into the supreme successor to *Two Gentlemen of Verona, As You Like It,* and *Twelfth Night.* I make the point not because one would expect or wish a dramatist simply to go on repeating his inventions, but to throw into prominence the peculiar distribution of differences with which we are presented in *All's Well.* For what we have instead of the page disguise is the pilgrim disguise and the bed trick, a mock death and a trick consummation. And the bed trick notoriously pleases no one. On the contrary, it crystallizes the general sense of impropriety, and throws into relief the split in critical opinion concerning Helena: saint or strumpet, and the near-unanimous critical repudiation of Bertram, tricker tricked, but not, it is felt, thereby improved.

For all these reasons the festive end is felt to be a flop, or a merely mechanical or superficial closure. And it lacks the grand harmonic completion the festive comedies have accustomed us to. The King, cured of his wasting disease in Act I, and 'of as able body as when he number'd thirty' (IV.v.77-8), remains unmatched, though the widowed Countess, it would seem, is an available and ideally suitable partner for him. 'You shall find of the king a husband', says Lafew, incorrigible matchmaker, already in line 6 of Act I, but that carefully planted option is not taken up. Nor is a mate found for the virtuous and good-hearted Diana. There is even another unmarried young woman, possibly jilted, in the wings at the play's end. The play provides all the constituents for a grand celebratory wedding closure in which 'individual fulfillment, marital intimacy and communal renewal are celebrated' (Wheeler, 3), but it is felt to be a question whether there are any truly festive marriages at all, or rather quite the contrary: a disillusioned rendering (for good or ill—some will praise the absence of illusion) of a cynical and sterile world. *All's Well,* it is generally agreed, has no commanding centre, does not integrate its realism (which is usually admitted to be of a power and veracity equal to Shakespeare's peak period) either with its folk-lore motifs—the Healing of the King, the Clever Wench, the Fulfilment of the Tasks[1]—or with conventional expectations, and produces an effect of unease and confusion.[2] *All's Well* is unable, it seems, to make up its generic mind. It is neither fish, flesh nor good red herring; neither comedy, tragedy nor romance.

I would like to submit that *All's Well,* so far from having to be apologized for, can be seen as a particularly interesting successor to the festive or, as it might be better to call them, the maturation comedies; that the critics' problems are often reflections of their own unaware masculine or feminine identifications, embodying defences and resistances which themselves repeat the conflicts dramatized in the play; and that therefore, the better to understand both critics and play, we must attempt to read, as we say, between the lines, and to hear with a third ear. The space between the lines is the psychic space of evocation and resonance shared by both audience and *dramatis personae.* It is the space of precipitation by the text into consciousness of the normally unconscious. It is there that we can find what Peter Brooks calls the 'complex history of unconscious desire, unavailable to the conscious subject but at work in the text' (516). This, 'the self's other story', is what we must set out to discover if we wish to do justice to the drama enacted in *All's Well* and to see as significant the anomalies mentioned above. The complaint, for example, of the Arden editor that the play lacks a 'central, acceptable, and unified viewpoint' to define its values, and to integrate its incompatibilities (xxxv), acquires a different kind of truth when we perceive that *All's Well* places itself at a node where three dreams cross: the dream of the elders, reliving their lives through their children, the dream of the young man escaping parental domination, and the dream of the young woman desiring a child and a father. And these dreams neither coincide nor harmonize.

In *All's Well,* still in outline and plan a courtship comedy, parents have become, if not central as in the romances, at least not completely instrumental. The point of view is predominantly of the young, but since the parents, with their own problems of ageing, of holding on and letting go, are not mere obstacle figures, their point of view is operative too. They exist within the play both in their own right, and as their wills, desires, fantasies and memories intermesh with those of the younger generation. This intermesh is a feature neither of the festive comedies nor of the romances, and it is what gives to *All's Well* its peculiar richness and density.

If there is a problem in this text, it is to be found in the unfinished business—unresolved tensions or repressed fears and desires which every play, every text, leaves in its wake to motivate the writing of the works to follow. But so far as its comic project is concerned, it quite triumphantly contains, while it also reveals, its potentially explosive and painful material.

. . . . .

Comedy, Chaplin once said, 'is at its best when it flirts with death, plays with it, mocks it, pokes its nose into it'. If there is validity in the view that comedy is the mode of drama which defers, denies, evades or overcomes death, then one can see the play's opening not as an abrogation of comic conditions, but as a foregrounding of them. The deaths of the two fathers are undone by the adoption of Bertram and of Helena by the King and Countess respectively. The initial mourning, already past as the play begins, suggests precisely such a denial, renewal or overcoming. But if death is thus vigorously defended against at the very start, its shadow remains to haunt the play. If we listen, as perhaps we always should, with half-closed eyes to the verbal texture of the opening scenes, we become aware of major themes which are the older generation's: nostalgia, the vulnerable body, the dereliction of time, impotence. 'In delivering my son from me', says the Countess, 'I bury a second husband' (I.i.1). The King's disease—that mysterious fistula—is immediately introduced, together with the wishful fantasy of his restoration to youthful fitness. A strangely skeletal image—'virtue's steely bones / Looks bleak i' th' cold wind' (I.i.101-2)—appears in Helena's defence of Parolles; the consequences she envisages should her gamble for Bertram fail are vividly imagined: 'Let the white death sit on thy cheek for ever' (II.iii.71). Parolles' adjurations on the subject of virginity not unexpectedly turn the age-old *carpe diem* theme into a very explicit *memento mori*: 'Your date is better in your pie and your porridge than in your cheek; and your virginity, your old virginity, is like one of our French wither'd pears: it looks ill, it eats drily; marry, 'tis a wither'd pear' (I.i.154-9).

The peculiar anxiety the play's body-language expresses lies in a vacillation between images of desire and of decrepitude. The passionate Helena, who has loved (though it was 'a plague' to do so) 'To see him every hour; to sit and draw / His arched brows, his hawking eye, his curls' (I.i.91-2), who longs to 'feed [her] eye . . . / To join like likes, and kiss like native things' (I.i.217, 219) grieves that 'wishing well had not a body in't / Which might be felt' (I.i.177-8). This vehemence is curiously echoed by Bertram, newly wed and in flight, as he parts from one of his new companions: 'I grow to you, and our parting is a tortur'd body' (II.i.36). We have the unvarnished plain speaking of Lavatch (of Touchstone's ilk) to drive the point home, as he seeks permission to marry his Isbel: 'My poor body, madam, requires it; I am driven on by the flesh, and he must needs go that the devil drives'; 'Service is no heritage, and I think I shall never have the blessing of God till I have issue a' my body; for they say barnes are blessings' (I.iii.26-8, 21-4). 'Issue of the body' is the leitmotif of the King's elegy for his own, and his old friend's, youth:

But on us both did haggish age steal on,
And wore us out of act . . .

(I.ii.29-30)

Would I were with him! . . .
"Let me not live", quoth he,
"After my flame lacks oil, to be the snuff
Of younger spirits, whose apprehensive senses
All but new things disdain; whose judgments are
Mere fathers of their garments . . ."
This he wish'd.
I, after him, do after him wish too,
Since I nor wax nor honey can bring home.

(I.ii.52, 58-65)

'Oil' for his flame, 'wax' or 'honey' for the hive, suggest that the loss of sexual potency underlies the melancholy of this Fisher King. We note his resigned reply to the courtier's 'You're loved, sir': 'I fill a place, I know't' (I.ii.67, 69). The lewd Lafew leaves no room for doubt about the nature of the King's disease, or at least of its symptomatic manifestation. He himself refers to his task—the bringing of the physician's daughter to her royal patient—as a pandar's role: 'I am Cressid's uncle / That dare leave two together' (II.i.96-7); describes what 'Doctor she' will achieve in language which barely cloaks its sexuality; and takes a salacious pleasure in persuading the melancholy King to attempt the cure:

O, will you eat
No grapes, my royal fox? Yes, but you will
My noble grapes, and if my royal fox
Could reach them. I have seen a medicine
That's able to breathe life into a stone,
Quicken a rock, and make you dance canary
With spritely fire and motion; whose simple touch
Is powerful to araise King Pippen, nay,
To give great Charlemain a pen in's hand
And write to her a love-line.

(II.i.68-77)[3]

It is precisely the King's virility that Helena restores. After his recovery, he is 'lustique' enough to lead his 'preserver' in a coranto (II.iii.41). 'Your dolphin is not lustier', Lafew informs us (II.iii.26). This restoration by the daughter of his old friend is the magic fulfilment of a wishful fantasy; but it also provides the King with—what? a surrogate daughter as well as a surrogate son? An Avishag for his declining years? A greater warmth, perhaps, than one would feel for one's physician is to be caught in the King's resolve to become her patient: 'more to know could not be more to trust' (II.i.205). His violent repudiation of the recalcitrant Bertram, the transformation of 'My son's no dearer' (I.ii.76) into

Check thy contempt;
Obey our will . . .
Or I will throw thee from my care for ever
Into the staggers and the careless lapse
Of youth and ignorance; both my revenge and hate
Loosing upon thee in the name of justice,
Without all terms of pity

(II.iii.157-66)

is the provision of the tyrannical *senex* of New Comedy with a vengeance. But if he is, as we intuit, more than half in love, not any longer with easeful death, but with a young woman who promises rejuvenation, it is not difficult to understand the intensity, and the ambivalence, of his emotional investment in this match.

By the same token we recall the words of the widowed Countess, as the play opens with the dispatching of Bertram to Paris: 'In delivering my son from me', says the Countess, 'I bury a second husband.' On the face of it, this is the patrician gesture of a dignified and courtly lady distancing with art a double sorrow. This second 'birth' is a second death, she says. But in the rhetorical condensation may we not descry a telltale parapraxis? The Countess is in mourning for her husband; she is also, we perceive, rather more than half in love with her son.[4]

The Countess's second exchange with her fool, which follows Helena's confession and her departure for Paris, is similarly revealing. She is sending him off in Helena's wake to the King's court and is prepared, with good-natured irony, to indulge his scapegrace effrontery. On the whole she treats his scurrilities with much the same matronly indulgence as Olivia does Feste's, but the open sexuality of his bawdry this time, it seems, is provocative of more than cool irony. His 'answer', he says, fits all questions 'like a barber's chair that fits all buttocks' (II.ii.16); is as fit

as ten groats is for the hand of an attorney, as your French crown for your taffety punk, as Tib's rush for Tom's forefinger, as a pancake for Shrove Tuesday, a morris for May-day, as the nail to his hole, the cuckold to his horn, as a scolding quean to a wrangling knave, as the nun's lip to the friar's mouth; nay, as the pudding to his skin. . . . From below your duke to beneath your constable, it will fit any question.

(II.ii.20-30)

'It must be an answer of most monstrous size that must fit all demands', is the Countess's reply; and then suddenly, in the midst of the thrust of parry and repartee, comes a striking *non sequitur*: 'To be young again, if we could' (37).

They are mourning their youth, this autumnal pair, it seems. And in consequence they are projecting upon their children (or their adopted children) their longing to relive their lives. It is no wonder that crossed currents of ambivalence will traverse this inverted family romance.

Read in this light the testing scene between the Countess and Helena becomes as iridescent as Helena's tears. The Countess receives the steward's confirmation of Helena's love for Bertram with an immediate, motherly empathy, shadowed, however, in its reference to 'faults', by the hint of a jealous reservation:

Even so it was with me when I was young;
. . . this thorn

Doth to our rose of youth rightly belong. . . .
Such were our faults, or then we thought them none.

(I.iii.123-5, 130)

The scene which follows is masterly in its representation of ambivalence, of simulation and dissimulation, between the two women, both contenders for Bertram's love. 'You know, Helen, / I am a mother to you' (I.iii.132-3) is the Countess's opening ploy, and it serves her purpose of eliciting response and testing intention excellently when Helena replies, with modestly disavowing emphasis, 'Mine honourable *mistress*' (my italics):

Nay, a mother.
Why not a mother? When I said "a mother",
Methought you saw a serpent. What's in "mother"
That you start at it? I say I am your mother,
And put you in a catalogue of those
That were enwombed mine. . . .
You ne'er oppress'd me with a mother's groan,
Yet I express to you a mother's care.
God's mercy, maiden! does it curd thy blood
To say I am thy mother? what's the matter,
That this distempered messenger of wet,
The many colour'd Iris, rounds thine eye?
—Why, that you are my daughter?

(I.iii.134-48)

The Countess exploits Helena's embarrassed feint—'The Count Rossillion cannot be my brother. . . . must not be my brother' (I.iii.150, 155) to point out that Helena as her daughter-in-law would solve the semantic problem, and she drives home her advantage:

God shield you mean it not! daughter and mother
So strive upon your pulse. What! pale again?
My fear hath catch'd your fondness; now I see
The myst'ry of your loneliness, and find
Your salt tears' head. . . .
Speak, is't so?
If it be so, you have wound a goodly clew.

(I.iii.163-7, 176-7)

She is playing the role of indignant matron that she has set herself. But in doing so, she is playing it out. The ambiguous irony of 'you have wound a goodly clew' allows us to register simultaneously the angry resentment she is professing, and the compensatory acceptance she is working her way towards. Since she cannot have a husband in her son, she will identify with the girl who would be his wife, and so transform her love for Bertram into a double maternal solicitude. This is an admirable solution: it is indeed the way of women in Shakespearean comedy to resolve their inner conflicts more successfully, more benignly, than do the men.

At the end of the scene, Helena has the Countess's leave and love and approval for her project. But in order to understand Helena in the testing scene we must retrace our steps.

The predicament that is developed in Act I of *All's Well* offers a powerful exemplification of Freud's observation upon family quadrangles. 'I am accustoming myself', he wrote in a letter to Fliess in 1899, 'to regarding every sexual act as an event between four individuals'. 'Every sexual thought' perhaps he should have said. Much of interest emerges when we turn our attention to the Countess's foster-daughter, also, like Bertram, in mourning for a father: 'The remembrance of her father never approaches her heart but the tyranny of her sorrows takes all livelihood from her cheek' (I.i.45-7), we are told. We are immediately riveted by a scene curiously reminiscent of the opening scenes of *Hamlet* but with the sexes reversed. 'I do affect a sorrow indeed, but I have it too' (50) is Helena's reply to the Countess's chiding: 'No more of this, Helena; go to, no more; lest it be rather thought you affect a sorrow than to have—' (47-9). Helena, it seems, like Hamlet, has something to hide, something that presses for utterance and chafes at the need for dissimulation. Helena, like Hamlet, as we speedily learn, is 'too much in the *son*':

I think not on my father,
And these great tears grace his remembrance more
Than those I shed for him. What was he like?
I have forgot him; my imagination
Carries no favour in't but Bertram's.

(I.i.77-81)

The lines are obscure, but possibly uncannily shrewd. To make sense of the antithesis we must read 'remembrance' as a metonymy for 'remains'—all that remains of her father is her memory of him. So: the great tears grace his memory more than those she shed at his funeral, tears shed 'for *him*', still, so to speak, present in the flesh. This is very condensed, more particularly since 'grace' carries with it its subliminal contrary—'disgrace'. Surely a considerable tinge of guilt colours Helena's acknowledgement of the displacement, in her passionate affection, of father by beloved. The denials, like most denials, are self-betraying. What the speech tells us is that she is very far from having forgotten her father; but that her love for Bertram has, quite literally, and not without guilt, taken the place of her love for her father, the one image overlaying the other. If so, it is no wonder that her love is perceived by her as unattainable, out of reach, never to be consummated. Yes, he is socially above her, and this provides the ostensible reason for her despair. But since nothing, we are told, is fortuitous in the world of the mind, Helena's choice of the object of her affections could be in accordance with a deeply ambivalent inner need. If it is her father she loves, and therefore a father that she seeks in the mate she chooses, the latter will be, for that very reason, impossible, untouchable, a forbidden *prince lointain*: ''twere all one / That I should love a bright particular star / And think to wed it' (I.i.83-5).

We are offered a great deal more data for the fathoming of Helena's complex motivation in the dialogue with Bertram's friend, Parolles, whom she loves 'for his sake' though she knows him for the liar, fool and coward that he is. With Parolles she enjoys a relationship of ironic equal-

Sharon Heldt as Mariana, Emma Richler as Townsperson, Lucy Peacock as Helena, Hazel Desbarats as Widow Capilet, Sally Cahill as Townsperson, and Kim Scarcella as Townsperson in Act III, scene viii of the 1988 Stratford Festival production of All's Well That Ends Well.

ity despite her lowly birth and his complacent patronizing. 'Save you, fair queen' is his greeting, and her reply, 'And you, monarch!' (I.i.104-5), shows, as does the flyting that concludes their conversation (187-200), that she can give as good as she gets in this power game. Helena is shrewd and self-reliant as the scene makes very clear: it ends with her bold resolve to seek the remedies that 'in ourselves do lie' (212):

> Who ever strove
> To show her merit that did miss her love?
> The king's disease—my project may deceive me,
> But my intents are fix'd, and will not leave me.
>
> (I.i.222-5)

She is also preoccupied, as the scene makes clear, with the very subject Parolles, with preternaturally cunning complicity, has chosen for their conversation.

Parolles is a mine of information on the subject of virginity, which is the topic he first provocatively launches. Helena parries his provocations to good effect, but in the process of enquiring of Parolles, who should know, how one may 'barricado it' against man the enemy, Helena also enquires, 'How might one do, sir, to lose it to her own liking?' (I.i.147). Parolles' diatribe against withered pears concludes with the challenge 'Will you anything with it?' (I.i.159-60), and is followed by an elliptical speech from Helena, perhaps half to herself, which has proved no less a challenge to interpreters:

> Not my virginity; yet . . .[5]
> There shall your master have a thousand loves,
> A mother, and a mistress, and a friend,
> A phoenix, captain, and an enemy,
> A guide, a goddess, and a sovereign,
> A counsellor, a traitress, and a dear.
>
> (I.i.161-6)

The ellipsis, a characteristic of Helena's which suggests a reflective inwardness, is open to a number of interpretations. Are we to hear an emphasis upon 'my' virginity? Is the implied other virginity, if any is implied, Bertram's? Is 'yet' temporal or concessive? Whatever is unspoken crystallizes finally upon what is evidently the dominant preoccupation—'your master': 'There shall your master have a thousand loves.' But where shall this take place? In Paris? Or in 'my virginity', the immediate antecedent for the anaphoric 'there'? However we read what follows, whether as an envious and ironic catalogue of sonneteering epithets (a denigration of the loves Bertram will find in Paris) or as an ardent outdoing even of the chivalric passions of the sonneteers (and so a valorization of the love that she can offer), immediately after 'a thousand loves' there occurs an oddity which we can surely only interpret as another astonishing slip of the text. What follows is 'a mother, and a mistress, and a friend'. For while one has encountered fantastic, hyperbolic, even outrageous, epithets in High Renaissance sonnets, even the most assiduous reader of these confections will be hard put to it to recall a mother among them. No occurrence, the Arden editor assures us, is on record.

Why has this 'mother' entered Helena's mind? Has she perceived the bond between the Countess and Bertram? And, seeking herself a father surrogate in her love, does her wise unconscious fear a contrary quest in Bertram? Or, on the contrary, is it her wish too to 'mother' Bertram? These are the questions which resonate further in the testing scene between the Countess and Helena, which we will consider now from Helena's point of view.

The Countess's outburst:

> does it curd they blood
> To say I am thy mother? what's the matter,
> That this distempered messenger of wet,
> The many-colour'd Iris, rounds thine eye?
> —Why, that you are my daughter?
>
> (I.iii.144-8)

receives the opaque reply, 'That I am not'. Helena, elliptical as ever, may mean by this 'I am not *that*', by way of emphatic disavowal, or 'Because I am not' by way of concession. How are we to read the elliptical Helena? Does she inadvertently reveal her true feelings, or cannily mask her feelings with a declarative equivocation? The reason she gives for her continued insistence is disingenuous: 'Pardon, madam; / The Count Rossillion cannot be my brother':

> My master, my dear lord he is; and I
> His servant live, and will his vassal die.
> He must not be my brother.
>
> (I.iii.153-5)

Embarrassed, Helena falls into confusion as she struggles between the Scylla of impoliteness or ingratitude and the hypothetical Charybdis of brother/sister incest:

> You are my mother, madam; would you were—
> So that my lord your son were not my brother—
> Indeed my mother! or were you both our mothers
> I care no more for than I do for heaven,
> So I were not his sister.
>
> (I.iii.156-60)

It can surely escape no one that Helena's double bind here is factitious. The Countess can be her mother only metaphorically. Certainly the semantic absurdity does not escape the Countess, who, as we have seen, uses it to drive home her advantage.

Helena's agitation serves the Countess's testing purposes, and she is trapped into the confession the Countess wants to hear. But we must seek a deeper reason for her extreme discomposure. Her ostensible reason—the desire not to be Bertram's sister since she wishes to be his wife—since it is absurd, can only be a screen upon which we can read an inner conflict. That she is made so nervous by the idea of being Bertram's forbidden sister could well be symptomatic of the deeper taboo. Daughter and mother so strive upon her pulse in a sense truer than the Countess knows: shall she continue to be her father's docile daughter, submissive and self-effacing, or become her lover's active pursuer, challenger and replacer of his mother? That it is the father's daughter which at this point dominates her mind is to be inferred from the posture of helpless, hapless adoration from afar that she expresses, in excess, one feels, of what is required to pacify the Countess, but in keeping with the masochistic note we have already heard ('The hind that would be mated by the lion / Must die for love', I.i.89-90):

> I know I love in vain, strive against hope;
> Yet in this captious and inteemable sieve
> I still pour in the waters of my love
> And lack not to lose still. Thus, Indian-like,
> Religious in mine error, I adore
> The sun that looks upon his worshipper
> But knows of him no more. . . .
> O then, give pity
> To her whose state is such that cannot choose
> But lend and give where she is sure to lose;
> That seeks not to find that her search implies,
> But riddle-like lives sweetly where she dies!
>
> (I.iii.196-202, 208-12)

Richard Wheeler says that Helena's main task is to overcome a difficulty 'that originates in Bertram's revulsion from her' (15). But this is surely not so. Helena's main task is to overcome a difficulty that originates in the Oedipal taboo. She is as passionate a woman as she is an affectionate daughter, but not yet able to break the father's spell. The phoenix image fantasizes a sublime self-immolation, but pursuit of Bertram to Paris is seductive too. The will to pursue Bertram to Paris under the guise of healing the King, since it is also the will to heal the King under the guise of pursuing Bertram, is for her a wonderfully composite and legitimizing wish-fulfilment. Using the craft of her own father, she will restore a proxy father-figure to health, and receive, at his grateful hand, a husband.

Helena consciously conceives her problem as a conflict between boldness and self-effacement, presumption and modesty, in terms both of the social hierarchies and the maidenly proprieties, but also in terms of chastity and sensuality. 'Loving dearly', for Helena, is no matter for platonic abstractions and Diana, her much invoked goddess, was, it will be recalled, the goddess of childbirth as well as of virginity. But it is Diana, not of the Ephesians but of virgins, whom she invokes in order to formulate her plight at this point:

> My dearest madam, . . .
> if yourself,
> Whose aged honour cites a virtuous youth,
> Did ever, in so true a flame of liking,
> Wish chastely and love dearly, that your Dian
> Was both herself and love—
>
> (I.iii.202-8)

Only later, and, typically, when she steels herself for possible humiliation in the self-exposure of the choosing scene, does she see herself as deserting Diana for 'imperial Love, that god most high' (II.iii.75).

Helena's fantasied plot of success, in which she will choose her man and the King-father will sanction her choice, fails. It is at the French court, following the triumph of her cure of the King, that humiliation—the 'Tax of impudence, / A strumpet's boldness, a divulged shame' (II.i.169-70) which, she told the King, she was ready to venture, in other words, had deeply feared, as the consequence instinctively associated for her with sexual love—becomes indeed her lot. In a way she has tempted Providence, for her replies to the reluctant courtiers are self-abasing: 'Love make your fortunes twenty times above / Her that so wishes'; 'I'll never do you wrong, for your own sake. / . . . in your bed / Find fairer fortune if you ever wed!'; 'You are too young, too happy, and too good, / To make yourself a son out of my blood' (II.iii.82-97). We conceive the drama that she has conceived, empowered by her father's power: the response she hoped for from Bertram would have reversed the situation, dignified her humility by triumphantly vindicating her intrinsic worth. But at her grand moment of choice, she is despised and rejected, punished, if you will, by a chauvinist text. The choice-of-a-suitor scene has understandably troubled critics, both on her behalf and on Bertram's. The latter indeed has troubles of his own, to which I now turn.

They interestingly mirror Helena's. For where Helena seeks, and struggles with, a father in her love, Bertram fears, and flees, a mother in his. Understanding this, we will understand the pathos of the crossed vectors of desire, the knot of conflicting needs which this comedy of maturation must untie.

Critics scold Bertram for being so unchivalrous about Helena, but we should surely register the authenticity of his resistance to a marriage forced upon him by a foster-father, to the socially inferior, and domestically familiar, receiver of his mother's patronage. Even to a kind of sister—Helena's anxiety on this score can alert us to his. That he chafes is hardly to be wondered at. Bertram has emerged from beneath the maternal wing only to fall under the sway of a new paternal authority. It is surely incumbent upon us to see the matter from his point of view when he bursts out with

> My wife, my liege! I shall beseech your highness,
> In such a business give me leave to use
> The help of mine own eyes.
>
> (II.iii.106-8)

And seeing it thus we may perceive the bind in which he is placed. It would hardly make things better for Helena if his repulsion were so great as to make him defy the King's threatened 'revenge and hate'. His surrender has been construed as abjectly, cynically opportunistic. But it could also be read as a bitter acceptance of *force majeure*:

> Pardon, my gracious lord; for I submit
> My fancy to your eyes. When I consider
> What great creation and what dole of honour
> Flies where you bid it, I find that she, which late
> Was in my nobler thoughts most base, is now
> The praised of the king; who, so ennobled,
> Is as 'twere born so.
>
> (II.iii.167-73)

It depends where we locate the irony, whether we monopolize that commodity as a critical prerogative, or allow the dramatized persona access to the sarcasm which is the defence of the powerless. And Bertram *is* powerless. That he is 'not yet old enough for a man, nor young enough for a boy' (as Malvolio says of Cesario in *Twelfth Night,* I.v.158-9) is the play's generational starting point.

Already in Act II Bertram's plight is presented as one of extreme frustration. He is

> commanded here, and kept a coil with
> "Too young", and "The next year" and "'Tis too
> early". . . .
> I shall stay here the forehorse to a smock,
> Creaking my shoes on the plain masonry,
> Till honour be bought up, and no sword worn
> But one to dance with.
>
> (II.i.27-33)

Seeking honour in battle, action, manhood, he is kept childishly at home by a King who is as patronizing as he is paternal. And this situation reaches a crisis when even freedom of marital choice is denied him.

But more is at stake for Bertram than freedom of marital choice. Lafew's comments throughout the scene of Helena's choice brand all the reluctant courtiers as beardless boys, objects of his macho contempt before their lackluster performance. 'Do all they deny her? And they were sons of mine I'd have them whipp'd, or I would send them to th' Turk to make eunuchs of' (II.iii.86-8). They are 'boys of ice. . . . bastards to the English; the French ne'er got 'em' (93-5). In particular he despises Bertram, and in terms which suggest the condescending arrogance of the grown man for the sexually immature youth.

'There's one grape yet. I am sure thy father drunk wine; but if thou be'st not an ass, I am a youth of fourteen; I have known thee already' (99-101).

In the scene which follows, the mutual hostility between Lafew and Parolles also hinges specifically upon the question of manliness: Lafew excoriates Parolles for his effeminate clothes—he is a 'good window of lattice' (II.iii.212)—and for his foppish airs and affectations—'I must tell thee, sirrah, I write man; to which title age cannot bring thee' (197-8). And his insinuations go further than aspersions cast merely upon Parolles' sartorial foppishness: 'Why dost thou garter up thy arms a' this fashion? Dost make hose of thy sleeves? . . . Thou wert best set thy lower part where thy nose stands' (245-8). To Lafew, aggressively male, Parolles is 'a hen'. As far as Lafew is concerned, it seems, Parolles is nothing but a male punk and he cannot stand him. Parolles for his part throws Lafew's 'antiquity' in his face, and, once Lafew is safely absent, swears 'Well, thou hast a son shall take this disgrace off me; scurvy, old, filthy, scurvy lord! . . . I'll beat him, by my life, if I can meet him with any convenience' (231-5). It is to this braggart 'sweetheart' that Bertram turns for sympathy when he enters, 'Undone and forfeited to cares for ever!' (263). Parolles' bravado, characteristic defence of the sexually and personally insecure, presents the refuge of a homosexual attachment as a valorization of the male cameraderie of warfare:

> To th' wars, my boy, to th' wars!
> He wears his honour in a box unseen
> That hugs his kicky-wicky here at home,
> Spending his manly marrow in her arms,
> Which should sustain the bound and high curvet
> Of Mars's fiery steed.
>
> (II.iii.274-9)

And off to the wars go the bachelor companions in perfect agreement that 'A young man married is a man that's marr'd' (II.iii.294).

For Bertram, frustrated by his forced marriage, Mars is a welcome substitute for Venus. But that a fear of impotence lies just beneath the surface of his martial posture is suggested not only by the Parolles connection but by his own tell-tale envoi:

> I have writ my letters, casketed my treasure,
> Given order for our horses; and tonight,
> When I should take possession of the bride,
> End ere I do begin.
>
> (II.v.23-6)

Effeminate Parolles, 'jackanapes with scarfs' (III.v.85), is Bertram's refuge from 'the dark house [a displaced image of female enclosure?] and the detested wife' (II.iii.288). The danger, bawdy Lavatch informs us, is in 'standing to 't': in battle, 'that's the loss of men'; elsewhere, 'the getting of children' (III.ii.40-1). Bertram, who runs away, the clown's irony seems to suggest, has double indemnity. Lavatch's caustic comment is important because it links the two masculine prerogatives, and puts them both in question *vis-a-vis* Bertram. But we must ask our own questions of the text that represents Bertram.

First of all, we note, the nearly universal critical prejudice against him leads to a cardinal misjudgment. Bertram does in fact exhibit prowess in battle. And he does not, at this stage at least, lie to Helena. He does not declare to her a love he does not feel. He will not kiss her even when they part, and she pleads for at least a formal embrace.

Moreover the riddle with which he sets Helena her impossible task: '*When thou canst get the ring upon my finger, which never shall come off, and show me a child begotten of thy body that I am father to, then call me husband*' (III.ii.56-8) is double-tongued, like all riddles. It states an apparent impossibility but represents an unacknowledged desire. To see this, one has only to suppose the conditional *form* changed, not the primary substance; to read instead of 'When thou canst . . .', 'If only thou couldst . . .'.[6]

And when he dispatches her to his mother, it is with almost a plea on his part for her understanding:

> And rather muse than ask why I entreat you;
> For my respects are better than they seem,
> And my appointments have in them a need
> Greater than shows itself at the first view
> To you that know them not.
>
> (II.v.65-9)

The need 'Greater than shows itself', as Richard Wheeler persuasively demonstrates, stems from the fact that Helena is ineluctably bound up in his mind with his mother: 'A son's affection for a mother is directed by Bertram toward the countess; a son's fears of female domination and of his own oedipal wishes are aroused in Bertram by Helena' (42). Hence 'I cannot love her nor will strive to do't' (II.iii.145). Wheeler concludes, however, that the play's 'comic purpose, to free Bertram from anxieties that originate in family ties', is not achieved. 'The action of *All's Well*', he says, 'dramatizes neither a liberation from nor a transformation of obstacles that obstruct the marriage to Helena' (80).

It is at this point that my own reading of *All's Well* diverges from Wheeler's. He reads into the play the problems of the Sonnets, with Helena as a screen figure for the humiliated and self-humiliating lover and Bertram as the Sonnets' young man, presented now with a savage mockery the self-excoriating author of the Sonnets could not permit himself. My own reading is dramatically opposed. I see these two as chiastic doubles, mirrors of each other. Where Helena seeks a (forbidden) father in her love, Bertram fears a (forbidden) mother; but the text also inscribes their shared desire for sexual enfranchisement, for fatherhood and motherhood, and provides the means for its attainment.

The reversals, which will make possible the happy ending, occur in the play's middle Act. Helena's great speech of renunciation is worth quoting at length for the subtlety with which it articulates a momentous transformation.

> Nothing in France, until he has no wife!
> Thou shalt have none, Rossillion, none in France;
> Then hast thou all again. Poor lord, is't I
> That chase thee from thy country, and expose
> Those tender limbs of thine to the event
> Of the none-sparing war? And is it I
> That drive thee from the sportive court, where thou
> Wast shot at with fair eyes, to be the mark
> Of smoky muskets? O you leaden messengers,
> . . . do not touch my lord.
> Whoever shoots at him, I set him there;
> . . . I am the cause
> . . . No; come thou home, Rossillion,
> . . . I will be gone;
> My being here it is that holds thee hence.
> Shall I stay here to do't? No, no, although
> The air of paradise did fan the house
> And angels offic'd all. I will be gone,
> . . . Come, night; end, day;
> For with the dark, poor thief, I'll steal away.
>
> (III.ii.100-29)

In the parting scene Helena begged for her kiss 'like a timorous thief, [who] most fain would steal' (II.v.81) what is legally hers. Now she will herself steal away, so only she be no obstacle to Bertram's return. It is to be noted, too, that in thus renouncing him she refers to him in his own patronymic right, as Rossillion. It is a turnabout for the determined young woman who has outfaced a king and a court to gain her end, and gained it. But what the accents of the speech tell us is that this self-abrogation, which springs no doubt from the masochism of infantile taboo, has undergone a transformation. Her guilt here is reality-tested, objective, since she really is the cause of Bertram's escape into soldiering. The tenderly maternal solicitude that we hear in this speech is a transference wonderfully, and movingly, caught. Helena has broken the spell of the father in this fantasy of herself as a mothering, protective figure to the man she desires.

It is for this reason, I suggest, that there is no page disguise in *All's Well.* Helena's problem has not been the sorting out, balancing and harmonizing of masculine and feminine components in her own personality as it was for her hermaphrodite sisters of the earlier comedies. They had to reconcile themselves to a woman's role without loss, if possible, of the adventurous, maverick male attributes they also possessed, and cherished. She has had to free her sexuality from the archaic bond of infancy, to undertake a pilgrimage into mature sexuality. It is beautifully in keeping with this trajectory of 'the other plot' that we are following that disguise as a girl called Diana, women's camaraderie, and the bed-trick mark her achievement of the passage from virgin chastity to marital sexuality. The bed-trick represents enabling fantasy for both partners. For Helena it offers camouflage—anonymity, invisibility—under cover of which she can transcend the inhibitions of a threatening sexuality. For men, conversely, bed-trick fantasies represent fears of being tricked in bed. But for Bertram the bed-trick is his sexual conquest of the woman he believes to be Diana and so fulfils an analogous liberation. Helena is dead. We do not know the nature of the change that came over Bertram when he received the news of Helena's death, but 'on the reading it he chang'd almost into another man' (IV.iii.3-4). Already in his wooing of Diana, he was liberated enough to be able to contemplate, and to exorcise by invoking, a primal scene: 'now you should be as your mother was', he says, 'When your sweet self was got' (IV.ii.9-10). Now, in bed with a light o'love—Fontybell!—and therefore unhampered by any honourable intentions whatsoever, 'he fleshes his will' (IV.iii.15), confirming his potency. Thus Bertram outgrows Parolles. Or rather, he is in a position to outgrow Parolles. His repudiation of his erstwhile 'sweetheart', however, is still to be brought about.

. . . . .

Parolles, often seen as a quasi-vice figure in a morality play contest with virtuous Helena, and about whom Wheeler, oddly, has very little to say, is perhaps the most brilliant dramatic invention in *All's Well.* Bertram's virtual sibling, brother-at-arms, alter ego, he is our essential vehicle for an understanding of Bertram's rake's progress as an authentic reflection of masculine adolescence. Perhaps too much so for the comfort of spectators, male and female, who cannot free themselves from masculine idealizations of romantic protagonists.[7] But let us examine the exposure of the inimitable Parolles.

The exposure of Parolles in Act IV marks, together with the bed-trick, the remedial phase of the Shakespearean comic plot. Characteristically, folly, become hyperbolically excessive, extrudes itself, exposes itself, or is exposed, exhausts and so eliminates itself.[8] The lords have a double remedial project in hand in the gulling scene. Parolles, 'most notable coward, an infinite and endless liar, an hourly promise-breaker' (III.vi.9-10), is to be openly and palpably disgraced, but Bertram too is due for chastisement for the brazen callousness with which he has received the news of Helena's death and for his seduction of 'a young gentlewoman . . . of a most chaste renown' (IV.iii.13-14). The French lords will 'gladly have him see his company anatomiz'd, that he might take a measure of his own judgments wherein so curiously he had set this counterfeit', and they economically set their trap so that each will be 'the whip of the other' (IV.iii.30-5). The first stage of the trap exposes Parolles, in sham pursuit of his lost drum, as the fraud and coxcomb, the 'counterfeit module' (IV.iii.96) and craven informer that he is. The second stage turns the tables upon the now indignant, and betrayed, Bertram. The latter appears, in extremely high spirits after his rendezvous with Diana, and that he deserves what he gets is underlined by his airy account of the 'sixteen businesses' he has dispatched (IV.iii.82-9) since the news of Helena's death.

Parolles, having surrendered unconditionally at the first syllable of the Lords' 'terrible language', is now beyond shame—'If ye pinch me like a pasty' (IV.iii.119-20), he says, he can betray no more military intelligence than he possesses, which, when it comes to a run-down on the French commanders, he is determined to embellish with details that will, he is confident, endear him to his interlocutors. Thus it comes about that the trickster Lords, including Bertram—'a foolish idle boy, but for all that very ruttish' (207)—hear no good of themselves. The blindfold removed, face to face with the objects of his 'pestiferous' slanders, Parolles' exposure is complete.

The 'cure' proves wonderfully effective; more so than Malvolio's even, perhaps because Parolles has had a measure of self-knowledge all along concerning at least his 'foolhardy tongue': 'Tongue, I must put you into a butter-woman's mouth, and buy myself another of Bajazeth's mule if you prattle me into these perils' (IV.i.41-3). But he goes on paroling himself into perils, and that it is by the Lords' gobbledegook—'choughs' language' (IV.i.19)—that a mean-spirited braggart is undone is no more than poetic justice. Or homeopathy. Self-knowledge, self-acceptance can hardly go further than that of Parolles, shamed beyond words, disgraced, despised, but alive:

> Yet am I thankful. If my heart were great
> 'Twould burst at this. Captain I'll be no more,
> But I will eat and drink and sleep as soft
> As captain shall. Simply the thing I am
> Shall make me live. . . .
> Rust, sword; cool, blushes; and Parolles live
> Safest in shame. . . .
> There's place and means for every man alive.
>
> (IV.iii.319-28)

But what of Bertram *vis-a-vis* his ex-alter ego? He repudiates him, of course. He is now, 'A pox upon him! . . . a cat' (IV.iii.254-5) whom he detests. But does he see anything of himself in this unmasking? 'What a past-saving slave is this!' 'Damnable both-sides rogue!' (IV.iii.135, 214), he says, failing to recall that the only after-thought he had about Diana was a fear of ever hearing of her again. We might adapt the courtier's rhetorical question regarding Parolles: 'Is it possible he should know what he is, and be that he is?' (IV.i.44-5). Is it possible that Bertram knows what Parolles is, and be as *he* is?

Bertram's own exposure, indeed, is still to come. At present he still 'thinks himself made' (IV.iii.16-17) by his battle honours and bed victories. If the gulling of Parolles dramatizes the demise in Bertram of Parolles the effeminate tongue-man, Parolles the feather-man remains to be demolished. Parolles himself, though he smells, is still very much alive—on handouts from the contemptuous Lafew. He must still run the gauntlet of Lavatch's olfactory insults, just as Bertram will run the gauntlet of the women's unmasking. The foppish kinship between them is neatly brought out by Bertram's affectation of a velvet patch (we have not heard that he was wounded) upon which Lavatch lavishes his scurrilous witticisms.

The final scene has the curious effect of a replay, only this time with the young women firmly in charge of the act. The elders are once more engaged in match-making, Lafew's daughter and Bertram this time, an opportune circumstance Bertram seizes with alacrity. Once more paternal benevolence turns into ferocity when Diana's possession of Helena's ring, given her, we recall, by the King as a pledge of his gratitude, makes the King suspect foul play, even murder, on Bertram's part.

And Bertram, trapped between rings, the inherited, patrilinear ring that he gave, the virginal, betrothal ring that he took? Yes, he lies, and wriggles and prevaricates. His snobbery is distasteful; chivalry was never his strong point. Like Parolles, in his recognition scene, he is disgraced, left with no face to save, his 'champion Honour' exposed for the broken reed it is.

But what, after all, do his critics expect? He is trapped, as he was at the beginning; he has a face, a life, to try to save.

He too is restored by Helena, who, like Mariana in *Measure for Measure,* wants no other, nor no better, man. Her 'O my good lord, when I was like this maid / I found you wondrous kind' (V.iii.303-4)[9] is, for his wounded ego, the one most restorative thing she could say. The bed-trick, it turns out, served his fantasy of virile masculinity, and trumped it. For he finds in the woman he seduced, the woman he fled—a nurturing, saving presence, a sexually compatible bride and the mother of his child. He is still bewildered when he says to the King, 'If she, my liege, can make me know this clearly / I'll love her dearly, ever, ever dearly' (V.iii.309-10). But I myself do not find his 'Both, both. O pardon!' (V.iii.302) necessarily perfunctory. Certainly an actor need not make it so.

Are they a mismatch? More, or less, than anyone else in life or in literature?

Is *All's Well* a 'problem' play, and as such deserving of relegation to second-class status? It has been my claim that no such special category is required for the elucidation of *All's Well.* It exhibits a firm structural family resemblance to the earlier maturation comedies. If it anticipates in certain aspects a late romance like *Cymbeline,* it is no more problematic for that reason than any other play in the Shakespearean opus (or any other), each play being manifestly transitional between its precursors and its successors.

Certainly the vicissitudes of motive and meaning caught and displayed in the web of its text engage our closest attention. If we allow its complexities, its psychological depth and finesse, their due, we might well admit it once more into the canon of Shakespeare's most admired plays. Where, to adapt once more Parolles' famous self-summation: simply the thing it is shall make it live.

The King, by the way, is still, at the end of *All's Well,* indefatigably in search of a marriage partner—this time for Diana Capilet.

Notes

1. See W. W. Lawrence, *Shakespeare's Problem Comedies.*
2. See e.g. Richard A. Levin, '*All's Well* and All Seems Well', *Shakespeare Studies,* 13 (1980), 131-42.
3. Richard Wheeler, p. 75, quotes Eric Partridge, *Shakespeare's Bawdy* (New York, 1955) on the sexual suggestiveness of 'stone', 'fire', 'motion', 'touch', '[a]raise', and 'pen'.
4. Otto Rank noted the Oedipal motif in the very first lines of the play as early as 1912, and found 'the tabooed relationship of mother and son underlying a good deal of the play'. See Norman Holland, 154. Literary critics, on the other hand, have made surprisingly little of suggested unconscious motivations. Significantly, however, Bernard Shaw, in whose 'deeper affections' the play was 'rooted', found the Countess 'the most beautiful old woman's part ever written': *Shaw on Shakespeare,* ed. Edwin Wilson (London, 1961), p. 10.
5. G. K. Hunter provides an account of the textual problem in his commentary on the lines in the New Arden edition.
6. Cf. Helena's 'riddle' in I.iii.212: 'But riddle-like lives sweetly where she dies', in which the wit masks a wish by way of the Elizabethan *double entendre* in 'dies'. Phyllis Gorfain, 'Puzzle and artifice: the riddle as metapoetry in *Pericles*', *Shakespeare Survey,* 29 (1976), makes the interesting suggestion that the paradoxes and contradictions out of which riddles are contrived constitute a 'schema of marriage'—children being born of male and female, and mediating between past and future. See also Freud's account of the *aliquis* 'riddle' in *The Psychopathology of Everyday Life* (*PFL* 5, 46-9).
7. G. K. Hunter admits Parolles' stage success as a humour character but finds no way to 'fit him into this play', or 'to balance him against the different kind of reality' of Helena (xlviii). But see Robert Rogers, *A Psychoanalytic Study of the Double in Literature,* ch. 8 and passim, for a very useful account of character 'doubling', especially the latent, 'secret sharer' kind, as 'a fundamental mechanism' for the representation of psychic conflict.
8. I have attempted to develop a theory of exorcist Shakespearean comic form in *Comic Transformations in Shakespeare* (London, 1980).
9. 'Sexually responsive' was one of the many nuances of the word in Elizabethan English, which included the archaic 'natural' and the modern 'well-intentioned' or 'good-natured'.

References

Brooks, Peter, 'Repetition, repression and return: *Great Expectations* and the study of plot', *NLH* (1980).

Frye, Northrop, *Anatomy of Criticism* (Princeton, NJ: Princeton University Press, 1957).

Holland, Norman, *Psychoanalysis and Shakespeare* (New York: Farrar, Straus, 1979).

Lawrence, W. W., *Shakespeare's Problem Comedies* (New York: Macmillan, 1931).

Mansfield, Katherine, *Journal,* ed. John Middleton Murry (London: Constable, 1927; repr. 1954).

Nicoll, Allardyce, *Shakespeare* (London, 1952).

Raysor, T. M., ed., *Coleridge's Shakespeare Criticism* (London: Dent, 1960).

Rogers, Robert, *A Psychoanalytic Study of the Double in Literature* (Detroit: Wayne State University Press, 1970).

Ure, Peter, *Shakespeare: The Problem Plays* (London: Longman, 1961).

Wheeler, Richard P., *Shakespeare's Development and the Problem Comedies* (Berkeley and Los Angeles: University of California Press, 1981).

CHARACTER STUDIES

Anthony Brennan (essay date 1980)

SOURCE: "Helena versus Time's Winged Chariot in *All's Well That Ends Well,*" in *Midwest Quarterly,* Vol. 21, No. 4, Summer, 1980, pp. 391-411.

[*In the following essay, Brennan discusses Helena in relation to the notion of time in* All's Well That Ends Well, *noting that she alone of the young people in the play has a strong connection with the older generation and that she actively struggles against the constraints of time to achieve her goals.*]

Time hath, my lord, a wallet at his back,
Wherein he puts alms for oblivion,
A great-sized monster of ingratitudes.
Those scraps are good deeds past, which are devoured
As fast as they are made, forgot as soon
As done. Perseverance, dear my lord,
Keeps honor bright; to have done, is to hang
Quite out of fashion, like a rusty mail
In monumental mock'ry.

(III, iii, 145-153)

These opening lines of Ulysses' great speech in *Troilus and Cressida* are the locus classicus of Shakespeare's constant preoccupation with the nature of time. The politician endeavours to arouse the lethargic Achilles by characterizing Time as an insatiable cannibal looming over us who can only be appeased by fresh deeds, fresh meat from the battlefield outside the Trojan walls. This image of Time as an implacable tyrant is presented with endlessly varied ingenuity by Renaissance writers. Of all the extraordinary changes that took place in this period the gradual emergence of a new attitude to time is one that has had far reaching consequences for subsequent history. Throughout the entire medieval period two concepts of time were in conflict—the cyclic and the linear. Because of the powerful influence of astronomy and astrology scientists and scholars for a long while emphasized the cyclic concept. The linear concept, which was ultimately to become triumphant, was promoted by the mercantile class and the development of a money economy. When power was concentrated in ownership of land the concept of time was associated with the unchanging cycle of the soil, a natural, recurring, beneficent rhythm, in which time was plentiful. The circulation of money led to the unlocking of that stable, even static way of life, led to mobility of goods, of people, of careers and reputation. Hence the difference in views of Falstaff and Hotspur on the subject of honour, Cassio's agony over his lost reputation, the precipitous crash of Othello whose 'occupation's gone.' Men pursue reputation but know it is 'a bubble.' It was in the fifteenth century that public clocks in Italian cities for the first time struck all twenty-four hours of the day. Just before Shakespeare came to London the attempt to fix time much more precisely was made with the introduction of the Gregorian calendar in March of 1582. And at the time when Shakespeare came to dominate the London stage, Johannes Kepler, formulating his three laws which changed man's world-view for ever, used a new concept of time as the fundamental variable. In the words of Ernst Cassirer:

> . . . the planets were dethroned as the ancient gods of time and fate, and the general view of time and of the temporal process was transferred from the image-world of the mythical-religious imagination to the *exact* conceptual world of scientific cognition.
>
> (p. 140)

The tempo of life was increasing, and time was considered to be something valuable that was slipping away continually. The singular concept that has such devastating effect in our technological society—namely that 'time is money' and must be used economically—emerged in Shakespeare's lifetime.

Erwin Panofsky has pointed out that in classical art time is represented as fleeting opportunity (Kairos) or as creative eternity (Aion) but in the Renaissance time is a destroyer, equipped with an hour-glass and a scythe. Panofsky argues that no period has been so obsessed with the horror and sublimity of time as the baroque, "the period in which man found himself confronted with the infinite as a quality of the universe instead of as a prerogative of God" (p. 92). The evidence of this uneasiness is found throughout Shakespeare's work. In stanza 133 of *The Rape of Lucrece* we are given an image of an assassin:

> Mis-shapen Time, copesmate of ugly Night,
> Swift subtle post, carrier of grisly care,
> Eater of youth, false slave to false delight,
> Base watch of woes, sin's pack-horse, virtue's snare,
> Thou nursest all and murder'st all that are:

Many characters in his plays lament their abuse of time or the pressure it puts on them. Anticipating Rilke's famous image we begin to get the impression that time is a bank deposit that must be withdrawn and wisely invested, otherwise we are subjected to cruel mockery—a position Richard II finds himself in when mewed up in Pomfret Castle:

> I wasted time, and now doth time waste me;
> For now hath time made me his numb'ring clock:
> My thoughts are minutes; and with sighs they jar
> Their watches on unto mine eyes, the outward watch,
> Whereto my finger, like a dial's point,
> Is pointing still, in cleansing them from tears.
> Now, sir, the sound that tells what hour it is
> Are clamorous groans, which strike upon my heart
> Which is the bell. So sighs and tears and groans
> Show minutes, times and hours.
>
> (V, v, 49-58)

There is a whiff of Samuel Beckett in this paralysis in face of the gorgon Time. But in solving the *angst* of 'la condition humaine' Shakespeare does not drift, as so many modern writers seem to do, towards catatonia. He has specific ideas on how to confront the assassin Time, and I want to look at those ideas in *All's Well That Ends Well.*

Mircea Eliade in *Myth and Reality* points out that "To cure the work of Time it is necessary to 'go back' and find the 'beginning of the world'" (p. 88). He points out in many of his books the strategies adopted by primitive societies to achieve cycles of eternal renewal. To conquer time you have to repeal it or reverse it—go back to the roots of your society. By the Renaissance, formally organized ritual methods of renewal were disappearing. In *All's Well That Ends Well,* we have the sense of a world of solid, firmly rooted values in decay, or being eclipsed by the newer world of pragmatic, political action willing to pay only lip-service to the old ideals. The new generation, eager to bustle in the world, cares little for a rooted tradition. It will snatch up any branches that are to hand and stick them in the ground. That the leaves on the branches may wither, that the garden will be laid waste is of less moment than the advantage they might gain in the immediate present. In pursuing the bubble reputation, they cannot afford true honour and honesty, only a semblance of it. There is no time for concern with how they might appear in their own eyes or in God's. But instead of conquering time, they become ever more slaves to it. Our hope in Shakespeare's comedies usually resides in the ability of the younger generation to grasp and reaffirm enduring values.

Helena is the only member of the younger generation who has strong, continuing links with the older generation. She has no difficulty getting along with the king, the Countess, or Lafew. As child of Gerard de Narbon, she is inheritor of ancient skills. The king, dying of a fistula, has respect for the old values, and yet, in the decline of his body, we see the decline of his society. His doctors have no skill, and he has no faith in them. Critics have often commented on the decayed nature of this French court, the shallow, young courtiers, the brooding atmosphere of death. There is an echo here of John of Gaunt on his deathbed facing Richard II and his court of rash, bavin wits, the world of Duncan being replaced by that of Macbeth, or Antony by Octavius, or old Hamlet's heroic times by Claudius' pragmatism. The age of heroes, of the Count Rousillon and Gerard de Narbon, may seem as irrecoverable as that of the Black Prince, but in comedy there is room for one green shoot to survive the new wintry world of shifting values.

The lines with which the Countess opens the play: "In delivering my son from me I bury a second husband" (I, i, 1-2) underlines a contrast that the play explores in detail. Bertram may be called a second husband, but he is not yet worthy to step into the shoes of the dead Count, who embodied the true, courteous, aristocratic ideal. In those past times miracles were almost possible, as she indicates in commenting on Gerard de Narbon's skill which "almost as great as his honesty; had it stretched so far, would have made nature immortal, and death should have play for lack of work" (I, i, 16-20). The parallelism of the two mighty ancestors of Bertram and Helena is important, for he betrays the memory of his father, while she inherits and practices Gerard's marvellous skills. That past age, however, was not inhabited by gods, as Lafew points out in his comment on Gerard: "He was skillful enough to have lived still, if knowledge could be set up against mortality" (I, i, 26-28). Yet we retain the impression that, though mortality could not be denied, the older world was not one in which Time was so easily triumphant. The king indicates to Bertram that the old Count was not one to alter his principles to suit the times but the embodiment of more enduring values:

> He did look far
> Into the service of the time, and was
> Discipled of the bravest. He lasted long,
> But on us both did haggish age steal on
> And wore us out of act. It much repairs me
> To talk of your good father; in his youth
> He had the wit which I can well observe
> To-day in our young lords; but they may jest
> Till their own scorn return to them unnoted
> Ere they can hide their levity in honor.
> So like a courtier, contempt nor bitterness
> Were in his pride or sharpness. If they were,
> His equal had awaked them, and his honor,
> Clock to itself, knew the true minute when
> Exception bid him speak, and at this time
> His tongue obeyed his hand.
>
> (I, ii, 26-41)

That wonderful final image indicates the defining quality of the lost golden age. The Count was like a self-regulating clock in that he responded only to his own interior standards of honour. The king goes on to say that the Count was able to show courtesy to those of humbler birth because of his security in his own honour and worth. Bertram, lacking any such rooted principles will respond with snobbery, and not with courtesy, to Helena.

We are not, of course, to assume that Shakespeare is totally in sympathy with this backward-looking lament, that the king's evaluation of the present decay is totally accurate. The king is a sick man, and his morbid distaste for the present is excessive. He is submitting to the power of death before he needs to do so. The action does indicate that things are pretty far gone at the French court, but the question Shakespeare attends to is the one he confronted all of his creative life—are they gone beyond redemption? In play after play he demonstrates that mere doting on that lost aristocratic world makes men vulnerable to the worst excesses of the new world that was so swiftly replacing it. To stem the tide and find a middle way before all is lost Shakespeare chooses Helena, who is not a born aristocrat, but who is, like so many other redeemers in Shakespeare, noble in spirit.

The new world she has to cope with is characterized most clearly by Lafew:

> They say miracles are past, and we have our philosophical persons, to make modern and familiar things supernatural and causeless. Hence it is that we make trifles of terrors, ensconcing ourselves into seeming knowledge when we should submit ourselves to an unknown fear.
>
> (II, iii, 1-6)

This scientific world resistant to mystery helps to make men vulnerable to time. If the world is a mechanism in which everything can be explained, the way is open for opportunists who understand the mechanism to work their way to the top. Such men act in feverish haste because the time at their disposal is limited. As Lafew asserts, this is a world of "Uncertain life and sure death" (II, iii, 23). And yet Lafew is, in fact, celebrating the miraculous recovery of the king by Helena's agency—an event which, in his view, makes scientific, mechanistic philosophies bankrupt. The king had had so little faith that he had not wanted to submit to the medicine, even though Lafew had claimed that it would bring King Pepin and Charlemain back from the dead—reminding us, perhaps, of the times when the raising of Lazarus was possible. The king asserted that nothing could "ransom nature / From her inaidable estate" (II, i, 118-119). Helena's cure is miraculous not merely because of the efficacy of her father's skill, not because it cures an illness, but because it recovers in the king a youthful vigour. In this reversal of time it seems, for a while, as if the irrevocable process of aging can be conquered.

Helena's revival of the king is an example of how faith (faith in her father's skill) can triumph. Her medicine is effective because she enlists God in her cause as the king's other doctors had not done:

Inspired merit so by breath is barred.
It is not so with Him that all things knows
As 'tis with us that square our guess by shows;
But most it is presumption in us, when
The help of heaven we count the act of men.

(II, i, 148-152)

The cure very specifically defeats time—it is accomplished in one day. But more than that, of course, Helena stakes her life on the cure. She asserts her faith by her disdain for death. In wrestling with Time's agent, Death, to release the king from its grasp, she willingly submits herself to its power. Like all of Shakespeare's heroines she asserts, in her aim to win Bertram, the transcendent power of love in her determination to hazard all for it: "If I break time or flinch in property / Of what I spoke, unpitied let me die" (II, i, 187-188). A world hag-ridden by time can be saved by enduring values of faith, hope, love, and the offer of self-sacrifice. We can see here a recovery on an archetypal level of the redemption of an aging Adam by a Christ-like willingness to sacrifice.

It is not the purpose of the play, however, to suggest that society can be saved by reviving old men, refurbishing those besmeared by sluttish Time. However firmly the old in this play may seem to have a grip on enduring values, they falter towards the end. True, their faltering is in the direction of compassion and forgiveness. When they decide to pull Bertram's chestnuts from the fire by marrying him off to Lafew's daughter, we are aware, as they are not, that he is not worthy of such an easy reprieve. Their decision is dotage not wisdom. The king is dangerously unstable, crotchety, all-forgiving, irascible, indulgent by turns. Society needs renewal not merely by miraculous reversals of time but by the infusion of new blood. It is necessary that those captivated by the temporal values of a fashion-conscious world be reclaimed or redeemed. Bertram's ill-angel, Parolles, is fired out, but the process of saving Bertram himself is not easy, and Shakespeare allows it considerable space.

It has often been noted that the career of Bertram bears some relation to the figure of an older morality drama, the prodigal son blundering into error by rejecting a complex of traditional values embodied in the elders of his society. Bertram is a figure who dashes here, there, and everywhere. The patience required in the extended series of inquiries to riddle out the truth about the rings is like that required in breaking a high-strung horse. The king makes a number of comments on how easily startled and frightened he is. Bertram spends most of the play darting away, rearing up against the idea of Helena as a mate, running abroad after glory and a mistress. There are moments, indeed, when he, too, seems to have reversed time by stumbling into Shakespeare's drama out of Peter Shaffer's play, *Equus.* To bring this runaway to a halt is no easy feat. Critics complain about the shallow, ill-defined quality of Bertram. It is that shallowness which is his defining quality. He is poorly developed; there is little stuff to him, for he is one of those young Renaissance bucks who pursue superficiality, mere fashion. One can often measure a man's solidity by the way he is capable of standing against the tide of time. Bertram simply bobs along like a cork with the tide. His snobbery leads him to sacrifice Helena, for he believes she would soil his reputation, and yet he persists in valuing Parolles, whose acquaintance brings him only dishonour, long after everyone else has seen through him.

Parolles figures as the polar opposite of the kind of courage embodied in the old Count Rousillon whom the king quotes:

'Let me not live', quoth he,
'After my flame lacks oil, to be the snuff
Of younger spirits, whose apprehensive senses
All but new things disdain; whose judgements are
Mere fathers of their garments; whose constancies
Expire before their fashions.'

(I, ii, 58-63)

The Count did not wish to live on into a world in which Parolles could offer Bertram advice on how to win friends and influence people:

Use a more spacious ceremony to the noble lords, you have restrained yourself within the list of too cold an adieu. Be more expressive to them; for they wear themselves in the cap of the time; there do muster true gate, eat, speak, and move under the influence of the most received star; and though the devil lead the measure, such are to be followed.

(II, i, 50-56)

All of Parolles' advice indicates that you have to be wide awake to keep up with the mad scramble of changing fashions, you have to know how to hit the market at the right time.

The play is full of vignettes of what happens when mere fashion reigns triumphant. The aging clown, Lavatch, is convinced that he has found a phrase, "O Lord Sir," which will serve every occasion, freeing him from having to accommodate himself to, or even pay attention to, the different situations he finds himself in. He tries it out on the Countess in Act II, Scene ii, but finds that it will not endure all inquiries. She wears out the usefulness of the phrase causing Lavatch to admit, "I see things may serve long, but not serve ever" (II, ii, 53). In commenting on the frivolity of the exchange, the Countess uses a metaphor that could be applied to the various ways in which the characters in the play are married to time: "I play the noble housewife with the time, / To entertain it so merrily with a fool" (II, ii, 54-55).

Time can be a nagging shrew. But one need not simply be a victim of time; there are different ways of using it. One can use it to develop, to grow into full manhood, or one can refuse to grow up. Bertram's resistance to marriage is unnatural. Full maturity in Shakespeare involves sharing one's fate with another. Bertram's resistance in this matter is almost as foolish as that of Katharine the shrew. His closest companion, Parolles, has not used time well. When Parolles mocks Lafew for being old, he gets the tart reply, "I must tell thee, sirrah, I write man, to which title age cannot bring thee" (II, ii, 197-198). When Parolles brings Helena news of Bertram's departure, he phrases it most particularly in terms of his world-view:

> Madam, my lord will go away tonight;
> A very serious business calls on him.
> The great prerogative and rite of love
> Which, as your due, time claims, he does acknowledge;
> But puts it off to a compelled restraint;
> Whose want, and whose delay, is strewed with sweets,
> Which they distil now in the curbed time,
> To make the coming hour o'erflow with joy
> And pleasure drown the brim
>
> (II, iv, 37-45)

Helena may have won the battle against time in curing the king, but time claims back the prize that she won by that act. Bertram itches to be off to submit to fashion in pursuit of battle glory rather than submit to a more enduring relationship figured in love. He is thus little better than Parolles, who seeks to escape the enduring value of honour.

Like Falstaff, Parolles has no concept of eternal values. He pursues short-term gains. His proposal to recover the drum is rooted not in the real world but in the illusory world of play acting. He will be happy enough to gain glory even though it only last a week. The First Lord says, "Certain it is that he will steal himself into a man's favor, and for a week escape a great deal of discoveries; but when you find him out, you have him ever after" (III, vi, 81-85). It will cost him two or three hours' sleep in a field and a few convincing wounds, which by Parolles' business calculations is a reasonable investment of time. This precise calculation of time is important, for it is utterly opposed to the older concept of honour, which a man held not for passing advantage but for an eternal assertion of the worth of his name. Maintaining the honour of a family name is valuable exactly because it is a statement of defiance against time, because no matter how time wears out individual men, honour passes from generation to generation. But Parolles' view is different. Lafew says, "the soul of the man is his clothes" (II, v, 42-43)—all exterior and no essence. Besides being a particularly vivid image of the decay of values, Parolles has an even more important function. He helps us to see that those who surround and torment him are not as noble as they pretend. He may be a slanderer and an inventive liar, but some of the mud that he throws in his blindfolded state sticks. Shakespeare structures this action very carefully by making Bertram the first object of Parolles' attack.

Parolles' protestations that he tried to save the virtuous Diana are certainly lies, but he does see very accurately into Bertram's lascivious nature. Bertram is nettled by the accurate description of him as an irresponsible wastrel. After he has hit this mark, we are liable to suspect that Parolles' comments on Captain Dumain and his brother may not be simple invention. The essence of his criticism is that they are opportunists, liars, frauds. Behind their noble exteriors, they are captives of the tyrant appetite. We may take this seriously or not, but we must remember two things. These are the young noblemen that the king and Lafew lamented were mere shadows of their parents. And the behaviour of the courtiers when Helena made her choice of husband indicated that Bertram was not alone in the shallowness of his values. Certainly they are able to see through Parolles as Bertram could not, but the delight they take in setting up the exposure of the coward has a kind of adolescent nastiness about it that is far from the courtesy of true aristocrats, who would hardly demean themselves by indicating irritation at such scurrilous detraction. So Parolles is merely the most visible evidence of a general decay. And he does, of course, win a measure of forgiveness by being true to his own existential values. He is willing to live in a dungeon, in the stocks, anywhere, so he may live. He will suffer no deep scars of humiliation:

> If my heart were great,
> 'Twould burst at this. Captain I'll be no more,
> But I will eat and drink and sleep as soft
> As captain shall. Simply the thing I am
> Shall make me live.
>
> (IV, iii, 307-311)

Here he speaks the true voice of the new age in which a man carries none of the excess baggage of idealism and traditional values. Life is a day to day affair in which the tyrant, Time, makes everything but mere survival irrelevant. Shakespeare does not submit to such a view, but by allowing Parolles, like Pistol before him, to declare his philosophy unashamedly, he acknowledges that such a strategy of life is becoming increasingly widespread. The fact that it is Lafew who intends to help him is significant. To Parolles he says, "though you are a fool and knave, you shall eat" (V, ii, 51). He intends, perhaps, to undertake his reform, but his capacity to forgive is a touch of the older, true, aristocratic courtesy.

The basest view of the relations between men and women is voiced by Parolles early in the play when he debates the subject of virginity with Helena. That Helena is willing to match wits with Parolles disturbs all those critics who adopt Shakespeare's heroines as their daughters and wish to bring them up amid the proprieties of a nice, middle-class home. The scene surely is meant to signal to us resilient and urbane qualities in the girl that will be amply demonstrated by her later actions. The nub of the argument is a juxtaposition of two attitudes to time. There is, after all, a great deal of poetry in this period which offers advice to young virgins on how to make much of time and how coy mistresses are to be winkled out of their infuriating shyness. The argument always has to do with a view of life as a process of wearing out. You can defeat time only by accommodating yourself to the fact that it will triumph eventually. Women are like baked goods which soon go stale, or like fashionable garments soon out of style. Because flesh ages, its appeal is merely transient. Wisely used, it can keep the world well supplied with virgins for which there is always a plentiful demand:

> Keep it not; you cannot choose but lose by't. Out with't! within ten years it will make itself ten, which is a goodly increase, and the principal itself not much the worse.
>
> (I, i, 141-144)

There are no absolute values. In this world-view, everything—love, honour, loyalty, faith—is a commodity. "'Tis a commodity will lose the gloss with lying: the longer kept, the less worth. Off with't while 'tis vendible; answer the time of request" (I, i, 148-50). This is how the world cuts itself off from transcendent values. Man has only a limited time to enjoy the fruits of this world because his enjoyment comes through appetite, through the senses, and the senses decay or wear out, so he has even less time than he thinks he has. So a woman has no time for nice considerations; she must jump into the market and sell herself right away. Parolles puts his point of view plainly enough towards the end of the scene: "When thou hast leisure, say thy prayers; when thou hast none, remember thy friends" (I, i, 205-206).

Though Helena does not share Parolles' view that prayers are useful only to fill an idle hour, she does not intend to rely simply on prayers, as she points out immediately:

> Our remedies oft in ourselves do lie,
> Which we ascribe to heaven. The fated sky
> Gives us free scope; only doth backward pull
> Our slow designs when we ourselves are dull.
>
> (I, i, 208-211)

Helena is an active agent, she will not be worn out by time. She aspires to one above her and yet uses the example of nature as her warrant. Critics have often found her too active in her own cause. Alarmed by what they seem to regard as a 'pushy' woman, they forget that that is a quality which defines so many of Shakespeare's heroines. Somebody has to push things in the right direction.

But we must not forget the crucial irony at the end of the play that relates back to this conversation with Parolles. Bertram, having refused to consummate his marriage, makes the loss of her virginity and a subsequent pregnancy a condition of his submission to the marriage he denies. Here we are in an upside down world—the woman who has chastely preserved her virginity for her husband cannot get rid of it. She did not offer it on the open market as Parolles counselled, but she cannot even make a lawful investment of it. Bertram, though married, is still free to range the market for maidenheads. The bed-trick that Helena plays on Bertram is appropriate payment for the unnaturalness of his behaviour. What he takes to be the sweets of an illicit union is lawful after all. Even as he supposed himself to be spreading his seed casually, in line with his submission to the urgency of the time, he was sealing himself into an eternal bargain—not a soldier's indulgence, but a husband's duty. That all this is validated with rings that are heirlooms passed down from one generation to another underlines the fact that Bertram, whether he knew it or not, was entering an enduring relation sealed by tradition and ending his submission to a life of ephemeral fashion.

When Bertram undertakes the assault of Diana, their debate echoes that earlier one between Helena and Parolles. Again we are focussed on that question of honour as it relates to time. Much of the behaviour involved in the courtly love code has to do with posing, a narcissistic self-regard, a pretence of eternal commitment to love as a way of gaining temporal advantage. Bertram, a married man, swears eternal faith in his adulterous designs, but Diana knows that he aims at only one night's pleasure. She asks for a marriage vow before God, the action of giving oneself 'as long as ye both shall live,' a bond which Shakespeare always asserts in face of the opportunism inherent in the courtly love code. Bertram's response is little better than the urgency of a little boy who wants to get to the bathroom: "Stand no more off, / But give thyself unto my sick desires" (IV, ii, 34-35). When asked for his ring as surety he offers to lend it, which indicates something less than long-term commitment. She can borrow his ring if he can borrow her body. Diana points out that she cannot lend since yielding up chastity is a permanent rather than temporary matter. Her chastity has to do with the honour of her family name, it is a jewel bequeathed down from many ancestors and so transcends time. Thus, Bertram is forced to yield up the ring which will ensnare him.

The definitive revelation of Bertram hag-ridden by time as he bustles in this busy world comes in the following scene:

> I have tonight dispatched sixteen businesses, a month's length apiece. By an abstract of success: I have congied with the duke, done my adieu with his nearest, buried a wife, mourned for her, writ to my lady mother I am returning, entertained my convoy, and between these main parcels of dispatch effected many nicer needs. The last was the greatest, but that I have not ended yet.
>
> (IV, iii, 80-86)

The eternal oaths sworn to Diana are reduced to this. She is a parcel, one item he has crossed off his checklist of business pending. The courtly lover commits himself to nothing beyond the satisfaction of his own body, trampling on the values of chastity, trust, honour, love, marriage. Shakespeare places this desecration of all values immediately before Parolles' breaking of trust with his friends. Bertram's outrage at this betrayal is, therefore, an example of the pot calling the kettle black.

At the beginning of this play, young love, as so often in comedy, was dammed up by Bertram's hasty departure. It has to find some subterranean passage, when Helena in the bed-trick pursues her deed of darkness, so that society, bound in submission to time and decay, can emerge into full daylight. In almost all the plays Shakespeare wrote in which women have to work hard to ensure that love finds a way, he gives them an important ally—the wisdom of nature. And this is a different interpretation of the effect of time. The enduring values are rooted in nature, which transcends the temporary aberrations of individual mortals. If we work in harness with what is natural, as Helena does in pursuing the sanctity of the marriage bond, then time becomes our ally, ensuring that by the process of maturing, things will turn out well. To make her point, Helena uses an image that underlines the inevitable cycle of nature:

> the time will bring on summer
> When briars shall have leaves as well as thorns,
> And be as sweet as sharp. We must away;
> Our wagon is prepared, and time revives us.
> All's well that ends well; still the fine's the crown.
> Whate'er the course, the end is the renown.
>
> (IV, iv, 31-36)

However, the difficulty Helena has in catching up with the French court almost brings us to believe that Helena will be defeated by a mere accident of time as, say, Romeo and Juliet were. Time, it seems, will heal all in the wrong way. The marriage arrangement that is fadged up with Lafew's daughter at the end to save Bertram is deliberately disturbing. The older aristocratic figures seem not to have learned from the sacrifice Helena has made. They revert to type and intend to seal up the usual alliance of noble households. Everyone is willing to forget and forgive Bertram's misdeeds. His sins were "done, i' th' blade of youth" (V, iii, 6). "The time is fair again" (V, iii, 36). The king is eager to make the most of time:

> All is whole;
> Not one word more of the consumèd time.
> Let's take the instant by the forward top;
> For we are old, and on our quick'st decrees
> Th' inaudible and noiseless foot of time
> Steals ere we can effect them.
>
> (V, iii, 37-42)

The attitude of not crying over spilt milk is a generous one, perhaps, but the haste is rather unseemly. Yet it is ultimately time itself that accomplishes Helena's purposes. It is their haste to bury the past that reveals the flaw in the design. Lafew asks for a favour to give his daughter, and Bertram yields up the ring that will unravel all his dark dealings in the past. By the time Helena arrives, Bertram's shame is public. But the miracle that Helena achieved in saving the king's life did not ensure a recovered state. The king may be vigourous, but he is prone to error still. He forgives Bertram; then he arrests him; he is sympathetic to Diana, and then he arrests her; he forgets Helena, and then he remembers her. He is a creature of caprice. Helena must effect another miracle. She must come back from the dead to claim her own, her blood must revive this decaying stock. She can do so because she is an amalgam of both the old and the new. She combines her father's almost magical skill and his sense of faith and sacrifice with a pragmatic ability to get what she wants.

In Shakespeare's comedies, the women, who usually have a much clearer perception than men of what is healthy and what is required to refertilize a sterile society, often have to go to extraordinary lengths to get what they want. The more devious are the means they have to use, the sicker is the society that they are trying to circumvent. Viola and Rosalynde have to go in disguise and take to the road to get what they want. But they do not have to get involved in bed-tricks as Isabella and Helena do. But then Illyria and the Forest of Arden are not as corrupt or decayed as Vienna or the French court. Horses for courses. And Helena is not simply a reincarnation of her father with his miraculous skills.

That world is gone. She wants marriage with someone who is above her social station. So that we may have no inclination to accuse her of social-climbing, she is endowed with near miraculous powers and with extraordinary tenacity. Her faith that Bertram, a decayed stem of a noble family, is not beyond redemption is admirable. But noble self-sacrifice, going on pilgrimages or down into death, would avail nothing. She has to bustle in the world. Is she then no better then the other young people in the play? Is she not merely an opportunist, no freer of the temporal, materialist philosophy than they? She is contrasted point by point with the others of her generation. She does not start off in all directions at once as Bertram does, she is not a prey to fashions. She pursues her goal undeviatingly and will never accept surface for essence. We can accept her opportunism because she is the only character in the play who exerts any energy to stop a bad situation from getting worse. At the end of the play we do not have the old world of the king's youth, of Count Rousillon and Gerard de Narbon recovered. But we do not have the shallow world of the feckless young courtiers or the ignoble Parolles triumphant. We have a new world achieved by a pragmatic determination to salvage some of the older values that men had once so easily taken for granted. The lengths to which Helena has to go to achieve a *via media* indicate that the world can not be set to rights by waving a magic wand. Indeed, if it could then when Helena cured the king, Bertram would have perceived her virtue, and the play could have ended right there. It does not help to say that Shakespeare found himself stuck with an awkward source story. He was no great respecter of his sources and altered them freely. What is, perhaps, significant is that at this point in his career he chose source stories, out of which he fashioned *Measure for Measure* and *All's Well that Ends Well,* that involve bed tricks. He did not have to choose those stories at all. He chose them, I suspect, precisely because he is at this point exploring how difficult it is for virtue to triumph in face of corrupt and decaying worlds. There is no twin brother who will show up at the appropriate moment to resolve all difficulties. Bertram, like Angelo and Isabella, is an inflexible figure who is changed not so much by persuasion but by being outflanked. The dark secret that he has buried is brought out publicly to shame him. Like Angelo, he has to recognize the tawdriness of his shameful attempts to deceive. Like Angelo, he tries to lie, bully, and brazen his way out of the situation to the very last minute. It takes considerable time and maneuvering for Helena to triumph, and when she disappears into the darkness, society almost manages to forget her. Quite clearly, all of these strategies are deliberate on Shakespeare's part, and they are designed to indicate how perilously close this world comes to a failure to achieve renewal. It is finally Helena's faith in marriage that provides stability in a shifting world of impermanent values and that allows her to triumph over "Time's winged chariot hurrying near."

Bibliography

Cassirer, Ernst. *The Philosophy of Symbolic Form,* Vol. II. New Haven, 1955.

Eliade, Mircea. *Myth and Reality.* New York, 1968.

Panofsky, *Studies in Iconology.* New York, 1962.

Christopher Roark (essay date 1988)

SOURCE: "Lavatch and Service in *All's Well That Ends Well,*" in *Studies in English Literature, 1500-1900,* Vol. 28, No. 2, Spring, 1988, pp. 241-58.

[*In the following essay, Roark asserts that Lavatch is an indicator of the failure of* All's Well That Ends Well, *noting that "[t]he fool fails to serve in the same way the play fails to serve."*]

> And let those that play your clowns speak no more than is set down for them; for there be of them that will themselves laugh, to set on some quantity of barren spectators to laugh too, though in the mean time some necessary question of the play be then to be consider'd. That's villainous, and shows a most pitiful ambition in the fool that uses it.
>
> (*Hamlet* III.ii.38-45)[1]

Of Shakespeare's wise fools, Lavatch in *All's Well that Ends Well* has been the most expendable in performance, and the most superfluous to critics. Tyrone Guthrie's 1953 production of *All's Well* at Stratford, Ontario, eliminated Lavatch's role.[2] Robert H. Goldsmith remarks, "he is unlike Shakespeare's other fools in that his role bears no significant relationship to the meaning of *All's Well.* He is in no way a measure of the play's meaning, as Touchstone, Feste, and Lear's fool are for their plays."[3] Hamlet's advice to the players tells us that fools like Lavatch are mere comic relief, provoking laughter which distracts the audience's attention from the play's necessary questions.

However, Jay Halio writes, "The clown's speeches pose some interesting problems of interpretation which scholarship has left almost entirely ignored; until they are worked out it seems wise to reserve comment on the true function of this character."[4] G. K. Hunter observes that "the action of the play is seldom allowed to make simple unimpeded effects, but is complicated throughout by a commentary, implicit as well as explicit, of which the principal agent is the clown." He notes that "we approach Helena's request to the Countess that she may pursue Bertram by way of Lavatch's request that he may marry Isbel." Later, the fool speaks of his growing distaste for Isbel at the same time the Countess reads Bertram's letter of rejection for Helena. The fool points to "the distinction between physical nurture and moral discipline so important to the play," as when Lavatch describes himself as "highly fed and lowly taught." Hunter wisely remarks in a footnote that "it is dangerous to assume that Shakespeare's clowning is making only obvious points."[5]

I submit that Lavatch's part, especially when it appears to be most superfluous, can add a crucial dimension to our understanding of *All's Well that Ends Well,* and is useful for focusing the critical debate about the play's unsatisfying resolution and other problems. Lavatch's fooling with the Countess about an answer that "serves all," a scene that occurs during the King's healing, has been particularly singled out as obscure. It has been called "silly stuff" by John Dover Wilson, "almost pointless" by Glynne Wickham, and omitted in modern productions directed by Henson, Benthall, Guthrie, and Willman.[6] Yet in this scene I believe Shakespeare is doing something odd to startle us into paying close attention. The fool goes through an elaborate buildup (twenty-eight lines) to an answer that will serve all men and fit all questions, though this only leads to a disappointing answer—nothing more than an exclamatory remark, "O Lord, Sir!" (II.ii.40). The long prologue and the answer are ridiculous, seem to serve no one, and appear to do nothing more than mock the play's occasional affected courtly talk. It also seems to confirm that Lavatch's part is tenuous.

But, if we begin to consider the scene within the larger dramatic context, it is at this crucial moment that the King's miraculous cure takes place, an answer that does serve all in the sense of serving the entire kingdom. When the King appears in the following scene, after some elaborate introductory remarks by Lafew and Parolles about Helena's miracle cure, it is a moment of festive celebration. Like the ending of many comedies, something heavenly or magical, beyond human comprehension, has restored things to their proper place, after earthly reason has failed.[7] The folktale origins of the play's story have been noted by W. W. Lawrence, with Helena as a virgin whose magical powers show "a heavenly effect in an earthly actor" (II.iii.24).[8] Following closely Lavatch's mock invocation to heaven, "O Lord, sir!" as the answer that serves all things, we have Helena's answer that also invokes providence, now to cure the King and thus serving all men. We expect her actions to lead to a happy marriage, the usual comic conclusion.

But like Lavatch's answer, Helena's cure does not really serve all men, especially Bertram. Her remedy for the King is with the help of heaven, but the cure for her love sickness is in stark contrast to the healing because it lies within her own designs:

Our remedies oft in ourselves do lie
Which we ascribe to heaven. The fated sky
Gives us free scope, only doth backward pull
Our slow designs when we ourselve are dull.

(I.ii.215-18)

Helena's thoughts are like the bastard Edmund's attitude in *King Lear*.[9] After Gloucester has attributed the kingdom's problems to heaven, Edmund also comments on false beliefs in providential control and such explanations for human behavior: "This is an excellent foppery of the world, that when we are sick in fortune—often the surfeits of our own behavior—we make guilty of our disasters the sun, the moon, and the stars, as if we were villains on necessity, fools by heavenly compulsion" (I.ii.121-25). Though it is an unflattering comparison, and though Helena does ally herself with heaven to cure the King, both she and Edmund forego dependence on providence and excel at the same kind of instrumental reasoning, employing various deceptions to rise in society. Both know providence cannot be depended upon and that "Our remedies oft in ourselves do lie." Whether it is for Bertram's own good or not, the ease with which Helena manipulates him to achieve her end is troubling, especially later in the play with the bed trick.[10] In spite of her professed admiration for Bertram, Helena's plot with the rings is based on an acute understanding of his weaknesses, on her knowledge that Bertram cannot control his lust, which she uses against him. I suggest that her manipulative reasoning, especially as it permits her to move up in society, was troubling for Shakespeare. In none of his other comedies do we find a marriage that attempts to cross such wide social boundaries, and those characters who dream of such things, such as Malvolio, are rudely put in their place. In the great tragedies to come, the skill with which Iago, Edmund, and Lady Macbeth are able to exploit the other characters' weaknesses helps to set the tragic wheels in motion. These characters also aspire to a higher social rank.[11]

Helena's manipulation of Bertram (even if it is out of love) so that he will recognize her new status (as the King and Countess do) is a basic problem in *All's Well that Ends Well* that reminds us more of Shakespeare's tragedies than his comedies. However, Shakespeare was aware of this problem and indicates this to us through the fool's discussion with the Countess during the King's healing. At the same moment that Helena is at the height of her heavenly powers, inherited from her father, the fool is also put to the "height" of his "breeding" (II.ii.2), invoking providence, "O Lord, sir!" as the answer that serves all. Helena, following the comic form, has also called upon providence to heal the King so that society can be reconstituted and her marriage follow. But like the fool, and as the action of the play bears out, Helena (and Shakespeare) discover that comic solutions, as Lavatch remarks, "may serve long, but not serve ever" (II.ii.55). The fool's "O Lord, sir!" is a glance at a comic solution by Shakespeare that parodies Helena's solution, points out its limits, and takes place at the same moment she is invoking her solution. The providential solution perhaps serves well for the pastoral ("Tib's rush for Tom's forefinger") and holiday references ("Shrove Tuesday, a morris for May day") that the fool invokes, but then fails to serve when the Countess reminds Lavatch that he is a fool, not a courtier, and that his low station makes him subject to whipping. In an odd way, the fool's difficulty is Helena's: invoking heaven, a comic solution, fails to treat the problem of his low station, and similarly Helena's heavenly healing of the King, also a comic solution, is unable to change her station in Bertram's eyes and lead to marriage.[12]

Like these two scenes, the characters in *All's Well that Ends Well* again and again offer answers that only partially, temporarily, or simply cannot serve the problems they encounter. In Lavatch's "silly stuff" we find a clue to a dominant characteristic of the play: time and again Shakespeare gives us elaborate buildups that often try our patience but lead only to answers that do not serve the problem at hand. Shakespeare takes every opportunity to reiterate this pattern, pointing toward the final episodes, especially Parolles's exposure (his answers only serve to damn him during the elaborate inquisition) and the play's exasperating final scene, where Bertram's "answers" (or rather lies) continually fail, and Helena's plan to reveal the truth seems to bring as many problems as solutions.

In the opening scenes, the characters also dwell on problems that seem unsolvable: first the King's incurable fistula; then the defense of virginity, discussed by Bertram and Helena; and later the servicc of "our young Lords," which the King holds to be inadequate. In all three cases, the answer is in a dead or lost past: Gerard de Narbon could cure the King, remaining a virgin was "formerly better," and the King finds the dead Count Rossillion's service superior to the young lords. With the exception of Helena's cure, often when characters do offer solutions, their answers are contradictory. When the Countess, to assuage Helena's sorrow, calls herself Helena's mother, Helena can only see herself as Bertram's sister, contradicting her wishes for married love (I.iii.158-63); or later in the scene when Helena desires to "Wish chastely and love dearly, that your Dian / Was both herself and love," we again have an answer to her problematic love for Bertram that is contradictory. Lavatch's elaborate answer to Helena's inquiry about the Countess's health, expressing that she is both well and not well, underscores this tendency (II.iv.1-13). His answer simply doesn't serve, and it prepares us for the same mutually exclusive answers that Parolles and Diana give in the play's last scene. Parolles's drum is another example: his elaborate complaints trap him with a problem he cannot solve. This is particularly highlighted when the Lords spy on the parasitical soldier ticking off five answers to his dilemma, all of which the Dumains observe are inadequate (IV.i.46-61).

An earlier example of this dominant pattern is Bertram's response to the marriage. Again, the play presents a curiously prolonged, and seemingly unneeded, buildup to the "answer," Helena's choice of Bertram (II.iii.63-101). Yet thinking that Helena's solution will not serve, but rather corrupt his bloodline forever (II.iii.115-16), he responds to her choice by going to war and serving the Duke of Florence, an answer which serves himself but not the King, his mother, or Helena. For Bertram's difficulties, Shakespeare again offers an instructive parallel with the fool that focuses a necessary question of the play. When we are introduced to Lavatch, Shakespeare presents us with Bertram's problem in reverse. No one is forcing the fool to marry and corrupt his bloodline; rather, the fool petitions the Countess to allow him to marry so that he can "have issue o' my body; for they say barnes are blessings" (I.iii.24-25). The fool is knowingly driven on by the flesh to marry so he may "repent"; Bertram is also driven by the flesh to repent, though unknowingly. The Countess contends that Lavatch should be married before he is wicked, which again recalls Bertram, who is unfaithful after he is married. Lavatch's final reason for marrying strikes us as an absurd answer, and an example of perverted service:

> *Clown*: I am out o'friends, madam; and hope to have friends for my wife's sake.
> *Countess*: Such friends are thine enemies, knave.
> *Clown*: Y'are shallow, madam, in great friends; for the knaves come to do that for me which I am aweary of. He that ears my land spares my team and gives me leave to in the crop; if I be his cuckold, he's my drudge. He that comforts my wife is the cherisher of my flesh and blood; he that cherishes my flesh and blood loves my flesh and blood; he that loves my flesh and blood is my friend. Ergo, he that kisses my wife is my friend.
>
> (I.iii.39-50)

The fool tells us that a man who cuckolds him does him service by cherishing what he cherishes. Even here, the fool's twisted logic relates to Bertram: cuckoldry is not just a problem with an unfaithful wife, but also a problem of awareness: that is, a cuckold is someone whose wife has sex with a man without the husband's awareness, which is what Bertram does when he has intercourse with Helena in Italy. In essence, Bertram cuckolds himself, and if we follow the fool's "logic," in doing so he becomes his own best friend. Yet our usual logic tells us that the man who cuckolds another's wife is the husband's worst enemy. Shakespeare is careful to emphasize at the opening of the last scene that in losing Helena, along with his seeming ill behavior toward Diana which is revealed moments later, Bertram "Did to his Majesty, his mother, and his lady / Offense of mighty note; but to himself / The greatest wrong of all" (V.iii.13-15). The irony of this, as we sense with the fool's twisted logic, is that Bertram has been at once his own worst enemy and his own best friend, both without his awareness. Lavatch's fooling exposes an uncomfortable contradiction about Bertram, emphasizing that the Count's worst desires, by Helena's trick, do him service, just as the fool's worst embarrassment, cuckoldry, by a trick with logic, does Lavatch service.

Excessive lust, cuckoldry, and the need for greater social status (for whatever reason), are all potentially tragic problems that are linked to service in *All's Well*. Lavatch's remarks show that service in the play is somehow perverted, especially as that service is related to marriage. In the festive comedies, Shakespeare controls problems with lust or status by relegating them to minor characters, such as Touchstone or Malvolio. But in *All's Well* these are Helena's and Bertram's difficulties. Our sense of disjunction about the play is summed up by the fool's banter about cuckoldry: we see a tragic problem solved by a trick with logic in a comic or humorous context, after an elaborate buildup, but it is not an answer that we feel satisfied with: it provokes more questions, as most "answers" in the play do, and calls attention to its own inadequacy.

It is with the peculiar behavior of the fool that Shakespeare underscores these difficulties and guides critical assessment of the play. The Countess's response that Lavatch will "ever be a foul-mouth'd and calumnious knave" (I.iii.56) uncomfortably echoes how easy it is to relegate him to a role of mere bawdy mockery or simple parody, as the other characters do. Unlike Touchstone and Feste, whose intelligence is recognized by both Rosalind and Viola respectively, Lavatch's relevance is unnoticed, except for Lafew's brief recognition of his shrewdness (IV.v.63). When Lavatch responds to the Countess's accusation by saying "A prophet I, madam, and I speak the truth the next way" (I.iii.58), he seems to know that his remarks, especially when the fool mentions a man at a women's command, foreshadow Bertram's problems later. Here Lavatch's part hints at the prophetic qualities of fools that become significant in *King Lear.*

The remark which continues Lavatch's discourse on cuckoldry is also prophetic, "If men could be contented to be what they are, there were no fear in marriage" (I.iii.50-51). Even the wit and wisdom of a Rosalind or Portia does not serve entirely to unite the divisive forces in Shakespeare's festive comedies; rather, it is the characters' recognition of their wisdom's limits and their ability to understand their own weaknesses, or simply be what they are and trust in providence, that enables difficulties to be overcome. Helena's intelligence, especially when she interrupts her pilgrimage and devises the bedtrick, allows her to escape confronting what she is, a skillful doctor's daughter whose station is abhorrent to the one she loves. But both Parolles and Bertram must be rudely introduced to themselves. The difference between Parolles's contented capitulation, and Bertram's final skepticism about whether or not he has been foolish (*"If* she, my liege, can make me know this clearly, / I'll love her dearly," V.iii.313-14) will be discussed later.

Clearly, though, Bertram's inability to recognize his shortcomings is an important problem. At the end of the play, we can still ask, as the Lords ask of Parolles, can Bertram know what he is and be what he is? During the reconciliation he stands isolated from the others, united to society by the same trick that has exposed his foolishness. He has been a man unknowingly "at a woman's command." Whether or not any harm's been done, as Lavatch also remarks (I.iii.91), is a troubling question which will be explored properly in the tragedies that follow, where Shakespeare is able to confront questions of self-awareness, sexuality, and human folly that he can only suggest here with Lavatch and others. In any case, with *All's Well that Ends Well,* it is a lack of self-awareness that serves Bertram, and also the play's plot and purpose of reconciliation, just as the soldiers who capture Parolles know how they are to serve that plot though ignorant of what they say to each other: "Not to know what we speak to one another, so we seem to know, is to know straight our purpose" (IV.i.17-19).

Another indication that *All's Well that Ends Well* is an interesting midwife between the festive comedies and the birth of Shakespeare's later tragedies is the fact that virginity, rather than something inviolately preserved until the play's end as in the festive comedies, becomes a means to trap Bertram. Providential aid does not serve to unite the protagonists in marriage, and likewise virginity and virtue in a woman no longer serve to attract a husband. It is because women are no longer virgins in the plays that Shakespeare must confront problems with procreation, heredity, and incest that figure so largely in the tragedies. Just as the comic form no longer serves the questions about self-awareness and service that Shakespeare is now asking, so virginity is "a commodity will lose the gloss with lying; the longer kept, the less worth" (I.i.154-55). Yet where Parolles only sees "rational increase" coming from the loss of virginity, the fool knows better; "The danger is in standing to't; that's the loss of men, though it be the getting of children" (III.i.41-42). Lavatch's previous desire to get married is gone after visiting court; perhaps like Bertram, he begins to sense the problems with procreation and marriage. Isbel and a family, like the play's comic solutions, no longer serve, giving way to lust: "I have no mind to Isbel since I was at court. Our old ling and our Isbels o' th' country are nothing like your old ling and your Isbels o'th'court. The brains of my cupid's knock'd out, and I begin to love, as an old man loves money, with no stomach" (III.ii.12-16). The clown recites this as the Countess reads Bertram's letter announcing his intention never to bed Helena and to roam the world. Lavatch's remarks parody Bertram's inability to recognize any domestic values and remind us that the spoils of war for him include the lusty pursuit of women.

Bertram's letter closes with an ironic twist; he signs off with "My duty to you," though his behavior is in violation of his proper duty to his mother's wishes. The problem at the heart of *All's Well* is that Bertram cannot recognize that his duty or service is only to himself, nor can he recognize the true service of others. Shakespeare carefully illustrates the contradiction between Helena's constant offers of humble service to Bertram (II.iii.103; II.iv.47, 51, 54; II.v.55, 73, 75, 87) and Parolles's declaration that Bertram, a count by inheritance, is nothing more than his equal (II.iii.186-93, 243-45, 260-63). In choosing to follow Parolles to war, rather than accept Helena in marriage, Bertram is choosing the answer that literally does not serve. Parolles is mere language and clothes that pervert true service. Lavatch does not only attack Parolles's apparent (except to Bertram) opportunism and pompousness (as Lafew also does), but also his service to the count: "Marry, you are the wiser man; for many a man's tongue shakes out his master's undoing. To say nothing, to do nothing, to know nothing, and to have nothing, is to be a great part of your title, which is within a very little of nothing" (II.iv.23-27). Parolles's banter is a "nothing" that Bertram, his master, follows. His talk both shakes out Bertram's undoing as it goads him to Italy, and then also undoes his master at the play's end, when Parolles's attempt to say nothing conclusively ties Bertram to his seeming crime against Diana (V.iii.257-64). Here, Parolles has been reduced to a fool-like servant who desires to say, do, and know nothing. The fool's remarks about Parolles, like his remarks about Bertram, precisely describe what is to come. They are underscored when Lavatch says to Parolles "much fool may you find in you, even to the world's pleasure and increase of laughter" (II.iv.36-37).

The fool's, the play's, and the critic's search for answers that serve well leads us also to consider Helena's service. Yet even her behavior, though obviously a better choice than Parolles, is hard to swallow because she so thoroughly traps and exposes Bertram. Helena's love does not allow her to remain simply his servant, but rather to have the "best wishes that can be forg'd in . . . thoughts be servants" to her as she pursues him (I.i.75-76). The service that her calculating thoughts do for Bertram makes us uncomfortable, and even her initial service to the King is tainted; she thinks of helping him only because it may give her an advantage with Bertram (I.iii.229-33). Similarly, Shakespeare is careful to repeat three times that Helena must pay for Diana's services, thus suggesting that no service in the play is without some sort of blatant self-consideration.[13]

Lavatch proclaims himself "A fool, sir, at a woman's service, and a knave at a man's." First, for his own lusty sake, he would "cozen the man of his wife and do his service," and then "give his wife my bauble, sir, to do her service" (IV.v.23, 27-28). All service, the fool tells us, is somehow perverted into self-service. Even the fool's desire to satisfy the cuckolded man's wife results in nothing more than her own self-serving masturbation. Lavatch also suggests the cause of *All's Well*'s corrupt service when he responds to Lafew's admonition that he should continue to serve the devil:

> I am a woodland fellow, sir, that always lov'd a great fire, and the master I speak of ever keeps a good fire. But, sure, he is the prince of the world; let his nobility remain in's court. I am for the house with the narrow gate, which I take to be too little for pomp to enter. Some that humble themselves may, but the many will be too chill and tender, and they'll be for the flow'ry way that leads to the broad gate and the great fire.
>
> (IV.v.47-55)

In contrast to Lavatch's narrow gate suggesting domestic values and service, Bertram remarks to the Countess in his letter as he flees marriage: "If there be breadth enough in the world, I will hold a long distance" (III.ii.23-24). Service in the court world, the fool suggests, is tainted, and often merely self-service.

Parolles is more parasite than braggart soldier, and the play's most obvious example of self-service.[14] And yet his response to the exposure of his false service, linked to the fool's remarks here, is one of the strangest moments in the play. Just as Parolles is the play's most blatant example of self-service, so also is he the only character who is forced to acknowledge his limitations, then be truly humbled and so transformed by them. Parolles's search for any answer to serve the enemy elaborately builds towards his invocation "O Lord, sir" (recalling Lavatch) before he is unmasked. Following this, his answer to "live / Safest in shame: Being fool'd by fool'ry thrive!" (IV.iii.340-41), is borne out when he returns after his exposure, now unrecognizable in the rags of a fool, and ready to enter Lavatch's narrow gate for domestic service. When he encounters Lavatch, the fool's earlier observations about him become true, "'Before a knave th' art a knave'; that's, 'Before me th' art a knave.' This had been truth sir" (II.iv.29-31). Parolles, by becoming a fool, has found Lavatch in himself: "Did you find me in yourself, sir? Or were you taught to find me? The search, sir, was profitable; and much fool may you find in you, even to the world's pleasure and the increase of laughter" (II.iv.34-37). Appropriately, Lavatch's last words bequeath Parolles to Lafew, "I do pity his distress in my similes of comfort, and leave him to your lordship" (V.ii.25-26).

Lafew enlists Parolles into service that recalls Lavatch's woodland fellow:

> *Parolles*: It lies in you, my lord, to bring me in some grace, for you did bring me out.
> *Lafew*: Out upon thee, knave! Dost thou put upon me at once both the office of God and the devil? One brings thee in grace and the other brings thee out . . . though you are a fool and a knave, you shall eat.
>
> (V.ii.47-55)

Like Lavatch, Parolles also serves a devil. Like the fool with the Countess, Parolles has been introduced to his real status; however, when he looks to a "lord" for grace he is saved. Parolles will humble himself and serve Lafew ("I'll make sport with thee") as Lavatch used to serve his old master ("My lord that's gone made himself much sport out of him"). Both characters forego the wide gate of pomp and reputation and enter into honest domestic service. Instead of interrupting Lafew with worthless courtly verbage, Parolles now humbly begs one single word to identify himself. His answer, "Parolles" (V.ii.40), is of course a fool-like pun, a play on a word that means "words," and also a contradiction like so many answers in *All's Well.* But importantly, this is a contradiction that serves: it leads to Parolles's recognition, and his service to Lafew. In an odd way Parolles's former vice of excessive language, exactly that which denoted his perverted service, literally now leads to his honest service, again showing that a character's vices, by a trick with a pun here, aid him, and allow the plot to be worked out. Later, Parolles, like a wise fool, exposes Bertram's folly with Lavatchian contradictory answers and thus does the count service. It is appropriately a humble domestic's service that forces Bertram himself into marriage, a bond that requires humble and honest service to another.

But to assess Parolles's importance, his exposure should be compared with Bertram's, especially as it bears on the play's understanding of service. Unlike Parolles, we do not see Bertram enthusiastically accepting his exposure, and we thus cannot be sure whether he can serve others. Parolles can both know himself and be himself, and in doing so can commit himself to serve others. But for Bertram this is one of the play's most nagging problems, and one that Shakespeare knows he cannot serve well in a comic context.[15] Since Bertram qualifies his last remark, ("*If* she, my liege, can make me know this clearly"), we simply do not know whether he can be himself and know himself, and thus whether he can commit himself to serve Helena and their marriage, or merely fall back on more self-service. Here we are returned to Lavatch's earlier proposition, "If men could be contented to be what they are, there were no fear in marriage" (I.iii.50). Our fear is that Bertram cannot recognize his shortcomings, much less correct them and serve another. Parolles can understand his limitations through a kind of comic self-consciousness; thus for him "there's place and means for everyman alive."[16] For someone to find his place, the play emphasizes, admitting one's limitations is crucial, exactly what Bertram fails to do again and again in the play's last scene, as he continually lies and returns to answers that don't serve. Bertram's one short request for pardon ("Both, both, O, pardon"), as noted, is quickly qualified by the "if" of his last remark.

Bertram's shortcomings, especially his vain lack of self-knowledge, are too much like those found in Shakespearean tragedy to be resolved here by anything more than artificial tricks which do not serve to correct the problem, as Shakespeare evidently knows. By titling the play *All's Well that Ends Well* he ironically underscores exactly what we do not feel at the play's close, for this title is an answer that does not serve, a proverb pasted over our discomfort as the play's resolution is pasted over Bertram's unconfronted problems.[17] Along with Helena's all too calculating entrapment, the play fails to find a satisfying response to Bertram's self-service of his selfish needs. If we accept that Parolles's transformation, and offer of service, is a gesture that counters Bertram's selfishness, then Shakespeare makes this a weak gesture at best.[18] Parolles's transformation prefigures those of Kent and Edgar, both fool figures who serve, but his, too late and too little, lacks the powerful tragic context that makes their sacrifices so unforgettable.[19] In the same sense, Bertram's vain lack of self-knowledge is an extremely muted version of Lear's slender knowledge of himself, as the comic context of *All's Well* continually mediates against the development of these tragic issues.

Lavatch himself, compared with Shakespeare's other wise fools, fails to serve. Although he does focus the play's necessary questions, he is more detached than Touchstone, Feste, and Lear's fool, and it takes a more careful search to understand how he highlights the other characters', and the play's, failure to serve. No other characters in the play have any hint of his curious relation to the larger action, and we wonder just how conscious Lavatch himself is of how his parodies or perverse remarks parallel the behavior of others. Touchstone's parody is more direct and obvious than Lavatch's, and unlike Feste and Touchstone, Lavatch is not in the play's final scene, when Parolles appears to take over his role. Again, as Parolles's final behavior reminds us of Kent and Edgar, in an oddly reductionistic way Parolles's fool anticipates Lear; like him, Parolles is also stripped of his position along with his clothes, and so takes on the missing fool's part.[20] That part means speaking the "truth," as Lavatch himself asserts; he foreshadows events and consistently focuses our attention on the play's problems. And yet, if Lavatch does have a fool's traditionally prophetic powers, it seems out of place in the realistic world of *All's Well.* In addition, with the exception of Lafew, the others cannot pun or play with language like Lavatch; they are little more than straightmen when speaking to the fool, unlike those who banter with Touchstone or Feste. On the whole, the play is barren of engaging battles of wit. The fool fails to serve in the same way the play fails to serve, for the answer that there are no answers that serve, which Lavatch's fooling reveals and the play itself consistently returns to, is not an answer that serves.

Do we then conclude that Shakespeare has failed? In a strict sense, he has with this play. The answer that there is no answer which serves well lies at the heart of our dissatisfaction with *All's Well.* If Shakespeare is claiming "no adequate answer" to the problems he has raised as the law, in the sense of an enabling poetic, of this play, then he is failing at what he has set out to do as a dramatic poet creating comedy, just as if critics claimed the same "no adequate answer." To explain the play as an experiment for what will receive proper attention in the forthcoming tragedies, especially *King Lear,* as I have in part done, is not really to interpret the play, but rather to assuage the failure by pointing to examples or other sets of laws outside of the play itself.[21] This is Hunter's strategy when he looks to the romances at the close of his introduction.[22] As critics, perhaps we can make the play "explainable," but strictly speaking the play lacks if it can only be understood by laws outside of itself or by examples from other plays. As a poem which contains the rules of its own interpretation, as Shakespeare's better plays do, *All's Well that End's Well* fails, and Shakespeare in the process calls attention to that failure, especially with Lavatch.

Given this problem, we must ask why Shakespeare wrote *All's Well.* On the one hand, with the admission that to say so we are not really interpreting the play, we can say that Shakespeare is experimenting; he purposely tries to resolve what are tragic motifs in a comic context, and so works with the problems that he will render with brilliance in his later tragedies. But it is the way he experiments, I think, that we must also try to understand, specifically his service as an artist as he confronts problems that turn out to be unresolvable in a comic context. Sigurd Burckhardt, in a study of Shakespeare's Prince Hal trilogy, argues that Shakespeare discovers "a lethal mixture of two mutually inconsistent and severally inadequate models of succession." Burckhardt makes this helpful comment in an effort to understand Shakespeare's solution:

> Some three centuries before Niels Bohr, Shakespeare discovered the need of complementarity—i.e., of operating with two mutually inconsistent and severally inadequate models because, and as long as, a single, consistent, and adequate model has not been found. Complementarity differs from and is superior to mixing because it remains aware of its "illegitimacy" and *pays the price* for choosing one model over the other. It does not pretend to be a solution, hence it does not close the road of discovery but on the contrary compels us to take the risk of following it. Its passionate demand for order forces us to leave the safe prison of a static, once-for-all world picture, to suffer the grief of imperfection and disorder, and the joy of genuine action and creativity. Complementarity, in short, asserts the value of *human action in time,* which is to say, of history, of drama.[23]

A compelling way, I think, to reconcile the problems of *All's Well* with Shakespeare's awareness of those problems is to say that he understood the illegitimacy of what he was doing and also its consequences, that he knew he was paying a price for choosing the comic model over the tragic for the treatment of Bertram's selfishness and lack of self-awareness, or Helena's self-regarding manipulation of the count. Shakespeare is leaving the safe prison of the comic genre and posing problems that, he discovers, he cannot pretend to solve convincingly with comic solutions, especially providential help. But his passionate demand for a humane solution to human difficulties, to problems of self-awareness, uncontrolled lust, lying, one character's questionable manipulation of another, and social status, all problems that block significant relations between people, required him *first* to try to solve these difficulties in a manner that would not exact the awful human destruction of tragedy. Before he could confront these problems in the most destructive of tragic contexts such as *King Lear,* Shakespeare, I would like to suggest, had to try to solve them in a benevolent comedy.

Shakespeare, I believe, understands his failure in *All's Well,* and carefully expresses this to us with Lavatch. He also underscores this failure in the play's final lines. Like Bertram, Helena, "the shadow of a wife," also begins her final remark with an "if" (V.iii.315). In addition, the King hedges about whether or not the ending is complete, "*if* this suit be won": it is exactly the "oneness" of Helena's and Bertram's marriage that troubles us. The King, like Parolles, is transformed to a humble "beggar" as he subtly thanks the audience for their patience, and asks them to put themselves in the actors' shoes, as the actors put themselves in the audience's place, "ours be your patience then, and yours our parts." While the King may have the audience "express content," one can't help but feel that the audience, like the King, senses the discontent, and has patiently endured the incomplete working out of the play's problems, and that Shakespeare is apologetically asking them to try to see it from the actor's point of view, whose service will "pay / With strife to please you, day exceeding day." The beggar-King's suggestion that the players will "pay" the audience uncomfortably echoes the fact that most of the service in the play is paid for rather than unselfishly given. The conclusion, then, is a tacit admission of *All's Well's* failure to serve the audience.

But service itself is an important idea for the ending of *All's Well.* Though there is no service that redeems the characters' severe problems or Shakespeare's failure to serve as a comic dramatist, Parolles hints that a character can free himself from false courtly artifice and deceit to serve honestly. But again, this does not tell us if Bertram can know himself and truly serve another or if Helena's manipulative intelligence, and the abuse that such control can lead to, will merely keep him "at a woman's command." Whether both can gain a comic understanding of their limits, and achieve an honest self-awareness, or whether their behavior will lead to tragic destruction, is an either-or proposition the play leaves us with, a problem of service and a question of complementarity insofar as the comic marriage and unresolved tragic problems clash. Burckhardt also writes:

> And the metaphor is one of *complementarity,* of either-or. It is neither a mixture nor a synthesis, but a metaphor: that strange entity which demands to be analytically dissolved because it *means* and creatively "made good" because it *is.* It is pregnant, hence promises birth; but the birth is never certain, while labor and pain *are* certain. Is even the father certain? Can we be sure of legitimacy? Will the offspring be the child of passion or of duty, of self-assertive lust or submissive routine? There are no guarantees, only the risk and the will—the need—to order.[24]

It is Bertram's inability to serve, and Helena's questionable methods of service, that lead to the pregnancy, an answer to the play that is literally and dramatically, and thus metaphorically, of questionable legitimacy. It is a clash of elements the play cannot resolve yoked together by pregnancy, by something with the potential to give birth both to good and bad. Shakespeare as dramatist has failed to serve because of this illegitimate answer, but the service itself that the play's creation also represents works metaphorically, a metaphor pregnant with possibilities that will be borne out in his great tragedies. As he wrote *All's Well that Ends Well* the birth of *King Lear* was not certain, but the labor and pain toward the highest achievements of drama, the "strife to please you," would be. The child in Helena now, of whom the father and the legitimacy is uncertain, is the child of both Bertram's lust and Helena's questionable service and duty, but what that child will turn out to be, and how the family and their love grows or is destroyed, is an either-or question the tragedies must answer as Shakespeare moves beyond complementarity to depict the clash of man's inhumanity with his humanity, of his selfish self-service with his service to others. It is a question that Shakespeare will serve with his greatest artistic skill, risking the road of discovery that leads to suffering, grief, and discord (especially as he questions the value of his own role as an artist), but also to the joy of genuine action and creativity.

The metaphor of pregnancy, it seems to me, is how we can understand this problem play: *All's Well that Ends Well* brings together clashing elements which lead to a product of questionable legitimacy. But the play itself is pregnant with questions which will be creatively made good in the great tragedies that follow, especially *King Lear,* where the necessary questions of duty and service, of both his characters and of the dramatist Shakespeare, will be presented along with the worst extremes of human destruction and self-service that poetic drama can portray, in a search for the questions and answers that will serve well. If Bertram's unresolved problem is his inability to recognize his limits, know himself, and serve others, and there is no adequate example in the play to counter his self-service (or something to counter Helena's self-regarding manipulation) then we must look ahead to Shakespeare's understanding of his role as an artist and his service to us in the later tragedies, as he leaves the seeming knowledge of comedy, of a static, once-for-all world picture, and submits himself and his characters to the unknown fear of tragedy. Miracles are past, and things unnatural and causeless must now be confronted head on.

Notes

1. All quotations from Shakespeare's plays are from *The Complete Works of Shakespeare,* ed. David Bevington (Glenview: Scott, Foresman, 1980).

2. Oscar James Campbell, ed. *The Reader's Encyclopedia of Shakespeare* (New York: Crowell, 1966), p. 17.

3. Robert H. Goldsmith, *Wise Fools in Shakespeare* (East Lansing: Michigan State Univ. Press, 1963), p. 60.

4. Jay Halio, "All's Well That Ends Well," *SQ* 15 (Winter 1964):35.

5. G. K. Hunter, introduction and notes to *The Arden Edition of All's Well That Ends Well* (London: Methuen, 1959), pp. xxxiv, xxxv, 47, 50.

6. J. L. Styan, *All's Well that Ends Well: Shakespeare in Performance* (Manchester: Manchester Univ. Press, 1984), p. 55.

7. Shakespeare takes pains to show that Helena's healing is an act of heaven. When she first argues with the King her language becomes religiously infused,

"So holy writ in babes hath judgement shown / When judges have been babes; great floods have flown" (II.i.138-39). She goes on to speak of "miracles" (141); "Him," referring to God (149); "the help of heaven" (152); and "of heaven not me make experiment" (154) to the King. All this stands in stark contrast to how she must win Bertram, "Our remedies oft in ourselves do lie, which we ascribe to heaven" (I.ii.215-16).

8. W. W. Lawrence, *Shakespeare's Problem Comedies* (New York: Ungar, 1960), pp. 35-63.

9. W. L. Godshalk writes that "religious references are replaced by the appeal to nature, an appeal frequently made in the play" in Helena's speech at the end of II.i. He continues, "Nature allows man to bridge the gaps made by Fortune; and, like Edmund in *King Lear,* Helena accepts Nature as her guide." See *All's Well That Ends Well* and the Morality Play," *SQ* 25 (Winter 1974):64.

10. David Scott Kastan writes, "In the problem comedies the contrivance is the character's own and is throughout too self-regarding, too unresponsive to the needs of others." See his fine essay "*All's Well that Ends Well* and the Limits of Comedy," *ELH* 52 (Fall 1985):579.

11. Helena's remark cited in note 7 which links her to Edmund can be compared to Viola's "O time, thou must untangle this, not I; it is too hard a knot for me to untie" (II.ii.40-41). Rosalind and Portia do deceive their husbands, not to win a love they already possess, but rather to expose follies which do not mar the close of their comedies. Helena's social position, and her method for advancing, is part of the larger issue of social mobility that needs further treatment in Shakespeare. However, as Lawrence Stone persuasively argues, we can say that the Elizabethans would have been sensitive to the aristocracy's "crisis" regarding social mobility, its "unprecedented" expansion during Shakespeare's age and the conservative backlash that sought to control it. For a thorough study of this problem, see Lawrence Stone, *The Crisis of the Aristocracy, 1558-1641* (Oxford: Clarendon Press, 1965).

12. Kastan's essay cited in note 10 is also concerned with the limits of comic solutions. However, he writes that the problem is "not Helena's social class or even Bertram's intractable snobbery but an inadequate conception of love—or, put differently, an inadequate conception of comedy, a conception that would exclusively formalize comic action, shaping comic characters and events to our desires" (p. 580).

13. Godshalk notes that "the fact that Helena is conducting a dubiously moral intrigue returns to haunt our excuses" each time Shakespeare reminds us that Helena is paying Diana (p. 65).

14. Hunter, p. xlvii.

15. See Phillip Edwards for an intelligent discussion of Bertram's behavior in *Shakespeare and the Confines of Art* (London: Methuen, 1968), pp. 113-15. Edwards points out that the count's "execrable" behavior is not a matter for critical debate: "The treatment of Parolles shows us a scoundrel changed by shame into a new recognition and a new way of life. Bertram is not so treated. Helena never saves Bertram. He is unredeemable: Shakespeare could not save him. It is not a matter of failing to write the lines that would have changed the soul of the play: it is a matter of not being able to force one's conscience to alter a character whose alteration would be, simply, incredible."

16. Shakespeare's wiser comic characters have an acute sense of their own folly, a comic and unpretentious appraisal of their failings, exactly what Bertram shows no trace of in the last scene especially, but also when the blind-folded Parolles anatomizes the count's bad behavior (IV.iii.216-37). M. C. Bradbrook's analysis, like Edwards's, makes it clear that Shakespeare intends little sympathy for Bertram: "The Elizabethan code of honour supposed a gentleman to be absolutely incapable of a lie. . . . To give the lie was the deadliest of all insults and could not be wiped out except in blood. . . . Alone among Shakespeare's heroes Bertram is guilty of the lie" and by such conduct "forfeits his claims to gentility"; see "Virtue and Nobility in *All's Well that Ends Well,*" *RES* 1.4 (October 1950): 289-301.

17. Ann Barton makes this insightful comment on the proverbial nature of the play's title: "Like the proverbs continually employed in the perverse and contradictory fashion by the bitter fool Lavatch—traditional bits of lore existing uneasily in a world grown too complex for such simplifications—it serves as a gentle reminder that fairy tales, ultimately, are not true." See her introduction in *The Riverside Shakespeare,* ed. G. Blakemore Evans (Boston: Houghton, Mifflin, 1974), pp. 499-503.

18. For an alternative view of Parolles's effect on the last scene, see Gerard J. Gross, "The Conclusion to *All's Well that Ends Well,*" *SEL* 23 (Spring 1983):275-76.

19. See Jonas A. Barish and Marshall Waingrow, "Service in *King Lear,*" *SQ* 9 (1958):347-55.

20. James Calderwood writes that Lear's fool's disappearance "makes foolish sense. When Lear has absorbed the fool's truths and begins to utter them himself, the fool becomes redundant." See "Creative Uncreation in *King Lear,*" *SQ* 28 (1986):10.

21. Sigurd Burckhardt, *Shakespearean Meanings* (Princeton: Princeton Univ. Press, 1968), pp. 296-98.

22. Hunter, p. lv.

23. Burckhardt, p. 183-84.

24. Burckhardt, p. 185.

Susan Snyder (essay date 1988)

SOURCE: "*All's Well That Ends Well* and Shakespeare's Helens: Text and Subtext, Subject and Object," in *English Literary Renaissance*, Vol. 18, No. 1, Winter, 1988, pp. 66-77.

[*In the following essay, Snyder probes the characterization of Helena as a sexually aggressive woman through instances of indirect and suppressed speech in the play.*]

I'm going to move into my speculations from two different directions. One point of departure is a set of gaps, disjunctions, and silences in *All's Well,* places where we lack an expected connection or explanation in the speeches or actions of the main character, Helena. The other is, on the contrary, an unexpected coincidence, a connection between that somewhat mysterious Helena and a character in another play which on the face of it is quite unlike *All's Well.*

Helena's career strangely mixes aggressive initiative and passivity. She begins *All's Well* in a state of social and psychological constriction: a physician's orphaned daughter silently in love with a young nobleman who cares nothing for her and is about to leave Roussillon for the court. Helena can only grieve passively. She is interrupted by Parolles, who engages her in a joking conversation, advancing the standard arguments against women retaining their virginity; and by the end of the scene she is suddenly resolved to go to Paris herself and offer a medicine of her father's to cure the desperate illness of the King. The initiative is a success, and brings the reward she dared to stipulate for her service, a choice of husbands from among the King's wards. But the chosen Bertram refuses to play his part in the fairy-tale match; he rejects her in outrage, and after the King terrorizes him into going through with the marriage, runs away with Parolles to the wars in Italy rather than consummate it. Bundled off to Roussillon at his order, Helena there receives by letter his cruel farewell: he will never accept her as his wife until she can get possession of his ancestral ring and conceive a child by him. He means the setting of impossible tasks as a total dismissal: "in such a 'then' I write a 'never'" (3.2.58).[1] She recapitulates her initial despair, blames herself for exposing him to danger on the battlefield, and vows to get out of the way so that he can come home. But almost immediately we find her as a pilgrim in Florence, where Bertram is, where she meets Diana, the girl whom he is trying to seduce. Helena again takes forceful control of the action, persuading the Widow to agree to the bed-substitution, instructing Diana, pursuing Bertram back to France, seeking an audience with the King, and manipulating the final revelation-scene to expose Bertram, prove her fulfillment of the impossible tasks, and claim her reluctant husband all over again.

The gaps and disjunctions I want to examine are associated with these shifts between assertion and self-abnegation. One of them occurs in the center of that early, apparently extraneous banter with Parolles about virginity. What moves Helena from hopeless assent to fate to the contrary proclamation that "our remedies oft in ourselves do lie, / Which we ascribe to heaven?" (1.1.212-13). Why should some bawdy conversation with a coarse braggart convert her from despairing withdrawal—"the hind that would be mated by the lion / Must die for love" (89-90)—to an energetic plan to follow Bertram to Paris and use this suddenly remembered medical remedy to win favor with the King? The answer is probably a complicated one, but we might look particularly at an odd break in the text at the very center of the conversation. Listening to Parolles' exuberant arguments against virginity, Helena has answered first, "I will stand for't a little, though therefore I die a virgin" (131-32); and after some more, "How might one do . . . to lose it to her own liking?" (147). Parolles argues further:

> Off with't while 'tis vendible; answer the time of request . . . your virginity, your old virginity, is like one of our French wither'd pears: it looks ill, it eats drily; marry, 'tis a wither'd pear. It was formerly better; marry, yet 'tis a wither'd pear. Will you anything with it?

Helena's response is disjointed, tangential:

> Not my virginity yet:[2]
> There shall your master have a thousand loves,
> A mother, and a mistress, and a friend.
> A phoenix, captain, and an enemy,
> A guide, a goddess, and a sovereign,
> A counsellor, a traitress, and a dear
>
> (150-66)

And so on through several more lines of epithets for the beloved lady familiar from the love sonnet tradition. Some textual commentators have denied any break here, reading something like "In *my* virginity, which is far from a withered pear, Bertram will find everything he ever wanted in a mistress."[3] But why should she suddenly reveal her love, kept secret from everybody, to this insensitive blabbermouth? And the epithets of the sonnet-lady tyrannizing over her enslaved lover—captain, enemy, goddess, traitress—are violently at odds with her habitual attitude to Bertram, expressed before and after this speech, which is the self-abasing devotion of one who feels herself inferior. It seems more likely that "there" means the court, where Bertram will find some all-consuming love. But what unenunciated pressure has brought up this powerful new mental vision?

Editors have speculated that the rest of the short line 161 has dropped out here, some reference to the court. Perhaps. The Folio copy for *All's Well* seems to have been especially messy, and recent textual work has uncovered signs of authorial second thoughts.[4] Yet even if we hypothesize a few missing words (Hanmer adds "You're for the court"; Gary Taylor conjectures "yet at the court"), Helena's transition from her maidenly defense against Parolles to imagining love-life at court is still abrupt, and it seems likely that the emotions suppressed here may figure in her larger transition in this scene from quiescent grief to active pursuit.

Textual corruption is not an issue in my second example. At court Helena has a hard time persuading the King, who has lost all hope of being cured. She argues professional skill (her father working through her), and the possibility of a miracle (God working through her). But the King maintains his steady resistance until he asks what she is willing to risk if she fails. He gets a strange reply:

> Tax of impudence,
> A strumpet's boldness, a divulged shame,
> Traduc'd by odious ballads; my maiden's name
> Sear'd otherwise; ne worse of worst, extended
> With vildest torture, let my life be ended.
>
> (2.1.169-73)

As in the Boccaccio story from which Shakespeare drew his plot, she risks death. That is what convinces the King. What he does not respond to, what is not in the source, is the kind of punishment she first feels compelled to propose: versions of public shame for immodesty and sexual boldness. Failure might convict her of professional or religious presumption, but why of being a strumpet? There is something operating here that she leaves unsaid.

In my next example, it is Shakespeare who leaves something unsaid, something very important. We are never told whether Helena deliberately pursues Bertram to Florence in order to fulfill his impossible demands or rather arrives where he is by accident and acts only on fortuitous opportunity. This is a deafening silence, all the more noticeable because the early acts have been so firmly centered in Helena's subjectivity: her soliloquies and her confidings in the sympathetic Countess, her foster-mother, keep us close to her feelings and motives. That centering is reasserted in the latter part of the play, when Helena finds new confidantes in Diana and the Widow. But at the crucial point Shakespeare opens a gap which prevents full understanding.

Helena's soliloquy after she hears of her husband's defection to Italy is all shame and withdrawal:

> And is it I
> That drive thee from the sportive court, where thou
> Wast shot at with fair eyes, to be the mark
> Of smoky muskets? . . .
> Whoever shoots at him, I set him there;
> Whoever charges on his forward breast,
> I am the caitiff that do hold him to 't;
> And though I kill him not, I am the cause
> His death was so effected. . . .
> I will be gone . . .
> Come night, end day.
> For with the dark, poor thief, I'll steal away.
>
> (3.2.105-29)

Bertram's own mother and friends have just condemned his conduct, but Helena locates all the guilt in her own action: pursuit of Bertram is equated with theft and murder. The new "action" she proposes is really a form of self-effacement: she will go away not with any particular destination but just to remove herself as an obstacle. Soon afterward we hear that she does have a destination, one that accords with her feelings of guilt:

> *I am Saint Jaques' pilgrim, thither gone.*
> *Ambitious love hath so in me offended*
> *That barefoot plod I the cold ground upon,*
> *With sainted vow my faults to have amended.*
>
> (3.4. 4-7)

At this point, however, we are not given Helena's direct speech but a letter she has left behind for the Countess; and we are further distanced from her thoughts by the letter's highly wrought sonnet form. As G. K. Hunter remarks, "by its various inversions and alliterations [it] produces an effect more archaic and formal than anything in *The Sonnets* or the early plays."[5] Purpose is conveyed to us without intimacy, at two removes. And in the next scene there is Helena—in Florence. Saint Jaques, later called Saint Jaques le Grand, is Saint James the Great, and Florence is considerably off the road from Roussillon in southern France to his shrine in northwestern Spain. Is the whole pilgrimage scheme simply a pretense, then, to cover her pursuit of Bertram? It is interesting that later one of the French Lords actually uses that word in describing her action.[6] Alas, the apparently pointed term doesn't point clearly in one direction: it could mean "false pretext" all right, but in Shakespeare's English it could equally well mean just "intention," with no deception implied (*OED* 3). In the same ambiguous way, while Helena's route to Santiago may raise suspicions in the audience, no one in Florence finds it odd. In fact, there are several pilgrims bound for the same place lodging there. Why this deliberate mystification, and how are we to fill in the gap it creates?

And now for my second point of departure. This mysterious Helena in *All's Well* is highly unusual among Shakespeare's comic heroines in that she not only loves before she is loved but actively, overtly, chases the man she wants. Even Rosalind and Portia, however spirited and ready to take control, wait to be wooed; in love, theirs are strategies of reception, not initiation. There is really only one other exception, in *A Midsummer Night's Dream*: a young woman who loves without response, who, after beginning in as passive and despairing a mode as the heroine of *All's Well,* turns to active pursuit and continues it even when pained and shamed by the rebukes of the man she pursues. And her name of course is Helena. The repetition of name and situation is striking, especially since as far as we know Shakespeare chose the names in both cases. He seems to have invented the *Midsummer* lovers and their story; and for *All's Well,* he deliberately rejected the name supplied by his source, Giletta, and substituted that of Helena or Helen.

We can't know what private associations the name Helena had for Shakespeare, if any, but the public one is unavoidable: Helen of Troy, the fought-over woman, the archetypal desired object in his culture's myth of origins. Did this legendary Helen influence Shakespeare's naming? It's not clear in *A Midsummer Night's Dream,* although the Helena there is of course Greek. In the play's one allusion to the legend, Theseus' scoff at the lover who "sees Helen's beauty in a brow of Egypt" (5.1.11), Shakespeare could well be glancing at Demetrius' earlier rejection of Helena's fairness for the dark complexion of her rival (Hermia, when out of favor, is called an Ethiop and a tawny Tartar). In *All's Well* it may be significant that, after first introducing his heroine as Helena, Shakespeare settled into a notable preference for the shortened form of her name, the form he always used for the archetypal queen.[7] But the play provides direct evidence for associating the two:

> *Steward*: May it please you, madam, that he bid Helen come to you; of her I am to speak.
> *Countess*: Sirrah, tell my gentlewoman I would speak with her—Helen I mean.
> *Clown: Was this fair face the cause, quoth she,*
> *Why the Grecians sacked Troy?*
>
> (1.3.63-68)

The Countess' "Helen I mean" is doubly superfluous: the Steward has just named Helen, and in any case she has no other attendant gentlewoman to confuse us. The name thus accented highlights the Clown's response, which is to sing a ballad of the Trojan War that had Helen's fair face as its object. This undoubted association may throw retrospective light on Parolles' first greeting to Helena, "Save you, fair queen"—a title she emphatically denies (1.1.104-07). Not only is she far from a queen in her social rank, so much lower than Bertram's, but she is an anti-Helen: not the desired one but the desirer. Shakespeare's own representation of Helen of Troy in *Troilus and Cressida,* a play probably near in time to *All's Well,* only sharpens the ironic contrast. She is argued about and fought over, but seen as an actual character only briefly, as a totally passive object.

I am suggesting, then, that the Helenas of the two comedies are linked by the name chosen for them, a name that ironically contradicts its prototype and thus underlines their peculiar situation as subject, the locus of active desire, rather than the usual "woman's part" as pursued object. Because the implications of this situation are clearer in *Midsummer* than in *All's Well,* for reasons I'll suggest later, I'm going to try the first play as a kind of subtext for the second, using what is manifest there to fill in the silences and suppressions surrounding the second Helena.

Helena in the first scene of *All's Well* goes from the threat of "old virginity" as a withered pear to a sudden sharp anticipation of Bertram in love with a court lady who has all she lacks, to the active quest for Bertram. Helena in the first scene of *Midsummer* is mopingly jealous of her rival, the favored Hermia: "Demetrius loves *your* fair . . . *Your* eyes are lode-stars" (1.1.182-83, emphasis mine). What spurs her to unwonted action is the news that Hermia is running off with Lysander to consummate her love, leaving her behind. Her course illuminates that of the second Helena, impelled by Parolles' reminder of time's passage and the fear of being left to wither, to the sharp realization that Bertram will find fulfilling love elsewhere, and to an answering urgency that propels her to act on her desires.

So Helena in *Midsummer* sets Demetrius in pursuit of the lovers and herself pursues him into the wild forest, beyond the walls of Athens and the accepted cultural constructions the city embodies. When Demetrius denounces her, the deeply rooted code of sexual difference speaks clearly:

> You do impeach your modesty too much
> To leave the city and commit yourself
> Into the hands of one that loves you not,
> To trust the opportunity of night
> And the ill counsel of a desert place
> With the rich worth of your virginity.
>
> (*MND,* 2.1.214-19)

Helena herself feels the deep unease of her reversal of cultural roles—"We should be woo'd, and were not made to woo"—but she persists in the radical venture:

> the story shall be chang'd:
> Apollo flies, and Daphne holds the chase;
> . . . the mild hind
> Makes speed to catch the tiger.
>
> (230-33)

The Helena of *All's Well* also leaves home to venture into alien territory. While she too has called herself a retiring hind, at court she "unnaturally" chases her lion instead of pining quietly away. The exchanges between Demetrius and Helena in *Midsummer* spell out her own unvoiced conflict as the shamed but persistently pursuing Daphne. She knows that healing the King is not her ultimate purpose but a means to achieving her sexual desire: she has already admitted to the Countess that but for loving Bertram she would never have thought of offering her father's medicine to the King.[8] Failure to win his gratitude would fully expose her cultural transgression. What should follow more inevitably than her public branding as an unwomanly woman, a shameless strumpet?

Success is shaming enough. She is embarrassed and self-denigrating when choosing among the King's wards, and almost can't go through with it.

> I am a simple maid, and therein wealthiest
> That I protest I simply am a maid.
> Please it your majesty, I have done already.
> The blushes in my cheeks thus whisper me:
> "We blush that thou should'st choose; but, be refused,
> Let the white death sit on thy cheek for ever" . . .
> Now, Dian, from thy altar do I fly,
> And to imperial Love, that god most high
> Do my sighs stream.
>
> (2.3.66-75)

If refusal of her self-offering would be the ultimate humiliation, she has to blush for the public choosing itself as a deep contradiction to the accepted image of "a maid." We might also remember that when Helena's love seemed hopeless she could claim to the Countess that "Dian / Was both herself and love" (1.3.207-08). But now that she has acted, chastity and love split apart. Helena's name, of course, associates her through the myth of Troy with Venus, the source of "imperial Love" and in Shakespeare's own most notable presentation the quintessential female pursuer of a reluctant Adonis.[9] But where Venus as a goddess can simply *be* desire, the socially conditioned human Helena is abashed by her public exposure as wooer. When she finally addresses Bertram, she does her best to deny her role as aggressive, desiring subject and to recast herself properly as object: "I dare not say I take you, but I give / Me and my service, ever whilst I live, / Into your guiding power" (2.3.102-04). Reshaping the situation with words, however, fails to disguise for either Bertram or Helena herself the radical reversal of male and female. He bitterly protests being the chosen rather than the chooser; and even before his desertion, she sees her act as illicit. She cannot claim her husband's kiss by right, because her marriage feels like a kind of robbery:

> I am not worthy of the wealth I owe,
> Nor dare I say 'tis mine—and yet it is;
> But, like a timorous thief, most fain would steal
> What law does vouch mine own.
>
> (2.5.79-82)

When Bertram runs off to the wars, escaping his unwanted wife and reasserting his threatened status as active male, the same sense of having usurped a role not rightfully hers shapes her self-reproaches: "with the dark, poor thief, I'll steal away." In her exaggerated guilt, Helena enacts on herself a form of the penalty for failure which she enunciated to the King, the "tax of impudence" for chasing her Apollo like a bold strumpet instead of withdrawing like a chaste nymph. The deeply imbedded, internalized story by which we are constituted in terms of sexual difference is not so easy to change.

In *A Midsummer Night's Dream* the story is in fact not changed. When Oberon observes the Athenian Daphne pursuing her Apollo, he intervenes forcibly to reconstruct the traditional pattern. It is not enough to make Demetrius reciprocate Helena's love. Puck must apply the love-juice so that their roles are truly reversed: "Fare thee well, nymph: ere he do leave this grove / Thou shalt fly him, and he shall seek thy love" (2.1.245-46). "Nymph" in this context implies a whole sexual ideology. As Louis Montrose points out, Oberon is enacting another version of his reassertion of patriarchal control over Titania.[10] Under his magic ministrations, Helena becomes an object with a vengeance, wooed furiously by both Demetrius and Lysander. Yet this does not make her happy. Instead, she feels used by the men, and she especially resents Hermia's perceived defection from their old sisterhood to support the men in objectifying her. In a long, moving passage (3.2.198-219) she recalls their self-mirroring girlhood friendship, a support of subjectivity now lost to her. The play sorts out its love-tangles into neat unions, but it never reinstates that close bond between Hermia and Helena. Rather, the passage marks what must be left behind in the process of growing up and being fully inscribed in the patriarchal order.

No so in *All's Well.* In that play Helena, as desiring subject, drives its plot onward. She inserts herself uninvited into Bertram's bed, and acts as her own Oberon to bring about her own order. No wonder Bertram has so little to say at the close, and no wonder that the ending in general has made critics so uneasy. Shakespeare was following his source, of course, but in giving an internal life to Boccaccio's externally-conceived characters, he created something much more subversive.[11] Did it make him uneasy too? He apparently revised the central husband-choosing scene in such a way as to underline Helena's feminine shame.[12] At the conclusion he gave Bertram no speech of full endorsement, and caused even the authoritative King to amend the play's affirming title into a more doubtful "All yet *seems* well" (5.3.327).[13] And he deliberately mystified the middle, leaving the thrust of purpose undefined.

Indefinition opens space for multiple interpretations, an especially useful effect for an unorthodox play. Fill in the gap with your own assumptions and needs, as you like it. Without claiming to be exhaustive, I shall propose two of interpretations, a "safe" one as well as a subversive one. For the first, I resort once more to *A Midsummer Night's Dream,* which questions culturally constituted sexual identities only to replace male subject and female object in a fully reaffirmed patriarchal system. Indeed, just because of that reversal the earlier comedy can voice more directly the conflicts that must remain half-submerged in the more problematic later one. The central actor in *Midsummer* is Oberon, who achieves his purposes by magic means unrecognized by those he works on. This godlike dominance may seem to offer no relevant subtext for *All's Well,* with its all-too-human Helena apparently in charge. Yet the characters there keep alluding to an offstage operative power, a supernatural manipulator who is as invisible to us as Oberon was to the lovers. When Helena's initiative in curing the King succeeds, everyone hails her, not as a good doctor, but as a channel of divine purpose. "A showing of a heavenly effect in an earthly actor . . . the very hand of heaven . . . in a most weak minister great power, great transcendence" (2.3.1-37). The age of miracles is not over, proclaims Lafew. Helena herself, when persuading the King to try her cure, dwells at length on scriptural examples of great deeds done by God through agents without power in themselves (2.1.135-40), and when successful presents herself as a tool of God: "Heaven hath through me restored the King to health" (2.3.64). In her pilgrimage to Saint James, proposed at the crucial juncture of blurred motivation, it is not hard to see her yielding to divine direction, which then guides her to Florence and the means of consummating her marriage. When it turns out that the money she can give for Diana's help will enable a poor girl to marry well, that is another providential sign, as she assures the Widow: "Doubt not but heaven / Hath brought me up to be your daughter's dower, / As it hath fated her to be my motive / And helper to a husband" (4.4.18-21). Helena's purpose must be God's purpose, since he has already signally intervened in the natural course of events to bring it about. The action is propelled by God's desire, not Helena's. Doubt not.

That's a safe way to fill in the silence. But Helena herself has pointed in a different direction when she said, "Our remedies oft in ourselves do lie, / Which we ascribe to heaven" (1.1.212-13). The text also invites a riskier reading, grounded in psychology rather than religion. Suppose Helena is drawn to Florence by Bertram's presence. We may still think something more than mere opportunity is needed to re-empower her as desiring self against the crippling guilt and shame that followed on her first action of pursuit. And in this respect we may notice different aspects of the scene (3.5) that introduces the Florentine women. Diana's mother and her neighbor Mariana discuss thoroughly Bertram's wooing of Diana, sizing him up realistically and counseling Diana in resistance, with her considered agreement. The female integrity of self they support, being predicated on Diana's chastity, is far more conventional than the kind Helena has earlier acted on; but there's a clear emphasis on it, and on the mutual support of women in maintaining it. What Helena walks into, and quickly joins, is a version of the kind of self-confirming female friendship that was so notably denied to the Helena of *A Midsummer Night's Dream.* In confirming the illicit nature of Bertram's own sexual initiative, this friendship allows her to project the felt guilt of her own different kind of transgression onto him, and makes renewed activity psychologically possible. But there are no fewer than three additional scenes of conference and mutual assurance among the women to remind us how important their solidarity is. Solidarity strengthens Helena; it empowers Diana to take complete control of the last scene, manipulating not only Bertram but even the King, who is nominally in control. The connection seems clear between the strength of a woman and the strength of women.

Does *All's Well* really "change the story?" I don't know. What it does do, I think, is to enact—by disjunction, indirection, and suppression as much as speech and action—the difficulties and conflicts of imagining a woman as active, desiring subject. It doesn't end unambiguously "well," and has trouble ending at all. That shouldn't surprise us.

Notes

1. Quotations from *All's Well that Ends Well* and *A Midsummer Night's Dream* are from the New Arden editions of G. K. Hunter (London, 1959) and Harold F. Brooks (London, 1979).
2. Folio punctuation; later editors have variously repointed according to their interpretations of the textual crux.
3. First advanced by Steevens in the 1773 Johnson-Steevens edition of the plays.
4. Fredson Bowers, "Shakespeare at Work: The Foul Papers of *All's Well that Ends Well,*" *English Renaissance Studies Presented to Dame Helen Gardner* (Oxford, 1980), pp. 56-73.
5. Arden ed., p. xx.
6. "Sir, his wife some two months since fled from his house. Her pretence is a pilgrimage to Saint Jaques le Grand" (4.3.45-47).
7. "The heroine of *All's Well that Ends Well* is called Helena four times in the Folio; three of these occurrences are in stage directions, only one in dialogue, a prose passage in the opening scene. . . . The occurrences in stage directions are in the opening direction and in two others in Act Two, Scenes Four and Five. . . . The short form of her name—Hel< l >en—occurs twenty-five times, sixteen of them in dialogue, both verse and prose. It seems that Shakespeare was initially rather inconsistent but that he eventually abandoned the long form": Stanley Wells, *Re-Editing Shakespeare for the Modern Reader* (Oxford, 1984), p. 47.
8. *Countess*: This was your motive / For Paris was it? Speak. *Helena*: My lord your son made me to think of this; / Else Paris and the medicine and the King / Had from the conversation of my thoughts / Haply been absent then (1.3.225-30). Even here she cannot fully enunciate her plan to win Bertram in marriage through service to the King. Similarly, as Bertrand Evans has observed, her soliloquy of determination at the end of 1.1 "does not make even her incidental purpose explicit—the cure of the king—let alone the deeper purpose to be served by that cure": *Shakespeare's Comedies* (Oxford, 1960), p. 151. For him this is an early hint of the drive and duplicity of a "relentless hunter," which the text only gradually reveals. Evans' obvious distaste for a woman in this role is a good example of the critical unease with *All's Well* I mention on p. 75 and the constructions of sexual difference that underlie it.
9. I am indebted to Professor Donald Cheney of the University of Massachusetts for calling to my attention the relevance of *Venus and Adonis* to Helena's situation. Among several points where play resonates with poem, we might notice especially Adonis' accusing Venus of immodesty (53), Venus' persistent plea for a kiss, his disdain of love in favor of manly exercise, and her lament when these pursuits lead to his death: "Love's golden arrow at him should have fled, / And not death's ebon dart to strike him dead" (947-48; cf. *All's Well* 3.2.106-07). The traditional opposition between Venus and Diana may have figured in Shakespeare's naming of the Florentine Diana who will be "most chastely absent" (3.7.34) while Helena takes her place to conclude the rites of love with Bertram.
10. Louis Adrian Montrose, "'Shaping Fantasies': Figurations of Gender and Power in Elizabethan Culture," *Representations,* 1:2 (1983), 82-83.

11. The Third Day of the *Decameron* is devoted to tales of those who gain what they desire by their wits; and the telling of Giletta's story stresses her clever *methods* of achieving her aim rather than what it feels like to be the desirer.
12. Bowers (p. 61) speculates on the basis of a misplaced stage direction that lines 66-73, which I discuss above, pp. 73-74, were added to 2.3 after the first writing.
13. Emphasis mine; cf. his less than confident appeal to the audience in the epilogue, "All is well ended if this suit be won, / That you express content."

GENDER ISSUES

Carolyn Asp (essay date 1986)

SOURCE: "Subjectivity, Desire, and Female Friendship in *All's Well That Ends Well,*" in *Literature and Psychology,* Vol. 32, No. 4, 1986, pp. 48-63.

[*In the following essay, Asp focuses on the reversal of power—inspired by Helena's desire—that allows Helena to succeed in her plans to win Bertram.*]

> *"That man should be at a woman's command and yet no hurt done!"*
>
> I.iii.92

According to prevailing opinion, *All's Well That Ends Well* is a "problem play" whose major difficulty is located in the very assertion that the title makes in summarizing the action. In the opinions of many critics the play does not "end well" because the resolution remains on the structural level rather than moving to the psychological level.[1] The frog prince remains a frog until the end and the princess chooses to overlook his slimy skin. If the reader or theatergoer expects the romance of heterosexual coupling that concludes Shakespeare's "high comedies," disappointment is inevitable.

Singular among the plays in Shakespeare's canon, *All's Well That Ends Well* is written out of the history of the female subject and this history is the history of her desire. The inadequacy of the male as subject is not only NOT repressed; it is emphasized. In this, the play challenges both culture and theory which both subordinate the issue of woman-as-subject-of-desire to the question of male subjectivity and desire. Renaissance notions of female inferiority (and consequent objectification) were largely based on physiological schemes. The cultural stereotypes that mandated female subordination were (and are) often legitimized by the appeal to the irreducible realm of the real, i.e., nature. Both Aristotle and Galen after him declared that the female is characterized by deprived, passive, material traits and is cold and moist (earthy) in her dominant humours. Because the female is less fully developed than the male, her sexual organs have remained internal; she is therefore incomplete in a teleological scheme that aims toward perfection, i.e., the male. Heat, associated with perfection on the physical level, is a male characteristic; it is the lack of heat in the process of generation that causes the genitalia of the female to remain internal and therefore imperfect. The male characteristic of heat thrusts out the genitalia and produces a perfect human specimen.[2] To round off the paradigm, this assumed frailty of body was thought to be accompanied by mental and emotional weaknesses which were the natural justification of the female's exclusion from responsibility and moral fulfillment. Although the explanations used to justify female subordination to patriarchal structures have become increasingly complex in our day, the figure of the female hero in Renaissance drama, a figure who, especially in the comedies, rebels against her "natural" inferior position (or better yet, pays it no heed), still serves as a model of self-determination, i.e., as the subject of her desire, not the object of another's. Because there was much of the new in the old, much of the old in the new, I wish to use certain paradigms from psychoanalytic theory that are congruent with Renaissance notions of the character and place of the female to discuss the complexities and ambiguities of the central female character in *All's Well That Ends Well.* Viewed from this perspective Helena can be seen as coming to independent womanhood by surmounting attitudes and theories of female deprivation and inferiority.[3] Psychoanalytic theory is a useful tool for such an investigation because it attempts to account for the phenomenon of female inferiority in terms of structural psychic formations and introjected cultural ideals; but it is also limited in that it insufficiently addresses itself to female psychic formation, i.e., to a female version of the Oedipal crisis. Until recently, despite Freud's late interest in the "pre-Oedipal phase," which stresses the mother-infant relationship,[4] psychoanalytic theory had largely ignored that stage of development. Helena, in her ambiguity, represents a challenging subject for the psychoanalytic critic in that she breaks out of both the cultural (historical) and psychic (transhistorical) strictures applied to women in both her time and our own. She does this by the assertion of desire, the refusal of objectification and by interaction with other women in the play.

According to psychoanalytic theory, particularly Lacanian theory, the inauguration of subjectivity and desire is based upon a male model, the model of the Oedipal crisis. That model stipulates the phallus as the signifier for the needs and drives which the subject must relinquish to gain access to the symbolic order, the order of language, culture, and symbolization. In the Lacanian scheme the phallus is not identifiable with the penis; it is, however, the signifier for the cultural privileges which define male subjectivity and legitimate his desire within the patriarchal order. The female subject remains isolated from this register, ironically, because she has no penis to lose or exchange for the phallus.[5] As Luce Irigaray comments: "All theories of the 'subject' will always have been appropriated by 'the masculine'. . . . The subjectivity denied to the woman is, without doubt, the condition which guarantees the constitution of any object: object of representation, of discourse, of desire."[6] The scene of "castration" has only one subject as the concept of penis envy implies; the little girl sees herself through the eyes of the boy as "lacking." The "truth" of female sexuality, therefore, is "truth-as-lack."

The male subject, on the other hand, gives up the penis (direct expression of his own sexuality) to attain the phallus (the privileges of the patriarchal order). The female subject does not succumb to as radical an alienation from sexuality but neither does she enjoy as full a participation in the patriarchal order. Female sexuality, then, is not represented by the phallus (power) but by "castration" or lack. Since female sexuality cannot be represented (it is lack or absence) it remains "a dark continent" that, according to male theory, threatens to overpower both the female and the patriarchal order. According to Antonia Fraser, this "menacing" aspect of female sexuality was well known and greatly feared by seventeenth century males. In addition to the testimony of countless dramatis personae, there is the witness of such men as Thomas Wythorne and poets from Wyatt to Lovelace.[7]

Although there is a nice logic about this paradigm it is contrary to common sense to assume that the female is outside of signification or that her sexuality is any less structured or repressed by culture than is the male's. In entering into meaning and symbolization the female makes a sacrifice analogous to that of the male, i.e., the sacrifice of the mother and the gratifications she supplies.[8] The difference is that the girl's sexuality is negatively rather than positively defined.[9] This definition occurs on a cultural level which assigns public power and prestige to the male. In developmental processes gender myths of female lack and male fullness are internalized and treated as "true" and identification with stereotyped characteristics takes place. On this cultural, or symbolic level, then, the both men and women are conditioned to think of the male as "all" and the female as "not-all" (Lacan, *Séminaire* III 198). Prior to the Oedipal crisis, however, the subject is bisexual (Freud, *SE* XX: 118) undetermined by gender myths. Although physiological lack may be used to justify the idea of female inferiority, it is not the cause. Penis-envy, such as it is, is symbolic rather than organic, referring to social power rather than to physical potency. Since the female functions as a signifier of lack in culture the male must accommodate himself to the fact of difference by either establishing the woman's unworthiness or by transforming her into a compensatory object. This objectification of woman (as castrated) is designed to annihilate the threat that she represents. Similar relief is found in the disparagement of women by which the male takes pleasure through control and punishment.

The subject's entry into the Symbolic Order (language, culture, power) displaces the mother as the central object of desire with the father; this transaction is of crucial importance in the constitution of the subject. The son identifies with the father as possessor of cultural power; the daughter with the mother as one who lacks such power. The result of such internalization is a profound sense of inadequacy both for the male and the female—the son can never be equivalent to the symbolic father (the position with which he identifies and with which he identifies the actual father); the daughter is denied even an identification with that position (Silverman 191).

This was especially true in matters of sexuality and marriage in Renaissance England where the role of female desire was widely held to be small, even non-existent. According to Lawrence Stone, the qualities most valued in a woman in the sixteenth and seventeenth centuries were weakness, submissiveness, charity and modesty: "the theological and legal doctrine of the time were especially insistent upon the subordination of women to men in general and to their husbands in particular."[10] Ian McLean, after an extensive review of the learned documents devoted to the discussion of women in Renaissance theory, comes to the conclusion that the single greatest force preventing fundamental changes in the notion of women in the Renaissance was the institution of marriage; in the eyes of Renaissance thinkers—all male, by the way—marriage is a divine, natural and social institution and any alternative is considered subversive (85). Rethe Warnicke states that ". . . women were expected to marry, and those who did not were denied the respect of their communities."[11] Any change in the position of the silent and submissive wife in relationship to her lordly husband would require a new vision of the mental and physical predispositions of the sexes; this was too radical even for such Utopian writers as Thomas More and Rabelais.

Renaissance handbooks on marriage speak of the "choice of a wife" but never the choice of a husband. It is the man—the suitor—who seeks, who chooses. He does not expect the woman to seek him or to take the initiative in declaring her love first. It was generally agreed by wise heads that both physical desire and romantic love were unsafe bases of an enduring marriage, since both were regarded as violent mental disturbances which could only be of short duration. Women were especially prone to fits of passion; a menacing aspect of female desire was the woman's suspected carnality as the sixteenth century mysogynist, Thomas Wythorne, states: "Though they be weaker vessels, yet they will overcome 2. 3. or 4 [sic] men in satisfying their carnal appetities" (qtd. in Fraser 4). Women were considered incapable of making a wise choice in the best interests of marriage. After arguing against "enforced marriages" in *The Anatomy of Melancholy,* Robert Burton adds: "A woman should give unto her parents the choice of her husband lest she be reputed to be malapert and wanton, if she take upon her to make her own choice, for she should rather seem to be desired by a man than to desire a man herself."[12] Somewhat later in the century (1688) Lord Halifax writes in his *Advice to a Daughter*: "It is one of the disadvantages belonging to your sex, that young women are seldom permitted to make their own choice; their friends' care and experience are thought safer guides to them than their own fancies, and their modesty often forbiddeth them to refuse when their parents recommend, though their inward consent may not entirely go along with it. . . . You must first lay it down for a foundation in general that there is inequality in the sexes, and that for the better economy of the world, men, who were to be law-givers, had the larger share of reason bestowed upon them, by which means your sex is better prepared for the compliance that is necessary for the better performance of those duties which seem to be most properly assigned to it" (Stone 278), i.e., the duties of marriage. This representative patriarchal statement implies that the duties of compliance and subservience which the marriage doctrine enjoins could only be performed by those limited by nature (biological determinism) to a lesser level of intelligence than man. As late as 1706 Mary Astell still laments; "A woman, indeed, can't properly be said to choose; all that is allowed her is to refuse or accept what is offered" (Stone 275).

Ruth Kelso, who has surveyed an impressive variety of treatises on female behavior in *The Doctrine of the Lady of the Renaissance,* finally speculates that such emphasis would probably not have been placed on the submission and obedience of women and the inborn superiority of men if women in general were not asserting themselves in the pragmatic sphere. According to Kelso, the womanly ideal as found in male writings represents a most unrealistic separation of theory from fact.[13] Joan Kelly adds another dimension to the pragmatic argument by quoting Lucrezia Marinella who speculates that the psychology of educated men (the authors and authorities) who both vituperated and idealized women was based on both the necessity of feeling superior to women and the displacement of sexual feelings.[14] The received opinion on the value and place of women in a male world was based on male psycho-sexual experiences, not on observation and truth to experience (Kelly 82). Learned treatises on the relations of the sexes and marriage were contaminated by the need to maintain male supremacy even if that meant flying in the face of truth. In the face of such bias, how was a true image of woman to be recovered?

It was in the drama in particular that a new portrait of the female began to emerge during the late sixteenth and early seventeenth centuries. No matter what the various guises in which she appears, this woman has one consistent trait: she does not think of herself merely as an appendage of man; she insists on making her own decisions. It is this insistence that is so threatening to the patriarchal prerogative; it sets her apart from the conventional woman and often subjects her to attack or disapproval. One of the most interesting types of female rebels is the one who, like Helena, insists on the right to choose her own husband, to assert her own desire. This was a radical demand. A woman's right to love and marry according to her own desires could not be admitted without upsetting an established order which regarded women as inferior beings who needed to be governed by the sex for whose pleasure and convenience they had been created. Yet with the recognition that woman as well as man was "a reasonable creature" came the acceptance of the fact that she should use her reason in one of the most vital concerns of her life—the choice of a marriage partner and her relations with him. To find this type of assertive woman very much alive and extremely articulate in Renaissance drama is surely a surprise given the repressive nature of the tracts and sermons. But it is a surprise that leads to a deeper understanding of what is actually new in what seems old; it also provides an interesting and often amusing instance of that gradual process by which new attitudes supplant old ones over a period of time and produce profound societal changes.[15]

Helena, in the opening scene, seems to have internalized the "lack" mapped onto the female body; she acquiesces in her own powerlessness as defined by her context and tearfully accepts Bertram's inaccessibility as a love object. In this scene she plays out her role as passive, even masochistic female. This problematic first appearance can be explained by looking at her behavior from the viewpoint of psychoanalytic theory which postulates that female masochism is connected with gender identity and sexual desire, both social products. When the girl completes the Oedipal crisis, she also, like the boy must renounce the mother, the first love-object, and turn to the father who will not affirm the phallus in her (as he does for the boy), but instead will give it to her. When she turns to the father, she represses the active part of her libido: "hand in hand [with turning to the father]" says Freud, "there is to be observed a marked lowering of the active sexual impulses and the rise of the passive ones. . . . The transition to the father is accomplished with the help of passive trends insofar as they have escaped from the catastrophe. The path of femininity now lies open to the girl" (Freud, *SE* 21:239). It is this path of powerlessness and dependence which Helena initially believes she must adopt in regard to her desire for Bertram.

The ascendence of passivity in the girl is due to her recognition of the futility of realizing her active desire and of the unequal terms of the struggle. A segment of erotic possibility (female desire) is constrained. This realization, reinforced by cultural norms, prompts Helena's excessive and according to the other characters, unspecified emotional response. The creation of "femininity" in women as they are socialized also leaves in them a resentment of the constraints to which they were subjected, but they have few ways of expressing this residual anger, even rage. Not only is passivity inculcated in the girl; masochism is as well. When she turns to the father because she must, she discovers that "castration" (lack of power) is the condition of the father's love, that she must be a woman (signifier of lack) to evoke his love. She therefore begins to desire to be castrated, or powerless, trying to turn a disaster into a wish. In finding her place in the sexual system, then, the woman is robbed of libido and guided into masochistic eroticism (Freud, *SE* XXII: 128).

Fiona Reid as Helena, Joseph Shaw as King of France, John Novak as Bertram, and Cheryl Swarts, Seana McKenna, and Lee J. Campbell as Ladies and Gentlemen of the Court in Act II, scene iii of the 1982 Stratford Festival production of All's Well That Ends Well.

Although Helena at first seems to embody these psychoanalytic paradigms of psychic masochism and powerlessness, she struggles at several points in the play to defy them and moves from tearful and powerless acceptance of her position—and a concomitant construction of herself as object—to an assertive desire of which she is the subject. How does this shift occur? In her bawdy and witty banter with Parolles on the subject of virginity they both speak of sexuality with the metaphors of warfare. This conversation brings with into contact with aggressivity and narcissism, thus establishing a contact with unconscious desire. Desire can be restricted within the bounds of societal gender myths or it can follow its own trajectory and operate independently of them. Helena quickly shifts into resolve rooted in desire and determines upon cunning, aggressive action: a woman need not always defend her virginity against attack, i.e., remain an object; she may in fact, go on the offensive and "lose it to her own liking" (I.i.145). Desire here overcomes both gender and class; under the impress of its mobile power the unpropertied, educated female had much to gain even though such a desirous woman was regarded as a usurper of the masculine function and prerogative. Filled with resolve she casts off abjection: "Who ever strove / To show her merit that did miss her love?" (I.i.218-219).

Helena is not alone in her struggle, however. In a canon in which mother-daughter relationships are so few, this play is unusual in having several. Although Helena is a ward of the Countess, it is obvious that the countess extends to her the love of a mother for a child: "you ne'er oppressed me with a mother's groan," she tells Helena, "yet I express to you a mother's care" (I.iii.140-141). Helena quibbles, rejecting a fraternal relationship with Bertram: not "daughter" but "daughter-in-law" is the title she desires. When Helena admits her love to the Countess as well as her scheme to cure the King, the Countess allows Helena to speak of her desire, gives her an empathetic hearing, and bids her success, promising what aid she can. Helena appeals to the Countess' own youthful female experience thus creating a bond of womanly desire that transcends class.[16] It is obvious that the Countess regards Helena as an appropriate wife for Bertram, but leaves the initiative to her (the King as Bertram's guardian, has the right to dispose of the young man). Once Helena has legally secured the reluctant Bertram and he rejects her, she returns to the Countess who verbally castigates her son but can do nothing to change the situation. The Countess functions as an emotional center who utters the correct—and truly felt—sentiments, but who is ineffectual to help Helena in any way except through verbal support. Albeit a kind and caring woman, a validator of Helena's desire, the Countess limits her effectiveness and accepts her position of dependence within the patriarchal order.

Helena leaves the maternal aegis of the Countess on the strength of her paternal inheritance; "prescriptions of rare and prov'd effects", male learning passed on to her as her dowry. She must leave the mother-figure to insert herself with a larger, public group and utilize the skill bequeathed her by her father. Armed with the patriarchal legacy of language and learning, she confronts and confounds "the schools" and attempts the king's cure. By curing the debilitating fistula (a sexually symbolic disease) Helena restores the king's manly vigor upon which the success of her project depends. But prior to the cure, she engages the royal honor: "Then shalt thou give me with thy kingly hand / What husband in thy power I will command" (II.i.194-95). It is in her best interest to restore power to the patriarchy which she plans to engage in her behalf.

This request, which depends upon patriarchal power for its implementation, paradoxically subverts the very order of patriarchy itself. Throughout history women, not men, have been sexual objects, gifts. The "exchange of women" expresses the social relations of a kinship system that specify that men have certain rights in their female kin and that women do not have such rights over themselves or their male relatives. In this system the preferred female sexuality is one that responds to the desires of others rather than one which actively seeks an object and a response (Lacan, *Séminaire II,* 306). We ask: "What would happen if a woman demanded a certain man as her gift rather than the other way around?" This play shows us what happens. The king's debt to Helena is reckoned in Bertram's flesh; he must become the sexual partner to her to whom he is "owed" as the reward for the restoration of the king's flesh.[17] Bertram resists this structural "feminization" loudly voicing the resentment that accompanies objectification, a resentment that arises from having been given no choice; "I beseech your highness, / In such a business give me leave to use / The help of mine own eyes" (II.iii.105-7).

The play contains a series of triangular exchange transactions of which this is the first. By power the king provides a substitute sexual partner for Helena who will function as his "stand in." It is obvious that he values and desires Helena more than any other male in the play—what man does not love the woman who restores his virility? But Helena is determined to have Bertram and the king, by virtue of his position, is outside the circuit of desire, Subject par excellence! Up to this point Helena attempts to control events less through her own sexuality and desire than through patriarchal gifts to her. These gifts come to her in language: prescriptions, learning, promises that will enable her to possess legally what she desires. Even though she is emboldened by desire, she is unable to evoke the desire of the other (Bertram), the ultimate goal in Lacanian psychic dynamics. So what she gets is a marriage in name only—an ironic reward—a marriage that Bertram never intends to honor with his flesh. The letter but not the spirit of the law is fulfilled. So her scheme has both succeeded and failed. This seems to be the limit for female desire that relies too heavily on even the best-intentioned of men.

After the check of Bertram's rejection Helena initiates a complex and indirect action for attaining her desire, an action in which she relies both on her own cunning and on bonding with other women. Taking up the apparently impossible conditions of Bertram's rejection as a challenge—"When thou canst get the ring upon my finger, which shall never come off, and show me a child begotten of thy body that I am father to, then call me husband, but in such a 'then' I write 'never'" (III.ii.56-59). Helena paradoxically weaves her net of capture by literally following his directives, turning his language into a trap. Her campaign initiatives arise from the very messages he sends denying her. Responding to his refusal to return to his ancestral lands "till I have no wife" she disguises herself as a pilgrim and sets out for Florence where it is possible she knows he is stationed. Ostensibly she appears submissive to his will, but her submission is also a strategy; her success from this point until the end is linked to her ability to assume a "feminized" (inferior, powerless) position and yet remain in cognitive control of the situation. This combination of positions is exceedingly potent and establishes her mastery in the second half of the play.

In the early part of the play the ideal that Helena thinks she sees in Bertram is not merely hidden; it is absent, lacking. She eventually must come to terms with this fact. Bertram is not a sufficient representation of the "virile object" that Helena sees only in her fantasy. We might wonder why she so desires him. In Lacanian terms, Helena is initially trapped in the level of consciousness called the Imaginary, i.e., the register in which opposition and identity are the only possible interrelationships between self and other. This "other" is usually someone or something which is thought to complete the subject or reflects back to him/her an ideal image (Lacan *Ecrits* 2-4). The Imaginary is the register of the ego, a construct that involves a purely dual either/or relationship that resembles that of the Hegelian master/slave paradigm. The predominance of the Imaginary in relationships results in the conversion of interdependent similarities and differences between man and woman into pathological identities and oppositions (as between images of man and woman). To enter into productive relationships it is necessary to transcend the oppositional relationships and reduce mastery to insignificance by means of this transcendence. During the course of the action Helena traverses this path of development, passing from the register of the Imaginary to that of the Symbolic Order (Lacan, *Séminaire I* 215). Early in the play she is almost overwhelmed by opposition in her relationship with Bertram; she can see only unbridgeable separations. Then she swings to the opposite, narcissistically identifying his desire with her own, never doubting her ability to win him. His severe rejection forces her to align herself with the limits of the possible. Finally she comes to a third position within the Symbolic Order, the register of similarities and differences, of the social and the cultural. She must accept the fact that his desire, whatever it may be, may be different from her own. Her original desire for Bertram seems to be displaced by her own maternity and by her return to the mother so that she is inserted into the larger cultural sphere of social and familial engagement. Paradoxically she does this by remaining true to her desire (is this type of maturation initiated, then, by desire within the register of the Imaginary?); as desiring subject she not only gets what she thinks she wants but more. And it is in this "more," this excess, that Helena's real triumph is located. This excess has to do with her increasing realization of the pragmatic and psychological support that female bonding provides for her in her erotic adventures.

In contrast to the Countess who is a very real but passive support, the Florentine women, a mother and daughter with whom Helena plots, are active on her behalf. Fallen from fortune, they must make their way in the world and struggle to defend their hard-earned gains. The precious jewel of her treasury is Diana's chastity, a "commodity" that commands a high price. As a consequence, these women have nothing but distrust and contempt for male language, especially the male language of seduction; instead, they rely on female lore: "My mother told me just how he would woo, / As if she sat in's heart" (IV.ii.69-70) says Diana, fore-armed against Bertram's vows. When these women show a willingness to believe her story, Helena grasps the opportunity to fulfill the letter of Bertram's law, an opportunity that Bertram's "sick desires" for Diana give her. In a scene of many exchanges she buys Diana's place with gold while Bertram thinks he is purchasing Diana's "ring" (genitals) with the patriarchal ring of Rosillon.[18] What occurs is a triangular transaction between women in the possession of a man. In this circuit of desire Diana remains aloof, Helena gets what she wants and Bertram gets what he does not know he does not want. Without cognitive power, Bertram assumes the role of a circulatable commodity; again he is "feminized."

In transactions of heterosexual desire, there can be hidden strategies of bonding which seem to occur here; the bond between Helena and Diana is cemented by means of sexual substitution. Earlier in the play (I.iii) there is an odd conversation between Lavatch and the Countess in which Lavatch describes the use he will make of Isbel to create "friends" for himself. Voluntary cuckoldry creates a bond among men with the "other" (the partner of the opposite sex) as the object to be exchanged among them. When the Countess remonstrates: "Such friends are thine enemies, knave," Lavatch points out to her this new type of bonding: "He that comforts my wife is the cherisher of my flesh and blood; he that cherishes my flesh and blood loves my flesh and blood; he that loves my flesh and blood is my friend; ergo, he that kisses my wife is my friend" (I.iii.43-47). Lavatch describes a literal series of heterosexual displacements in which implicit homoerotic desire is represented as heterosexual adultery. Isbel will mediate a communion among males. Is Lavatch a fool or a knave or neither? He describes himself as involved in triangular sexual transactions in which he maintains control through knowledge and manipulation. As either thief or distributor he regards women as circulatable commodities, objects of desire. His song invoking Helen of Troy underlines this paradigm of the shared woman, the common ground of male desire.

Helena's sexual experience with Bertram, in which she substitutes her body for that of the desired Diana's, leaves her with the conviction of the impersonality of the act. "Strange men"—in several senses of that word—make sweet use of what they hate, i.e., the female body with its threatening lack. "Lust doth play / With what it loathes" (IV.iv.24-25) in the darkness which hides both the particularity (subjectivity) of the woman and the place of castration. Lacan explains this imbalance by commenting that what man approaches in the sexual act is the cause of his desire (lack). The male identifies the woman with what he has repressed in himself and makes love to complete himself in her. Thus the woman's specificity is subordinate to the man's quest for this own fulfillment (Ragland-Sullivan 292). Helena seems both shocked and disillusioned by this experience of sexual objectification in which she is not seen and in which she may not speak. Yet from this place of apparent lack (her genitals) and seeming powerlessness she traps the cozened Bertram's wild desires and lures them into consummating the legal bond. Publicly commenting on her experience later in the play, Helena admits that Bertram's sexual performance was "wondrous kind" (V.iii.305), gentle and natural.

After Helena has fulfilled Bertram's stipulations, the ensuing action is excessive, almost gratuitous. I believe that it is only at this point that Helena moves beyond the Imaginary (projected idealizations) with respect to Bertram and begins to see him as he is. All traces of psychological masochism vanish from her character and she begins to express a residual anger toward him, a desire to punish him for having rejected her desire and objectified her. It becomes clear that she has his public humiliation in mind since she now has achieved a cognitive leverage over him which gives her power. She has sent back word to France that she is "dead," i.e., she represents "castration" or loss as the ultimate lack or absence. Paradoxically it is from this position of "castration" or loss that she is able to achieve her greatest power as an active subject.[19] What is thought to be absent can be ignored; what is regarded as lost can be thought of as without power. Yet the very veil of disappearance allows the subject room to act with impunity. Once again she enlists the aid of the Florentine women to carry out her project.

Having arrived in France Helena sends a letter ahead to the King via messenger. Because of the unforeseen concatenation of events, it becomes clear that this letter had been prepared in advance by Helena although it is signed with Diana's name. It lays claim to Bertram as a fair exchange for the latter's honor. What becomes increasingly apparent is that Helena is preparing a public confrontation between Diana and Bertram based on a non-event, i.e., an absence that will entrap him in a web of signs (rings) and language (lies) from which he will be unable to escape. The effectiveness of Diana's script turns upon an exchange of rings prior to the bed trick. Here the plot becomes increasingly dense since neither the audience nor most of the characters knows the history of the rings. The disclosure that the ring Diana gave to Bertram had been given to Helena by the King is a shocking surprise. What is even more disquieting is the fact that Helena had given it to Diana explicitly to exchange for Bertram's patriarchal ring, a transfer that indicates Helena's intent to entrap, since encoded in this ring is a secret message to the King: she is in need of his help. The sight of Bertram wearing this ring coupled with Helena's fictional account of her own death leads the King to suspect Bertram of foul deeds. On the defensive, Bertram entangles himself more and more tightly in the snare; brazenly lying, he repudiates Diana and denies any knowledge of Helena. As the *pièce de résistance* Diana produces Bertram's ring, alleging that with it he purchased her honor. Although like Parolles, Bertram may play with language, he cannot deny the object, irrefutable proof of his complicity. Publically revealed as a liar, a coward and a faithless husband, Bertram has no choice but to stand shamed and endure humiliation. At this point Helena enters triumphant as the *dea ex machina* to clarify and forgive.

By reading events of the second half of the play backwards, so to speak, we can see Helena's complex plan to turn Bertram's desires and fears against him and then make his weakness, perfidy and ignorance public through the accusations of others, herself remaining aloof.[20] It is evident that there is little romance in Helena's attitude toward Bertram at the end of the play; when she greets him she merely makes known her fulfillment of his conditions. When he further questions her, her final words to him are distant and almost foreboding: "If it appear not plain and prove untrue / Deadly divorce step between me and you" (V.iii.314-315). This marriage is an unknown item, a risk whose outcome is to be determined beyond the limits of the play. In contrast her greeting to the Countess is warm and affectionate: "O my dear mother, do I see thee living?" (V.iii.316). These, her last words in the play, seem to indicate that she has re-adjusted the focus of her desire.

Along with the power shift that occurs in the second half of the play there seems also to be a psychological reversal. I would go so far as to say that lurking behind Helena's apparent psychological masochism of her initial attitude towards Bertram lies its opposite, i.e., anger or rage at having been denied subjectivity by him and a willingness to inflict pain, a psychological form of sadism.[21] In some ways her reversal is quite shocking but it certainly is not an unusual female paradigm. As mentioned earlier in this essay, the constraint of female desire in a patriarchal system leaves a residual resentment and anger in the woman which most women, unlike Helena, do not have the opportunity to act on. Granted, her action is indirect, even cunning, but for all that, it is eminently effective. As Helena moves from object position into subject status, from passive to active (the latter associated with the masculine "position") she concomitantly exchanges psychological masochism for a certain degree of willingness to inflict pain or humiliation in the assertion of mastery. Shakespeare manages to put Helena in the subject (sadistic) position without depriving her of our sympathy by shielding her behind the accusations and anger of others whom she has convinced to act in her place. Her agency has been displaced, certainly veiled. We cannot deny that Bertram deserves the punishment she arranges; our puzzlement is reserved for the "reconciliation" on which the play ends. If there is a reconciliation, then how does it come about and whose attitudes must change?

Helena's shift occurs in two phases in an encounter with the Real, i.e., the given field of existence, nature in self and in the world. The first phase is Bertram's rejection and abandonment of her which forces her to see him as he is; the second is her sexual encounter with him which is lustful and procreative rather than romantic. These encounters with the Real shake her out of the narcissism and the false perceptions associated with the Imaginary register and precipitate her into positioning herself within the Symbolic Order as a viable alternative to the delusory projections of the early part of the play. There is loss but there is also gain. Her position in culture and the collective is ratified by her obvious "wife-li-ness" and maternity. She is the fleshly sign of the link between the generations and as such holds a secure place in the Symbolic Order (Welsh 21). Helena has successfully rejected the powerlessness of her original position in the Imaginary, emerging from it at another level, carrying the signs of her transaction. It is she, not Bertram, who has both the ring and the child and she will exchange both for his acceptance of her as his wife and mother of his child. Helena's desire now locates itself within the social order—the child in her womb is the heir—but that order is not exclusively patriarchal. In the process of pursuing her desire for Bertram, Helena has come to experience the loyalty, support, and kindness of women who not only never doubted her but who never failed her. What began as a pursuit of a man developed into a transaction among women. With skill, intelligence and cunning they use Bertram's very desires to bind him to what his position and phallic potency demand of him. Through the trajectory of desire he becomes the victim of the trick. But the paradox does not operate only in Bertram's case. Let us entertain the possibility that in the pursuit of a husband Helena has actually found a mother, has discovered the power of feminine bonding. Although she carries the sign of her heterosexual eroticism and Bertram's potency, her desire seems to have transcended the narrow limits of such eroticism and moved into the larger sphere of female affectivity. Her sexual experiences and her own maternity seem to create a new awareness of and desire for the maternal body.

Is Helena's turning to women at the end of the play unusual in her immediate social context? Or does it signal some kind of change in sensibility that was actually occurring at the time? Although there has not yet been much investigation of primary documents relating to the bonding of women in the Renaissance, there are many collateral sources which refer to this phenomenon, including works of poetry, fiction and drama which depict strong, loyal, and loving relationships between and among women. In addition, it seems likely that in a society so constrained by rigid gender-role differentiations there would be both the emotional segregation of women from the male world and a corresponding development of bonding within the female circle. It is certainly true that biological realities centered around incessant pregnancies and childbirth traumas bound women together in intimacy. Supportive female networks paralleled the social restrictions on intimacy between men and women. Courtesy books, advice books, sermons, and other male-originated texts all stress gender-role differentiations as well as the social segregation characteristic of the culture.[22]

Although generally speaking the mother-daughter relationship is at the heart of the female world, in Renaissance literature we see bonds of kinship and service forming the basis of intense friendships. The literature frequently depicts a "conspiracy of women" that organizes itself around female desire. When the male is indifferent or hostile to such desire, the female characters find support in female kin, friends, or servants. Celia conspires with Rosalind; Emilia defends Desdemona to the death; Paulina refuses to abandon Hermione; Cleopatra surrounds herself with her women in the hour of her final triumph. This woman's world has a dignity and integrity that spring from mutual affection and the shared experiences of being a woman in a man's world. The drama of late sixteenth and early seventeenth century England, then, provides many examples of not only strong women but of strong friendships between women. According to Juliet Dusinberre, the struggles of many of the heroines in Shakespeare's plays are struggles against the male idea of womanhood; they are efforts to be considered human in a world that sees them only as female, i.e., as powerless, "castrated" devoid of initiating desire. In these conflicts women are intimate not just as individuals but as women; they develop a loyalty to their sex which can express itself in confederacy, even cunning.[23] For example, in the play under consideration, the Countess is more sympathetic toward Helena than she is to her own son. She assures Helena: ". . . be sure of this / What I can help thee to, thou shalt not miss" (I.iii.248-49).

Helena succeeds in her scheme because she heeds and follows her desire even though the caveats of internalized gender values and the constraints of society make her task seem impossible. Frequently she occupies the so-called male position, the position of knowledge and power, through the very paradox of her "castration"; in this position she sets up the exchanges upon which society depends for its continuation. By the play's end she has come to value and depend on the world of women whose power Bertram, with some humility, is forced to acknowledge. Her success argues for a re-evaluation of the patriarchal denigration of female desire and a reconsideration of that desire's power and validity in the social order. Through Helena's single-minded action a redefinition of gender prerogatives has occurred and as a consequence the patriarchal order is modified, if ever so slightly.[24] Fired by her desire, Helena refuses to submit to gender myths that link the female with loss unless that loss can be turned to gain. The play ends as well as it can—all only "seems well" the king states at the conclusion—given the fact that sexual relations will never be harmonious, that psychic unity is tenuous at best.[25]

Notes

1. Paula S. Berggren, "The Woman's Part: Female Sexuality as Power in Shakespeare's Plays," in *The Woman's Part,* ed. Carolyn Lenz, Gayle Greene and Carol Neely (Chicago: University of Illinois Press, 1980). pp. 22-23; G. K. Hunter, "Introduction" to *All's Well That Ends Well,* Arden Edition (Cambridge, Mass: Cambridge University Press, 1959), xxix-xxxi; Hunter also comments (liv-lv) that "in these plays (the problem plays) the strand of psychological realism makes the absence of personal reconciliation seem wanton and careless." Richard Wheeler states that the ending of the play is not a true resolution but merely a superficial denial of the hero's rebellion: "Marriage and Manhood in All's Well That Ends Well," *Bucknell Review,* 21 (1973), 103-24. Roger Warren in "Why Does It End Well?: Helena, Bertram and the Sonnets", *Shakespeare Survey* 22 (Cambridge: Cambridge University Press, 1969), 79-92, faults Shakespeare for failing to provide a "powerful and reassuring speech" for Helena at the finale, a definite dramatic weakness in his opinion.

2. Ian McLean, *The Renaissance Notion of Woman* (New York: Cambridge University Press, 1980), p. 33.

3. Warren sees Helena as "unbearably poignant" and tends to idealize her masochistic tendencies; my argument follows Hunter's insight that "to fit Helena into the play or to adapt the play to Helena is obviously the central problem of interpretation" (xiviii). I agree with Hunter that "her role is a complex one, but there is an absence of adequate external correlatives to justify this complexity; we are drawn to regard her as an isolated, complex individual" (xlix). In his enlightening study of the play, Wheeler (*Shakespeare's Development and the Problem Comedies,* (Berkeley: University of California Press, 1981)) keeps to a middle ground when he asserts both her humble, adoring love for Bertram and her "vigorous, cunning and determined pursuit" of him.

p. 63. Psychoanalytic theory can provide paradigms to account for her complex attitudes and behaviors.

4. Sigmund Freud, *The Standard Edition of the Complete Psychological Works,* ed. James Strachey (London: The Hogarth Press, 1964), XXII, 112-135. Nancy Chodorow in *The Reproduction of Mothering* (Berkeley: The University of California Press, 1978) has developed this theory in great detail.

5. Jacques Lacan, *Ecrits: A Selection,* trans. Alan Sheridan (New York: Norton, 1977), p. 66.

6. Luce Irigaray, *Speculum de l'autre femme* (Paris: Minuit, 1974), p. 165.

7. Antonia Fraser, *The Weaker Vessel* (New York: Knopf, 1984), p. 4.

8. Ellie Ragland-Sullivan, *Jacques Lacan and the Philosophy of Psychoanalysis* (Chicago: The University of Illinois Press, 1985), pp. 297-98.

9. Kaja Silverman, *The Subject of Semiotics* (New York: Oxford University Press, 1983), p. 198.

10. Lawrence Stone, *The Family, Sex, and Marriage in England: 1500-1800* (New York: Harper and Row, 1977), p. 199.

11. Rethe Warnicke, *Women of the English Renaissance and Reformation* (Westport, Conn.: Greenwood Press, 1983), p. 178.

12. Robert Burton, *The Anatomy of Melancholy* (New York: Vintage, 1932), "Third Partition", p. 238.

13. Ruth Kelso, *The Doctrine of the Lady in the Renaissance* (Urbana: The University of Illinois Press, 1978), p. 208.

14. Joan Kelly, *Women, History and Theory* (Chicago: University of Chicago Press, 1984), p. 81.

15. Jean Gagen, *The New Woman* (New York: Twayne, 1954), p. 119.

16. Carol McKewin, "Counsels of Gall and Grace: Intimate Conversations between Women in Shakespeare's Plays," in *The Woman's Part,* pp. 117-132.

17. Eva Sedgewick, "Sexualism and the Citizen of the World," *Critical Inquiry* (December, 1984), p. 233. See also Wheeler, pp. 49-51 on the deflection of male sexual interest from women to men.

18. Alexander Welsh in "The Loss of Men and the Getting of Children: *All's Well That Ends Well* and *Measure for Measure,*" *Modern Language Review,* Vol. 73, Part I (January, 1978), argues against Wheeler and later Kirsch (*Shakespeare and the Experience of Love* (New York: Cambridge University Press, 1981)) in their emphasis on the "threat of castration inherent in the Oedipal situation," i.e., Bertram's identification of Helena with her mother. He asserts that "inheritance and succession are far more important concerns than Oedipal jealousies" p. 21. Although my focus is not on Bertram, I agree with Welsh that the Oedipal argument is quite weak and unconvincing. Aside from the "punning" scene between the Countess and Helena, there is no reference to such a motive in the play. In that scene Helena specifically and somewhat playfully, refers to brother/sister incest.

19. Here I disagree with Hunter (xxxii) on the power of coincidence and submission to supernatural forces as the dynamic forces of the second half of the play. Helena actively uses and arranges the circumstances that lead to her success.

20. R. B. Parker, "War and Sex in *All's Well That Ends Well,*" *Shakespeare Survey* (New York: Cambridge University Press, 1984), 37: 111-112.

21. Wheeler states that "the exposure of Bertram releases a righteous feeling of moral outrage and with it a kind of vindictive pleasure that corresponds to the sadistic attack on the internalized object lost in reality described by Freud", pp. 72-73.

22. Carroll Camden in *The Elizabethan Woman* (New York: Elsevier Press, 1952) quotes from many such treatises which lead us to believe that women spent a great deal of time together. In his satirical pamphlet, *The Gossips Greeting,* Henry Parrot inveighs against talkative and outgoing women. Burton also refers to gossiping among women as "their merrie meetings and frequent visitations, mutual invitations in good towns . . . which are so in use." A Dutch traveller named Van Meteren found this mode of entertainment a notable one among Elizabethan women. He writes: "all the rest of their time they employ in walking and riding, in playing cards or otherwise, in visiting their friends and keeping company, conversing with their equals and their neighbors and making merry" (162). Educated women also spent time carrying on an extended correspondence with their female friends.

23. Juliet Dusinberre, *Shakespeare and the Nature of Women* (New York: Macmillan, 1975), p. 282.

24. Even at the end of the play the king proposes to repeat the process he inaugurated with Helena by finding Diana, the professed virgin, a husband. Lefew's daughter is offered to Bertram and then summarily withdrawn without any consultation with her. The tableau of women at the end of the play is intriguing; it ranges from Diana, who has vowed not to marry, to "fair Maudlin" who is given and taken back. The widow Countess stands with the newly restored wife-mother, Helena. What seems to be emphasized is the lack of or problematic nature of heterosexual relationships.

25. Jacques Lacan, *Séminaire XX,* ed. Jacques-Alain Miller (Paris: Seuil, 1973-74), p. 14. Other references to the *Séminaires* in the text refer to the French editions published by Seuil and edited by Miller.

Barbara Hodgdon (essay date 1987)

SOURCE: "The Making of Virgins and Mothers: Sexual Signs, Substitute Scenes, and Doubled Presences in *All's Well That Ends Well,*" in *Philological Quarterly,* Vol. 66, No. 1, Winter, 1987, pp. 47-71.

[*In the following essay, Hodgdon examines the gender theme on a structural level, revealing how Shakespeare's use of the various instances of doubling and substitution—most notably in the bed-trick scene—help to bring about the marital compromises that conclude the action of the play.*]

In *All's Well That Ends Well,* Helena stands, much like *As You Like It*'s Rosalind, at the center of the internal drama as well as the critical drama—that is, its critical controversies concerning meaning and language.[1] Both plays share significant story elements; both are fictions of an ordinary woman who becomes extraordinary. Both Rosalind and Helena disguise their sexuality—the one by assuming a mask which permits her to explore male as well as female roles and attitudes through verbal wit and situational jokes; the other by foregrounding—even flaunting—her most vulnerable quality—her virginity. Both achieve their ends (Is it possible to talk of sexuality without creating a secondary sexual discourse?) by taking on the drive and ambition usually associated with males, by insisting on their intelligence, by using themselves (and their "magical" powers) in order to gain and to preserve their imagined loves.[2] And both dramas endow their heroines' explorations of desire with stature and conviction.

Critical discussions of both plays, however, often ignore if not erase such similarities and focus on the differences between the two, engaging enthusiastically with Rosalind's fabular androgyny but questioning—even condemning—Helena's motives as well as the "unlawful" means through which she "doubly wins" a husband. *As You Like It* may offer jibing critiques of Petrarchan ideals or the foolishness of love at first sight, may provide glimpses of alternative perspectives on sexual desire as a potential threat to individual relationships or to the community fabric; but its close places these features within an idealized construct that celebrates desire and mutuality. In *All's Well,* however, sexuality appears, on the one hand, as a blatant preoccupation of the play and, on the other, assumes the convenient disguise of plot and character conventions associated with fairy tale and romance. Much like the screwball film comedies of the late 1930s and early 1940s, *All's Well* conveys its concern with sexuality paradoxically by means of prohibitions of representation and language[3]—by what it does not say or show, by avoiding areas or topics to which it has access. And although *All's Well* journeys toward a celebratory ending similar to that of *As You Like It,* this paradox generates a complex of meanings that compromises the arrival. Whereas *As You Like It* bears us away, *All's Well* bears pondering.

Let this pondering take the form of a *bricolage* of at least three voices. One re-examines Shakespeare's transformation of Boccaccio's tale; another explores how sexual signs are articulated in character and event; yet another discloses how what I call substitute scenes and doubled presences function to sexualize its narrative structure.[4] Although I will be moving somewhat freely among these voices or perspectives, my re-reading of *All's Well* approaches the play primarily from Helena's point of view. And because her virginity—and the "use" she makes of it—lies at the heart of both the drama and its critical history, I begin by raising that issue in conjunction with another, *All's Well*'s re-naming of Boccaccio's heroine.[5]

Why does Shakespeare change Giletta's name? Rather than, as with Beltramo, simply anglicizing her name to Juliet or Julietta, thus suggesting comparisons to the heroine of his romantic tragedy (or tragical romance), *Romeo and Juliet,*[6] he chooses to call her Helena, thus signalling particular sexual, as well as social and metadramatic, connotative possibilities. By association, her name evokes both the adulterous Helen of Troy and the lonely, virginal, left-out Helena of *A Midsummer Night's Dream,* strongly locked on a single object of desire. In name alone, then, Helena embraces a paradox, one insistently reenforced by the text. Through extremely economical means, Shakespeare's renaming of his heroine encompasses her sexual awareness, her obsessive desire and her virginity. And this latter quality the playtext underscores further, first in her conversation with Parolles (1.1.104-211)[7] and then by linking her to Diana, the name and symbol of chastity itself.

The dialogue Helena shares with Parolles separates two soliloquies. In the first, she declares that Bertram has replaced her father in her imagination and that she is "undone"—even dead: "there is no living, none, / If Bertram be away" (1.1.80-81); in the second, cued by Parolles' exit line—"Get thee a good husband, and use him as he uses thee. So, farewell" (1.1.206-7)—she exchanges her former sense of lifelessness for a fixed resolve, a "project" involving the King's disease which, although she avoids specific reference to Bertram, presumably will help to win him. Helena's initial position is comparable to that of Ophelia in *Hamlet*—if Hamlet had returned to Wittenberg or gone off to the Norwegian court. As others have noted, much about *All's Well*'s opening recalls Hamlet; indeed, the entire first scene reads almost like *Hamlet* from Ophelia's point of view, although the advice Helena receives from Parolles is exactly opposite to that which Laertes gives Ophelia just as he leaves, coincidentally, for Paris. Helena, however, speaks not with a brother, a desired lover or even (as Rosalind does with Celia) a close friend but with a man she identifies as a liar, a fool and a coward—but nevertheless a substitute for Bertram, a man she will love for Bertram's sake. Their exchange represents the only sign of her willingness to engage in sexual banter, and the implicit questions raised here press Helena—and the narrative—on.[8] Why is virginity humiliating, laughable—"a desperate offendress against nature," "out of fashion," "a wither'd pear?" Why worthless until used? Why, or to what extent, is marriage thought to justify its "use?" And, of course, Helena's own explicit question, "How might one do, sir, to lose it [virginity] to her own liking?" (1.1.147). Although Helena states the text's hermeneutic question directly, without metaphoric double entendre, thus placing her in a position of sexual power, from this point on the text consistently masks her sexual awareness with riddles or with language that betrays her deep mistrust, even fear, of sexuality. Only her actions express her desires frankly, moving her toward a husband as well as toward an initiatory sexual experience that is hurried, cloaked by night and silence and set up through deceit and trickery—however "lawful" that deceit may be. At the same time, the text represents her as a miraculous and virginal minister of healing grace, capable of restoring her King to sexual health and her future husband to (presumably) sexual wealth.

Helena herself, speaking to the Countess, outlines the paradox:

> . . . but if yourself,
> Whose aged honour cites a virtuous youth,
> Did ever, in so true a flame of liking,
> Wish chastely and love dearly, that your Dian
> Was both herself and love—O then, give pity
> To her whose state is such that cannot choose
> But lend and give where she is sure to lose;
> That seeks not to find that her search implies,
> But riddle-like lives sweetly where she dies!
>
> (1.3.204-12)

To be both Dian and love; to give and to lose; to live and to die: the narrative process seeks to explore—and finally to integrate—these absolute oppositions. Toward this end, the play gives Helena two doubles—Diana and Lavatch. In linking her to Diana, the text again particularizes its narrative source: Boccaccio's substitute for Giletta in the bed trick remains nameless, plays her purely functional role, is rewarded with a dowry and leaves the city. Shakespeare's text not only highlights (ironically) notions of idealized chastity by naming her Diana but also firmly establishes her within a community of women as Helena's ally, not her possible rival; and the riddling language the two share further reinforces their correspondence. Thus Helena's "maiden pilgrimage" to Saint Jaques' shrine takes her "from Dian's altar" to "imperial Love" by way of the literal Diana; and Helena's loss (or giving "use") of her own virginity preserves Diana's chastity, which becomes a crucial feature in the play's final revelations.

Helena's link to Lavatch, though less precise—comparable to the implicit relationship between Cordelia and Fool in *King Lear* in that, just as Fool replaces the banished Cordelia, so does Lavatch replace Helena as the Countess's companion—provides one means of sustaining a level of witty playfulness about sex that disappears, after her conversation with Parolles, from her role. Reading Lavatch as Helena's substitute, surrogate or double enriches both their presences: that his first appearance separates Helena's initial statements of her desire for Bertram and her confession of that desire to the Countess and that he speaks of what occupies her mind—marriage—further join the two. The Clown's persistent theological references, which parody, within a bawdy context, the court's pious sentiments on honor, virtue and fortune,[9] also suggest Lavatch's correspondence with the religious aura surrounding Helena. His "holy reasons" for marrying—that he is "driven on by the flesh" and seeks to marry in order to repent—preface a sustained parody of the Epistle for the marriage service (1.3.44-53).[10] This double, rather perverse, view of marriage as fulfilling male hopes and fears—giving sensual satisfaction but also leading to cuckoldry—suggests a potential register of Helena's suppressed discourse, one that critics, anxious to stress her selfless, saint-like perfection and humility (and thus aiding their defense of her forthright and devious "male" behavior), have themselves suppressed. And it is Lavatch who also evokes Helena's link to Helen of Troy, "corrupt[ing]" his ballad by juggling the proportion of good men in order to "purify" the number of good women (1.3.57-84). This rather backhanded compliment, as well as the words just preceding his exit—"That man should be at woman's command, and yet no hurt done!" (1.3.87-88)—surely suggest Helena's situation, which the Steward outlines for the Countess just before Helena enters.[11] I shall return to Lavatch, but now I should like to turn, as the narrative does, to the King's healing.

As many of its critics have noted, *All's Well,* like *The Winter's Tale,* falls into two halves: each contains a miraculous and sexually charged transformation, and each transformation is doubled—that is, each generates its own medium of exchange. Linked to death as well as to new or renewed life on both literal and metaphoric levels, transformation not only threatens the integrity of the individual but also becomes a means to register sexual events. In the first such transformation in the play, Helena restores the King's health in order to get the man she desires, Bertram. Yet, although Lafew's comments about Helena's ability to "araise King Pippen" and "To give great Charlemain a pen in's hand / And write to her a love-line" (2.1.75-77) preface their confrontation, the formal, rather distanced, riddling couplets articulating their exchange as well as Helena's presentation of herself as one possessed not only of purely natural healing properties (inherited from her father) but also of God's grace and the help of heaven strongly counter this particular level of sexual suggestiveness. And again, the playtext differs significantly from the source text.

In Boccaccio, the King, after deciding to permit Giletta to work her cure, asks her to set the terms of her failure:

> "Damosel, if thou does not heale me, but make me to breake my determination, what wilt thou shal folow thereof." "Sir," said the maiden: "Let me be kept in what guard and keeping you list: and if I do not heale you within these eight dayes, *let me be burnt*: but if I do heale your grace, what recompence shall I have then?" To whom the kinge aunswered: "Because thou art a maiden and unmaried, if thou heale me according to thy promise, I wil bestow thee uppon some gentle-

> man, that shalbe of right good worship and estimation." To whom she aunsweared: "Sir, I am very well content that you bestow me in mariage: But I beseech your grace let me have such a husband as I myselfe shall demaund, without presumption to any of your children or other of your blood." Which request the king incontinently graunted.[12] [my emphasis]

In *All's Well*'s source, the idea of rewarding Giletta with a husband comes from the King; in Shakespeare's text, Helena sets the terms of the bargain herself, a change that foregrounds her sense of her own power. More remarkable, though, is how the playtext transforms Giletta's suggestion that she be burned (the fate of witches) if she fails to heal the King.

> *King.* Upon thy certainty and confidence
> What dar'st thou venture?
> *Helena.* Tax of impudence.
> A strumpet's boldness, a divulged shame,
> Traduc'd by odious ballads; *my maiden's name*
> *Sear'd otherwise*; ne worst of worst extended
> With vildest torture, let my life be ended.[13]
>
> (2.1.164-73 [my emphasis])

Shakespeare's playtext transfers the notion of burning (which looks back to the "flame of liking" in 1.3) to Helena's maiden name, adding the ideas of torture and death as circumstances which extend the other risks: impudence, boldness, shame, traduction. Helena foregrounds the threat to her virginity, links that idea to her worst fears, and places herself in a position of abjection, substituting the literal mention of death as a cover for its metaphorical sense.

That Helena's cure of the King as a means of forwarding her own desires and that her language—both consciously and subconsciously—reflects those desires seems clear enough. But what of the King? Lafew's remark, "I am Cressid's uncle / That dare leave two together" (2.1.96-97) suggests reading the scene as an illicit encounter; the exchange of vows, sealed with a handclasp, and the absence of a "love scene" so far in a play concerned with romance further invite reading at least an implicit current of sexual attraction between Helena and the King.[14] Initially, however, he rejects Helena's aid until she evokes the help of heaven and repeats her vow to hazard her life: "Not helping, death's my fee" (2.1.188). And the only phrase he speaks that approaches double entendre—"Thy will by my performance shall be serv'd" (2.1.201)—gains a potential sexual resonance more from Helena's (and an audience's) hearing than from its literal context. The BBC-TV production pushed that potential by closing the scene with Angela Down's Helena bending over Donald Sinden's King, who sucked life from his restorer in a passionately consuming kiss, over which the camera lingered. Representing the King's cure as initiated by a shared sexual attraction anticipates and supports the courtiers' elliptical remarks when, fully recovered, he dances with Helena (2.3). Yet the playtext chooses other means—the first of several substitute scenes—to signal the King's reawakened sexual powers.

With this scene (2.2) the narrative returns to Rossillion and to some comic banter between the Countess and Lavatch. On the surface, their dialogue does little more than simply fool away the time: the usual thematic reading focuses on pointing the distinction between physical nurture and moral discipline and as Shakespeare's familiar commentary on the emptiness of courtiers. Read as a narrative substitute for the King's healing, however, its heavily suggestive double entendre not only articulates offstage events but also further supports the notion that Lavatch functions as Helena's double. Although the Countess opens the exchange with a line that glances at Helena's role—"Come on, sir: I will now put you to the height of your breeding" (2.2.1-2)—Lavatch's claim—"I have an answer will serve all men" (2.2.14)—puts him more directly in her position as "healer-virgin." And the Countess's questions and comments evoke the King's earlier verbal behavior. At first she seems to ignore Lavatch's bawdy play on "it," yet she does not reprimand him but, rather, repeats her questions.

> *Count.* Have you, I say, an answer of such fitness for all questions?
> *Lav.* From below your duke to beneath your constable, it will fit any question.
> *Count.* It must be an answer of most monstrous size that must fit all demands.
> *Lav.* But a trifle neither, in good faith, if the learned should speak truth of it. Here it is, and all that belongs to't; ask me if I am a courtier; it shall do you no harm to learn.
> *Count.* To be young again, if we could, I will be a fool in question, hoping to be the wiser by your answer.
>
> (2.2.27-38)

The Countess's wish here is exactly consonant with what is happening to the King in these moments. Moreover, she herself not only indulges in but seems to enjoy this juvenile wit play, encouraging Lavatch's riff on "O Lord, sir!" until he says, "Nay, put me to't, I warrant you" (2.2.45)—at which point she reminds him of whipping (Does Helena's mention of torture as an alternative echo here?). Although straining exact substitutions—Lavatch for Helena; the Countess for the King—risks overprivileging this exchange, the Countess's wish for youth and her momentary indulgence in sexually playful talk at this particular point in the narrative do function as verbal substitutes for unrepresented events.[15] The next scene fulfills her wish: Helena's cure restores the King's youth. Although thought to be miraculous—"A showing of a heavenly effect in an earthly actor" (2.3.23-24)—his cure also results from double entendre, from the text's own sexual play with the power of language as representation.[16] Lafew first stresses the King's youthfulness—"Why, your dolphin is not lustier"; his next comment registers a more precise sexual connotation: "Lustique, as the Dutchman says. I'll like a maid the better whilst I have a tooth in my head. Why, he's able to lead her a coranto" (2.3.26-27; 41-43).

Once again, the playtext's stress on the King's sensual health transforms Boccaccio's details. In the tale, Giletta, once married to Beltramo, wins the love and affection of her husband's subjects for returning order to Rossiglione, for restoring "all the countrie again to their auncient liberties." Her sociopolitical concern for the subjects' welfare prompts her to assemble the "noblest and chiefest of the country" to announce that she will leave Rossiglione for pilgrimages and devotion.[17] In Shakespeare's playtext, ordering the social and political aspects of the state becomes linked to the reawakening of the King's sexual powers, thus foregrounding Helena's ability to restore a dying world to life. But the most important narrative results of the King's restoration are that it not only produces a couple, Helena and Bertram, but that Helena gains from the King the "honor and wealth" that make her Bertram's equal. Here, too, the playtext manipulates Boccaccio's details. Whereas Giletta is fatherless and rich and refuses many husbands with whom her kinsfolk would have matched her, Helena, though she is also fatherless, is neither rich nor sought after but, like the nameless gentlewoman in Boccaccio's tale who becomes her bed-trick substitute, "very poore and of small substance, nevertheless of right honest life and good report, who by reason of her poverty was yet unmaried."[18] And Shakespeare's playtext transforms Giletta's refusal of many husbands into a miniature occasion that foregrounds Helena's undesirability, not her eligibility, by surrounding her with a whole group of unwilling potential husbands (and sympathetic, if not willing, older men—surrogate fathers) from which Helena chooses (as we know she will but the King does not) the singularly unwilling Bertram. Further, the King assumes a father's role in granting Helena both a title and a dowry, which both validates her marriageability and transforms her virginity into a medium of exchange. And it is precisely through this exchange, through the King's "raising," that Helena acknowledges her desire and effects her second miracle. But first, some talk of the happy couple.

Assuming that dialogue between lovers functions as a form of discourse that substitutes for sexual foreplay, the talk that Helena and Bertram share represents the confined and sexually constrained (or silent) nature of their relationship. As the King formalizes their marriage contract, Bertram and Helena speak only to him, not to one another. Here as well as in the next few scenes, they speak only through intermediaries—the King, Parolles—meeting (in 2.5) only to say goodbye, a point at which the text inscribes an acute lack of mutuality. Bertram rejects Helena's words, her obedience, her very physical presence; he ignores and/or turns away from her wish to "steal" a parting kiss: neither her body nor her language can transform his silence into either sexual discourse or gesture. Yet that silence functions in conjunction with what they do say to one another (and what other characters say, not only to them and about them but to others) as a structuring absence: in this text, avoiding access to sexuality constitutes a mode of paying heightened attention to it. In representing Helena and Bertram's relationship, the text articulates a tension between the obsessive frankness of highly playful double entrendre and a repressive discourse centering on ideal notions of love, virtue and honor. And the narrative structure further represents this tension between obsessiveness and restriction by masking heightened sexual events with substitute scenes which cover but do not silence their presence.

When with Parolles, Helena speaks straightforwardly of losing her virginity; when alone, she expresses her desire for Bertram in romantic metaphors, seeing him as "a bright particular star" and herself as "the hind that would be mated with the lion"; she talks of dying for love (1.1.84; 89-90). When with Bertram, however, she suppresses both modes of speech. Like Helena, Bertram would preserve his virginity—"lose it to [his] own liking"; also like Helena, he speaks most freely with Parolles, his double. Just as Lavatch's comments reveal the underside of Helena's sensuality, Parolles' remarks disclose Bertram's sexual preoccupations in the conventional bawdy glaze of locker-room juvenilia. At Parolles' urging, Bertram substitutes the romance of the Tuscan wars for the marriage bed—"Wars is no strife / To the dark house and the detested wife" (2.3.287-88)—later shifting that desire onto Diana. Ironically, his attempt to refuse the story scripted for him by the King and to introduce a new, and forbidden, sexual narrative leads him to legitimize Helena's desire.

As Helena and Bertram leave the stage to be married, the narrative parts them. That the text avoids the sort of bawdy substitute for Helena and Bertram's marriage that it provides for the King's cure measures the coldly contractual, nearly asexual nature of their union. Yet the moment does receive a substitute: Lafew's ridicule of Parolles masks the ceremony, and the text foregrounds the coincidental timing by Lafew's exit and immediate return with the news of Helena and Bertram's marriage. Parolles, by not even acknowledging the marriage but instead demanding "reservation" of the "wrongs" in Lafew's statement about his "lord and master," mirrors Bertram's refusal to accept Helena, to be "mastered," except by God (2.3.238-60). Their exchange functions doubly, exposing Bertram's unworthiness by showing Parolles' emptiness and self-concern and by preserving Bertram from immediate judgment by displacing that potential for judgment onto Parolles. When Bertram does enter, his absolute refusal of Helena, set against Parolles' ingratiating, almost nanny-like support of the wars as an alternative to marriage,[19] locates honor in sexually explicit terms:

> He wears his honour in a box unseen
> That hugs his kicky-wicky here at home,
> Spending his manly marrow in her arms,
> Which should sustain the bound and high curvet
> Of Mars's fiery steed.
>
> (2.3.275-79)

In his willingness to exchange the use of his "manly marrow" in his wife's arms to pursue "honour" in the wars, Bertram, like Helena in her bargain with the King, views possible death as an alternative to consummating what he views as illegitimate desire. And when Helena next appears (2, 4), the text sets her concern for the Countess and her desire to conform to Bertram's will sharply against Bertram's hatred of the King's "present gift" and his resolve to send her to her "single sorrow"—a state she will share, if briefly, with his mother. Helena's exit with Lavatch, after hearing Parolles' flowery (and prophetic) excuses for Bertram's delay in consummating the marriage, strengthens the earlier suggestions of their doubling, equating their fool-likeness. Their shared silence here foregrounds the defeat of both verbal aspects of Helena's sexuality: against that of the man of words, Parolles, neither form of discourse has power. In Trevor Nunn's 1982 Royal Shakespeare Company production of *All's Well,* Helena's slow exit, holding hands with the stooped and limping Lavatch, movingly evoked their relationship as well as her extreme vulnerability.

Following a brief scene that sets up the war, the narrative now focuses on that vulnerability by further outlining the threatening territory of death and dying that Marjorie Garber suggests as a pervasive grounding for Shakespearean comedy.[20] Soon, Helena will begin to question both Bertram's sexuality and her own; but now, again in banter with the Countess, Lavatch glances at Helena's position. He thinks not of his desire, Isbel: "The brains of my Cupid's knock'd out, and I begin to love as an old man loves money, with no stomach" (3.2.14-16). Lavatch leaves for the reading of Bertram's letter, which tells the Countess of his "undoing" and his flight, returning to outline the life and death issues. In so doing, he links Bertram's vulnerability with Helena and identifies his "danger" specifically in terms of sexual encounters.

> *Lav.* Nay, there is some comfort in the news, some comfort; your son will not be kill'd so soon as I thought he would.
> *Count.* Why should he be kill'd?
> *Lav.* So say I, madam—if he run away, as I hear he does; the danger is in standing to't; that's the loss of men, though it be the getting of children.
>
> (3.2.35-41)

As Alexander Welsh points out, the play takes seriously the joke on "standing to't": the only way Helena can call Bertram husband is to turn him into the father of her child.[21] But as the play's first half ends,[22] Helena's soliloquy expresses her fears of Bertram's death in battle; imagining herself as the potential cause of his death, she resolves to substitute her absence for his return to Rossillion. She sees herself, as when she earlier sought Bertram's farewell kiss, as "a timorous thief" who has stolen the title of wife. At this mid-point, closing (as it began) on notes of death and loss, of humiliation and self-sacrifice, Helena's sexuality has no potentially expressive means: denied as both virgin and wife, she is nothing.[23]

The opening of the second half, by rhyming on the play's first scene, where Bertram leaves for Paris, initiates some expectation that the narrative will now follow his military career. Instead, the text explores his sexuality, exposing his faults and then betraying him to himself, thus confirming Helena's view of him as a worthy object of desire. Although the second part of the narrative analyzes Bertram's experience as well as the patriarchal conventions he attempts to put into play, its affective center affirms Helena's control and power as a counter to those conventions. The narrative overturns the vowed absences of both characters, transforming these lacks into presence.

After Helena leaves, her letter to the Countess, blessing Bertram and vowing to sanctify his name, concludes:

> He is too good and fair for death and me;
> Whom I myself embrace to set him free.
>
> (3.4.16-17)

Most editors gloss "whom" as "death," which limits the possible play in her phrase. The words riddle prophetically: she will embrace both herself (in the person of Diana) and death (literally, by forging her own, and metaphorically, by embracing Bertram). That embrace will free Bertram from literal to metaphoric death, which, in turn, will eventually free him to her. Strikingly, she betrays her suppressed preoccupation with sexual dying by positioning herself (as she had before the King) as a substitute for death.

Increasingly, Helena's language elides both the actors and the actions of desire, compressing her thought into cryptic phrases that mask self-revelation.[24] After arranging the bed trick, for instance, taut, riddling couplets formalize and cap her resolve:

> Let us assay our plot; which, if it speed
> Is wicked meaning in a lawful deed,
> And lawful meaning in a lawful act,
> Where both not sin, and yet a sinful fact.
> But let's about it.
>
> (3.7.44-48)

Glossing Helena's phrases not only suggests their complexity but reveals her attempt to legitimize her "plot," to transform "wicked meaning" (Bertram's intended adultery as well as, perhaps, her own ruse) to "lawful deed" (Bertram's marriage duty to Helena) and to enclose "lawful meaning" (Helena's rights as a wife) in a "lawful act" (marriage) which erases the "sin" of both. But Helena's argument, which reflects the intricate and delicate play between forbidden and legalized sexuality in purposefully antithetical absolutes, cannot so transform Bertram's attempted adultery; rather, "and yet" separates that "sinful fact" from the rest of her thought, signalling its transgressive nature. Nevertheless, her impersonal terms and strong end rhymes press toward action and aftermath: intent upon *meaning, deed, act* and *fact,* she seems distanced, apart, speaking more for the playtext's mechanism than for herself.[25]

Although Helena's last words—"But let's about it"—anticipate that the bed trick will follow directly, the text elides it, substituting a noisy mask for the promised silence of the sexual encounter. Two scenes of foreplay introduce the centerpiece. Parolles' capture and blindfolding, where his captors taunt him (appropriately, with meaningless languages), repeat and intensify the earlier substitution for Helena and Bertram's wedding—Lafew's attack on Parolles (4.1). And again, the moments function doubly, to suggest Bertram's position by showing Parolles' blindness, his fear and his concern for his life; and to emphasize not only the artificiality of language but also its inability to convey meaning.[26] Diana's claims for true vows continue and extend this mockery, exposing and ridiculing Bertram's reliance on conventional sonnet epithets and on his *carpe diem* argument, recalling Parolles' earlier words to Helena—"Loss of virginity is rational increase, and there was never virgin got till virginity was first lost" (1.1.125-27). Prophetic in his "sick desires," he gives Diana his ring and vows, "My house, mine honour, yea, my life be thine / And I'll be bid by thee" (4.2.52-53). Hearing Diana's "You have won / A wife of me, though there my hope be done" only through the immediacy of desire, he transforms her thought to his own sexual fantasy: "A heaven on earth I have won by wooing thee" (4.2.64-66).[27]

The bed trick itself constitutes the most complex substitute scene in the narrative, linking betrayal, exposure and death. The first speakers, Bertram's fellow-officers, blame him for shaking off his worthy wife, for incurring the displeasure of the King and for perverting a young gentlewoman in Florence. Just at this moment, they say, Bertram "fleshes his will in the spoil of her honour" (4.3.15), an action the Lords condemn: "Now, God delay our rebellion! As we are ourselves, what things we are!" "Merely our own traitors," replies the Second Lord (4.3.18-20). Again the time is mentioned, a precision Shakespeare's texts rarely employ except to emphasize its particular significance. The Lord's conversation turns briefly to Parolles' anticipated unmasking, then to the war's peaceful conclusion and finally to Helena's pilgrimage and the news of her death: "the tenderness of her nature became as a prey to her grief; in fine, she made a groan of her last breath, and now she sings in heaven" (4.3.49-51). Once more, as when double entendre masked the King's cure (2.2), the text articulates, on the level of social gossip, the progress of offstage events. The report of Helena's death coincides with the moment that Bertram consummates what he thinks is his desire for Diana and what we know is the "lawful act" of marriage.[28] The shrine of "imperial Love" blurs the distinctions between literal and metaphoric dying: it is both a kind of brothel and a heaven of peace.

The possibility of Bertram's honor being "used up" by his death at the hands of war becomes replaced by Helena's metaphoric death, by what she later refers to as the "sweet use" of her virginity. In *All's Well* the exchange is much less cruelly mechanical than the exchange of head for maidenhead in *Measure for Measure*.[29] Nevertheless, the moments produce a similarly problematic life and death context, tainted by betrayal. For Helena has surely "betrayed" Bertram into her bed under the cover of darkness, just as the Lords have lured Parolles to "betray[ing] us all unto ourselves" (4.1.92). Like Angelo in the final scene of *Measure*, and like Bertram and Helena in this play, Parolles is threatened with torture and death and then allowed to live. And, in another startling reminiscence of the earlier substitute scene, his "O Lord, sir, let me live, or let me see my death!" echoes Lavatch's riff on the answer of "fitness for all questions" (2.2).

However dazzling and satisfying this purge of Parolles/ Bertram, Bertram's own responses to facing his doubled death seem puzzlingly muted. In cataloguing the "sixteen businesses" he has dispatched, he summarily dismisses Helena's death and his mourning and makes only an elliptical reference to the "business" of his sexual pleasure—"the last was the greatest, but that I have not ended yet" (4.3.88-89)—which yields almost immediately to his fear that Diana will claim him as her husband. Even when he hears himself described as "ruttish," a "dangerous and lascivious boy, who is a whale to virginity, and devours up all the fry it finds," and when Parolles' verse letter exposes his half-made oaths and inability to pay what he owes, he condemns Parolles only briefly (4.3.212-23). Like Helena in 2.2, who approaches the four Lords with a careful balance of rhyming wit and commonplace blessings that masks her feelings about choosing a husband publicly, Bertram's comments on Parolles' gulling cover the extent of his own exposure: of all the participants in this mass confessional, he remains most distant. Whereas the text might have given him either a long aside or a soliloquy,[30] instead *Parolles*, his double, speaks in self-acknowledgment—"Simply the thing I am / Shall make me live. . . . There's place and means for every man alive" (4.3.322-28)—delaying knowledge of Bertram's own awareness.

If this substitute for privileging Bertram's point of view frustrates rather than reassures, Helena's level of awareness is equally problematic. Although the easy trust among the play's community of women purposefully counters the men's betrayal of themselves and of Parolles, Helena's words reveal her distance:

> But, O strange men!
> That can such sweet use make of what they hate,
> When saucy trusting of the cozen'd thoughts
> Defiles the pitchy night; so lust doth play
> With what it loathes for that which is away.
>
> (4.4.21-25)

She views her hour with Bertram not as giving sexual pleasure but, paradoxically, as a "sweet use" which prompts her to analyze the mental operations of hatred, wantonness and lust, producing a discomforting commentary on male sexuality. As before, she elides subject and object. But here, her thought process completely represses the female presence, transforming it into "what they hate," "what it [lust] loathes," "that which is away." Finally, she masks the future with proverbial notions:

> All's well that ends well; still the fine's the crown.
> Whate'er the course, the end is the renown.
>
> (4.4.35-36)

Both Bertram and Helena turn toward the results of their experience, toward endings. Bertram elides any analysis of his sexuality, suggesting both his deep privacy and his self-concern. Helena, puzzled by men's strangeness, tries to comprehend a male point of view; characteristically, she does so by denying self and without conveying specific blame. The strongest impression of both, however, is that their metaphoric death produces stillness and verbal silence: sexuality seems suspended, momentarily in a kind of limbo, following its "use."

Lavatch's appearance following the bed trick reflects this suppression. His sexual wit play gone, his comments glance at both Helena and Bertram as he rues her death and professes himself "a fool . . . at a woman's service, and a knave at a man's" (4.5.1-22). His view of the world has shrunk:

> I am a woodland fellow, sir, that always loved a great fire, and the master I speak of ever keeps a good fire; but sure he is the prince of the world; let his nobility remain in's court, I am for the house with the narrow gate, which I take to be too little for pomp to enter; some that humble make themselves may, but the many will be too chill and tender, and they'll be for the flow'ry way that leads to the broad gate and the great fire.
>
> (4.5.44-52)

This apocalyptic glimpse glances precisely at how Lavatch views a world lacking Helena's redemptive presence.[31] Although Lavatch's despair causes Lafew to dismiss him and the Countess to apologize for him, the text continues to support his link to Helena. Significantly, in his absence, Lafew introduces the idea of Bertram's marriage to his daughter, Maudlin, just before Lavatch returns to announce Bertram's arrival. And in the final moments of his role, he faces and insults his opposite double, the muddy (and smelly) Parolles, before leaving him with Lafew.[32] His absence in the final scene signals the repression of his particularly incisive, misanthropically proverbial wit and his replacement with his now-transformed double, Helena. For one function of the closing scene is to remove the taint of Helena's deception, likening her to Bertram and Parolles, and to substitute another likeness.

The final scene recalls and reproduces the whole narrative, transforming each repeated event in a series of astonishing volte-faces. These features suggest its likeness to a play-within-a-play, yet it provides not just a contrapuntal inset mechanism but a full and tough-minded analysis of grief, confession, lies and accusations, justifiable anger and reconciliation. All of these mirror, though not in their precise ordering in the playtext's process, the stages Elisabeth Kübler-Ross identifies as those we pass through in accepting death.[33] That acceptance of literal as well as metaphoric death grounds one function of the sexual signs operating here. On another level, the text reconfirms and equates virginity with miraculous capabilities; further, elaborate doublings validate virginity as well as marriage. Although to some extent, metaphorical, mythical and miraculous constructs here displace those of actual human behavior, such fairy-tale signs have been integrated, throughout the play, with signs of the real, and the close continues that seeming paradox.

First, a summary of Boccaccio's ending. Having executed the impossible tasks—getting Beltramo's ring and a son begotten by him—Giletta appears at a feast Beltramo gives on All Saints' Day. Just as the company prepares to sit down at table, she enters, bearing her twin sons in her arms, identifies herself and asks (since she has fulfilled his conditions) to be received as Beltramo's wife. Beltramo, "greatly astonned," recognizes the ring and "the children also, they were so like hym." As she retells her story, Beltramo instantly knows that she speaks the truth and, "(perceiving her constant minde and good witte, and the twoo faire young boyes)," accepts Giletta as his lawful wife, honoring her and "abject[ing] his obstinate rigour," not only in order to keep his promise but also to please his subjects.[34]

Whereas Boccaccio focuses on Giletta's constancy and cleverness as a way to acknowledge and affirm the legitimacy of the social order, Shakespeare's text uses these emphases only as a frame to join the play's oppositions—virginity and marriage, giving and losing, life and death. Two of Boccaccio's most striking details, however, are foregrounded: the mention of All Saints' Day and Beltramo's twin sons. One has a limited "presence," in that it acts as a pre-text only for some elements of the closing scene; the other pervades the entire play.

All Saints' Day, the festival celebrating the saints in heaven, becomes not only a possible antecedent for Helena's reference to herself as "but the shadow of a wife" but also lies securely behind an ending celebrating her return from the dead. *All's Well* certainly evokes the spirit, as well as a remembrance, of both the Epistle and the Gospel for All Saints' Day. The Epistle, from Revelation 7:2, concerns the appearance of a multitude standing before the throne of the Lamb clothed in white robes. When an elder asks who they are, he receives this reply:

> These are they which came out of great tribulation, and have washed their robes, and made them white in the blood of the Lamb. Therefore are they before the throne of God, and serve him day and night in his temple; and he that sitteth on the throne shall dwell among them. They shall hunger no more, neither thirst any more; neither shall the sun light on them, nor any heat. For the Lamb which is in the midst of the throne shall feed them, and shall lead them unto living fountains of waters: and God shall wipe away all tears from their eyes.

Do Lafew's tears—and the Countess's—also recall this passage? And as a pre-text for the religious undertones here, the Gospel for All Saints' Day—Matthew 5:1, the beatitudes—prefaces Christ's call to perfect love.

All's Well transforms Beltramo's twin sons into a series of resonant doublings: Bertram/Parolles; Helena/Diana;

Helena/Lavatch; Helena/Maudlin (a "shadowed" doubling prompting Bertram's avowal of Helena's worth); Helena's double cures of the King and Bertram; the doubled rings; doubled "deaths"; Bertram's double "winning." In addition, the closing scene produces further doubles. In denying that the ring he gives to Maudlin was Helena's, Bertram prompts the King to accuse him of Helena's literal, not her metaphoric, death. Momentarily, then, he again faces consequences similar to those Helena was willing to suffer if she failed to cure the King. Further, Bertram's initial rejection of Diana repeats, with a difference, his earlier rejection of Helena. Diana, insistent on her "right," vows "That she which marries you must marry me— / Either both or none" (5.3.173-74), words that introduce the equation of virginity with married chastity, which Helena's later appearance confirms. Pressed on all sides, but especially by the threat of exposure from Parolles, Bertram finally acknowledges that he "boarded her i' the wanton way of youth," idealizing his own role in the encounter and blaming her "restraint" for "madding" his eagerness (5.3.210-12). These statements, together with Parolles' remarks that Bertram "Lov'd her, and lov'd her not" and that he, Parolles, "knew of their going to bed and other motions" (5.3.245; 257-58) are the most explicit sexual signs in a discourse where sexuality is confined to its symbols—the rings—and endowed with an ability, once openly recognized, to regenerate the past, heal the present and provide for the future.

Diana's forthrightness here, like Helena's as she proposed to cure the King, threatens her with death. Lafew assumes, from Diana's answers, that she is a whore: "This woman's an easy glove, my lord; she goes off and on at pleasure" (5.3.271-72), recalling Helena's similar positioning of herself if she failed to cure the King—either a strumpet (her "maiden name sear'd") or a wife. Denying that she is a strumpet, Diana assumes Helena's magical qualities, sets up the riddle that solves her own riddling ambiguities and produces Helena. In turn, as Helena produces Bertram's ring and the letter, her double winning of her husband validates Diana's chastity. And Bertram faces, in his moment of revelation, not twin sons, replicas of himself, but doubled presences of chaste virtue. And, as the King promises to provide Diana with a dowry and the husband of her choice, she (as well as what she stands for) becomes additionally powerful—the means for the story to be repeated once again.

Throughout, Shakespeare's text complicates the characters' sexual psychology beyond Boccaccio's details, generating suggestions of Helena and Bertram's potential incest as well as creating the expectation that the King and the Countess may marry.[35] The close, however, evades both notions. The King, in accepting Bertram and providing Helena with a dowry, does become a surrogate father for both, but the text does not couple him with the Countess, thereby eluding the creation of a family joined by metaphorical, if not literal, incest. The final words of his role stress his presence as "lord" and "liege" to Helena and Bertram, and his fatherly function transfers from them to Diana, for whom—*if* she proves herself a virgin—he will provide a dowry.

These last-minute transfers and transformations suppress the Countess's verbal role: she functions as an observer, providing explanatory asides and confirming significant information, such as the ring's provenance. Although Bertram neither greets her nor acknowledges her commentary, Helena does respond: "O my dear mother, do I see you living?"[36] In Nunn's production, the Countess's weeping prompted Helena to embrace her, reaching beyond the formally achieved marital and social resolutions articulated by the text toward an emotional expression of reconciliation. Only Lafew's tears fill the silence that marks the text's final riff on doubled presence: one mother faces (and/or embraces) her replacement on the crowded, uncoupled stage, recalling Helena's early wish:

> The mightiest space in fortune nature brings
> To join like likes, and kiss like native things.
>
> (1.2.218-19)

Finally, the play positions women either as virgins ready for marriage or as mothers. Implicitly and explicitly, the woman who acknowledges her own sexual desire becomes transformed into one or the other.

This transformation marks Helena's willingness to relinquish her independent identity for the dependency of marriage and motherhood, to (some would say) sacrifice herself to these institutions. Yet she has already passed through the sacrificial fire that would sear her maiden name; in winning through to her desire, she is, unlike her namesake from Troy, neither war booty, ransom, nor gift. Unlike many Shakespearean heroines, she does not lapse into silent consent at the close. Rather, the text displaces that potential onto Diana, who remains silent at the King's offer of a dowry if she proves to be a virgin—in other words, a substitute for what Helena was. Thus, although the close foregrounds conformist ideology by placing Helena as a socially and sexually legitimate wife and mother, it also generates another virgin who may attempt to use the patriarchal system in order to gain power—much as Queen Elizabeth used patriarchal codes by speaking a discourse of apparent abjection and vulnerability.[37] By articulating a cogent analysis of female (and male) sensibility, Shakespeare's text generates an incipient critique of patriarchal systems as well as a model of feminized power. But that is another essay.

I began this essay by saying that Helena lies at the center of the internal as well as the critical drama of *All's Well.* At the close, however, the critical emphasis shifts away from Helena to express widespread disappointment and dissatisfaction with Bertram's truncated and insubstantial replies to Helena, objections that level at what I read as signs of realism (albeit expressed through highly controlled artifice) in a non-realistic text and seem to be grounded in a romantic expectation that Shakespearean characters will not only say exactly the "right thing"—that is, that they will speak expressively, preferably at some length and with rhetorical fluency—but also that this particular character, Bertram, will finally accept Helena with a bit more enthusiasm.[38] Listen to their final exchange with the King:

> *[Re-]enter Widow* [with] *Helena*
> *King.* Is there no exorcist
> Beguiles the truer office of mine eyes?
> Is't real that I see?
> *Helena.* No, my good lord;
> 'Tis but the shadow of a wife you see;
> The name and not the thing.
> *Bertram.* Both, both. O pardon!
> *Helena.* O my good lord, when I was like this maid
> I found you wondrous kind. There is your ring,
> And, look you, here's your letter. This it says:
> *When from my finger you can get this ring*
> *And is by me with child, & c.* This is done;
> Will you be mine now you are doubly won?
> *Bertram.* If she, my liege, can make me know this clearly
> I'll love her dearly, ever, ever dearly.
> *Helena.* If it appear not plain and prove untrue
> Deadly divorce step between me and you!
>
> (5.3.299-312)

Helena first speaks to Bertram through the King, echoing her earlier inability to address him directly. Yet by completing her verse line, Bertram's response joins his thought to hers: in the compression and elision characteristic of his (and Helena's) role, he gives her the name of wife, acknowledges that she is no longer "nothing" but "the thing itself" and asks for pardon. Helena's words seek further surety, reminding him, first, of their encounter and then, more specifically, that the terms of her acceptance were his. Her question—"Will you be mind now you are doubly won?"—in its pun on *won/one,* recalls the twins of the source and invites Bertram to reconfirm her presence in terms of a unity that includes them both. And again Bertram cues his speech to hers, addressing her through the King in words that pick up, in his repetition of *ever* and *dearly,* her notion of "doubly won"—and thus acknowledge his willingness. Helena's response continues and confirms the paired notions that, alone, make their exchange noticeably extraordinary. Her thought first rests on plainness, on constancy. Now, she links divorce to death, rephrasing her initial oppositions—to be both Dian and love, to give and to lose, to live and to die. But she no longer bears death alone; she transfers it to divorce, to what may "step between me and you." And she repeats Bertram's conditional preface, grounding her answer in negatives—"not plain," "prove untrue"—that can transform into positive terms only through a similar operational instruction, a potential "if." The exchange, sounding more like the terms of a bargain (and a fictional one at that) than the romantic language of our expectations, articulates—in this text, for these characters—a startling mutuality.

Finally, for Helena and Bertram, their commitment to their shared sexuality becomes hesitantly apparent, more in silence than through extravagant speech or romantic gestures, as the possibility of kindness and love. Trevor Nunn chose to open his production of *All's Well That Ends Well* with a couple waltzing in half-light to a haunting tune and to deny a similar image at the close but rather to have Helena and Bertram exit—after the King's epilogue and after the others had left the stage—slowly, together but without touching one another. His staging privileges those features of the close suggesting that all only *seems* well—for the characters as well as for the comedy—given the problematic "ifs" of Bertram, Helena and the King, which acknowledge the conditional nature of human sexual behavior in marriage and of fictions about marriage. This close celebrates compromise, the text's final real-izing of romance.

Notes

1. I borrow this construct from Jacqueline Rose, "Sexuality in the Reading of Shakespeare: *Hamlet* and *Measure for Measure,*" in *Alternative Shakespeares,* ed. John Drakakis (London: Methuen, 1985), pp. 95-118.

2. For these notions of story elements, see Molly Haskell, *From Reverence to Rape: The Treatment of Women in the Movies* (Baltimore: Penguin Books, 1974), see especially pp. 138-19, 160-61 and 230.

3. Brian Henderson, "Romantic Comedy Today: Semi-Tough or Impossible?" *Film Quarterly* 31, no. 4 (Summer 1978): 11-23.

4. In reading the play's structure, I draw from the following: V. I. Propp, *Morphology of the Folktale* (1928), trans. Laurence Scott (U. of Texas, 1958); A. J. Greimas, "Elements of a Narrative Grammar" (1969), *Diacritics* 7 (1977): 23-40; and Roland Barthes, *S/Z* (1970), trans. Richard Miller (New York: Hill and Wang, 1974).

5. Although some have not been cited, I should like to acknowledge a general debt to the following studies: Nicholas Brooke, "*All's Well That Ends Well,*" *Shakespeare Survey* 30 (1977): 73-84; James L. Calderwood, "Styles of Knowing in *All's Well,*" *MLQ* 25 (1974): 272-94; Howard C. Cole, *The All's Well Story from Boccaccio to Shakespeare* (U. of Illinois Press, 1981); Ian Donaldson, "*All's Well That Ends Well*: Shakespeare's Play of Endings," *Essays in Criticism* 27 (1977): 34-55; R. A. Foakes, *Shakespeare: The Dark Comedies to the Last Plays* (U. Press of Virginia, 1971); Northrop Frye, *A Natural Perspective* (Columbia U. Press, 1965); Marjorie Garber, *Coming of Age in Shakespeare* (London: Methuen, 1981); Robert G. Hunter, *Shakespeare and the Comedy of Forgiveness* (Columbia U. Press, 1965); Arthur C. Kirsch, *Shakespeare and the Experience of Love* (Cambridge U. Press, 1981); G. Wilson Knight, *The Sovereign Flower* (London: Methuen, 1958), pp. 95-160; W. W. Lawrence, *Shakespeare's Problem Comedies,* 2nd edition (New York: Frederick Ungar Publishing Co., 1960); Joseph G. Price, *The Unfortu-*

nate Comedy (U. of Toronto Press, 1968); A. P. Rossiter, *Angel with Horns* (London: Longman's, Green and Co., Ltd., 1961); R. L. Smallwood, "The Design of *All's Well,*" *Shakespeare Survey* 25 (1972): 45-61; E. M. W. Tillyard, *Shakespeare's Problem Plays* (U. of Toronto Press, 1971); Roger Warren, "Why Does It End Well? Helena, Bertram and the Sonnets," *Shakespeare Survey* 22 (1969): 79-92; Richard C. Wheeler, *Shakespeare's Development and the Problem Comedies* (U. of California Press, 1981).

6. All references to Boccacio's tale are from William Painter's version (1575) as reprinted in Geoffrey Bullough, *Narrative and Dramatic Sources of Shakespeare* (London: Routledge and Kegan Paul, 1958), 2:389-96.

7. All text references are to the Arden edition of *All's Well That Ends Well,* ed. G. K. Hunter (London: Methuen, 1962).

8. G. K. Hunter sees Helena's dialogue with Parolles as a "free and frothy play upon the ideas which are fermenting . . . in Helena's (or rather Shakespeare's) mind" and as "germane" to Helena's situation. (Arden Introduction, p. xlii.) Free and germane it certainly is, but that Helena confirms her determination to put her virginity to use through joking with Parolles seems more disturbing than frothy.

9. See G. K. Hunter, Arden Introduction, pp. xxxiv-xxxvi.

10. Arthur C. Kirsch notes the liturgical parody and provides a cogent analysis, p. 140. In discussing these moments, Joseph G. Price reminds readers that the Clown's parody must be seen in its overall thematic context and that we are not to take it seriously, for seeing him as a choral commentator on Helena's love ignores both the text and the role of the clown in Shakespeare's plays (Price, pp. 146-47). But by so limiting Lavatch's (or any clown's) verbal presence, he becomes simply an incidental figure whose role functions only to express a dramatic convention.

11. G. K. Hunter, the Arden editor, notes the glance at Helena's situation, p. xxxv.

12. Bullough, pp. 390-91.

13. I have adopted the Folio punctuation here, which, rather than making "extended / With vildest torture" parenthetical, suggests the rush of Helena's thought.

14. Like Angelo in a more avowedly perverse love scene in *Measure for Measure* (2.4), the King seems attracted to Helena's virtuous qualities.

15. For a full discussion of unrepresented events in *The Winter's Tale,* see Howard Felperin, "'Tongue-tied our queen?': The Deconstruction of Presence in *The Winter's Tale,*" in *Shakespeare and the Question of Theory,* ed. Patricia Parker and Geoffrey Hartman (London: Methuen, 1985), pp. 3-18.

16. In Roland Barthes' view, from the pleasure of the text. *The Pleasure of the Text* (1973), trans. Richard Miller (New York: Hill and Wang, 1975).

17. Bullough, p. 392. A similar concern for the country's welfare and for its *mis*use of "liberty" prompts Duke Vincentio to assume the disguise of a friar. Unlike Giletta, however, he tells no one except another friar where he is going or why. *Measure for Measure* may be indebted to *All's Well*'s source for these details.

18. Bullough, p. 393.

19. Cf. Juliet's nurse advising her to marry Paris, *Romeo and Juliet* 3.5.214-27.

20. Marjorie Garber, "'Wild Laughter in the Throat of Death': Darker Purposes in Shakespearean Comedy," in *Shakespearean Comedy,* ed. Maurice Charney (New York: New York Literary Forum, 1980), pp. 121-26.

21. Alexander Welsh, "The Loss of Men and Getting of Children: *All's Well That Ends Well* and *Measure for Measure,*" *MLR* 73 (1978): 17-28.

22. See Emrys Jones, *Scenic Form in Shakespeare* (Oxford U. Press, 1971), esp. pp. 66-88, for a full discussion of two-part structure.

23. Cf. Mariana in *Measure for Measure,* 5.1.172-79.

24. Nicholas Brooke's essay, "*All's Well That Ends Well,*" gives extremely sensitive readings of the operations of language in the play.

25. As does *Measure*'s Duke Vincentio at similar points in that play's narrative (3.2.254-75; 4.1.71-76). "Who is speaking here?" Barthes would ask. *S/Z* (1970), trans. Richard Miller (New York: Hill and Wang, 1974), pp. 41-42.

26. Price, p. 163.

27. Several cruxes of language in 4.2 have long puzzled editors. First, Bertram's opening line, "They told me that your name was Fontybell." G. K. Hunter reports Thiselton's conjectural reference to the fountain with a statue of Diana erected at Cheapside in 1596 but comments on the lack of evidence that it was ever called *Fontybell* or *font bel.* He adds, "Even if it had been, why should Bertram be told that his beloved had the name of a fountain?" (pp. 100-1, n.). Even though Bertram, a few lines later, calls Diana "no maiden but a monument" (which supports the statue reference), does not his question, in the situation literally an opening "line," function as double entendre? Surely he knows Diana's name and is attempting to transform her into the "beautiful fount" of his imagined desire, testing her sexual willingness. If so, Diana will not play the game and silences Bertram's initial approach: "No, my good lord, Diana." Refusing to be seen as an available object, she reminds Bertram that she has the name of chastity herself. Returning to Ovid's Diana, it is tempting to suggest

that Actaeon's fate upon seeing Diana "naked in his sight," bathing in "a lively spring with Christall streame" underlies this exchange. In Ovid, Diana sprinkles water on Actaeon's head and face and says, "Now make thy vaunt among thy mates, thou sawste Diana bare. / Tell if thou can: I give thee leave: tell heardly: do not spare." And then she places the hart's horns on his head. *Shakespeare's Ovid,* ed. W. H. D. Rouse (Southern Illinois U. Press, 1961), Bk. 3, ll. 188; 220-30. It would, however, be a strain to push a full correspondence between the two situations and the two texts. Diana does not seek as thorough a revenge on Bertram (she is, after all, not seen naked but prevents that), and the usual threats of cuckolding are absent from the text.

Second, I would like to add a new possibility to those offered by editors for the crux of 4.2.38: "I see that men make rope's in such a scarre." Might "I see that men may rope's in such a scarf" make good sense? It certainly has the advantage of re-calling Parolles, whom Diana has described as "that jackanapes with scarfs" (3.5.85)—a further reminder of his position as Bertram's double, and sexual mentor, in this crucial scene.

28. Welsh also notes this conjunction, p. 20.

29. Jan Kott, "Head for Maidenhead, Maidenhead for Head: The Structure of Exchange in *Measure for Measure,*" *Theatre Quarterly* 8:31 (1978): 18-24.

30. Similarly, Helena, following Bertram's rejection in 2.4 or 2.5, might have spoken in soliloquy, as she did at the close of 3.2.

31. Northrop Frye overstates the case, I think, in calling this a vision of "the mass of humanity moving witlessly, like lemmings, to its own annihilation" that summarizes the "blind and deluded movement that sent Bertram out to the wars" and that anticipates the final action that brings him home (Frye, pp. 105-6).

32. Lavatch's final line, "I do pity his distress in my similes of comfort, and leave him to your lordship" (5.2.24-25), is not unlike Fool's last comment on the situation to his double, Lear: "And I'll go to bed at noon" (*King Lear* 3.6.83).

33. Garber, "Wild Laughter." See also Elisabeth Kübler-Ross, *On Death and Dying* (New York: Macmillan Co., 1969) and Edwin S. Shneidman, "Death Work and Stages of Dying," in *Death: Current Perspectives,* ed. Edwin S. Shneidman, 2nd. ed. (Palo Alto: Mayfield Publishing Co., 1980), pp. 305-11, in which he argues that the stages Kübler-Ross indentifies do not of necessity follow the exact progression she outlines.

34. Bullough, p. 396.

35. As Marjorie Garber points out, the play's first line is the Countess's ambiguous remark, "In delivering my son from me, I bury a second husband." Bertram, at once a newborn son and his mother's (forbidden) husband, leaves for the King (in whom, Lafew promises, his mother will find a husband and he a father) and male companionship in the wars, apparently fleeing a household dominated by women. Clearly, Bertram associates Helena with his mother, speaking to her as though she were a sister; Helena herself rejects this role when the Countess offers to be a mother to her by declaring that she desires not a mother but a mother-in-law (*Coming of Age,* pp. 41-42).

36. The moment has a parallel in *As You Like It* that can easily go by unnoticed, both on the page and in performance. Directly following Hymen's wedding song in 5.4, Duke Senior says, "O my dear niece, welcome thou art to me, / Even daughter, welcome, in no less degree!" (5.4.141-42). Juxtaposing the divine with a simpler emotional response translates what is universal to a particularized human intensity: enabling people to co-exist, honored, in families, is one lasting residue of the "blessed bond of board and bed."

37. See Michael Calvin McGee, "The Origins of 'Liberty': A Feminization of Power," *Communication Monographs* 47, no. 1 (1980): 23-45; Michael Calvin McGee, "On Feminized Power," The Van Zelst Lecture in Communication, Northwestern University School of Speech, May 1985.

38. In *Measure for Measure*'s final scene, the gender expectations are reversed, as the continuing debate over Isabella's consent or non-consent to Duke Vincentio's rather badly timed proposal demonstrates. The critical dramas surrounding both plays, however, are heavily weighted by individual critics' assumptions about (for examples) comic form, closural conventions, the sanctity (or non-sanctity) of marriage and gender-specific behavior.

David McCandless (essay date 1997)

SOURCE: "*All's Well That Ends Well,*" in *Gender and Performance in Shakespeare's Problem Comedies,* Indiana University Press, 1997, pp. 37-78.

[*In the following essay, McCandless focuses on the evolving gender roles of Helena and Bertram in* All's Well That Ends Well, *discussing Shakespeare's handling of the bed trick as a tool for exploring gender myths.*]

The starting point for my discussion is Susan Snyder's recent characterization of *All's Well* as a "deconstructed fairy tale":[1] lurking beneath the folkloric narrative of the poor physician's daughter who deploys magic and cunning in order to overcome a dashing Count's disdainful resistance are the unrepresentable spectres of female sexual desire and male sexual dread. Indeed, the play invests the fairy tale motifs that W. W. Lawrence believes undergird

All's Well—"The Healing of the King" and "The Fulfillment of the Tasks"—with potent erotic subtexts.[2] In adapting "The Healing of the King," Shakespeare, like his model Boccaccio, departs from tradition in making the King's healer a woman. Lawrence barely mentions this innovation, but it seems highly significant, especially since Shakespeare, unlike Boccaccio, makes Helena's gender—more particularly, her sexual ardor and allure—indispensable to the cure.

Integral to the narrative of "The Fulfillment of the Tasks" is the bed-trick, an explicitly sexual event in which a disprized wife wins back her husband by making love to him incognito, taking the place of another woman (in some versions the wife herself in disguise) whom he has wooed. *All's Well* deconstructs this folkloric device by wedding it to genuine sexual perturbation. The bed-trick is not simply the consummation of a marriage, in which Helena cleverly satisfies Bertram's seemingly impossible conditions, but an act of prostitution, in which Helena services Bertram's lust and submits to humiliating anonymous "use," and a kind of rape, in which Helena coerces Bertram into having sex with her against his will.

Yet, as many critics have noted, the play seems to suppress its own erotic subdrama.[3] Certainly Shakespeare idealizes and mystifies the sexual arousal that empowers Helena's cure of the King. He lends Helena magical and hieratic powers, giving her the capacity to effect a supernatural cure. He similarly desexualizes her erotic agency in the bed-trick, allowing Diana to serve as Helena's sexualized double. Diana also suffers Bertram's degrading slander in the play's final scene, allowing Helena to reenter the play as a saintly, resurrected figure whose visible pregnancy sanctifies her sexuality and who elicits an instantaneous reformation from Bertram. The bed-trick becomes a transcendent event, vastly removed from groping bodies in the dark, from the kind of event imaged as "defil[ing] the pitchy night" (4.4.24).[4]

I propose in this piece to stage the play's erotic subdrama, to push it further to the surface, for the purposes of tracing the play's provocative interrogation of gender. Helena and Bertram are both inextricably entangled in gender's constrictive myths. Helena performs and seeks to reify a normative femininity that her aggressive desire contradicts, while Bertram enacts a normative masculinity that his model, the meretricious Parolles, radically destabilizes. The reading I wish to stage adumbrates a theatrical staging that I will extend by citing and imagining corroborative directorial choices. I will consider, in particular, how the circulation of the look reinforces or disrupts gender roles. My investigation of performance will focus most heavily on the implications of performing the unperformed bed-trick. In performance, the bed-trick constitutes a "lack" in the play's narrative because it is unperformed, not part of the play's visceral, theatrical life, a plot mechanism scarcely capable of disconcerting spectators to the degree that it has critics. I want to examine the extent to which staging the bed-trick can assist in dramatizing the "deconstructed fairy tale" that lies at the heart of *All's Well*—can assist, that is, in bringing to the surface the erotic subdrama that the play represses, and, in so doing, deepen the play's deconstruction of gender. Indeed, a staged bed-trick demystifies and substantiates a female sexuality that the play elsewhere mystifies and evades, and thus begins to redress the "lack" not only in the play's performed life but in a representational economy in which woman figures only as absence.

Helena's Femininity: Subject vs. Object

Helena has been such a puzzle and provocation to critics because she occupies the "masculine" position of desiring subject, even as she apologizes fulsomely for her unfeminine forwardness and works desperately to situate herself within the "feminine" position of desired object.[5] At the same time, Bertram poses problems because he occupies the "feminine" space of the objectified Other, even as he struggles to define himself as a man by becoming a military and sexual conqueror. He is the desired object, the end of the hero's (or, in this case, heroine's) gendered journey of self-fulfillment.

Helena's opening soliloquy conveys the plight of a woman trapped between active ("masculine") and passive ("feminine") modes of desire. She clearly expresses her desire to consummate a sexual love, calling herself a "hind" who wishes to be "mated by the lion" (1.1.85-92). At the same time, she adopts a "feminine" posture: she cannot mate but only be "mated." Furthermore, as a hind desiring a lion, she cannot mate at all. Helena thus naturalizes the culturally established distinctions of gender and class that make Bertram a forbidden object. In addition, Helena trains a desiring look on Bertram, submitting her "curled darling" to rapturous objectification, only to affirm a "feminine" helplessness, lamenting the impossibility of eliciting his returned look.[6]

> 'Twas pretty though a plague,
> To see him every hour, to sit and draw
> His arched brows, his hawking eye, his curls,
> In our heart's table—heart too capable
> Of every line and trick of his sweet favour.
>
> (1.1.92-96)

Her look manifests lack and insufficiency, conveying a masochistic fixation: it was pleasurable torment—"pretty though a plague"—to survey his beauteous, unattainable form "every hour" (1.1.79-98).

Once galvanized by Parolles' bracing anti-virginity jape, however, Helena resolves to "feed" her desirous look, to make the object of worship an object of consumption:

> What power is it which mounts my love so high,
> That makes me see and cannot feed mine eye?
> The mightiest space in fortune nature brings
> To join like likes, and kiss like native things.
>
> (1.1.220-23)

That Helena imagines a sexual feeding here seems plausible, given the imagery of "joining" and "kissing," not to mention the suggestive phraseology of "mount[ing] my love." The "space" separating her and Bertram she portrays as a product not of nature, which favors their "joining," but of "fortune," which seems here to mean "standing in life" (*OED* 5) and thus to represent culture.

The language Helena employs is characteristically elliptical, stemming from her guarded, coded, sexually charged dialogue with Parolles. The obscurity of her discourse perhaps reflects the unspeakability of her desire. Her exchange with Parolles begins as a theatrical "turn," with Helena playing "straight man" for the swaggering poseur. As straight *man,* Helena translates her unspeakable desire into the discourse of male bawdry, seeking a kind of release through the sublimated pleasures of naughty talk, even if her lines serve principally as cues for Parolles' ribaldry.

Helena's salacious banter with Parolles marks her first explicit deviation from normative femininity, marks her as provocatively "open" in a social spectacle that, in Shakespeare's time, demanded female "closedness."[7] Lisa Jardine asserts that Helena reveals herself as "too [sexually] knowing for the innocent virgin she professes to be."[8] Yet Helena does not profess to be anything at all in the play's opening scene. Rather, she challenges the spectator's attempt to hold her to a stable identity. She appears a grieving daughter, reveals herself a despairing lover, and finally emerges a resolute wooer, signaling a subjectivity that eludes a coherent singleness.

Certainly Parolles regards Helena as sexually knowing and therefore "open" to ravishment. Performance could make clear that Parolles not only jests with Helena but cheekily flirts with her, launching, behind the cover of licentious badinage, an assault against her own virginity. The two of them may actually engage in some version of the erotic combat they describe: Helena "blows up" (arouses) Parolles, and Parolles seeks an opportunity to "blow up" Helena (make her pregnant). Although Parolles casts Helena as desired object, she maintains her status as desiring subject, rejecting subjection to his controlling look. Her objection to his greeting—"save you, fair queen" (106)—registers a protest against being treated like a "quean." She claims the right to control her own sexual destiny, resisting Parolles' injunction to "answer the time of request," and thus rejecting the notion that a woman must not exercise choice but must make herself the object of a man's. If Helena initially agrees to play the role of imperiled virgin, she ends the scene by emasculating Parolles, not simply by declining to gratify his desire but by mocking his cowardice and thereby undermining his masculine honor, provoking his retributive threat to return in order to "naturalize" (i.e., debauch) Helena.

Helena's query, "how might one do, sir, to lose [virginity] to her own liking?" (150-51) conveys something more than a rebuff of Parolles' lecherous overtures. By invoking the possibility of fulfilling her own desire, Helena begins to take seriously Parolles' aspersion of virginity—or, more specifically, his vision of the naturalness and regenerativeness of sexuality. She steps outside the scene's theatrical frame and trades the role of "straight man" for that of surprised convert. She disregards his censure of her wish to choose rather than be chosen and answers his challenge, "will you anything with it?" decisively if obscurely:

> Not my virginity yet:
> There shall your master have a thousand loves,
> A mother, and a mistress, and a friend,
> A phoenix, captain, and an enemy,
> A guide, a goddess, and a sovereign,
> A counsellor, a traitress, and a dear.
> His humble ambition, proud humility;
> His jarring concord, and his discord dulcet;
> His faith, his sweet disaster; with a world
> Of pretty, fond, adoptious christendoms
> That blinking cupid gossips.
>
> (165-75)

Modern editors have been inclined to assume a missing line between Helena's terse defense of virginity and her expansive list of lovers' endearments. "There" is usually taken to mean "at the court," and the speech is explained as Helena's anxious contemplation of courtly rivals whose enchantments may well stir Bertram's desire. The speech might be better understood, however, as a coded disclosure of Helena's own erotic stirrings. Her need to speak cryptically and elliptically not only betrays a compulsion to conceal her sexual passion but also reflects the difficulty of representing female sexuality within an oedipal plot that typically idealizes or erases it. If one gives up the idea of a missing line, the sense of Helena's response is captured in G. Wilson Knight's paraphrase, "I shall not part with my virginity to anyone yet, because therein your master has an infinite love."[9] Knight, however, backs away from the aggressively sexual connotations of this decoding, asserting, "I do not think, at this early stage in her story, it can mean 'in giving your master my virginity I shall give him a thousand loves,' since she has no good reason at this stage to expect such an event."[10] Helena's lacking a reason to expect "such an event" is surely beside the point; she clearly desires to "mate" with Bertram and, stoked by Parolles' libidinous exhortations, she presumably builds on the tantalizing possibility of losing her virginity to her own liking—that is, to Bertram. The speech becomes the link between this heretofore unthinkable idea and the conception of her bold plan for winning him.

She wishes Bertram well, she tells Parolles, but would rather *do* him well—"show what we alone must think." She would like to give her well-wishing (that is, her love) a "body" which "might be felt" (180-81). Her wish that Bertram feel the body of her love foreshadows the offering of her body in the bed-trick and in marriage. Perhaps "at the court" has seemed the best candidate for Helena's imagined "there" because virginity—or rather the unpenetrated female territory it predicates—has been perceived, within a phallocentric register of meaning, not as a "there" but as a "nowhere," a "nothing-to-be-seen" in Irigaray's striking phrase.[11] In a Shakespearean sense, the virgin "knot" connotes a "not."[12]

Thus the key to the speech may lie not in a missing line but in a missing language—one that embodies a woman's "thereness" and enables the expression of female desire. Helena appears trapped within the phallocentric linguistic system that Lacan describes, in which female desire is literally unspeakable, always already reconfiguired as the desire for male desire.[13] The unspeakability of Helena's passion compels her to speak it evasively and mystically. She thus characterizes her "virginity" as a kind of philosopher's stone (5.3.102), a "tinct and multiplying medicine" that blesses Bertram with a supernally expansive love and allows her, for his sake, to assume all the guises of the courtier's beloved—to become a kind of shape-shifting superwoman. "I am his anything," Helena seems to say, as though embracing the status of possession that Petruchio prescribes for Kate when he calls her "my any thing" (3.2.332).

In addition, Helena continues to believe that she must be "mated": she cannot unleash this mystical female power, cannot become Bertram's idealized courtly lover, until Bertram "has" her maidenhead, discovers her wonders "there." Bertram will, in effect, give birth to her as a woman, becoming the fount of signification, a father as well as husband, confirming a transference implied in Helena's earlier assertion that his image had supplanted her father's (79-83). Once more the play seems to dramatize the contradiction of female subjectivity: Helena expresses an active ("masculine") longing to consummate her passion but in terms that betray a "feminine" urge to empower and sustain Bertram, to fit herself to his fantasies—or at least to his received images of femininity. Helena's feminine hope that Bertram might love her once he knows her (sexually) eventually impels her "masculine" orchestration of the bed-trick.

Helena continues to feminize her desire throughout her campaign to win Bertram, offering compensatory performances of exemplary chastity to atone for the unchaste boldness of her plan.[14] Her urge to simulate a normative femininity furthers an oedipal narrative that depends upon muting her sexual provocation. Forced by the Countess to confess her love for Bertram, Helena disclaims the desire to win him that we know she harbors, reviving the self-abasing hopelessness of her first soliloquy, once more portraying Bertram as an unattainable heavenly body that she worships (1.3.204-207). In a conversation with the King, she betrays a similar compulsion to appear normatively chaste. After Lafew does his best to mark their meeting as a sexual tryst, Helena precipitously withdraws her suit when the King taints her proffered cure with imputations of prostitution, "humbly entreat[ing]" a "modest thought"—requesting his belief in her chastity—as she prepares to take her leave (2.1.127-28). Her willingness to suffer a prostitute's punishment if her cure fails (2.1.170-73) seems designed to dispel any lingering suspicions of unchastity, to distance her holy magic from wanton witchery.[15]

In 2.3, the scene in which Helena is to choose a husband, her status as desiring subject becomes public. The King, submitting a batch of eligible wards for her inspection, formally confers "looking power" upon her: "fair maid, send forth thine eye. . . . peruse them well" (52, 61). He also lends her the masculine privilege of choice: "Thou hast power to choose, and they none to forsake" (56). Her public position as dominant woman is so unprecedented that Lafew mistakenly believes that the young lords have rejected her rather than vice versa: as a woman, she cannot be the chooser but only the object of choice.[16] Helena's singular ascent requires another compensatory performance of "femininity." Although she has, in fact, "command[ed]" the King to grant the fulfillment of her desire (2.1.194), she protests her chastity to the assembled suitors and blushingly retires before the King ratifies her authority and compels her to continue.

Helena has come a long way from her earlier masochistic fixation on Bertram. In surveying the undesired suitors, her look frees itself from libidinal investment and so emulates the gaze by marking them as signifiers of her power (over the King), as participants in her spectacle. At the same time, Helena also derives power from being looked at, from being the center of attention, the belle of the ball. Her "to-be-looked-at-ness"—in cinema a signifier of female "lack," according to Laura Mulvey[17]—becomes in the theater an attribute of power, a specularity that approximates the gaze rather than marking her as its object. As Lacan puts it,

> At the level of the phenomenal experience of contemplation, this all-seeing aspect [of the gaze] is to be found in the satisfaction of a woman who knows that she is being looked at, on condition that one does not show her that one knows that she knows.[18]

Within the theatrical frame, the looked-upon central performer and her observers do indeed collude in the kind of disavowal of specularity that Lacan describes. Of course, Helena (or the actress performing her) is looked at not simply by the other figures on stage but by the play's spectators as well. Yet here, too, she may escape a fetishizing look by availing herself of a strategy inaccessible to the film actress: returning the look. In this particular scene, such an effect could be achieved by placing the prospective suitors within the audience, so that when Helena sends forth her eye, she surveys "us" as well as them, bringing us into spectacle by breaking the fourth wall—by determining us, the audience, as lacking by linking us with those desiring suitors whom she rejects. Even in relation to the audience, then, Helena may represent not "to-be-looked-at-ness" but "looking at to-be-looked-at-ness."

When she finally claims Bertram, as Snyder observes, "she does her best to deny her role as aggressive desiring subject and to recast herself properly as object":[19] "I dare not say I take you, but I give / Me and my service, ever whilst I live, / Into your guiding power" (102-104). Bertram, however, discerns and resists this implicit emasculation, dismissing her protestations of vassalage and reclaiming the masculine privilege of looking: "I shall beseech your highness, / In such a business give me leave to use / The help of mine own eyes" (106-108). Bertram refuses to let Helena function as gaze for him. He breaks the stage picture of the happy affianced couple that Helena, in collusion with the King, has created. Indeed, if Bertram takes his protest to a King enthroned upstage right, and the humiliated Helena drifts downstage left, her stage observers shift accordingly, "facing out" in order to look at her. Helena takes a vulnerable position and accepts the status of "to-be-looked-at" as the audience no longer looks at her but looks at her being looked at. She is now clearly the object of the male look, the pawn in a male power struggle, standing by mutely as the King and Bertram proceed to debate her worth. If Helena is born to femininity and at certain moments compelled to achieve it, here it seems thrust upon her.

To call attention to Helena's "performative" femininity is not to accuse her of hypocrisy or willful deception. To point out that her self-effacements are self-serving is not to rehearse the tired, limited characterization of her as a two-faced, manipulative man hunter.[20] It seems to me more helpful to understand Helena's hyperfemininity as a kind of *misrecognition* that she persists in enacting. Helena can perform femininity with such conviction because she has successfully internalized a culturally imposed image of Woman. When Helena seems to affect femininity for the sake of covering her unfeminine, predatory tracks, she may not be crudely dissembling but, like a good method actress who loses herself in the role, truthfully simulating, thereby authenticating the role demanded of her. As Butler suggests,

> gender is . . . a construction that regularly conceals its genesis; the tacit collective agreement to perform, produce, and sustain discrete and polar genders as cultural fictions is obscured by the credibility of those productions.[21]

Helena challenges a restrictive standard of feminine chastity but, while doing so, she must answer to the chaste self-image shaped by patriarchal society. As John Berger puts it, a woman is "almost continually accompanied by her own image of herself."[22] One reason, no doubt, that Helena has elicited such contradictory critical assessment is that she so vividly embodies the contradiction foundational to female subjectivity in a phallocentric system of meaning—that between self and cultural mirror, woman and Woman.[23]

In performance, one way to call attention to that contradiction would be to assign two actors to the role of Helena: a woman accompanied by a man in drag who would step in whenever Helena "acts feminine." These two Helenas would then take turns, sometimes within the same scene (Helena's interview with the King in 2.1, for instance) or even the same speech (for example, the first soliloquy), while at other times a single Helena would dominate (the female for Helena's combative exchanges with Parolles, the cross-dressed male for her doleful evasions of the Countess). In a modern-dress production of *All's Well,* costuming could accentuate this duality, with the cross-dressed male (as cultural mirror) far more unerringly "feminine" in appearance than the female, whose attire could be freer and more individualized, even androgynous. This prettified, feminine, male-constructed Helena then becomes kin to the lavishly festooned Parolles, a culturally constructed gender image compelling imitation. Such a choice dramatizes the process of misrecognition, exposing the performativity of gender in a manner congruent with much of feminist theater theory.[24] Director/theorist Jill Dolan took a similarly deconstructive approach to her staging of *A Midsummer Night's Dream*:

> [W]hen Helena prostrated herself and pleaded with Demetrius to "beat me," Puck halted the action, directing "ACT-UP" fairies to reconfigure Helena's masochistic desires by taking over for her and Demetrius. The male and female actors moved in and out of the Balinese-derived masks which indicated these two roles, suggesting the construction of gender and the representational constraints placed on women.[25]

In addition, Dolan underlined the theatricality of gender by cross-dressing Theseus and Hippolyta in the final scene and by "cross-casting" Oberon and Titania: the fairy king was a mustachioed woman in suit and hat, the queen a man in high heels, leather miniskirt, and rhinestone-studded bra.

The two-actor approach I describe might, however, have the regrettable effect of collapsing Helena's core self with a "masculine" desire as symptomatic of cultural influence as her "feminine" self-abjection. The director may therefore prefer to capture Helena's doubleness not through double-casting but through the concentration of its contradictory effects in a single actress—an actress capable of projecting a core self that dramatizes the contradiction as a symptom, preventing the role from sliding into static incoherence. Helena thus becomes as self-possessed and unself-consciously sensual in her active moments as she is self-effacing and studiously chaste in her passive ones. Traditional criticism has tended to portray Helena as either long-suffering Griselda or cunning vixen (thinly veiled versions of "madonna" and "whore"), either glossing over her audacious desire and celebrating her virtue or reading her virtue as a mask for audacity and regretting or deploring her duplicity. A characterization keyed to Helena's doubleness invalidates these reductive caricatures, underscoring the inadequacy of phallocentric constructs to an understanding of Helena's complex subjectivity. This approach challenges audiences to reconcile Helena's indomitable sexuality with her obsequious femininity, to account somehow for a nice girl who seeks and obtains what has traditionally been considered the bad girl's pleasure.

Helena's doubleness manifests itself unmistakably in her one scene with Bertram (prior to the play's final moments).

In one sense, she savors "feminine" subservience as the reward for her "masculine" boldness, embracing wifely subjugation with a fervor that mortifies Bertram. "Come, come, no more of that," he protests when she pronounces herself "his most obedient servant" (72). She seems to accept—even to flaunt—a neutered passivity for the sake of eliciting male love.[26] At the same time, her lavish self-effacements seem designed to compensate for her irrepressible, potentially transgressive desire. In asking Bertram for a kiss, she offers a muted sexual overture and claims some measure of her conjugal rights—yet in language so elliptical that it virtually negates the desire it manifests. When Bertram demands, "what would you have," she answers,

> Something, and scarce so much; nothing indeed.
> I would not tell you what I would, my lord.
> Faith, yes:
> Strangers and foes do sunder, and not kiss.
>
> (2.5.83-86)

Once more Helena struggles with the unspeakability of her desire, managing to speak it only indirectly and negatively. It is "something" which quickly becomes "nothing," something she would *not* tell. Although she shifts back into affirming it ("yes") she quickly subsides into a pause, manifesting her search for a language expressive of her desire. As though confirming the impossibility of finding it, she proceeds to describe the desired kiss as something strangers and foes do *not* do.[27]

As noted, Helena's "masculinity" is as much a construct as her "femininity" for, as Foucault has argued, sexual desire is as much culturally engendered as naturally derived.[28] Accordingly, Helena's desire is directed toward the culturally approved end of marriage, an institution that, at least according to the puritan propaganda of Shakespeare's time, confirms a woman in femininity by delivering her to permanent chastity and subservience.[29] Helena herself seems to affirm her belief in this ideal of redemptive marriage when, in an attempt to enlist the Countess' sympathies, she assesses the impossible alternatives imposed by a marriageless life:

> if yourself,
> Whose aged honour cites a virtuous youth,
> Did ever in so true a flame of liking
> Wish chastely, and love dearly, that your Dian
> Was both herself and Love, O then give pity
> To her whose state is such that cannot choose
> But lend and give where she is sure to lose;
> That seeks not to find that her search implies,
> But riddle-like lives sweetly where she dies.
>
> (1.3.209-17)

Helena presents the "feminine" alternative to marriage as the "sweet death" of terminal sexual pining, the "masculine" as the "loss" of chastity that attends "lending" and "giving" her body. She implies that she must choose between fruitlessly preserving her virginity or fruitlessly expending it. Marriage, by contrast, offers the fruitful option of expending *and* preserving her virginity—or at least preserving the virginal purity that chastity commends. In marriage, Dian is both herself, the goddess of chastity, and Love (or Venus), the goddess of desire. In marriage, that is, a woman may be both sexual and chaste, "living sweetly where she dies" in quite a different sense. This speech suggests that Helena wishes to channel her sexual desire into culturally idealized marital chastity.

Yet Bertram annuls the marriage that Helena takes such pains to make, and in terms that aim at quashing her desire, imprisoning her in the female negative, in the land of "not" and "never." "I have wedded her, not bedded her," he informs his mother, "and have sworn to make the 'not' eternal." In his letter to Helena, he does indeed afflict Helena with an "eternal not": "in such a then I write a never." In so doing, Bertram swears to make Helena's virgin knot eternal, demanding that she remain lacking, accepting her status as the negative signifier of his masculine positive. Indeed, the "dreadful sentence" that Bertram hands Helena demands the very sexual renunciation that she undertakes in her pilgrimage. She embraces a monastical chastity, reconfiguring herself as a penitent whore getting herself to a nunnery, disavowing her desire and receding into iconicity, inspiring the Countess to compare her to the Virgin Mary (3.4.25-29).

From this perspective, Helena's pilgrimage becomes the ultimate compensatory performance of femininity. Some commentators have regarded the pilgrimage as a ruse for renewed pursuit of Bertram.[30] While it is tempting to read her farewell sonnet as yet another coded disclosure of desire, its tone and content accord exactly with the masochistic, grief-stricken, guilt-ridden soliloquy in which Helena announces her intention of fleeing France in order to secure Bertram's return. Shakespeare transforms what had been, in Boccaccio's story, a relentless pursuit into a pilgrimage converted to pursuit by virtue of a miraculous coincidence. Once more Shakespeare seems to mystify Helena's sexuality, portraying her as the prodigious recipient of another heavenly favor that works to validate her desire.

Helena's sexual renunciation ends when she locates another mirror of misrecognition: Diana, who defines femininity for Helena by virtue of her attractiveness to Bertram. As Catharine MacKinnon asserts, "socially, femaleness means femininity, which means attractiveness to men, which means sexual attractiveness, which means sexual availability on male terms."[31] In order to win Bertram, Helena, the devoted would-be wife, must refashion herself as sexual object. Her goal shifts from the fulfillment of desire to the achievement of desirability.[32] Her desire is no longer simply the desire to wed but the desire to be desired. She thus identifies with, and acts through, the woman whom Bertram covets. Helena says not "I wish to become a woman" but, rather, "I wish to be like her whom I recognize as a woman," mimetically replicating a gender ideal.[33] Helena's deputization of Diana offers an extreme instance of her need to conceal her desire. Only when Helena secures the services of a surrogate who agrees to embody that desire and risk the "tax of impudence" that Helena herself carefully dodges does she manage to secure Bertram.

Helena's employment of Diana allows her to remain on a kind of pilgrimage—away from patriarchy's center (represented by the King) to a position on its margins where she can operate more daringly. She gets herself to a kind of secular nunnery, joining a confederacy of women who assist her in an intrigue that leads to her rebirth into patriarchal culture as wife and mother. Yet she must still take pains to prove her femininity, assuring the Widow of the lawfulness of her seemingly unchaste plot. She also continues to refer her power to the King ("That you may well perceive I have not wrong'd you / One of the greatest in the Christian world / Shall be my surety" [4.4.1-3]) and to invoke Heaven, mystifying her bribery of the Countess as an implement of divine providence ("Doubt not that heaven / Hath brought me up to be your daughter's dower" [4.4.18-19]). Having, in effect, pimped Diana by exposing her to censure as a whore (a censure she actually suffers in the final scene) Helena undertakes to redeem Diana by reversing the mirroring process and turning her into an image of herself, a virgin positioned for advantageous marriage, a status the King ratifies in the final scene by extending to Diana the same privilege of choosing a husband that he once conferred upon Helena (5.3.327-28)—a position seemingly contrary to her wishes to "live and die a maid" (4.2.74).

Bertram's Masculinity: Rite of Passage

One must understand Bertram's treatment of Helena in light of his quest for normative masculinity. He begins the play as a liminal figure, an "unseason'ed," uninitiated male caught in the limbo between boyhood and manhood. In the play's opening lines, his mother, the Countess, not only heralds but laments his passage into manhood—"in delivering my son from me, I bury a second husband"—registering his birth as a man as the death of a husband-surrogate, as though regretting her powerlessness to hold him in perpetual boyhood. The incest she evokes may be metaphorical but, within the oedipal plot enveloping Bertram's development, it raises the specter of maternal engulfment threatening to his masculinity. His quest for manhood meets with two principal obstructions: an absence of men willing and able to help him achieve it and the continued presence of Helena, who, in consort with his mother, launches a campaign to marry him and (at least from his perspective) return him to maternal dominance.

Bertram seems adrift in a world of strong women and weak men, men who fail him as father figures. His own father is dead and cannot instruct him in courtly or military arts. Lafew, despite an explicit promise to the Countess to advise Bertram (1.1.71-73), makes little attempt to do so, and on occasion even evinces scorn for his charge (2.3.99-101). The King, a surrogate father, seems rather to block Bertram's passage into manhood, shaming him with marriage to Helena and excluding him from the wars.

The histrionic Parolles happily fills the void, embodying a fiction of masculine grandeur that Bertram attempts to actualize, a mirror of misrecognition in which Bertram insists on seeing himself, a narcissistic reflection of an idealized self that confers an illusion of wholeness. In particular, the supposedly battle-tested, sumptuously plumed Parolles offers Bertram an image of military glamor and promotes participation in the Italian war as a rite of passage into manhood. Thus he praises Bertram's determination to fight as evidence of potency: "Why, these balls bound, there's noise in it. 'Tis hard!" (2.3.279-83).

Yet the Countess and King both define manhood for Bertram as an imitation of his father, the true "perfect courtier" (1.1.60-61, 1.2.19-22). They admonish him to live up to his father's memory. Parolles becomes a rival father figure whom Bertram's own father, speaking through the King, indirectly disparages with his criticism of meretricious fashion-mongers who beget nothing but clothes ("whose judgments are / Mere fathers of their garments"). Later, Lafew implies that Parolles was begot *as* clothes, that he was not born but made by a tailor (2.5.16-19). These images impute to Parolles and his like sterility, unmanliness, and—through the emphasis on costume—imposture and barren theatricality. Indeed, by Lafew's reckoning, Parolles constructs a persona that displays attributes of a social rank and gender to which he has no legitimate claim. By insisting on calling Parolles a "servant," Lafew disputes his nobility (2.3.186-95, 242-51), and by referring to him as a "hen" (213), denies his masculinity. Indeed, Lafew tells Parolles, "I write man, to which title age cannot bring thee" (198-99) and casts similar aspersions when the King summons Parolles to testify against Bertram: "I saw the man today, if man he be" (5.3.203). Yet Parolles' histrionics problematize the notion of a masculine essence implicit in Lafew's disparagements. He functions as a symptom of the tailoredness of gender, performing a masculinity that seems as much a caricature of the cultural norm as the performed femininity of Helena. In following this counterfeit soldier-courtier, Bertram appears to be doing what Helena has already done: internalizing and authenticating a culturally inscribed myth of gender, saying not "I'm a man" but, rather, "I'm like him whom I recognize to be a man."

His father's masculinity, such as Bertram confronts it, may be no more authentic than that of Parolles, for it is also derived from a performance, from the King's dramatic death-bed celebration of the Count. The King constructs an exceptional figure, a hero/courtier of fabulous proportions, who seems partly a product of the King's intense nostalgia for a lost youth. The King not only draws the Count's character for Bertram to emulate but, at one key moment, speaks for him ("'Let me not live,' quoth he"). In a sense, the King impersonates Bertram's father, giving the Count's melancholic reflection on mortality a particularly dramatic recitation by turning it into his own death-bed speech—his own enactment of a father's dying advice to his son. Indeed, with one foot in the grave, the King becomes a virtual medium for the deceased Count's spirit.

His line, "methinks I hear him now," could refer not only to a recollected worldly voice but to a newly audible, other-worldly one. The King functions as the ghost of Bertram's father, whose underlying message is, "remember me." Yet the "me" that Bertram is asked to remember is so mystified and glorified that he appears to be left with a choice between two equally fantastical images of manhood: the inaccessibly legendary and the insidiously fashionable.

Despite exhorting Bertram to emulate his father, the King denies him the opportunity to do so by forbidding his soldiership, rendering him unable to prove himself "the son of a worthy Frenchman" (2.1.11-12). Bertram implicitly equates exclusion from the war with emasculation:

> I shall stay here the forehorse to a smock,
> Creaking my shoes on the plain masonry,
> Till honor be bought up, and no sword worn
> But one to dance with.
>
> (2.1.30-33)

Bertram accuses the King, who ought to have initiated him into manhood, of prolonging his boyhood by consigning him to the company of women, precluding his purchase of masculine honor, leaving him with a permanently sheathed, ornamental sword rather than a phallic weapon. His affected farewell to the departing soldiers also conveys his sense of emasculation: "I grow to you, and our parting is a tortur'd body" (2.1.36-37)—an image highly suggestive of castration.

Moreover, in imagining himself the "forehorse to a smock," Bertram imagines himself a woman's beast of burden, an animal she drives and whips. He thus protests the emasculating reversal of the roles of man/woman, rider/horse, master/slave that had become homologous in Shakespeare's England.[34] Bertram's paranoid fantasy seems to be almost instantly fulfilled. Upon choosing Bertram as husband, Helena offers her "service," but, by coercing him into being her sexual partner, she implicitly commands Bertram to do her "service." Rather than being allowed to "woo" and "wed" honor, as the King commands the departing soldiers, Bertram becomes an object of a woman's wooing and wedding. The King, at Helena's behest, subjects Bertram to the very calamity he had urged his soldiers to avoid—bondage to female sexuality:

> Those girls of Italy, take heed of them.
> They say our French lack language to deny
> If they demand. Beware of being captives
> Before you serve.
>
> (2.1.19-22)

Bertram is "captive before he serves," in thrall not to one of "those girls of Italy" whom the King stigmatizes, but to the girl from Rossillion, the girl next door, with whom he grew up. While he is primed to resent any imposed responsibility that keeps him from going a-soldiering, marriage to Helena is, from his perspective, the very worst of fates, regressing him even further into boyhood by returning him to the maternal domination he presumably escaped when ending his constrictive "marriage" to the Countess.[35]

Perhaps the best demonstration of the distance between Bertram and Helena comes when Parolles, urging Bertram to "steal away" to the wars in order to avoid the emasculation of marriage, characterizes Helena's virginity in terms radically different from her own:

> He wears his honor in a box unseen
> That hugs his kicky-wicky here at home,
> Spending his manly marrow in her arms,
> Which should sustain the bound and high curvet
> Of Mars' fiery steed.
>
> (2.3.279-83)

The site of Helena's miraculously generative sexual love becomes a lack, an unseen box, a black hole that consumes Bertram's manly essence, an effeminizing, contemptible "kicky-wicky." The opportunity to mount Mars' fiery steed in manly combat rescues Bertram from his emasculating role as forehorse to a smock.

That Bertram's rejection of Helena stems more from sexual dread than class prejudice seems borne out by his dismissal of the King's promise to endow her with title and dowry. If Bertram were concerned solely with social status, marriage to the King's favorite would seem distinctly advantageous. The King, after his lengthy lecture equating honor with virtue, puts thc matter quite plainly: "if thou canst like this creature as a maid, / I can create the rest." Bertram's response is equally unambiguous: "I cannot love her, nor will strive to do't" (2.3.142-43, 145).

Bertram "cannot" love Helena. She cannot be an object of his sexual desire, cannot be a "real girl" in Havelock Ellis's terms.[36] This fact is striking, as she so easily achieves that status with the other men in the play, sexually provoking Parolles, Lafew, and the King alike. Lafew considers Helena so much a "real girl" that he would like to consign those seemingly standoffish suitors to the fate of castration (2.3.86-88). From Lafew's perspective, anyone who would not consider Helena a "real girl" is not a real man.

From a psychoanalytic perspective, Bertram cannot love Helena because she is a forbidden object. The Count's responsibility for "breeding" Helena (2.3.114) reinforces her status as a sister figure. The Countess's sponsorship of her matrimonial campaign makes her a kind of mother-surrogate as well. The Countess sees in the passionate Helena an image of her younger self (1.3.128-31). By colluding in Helena's plot, the Countess aims to help Helena secure her son as husband, to revive by proxy the relationship she herself has lost.[37] Helena also may be considered a maternal figure by virtue of her status as partner to the King, Bertram's surrogate father. In an apparent reversal of the oedipal plot, in which the son sacrifices the mother as the price of masculine autonomy, the King blocks Bertram's achievement of manhood by forcing upon him the object of his own sexual interest ("follows it, my lord," Bertram protests, "to bring me down / Must answer for your raising?" [111-13]).[38]

In addition, the first of the identities Helena hopes to derive from marriage to Bertram is the one conspicuously removed from the realm of courtly love that engenders them: mother ("There shall your master have a thousand loves, / A mother, a mistress, and a friend").[39] On one level, of course, Helena simply invokes a biological fact: she may become pregnant as a consequence of intercourse with Bertram. Indeed, motherhood is an essential requirement of Bertram's impossible conditions for marrying her ("when thou canst . . . show me a child begotten of thy body that I am father to"). On another, she explicitly identifies with the very maternal image that repels Bertram and, by raising the spectre of castration, drives him to the wars. Within an oedipal framework, Helena's maternal associations make her a forbidden object, a mystified (m)other both attractive and repellant to Bertram. In one sense, then, his military campaign represents a retreat: Parolles, he "runs away for advantage when fear [in this case fear of Helena's sexuality] proposes the safety" (1.1.201-203).

Lavatch later characterizes Bertram's campaign in precisely the same terms. Bertram will not be "killed"—his manhood will not be "lost"—because he runs away from Helena: "The danger is in standing to't; that's the loss of men, though it be the getting of children" (3.2.37-42). If the swaggering, ornamental Parolles mirrors the glamorous masculinity for which Bertram strives, the wisecracking, enigmatic Clown voices the sexual anxiety that underlies it.[40] His first jest portrays female sexuality as a force that deflates male sexuality in its insatiable demand for "service," hence the Clown's preposterously cheerful acceptance of cuckoldry: "the knaves come to do that for me which I am a-weary of. He that ears my land spares my team, and gives me leave to inn the crop" (1.3.43-45). Thus Lavatch celebrates his nonsexual servitude to the Countess: "that man should be at woman's command and yet no hurt done!" (1.3.92-93).

In addition, the Clown parallels Bertram's course by presenting himself as a man recoiling from marriage and female sexuality ("I have no mind to Isbel since I was at court . . . the brains of my Cupid's knock'd out, and I begin to love, as an old man loves money, with no stomach" [3.2.12, 14-16]). When Bertram returns from the wars, having embraced the sexual experience that Lavatch eschews, the Clown suggests that the patch upon his cheek conceals syphilitic scars, reading the patch as a signifier of Bertram's corruption by female sexuality ("it is your carbodano'd face" [4.5.101]).

Lavatch seems to function as Bertram's secret sharer in a second sense: his scant commentary on Helena indicates a comparable need to construct her as a sexless madonna. Late in the play, thinking Helena dead, Lavatch affectionately eulogizes her as "the sweet marjoram of the sallet or rather the herb of grace" (4.5.16-17). This remark suggests that his earlier misogynistic ditty decrying female turpitude and seemingly linking Helena with Helen of Troy might actually mark her as the unnamed "one good woman" exempt from his slanders, dissociated from her notorious namesake and the corrupting female sexuality she epitomizes (1.3.70-79). Lavatch's need to desexualize Helena provides a subtext for his only direct speech to her, in which he offers the seemingly arbitrary anti-joke about the Countess's "wellness." In locating "wellness" in the other world, Lavatch may be admonishing Helena for her excessively worldly (that is, sexual) conduct, urging her to a monastical chastity, implicitly scolding her unchaste entrapment of Bertram. His later eulogy celebrates her seeming compliance, her expiration at the end of her penitential trek to a holy shrine, her ascension to saintly martyrdom.

Bertram so distinguishes himself in the Florentine wars that he ascends to the position of "general of our horse" and wins the masculine honor he had so craved. The scene of his ascension (3.3) often has been cut in performance but it affords an opportunity for staging a grandiose military ceremony dramatizing Bertram's ritual birth as a man, as young warrior-god. The ceremony could center on Bertram's reception of a sword, symbolizing his supposed acquisition of the phallus. In such a staging, the Duke unfurls the sword, raises it high, executes some histrionic sword salute—collectively seconded by a troop of sword-wielding soldiers—then lowers it to a kneeling Bertram, who takes hold of it, kisses it, then rises to receive it. Perhaps a pounding of drums accompanies the ceremony, which climaxes in multiple gun shots. As the thunderous volleys cease, Bertram steps forward and declares, "Great Mars, I put myself in thy file; / Make me but like my thoughts, and I shall prove / A lover of thy drum, hater of love" (9-11).

Bertram occupies the same position that Helena did in 2.3: the center of attention, the object of an admiring, even fetishizing, male look. Like Helena, Bertram functions as both spectacle (to be looked at) and simulated gaze (determining through looking). He is the glittering, glamorous presence who constitutes the others as lacking, as needing to be seen by him. Like Helena, Bertram may function as gaze for the play's spectators as well, if they are joined by soldiers extending the lacking army beyond the proscenium arch.

If the ceremony seems sufficiently overwrought and theatrical, it may begin to convey the extent to which Bertram delivers himself to a role, embracing a mythical masculinity and effectively becoming his own Parolles, who ought to be exiled to the periphery during this scene. Bertram's birth as a man coincides with his willing entrance into spectacle, his assumption of the image of ruthless warrior after rejecting that of domesticated husband.

If Bertram, contrary to the Clown's insinuations about his patch, sustains a bleeding wound—either in battle or in ritual—his ascent to manhood can include a ceremonial purgation of femininity familiar to tribal rites of passage: the bleeding wound symbolizes a male vulva that enables a masculine rebirth superseding his original birth through woman. By spilling blood and voicing rage (declaring himself a lover of Mars' drum and a hater of love), Bertram "gets the woman" out of himself and achieves manhood.[41]

At the mid-point of the play, Bertram and Helena appear to have achieved the extremes of emblematic masculinity and femininity. One could underscore this polarity in performance by creating a tableau at the end of 3.4. (invariably the end of "Act One" in performance), presenting Bertram as gilded, sword-brandishing military hero and Helena as supplicating, saintly madonna. Barbara Dameshek's 1993 production for Shakespeare Santa Cruz extended this idea, counterpointing a soldiers' chorus chanting in rap style "lover of thy drum, hater of love" with the ethereal singing of women dressed in white who assisted Helena in a highly stylized donning of her pilgrim's costume: as the Countess read her letter, Helena walked down a path of white gauze fabric while wrapping around her waist a banner that contained the first line of her sonnet ("I am Saint Jacques' pilgrim, thither gone" [4]).

Some critics have attempted to justify Bertram's rejection of Helena, or at least to present it sympathetically, as an understandable rebellion against a degrading forced marriage.[42] This laudable championing of Bertram's cause ignores the fact that a character must first become a subject before an audience can take offense at his or her being treated as an object. Theatrically speaking, Bertram has not yet become enough of a subject for the spectator to perceive his injury when the play's sympathetic heroine chooses him as husband. His first two scenes are public, dominated by his elders, allowing him little opportunity to display an individuated character. In the first, eager to leave for Paris, he struggles to play the dutiful, respectful son. In the second, he strives to make a favorable impression on the King. Only in his third appearance, free of his elders and petulantly protesting his exclusion from the war, does he exhibit a discernible subjectivity. Yet this effusion of personality is unlikely to win him many admirers. Nobody likes a whiner.

Most critics have found Bertram manifestly unworthy of Helena's devotion.[43] Certainly his conduct alienates the play's other characters, each of whom defames him at one time or another. He humiliates and abandons Helena, defies and enrages the King, and so offends his mother that she resolves to disown him and later endorses the King's threat to punish him—possibly even to execute him. His callous treatment of Diana repulses his comrades-in-arms. Offered an unearned second chance to regain the favor of his benefactors, he instead renews their ire—particularly the King's—and to save himself from censure and disgrace, he contemptuously scorns the woman to whom he had sworn eternal love. An unremittingly unsympathetic Bertram poses considerable problems for performance, however: Helena appears hopelessly foolish and deluded if the object of her pursuit is a thoroughly disagreeable clod who unequivocally disdains her. Since the play clearly derives dramatic interest from the discrepancy between Helena's unquestioning desire and Bertram's questionable desirability, the crucial question for the director to address is this: just how bad is Bertram? To what extent should he be seen as "worth it?" To what extent should one mitigate his defects in performance? Should the audience perceive something potentially redemptive in his character or potentially receptive in his attitude toward Helena? A performance that predicates Bertram's unequivocal inadequacy generates less tension and conflict—ingredients essential to dramatic interest—than one that leaves the question of Bertram's worth unresolved. Who wants to watch a play about a terminally besotted girl pursuing an insufferably churlish boy? In such a production, the play's ending becomes an unambiguous anti-climax, confirming what the audience could be presumed to have known all along: that Bertram is a boor, Helena a masochist, and their marriage an almost certain catastrophe. Such an approach does not so much deconstruct the comic love story as decisively preempt it. Indeed, the play's notorious open-endedness depends upon preserving the possibility of a comic resolution—which in turn requires the possibility of Bertram's reformation, which requires presenting him as reformable, or at least worth reforming, and therefore worth attending to as the play progresses.

Directors have employed various means to mitigate Bertram's obnoxiousness. Some have cast a physically striking, charismatic actor (such as Mike Gwilym, who played the part for Trevor Nunn) in order to make Helena's attraction credible, while others have opted to accent Bertram's youthfulness in order to make his trespasses tolerable. Paul Venables, for instance, who played the part in Barry Kyle's 1989 RSC production, was "baby-faced," "guileless," and "slightly goofy": "the sense that his errors and offenses were committed in a blissfully naive thoughtlessness . . . made him ultimately forgivable at the play's end."[44]

Directors have also aimed to redeem Bertram by lending him a subtextual complexity that qualifies and complicates his mistreatment of Helena. In Peter Hall's recent RSC production, for instance, Toby Stephens's callow, self-involved Bertram begins to mature in the second act when tested by the ravages of war and the first confused stirrings of sexual passion. The actor's subtext registered strongly with one critic who wrote, "[Bertram] doesn't seem to know what to feel, but it's clear he's feeling *something* deeply, for the first time."[45] Helena thus became the jewel in the crown of his hard-won maturation.

Trevor Nunn devised a different subtext for Bertram in his 1981 production, drawing on a psychoanalytic reading of repressed desire. According to Harriet Walter, who played Helena,

> In Trevor's scenario, Bertram had funny dreams about Helena. She's someone who's been raised in the

> household but is only the daughter of a family retainer. So he's somehow disturbed by her because he *mustn't* love her. He doesn't like the effect she has on him so he cuts her out.[46]

In Nunn's view, according to Walter, "Bertram had loved Helena all along but discovered it too late."[47] Yet Gwylim, Nunn's Bertram, objected to this interpretation and consequently keyed his performance to the dismissive gestures on the surface rather than the messier emotions underlying them.[48]

Nunn's choice offers the actor playing Bertram an emotional investment in Helena that adds drama and intrigue to his mistreatment of her, creating and heightening the conflict on which drama depends. Such a subtext could establish that Bertram struggles against feelings for Helena that confuse and unnerve him, that he rejects her not out of contempt but out of fear. Some directors have flirted with this interpretation, in particular turning Helena's request for a kiss into a stimulus for feelings that belie Bertram's apparent disdain for her. In Noel Willman's (1953) and Tyrone Guthrie's productions (1959), Bertram seemed ready to grant the kiss until, reminded of Parolles' presence, he recoiled and brusquely dismissed Helena, as though admonished by Parolles' image of uncompromised masculinity.[49] In John Houseman's production, as well as in Kyle's, Bertram willed himself to reject Helena and then remorsefully sought to make amends, turning to her as if to speak a kind word in Houseman's show, seeming tempted to hug her in Kyle's.[50] In all four cases, an agitated and uncertain Bertram evinces feelings that undermine the genuineness of his rejection. He seems motivated by a need to defend himself, not only against the force of her passion but also against the unseemliness, the unmanliness, of his own.

These choices illustrate the directorial necessity of planting in earlier scenes effects necessary to those in later ones. A bitter and hateful Bertram in 2.5 may so alienate the audience as to foreordain an unambiguously dissatisfying ending instead of a provocatively ambiguous one. In Elijah Moshinsky's BBC production, for instance, Ian Charleson's Bertram dismissed Helena harshly and disdainfully, as though her request for a kiss mortally offended him. Indeed, Charleson, normally a resourceful actor, was so narrowly sulky and conceited as Bertram, and Angela Down so relentlessly downcast as Helena, that long before their final pairing off, which Moshinsky seemingly wished to portray as a touching reconciliation, I had lost interest in them. A reconciliation of such antithetical forces can only be untenably miraculous or preposterous rather than intriguingly, even irritatingly tenable. A Bertram with some measure of merit or appeal or mitigating "unseasonedness" not only keeps the ending open but also helps ensure that Helena will appear uncomfortably obsessed rather than foolishly deluded.

Drama of Difference: Old and New Tales

Bertram constructs a narrative of initiation that essentially subsumes the oedipal plot in which woman functions as both figure of obstruction (Helena) and figure of closure (Diana). Bertram's ascension to manhood requires that he prove himself a sexual as well as military conqueror. So he sets his sights on Diana, a "real girl," a sexual object safely removed from the maternal realm. Bertram's oedipal plot intersects with what feminist critic Susan Griffin considers the quintessential pornographic plot: despoiling an idolized virgin.[51] For Bertram, who worships and supplicates Diana as a goddess but means to use her as a whore, the bed-trick becomes a mostly auto-erotic exercise. His lust reduces Helena and Diana to interchangeable embodiments of *Woman,* functioning as passive, anonymous receptacles. Of course, Helena's plot *requires* her willingness to become *Woman,* to enter the bed-trick having assimilated the fantasy image of Diana that Bertram projects. Through the bed-trick, Helena does not so much negate as revise Bertram's oedipal narrative, substituting herself as both bed-mate and figure of closure.

In appointing Helena her impossible tasks, Bertram sets up a fairy tale framework only for the sake of demolishing it. While the tasks themselves present a fairy tale challenge—do these things and "then call me husband"—his decoding of them precludes a fairy tale solution: "But in such a 'then' I write a 'never'" (2.4.57-61). Helena, however, insists on the fairy tale framework, reading his metaphor of rejection as a scenario of acceptance and orchestrating the bed-trick, a folkloric convention, in order to secure him as husband. Helena, however, describes the actual event in anything but fantastical terms:

> O strange men,
> That can such sweet use make of what they hate,
> When saucy trusting of the cozen'd thoughts
> Defiles the pitchy night; so lust doth play
> With what it loathes for that which is away.
>
> (4.4.21-25)

Helena's language is again elliptical: her assertion that strange men make sweet use of *what* rather than *whom* they hate evokes once more her hidden, forbidden sexuality, the "there" of her previous conjurings. Her disillusioned look transforms Bertram from curled darling to lustful debaucher. Just as she had predicted, his incontinent passion impels him to surrender his ancestoral ring ("in his idle fire, / To buy his will, it would not seem too dear" [4.1.26-27]). Her recent trials seem to have curbed her rapt idealizations. Helena temporarily releases Bertram from his position of substantiating mirror, the Prince Charming who enables her fantasy of ascent to love and esteem. She now configures him as Other, as personification of difference, a creature from whom she is *estranged.* She redirects her energies to overcoming this estrangement, straining against her disillusioning knowledge to reconfigure Bertram as curled darling. If, in the play's first half, Helena follows a fantasy image of Bertram, in the second half she undertakes to subdue the real Bertram to it—to facilitate or fabricate his transformation back into the creature of her fancy and so solidify her preferred image of herself.

In addition to the folkloric tropes that Lawrence identifies, *All's Well* also discloses affinities with other "old tales" that more directly address this problem of "strangeness." I am thinking, in particular, of The Loathly Lady, which deals with male fear of female sexuality, and Beauty and the Beast, which dramatizes the female's struggle with male sexuality. In each story, the protagonist's love—acceptance of the loathliness or beastliness (that is, sexual difference) of his or her opposite—converts ugliness into beauty. Beauty and the Beast depicts a young woman's transference of love from father to Beast, the sexually menacing male Other. According to Bruno Bettelheim, "only after Beauty decides to leave her father's house to be reunited with the Beast—that is, after she has resolved her oedipal ties to her father—does sex, which before was repugnant, become beautiful."[52]

At the start of the play, Helena has already made this transference. "What was [my father] like?" Helena muses. "I have forgot him. My imagination / Carries no favor in't but Bertram's" (1.1.81-83). Moreover, far from fearing male sexuality, Helena initially embraces Bertram's beastliness, portraying him as a lion with whom she wishes to mate. Indeed, by portraying herself as a hind, Helena both affirms her own sexuality and evokes a fundamental difference in "kind" that divides them. The bed-trick forces Helena to confront the un-kind Beast within Bertram and to undertake his taming. Bertram, by contrast, recoils from Helena's loathliness, her menacing sexual difference ("what [he] hate [s]"), seeing in her an image of the old crone or castrating mother.

Helena's story—and, by implication, *All's Well* itself—also sports intriguing parallels to what Jane Yolen identifies as the common incidents of the traditional tale of Cinderella: "an ill-treated through rich and worthy heroine in Cinders-disguise; the aid of a magical gift or advice by a beast/bird/mother; the dance/festival/church scene where the heroine comes in radiant display; recognition through a token."[53] Helena fits this profile to a significant degree: a worthy yet socially undesirable young woman who finds herself, thanks to a magical gift, miraculously conveyed to, and radiantly displayed at, a royal public ceremony. ("Mort du vinaigre!" exclaims Parolles, apparently stunned by her glamorous appearance, "is not this Helena?" [2.3.44].) It is surely no accident that both Tyrone Guthrie and Trevor Nunn, directors of two celebrated modern productions of *All's Well,* staged this scene as a lavish ball and costumed the poor physician's daughter in an elegant gown, effectively portraying her as Cinderella-turned-princess. And, while she fails to enchant the prince at first, she does become the object of his desire at another clandestine encounter, which she proves publicly by means of a token that seals their marriage. The token in this instance is a ring, as it is in several versions of the traditional tale.[54]

In psychoanalytic terms, the traditional tale presents a heroine who comes to terms with her own sexuality. Her cinders-guise externalizes her dread of the dirtiness of her own sexual drives. Her awareness of the underlying dirtiness impels her to exit the dance prematurely three times,

Mrs. Ternan as Countess Rousillon and Mr. Lewis Ball as Clown, engraving.

unable to yield to her sexual longing for the reciprocally desirous prince (the midnight deadline that impels her departure is not part of the traditional tale but, rather, the invention of Charles Perrault, whose seventeenth-century version provides the source for the well-known Disney movie). In the climactic scene, she affirms her sexuality by meeting the prince in her cinders-guise and, in an overtly "phallic" gesture, triumphantly inserting her foot into the slipper.[55] In *All's Well,* by contrast, the prince runs from the heroine, whose active sexuality begrimes her chastely feminine persona. She wins the prince by catching him and taking him into the cinders with her.

Traces of Beauty and the Beast and Cinderella may be found in the romance novel, a kind of contemporary fairy tale that also sports parallels to *All's Well.* The "new heroine" of those novels

> is no longer split between two archetypal female characters: the plain-naive-domestic-selfless-passive-chaste heroine and the beautiful-sophisticated-worldly-selfish-assertive-sexually active Other Woman. Instead, the New Heroine is both good and sexual.[56]

Helena holds in unresolved tension the roles of good girl and sexual adventuress that the "new heroine" has apparently successfully assimilated. A motif of taming the beast figures prominently in these contemporary tales: a seemingly beastly (i.e., hard and unyielding man) loses his heart to the worthy heroine and becomes a sensitive lover. As though ruled by this fantasy, Helena endeavors, through the power of her love, to transform the beastly Bertram into the Prince Charming of her fantasy. Helena's own narrative of self-fulfillment—and a narrative pressure of the play itself—resembles a romance novel in which the cruel hero's callous disregard of the desirous heroine masks a depth of adoration he ultimately avows.[57] The romance novel—and possibly *All's Well* as well—predicates a retributive fantasy of benign dominance-and-submission. As Tania Modleski puts it,

> A great deal of our satisfaction in reading these novels comes, I am convinced, from the elements of a revenge fantasy, from our conviction that the woman is bringing the man to his knees and that all the while he is being so hateful, he is internally groveling, groveling, groveling.[58]

One may say that Helena seeks to transform Bertram's fantasy by enabling it, replacing the pornographic narrative of violating an idealized virgin with the romance-novel plot of eliciting a redemptive kindness from an unyielding male.[59]

Staging the Bed-Trick

Indeed, if the bed-trick were dramatized, it would literally dislocate the narrative of Bertram's debauchery: "I will tell you a thing," the Second Lord confides to this brother, "but you shall let it dwell darkly with you" (4.3.10-11). This report of one woman's degradation would then give way to the dramatization of another woman's desire. Within the oedipal plot, says de Lauretis, "the place and time of feminine desire" are "nowhere" and "now," which are representable only from an "elsewhere of vision" and within "a different narrative temporality."[60] In virtually every performance of *All's Well,* the place of the bed-trick is precisely "nowhere" or "elsewhere." Its narrative temporality is *other* than the play's—parallel but not precisely coincident with that of the French Captains' gossip. Indeed, the literal death they ascribe to Helena becomes the only means of registering the metaphorical "death" of sexual pleasure she experiences during the bed-trick (4.3.47-59).[61] Through the bed-trick, Helena arrests Bertram's teleological quest for manhood and forces it into the atemporal "now" of her desire, replacing the march of "masculine" time with the occupation of "feminine" space. This hitherto unrepresented space of the bed-trick emblematizes a female difference unrepresentable within a phallocentric framework that associates that space with a "nothing-to-be-seen." If Helena's goal in the bed-trick is to undo the "knot" that Bertram vowed to make eternal, a staged bed-trick can begin to undo her "not," to deliver her from the constraints of a "lacking" femininity.

The staged bed-trick serves as a powerful gestus by creating an alternative space (not but) of female erotic agency, defamiliarizing Helena by unveiling her persistently veiled desire, enabling her to embrace unapologetically the status of sexual subject. Far from resolving her baffling doubleness, the staged bed-trick exacerbates it, intensifying the aggressiveness that belies Helena's habitual self-abjection, stressing not only her contradictory status within the play's narrative but the contradictory status of women assimilated to a phallocentric construct of idealized femininity to which they are always already unassimilable. This effect of heightened contradiction is precisely what de Lauretis identifies as the hallmark of the most effective feminist art:

> [I]t should be possible to work through [narrative] codes in order to shift or redirect identification toward the two positionalities of desire that define the female's oedipal situation; and if the alternation between them is protracted enough . . . the viewer may come to suspect that such duplicity, such contradiction cannot and perhaps even need not be resolved.[62]

By accentuating Helena's doubleness, the staged bed-trick underscores her nonmimetic subversiveness, her assertion of a difference ultimately unconforming to oedipal femininity. It brings her closer to hysteria, to a realm outside the oedipal plot where she must serve as the source of her own signification.

This outside realm, this elsewhere, substitutes unscripted body language for sanctioned verbal text, allowing Helena to replace the passive silent body Bertram expects with her own powerful "speaking body." She controls "elsewhere" by controlling its speechless discourse, effectively inscribing a condition of lack on Bertram's body. The circumstances that she stipulates—silence and darkness—deprive him of the operations that define him as masculine subject: speech and dominating look. Helena positions Bertram so that he lacks language to deny what she commands, transforming him into precisely what he sought in Diana: a masterable body.

An often overlooked marker of Helena's mastery is her curious post-coital detention of Bertram. "When you have conquer'd my yet maiden bed," Diana says on Helena's behalf, "remain there but an hour, nor speak to me" (4.2.57-58). What, one must ask, is the point of this detention? What takes place during that hour? Surely the two lovers do not simply lie there together, not seeing, not speaking, not touching. It seems that Bertram is being set up for something—but that something is never explicitly revealed. Does the dilation of the trick express a desire on Helena's part for a more sustained intimacy, for an extension of "now," for satisfaction on *her* terms? Does it aim beyond mere sexual intercourse for the "something more" of *jouissance*? Does it portend Bertram's unknowing immersion in the space he sought to penetrate and withdraw from, his submergence in the neverland of "there"? In arranging the assignation with Diana, Bertram wishes for nothing more than the performance of sex, a "trick" in another sense of the word. Helena not only offers him a different kind of trick but attempts to elicit a different kind of performance, one that transcends a merely performative sexuality. This curious ellipsis not only offers another veiled glimpse of Helena's erotic agency but also evokes her need to tame the beast, to transform a one-night stand into a foretaste of conjugal love.

The moments preceding Bertram's entrance could parallel those of Helena's aborted wedding night, which one could dramatize by cutting the Clown from 2.4. and setting the scene in a bedchamber, showing Helena readying herself for Bertram's arrival, attended by women who hasten away upon hearing a knock at the door. Helena then walks to the door and opens it, admitting not the longed-for Bertram but his leering emissary Parolles, who reports that Bertram must postpone "the great prerogative and rite of love" (2.4.41). One could then repeat this staging for the later scene: once more Helena readies herself, attended by women (this time her coconspirators Diana, the Widow, and Mariana), but this time she too flees upon hearing the knock, leaving Diana to welcome her wayward husband.

The trick itself could begin with Diana's placing a blindfold on Bertram and yielding her place to Helena. The blindfold not only provides a realistic explanation for Bertram's inability to distinguish her from Diana but also visually links him with his double, Parolles, who is likewise blindfolded and tricked in the very next scene. The blindfold would both deprive Bertram of the look and signify his blindness to the threat of castration that originally drove him from Helena. Diana could plausibly place the blindfold on Bertram if the first part of the scene were staged as a playful chase, a physicalization of the verbal cat-and-mouse game that characterized their last meeting. At some point, Helena could literally emerge from the shadows and replace Diana as the object of Bertram's pursuit.

Extending the implications of Bertram's post-coital detention, Helena could then initiate a kind of suspended foreplay, deflecting Bertram's lust-driven energies into more dilatory, sensual rhythms, indicating a desire for "something more" and ultimately turning his hasty act of undressing into a sustained performance for her benefit. If one positions Helena upstage of Bertram, the audience perceives her as looking subject and Bertram as looked-upon object. Helena emulates the gaze by making a spectacle of Bertram, constituting him as lacking through the projection and control of her desiring look. One could underline this powerful "gaze" by visually contrasting it with her earlier powerless look: during her woebegone first soliloquy she could actually watch Bertram watch himself in a mirror as he finishes dressing for his journey to Paris. In the bed-trick, by contrast, he undresses in the mirror of Helena's preemptive look. Here, as in the husband-choosing ceremony, Helena signifies not "to-be-looked-at-ness" but "determining-through-looking." In both scenes, she elicits and manages male desire, drawing a look that manifests lack. But now she looks back, unaided by the King's authority, desiring the man who desires her despite himself, functioning as the gaze for him as he previously did for her.

The play provides other possibilities for reinforcing this look. In 3.5, for instance, Diana, her mother, and Mariana all position themselves as spectators to the triumphal procession of soldiers. Diana "sends forth her eye" over these glistening combatants and lights on Bertram as desired object. The previously all-male military world admits female spectators who watch a display of macho glamor that once more positions Bertram as "to-be-looked-at" male.

Similarly, one could turn Bertram's attempted seduction of Diana (4.2) into a spectacle by positioning Helena, the Widow, and Mariana as spectators, concretizing the female frame of reference that contains the scene. Within this play-within-a-play, Diana acts the part of sexual tease, defamiliarizing the role of "the girl-who-says-no-but-means-yes" by exposing it as performative, presenting herself instead as "girl-who-says-yes-but-means-no." The concealed female audience also marks Bertram's incipient masculinity as performative. "My mother told me just how he would woo," exclaims Diana, "As if she sate in 's heart. She says all men / Have the like oaths" (4.2.69-71). Like Helena in her hyperfeminine mode, Bertram enacts a culturally inscribed script without knowing it, affirming his kinship with "all men" by venting unctuous oaths and fulsome endearments in order to arrange a one-night stand. Because the play's audience watches not only Bertram's performance but also the women watching it, the scene parallels that of Parolles' capture, in which concealed pranksters also watch their victim walk into a trap. One could extend this staging of the female look in the bed-trick, with Diana, the Widow, and Mariana joining Helena as spectators to Bertram's striptease.

In addition, Helena's reanimation of the King provides a parallel opportunity to accent her sexual power and to stage the unstaged. The cure, like the bed-trick, constitutes a significant "lack" in the play's narrative, its absence similarly serving to mask Helena's sexuality—at least insofar as the play strongly hints that the cure is sexual in nature, that Helena revives the King by arousing him.

Indeed, Helena's interview with the King functions as a kind of antecedent bed-trick. Often set in a bedchamber, it is an erotically charged, intimate meeting that forges the contract that the bed-trick ultimately fulfills. Calling himself Cressida's uncle, Lafew insinuates that Helena's medicinal powers derive from her sexual allure and later attributes the King's revival to an increase in lustiness, an interpretation Bertram seems to share in calling it a "raising" (2.1.72-78, 97-98; 2.3.41). The King suggests that entertaining Helena's cure would be tantamount to prostitution and ultimately yields to her in terms that connote an assent to sexual union: "sweet practicer, thy physic I will try, / That ministers thy own death if I die" and "thy will by my performance shall be serv'd" (2.1.185-86, 201). In addition, while the King claims his "heart owes the malady," the association of "fistula" with the anus makes Helena's attempted cure a particularly intimate act and connects *All's Well's* stricken monarch with the Fisher King, whose wound "between the thighs" (suggesting emasculation) seems similarly sexual in origin.[63] The sexual symbolism of the King's ailment, combined with the sexual language surrounding its proposed cure, give the impression of a sexually contracted or sexually disabling disease. If the King is so afflicted, poised to die because infected by a woman, his warning to departing soldiers to avoid Italian girls, combined with the Clown's suggestions that Bertram's patch conceals a syphilitic scar, circulates even more widely the fear of female sexuality that shadows Helena's pursuit of Bertram.

More to the point, it burdens Helena with the weight of male sexual dread, necessitating the vindication of her chastity. Although this scene comes the closest of any in the play to affirming Helena's erotic agency, it nevertheless shrouds that agency in mystical incantation and miraculous faith healing. The director may therefore extend the feminist gestus simply by judiciously demystifying Helena's hieratic ministrations to the King, making clear in performance the extent to which she not only persuades and inspires but sexually excites him, inducing appreciable gains in vigor as the scene progresses. This preliminary rejuvenation both anticipates and initiates the actual healing. It could even be said to substitute for it.

Some directors have attempted, with varying results, to bring the scene's sexual undercurrents to the surface, to suggest that Helena secures Bertram as bed-mate by, figuratively speaking, going to bed with the King. In John Barton's 1967 production, Helena was reduced to a "tease of a girl" who titillated the King by sitting on his bed and fluffing up his pillows,[64] and in Moshinsky's BBC version she was a proper young woman whose erotic effect on the King—culminating in a lingering kiss—seemed both incongruous and unintentional. Closer to the mark perhaps was Barry Kyle, who, in his 1989 RSC production, attempted to preserve the scene's mysticism as well as accent its eroticism: his Helena "kick[ed] off her shoes to perform a circling, energetic, sexually assertive, slightly fey dance," exuding an aura of "white witchery."[65]

My own choice would be to extend the erotics of Helena's encounter with the King into a staging of the cure itself, first by eroticizing the gesture of "laying on hands" suggestive of faith healing.[66] At the half-line, "my art is not past power," Helena could pause, reach under the King's nightshirt, and place her hand on his chest, a gesture at once sensual and clinical, disclosing Helena's mode of diagnosis: "nor you past cure." Given that more intimate areas of the King's anatomy might require a healing touch, one could also capture the scene's peculiar mixture of sex and witchery by having Helena perform a kind of mystical sensual massage, moving her hands soothingly and rhythmically around the stricken parts of his body without actually touching him, an image that extends the conflation of faith healing with sexual stimulation. If one dispenses with the arguably dispensable interview between the Countess and the Clown (2.2), one could extend this mystical therapy into a dramatization of the cure itself. Having regained full vigor at Helena's hands, the King could rise from his sickbed and continue to respond to Helena's gestural stimulations, initiating a pattern of rhythmic movement that could slowly shift into a celebratory, intimate dance, setting the stage for their dancing entrance in the next scene.

Of course, these displays of female erotic power have their limitations. The dominating, objectifying look afforded Helena by the staged bed-trick reverses rather than replaces a masculine-feminine polarity, supporting asymmetrical power relations. Moreover, to the extent that Helena secures control of the King and Bertram by withholding satisfaction of the desire she elicits, she claims the only kind of power seemingly available to women in a phallocentric economy: the power derived from the excitation and frustration of male desire, from "blowing up" men and thereby inducing surrender to their will.

Nevertheless, the powerful position of speaking body/looking subject that Helena achieves through a staged bed-trick has the subversive effect of freeing her desire from "feminine" constraint, defamiliarizing the disabling gender roles with and against which Bertram and Helena struggle. By decisively (if only temporarily) giving up the "feminine," Helena establishes the limits of gender-typing and thus evokes a more nuanced enactment of gender than the oedipal polarity permits. In addition, by releasing Helena's repressed erotic energies and suggesting her longing for the "something more" of *jouissance,* by accentuating the anxiety and incongruity that attain to her pursuit of Bertram, the staged bed-trick potentially restores the female difference that Bertram—and the play—so fretfully elides.

Final Scenes: Unresolved Tension

The drum-trick parallels the bed-trick in several key respects and so functions as an ironic substitution scene: both Bertram and Parolles lack language to deny their captors' schemes; both transgress in intention but not in fact; both mistake the familiar for the strange; and both succumb to primitive drives (fear in Parolles' case, lust in Bertram's).[67] In addition, by subjecting Parolles to humiliating exposure, the drum-trick also forecasts Bertram's own humiliation in the final scene. Parolles' discasing functions as a warning that Bertram fails to heed, an emasculation that fails to threaten his masculinity because he has already actualized the image of military and sexual conqueror that Parolles merely projected. Bertram perceives no threat in the wreckage of a discarded model.

One could stage the moments following the removal of Parolles' blindfold as a court-martial, a ritual emasculation, in which Bertram and the French Captains, before contemptuously dismissing him, ceremoniously strip Parolles of his sword, his insignias, and his extravagant military costume, leaving him virtually naked. To the accompaniment of a drum roll—ironically underscoring the agency of his demise—Parolles suffers the destruction of his carefully constructed masculine facade. Like Bertram in the staged bed-trick, Parolles submits to the feminization and specularization of his body, but as object of shame rather than desire. Parolles also takes Bertram's place as center of attention in a military pageant whose staging could parallel that of the general-of-our-horse ceremony. The collective male look strips Parolles of manhood even as it had conferred it on Bertram.

Parolles' near-nakedness lends his final speech added significance:

> Simply the thing I am
> Shall make me live. . . .
> Rust sword, cool blushes, and, Parolles, live
> Safest in shame! Being fool'd, by fool'ry thrive!
> There's place and means for every man alive.
>
> (4.3.333-39)

The "thing" that Parolles is becomes the "place" that he fills. His resolution to thrive by foolery may thus be read as a wish to find employment as a professional jester. The human actor requires a role—a Lacanian "screen"—in order to enter into the spectacle of the world.[68] Stripped of his macho soldier's garb, Parolles seeks a fool's motley, aiming to reconstitute himself by recostuming himself. Lafew seems to have been right all along: the soul of this man *is* his clothes.

Before reentering the Symbolic Order at the play's end, Parolles passes through an (undramatized) limbo of statuslessness and genderlessness in which, as Lavatch had predicted, he signifies nothing (2.4.23-27). One might stage this liminal phase by arranging for Parolles to cross paths with Helena and her women as they journey home to France. If, like Kyle, the director portrays Helena's group as a "little female army behind their wooden cart,"[69] the hungry, outcast Parolles—perhaps transformed by his derelict wanderings into the semblance of a bare, forked animal—could join their army, gratefully donning a dress that one of the women extracts from a trunk in order to cover his bare limbs. Such cross-dressing could underline Parolles' genderless status, his consignment to ranks of not-men, confirming Lafew's disparagements of him as a "hen," one who cannot "write man."

Parolles' feminine attire could also sharpen the additional shaming he receives from the Clown and the old Lord, each of whom had earlier seen through his macho impostures (2.4.23-37; 2.5.45-46). Parolles acquiesces in his own humiliation for the sake of gaining entry into the Symbolic Order. Since he can no longer be a soldier or courtier or even a man, he becomes a "tame" one to be kept (2.5.45-46), accepting a permanently liminal, "lacking" status. His appearance in the final scene in full fool's regalia marks his debut as professional jester. Indeed, his equivocating testimony at Bertram's trial may easily take the form of a fool's quibbling word games. Ultimately, Parolles demonstrates the constructedness not only of gender but of subjectivity, the cultural regulation to which a core self is subject. The audience discerns that role-playing is foundational to Parolles' subjectivity even as, thanks to the actor, it grasps a "Parolles" separable from the roles he plays. His descent to the status of fool may therefore be read as an act of self-preservation rather than self-evacuation, a survival artist's anti-heroic adaptation to a cultural order that would otherwise erase him.

In the final scene, Bertram, despite disowning his disgraced double, suffers a comparable shaming, a comparable assault on his constructed masculinity and capitulation to those he formerly scorned. Helena avenges her earlier humiliation at Bertram's hands by orchestrating his utter ruination: he is censured, disgraced, and threatened with execution. The drama that she oversees virtually reenacts the earlier scene. Once more the King tries and fails to make a match for Bertram (Lafew's daughter Maudlin). Once more Bertram scorns and humiliates a prospective wife (Diana), a threateningly desirous stand-in for Helena who claims him as husband. Once more the would-be wife suffers transformation from subject to disprized object. Indeed, Bertram might repeat his earlier beseeching move upstage to the enthroned King in an attempt to make a spectacle of Diana, reinforcing his efforts to put her on trial, to portray himself as her victim, a helpless male preyed upon by female cunning (5.3.210-19).

Bertram tries to align himself with the King, whose royal look approximates a gaze. In fact, Helena functions as gaze in this final scene. She establishes and orchestrates the spectacle. Hers is the all-seeing unseen eye for whose sake the others perform. One might even position Helena as concealed spectator to the play's final scene in order to foreground this function. When Helena herself enters the spectacle, she decisively resumes the position she previously secured in the husband-choosing scene, the all-observing observed of all observers. Helena-as-gaze thus makes a spectacle of Bertram, turning his triumphant homecoming into a trial, foiling his attempt to act the part of prodigal son, the reformed rake reconciling with a forgiving father (the King). She also prevents the fatherless Bertram from gaining Lafew as father-in-law by ruining his hopes of marrying Maudlin. Helena dominates the play's final scene but, characteristically, she is not physically present—not "there"—until its final moments.

She embodies herself—and her desire—through two rings which, once introduced, turn the tide quickly and overwhelming against Bertram. The first ring, which Helena places on Bertram's finger during the bed-trick, functions both as a wedding ring, signifying her consummation of the marriage, and as a symbol of Bertram's bondage to the female sexuality he had previously abhorred. The ring around his finger signifies the (k)not that Helena has tied around his body, the "there" in which Bertram seemingly loses himself during the bed-trick and from which he cannot escape. The ring, a gift from the King, also represents Helena's power to "command" patriarchal authority, to enlist the King's assistance once more in winning Bertram as husband (5.3.83-86). Its introduction thus induces the King to turn violently against Bertram, leaving him vulnerable to Helena's further manipulations. The second ring, which Bertram surrenders to Diana in exchange for (he thinks) her sexual favors, also signifies Helena's dominance, her success in securing Bertram as permanent sexual partner by fulfilling his conditions for marriage. By surrendering the token of his masculine honor, Bertram further binds himself to a dominant female sexuality.

These rings restore Helena's dominance not only covertly but, as tokens of her unrepresentable sexuality, nonmimetically as well. Certainly they play havoc with the King's attempt to conduct an orderly investigation into their origins and meanings. Although a careful reader can keep track of them, the rings' dizzying trajectories in performance render them virtually nonreferential, or at least unstable and ungraspable, signifiers without a clear signified. The King goes so far as to suggest that Helena's ring possesses alchemical properties, conjuring multiple owners just as its elusive referent ("there") generated multiple identities for Helena (5.3.101-106).

Diana's evasions and equivocations concerning the rings further destabilize meaning, transporting the King to the realm of "Not": "It was not given me, nor I did not buy it. . . . It was not lent me neither. . . . I found it not. . . . I never gave it him" (5.3.272-76). Diana diverts the King's investigation into the unraveling of a riddle, initiating the kind of representational shell game imagined by Irigaray in her description of a nonmimetic "hystera theater": "[Y]ou will always already have lost your bearings as soon as you set foot in [it]."[70] Trying to explain her acquittal of Bertram, Diana makes the riddle explicit, evoking the hidden secrets of the nonmimetic bed-trick:

> he's guilty and not guilty.
> He knows I am no maid, and he'll swear to't;
> I'll swear I am a maid, and he knows not. . . .
> He knows himself my bed he defil'd,
> And at that time he got his wife with child.
> Dead though she be, she feels her young one kick.
> So there's my riddle: one that's dead is quick.
> And now behold the meaning.
>
> (5.3.189-91, 300-304)

Diana's "hysterical" discourse confounds distinction, deranging the binary logic on which language—and mimesis—depends. Her words insist on an impossible two-in-oneness, a meaning capable of unifying opposites, of reconciling positive to negative. This assertion of the "not-one" proves an "abuse" to the King's ears until Helena steps forward and offers herself as unambiguous signified, the answer to the riddle, the "meaning" of the spectacle, the "one" who dissolves contradiction.

Yet Helena herself continues to be impenetrably contradictory. For one thing, she continues to mystify her power and desire, staging her return as a miraculous resurrection that once more casts her as necromancer—or, in this case, "exorcist" (5.3.304). To ensure her reception as savior, she positions Bertram as redeemed sinner, masking the elements of revenge and erotic conquest that also mark her homecoming.[71] Like Duke Vincentio, who resolves to make Isabella "heavenly comforts of despair," Helena sanctifies her scheme to rescue Bertram from the calamity she herself has created—presumably in order to elicit feelings of indebtedness conducive to capitulation.

Moreover, Helena reaffirms doubleness in calling herself, essentially, a wife and no-wife ("the shadow of a wife, . . . / The name, and *not* the thing" [5.3.307-308, emphasis mine]), thereby perpetuating rather than dissolving contradiction. Bertram affirms that she is both "name" and "thing" and begs her pardon, as though ready to accept her as wife and end her riddling self-division. Yet he follows his seemingly unequivocal affirmation with a more conditional one: "[I]f she, my liege, can make me know this clearly, / I'll love her dearly, ever, ever dearly" (315-16). Characteristically, Helena affirms her claim to have met his conditions in negative terms: "[I]f it appear not plain and prove untrue, / Deadly divorce step between me and you"—once more raising the spectre of a permanent "not," the "never" of Bertram's original formulation. If Helena does indeed succeed in securing Bertram as husband, the marriage she makes can represent, at best, a double negative: she successfully negates Bertram's negation of their wedding. She proves herself not a not-wife. Whether she can truly achieve the status of wife remains provocatively questionable.

Equally questionable is precisely what it would mean to achieve it. What does "the thing" signify? The suspicion that "wife" connotes "safely nullified female" haunts the play's final scene. On one hand, Helena no longer feels compelled to simulate normative femininity. She does not disclaim dominance of Bertram by fulsomely protesting subservience. She does not hesitate to call the Countess "mother" (5.3.119). At the same time, given her previous displays of obsequiousness, given the wife's submissive status in marriages of Shakespeare's time, to become "the thing" of wife may mean to erase permanently those aspects of herself at odds with normative femininity, to end doubleness at the expense of self-erasure. From this perspective, her dominance of Bertram ultimately enables her to submit to him in marriage. Ever in thrall to Bertram, she wins him only by putting him temporarily in her thrall so that she can put herself permanently in his. Although Helena's narrative dominates Bertram's, allowing her to construct him as the Other out of whom she creates herself, at the same time her fundamental, culturally prescribed desire is to become the object of his desire, the Other out of whom he creates himself:

> The end of the little girl's journey, if successful, will bring her to the place where the boy will find her, like Sleeping Beauty, awaiting him, Prince Charming. For the boy has been promised, by the social contract he has entered into at his Oedipal phase, that he will find woman waiting at the end of *his* journey.[72]

The fulfillment of Helena's quest for womanhood depends upon fulfilling Bertram's quest for manhood, functioning as figure of closure for his oedipal plot. Despite persistently demonstrating her divergence from lacking femininity, Helena ultimately appears to embrace it, to read her worth and constitute her identity in the returned look of her Prince Charming, to resolve her doubleness by submitting to his "one."

Helena aims to deliver both herself and Bertram to a fairy tale denouement that safely reinscribes a masculine-feminine polarity, submitting difference to a symbolic opposition that turns Bertram into her substantiating mirror. In the immediate aftermath of the bed-trick, Helena recoiled from male lust and affirmed Bertram's difference ("O strange men, / That can such sweet use make of what they hate" [4.4.21-22]). In the play's final scene, however, she emphasizes his likeness to her, his "kindness" ("O my good lord, when I was like this maid, / I found you wondrous kind" [5.3.309-10])—a word that connotes kindredness as well as gentleness or generosity.[73] Helena needs to claim Bertram as one of her own kind, to create him in her own image—the same image she has sought doggedly to impose despite all his obstinate assertions of alienness. In the final scene, Helena tries to confirm Bertram in kindness by "crush[ing] him with a plot." She replaces his prodigal-son narrative with a version of the romance-novel retributive fantasy, aiming to bring him to his knees (a posture he has assumed literally in more than one production), abusing him in order please him, positioning him to savor the bondage he initially abhorred.[74] She succeeds only to the extent that she elicits an apology and a capitulation that approximate and promote the kindredness she covets. The play, however, offers no assurances that Bertram has truly accepted transformation from Beast to Prince Charming or that he can ever hope to match Helena's idealized vision of him.

Critics have long lamented the paltriness of Bertram's conversion speech, but the problems with the play's final scene run much deeper.[75] Because Bertram has twice before falsely professed admiration for Helena (2.3.167-73; 5.3.44-55), no words of his, no matter how eloquently or torrentially penitential, could ever suffice to confirm his sincerity. Nor, for that matter, could his actions. Even the most extravagant, self-abasing gestures may be symptoms simply of feverish gratitude rather than of genuine conversion. Helena may be able to work up feelings in Bertram that simulate and even enable love but do not actually generate it. And, of course, Bertram may simply cunningly simulate a penitential swoon. In either case, Helena manipulates Bertram into affecting a kind-ness that he may quickly discontinue upon resuming his male prerogatives in marriage. Perhaps Bertram functions here as a male Kate—a seemingly tamed lout who performs the submissive part his dominant spouse has taught him but who may, after all, only be performing. Because, in the play's second half, Helena's aim seems to shift from wedding Bertram to eliciting his desire—from being the "name" to being the "thing"—it may be that, for the second time in the play, her goal eludes her even as she appears to achieve it.[76]

Moreover, Helena's attempt to embrace femininity is scuttled not simply by Bertram's uncertain response but by her own unfeminine excess, her embodiment of a doubleness that resists reduction to a legible unity. Even as she attempts to accommodate herself to the oedipal plot, she remains elsewhere. Even as her pregnant body allows her to inscribe herself as "wife" and "mother" within the patriarchal order, it also projects the nonmimetic *jouissance* of the bed-trick.[77] On one hand, that is, Helena's pregnant body assimilates her sexuality to a reassuringly feminine, maternal image that evidences Bertram's potency and paternity. On the other, it manifests her sexual dominance, serving as the text of Bertram's fulfilled conditions—and thus as the cause of his capitulation. It also speaks of her own desire and pleasure, reaffirming the active sexuality transgressively alien to the oedipal plot.

Let's look at this double effect in greater detail: on one level, Bertram's apparent readiness to accept Helena's satisfaction of his conditions invites a revisionist reading of them as coded desire, embedding a fantasy of merger with the dreaded but desired female other.[78] The conditions are themselves provocatively contradictory, both prescribing and prohibiting sexual intercourse with Helena. Indeed, assuming that Bertram harbors a hidden desire for Helena, the conditions themselves constitute a riddle: how can I have sex with you without suffering shame or emasculation? How can you have sex with me without contaminating yourself or surrendering maternal purity? Helena's answer is the bed-trick, which allows Bertram not only to fulfill his forbidden desire for her involuntarily but to overcome a disabling, contradictory apprehension of female difference: through the bed-trick Helena assimilates for Bertram's sake the seemingly unassimilable roles of wife and lover, (m)other and "real girl" and, in so doing, appears to become "one" with the oedipal plot.

The finale of *All's Well* could therefore be said to dramatize (at least on one level) the amelioration of castration anxiety—the dread of loss and lack that attends Bertram's aversion to Helena. Helena presents herself as uncastrating, one who has already "had" Bertram sexually without damaging him. She steps forward as the eroticized mother figure of his dreams. Her "resurrection" at the play's end represents the final mystification of her own sexuality, an unthreatening eroticizing of the saintly guise she assumed for the pilgrimage. She replaces her own degraded double, sanitizing the wayward desiring self that the beleaguered Diana personifies. Her visible pregnancy—her status as mother—purifies the sexuality it affirms. It also ratifies Bertram's manhood, signaling his conquest of her, his success in "blowing her up." Moreover, given the belief circulating in Shakespeare's day that a woman could conceive only if she experienced an orgasm,[79] Helena's pregnancy serves as proof not simply of his sexual potency but of her satisfaction by him. Also, by helping him to become a father, Helena promotes Bertram's resemblance to the father he was urged to emulate from the outset.

The bed-trick becomes Bertram's initiation into manhood, with Helena serving as his initiator, the womb or matrix through which he is reborn, negating his attempt to "get the woman out," to undergo a rite of passage symbolically affirming his separation from woman. His "second birth" repeats rather than replaces the first, affirming his maternal origin. In this world of absent fathers, no viable model of manhood exists for Bertram. Helena essentially takes the place of Bertram's father, as her possession of his ancestral ring suggests. Bertram becomes her creation rather than the Count's. In marrying Helena, Bertram finds his masculinity affirmed through a reassuring maternal presence, getting what he may have wanted all along: a wife/lover/mother who allows him to become a man by remaining a boy.

On another level, Helena's difference is not so easily assimilated, and the impossible conditions represent not a fantasy to fulfill but a law to countermand. By consigning Helena to the realm of Not, Bertram reinscribes the Law of the Father, dismissing her body as nothing-to-be seen, erasing her by textualizing her, subduing her to the patriarchal symbolic. By seeming to return from death—the realm of permanent "not"—Helena underscores her resistance to symbolic erasure, her subversive unassimilability to the lack culturally assigned her. The body Bertram used and disposed of proves itself indisposable; the invisible object of the bed-trick becomes formidably subjective and visible, returning in the person of a would-be wife, a once and future lover, who claims him like an avenging spirit.

Helena defeats the phallocentric negation embedded in Bertram's text by offering the text of her own pregnant body as proof of her indisposability, a text whose meaning exceeds the limits of the conditions it fulfills and the symbolic categories (wife, mother) to which it is subject. By bearing material traces of the nonmimetic bed-trick, by textualizing her own aspiration to *jouissance,* Helena records a difference irreducible to anatomy. Her body becomes not the source of a prediscursive, universal female meaning in which she shares but a signifier of her own elusive subjectivity, the text of her own persistent riddle. Helena brings Bertram, however obscurely, new knowledge of herself, offering allusions to their time in bed and visible proof of their mutual gratification—allusions both tantalizing and confounding. Her body claims knowledge of Bertram and attributes to him a knowledge of her that contradicts and challenges his lack of knowledge, sparking the desire to know more. When Bertram declares, "if she, my liege, can make me know this clearly," the "this" he wishes to know surely encompasses a good deal more than the details of Helena's fulfillment of his conditions: it must include the mystery of female difference, of an otherness he may now perceive as other than "nothing-to-be-seen," other than Other, distinct from the culturally promised Woman awaiting him at his oedipal journey's end. To desire to know more of Helena is to desire *her,* to regard her as a riddle worth solving. The "this" that Bertram's wishes to know becomes homologous with Helena's "there," suggesting that the performance of sex has solved his problem with sexuality, that he loves her and loves her knot—to rework Parolles' definition of a gentleman's love for a woman. Yet this solution, and the desire for knowledge it predicates, are simply intriguing possibilities. As the play ends, Helena remains elsewhere, suspended somewhere between known and not known. By recurrently transcending the lacking femininity she seemingly strives to embrace, Helena moves beyond the realm of "not" to the elsewhere of "not, but," paradoxically inserting herself into the oedipal plot as the source of her own meaning, hysterically coexisting with her own negation.

The play's refusal to dissipate its tensions or substantiate its tentative resolutions leaves its drama of sexual difference suspended, arrested in an unresolved but provocative, even poignant, tension. Helena remains a mystery to be solved by the reader and spectator as well. So, too, does Bertram. Both characters aim to ground themselves in genders that the play suggests are groundless—or at least unstable, fluid, performative. Neither manages to forge a stable identity or secure a clear destiny. Modern performance could underline Helena's and Bertram's status as subjects-in-process, active agents inextricably engaged with subjugating myths of gender. In particular, a staged bed-trick, by fetishizing the male body and empowering a female gaze, could underline the instability of those genders they seek to stabilize, taking the play's provocative dramatization of difference to startling and invigorating lengths.

The play itself also remains a riddle to be solved. It interrogates the happy ending it provisionally enacts by refusing to exorcise the doubts that have clouded Helena's pursuit of Bertram from the outset. It seems almost deliberately designed to force the audience to confront the implications of its need for a comic love story in which imperiled protagonists happily transcend all conceivable obstacles and vexations. Even as Helena finally secures Bertram as husband, the play stokes doubts about the sincerity of his conversion and the seemliness of their union. Does their reconciliation evidence the flourishing of mutual love and desire or the wedding of delusion and opportunism?

The play gestures toward comic closure while refusing to harmonize its anti-comic discordances. For this reason, the director may wish to insert Lavatch into the final scene as a signifier of that anti-comic spirit. The Clown's strained and dissociated jesting manifests not only sexual but metaphysical anxiety. His jokes "keep touching religion like a sore tooth."[80] On at least three occasions he addresses issues of salvation and damnation (1.3.28-37; 2.4.1-13; 4.5.36-55). When Lafew, unnerved by such apocalyptic raillery, calls Lavatch "a shrewd knave and an unhappy," the Countess concurs, "So 'a is. My lord that's gone made himself much sport out of him; by his authority he remains here, which he thinks is a patent for his sauciness" (4.5.60-63). In this brief exchange, one not only hears of Lavatch's bitter and melancholic disposition but deduces their probable source: the death of the Count, to whom the Clown was evidently much attached. Lavatch is a walking symptom—of the fear of female sexuality, of the dread of mortality, of the instability surrounding the death of the father. In the midst of a narrative straining to resolve itself comically, he personifies that principle in experience that resists comic idealization.

Lavatch might be placed as brooding, skeptical spectator to the play's final events, signaling the stubborn persistence of his personified question. Can dread of female sexuality be so easily exorcised? Can the unruliness of male sexuality be so safely assimilated to a redemptive marriage of the very sort that Lavatch mocked in his opening scene? Can any of these characters achieve "wellness"? Can the play itself achieve it, mired as it is in a truculently realistic anxiety? The melancholy jester/scourge sticks like a burr to this play. One could close the play with the King's summoning his subjects offstage, leaving Bertram and Helena alone at last, sealing their marriage with a kiss. Upstage of them, standing in the shadows but perturbingly visible and intensely observant, is Lavatch, an unanswered, perhaps unanswerable question mark. The play ends by directing focus to a doubting look that disrupts Bertram's and Helena's attempt to signify "happily married couple" in the spectacle of the world.

In the play's epilogue, the actor/King declares, "The king's a beggar, now the play is done; / All is ended well if this suit be won, / That you express content" (Epi. 1-3). The play ends well if we say that it does. Remembering Lavatch's definition of "wellness" as a state of grace beyond human experience, one must perhaps admit that, given the play's engagement with that often unlovely and dispiriting experience, it ends as well as it can.

Notes

1. *Bulletin of the Shakespeare Association of America* 16 (July1992), 4.
2. *Shakespeare's Problem Comedies* (New York: Macmillan, 1931). Although Lawrence insists that these plays should be accepted simply as stories, requiring the same level of unsophisticated reception as the widely known traditional tales from which, by his reckoning, they were derived (73-77), folklore scholars have for some time uncovered the potent cultural and psychological dramas that such tales encode. See, for instance, Alan Dundes, "The Psychoanalytic Study of Folklore," in *Parsing through Customs: Essays by a Freudian Folklorist* (Madison: U of Wisconsin P, 1987), 3-46. *All's Well* may be considered a play that pushes the folktale's subterranean psychic drama provocatively close to the narrative surface, threatening the uncomplicated unfolding of the oedipal plot and the gender ideology it encodes. A feminist gestus aims to heighten the drama of that threatened rupture by staging the play's repressed contents.
3. See, for example, Janet Adelman, *Suffocating Mothers: Fantasies of Maternal Origin in Shakespeare's Plays, Hamlet to The Tempest* (New York: Routledge, 1992), 84-86; Barbara Hodgdon, "The Making of Virgins and Mothers: Sexual Signs, Substitution Scenes, and Doubled Presences in *All's Well That Ends Well*," *Philological Quarterly* 66 (1987) 47-55; Susan Snyder, "'The King's Not Here': Displacement and Deferral in *All's Well That Ends Well*," *Shakespeare Quarterly* 43 (Spring 1992); and "*All's Well That Ends Well* and Shakespeare's Helens: Text and Subtext, Subject and Object," *English Literary Renaissance* 18 (1988), 73-77.
4. References to *All's Well That Ends Well* are based on *The Riverside Shakespeare,* ed. G. Blakemore Evans et al. (Boston: Houghton Mifflin, 1974).
5. I italicize *feminine* and *masculine* in order to make clear that I use the terms to denote modes of desire (passive and active) while distancing myself from the Freudian view that such modes are rooted in the biological difference between male and female.
6. I borrow the resonant phrase "curled darling" from Robert Ornstein, *Shakespeare's Comedies: From Roman Farce to Romantic Mystery* (Newark: U of Delaware P, 1986), 182. Carolyn Asp, in her fascinating psychoanalytic account of the play, also notes Helena's initial embrace of masochistic femininity, "Subjectivity, Desire and Female Friendship in *All's Well That Ends Well,*" *Literature and Psychology* 32 (1986), 52.
7. For an extremely helpful discussion of the paradigm of "closed femininity," see Peter Stallybrass, "Patriarchal Territories: The Body Enclosed," in *Rewriting the Renaissance: The Discourses of Sexual Difference in Early Modern England,* ed. Margaret W. Ferguson, Maureen Quilligan, and Nancy J. Vickers (U of Chicago P, 1986), 123-42.
8. "Cultural Confusion and Shakespeare's Learned Heroines: 'These Are Learned Paradoxes,'" *Shakespeare Quarterly* 38 (Spring 1987), 1-18.
9. *The Sovereign Flower: On Shakespeare as the Poet of Royalism Together with Related Essays and Indexes to Earlier Volumes* (London: Methuen, 1958), 137.
10. Knight, *The Sovereign Flower,* 138. In a sense, Knight extends Helena's (or Shakespeare's) mystification of virginity: "the love is infinite, 'a thousand loves'; it is the window to a great insight. It may be related to the state of perfect integration from which poetry is born."
11. "Blind Spot of an Old Dream of Symmetry," in *Speculum of the Other Woman,* trans. Gillian C. Gill (Ithaca, N.Y.: Cornell UP, 1985), 50.
12. Cf. Mariana in *Pericles*: "If fires be hot, knives sharp, or waters deep, / Untied I still my virgin knot will keep" (4.2.146-47).
13. See Jacques Lacan, *Feminine Sexuality,* trans. Jacqueline Rose (New York: Norton, 1985), 144-45.

14. Jardine perceives a more fundamental split in Helena's behavior: her exemplary passivity in the play's second half atones for her transgressive forwardness in the first. "[T]he sexually active Helena of the first part of the play [becomes] the virtuously knowing, ideal wife" ("Cultural Confusion and Shakespeare's Learned Heroines," 11). I would contend that Helena is consistent throughout the play in mitigating her audacity with displays of "femininity," that her recession in the play's second half simply extends her strategy—or habit—of compensatory self-effacement. Her urge to assume an exemplary femininity reflects Shakespeare's need—or, rather, a cultural need working through him—to purify and mystify female sexuality in order to neutralize its provocations. Hence, the possible value of a staged bed-trick that foregrounds and demystifies female desire.

15. As Jardine points out, the infamy that Helena courts, if realized, could "ostracize [her] from the community, recasting her wisdom as witchcraft" ("Cultural Confusion and Shakespeare's Learned Heroines," 10).

16. Some commentators believe that the young lords are indeed standoffish. See, for instance, Joseph Price, *The Unfortunate Comedy: A Study of* All's Well That Ends Well *and Its Critics* (Liverpool UP, 1968), 155-56. I find it difficult to credit this reading because of the unlikelihood of the wards' openly flouting the King's formidable demands for cooperation (2.3.56, 72-73). It is far more likely that Lafew takes a position peripheral to the proceedings and so misconstrues their meaning.

17. "Visual Pleasure and Narrative Cinema," *Screen* 16, no. 3 (1975), 11-12.

18. *The Four Fundamental Concepts of Psycho-Analysis,* trans. Alan Sheridan (New York: Norton, 1978), 75.

19. "*All's Well That Ends Well* and Shakespeare's Helens," 11.

20. While relatively few modern critics have subscribed to such an extremely negative view of Helena (see, however, Bertrand Evans, *Shakespeare's Comedies* [Oxford UP, 1960], 145-66; and Richard A. Levin, "*All's Well That Ends Well* and 'All Seems Well,'" *Shakespeare Studies* 13 [1980], 131-44), many have felt compelled, until very recently, to *judge* Helena's character in some measure, and have often found cause to indict or at least regret the duplicitous and predacious tactics that belie her celebrated virtue. See E. K. Chambers, *Shakespeare: A Survey* (London: Sidgwick and Jackson, 1925), 200-207; Clifford Leech, "The Theme of Ambition in *All's Well,*" *ELH* 12 (1954), 17-29; Alexander Leggatt, *Modern Language Quarterly* 32 (1971), 22-41; W. L. Godschalk, "*All's Well* and the Morality Play," *Shakespeare Quarterly* 25 (1974), 61-70; David Scott Kastan, "*All's Well That Ends Well* and the Limits of Comedy," *ELH* 52 (1985), 575-89. Critics, of course, have also judged in Helena's favor. See my own earlier essay, "'That Your Dian / Was Both Herself and Love': Helena's Redemptive Chastity," *Essays in Literature* 17 (1990), 160-78. Judgments of Helena perhaps follow inevitably from a formalist focus on the play's "genre trouble" rather than its "gender trouble" (to borrow Judith Butler's term).

21. *Gender Trouble: Feminism and the Subversion of Identity* (New York: Routledge, 1990), 140.

22. *Ways of Seeing* (New York: Viking, 1973), 121.

23. De Lauretis discusses this contradiction in especially helpful terms in *Alice Doesn't,* 156-59.

24. See, for instance, Janelle Reinelt, "Feminist Theory and the Problem of Performance," *Modern Drama* 32 (March 1987), 48-57.

25. Stacy Wolf and Michael Peterson, review of *A Midsummer Night's Dream, Theatre Journal* 42 (May 1992), 228.

26. See Sigmund Freud, "Femininity," in *The Standard Edition of the Complete Psychological Works,* ed. James Strachey (London: Hogarth, 1964), 22, 112-35. According to Freud's reductive biological model, the little girl's desire shifts from wanting a penis to wanting the one who possesses it. She thus surrenders or represses the active part of her libido ("masculine" desire) in return for her father's (i.e., male) love, consenting to her condition of "lack," of passivity and dependence.

27. I am indebted to Ralph Alan Cohen for pointing out the pervasiveness of the negative in the language of *All's Well* in "The (K)notty Discourse of *All's Well That Ends Well,*" unpublished manuscript, presented to the Shakespeare Association of America, 1993.

28. "Sexuality must not be thought of as a kind of natural given which power tries to hold in check, or as an obscure domain which knowledge tries gradually to uncover. It is the name that can be given to a historical construct: not a furtive reality that is difficult to grasp, but a great surface network in which the stimulation of bodies, the intensification of pleasures, the incitement to discourse, the formation of special knowledge, the strengthening of controls and resistance, are linked to one another, in accordance with a few major strategies of knowledge and power" (*The History of Sexuality, Volume I: An Introduction,* trans. Robert Hurley [New York: Random House, 1978], 105-106).

29. Although she overestimates the liberating effects of Elizabethan marriage for women, Juliet Dusinberre nonetheless gives a good account of the ideal of marital chastity with which Puritan reformers sought to displace a monastical (catholic) one (*Shakespeare and the Nature of Women* [London: Macmillan, 1975], 20-63).

30. Richard A. Levin offers the most extreme version of this view, essentially arguing—seldom with textual support—that everything that happens in the play is the direct result of her indefatigable conniving (*"All's Well That Ends Well* and 'All Seems Well'").

31. "Feminism, Marxism, Method, and the State: An Agenda for Theory," *Signs* 7 (Spring 1982), 530-31. While MacKinnon's comment offers a useful gloss on Helena's predicament, it can hardly be taken as universally true; female sexuality is surely far too powerful, multifaceted, and complex to suffer reduction to the simple task of attracting and pleasing men.

32. James Hillman suggests that Helena never gives the slightest indication that she cares whether Bertram desires her or not; she wishes to construct herself out of her construction of him and so aspires only to render him powerless to reject the image she wishes to project onto him (*William Shakespeare: The Problem Plays* [New York: Twayne, 1993], 67). Although I agree that Helena positions Bertram as self-substantiating Other, I would argue that her alliance with Diana bespeaks a need not merely to stand in for but to *become* the object of Bertram's desire, to present herself at play's end as, among other things, a body bearing physical evidence of its antecedent desirability.

33. "The statement, 'I am a man,' . . . at most can mean no more than, 'I'm like he whom I recognize to be a man, and so recognize myself as being such.' In the last resort, these various formulas are to be understood only in reference to the truth of 'I is an other,'" Jacques Lacan, "Aggressivity in Psychoanalysis," in *Ecrits: A Selection,* trans. Alan Sheridan (New York: Norton, 1977), 23.

34. Lynda E. Boose discusses this homology in her stunning essay "Scolding Brides and Bridling Scolds: Taming the Woman's Unruly Member," *Shakespeare Quarterly* 42 (1991), 199-200; also Stallybrass, "Patriarchal Territories: The Body Enclosed," 126.

35. For a superb psychoanalytic account of Bertram's fear of Helena's engulfing maternalism, see Adelman, *Suffocating Mothers,* 79-86.

36. "But only the girl with whom one has not grown up from childhood, and become accustomed to, can ever be to us in the truly sexual sense, a real girl. That is to say, she alone can possess these powerful stimuli to the sense of sexual desirability, never developed in people one has grown unconsciously used to, which are essential to the making of a real girl," in *Sex and Marriage* (Westport, Conn.: Greenwood, 1977), 42.

37. Ruth Nevo contends that the Countess is "rather more than half in love with her son," and "since she cannot have a husband in her son, she will identify with the girl who would be his wife, and so transform her love for Bertram into a double maternal solicitude" ("Motive and Meaning in *All's Well That Ends Well,*" in *"Fanned and Winnowed Opinions": Shakespearean Essays Presented to Harold Jenkins,* ed. John W. Malion and Thomas H. Pendleton [London: Methuen, 1987], 33, 35). My argument is closer to that of Adelman, who identifies a "binding maternal power" in the Countess which Helena enacts and extends (*Suffocating Mothers,* 79-80).

38. For a brilliant discussion of the oedipal conflict between Bertram and the King, see Richard P. Wheeler, *Shakespeare's Development and the Problem Comedies,* 35-45.

39. Nevo also notes the strangeness of "mother" within the menu of lovers' epithets, "Motive and Meaning in *All's Well That Ends Well,*" 37-38.

40. Other critics have noted the Clown's role as Bertram's double (see, for instance, Snyder, "'The King's Not Here,'" 23-24), though none that I know of has argued that the parallel encompasses an ambivalent attitude toward Helena.

41. The way in which male initiation rites tend to exclude women and often require the reception of a wound that constitutes a male vulva has been noted by, among others, Mircea Eliade, *Rites and Symbols of Initiation: The Mysteries of Birth and Rebirth,* trans. Willard R. Trask (New York: Harper & Row, 1975), esp. 21-40; and Bruno Bettelheim, *Symbolic Wounds: Puberty Rites and the Envious Male* (Glencoe, N.Y.: Free Press, 1954; rpt. New York: Collier), esp. 90-121.

42. See, for instance, Ornstein, *Shakespeare's Comedies,* 183.

43. David Haley's recent study, *Shakespeare's Courtly Mirror: Reflexivity and Praxis in All's Well That Ends Well* (Newark: U of Delaware P, 1993), offers perhaps the most thorough defense of Bertram, arguing that his character can be understood only in the context of aristocratic "praxis" and not individual psychology. Haley argues that Bertram, like Hal, becomes the heroic nobleman he was destined to be from the outset: "[T]he playwright has fashioned the character primarily with a view to the character's heroic end. Bertram must be conceived as the nobleman he will ultimately be" (218). Haley's confidence in Bertram's maturation—and concomitant elision of his inadequacies—strikes me as problematic, as does his reification of an heroic code that the play seems to destabilize. Although Haley resists psychoanalytic interpretations, his notion of "mirroring" lends itself to Lacanian translation: Bertram must identify with a culturally imposed image that allows him to signify within the cultural (courtly) spectacle, must fit himself to the screen that enables capture by the gaze. That such identification constitutes a *misrecognition* seems apparent from the insubstantiality of the models to which Bertram is subject: the militaristic flummery of Parolles and the nostalgically mythologized courtliness of his father, the Count.

44. Robert Smallwood, "Shakespeare at Stratford-upon-Avon, 1989, Part II," *Shakespeare Quarterly* 41 (Winter 1990), 494.

45. Steve Vineberg, "Problem Plays," *Threepenny Review* 52 (Spring 1993), 32.

46. Carol Rutter, *Clamorous Voice: Shakespeare's Women Today* (London: Women's Press, 1988), 81.

47. Rutter, *Clamorous Voices,* 88.

48. Rutter, *Clamorous Voices,* 88.

49. J. L. Styan, *All's Well That Ends Well: Shakespeare in Performance* (Manchester UP, 1984), 72.

50. See Price for an account of Houseman's staging (*The Unfortunate Comedy,* 67), and Smallwood for a description of Kyle's ("Shakespeare at Stratford-upon-Avon, 1989," 494).

51. *Pornography and Silence: Culture's Revenge against Nature* (New York: Harper, 1981), 22. Griffin offers compelling evidence of the consistent recurrence of this plot, although her association of women with nature and her affirmation of a natural sexuality seem problematically essentialist.

52. *The Uses of Enchantment: The Meaning and Importance of Fairy Tales* (New York: Random House, 1975), 308.

53. "America's Cinderella," in *Cinderella: A Folklore Casebook,* ed. Alan Dundes (New York: Garland Publishing, 1982), 298.

54. Yolen, "America's Cinderella," 296.

55. My reading of the traditional tale of "Cinderella" is indebted to that of Bettelheim (*The Uses of Enchantment,* 260-72), who regards the climactic insertion of foot into slipper as both an affirmation of female sexuality and a palliation of a male castration anxiety symbolized by the Prince's inability to observe the blood from the amputated parts of the step-sisters' feet. The limits of Bettelheim's reading reflect the limits of its Freudian predicates: to characterize Cinderella as an "uncastrated woman" whose dangled foot expresses a "desire for a penis" presupposes the embeddedness of "penis envy" in the female psyche and the experience of "lack" as a biological condition rather than a patriarchal construction. The point seems worth stressing because, shorn of its biological determinism, Bettelheim's reading of "Cinderella" applies most intriguingly to *All's Well*: through the bed-trick, Helena both affirms her sexuality and ameliorates Bertram's castration anxiety—the dread of loss and lack that accompanies his aversion to her. Helena not only gives Bertram a taste of the sexuality that Cinderella symbolically evokes but presents herself at the end as uncastrating (rather than uncastrated), one who has already had Bertram sexually without damaging him.

56. Carol Thurston, *The Romance Revolution: Erotic Novels for Women and the Quest for a New Sexual Identity* (Urbana: U of Illinois P, 1987), 8.

57. Thurston points out that the callous male who learns to be sensitive has recently been challenged by a "new hero" whose sensitivity is manifest from the outset (*The Romance Revolution,* 72).

58. Tania Modleski, *Loving with a Vengeance: Mass-Produced Fantasies for Women* (New York: Methuen, 1982), 45. As a genre of contemporary fiction written almost exclusively by and for women and, as a recent site of feminist criticism, the romance novel seems a valuable referent for a male critic/director pondering the narratives—both old and new—that intersect with *All's Well's* drama of sexual difference. For a spirited and compelling defense of linking Shakespeare to popular culture, see Harriet Hawkins, *Classics and Trash: Traditions and Taboos in High Literature and Popular Modern Genres* (U of Toronto P, 1990). For a very different critical use of the romance novel, see Linda Charnes, "What's Love Got to Do with It? Reading the Liberal Humanist Romance in Shakespeare's *Antony and Cleopatra,*" Textual Practice 6 (Spring 1992), 1-17. Charnes discerns a romance-novel sensibility not in Shakespeare's play but in the "traditional liberal-humanist" reading of it, in which "'love' will proleptically revise and make emotional sense of all preceding experience, no matter how violent and disjunctive" (11).

59. "In both [*All's Well That Ends Well* and *Measure for Measure*], the bed-tricks are employed to cure or transform male fantasy through its apparent enactment" (Carol Thomas Neely, *Broken Nuptials in Shakespeare's Plays* [New Haven: Yale UP, 1985], 92). Although Neely sees the bed-trick as primarily humiliating for Helena (as I do not), she does acknowledge Helena's affirmation of the "sweetness of her pleasure and the growth that will ensue: 'the time will bring on summer, / When briars shall have leaves as well as thorns, / And be as sweet as sharp'" (4.4.31-33), 80.

60. *Alice Doesn't,* 99, 83.

61. See Neely, *Broken Nuptials,* 73, and Hodgdon, "The Making of Virgins and Mothers," 60.

62. *Alice Doesn't,* 153, 157.

63. For a helpful discussion of the King's fistula, see F. David Hoeniger, *Medicine and Shakespeare in the English Renaissance* (Newark: U of Delaware P, 1992), 293-98. Surveying contemporaneous medical treatises, Hoeniger concludes that Shakespeare's audience would have assumed that the King's fistula was *in ano.* Hoeniger believes that the cured King's reference to "this healthful hand, whose banished sense / Thou hast repealed" indicates that the wound might actually have been located in his hand, as though Shakespeare were playing a joke on an audience inclined to believe that the fistula was *in ano.* This single line, however, does not provide strong enough evidence that Shakespeare wished to contradict the audience's assumption. The Fisher King "had

been crippled by a spear-thrust in the thighs. It seems clear that the words usually translated 'wounded through his two thighs' were intended to mean 'wounded between his two thighs.' In plain language, he was emasculated. The Fisher King is impotent and his land is threatened with ruin," Robert Cavendish, *King Arthur and the Grail: The Arthurian Legends and Their Meaning* (London: Weidenfeld and Nicolson, 1978), 140.

64. See Styan, *All's Well That Ends Well,* 25, 52.

65. Smallwood, "Shakespeare at Stratford-upon-Avon, 1989," 494.

66. Guthrie's production offered a purely mystical example of faith-healing. See Styan, *All's Well That Ends Well,* 54.

67. I am essentially paraphrasing Snyder here ("'The King's not here,'" 27).

68. See Lacan, *Four Fundamental Concepts,* 96-97. As Silverman explains, Lacan is "concerned with the process whereby the subject assumes the form of a representation, or—to state the case somewhat differently—*becomes a picture,* a process which involves *three* rather than *two* terms: subject, screen, and gaze," in *Male Subjectivity at the Margins,* 148.

69. Smallwood, "Shakespeare at Stratford-upon-Avon, 1989," 495.

70. *Speculum of the Other Woman,* 244, 292.

71. Some critics have contended that the play itself resembles a morality play. See, for instance, Knight, *The Sovereign Flower*; Robert Grams Hunter, *Shakespeare and the Comedy of Forgiveness* (New York: Columbia UP, 1965); and William B. Toole, *Shakespeare's Problem Plays* (The Hague: Mouton, 1966), 130-51.

72. de Lauretis, *Alice Doesn't,* 133.

73. For an excellent discussion of the implications of the word "kind" for Shakespeare's audience, see Arthur Kirsch, *Shakespeare and the Experience of Love* (Cambridge UP, 1981), 142.

74. Asp also identifies Helena's veiled sadism: "I would go so far as to say that lurking behind Helena's apparent psychological masochism of her initial attitude towards Bertram lies its opposite, i.e., anger or rage at having been denied subjectivity by him and a willingness to inflict pain, a psychological form of sadism" ("Subjectivity, Desire, and Female Friendship," 58). Asp, however, sees Helena as more unequivocally altered and triumphant than I do, arguing that she decisively shifts from a deluded idolization to a realistic assessment of Bertram, giving up an obsessive desire for otherness rooted in the Imaginary for structural coherence as wife and mother within the Symbolic. In my reading, neither of these shifts is clear-cut: Helena's desire continues unabated, implicating Bertram as Other and exceeding the maternal and wifely roles she claims.

75. G. K. Hunter speaks for many critics: "[T]he mere substitution of Bertram's cryptic fustian . . . for the elaborate recognitions of the earlier comedies does not remove from our minds the desire for some expression of what is being resolved," Introduction to *All's Well That Ends Well,* in *The Arden Shakespeare* (London: Methuen, 1959), lv.

76. In Susan Snyder's Lacanian reading of *All's Well,* Helena's goal eludes her because it is essentially illusory: "'the bright particular star' she pursues is her own fantasy, a far cry from the increasingly soiled and compromised actuality of Bertram. . . . The whole shape of the story thus enacts desire in Lacanian terms: at best you get a flawed, imperfect substitute for the image that drives you" ("'The King's Not Here,'" 30). I see more ambivalence and ambiguity in the play's ending, owing to Bertram's possible awakening to Helena's difference which, while not redeeming his demonstrable inadequacies, nevertheless points him to a new and enabling knowledge.

77. It seems clear that Helena must be *visibly* pregnant in the play's final scene, not simply because Diana's testimony that she "feels her young one kick" places the pregnancy in its advanced stages but because Helena's claim to have fulfilled Bertram's conditions would otherwise lack substance. The claim is still problematic, of course, given that Bertram actually requested a child (in the source, Giletta presents Beltramo with twin boys) and that Helena could be carrying another man's baby. Still, it seems unlikely that Helena would claim fulfillment without visual corroboration. I am also intrigued by the possibility that, if Helena is indeed visibly pregnant, her line "When I was like this maid" could be heard as "when I was like this made."

78. See Adelman, *Suffocating Mothers,* 85; Nevo, "Motive and Meaning," 44; and Kay Stockholder, *Dream Works: Lovers and Families in Shakespeare's Plays* (U of Toronto P, 1987), 75-76 for corroborative readings of the wish-fulfillment fantasy encoded in Bertram's impossible conditions.

79. See Thomas Laqueur, *Making Sex: Body and Gender from the Greeks to Freud* (Cambridge, Mass: Harvard UP, 1990), 1-9.

80. Helen Wilcox, "'Help of Heaven' or 'Act of (Wo)Man'?: Sacred and Secular in *All's Well That Ends Well,*" unpublished manuscript, presented to the Shakespeare Association of America, 1993.

MARRIAGE

Margaret Loftus Ranald (essay date 1963)

SOURCE: "The Betrothals of *All's Well That Ends Well*," in *Huntington Library Quarterly*, Vol. 26, No. 2, February, 1963, pp. 179-92.

[*In the following essay, Ranald discusses the nature of Elizabethan matrimonial contracts in order to elucidate the marriage theme of* All's Well That Ends Well.]

Of Shakespeare's three so-called problem comedies, *All's Well That Ends Well* has been the most neglected. Some of the situations (notably the bed trick) undoubtedly do repel some readers, and scholars have largely concentrated on explaining their significance to the play. One allied topic has, however, gone almost unnoticed: the betrothals and resultant matrimonial situations. Certainly W. W. Lawrence discusses them in his study of this play, and G. K. Hunter appends some thought-provoking annotations to the new Arden edition of Shakespeare; but in general too much attention seems to have been paid to the bed trick, while the nature of matrimonial contracting, a topic which appears continuously throughout the play, has been largely ignored.

The aim of this paper is, therefore, to study the somewhat confused yet generally accepted laws surrounding Elizabethan matrimonial practice and to examine their relevance to the marriage of Bertram and Helena. The marriage contracts seem to be largely representative of English practice, so it would appear that Shakespeare has "Englished" his source (Boccaccio) in this way also. Thus through an understanding of Elizabethan matrimonial law some of the material in Act II may become more clear, and some of the immense confusion of Act V may be seen to have an underlying order and dramatic significance.

Many of the difficulties of *All's Well* were admirably solved by W. W. Lawrence when he showed how much of the action of the play had its roots in the conventions of folk and fairy tale. But despite Lawrence's assurance that "The Elizabethan audience would have accepted these 'tricks' [of Helena] as valid without question; that Bertram's sudden change of heart was a convention of mediæval and Elizabethan story, which must be expected to follow Helena's triumph,"[1] critics have still had difficulty in matters of characterization and meaning and often end by merely classifying the play as a "problem comedy." Yet, as Madeleine Doran remarks, "the only 'problem' in it is Helena's problem of getting the man she wants for a husband."[2] Certainly, as John F. Adams points out, Helena is no cold virgin. She is a virtuous woman whose aim in the play is to fulfill her function of procreation by losing her virginity through marriage to a man who pleases her.[3] This motivation makes of Helena a really "clever wench" in her interestingly legal attempts to gain Bertram's person and his love.

The first move in any Elizabethan arrangement, after the financial details were settled, was the betrothal, or the espousal. This ceremony was of such great importance in both civil and ecclesiastical law that it was surrounded with specific official formulas, chiefly concerning the promises which the Church of England recommended that its members make in public and before witnesses.[4] Elizabethan law recognized two different kinds of betrothal. The first of these was *sponsalia per verba de praesenti,* which meant an exchange of consents in words of the present tense, preferably spoken in public. This espousal in effect created the status of marriage immediately and was indissoluble except in cases of diriment impediments,[5] earlier contract to another, or adultery committed by one of the parties to the unconsummated contract.[6] Though the *sponsalia per verba de praesenti* did not confer the sexual privileges of marriage, it was treated almost like a valid marriage and could be upheld in the courts.[7] The second kind of betrothal was *sponsalia per verba de futuro,* which meant an exchange of consents in words of the future tense, preferably spoken in public, and merely entailed an obligation to marry at some later date. At that time a public exchange of consents in the present tense would take place *in facie ecclesiae.*[8] Consent was therefore recognized as the basis of matrimony, but the view of Gratian was still upheld even in post-Reformation England: the contract effected *matrimonium initiatum* only, and consummation was required for *matrimonium ratum,* a marriage made quite indissoluble by sacramental symbolism.[9]

Consent could also be given subject to conditions, providing that they were not impossible, frivolous, involving grave sin, or concerned with necessary natural conditions such as "if the sun rise tomorrow."[10] If, however, the parties to the conditional contract later expressed their mutual consent in words of the present tense, they were considered joined in simple matrimony.[11] Again, if the parties to a conditional espousal later had carnal knowledge of each other before the fulfillment of the condition they were then considered to have renounced the condition.[12] In short, carnal knowledge of the contracting parties meant that they had contracted simple matrimony.[13]

The ceremonies of public espousal included the exchange of consents by the contracting parties before sufficient witnesses (at least two) and, generally, handfasting. The exchange of nuptial kisses and rings was also considered important, and rings were sometimes exchanged even in cases of secret and unsworn espousals.[14] This last point ought to be remembered in the study of *All's Well.*

The state of mind of the parties was also important. As William Harrington said in 1528, "it is to be knowen that man and woman dothe entre this holy ordre and sacramente of matrymony by expresse and free consente of both partyes."[15] This insistence on free and unforced consent was often paid only lip service in Elizabethan arranged matches, but consent given through intimidation caused by threats sufficient to put the fear of death into a strong man (*metus qui posset in virum constantem cadere*), could render a marriage null and void *ab initio* even if it had been consummated.[16]

This situation is important in *All's Well* because Bertram is the ward of the king and is forced into marrying Helena. Certainly under Elizabethan law the king is within his rights in choosing Helena for Bertram, or rather in agreeing to her choice of Bertram; but he follows the often castigated practice of Elizabethan guardians by unjustly exercising his prerogative and forcing his will upon an unwilling ward "by the rigour of the law."[17] As Glenn H. Blayney notes, this occurrence is extremely important to the later development of the play: "The enforcement motif has been heightened in Shakespeare, and Bertram's neglect of Helena follows more dramatically from this motivation. . . . Perhaps we should today regard Bertram in the light of seventeenth-century attitudes which explained his behavior as a victim of a king's will unjustly imposed through the prerogatives of wardship."[18]

The actual scene of choice and espousing in II.iii seems to follow contemporary Elizabethan practice and to reproduce most of the legal requirements of betrothal. The espousal actually begins when Helena approaches Bertram with these words:

> I dare not say I take you; but I give
> Me and my service, ever whilst I live,
> Into your guiding power. This is the man.
>
> (II.iii.109-111)[19]

Obviously in this speech we have a classic statement of a *de praesenti* espousal with the slight distinction humbly made by the young lady in the first line. Customarily in espousals one would say "I *take* thee for my wife, or husband." Here Helena seems almost too conscious of the social difference between her and Bertram and therefore she changes the words slightly, though the meaning is doubtless the same.

The king, standing *in loco parentis,* promptly gives his blessing and consent to the match: "Why, then, young Bertram, take her; she's thy wife" (II.iii.112). The use of the word "wife" here is noteworthy, because although espousals did not confer all the rights of marriage, the titles "wife" and "husband" were frequently used for betrothed couples.[20] Bertram's reply is one that has on occasion incensed critics:

> My wife, my liege! I shall beseech your Highness,
> In such a business give me leave to use
> The help of mine own eyes.
>
> (II.iii.113-115)

It must not be forgotten, however, that Bertram is really asking for nothing more than the elemental right to choose his own wife rather than to have one forced upon him. The young ward, with some justice, fails to understand why he should pay the price for his guardian's cure. Almost in desperation he concocts reasons which might make the match unsuitable, beginning with the difference in rank and fortune:

> I know her well;
> She had her breeding at my father's charge.
> A poor physician's daughter my wife! Disdain
> Rather corrupt me ever!
>
> (II.iii.120-123)

The king promptly dismisses that reason by offering to give Helena a title and money, while at the same time rebuking Bertram for his false values in equating nobility with rank and wealth instead of with virtue. The king also takes care to state Helena's fitness to be Bertram's wife:

> She is young, wise, fair;
> In these to nature she's immediate heir,
> And these breed honour. That is honour's scorn,
> Which challenges itself as honour's born
> And is not like the sire. Honours thrive,
> When rather from our acts we them derive
> Than our foregoers. . . .
>
> . . . . .
>
> If thou canst like this creature as a maid,
> I can create the rest. Virtue and she
> Is her own dower; honour and wealth from me.
>
> (II.iii.138-151)

Obviously he considers Helena more than a fit match for his stubborn and unappreciative ward, and most Elizabethan courtesy books would agree.

Bertram then seeks for another reason: "I cannot love her, nor will strive to do't" (II.iii.152). At this point Helena attempts to withdraw her offer; but by now the king's anger is aroused at the flagrant disobedience of his ward, and he exercises his prerogative as a guardian to enforce Bertram's consent, even to the extent of threatening the young man with punishment and the loss of royal favor (II.iii.156-173).

The king's threat speedily brings Bertram to heel. All his objections are overruled and the quality of "liking" or "fancy" is all that is lacking. So, with a very bad grace, Bertram acquiesces:

> Pardon, my gracious lord; for I submit
> My fancy to your eyes. When I consider
> What great creation and what dole of honour
> Flies where you bid it, I find that she, which late
> Was in my nobler thoughts most base, is now
> The praised of the King; who, so ennobled,
> Is as 'twere born so.
>
> (II.iii.174-180)

Bertram then takes the lady's hand, saying merely "I take her hand" (II.iii.183). It is evident that the king considers this act one of hand-fasting and takes it as an outward sign of consent. This situation would presumably equal a binding contract because, as Henry Swinburne notes:

> . . . albeit neither of the Parties express any words at all, but some *third* person recite the words of the Contract, willing them if they be there-with content, to joyn their hands together, or to embrace each other; the Parties so doing, the Contract is of like Efficacy, as if they themselves had mutually expressed the words before recited by the third Person.[21]

The king then gives his blessing and consent as guardian, taking the joining of hands as consent on the part of the two betrothed, and the rest of the court act as witnesses. Apparently neither nuptial kisses nor rings are exchanged, but the words of the king indicate that he considers a contract to have been made:

> Good fortune and the favour of the King
> Smile upon this contract, whose ceremony
> Shall seem expedient on the now-born brief,
> And be perform'd to-night. The solemn feast
> Shall more attend upon the coming space,
> Expecting absent friends. As thou lov'st her,
> Thy love's to me religious; else does err.
>
> (II.iii.184-190)

Such a ceremony of espousing was, of course, followed by a religious ceremony *in facie ecclesiae*. Usually, in Elizabethan England, banns would have been called; but in many cases, including Shakespeare's own marriage, the banns were dispensed with. It was this ceremony *in facie ecclesiae*—and not the *sponsalia per verba de praesenti*—that actually conferred all the rights and privileges of matrimony.[22] William Harrington's statement of 1528 was also true of Shakespeare's day:

> . . . yet the man maye not possesse the woman as his wyfe / nor the woman the man as her husbonde / nor inhabyte / nor flesshely meddle togyther as man and wyfe: afore suche tyme as that matrymony be approved and solempnysed by oure mother holy chyrche / and yf they do in dede they synne deedly. . . .[23]

If, however, a betrothed couple did consummate their contract before the church ceremony, the sin was generally considered venial rather than mortal because of the existence of the contract.[24] Nevertheless the Church would still insist upon the ceremony, and ecclesiastical penalties could be imposed.

The king proposes that the church ceremony be held that very evening and that the wedding banquet, a purely social appendage, be postponed until a later date. Apparently the religious service takes place almost immediately, because later in the same scene Lafeu enters with "Sirrah, your lord and master's married; there's news for you. You have a new mistress" (II.iii.257-258). Bertram also reinforces this evidence that the public espousals have been ratified *in facie ecclesiae*:

> *Ber.* Although before the solemn priest I have sworn, I will not bed her.
> *Par.* What, what, sweetheart?
> *Ber.* O my Parolles, they have married me! I'll to the Tuscan wars and never bed her.
>
> (II.iii.286-290)

This action has also been used to paint Bertram as a singularly nasty young man, but as Blayney says, "We may find an excuse for his treatment of Helena in the contemporary attitudes and conduct which accompanied wardship and the enforcement of marriage."[25]

Bertram seems, in fact, to be taking the only course open to him. The religiously ratified *de praesenti* matrimonial contract that he has just entered into is binding and almost indissoluble, but the important element of consummation is lacking. Should Bertram avoid cohabitation and refuse to consummate the marriage, then he would still have the possibility of escape on several grounds: (1) consent obtained by threats sufficient to arouse fear in a strong man; (2) consent obtained through respect for authority (*per metus reverentialis*); (3) mental reservation at the time of the ceremony;[26] (4) refusal to consummate the marriage indicated by a three-year absence from the province, or a two-year absence within the province.[27] Therefore one may say that by refusing to go to bed with Helena, Bertram is doing the only sensible thing possible under the circumstances, because the act of consummation would be considered the outward sign of consent on both sides. He would then be condemned without recourse to indissoluble marriage with his unwanted, unloved wife. It is interesting to note that Bertram can on occasion disobey the king, but only in his guardian's absence. In both the espousal scene of Act II and the concluding scene of Act V he is quite unable to protest satisfactorily when the king is present.

The central emphasis in the matrimonial affairs of the play now shifts from Bertram to Helena, and the remainder of the plot is concerned with what W. W. Lawrence called the theme of the "clever wench" or "the fulfilling of the task." In the manner of a truly obedient wife, Helena at first acquiesces in Bertram's desire to postpone consummation of the match. She then leaves the court to return to the only home she has ever known, Roussillon, where she is shown to have gained the consent of the countess herself, who also stands *in loco parentis* to Helena: "It hath happen'd all as I would have had it, save that he comes not with her" (III.ii.1-2). At this time Shakespeare plays on the sympathies of his audience by having even the countess comment disparagingly on the conduct of her own son and praise the virtues of Helena. All blame is now fastened on Bertram, and Helena is all-praised—and decidedly resourceful.

Bertram's letter to his mother is exactly what one would expect, and it is significant that this is the first time the young man has put a statement of his attitudes and proposed actions in writing:

> "I have sent you a daughter-in-law; she hath recovered the King, and undone me. I have wedded her, not bedded her; and sworn to make the 'not' eternal. You shall hear I am run away: know it before the report come. If there be breadth enough in the world, I will hold a long distance. My duty to you."
>
> (III.ii.21-27)

This letter is Shakespeare's addition to the Boccaccio source and it serves two purposes: it could be excellent evidence for the annulment of the marriage, and it gains further sympathy for Helena when she reads Bertram's accompanying letter of conditions:

> "When thou canst get the ring upon my finger which never shall come off, and show me a child begotten of thy body that I am father to, then call me husband; but in such a 'then' I write a 'never.'"
>
> (III.ii.59-63)

Such conditions are of course typical of those in the "clever wench" genre of folk tales so admirably described by Lawrence,[28] but the letter can also be read as a conditional espousal added to the earlier, public and unwilling one. It will be recalled that such conditions were not supposed to be impossible or to cause grave sin, and Bertram is saying nothing more than that he will refuse to accept the *title* of husband until he has *acted* as Helena's husband, consummated the marriage—which he has so far obstinately refused to do—and begotten a child on Helena. All that Helena does from that time is to find a way to fulfill Bertram's conditions, to obtain her conjugal rights and to lose her virginity to her own "liking," a situation entirely different from that described in *Measure for Measure.* We now have the picture of a woman desperately in love who wants quite frankly to consummate her marriage and is prepared to go to almost any lengths to do so. Certainly the means she uses to obtain her end seem to arise rather too much from coincidence—but then Shakespeare was following his source. It is the treatment of this part of Boccaccio's tale that is important, and one cannot fail to note how carefully Shakespeare seems to make his material fit the Elizabethan patterns of espousing. This statement is particularly true of Bertram's relations with Diana, the maiden whom the young man solicits, and it seems to serve as a key to many of the problems surrounding the conclusion of the play.

At the opening of Act V the entire court is mourning the supposed death of Helena, and in a situation reminiscent of *Much Ado about Nothing* we have a second match suggested as a consolation prize for the young man who has learned the worth of his jilted lady too late:

> she whom all men prais'd and whom myself,
> Since I have lost, have lov'd, was in mine eye
> The dust that did offend it.
>
> (V.iii.53-55)

As in the case of Claudio, these lines should be taken at their face value. What is lost is now loved. Bertram is also more mature and less hasty. In the public espousal scene which follows and which parallels that of II.iii his behavior shows considerable alteration. Instead of protest we have deference and obedience to his guardian's wishes (V.iii.28-31). The king expresses a desire for the match, and "The main consents are had" (V.iii.69). In other words, the king and the countess of Roussillon as guardian and parent, Lafeu as the father of the young lady, and Bertram himself have all agreed, and Maudlin has been reported as consenting to the match. Lafeu then asks for the usual token, and Bertram naturally gives a ring—but it is the ring given him by the supposed Diana, and both Lafeu and the king instantly recognize it as the king's gift to Helena.

Thus at the moment of what would seem to be Bertram's success his bubble is pricked, and the young man's pride is broken. Bertram seizes upon the first plausible lie, but the king's suspicions are aroused to the extent of wondering whether the unwilling bridegroom might not have done away with his unwanted wife, Helena (V.iii.115-120). On top of these revelations Shakespeare produces a letter from Diana in which she claims, in the best legal manner, that Bertram is now contracted irrevocably to her:

> "Upon his many protestations to marry me when his wife was dead, I blush to say it, he won me. Now is the Count Roussillon a widower; his vows are forfeited to me, and my honour's paid to him. He stole from Florence, taking no leave, and I follow him to his country for justice. Grant it me, O king! In you it best lies. Otherwise a seducer flourishes, and a poor maid is undone. Diana Capilet."
>
> (V.iii.138-146)

Immediately upon this discovery Lafeu withdraws his offer of Maudlin, whom we never see.

Shakespeare has of course already prepared us for Bertram's discomfiture when in the preceding act he has Diana propose an exchange of rings as her price for entertaining Bertram:

> When you have conquer'd my yet maiden bed,
> Remain there but an hour, nor speak to me.
> My reasons are most strong and you shall know them
> When back again this ring shall be deliver'd;
> And on your finger in the night I'll put
> Another ring, that what in time proceeds
> May token to the future our past deeds.
> Adieu, till then; then, fail not. You have won
> A wife of me, though there my hope be done.
>
> (IV.ii.57-65)

This careful doubling of the rings is original with Shakespeare, and G. K. Hunter appends the following perceptive comment:

> The exchange of rings was part of the ceremony of betrothal . . . ; since Diana claims Bertram as her husband in v.iii perhaps the exchange is thought of as having a similar force here. . . ."[29]

Diana also uses the word "wife" in referring to herself and in IV.ii.71-72 notes that Claudio

> had sworn to marry me
> When his wife's dead. . . .

In her statements Diana seems to describe a conditional and secret espousal with an exchange of rings. The fulfillment of the condition (i.e., the death of Helena) would therefore leave Bertram contracted to Diana, although in secret. Consummation of such a relationship would of course ratify the contract, constituting a putative marriage recognizable under law. Admittedly the espousals are clandestine, being sworn in secret and lacking the religious ceremony *in facie ecclesiae,* but this kind of secret marriage could be, and in fact was on occasion, upheld in court, although ecclesiastical penalties and sometimes temporal punishment could be imposed because of the irregularity of the contracting.[30]

At this point in the play Diana almost seems to be the instigator of much of the succeeding action, a fact which contributes to the character of Helena, who does not therefore appear to be a relentless plotter. After all, as Harold Wilson says, "the controlling idea of the play that emerges is the conception of Helena's love as far stronger than Bertram's arrogance, a love which works unobtrusively and with humility toward an end that heaven favors."[31] The complication of the play has now reached its climax, and the great confrontation scene now takes place. Shakespeare does not make it clear which of the two ladies, Helena or Diana, is responsible for the planning of this scene, but it serves a highly useful purpose in motivating the repentance of Bertram and showing that by the end of the play he has gained sufficient self-knowledge and maturity to comprehend the true nobility of Helena. Only then can he be remotely worthy of her.[32]

On Diana's appearance Bertram is backed into a corner; his accomplice in what he would seem to have considered a mere soldier's flirtation has now come to claim him. And by Elizabethan law and practice Bertram would have been bound to her because of the promise, the exchange of rings, and the consummation of the relationship. Most unchivalrously he attacks Diana's reputation, at which point the girl produces Bertram's ancestral ring as evidence both of the contract and of his perfidy. This blow is the culminating one in a long series of shocks to the young man's pride, beginning with the marriage to Helena, continuing with the unmasking of Parolles, and culminating in this scene. By now Bertram's pride is completely crushed. All he can do is gibber wildly in an undignified attempt to cover up for himself, while Diana relentlessly uncovers each lie. Bertram must finally confess that he received the ring from "Diana" and stand by while the foul-mouthed braggart Parolles tells all. The behavior of Diana at this point seems rather strange, and critics since Johnson have objected to this part of the scene. It is important, nevertheless, because her stalling and her pert answers to the king forfeit any sympathy she might gain from the court or the audience. Further, it is dramatically necessary that Bertram be given a very real scare. His shortcomings in preferring Diana to his lost wife, who loved him for himself, must be revealed. Bertram, now knowing himself for what he is, can then react positively when Helena comes to announce the fulfillment of the conditions he had set her.

With the appearance of Helena, the now humbled young man rejoices. Some of his joy may also be dictated by the fact that she is undoubtedly saving him from the undesirable match in which he had believed himself trapped. The existing contract with Helena, though consummated by a trick, has now become binding, indissoluble matrimony; and it certainly outweighs any later contract into which Bertram might have entered. He has now been "doubly won" and his lines

> If she, my liege, can make me know this clearly,
> I'll love her dearly, ever, ever dearly
>
> (V.iii.316-317)

may bear the added meaning of gratitude towards his lady. Bertram can now compare the love and forgiveness of Helena with the almost shrewish insistence of Diana. He is still understandably confused, however, since he has only riddling words as a guide. This time he goes with relief into what he had formerly considered "loathsome bondage" with Helena, now apparently giving "free and unforced consent."[33]

Thus the play ends happily with a reconciliation scene, accomplishing that transition from sorrow to joy characteristic of Shakespearean comedy. Bertram, the immature young man of Act II, has discovered through his own experience the nature of love and marriage and has as a result become worthy of the resourceful, faithful, and forgiving Helena. Shakespeare is not, of course, merely using this play to illustrate and criticize aspects of Elizabethan wardship and matrimonial practice;[34] he is employing matrimonial material that was probably familiar to his audience to point up the motivations and explain the actions of some of the principal characters. And certainly a knowledge of this sixteenth- and seventeenth-century material helps to rehabilitate the character of Bertram. In like manner the problems surrounding the function of Diana and the plot of the bed trick partially disappear. One may therefore say with justice that a study of the nature of Elizabethan matrimonial contracting helps to explain many of the apparent inconsistencies in *All's Well That Ends Well* and leads to the discovery of added meaning in this so-called problem comedy.

Notes

1. William Witherle Lawrence, *Shakespeare's Problem Comedies* (New York, 1931), p. 38.

2. Madeleine Doran, *Endeavors of Art: A Study of Form in Elizabethan Drama* (Madison, 1954), p. 251.

3. John F. Adams, "*All's Well That Ends Well*: The Paradox of Procreation," *Shakespeare Quarterly,* XII (1961), p. 262.

4. There were of course completely secret *de praesenti* espousals which could be upheld in the courts as valid matrimony; cf. *The Duchess of Malfi.* The Church vigorously opposed this practice and insisted upon the religious ceremony.

5. Diriment impediments were quite indispensable and could, when they were discovered, dissolve an existing union, even if it had been consummated. They included, among other things, impotence and relationship within the prohibited degrees.

6. Henry Swinburne, *A Treatise of Spousals, or Matrimonial Contracts* (London, 1686), pp. 236-239. This book was actually written ca. 1600.

7. 2 & 3 Edward VI, c. 23. In *Statutes* of *the Realm,* ed. Alexander Luders et al., IV, Pt. 1 (London, 1819), 68-69.

8. Swinburne, pp. 12-15; see also Alexander W. Renton and George G. Phillimore, *The Comparative Law of Marriage and Divorce* (London, 1910), p. 18.

9. George Hayward Joyce, S. J., *Christian Marriage: An Historical and Doctrinal Study,* Heythrop Series, I (London, 1948), 58. This distinction was raised in the matter of the marriage, and later the divorce, of Henry VIII and Catherine of Aragon. Had the marriage between Catherine and Arthur, Prince of Wales, been *matrimonium ratum,* an indissoluble diriment impediment would have existed on grounds of affinity.

10. Swinburne, pp. 114-121.

11. Ibid., p. 122.

12. Ibid., p. 121.

13. Ibid., pp. 150-151.

14. Chilton Latham Powell, *English Domestic Relations, 1487-1653* (New York, 1917), p. 17. Canonical opinion seems to have been divided over the question of whether a mere exchange of rings without accompanying words constituted an espousal. See Swinburne, p. 209.

15. William Harrington, *In This Boke Are Conteyned the Commendacions of Matrymony* (London, 1528), sig. A3r.

16. Joyce, p. 80.

17. See Swinburne, pp. 216-217.

18. "Wardship in English Drama (1600-1650)," *Studies in Philology,* LIII (1956), 478.

19. All quotations and citations from Shakespeare are from *The Complete Plays and Poems of William Shakespeare,* New Cambridge edition, ed. William Allan Neilson and Charles Jarvis Hill (Boston, 1942).

20. Cf. *The Taming of the Shrew,* III.ii.19-20:
Lo, there is mad Petruchio's wife,
If it would please him come and marry her!

21. Swinburne, p. 206.

22. See Davis P. Harding, "Elizabethan Betrothals and *Measure for Measure,*" *JEGP,* XLIX (1950), 139-158.

23. Harrington, sig. A[4^v].

24. Cf. *Much Ado about Nothing,* IV.i.49-51:
If I have known her
You will say she did embrace me as a husband,
And so extenuate the 'forehand sin.

25. Blayney, "Wardship," 477.

26. Joyce, pp. 75-82; Swinburne, pp. 236-239.

27. Swinburne, p. 237.

28. William Witherle Lawrence, "The Meaning of *All's Well That Ends Well,*" *PMLA,* XXXVII (1922), 427-436.

29. *All's Well That Ends Well,* new Arden edition (London, 1959), pp. 103-104*n.* Swinburne, *A Treatise* (p. 209) believes that the exchange of rings confirms whatever contract the words then spoken import. Should there be any doubt whether the contract be considered matrimony or espousal "it is to be judged matrimony" in law.

30. Joyce, pp. 106-107. Under English civil law certain property rights, in particular the widow's right to dower, could not be granted unless assigned formally at the church door.

31. Harold S. Wilson, "Dramatic Emphasis in *All's Well That Ends Well,*" *HLQ,* XIII (May 1950), 239.

32. Kenneth Muir, *Shakespeare's Sources,* I (London, 1957), 100-101.

33. Blayney, "Wardship," 478, maintains that "The reconciliation of Bertram and Helena is not the triumph of romantic love, but obedience to a royal command at the time of their marriage."

34. Glenn H. Blayney, "Enforcement of Marriage in English Drama (1600-1650)," *Philological Quarterly,* XXXVIII (1959), 463-464 remarks that ". . . Shakespeare in *All's Well That Ends Well* fused realism and romance by adapting two romantic plots to disguise and yet illustrate the social problem of wardship and resulting enforced marriage."

W. Speed Hill (essay date 1975)

SOURCE: "Marriage as Destiny: An Essay on *All's Well That Ends Well,*" in *English Literary Renaissance,* Vol. 5, No. 2, Spring, 1975, pp. 344-59.

[*In the following essay, Hill explores how familial relations and marriage eventually enable Bertram to assume his proper role within the comic plot of* All's Well That Ends Well.]

Shakespeare's plays persistently treat familial relationships. Neither Jonson's nor Marlowe's do, except incidentally, and from the perspective of Shakespeare, their avoidance is odd. The only characters in *The Alchemist* who are related to one another in ways prior to the gullings that summon all to the house of Lovewit are Kastril and Dame Pliant, and their relation as brother and sister remains essentially unexplored. The isolation of Faustus is defined by a lack of familial ties: he is a man without parents, siblings, spouse, or children—everyman, yes, but no man, too. By contrast, Webster's Duchess of Malfi, whatever her social isolation as a result of her marriage to Antonio, is seen relationally: the central conflict in that play is between rival family and marital relationships—marriage to her steward versus her sibling-tie to Ferdinand. The dramatist has every reason to exploit these ties, universal in occurrence and primal in strength; the critic finds in family relationships and their reconstitution in marriage useful differentiae for comedy and tragedy.

Tragedy, which ends in death, deals in familial relationships that have gone sour, become incapable of change, and hence destructive of the individuals that constitute the family unit. Comedy, which ends in marriage, argues the possibility of change through the agency of new and compensatory familial constellations. In tragedies the promise of marriage is characteristically frustrated or illusory. Othello's marriage to Desdemona, that archetypically romantic union of opposites—black with white, native with exotic, age with youth, military activity with domestic passivity—is destroyed by an agent of the old order of things, whose contempt for women, for authority, and for marriage is provoked by the new relationship that Othello has forged with Desdemona. In *Hamlet* there are two marriages, one in fact, the other in prospect; but Gertrude's with Claudius is at once incestuous and adulterous, the occasion if not the cause for murder, a retrograde step that blights the future hopes of Prince Hamlet and undoes the past accomplishments of his father; and Hamlet's own with Ophelia is undone by Polonius. In *Lear,* a classic instance of marriage as parental compensation goes forward in the first scene, as France accepts with gratitude the very daughter that Lear has just disowned in rage. But the exigencies of the political overplot banish France, and it is as the daughter of Lear that Cordelia returns to England, not as Queen of France. The death that concludes all in tragedy is thus the death of any possibility that conflicts intrinsic to the human situation—conflicts most intimately experienced within the context of familial relationships—shall be resolved through marriage.

Conversely, the marriages that conclude Shakespeare's comedies are emblems of hope, secular miracles, affirmations of the possibility of growth, yes, but precisely in those relationships where familial conflict is most acute. To take two especially symmetrical examples: in *Romeo and Juliet,* friendship (male-male loyalty) and marriage (male-female love) are presented as irreconcilable opposites; in *The Merchant of Venice,* the reverse is true. The marriage of Romeo and Juliet promises to end the traditional hatred of Capulet and Montague, but it is destroyed by Romeo's impulsive loyalty to Mercutio, for in the instant that Romeo determines upon the murder of Tybalt in revenge for the death of Mercutio, he irrevocably destroys the marriage he has just celebrated with Juliet. In the *Merchant,* however, the friendship of Bassanio with Antonio—Bassanio has no family but Antonio—subsidizes his courtship of Portia, whose father is dead and whose mother goes unmentioned, and the marriage of Portia and Bassanio saves Antonio's life and preserves his friendship with Bassanio. Characteristically, the change of venue common to so many of the comedies involves a removal of the participants from rigid and impacted social and familial situations, frequently associated with royal courts, to locales nearby (a wood near Athens, the Forest of Arden, Belmont, Bohemia, Bermuda) in which more symmetrical and more satisfying relationships may flourish. In the Forest of Arden, the fratricidal rivalry of Oliver and Orlando metamorphoses into parallel marriages to Celia and Rosalind, cousins. In *Othello,* the removal to Cyprus promises, but does not fulfill, the same expectation. The pattern is so familiar that it scarcely deserves note. Still, it is operative in plays that are formally comedies—that is, that conclude in marriage, not death—yet are neither obviously romantic nor particularly risible. Such generically are the so-called problem comedies, and in particular *All's Well That Ends Well,* of which the best that is said of it is that it was a staging ground for *Measure for Measure.*[1] An analysis of the familial basis for the marriage of Bertram and Helena, however, shows a play at once more coherent in itself and more of a piece with other Shakespearean plays than is commonly acknowledged.

II

Some bracketing definitions are in order. (1) Whatever the laugh-quotient, the play is a comedy by any Shakespearean standard. That is, it ends happily, in the marriage of its principals, though the dénouement is not so much the marriage itself, for that is concluded in II.iii, as it is the consummation of that marriage, its public acknowledgment, and the evidence of Helena's pregnancy. The essential movement of the play, then, is from a *de jure* to a *de facto* marriage, from social arrangement and dynastic continuity to sexual commitment and emotional fulfillment.

(2) The title suggests obliquely—as others of Shakespeare's comedies do directly—that the play has to do with the realization of wishes, desires, hopes, of which romantic love and its celebration in marriage are, respectively, the personal and social symbols. The theme of "what you will" is perfectly explicit for Helena, for whom marriage with Bertram is avowedly a matter of life and death—hers and the King's; it is less so for Bertram, for whom marriage with Helena is decidedly not "as you like it." Bertram regards it as a death to him of his hopes: "Undone and forfeited to cares for ever!" (II.iii.263). Risking death he rushes off to war to avoid it: "I'll to the Tuscan wars and never bed her" (l. 269). Only after the convolutions of the plot have been worked out does he come to accept his marriage to Helena as—potentially, at least—the positive and self-fulfilling relationship that it is.

(3) The intellectual quality of the play links it equally with the happy comedy of *As You Like It* and the problem comedy of *Measure for Measure*. The themes of virtue, ambition, and nobility have each provoked extended commentary. But there are various other themes, drawn similarly from Renaissance conduct books and romance tradition, that inform the texture of thought and shape the action in the play. Like *Hamlet, All's Well* is concerned with the congruence of word and deed, intention and act. The twin themes of fortune (fate) and free will (nature) occupy the minds of Helena and Bertram in equal but asymmetrical measure. Helena is fated to love Bertram without apparently being able to marry him, and Bertram is fated to marry Helena without being the least in love with her. Youth versus age (Lafew and the King, Bertram and Parolles; the Countess and Helena), appearance and reality, wisdom and folly, nature and supernature, the individual and society—the list reads like a litany of Shakespearean themes. The problem for the critic, of course, is to see in the play the underlying pattern that animates it, that organizes the multiplicity of its intellectual motifs about a coherent and meaningful center of concern and urgency.

It is precisely here that the prior familial constraints that provoke the marriage are crucial. Bertram and Helena have each recently lost fathers: Helena so recently that her tears are mistaken as for him and not for Bertram; Bertram, that the household of the Countess is in mourning, "*all in black*" (I.i.*s.d.*). Both fathers are ideal figures. Whereas in Shakespeare's source, "the Counte of *Rossiglione* . . . was sickely and diseased" (Arden ed., p. 145), in the play he is "such a man [as] / Might be a copy to these younger times," famous alike for his "moral parts," his soldiership ("He did look far / Into the service of the time, and was / Discipled of the bravest"), and his social graces: "So like a courtier, contempt nor bitterness / Were in his pride or sharpness . . ." (I.ii.45-46, 21, 26-28, 36-37; cf. 38-45). Like Prince Hamlet, whom he resembles in ways more than adventitious, Bertram has the equivocal blessing, the good "fortune," to have a father at once ideally virtuous and definitively distant, whose reputation serves as a spur to achievement, but whose absence in death renders him incapable of serving as the model his son needs for that achievement. For this reason, Bertram departs for the royal court at Paris, and for this reason, too, he falls under the influence of Parolles, who plays Falstaff to his Hal. Lafew, the Lord Chief Justice of the piece, early on disqualifies himself as paternal model by his put-down—"I would it were not notorious" (I.i.33)—the moment Bertram opens his mouth, and Bertram rejects the King precisely for his role in forcing Helena upon him. The obligation to live up to his father's example as his lineal successor, to show the nobility of his birth in virtue as well as *virtù,* in deed as in word, in fulfillment as in promise, rings again and again in Bertram's ears. The greeting of the King echoes his mother's parting advice: "Youth, thou bear'st thy father's face; . . . thy father's moral parts / Mayest thou inherit too!" (I.ii.19-22; cf. I.i.57-60). But in the event, self-affirmation and a virtuous conformity to paternal example are rival, not congruent, impulses in Bertram's mind and will.

III

The first line of the play abruptly and cryptically announces the theme. Entering in mourning, the Countess announces: "In delivering my son from me, I bury a second husband" (I.i.1-2). Here it is not a marital union that compensates for a familial loss (as in France's grateful betrothal to a Cordelia whom Lear disinherits in his fury), but the other way around. It is the compensation of her son's presence, the now Count Rossillion, for her late husband that the Countess is here renouncing; and the separation, a *rite de passage* for the young Bertram, is as the death of a "second husband" to his widowed mother. Still, there are compensations. The King will substitute for the absent Count as both father and husband: "You shall find of the king a husband, madam," says Lafew, and "you, sir"—addressing Bertram—"a father" (ll. 6-7). In departing, Bertram acknowledges his formal dependency upon the King: "I must attend his majesty's command, to whom I am now in ward, evermore in subjection" (ll. 4-5). But if Bertram has reason now to grieve the loss of a father—"weep o'er my father's death anew" (ll. 3-4)—we may suppose that he will later have cause to resent wardship to a man whose frailty and imminent death threaten a repetition of that abandonment. The King's precarious health thus becomes the topic of the dialogue that follows. We learn that Helena, too, has lost a father—one, too, of ideal stature, "whose skill was almost as great as his honesty," that "had it stretch'd so far, would have made nature immortal, and death should have play for lack of work" (ll. 17-20). Here is a potential countermovement to the "common theme" of the "death of fathers" (*Hamlet* I.ii.103-04). Like Bertram, Helena is "sole child" of her father, but unlike him, she is quite prepared to substitute a husband when she has lost a father. Her tears, we soon find out, are ambiguous: to others, they are for her dead parent; to her, for the departing Bertram. This she makes explicit in her soliloquy, which she speaks after the Countess has bid her son a ritual farewell, has given him, like Polonius to the departing Laertes, both blessing and advice (cf. ll. 57-66):

> *Helena.* I think not on my father,
> And these great tears grace his remembrance more
> Than those I shed for him. What was he like?
> I have forgot him; my imagination
> Carries no favour in't but Bertram's.
>
> (ll. 77-81)

(Her confusion of pronoun reference, "his . . . him . . . he . . . him," mirrors the conflation of the two men in her mind.) But the social disparity is too great, however vital the bond—"there is no living, none, / If Bertram be away" (ll. 82-83)—and Helena concludes: "Th'ambition in my love thus plagues itself: / The hind that would be mated by the lion / Must die for love" (ll. 88-90).

As Bertram is ward of the King, so is Helena of the Countess, "bequeathed," as the Countess says, "to my overlooking" (ll. 35-36). As her natural mother goes unmentioned, the Countess becomes one: "You know, Helen, / I am a mother to you" (I.iii.132-33; cf. ll. 134-49). Through familial intimacy quite as much as native virtue, Helena acquires the social promotion her birth has denied her. The nature of this relationship is made explicit in the interview in I.iii in which she confesses her love for Bertram when she rejects the maternal offers of the Countess, lest incest bar marriage. Indeed, the Countess is more maternal in her adoptive relationship with Helena than she is with her natural son. Him she can but "deliver" up to the court, but her maternal energies find a natural and needed outlet in her role as confidante and patroness of Helena. Its basis is the strong identification she feels for Helena, of age for youth, in Helena's apparently desperate love for the absent Bertram:

> Even so it was with me when I was young;
> If ever we are nature's, these are ours; this thorn
> Doth to our rose of youth rightly belong;
> Our blood to us, this to our blood is born:
> It is the show and seal of nature's truth,
> Where love's strong passion is impress'd in youth.
> By our remembrances of days foregone,
> Such were our faults, or then we thought them none.
>
> (ll. 123-30)

It is a speech of conspicuous generosity of feeling, one that renders the niggardly behavior of her son all the more repellant. Her willingness to extend a merely formal wardship into a substantive and explicitly parental tie, to overlook the rivalry in love the two women have for Bertram, raises the naturally gifted Helena—"She is young, wise, fair; / In these to nature she's immediate heir, / And these breed honour" (II.iii.131-33)—to a position of familial and hence social equality with Bertram. It is a process that the King will continue and complete: "all that life can rate / Worth name of life in thee hath estimate: / Youth, beauty, wisdom, courage—all . . ." (II.i.178-80). In a testing of the genuineness of Helena's love, of which she has been earlier informed by her Steward (no mother wants her son vamped by someone merely ambitious to be the next Countess), she forces Helena to confess to the strength—and hopelessness—of her passion. She does so, in effect, by asking Helena to choose between the two of them. Helena's dilemma is that she wants the security of being the Countess' adoptive daughter, but not at the cost of losing Bertram. "Daughter and mother / So strive upon [her] pulse . . . ," the Countess remarks, and, as Helena realizes, only through separation from her adoptive brother will the definitive bar of incest be removed: "Pardon, madam; / The Count Rossillion cannot be my brother" (I.iii.149-50). On her knees in submission and supplication, Helena begs that they not be regarded as rivals: "My dearest madam, / Let not your hate encounter with my love, / For loving where you do" (ll. 202-04). Instead, she invokes (as the Countess had earlier) their essential commonalty of purpose, experience, and love:

> . . . but if yourself,
> Whose aged honour cites a virtuous youth,
> Did ever, in so true a flame of liking,
> Wish chastely and love dearly, that your Dian
> Was both herself and love—O then, give pity
> To her whose state is such that cannot choose
> But lend and give where she is sure to lose;
> That seeks not to find that her search implies,
> But riddle-like lives sweetly where she dies!
>
> (ll. 204-12)

Like the would-be wooer of Portia, Helena is prepared to "give and hazard all she has," in the name of a love that is not more precious to her than it is impossible of fulfillment.

Though she is folk heroine, not social climber (no one except Cinderella's stepmother would accuse *her* of "ambition"), there are limits to the exercise of pure will: "Who ever strove / To know her merit that did miss her love?" (I.i.222-23). Still her impulse to follow Bertram is underwritten by the happy coincidence that the most effective medicine her father left her is a specific for the ailing King's "fistula." More than coincidence, really, as she herself acknowledges:

> There's something in't
> More than my father's skill, which was the great'st
> Of his profession, that his good receipt
> Shall for my legacy be sanctified
> By th' luckiest stars in heaven. . . .
>
> (I.iii.237-41)

Even the best of nature requires the providential concurrence of powers beyond natural ken. But Helena is more than willing to stake her all on its success: "I'd venture / The well-lost life of mine on his grace's cure / By such a day, an hour" (ll. 242-44). Won over, the Countess gives her blessing, "my leave and love, / Means and attendants, and my loving greetings / To those of mine in court" (ll. 246-48). If one so interested in Bertram's well-being as his own mother, one so close to him that he has supplied for her the place of her own absent husband, can give her blessing upon the tie, we cannot very well interpose our own objections.

IV

Helena belongs to that class of active, intelligent, and aggressive Shakespearean heroines who don male disguises—assume the "masculine" initiative—in pursuit of their fulfillment as married women. This point is made explicit in Helena's interview with Parolles on the subject of her virginity, her social "honour," her marital capital, which she would "lose"—invest—"to her own liking" (I.i.147). There is a paradox here: how can one actively be passive? how, given her dependent status as woman and ward, translate thought into deed, wish into actuality, love into marriage? "'Tis pity—," she muses; "What's pity?," Parolles asks, to which she replies:

> That wishing well had not a body in't
> Which might be felt, that we, the poorer born,

> Whose baser stars do shut us up in wishes,
> Might with effects of them follow our friends,
> And show what we alone must think, which never
> Returns us thanks.
>
> (ll. 175-82)

She is "not in his sphere," as she—and we—realize, and the first half of the play is construed to minimize that disparity. But discrepancy of rank and birth symbolizes a greater and more germane distance: first, between the two principals (even as they are joined socially, they are divorced sexually) and, second, within each as individuals (as between thought and deed, wish and fulfillment of that wish, personal self and social role). The problem of the play is to orchestrate the simultaneous and reciprocal resolution of these conflicts—the reduction of distance, the creation of a viable intimacy, within and between Helena and Bertram, both as individuals and as a couple, all in the context of an arranged marriage.

Helena's case is evidently the easier of the two. She has but to secure the alliance of the Countess. So authorized, she can travel to Paris to seek out Bertram, not as her rival but as her emissary and adoptive daughter. And it is as her father's daughter that she cures the King, bringing the dead back to life, restoring him to potency and power. Lafew's comment strikes the proper note here. "I have seen a medicine," he tells the King,

> That's able to breathe life into a stone,
> Quicken a rock, and make you dance canary
> With sprightly fire and motion; whose simple touch
> Is powerful to araise King Pippen, nay,
> To give great Charlemain a pen in's hand
> And write to her a love-line.
>
> (II.i.71-77)

The phallic imagery is nicely understated, but the tenor is clear enough: that which was dead shall rise again. In effect, in restoring the King to health and potency, Helena reacquires a father who can, in turn, bestow her in marriage. The cure is, naturally, a miracle, "the rarest argument of wonder that hath shot out in our latter times," completely of a piece with the ordinary matter of Shakespearean comedy:

> He that of greatest works is finisher
> Oft does them by the weakest minister.
> So holy writ in babes hath judgment shown,
> When judges have been babes. Great floods have flown
> From simple sources, and great seas have dried
> When miracles have by the great'st been denied.
> Oft expectation fails, and most oft there
> Where most it promises, and oft it hits
> Where hope is coldest and despair most fits.
>
> (ll. 135-43)

Helena risks her honor and her life on her cure, and in her success she is allowed the choice of her husband. By supernatural intervention and royal prerogative, woman is authorized to play the man—to choose, not be chosen, in marriage. Those who puzzle as to why Helena should love Bertram in the first place and choose to stay with him in the second ignore what parentally the two have in common: in the Countess they share the same mother; their fathers are dead; and in the King they share the same adoptive surrogate. Given the romance element of the play, it is surely expressive of Helena's deepest wishes that she be able to bring back to life, to restore to potency, power, and authority, a father who will grant her her wish and bestow upon her Bertram.

But so delicately poised is this marital equation that what is appropriate to *her* deepest wishes is directly contrary to Bertram's. For the father whom she re-creates for herself is not one that Bertram is disposed to obey. He asserts his traditional right "in such a business . . . to use / The help of mine own eyes" (II.iii.107-08). Whatever right a king may have in disposing a minor ward in marriage, dramatically our sympathies go to Bertram in his wish, in matters as intimate as love and marriage, to choose for himself. There is some question, however, as to whether he is, in fact as well as intention, capable of acting in his own best self-interest. Objectively, Helena is a marital prize of the highest order, and Bertram must obey his King. True self-interest, marriage to Helena, and submission to royal authority, distinct as all three are in Bertram's mind, are clearly congruent in the play. When Helena withdraws her petition upon Bertram's rejection—"That you are well restor'd, my lord, I'm glad. / Let the rest go" (ll. 147-48), the King forces the issue by threatening to withdraw his support from Bertram, to abandon him to his own self-destructive devices:

> Check thy contempt;
> Obey our will which travails in thy good;
> Believe not thy disdain, but presently
> Do thine own fortunes that obedient right
> Which both thy duty owes and our power claims;
> Or I will throw thee from my care for ever
> Into the staggers and the careless lapse
> Of youth and ignorance. . . .
>
> (ll. 157-64)

A fatherless son, threatened here with abandonment by his adoptive father—"Welcome, count; / My son's no dearer" (I.ii.75-76)—Bertram acquiesces in the marriage:

> Pardon, my gracious lord; for I submit
> My fancy to your eyes. When I consider
> What great creation and what dole of honour
> Flies where you bid it, I find that she, which late
> Was in my nobler thoughts most base, is now
> The praised of the king; who, so enobled,
> Is as 'twere born so.
>
> (II.iii.167-73)

Helena has been granted the fulfillment of her wishes; in equity Bertram demands no less. The challenge, of course, is whether these two, meant for each other no less than Beatrice and Benedick, can, on their own initiatives and left to their own devices, acting on self-perceived motives of apparent self-interest, come together and stay together. For the moment, the answer is no. It is one of the components of the myth of romantic love that the individual partners shall have freely chosen one another, independently of any social or familial matrix of which they are a part. The enforced passivity of his role in the marriage contract galls Bertram beyond tolerance, and he naturally resists the obvious truth that he could not possibly have chosen better for himself than others—the Countess, the King, Helena—have chosen for him. (In this regard, Helena's love for Bertram is less problematic: it is simply there from the beginning, a *donné* of her person and her situation at Rossillion.) Thus, as soon as the marriage is celebrated, Bertram escapes to the military. Abetted by Parolles, whose elective counsel Bertram pointedly prefers to that of either Lafew or the King, he lies to his King and his wife and sets off for Florence. There he is improbably given the generalship of the cavalry—the horse, "Mars's fiery steed," is Bertram's emblem in this play[2]—and wins back in war the honor he feels he has lost in marriage. As corollary to war-making (and through the adroit pimping of Parolles), he seeks the conquest of the virgin Diana, poor but nobly born.

Meanwhile, Helena returns to Rossillion, where she receives from Bertram the impossible conditions of their reunion. Despite her credentials as the daughter of Gerard de Narbon, there are limits to the powers of will: she can restore an aged king to potency; she can secure a husband far beyond her own social rank; but there is simply no way she can will her own impregnation. Conversely, though he will wed her but "not bed her," it is not sex that drives Bertram from Helena, but the element of social and sexual compulsion which marriage to her represents. Bertram is decidedly not lacking in masculine force, despite his susceptibility to consolation in the company of the befeathered Parolles. He is an exemplary soldier, and he is clearly attracted to Diana. But he treasures the model of masculine love as simultaneously self-assertive *and* self-fulfilling, where in his own particular it is not. Exactly the same is true of Helena, and in this respect the pair are ideally matched. But where Bertram thrashes about in the random aggression of the battlefield and the bedroom in the company of the coward Parolles, Helena embarks upon a solitary pilgrimage to St. Jaques le Grand (cf. III.ii.102-29). The journey is professedly in penance for her marital "ambition"; in fact, it expresses her frustration—and consequent self-blame—at her inability to do for Bertram what she had done with such singular success for the King: to create, out of the intensity of her love and wholeness of her own self-giving, the entire substance of a relationship with another person. Her travels bring her to Florence together (later) with the news that she has died. The exchange is arranged with Diana, and like Mariana in *Measure for Measure,* she forgoes her very identity to consummate the wished-for union with her Angelo. From the extremes, then, of willed self-assertion—the restoration to life of a dead father and the securing of a husband—she passes to the converse extreme, complete self-abnegation, total loss of personal identity and will in love, and a symbolic death. But marriage, with its inevitable compulsions, its necessary curbing of unbridled individualism, continues to spook the skittish Bertram, and he flees Diana the instant the news of Helena's death reaches him: that is, the very moment—and the very news—that would have made it possible for him to fulfill his promise to marry her. Evidently, whether we are a Helena or a Bertram, we must be careful what we wish for, lest we get it.

If we ask further why Bertram should reject out of hand the "young, wise, fair" Helena, whose very name connotes the loveliest woman in the world, the answer must be because she is to him such a transparent stand-in for his own mother, the Dowager Countess. The marriage is what *she* had been wishing for all along, but to Bertram it simply constitutes submission to her will. "It hath happen'd all as I would have had it, save that he comes not along with her" (III.ii.1-2), the Countess remarks at Helena's return. And when Bertram's impossible letter is read, her response is unequivocal: "He was my son, / But I do wash his name out of my blood / And thou art all my child" (ll. 66-68). Like Gertrude, the Countess is a powerfully maternal figure, even matriarchal, and like King Hamlet, the old Count is dead. Such a marriage to the adoptive daughter of one's own mother has its own terrors, and insofar as Bertram is truly his mother's own son, we may assume that he wants—and fears—that transposed intimacy in equal measure. That circumstances beyond his control should enforce this unacknowledged wish upon him precisely through the agency of his King and guardian fills him with understandable anxiety, for the warmth and promise of intimacy that have attracted Helena to the Countess repel her son from Helena with equal force. Rather than wonder why Helena should love a Bertram and Bertram should reject a Helena, we should recall what happened when a similarly compensatory marriage between Ophelia and Prince Hamlet was blocked by Polonius, despite Gertrude's apparent encouragement and support, on grounds identical to those on which Bertram rejects Helena.

V

In war, Bertram finds the honor he seeks, earning the praise of the Duke of Florence and the promise of letters of recommendation for his courtly dossier that puts him on an equal and autonomous footing with his esteemed father. But war and the courtship of death have their limitations as a mode of self-fulfillment, as Helena, who takes upon herself the guilt of any danger that the reckless Bertram might risk, is the first to realize:

> Poor lord, is't I
> That chase thee from thy country, and expose
> Those tender limbs of thine to the event
> Of the none-sparing war? . . .
> better 'twere
> I met the ravin lion when he roar'd
> With sharp constraint of hunger; better 'twere

That all the miseries which nature owes
Were mine at once. No; come thou home, Rossillion,
Whence honour but of danger wins a scar,
As oft it loses all. . . .

(III.ii.102-05, 116-22)

After war, sex—as practiced by the predatory Bertram upon the vulnerable Diana—is equally destructive. For an hour's encounter in which no words pass, Bertram barters away the very family honor he had invoked in rejecting Helena. And for all our distaste for the bed-trick, it remains the perfect emblem of the joyless encounter that Bertram is in fact seeking. In return for the ring of his father's that has been passed down for six successive generations and that betokens the unexceptioned legitimacy of his inherited honor, he accepts the ring from off Helena's finger, thus affiancing himself to his own wife as a condition of fathering his own successor.

Surely Bertram's youth is crucial here. Scarcely an adolescent, packed off to the court to complete his education but dependent upon the King and too young to be sent to Italy, passion and self-restraint ("blood and virtue") are precariously poised in him. "My Lord," the Countess had said to Lafew, "'Tis an unseason'd courtier; good my lord, / Advise him" (I.i.66-68). Bertram's education as a courtier is the essential subject of the play, and that means learning to be a son to his mother, the son of his father, a subject to his King, a husband to his wife—and, in the future beyond the play, a father to his own son. What is unusual, in the context of Shakespeare's treatment of courtship and marriage, is that the *education sentimentale* proper to courtship must here emerge *after* the marriage has been irrevocably established. Bertram must come to accept that marriage to Helena is in fact in his own best self-interest, that whatever he *thinks* he wants, he actually desires her far more intensely than he is prepared to admit to himself. Hence the importance of their union in the dark, for darkness conceals not only Helena's identity from him but also his own deepest desires from himself. Only under these improbable circumstances can his impossible demands upon her—and his own inadmissable wishes for himself—be simultaneously fulfilled. This is true equally of his explicit demand (secure my ring, bear my child) as it is of his unconscious one (be to me as my mother was to my father). Just as Helena's marital destiny could finally be realized only through an act of supreme self-abnegation, so with Bertram. The difference lies in the fact that Helena is conscious of that necessity, while Bertram is not. Helena sleeps with Bertram knowing that he is her husband and because she loves him. He sleeps with her—indeed, can *only* sleep with her—under the condition that her identity remain hidden. Because he cannot, of his own volition, bring himself to take his father's place with respect to his mother's stand-in, Helena, he sleeps with her thinking she is Diana, a girl to whom he promises marriage, betroths himself, and whom he then betrays. Perhaps Laertes' advice to Ophelia was not so out of place after all.

Helena contrives Bertram's exposure by doing exactly as he demands. For all her force of will, she is capable of equally great submission: "Sir, I can nothing say / But that I am your most obedient servant" (II.v.71-72). She returns to the King for the husband she had earlier won. In the interim, however, she has herself learned the limits of will and the qualifications of desire; that marital relations, unlike the parental and filial ones on which they are based, are reciprocal and interlocking. Bertram has yet to learn much the same lesson. The exchange of rings trips him up, and he is obliged to admit in public what he has done in private. Under the scrutiny of the assembled court, deed must now match word; act, intent; social role, private self. Sex and society must be incorporated in a marriage both *de facto* and *de jure*. Caught in the toils of his own duplicity—as much self-deceit as deceit of others—it comes as an enormous relief to Bertram to learn that he has in fact committed adultery with his own wife, that he has betrayed, not the virtuous virgin of Florence, Diana, but only himself—less virtuous, perhaps, but as Count Rossillion, just as virginal.

VI

In this, a comedy, it is not for Shakespeare to articulate the process by which Bertram can come to say, "If she, my liege, can make me know this clearly / I'll love her dearly, ever, ever dearly" (V.iii.309-10). Whatever else he may share with Hamlet, the youthful Bertram has none of the latter's introspection (itself by no means an infallible guide), and the dramatic sleight-of-hand by which Helena and Bertram are brought together does not wholly make explicit the substantive basis they have for finding in marriage to the other their own true self-interests. But it is simply churlish to contradict Helena when she says, "O my good lord, when I was like this maid / I found you wondrous kind" (ll. 303-04), where "kind" invokes Bertram's solicitude as well as his natural condition. None of us was there, and we must take Helena's word for it. Still, if their marriage is recognized as the favorable—and wished-for—compensation for prior familial imbalances and parental asymmetries, then its rationale is evident and agreeable. In marriage to Helena, Bertram secures a relationship at once socially acceptable and sexually satisfying, a way of marrying his mother *and* obeying his father (he makes no complaints about "Diana" afterwards, and it was certainly not because of sexual inadequacy that he originally deserted her). In her marriage to Bertram, Helena finds the father she has lost and, as the Countess' daughter-in-law, the mother she has never had. En route, she fulfills her own deepest desires as a woman: as a daughter to restore new life to the old King and so vindicate her father's memory, and as a wife to bear Bertram's child, desires parallel to Bertram's for military success and glory. Only the literal-minded will begrudge the substantive foundations of this union. Plausible, it is not; social barriers impede it; there is frankly an element of compulsion in it, both as presented to Bertram by the King and by Shakespeare to us. But we too can rejoice in it if we see that the marriage symbolizes on both parts an acceptance of their own faulty parental experiences; that it is no less what Bertram most deeply desires than it is what Helena so explicitly wants; and that it is no less life-giving, restorative, divinely sanctioned, and royally beneficent to him than to her. For Bertram, in his youth, his native rebelliousness, his justifiable fear of the enveloping maternalism of the Countess, and in the absence of his own father, is simply not prepared to admit to himself truths that are self-evident to others. It is to this boundary of self-awareness, self-admission, and self-acceptance that the reluctant Bertram must be brought by the plot-machinery of romance. And with this, Shakespeare draws the curtain. Let Helena's first words be our last:

> The mightiest space in fortune nature brings
> To join like likes, and kiss like native things.
> Impossible be strange attempts to those
> That weigh their pains in sense, and do suppose
> What hath been cannot be.
>
> (I.i.218-22)

Notes

1. Cf. G. K. Hunter, ed., *All's Well That Ends Well,* The Arden Shakespeare (1959; rpt. London, 1967), pp. xxiii-xxiv. All quotations are from this edition.

2. Cf. the following (italics mine):

   Bertram. I shall stay here *the forehorse* to a smock. . . .

   (II.i.30)

   King. Check thy contempt; . . .
   Or I will throw thee from my care for ever
   Into *the staggers* and the careless lapse
   Of youth and ignorance. . . .

   (II.iii.157, 162-64)

   Parolles. He wears his honour in a box unseen
   That hugs his kicky-wicky here at home,
   Spending his manly marrow in her arms
   Which should sustain *the bound and high curvet*
   Of Mars's fiery steed. To other regions!
   France is a *stable*; we that dwell in't *jades.*

   (II.iii.275-80)

   Duke of Florence. The general of our horse thou art. . . .

   (III.iii.1)

   King. You *boggle* shrewdly. . . .

   (V.iii.231)

Susan Bassnett-McGuire (essay date 1984)

SOURCE: "An Ill Marriage in an Ill Government: Patterns of Unresolved Conflict in *All's Well That Ends Well,*" in *Shakespeare-Jahrbuch*, Vol. 120, 1984, pp. 97-102.

[*In the following essay, Bassnett-McGuire suggests that* All's Well That Ends Well *reflects post-Reformation views of the marriage contract and also comments on the individual's relationship to the state.*]

All's Well That Ends Well occupies one of the minor positions in the Shakespeare canon, and the map of its critical history reveals a text often held to be problematic, described variously as incomplete or inadequate, and perhaps dismissed most tellingly by Logan Pearsall Smith who declared that "it reads like hack-work."[2] Overall, critical opinions of the play have tended to see it as a flawed text in which disparate element sit uneasily together.

In the eighteenth century a resolution was found by placing emphasis on the farcical elements within the text, and after Garrick's 1756 adaptation for the stage the figure of Parolles acquired central status and was frequently seen as a comic figure rivalling Falstaff in stature. By the end of the eighteenth century the emphasis had shifted to focus this time on Helena, described by Coleridge as Shakespeare's "loveliest character"[3], a pattern that was to continue with the advent of an acting style based on concepts of psychological realism. The sentimentalization of the play in the early nineteenth century moved away from the earlier farcical reading, a process further compounded by the views of A. W. Schlegel who saw the play as linked to the traditional fabliaux of the triumph of woman's patience against all odds.[4]

More recently *All's Well That Ends Well* has been re-evaluated somewhat more favourably. Muriel Bradbrook has seen it as a moral play that undertakes "a grave discussion of the question of what constituted true nobility and the relation of birth to merit"[5], while Clifford Leech has considered the play as a satire on the Elizabethan duality towards love and ambition[6], but it remains less frequently performed than most of Shakespeare's other comedies and far less frequently discussed.

Yet as soon as we move away from a reading that lays undue emphasis on story-line or characterisation of protagonists, patterns begin to emerge in the play that compel us to consider it more seriously and to look more closely at the society it depicts. The settings are aristocratic—the court of the king of France, the court of the Countess of Roussillion and the court of the Duke of Florence, with the sole exception of the Widow's house in Florence and the scene in the soldiers' camp. Moreover, all these courts are stricken with some kind of pestilence—the King of France is sick with an apparently incurable malady; the Court of Roussillion has suffered the double loss of the Count and the youthfulness of Bertram the heir, who cannot succeed his father directly but "must attend his majesty's command," to whom he is now "in ward, evermore in subjection" (I, 4 f.) and the Duke of Florence is at war with the Siennese. The action of the play is set against this background of death, and the opening lines, spoken by the widowed Countess remind us that all is set in motion by the loss of her husband: "In delivering my son from me, I bury a second husband." (I, 1, 1) The private loss is followed immediately by a second loss, one dictated by the terms of feudal law, under which the son inherits but is bound to the overlord until his majority and then by an oath of realty, unable to act for himself without his Lord's permission.

Against this dark background, the story line follows the fortunes of two figures: Helena and Parolles, who move across class lines in diametrically opposite ways. Helena, in love with Bertram whom she perceives as hopelessly above her socially, achieves preferment from the King through her magical healing powers. Having cured the incurable, she is then granted the impossible—the right to choose her own husband regardless of his status or inclination. She chooses Bertram, who rejects her and flees from both wife and Lord to the Florentine wars, pausing only before he leaves to issue her with a seemingly hopeless task to fulfill: "When thou canst get the ring upon my finger, which shall never come off, and show me a child begotten of thy body that I am father to, then call me husband: but in such a 'then' I write a 'never'." (III, 2, 56-60)

Miraculously, just as Helena cures the incurable King, so she succeeds in tricking Bertram to give her both his ring and a child, and after all her trials is restored to the King's protection at the end of the play.

There are no miracles in the Parolles story line, however, which charts his fall from a position of arrogance to rejection and degradation where he can state of himself that "Simply the thing I am / Shall make me live" (IV, 3, 322 f.) The insecurity of social status of anyone who is not part of the hereditary aristocracy reveals a society in turmoil, where one turn of the wheel of fortune can make or unmake an individual irrevocably.

Weaving through the rise of Helena and the fall of Parolles is the Florentine-Siennese war. In I, 2 when we first meet the King, he is despatching Gentlemen to observe "either part". Later, in II, 1 when the Gentlemen meet the Duke of Florence, they are at pains not to give a precise opinion as to the rights and wrongs of the conflict, but note that

> the younger of our nature
> That surfeit on their ease will day by day
> Come here for physic.
>
> (III, 1, 17-19)

And of course this is precisely what Bertram does, when he flees from the French King's court. Arriving in Florence, he is given a command and becomes a military hero. There is therefore a clear contrast between the relationship of fealty to the Overlord on the one hand and the idea of foreign wars as places of entertainment and self-trial for bored young aristocrats, deprived of any significant power by their oath of fealty. What emerges from this contrast is a view of two worlds in opposition—the pre-Machiavellian world of the old King and the post-Machiavellian world of young Bertram. The thrust of the play is therefore to show two ideologies in conflict and the lack of clear cut resolution at the end only reinforces the sense of crisis and tension within the aristocratic world.

The image of Bertram as military hero, described by the women in III, 5 is in contrast to that of the sullen young husband in the earlier part of the play. Readings of Bertram's character have been greatly influenced by Dr. Johnson's famous dismissal of him as "a man noble without generosity, and young without truth; who marries Helena as a coward and leaves her as profligate: when she is dead by his unkindness, sneaks home to a second marriage, is accused by a woman whom he has wronged, defends himself by falsehood, and is dismissed to happiness."[7] A major problem for directors of *All's Well That Ends Well* is indeed presented by the figure of Bertram, for if Dr. Johnson's view is shared, the question must be asked as to what a woman so virtuous, beautiful and noble-spirited as Helena could ever find to love in such a man? It would seem that his rashness and extravagance should be conceived of as *virtù* in Machiavelli's sense of the term so that when he appears at the head of the Florentine army, he comes as the conquering hero, the Renaissance Prince, a dominant stage figure described by Diana as a "most gallant fellow". In V, 3 it is hard not to admire the skill with which Bertram tries to argue himself out of his increasingly complicated predicaments, when he lies about the ring, blackens Diana's name and rejects Parolles, and finally only concedes defeat when Helena appears, that is, when dealt a blow by fortune that individual cunning cannot counter. Even at this stage, however, Bertram is by no means unequivocal. Challenged directly by Helena with "Will you be mine now you are doubly won?" (V, 3, 308), he replies not to her but to the King, in a weak couplet hinging on a conditional clause:

> If she, my liege, can make me know this clearly
> I'll love her dearly, ever, ever dearly.
>
> (V, 3, 509 f.)

Helena retorts immediately, in a strong rhyming couplet, with another conditional, addressed directly to Bertram:

> If it appear not plain and prove untrue
> Deadly divorce step between me and you.
>
> (V, 3, 511 f.)

It is interesting to note that Helena talks about divorce at this point in the play, the moment when seemingly all wrongs are righted and husband and wife are united at last under the king's protection. It is also somewhat curious, since divorce has been notably absent from the play up to this moment. Bertram, when lamenting his fate to Parolles in II, 3 talks about the indissolubility of his marriage.—"Undone and forfeited to cares forever" (II, 3, 263) and chooses flight from France as his only hope of avoiding a wife he does not want. Helena's reference to "deadly divorce" in her final lines carries a weight that cannot be overlooked.

Divorce in Reformation England was by no means a clear cut issue. The Church recognized divorce on grounds of consanguinity or affinity within the prohibited degrees of marriage or for permanent impotence. It also recognized separation *a mensa et thoro,* for cases of adultery or extreme cruelty, but in both categories remarriage was forbidden.[8] In this respect, the Anglican Church differed from most of the other Protestant churches, which allowed remarriage for the innocent party following a divorce, and the divorce debate reached a climax in 1604, (N.B. George Hunter dates *All's Well* tentatively as being produced in 1603-04)[9] when No. 107 of the Canons finally forbade the remarriage of divorced persons conclusively.

In her essay on *Arden of Faversham,* Catharine Belsey sums up the political significance of the divorce issue in Elizabethan England: "The importance of the divorce debate lies in its polarisation of conflicting definitions of marriage. Broadly, the Anglican position was that marriage was indissoluble, that couples were joined by God for the avoidance of fornication and the procreation of children, and that there was no remedy for marital disharmony and discontent . . . Equally broadly, the Puritans held that marriage was a civil covenant, a thing indifferent to salvation, that it depended on consent, and that where this was lacking the couple could not be said to be joined by God, and could therefore justly be put asunder. . . . The contest for the meaning of marriage cannot be isolated from the political struggles which characterize the century between the Reformation and the English Revolution."[10]

Reading *All's Well That Ends Well* in the light of that divorce debate and the political implications of dissolubility of marriage throws the supposedly fairy tale world of the play into different focus. Throughout the play, a major structural feature is the contract-oath, and this binding nature of marriage is explored together with the bond between Lord and subject. Both relationships come together in Bertram, the new self-willed aristocrat, recently come into his inheritance but blocked from expressing his will either in public or in private by his overlord, the King. In II, 3, ordered by the King to take Helena as his wife, Bertram accepts in a speech of bitter irony, professing subjection to the King's will while at the same time questioning the basis of the King's power over him:

> Pardon, my gracious lord; for I submit
> My fancy to your eyes. When I consider
> What great creation and what dole of honour
> Flies where you bid it. I find that she, which late
> Was in my nobler thoughts most base, is now
> The praised of the king; who, so ennobled
> Is as 'twere born so.
>
> (II. 3. 167-173)

At this moment of supposedly bowing to the King's wishes, Bertram chooses to talk in terms of his own subjection to the power the King exercises over him, and, again describing Helena as "she", refers to the social gulf between them both. She, Helena, being the favoured of the King, is as good as ennobled, is the surface message of Bertram's speech, but the deep structure reveals the irony beneath his words. His very acknowledgement of the relationship of fealty between himself and the King is an assertion of his belief in the binding nature of that contract, a contract made by virtue of his aristocratic birth alone, and that belief negates any statement he may make about the ennobling of Helena through actions rather than through blood. Even while appearing to accede to the King's wishes, he is challenging the fundamental premise on which the King's command is being made.

The relationship between King and subject is presented as being based on the subject's acceptance of the King's absolute power, and in the same way the relationship between husband and wife is shown as an indissoluble contract. Bertram enters into two such contracts—publicly, with Helena, and privately, through the exchange of rings with the woman he thinks is Diana. The validity of that private marriage is not called into question—when she sees the ring on Diana's finger, the Countess declares

> Of six preceding ancestors, that gem
> Conferr'd by testament to th'sequent issue,
> Hath it been owed and worn. This is his wife:
> That ring's a thousand proofs.
>
> (V. 3. 195-198)

The value conferred on the ring by heredity becomes a sign to the Countess of Bertram's sincerity, and again the link is made in the text between the inherited power system of the aristocracy and marriage, regardless of whether that marriage has been celebrated before a priest or not. The marriage contract is presented as having an intrinsic value of its own, like the blood relationship of father and son, that cannot be challenged.

It is significant that neither of the marriages are presented on stage. We hear about them both, *post facto* but do not see them take place. Instead, what we do see is the exchange of vows between Helena and the King, when she promises healing and he promises to allow her to choose a husband "from forth the royal blood of France," (II. 1. 196) and this scene is strongly reminiscent of a marriage. Helena swears an oath that has both a temporal and spatial dimension, showing her total commitment to her task in the following lines:

> If I break time, or flinch in property
> Of what I spoke, unpitied let me die,
> And well deserv'd.
>
> (II. 1. 186-188)

This oath is the only one that is actually kept. Bertram allows his private passions to continually over-ride public declarations of loyalty, hence in his marriage to Helena he has no qualms about declaring his contract before a priest but then refusing to consummate the pact and likewise he is willing to consummate but not publicly acknowledge his contract with Diana.

In the decaying courtly world of this play, the whole question of public and private contract is thrown into confusion. What we have is a picture of a society in turmoil, self-destructive, as the old moral idealism of the feudal hierarchy is threatened by the new opportunistic ethos. Bertram struggles to reject feudal authority when it extends into his private life, but fails because his opposition is rooted in an equally hierarchical conception of the world. All he can do is take flight to another court and play at being a military hero. In the end he is forced to accept the authority of his overlord and publicly acknowledge not only a wife but the heir she presents him with, who offers him the possibility of consolidating his own social position in time future. It is a compromise, but an inevitable one if the courtly class position is to be maintained.

Likewise, Helena's final solution is also a compromise. She has pushed through a contract in spite of the other partner's opposition and in the process has replaced the pre-Reformation idealisation of virginity with a marriage that ensures her a high social status as she is accepted into the aristocracy. What she does not get is commitment from her partner, and at the end of the play is as far away from a marriage as a union of equal minds as she has ever been. She is bound to Bertram in a power relationship, quite unlike Milton's idealised vision of marriage as "a covenant, the very being whereof consists not in a forced cohabitation, and counterfeit performance of duties, but in unfeigned love and peace."[11]

Helena's reference to "deadly divorce", seen in terms of the inter-relatedness of public and private contracts in *All's Well That Ends Well,* and set against the ongoing debate in England about the social basis for divorce is therefore a crucial moment in the play. The Anglican orthodoxy feared divorce as leading to disorder, and as setting a dangerous precedent that might cause other types of contract to be questioned, most particularly that existing between prince and subject. Divorce, in short, was dangerously revolutionary, and it is hardly surprising that Milton should have argued for liberty within marriage as reflecting man's right to liberty within the state: "He who marries intends as little to conspire his own ruin, as he that swears allegiance: and as a whole people is in proportion to an ill government, so is one man to an ill marriage. If they, against any authority, covenant or statute may, by the sovereign edict of charity, save not only their lives but honest liberties from unworthy bondage, as well may he against any private covenant, which he never entered to his mischief, redeem himself from unsupportable disturbances to honest peace and just contentment."[12]

At a time of growing disquiet and economic crisis, with the passing of Elizabeth and the accession of James bringing sharply into focus the relationship between Monarch and religious groups, Shakespeare wrote a play that offers both an analysis of the complexities of the post-Reformation views of the marriage contract vis-à-vis the State and is also a warning to a class that has grown too complacent in its demands for absolute power. *All's Well That Ends Well* is a signpost on the road to the English Revolution.

Notes

1. Beitrag zum Kolloquium der Shakespeare-Tage in Weimar, vorgetragen am 23. April 1983.
2. Logan Pearsall Smith, *On Reading Shakespeare,* London 1933, p. 58.
3. T. Middleton Raysor (ed.), *Coleridge's Shakespeare Criticism.* London 1930.
4. Cf. A. W. Schlegel, *Lectures on Dramatic Art.* London 1883.
5. Muriel Bradbrook, *Shakespeare and Elizabethan Poetry.* London 1951, p. 162.
6. Cf. Clifford Leech, "The Theme of Ambition in *All's Well That Ends Well*'", in: *English Literary History* 21 (1954) 3, pp. 17-29.
7. Samuel Johnson, *The Plays of William Shakespeare,* London 1765.
8. Cf. Lawrence Stone, *The Family, Sex and Marriage in England, 1500-1800.* London 1977, p. 37.
9. Arden Edition. London 1967, Introduction p. XXV.
10. Catherine Belsey, "Alice Arden's Crime", in: *Renaissance Studies No* 13, Spring 1983. I am indebted to Catherine Belsey for first drawing my attention to the political significance of the divorce debate in the sixteenth century in a version of this article presented at the University of Southampton in 1982. Without the inspiration of her paper, mine would not have been written.
11. John Milton, *The Doctrine and Discipline of Divorce.* In: *Milton's Prose Writings.* Ed. by K. M. Burton. London 1958, pp. 247-319.
12. Milton, ibid.

Peggy Muñoz Simonds (essay date 1989)

SOURCE: "Sacred and Sexual Motifs in *All's Well That Ends Well,*" in *Renaissance Quarterly,* Vol. 42, No. 1, Spring, 1989, pp. 33-59.

[*In the following essay, Simonds examines several matrimonial texts that were available to Shakespeare and his contemporaries in order demonstrate how Shakespeare's audience might have reacted to the characters of Bertram and Helena.*]

Whatever scholars may think of its value as a work of poetic literature, Shakespeare's *All's Well That Ends Well* is remarkably entertaining in the theater. Perhaps this is so because it fulfills the fundamental generic responsibility of comedy; it overcomes the death of the fathers through a bawdy emphasis on youthful sexuality and love, and it manipulates mythical plot elements that are subconsciously familiar to any audience in Western civilization. The play skillfully diverts our attention from death and burial to the "little death" of sexual orgasm, from age, illness, and the destruction of war to marriage and the joy of new life. Above all, it is not so much a "problem play" in the Shavian sense as it is a typical work of Renaissance comic art that attempts to unite both the physical and the spiritual elements of human existence within a single structure of the imagination.

In this essay, I shall examine certain intertextual relations concerned with the subject of matrimony that may help to shed some light on the play's meaning or meanings to a Renaissance audience. Specifically, I shall compare certain aspects of *All's Well* with: (1) the so-called "Greek Epithalamium" by Catullus; (2) the colloquy "Proci et Puellae" by Erasmus; (3) the text of the 1559 marriage liturgy we may presume was used in the offstage wedding of Helena and Bertram; (4) an important scriptural use of the bed-trick to fulfill the obligations of the marriage contract; and (5) a sermon by a leading Anglican divine of the period. Of course, I am not concerned here with proving that any of these texts was a direct source for the comedy. All of them were familiar to literate men and women of the English Renaissance; they all formed part of a common cultural context for the work of William Shakespeare and other creative artists of the period.

My thesis is that *All's Well That Ends Well* ought to be experienced in the theater and in the study as a play that is not so much ambivalent in meaning, as is often suggested, but simultaneous in its thematic implications. Among its many themes—and I will consider only the marriage topos in this paper—the play simultaneously discusses both sexual and sacred matters without essential conflict between them; therefore, any final thematic statement about *All's Well* must include the two elements, not simply one or the other. My purpose here is to attempt a Renaissance rather than a modern reading of the play, even though such a reading may seem remote from contemporary interests and socio-political doctrines.

It seems to me that what primarily disturbs the modern reader of *All's Well* (dated 1602-3 by Anne Barton) is the intimate relation we note between the language of sexuality and the language of spirituality or Protestant theology within the text. Since many modern readers are offended by the pervasive Renaissance tendency to see constant analogies between the everyday physical life of men and women and the hope for a spiritual life to come, we usually focus on Shakespeare's bawdry and thus overlook certain eschatological elements in the comedy, i.e., the poetic references to "last things," to humanity's final destiny after death. But even Shakespeare's title, *All's Well That Ends Well,* would have immediately evoked thoughts of death and the Last Judgment in the minds of his audience. Of course, we do not know what Shakespeare personally thought about the quarrelsome Christianity of his age and culture. We do know, however, that he earned his livelihood by writing plays for a Christian audience. This audience could be expected to understand and respond to any theological resonances they heard in the theater, especially since open discussions of religious doctrine were forbidden on the public stage by the political authorities. I believe it is precisely the *subversive* presence of sacred concerns running parallel to, and often interpenetrating, the lusty sexuality of the play that makes *All's Well* seem "dark" to us, but that might well have ensured a commercial success for the playwright in early seventeenth-century England. Furthermore, in discussing this play, we must always keep in mind that England was then governed by a childless and elderly Protestant queen, who might have recently died by the time the play was first performed. All this provides an "interesting" context for a serious comedy, or tragicomedy, on sex, forced marriage, reproduction, illness, apparent death, and joyful resurrection.

Morris P. Tilley has already called our attention to the proverb that may lie behind the sexual implications of the title: "All shall be well, and Jack shall have his Jill."[1] And, since the continuity of physical life on earth does indeed depend on Jack's having Jill and vice versa, one entire level of the comedy is definitely concerned with coaxing the younger generation into bed—within a socially acceptable context—in order to fulfill its reproductive duties, which England's Virgin Queen had refused to do. At no point, however, is sexuality romanticized or glorified in this comedy; it is simply taken for granted as a necessary element of human life and a duty for married people. That the tempting pleasures of sex outside of marriage may lead the young morally astray is taken for granted as well, so that most of the bawdry in this play is notably rough and cynical in nature. Indeed, there is a dark Augustinian cast to the sexual jokes throughout *All's Well* ("so lust doth play / with what it loathes," IV.vi.24-25) in subtle opposition to Helena's personal promise of curative beauty, love, and fruitfulness, thus suggesting a typical Protestant viewpoint keyed to the beliefs of an Anglican audience. But the value of marriage itself as a mysterious source of purification and regeneration is emphasized again and again within the structure of the play, and this too is typical of sixteenth-century Protestantism.[2] According to Mary Beth Rose, "The fact that romantic comedy, a dramatic form which celebrates erotic love and marriage, flourished in the environment of a new sensibility which embraced marriage both as the spiritual foundation of society and as the repository of hope for personal happiness, strongly suggests a parallel development between the increasingly complex, optimistic comic representations of eros that followed Lyly's plays and the more positive moral conceptions of sexual love and marriage that were beginning to be articulated in Protestant conduct literature."[3]

Since *All's Well That Ends Well* is the most eschatological title in the entire Shakespearean canon, the play must also have something to do with sacred love, or salvation on a cosmic level, as G. Wilson Knight and others have argued.[4] But, as I have previously suggested, the modern mind seems to find it difficult to consider sex and salvation at the very same time, since—unlike the Elizabethans—we strive to keep Saturday night and Sunday morning carefully apart.

In contrast to our own lingering Puritanism, the use of erotic religious metaphors was a commonplace for the Renaissance. We need only recall, for example, Titian's erotic painting entitled *Venus and Cupid With Organist* (Madrid, Museo del Prado), which depicts a musician playing an organ while staring fixedly over his shoulder at a reclining and naked Venus, whose infant son's arms are twined about her neck from behind the couch.[5] The organ is both a sexual reference and the most divine of musical instruments because it can sound all the chords of "World Harmony."[6] Significantly, Titian also portrays two different worlds in the same picture plane on his canvas (indeed, sharing the same couch)—the human world of the musician dressed in his fashionable Renaissance clothes and the divine world of the nude Venus and Cupid.[7] He suggests thereby a marriage between heaven and earth, between historical specificity and eternal values, within the same work of art.[8] It seems to me that Shakespeare employs a similar Renaissance aesthetic in *All's Well That Ends Well.*

. . . . .

Ordinary human marriage requires sexuality—the physical loss of virginity and the spiritual loss of innocence for both sexes in order to bring fertility into the wasteland. Although usually advertised as pleasurable, this loss can be frightening and indeed painful for young people, especially for girls. But in *All's Well,* the loss of virginity appears rather surprisingly to disturb Bertram even more than Helena, who is willing to give all for the love of her childhood playmate. In contrast, Bertram runs away from a marriage he has religiously sworn to consummate, and later he pursues not a camp follower but an honest Florentine lady named after the pagan goddess of virginity and marital chastity, Diana. Apparently he worships this goddess, as did Hippolytus, perhaps because he is still too young to face the challenge of Venus, or of her mythic priestess, Helena. We must remember that only Parolles, "a notorious liar" (I.i.100) and traitor, accuses Bertram of being "a foolish idle boy, but for all that very ruttish" (IV.iii.215-16), and then he clearly libels the master he knows has run away from a virgin by announcing that, "I knew the young Count to be a dangerous and lascivious boy, who is a whale to virginity, and devours up all the fry it finds" (IV.iii.219-21).[9] At this point, Bertram himself protests the lie, although it might be expected to enhance his masculine reputation in a military camp. He calls Parolles a "Damnable both-sides rogue" (IV.iii.222). It should be noted that Helena, as well as Parolles, uses the word "idle" in respect to Bertram, but she seems to confirm his continued virginity when she calls his awakening sexuality so far an "idle fire" (III.vii.26). What Bertram wants at this point is "To buy his will" (27), that is, to gain sexual experience his own way, without any emotional or social commitment whatsoever.

At the same time, the audience can only feel sympathy with Bertram's rebellion against the notorious ward system that allows his king to force him to marry *against* his will. Lawrence Stone states that "up to 1640 the landed classes continued to endure, although with increasing discontent, the practice of wardship, by which the marriages of young fatherless heirs and heiresses of landed property were put up for sale by the Crown. The Court of Wards was tolerated as long as the society upon which it levied its tribute had itself little respect for individual freedom of choice, and treated its own children with as little consideration for personal feelings as did the Court itself."[10]

In *All's Well,* the king rather cynically uses Bertram to pay off his medical bill, even after the physician Helena withdraws her request for the young man as her husband once she sees his distaste for the match. Nevertheless, Bertram's social snobbery and subsequent dash for freedom on his wedding night reveal him to be a spoiled adolescent unworthy of our sympathy and of the bride his mother approves for him.

Helena, of course, is far more mature. Just before her famous virginity debate with Parolles, the heroine tells us in a soliloquy of her very physical love for Bertram, for "His arched brows, his hawking eye, his curls" (I.i.11). She admits her desire to "die" for him, in both senses of the word, since "The hind that would be mated by the lion / Must die for love" (91-92). Helena understands sexual intercourse to be—in terms of a popular medieval topos—the culmination of a cruel hunt, but she accepts it willingly as the price of love. Thus, Shakespeare clearly means us to catch the irony of Parolles's impudent question as he strides onstage: "Are you meditating on virginity?" (110). The very opposite is true. Where Bertram seems to fear sexuality until he has proved himself as a soldier, after which he makes conventional and boyish attempts to seduce the impoverished maiden Diana (a common appellation for the Virgin Queen), Helena is now ready to fly from the altar of divine Diana and to dedicate herself "to imperial Love" (I.iii.74-75).

The virginity debate that follows between Helena and Parolles seems politically daring in Elizabeth's England, although it is based on an ancient topos in marriage songs. One of the oldest literary examples of it we have today appears to be the "Greek Epithalamium," *Carmen* LXII, by Catullus, and this is the first intertextual relationship I wish to discuss.[11] In this song, Catullus introduces a group of maidens who debate with a group of youths on what Peter Demetz has called "the gains and losses of marriage."[12] Much as Helena in *All's Well* initiates the Shakespearean discussion with her complaint that "Man is enemy to virginity; how / may we barricade it against him? (I.i.12-13), the Roman maidens in *Carmen* LXII compare the bride's virginity to a city that can no longer defend itself against enemy attack:

Antoni Cimolino as Soldier, Kim Scarcella as Townsperson, Michel LaFleche as Porter, Robert Smith as Soldier, Keith Thomas as Lord Dumaine Elder, Emma Richler as Townsperson, Tony Martin as Soldier, David Brown as Rinaldo, Susan Wright as Countess, Allan Gray as Lavatch, and Richard Curnock as LaFew in Act I, scene i of the 1988 Stratford Festival production of All's Well That Ends Well.

> Hesperus, what more cruel fire than thine moves in the sky? for thou canst endure to tear the daughter from her mother's embrace, from her mother's embrace to tear the close-clinging daughter, and give the chaste maiden to the burning youth. What more cruel than this do enemies when a city falls?
>
> (87)

Parolles in *All's Well* tells Helena bluntly that the only defense against man is to "Keep him out" (I.i.114), to which she replies:

> *Hel.* But he assails, and our virginity though valiant, in the defense yet is weak. Unfold to us some war-like resistance.
> *Par.* There is none. Man, setting down before you, will undermine you and blow you up.
>
> (I.i.115-19.)

Although the profanely sexual military analogy continues throughout the virginity debate in *All's Well,* the Roman maidens of Catullus then shift to vegetation imagery in their lament for the bride's imminent defloration:

> As a flower springs up secretly in a fenced garden, unknown to the cattle, torn up by no plough, which the winds caress, the sun strengthens, the shower draws forth, many boys, many girls, desire it; when the same flower fades, nipped by a sharp nail, no boys, no girls desire it: so a maiden, whilst she remains untouched, so long is she dear to her own: when she has lost her chaste flower with sullied body, she remains neither lovely to boys nor dear to girls.
>
> (89)

But the chorus of youths answers with a similar plant analogy that points out the need for husbandry to make a vine fruitful:

> As an unwedded vine which grows up in a bare field never raises itself aloft, never brings forth a mellow grape, but bending its tender form with downward weight, even now touches the root with topmost shoot; no farmers, no oxen tend it: but if it chance to be joined in marriage to the elm, many farmers, many oxen tend it: so a maiden, whilst she remains untouched, so long is she aging untended; but when in ripe season she is

> matched in equal wedlock, she is more dear to her husband and less distasteful to her father.
>
> (89)

Each verse concludes with the refrain, "Hymen, O Hymenaeus, Hymen, hither, O Hymenaeus!"—a formal evocation of the god of marriage. The young men obviously win the argument with their claim that a husband is like a tree (the family tree) to which a delicate maiden, like a tender vine, may cling and become fruitful with his support. But if a virgin does not marry, she will be forgotten and die unknown. The main reason for marriage is therefore fruitfulness, according to Catullus, and not the romantic love of golden lads and lasses. Demetz (527-28) calls our attention to the almost literal translation of the epithalamium by Shakespeare's contemporary Ben Jonson in his 1606 *Hymenai, or The Solemnities of Masque and Barriers at Marriage.*

Although in *All's Well* Parolles lures Bertram away from fruitful marriage to the destruction of war, he also makes a witty personal attack on Helena's virginity in I.i, just as he later tries to win Diana for himself in Florence. In answer to Helena's defense of her chastity until she can offer it to the man of her choice, Parolles replies with the argument of the Roman youths that it is "against the rule of nature," to which he adds some Christian elaborations:

> He that hangs himself is a virgin; virginity murthers itself, and should be buried in highways out of all sanctified limit, as a desperate offendress against nature. Virginity breeds mites, much like a cheese, consumes itself to the very paring, and so dies with feeding [its] own stomach. Besides virginity is peevish, proud, idle, made of self-love, which is the most inhibited sin in the canon. Keep it not, you cannot choose but lose by't. Out with't!
>
> (I.i.138-46)

Curiously enough, Parolles personifies virginity here in male as well as female terms. Indeed, what better description do we have of Bertram than that of a young man who is "peevish, proud, idle, made of self-love"?

After Helena assures Parolles that she will do nothing with her "virginity yet" (I.i.165), she makes a speech that has been widely interpreted as a list of conventional poetic references to the loves Bertram will find at court. I tend to agree, however, with those who believe Helena is referring here to the gifts Bertram will receive when she relinquishes her virginity to him as his wife. The first word, "There," is the source of her sexual powers, the city she continues to defend against others. She tells Parolles prophetically that

> There shall your master have a thousand loves,
> A mother, and a mistress, and a friend,
> a phoenix, captain, and an enemy,
> A guide, a goddess, and a sovereign,
> A counsellor, a traitress, and a dear;
> His humble ambition, proud humility;
> His jarring concord, and his discord dulcet;
> His faith, his sweet disaster, with a world
> Of pretty, fond, adoptious christendoms
> That blinking Cupid gossips.
>
> (I.i.166-75)

Lines 171-73 appear to be subtextual allusions to the varying pleasures of sexual intercourse for the male, followed by the fruitful results for the female. To "gossip" once meant to "godparent"; thus Cupid himself godparents the results of a union between Bertram and Helena. The apparent discrepancy between the words of superior power and command in these lines referring to the privacy of sexual dominion ("captain,""sovereign,""traitress,"etc.) and Helena's humble attitude toward Bertram in public merely reflect the unfortunate social realities of an Elizabethan marriage in which the wife was indeed a "clinging vine," a legal dependent of her husband and lord, although equal to him as the "heart" of a household in which he was the "head."

Helena accepts a certain loss of dignity and independence through her marriage, but Bertram angrily struggles against his own legal subservience as a mere "ward" to the king. He announces petulantly, "I cannot love her, nor will strive to do't" (II.iii.145), which then forces the king to "produce [his] power" (150). In the security of the home, a loving woman may indeed offer the variety of experience for which Bertram is not yet sufficiently mature, as Richard P. Wheeler has convincingly argued in terms of modern psychology.[13] Until the virginal Bertram is ready for the delights that the virginal Helena wishes to offer him, he is much like the equally immature Demetrius in *A Midsummer Night's Dream,* who—pursued by another determined, aggressive Helena—finally admits that

> . . . all the faith, the virtue of my heart,
> The object and the pleasure of mine eye,
> Is only Helena. To her, my lord,
> Was I betrothed ere I [saw] Hermia;
> But like a sickness did I loathe this food;
> But, as in health, come to my natural taste,
> Now I do wish it, love it, long for it,
> And will evermore be true to it.
>
> (IV.i.169-76)

Similarly Bertram—called a "boy" by his mother, Parolles, and the king, who considers him too young to go to war—admits that his assault on the chaste Diana is based on "sick desires" (IV.ii.35), or on a boyish need for forbidden and irresponsible sex. At the same time, he has carefully chosen as the object of those desires a lady most unlikely to be bought. Fortunately, Shakespeare's Helena is a healer, one willing to risk her reputation and her life in order to cure the sick king and her equally sick beloved.

. . . . .

In the early sixteenth century, Catullus's *Carmen* LXII was wittily Christianized by the humanist priest Desiderius Erasmus in his Latin colloquy "Proci et Puellae" ("Suitors and Sweethearts"), and G. K. Hunter briefly footnotes in the Arden edition of *All's Well* some striking similarities between this humanist dialogue and the virginity debate in the play.[14] Erasmus's "Proci et Puellae" was translated into English by "N. L." (thought to be Nicholas Leigh) in 1568. Like the Catullus epithalamium, this colloquy is concerned with the contradiction between the value of virginity in itself and the necessity of losing it in a fruitful marriage, which is to say that both texts are concerned with the paradoxical nature of marriage itself. Matrimony exchanges the value and power of virginity for the value and power of fecundity. As Parolles so crudely explains of bartered virginity, "Within t' one year it will make itself two, / which is a goodly increase, and the principal itself not / much the worse" (I.i.147-49).

"Proci et Puellae" is an ironic dialogue between the lover Pamphilus and a witty virgin named Maria. Like Erasmus's more famous *The Praise of Folie,* this charming colloquy has both profane and sacred levels of meaning. Even the names of the characters are suggestive. The eager Pamphilus, much in love with Maria's outward appearance, first attempts to seduce her by a rhetorical "appeal to pity," insisting that her beauty has murdered him and that only she can raise him up to life once more. Hunter first notes the similarity of the greeting between Parolles and Helena, who address each other as "fair queen" (I.i.106) and "monarch" (I.i.107), and Pamphilus's promise to Maria that "I shall be to you a King, and you shall be to me a Queene."[15] Just as Maria first refuses Pamphilus's invitation to royalty in return for her body, so Helena and Parolles jokingly refuse one another's proffered crowns.

Pamphilus in *A Modest Meane to Marriage* informs his reluctant sweetheart that she should be called *Martia* rather than Maria:

> *Mar.* And why so I beseech you? what have I to doe with Mars?
> *Pam.* For as that God counteth it but a pastime to murther and kill me, even so doe you. Herein yet more cruell than *Mars,* for you murther him that hartily loveth you.
>
> (Erasmus, sig. Avi)

Shakespeare also refers to the god Mars in *All's Well* I.i, but he changes the application for ironic purposes to a jest on cowardice. This allows Helena to "undermine" Parolles rather than vice versa:

> *Hel.* Monsieur Parolles, you were born under a charitable star.
> *Par.* Under Mars, I.
> *Hel.* I especially think, under Mars.
> *Par.* Why under Mars?
> *Hel.* The wars hath so kept you under that you must needs be born under Mars.
> *Par.* When he was predominant.
> *Hel.* When he was retrograde, I think rather.
> *Par.* Why think you so?
> *Hel.* You go so much backward when you fight.
>
> (I.i.190-99)

Helena's insult foreshadows Bertram's later sexual cowardice in respect to marriage, backward behavior that is directly analogous to Parolles's cowardice on the battlefield and possible homosexuality. Indeed, the King later comments ironically on Bertram's sexual backwardness when he says, "I wonder, sir, [sith] wives are monsters to you / And that you fly them as you swear them lordship, / Yet you desire to marry" (V.iii.154-57); and Parolles assures Helena that she can lose her virginity "to her own liking" if she will "Marry, ill, to like him that ne'er it likes" (I.i.151-53). Much of the malaise of the present court seems to consist of such fearful backwardness, as the king points out in his eulogy of Bertram's father: "Such a man / Might be a copy to these younger times / Which followed well, would demonstrate them now / But goers backward" (I.ii.45-48). In contrast to Bertram's cowardice, a normal adult male must imitate Mars when in bed with his bride and courageously storm the city gate, for as Erasmus's Maria reminds us, "virginite would seeme alwayes to be taken with violence, yea though sometime we love the partie most earnestly" (sig. Ciii).

But while Shakespeare's Parolles uses the military metaphor to explain to Helena how men "undermine" the city gates and "blow up" virgins, Pamphilus in *A Modest Meane* instead complains to Maria about virgins triumphing over the dead bodies of their suitors slain by unrequited love:

> *Mar.* Oh queint handsome, nice dead body: when shall your funerals be prouided for?
> *Pam.* Sooner than you thinke ywisse, except you remedie in time.
> *Mar.* I remedie good Lord? am I able to do such a cure?
> *Pam.* Yea surely: all were I deade, it lyeth in you to rayse me up againe to life, and that with a light thing.
>
> (sig. Bii^{v})

There are obviously both sexual and eschatological insinuations in this teasing exchange, which may remind us of Helena's poignant plea to the Countess:

> O then give pity
> To her whose state is such that cannot choose
> But lend and give where she is sure to lose;
> That seeks not to find that her search implies,
> But riddle-like lives sweetly where she dies.
>
> (I.iii.213-17)

The motif is eventually literalized through Helena's own later resurrection (in a state of pregnancy) from supposed physical death. Not only is she restored to her reluctant husband, but new life also proceeds from the "little death" of the bed-trick which has finally joined her with Bertram.

The resurrection motif is literalized as well when Helena raises the king of France from his sickbed with her beauty, her faith, and her medicine—a miraculous cure that leads the Clown to call her "the herb of grace" (IV.v.17), or that rue which restores life to the soul. On the sexual level, however, Lafew claims that Helena's youth and beauty are powerful enough medicine in themselves to "araise King Pippen" and to "give Charlemain a pen in's hand / And write to her a love line" (II.i.76-78).

In *A Modest Meane,* when Maria is asked to revive Pamphilus, she replies, "As you say, peradventure I might doe it, if some bodye woulde helpe me to the herbe *Panaces,* whereunto they ascribe so great a vertue." But Pamphilus will not be lured into medical discussions at this point. He tells her that "There needeth none herbes to doe it, only vouchsafe to love againe, what is more easie to be perfourmed? nay rather what is more due and just? otherwise you shall never acquite your selfe of manspilling" (sigs. Bii and Bii^{v}). When he is unable to persuade Maria to have an affair with him, however, Pamphilus proposes marriage with equal enthusiasm. But Maria is still unconvinced since "that thing requireth long deliberation, and much advisement, which when it is done cannot be undone againe" (sig. Bv). For the Renaissance, marriage was a serious commitment that men like Shakespeare's Bertram violated at their own peril.

Pamphilus then assures Maria in *A Modest Meane* that he does love her, and for all the right reasons, in the kind of speech we would wish Bertram to make to Helena: ". . . I have knowne for the space of certain yeares the verteous and honest behauior of your parents, that is a birde [sic] not least to be regarded (I think) to come of good stock. Moreover, I am not ignorant with what wholesome instructions, and verteous examples you haue bene traded and brought up by them. And truely good education is of more effect than good parentage" (sig. Bv^{v}). Not surprisingly, however, the "boy" Bertram must first "breed" his personal honor and courage through victory in the battlefield before he can successfully encounter Helena's female perfections in the marriage bed.

The young people in *A Modest Meane to Marriage* discuss the paradox of virginity in vegetation imagery that clearly echoes the "Greek Epithalamium" of Catullus. For example, Pamphilus asks Maria "whether is it a better sight for a Vine to lye uppon the grounde and rot, or the same to embrace a poale, or an elme, and lode it full with purple grapes?" (sig. Bvii). But Maria, like the Roman maidens, sees only the moral paradox of virginity, which she is still reluctant to lose even by way of an honorable marriage:

> *Mar.* . . . for all your saying, virginity is a thing much beloved and lyked with all men.
> *Pam.* I graunt you, a young woman, a virgine, is a fayre, a goodly thing, but what by course of kind is more unseemly than an old wrinkled maide? Had not your mother been contented to lose that flower of hir virginitie, surely we had not had this flower of your beautie. So that in case (as I hope) our mariage be not barren for the losse of one virgine we shall paye God manye.
>
> (sig. Bvii^{v})

Parolles makes exactly the same points during his virginity debate with Helena in *All's Well*: "It is not politic in the commonwealth of nature of preserve virginity. Loss of virginity is rational increase, and there was never virgin got till virginity was first lost. That you were made of is metal to make virgins. Virginity by being once lost, may be ten times found; by being ever kept, it is ever lost" (I.i.126-32).[16]

If Queen Elizabeth were still alive when *All's Well* was first performed, we ought to be amazed at Shakespeare's political daring in allowing his comic character such pointed remarks on aging virginity. Parolles also criticizes "old wrinkled" virgins in language even more explicitly sexual than that of Pamphilus or the Roman youths: "Your old virginity, / is like one of our French wither'd pears, it looks ill, / it eats drily, marry, 'tis a wither'd pear" (I.i.160-63). Helena replies, nevertheless, that she will keep her virginity a little while longer.

Although Maria finally grants Pamphilus leave to address her parents in *A Modest Meane,* she also advises him to consider well what he is doing. She reminds him that marriage is not only a license for sexual pleasure but a serious religious contract as well, a sacrament that Christians believe has a bearing upon the afterlife:

> *Mar.* And do not take into your counsaille, this blind affection borne towardes my person, but rather reason, for that which affection decerneth is liked for a ceason, but that which reason aviseth is never mislyked.
> *Pam.* Certes, thou speakest like a wittie wench; wherefore I intend to follow thy counsayle
>
> (sig. Ciii).

Although Maria counsels "reason" over sexual attraction as a basis for marriage, she also undoubtedly alludes to Saint Paul's often quoted *reason* for Christians to marry at all—"if they cannot contain, let them marry: for it is better to marry than to burn" (I Cor. 7:9)—or Pamphilus would not otherwise call her a "wittie wench" and assent so cheerfully to her advice.

Shakespeare's Bertram, in contrast to Pamphilus, refuses to listen to the king's attempts to reason with him in *All's Well,* preferring war and sexual freedom to the lawful (and sacred) estate of marriage. His behavior is strikingly parodied in I.iii by the Clown, who asks formal permission from the Countess to marry her serving maid Isabel. Lavatch plays the part of the Christian fool as presented by Erasmus in *The Praise of Folie* when he does so.[17] The allusion to Corinthians is of course very clear in this passage:

> *Count.* Tell me thy *reason* why thou wilt marry.
> *Clown.* My poor body, madam, requires it. I am driven on by the flesh, and he must needs go that the devil drives.
> *Count.* Is this all your worship's *reason*?
> *Clown.* Faith madam, I have other *holy reasons,* such as they are.
> *Count.* May the world know them?

Clown. I have been, a madam, a wicked creature, as you and all flesh and blood are, and indeed I do marry that I may *repent.*

(I.iii.27-37; italics mine)

Some twentieth-century critics have been so titillated by the Clown's sexual pun on "holey raisings" (a not unimportant aspect of marriage) that they have failed to recognize the eschatological seriousness of this scene. The pun may also refer, after all, to the Elizabethan belief in the end of the world when all men and women shall be raised from their graves to stand judgment. Despite our modern skepticism about the afterlife, we have no reason to think that Shakespeare's Clown is anything but sincere when he proclaims that he wishes to marry "that I may repent," thus implying that his marriage may lead to his ultimate salvation.

As Arthur Kirsh reminds us in a recent study of love in selected Shakespearean plays, the reference to "holy reasons" in *All's Well* is far more than a bawdy joke: "Even for Shakespeare the blend of obscenity and revealed truth in these lines is remarkable, but it is a mistake to conclude that the result is an ironic depreciation either of Helena's quest or marriage itself. On the contrary, the obscene point is also the theological (and psychological) one."[18] In fact, the sources of the Clown's argument for repentance through marriage can be found in Saint Paul's assurance that "the unbelieving husband is sanctified by the wife, and the unbelieving wife is sanctified by the husband: else were your children unclean; but now they are holy" (I Cor. 7:14). Paul also reminded the Corinthians, "For what knowest thou, O wife, whether thou shalt save thy husband? or how knowest thou, O man, whether thou shalt save thy wife?" Apparently the Countess recognizes these scriptural allusions in the Clown's *reasons* and grants his request to marry: "Thy marriage, sooner than thy wickedness" (I.iii.38).

On the other hand, I do not wish to overemphasize in turn the sacred or eschatological point of view, since the comedy of the scene is clearly based on a double entendre, and the Countess's reply is deliberately ambiguous. The sexual import of her remark is that the Clown will repent not his sins but his marriage, which even he admits will soon become little more than weary physical labor in a fallen world and which will probably end in his becoming a cuckold. Lavatch adds, however, a delightful encomium to the sacred brotherhood of cuckoldry, once again in a Bottom-like parody of Saint Paul: "He that ears my land spares my team, and gives me leave to inn the crop. If I be his cuckold, he's my drudge. He that comforts my wife is the cherisher of my flesh and blood; he that loves my flesh and blood is my friend: *ergo,* he that kisses my wife is my friend" (I.iii.45-50). The relevant passage from Saint Paul forms part of the Elizabethan marriage ceremony in *the Book of Common Prayer 1559*: ("So men are bound to love their own wives as their own bodies. He that loveth his own wife, loveth himself. For never did any man hate his own flesh, but nourisheth and cherisheth it, even as the Lord doth the congregation: for we are members of his body, of his flesh and of his bones."[19]

Because profane parody of the sacred intensifies audience response to that which is parodied, the Clown's foolery reminds us—within the context of a secular theatrical performance—that the marriage union itself is sacred and that it concerns both the physical and spiritual life of the community around us. "The mystery is great," Paul adds, "but I speak of Christ and of the congregation." So, I believe, does Shakespeare in *All's Well That Ends Well,* as I shall explain.

Pamphilus in *A Modest Meane to Marriage* agrees, as does Shakespeare's Clown, to follow the path of reason in order to gain his desire and to request Maria's hand in marriage. In this case, the maiden hastens to assure her suitor that he will have no cause to repent his decision.

Mar. You shall not repent you thereof, but howbe sirha there is now fallen in to my minde a doubt, which bereth mee fore.
Pam. Away with all such doubtes for Gods sake.
Mar. Why will you haue me marry myself to a dead man?
Pam. Not so, for I will reuive againe.

(sig. Ciii^{v})

Here Erasmus permits us to smile at the lover's naughty allusion to sexual resurrection, but the eschatological significance of Pamphilus's assertion is clear as well. The lover's marriage to Maria involves participation in a sacrament that will eventually help him to achieve spiritual resurrection, as the Clown in *All's Well* also suggests.

Erasmus brings his ironic colloquy to a close with one last attempt by Pamphilus for extra-marital sex:

Mar. I pray God guie you a good night, why fetch you such a sigh man?
Pam. A good night say you? I woulde to God you would vouchsafe to giue me that, which you wish mee.
Mar. Soft and faire, I pray you, your harvest is yet but in the greene blade.

(sig. Ciii^{v})

Not only does Maria's reference here to harvesting have an eschatological ring to it, but it reminds us as well of a similar line in Shakespeare's comedy. The Countess begs the King in the last act of *All's Well* to forgive Bertram's folly as no more than "Natural rebellion, done i' th' blade of youth" (V.iii.6). But the grim blade of the harvester Time will eventually cut down all such blades, whether still green or ripe with age.

Marriage, however, offers a defense against the harvester's blade, first through its physical promise of new life in this world, and secondly, through its sacramental promise of new life for the human spirit after death. For this reason, Kirsch correctly finds the text of the marriage liturgy in the 1559 *Book of Common Prayer* crucial to our understanding of many Shakespearean plays.[20] It is important to remember that in *All's Well* Bertram does actually marry Helena in a formal ceremony offstage. He then runs away from his sacred promise to worship Helena with his body, telling Parolles that "Although before the solemn priest I have sworn, / I will not bed her" (II.iii.268-70). We should note that Bertram does not describe his *vow* as "solemn" but the *priest,* thus indicating a disturbing failure to understand the ordinary patterns of language or of religion. In a similar inversion of convention, Bertram—rather than his bride—now becomes the virgin who murders his own posterity (in the sense of Parolles's previous warning to Helena) by refusing to have sexual intercourse with his wife in direct violation of his religious vows: "With this ring I thee wed: with my body I thee worship: And with all my worldly goods I thee endow. In the name of the Father, and of the Son, and of the Holy Ghost" (293). Thus he breaks divine law as well as the social law of the sixteenth century when he withholds his family ring, his body, and his seed from his bride. Bertram's refusal to consummate his marriage, even to kiss Helena, also has an important religious significance for the congregation which has just witnessed the ceremony.

First, the state of matrimony was deemed analogous by Renaissance Christians to the mystical union between Christ and his people or the Church. The Anglican marriage liturgy of the period includes the following prayer: "O God, which hast consecrated the state of matrimony to such an excellent mystery, that in it is signified and represented the spiritual marriage and unity betwixt Christ and his Church, look mercifully upon these thy servants, that this man may love his wife, accordingto thy Word (as Christ did love thy spouse the Church, who gave himself for it, loving and cherishing it even as his own flesh)" (296). Sexuality within the marriage bond thus becomes a religious "mystery." As Christ died for his people or congregation in order to give them everlasting life, so a husband must be willing to "die" sexually for his wife in order to make her fruitful and to provide new physical life for both the family and the community. For this reason, the king formally exhorts Bertram, "As thou lov'st her. / Thy love's to me religious; else does err" (II.iii.182-83).

We should note here the curious fact that Renaissance males did indeed believe that they shortened their own lives each time they had intercourse, since they still held the classical belief that semen (thought to carry the family *genius*) originated in the marrow of the bones and was irreplaceable once spent. The belief is referred to in Emblem 77 of *The Theater of Fine Devices,* Thomas Combe's 1593 English translation of Guillaume de la Perrière's *Le Théatre des bons Engins* (1539). The *incriptio* of the emblem states that "All those that love do fancie most, / But lose their labour and their cost." The *pictura* shows a young man pouring water from a pitcher through a sieve held out to him by a blindfolded Cupid. . . . According to the *subscriptio* or verse,

> Fond love is chiefly likened to a sive,
> In which the more you poure the water in,
> The more is spilt, by letting thorow driue,
> And you no neare then when you first begin.
> Ev'n so for love when yong men frankly give,
> Till oft they leave themselves not worth a pin:
> When all is spent, and they live by the losse,
> They turne againe at last by weeping crosse.[21]

Shakespeare refers to this belief twice in *All's Well.* First, Parolles encourages Bertram to risk his life bravely at war rather than to waste it slowly at home with his wife in bed:

> He wears his honor in a box unseen,
> That hugs his kicky-wicky here at home,
> Spending his manly marrow in her arms,
> Which should sustain the bound and high curvet
> Of Mar's fiery steed
>
> (II.iii.279-83.)

Later the Clown makes a similar statement when he suggests that marriage is more dangerous than war, which is why a man enters into such a union only for the most serious reasons. After hearing that Bertram has run away from his bride and his solemn vow, the Clown tells the Countess the following:

> *Clown.* Nay there is some comfort in the news, some comfort. Your son will not be kill'd so soon as I thought he would.
> *Count.* Why should he be kill'd?
> *Clown.* So say I, madam, if he run away, as I hear he does. The danger is in standing to 't; that's the loss of men, though it be the getting of children.
>
> (III.ii.36-42)

Yet Bertram has in fact sworn before God and the congregation to imitate in sexual terms Christ's sacrifice of the flesh and to "die" for new life within his marital union. He religiously owes Helena the "great prerogative and rite of love" (II.iv.41). When he runs away, Bertram violates the sacred mystery of the covenant between God and man. The implied theological analogy would have been clear to a Renaissance audience. If a nobleman and a ward to the king refuses to give new life to his family and to his society, Christ may not keep his promise to provide an afterlife for the congregation which has witnessed Bertram's vows. As one prominent sixteenth-century English clergyman reminded the faithful, "A Household is as it were a little common wealth, by the good govarnment whereof, Gods glorie may be aduaunced."[22]

In striking contrast to Bertram's fear of losing a little life through the sexual aspect of marriage, Helena feels that her own love is inexhaustible:

> I know I love in vain, strive against hope;
> Yet in this captious and intenible sieve
> I still pour in the waters of my love
> And lack not to lose still.
>
> (I.iii.201-04)

Thus Shakespeare uses the sieve image in *All's Well* not to symbolize the waste of youth through lust, as in Combe's emblem, but to reinforce the idea of love as a source of eternal replenishment of life, as "A fountain of gardens, a well of living waters . . ." (Song Sol. 4. 15). As far as Helena is concerned, however, the image of the sieve was also a popular symbol of chastity, a symbol deriving from the story of the Roman Vestal Virgin Tuccia. . . .[23]

Secondly, in respect to the significance of the marriage liturgy, the priest reminds the congregation and the couple of Paul's commandment to all married men in Ephesians 5: "Ye husbands love your wives, even as Christ loved the Church, and hath given himself for it, to sanctify it, purging it in the fountain of water, through thy Word, that he might make unto himself a glorious congregation, not having spot or wrinkle, or any such thing, but that it should be holy and blameless" (297). Let us recall once more Parolles's threat that if Helena remains a virgin, she will become "like one of our French wither'd pears." The sacred significance of marriage implies that a husband's love has the important function of keeping his wife beautiful and blameless in the eyes of God. He helps her gain salvation, as she helps him in turn.

Thirdly, according to the Anglican liturgy of Shakespeare's time, the main purpose of marriage was "the procreation of children," although the Church also agreed with the Clown's reasons for marrying as "a remedy against sin, and to avoid fornication," as well as a source of "mutual society, help, and comfort" (290-91). In denying Helena his bodily worship, Bertram obviously denies her children too. At the same time, Helena is enjoined by her marriage vows to submit to the will of her husband, to think of him as her lord in the sense that Christ is Lord over the Church.[24] Since Bertram wills not to love her, Helena must then find a way to make herself worthy. She therefore sets out on a pilgrimage to atone for her pride in desiring a noble marriage, striving as well to complete the impossible labors her lord has set for her in his letter: "When thou canst get the ring upon my finger, which never shall come off, and show me a child begotten of thy body that I am father to, then call me husband; but in such a 'then' I write a 'never'" (III.ii.57-60). While Bertram subsequently magnifies himself in pride by conquering the Sienese army, Helena conquers herself and her natural pride by religious penance. In addition, she accepts the total humiliation of playing the whore for her husband in the dark as the only possible means of consummating their marriage.

I shall not review here the many modern critical objections to the folkloric and "unbelievable" bed-trick which allows Helena to fulfill her tasks and thus her wedding vows.[25] In the play Diana tells us the correct moral response when she observes of her own part in obtaining Berram's signet ring and his seed for Helena: "I think't no sin / to cozen him that would unjustly win" (IV.ii.75-76). Moreover, the bed-trick has a very respectable precedent in the Judeo-Christian heritage, as I have shown elsewhere.[26] The story is told in Genesis 38, a chapter read aloud each January 21 in Elizabethan churches, of how the widowed Tamar tricks Judah into sleeping with her in fulfillment of his neglected patriarchal obligation to provide her with an heir to Israel. Disguising herself as a prostitute, Tamar demands of Judah his cloak, his staff, and his *signet* in pledge for the payment of her fee. The Geneva Bible indicates that Judah's failure to recognize Tamar at this time is an act of providence. The marginal gloss states that "God had wonderfully blinded him that he colde not knowe her by her talke," although Judah finally admits the signet as his and the righteousness of Tamar's deed. She later brings forth twins from this union with the eponymous ancestor of Judea. His first-born son is Pharez or Perez, direct forebear of King David and thus of Christ (Matt. I).

In the biblical story, as in *All's Well,* a signet ring is the controlling token of a legitimate legal claim on the reluctant male who rebels against the rights of a female. First, Helena remarks that Bertram's ring comes to him from "the first father" (III.vii.25). Bertram himself then tells Diana that his ring "is an honor 'longing to our house, / Bequeathed down from many ancestors / Which were the greatest obloquy i' th' world / In me to lose" (IV.ii.42-45). Yet, paradoxically, tradition tells us that the ring must be given away (in *The Merchant of Venice* also); worldly honor must be risked for justice to be done. And in all such mythic cases, divine providence sees to it that the ring is given lawfully to the right person.

Thomas Malory also relates two important examples of the bed-trick in British legendary history, one perpetrated by a male, Uther Pendragon, and one by a female, the Lady Elaine.[27] The first results in the conception of King Arthur, savior of Britain, and the second results in the conception of Sir Galahad (Gilead), a knightly Christ-figure, who miraculously cures the maimed Fisher King, much as Helena mysteriously cures the King of France in *All's Well.* The bed-trick convention was thus a familiar symbol to the Elizabethans of providence at work in human affairs and was meant to be understood as necessary rather than as immoral. Certain children must be born into the world.

To be sure, by Shakespeare's time scepticism was already eating into earlier belief in supernatural miracles. The arguments of both the alchemists and—quite unintentionally—the Lutherans were causing this erosion of faith in miracles, a fact carefully brought to our attention by the dramatist in *All's Well* II.iii when Lafew remarks to Bertram: "They say miracles are past, and we have our philosophical persons, to make modern and familiar, things supernatural and causeless. Hence is it that we make trifles of terrors, ensconcing ourselves into seeming knowledge, when we should submit ourselves to an unknown fear (II.iii.1-6). Lafew apparently refers here to the eschatological realm, to reverence for mysteries and possibly to a prudent fear of the Last Judgment. He then reads aloud the providential title of a current broadsheet: "A showing of a heavenly effect in an earthly actor" (II.iii.23-24). Shortly after this, Helena enters with the King, whom she has just raised up from his sickbed and marvelously cured. We do not know exactly how she has done this, any more than we know how Paulina brings the statue of Hermione to life in *The Winter's Tale*. The miracle is to be accepted, not understood. As Helena and the King stand onstage together, they are a visual emblem of what Lafew calls the "very hand of heaven" (II.iii.31) still at work in Shakespeare's time—at least in the theater. After so pointedly dramatizing this example of a providential miracle, the playwright then assumes in all probability that his audience will accept the equally providential nature of the bed-trick.

Both the curing of the King and the bed-trick provide a familiar religio-mythic infrastructure for the plot of *All's Well.* The comedy begins with death and disease, continues with the offer of a cure for present illness in return for a marriage with all its sacred overtones, and ends with the unexpected appearance onstage of a pregnant woman previously believed to be dead. This woman—Helena, or love in all its most luminous aspects—is the physical and spiritual emblem of new life indeed, and her story resonates far beyond the structural confines of the comedy and of the theater itself in the best traditions of dramatic art. The chaste Diana, as "presenter" in act V, clearly states in a primitive poetic form the sacred-sexual paradox inherent in both the play and the marriage: "Dead though she be, she feels her young one kick. / So there's my riddle: one that's dead is quick" (V.iii.302-303).

At this point Helena reappears onstage, as if literally resurrected from the dead, which prompts the King to question her reality. She rather strangely replies, "No, my good lord, / 'Tis but the shadow of a wife you see, / The name and not the thing" (V.viii.306-08). Since Helena is seen by all to be pregnant and is about to prove by her possession of the signet ring that Bertram is the father of her child, she is presumably not just the shadow of a wife in the usual sense of the word. However, the Anglican minister Henrie Smith employed the very same term in a sermon to refer to the taking of a second wife or concubine: "another sayth, that the name of his second doth signifie a shadow, because she was not a wife, but the shadow of a wife: For this cause the Scripture never biddeth man to love his wives, but to love his wife, and sayth, *They shall be two in one flesh,* not three, nor foure, but onely two."[28] It seems probable then that Helena is here reprimanding Bertram for making love to her when he thought her a concubine in Florence rather than fulfilling his duties on their true wedding night. The paradox is that, although the pregnant woman onstage is still Bertram's wife, Helena, she is also the second woman after his marriage to be taken by Bertram, in this case when—in the dark—he believed her to be Diana. She is therefore the shadow of a wife, or pregnant as his second wife or concubine. Confused, and already publicly shamed as a would-be adulterer, Bertram quickly promises to love Helena "dearly," if she can make him understand the paradox and her trick, or "to know this clearly" (V.viii.315).

Helena then mischievously threatens him with "deadly divorce" if she cannot do so. If Bertram is *not* the father of her child, not only has he been unfaithful, but she also is guilty of adultery, which was the only ground for divorce accepted by the Church: "As God hath ordained remedies for every disease, so he hath ordained a remedie for the disease of marriage. The disease of marriage is adultrie, and the medicine hereof is divorcement."[29] The play has indirectly circled back to the possibility of disease, but this time the cure lies in the hands of Bertram himself—*if* he chooses to exercise this means of escape from marriage and to be further shamed publicly as a cuckold. An Elizabethan audience would undoubtedly have caught the joke on the young rake bested in this way by his "clever wench" and have agreed that this marriage would indeed last, especially since the couple had evidently enjoyed the Florentine sexual consummation of their earlier enforced sacramental wedding.

Much as Greek and Roman comedy, a religious genre for the ancient world, always celebrated a wedding, or a resurrection, or both, so does Shakespeare's *All's Well That Ends Well.* The play is consistently evocative of the interaction between sexual love and sacred love in the lives of individuals and communities through their participation in the mystery of matrimony. At once obscenely physical and profoundly spiritual, a fruitful marriage represented for the Renaissance the central Christian mystery of the Incarnation, or the philosophical doctrine that humanity itself transcends the limitations of bodily existence and partakes of the divine nature. The strange enigmas of the marriage between spirit and body, of eternal redemption intersecting the waste of time, of life arising from sickness, loss, and death, all echo and re-echo throughout a play as provocative to an audience as is Titian's painting of *Venus and Cupid with an Organist.*

Finally, if Shakespeare's King will only say in the end that "All yet *seems* well" (V.iii.333; italics mine), it is not only because he feels concern for the marital happiness of Helena and Bertram, but because the final judgment is not *his* to make. In his own role as King, he too must face the Last Judgment by a higher authority. The Globe audience was very familiar with Juan Vives's analogy between the stage and the world, the audience and the gods, which gave their theater its name. It is for this reason that, in one of Shakespeare's most poignantly eschatological epilogues, the player king employs the familiar theater metaphor to remind us that even "The king's a beggar, now the play is done" (V.iii.I).

Notes

My thanks to Susan Snyder, who kindly read an earlier version of this essay and provided many helpful suggestions, and to Richard P. Wheeler, who did the same on behalf of *Renaissance Quarterly.* The section on Erasmus and Shakespeare was previously read at the South Atlantic Modern Language Association meetings in Atlanta in fall 1984. The original version of this paper was presented at the Shakespeare Association of America meetings of 1983 in Ashland, Oregon.

1. *A Dictionary of the Proverbs in England in the Sixteenth and Seventeenth Centuries* (Ann Arbor, 1950) A 164.

2. See Lawrence Stone, *The Family, Sex and Marriage in England 1500-1800* (New York, 1977) 135-36; Heinrich Bullinger, *The Golden Booke of Christian Matrimony,* trans. Miles Coverdale (London, 1560); Henrie Smith, "A Preparative to Marriage," in *The Sermons of Maister Henrie Smith, Gathered into one volume* (London, 1594) 1-3; Thomas Becon, *Workes,* 3 vols. (London, 1560); and Robert Cleaver, *A Godlie Forme of Householde Government: for the Ordering of Private Families* (London, 1598).

3. "Sexual Love in Elizabethan Comedy," *Renaissance Drama,* 15 (1984): 1-29.

4. G. Wilson Knight, *The Sovereign Flower* (London; 1958) 131-57. M. C. Bradbrook notes that "the language of religion is used with particular frequency by Shakespeare in this play," in her fine thematic study "Virtue is the True Nobility," repr. in *Shakespeare, The Comedies,* ed. Kenneth Muir (Englewood Cliffs, NJ, 1965) 131. See also the theological interpretations of Robert Grams Hunter, *Shakespeare and the Comedy of Forgiveness* (New York, 1965), and of Jay Halio, who rightly calls Helena a "Minister of Providence" in "*All's Well That Ends Well,*" *Shakespeare Quarterly,* 15 (1965):33-43. Much less convincing is David S. Kastan, "*All's Well That Ends Well* and the Limits of Comedy," *English Literary History,* 52 (1985):575-89. Aside from ignoring the tragicomic precedent of Euripides' *Alcestis* in theater history, Kastan joins a long line of male critics, including Richard A. Levin, in finding the play unpleasant because he finds Helena's tenacity "predatory" (p. 579). One suspects that a similar tenacity in achieving his goal by a dramatic *hero* would be praised by this critic and others as commendable heroic determination. But Shakespeare seems to be more tolerant than his critics of women in love, and he makes the majority of his most attractive romantic heroines into notably aggressive man-chasers, which is about all they were allowed to chase in the sixteenth and seventeenth centuries: witness Rosalind, Viola, Imogen, as well as Hermia and Helena of *A Midsummer Night's Dream.*

5. Although Venus inspires music and the arts in her celestial form, the presence of Cupid in the painting accentuates as well her earthly fecundity. The dominion of Venus over the vegetable world and human sexuality is symbolized in the background of the picture by the garden with its satyr fountain, the leaping deer, and the pair of lovers strolling away from the viewer.

6. See Leo Spitzer's comprehensive study, *Classical and Christian Ideas of World Harmony* (Baltimore, 1963). The organ is also an attribute of Saint Cecilia and thus can stand alone as a symbol of music and of the sense of hearing.

7. Edgar Wind emphasizes the manner in which Titian differentiates between the two types of beings which occupy the same couch: "In the Holkham *Venus* (Metropolitan Museum of Art, New York) and the corresponding paintings by Titian in Madrid and Berlin, the disparity between mortal and goddess is heightened by a paradox of posture. While the courtier plays music under the inspiration of love (cf. Erasmus, *Adagia* s. v. *Musicam docet amor*), he does not face the goddess directly, but turns his head over his shoulder to 'look back' at her; he thus enacts the Platonic . . . reversal of vision by which alone a mortal can hope to face transcendent Beauty" (*Pagan Mysteries in the Renaissance,* rev. ed. (London, 1968) 143, n.7. See also the somewhat different views of Erwin Panofsky, *Problems in Titian, Mostly Iconographic* (New York, 1969) 122-25.

8. Panofsky's *Early Netherlandish Painting: Its Origin and Character* (Cambridge, MA, 1953) remains one of the best studies of Renaissance aesthetics with its meticulous surface realism in juxtaposition with elaborate symbolism and religio-mythic allusions. A recent essay by John N. Wall, Jr., has enlarged on Panofsky's insights by pointing out that the realistic *style* and iconographic *content* of pictures such as Jan van Eyck's *Amolfini Wedding Portrait* actually work together as a Renaissance proclamation that Christian "abstractions have significance *only* in their specific and particular manifestations." As Christ entered into "historical specificity" in order to redeem fallen humanity, so the moral behavior of specific individuals in later time repeats the Fall and then does or does not merit the Redemption. See Wall, "*The Amolfini Wedding Portrait* as Christian Proclamation," *Renaissance Papers* (1981):71-81.

9. All quotations from Shakespeare are taken from *The Riverside Shakespeare,* ed. G. Blakemore Evans (Boston, 1974).

10. Stone, *Family, Sex, Marriage* 182.

11. See *The Poems of Catullus,* trans. F. W. Cornish, Loeb Classical Library (New York, 1918) 85-89. Further references to this poem will be noted in the text.

12. Peter Demetz, "The Elm and the Vine: Notes Toward the History of a Marriage Topos," *PMLA,* 73 (1958): 521-32. Further references to this article will be noted in the text.

13. "Imperial Love and the Dark House: *All's Well That Ends Well,*" in *Shakespeare's Development and the Problem Comedies: Turn and Counter-Turn* (Berkeley, 1981) 35-91.

14. *All's Well,* ed. Hunter (London, 1959) 9 n. 104-105, 10 n. 126-27, 12 n. 148.

15. Erasmus, *A Modest Meane to Marriage,* trans. N. L. (London, 1568), sig. Ci[v]. The sexual desires of Pamphilus can be summed up in the following line: "As for myselfe, if God so woulde, it were unto me a pleasure, even to end my life in your armes" (sig. Cii). Since the beloved is named Maria, the remark simultaneously evokes an image of the Pietà. All further signatures from this work by Erasmus will be noted in the text.

16. According to Hunter in the Arden ed. of *All's Well* 10-11 n. 126-27. "The idea probably goes back to Jerome's 'Laudo nuptias, laudo coniugium, sed quia mihi virgines generant.'" Hunter also notes that the same argument that virgins bring forth virgins is used by Venus in Shakespeare's *Venus and Adonis* (lines 203-204) and by Ferardo in Lyly's *Euphues.*

17. For a persuasive study of Shakespeare's Erasmian ideas, see R. Chris Hassel, Jr., *Faith and Folly in Shakespeare's Romantic Comedies* (Athens, GA, 1980).

18. *Shakespeare and the Experience of Love* (Cambridge, 1981) 140.

19. John E. Booty, ed., *The Book of Common Prayer 1559* (Charlottesville, VA, 1976) 293. Further page references to this work will be noted in the text.

20. Kirsh, *Experience of Love* 10.

21. I have used the Huntington Library copy (STC 15230) of Thomas Combe, *The Theater of Fine Devices* (London, 1614).

22. Cleaver, *Godlie Forme,* 13.

23. See Cesare Ripa, *Iconologia* (Padua, 1611; New York, 1976) 74.

24. Smith, "Preparative to Marriage" 28.

25. See G. K. Hunter, introduction, *All's Well,* Arden ed., xliv.

26. See my note "Overlooked Sources of the Bed Trick," *Shakespeare Quarterly,* 34 (1983):433-34, and John E. Van Domelen, "Genesis, Boccaccio, and Shakespeare," *The Shakespeare Newsletter* (May 1965):24, which unfortunately never appeared in the indexes.

27. For the story of the bed-trick as practiced by Uther Pendragon on the Duchess of Tyntagil, with the help of the enchanter Merlin, see Book I of "The Tale of King Arthur" in Thomas Malory, *Works,* ed. Eugene Vinaver, 2d ed., (London, 1971) 3-6. Sir Lancelot is similarly enhanted into spending a fruitful night with Elaine, daughter of the Fisher King. According to the prophecy, the parents of Galahad (the perfect knight and a second Christ) were to be descendants of Joseph of Arimathea and the Fisher King, which meant Lancelot du Lac (who would sleep only with Queen Gwenyver) and the Lady Elaine. The story is told in "The Booke of Sir Tristram de Lyones" of how Sir Lancelot is shown a ring belonging to the queen "lyke as hit had com frome her" (480). He is told where to meet her, and then is given wine to prevent him from recognizing the substitution in the bedchamber of Elaine (479-80). Galahad is named after Gilead, whose balm was a universal "panacea," like Helena's. In this case, the "balm of Gilead" is the blood of Christ, which Galahad later applies to the wound of the Fisher King to cure him.

28. Smith, "Preparative to Marriage" 6.

29. *Ibid.,* 36.

FURTHER READING

Criticism

Beauregard, David N. "'Inspirèd Merit': Shakespeare's Theology of Grace in *All's Well That Ends Well.*" *Renascence* 51, No. 4 (1999): 218-39.

Argues that a Roman Catholic theology of grace influenced the plot and dialogue of *All's Well That Ends Well.*

Bradbrook, M. C. "Shakespeare's Hybrid: *All's Well That Ends Well.*" In *Muriel Bradbrook on Shakespeare,* pp. 84-98. Sussex: The Harvester Press, 1984.

Contends that *All's Well That Ends Well* is a dramatic failure in that Shakespeare attempted to write a moral play but only succeeded in creating characters as moral stereotypes.

Ellis, David. "Finding a Part for Parolles." *Essays in Criticism* 39, No. 4 (October 1989): 289-304.

Discusses Parolles's various roles in *All's Well That Ends Well,* contending that ultimately the character defies categorization.

Huston, J. Dennis. "'Some Stain of Soldier': The Functions of Parolles in *All's Well That Ends Well.*" *Shakespeare Quarterly* 21, No. 4 (Autumn 1970): 431-38.

Focuses on the various roles of Parolles, noting that his main function is to represent the youthful energy capable of transforming the world in *All's Well That Ends Well.*

Lewis, Cynthia. "'Derived Honesty and Achieved Goodness': Doctrines of Grace in *All's Well That Ends Well.*" *Renaissance and Reformation* 26, No. 2 (Spring 1990): 147-70.

Discusses *All's Well That Ends Well* as Shakespeare's interpretation of the theological controversy regarding whether grace is granted through election or through a gradual process of enlightenment.

Love, John M. "'Though Many of the Rich Are Damn'd': Dark Comedy and Social Class in *All's Well That Ends Well.*" *Texas Studies in Language and Literature* 18, No. 4 (Winter 1977): 517-27.

Comments on the role of social class in *All's Well That Ends Well,* noting that the ultimate fate of Helena and Bertram is determined by their class.

Palmer, David J. "Comedy and the Protestant Spirit in Shakespeare's *All's Well That Ends Well.*" *Bulletin of the John Rylands University Library of Manchester* 71, No. 1 (Spring 1989): 95-107.

Illustrates how Shakespeare interwove elements of comedy and Puritan theology into the plot and characterizations of *All's Well That Ends Well.*

Price, John Edward. "Anti-Moralistic Moralism in *All's Well That Ends Well.*" *Shakespeare Studies* 12 (1979): 95-111.

Asserts that *All's Well That Ends Well* is an antimoralistic play, in which Helena and Bertram expose the empty rhetoric of the older generation through their struggle to gain their freedom and to establish their individual identities.

Richard, Jeremy. "'The Thing I Am': Parolles, the Comedic Villain, and Tragic Consciousness." *Shakespeare Studies* 18 (1986): 145-59.

Contends that *All's Well That Ends Well* bridges Shakespeare's comedies and tragedies, and discusses the role of Parolles in terms of his evolution from comic villainy to self-consciousness in the play.

Rothman, Jules. "A Vindication of Parolles." *Shakespeare Quarterly* 23, No. 2 (Spring 1972): 183-96.

Attempts to vindicate Parolles from critical censure, maintaining that his character is the prime source of humor in *All's Well That Ends Well.*

Schork, R. J. "The Many Masks of Parolles." *Philological Quarterly* 76, No. 3 (Summer 1997): 263-69.

Discusses the role of Parolles in *All's Well That Ends Well,* pointing out that his characterization draws on two popular types from the classical comedies of Plautus.

Simpson, Lynne M. "The Failure to Mourn in *All's Well That Ends Well.*" *Shakespeare Studies* 22 (1994): 172-88.

Argues that in pursuing Bertram as a substitute for her deceased father, Helena "in effect denies the death of the father by 'forgetting' him despite the prominent and constant reminders of those around her."

Snyder, Susan. "Naming Names in *All's Well That Ends Well.*" *Shakespeare Quarterly* 43, No. 3 (Fall 1992): 265-79.

Explores the significance of various names in *All's Well That Ends Well,* emphasizing the mythic role that Helena and Diana play in the action.

Solomon, Julie Robin. "Mortality as Matter of Mind: Toward a Politics of Problems in *All's Well That Ends Well.*" *English Literary Renaissance* 23, No. 1 (Winter 1993): 134-69.

Illustrates how Shakespeare's use of contemporary discussions about the limits of medical knowledge and the interplay between nature and culture inform the themes of *All's Well That Ends Well.*

Taylor, Michael. "Persecuting Time with Hope: The Cynicism of Romance in *All's Well That Ends Well.*" *English Studies in Canada* 11, No. 3 (September 1985): 282-94.

Focuses on Shakespeare's ironic treatment of the idea of romance in *All's Well That Ends Well.*

Wheeler, Richard P. "Imperial Love and the Dark House: *All's Well That Ends Well.*" In *Shakespeare's Development and the Problem Comedies: Turn and Counter-Turn,* pp. 35-91. Berkeley: University of California Press, 1981.

Focuses on the relationship between Bertram and Helena as it effects Bertram's quest for a social and sexual identity in the play.

Henry VI, Parts 1, 2, and *3*

For further information on the critical and stage history of *Henry VI, Parts 1, 2,* and *3,* see *SC,* Volumes 3, 24, 39, and 56.

INTRODUCTION

Classified among Shakespeare's earliest works, the chronicle history plays designated as *Henry VI, Parts 1, 2,* and *3* detail the late medieval conflict between England and France, as well as the Wars of the Roses—the long civil war between the houses of York and Lancaster in fifteenth-century England. Characterized by frequent artistic lapses and an episodic structure, the *Henry VI* plays were, until the mid-twentieth century, the subject of considerable dispute concerning their authorship, with a number of critics arguing that Shakespeare collaborated with contemporary playwrights in composing these works. By the late-twentieth century, however, doubts concerning Shakespeare's role in writing the three parts of *Henry VI* had almost entirely been put aside; scholars instead focused on the diverse array of issues raised in the plays. Principal among these continues to be a prevailing interest in Shakespeare's treatment and manipulation of historical fact. Critics acknowledge that the dramatist inverted historical order, transferred events and characters, and compressed and expanded the material he found in his sources—including his principal text, Edward Halle's chronicle of English history entitled *The Union of Two Noble and Illustre Families of Lancaster and York* (1548). Others have identified numerous scenes and incidents—for example, the love affair between Margaret and Suffolk—which Shakespeare likely invented to suit his artistic goals. These and other dramatic alterations of history continue to intrigue scholars. A number of modern critics have also been drawn to thematic and structural aspects of the plays, such as the overall design and artistic integrity of the dramas, as well as their significant comic aspects. Finally, Shakespeare's representation of women in *Henry VI, Parts 1, 2,* and *3,* especially his dramatic treatment of Margaret of Anjou and Joan la Pucelle (the historical Joan of Arc), remain popular subjects among contemporary feminist commentators.

Shakespeare's interpretation and reorganization of history in the *Henry VI* plays has elicited considerable interest among critics, many of whom have sought to understand the dramatist's method of historiography and broad view of English history as it is illustrated in these early works. By seeing *Henry VI, Parts 1, 2* and *3* as works of history rather than simply imaginative literature, Philip Brockbank (see Further Reading) concentrates on the theme of civil dissension leading to anarchy, and observes the ways in which Shakespeare reshaped history. Wayne L. Billings (1972) regards the subject of history in *Henry VI* through the lens of heroic irony, discussing the principal figures in these works as disastrously flawed embodiments of the heroic ideal who lead England into turmoil by demonstrating cowardice and disgraceful behavior. Thomas Cartelli (1994) studies social history in *Henry VI, Part 2* by probing the doomed peasant revolt headed by Jack Cade as an intriguing look into the class dynamics of early modern England. Gwyn Williams (1974) examines Shakespeare's free interpretation of history in regard to his invented love affair between Margaret and Suffolk. While noting that historical evidence for such a romantic involvement is slight, Williams sees the relationship as a significant early example of tragic Shakespearean lovers, and an apt illustration of historical veracity subordinated by dramatic necessity.

By examining the design and thematic texture of *Henry VI, Parts 1, 2* and *3,* contemporary critics have sought to discern in the plays sources of artistic unity and thematic cohesiveness. Acknowledging the flawed and episodic state of the dramas, E. Pearlman (1992) nonetheless observes unifying themes in Shakespeare's depiction of Henry's personal shortcomings and in the dramatization of the decline of the House of Lancaster. Sigurd Burckhardt (1968) views *Henry VI, Part 1* as a dramatic whole, connected by the theme of troubled monarchical succession and by the ceremonial mode principally demonstrated in the noble figure of Talbot. Faye L. Kelly (1973) approaches all three of the *Henry VI* plays via the theme of oaths, seeing the making and breaking of formal pledges as a central structural element. Turning specifically to *Henry VI, Part 3,* Raymond V. Utterback (1978) remarks on the subject of legitimate kingship, while Maurice Hunt (1999) points to the drama's thematic integrity by tracing the sustained motif of unnatural acts perpetrated against family, country, and God.

Other topics of contemporary critical interest in *Henry VI, Parts 1, 2,* and *3* include the works' comic elements and the integral role of women in these narratives. Addressing comedy, Waldo F. McNeir (1974) sees a pattern of comic resolution in the dramas when viewed as a whole, and finds significant sources of laughter and stage spectacle throughout. Donald G. Watson (1978) perceives another dimension of comedy in the *Henry VI* plays by concentrating on the macabre, grotesque, and elements of black humor, noting that these elements are especially apparent in stage performance. The dark portrayal of the chief female characters in the plays continues to educe commentary as well. Nancy A. Gutierrez (1990) highlights Joan de Pucelle's relegation to an inferior position, based upon her gender, in the male-defined cultural conflict between England and France in *Henry VI, Part 1*. Kathryn Schwarz (1998) explores male fears concerning the disruptive and enigmatic power of the feminine in the trilogy as they are personified in the figures of Joan and Queen Margaret.

OVERVIEWS AND GENERAL STUDIES

E. Pearlman (essay date 1992)

SOURCE: "The First, Second, and Third Parts of *King Henry the Sixth*," in *William Shakespeare: The History Plays*, Twayne Publishers, 1992, pp. 22-47.

[*In the essay below, Pearlman summarizes the action, major themes, and principal characters of* Henry VI, Parts 1, 2, *and* 3.]

The three parts of *Henry the Sixth* appear in consecutive order in the great 1623 folio collection of Shakespeare's works. They are placed between *The Life of Henry the Fifth* and *The Tragedy of Richard the Third.* It is generally agreed that the three plays were written during the very first years of the 1590s. There is a small body of opinion that denies exclusive authorship of these plays to Shakespeare and argues that they result from a collaborative effort in which Shakespeare played a leading role. There is even a well-developed theory that *1 Henry VI* was written after *Parts 2* and *3* and is therefore what has lately come to be called a "prequel." For present purposes, the three plays will be discussed as if they were composed in the order in which they appear in the folio and as if they are all among Shakespeare's very earliest writings.

The First Part of King Henry the Sixth begins with a procession of noblemen who have assembled to mourn the death of Henry V, hero of Agincourt and conqueror of France. The Duke of Bedford grieves for his late kinsman in words that may be imagined as the first piece of historical writing to which Shakespeare ever bent what he would later call his "rough and all-unable pen." Shakespeare was not a prodigy and Bedford's address does not mark a turning point in the history of English literature. It is nevertheless a workmanlike piece of dramatic poetry: "Hung be the heavens with black," Bedford says, expanding his private sorrow into a universal lament:

> yield day to night!
> Comets, importing change of times and states,
> Brandish your crystal tresses in the sky
> And with them scourge the bad revolting stars
> That have consented unto Henry's death—
> King Henry the Fifth, too famous to live long!
> England ne'er lost a king of so much worth.
>
> (1.1.1-7)

Bedford's rhetorical style leans heavily on abstraction and generalization. When he makes his appeal to such impersonal entities as the heavens, the day, and the comets, he fails to lend distinctiveness to his own character or particularize his grief. None of his injunctive verbs ("yield," "brandish," "scourge") quite hits the mark. The notion that the stars have rebelliously agreed to the death of King Henry succeeds only in paying distant homage to a commonplace. Bedford's conclusion is anticlimactic and weak, especially the final phrase "of so much worth," in which Shakespeare misses the chance to complete the measure with the concrete detail or vivid metaphor that might have brought both the orator and his abundant sorrow to life.

Although the verse is flat and artificial, the passage is not without resonance to audiences or readers of Shakespeare's history plays. Not even the most prescient and insightful hearer of these lines could guess that the twenty-five- or twenty-six-year-old William Shakespeare who wrote them would devote a great part of his intelligence and working life in the decade of the 1590s to the composition of a series of eight plays that pivot around the heroic life and untimely death of the King Harry who is memorialized by Bedford. Four of these plays (the so-called first tetralogy consisting of the three parts of *Henry VI* and their sequel *Richard III*) would deal with the consequences of King Henry's early death. Four others (the second tetralogy of *Richard II*, the two parts of *Henry IV*, and *Henry V*) would examine the events that culminated with the reign of the "too famous" king celebrated in Bedford's eulogy. It is pleasing though illusory to imagine that Shakespeare intuitively understood that the death of the hero king could be dramatized as the crucial event of the hundred years of English history—from the deposition of Richard of Bordeaux to the violent death at Bosworth field of Richard of Gloucester—which the poet would claim as his particular province. Nevertheless, it was with Bedford's first speech that Shakespeare initiated the epic circular journey that both begins and ends with Henry's death. In the three parts of *Henry VI*, Shakespeare dramatized the loss of France, the bleeding of England, and what he would later remember in the last and most eloquent chorus in *Henry V* as the "blasting" of the "world's best garden . . . which oft our stage has shown" (Epilogue, 1. 7).

Shakespeare's first history, although to modern eyes the least of his accomplishments, must have had an extraordinary impact in its own time. The popularity of *The First Part of Henry the Sixth* is seen not only in its amazing succession of sequels but also in contemporary testimony. Shakespeare's sometime rival Thomas Nashe used an example from this play to demonstrate that the threater has moral value and may function as "a reproof to these degenerate effeminate days of ours": "How would it have joyed brave Talbot (the terror of the French) to think that after he had lain two hundred years in his tomb, he should triumph again on the stage, and have his bones new embalmed with the tears of ten thousand spectators at least (at several times), who, in the tragedian that represents his person, imagine they behold him fresh bleeding" (Salgādo, *Eyewitnesses,* 16). Nashe captures the immediacy and excitement of a new kind of theatrical experience for an audience that had not yet been sated with innumerable bland historical dramas.

Despite Nashe's enthusiasm *1 Henry VI* seems shapeless and unfocused. The play is a hodgepodge of competing actions. The language lacks variety; long swatches consist of formal, sometimes stilted, and occasionally monotonous blank verse that do not display the rich metaphorical and imagistic complexity that becomes Shakespeare's hallmark. The characters are not effectively differentiated. Except for Talbot himself, the earls and dukes all speak in the same florid and excited idiom. Moreover, the plot lacks resolution and comes not so much to a climax as to a halt. It would be idolatrous to deny that these (and other) flaws make it difficult to give one's wholehearted support to *1 Henry VI,* but they do not make it either unapproachable or unrewarding.

1 Henry VI consists of a number of separate actions that are not so much integrated as they are intertwined. The most coherent and important of these is the series of English sieges, thrusts, and counter-attacks aimed against the forces of France. Shakespeare draws with some care the contrast between English John Talbot, the commander of one side, and Joan of Arc, the inspiration of the other. A second major action is the dynastic squabble between Richard Plantagenet (later the Duke of York) and the party of the white rose, and their antagonists the Lancastrians, the party of the red rose, led in this play by the Earl of Somerset. Still a third action is the continuing antagonism between the protector Humphrey, the good Duke of Gloucester, and his uncle the ambitious clergyman (later bishop) Winchester. Finally, at the end of the play, the Earl of Suffolk emerges as a major figure when he arranges a marriage between King Henry and Margaret, the powerful queen whose furious intensity dominates so many scenes during the three subsequent plays in the first tetralogy. The play is certainly episodic, but each episode has its own rewards.

The most memorable character, to Nashe as well as to modern audiences, is the heroic Talbot, in whom is embodied the most cherished values of chivalric civilization. Against Talbot are arrayed two very powerful groups of enemies. The first consists of the forces of France, inspired and led by the witch Joan, who are eager to reclaim lands recently taken from them by the great Henry V. The second and ultimately more dangerous enemy is the inability of Talbot's fellow nobles to set aside private grudge, petty antagonism, and dynastic rivalry in order to support the grander national purpose. The combination of external wars and domestic subversion leads both to Talbot's death and to the near anarchy dramatized in the later plays.

Talbot's world, very much idealized in this play, is built on values that remind us that Shakespeare exalts a civilization that we need not sorrow to have lost. Feudal society is erected on sharp distinctions between nobility and commoners. It is marked by loyalty and fidelity to the king or leader; although betrayal is frequent, it is always greeted not only with condemnation but also with shock and surprise. Status is ascribed rather than earned—that is, dependent on birth rather than achievement. Courage and skill in battle are principal virtues. Great value is attached to political and military leadership, especially that which is revealed in oratorical performance. The giving and taking of oaths is extremely important. Those who give their bond are expected to keep it; oath breakers are, like those who show cowardice, roundly contemned and scorned. The aristocrats like Talbot who embody these virtues are accustomed to command and are consequently distinguished by their overbearing manners and extremely short tempers. They are always on the verge of emotional explosion and their swords are never far from their hands. They are sensitive to insults to their birth, status, and courage, and they routinely subordinate private and domestic relationships to public and military performance. In Shakespeare's feudal world, the roles alloted to women are clearly demarcated, and as a result the occasional woman who intrudes into the world of soldiership and government must be regarded as perverse or unnatural. Chivalric notions underlie not just this play but every one of Shakespeare's histories.

A definitive statement of these values occurs during the encounter in act 4 between Falstaff and Talbot. Falstaff has run from battle once again, and Talbot fulfills his threat to humiliate him by stripping the garter (the insignia of his knightly order) from his leg. Talbot blames Falstaff for the loss of the battle and for the deaths of twelve hundred men. He is shocked that "such cowards" are allowed "to wear / This ornament of knighthood" (4.1.28-29), and he proceeds to construct a mythic history of a favorite ideology:

> When first this order was ordained, my lords,
> Knights of the Garter were of noble birth,
> Valiant and virtuous, full of haughty courage,
> Such as were grown to credit by the wars;
> Not fearing death nor shrinking for distress,
> But always resolute in most extremes.
> But he that is not furnished in this sort
> Doth but usurp the sacred name of knight,
> Profaning this most honorable order,
> And should (if I were worthy to be judge)
> Be quite degraded, like a hedge-born swain
> That doth presume to boast of gentle blood.
>
> (33-44)

Talbot knows that true knights are both courageous and noble by nature and are most resilient when most in peril. If they betray their heritage and show cowardice, they must be, as Talbot says, "degraded"—that is, reduced in rank—to the level of a presumptuous "hedge-born swain" or homeless peasant. He also knows that the Order of the Garter was not established after a secular manner, but rather "ordained"—a carefully chosen word that is resonant with spiritual and religious significance. The implications of "ordained" are extended in the contrast between the "sacred" name of the order and its "profaning" by cowardice. Throughout Talbot's speech a holy and romanticized past contrasts with a fallen present.

It is around such notions that Shakespeare organizes the conflict between Talbot and Joan and between England and France. Talbot embodies the ideals of chivalry. When he and his six thousand troops are surrounded by twenty-three thousand Frenchmen, Talbot "enacted wonders with the sword and lance" (1.1.122), only to succumb when "a base Walloon . . . / Thrust [him] with a spear into the back" (137-38). Shakespeare gives credence to the myth that an individual knight armed with traditional weapons can carry the day in a field of thirty thousand soldiers, and that only a "base Walloon" would lower himself to the indignity of an attack from the rear. When captured by the French, Talbot "craved death / Rather than [be] so vile esteemed" (1.4.32-33) as to be exchanged for anyone but his social equal. When the French enemy wisely rest in safety behind their fortifications, Talbot thinks their unchivalric tactics are rude and unsportsmanlike: "Base muleteers of France! / Like peasant foot-boys do they keep the walls / And dare not take up arms like gentlemen" (3.1.68-70).

Orthodox and reverent, Talbot expresses contempt for enemies who are led by a woman and are presumed to consort with devils: "Let them practice and converse with spirits. / God is our fortress" (2.1.25-26). Talbot is most moved by the "chance" (1.4.71) death by cannon fire of Salisbury, that great "mirror of all martial men" (74). His violent longing for revenge takes the form of hyperbolical and sadistic invective perhaps characteristic of feudal aristocracy but difficult to honor today: "Pucelle or pussel [i.e., pizzle, prick], Dolphin or dogfish, / Your hearts I'll stamp out-with my horse's heels / And make a quagmire of your mangled brains" (107-9). Talbot is proud to kill five Frenchmen for every drop of blood lost by Salisbury.

Yet the same Talbot so furious in war is also capable of courtly deference to his sovereign:

> This arm that hath reclaimed
> To your obedience fifty fortresses. . . .
> Lets fall his sword before your highness' feet
> And with submissive loyalty of heart
> Ascribes the glory of his conquest got
> First to my God and next unto your grace.
>
> (3.4.5-6, 9-12)

While Talbot does not forget to vaunt his conquests, he can also allow his sword to fall before weak King Henry's feet and proudly acknowledge that his submission and loyalty are not of the surface but from the heart.

Opposite to Talbot in almost all respects is Joan of Arc, who is not male but mannish, demonic rather than Christian, ambitious rather than deferential, unchaste or at least the constant target of sexual innuendo, and, worst of all, unequivocally base-born. Joan embodies the polar opposite of the orderliness and orthodoxy of chivalric tradition. As a consequence, Shakespeare depicts her in extraordinarily unflattering terms. Joan's successes on the battlefield are ascribed not to military prowess but to "hellish mischief" (3.2.39). The appeal to French nationalism that attracts waffling Burgundy to her side is dismissed as mere playacting. In her last appearance, Joan first repudiates her shepherd father, then attempts to forestall her own execution by claiming to be with child by either the Dauphin, or Alencon, or Reignier. She is offered no compassion by the English or by Shakespeare and, condemned as a witch and strumpet, leaves the stage while York abuses her as a "foul accursèd minister of hell!" (5.4.93). It is an ugly scene.

Even though Joan is the antithesis of Talbot and is allowed a few temporary military successes, the play makes it clear that the real cause of the English failure is internal division. Consumed by their own ambitions, the English nobles cannot refrain from petty squabble, from name-calling and duels, or from countermining each other's achievements. The fault is not in chivalry itself, but in the failure of its nobility to live up to the ideals they profess. In the first scene of the play the noble Bedford utters a prayer that his peers will all too often ignore: "Henry the Fifth, thy ghost I invocate: / Prosper this realm, keep it from civil broils" (1.1.53-54). The King himself, exasperated but powerless to intervene between Winchester and Gloucester, recognizes that "Civil dissension is a viperous worm / That gnaws the bowels of the commonwealth" (3.1.72-73). Eventually, Talbot finds himself defeated by the forces of the French while his would-be allies Somerset and York debate over who is most at fault for abandoning him. Exeter asserts that

> no simple man that sees
> This jarring discord of nobility,
> This shouldering of each other in the court,
> This factious bandying of their favorites,
> But sees it doth presage some ill event.
>
> (4.1.187-91)

Sir William Lucy (a character who is little more than a choric voice) expands on this important lesson. "The fraud of England, not the force of France, / Hath now entrapped the noble-minded Talbot (4.4.36-37). "The vulture of sedition" (47), he concludes, has betrayed "The conquest of our scarce-cold conqueror / That ever-living man of memory, / Henry the Fifth." (4.3.51-53). The heirs of the great Henry, whose revered memory hangs heavy over each event of this long play, have destroyed themselves with sloth and sedition.

1 Henry VI focuses on the decline of chivalric civilization and the disorder in England. Yet audiences are likely to be struck not so much by the ideological coherence of the whole as by a few memorable scenes. The most striking event in the play is the sequence of scenes in act 4 in which both Talbot and his son young John Talbot meet their deaths. The two compete in self-sacrifice and familial loyalty. Their devotion to each other is highly stylized and mannered, exemplary rather than realistic. The Talbots' mutual reverence directly contrasts with the antagonism in other aristocratic English families and with the parody of family loyalty in the nasty encounter between Joan and her peasant father. The embrace of Talbot and his equally noble son may be artificial and too highly patterned, but it is also a daring and pioneering piece of writing, if only because Shakespeare attempts to embody the theme of loyalty in a dramatic action.

For many readers the Temple Garden scene is another instance in which the young Shakespeare can be observed writing with unusual authority. In this scene Shakespeare momentarily liberates himself from too exact fidelity to the chronicles. He imagines an event (for which his sources offer no precedent or clue) in which a set of young and passionate noblemen who are engaged in legal study enlarge a disagreement over some "nice sharp quillets of the law" (2.4.17) into a conflict that threatens the entire kingdom. At first the bystanders try to neutralize the combatants Plantagenet and Somerset by making jest of their disagreements. But the conflict uncontrollably escalates and one by one the bystanders are forced to choose a side. Each party accuses the other of cowardice and fear. Plantagenet raises the stakes when he calls Somerset a "peevish boy" (76); Somerset, equally unrestrained, responds by describing Plantagenet as a "yeoman." Insults to manhood and ancestry lead directly to "blood-drinking hate" on both sides. Warwick is left to prophesy that "this brawl today, / Grown to this faction in the Temple garden, / Shall send, between the red rose and the white, / A thousand souls to death and deadly night" (124-27). The scene is richly theatrical. The quarrel is about nothing, and the young men are filled with hot tempers and adolescent energy. Ritual plucking of roses edges the scene toward the arena of allegory, while vigorous flyting frees the language from the steady thump of iambics, and for a welcome moment drums and guns and wounds give way to a promising symbolic psychology.

In another scene that stands out (4.1), Shakespeare makes a first attempt at a practice that he raises to a fine art in later plays. He places in close juxtaposition a series of events that have a common thematic subject—in this case an exploration of feudal values. First the Governor of Paris swears an oath of fidelity to King Henry. Then Talbot strips Falstaff of the garter and comments on the history of chivalry. Just as Falstaff is banished, the news arrives that Burgundy has repudiated the oaths that have bound him to the English king. Gloucester, ever the true believer, is shocked: "Can this be so? / That in alliance, amity, and oaths / There should be found such false dissembling guile?" (4.1.61-63). Following hard upon this revelation, Vernon and Basset, servants respectively of Gloucester and Winchester, come storming onto the stage to ask that they be allowed to tilt or duel because of the insults that each feels he has suffered. The good but ineffectual king is once again shocked: "what madness rules in brainsick men / When for so slight and frivolous a cause / Such factions emulations shall arise!" (111-13). The king attempts to adjudicate the quarrel but in the process commits some grave procedural errors. The whole sequence—the taking of oaths and their repudiation, Talbot's high-minded exaltation of the theory of chivalry and its deficient application in the case of Vernon and Basset—shows Shakespeare for the first time learning to represent ideas in dramatic form. His intelligent experimentation points to better things to come.

2 Henry VI

1 Henry VI focuses on wars of territorial conquest in France but also depicts a rivalry among the major aristocratic families that is both ferocious and unending. In *2 Henry VI,* competition between England's two great aristocratic families has become the dominant concern. The pious and inattentive Lancastrian king, Henry VI, proves to be far too weak to control his aspiring wife, Margaret of Anjou, and her self-serving advisors, while Richard Plantagenet, now the Duke of York, has emerged as an ambitious politician who is unencumbered by moral scruple. The rivalry of King and Duke is continuous. The background against which the dynastic squabble is played out has also changed. The principal tension in *2 Henry VI* is no longer between the English and the French but between the governing aristocratic oligarchy on the one hand and the commons on the other. Out of this conflict arises the political design and political meaning of the play.

The most memorable figures in *1 Henry VI* were English John Talbot and the French witch Joan; the most memorable figure in *2 Henry VI* is the Kentish rebel Jack Cade, who leads a revolt against the feudal establishment. Cade's rebellion succeeds militarily for a tense interval but collapses without leaving a permanent mark. It is a much tougher challenge to depict a domestic revolt than to mount the easy appeal to national pride that distinguishes (or disfigures) *1 Henry VI.* In the first play, the English cause is unquestionably just while the French are cowards or demons. In *2 Henry VI* the enemy may be impoverished, uneducated, and contemptible, but it is still English. Shakespeare pillories Cade and his followers and unequivocally supports established government, but he allows powerful popular forces a great deal of scope and play before repudiating them. He flirts with very dangerous material. It is only at the end of the play, the revolt suppressed and order restored, that an orthodox monarchist perspective is again asserted.

In *1 Henry VI* the common people appear only intermittently: among those who take their turn on the stage are the gunner's boy who is responsible for the death of old Salisbury, the servants of Gloucester and Winchester who stone each other in the streets, and the French sentinels at Orleans, "poor servitors, / When others sleep upon their quiet beds, / Constrained to watch in darkness, rain, and cold" (2.1.5-7). In *2 Henry VI,* Shakespeare takes a great step forward when he transforms the commons into an important constituent of the polity. (It is not always clear to whom the word "commons" refers. Sometimes Shakespeare seems to mean commons as in House of Commons—i.e., prosperous landowners, merchants, lawyers; at other times, "commons" seems to refer to butchers, clothiers, beggars, soldiers.) Shakespeare prepares his audience for Jack Cade's rebellion by representing a series of encounters between rich and poor. A few humble villagers attempt to deliver a petition to Gloucester early in the play; Horner, a tradesman, is charged with treason by his apprentice and brought before the court; Simpcox the beggar's boast that he has been miraculously healed is publicly examined; the disgraced Duchess of Gloucester is forced to walk penitentially among the "rabble"; Suffolk, banished from England at the behest of the commons, is murdered by pirates; finally, Jack Cade leads a rebellion of the poor. More than any other of Shakespeare's plays, *2 Henry VI* explores the conflicts between the social classes.

Although the play represents the tension between rich and poor, it is noteworthy that neither class is monolithic in its attitude to the other. The aristocracy itself is severely divided. While there is no question but that rebellion, or even the merest trace of uppity behavior, must always be thoroughly reprehended, aristocrats disagree in major ways about the plight of the poor. On the one side is the faction that is led by Gloucester and that sometimes includes Warwick and Salisbury. This group is on the whole alert and responsive to members of the underclass. The other faction, of which Winchester, Suffolk, and Queen Margaret are the most prominent members, is largely contemptuous of the poor and indifferent to their welfare. Winchester and Gloucester are distinguished not by differences of opinion about national policy but by their capacity for human empathy.

Gloucester, the "good Duke Humphrey" of legend, is sympathetic from the very first scene, primarily because he is shocked not only by the fatal marriage between the naive King Henry and the remorseless Margaret but also by the accompanying loss to England of the French provinces of Maine and Anjou. The audience would immediately understand that he is stung not for his private interests but for what he perceives as treachery to the community of England. Gloucester laments "the common grief of all the land" (1.1.75). Cardinal Winchester responds to the loss not as a public but as a personal tragedy. The distinction between the good Duke and the imperious Cardinal is made very clear when Winchester describes Gloucester in these envious terms:

> Let not his smoothing words
> Bewitch your hearts; be wise and circumspect.
> What though the common people favor him,
> Calling him "Humphrey, the good Duke of Gloucester,"
> Clapping their hands and crying with loud voice
> "Jesu maintain your royal Excellence!"
> With "God preserve the good Duke Humphrey!"
> (154-60)

Winchester bristles with the Tory suspicion that anyone loved by the populace must be either a hypocrite or a demagogue. His sentences succinctly establish the lines of conflict between Duke and Cardinal: Gloucester enjoys the support of the common people of whom Winchester is contemptuous. Gloucester's England comprehends all the classes while Winchester's includes only his social equals. This is no trivial distinction, but it is difficult to be certain exactly how it should be evaluated. Official Elizabethan ideology is deeply distrustful of the people, who are, in this play as in others, inconsistent, disloyal, wavering, thoughtless, emotional. Yet it is difficult to believe that Winchester's condemnation of Gloucester would not have been heard as praise by all but the most haughty ear.

It is certainly no surprise that the common people address Gloucester, not Winchester, in time of trouble. In the third scene of the play, Shakespeare allows members of one class to confront the other. Two petitioners come forward to present their grievances to Duke Humphrey. Their reverence for Gloucester confirms Winchester's worst fears. A petitioner speaks: "Marry, the Lord protect him, for [Gloucester's] a good man, Jesu bless him" (1.3.4-5). The first petitioner protests that he has been mistreated by Winchester; the second makes similar charges against Suffolk. Bad luck causes the petitions to miscarry and come into the hands of Suffolk himself. He reads them aloud: "'Against the Duke of Suffolk, for enclosing the commons of Long Melford.' How now, sir knave?" (19-21). The brief episode exhibits Suffolk's hostility to the commons and his indifference to legitimate grievance. It also brands him as an encloser. Enclosure—essentially the conversion of land from common to private use—was the focus of the perennial conflict between those who control and those who work the land. There had been over one hundred enclosure riots of all kinds during the reign of Elizabeth. Shakespeare's use of the word "enclosure" would certainly stimulate an awareness of contemporary grievance. Clearly the petitioners had hoped to gain the support of Gloucester against the repressive effects of Suffolk's stewardship. The distinction between the parties has been suggestively but clearly drawn.

A second instance that serves to discriminate among aristocratic attitudes occurs in the unmasking of the beggar Saunder Simpcox. Simpcox claims that he has been crippled and blind from birth and that his sight has been suddenly and miraculously restored. This scene, which is superfluous to the plot, seems to be designed for two primary purposes. The first is to demonstrate that Gloucester indeed displays the characteristics that Shakespeare found in John Foxe's *Acts and Monuments* (the source for this episode)—"a head, to discern and dissever truth from forged and feigned hypocrisy" (Bullough, *Sources,* 3:128). It is also one of the many events in this play (and in others in the tetralogy) in which the question of divine meddling in human affairs is raised and pondered. But primarily the scene reflects on the relation between rich and poor, especially in its conclusion when Simpcox, exposed by Gloucester as a charlatan, is whipped until he finds his legs and jumps over a stool. Shakespeare concludes the scene by inventing a spectrum of moral responses to his exemplum:

> *King.* O God! seest thou this, and bearest so long?
> *Queen.* It made me laugh to see the villain run.
> *Gloucester.* Follow the knave, and take this drab away.
> *Wife.* Alas sir, we did it for pure need.
> *Glou.* Let them be whipped through every market town,
> Till they come to Berwick, from whence they came.
>
> (2.1.146-50)

King Henry is characteristically pious; he appeals to the Lord and projects his own passivity onto the diety. Queen Margaret, speaking as a member of the party of Suffolk, is typically heartless and cruel. Gloucester may seem harsh by modern standards, but he stands for justice uncontaminated by the lenity that Elizabethans so feared. His command that the two perpetrators of the fraud be whipped reminds us that there is a long distance between Elizabethan justice and modern liberal sensibility. The Wife's remark is most troubling. Shakespeare, who has already added the leaping, stool, beadle, and whip to his source, also adds the deeply humanizing cry: "Alas, sir, we did it for pure need." The line is simple but not without eloquence. "Alas" signals genuine despair; "sir" is informed with sufficient deference to reassure a worried audience that the beggars are free of social assertion; "we" indicates that the wife will not abandon her husband; "pure need" tells any sympathetic hearers that the fraud was a consequence of the absolute necessity of the need to eat. If nothing else, the Wife's line sharpens the distance between Beggar, Duke, and Queen.

The definition of Gloucester's political position in the commonwealth of England is further complicated by the events surrounding the revelation that his wife has been consorting with magicians and spirits. The penalty for the fallen Duchess (who has been entrapped by Winchester) is public humiliation; Gloucester attempts to console her:

> Sweet Nell, ill can thy noble mind abrook
> The abject people gazing on thy face,
> With envious looks laughing at the shame,
> That erst did follow thy proud chariot wheels
> When thou didst ride in triumph through the streets.
>
> (2.4.10-14)

The painful ceremony plays on the nobles' fear of exposure and their hostility to the lower classes. Here, as elsewhere, Shakespeare knows that he can draw tears from his audience by dwelling on the pathos that attends the fall of princes (or, in this case, princesses). He plucks this string shamelessly when he allows the Duchess to lament,

> Methinks I should not thus be led along,
> Mailed up in shame, with papers on my back,
> And followed with a rabble that rejoice
> To see my tears and hear my deep-fet groans. . . .
> . . . a wonder and a pointing-stock
> To every idle rascal follower.
>
> (30-33; 46-47)

On the side of the commons, hostility and vengeance; on the side of the nobility, fear of contamination and contact. It is not a pretty picture. The political meaning is clear: even the wife of the good Duke of Gloucester is not exempt from the antagonism implicit in the hierarchical system. It is remarkable that Shakespeare does not allow Gloucester to share the Duchess's antagonism to the commons, nor does he put expressions in the Duke's mouth that would apologize for the people's passion.

One of the most interesting encounters between the classes occurs when the banished Suffolk is taken by pirates. Suffolk masquerades as a commoner, but he is incapable of disguising his aristocratic personality and immediately betrays himself. He speaks to his captors in language that demonstrates that he would rather preserve his identity than his life: "Obscure and lousy swain, King Henry's blood, / The honorable blood of Lancaster, / Must not be shed by such a jaded groom" (4.1.50-52). Nor can he resist an ostentatious display of privilege; he treats Walter Whitmore, whose prisoner he is, not as an individual but as a representative of a class he despises:

> Hast thou not kissed thy hand and held my stirrup?
> . . .
> How often hast thou waited at my cup,
> Fed from my trencher, kneeled down at the board,
> When I have feasted with Queen Margaret?
>
> (53, 56-58)

It is left to Whitmore's companion, a nameless yet eloquent (and remarkably well-informed) Lieutenant, to respond to Suffolk. Once again Shakespeare reiterates the idea that the common people are also injured when aristocrats act in their own interests and without regard for the community of England. The Lieutenant attacks Suffolk for the indulgent marriage of Henry to the French temptress, for the loss of Anjou and Maine, for the wars that monopolize the attention of Warwick and his Neville relations, and for the dissension of York and the Kentish rebels. Suffolk gives no sign that he understands the damage for which he is responsible, nor can he broaden or humanize his very narrow interpretation of the aristocratic values which paralyze him:

> Suffolk's imperial tongue is stern and rough,
> Used to command. . . .
> No, rather let my head
> Stoop to the block than these knees bow to any
> Save to the God of heaven and to my king; . . .
> True nobility is exempt from fear.
> More can I bear than you can execute.
>
> (122-23, 125-27, 130-31)

But Suffolk's unbending manner and imperial tongue fail to impress his captors, and moments later, his imperial head is cut off: "Great men oft die by vile bezonians, . . . and Suffolk dies by pirates" (135, 139). Shakespeare has made it clear that the pirates speak with the authentic voice of the entire English community and not of the commons alone. It is impossible to imagine that Suffolk's death did not cheer the audience.

When in act 4 Shakespeare at last turns to Cade's rebellion, distinctions of attitude among the nobles no longer matter. Whether or not the commons have been provoked is immaterial; their insurrection is illegitimate and purposeless. Moreover, it is placed under the control of the Duke of York, who is the enemy of the people. York had described his plan in considerable detail:

> I have seduced a headstrong Kentishman,
> John Cade of Ashford,
> To make commotion, as full well he can,
> Under the title of John Mortimer. . . .
> This devil [Cade] here shall be my substitute; . . .
> Say that he thrive, as 'tis great like he will;
> Why, then from Ireland come I with my strength
> And reap the harvest which that rascal sowed.
>
> (3.1.356-69, 371, 379-81)

By making him a tool of York, Shakespeare eliminates the possibility that Cade can lay claim to the slightest political credibility.

Cade himself is no simple figure. In Hall's history, he is merely "a certayn young man of a goodly stature and pregnant wit" (Bullough, *Sources,* 3:113). Shakespeare complicates the picture. York describes Cade as both duplicitous and close-mouthed, and adds that in battle he fought so long

> that his thighs with darts
> Were almost like a sharp-quilled porpentine;
> And in the end being rescued, I have seen
> Him caper upright like a wild Morisco,
> Shaking the bloody darts as he his bells
>
> (362-66).

These lines portray Cade as someone to be feared but not admired. He is alien after the manner of an ecstatic morris (i.e., Moorish) dancer, while his indifference to pain makes him as exotic as that oddity the porcupine. Cade may be a formidable enemy but he is not an adversary who can be respected by knight or aristocrat. In this respect he is like Joan, who is also treated as the outsider or "the Other." Joan is a foreign and female soldier and therefore a sorceress; Cade is a weaver warrior and not quite human.

Cade's followers, on the other hand, are allowed to express their own motives. Shakespeare precedes Cade's first appearance with a brief choral introduction:

> *1. Rebel.* I tell thee, Jack Cade the clothier means to dress the commonwealth and turn it and set a new nap upon it.
> *2. Rebel.* So he had need, for 'tis threadbare. Well, I say it was never merry world in England since gentlemen came up.
> *1. Rebel.* O miserable age! Virtue is not regarded in handicraftsmen.
>
> (4.2.4-10)

The two "rebels" stand apart from the insurrection; they observe but do not participate. While they are not allowed to be perfectly logical, neither are they clowns; they are alert to inequity. They know that the commonwealth is "threadbare" and needs to be turned inside out; they know that there was once a "merry world" when Adam delved and Eve span and before the community was separated into gentle and common; they know the Biblical injunction that all work is of value, although they twist it to reflect a revolutionary intent. These are the sentiments of the leveler underground—the tavern intellectuals whose egalitarian and heterodox notions were kept in check by repressive governments until they burst out of control during the revolutionary years of the next century.

It is therefore no surprise that the attitude of the commons toward Cade is complex. Some of Cade's more egregious pretensions are regularly undermined by the statements of his more restrained followers. Much of the dialogue is in a form in which Cade makes an absurd assertion which is counterpointed by the good sense of one of his allies:

> *Cade.* My father was a Mortimer—
> *Butcher.* [*Aside.*] He was an honest man, and a good bricklayer.
>
> (4.2.35-37).

Cade is no philosopher, but his primitive radical vision that "all the realm shall be in common" (62) must have sounded terrible to the ears of the audience. Cade imagines an egalitarian utopia when England comes under his rule:

> All the realm shall be in common . . . there shall be no money; all shall eat and drink on my score; and I will apparel them all in one livery, that they may agree like brothers, and worship me their lord.
>
> (4.2.62, 66-69)

To which the Dick the Butcher replies with the immensely practical injunction that has become the play's most famous saying: "The first thing we do, let's kill all the lawyers" (3.2.73).

The rebellion itself is portrayed as idiotic know-nothingism. The rebels murder a clerk because he knows how to read and write and hang Lord Say (historically, a detested landowner) because he can speak Latin; a soldier is beaten to death for calling Cade "Cade" and not Mortimer. Cade is made to betray his own values. Although he asks more than once that all things be held in common, he demands absolute authority for himself. Yet Cade can transcend his absurdity and rise to the occasion. His greatest moment comes just before his followers turn tail. Facing the multitude, he addresses them not, for once, as a clown, but as a dangerous and fiery leader and demagogue:

> I thought ye would never have given out these arms till you had recovered your ancient freedom. But you are all recreants and dastards, and delight to live in slavery to the nobility. Let them break your backs with burdens, take your houses over your heads, ravish your wives and daughters before your faces. For me, I will make shift for one; and so God's curse light upon you all!
>
> (4.8.24-31)

It is only by invoking the glorious memory of Henry V and by turning attention from local injustices to the prospect of renewed French wars that the aristocrats can quiet the crowds and persuade them to abandon their popular leader. Cade is forced to flee. In the last scene of act 4, he stumbles into the garden of the squire Alexander Iden. In historical fact, both Cade and Iden were Kentish gentlemen, but Shakespeare has degraded and vilified the one and idealized the other. Iden speaks in tones that have not before been heard in this play:

> Lord, who would live turmoiled in the court
> And may enjoy such quiet walks as these?
> This small inheritance my father left me
> Contenteth me, and worth a monarchy.
> I seek not to wax great by others' waning,
> Or gather wealth, I care not with what envy.
> Sufficeth that I have maintains my state
> And send the poor well pleasèd from my gate.
>
> (4. 10. 15-22)

His soliloquy creates a world that is antithetical in almost every respect to what Shakespeare had until this moment been at such pains to delineate. The England of *2 Henry VI* is packed with restless ambition and intrigue; the world of Alexander Iden is one in which a good man is content with his place. Enclosure, antagonism between the classes, hungry beggars, and popular revolt are superseded by a serene pastoralism in which the poor are "well pleased" with alms from the rich. Iden's unsullied "quiet walks" and "small inheritance" are preferablc to kingship itself. The passage celebrates the classical ideal of riches left, not got with care. If simplicity and peace already flourish in Cade's utopian garden, what possible reason can there be for all this noise and commotion? Iden duels with Cade and kills him. In the scene that follows, Iden takes Cade's head to the King and is knighted and granted a bounty of one thousand marks. Shakespeare has no other means to express congratulation than by the cash and courtesies that Iden had so recently disdained. Iden's confrontation with Cade rings hollow. Shakespeare pits a clownish rebel whose every word smacks of self-betrayal against an idealized squire who speaks in the language of official political allegory. Cade and his rebels stand for a real disease and Iden for an inauthentic and inadequate remedy.

3 Henry VI

The Third Part of Henry VI is so thick with incident and event that it is difficult to follow, remember, or summarize. Declamations, battles, reversals of fortune, betrayals, and atrocities fill a very crowded stage. The play begins at the battle of St. Albans (where *2 Henry VI* had concluded). The party of York, led by the forceful Earl of Warwick, is temporarily triumphant. In order to retain the kingship during his lifetime, the captured Lancastrian sovereign Henry VI is compelled to entail the crown to Richard, Duke of York. But the solemn agreement does not outlast the first scene. Henry's Queen Margaret, protesting the disinheritance of her son, spreads her colors; almost simultaneously, York's sons argue that "for a kingdom any oath may be broken" (1.2.16). Shortly thereafter, the two sides meet at Sandal Castle and Margaret's forces are victorious. York's son Rutland, unhistorically represented as a child, is murdered; immediately after, York himself is tormented and eventually stabbed to death by Margaret and her chief confederate Clifford. The Lancastrian ascendancy lasts only until Towton (2.6.3-6), where Clifford is killed, Henry escapes to the north of England (where he is soon captured and returned to London), and Margaret takes refuge in France. Edward (York's oldest son and now the standard bearer of his line) proceeds to London "to be crowned England's royal king" (2.6.88). Warwick, still a partisan of the Yorkists, goes to the French court to arrange a marriage for his new king, only to discover that "lascivious Edward" (5.5.34) has embarrassed and betrayed him by his hasty marriage to the widow Lady Elizabeth Grey. Shamed, Warwick suddenly changes sides; he allies himself to Queen Margaret and returns to England "to seek revenge on Edward's mockery" (3.3.265). When the news comes that Warwick and Margaret are in the field, Edward's brother Clarence switches to the Lancastrian side. But the apparently inevitable encounter between the two families is forestalled when Warwick raids Edward's camp, captures the Yorkist King, and sends him as a prisoner to his brother the Archbishop. Warwick then sets out to free Henry from imprisonment in London. The news that the Edward has escaped sours the celebration of King Henry's restoration to the throne. Edward heads for York once again to "interchange my wanèd state for Henry's regal crown" (4.7.4). Yet one more time Lancastrians under Warwick and Margaret face Edward and his allies. The momentum shifts to the party of York when "perjured George" (5.5.34) changes allegiance again, this time rejoining his brothers. At Barnet, Warwick, "proud setter up and puller down of kings" (3.3.157), is killed. Soon afterwards, "misshapen Dick" (5.5.35) joins his two brothers in stabbing young Edward (the son of Henry VI and Margaret). Finally, Richard rushes off to London to kill the remaining Lancastrian, Henry VI, and the triumph of the house of York is apparently complete.

Shakespeare drew a great deal of his story from Edward Hall's *The Union of the Two Noble and Illustre Famelies of Lancastre and Yorke*. Hall's story is also long and complicated, bristling with facts, but it is not without its reflective moments. Hall offered two different explanations for Henry's inadequacies as a king. The first can be called "providential." It affirms that the misfortunes of Henry's reign must be ascribed not to weaknesses of human personality or to the flaws of social institutions, but to divine intervention. Hall says that the tribulation of England can be attributed

> only to the stroke and punishment of God, affirming [that] the kingdom, which Henry the IV his grandfather wrongfully gat, and unjustly possessed against King Richard II and his heirs, could not by very divine iustice, long continue in that injurious stock; and that therefore God by his divine providence, punished the offence of the grandfather, in the son's son.[1]

In this version of history, the murder of Richard II and the usurpation of Henry IV constitute a crime against heaven that can be expiated only by a return to legitimate monarchy. Hall's phrase, which consciously echoes biblical language, that God punished "the offence of the grandfather, in the son's son" is constantly reflected in the dramatic and narrative structure of this and other plays in the cycle. Prophesies, predictions, dreams, revelations, and the assertion of God's intervention are regularly trundled forth by the actors of these secular events in order to assert eternal providence. Shakespeare is so generous about supplying such material that it has not proved difficult to interpret this play, as well as the entire sequence of eight plays from *Richard II* to *Richard III,* as an acting out of God's darker purposes.

But Hall is not tied to a single interpretation of these complex events. He offers a second explanation, equally persuasive, and given equal weight, for King Henry's "ill chance and misfortune." Hall succinctly evaluates Henry's personal and moral characteristics:

> he was a man of no great wit, such as men commonly call an innocent man, neither a fool, neither very wise, whose study always was more to excel, [rather] in Godly living and virtuous example, than in worldly regiment or temporal dominion, in so much that in comparison to the study and delectation that they had to virtue and godliness, he little regarded, but in manner despised all worldly power and temporal authority. . . . But his enemies ascribed all this to his coward stomach.
>
> (Cairncross, *3 Henry VI* p. 166)

Hall has no difficulty giving equal credence to the one idea—that God's hand is responsible for the punishment of England and the Henry—as the other, that the king's flaws of character (unworldliness, simplicity, cowardice) are also the cause of the trouble. Shakespeare's sources license him to explore these two different systems of interpretation and causation.

Shakespeare continually demonstrates King Henry VI is unsuited to monarchy. He is perpetually youthful and immature, dominated first by his uncles and later by his wife Margaret. He is feeble in war and always more drawn to prayer than politics. In the first two plays that bear his name, "bashful Henry" (1.1.41) had been distinctly subordinate to his obstreperous uncles. To the dangerous rebellion led by Cade, his response was merely to wring his hands. In *3 Henry VI,* Shakespeare gives greater dimension to the character of the King. While he does not become more active or stronger, he does become more coherent, more sensitive, more affecting—a precursor, perhaps, of Richard II.

Henry makes his most memorable appearance at the battle of Towton. Shunted to a corner by the fierceness of the combatants, he sits and reflects on war and society while the two sides skirmish. He is withdrawn and passive, indifferent to the partisanship that drives all other characters: "Here on this molehill will I sit me down. / To whom God will, there be the victory" (2.5.14-15). He indulges in an escapist fancy in which he is a "homely swain" or shepherd who has nothing to do but count the hours until his ewes will yean and their fleece can be sheared. The delicious solitude of the rural world is contrasted to the care and corruption of the busy haunts of men:

> Ah, what a life were this! how sweet, how lovely!
> Gives not the hawthorn bush a sweeter shade
> To shepherds looking on their silly sheep,
> Than doth a rich embroidered canopy
> To kings that fear their subjects' treachery?
>
> (41-45)

But all the while, the audience knows that it is a sign of dereliction when kings enjoy bucolic bliss. Henry's principal vice has been what Elizabethans called "lenity"—"harmful pity" in Clifford's definition—or softness in dealing with antagonists.

To this very long, self-indulgent meditation, Shakespeare opposes a scene designed to dramatize the limitations of Henry's views. As Henry looks on, a "Son" enters with the body of a man he has killed, and as he rifles it searching for "crowns," he discovers that he has killed his own father. He laments: "O heavy times, begetting such events" (63). But it is soon revealed that the fault is not just in the times but in Henry himself. "From London by the King was I pressed forth" (64). The King, always compassionate to suffering, understands that he must share the blame: "While lions war and battle for their dens, / Poor harmless lambs abide their enmity" (74-75). The Arcadian fantasy of shepherds and their silly sheep has been revealed to be a world where lambs lie down with lions at their peril. Shakespeare proceeds to drive home the point. "*Enter a Father that hath kill'd his Son, with a body in his arms.*" After the father's lament, which mirrors too exactly the son's speech that preceded it, Henry moralizes what he has just observed. He accepts personal responsibility for the destruction of English families. (He does not notice that Shakespeare replicates in the common people the exact pattern of the murdering of fathers created by dynastic rivalry.) Once again his grieving is poignant but misguided:

> The red rose and the white are on his face,
> The fatal colors of our striving houses.
> The one his purple blood right well resembles;
> The other his pale cheeks, methinks, presenteth.
> Wither one rose, and let the other flourish.
> If you contend, a thousand lives must wither.
>
> (97-102)

Henry's strengths and weaknesses as a leader reveal themselves in this highly metaphorical statement. He acknowledges that the marks of civil dissension are allegorized in the faces of its victims, and he is sensitive to the suffering of his people. But neither the willingness to embrace martyrdom nor indifference to the outcome of the contention signals an effective leader. In the end, he is reduced to hopeless sentimentality: "Sad-hearted men, much overgone with care, / Here sits a king more woeful than you are" (123-24).

Eventually, Henry is stabbed to death by Richard of Gloucester, who emerges as the dominant figure in the final act of the play. Henry knows that he is about to be murdered, but he is still concerned about the people of England, and prophesies to Richard that "Men for their sons, wives for their husbands, / Orphans for their parents' timeless [i.e. untimely] death— / Shall rue the hour that ever thou wast born" (5.6.41-43). Henry dies at the moment in which his language is at its most animated.

Despite this moment of passion, the character of Henry remains relatively static through the three plays. On the other hand, Richard of Gloucester is nondescript at the outset of *3 Henry VI,* but its dominant figure at last. Shakespeare seems hesitant about what to do with Richard. At first, it appears as though he will be cast as an overreacher in the Marlovian mode. When, in the first act, he urges his father York to seek the kingship, Richard speaks in the tones of Tamburlaine:

> father, do but think
> How sweet a thing it is to wear a crown,
> Within whose circuit is Elysium
> And all that poets feign of bliss and joy.
>
> (1.2.28-31)

In the second act, Shakespeare takes another tack. Now he casts Richard as an avenger out of a revenge play like Kyd's immensely influential *Spanish Tragedy.* At the battle of Towton, in the midst of the excursions, strokes, and blows of combat, young Richard arrives with a message for Warwick, the leader of the party of York, to tell him that his half-brother (actually his bastard half-brother Salisbury) has been killed by Clifford:

> Thy brother's blood the thirsty earth hath drunk,
> Broached with the steely point of Clifford's lance;
> And in the very pangs of death he cried,
> Like to a dismal clangor heard from far,
> "Warwick, revenge! Brother, revenge my death!"
>
> (2.3.15-19)

At this point in his development Richard's language is far removed from the jaunty mockery that eventually becomes his hallmark. He speaks in the popular style of the early 1590s at its windiest. His language is marred by too ample alliteration ("brother's blood," "broach'd"), mandatory adjectives ("thirsty earth," "steely point," "dismal clangor"), and unfortunate vaguenesses when specificity is sorely needed ("heard from afar"). This is the kind of writing that Shakespeare would later mock by putting it in the mouths of Bottom/Pyramus and Pistol.

It is only in act 3, scene 2, that the familiar figure of Richard begins to emerge. The remarkable scene in which this occurs is comprised of two sections. In the first part, Richard's older brother Edward, now Edward IV, woos the widow Lady Elizabeth Grey. Richard and his brother George comment aside on Edward's sexual aggressiveness. After Elizabeth accepts Edward's offer of marriage, Richard remains on stage. In the course of a long soliloquy, his new character—theatrical, comic, wicked, angry, ironic—springs to life.

Edward is attractive to women and something of a philanderer (Hall says that he "loved well both to look and to feel fair damosels" [Cairncross, *3 Henry VI,* 159]). Elizabeth, whose husband was slain fighting for Edward at St. Albans, approaches Edward with a suit to repossess her alienated lands. Edward hints that the lady offer her virtue in trade for her property. Richard, overlooking, makes a series of prurient comments: "I see the lady hath a thing to grant"; "Fight closer or, good faith, you'll catch a clap"; "Ay, good leave have you, / Till youth . . . leave you to the crutch" (3.2.12, 23, 34-35). Elizabeth does not yield easily, and Edward, smitten, asks her to be his wife. This is the worst possible outcome for Richard. He is jealous of Edward's attractiveness to women, and he knows that a fruitful marriage will imperil his chance of succeeding to the throne.

Close observation of his brother catalyzes Richard. He reacts violently to the prospect of his brother's marriage: "Ay, Edward will use women honorably. / Would he were wasted, marrow, bones and all, / That from his loins no hopeful branch may spring" (124-26). Richard reveals his ambition and admits that it is unlikely that he will become king. He only "dream[s] on sovereignty." But when he dismisses the prospect of kingship, an alternative suddenly arises. "Well, say there is no kingdom then for Richard; / What other pleasure can the world afford?" (146-47). Richard scornfully dismisses the possibility that he could succeed with women as his brother does. "I'll make my heaven in a lady's lap, / And deck my body in gay ornaments / And witch sweet ladies with my words and looks. / O miserable thought." Hall had described Richard in most unflattering terms: "little of stature, evil featured of limbs, crook-backed, the left shoulder much higher than the right, hard favored of visage, such as in estates is called a warlike visage, and among common persons a crabbed face" (Cairncross, *3 Henry V,* 174). Shakespeare, interested in the psychology of his character, transforms Richard's deformity first into self-loathing and then into motive:

> Why, Love forswore me in my mother's womb; . . .
> To shrink mine arm up like a wither'd shrub;
> To make an envious mountain on my back . . .
> And am I then a man to be beloved?
>
> (3.2.153, 156-57, 163)

Richard resolves not to seek heaven in a lady's lap (in the Petrarchan language he parodies) but instead resolves, "I'll make my heaven to dream upon the crown" (168).

Shakespeare then introduces still another novel element when Richard begins to draw on the familiar image of the vice of the morality plays, one of whose roles is to dissemble and pretend. "Why, I can smile, and murder whiles I smile, / And cry 'Content!' to that that grieves my heart, / And wet my cheeks with artificial tears" (182-84). Shakespeare has now provided Richard with a motive (an acute consciousness of his deformity and uniqueness), an objective (the crown), and a borrowed and transformed morality play inheritance that allows him to toy with his enemies while revealing himself to the audience. As he brings the soliloquy to a conclusion, Richard adds the modern (and anachronistic) horror of Italian intrigue: he will "set the murderous Machiavel to school" (3.2.193). Shakespeare has left the preliminary gestures toward Kyd and Marlowe far behind and created a character infinitely more complex and sinister than his predecessor playwrights could possibly imagine.

The most famous lines in *3 Henry VI* occur in Richard of Gloucester's last soliloquy. Richard has stabbed King Henry, who has been "famed for mildness, peace, and prayer" (2.1.156); he turns to the audience in the speech beginning "I, that have neither pity, love, nor fear" (5.6.68) and makes the chilling assertion that

> I have no brother, I am like no brother;
> And this word "love," which greybeards call divine,
> Be resident in men like one another,
> And not in me. I am myself alone.
>
> (80-83)

These phrases define Richard's emerging amorality. Explicit atheism, scandalous to the orthodox among the spectators, comes to the fore in the contemptuous dismissal of "love" as an idea to which only the old-fashioned would cling. The accompanying word "divine" makes it clear that Richard repudiates not only the love of man but the love of God. Over and above his rejection of traditional religion, Richard also claims to be set apart from the larger community of men. He is "alone"—an individual, an isolate, concerned not with the public good or communal morality, but only with personal and private needs and desires. In these few vivid and condensed words of self-revelation, Richard manages to repudiate ancestral standards of both religious and social behavior.

Even more resonant is "I have no brother, I am like no brother." All of Shakespeare's histories pay homage to dynastic and family loyalty; *3 Henry VI* sometimes seems to have no other subject. Taken literally, Richard's announcement that he has no brother is of course simply untrue. Richard has three brothers: Edward, the Earl of March, succeeds his father as Duke of York and achieves the throne as Edward IV; feckless George, Duke of Clarence, wanders from the Yorkist side to the Lancastrian and back again; and Edmund of Rutland, the "innocent child" (1.3.8), is murdered by "bloody Clifford" (2), in one of the drama's more gruesome atrocities. Richard does not pretend that he has no legal or literal brother. The denial that he has a brother means that he is not tied to the community of England by fraternal or familial bonds; that there is no one, not even a brother, with whom he shares a common humanity; and finally, that he has no use for the tenderness that other human beings acknowledge toward their most intimate friends and relations. When Richard says that he has no brother, he certainly suspends his loyalty to Edward, George, and Edmund, but he also means that he no longer participates in the brotherhood of man. His literal lie reflects a deeper truth—and from this truth both the murder of his brother Clarence and the conscienceless villainy that mark his subsequent career inevitably follow.

Notes

1. Cited in *The Third Part of 3 Henry VI,* ed. Andrew S. Cairncross (London: Methuen, 1964), 166-67.

CHARACTER STUDIES

Nancy A. Gutierrez (essay date 1990)

SOURCE: "Gender and Value in *1 Henry VI:* The Role of Joan de Pucelle," in *Theatre Journal,* Vol. 42, No. 2, May, 1990, pp. 183-93.

[*In the essay below, Gutierrez examines Shakespeare's representation of Joan de Pucelle in* Henry VI, Part 1 *as a problematic, feminine scapegoat used by men to gain power. Gutierrez notes that such a representation reflects a patriarchal desire to eliminate female threats by transforming them into actions that bolster male power.*]

Among the many critical problems resulting from the uncertain text of Shakespeare's *1 Henry VI* is the theatrical presentation of Joan de Pucelle, history's Joan of Arc. She is, at various times in the play, a divinely-commissioned peasant girl who dons soldier's garb for the glory of God's mother, a glorified camp follower, a master orator in defense of her country, a conjuring witch, and an abject traitor. Most recently, Gabriele Bernhard Jackson argues that Shakespeare's presentation of Joan, as "partially continuous and partially disjunct," is deliberate, for the playwright exploits the "varied ideological potential inherent in the topically relevant figure of the virago," and shows her "first as numinous, then as practically and subversively powerful, and finally as feminized and demonized."[1]

While I am persuaded by Jackson's argument about the topicality of Joan's depiction, I also see in Shakespeare's representation of Joan's relationship with her French allies and English enemies a deliberate gendering that demonstrates the patriarchy's need to defuse and neutralize any female threat by transforming it into a reinforcement of the male prerogative. The political tension between the

Jean-Louis Roux as Burgundy, Martha Henry as Joan la Pucelle, and members of the Festival Company as French Soldiers in Act III, scene iii of the 1966 Stratford Festival production of Henry VI.

English and the French, and between Joan and both her French allies and English enemies, further demonstrates the cultural use of gender as a value-laden metaphor descriptive of both political and moral issues: biological difference becomes the site for cultural conflict.[2] Let me emphasize that I am interested here in representation, not in characterization, in *how* Joan is depicted by the dramatist through her own words and actions and through what other characters say about her, not in *what* the dramatist might understand as her so-called psychologically-coherent inner being. Thus, while Jackson argues that "a positive militaristic reading [of Joan]" and "a negative misogynist one [neglect] both the play's topicality and the historical moment's ideological complexity," the case is rather that these readings are incomplete accounts of the play's binarization of gender, a cultural construct that facilitates the representation of political and ideological antagonisms.[3] This metaphoric use of gender is further accommodated by Shakespeare's dramatic technique of presenting Joan's character to the audience through the perspective of other characters, an operation that forces the audience into collusion with the patriarchal point of view.

Shakespeare's first tetralogy dramatizes the struggle of men to assert individual legitimacy and authority, in other words, the struggle of fathers to pass on their paternity, and the struggle of sons to accept and validate it. One might assume that in such a conflict of patriarchal claims there would be no place for women, but as a matter of fact, women play significant roles in the enactment of the plot, both in supporting their male relatives who are centers of the conflict, and in actively fighting those men who are their enemies (Margaret of Anjou is, of course, the most prominent example, but also consider the less successful activities of the Duchess of Gloucester and Queen Elizabeth). These plays support Gayatri Chakravorty Spivak's observation that it is through women that men assert their prerogative and assume power: "the institution of phallocentric law is congruent with the need to prove paternity and authority, to secure property by transforming the child into an alienated object named and possessed by the father, and to secure property by transforming the woman into a mediating instrument of the production and passage of property."[4] While Spivak here is addressing the way men co-opt woman's reproductive powers as their own vehicles to power, this dictum applies as well to the French use of Joan the soldier, as a medium through which to lay claim to France. Joan becomes a battleground on which the French and English enact their power struggle, and her ultimate execution at the hands of the English makes explicit the masculine use of woman as scapegoat for sexual (and here, cultural) inadequacies.

Act 1, scene 2, the scene in which Joan first comes on stage, initiates this power struggle between the sexes. During this scene, several related actions occur: the French are first seen boasting about their military gains and denigrating the English counterattempts; they leave the stage for battle and return, beaten back and surprised by the heroism of the English army; Joan is introduced as a holy maid sent to help the French; as she enters, she recognizes Charles, the Dauphin, in spite of a ruse the French had contrived to fool her; she overcomes Charles in a sword fight, he vows love to her (a love Joan puts off because she has taken a vow of chastity because of her calling); and Joan is awarded a place in battle.

This superficial account of the action, an action which seems to conclude with Joan's victory over her male doubters, is called into question, first by the notions of gender underlying the various interrelationships; second, by the inherent ambiguities of meaning in the language of certain characters; and finally by the obvious metadrama in the last part of the scene. These literary strategies of indirection continue in other scenes with Joan, until the final act of the play. At this point, what had heretofore been artifice becomes reality: Joan's construction as whore and witch by her male cohorts and male enemies—a construction ever obvious to the viewing audience—is presented to the audience for the first time without the guiding interpretation of chorus-like male characters.

In *1 Henry VI,* as in all of Shakespeare's plays, stage directions are minimal, so that Shakespearean discourse *is* primarily language. The case of Joan of Arc, however, is a special one: she is presented as a woman who "cross dresses," who dresses like a man. Such a violation of order may or may not be threatening to the patriarchal status quo, depending on the context, as scholars such as Natalie Zemon Davis, Lisa Jardine, and Linda Woodbridge have pointed out.[5] In any case, Joan's situation is different from many other cross-dressing stage heroines, in that she openly admits the disjunction between sex and costume. Consequently, the play's cultural anxiety about gender difference is not dramatized in her language, as it is in the language of Shakespeare's cross-dressing comic heroines, but rather is displayed in the strategies—linguistic and behavioral—by which the other characters in the play (all male, as it turns out) react to Joan.[6]

When they first enter the stage in this scene, Charles and his French nobles are complacent about their military situation: they have possession of the most significant towns, the English have lost heart and offer battle reluctantly, and most significantly, the English heroes are neutralized: Talbot is prisoner and Salisbury is "mad-brained."[7] Mars, the god of war and male power "is smiling" on the French, while the English are virtually emasculated, being "pale ghosts" and "drowned mice," and are explicitly said to lack manpower (I. ii. 4, 7, 12, 17). This gendering of sides shifts in the off-stage battle that follows. The French return, complaining that the French army is full of "Dogs, cowards and dastards" (I. ii. 23), who have fled before the English. On the other hand, the English are "lions," "Olivers and Rolands," "Samsons and Goliases," "hare-brain'd slaves," who will tear down the walls with their teeth (I. ii. 27, 30, 33, 37). Now it is the French who are depicted as effeminate, and the English who have masculine strength and power.

The values accorded to "masculine" and "feminine" behavior are obvious in this half-scene. First of all, these terms do not refer to biology, but to "attitudes." "Masculine" refers to the physical ability to control and dominate, to take action and to create or change the world, while "feminine" means just the opposite: to lack physical prowess and the ability to change or create, to be unable to dominate or control, to be able only to react. Further, both terms are invested with moral overtones: "masculine" behavior is significant and "feminine" behavior is trivial; "masculine" behavior is admirable and praiseworthy and "feminine" behavior is pathetic and embarrassing.

The assigning of positive values to masculine activity, and of negative values to feminine is, of course, one of the most basic forms of patriarchal domination. Critics as different as David Bevington and Coppélia Kahn have noted that the feminization of the French is one means by which Shakespeare simultaneously denigrates the English enemy and celebrates his own country.[8] However, because this assigning of gender is a continuous activity in the play, the meaning of the gender ascription shifts according to its context, thus rendering such a static interpretation invalid. The next half of this scene very quickly demonstrates this point.

Jean, Count Dunois, the Bastard of Orleance, comes on the stage, a man whose birth has both denied him his paternity of the French crown, and placed him outside the social and political order. While he is not a malcontent, but a loyal Frenchman, his very name nevertheless signals his alien nature, and for the English audience he becomes a paradigm of France itself: an illegitimate political upstart. Thus, it is interesting that he is the one who first tells Charles, the legitimate heir of France, about Joan. In this detail, Shakespeare departs from Holinshed and Hall, who state that Joan was introduced to the Dauphin by Peter Baudricort, Captain of Vaucouleurs.[9] In Shakespeare's version, a bastard introduces a cross-dressing woman: an outsider by birth introduces a sexually-ambiguous creature, who by such gender indeterminacy is an outsider as well.

What follows is an inverting of the scene's first actions. Just as the French at the beginning of the scene assert their position of masculine mastery over the feminized English only to find these positions and gendering reversed, Joan too asserts her masculine authority over the French, only to have it subverted at the end of the scene, where she is returned to a feminine position in relation to the soldiers she wants to lead. This reversal is accomplished through language: while the French speak to one another in the first part of the scene in a discourse that clearly reflects their shared experience, in this second part of the scene language is not at all monolithic, and has different meaning for different characters, and often several simultaneous meanings for a single character. Consequently, language becomes the site of conflict.[10]

The Bastard describes Joan as a messenger from heaven: with the help of God's mother, she has the gift of prophecy and the ability to rid France of the English. This idealized description is obviously Joan's own self-fashioning of her identity. Her dress of masculine armor, which strikes the audience immediately as she walks on the stage, dramatically reinforces this reported discourse. Also reinforcing her self-representation is her identification of the real Dauphin, in spite of Charles's attempt to deceive her, in a kind of hearty language and tone that one of the onlookers describes as "dash" (I. ii. 71). This masculine behavior and style of speech is Joan's own redefinition of the concept "holy maid," a term which in religious and patriarchal convention suggests the feminine virtues of chastity, silence, and obedience, linked with religious virtues of humility and selflessness.

Joan takes Charles aside and in her conversation with him offers yet another self-description. She calls herself "a shepherd's daughter" (I. ii. 72), emphasizing both her class and her pastoral roots. Her very departure from these roots threatens the hierarchical nature of the patriarchal system. She goes on to assert that she is "untrained in any art," a logical result of her parentage. However, she then claims the power of "Heaven and Our lady," significantly a power derived from "female," not male divine powers. Joan comments on "Our Lady's" power by claiming that she used to be "black and swart" but now has beauty, and that she now has both the gift of prophecy and a courage beyond her sex. In short, Joan defines herself as coming from a marginalized group in society with no access to the ruling power structure; however, divine *female* forces accord her powers valued by the ruling structure—physical prowess equal to a man (symbolized by her armor), external feminine beauty, and superhuman intellectual powers.

Such a creation as Joan describes herself to be has no place in the male-defined world of the play. However, the impulse to categorize, an impulse usually ascribed to the masculine mindset, controls the response of the male characters to Joan in this scene, and in those scenes with the English which follow.

Charles picks up on the ambiguity of meaning in Joan's challenge to him: when she asks him to "try [her courage] by combat" so that she might become his "warlike mate" (I. ii. 89, 92), the words point not only to swordfighting, but to sexual play as well. Whether Joan intends the sexual suggestiveness of her speech is not absolutely clear (see n. 10), but she does, in fact, insist on her physical prowess. In any case, the Dauphin uses Joan's rhetoric, demanding that she "buckle with me"—a phrase meaning to engage in a swordfight, or to make love—to prove her divine mission. When Joan overcomes him, his language immediately loses its ambiguity. He retains the military wording, but now clearly uses it in the service of "love," as he takes on the role of Petrarchan lover, a man at the mercy of his mistress: he has literally been overpowered by Joan's skill with the sword, and he metaphorically proclaims his "thralldom" to her love. In doing so, the Dauphin, as representative of the French, proclaims his lack of manliness. Earlier he had been defeated by a superior English army and had shown himself a coward by running away; now, he begins to insinuate with words, to use language for the purposes of deceit. Such effeminacy proves his inferior standing—not only morally, but also politically and socially—and, as a corollary, affirms the superiority of the English.

Joan's victory over Charles may also be seen to be a deviation from the conventional depiction of warrior women. As Simon Shepherd reminds us, the battle between a warrior woman and her lover is the climax of the woman's career.[11] After this battle, no matter what its outcome, the warrior woman usually submits to her lover in marriage. In Joan's case, this victory over a man who proclaims his intention to be her lover is instead her initiation as a warrior, and marriage or sexual partnership is delayed. Apparently this battle is Shakespeare's invention, for nothing like it is found in the sources.[12] Shakespeare seems to be deliberately inverting the convention, signaling both man's culpability for allowing the intrusion of woman into his world, and, at the same time, the comic situation of such an occurrence. Besides being good theater, the battle clearly demonstrates the questionable nature of the French cause.

The Petrarchan discourse consequently appears to be congruent with Joan's discourse of costume: the cross-dressing woman dominates the "effeminate" lover; gender roles are reversed as the woman takes charge. However, this apparent transference of power is undercut by the very Petrarchan discourse used by the Dauphin. This fictionalized construct may place a man at the mercy of his lady, but as maker of his poetry, the male poet gives life and meaning to his mistress: she is defined by his power of language. Further, Petrarchan discourse objectifies the lover's mistress, for she becomes the means by which he reaches a higher state: "Rendered passive and chaste, [the Renaissance lady] merely mediates the courtier's safe transcendence of an otherwise demeaning necessity."[13] Thus, although the Petrarchan lover is literally at his mistress's mercy, he is subtly—and more realistically—in control. The Dauphin effectively takes away Joan's victory over him by placing her within this patriarchal discourse. Indeed, we can probably say that Joan was beaten from the beginning, since her weapon—Petrarchan language and/or the phallic sword—was really her enemy's.[14]

Joan's apparent assertion of power is further undermined by the interpretation given to her private conversation with Charles by the other French nobles. While Joan denies her place in the Petrarchan discourse, a denial heard by the audience, the onlooking Frenchmen who cannot hear what is being said describe what they see as verbal sexual foreplay. Alanson, for example, jokes that the long conversation suggests that Charles is "[shriving] this woman to her smock" (I. ii. 119), making love to her. Such a comment indicates that the French view Joan simply as a sexual object. She might be a cross-dressing woman whose sex is supposedly confused, but she provides no ambiguity for the Dauphin's followers: her armor is invisible and her female body is obtrusively present. Although the perspectives of Charles and his soldiers seem entirely different—Charles idealizes Joan in his Petrarchan rhetoric while his soldiers essentialize her—these perspectives are actually two versions of a single conception: woman as sexual object used by man for his own purposes. In essentializing Joan, the French have reacquired the masculine identity they had lost in battle with the English.

This part of the scene functions much like a play within a play, in that Joan and Charles play out a scene which other characters interpret, while the actual audience measures the onlookers' comments against their own experience of the scene. While this metadramatic device lacks the complexity of such future inset "plays," like those in *Hamlet* and *Troilus and Cressida,* it nevertheless works to "stylize," to emphasize the artifice of the so-called scene.[15] It calls attention to the act of interpretation practiced by the French nobles and their prince: the character of Joan is represented to the English audience through the filter of the French perspective. To the English of Shakespeare's day, Joan was no Catholic saint, no Shavian symbol of individualism, but instead an unnatural woman, definitely a witch, probably a whore.[16] Consequently, when the French nobles watch Charles and Joan together and interpret Joan as a woman on the sexual prowl, they are effectively representing the English audience and voicing its probable reaction.

The scene-within-a-scene also functions on another level. As Laura Mulvey points out, "in a world ordered by sexual imbalance, pleasure in looking has been split between active/male and passive/female."[17] Just as the Petrarchan lover creates his mistress with his poetry, the spectator creates the picture's meaning by his gaze. While Mulvey discusses the phallocentric nature of the camera in cinema, her theory illuminates the subtextual *agon* of this scene: if woman functions naturally as erotic object, if her very presence connotes "to-be-looked-at-ness," then Joan's exhibitionist cross-dressing emphatically invites the same kind of response. Furthermore, if the camera highlights the voyeuristic aspect of the male gaze, then the metadrama operating in this scene plays the same function, for Charles and Joan's interaction is interpreted solely in erotic terms. The "male" gaze of the French nobles reinforces the real audience's place as patriarchal overseer and approver. Such congruence of perspective demonstrates the bonding of men, or in this case of patriarchally-defined cultures: The French soldiers and the contemporary English audience, normally "natural" enemies, become allies when threatened by a woman.

The English in the play show this coherence of view almost immediately. When the English hero Talbot first hears that the French are being aided by "a holy prophetess," he questions whether she is "pucelle or puzzel," that is, virgin or whore, transforming Joan's self-definition as the embodiment of chastity into its opposite, sexual promiscuity. He likewise transforms the Dauphin or Dolphin from the highest fish on the chain of being to dogfish, the lowest. In both cases, he places the enemies of the English into positions of moral and hierarchical devaluation.

When Talbot meets Joan in battle, he continues his labeling of her: she is "a woman clad in armor," a "devil or devil's dam," "a witch," "a high-minded strumpet" (I. vi. 3, 5, 6, 12). In so naming her, Talbot essentially "creates" Joan as these very creatures: she has no choice but to *be* what Talbot says she is because he will acknowledge no other identity.[18] He also rationalizes the defeat that the English are suffering: where earlier the French had genderized both themselves and the English into masculine and feminine categories, Talbot now does the same. The English no longer exhibit the "fierceness [of] dogs," but are "whelps [who] crying run away," are sheep instead of lions, slaves instead of masters (I. vi. 26, 28-31, 32). The reason for the transformation of the English from a masculine to feminine position is the intrusion of Joan into the world, a creature known to be from hell because of the confusion of gender she embodies. Talbot's language, like that of the Dauphin in I. ii, demonstrates the equivalence of gender and politics in determining value and power within social groups.

In summary, the French, who are stripped in battle by the English of any courage and manliness they might have had, are revitalized by Joan's entrance, but not as Joan would wish—at first they are skeptical, and then they define her as a woman to be sexually encountered. In other words, they ignore her sexual ambiguity entirely and create her as they wish her to be.[19] Joan wins her right to lead the French in this scene, physically conquering a man in the process, but in no way can we say that she is empowered, for she is not the one who controls how the characters look at the world. Likewise, she is always the object of looking herself, never the subject, and therefore never in control. Her "discourses" of costume (armor), language (Petrarchan speech), and action (dueling with a sword), because of their very nature as patriarchal weapons, and because of their inherent function as objects of curiosity *to be looked at,* cannot overcome the preconceived and pre-locked mindsets of the French about woman. In fact, the use of these discourses by a woman results in what Alice Jardine calls *paranoia,* the reinforcement of sexual differences.[20]

This scene serves as a paradigm for Joan's relationship with the French in the rest of the play, as she becomes a vehicle by which the French regain their country and, more importantly, their own identity as the masculine and virile sex. In I. vi, after Joan's first victory over the English, the French honor her as "Divinest creature, Astraea's daughter," "France's saint" (I. v. 4, 29): she has interceded for them and facilitated "the joy that God has given [them]" (I. vi. 14). This language of religious worship is echoed on other occasions when Joan succeeds militarily, particularly in her initial victory at Roan and in her scene with Burgundy (III. ii, III. iii).

More often, however, the French locate Joan not in a numinous position, but very specifically in a "feminine" position. In Act 2, scene 1, for example, a scene in which Joan and Charles come onstage together in the middle of the night, the Bastard immediately interprets their being together as a sexual liaison, and Charles offers a weak excuse for their association, therefore implying that the Bastards's inference is accurate. Although it is highly probable that Joan and Charles indeed were together, Joan presents herself not at all as Charles's mistress. Rather, she vehemently defends herself against the Dauphin's attacks of misloyalty, and challenges the military watchfulness of the French soldiers. The scene ends with her briskly trying to put an end to the bickering when an English soldier enters and scatters the French. In this scene, as in all the later scenes in the play until Act 5, she presents herself as loyal retainer of her prince, courageous in battle and wily in military strategy. But, as in I. ii, Joan's male colleagues see only her sexual nature and define her accordingly.

Even when Joan fights for her country, her strategies for victory, which the French encourage, are invariably "feminine." First of all, she takes Roan by duplicity, disguising herself and the French soldiers so they can enter the city secretly. Such indirection is "treachery" and "treason" to the English, and Talbot challenges the French soldiers to "take up arms like gentlemen" (III. ii. 36, 37, 70), that is like "men." Of course, they would be "fools" to do so, as Joan points out (III. ii. 62). Joan's second "victory" is also a result of "feminine" strategy, a power of persuasion that is likened to witchcraft: she determines "by fair persuasions, mix'd with sug'red words, / [to] entice the Duke of Burgundy" to change sides and ally himself with the French (III. iii. 18-20). Charles encourages her to "enchant" the Duke, and the Duke himself feels "she hath bewitch'd me with her words" (III. iii. 40, 59). Finally, Joan's antiheroic response to Lucy's idealized verbal monument to the dead Talbot challenges the carefully-constructed structure of chivalry so valued by the "manly" English.[21]

That these feminine and deceitful strategies are encouraged by the French is made obvious by their collusion in them. More direct evidence is provided by the Bastard's pointed request to Joan to "Search out thy wit for secret policies," and by Alanson's echo to "Employ thee then . . . for our good" (III. iii. 12, 15). Consequently, as much as Joan might assert her masculine prowess by her masculine dress, she is invariably placed by her French allies into "feminine" positions which they then exploit for their own purposes.

When she is finally captured by the English at the end of the play, she has just been abandoned by devils she has conjured, demonstrating emphatically the demonized nature the English have attributed to her throughout the play. This is the only scene in the entire play in which the audience actually sees Joan practice witchcraft. Furthermore, it is the only scene in which Joan is presented to the audience without the filter of the perspective of her French allies. The absence of a choral perspective in this particular scene is both striking and significant.

While the French, throughout the play, have "constructed" Joan as a cross-dressing whore, and the English have "constructed" her as a witch from hell, Joan's words and actions have suggested that she is neither. However, the perspectives of both the French and the English have been presented to the audience as providing the correct interpretations of Joan. From the very beginning, Joan has no power to impose her self-fashioned identity upon the world of the play, for the masculine mindset both of her allies and of her enemies refuses to grant her the freedom of such self-creation. Likewise, she has no power to influence the audience, because she is trapped in the paradigmatic configuration of the female/passive object of the male/active gaze.

Act 5 shows Joan finally and irrevocably as the male characters and the audience have fashioned her. Whatever options she had as a character—and these options are evident in the kind of disjunction noted by so many critics, and explained so well by Jackson in her discussion of Joan's topical meaning as virago—these options are narrowed to the one meaning acceptable to the patriarchal construct of the play: in V. iii, Joan is represented as a witch, unsuccessfully calling upon hell for aid, and cursing her human persecutors; in V. iv, she rewrites her past, renouncing her pastoral roots and claiming power from a fulfilled sexuality (she pretends to be pregnant). In refashioning herself in this way, she becomes a conventional female threat, and she is treated conventionally: she is burned.

While the English may perceive the French as effeminate because of the French exploitation of Joan's female strategies, with her help the French recapture their country from the English. In actuality, the land empowers the French. With her death, Joan removes from the French consciousness a reminder of its earlier ineffectuality and reinvests the French fully with their lost masculinity: she is a sexual scapegoat for their political and military identities. On the other hand, the English "conclude effeminate peace," emasculated "by treason, falsehood, and by treachery" (V. iv. 107, 109). Her name is not mentioned in the council between the French and the English, but Joan's influence remains; the French agree outwardly to a truce, while privately planning to thwart the English with policy. Thus the French retain "feminine" strategies as the means to "masculine" identity, while the English do the opposite. The clash of moral values in these gender categories mirrors the antagonism in the play between realistic observation and romantic posturing, between practical behavior and quixotic gesture, between pragmatism and honor.

As both battleground and cultural scapegoat, a *medium* by which men gain power and a touchstone by which gender stereotypes are reinforced, the theatrical representation of Joan demonstrates how the masculine mindset transforms what it perceives as a female challenge into a reinforcement of the patriarchate. Furthermore, it reveals the binarization of gender as cultural expression of value. The sexual tension between Joan and both her French allies and her English enemies parallels the political antagonism between the French and the English, and the power politics practiced by each side in these two clashes rests on gender ascription. Ultimately, however, the moral worth assigned to "masculine" and "feminine" categories in the play is compromised, not because Shakespeare is ahistorically feminist, but because the play depicts a grey, ironic world, in which such black and white categories are obvious and fragile fictions of a human mind attempting to find order and meaning.

Notes

1. Gabriele Bernhard Jackson, "Topical Ideology: Witches, Amazons, and Shakespeare's Joan of Arc," *English Literary Renaissance* 18 (1988): 44, 64-65. For a topical interpretation of Joan complementary to Jackson's, see Leah S. Marcus, *Puzzling Shakespeare: Local Reading and Its Discontents* (Berkeley: University of California Press, 1988), 51-96.

2. This intersection of gender and politics provides for *1 Henry VI* a practical intratextual method of interpretation by which to reinforce topical readings

such as Jackson's. While there might seem to be a radical dislocation between a theoretical feminist discourse and a topical discourse such as Jackson's, the historical pluralist tendency of feminist criticism provides both a justification and a precedent. See, for example, Annette Kolodny, "Dancing Through the Minefield: Some Observations on the Theory, Practice, and Politics of a Feminist Literary Criticism," in *Feminist Criticism: Essays on Women, Literature, and Theory,* ed. Elaine Showalter (New York: Pantheon Books, 1985), 144-67 (first published in *Feminist Studies* 6 [1980]: 1-25); Elaine Showalter, "Feminist Criticism in the Wilderness," Ibid., 243-70 (first published in *Critical Inquiry* 8 [1981]: 179-205); and Carol Thomas Neely, "Feminist Criticism in Motion," in *For Alma Mater: Theory and Practice in Feminist Scholarship,* ed. Paula A. Treichler, Cheris Kramarae, and Beth Stafford (Urbana: University of Illinois Press, 1985), 69-90.

3. Jackson, "Topical," 47. Jackson provides a brief overview of this criticism; see 40-47, especially 40-41 and 47.

4. Gayatri Chakravorty Spivak, "Displacement and the Discourse of Woman," in *Displacement: Derrida and After,* ed. Mark Krupnick (Bloomington: Indiana University Press, 1983), 184.

5. See, for example, Natalie Zemon Davis, "Women on Top," in *Society and Culture in Early Modern France* (London: Duckworth, 1975), 124-51; Lisa Jardine, *Still Harping on Daughters: Women and Drama in the Age of Shakespeare* (Sussex: Harvester Press, 1983); and Linda Woodbridge, *Women and the English Renaissance* (Urbana: University of Illinois Press, 1984).

6. On cross-dressing heroines in Shakespearean drama, see for example, Phyllis Rackin, "Androgyny, Mimesis, and the Marriage of the Boy Heroine on the English Renaissance Stage," *PMLA* 102 (1987): 29-41; Mary Beth Rose, *The Expense of Spirit: Love and Sexuality in English Renaissance Drama* (Ithaca: Cornell University Press, 1988), 43-92; and Jean Howard, "Crossdressing, the Theatre, and Gender Struggle in Early Modern England," *Shakespeare Quarterly* 39 (1988): 418-40.

7. *1 Henry VI,* I. ii. 15, in *The Riverside Shakespeare,* ed. G. Blakemore Evans et al. (Boston: Houghton Mifflin, 1974). All subsequent references to this play will be cited in the text.

8. David Bevington, "The Domineering Female in *1 Henry VI,*" *Shakespeare Studies* 2 (1966): 53-54; Coppélia Kahn, *Man's Estate* (Berkeley: University of California Press, 1981), 55.

9. *Hall's Chronicle,* in *Narrative and Dramatic Sources of Shakespeare,* ed. Geoffrey Bullough (London: Routledge and Kegan Paul, 1960), 13: 56-57; *Holinshed's Chronicles, Narrative and Dramatic Sources,* 75.

10. In her discussion of Julia Kristeva, in *Sexual/Textual Politics* (London: Routledge, 1985), Toril Moi makes a point that opens up this linguistic "encounter" between Joan and Charles: "[Non-essentialist feminist analysis of language] posits that we all use the same language but that we have different *interests*—and interests must here be taken to mean political and power-related interests which intersect in the sign. The *meaning* of the sign is thrown open—the sign becomes 'polysemic' rather than 'univocal'—and though it is true to say that the dominant power group at any given time will dominate the intertextual production of meaning, this is not to suggest that the opposition has been reduced to total silence. The power struggle *intersects* in the sign" (158, Moi's emphasis).

11. Simon Shepherd, *Amazons and Warrior Women: Varieties of Feminism in Seventeenth-Century Drama* (New York: St. Martin's Press, 1981), 12.

12. See Bullough, *Narrative,* 3:57 (Hall), and 75-76 (Holinshed).

13. Joan Kelly-Gadol, "Did Women Have a Renaissance?" in *Becoming Visible: Women in European History,* ed. Renate Bridenthal and Claudia Koonz (Boston: Houghton-Mifflin, 1977), 159.

14. In *Wooing, Wedding and Power* (New York: Columbia University Press, 1981), Irene G. Dash makes exactly this point in her chapter on the women characters in the first tetralogy (155-207). However, because Dash focuses on the interrelationships among women, she leaves Joan out of her discussion.

15. In Christopher Marlowe's *Edward II,* a similar scene is played out between Mortimer and Isabella early in the play. In this scene, Isabella convinces Mortimer to recall her husband's favorite from exile, apparently by suggesting that he could then be assassinated. While the interchange between Mortimer and Isabella is not heard, unlike the dialogue between Charles and Joan, both inset scenes are interpreted by onlooking French nobles. These scenes are also similar in that the female characters in both plays share a history of negative scholarship, in which these scenes in particular are offered as evidence, scenes in which a woman's actions are interpreted by male onlookers. For a more reasoned analysis of Isabella's motivation in the scene, see T. McAlindon, *English Renaissance Tragedy* (London: Macmillan, 1986), 114-17.

16. However, see Jackson, "Topical," 58, n. 53, for evidence of Joan's occasional representation as heroic during this period.

17. Laura Mulvey, "Visual Pleasure and Narrative Cinema," *Screen* 16 (1975): 11.

18. This power of verbal construction supports Rackin's argument, in "Anti-Historians: Women's Roles in Shakespeare's Histories," *Theatre Journal* 37 (1985),

that the "masculine voice of history" clashes with feminine subversion in the history plays, and that in *1 Henry VI* in particular, "the contest [is] between English words and French things, between the historical record that Talbot wishes to preserve and the physical reality that Joan invokes to discredit it" (329, 331).

19. Howard, recalling Annette Kuhn's discussion of sexual disguise in film, reminds us that "in certain circumstances crossdressing intensifies, rather than blurs, sexual difference" ("Crossdressing," 434).

20. Alice Jardine, *Gynesis: Configurations of Women and Modernity* (Ithaca: Cornell University Press, 1985), 48, 97-102.

21. This point is made by Rackin, "Anti-Historians," 332-33.

Kathryn Schwarz (essay date 1998)

SOURCE: "Fearful Simile: Stealing the Breech in Shakespeare's Chronicle Plays," in *Shakespeare Quarterly,* Vol. 49, No. 2, Summer, 1998, pp. 140-67.

[*In the excerpt below, Schwarz studies the complex portrayal of women in* Henry VI, Parts 1, 2, *and* 3, *focusing on the depiction of Joan as an outsider and as a contradictory embodiment of extremes. Schwarz also analyzes the portrayal of Margaret as both a conventional object of desire and a disruptive role-player.*]

To Be

Henry VI, Part 1 defines Joan with relentless thoroughness as an outsider. Opposed to an English male aristocratic ideal, she is a woman, a peasant, a virgin, a whore, a saint, a witch, an Amazon, and French. Her threatened invasion, while it challenges English idealizations of heroic significance and physical space, could consolidate those ideals; if the English, at the end of *1 Henry VI,* return to a smaller England, they bring with them a clarified sense of what Englishness means. Such a process appears to reiterate a convention of subjectivity, a negotiation of the relationship between familiar and strange that produces identity through difference; the multiplication of Joan's alien identities not only reflects that which is not English but comes, through that opposition, to define Englishness itself. Recognition of Joan, and violent disassociation from her, construct the male heroic subject, or, in Rackin's historiographic terms, male heroic abstractions are opposed to the insistence of female bodies: "[T]he whole issue of physical presence vs. historical record, dramatized in *1 Henry VI* as a conflict between English men and French women, is central, not only to this particular play, but to the history play genre itself."[1] Joan's "femaleness," however theatrically contingent, is an ideologically absolute condition against which the play constructs its privileged terms. *Henry VI, Part 1* stages the processes of deliberately oppositional self-construction, what Butler, in her theory of "sex" as a function of sociality and power, describes as "a repudiation which produces a domain of abjection, a repudiation without which the subject cannot emerge." Butler goes on to argue, "This is a repudiation which creates the valence of 'abjection' and its status for the subject as a threatening spectre."[2] But if Joan is abject and her threatening otherness useful, I would argue that her utility is complicated by the relationship it sets up between who she is and what she does. The play most effectively equates identity to performance in a figure who is neither English nor male nor conventionally heroic; the essentializing rhetoric that surrounds Joan both mirrors and parodies the play's various representations of essential connections between maleness and masculinity, between kingship or heroism and authority. If the play's resolution, defined in terms of nationalism, gender, or individual subjectivity, depends on a return to naturalized causalities, that return is proleptically disrupted in the characterization of Joan herself. The threat posed by Joan is not simply her evident otherness—which might, after all, only tell the hero what he wants to know—but is also the sense in which that otherness produces a more efficient claim to embodied referentiality than that posed by English male heroic authority itself.

The representation of Joan is thus ideologically useful in that it clarifies categorical and hierarchical structures by defining her against them; at the same time, because her role draws together gendered conventions identifying both the powerful and the abject, it might call into question the discretion and the privileged position of defining structures themselves. *Henry VI, Part 1* insists on the verb of equation that links Joan to terms of description: Joan "is" a range of things, contradictory but always extreme, and in the spaces between them domesticity, as a nationalist and ultimately a familial ideology, is constituted. In her first encounter with the Dauphin, Joan offers a challenge and a warning: "My courage try by combat, if thou dar'st, / And thou shalt find that I exceed my sex" (1.2.89-90) [Quotations from the *Henry VI* plays follow *The Complete Works of William Shakespeare,* ed. David Bevington, 4th ed. (New York: Harper Collins, 1992).] That trial prompts the Dauphin's own statement of definition, the implications of which will follow Joan throughout the play. "Stay, stay thy hands! Thou art an Amazon, / And fightest with the sword of Deborah" (ll. 104-5). The Dauphin here conflates what Joan is, what she has, and what she does, suggesting an economy within which signification does not float but remains firmly anchored to the conditions of its production. Joan's body may not display the monomastic utility invoked by "Amazon," but it has been nonetheless modified for her purpose, transformed by her encounter with divine grace. She says, "And, whereas I was black and swart before, / With those clear rays which she infused on me / That beauty am I blessed with which you may see" (ll. 84-86). And her sword, if not actually the sword of Deborah, has been chosen by supernatural intervention, placed in her hands by a force that is not her own. The curious literalism of what should be metaphor gives Joan a singularity of function even as she is doubly read; throughout *1 Henry VI* her identity will be defined by equation, by the rhetoric of "I am" and "you are." "Assigned am I to be the English scourge" (l. 129), she says. For the admirers and the objects of this scourging, its outcome may be differently valued but its processes look much the same.

It is this gap—between the recognized efficiency of Joan's acts and the dispute over their value—that complicates negotiations of relationships among men. True to theatrical form, *1 Henry VI* privileges an almost exclusively homosocial universe; Howard and Rackin characterize the history play as "a specifically masculine genre" and argue that "its masculinity was identified with its function as an ideological apparatus for the construction of an emergent national consciousness."[3] Women in such a context are defined most logically as the matter from which homosocial bonds are built, and this function is as important in the consolidation of hostility as it is in the making of friendship. Figured as individual chivalric conflicts or as wars between nations, battles between men (like alliances) display women as prize, as motive, and as cause. More than anything else, such displays require that the task of defining women in terms of sexual value must rest with men; that value may shift—Helen of Troy may look different to the Trojans than she does to the Greeks—but women themselves are always excluded from its determination. Fighting for or through or because of women gives logic to a male homosocial universe only as long as the place of women themselves remains constant, and in *1 Henry VI* such constancy is an impossible fiction. Rather than being fought for, Joan la Pucelle is fought against, entering into the play's privileged masculine terms through the condition of masculinity itself. The resulting clash of conventions creates a kind of exemplary chaos, in which Joan is defined in terms that variously respond to evidence of her own agency rather than demonstrating the determinative power of men. When the French argue among themselves or with the English over her value, the terms of disagreement suggest that the relationship between her sexual and martial roles upsets the conditions through which the place of women is defined: is she given to the Dauphin as a gift or brought to him as an ally? Is she like the French in fighting for their cause, or are the French and the English, alike in being men, united against her? Are her grounds of battle those of nationalism, chivalric heroism, or some odd, early version of what we might now term women's rights? Responses to the play have suggested that Joan's presence onstage unites the English against the French, the men against the woman, the audience against the French, the audience and the English and arguably the French against Joan;[4] the multiple gestures toward some consolidation of alliances suggest that Joan la Pucelle has anything but a consolidating effect.

The shifting values attached to her produce a constellation of names that trace the failure of consensus: in his introduction to *Saint Joan* George Bernard Shaw writes, "She is the most notable Warrior Saint in the Christian calendar, and the queerest fish among the eccentric worthies of the Middle Ages."[5] The oddity of her iconography inflects Shakespeare's representation as well as those that precede and follow from it. In *1 Henry VI* she is "a holy maid" (1.2.51), "an Amazon" (l. 104), "Pucelle or pussel" (1.4.107), "a witch" (1.5.6), a "high-minded strumpet" (l. 12), "Divinest creature, Astraea's daughter" (1.6.4), "France's saint" (l. 29)—and this is only in Act 1. In the multiplicity of epithets and encomia, Shakespeare echoes his sources; for Hall, in particular, Joan requires an agility of description which, even as it condemns her as "monster" and "orgayne of the deuill," gives rhetorical space to her own claims. Speaking of "[t]his wytch or manly woman, (called the maide of GOD)," Hall ascribes her virginity (if it exists) simultaneously to her "foule face" and to her own agency, making her at once a sign of the depravity that is Frenchness and a deceiver of noble rulers, "wise men," and "lerned clarkes." He writes, "O Lorde, what dispraise is this to the nobilitie of Fraunce: What blotte is this to the Frenche nacion?"[6] The historical fact of Joan disrupts any rhetoric of analogy between Englishmen and Frenchmen; France may, in Hall's reading as in Shakespeare's, be outside whatever is English, but Joan la Pucelle represents a clear threat not only to Englishness but also to anything redeemably male in that which is French. Joan disrupts the rhetoric that connects men to men; and if the French seem willing to privilege her utility over her threat to their own masculinity, it is nonetheless true that even their praise marks her difference. The sense in which that difference both separates her from men and divides men from one another becomes explicit when she persuades Burgundy to abandon the English cause for that of the French. "Done like a Frenchman—[*aside*] turn and turn again!" (3.3.85), she says, and suddenly Burgundy's relationship to national identity, whether French or English, is not connection and self-definition but treason.

"Amazon," perhaps the most imaginatively powerful of Joan's identities, might encompass all of her extremes: a mythological structure that accommodates Penthesilea, chaste hero of Troy, beside the sexually ravenous cannibals of the New World can surely find space for a saint who is also a high-minded strumpet. Indeed, martial chastity and sexual excess are often invoked simultaneously to *define* the Amazon, providing a logic for Joan's doubleness. Gabriele Bernhard Jackson reads such doubleness as the play's insistence on the shiftiness of iconographic value: "In my reading of *1 Henry VI,* the disjunctive presentation of Joan that shows her first as numinous, then as practically and subversively powerful, and finally as feminized and demonized is determined by Shakespeare's progressive exploitation of the varied ideological potential inherent in the topically relevant figure of the virago. . . . At no stage is the allocation of value clearcut."[7] Virgin and whore, saint and witch, ideal and debased, masculine and feminine, Joan makes inevitable the punning paradox of Talbot's "Pucelle or pussel." Readings of her iconography point to anxieties concerning women which range from demonic possession to Catholicism to martial violence to sexual excess to the presence of a queen on the throne; behind each of these readings is the recognition that Joan's conflation of sexual and martial agency, like that represented in stories about Amazons, interrupts the privileged system of homosocial masculinity, rather than being defined by its terms. In the constellation of terms attached to female martiality, the strategies of definition locating women in a particular social place are still in play; but their efficacy comes into question when women can also take the place of men.

Definitions of Joan do not converge even in the name of patriotism; if for Hall and for Holinshed her monstrosity is demonstrably un-English, for other contemporary writers the nationalist distinction is less simple. Agrippa, in *Female Pre-eminence,* writes, "The *English Nation* were most ungratefull, should they ever forget their Obligations to this Sex," but oddly follows this with a brief history of Joan, describing what she has done for the French: "taking *Arms* like an *Amazon,* [she] *arrested* their fortune, put a stop to the *torrent* of their victories, and by degrees restor'd the *withering de Luces* to their former lustre."[8] Christopher Newstead's *Apology for Women* follows Agrippa both in praising Joan and in invoking her in a context that fails to privilege nationalist agendas. He offers an exemplary catalogue of warlike women that places her in the company of Artemesia, Semiramis, Boadicea, and the Amazons of classical mythology.[9] And Thomas Heywood, again like Agrippa, brings her analogically close to Englishness, offering a chapter in his *Gynaikeion* titled "Of English Viragoes. And of *Ioan de Pucil.*"[10] Each of these accounts accepts the militant virginity that *1 Henry VI* places radically in question; each recognizes militance itself as a mode of nationalism not incongruously embodied in women. Still, though, such accounts suggest a certain ambivalence of their own: not everyone would agree with Newstead that Amazons make good exempla; not everyone would wish to return to the female heroic past celebrated by Agrippa, who himself calls Joan a "strange ridling Prodigy";[11] and Heywood mediates his praise of Joan through her claims and those of her chroniclers, giving her history few of his own words and little of his authority. Joan "would report to diuerse" concerning her divine visitation; "The French Chronicles affirme" her acts of heroism; "she was proclaimed a Virago" in a declaration from the pope.[12] Such gestures of ambivalence and mediation show that, while Joan's power to signify goes unchallenged, the question of *what* she signifies remains unclear. Both the accounts that praise her and those that deplore her do so in ways that allow the spectacle of female masculinity to rhetorically displace the importance of national boundaries. In *1 Henry VI,* whatever fighting against Joan does or does not prove about being masculine, it at least demonstrates the fact of being English; but her exemplary function in early modern texts suggests that even this process of consolidation may be obscured by the shifting terms in which she is read.

Rather than continuing to focus on the ways in which accounts of Joan differ, I would like to turn to the sense in which they seem always to produce the same effect. Whether we imagine the grammatical condition of *and* or *or*—whether Joan exists simultaneously through contradictory identities or moves through a range of registers or "is" one thing but is erroneously read as another—the extremes of characterization preclude what is in between. No matter what we accept or reject about her claims of virginity and pregnancy, Joan cannot function conventionally as chaste daughter, generative mother, or nurturing wife; she is dislocated throughout this play from the domestic universe in which the roles played by women materialize the connections among men.[13] Though her virginity is, according to her, absolute, it has no iconographic power to save her; Vives writes, "We haue redde of wome[n], that haue ben taken & let go agayne of the moste vnruly soudyours [soldiers], only for the reuerence of the name of virginitie, bicause they sayde that they were virgins,"[14] but such logic does not work for the soldiers who capture Joan. She has no recognized value on which men can agree; the representational force of her virginity is opposed to, without being mediated by, her own claims to sexuality and the English definition of her as a whore. The categories are less confused than insisted upon as separate but equal. The rhetoric that condemns her, recalling Talbot's pun on her name, reiterates the paradox rather than demanding a single "truth": "Now heaven forfend! The holy maid with child?" (5.4.65); "And yet, forsooth, she is a virgin pure! / Strumpet, thy words condemn thy brat and thee" (ll. 83-84). Joan's death, like her martial success and her iconographic effect, is a result of being at once neither and both. The space *between* virgin and whore, the complicated negotiation that produces the terms of the domestic, is precluded both by what others say about Joan and by what Joan says about herself; her ability to remain so relentlessly *outside,* however broadly the inside is defined, emerges from this sense in which she is never imaginably at home.

This becomes explicit when Joan tries to find some space within the *heimlich;* her final claim to be pregnant is an attempt to become recognizable as a commodity, a woman defined in terms of specific social value. Having witnessed the failure of her insistence on virginity and nobility, Joan performs what readers have always found to be a startling reversal, not only claiming pregnancy but revealing a disconcerting flexibility about the question of paternity. This, I would suggest, is a belated and doomed attempt to enter into the system of male bonds in conventionally feminine terms, to literally embody the condition that connects men to one another; and if her captors do not value the Dauphin's child, Joan is willing to change her story through the invention of a series of fathers until her body performs an acceptable role. But as the play makes clear, the attempt to rewrite this particular body as doing socially conventional work cannot succeed. What is perhaps most interesting here is that the men of the play do not *care* whether Joan's claims are true or false, whether she is indeed the mother of a child and, if so, whose child; in an ideological sense the question is not worth asking, for the literal fact of pregnancy could not, for Joan, be equated with the social value of maternity. Joan is defined by and as the frustration of the bonds that her final narrative attempts to form, and hers is not an identity that can be revised. Like the stories of amazonian maternity narrated by early modern authors, in which Amazons kill, cripple, or enslave their male children or return them to anonymous fathers, Joan's version of maternity cannot be translated into patriarchal terms. Her last desperate claim, and the death that follows, have been read as feminization, putting her body back into a recognizable social place; yet I think that this ending demonstrates more explicitly than any other element of Joan's story that for her such a place does not exist.[15]

Joan's threat to the male homosocial systems of the play rests on this dislocation; her identity as a woman is not socializable, and her martial performance threatens to make conventions of masculinity inscrutable as well. Battling each other, men affirm what masculinity is; battling Joan, whose doubleness is relentlessly legible, they have difficulty knowing what it means. When Bedford asks, "A maid? And be so martial?" he points to the fact that Joan's martial acts do not constitute a transvestite disguise plot; there is no moment of redeeming revelation and refeminization, for the female body is always visibly the referent of masculine acts.[16] "Where is my strength, my valor, and my force?" asks Talbot; "Our English troops retire; I cannot stay them. / A woman clad in armor chaseth them" (1.5.1-3). If Talbot conventionally marks the center of English male chivalric valor, he finds in Joan's female masculinity the potential unwriting of the referential structure that defines him; his statement "I know not where I am nor what I do" (l. 20) suggests that Joan's presence unravels the naturalized connection between masculinity and men. It is not Joan who kills him; indeed, they are not even opposites in the representational logic of *1 Henry VI* but are rather two objects that cannot occupy the same space at the same time. Rackin writes that "Talbot, the English champion, and Joan, his French antagonist, speak alternative languages."[17] When the English scourge speaks her deflating words over the English champion, she proves that he has come too far into her field of discourse.

Readers have theorized Joan's difference in many ways, from the mythological to the sexual to the economic to the theological, but her opposition to the play's martial, male, English center seems clear.[18] Indeed, in recalling her abortive battle with young Talbot, Joan herself sees it as a convention, a set of oppositions always already in quotation marks.

> Once I enountered him, and thus I said:
> "Thou maiden youth, be vanquished by a maid."
> But with a proud, majestical high scorn
> He answered thus: "Young Talbot was not born
> To be the pillage of a giglot wench."
>
> (4.7.37-41)

The maid is opposed to the "giglot wench," the French to the English, the Amazon to the would-be conqueror, the woman to the man. And yet such lines might be obscured by the image of Joan, and the distinction between outside and in threatens at times to disappear entirely; England itself is not safe from the effects of Joan's iconography. Bedford articulates this vulnerability in one of the play's earliest speeches, while the body of Henry V still lies onstage: "Posterity, await for wretched years, / When at their mothers' moistened eyes babes shall suck, / Our isle be made a nourish of salt tears, / And none but women left to wail the dead" (1.1.48-51). England in this image becomes a place of women, a space defined by the loss of men; the land of Amazons is always, such rhetoric implies, closer than you think.

Or perhaps the *heimlich* is simply farther away. The moments at which the terms of the center are threatened suggest less an invasion than a dispersal; Joan la Pucelle, with all the strangeness she signifies, never comes close, but the various elements that converge to produce familiarity can always move apart. Leah Marcus takes this possibility to its logical extreme when she finds in Joan an image of Queen Elizabeth I:

> In *Henry VI, Part 1,* Joan La Pucelle functions in many ways as a distorted image of Queen Elizabeth I. She, like Elizabeth, is a woman who "acts like a man." She collects about her a markedly similar set of idealized symbolic identities. Yet she belongs to the enemy camp. The figure of Joan brings into the open a set of suppressed cultural anxieties about the Virgin Queen, her identity, and her capacity to provide continuing stability for the nation.[19]

If Joan looks like Elizabeth, if Elizabeth looks like Joan, this is not a domestication of the strange but an estrangement of the domestic; the metonymies that lead from queen to biblical heroine to classical goddess should never be pursued to the borders occupied by devils and witches and whores. Understood in the terms that define Joan la Pucelle, Queen Elizabeth I would figure a revision of royal iconography in which the sovereign, rather than embodying the bond that draws men together, makes monstrous the hierarchical connection of monarch to male subject and thus disrupts the lateral connections that define unified male subjectivity itself. Such disruption, *1 Henry VI* suggests, is the danger posed by female martiality; in the set of associations traced by Marcus, that danger is unimaginably escalated in the figure of a martial female queen.

Henry VI, Part 1 ultimately resists the identification of Queen Elizabeth with Joan, or at least distorts the mirror image to the point of unrecognizability; there remains a powerful impulse to keep the figure of Joan la Pucelle outside the terms of the familiar. It is an impulse that has driven readings not only of dramatic structure but of canon: if Joan is definitively not English and in some sense not French, she is also sometimes not Shakespeare's. Tillyard, in *Shakespeare's History Plays,* describes this argument as he dismisses it:

> Apart from the queer reluctance to allow Shakespeare to have written ill or like other dramatists when he was

> immature, the chief reason why people have been hostile to Shakespeare's authorship [of *1 Henry VI*] is the way he treats Joan of Arc. That the gentle Shakespeare could have been so ungentlemanly as to make his Joan other than a saint was intolerable. This is precisely like arguing that Shakespeare could not have written *King John* because he does not mention Magna Carta.[20]

Not, perhaps, precisely. The gesture that defines Joan la Pucelle as "not Shakespeare's" is not merely a defense of chivalry or good historicism but a symptomatic reproduction of the play's own logic, logic that identifies the familiar through the power of the contrary example: if idealized Englishness is constructed against France's Joan, then the idealized Shakespeare, in controversies over the authorship of this play, has been constructed against a Joan who belongs to someone else entirely. By this logic, to allow Joan into the canon is to endanger the most important bond of all—that which links Shakespeare to his readers and thus to the "Shakespearean." In metatextual negotiations, as with those that take place onstage, the terms in which Joan is defined suggest the fragility of privileged systems of connection.

To Have

Possession may, as Lacan asserts, always be an illusion; it is also, however, a way of articulating the relationship between agency and desire that structures the representation of women in *Henry VI, Part 2.* As York speaks his last line to Joan—"Curse, miscreant, when thou com'st to the stake" (*1HVI,* 5.3.44)—the statement of finality, punctuated by the stage direction "*Exeunt,*" is immediately undermined by another stage direction: "*Enter Suffolk, with Margaret in his hand.*" For Joan, being a Frenchwoman in the hands of the English is an experience of violence that demonizes sex; for Margaret, literally in the hand of Suffolk and metonymically in the hands of the king, the position is more conventionally eroticized, her body defined as a commodity well worth the effort expended to acquire it. "She's beautiful, and therefore to be wooed; / She is a woman, therefore to be won," says Suffolk (ll. 78-79); and where Joan's beauty had been, like her sword, a weapon divinely bestowed, Margaret's is read as a commodity adding to her value and lending agency to the men who look at her. Immediately recognizable as an object of desire, Margaret is given a version of power which, like the power of all Petrarchan objects, returns itself to the man disempowered by her beauty. "Fie, de la Pole, disable not thyself," Suffolk says,

> Hast not a tongue? Is she not here?
> Wilt thou be daunted at a woman's sight?
> Ay, beauty's princely majesty is such
> Confounds the tongue and makes the senses rough.
>
> (ll. 67-71)

The hint that Margaret might possess the power to disable men—a hint to which the play will come back with, quite literally, a vengeance—is here transformed into a conventionally self-authored loss of speech analogous to that suffered by Sidney's Astrophil.[21]

The tropes that link sexual and political economies define Margaret's place onstage, making her at once a prize of war and a prisoner of love. "To be a queen in bondage is more vile / Than is a slave in base servility, / For princes should be free," she tells Suffolk, and he replies, "And so shall you, / If happy England's royal king be free" (ll. 112-15). The equation of sovereign privilege and erotic power will return to haunt the men who desire Margaret; for the moment, though, such shifts in agency and literalization are remote, and Suffolk constructs success from the familiar materials of Petrarchan language.

> Solicit Henry with her wondrous praise;
> Bethink thee on her virtues that surmount,
> And natural graces that extinguish art;
> Repeat their semblance often on the seas,
> That, when thou com'st to kneel at Henry's feet,
> Thou mayest bereave him of his wits with wonder.
>
> (ll. 190-95)

Agreeing to function as the connection between men, Margaret enables Suffolk to conquer his king, bringing Henry not only to desire but to dependence: "So am I driven by breath of her renown / Either to suffer shipwreck or arrive / Where I may have fruition of her love" (5.5.7-9). And yet, we should perhaps remember, triangles work in a number of directions; if Suffolk reads Margaret as a mediating term, for Margaret herself Suffolk mediates effectively—and briefly—between a position of disadvantage and one of extraordinary power. Margaret's body does not long remain a passive text, and Shakespeare's own text is governed less by Petrarchan conventions of desire than by the anxieties of a more material fragmentation. *Henry VI, Part 2* stages the shift from "Queen Margaret, England's happiness!" to the "blood-bespotted Neapolitan, / Outcast of Naples, England's bloody scourge!" of York's accusation (1.1.37; 5.1.117-18). Margaret, aggressively conventionalized as the matter of male bonds, becomes instead the cause of their most radical dissolution, precipitating the representational violence not of sonnets but of civil war.

Echoes of a familiar rhetoric attach themselves to Margaret long before York's reinvocation of the English scourge. "Such commendations as becomes a maid, / A virgin, and his servant, say to him," she instructs Suffolk at the end of *1 Henry VI* (5.3.177-78), immediately recalling that other maid who has scarcely left the stage.[22] But if Margaret's body—female, French, desirable, and of dubious lineage—recalls Joan la Pucelle, her performance is markedly different. She moves inward as decisively as Joan remains outside, her body focusing projections of the future as the body of Henry V had summoned nostalgia for the past. "Her valiant courage and undaunted spirit, / More than in women commonly is seen, / Will answer our hope in issue of a king" (*1HVI,* 5.5.70-72). Even here, in Suffolk's early words, Margaret is already both in and curiously out of place, her courage and spirit analogous to the conquests of Henry V, while Henry VI stands in a mediated relationship to both: "For Henry, son unto a conqueror, / Is likely to beget more conquerors, / If with a lady of so high resolve / As is fair Margaret he be linked in love" (ll. 73-76). The dynamics of this triangle, from the perspective of the living English male sovereign authority, have already gone wrong, as will those of the triangle formed by Margaret, Suffolk, and Henry VI. "She should have stayed in France and starved in France" (*2HVI,* 1.1.133), Gloucester says, but such literal marginalization, like the categoric strategy on which it relies, does not work for Margaret as it did for Joan. Identified as mother, queen, and wife, Margaret embodies a range of conventionally feminine obligations and transgressions that locate her in the midst of English nationalist negotiations, not despite but because of their aggressively domestic terms.

It is important to note that the disruptive effect of women in this play stems not from any rebellion against convention but from full participation in it. The Margaret of *2 Henry VI* plays out a woman's part: if the first play of this tetralogy presents the materiality of Joan's body iconographically, the second defines Margaret's body in terms of its utility, representing her first as an object and finally as an agent of acquisition. That shift in agency structures Margaret's appearances in the play, as the qualities that make her desirable to Suffolk and to Henry become the means through which she herself claims the agency of desire. Imagined as a royal accessory, she is acquired at a cost, gaining control of the English succession even as England loses control of France. The marriage, which Henry reads as a triumph of desire and Suffolk as a strategic climax, is for Margaret only the beginning. "Margaret shall now be Queen and rule the King; / But I will rule both her, the King, and realm" (5.5.107-8), Suffolk says at the end of *1 Henry VI.* It is a prophecy perhaps best answered by a stage direction from *2 Henry VI* that uncannily parallels Suffolk's entrance "*with Margaret in his hand*": "*Enter the King with a supplication, and the Queen with Suffolk's head . . .*" (4.4, s.d.).

And *why,* we might briefly pause to wonder, is she carrying his head? Margaret does not directly cause Suffolk's death. But as she walks onstage, she has an odd effect on the doubled convention, erotic and political, of fragmentation-as-synthesis: the metaphor that presents the ruler as the head of the body politic, like the Petrarchan tropes that dissect the body of the mistress for the pleasure of other men, is displaced by this economy in which bodies, *men's* bodies, literally come apart. Margaret's mourning takes a darkly comic form—"Here may his head lie on my throbbing breast, / But where's the body that I should embrace?" (ll. 5-6)—as it materializes Suffolk's earlier conceit:

> If I depart from thee, I cannot live,
> And in thy sight to die, what were it else
> But like a pleasant slumber in thy lap?
> Here could I breathe my soul into the air,
> As mild and gentle as the cradle babe
> Dying with mother's dug between its lips. . . .
>
> (3.2.388-93)

"Leaving you would kill me," the Petrarchan lover routinely tells his mistress, claiming her through her claim on him; but the dynamics of power look rather different if he is right. Objectified in such conventional terms, Margaret figures the ways in which conventions themselves might go wrong, reentering the representational space of *2 Henry VI* with the fragmented body of her object of desire.[23] And Suffolk's death marks the first explicit displacement of King Henry as well: "His body will I bear unto the King. / If he revenge it not, yet will his friends; / So will the Queen, that living held him dear," says the courtier who picks up the pieces (4.1.146-48). Imported to connect Suffolk to his king, Margaret transforms that connection into an image of violence and loss; in Margaret, Henry gets rather more than Suffolk had bargained for.

"These are no women's matters" (1.3.117), Gloucester tells the queen as dissent threatens England, but the fragmentation central to *2 Henry VI* is precipitated first by male attempts to acquire Margaret and finally by Margaret's own strategies of acquisition, transforming passion into action, an object to an agent within explicitly feminine conditions of performance. Margaret effects disruption through adultery, envy, lust, shrewishness, extravagance, and conceit, her excesses conventionalized even as they are held responsible for the increasingly precarious state of England. Gloucester's wife Eleanor, who, like her husband, will fall victim to Margaret's revenge, recognizes her power of categorical upset, telling Henry: "Look to't in time. / She'll hamper thee and dandle thee like a baby. / Though in this place most master wear no breeches, / She shall not strike Dame Eleanor unrevenged" (ll. 144-47). But again, as in the Petrarchan fantasies of Suffolk and of King Henry himself, reading Margaret proves a dangerous business. The structures of power may be clear, but positions within them shift without warning; and Eleanor finds herself the object rather than the agent of revenge.

> Not all these lords do vex me half so much
> As that proud dame, the Lord Protector's wife.
> She sweeps it through the court with troops of ladies,
> More like an empress than Duke Humphrey's wife.
> Strangers in court do take her for the Queen.
>
> (ll. 75-79)

No one in Queen Margaret's court should look too much like Queen Margaret. But this is not the "Captain Margaret" of *3 Henry VI,* who emasculates her husband by taking command of his armies; this is instead a figure of specifically feminine pique, whose physical violence is limited to the stage direction "*She gives the Duchess a box on the ear*" (*2HVI,* 1.3.138, s.d.).

Margaret, in short, is dangerous in this play *because* she is conventional, because desire for her makes her husband an effeminate cuckold and because her own feminine vanity makes her a formidable political conspirator. The synthesis of desirability and agency disrupts the hierarchical relationship between homosocial privilege and the heterosexuality through which it is reproduced; Henry's marriage guarantees not the promised continuity of father and son but the intervention of women in the negotiations among men. Thus Gloucester falls as a consequence of both Margaret's ambition and his own conjugal indulgence, much as Henry falls to his own desire, for in the world of this play, men are victimized by Margaret's performance of femininity as effectively as York will be by her sword. Coppélia Kahn has argued that, in history plays, "liaisons with women are invariably disastrous because they subvert or destroy more valued alliances between men."[24] Such an effect, naturalized through repetition in the *Henry VI* plays, is in fact distinctly *un*-natural; it suggests that heterosexuality, rather than playing its proper part in the perpetuation of male homosocial systems of power, violates the hierarchical relationship on which that power is based, invading rather than delineating the space between men. Instead of the logic that draws men together through the processes of evaluation and exchange, these plays offer an alternative logic in which female agency disrupts male control over the significance of conventional roles. The terms of the *heimlich,* of domestic convention itself, thus become signs of disjunction rather than consolidation; in *2 Henry VI* the enemy is at home, and Henry's marriage, which Joyce Green MacDonald calls "a marriage contradicting in every particular the patriarchal mandate for the union of a prince," systematically strips him of the conditions of agency which, for the space of *3 Henry VI,* Margaret will take on.[25]

Henry's marriage to Margaret does not merely unman him but places him in a distinctly precarious relationship to the crown; echoing the chronicles, Gloucester holds that union responsible for the fragmentation of England itself.

> O peers of England, shameful is this league!
> Fatal this marriage, canceling your fame,
> Blotting your names from books of memory,
> Razing the characters of your renown,
> Defacing monuments of conquered France,
> Undoing all, as all had never been!
>
> (1.1.96-101)

Margaret erases the glory of England as Joan la Pucelle had deflated posthumous Talbot's catalogue of glory—"Him that thou magnifi'st with all these titles / Stinking and fly-blown lies here at our feet" (4.7.75-76)—but here what Rackin has described as women's "anti-historical" effect is generated and articulated from within. Both Joan and Margaret threaten to obscure the terms through which men recognize one another and thus identify themselves, but in *2 Henry VI* history is obscured not by a battle but by a marriage. "My wife was wise and good had she bene rightly sought, / But our vnlawful getting it, may make a good thing nought," Henry says in *The Mirror for Magistrates.*[26] In *2 Henry VI,* Margaret, the "thing" to be "got," recoils upon the getter, turning the structures of acquisition and desire into her own narrative tools. Wanting to be queen, she marries Henry; wanting to be first in importance, she ousts Gloucester; simply, apparently, wanting, she acquires Suffolk, in whole and then in part. There is an insistently conventional femininity not only in the nature of these transgressions but in Margaret's mediated participation in them: as a desiring subject, she works indirectly, appropriating to her uses the structures and the desires of men. If Joan la Pucelle might consolidate an English male aristocratic ideal through opposition, Queen Margaret gets under its skin.

Domesticity, in this context, fails to reassure; there is no space, literal or mythological, between Margaret and England as there is between England and Joan, and Margaret's implication in nationalist and familial tropes fragments the political state even as she appropriates the rhetoric of statecraft. Margaret's presence is inescapably quotidian: where Joan's iconographic identities exist in synchronic contradiction, Margaret's have a diachronic utility. Chastity makes her a wife, sexuality makes her a queen, maternity makes her the mother of a prince, and, in *3 Henry VI,* martiality will make her an effective king. Because her roles begin in femininity and persist into usurpation, Margaret is difficult to put in her place; even Heywood, who places her among his "English Viragoes," prefers to say as little as possible, stating only that iconographic rhetoric lacks words to contain her.

> Of queene *Margaret* the wife of *Henrie* the sixt, her courage, resolution, and magnanimitie, to speake at large, would askc a Volumc rather than a compendious discourse, to which I am strictly tyed. And therefore whosoever is desirous to be further instructed in the successe of those many battailes fought against the house of Yorke, in which she was personally present, I referre them to our English Chronicles, that are not sparing in commending her more than womanish spirit, to euerlasting memorie.[27]

As Heywood's catalogue of exempla directs the reader to the chronicles, diachronic action again displaces synchronic definition; Margaret must be read less according to what she is than to what she does. The privileging of action—or, in the context of Shakespeare's plays, of acting—is implicit in Margaret's adroit deployment of femininity in the second part of *Henry VI;* it will emerge fully in the aggressive seemings of the third.

To Seem

As *3 Henry VI* begins, Margaret no longer stands in a mediated relationship to sovereign power. The king has become "Base, fearful, and despairing Henry!" (1.1.178), and Margaret claims the space of government. The claim, again, is based on an invasion that has already taken place. When Henry, yielding to York, disinherits his own son, Margaret first desires to disclaim her relationship to national and familial domesticity altogether: "Ah, wretched man! Would I had died a maid / And never seen thee, never borne thee son, / Seeing thou hast proved so unnatural a father!" (ll. 216-18). Margaret here wishes herself back in the position of Joan, the maid opposed to rather than implicated in the political and erotic terms of Englishness. But if for Joan that distance is always potentially an illusion, for Margaret it is not even that. Playing the roles of mother and wife, she chastises Henry for his own more tenuous connection to their son and by extension to kingship itself:

> Hadst thou but loved him half so well as I,
> Or felt that pain which I did for him once,
> Or nourished him as I did with my blood,
> Thou wouldst have left thy dearest heart-blood there,
> Rather than have made that savage duke thine heir
> And disinherited thine only son.
>
> (ll. 220-25)

Constructing a causal relationship between maternity and good sovereignty, Margaret excludes the king, displacing him simultaneously in marital and martial terms: "I here divorce myself / Both from thy table, Henry, and thy bed. . . . The northern lords that have forsworn thy colors / Will follow mine, if once they see them spread" (ll. 247-48, 251-52). If generative heterosexuality identifies Margaret as the means through which Henry is connected to and reproduced in his son, here the means becomes an end; Margaret's declaration of agency, rather than her passively maternal body, reasserts the identity of Prince Edward as that identity is threatened by the king's paternal failure. Her martiality does not replace the conventional femininity of maternal obligation but emerges from it; with her claim to Henry's armies, Margaret makes violence itself domestic. Henry articulates the causality: "Poor Queen! How love to me and to her son / Hath made her break out into terms of rage!" (ll. 264-65), he says, revealing the sense in which the conventionalized femininity of *2 Henry VI* leads inexorably to the "ruthless queen" of *Part 3.* Margaret seems always to be between men in these plays, but as she shifts her investment from Suffolk to Henry, from Henry to his son, the dynamics of power implicit in that position become distinctly double-edged.

For the chroniclers Henry is "a ruler not Ruling," and Margaret, in consequence, becomes "quene Margarete his wyfe, in whom the whole rule of the realme consisted"; "The Quene, which bare the rule"; "the Quene, whiche then ruled the rost and bare the whole rule"; "Quene Margarete, whose breath ruled."[28] In such accounts Margaret's agency, however aggressively defined, results from the king's abdication; Hall writes, "[T]he Quene encouraged her frendes, and promised great rewardes to her helpers: for the kyng studied nothing but of peace, quyet and solitarie life."[29] Because there is no king, there must be Queen Margaret. Howard and Rackin suggest that this causality structures *3 Henry VI:* "Margaret's prominence in the action immediately suggests a weakness in the patriarchal structures that should have rendered her less visible and less powerful"; they conclude, "The scandal of *Henry VI, Part III* is not that a woman is a general, but that a man, and an anointed king to boot, can perform none of the actions expected of a father and a king."[30] But I think that for Shakespeare the construction of Queen Margaret is a more deliberate process: as it conflates claims to maternal and martial agency, her statement "I here divorce myself" takes on the force of a speech act, creating a role that exceeds the space left empty by the king. Accused of playing the Amazon, Queen Margaret figures an agency that is constructed without being contingent. Within the terms of amazonian logic, women may assume power through the absence of men, but in so doing, they alter the conditions of power itself, making it difficult if not impossible for the conventional relationships between agency and maleness to return. As she brings the spectacle of female martiality into England and into the play's national and familial structures, Margaret appropriates a kind of editorial control over what the roles of king and queen, husband and wife, man and woman can be understood to *mean,* closing down the imaginative possibility of a naturalized reinscription of hierarchy. The terms through which Margaret becomes amazonian are those of recognizing something already in place, not of discovering something new. Conventional domesticity does not provide a space of safety in *3 Henry VI,* for both Margaret's rhetoric and that which describes her suggest that martial women are not born but can be made.

"I would Your Highness would depart the field. / The Queen hath best success when you are absent," Clifford tells Henry, and Margaret adds, "Ay, good my lord, and leave us to our fortune" (2.2.73-75). This differs subtly but significantly from the account given by the chronicles, in which Margaret's success contextualizes Henry's failure: "Happy was the quene in her two battayls, but vnfortunate was the kyng in all his enterprises, for where his person was presente, ther victory fled euer from him to the other parte, & he commonly was subdued & vanqueshed."[31] In *3 Henry VI* Margaret's possessive—*our* fortune—exiles Henry from the condition of England; he does not lose the battle so much as vanish from its terms of representation, as when his son tells him, "When I return with victory from the field, / I'll see Your Grace. Till then I'll follow her" (1.1.261-62). The dyad of mother and son, like that of sovereign and subjects, excludes the king, for the Margaret of *3 Henry VI* is no longer constructed through triangles. Her roles draw substance from familial and political connections, but her relationship to agency is not contingent on third terms. Having consolidated the functions of domesticity, Margaret makes maternal and national obligation the same thing: to fight for her son is to fight for the integrity of England itself. "A woman's general. What should we fear?" Richard asks; but in the world of *3 Henry VI,* in which Margaret's synthesis of martiality and maternity intervenes in the connections and actions conventionally reserved for men, his question contains a differently self-evident answer than he imagines.

Where Joan la Pucelle embodies contradictory iconographic positions by literalizing a series of tropes, Margaret consolidates contradiction through the explicitness of playing, her masculine performance inseparable from the fictional female body she presents onstage. For Margaret's role-playing, even when referred to what seem the most essential of causes, is relentlessly performative; having appropriated the terms of Englishness, she disrupts them through a theatrical presence that confounds materiality and illusion. Butler writes, "[T]he regulatory norms of 'sex' work in a performative fashion to constitute the materiality of bodies and, more specifically, to materialize the body's sex, to materialize sexual difference in the service of the consolidation of the heterosexual imperative. . . . what constitutes the fixity of the body, its contours, its movements, will be fully material, but materiality will be re-thought as the effect of power."[32] On the early modern stage such apparently counterintuitive causalities of embodiment reflect dramatic necessity, and for history plays the relationship between performative agency and political power poses questions that are particularly acute. For *3 Henry VI* those questions are at once focused and redoubled as the concerns of politics and sex converge in Queen Margaret. The connections among power, performance, and heterosexual imperatives produce a female sexual body that is not only a theatrical but a political intervention. And if, as Butler suggests, heterosexual sociality constructs and makes use of certain kinds of bodies, the manifestly constructed body of Margaret makes effective use of heterosexual sociality itself. A boy-actor in a woman's part, a Frenchwoman who becomes England's queen, a queen who acts as a king, a mother who defends the patrilineal rights of her son by standing in a father's place, Shakespeare's Queen Margaret constructs agency through a revision of the relationship of bodies to acts and of women to the systematic conventions of masculine identity.

Because these plays attempt to identify the center against what it is not—or, in the case of Queen Margaret, what it should not be—the space of English male subjectivity is defined by the performances of women. And, with Margaret's various deployments of domesticity, that space becomes ever more claustrophobic. As I have suggested, her domestic sphere is national as well as familial, a conflation that inflects the play more generally. Thus, having captured York, Margaret brings home the frustration of his political ambition through a death in the family: "Look, York, I stained this napkin with the blood / That valiant Clifford, with his rapier's point, / Made issue from the bosom of the boy" (1.4.79-81). Rutland's death, which is for Margaret a logical consequence of this kind of war, represents for his father a monstrous crossing of lines:

> O tiger's heart wrapped in a woman's hide!
> How couldst thou drain the lifeblood of the child,
> To bid the father wipe his eyes withal,
> And yet be seen to bear a woman's face?
> Women are soft, mild, pitiful, and flexible;
> Thou stern, obdurate, flinty, rough, remorseless.
>
> (ll. 137-42)

York here attempts to re-separate, to oppose "women" to "Margaret" and prove through her acts that she is not one; calling on conventions of femininity, he rhetorically returns women to their place. Yet Margaret's performance disrupts the masculine structures that give such conventions authority, denaturalizing the distinctions on which York insists; and even his own language mirrors Margaret's privileging of playing, of seeming over being seen to be. The verb of equation linking Margaret to the qualities she does or does not possess connects her to adjectives rather than to nouns; where Joan is Amazon, witch, strumpet, scourge, Margaret is stern, obdurate, flinty, rough, remorseless. Margaret does not *seem as, act as* she should, and York's metaphor of the "tiger's heart wrapped in a woman's hide," figuring the female body as a costume, implicates sexual essentialism itself in the rhetoric of performance.

According to York, Margaret epitomizes all that women and queens should not be: "But that thy face is, vizardlike, unchanging, / Made impudent with use of evil deeds, / I would assay, proud queen, to make thee blush" (ll. 116-18). According to early modern monitory texts, however, she acts precisely as women and queens always threaten to do; *The English Gentlewoman,* for example, describes predictable disillusion rather than monstrous wonders but echoes York's rhetoric closely nonetheless. "What prodegy fuller of wonder, then to see a woman thus transformed from nature?" Brathwait writes. "Her *face* is not her owne, note her *complexion;* her *eye* is not her owne, note her *straid motion;* her *habit* is not her owne, eye her *strange fashion.* Whilest *loose weares* imply *light workes;* and thin cobwebbe couers promise free admittance to all sensuall louers."[33] In such clichés, as in Shakespeare's first Henriad, female excess, inherently theatrical, is at once a snare for men and an appropriation of apparent maleness. Cosmetics and clothes produce a strangely masculine monster, and exposure of the essential woman holds as many unpleasant surprises as does the armor of feminine convention. Joan Riviere refers to "the conception of womanliness as a mask, behind which man suspects some hidden danger."[34] In *3 Henry VI* the danger is doubled: to interrogate one masquerade is to be confronted by another, and any attempt to see *either* the woman *or* the warrior results only in the reminder that Margaret, at any given moment, quite efficiently seems to be both. "Tell him my mourning weeds are laid aside / And I am ready to put armor on" (3.3.229-30), she says in response to Edward's challenge; her response, like Joan's encounter with young Talbot, is later mediated by quotation marks. The Post relays the message—"'Tell him,' quoth she, 'my mourning weeds are done, / And I am ready to put armor on'"—to which Edward replies, "Belike she minds to play the Amazon" (4.1.104-6).

The anxiety produced by such playing emerges fully in the only simile of York's great speech: "How ill-beseeming is it in thy sex / To triumph, like an Amazonian trull / Upon their woes whom fortune captivates!" (1.4.113-15). The term that finds a logical referent in Joan la Pucelle is attached only fearfully and contingently—"*like* an Amazonian trull"—to England's queen. If Margaret is "Amazonian," the adjective attaches itself uneasily; for if she marks the space "beyond"—beyond Englishness, maleness, a constant and referential understanding of power—she does so from so far inside the structures defining those terms that it is not clear where the English male aristocratic hero can safely go. "[Y]ou are more inhuman, more inexorable, / O, ten times more, than tigers of Hyrcania. / See, ruthless Queen, a hapless father's tears!" says York (ll. 154-56); the "inhumanity" of Margaret's performance lies in its exposure of the transgressive potential of women's roles, its playing out of the anxious possibility of literalization. Margaret gives York the blood of his son, identifying it by defining the paternal connection that he cannot recognize without her help. Metaphorically articulated, such an act precisely enables male bonding, using women to materialize fantasies of parthenogenesis. Literalizing the rhetoric of those fantasies in an act of violence, Margaret dismantles patrilineal systems of connection.

This is the threat posed by the amazonian in *3 Henry VI:* the play does not attack the conventions that define women's roles but performs them, demonstrating their vulnerability to revision from within. Margaret's transgressions gain force from their revelation that the logic of transgression is already in place, for in fact the terms of seeming—or, to take up York's term, ill-beseeming—that attend Margaret's performance are not alien but familiar. As John Knox's rhetoric in *The First Blast* suggests, female dominance might always shift from the political to the personal and back again; Knox's notorious observation that those seeing England under female rule "should judge the whole world to be transformed into Amazons" is followed by a detailed discussion of the Amazon at home.

> To the further declaration of the imperfections of women, of their natural weakness and inordinate appetites, I might adduce histories proving some women to have died for sudden joy, some for unpatience to have murdered themselves; some to have burned with such inordinate lust that, for the quenching of the same, they have betrayed to strangers their country and city; and some to have been so desirous of dominion that, for the obtaining of the same, they have murdered the children of their own sons. Yea, and some have killed with cruelty their own husbands and children.[35]

Women, Knox argues, are always potentially excessive, always potentially amazonian: women make bad enemies; women will betray their countries; women will become dangerous within the family, killing their children and their men. The Margaret of *3 Henry VI* emerges from this tradition of anxious polemics, in which the amazonian is linked to the domestic through terms of violence. The most logical victims of that violence are the husbands and children whose identity conventional femininity should work to mediate and define.

As Margaret's first victim, King Henry VI is identified in terms of his vulnerability to revision; in Warwick's words,

> The proud insulting Queen,
> With Clifford and the haught Northumberland,
> And of their feather many more proud birds,
> Have wrought the easy-melting King like wax.
>
> (2.1.168-71)

Describing himself as "the hapless male to one sweet bird" (5.6.15), Henry can be understood only in relation to the desires and intentions of his wife. Conquering her husband erotically and aesthetically, Margaret literalizes the fantasy of female power articulated by Suffolk and by Henry himself in conventionally Petrarchan terms; the revelation of *3 Henry VI* is that Petrarchan fictions have real consequences, leading as naturally to "Captain Margaret" as they do to the rhetoric of desire.[36] And Warwick, describing Henry as "My sovereign, with the loving citizens, / Like to his island girt in with the ocean, / Or modest Dian circled with her nymphs" (4.8.19-21), suggests that a woman who appropriates the power ascribed to her by the language of courtship does so at the expense of men. Explicitly feminized, aestheticized, and made chaste, a Diana more modest than martial, Henry himself becomes a Petrarchan object, protected from the obligations of maleness and of kingship. As Diodorus writes of the Amazons, "Theire husbondes stonde in like condition as women and wives doo among vs in oure contrey, ordeyned of purpose to kepe the house at home, to be buxom and obedient vnto theire wives, clerely discharged from all maner of warre, beryng no rome nor office of worship in theire contrey."[37]

Richard wishes of Margaret "That you might still have worn the petticoat, / And ne'er have stol'n the breech from Lancaster" (5.5.23-24), but King Henry, mediating between memories of his father and hopes for his son, is always contingent—the significance of his death divided between foreshadowing and afterthought, the death itself a virtual aside. Prince Edward, too, represents a presence substantiated only through nostalgia and anticipation. Thus Oxford says of him, "O brave young prince! Thy famous grandfather / Doth live again in thee: long mayst thou live / To bear his image and renew his glories" (5.4.50-54). But for Prince Edward, as for his father, the connection to Henry V is displaced, his past and future defined and circumscribed by a body that is still onstage. Howard and Rackin argue that "the play also demystifies the idea that patriarchal blood lines, even ones unadulterated by bastardy, guarantee the valor or worth of the father's descendants. . . . Edward claims the throne in his father's name, but he does so in his mother's spirit."[38] Edward—the other Edward—calls Margaret "You, that are King, though he do wear the crown," and the crown prince is most recognizably his mother's son. In Richard's words, "Whoever got thee, there thy mother stands; / For well I wot thou hast thy mother's tongue" (2.2.90, 133-34).

The multiple representations of Margaret turn against her son even as they are turned to his cause; her role-playing itself precludes the return of kingship to any uncontested state. When Prince Edward appropriates the rhetoric of sovereignty, he does so through an essentialist logic that is newly fragile, his contested position as male heir figuring the play's detachment of referentiality from men. In response to Warwick's "Injurious Margaret!" Prince Edward asks, "And why not Queen?" Warwick's reply reveals that such signifiers are not firmly fixed: "Because thy father Henry did usurp; / And thou no more art Prince than she is Queen" (3.3.78-80). Relying on primogeniture, Prince Edward is vulnerable to the failure of that term; and his connection to Henry V, like his father's, is ultimately a false trail, or at least one obscured by Margaret's intervention. The impossibility in this play of returning to an unproblematic condition of patrilineal logic results directly from her attempt to stage-manage such a return. When women cease to be objects proving a connection among men and become instead agents attempting to impose it, the register of the connection necessarily shifts from the natural to the constructed. This is the lesson that Prince Edward does not learn; where Margaret inverts sovereignty through a consolidation of roles, her son reads it as self-evident. And, in *3 Henry VI,* in the newly formed court of the rival King Edward IV, he reads it wrongly. His body recalls not a heroic past but the presence of his mother, and the terms of his death—Edward's "Take that, thou likeness of this railer here"—insist that his mother's body signifies as his father's name does not. This is a mirror game not between two King Edwards but between mother and son, and it is distinctly unhealthy to be the son of an Amazon.[39]

Margaret's rhetoric of mourning is at once conventionally maternal and a sharp reminder of another, earlier moment of violence. Comparing her son's death to that of Caesar, she says, "He was a man; this (in respect) a child, / And men ne'er spend their fury on a child" (5.5.51-57). Men may not; Margaret already has. And the death of Rutland reappears, not only as a linguistic ghost in a metatheatrical revenge plot but as a reminder that, through Margaret, domestic violence connects the fragmentation of families to that of England itself. *Henry VI, Part 3* does not present a dynamic in which essentialized femininity gives way to martial agency only to collapse back into maternal helplessness. Instead, the conditions of martiality are always those of maternity, and the female body is itself staged as performance.[40] Grieving mother, like grieving wife, is a role, neither more nor less genuine than the condition of being beautiful or amazonian or tiger-like. "Here sheathe thy sword. I'll pardon thee my death" (l. 70), Margaret tells her tormentors. Even physical vulnerability is a trope, a reminder of the fact that both rape and death here operate at the level of metaphor and that such metaphorical swords always cut both ways.

As it makes visible the constructedness of dramatic conventions and gender roles, Margaret's amazonian performance precipitates the disjoining of men from one another and from any essentialized condition of masculinity. By the play's conclusion, her presence seems necessary for masculinity to be connected to men at all. Before the final battle, it is not Prince Edward's presence or the king's name but Margaret's rhetoric that clothes men in the performativity of heroism, as the prince himself observes: "Methinks a woman of this valiant spirit / Should, if a coward heard her speak these words, / Infuse his breast with magnanimity, / And make him, naked, foil a man at arms" (5.4.39-42). This is only a local example of Margaret's larger implication in the structures of violence; from the beginning the play is explicit about her responsibility not only for individual performances of masculine martiality but for martial conflict itself. According to Edward, duke of York, it is her role-playing that brings England to irrecoverable self-fragmentation: "For what hath broached this tumult but thy pride? / Hadst thou been meek, our title still had slept; / And we, in pity of the gentle King, / Had slipped our claim until another age" (2.2.159-62). Having brought England to civil war, Margaret bears a responsibility that is theatrical as well as political and identifies her as the cause of the play: "Hadst thou been meek, our title still had slept"—or, in Edward's final condemnation, "No, wrangling woman, we'll no longer stay. / These words will cost ten thousand lives this day" (ll. 176-77). Margaret is thus conventionally feminized as a "wrangling woman" even as she plays her most martial role. Her own rhetoric of inspiration participates in the conflation of nationalist impulses with her position as a grieving wife: "Lords, knights, and gentlemen, what I should say / My tears gainsay; for every word I speak, / Ye see, I drink the water of mine eye" (5.4.73-75). Because her domestic chaos coincides with England's own, Margaret anticipates the state of disconnection toward which the tetralogy tends. Relationships defined in nationalist or familial terms are relentlessly denaturalized by her performative play. At the moment of victorious consolidation, Edward IV finds it difficult to banish this ghostly reminder of contingency and loss, as his proliferation of insistences suggests: "Away with her. Go, bear her hence perforce"; "Away, I say! I charge ye bear her hence"; "Away with her, and waft her hence to France." (5.5.68, 81; 5.7.41). The last question in this play full of questions—"What will Your Grace have done with Margaret?" (5.7.37)—suggests that disposing of an amazonian queen is a difficult speech act indeed.

The answer to this question is, I think, another question: as he contemplates the captive Margaret, Richard asks, "Why should she live, to fill the world with words?" (5.5.44). The image has a particularly historical—or perhaps, in Rackin's term, antihistorical—referent, for Margaret will indeed live on ahistorically into the England of *Richard III,* continuing to offer political forecasts long after she should have died in ignominious exile. Rather than disappearing in response to Edward's slightly hysterical orders, Margaret brings into the world of *Richard III* the economy of fragmentation and loss that had so distressed York, an economy in which kings are traded for kings, husbands for husbands, sons for sons:

> Though not by war, by surfeit die your king,
> As ours by murder, to make him a king!
> Edward thy son, that now is Prince of Wales,
> For Edward our son, that was Prince of Wales,
> Die in his youth by like untimely violence!
> Thyself a queen, for me that was a queen,
> Outlive thy glory, like my wretched self!
>
> (1.3.197-203)

Through the anomalous presence of Queen Margaret, the language of reciprocity, which defines men as the tokens and the victims of exchange while women survive to count the costs, persists into *Richard III.*[41] Having survived the three parts of *Henry VI,* Margaret in this final play explicates the conflation of the political and the domestic that she has so disruptively performed, theorizing the narrative of loss that equates civil war and family feud.

To return to Clarence's question, what is to be done with Margaret? Edward's response at the end of *3 Henry VI* is a refusal of circles or mirrors, a statement that historical spectacles always move forward:

> And now what rests but that we spend the time
> With stately triumphs, mirthful comic shows,
> Such as befits the pleasure of the court?
> Sound drums and trumpets! Farewell sour annoy!
> For here, I hope, begins our lasting joy.
>
> (5.7.42-46)

Edward is notoriously wrong here, and the failure to evade images and repetitions of the past, figured through the persistent presence of Queen Margaret, haunts not only *Richard III* but literary history itself. Robert Greene, in his notorious critique of Shakespearean originality, returns to what seems to have become a kind of historical primal scene:

> trust them not: for there is an vpstart Crow, beautified with our feathers, that with his *Tygers hart wrapt in a Players hyde,* supposes he is as well able to bombast out blanke verse as the best of you: and beeing an absolute *Iohannes fac totum,* is in his owne conceit the onely Shake-scene in a countrey.[42]

Greene's misquotation is a near-quotation that replaces "woman" with "player" in a gesture that is no substitution at all. In playing, in seeming, in the ruthless appropriation of text, Shakespeare is equated with the Queen Margaret of his own reinvention.[43] If Joan la Pucelle has been taken to identify *1 Henry VI* as "not Shakespeare's," Margaret here becomes the sign that Shakespeare's text was never his to begin with—or perhaps such conventions of ownership, like Margaret's own paradoxical conventionality, produce only an infinite circularity, for what does it mean to attack Shakespeare for having no words of his own if the attack is formulated in Shakespeare's own words? Here again an attack from outside takes the form of that which is already inside; again the terms of alienation reproduce even as they invade the *heimlich;* and again Margaret, brought to England to articulate a relationship among men, becomes less the matter of that relationship than the sign of its radical failure.

Notes

1. Phyllis Rackin, "Anti-Historian: Women's Roles in Shakespeare's Histories," *Theatre Journal* 37 (1985): 334. For an earlier version of this opposition of material to spiritual, see [David] Bevington's claim that "Talbot triumphantly demonstrates the ascendancy of the truest sort of masculinity—not man's body but his mind and soul—over the trammels of the flesh" ("The Domineering Female in *1 Henry VI,*" *Shakespeare Studies* 2 (1966): 55).

2. Judith Butler, *Bodies That Matter: On the Discursive Limits of 'Sex'* (New York: Routledge, 1993), 3.

3. Jean E. Howard and Phyllis Rackin, *Engendering a Nation: A Feminist Account of Shakespeare's English Histories,* (London and New York: Routledge, 1997), 47.

4. See for example [Nancy] Gutierrez's argument concerning Joan's effect on the audience: "The French soldiers and the contemporary English audience, normally 'natural' enemies, become allies when threatened by a woman" ("Gender and Value in *1 Henry VI:* The Role of Joan de Pucelle," *Theatre Journal* 42 (1990): 190).

5. George Bernard Shaw, *Saint Joan* (1924; rpt. New York: Random House, 1956), 3.

6. [Edward] Hall, *The Vnion of the two noble and illustrate famelies of Lancastre and York beeyng long in continual discension for the croune of this noble realm* (London, 1548), fols. Cvii^{r} and Cxiii^{v}. On the relationship between Shakespeare's portrayal of Joan and the chronicles', see Richard F. Hardin, "Chronicles and Mythmaking in Shakespeare's Joan of Arc," *Shakespeare Survey* 42 (1990): 25-35.

7. Gabriele Bernhard Jackson, "Topical Ideology: Witches, Amazons, and Shakespeare's Joan of Arc," *English Literary Renaissance* 18 (1988): 40-65, esp. 64-65. See also Clayton G. MacKenzie, "Myth and Anti-Myth in the First Tetralogy," *Orbis Litterarum* 42 (1987): 1-26, esp. 2-3.

8. Henry Cornelius Agrippa, *Female Pre-eminence: or the Dignity and Excellency of that Sex, above the Male* (1509), trans. H[enry] C[ase] (London, 1670), 66-67.

9. See Christopher Newstead, *An Apology for Women: or, Womens Defence* (London, 1620), 17-18.

10. See Thomas Heywood, *GYNAIKEION: or, Nine Bookes of Various History Concerninge Women* (London, 1624).

11. Agrippa, 66.

12. Heywood, 236. Christine de Pizan, whose *Le Ditié de Jeanne d'Arc* was the first poem praising Joan of Arc and the only one written during Joan's lifetime, celebrates her martial conquests without apparent ambivalence; for Christine de Pizan, of course, neither Joan's nationality nor her sex gave cause for concern. For one reading of this poem in the context of Christine's life and other writings, see Charity Cannon Willard, *Christine de Pizan: Her Life and Works* (New York: Persea Books, 1984), 204-7. For a discussion of the poem in the context of other early

literary representations of Joan of Arc, see Deborah Fraioli, "The Literary Image of Joan of Arc: Prior Influences," *Speculum* 56 (1981): 811-30.

13. On the confusion of categories, see Jeanne Addison Roberts, "Birth Traumas in Shakespeare," *Renaissance Papers* (1990): 55-66, esp. 62.

14. Johannes Ludovicus Vives, *A very Frutefull and pleasant boke called the Instruction of a Christen Woman,* trans. Richard Hyrde (London, 1541), G2^{r}.

15. For a reading of Joan's feminization as a trope of woman-taming, see Jackson, 60.

16. Shaw calls Joan "the pioneer of rational dressing for women" (3). On the visual doubleness of female body and masculine armor, see Marcus, 100; Gutierrez, 185; and Jackson, 54.

17. Rackin, "Anti-Historians," 331. Catherine Belsey reads Joan in the context of such "extrahuman" figures as Cleopatra and Lady Macbeth; see *The Subject of Tragedy: Identity and difference in Renaissance drama* (London: Methuen, 1985), 185.

18. See, for example, Hardin, 35; [Christopher] Pye, "The Theater, the Market, and the Subject of History," *English Literary History* 61 (1994): 511; and John D. Cox, "Devils and Power in Marlowe and Shakespeare," *The Yearbook of English Studies: Early Shakespeare Special Number* 23 (1993): 46-64, esp. 61.

19. Marcus, 53.

20. E. M. W. Tillyard, *Shakespeare's History Plays* (London: Chatto and Windus, 1948), 162. Shaw suggests that even if the play is Shakespeare's, the intention is not, a possibility that displaces guilt while maintaining authority: "The impression left by it is that the playwright, having begun by an attempt to make Joan a beautiful and romantic figure, was told by his scandalized company that English patriotism would never stand a sympathetic representation of a French conquerer of English troops, and that unless he at once introduced all the old charges against Joan of being a sorceress and harlot, and assumed her to be guilty of all of them, his play could not be produced. As likely as not, this is what actually happened" (24).

21. This conceit, that looking at the beloved object causes a loss of language which nonetheless produces poetry, runs throughout such sonnet sequences as *Astrophil and Stella.* See, for example, the famous concluding lines of Sonnet 1: "Thus great with child to speak, and helpless in my throes, / Biting my truant pen, beating myself for spite, / 'Fool,' said my Muse to me, 'look in thy heart and write'" (*Sir Philip Sidney: Selected Poems,* ed. Catherine Bates [New York: Penguin Books, 1994], ll. 12-14).

22. Lee, in her account of the ways in which Margaret is iconographically connected to Joan, quotes Pius II: "They said that the spirit of the Maid, who had raised Charles to the throne, was renewed in the Queen" (199).

23. For readings of this stage direction, see Janet Adelman, *Suffocating Mothers: Fantasies of Maternal Origin in Shakespeare's Plays,* Hamlet *to* The Tempest (New York: Routledge, 1992), 8; and Rackin, "Historical Difference," 42.

24. Coppélia Kahn, *Man's Estate: Masculine Identity in Shakespeare* (Berkeley: U of California P, 1981), 55.

25. Joyce Green MacDonald, "'Hay for the Daughters!': Gender and Patriarchy in *The Miseries of Civil War* and *Henry VI,*" *Comparative Drama* 24 (1990): 193-216, esp. 209.

26. "How king Henry the syxt a vertuous prince, was after many other miseries cruelly murdered in the Tower of London" in *The Mirror for Magistrates* (1559), ed. Lily B. Campbell (Cambridge: Cambridge UP, 1938), 216.

27. Heywood, 239-40. It is worth noting that reticence verging on disavowal characterizes the end of Heywood's list of viragoes: Joan la Pucelle, of whom he would prefer to say nothing that others have not already said, is followed by Emma, of whose slaughter of the Danes he says, "though it after prooued ominous, and was the cause of much miserie and mischiefe, yet it shewed in her a noble and notable resolution"; and Emma is followed by Margaret, the last item in his catalogue, of whom he would apparently prefer to say nothing at all. Here, as in the *Henry VI* plays, even the encomiasts show a certain ambivalence. For Heywood in particular this ambivalence appears to exercise its own fascination; in his 1640 catalogue of female worthies, *The Exemplary Lives and Memorable Acts of Nine the Most Worthy Women of the World,* he will return to Queen Margaret, making her his second Christian and his penultimate queen, to be followed only by Queen Elizabeth herself.

28. Hall, fols. Clij^{r}, Cliiij^{r}, Clix$^{r\text{-}v}$, Clxvij^{v}, and Clxx^{v}. For readings of a possible connection between such descriptions of Margaret and representations of Queen Elizabeth I, see Lee, 214-17; and Marcus, 89-93.

29. Hall, fol. Clxxvj^{v}.

30. Howard and Rackin, *Engendering a Nation,* 84 and 85. See also Kahn's statement, "From this point on, it is Margaret who takes charge of the Lancastrian cause, a woman stepping into the vacuum of authority left by a weak man" (60-61).

31. Hall, fol. Clxxxiiij^{r}.

32. Butler, *Bodies That Matter,* 2.

33. Brathwait, 123.

34. Joan Riviere, "Womanliness as a Masquerade" (1929) in *The Inner World and Joan Riviere: Collected*

Papers 1920-1958, ed. Athol Hughes (London: Karnac Books for the Melanie Klein Trust, 1991), 90-101, esp. 101.

35. John Knox, *The First Blast of the Trumpet Against the Monstrous Regiment of Women* (1558) in *The Political Writings of John Knox,* ed. Marvin A. Breslow (Washington, DC: The Folger Shakespeare Library, 1985), 37-80, esp. 44-45.

36. On the relationship between male tyranny and female sexual excess, see Rebecca Bushnell, "Tyranny and Effeminacy in Early Modern England" in *Reconsidering the Renaissance,* Mario A. di Cesare, ed. (Binghamton, NY: Medieval and Renaissance Texts and Studies, 1992), 335-54, esp. 343.

37. Diodorus Siculus, *The Bibliotheca Historica,* trans. John Skelton, 2 vols. (London: Oxford UP, 1956), 1:287-88.

38. Howard and Rackin, *Engendering a Nation,* 87.

39. For accounts of Amazon violence against male children, see Diodorus Siculus, 200; and Strabo, *Geography of Strabo,* trans. Horace Leonard Jones, 8 vols. (London: William Heinemann, 1918), 5:235. Amazonian maternity is, in this sense, always about breaking the bonds among men.

40. For readings of Margaret's grief as feminization, see Howard and Rackin, *Engendering a Nation,* 97; and Irene G. Dash, *Wooing, Wedding, and Power: Women in Shakespeare's Plays* (New York: Columbia UP, 1981), 191.

41. For samples of the ongoing debate over Margaret's agency—do curses make history or merely take advantage of hindsight?—see Marcus, 95; and Rackin, "Anti-Historians," 337. For a historical view of the contingency of Margaret's power, see Lee, 192.

42. Robert Greene, *Greenes Groatsworth of witte, bought with a million of Repentance* (London, 1592), F1^{v}.

43. For readings of the relationship between Margaret and Shakespeare as suggested by Greene, see Howard and Rackin, *Engendering a Nation,* 96; see also Marcus, 96.

HENRY VI AS COMEDY

Waldo F. McNeir (essay date 1974)

SOURCE: "Comedy in Shakespeare's Yorkist Tetralogy," in *Pacific Coast Philology,* Vol. 9, April, 1974, pp. 48-55.

[*In the essay below, McNeir recounts numerous elements of comedy in* Henry VI, Parts 1, 2, *and* 3 *and* Richard III.]

The pattern of English history from Richard II to Richard III is comic in the sense that it includes usurpation, troubles, a respite, suffering, expiation, deliverance. Because the form of the cycle is all-inclusive, Shakespeare incorporates the condition of the damned into the comic pattern. This produces a variety of parallels and contrasts: double plots and double-dealing, incongruent elements of the pathetic and the risible, mixed modes of character portrayal and development. Comic elements in the Yorkist tetralogy have received little attention.

Henry VI, Part 1 offers opportunities for comic stage spectacle. It calls for almost as much acrobatic leaping about on the walls of Orleans and Rouen, climbing up and jumping down, demanding as many gymnastic stunts as were required by the catwalk, trapezes, and swings used in Peter Brooks's recent production of a *A Midsummer Night's Dream.* Some of the stage directions could hardly be carried out except comically, as when "The French leap over the walls in their shirts," appear half-undressed, and then "fly, leaving their clothes behind" (II.i).

The episode in which Talbot outwits the threatening Countess of Auvergne, as Shakespeare handled it, isn't in Hall's *Union* or Holinshed's *Chronicles* (II.iii). S. L. Bethell is mistaken when he writes, "All of the incidents given comic treatment [in the Yorkist plays] are to be found in the sources.[1] As the Arden editor suggests,[2] this incident may be derived from the Robin Hood cycle; if so, it is related to Munday's two-part play on Robert Earl of Huntingdon (1598), and to the earlier lost *Comedy of Robin Hood and Little John* (1594). Most of the comedy in the Yorkist plays is black, but Talbot's turning the tables on the Countess is light, the comic *topos* of the trickster tricked. Talbot can't be physically anything like the Countess's description of him: "a child, a silly dwarf! . . . this weak and writhled shrimp" (22-23); he jokes with the Dragon Lady and forgives her. Richard Burbadge probably played Talbot. If the Countess is a boy on stilts, that could give her a Brobdingnagian perspective, and the humor of the encounter would take on another dimension.[3]

In the Parliament House scene (III.i) the servants of the bitter enemies, the Bishop of Winchester and the Duke of Gloucester, pelt each other with stones that are called "pebbles" by the ineffectual Mayor, hardly missiles to "pelt so fast at one another's pate / That many have their giddy brains knock'd out" (82-83). The servants keep skirmishing despite attempts to stop the uproar (stage direction: "Enter in skirmish with bloody pates"). The first two servants withdraw to a surgeon's, and the third "to see what physic the tavern affords" (146-48). This boisterous scene is thematic like the opening street brawl between the servants of the Montagues and the Capulets. Shakespeare was already attracted by the paradoxes we find in his more mature work.

The treatment of Joan La Pucello was comic to an Elizabethan audience. It appealed to jingoism, terror of traffic with spirits, and male chauvinism. The heroic

Amazon of the French is a villainess to Shakespeare's audience. She communes with fiends, and so she is a witch; she humiliates Englishmen with her unnatural masculine power, and so she must be extirpated as a threat to male sovereignty. Spenser's Britomart is an Amazon with a magic spear, seeks aid from Merlin, and humiliates many of her male opponents. But Britomart never loses her femininity; she uses a magic weapon and magic advice for good, and she is always in quest of her beloved Artegall. Hence no comparison can be made between the two. The real parallel is between Joan and Spenser's Radagon, both intolerable women's libbers. Joan's capture, confession, and condemnation are a satisfying retribution brought upon an unsexed monster.

The cowardice of Sir John Falstaff in *Henry VI, Part 1* (he is so called throughout in the first Folio) shames him, but not his successor of the same name in the *Henry IV* plays. When Shakespeare had to think of a substitute for Oldcastle in the *Henry IV* plays, he thought of Falstaff in *Henry VI, Part 1.* To the Elizabethans, cowardice was a comic vice, as seen in Udall's Ralph Roister Doister, Lyly's Sir Thopas, Sidney's Dametas, Spenser's Braggadochio, and later in Shakespeare's Parolles.

In *Henry VI, Part 2,* adulterous Margaret of Anjou succeeds Joan La Pucelle as England's scourge and becomes its Queen. Incongruously, she is the wife of saintly King Henry. Such incompatibility as theirs is a source of marital jokes about recalcitrant wives and patient husbands from the Noahs in the Corpus Christi cycles to Maggie and Jiggs. Margaret chafes at Henry's holiness; her contempt for religion parallels La Pucelle's "false" piety and is in contrast with it. Margaret's and Henry's union mocks matrimony, reducing it to absurdity. Shakespeare has only to follow his historical sources to make us want to throttle Margaret and kick Henry. She is more blatant in her relations with her lover, the Duke of Suffolk, than Edward II's Queen Isabel with the younger Mortimer in Marlowe's play, later than Shakespeare's and influenced by it. Margaret's tantrum of self-pity, when Gloucester is murdered and Suffolk is banished, is an overwrought tapestry of lies (III.ii). Her parting from Suffolk has been compared to the parting of Edward II and Gaveston, Richard II and his Queen, and Romeo and Juliet; but it is more turgidly melodramatic than any of these, and in the context of a debauched society a satiric revelation of their grotesque fantasy of themselves. After stiff-necked Suffolk's execution, done by politically wise pirates (IV.i), when his severed head is delivered to Margaret and she cuddles it and waters it with her tears in her husband Henry's presence, she outdoes Boccaccio's and Keats's Isabella. La Pucelle was a comic witch; Margaret is a comic bitch.

The Duchess of Gloucester's seance is serious because she is doomed to suffer the fall that in her *hubris* she plans for others, but it has its comic side. I suspect a burlesque intent in the conjuring scene that occurs in the Duke of Gloucester's garden (I.iv), as his termagant Duchess is duped by trashy hirelings and brings about her own and her husband's downfall. Greene may have thought that Shakespeare was encroaching on his patented stage magic, and this may be one reason why he attacked the "upstart crow" in *A Groatsworth of Wit* (1592). The Duchess's kleptomania in stealing occult information that she can't use adds a peculiar twist to crass political anomalies. Her husband Gloucester's good intentions can't cope with a tough, pragmatic world; the Duchess compounds his difficulties by prying into the cloudier supernatural world.

Gloucester's ruthless exposure of the ludicrous imposter Simpcox (II.i) also exposes the King's credulity. Henry wants to believe in pious miracles; the Duchess of Gloucester wants to believe in impious marvels. "Blind" and "crippled" Simpcox is as palpable a fraud as the Duchess's conjurer, witch, and priests. The bogus "miracle" of St. Alban is a comic anecdote, like a fabliau or a Canterbury tale. Its source in Foxe's *Book of Martyrs* is as completely humorless as most of Foxe's stories, although, as Curtius shows,[4] in the medieval *vita sancti* jest penetrated earnest in a way that it could not in Reformation propaganda. As Gloucester forces the King to see the unwelcome truth when the blind cripple runs away after the Beadle has hit him once, another irony becomes apparent, that of Gloucester's own inability to see his Duchess's drift. I think Margaret's response to the exposure of Simpcox, "It made me laugh to see the villain run," would be that of any audience, regardless of their feeling about her.

Act II, scene iii, contains two travesties of justice: the removal of Gloucester as Protector and the sentence of his Duchess, which are not comic; and the ridiculous trial by combat between the cowardly Peter Thump and his drunken boss Thomas Horner, which parodies chivalric ceremony[5] and carries the same thematic import as the brawling servants in *Henry VI, Part 1.* Contrasting effects in these juxtaposed episodes illustrate Shakespeare's technique of putting together disparate developments.

The court-martial of Suffolk under commoners turned pirate is good riddance of anarchistic self-interest among the upper classes. In another significant placing of scenes, the insurrection of Jack Cade and his land pirates follows immediately and fills the remainder of Act IV (ii-x) with chaos. Cade's rebellion is satiric comedy which breaks down customary associations; yet these scenes are preceded by the same thing with the collapse of government in the hands of a predatory aristocracy, similar to the breakdown of order when Goneril, Regan, Cornwall, and Edmund seize power in *King Lear.* Cade's revolt is a logical outcome of prevailing conditions founded on illogic. This is not what S. L. Bethell means when he says, "The theme of disorder, confusion, inversion, topsyturvydom, is expressed through a deliberate and witty use of logical and rhetorical fallacy."[6] He forgets the prentices in the pit, his pedantic analysis of "the techniques of logic and rhetoric, so well understood by the Elizabethans" suggesting that expertise in these matters was necessary to understand the monstrosity of Cade's rebellion. More to the point is Willard Farnham's book, *The Shakespearean Grotesque,* with a chapter on "Diabolic Grotesqueness" in which he remarks: "Behind Caliban as launcher of revolution there is the early clown Jack Cade in *Henry VI, Part 2.* But in him there is little that points forward to Caliban's kind of grotesqueness . . . The dramatic treatment of Cade in his pretentious bid for kingship is one of harshly satiric rejection, not one of comic acceptance."[7] One may agree with this but still question the suggestion that satiric rejection cannot be comic.

Jack Cade plans to make England into an alternative university with no entrance requirement other than illiteracy, open class rooms, unstructured courses in such vocational subjects as meat-cutting, basket-weaving, death to the peerage, and book-burning. Clearly a Lord of Misrule with a jaunty air, he is hardly festive. The rebels make headway and shake the shaky Establishment. A grisly sight is the heads of Lord Say and his son-in-law carried atop poles and made to kiss at every corner, more shocking than the sight of Macbeth's head carried on a pole where it belongs. But disorder does not triumph. Mere mention of a French invasion turns Cade's fickle followers against him, and he slinks away to an ignominious end from one Alexander Iden, Esq., a small landowner of Kent and a thoroughgoing prig.

How are we to respond to Jack Cade's homicidal demagoguery? Not with the simple-minded moralizing of his ghost in *The Mirror for Magistrates* (1559), ruminating on the God-given power of reason to keep lust and will in check so that men will not aspire to rise above their place, and especially never to "presume our princes to resist." This Tiny Tim philosophy is as much out of character for the cutthroat Cade as for the overweening nobles whom he threw into panic. The comic catharsis of Cade's rebellion is the same as that of Gulliver's discovery that both High-heels and Low-heels, like Shakespeare's Haves and Have-nots, are pernicious rodents. Once the threat of Cade has passed, Yorkists and Lancastrians fall to carving each other up at the Battle of St. Alban's.

The last of the *Henry VI* plays refines the comedy of gangsterlike deceit and treachery. Bethell says that *Henry VI, Part 3* has "no comedy at all."[8] He can't be right, if laughter and tears are psychological cousins; or if comedy and tragedy alike sprang, both in ancient Greece and medieval Europe, from rites developing in different directions; or if we believe, in any sense, that Hamlet's intellectualizing and agonizing make him a potentially ridiculous fellow, saved from being so because Polonius is Hamlet turned comic-side out, or that *Antony and Cleopatra* is a see-saw affair that celebrates the triumph of Love and the triumph of Folly as inseparable. Shakespeare had no monopoly on the "funny/tragic," which was present in Elizabethan and Jacobean drama from *The Spanish Tragedy* to *'Tis Pity She's a Whore.* But the Yorkist plays are political history, you say. To put the matter in contemporary terms, they have a serio-comic aspect if the Watergate break-in and the erased tapes are comic, as they are to Art Buchwald, Bill Mauldin, and many others who are neither columnists nor cartoonists. In *Henry VI, Part 3,* the sinister comedy of the two preceding plays comes to a head before it erupts in *Richard III.*

King Henry, thirty-four years old when his last play begins, remains a retarded child. He cravenly yields to York's demands and disinherits his son (I.i). How the lamb ever got a son on "the she-wolf of France" is puzzling. Henry's reluctance to give up a crown that he is unfit to wear recalls the witless surrender of Mycetes in *1 Tamburlaine.* At the insistence of his own adherents, because he brings nothing but bad luck to his own cause (II.ii), Henry retires before the Battle of Towton to his molehill—he is a mole in the Great Chain of Being—to indulge in pathological yearning for the "soft" primitivism, to use a term of Lovejoy and Boas, that he imagines to be the condition of pastoral life (II.v). His battlefield speech has been called "flat, fatuous."[9] When captured by gamekeepers (III.i), he blames the inconstancy of the humble hinds he envied and wanted to join; he is oblivious of the ironical joke that history has played on him, but Shakespeare isn't. Henry goes down, up, and down for the last time, like a Cartesian diver, when he is murdered in the Tower by Richard Crookback. One critic remarks, "Richard is almost justified in getting rid of such a bore."[10]

The ingenuity of some directors fails them with the part of Henry, for the same reason that the Morality hero is less interesting than the unequivocal Vices. This need not be so. The portrayal of Henry gains in realism as his unfitness to rule clashes glaringly with the determination of Clifford, Margaret, and Warwick to keep him on the throne that he doesn't want, and also as it clashes with the determination and success of the Yorkists in elevating the unfit Edward as a foil who is lecherous, self-indulgent, egoistic, and ambitious—all that Henry isn't. To Shakespeare, vacuity is as entertaining as viciousness; and Golding should be as entertaining as Francis Quicksilver in *Eastward Ho!*

As Henry burrows deeper, like one of Beckett's characters, digging his own grave, Margaret fights against interment with him, flourishing for a while as Lancastrian general, more Amazonian than Joan La Pucelle but without the extenuating shadow of Joan's unifying nationalism. Only the loss of a loved son and an unloved husband can reduce Margaret to a feminine role in *Richard III,* broken and forlorn. Shakespeare shapes history to this end for her; unlike Thomas Hardy, he needs no Spirits Sinister and Ironic as commentators. In the Yorkist tetralogy Margaret emerges from the chronicles as a throbbing human being in her life story of victory and defeat. In the course of her career she is as timidly deceitful as Bianca, more shrewish than Katherina, as resourceful as Portia, more sentimental than Olivia, as managerial as Rosalind, as shameless as Helena, as viperish as Cleopatra, and finally more possessively ruinous than Volumnia.

At the zenith of Yorkist power, King Edward begins to rut for Lady Grey, a widow with three grown or half-grown sons. Since she declines to become his mistress, but so coyly that she whets his appetite, he foolishly decides to make her his Queen. His blunt declaration, "I aim to lie with thee," calls for lascivious pawing and feeble defense. This spectacle draws twelve sardonically bawdy asides from Edward's brothers Clarence and Richard. Division between York's sons is foreseen at the turning point of the play (III.ii). Edward's folly is as disastrous as Henry's in marrying Margaret. Henry marries with illusions that he soon loses. Edward is a confirmed wencher and marries without any illusions, which makes him the bigger fool.

The scene in which news of Edward's haste to bed with Lady Grey reaches the French court (III.iii) develops into a parody of the dynastic marriage game, which is as ruthless as that played at Netherfield Park, but much more dangerous. Pride and prejudice are present in the game at the French court, and they are laughable there, too. King Lewis does a double reversal, at first stalling about foreign aid to defeated Queen Margaret and her son, hedging his oath to support Henry, then pleasantly venal in giving his sister Bona to King Edward as a wife, and finally when furiously affronted he promises Margaret any aid to overthrow perfidious Edward. Lewis is almost as disgusting as Octavius Caesar bestowing his chaste sister Octavia on the libertine Antony. Margaret needs more help than Lewis can, or will, give. Bona is spiteful from disappointment. Warwick changes sides because Edward's move without consulting him mocks his conception of his own importance. Most surprising is the temporary rehabilitation of Margaret, who comes off best, and without trying to run the show for a change. Yet the ease with which she embraces the turncoat Warwick shows her unscrupulousness. If this scene were merely domestic in context, its exhibits of venality, pique, deflated ego, and opportunism, along with its brilliant control of reversals and ambivalences would place it with the best scenes in the city comedies of Jonson, Middleton, and Massinger.

As critics have come to realize, *Henry VI, Part 3,* like its predecessors, sustains interest in a variety of situations and personalities. The counterpoint of character and political issues is complex. Comic incidents are identifiable within a great range, and these, it seems to me, have contributed to the success of these eminently actable plays in both Elizabethan and modern times before a Shakespearean audience attuned to ironic peripeties accompanying political tensions, and incongruous disparities between the pretensions of policy (saying) and the actualities of outrage (doing), along with "the common curse of mankind—folly and ignorance."

Before going on to the last and greatest play of the Yorkist tetralogy, I should like to mention the compulsive categorizing of Northrop Frye, who doesn't know what to do with the Elizabethan history play. He drags it into his *summa,* which has sometimes been confused with that of St. Thomas Aquinas, under a sub-subheading called "The Rhythm of Association: Lyric," where it gets two paragraphs. The gist of it is that history merges easily with tragedy, but "There seems to be a far less direct connection between history and comedy: the comic scenes in [Shakespeare's] histories are, so to speak, subversive."[11] They are, indeed, as I have suggested in describing the main import of the comic scenes in the *Henry VI* plays. But I suspect that Frye is thinking of the subversiveness of Falstaff in the two parts of *Henry IV.*

Richard III, as a whole, is a subversive play. As I have pointed out elsewhere,[12] Shakespeare's portrayal of its protagonist begins at the end of *Henry VI, Part 2* (V.i), where Richard has no right to be, gradually develops, and becomes clear in his soliloquy in the middle of *Henry VI, Part 3* (III.ii), where the histrionic Richard makes his bow, already acting as he ticks off the assets of his dissimulative skills in double-dealing. He does not overestimate himself. It has been observed that, "Throughout *Henry VI, Part 3,* Richard usurps the pivotal, initiatory role that had been played by the women of the earlier plays—Joan . . . and Margaret."[13] Hapless Henry, before Richard murders him at the end of *Henry VI, Part 3* (V.vi), calls him "Roscius," a Renaissance byword for versatility in role-playing.

Richard lives up to this accolade in his own play, with his own scenario and casting. He always acts for two audiences: for his dupes and accomplices in the play which he directs on the stage, and for us in the theater. We become his confidants in crime, forced into *our* roles by Shakespeare's calculated concentration of four of Richard's five self-revealing soliloquies in the first three scenes of the play. As he winks at us, smiles, snorts, chuckles, and hugs himself in gleeful anticipation, we become prepared to enjoy with him his virtuosity in villainy. The stripping of our defenses lays bare our "unofficial" selves—George Orwell's term, quoted by Tillyard[14]—the same selves to which Falstaff strongly appeals in the *Henry IV* plays.

Richard's outrageous performance when he wins Lady Ann in the second scene, nothing of which appears in the chronicles, wins us as well as her. We watch in fascination as his other dupes, such as the fatuously overconfident Hastings, fall like duck pins. His triumph as both actor and politician (III.vii) occurs when he is persuaded, against his will, to accept the crown. He and Buckingham stage what I have called "an Im-morality play of the first order."[15] Richard is posed "aloft" between two bishops with a prayer book in his hand, a stylized grouping which Alice Venezky likens to the familiar tableau of a pageant sovereign surrounded by personified virtues.[16] It is the kind of show designed to appeal to bourgeois piety. Richard is the prince of players, and the anti-prince of princes. Thomas More in his *History of King Richard III,* incorporated by Holinshed into his *Chronicles,* and Shakespeare's main source, draws an extended analogy between this episode and a stage play.[17] The stage metaphor, a favorite of More's,[18] must have impressed Shakespeare.

We see Richard's mastery of as many character parts as Roscius played to bedazzle everybody, as he switches

Scene from Henry VI, Part 2, *engraving.*

rapidly from one role to another. He is a witty villain amused at the cleverness of his multiple deceptions. Toward the end, of course, his continuous play-acting fragments him, and he loses cohesion as an individual. He begins to break immediately after he becomes King, a microcosmic reflection of the macrocosmic destruction of normal values in the police state. The doom-saying Margaret, now a vengeful crone, has witnessed what she calls "A dire induction," and she hopes "the consequence will prove as bitter, black, and tragical" (IV.iv.1-7). Her hope is more than fulfilled, but she is not around to see it. When the ghosts of all Richard's victims appear to him in his nightmare (V.iii), he is deep in schizophrenia, the occupational neurosis of actors; but his nightmare has a therapeutic effect. Histrionic to the end, he rallies for a final appearance, or farewell performance, at Bosworth Field that is as theatrical as if he and not Shakespeare had staged it.

The Lancastrian plays are not my subject here, but I will venture the opinion that much of their humor is not different in kind, but only in degree, from the comedy in the Yorkist plays. The later histories are equally ironic but less sardonic, as I have recently tried to show in connection with the new tone of the comedy that crops up near the end of *Richard II* (V.ii-iii), in the handling of the Oxford conspiracy, which genially descends from the serio-comic to the farcical.[19] Almost inevitably, when we think of the Lancastrian plays, we think of them as graced by the disgraceful Falstaff, who would score so high on the GRE verbal-aptitude test that he wouldn't be admitted to Jack Cade's kind of alternative university, if he deigned to apply; but of course he would scorn it because he is Dean of the one of his own design already in operation.

If *The Comedy of Errors* and an early version of *Love's Labor's Lost* preceded the Yorkist tetralogy (1588-1592), these comedies give few hints of the overreaching greed, incalculable chicanery, and preposterous incongruity in character and event of the plays dealing with the dark period of English history from 1420 to 1485. When Shakespeare, after a lapse of several years, resumed his sequence at the wrong end with the plays covering English history from 1398 to 1420, he had behind him the two earlier comedies, and also *The Taming of the Shrew,* and *The Two Gentlemen of Verona.* Moreover, it is likely that interspersed between *Richard II* (1595) and *Henry V* (1599) are *A Midsummer Night's Dream, The Merchant of Venice,* and *Much Ado About Nothing.* In any event, such speculation aside, Shakespeare from the beginning was capable of the detachment required for the integration of a comic perspective and history, just as he later injected a comic perspective into most of his tragedies.

Notes

1. "The Comic Element in Shakespeare's Histories," *Anglia* 71 (1952), 82.

2. Andrew S. Cairncross, ed., *The First Part of King Henry VI* (London, 1962), p. 40, note.

3. The role of the Countess is assigned by T. W. Baldwin to William Eccleston, who was probably apprenticed to the comedian William Kemp, and who played comic ladies; *The Organization and Personnel of the Shakespearean Company* (Princeton, 1927), Appendix VII, pp. 416-22.

4. Ernst R. Curtius, *European Literature and the Latin Middle Ages,* trans. Willard Trask (New York, 1953), Excursus IV, "Jest and Earnest in Medieval Literature," pp. 425-28.

5. See my "Trial by Combat in Elizabethan Literature," *NS* 15 (1966), 101-12.

6. Bethell, pp. 89-92.

7. (Oxford, 1971), pp. 153-54.

8. Bethell, p. 82.

9. H. M. Richmond, *Shakespeare's Political Plays* (New York, 1967), p. 57.

10. *Ibid.*

11. *Anatomy of Criticism* (Princeton, 1957), pp. 283-84.
12. "The Masks of Richard the Third," *SEL* 11 (1971), 167-86.
13. Richmond, p. 60.
14. E. M. W. Tillyard, *Shakespeare's History Plays* (London, 1944), pp. 289-90.
15. "The Masks," p. 181.
16. *Pageantry on the Shakespearean Stage* (New York, 1951), pp. 131-132, 168.
17. Raphael Holinshed, *Chronicles of England, Scotland, and Ireland* (London, 1808; repr. New York, 1965), III, 396.
18. Richard S. Sylvester, ed., *The History of King Richard III,* in *Complete Works of St. Thomas More* (New Haven, 1963), II, 258.
19. "The Comic Scenes in *Richard II:* V.ii and iii," *NM* 73 (1972), 815-22.

Donald G. Watson (essay date 1978)

SOURCE: "The Dark Comedy of the *Henry VI* Plays," in *Thalia,* Vol. 1, No. 2, Autumn, 1978, pp. 11-21.

[*In the essay below, Watson traces the farcical, sardonic, and grotesque patterns of* Henry VI, Parts 1, 2, *and* 3.]

Although the three parts of Henry VI have always offered more than their fair share of grist for the mills of historical scholarship, only recently have they attracted much appreciation or critical interest *as* plays. After several fine productions and interpretive essays, it no longer seems necessary to excuse them as the products of composite authorship, an inchoate genre, or a young playwright's apprenticeship. This essay will explore their theatricality, concentrating upon those scenes which are essentially comic or whose ironic, macabre, or grotesque tone places them very near the comic. As the comedy in the first tetralogy progressively darkens from the laughter of derision in Part 1 to the macabre violence of *Richard III,* its place in each play expands from pervasive but limited farce and mockery to grotesque villainy and satanic horror. Often grim, sometimes savage, this farcical humor, I believe, is central to an understanding of the plays, not merely because it creates effective theatre but also because it deliberately and aggressively challenges the audience's assumptions about the relationship of politics and morality.[1]

I

In Thomas Nashe's words, *1 Henry VI* is the tragedy of "brave Talbot (the terror of the French)" whose "bones" are "new embalmed with the tears of ten thousand spectators at least, (at several times) who, in the Tragedian that represents his person, imagine they behold him fresh bleeding."[2] But the play is more than that: Talbot's "tragedy" is but a moment in a play otherwise filled with derisive laughter, knockabout farce, disorder that is more comic than tragic, irony that is more sardonic than sympathetic. Talbot, a monumental and thoroughly admirable epic hero, dies before the end of Act IV, and his pathetic though somewhat stagy death is followed by the undeniably comic humiliation of Joan La Pucelle (V.4) and the ominous ironies of Suffolk's plotting to rule Henry VI and England through Margaret of Anjou (V.5.) Joan's condemnation is but the last scene in a sequence of alternations of victory and defeat in the wars, and the play's final scene extends a related pattern of false reconciliations between the English and the French and especially among factions within the English nobility, a pattern whose ironies are comic in their evocation of knowing superiority in the audience rather than active sympathy for the characters.

In the first scene of *1 Henry VI* we are introduced to a fallen world, fallen heroically and historically more than morally and theologically, by the lamentations of Henry V's brothers and uncles over his death. Three messengers announce progressively more disastrous defeats for the English in France; even the brave Talbot has been taken prisoner. The Bastard of Orleans in the next scene introduces a "holy maid" with visionary powers to accelerate this process of driving "the English forth the bounds of France" (I.2.51-54).[3] The "overtones of the comic occur when she first appears," writes Ernest W. Talbot of Joan. "The love rhetoric of Charles is amusing in its absurdity. It also agrees with a comic conception that will place Charles and Joan in situations reminiscent of the braggart and the prostitute, as well as the ugly, rustic, brawling wench."[4] There is never any real tension between Pucelle and Puzzel; from the beginning Joan's claim to heavenly assistance and holy chastity is undermined by the amorous dalliance, bawdy innuendo, and double-entendre. Although the comedy of Joan La Pucelle reaches its culmination in the total unmasking of the play's penultimate scene, it is openly derisive comedy all along.

Even if we set apart twentieth-century admiration for Joan of Arc, we are likely at first to think the laughter at her expense rather cheaply extracted through chauvinistic characterization. The matter, however, is more complex, for if Joan is exposed and led off to execution, Talbot, the last loyal soldier, is dead as well, and the English have sacrificed their national unity while losing their French provinces. Even this incongruity, followed by the ironic gap between Suffolk's loyal rhetoric and ambitious intentions in the last scene, cannot completely contain the comic process involved in the La Pucelle part of the play.

Part of the comedy of the Joan plot comes from simple dramatic recognition of incongruity through the superior knowledge provided by irony. This superiority, augmented by nationalistic bias, produces derisive laughter, the kind of laughter most often defined by Elizabethan rhetoricians and psychologists.[5]

The comedy of La Pucelle begins and ends with it; what complicates the audience's response in between is the internalization of derision within the play. If we share in the English lords' mockery of Joan, her exultation over her victories and scoffing over Talbot's corpse are, if not painful, at least unpleasant, and unpleasant in proportion to the audience's identification with the English forces. One such scene occurs after Joan's capture of Rouen through the stratagem of disguising herself and her men as peasants selling corn. She and the French lords stand on the walls of Rouen, illustrating theatrically their superiority; on the stage the dying Bedford is "brought in sick to a chair":

> PUCELLE. *Good morrow, gallants!*
> *What ye corn for bread?*
> *I think the Duke of Burgundy will fast*
> *Before he' ll buy again at such a rate.*
> *'Twas full of darnel; do you like the taste?*
> BURGUNDY. *Scoff on, vile fiend and shameless courtesan!*
> *I trust ere long to choke thee with thine own*
> *And make thee curse the harvest of that corn.*
> DAUPHIN. *Your grace may starve perhaps before that time.*
> BEDFORD. *O, let no words, but deeds, revenge this treason!*
> PUCELLE. *What will you do, good graybeard?*
> *Break a lance,*
> *And run atilt at death within a chair?*
>
> *III.2.41-51*

It is not easy to know how to respond to the cruel humor here or later to that of Pucelle's response to Lucy's request for Talbot's body:

> *I think this upstart is old Talbot's ghost,*
> *He speaks with such a proud commanding spirit.*
> *For God's sake, let him have him; to keep them here,*
> *They would but stink and putrefy the air.*
>
> *IV.7.87-90*

Lucy's rhetoric of titles is sarcastically mocked as a "silly stately style" (72), and the Dauphin's conclusion—"All will be ours, now blody Talbot's slain" (96)—is unfortunately and correctly prophetic. That York's and Somerset's unchivalric refusals to send Talbot reinforcements are more responsible for his death than Pucelle's prowess or magic further complicates the scene. The English have embarked, as Gareth Lloyd Evans says, upon a sea of "national decadence,"[6] and the French derision is justified; even the "barbs" of Joan's "searching indictment of English hypocrisy (V.4.36ff)," as J. P. Brockbank points out, cannot "be removed by the spectacle of her converse with evil spirits."[7] The English finally must share in the derision, and the audience's superiority is taken away. The heroism of the Talbots is at least partially cancelled by the final scenes which promise the ascendancy of Suffolk; there, Brockbank explains, in a "parody" of the "absurdities of political romance" in the "style of a professional philanderer," the "treacheries exercised in the politics of flirtation are as sinister as they are amusing—the betrayal of trust must have evil consequences in the harsh chronicle setting."[8] The wry mockery of La Pucelle contributes to the sardonic irony of the last scene by telling truths about the faded martial glory and chivalry of the English. With Suffolk and Margaret returns the comic combination of lovemaking, politics, and warfare which characterized the first scene between Charles and Joan; only the irony has darkened. Margaret promises to succeed Joan as the scourge of England, and Henry VI's cuckolding will be an ironic counterpoint to Joan's promiscuity; the force of Talbot has given way to the fraud of France and the descent into effeminacy, cunning, and decadence is accelerating.

The ironic pattern of false reconciliations adds to the savage farce of politics. The war with France is made more difficult by the factionalism within the English nobility, Henry VI's uncles and great-uncles. The third scene of the play introduces the bitter feud between Gloucester and Winchester in a way which can only look like farce on the stage. Gloucester's men in blue coats give Winchester's men in tawny coats a beating which is interrupted by the Mayor of London and his officers and then begins again. Again the tone is derisive, most of the insults coming from Gloucester, who is far from the wise counsellor, judge, and Christian humanist of Part 2. If Winchester comes off the worse in this flyting, it is because of the anti-papal nature of Gloucester's diatribe and the Mayor's comment that "This cardinal's more haughty than the devil" (85). The skirmishes of the men are farcical, and the exchange of insults simple, bad-natured, and coarse. When again in III. 1. the two exchange defiant insults and puns and their serving-men again "skirmish" three separate times in this scene, the farce deepens, for not even Henry VI himself can stop these irreverent and violent factions:

> KING. *We charge you, an allegiance to ourself,*
> *To hold your slaught' ring hands and keep the peace.*
> *Pray, uncle Gloucester, mitigate this strife.*
> FIRST SERVINGMAN. *Nay, if we be forbidden stones, we'll fall to it with our teeth.*
> SECOND SERVINGMAN. *Do what ye dare, we are as resolute.*
> *Skirmish again.*
>
> *III.1.86-92*

Even the King cannot control this anarchy, and their "resolute" animosity and "bloody pates" mock any pretense to order. After peace has finally been restored, and several servingmen head for the surgeon's, and one to "see what physic the tavern affords" (149), the King creates the potential for more havoc by making Plantaganet Duke of York. The reconciliation of Gloucester and Winchester is only a show, and each has a one-line aside to underscore the insincerity of their intentions to remain at peace. The choric Exeter ends the scene with a prophecy of more "base and envious discord" (III.1.190-92).

In IV.1. Vernon and Basset crave combat in the factional dispute over the proper color of roses to wear as badges. Henry attempts to resolve the quarrel by putting on a red rose and making York regent of France; the "solution" provides another false reconciliation and aggravates the division. Warwick sarcastically remarks that Henry "Prettily, methought, did play the orator" (175), York rankles, and Exeter ends the scene with another choric soliloquy prophesying "More rancorous spite, more furious raging broils" (185). Finally, the last two scenes present an obviously phony reconciliation between the English and the French—no one intends to keep the "solemn peace" concluded—and an ominous agreement among the English lords to Henry's marriage to Margaret of Anjou. The pattern which started with the farcical flyting of Gloucester and Winchester and the fisticuffs, rock-throwing, and bloody pates of the blue coats and tawny coats has darkened into the tragic probability of civil war and the ironic machinations of William de la Pole, Duke of Suffolk, member of neither family yet ambitious to rule all through an adulterous liaison:

> *Margaret shall now be queen and rule the king;*
> *But I will rule both her, the king, and realm.*
>
> *V.5. 107-8*

These scenes drain the dignity and significance of diplomacy from the ritual of politics and present a king totally manipulable, almost ludicrously unaware of the insincerity of his counsellors—no one but he believes in the reconciliations—and naively and ironically responsible for aggravating the factionalism which will ruin his kingdom. The audience is kept aware of every motive through the asides and Exeter's soliloquies; for everyone but Henry, all intentions have a remarkable clarity. The irony is what makes these false reconciliations dramatic. C. L. Barber makes a distinction useful to our consideration of this pattern:

> *The Renaissance. . . . was a moment when educated men were modifying a ceremonial conception of human life to create a historical conception. The ceremonial view, which assumed that names and meanings are fixed and final, expressed experience as pageant and ritual—pageant where the right names could be changed in the right, the proper way. The historical view expresses life as drama. People in drama are not identical with their names, for they gain and lose their names, their status and meaning—and not by settled ritual: the gaining and losing of names, of meaning, is beyond the control of any set ritual experience.*[9]

1 Henry VI becomes dramatic by emptying ritual of meaning, by clearly revealing the gap between professed intention and true motive; Henry himself naively believes in the capacity of ritual to order the world and abuses its power to confer name and status by making Plantaganet Duke of York and later regent of France.

The audience is left feeling uncomfortably superior to the naive Henry VI, a position in accord with the general reduction of the heroic to rock-throwing servingmen, braggart noblemen, empty ritual, and amatory politics. The sense of Henry's imperceptiveness is cumulative and also leads from comedy to a darker irony at the end. As with Joan La Pucelle, the audience feels superiority, not sympathy; and this feeling belongs essentially to comedy rather than tragedy. The world of *1 Henry VI* is an inverted world, and Henry acts as if it were not.

David Bevington examines one aspect of this inversion, the dominance of masculine principles by feminine ones, and finds Henry himself wilfilly submitting "uproariously to the Amazonian disgrace with which the play ends."[10] This dominance forms a clearly comic pattern; indeed, this is one way Sidney defines comedy in his *Defense of Poesy:*

> *So in Hercules, painted with his great beard, and furious countenance, in a womans attyre, spinning, at Omphales commaundement, it breeds both delight and laughter: for the representing of so straunge a power in Love, procureth delight, and the scornfulnesse of the action, stirreth laughter.*[11]

Shakespeare's comedy is not so farcical but the principles are the same, as the Venus and Mars and Helen and Paris allusions of the play suggest. Joan La Pucelle, as Bevington says:

> *is not interested in sex for its own sake; she yields her body for power. This discrepancy between appearance and intention is treated by Shakespeare as a comic discrepancy, and produces an emphasis on salacious double entendres throughout her conversations. The pun is not simply an undignified form of wit intended to provoke coarse laughter, but a thematic device. In virtually every instance, the point is that sexual war is replacing military war.*[12]

Only Talbot is really exempt from feminine dominance; even Winchester is accused of being "froward by nature. . . . Lascivious, wanton" (III.1.18-19). Margaret captivates Suffolk while confessing her helplessness, "Tush, women have been captivate ere now" (V.3.107); she will make the best out of a situation which she has not chosen. That she clearly recognizes the nature of Suffolk's wooing and his intentions shows her his equal if not better in wit and craft; the mere presence of her beauty confuses Suffolk into betraying his better instincts as a loyal husband, and the proposed marriage results in Henry's taxing "the people. . . . a tenth" to fetch her and her worthless titles.

The ironies of *1 Henry VI* turn sardonic again in the last act, yet the memory of the brave Talbots and the comic relish of Joan's exposure and condemnation provide enough true heroic idealism and sheer comic laughter to mitigate the darkness somewhat. The undeniably traditional comic gambits of unmasking—stripping the cowardly Falstaff's garter, as well as exposing Joan's imitation of the Virgin Mary—and of the trickster tricked—the Countess of Auvergne and Joan—evoke the traditional responses of superiority and varying degrees of derision. Nevertheless, in the end the audience is left feeling superior to the imperceptive (and now wilful) king and sympathetic to no one but the dead Talbots. The sequence of false reconciliations threatens to make Henry VI into a comic butt, yet his unintentional mistakes in setting up his enemy, the Duke of York, and his unconscionable tax on the people actively involve him in the sardonic muddle of errors which will lead to the savagery of the Wars of the Roses and to Cade's rebellion in Part 2. All that, however, is to come, and to point in the direction of the escalation of violence in the remainder of the first tetralogy should not blind us to the lighter atmosphere of Part 1.

II

The general comic patterns of Part 1 are intensified in Part 2: what begins in physical farce and uncomplicated laughter darkens into some sour and even more savage ironies. Like *I Henry VI,* the second part has a clearly admirable character, Humphrey Duke of Gloucester, who, though still at odds with the Bishop of Winchester, is no longer Part 1's master of insults and leader of rock-throwing, head-thumping serving men. Now the Christian humanist, loyal, wise, and beloved by the people, Gloucester resists the ambitious scheming of the new Machiavels.[13] The people optimistically petition him and react furiously to his death (III.2). Like Talbot's, his absence from the play leaves a vacuum which is filled with anarchy and violence. Lord Say, his would-be humanist successor, can do nothing with Cade and his rebels; however eloquently he reasons with them, like Bérenger in Ionesco's *Tueur sans gages,* he is doomed.[14] Shakespeare, it would seem, has deliberately gone back to the Tyler rebellion of 1381 in fashioning Cade's attack on literacy, the very core of humanism in Tudor England.

In Part 2 the scenes in which Peter and Horner, Saunder Simpcox, and Jack Cade appear are clearly comic in some way; of the three, only the Simpcox scene does not turn sardonic and grotesque, and even this scene has several ambivalent resonances. It illustrates Gloucester wisely and goodnaturedly handling the charlatan Simpcox and thereby usefully serving his king. It provides the audience a few good laughs, but it also gains their sympathy for Gloucester who is to be killed in the next act. More important than the unmasking of Simpcox itself are the responses of the little audience of Gloucester's shrewd exposure. The mayor and his brethren cry "A miracle!" The beadle "with whips" beats Simpcox over the head and chases him offstage. Henry VI's response is totally absurd: "O God, see'st thou this, and bearest so long?" (153). Margaret completes this range of purely comic responses: "It made me laugh to see the villain run" (154). But then Simpcox's wife foreshadows the Cade rebellion, which however anarchic has some basis in social discontent, "Alas, sir, we did it for pure need" (156). Gloucester wants them "whipped through every market town / Till they come to Berwick, from whence they came" (157-58), a rather severe punishment. The scene now turns rather sour, as the animosity of Gloucester towards Winchester and Suffolk flares up again:

> CARDINAL. *Duke Humphrey has done a miracle today.*
> SUFFOLK. *True—made the lame to leap and fly away.*
> GLOUCESTER. *But you have done more miracles than I:*
> *You made in a day, my lord, whole towns to fly.*
>
> *159-62*

Buckingham at this point arrives with the Cardinal's revenge for this insult—news of Eleanor's traffic with spirits and "conspiracy" against "King Henry's life and death" (173).

The Peter Thump-Thomas Horner scenes work very much in the same manner. The combat of the prentice and the armorer is set up in I.3, and promises to be a farce. Peter's confusion of "usurer" and "usurper" deliberately combines simple comic wit and thematic relevance; the whole matter is indeed rather clear when reduced to such a verbal mistake:

> QUEEN. *What say' st thou? did the Duke of York say he was rightful heir to the crown?*
> PETER. *That my master was? No, for sooth; my master said that he was, and that the king was an usurer.*
>
> *29-32*

(Henry has, we might recall from Part 1, taxed the commons a tenth.) The entire ceremony of politics is thus diminished to an armorer's ability to confer name and status.

When the two combatants return to fight it out in Henry's hall of justice, the audience is led to expect great fun. The farce begins with the quite drunk Horner and his neighbors entering at one door and Peter and the quite drunk prentices at the other, both warriors equipped with staffs and sandbags. Peter makes his last testament verbally, giving away his hammer, apron, and money. The fight begins, and the farce is over: Peter kills his master! It is indeed "a grim comedy," as Clifford Leech says. "Moreover," he continues, "the formal combat between the armourer and his man is a parody of chivalric encounter: in a way remarkably sophisticated for this early drama, it implies a critical attitude towards the warring nobles whose quarrels are grotesquely mirrored in this fight between two simple men, one terrified, one drunk."[15] Again, Henry VI's response seems comically incongrous:

> *Go, take hence that traitor from our sight;*
> *For by his death we do perceive his guilt:*
> *And God in justice hath revealed to us*
> *The truth and innocence of this poor fellow,*
> *Which he had thought to have murdered wrongfully.*
>
> *101-105*

In both scenes, the King's "pious credulity" adds to his characterization; we are also reminded that Suffolk's little scheme has worked: "With comic irony," Talbert says, "Suffolk finds [in I.3] that the petition of a whole township is against himself for enclosing the commons, but he seizes upon Peter's petition as matter that can be used against York." If the "scene undoubtedly provided an amusing interlude for Elizabethans,"[16] as he claims, their amusement must have been mixed with this sardonic irony, for Horner, a simple man unwittingly involved in Suffolk's machinations, is dead, the English king ludicrously serious in his obliviousness to the situation, and the values of politics and chivalry grotesquely diminished.

The Cade scenes similarly begin in a mixture of nonsense, sensible social comment, and laughable farce and end by turning savagely brutal. James Sandoe produced *2 Henry VI* for the Oregon Shakespeare Festival in 1954 and wrote about his audience: "Their response to the Cade scenes was distinct: they began by laughing as we all expected but thereafter the ferocity of Cade and the little sprawl of mob caught their fun in the throat and turned it sour, especially as the second scene culminated in the harrowing of the wretched Lord Say and his haling offstage to be brought back (a head on a pike) an instant later, the mob growling and giggling madly. . . . The Simpcox sequence allows them one or two clear laughs, but Cade only lets them begin so, then bottles them up in horror."[17] The ridiculous genealogy, the mock-nobility, the bombastic heroism are at first amusing, and Dick the Butcher's running commentary adds to the laughs, but Cade's rebellion, whatever its virtues of reform, turns vicious and indiscriminately savage as the Clerk is led off to be hanged for his literacy. The sequence leads to the macabre butchery of Lord Say and his son-in-law, Sir James Cromer, whose heads are brought on stage to the shout of Cade's men, "O Brave!", and to Cade's mockery:

> *But is not this braver? Let them kiss one another, for they loved well when they were alive. Now part them again, lest they consult about the giving up of some more towns in France. Soldiers, defer the spoil of the city until night: for with these borne before us, instead of maces, will we ride through the streets; and at every corner have them kiss. Away!*
>
> *IV.7.131-38*

We also should recall that York has encouraged all this anarchy, just as Suffolk had used the Peter-Horner combat to get at York, and before we generalize about Shakespeare's conservatism we should recall also that the Commons at Bury St. Edmunds had forced Henry VI to banish Suffolk for conspiring in Gloucester's death.

The three comic sequences of Peter and Horner, Saunder Simpcox, and Jack Cade each begin in farce and end in grotesqueness of one sort or another. Their place in determining the general tone of the play can hardly be underestimated, yet even so the nastiness of the play's comedy is not confined to these scenes. In I.3. the king and his counsellors dispute the "regentship" of France—Somerset or York—and suddenly turn on Gloucester who wants Henry and not Margaret to decide the issue. Suffolk, Winchester, Somerset, and Buckingham insult both Humphrey and Eleanor, and Margaret gives Eleanor "a box on the ear." The trivial violence here is grotesque in its gratuitousness and malice and prompts the usual threat of revenge. Though Eleanor loses in her struggle for power, so does Margaret suffer for her liaison with Suffolk. In IV.4. with her husband, Buckingham, and Say pondering the rebellion of Cade, Margaret laments Suffolk's death, carrying his head about the stage. The juxtaposition is macabre, not pathetic, no matter what we think of the parting scene (III.2.). Sandoe was puzzled, "All sorts of special doubts crowd in, notably as to the handling of the scene in which the Queen fondles Suffolk's severed head (wrapped in red taffeta). I don't know, still, how far it's effective and tonight's audience didn't teach me much."[18] Indeed, how are we to react? What effect is wanted? The response is made more problematic by the scenes on either side: Jack Cade's putting on the dead Sir Humphrey Stafford's armor and promising to drag the Staffords' bodies "at my horses' heels till I do come to London" (IV.3) and Cade's ordering the death of a soldier for crying "Jack Cade" instead of "Lord Mortimer" (IV.5).

Finally, in York Shakespeare presents a touch of that gleeful mockery which he later makes so integral a part of Richard Crookback's character. The Cardinal, Somerset, Suffolk, and Margaret get rid of Gloucester for him and make him regent of Ireland; they are almost as naive as Henry VI was in Part 1. York is exultant:

> *Well, nobles, well: 'tis politicly done,*
> *To send me packing with a host of men*
> *'Twas men I lacked, and you will give them me:*
> *I take it kindly: yet be well assured*
> *You put sharp weapons in a madman's hands.*
>
> *III.1.341-47*

The next thirty-five lines outline in detail his instigation of the Cade rebellion in an unambivalently joyful, machiavellion tone.

The dominant atmosphere of *2 Henry VI* is darker, more savage, more grotesque than that of *1 Henry VI;* we have passed far beyond the sardonic. John Russell Brown objected to John Barton's and Peter Hall's production of a shortened version of the first tetralogy at Stratford in 1964 because they had conceived of the plays as forming "a relentless horror comic."[19] But that aspect of the tetralogy seems the ruling conception in *2 Henry VI.* In the first part Shakespeare leaves us uncertain about how to respond to the sardonic ironies of a world of fallen glory; in the second he explores that insecurity by asking us to respond to a grotesque combination of the comic and savage.

III

If the influence of Marlowe is apparent in many of these scenes from both of the first two parts, the grotesque is yet more complicated than in the Marlovian *Schadenfreude,* the "delight in someone else's misfortune which is central to derisive laughter."[20] In Marlowe's *Tamburlaine, Jew of Malta,* and *Massacre at Paris,* there are no characters who approach Talbot, Humphrey Duke of Gloucester, or Lord Say in their positive virtues, and the mixture of mockery and savagery occurs in a locale distinct from England and less immediate in its historical basis. The victims of The Guise and the virgins of Damascus are only sketches; Gloucester is killed by English lords not by a Tamburlaine or Barabbas; Lord Say is paralyzed before the English social reformer-anarchist, Jack Cade. The scenes of humorous farce turning perversely cruel are more extensive and carefully elaborated than any of Marlowe's; they seem to be deliberately calculated to force upon the audience something very near what Eliot called Marlowe's "savage comic humour"[21] while taking away some of the defense mechanisms against horror and atrocity which lessen the farcical cruelty in Marlowe's plays.

This grotesque comedy is further escalated in *3 Henry VI.* Sir Barry Jackson, in attempting to produce the second and third parts of *Henry VI* at Birmingham in 1952, found that the line "between the risible and the serious is of such infinitesimal breadth that the reaction of the audience can never be foretold."[22] These kinds of difficulty begin with the first scene in Part 3: in the first few lines the York family exults in their victories at St. Alban's, the father boasting, Edward waving his bloody sword, and Richard crying

> *Speak thou for me, and tell them what I did.*
> *[Throws down the Duke of Somerset's head]*
>
> *I.1.16*

His bouncing this severed head onto the floorboards of any stage is as likely to elicit laughter as it is shock. It would seem equally difficult later not to enjoy the mockery of the captured and soon-to-be-executed York who Queen Margaret places on a molehill, crowns with a paper coronet, and taunts; or not to relish the savage sarcasm of the three York sons' stichomythic mock-shriving of the dead Clifford; or not to smile at the asides of Richard and Clarence when brother Edward is trying to seduce Lady Grey in the most coarse, bawdy, and clumsy manner. It is, to be sure, grisly comedy and goes beyond anything in the first two parts of *Henry VI.*

Several patterns emerge from the grim scenes in Part 3, the most obvious of which is the ritualization of the grotesque. In Part 1, the repetition of scenes of false reconciliation reveals an ironic discrepany between appearances and intention which makes politics a farce; in Part 2 the ritual trial by combat leads from the farcical drunkenness and sandbags-and-staffs to Horner's death, and Cade the mock-king dons Stafford's armor and leads a procession through London with the severed heads of Say and Cromer kissing at every corner. Ritual and ceremony become dramatic, it would seem, only when broken, challenged, violated, mocked, and misapplied. The first scene opens with a deliberate mockery of ceremony: York installs himself on the throne, and Henry VI and his counsellors enter in what becomes almost the role of suppliants. Sheer power makes this usurpation possible; Richard asserts the authority of force in a comically sarcastic boast: "Sound drums and trumpet, and the king will fly" (I.1.118). Even Henry sees his powerlessness here, and his concern for the sanctity of ceremony thereby appears rather comically delicate:

> *Far be the thought of this from Henry's heart,*
> *To make a shambles of the parliament house.*
>
> *70-71*

The private quarrel between Henry and Margaret, husband and wife more than king and queen, dramatizes by contrast just how thoroughly the foregoing scene of compromise (and false reconciliation) has inverted the ideals of chivalry, loyalty, royalty, and fatherhood.

This usurpation of ceremony prepares the audience's emotional expectations for Margaret's revenge at Wakefield. Brockbank, whose analysis of this scene is very suggestive, says that "the paper crowning (I.iv), mutilates the idols of Knighthood, Kingship, Womanhood and Fatherhood." By "making a ritual of the atrocity," Shakespeare "imitates the history" of the chroniclers and intensifies the venomous comedy of their accounts.[23] Margaret, who even in Part 1 defended herself with a witty "quid for quo" (V.3.109), exults in her vengeance with a savage sarcasm. The blasphemous analogy of York's paper crown to Christ's crown of thorns suggests the tone of the queen's sardonic taunting. John Russell Brown's description of Dame Peggy Ashcroft's performance in this scene (Stratford, 1964) defines its effectiveness:

> *The cruel humour of the lines was played close to hysteria: 'I prithee grieve to make me merry.' (line 86) was an almost necessary request to excuse Margaret's impulse towards helpless laughter, a physical and emotional relief and a breakdown of control. Margaret was constantly changing her stance and position as if instinctively; her taunts were controlled and insistent so that only her body, moving repeatedly, could show the inward instability. As York replied in pain and passion, Margaret was silent, after one last, and now forced, laugh. When she stabbed him it was with a quick movement, and then she wept. And then the tears stopped with a wild, painful cry. In this scene the violent was emphasized as much as anywhere, but there was also rhetorical and musical control and a daring, emotional performance.*[24]

This interpretation of the scene rings true: Margaret's passion has pushed her beyond suffering into that Ovidian hysteria which also characterizes *Titus Andronicus.* Only, the ritualization of this excess makes it dramatically grotesque rather than theatrically shocking, as a comparison with the crude and perverse wit of Marlowe demonstrates:

> LORD HIGH ADMIRAL. *O let me pray before I dye.*
> GONZAGA. *Then pray unto our ladye, kisse this crosse.*
> Stab him
>
> (lines 305-6; cf. 345-7, 358-64)[25]

The Massacre at Paris is a crude, mangled fragment, but one can find much the same sort of theatrical, dance-of-death, comic humor in the other plays.

The ritual of the atrocity makes Shakespeare's scene more effectively grotesque; carefully orchestrated, the excessive cruelty becomes not merely perversely comic but also ceremonious and revolting. The ambivalence of response is conditioned by the odd mixture of stylized rhetoric and colloquial insult, of ceremony and brutality, of humor and horror. The Yorks have their turn again at Towton, and again a ritual is blasphemously parodied; the dead Clifford is offered confession for his sins.

RICHARD. *Clifford, ask mercy and obtain no grace.*
EDWARD. *Clifford, repent in bootless penitence.*
WARWICK. *Clifford, devise excuses for thy faults.*
CLARENCE. *While we devise fell tortures for thy faults.*

II.6.68-71

To borrow Brockbank's phrase, this is a "sophisticated savagery."[26] The heartless indifference allows the brutality to be treated as matter for the play of ironic wit and elegant sarcasm; murder and blasphemy are stylized. The laughter which should act as a kind of relief or defense mechanism turns into revulsion and horror, yet the iconoclasm and energy exert a fascination if not an attraction which intensifies the ambivalence of response.[27]

One might object to this sort of analysis by pointing to the comic horror as conventional and cite the Herods of the mysteries, the Vices of the moralities, the titanic monster-heroes of Marlowe, the scurrilous Marcolfs and Scogins of farce and jest book. But to see one or all of these characters or personifications in the Yorks and Lancasters is not to dismiss the disturbing quality of the grotesque scenes. Shakespeare closes the aesthetic distance by drawing upon these conventions for the history play and by making rituals out of the mockery of people and politics. The derision is placed within the play, and the audience finds itself not only laughing *at* the characters who deserve scorn but laughing *with* deriders on stage who mock them. Edward's wooing of Lady Grey is another example. Richard and Clarence, apparently out of earshot of the conversation, comment upon their brother's crudeness and bluntness. For them the scene is a parodic mime of the ritualistic gestures of courtship; for us it is that and more—a ritualized bargaining to exchange Lady Grey's sons and lands for her chastity. The irony of Edward's having to seize her property and threaten her sons' lives to have anything to negotiate with deepens the sardonic tone, while Richard and Clarence encourage us to laugh. The brothers use the imagery with which they had mocked the dead Clifford—

RICHARD. *[Aside to Clarence]*
The ghostly father now hath done his shrift.
CLARENCE. *[Aside to Richard]*
When he was made a shriver, 'twas for shift.

III.2.107-08

—thus linking the anti-Lancaster sarcasm with their scorn for their own brother.

In the next scene another amatory ritual is underway in the King of France's palace with Warwick wooing Lady bona for Edward and Margaret pleading for Henry's right. Although there are neither grimaces nor guffaws here (unless a smile of knowing superiority at Margaret's "Henry, sole possessor of my love"), the mockery of the whole business of politics as a muddle of errors is clearly intended. The Post's message breaks into this ritual of diplomacy and causes Warwick's complete reversal; Edward has duped him.

From this chaos of the political jungle emerges the grand manipulatory of all appearances, the Protean Richard Crookback. Already characterized by his military brutality, sarcastic wit, and physical deformity, in III.2 of Part 3 he picks up the gleeful mockery of his Marlovian and Machiavellian father and combines it with the wry Satanism of the morality Vice. The audience's participation in the sardonic relish of a Richard Crookback has not always been sufficiently examined; here again, the Marlovian parentage is worth commenting upon. Clifford Leech points out that Tamburlaine's rhetoric of assertion and brutality is often comic in a painful way: "The residual gap, between what even this man is and what he says and does, is enormous, terrifying, absurd."[28] So too with Barabbas and even Faustus. If Richard's aspirations sound Marlovian in their overblown rhetoric, this Shakespearean chameleon is more changeable than Marlowe's overreachers, and the effect, even in *3 Henry VI,* of his ruthless viciousness and comic diabolism is more complex than that of Marlowe's heroes because of his multi-faceted self-consciousness.

However, one must not succumb to the temptation to conflate the last two acts of *3 Henry VI,* with *Richard III.* The whirligig of battles and betrayals allows Richard little room to exercise his virtuosity. He runs from Warwick (IV.3), rescues brother Edward (IV.5), stabs young Prince Edward (V.5), and kills Henry VI (V.6). Although he occasionally adds a sardonic remark, an aside about his ambition to reign, and a final declaration of his resolve, none of these actions demonstrates very fully the demonic humor of Richard III. The only real subtlety in *3 Henry VI* lies in Richard's ignoring Edward's offer of amnesty to young Prince Edward. The obstacles in his path to the throne have begun to fall—though plenty are left for *Richard III*—but what happens in the last two acts of *3 Henry VI* is not much like what happens in *Richard III.*[29] Of the fifteen scenes of Acts IV and V most are outside of London; three are set in the royal palace in London: the first has Edward king (IV.1), the second Henry (IV.4), and the third is the final scene (V.7) with Edward again king. Except for Richard's murders of young Edward and Henry VI, there is little violence—Warwick is wounded offstage though he dies onstage—yet the sense of the confusion of the battlefield is strong between IV.2 and V.6. Everyone is conferring or scurrying off somewhere, and without a climactic battle like St. Alban's what stands out theatrically is Warwick's uncrowning of Edward and Edward's uncrowning of Henry (IV.3 and 8), Henry's prophecy of Richmond's glory and his self-justification in terms of pity, mildness, and mercy (IV.6 and 8), Montgomery's throwing down his gauntlet to all Lancastrians—a ludicrous chivalric gesture at this point in the anarchy (IV.7), Warwick's dying speech and Margaret's lamentation (V.2 and 4), and Richard's murders (V.5 and 6). Except for Montgomery's absurd heroics, perhaps, none of these scenes is humorous; except for Richard's stabbings, none is horrible. Yet the very busy-ness of the last two acts makes them a dramatic embodiment of the anarchy of the War of the Roses. Nothing is very fully developed; yet the uncrownings, Montgomery's inappropriate gauntlet, Henry's making Clarence and Warwick his "protectors"

(IV.6), and the irony of the ceremonious final scene continue the mockery and parody of ritual and contrast with the absence of ceremony in the battlefield scenes.

In the midst of all this chaos Henry VI gains some sort of stature, but his devout piety and resignation to the powerlessness of his own unkingly character—however sincere—are not wholly admirable. Much has been written about the lyrical and pastoral Henry, yet in the theatre he almost disappears until his encounter with Richard in V.6. As the play's only sympathetic character, he does illuminate the issues involved: like Gloucester in Part 2, he is well-intentioned, virtuous, humanistic, religious—and ineffective. In the last half of Part 3, Shakespeare has dropped the comic qualities of his role—his marital difficulties with Margaret, his contributions to his own ruin, his ludicrously naïve responses to events. He has taken on the choric commentary and prophecy of the chronicle narrator which had been assigned to Exeter in Part 2. Through this very detachment and resignation, however, the demonic savagery of Richard is emphasized by contrast; his withdrawal into unworldliness repeats the pattern of the futility and destruction of the good seen in the similarly isolated figures of Talbot and Gloucester, while Richard is the culmination of the patterns of triumphant villainy seen in Suffolk and York and of demonic anarchy seen in Joan La Pucelle and Jack Cade.

The escalation of grotesque violence within the *Henry VI* plays is dramatized most effectively and clearly by the comic scenes. If there is an undeniable pathos and horror in the murders of the young prince and the weak king at the end of *3 Henry VI,* the Machiavellian Richard's invitation to the audience to share in his knowing superiority is uncomfortably appealing. Indeed, what place do "pity, love, and fear" have in the farce of politics? The gap between appearance and intention widens with each play, until in the final scene of *3 Henry VI* sharing the irony with Richard the ruthless comedian becomes irresistible. For the reader or audience of the other *Henry VI* plays, the scene grotesquely repeats the ironies of mocking exultations over defeated enemies, temporary triumphs and hopes of stability, and false reconciliations. Shakespeare has temporarily silenced our moral judgment; we laugh *with* rather than *at* the evil and deformed.[30]

IV

Several patterns we have seen in the first three plays are repeated and given a different twist in *Richard III,* and most of these variations result from Richard's comic dialectic with the audience. Most prominent is what I have called the internalization of derisive laughter; like Joan and Cade, Suffolk and York, and like Margaret in the Paper Crown scene, Richard exults in the power he has over his enemies. The scorn and superiority which usually belong primarily to the audience alone must, therefore, be shared (or withheld) from the public mocker of human weakness or powerlessness. Nicholas Brooke describes the "special emphasis" of this relationship quite well: Richard "alone has any direct contact with the audience at all. . . . Everyone else is distanced from the audience, is in a sense taking part in a play within a play of which Richard is the presenter. We are forced to know them as actors acting just as, when Richard joins them, he is (more obviously) an actor acting." We have a "double view of what is happening," and the critical detachment limits the possibility of sympathy for his victims.[31] From the opening speech of the play, Richard makes us collaborators in his conspiracy against everyone within the play, and since his victims are without conscience or without political savvy, we enjoy his comic exposure of their mental and moral weaknesses and "rejoice in their stultification."[32]

The special relationship of Richard to the audience and to the other characters allows him to manipulate freely the comic techniques we have seen in the *Henry VI* plays. He manages the ironies of the already phony reconciliation of the Woodvilles and the Hastings-Buckingham faction by breaking the ceremony around Edward's sickbed (II.1), only one instance of his constant unmaskings. Lady Anne's ritual lamentations are crudely but effectively silenced and revealed as empty words; the knighting of all these "sly, insinuating Jacks" (I.3.53) is called the ruse it is; his asides puncture the ritual of sorrow in which the Queen, the Duchess of York, and Margaret indulge. On the other hand, he usurps the trappings of ceremony without believing in them and without filling them with any substance: the condemnation of Hastings, the appearance between the reverend fathers, the blasphemous parody of the Election Scene, even the denial of the earldom promised Buckingham—these and other mockeries of ritual illustrate Richard's sure sense that he who controls ceremony controls the state. Again, as in the *Henry VI* plays, the ceremonial view of the world becomes historical and thus dramatic through parody and mockery. The *tour-de-force* of Anne's wooing demonstrates that whoever controls the ritual—the ritual of courtship and betrothal here displacing the ritual of funeral procession and lamentation—can assign roles and make people play them. The deflating mockery of Richard's "Was ever any woman in this humor wooed? / Was ever any woman in this humor won?" (I.2.227-8) can be measured against Joan's mockery of Burgundy after she has talked him into joining the French: "Done like a Frenchman: turn and turn again!" (Part 1: III.3.85). The dramatic structure is the same, but Shakespeare has greatly complicated the irony.

To use A. P. Rossiter's phrase, at some point probably even "the Elizabethan spectator began to back out."[33] The separation of aesthetic and intellectual interests from moral instincts becomes uncomfortable—no matter how enjoyable the pleasures of the grotesque—long before the murder of the little princes. The audience "backs out" of the conspiracy, yet to describe its response in this way does not defuse the anxiety (or even guilt) created by its sharing in Richard's diabolism. Several aspects of the play counter Richard's ruthlessness: the pattern of curses and prophecies concerning the retributive justice of God's Providence, the natural nemesis involved in the self-consuming nature of evil, and the appearance of the Godly King to replace the Devil-King on the English throne. Each helps the audience to see the events of the play from a perspective different from and alien to Richard's, but none can totally free the spectator from the tension of incompatible responses prompted by the grotesque comedy centered around Richard's violence. The retribution Margaret and the Duchess of York call for is defined by the unattractive rhetoric of their ritualized curses and is personalized into a rather mechanical desire for vengeance: for Margaret, Providence means that God will wipe all Yorks off the face of England; for the Duchess it means all Lancasters and her own Richard. The pattern of natural nemesis certainly exists within the play, yet even so the self-destructiveness of evil fails to satisfy us aesthetically. We would perhaps have preferred to see the creative good struggling with the destructive evil, but the evil defeats itself almost before the good appears.

This brings us to Henry VII and the Tudor myth. Richmond's appearance in his own terms makes the first tetralogy a kind of Divine Comedy in which everything is set right again, yet some recent critics of the play have refused to be convinced. As the scourge of England, Richard plays into the scheme of Divine Providence; such is the old argument of Tudor propaganda, and it is marvellously ironic: all the evil the Devil can do is turned to good. The final act of *Richard III,* however, remains the one event of British history which Shakespeare could not alter, reorganize or ignore, the *terminus ad quem* fixed for all time. That Henry Richmond is treated almost emblematically makes the conviction behind the ending suspect. Michael Manheim says of the first tetralogy that the *Henry VI* plays "feed an audience state of intense frustration, and relief from the frustration is nowhere to be found, unless it be in the catharsis successful dramatic experience provides."[34] The same is true of *Richard III* and is true of the darker kind of comedy which Clifford Leech describes as "ruthless" and I have called "grotesque." Leech writes that in contrast to the "smaller kind of comedy that leaves us feeling fortified and near to society's heart," there is "a more ambitious kind of comedy which refuses us the purge." He uses *Volpone* and *The Alchemist, Measure for Measure,* Chekhov's plays and Ibsen's *Wild Duck* as examples: "In such comedies, and surely they are the most ambitious, there is no catharsis: at their endings we look about in uncertainty, we see that there have been no scapegoats to take away our guilt."[35]

No catharsis to take away our guilt, our anxiety: the grotesque comedy of the first tetralogy is radically aggressive. The whole fabric of Renaissance humanism is under challenge: concern with the ease in which man's weakness can be exploited and with the moral casualties which result threatens the belief the humanists had in their programs to create the virtuous through education; questioning the providential view of history suggests the need to jettison almost every sixteenth-century chronicle; dramatizing the irrelevance of ethics in politics makes much of the political theory obsolete. If man has power to shape his own laws, a Richard III stands these notions on their head: in his own way he believes in the nobility of merit over birth and in the humanist motto of Giannozo Manetti: *agere et intelligere,* to know how and to be able to govern the world which was made for man. The proportion of the comic and the horror-ful, of laughter and tears, and, to use Ruskin's terms for the grotesque, of the ludicrous and the fearsome, of the sportive and the terrible, depends upon individual perception and response. For the orthodox Elizabethan, perhaps the return of Henry Richmond, the order reimposed by the Tudors, and the self-destructiveness of evil would have accommodated the guilt of his brotherhood with Richard and the anxiety of the farcical jungle of political history in which the most vicious seem to prosper. For others the unrelenting comic horror of the first tetralogy intensifies the anxiety that they live in an irrational, incomprehensible, absurd, and terrible universe. The first tetralogy is neither the Homilies nor Hall, nor is it Camus or Beckett.

In *The Grotesque in Art and Literature* Wolfgang Kayser reaches "a final interpretation of the grotesque: an attempt to invoke and subdue the demonic aspects of the world."[36] The demonic once invoked, however, is not so easily subdued; we can laugh *at* it, accept the invitation to laugh *with* it, and cringe when it turns and laughs at *us.* Each of these experiences of the comic and the grotesque is likely to prove unpleasant. By exorcising the demons which the orthodox and complacent suppress, Shakespeare increases the discomfort that is not so easily laughed away. This ambivalence in response to the plays' dark comedy is, I think, a measure of the achievement of the first tetralogy.

Notes

1. The traditional critical view has been that the first tetralogy reflects Shakespeare's adherence to the Tudor myth and his fear of disorder. Shakespeare's political conservatism still explains these plays for many readers, including Alvin Kernan, who writes about them as "rituals of the conservative view of history and the ethic of order, counselling obedience and submission to the old ways and showing the dreadful consequences of rebellion and usurpation." In *The Revels History of Drama in English. Volume III: 1576-1613* (London: Metheun, 1975), p. 264.

2. *Pierce Pennilesse, His Supplication to the Divell* (London, 1592), p. 87.

3. All references are to the Arden editions of the *Henry VI* plays, edited by Andrew S. Cairncross.

4. *Elizabethan Drama and Shakespeare's Early Plays* (Chapel Hill: University of North Carolina Press, 1963), p. 183. Talbert's chapter on the *Henry VI* plays is the best treatment of their comic elements.

5. See, for example, Thomas Wilson, *The Arte of Rhetoricke* (London, 1553), p. 135-36, and Timothy Bright, *A Treatise of Melancholie* (London, 1586), pp. 82-83.

6. *Shakespeare I: 1564-1592* (Edinburgh: Oliver and Boyd, 1975), pp. 37-39.

7. "The Frame of Disorder: *Henry VI,*" in *Early Shakespeare,* ed. J. R. Brown and B. Harris, Stratford-upon-Avon Studies, 3 (London: Edward Arnold, 1961), p. 80.

8. *Ibid.,* pp. 80-81.

9. *Shakespeare's Festive Comedy* (Princeton: Princeton University Press, 1959), p. 193.

10. "The Domineering Female in *1Henry VI,*" *Shakespeare Studies,* 2 (1967), p. 57.

11. *Prose Works,* ed. Albert Feuillerat (Cambridge, 1917-24), III, p. 40.

12. Bevington, p. 53.

13. See Michael Manheim, *The Weak King Dilemma in the Shakespeare History Play* (Syracuse: Syracuse University Press, 1973), pp. 90-92. Manheim speculates that "to the theatre audience of the 1590s the image of the humanist is that of a loser in politics."

14. In James Anderson's 1864 production for the tercentenary, the same actor played both roles—Humphrey and Say—graphically illustrating the paralysis which followed ineffectiveness. This emphasis was not, however, mentioned by the reviewer in *The Athenaeum,* 30 April 1864. Reprinted in *Eyewitnessess to Shakespeare,* ed. Gamini Salgado (Susses: Sussex University Press, 1975).

15. William Shakespeare: *The Cronicles* (London: The British Council, 1962), p. 17.

16. Talbert, pp. 190, 194.

17. "*King Henry VI, Part 2:* Notes During Production," *Theatre Annual,* 13 (1955), pp. 45-46.

18. *Ibid.*

19. "Three Kinds of Shakespeare," *Shakespeare Survey,* 18 (1965), p. 149.

20. The definition is Erich Segal's, from his essay, "Marlowe's *Schadenfreude:* Barabbas as Comic Hero," in *Veins of Humor,* ed. Harry Levin, Harvard English Studies, 3 (Cambridge, Mass.: Harvard University Press, 1972), p. 75.

21. "Notes on the Blank Verse of Christopher Marlowe," in his *The Sacred Wood* (London: Metheun, 1920), p. 92.

22. "On Producing *Henry VI,*" *Shakespeare Survey,* 6 (1953), pp. 49-52.

23. Brockbank, p. 95.

24. Brown, p. 152.

25. *The Works of Christopher Marlowe,* ed. C. F. Tucker Brooke (Oxford: Clarendon Press, 1910), pp. 454-55.

26. Brockbank, p. 98.

27. Recent interest in the aesthetics of the grotesque is relevant here. For the rhetorical uses of the grotesque to disturb and disorient the reader, see Philip Thomson, *The Grotesque,* The Critical Idiom, 24 (London: Metheun, 1972), pp. 58ff. For an approach to the psychology of aesthetic response, see Michael Steig, "Defining the Grotesque: An Attempt at Synthesis," *Journal of Aesthetics and Art Criticism,* 29 (1970), pp. 253-60. Also Frances K. Barasch, *The Grotesque: A Study in Meanings* (The Hague: Mouton, 1971). Muriel C. Bradbrook sees Marlowe's combination of the comic and the terrible as a variation within the "eldritch" tradition and links Marlowe's grotesque (she doesn't use the term, however) with medieval mystery and morality plays, poems like *Jacob's Well,* Tudor jest books, and anti-Catholic prose. In "Marlowe's *Doctor Faustus* and the Eldritch Tradition," *Essays on Shakespeare and the Elizabethan Drama,* ed. Richard Hosley (Columbia, MO.: University of Missouri Press, 1962), pp. 83-90.

28. "When Writing Becomes Absurd," in his *The Dramatist's Experience* (London: Routledge Kegan, 1970), p. 65.

29. On the last act the comments of J. P. Brockbank are brief but suggestive. See his "Shakespeare: His Histories, English and Roman," in *English Drama to 1710,* ed. Christopher Ricks, Sphere History of Literature in the English Language, Volume 3 (London: Barrie and Jenkins, 1971), p. 173.

30. Cf Wilbur Sanders, *The Dramatist and the Received Idea* (Cambridge: Cambridge University Press, 1968), pp. 90. ff.

31. *Shakespeare's Early Tragedies* (London: Metheun, 1968), pp. 57-58. See also A. P. Rossiter's essay on *Richard III* in *Angel with Horns,* ed. Graham Storey (London: Longmans, 1961).

32. Rossiter, pp. 15-16.

33. *Ibid.,* p. 16.

34. Manheim, p. 115.

35. "Catharsis in English Renaissance Drama," in *The Dramatist's Experience, pp. 142-43.*

36. *The Grotesque in Art and Literature,* trans. Ulrich Weisstein (New York: McGraw-Hill, 1966), p. 188. First published in 1957.

PLAYING WITH HISTORY

Wayne L. Billings (essay date 1972)

SOURCE: "Ironic Lapses: Plotting in *Henry VI,*" in *Studies in the Literary Imagination,* Vol. 5, No. 1, April, 1972, pp. 27-49.

[*In the essay below, Billings links the historical failures of the characters in* Henry VI, Parts 1, 2, *and* 3 *to Shakespeare's theme of a decline in heroic virtues and ideals, and examines the structural role of heroic irony in the plays.*]

Henry VI ironically adapts the conventions of heroic drama to the matter of the Lancastrian losses, first of France and secondly of England. So dominant are the irony and the heroic conventions that the Tudor propaganda of Hall's *Union* and Holinshed's *Chronicles*[1] is obscured by the characters' sense of heroic duties and by the frequent frustration both of heroic intent and fulfilment of duty. Although the Tudor historians and Shakespeare show that civil dissensions weakened England and contributed to the losing of France, Hall, and Holinshed after him less insistently, assigns blame to human folly and weakness. In Shakespeare's trilogy, however, English reverses are most often the result of a failure in the heroic stance. Where the historians sometimes considered misfortune or simple lack of foresight the cause of adversities, Shakespeare presents the failures as the results of unmanly mildness, amorous entanglement, dishonorable choices of the lesser glory, or cowardice. Neither a politics without valor nor a valor without political nobility has a chance of lasting success in the world of *Henry VI,* in which most of the characters act out flawed versions of the heroic ideal.

In part the differences between the chronicle sources and the historical trilogy come from the narrower range of the three plays—from the death of Henry V in 1422 to the murder of Henry VI in 1473, a half-century in which no single hero or saint or villain dominated. Ironic defeat of expectation rather than triumph was more natural for treating this time. Despite Henry VI's prophecy over the future Henry VII, there was little opportunity for Shakespeare to take the longer view and to show dramatically that disorder and intrigue had some good ultimate end.[2] Having no single dominant figure around whom to build the trilogy, Shakespeare yet had the Elizabethan dramatic method of presenting a conflict rather than a single protagonist, with episodic scenes alternating among several groups of characters. In this way he could equal Hall's narrative long view with an ironic distance created by contrasts between the parties to contention. Further, the meanings of most of these actions could be indicated by implicit contrast with a heroic ideal, so that the episodic actions could be seen as consistently relevant to a single broad context of values.

The conventions of heroic drama had already been used in plays dealing with civil as well as foreign war. Lodge's *The Wounds of Civil War* (1589), Peele's *The Battle of Alcazar* (1589), and *The Troublesome raigne of John, King of England* (printed 1591) deal mainly with civil war;[3] the first two are quite clearly influenced by the language and grand dauntlessness found in Marlowe's drama of heroic conquest, *Tamburlaine.* Even while the trilogy was in progress, probably in 1591 and 1592, *Locrine,* a historical-heroical tragedy also influenced by *Tamburlaine,* was very likely being composed in its first version.[4] *Locrine* also featured a civil war and, like *The Troublesome raigne,* dramatized the repulse of invaders. The heroic drama presented Herculean protagonists with a martial code set in contrast both with conventional morality and with characters motivated by considerations other than the irascible passions and the glories of power.[5] From a conventional point of view, such a code and such characters are ambiguous, according to their service of established goods.[6] The ambiguity gave the playwrights an opportunity of dramatizing what may happen in war—the defeat of the good and the triumph of the unrighteous. Peele did try to slant *The Battle of Alcazar* so that the usurper is cowardly and treacherous as well as ambitious, while the true heir of Morocco is godly as well as wise and courageous; but the Christians in the battle, King Sebastian and Stukely, happen to be on the usurper's side and are slain despite their bravery and good intentions. In Lodge's *The Wounds of Civil War* both Sulla and Marius are heroic but destructive of the state. In the anonymous *The Troublesome raigne,* the Bastard Falconbridge, though inspired by the glory of his own Plantagenet heritage, is irreverently alert to his Plantagenet king's weaknesses. Locrine sins against the moral as well as the heroic code by serving his lust for his concubine rather than his duty to his wife, her family, and the kingdom; yet he fights to the death against those he has outraged, and never repents his wrongdoing. Even in these dramatic discrepancies between heroic *virtù* and conventional rules of conduct, there are ironies directed against the simple equations of political success with moral worth and of political failure with moral turpitude. The man of war may not achieve political order, and the man who forsakes the code of war and honor may lose his political power as Locrine does.

Shakespeare in *Henry VI* likewise rejects this simple correlation of political with moral qualities, so that no political prediction can be made from moral virtues. The well-meaning King Henry quite lacks *virtù* and love of glory, admits the weakness of his dynastic claim, and finally leaves the defense of England and the Lancastrian cause to his wife. His prime adversary, the Duke of York, is valiant in war but deceptive and intriguing in peace; yet he is defeated in war by his own excess of valor rather than by his dishonorable share in intrigues. Talbot, the only major character of unstained virtue, both military and patriotic, is stripped of all but his honor in a defeat caused by his own countrymen's failure to rescue him. The defeat of the well-meaning, the flawed, and the stainless never alone becomes the unifying purpose of the action. These repeated defeats instead contribute to a unifying political purpose, to show that two categories of value, the heroic and the conventional, are necessary to the ordering of the realm. The purpose is not simply to show a frame of disorder,[7] but a disorder that pits two incomplete kinds of ability against each other.

The heroic play contributed to the situations and characterizations of *Henry VI* as well as to the theme. The plots of heroic plays normally turn upon an emulous rivalry between the central figure and one or more adversaries. Properly the rivalry is to be resolved by one or more battles. Failure to do battle at an early opportunity is, of course, a lapse from the heroic. Heroic figures are mainly moved by irascible passions rather than righteousness, and in some heroic plays like *Tamburlaine* and *Locrine* there is tension not only between the heroic rage and unwarlike values but also between irascible and concupiscent passions. Love and mercy would also keep a man from going to war and thus from his manly glory. Tamburlaine resists but Locrine yields to softness of heart for weeping, lovely women. When circumstances prevent conflict, the hero must keep up the struggle with words and dauntless attitudes. In any case the heroic struggle should be open and conducted against armed adversaries without underhanded efforts to lessen the risk. Locrine and the usurping Moor in *Alcazar* underhandedly betray loyal comrades in arms, unlike Tamburlaine, who openly turned against Cosroe and met him in the field to fight for the crown of Persia. Both Sulla and Marius kill unarmed political enemies (who meet death unflinchingly and with reproofs) until Sulla is so moved by one honorable suicide of an enemy that he gives up his power and his authority. This interpretation of Sulla's act is, by the way, Lodge's own rather than one of the views he found in Appian or Plutarch.[8] In *The Troublesome raigne,* King John's supposed murder of the youthful Prince Arthur provokes the nobles into a rebellion. Not only dishonorable shedding of blood but non-combat, an unheroic failure to fight, had appeared in heroic drama before *Henry VI.* Marlowe treats Mycetes' cowardice comically in *I Tamburlaine,* but in *II Tamburlaine* the effeminacy of the conqueror's son in abstaining from battle gives occasion for a grim and shocking lesson in heroic conduct. Likewise the Bastard Falconbridge's intimidations of his weakly half-brother and blustering Lord of Austria stress the heroic obligation to fight or threaten at every provocation to honor.

Henry VI in every part is complicated by manifold rivalries and by varied forms of the heroic situations already suggested. Talbot tirelessly struggles against Joan of Arc; the Duke of York against King Henry; the Duke of York and afterward his sons Edward and Richard against Queen Margaret and her son Prince Edward. In addition to these central rivalries, which all eventuate in battles, there are unheroic failures to do battle or to face the rival openly; these lapses nonetheless alter the balance of power between the main contestants. The animosity between Somerset and York in *Part I* never produces an armed struggle in that play, but leaves Talbot fatally weak against Joan and the French power. The long wrangling between the Cardinal-Bishop of Winchester and the Duke of Gloucester is ended underhandedly by political maneuvering and murder. King Henry is left without the latter's support in the battle against the Duke of York, and one has the impression that Henry's defeat is promoted by his earlier loss of the Duke of Gloucester. In *Part III* Shakespeare uses a more schematic method: promise-breaking repeatedly breaks an uneasy peace and alters the military situation; there being no absolute loyalties, there can be no solidarity in any heroic triumph. Until the last promise-breaker and the last man with a private grievance be dead, military victory is likely to be followed by a breach of loyalty and a new cause of warfare. In *Part III,* then, Shakespeare does not dramatize the corrupting of heroic endeavor by unheroic maneuver; he dramatizes the decline of heroic honor into a self-regarding dream of private satisfactions. Throughout the trilogy, too, there are tensions between concupiscence and irascibility. Concupiscence is, of course, another self-regarding motive. Talbot resists the lures of the (unhistorical) Countess of Auvergne, while his French enemies are seduced by Joan, and his sovereign, Henry, is ensnared by the beauties of Margaret of Anjou. In *Part II,* Margaret's vanity and ambition to be first lady of the court prompt her to conspire against the Duke of Gloucester; and her desire for a gallant, decisive lover and ally overrides the evident worthlessness of Suffolk (and, after him, Somerset) in command. In *Part III,* King Edward's lust for the chaste Lady Grey prompts him to take the more convenient course of marrying her rather than the Lady Bona, to whom he had made overtures. Her brother, the King of France, and Edward's emissary, Warwick, are quite naturally angered by such trifling with their honors and turn against the English king. In heroic encounters, in faulty, dishonorable, or lascivious motives, the trilogy seems repeatedly to echo the situations of heroic drama.

The ironies created by Shakespeare's construction, however, set up situations of considerable moral complexity. It is not possible to assign a constant value to one kind of behavior or to one character, for value is affected by dramatic context. For example, in heroic drama circumstances such as bodily weakness or captivity might prevent the required passage of arms, as a mortal wound keeps Stukely in *The Battle of Alcazar* from continuing in battle, or as enslavement forces the kings drawing Tamburlaine's chariot to content themselves with invective. In *I Henry VI* it is apparently a point of honor for Talbot to have wrenched up cobblestones to throw at his French captors, and so also it must have seemed a matter of honor for the servants of Winchester and Gloucester to continue their masters' quarrel with stones after being forbidden to bear weapons. Although both Talbot and the servants show a manly firmness of will, the soldier has been engaged in a nobler struggle than the street-brawling servants. In a way the servants parody Talbot as well as their masters. Likewise the future Duke of York, supporting his dying uncle, Mortimer, and resolving to carry on the dynastic claims of the family, acts out both a heroic duty and a parody; for while York may resemble the young Locrine receiving the dying Brutus' benediction and testament, he also resembles the defeated Talbot embracing his dying son, who has with his father secured the family's claim to a deathless glory. It is hard to see how the heir of York and Mortimer could have relinquished the ancestral claim without also relinquishing honor and an absolute fidelity to family; yet it is also clear that he is not prepared to be as magnanimous as the Talbots. Political circumstances prevent his open declaring of a claim to the throne. The need to be secret until he has the power to strike is in fact what compromises his honor until the last act of *II Henry VI.* He must engage in unworthy intrigues. Yet again, however, his motives and dramatic circumstances distinguish him from other intriguers. Unlike them, for example, he is angered by the loss of French territories because he is ambitious to rule, not simply because he wants more sway at court. His secret intriguing is improved also by the greater complexity of the situation in *II Henry VI* than in some other heroic plays. No naive single combats like that by which Alphonsus of Aragon regains his patrimony would have served to wrest political and military power from a court composed of several factions. In *III Henry VI,* too, the moral judgments are not simple. Queen Margaret, who had seemed unheroic as well as unwomanly in taunting the captive York with the blood of his son, comes later to seem, by contrast with King Edward IV and Richard of Gloucester, a genuinely heroic figure still inspired by resolution and loyalty to her own son. Finally, King Henry VI himself has no constant value in the trilogy, even though Shakespeare gives him a consistent character. His amiability and moral purity appear to best advantage when he justly appreciates a temperament different from his own. In *Part I* he gives the heroic Talbot due praise and friendly audience. In *Part III* he fearlessly but without rancor anatomizes the villainous Richard of Gloucester, who has Henry at his mercy. But when his moral purity leads him to overrate a Somerset's or a Winchester's good intentions, or when his amiability prompts him to shrink from unavoidable conflicts with his queen's strong will, he appears weak and almost complicit with disorder.

To show that this trilogy is indeed a "frame of disorder" unified by consistent relationship to heroic conventions, we may first consider what, in three specific instances, Shakespeare has done with his sources. The foregoing examples have illustrated general resemblances, and although Hall and Holinshed do suggest the general outlines of Henry's, Talbot's, Margaret's, and Richard of Gloucester's characters, the historians do not suggest the content of scenes involving these and other characters. Comparison of scenes with both historical sources and heroical analogues will more clearly show that the heroical patterns modified the handling of history. Because the order of composing the three parts remains uncertain, we need not assume that considering scenes from *Parts I, II,* and *III* respectively shows any trend or development of Shakespeare's imagination. (This incidentally is the moment to say that all of the arguments against Shakespeare's authorship of the trilogy prove only that the author was not very careful of details, that the author did not write consistently in the style of Shakespeare's more mature historical plays, and that Greene was a rival of the actor William Shakespeare.[9] This evidence does not overturn the fact that Shakespeare's associates included the trilogy in the Folio, or the fact that from 1593 or 1594 to 1600 Shakespeare—*not* Greene, Nashe, Peele, Marlowe or any other possible author—was so deeply interested in English history that he wrote six plays on the matter of England; no other dramatist seems to have cared so much for the subject.[10] Whatever other play or plays may have been written before 1593 about the life and times of Henry VI, it seems reasonable to suppose that Shakespeare did his own reading in the chronicles and was responsible for the rehandling of history in *Henry VI.*)

Rather than choosing passages that best support a thesis, we may look at scenes important to the action of the plays. A little past the midpoint of each part, Shakespeare sets a scene of consultation that decisively changes the course of events. As the balance of forces is changed in the scenes, so expectations are defeated. The question to be asked is, Are these scenes to be understood as simply an effort to dramatize history, or also as ironic dramatizing in terms of heroic conventions? In *I Henry VI,* III.iii, Joan la Pucelle persuades Burgundy to join the French. The pivotal scene in *II Henry VI* is III.i, in which the accusers of the Duke of Gloucester decide to murder him and also to send York to put down an Irish uprising, so that King Henry loses his strongest loyal ally while his most dangerous enemy gains an army. In *Part III,* both III.ii and III.iii are decisive, for in the former King Edward persuades himself to marry Lady Elizabeth instead of Lady Bona, and in III.iii, King Lewis is prompted by Edward's default to ally himself with Queen Margaret's party. I shall consider each of these pivotal scenes, except for the scene of self-persuasion (*Part III,* III.ii).

The Duke of Burgundy's withdrawal from the English cause followed a very gradual disaffection, according to Hall.[11] Joan had been condemned and executed some four years before Burgundy's final break, and so she had no historical part in persuading him. The Duke's main grievances were King Henry's claim to full authority in France and the Duke of Bedford's refusal to grant the city of Orleans to Burgundy. He was persuaded finally to make peace with the French at the Council of Arras in 1435, after the English representatives had failed to reach an agreement with the French. Hall ascribes two main motives to the Duke: jealousy *vis-à-vis* Bedford, and a belief that his interests were French as well as Burgundian:

> But when it happened, contrary to his expectacion, that the kyng of Englande, by the right course of inheritaunce, tooke vpon hym the whole rule and gouernaunce, within the realme of Fraunce . . . & that the duke iudged, that he was not had in great confidence, nor in perfite truste, as he thought, because the Duke of Bedforde, would not suffre the toune of Orleaunce, to be rendered to hym (as you before haue heard): He therfore imagined, & determined with hymself, to returne into the pathe again, from the whiche he had straied and erred, and to take part, and ioyne with his awne bloud and nacion . . .

provided that the return should seem not to be of his own choosing.[12]

In *I Henry VI* Shakespeare makes Burgundy's defection occur on the battlefield at the instigation of la Pucelle. Immediately after an English success at Rouen, while the armies still are marching from the field, Joan detains Burgundy and offers arguments roughly the same as those which Hall had ascribed to the Duke himself:[13]

> Who join'st thou with but with a lordly nation
> That will not trust thee but for profit's sake?
> When Talbot hath set footing once in France,
> And fashion'd thee that instrument of ill,
> Who then but English Henry will be lord,
> And thou be thrust out like a fugitive?
>
> (III.iii.62-67)

There follows an anachronistic reference to another grievance, the English release of Burgundy's enemy, the Duke of Orleans, which occurred later, in retaliation for Burgundy's defection. Then Joan echoes Hall's metaphor of straying from the path: "Come, come return; return, thou wandering lord" (76). Until this moment, there have been no hints of ill will between Burgundy and the English, and no mention of a Duke of Orleans. As for Bedford, Shakespeare had already dramatized his death in III.ii to make way for Talbot's pre-eminence. So far Shakespeare's handling of history only accentuates the suddenness of Burgundy's change and further builds up Joan's role in opposition to Talbot's. But her speech has earlier included a topic, the devastation of France, which was the motive not of Burgundy but of Pope Eugenius, who sought to initiate peace conferences. It is this topic that first weakens the Duke, and Shakespeare has expressed it in imagery of his own:

> look on fertile France,
> And see the cities and the towns defac'd
> By wasting ruin of the cruel foe;
> As looks the mother on her lowly babe
> When death doth close his tender dying eyes,
> See, see, the pining malady of France;
> Behold the wounds, the most unnatural wounds
> Which thou thyself hast given her woeful breast.
> O, turn thy edged sword another way;
> Strike those that hurt, and hurt not those that help!
> One drop of blood drawn from thy country's bosom
> Should grieve thee more than streams of foreign gore.
> Return thee therefore with a flood of tears,
> And wash away thy country's stained spots.
> Burgundy. [*Aside.*] Either she hath bewitch'd me with her words,
> Or nature makes me suddenly relent.
>
> (III.iii.44-59)

La Pucelle's later contempt for his relenting ("turn and turn again") shows that we, too, may consider it dishonorable. Further, the very images of Joan's exhortation, *mother, babe, flood of tears,* have already been treated with the scorn that the heroic resolve feels for melting moods. Bedford's lament for Henry V uses the same imagery:

> Posterity, await for wretched years,
> When at their mothers' moist eyes babes shall suck,
> Our isle be made a nourish of salt tears. . . .
>
> (I.i.48-50)

And in the same scene he rejects such talk:

> Away with these disgraceful wailing robes!
> Wounds will I lend the French instead of eyes,
> To weep their intermissive miseries.
>
> (I.i.86-88)

Burgundy has not rejected such persuasion as unmanly. The scene is one in which a heroic resolve clearly seems required and then fails to appear. Shakespeare's adaptations of history not only magnify Joan's role but are shaped ironically to prove Burgundy no true hero, or just possibly a victim of bewitchment.

Persuasion may give a man of war and honor a chance to make a heroic choice only when he may gain a greater glory by changing his course, as Theridamas does when he forsakes the Persian king to follow Tamburlaine's far stronger leadership. Sebastian of Portugal is persuaded to fight at Alcazar by his hope of establishing the Christian faith in Africa. But in such cases weeping nations are not to be convincing topics. Although the historical Duke Philip of Burgundy prospered after breaking with England, Shakespeare shows that he was undone morally, as Talbot was never directly undone, by a woman's persuasions.

A woman has undue influence also in the pivotal scene of *II Henry VI,* in which the Duke of Gloucester is doomed while the Duke of York gains the army his ambition will require to gain its ends. The woman is Queen Margaret, to whom Hall does ascribe a commanding role in bringing down Gloucester. Although Shakespeare does not widely depart from the chronology and relationships of history, he not only compresses events but emphasizes York's complicity in all of them. The events were these.[14] At the instigation of the Queen, Gloucester was removed from the protectorship in the twenty-fifth year of Henry's reign and was made the victim of various accusations in council; in the same year, the Duke was made to answer formal charges before a Parliament at Bury, but was murdered before a verdict could be rendered. Within a year afterward, the Cardinal-Bishop of Winchester died. The Duke of York began to feel out support for his own claim to the throne. During the next two years, the twenty-seventh and twenty-eighth, the Duke of York put down a rebellion in Ireland, but the Duke of Somerset was totally unsuccessful in his efforts to keep Normandy out of French control. Margaret was behind the intrigues against Gloucester, and presumably consented to the later appointments of Somerset and York.

Shakespeare's scene, III.i, rearranges some of these events and omits York's solicitation of support, which has already been dramatized in II.ii. The loss of Normandy is announced near the beginning of the scene, the condemnation of Gloucester takes up the middle portion, and the announcement of an Irish rebellion comes near the end. The discovery of the murdered Gloucester opens the following scene, III.ii. The early discrediting of Somerset is less important than the introduction of York as a main participant in the Queen's intrigue against Gloucester. Hall does not give the Duke of York such a role, and indeed his narrative suggests that York did not begin to aspire to the throne until he had seen "the destruccion of the good duke of Gloucester, and exaltacion and advauncement of this glorious man [the vainly-ambitious Suffolk]" (p. 210). Shakespeare has made York a less patriotic figure, whose solicitations of the Nevilles in II.ii anticipate that the fall of Gloucester will clear the way for a Yorkist triumph.

He has also made King Henry a more deplorable, less manly figure by introducing him into this scene, apparently to show that Gloucester's doom is made possible by Henry's ineffectual resistance. Apparently ignorant of the plan to bring charges against his uncle, Henry at first only protests that Gloucester must be innocent as "the sucking lamb or harmless dove" (III.i.71). He scarcely objects while accusations are made in quasi-allegorical, emblematic terms, and then weakly proposes to withdraw. His state of mind is expressed in images like those of Joan's false persuasion and Bedford's ignominious grief:

> my heart is drown'd with grief,
> Whose flood begins to flow within mine eyes,
> My body round engirt with misery.
>
> . . . . .
>
> And as the dam runs lowing up and down,
> Looking the way her harmless young one went,
> And can do nought but wail her darling's loss;
> Even so myself bewails good Gloucester's case
> With sad unhelpful tears, and with dimm'd eyes
> Look after him, and cannot do him good;
> So mighty are his vowed enemies.
>
> (III.i.198-200, 214-20)

Here again is weeping that swamps the active principle, and maternal grief; because the imagery of this scene has been predominantly composed of animal emblems, the mother here is a cow.

Henry's weakness and the conspirators' duplicity are dishonorable; only York's furious ambition emerges in the closing soliloquy as the one heroic possibility of the scene. The opening words of the speech are a call to valorous purpose:

> Now, York, or never, steel thy fearful thoughts,
> And change misdoubt to resolution:
> Be that thou hop'st to be, or what thou art
> Resign to death; it is not worth th' enjoying.
>
> (III.i.331-34)

But although this resembles Bedford's own resolve in *Part I,* York speaks of himself here as having a brain busier "than the labouring spider" (339) and as being a "starved snake" (343) foolishly revived by the Queen's party. And when he considers his new army "sharp weapons in a madman's hands" (347), the image suggests Bedlam rather than the maddened Ajax Telemonius, to whom he alludes two acts later (V.i.26 f.). Only with the imagery of storm and sun does York return to metaphors for power and glory worthy of a hero:

> I will stir up in England some black storm
> Shall blow ten thousand souls to heaven, or hell;
> And this fell tempest shall not cease to rage
> Until the golden circuit on my head,
> Like to the glorious sun's transparent beams,
> Do calm the fury of this mad-bred flaw.
>
> (III.i.349-54)

Because one cannot speak sardonically of oneself as snake and madman without ironic contrast with the vaunting speech about oneself as tempest and golden-crowned king, York's soliloquy must be perceived as an imperfectly-heroic set speech of review and planning.

We must also give some attention to the fall of Gloucester, whom Shakespeare has gone to some trouble to establish, in *Part II,* as the good governor of himself and of the state.[15] Despite his antagonism to Winchester, he has never been a participant in heroic or honorable combat but has instead sought the honor of himself and the state through legitimate political means. He corresponds most closely to those senators in *The Wounds of Civil War* who like Antonius insist that their service is alone lawful and beneficial to the state, and who morally defy their armed accusers and destroyers:

> Can then your eyes with thundering threats of rage,
> Cast furious gleames of anger vpon age?
> Can then your harts with furies mount so hie,
> As they should harme the Romane Anthonie?
> I farre more kinde than sensles tree haue lent
> A kindly sap to our declining state,
> And like a carefull shepheard have foreseene
> The heauie dangers of this Citie Rome
> And made the citizens the happie flocke
> Whom I haue fed with counsailes and aduice.
>
> (1855-64)

This portrayal of his own good qualities does not arouse pity alone because it is part of an accusation against his destroyers' tyranny. The effect is a kind of heroical pathos, created by the clash between heroic ambition and political nobility. Gloucester exhibits the same kind of resolution and defiance:

> And if my death might make this island happy,
> And prove the period of their tyranny,
> I would expend it with all willingness.
>
> . . . . .
>
> Beaufort's red sparkling eyes blab his heart's malice,
> And Suffolk's cloudy brow his stormy hate;
> Sharp Buckingham unburthens with his tongue
> The envious load that lies upon his heart;
> And dogged York, that reaches at the moon,
> Whose overweening arm I have pluck'd back,
> By false accuse doth level at my life.
>
> (III.i.148-50, 154-60)

In *The Wounds of Civil War* the effect of heroical pathos from the dying or doomed senators is to limit the claims of heroical ambition. In this scene in *II Henry VI,* Gloucester's defiant self-vindication not only contrasts with

Henry's timorous reproaches but also shows that legitimate authority may have more magnanimity than ambition can.

The heroic motive in *Part II* must work within a political context even more sharply defined than that of *Part I.* While a Tamburlaine need not concern himself with his title to a crown, the heroic ambition of a York must be supported by a legitimate claim as well as by a glorious vision of royal estate. York has already recited his genealogy in this play, but he has not yet had occasion to demonstrate the kind of political righteousness Gloucester has shown.

Neither does York conclude with this anticipation of the sun-like crown, but goes on instead to describe his plan to use Jack Cade as a catspaw. Certainly the audience must be forewarned that Cade is an imposter, and that York has instigated his uprising. There is no reason, however, that this information must come at the end of a set speech in which York reviews his situation and incites himself to plan and to take future action. This placement of this exposition—the only matter in this soliloquy that is firmly grounded in the historical source—strengthens the effect of a heroic resolve much modified by cunning and malice. Shakespeare's compression of events has presented Henry's default, Gloucester's fall, and Margaret's conspiracy as the ignoble conditions of success for York's long-standing and deep-laid plot, and has presented York as consciously turning these conditions to his own advantage. Intrigue, not martial confrontation, is York's strategy. The release of resentments as well as ambition of glory is his motive.

We may contrast this moment with the occasions on which other heroes turn upon an ally or upon an unoffending kingdom to gain power. In every case—in *I Tamburlaine,* in *Locrine,* in *The Battle of Alcazar*—the hero leads in his own person, not by a substitute. In every hero—Tamburlaine, Humber (the invader of Locrine's kingdom), and Sebastian—the motive of glory is uppermost. Tamburlaine persuades himself and his followers to turn upon Cosroe by dwelling upon the splendor of kingship. Humber, determined to possess a land he finds rich and lovely, anticipates with bloody-minded longings the joys of war in that land:

> Me thinkes I see both armies in the field:
> The broken launces clime the cristall skies;
> Some headless lie, some breathless on the ground,
> And euery place is straw'd with carcasses.
> Behold! the grasse hath lost his pleasant greene,
> The sweetest sight that euer might be seene.
>
> (*Locrine,* III.ii.16-21)

Sebastian has less bloodthirsty sentiments but more ambitions:

> And thrive it so with thee as thou doest meane,
> And meane thou so as thou doest wish to thrive,
> And if our Christ for whom in chiefe we fight,
> Heereby to inlarge the bounds of christendome,
> Favor this warre, and as I do not doubt,
> Send victorie to light upon my crest,
> Brave Moore I will advance thy kingly sonne,
> And with a diademe of pearle and golde,
> Adorne thy temples and inrich thy head.
>
> (*The Battle of Alcazar,* 914-22)

It is not amiss for a hero to think of suffering and treachery, but he must not be moved by anything less than a glory for which he personally would lead his armies in battle. York's speech just sufficiently resembles these other models that his lapses from them might well have been felt as unwitting irony.

In *III Henry VI* one pivotal scene, III.iii, may seem quite without mean-mindedness and irony, for Warwick and King Lewis seem moved by honor to drop their alliance with King Edward in order to support the creditable cause of Queen Margaret and Prince Edward. Shakespeare has created an imaginary encounter between Warwick and Margaret at the French court, and the meeting gives opportunity for the rival Yorkist and Lancastrian claims to be debated before a royal, though French, audience; before the debate is ended, news of Edward's sudden marriage to Lady Grey piques Warwick into forsaking Edward, and provokes the Lady Bona to move her brother Lewis to join Margaret. Historically, Warwick's and Lewis' reactions to Edward's marriage were much less prompt. Warwick left France highly rewarded, says Hall, "& for the great & noble corage that was in him, he obteyned such fauor of the kynge, the quene and the nobles of Fraunce that when [five years later] he fled out of England, he was there honorably receiued . . ."; the Earl did not reveal his resentment upon his return to England in 1465.[16] Moreover, he kept his rebellion native until it had been defeated at Losecoat Field in 1470; at that time he withdrew to France, and formed his alliance with Lewis and Margaret. In Shakespeare's play, Warwick's motive is after all personal pique, as his closing soliloquy makes clear:

> Had he [Edward] none else to make a stale but me?
> Then none but I shall turn his jest to sorrow.
> I was the chief that rais'd him to the crown,
> And I'll be chief to bring him down again:
> Not that I pity Henry's misery,
> But seek revenge on Edward's mockery.
>
> (III.iii.260-65)

With the absence of praise for Henry and with the lack of private reference here to his earlier public expression of concern for the "strength and safety of our country" (211), Warwick's motives even in the foregoing dialogue come in this soliloquy to seem clearly less than grand. Shakespeare has created a scene in which the likeliest figure to make the required heroic response to Edward's fickle concupiscence does not fully do so.

Certainly the scene is sufficiently formal in execution and weighty enough in manner to call forth ambitious hopes and grand attitudes. Shakespeare sets up a formal balance of characters—three French (Lewis, Bona, and the mute figure, Bourbon); three Lancastrian English (Margaret, Prince Edward, and Oxford); and the pivot, Warwick. Before Warwick enters, there is some discussion whether sitting or standing is more suitable to honor, just as there is some discussion of sitting and standing in *I Tamburlaine* when the evenly-balanced Scythian and Turkish royal parties meet. After Lewis and Margaret are seated side by side, their respective parties presumably being grouped on either hand, Margaret broaches her weighty mission in heavily end-stopped verses. Warwick's entry breaks the symmetry, for while Margaret rises, Lewis descends to meet his guest and may be thought to draw Bona and Bourbon after him. Warwick's mission, the proposed marriage, is also a matter of importance, which soon requires that he debate still another grave question, Edward's right to rule. And yet through all these formalities and verbal contentions run the retrospective note, sometimes elegaic, sometimes captious, that suggests that heroic endeavor lies in the past, not the future. "I was, I must confess," remembers Margaret, "Great Albion's Queen in former golden days" (III.iii.7). Oxford recalls

> great John of Gaunt,
> Which did subdue the greatest part of Spain;
> And after John of Gaunt, Henry the Fourth,
> Whose wisdom was a mirror to the wisest;
> And after that wise prince, Henry the Fifth,
> Who by his prowess conquered all France:
> From these our Henry lineally descends.
>
> (III.iii.81-87)

About Henry little can be said, and Oxford does not improve upon his own silence. But he does recall his own father's death by order of Edward, "Even in the downfall of his mellow'd years" (104), while Warwick remembers times when a gentler passion overtook Edward:

> this his love was an eternal plant,
> Whereof the root was fix'd in Virtue's ground,
> The leaves and fruit maintain'd with Beauty's sun,
> Exempt from envy, but not from disdain,
> Unless the Lady Bona quite his pain.
>
> (III.iii.124-28)

When we recall that Edward subsequently accepted Lady Grey without a wince, we may conclude that all this imagery of nobility, virtue, and splendor seems to refer to what never was or to what never may be recovered.

The retrospective note is not that of *The Mirror for Magistrates,* in which the dead with hindsight analyze their errors. There is hardly any moral self-recrimination in this scene, except for Warwick's recital of Edward's offenses against himself, offenses we have never heard of before (186-88). The tone is that of the dying Brutus in *Locrine* recalling his conquests before handing on the sovereignty to his son; or perhaps Warwick's allegorical talk about Edward's love could resemble not only a sonnet-conceit but also Tamburlaine's allegorical description of the assault of Zenocrate's tears upon his irascible spirit; but here the review of the past is not completed by a prospective view of things to be won. The golden age is chiefly to be remembered, not realized.

In these pivotal scenes of heroic irony, Shakespeare alters the interpretation as well as the facts recorded in his sources. A mere desire to compress material does not wholly account for what was done with the facts. Had Shakespeare merely wanted to follow the historical view of Burgundy, it would have been easy to have a French lord rather than Joan appeal to Burgundy's pride—rather than to his pity. Had Shakespeare wanted only to present Gloucester's fall from power, he could have kept York out of the proceedings and could instead have had Queen Margaret name York *in absentia* as the commander in Ireland. If Shakespeare had thought merely to dramatize the disaffection and the new purpose of Warwick, he could have composed quite a different scene in which Warwick, returned from France, persuades the Duke of Clarence to Queen Margaret's cause. But what the dramatist seems to have wanted were opportunities to dramatize failure, perfidy, and even anger as imperfect approximations to or fallings-away from a heroic code.

None of these pivotal scenes is a battle scene, and therefore it may be argued that we have been looking in the wrong place for signs of the true heroic spirit. Because Shakespeare seems never to have had misgivings about the value and necessity of foreign war, we may consider how he handles combat in the trilogy. The heroic figure and his code expressed themselves most fully and properly in scenes of flyting and swordplay, and in those scenes of triumph or death that called for set speeches. We shall find, however, that even these do not have their full value in these plays.

Heroic set speeches of the defeated or the dying were a way of reiterating their tireless valor, their grandeur of ambitions, and their singleness of mind. There were two or three common topics for such speeches in Elizabethan drama. One theme was, If I fall, let the world fall with me. In this vein is Humber's speech cursing the universe that gave him birth, and another example is the Moor's very similar itemizing and blasting of all the causes of his being, in *The Battle of Alcazar:*

> Where shall I finde some unfrequented place,
> Some uncouth walke where I may curse my fill,
> My starres, my dam, my planets and my nurse,
> The fire, the aire, the water, and the earth,
> All causes that have thus conspirde in one,
> To nourish and preserve me to this shame. . . .
>
> (1268-73)

Nothing of the sort happens, of course, in *The Battle of Alcazar* or in *Locrine.* This is simply a way of saying that he wishes not to have lived to have been so disgraced by defeat. Another topic might have said the same thing, but not with suggestive cosmic references. This theme is also worked by Theridamas, Techelles, and Usumcasane in their lamentations of Tamburlaine's imminent death.

Another, second topic merely varies the first: If I fall, let heaven or earth (or both) drop down upon my enemy. So the captive Bajazeth wishes night and the terrors of the earth and skies to overtake Tamburlaine, and the three captive kings who pull the chariot in *II Tamburlaine* invoke heavenly and infernal powers upon their conqueror. Again, although neither heaven nor hell is moved, these speeches not only show the unbroken spirits of the defeated but also measure the kind of force needed to overcome the victor. A third theme of speeches on the occasion of death or defeat has a better chance of being borne out by events: If I fall, let my heirs take up my fight. Tamburlaine after reconciling himself to his own death bequeaths his fiery spirit and his search for new dominion to his sons. Brutus bestows his rule and his kingly duties upon his son, Locrine. Abdelmelec, dying at the outset of battle, resigns his soul to God and the struggle for Morocco to his heirs. In such moments as these, handing on the cause not only reiterates the great and unbowed spirit of the fallen leader but also provides a way of emphasizing the primacy of honor over milder passions, such as grief or fear. "Let not thy love exceed thine honour" (*Part II,* V.iii.199), Tamburlaine warns his grieving son.

In *I Henry VI* there are certainly speeches in both the heaven-invoking and the heir-inciting manners, but Shakespeare seems to withhold the dramatic endorsement that gives a set speech full emphasis. In scene one, instead of letting the lamentations of Gloucester and Bedford and Exeter move unbrokenly into self-incitement to pursue the French conquests of the dead Henry V, Shakespeare provides first a quarrel and then a series of three messengers with bad news from France. The lamentations therefore seem somehow improper in retrospect. The practice that eventually becomes almost a convention emerges here, so that the audience may well feel from the beginning a distrust of fine language and rhetorical ornament whenever it is not seconded by timely and effectual action. Of course it would in real life be unfair to fault Gloucester and the others for mourning instead of attending to the bad news they could not know was coming; but in drama we look to the stage-effect, which is that of men quite unready at first to deal with challenge and defeat. Moreover, the finest hero of this play, Talbot, never orates when occasion is about to call him to act. He generally speaks a plain idiom of command. The scenes of his last battle, at Bordeaux, and of his death (*I Henry VI,* IV.v and vi) are times for his son to give effective though finally unavailing support, and for the father to rescue the son. These scenes are composed in couplets with some stichomythia, but are not otherwise greatly ornamented. In place of Marlovian and Spenserian imagery in the opening scene, there is only the single image of Young Talbot as Icarus in a sea of blood to remind us of other aspirations. Talbot seldom suggests that the stars are somehow involved with his fate. Once he blames them, but later he quite sensibly blames York, the English Regent of France, for failing to supply aid. It is Talbot's way to keep to the facts that define his valor, so that in dying with the body of his son in his arms he may claim that their valor is proven and will outlast death.

It is true that Talbot delivers a short eulogy over the mortally wounded Salisbury, and vows revenge on his behalf, and further, that the vow is embellished with one of the grislier stock images of heroic determination: "Your hearts I'll stamp out with my horse' heels / And make a quagmire of your mingled brains" (*I Henry VI,* I.iv.107-08). It is also true, however, that this warlike revenge is at once frustrated by the loss of Orleans, and that Talbot momentarily wishes to be dead like Salisbury. The regaining of Orleans is businesslike and embellished mainly by the use of scaling-ladders rather than metaphors, amplifications, allusions, or other figures. The victorious Talbot, satisfied that sufficient French dead have paid for Salisbury's death, chooses to mark his revenge concretely with a tomb, "that hereafter ages may behold / What ruin happen'd in revenge of him" (*I Henry VI,* II.ii.11-12). In this play effective action rather than words is the mark of a hero in the presence of death; and without action, no words will suffice.

In the next two parts of the trilogy the set speeches by the defeated and by their allies have been much more elaborated. As in *Part I,* these speeches in *II* and *III Henry VI* lack full dramatic endorsement: no one seconds them; events immediately following contradict them; and most importantly the speeches do not support fully the heroic image that should be proper to the speaker.

Although Henry's regretful longing in *Part III* to be a shepherd is the most obvious instance of lapse from the stance proper to a hero during a battle, Warwick's death-speech also relinquishes the power he has fought for:

> Lo now my glory smear'd in dust and blood!
>
> . . . . .
>
> Why, what is pomp, rule, reign, but earth and dust?
> And live we how we can, yet die we must.
>
> (V.ii.23, 27-28)

Among heroic figures in Elizabethan drama, only Sulla before this had abruptly repudiated the earthly glory he had fought for. Heroic plays and heroes—even Talbot—ignore the ironic possibility of an eternity inhospitable to the claims of earthly greatness. York's long and formal invective against those who have slain his youthful son does not precisely condemn the mutable world, but it does dwell on the vileness of those who have won, Queen Margaret and Lord Clifford:

> There, take the crown, and with the crown my curse;
> And in thy need such comfort come to thee
> As now I reap at thy too cruel hand!
> Hard-hearted Clifford, take me from the world:
> My soul to heaven, my blood upon your heads!
>
> (I.iv.164-68)

When Clifford's turn comes to die, he makes no complaint against his fate, but even gives over his grief at the waste of all his valor and strength in behalf of Lancaster:

> And, Henry, hadst thou sway'd as kings should do,
> . . . . .
> I, and ten thousand in this luckless realm
> Had left no mourning widows for our death;
> And thou this day hadst kept thy chair in peace.
> . . . . .
> Bootless are plaints, and cureless are my wounds;
> No way to fly, nor strength to hold our flight:
> The foe is merciless and will not pity;
> For at their hands I have deserv'd no pity.
>
> (II.vi.14, 18-20, 23-26)

This admirable analysis of the reasons for Henry's and Clifford's present woes tacitly renounces the cause—Lancastrian supremacy and personal revenge—for which Clifford had fought against and murdered the Duke of York. The dying lord does not leave his curse to his enemies or his cause to his allies: "Come, York [Edward] and Richard, Warwick and the rest; / I stabb'd your fathers' bosoms: split my breast" (*III Henry VI,* II.vi.29-30). So they do, but they do not discover Clifford until he is dead and must content themselves with ignominious abuse of a corpse. In various ways, York's, Clifford's, and Warwick's speeches—for which neither Hall nor Holinshed gives any hints—show Shakespeare departing from the usual formulas for the valedictories of heroes. While a Talbot may find his valor affirmed by his and his son's deaths, the participants in civil war find nothing in their time of dying to affirm the glories of their causes. For the audience, too, nothing ever seems secured by victory in the *Henry VI* plays.

Although Talbot secures his fame, he is not vindicated by an English triumph, and York's victory over Joan la Pucelle in *Part I* soon is followed by an unreliable peace. Although both York and Lancaster win victories, each victory is followed by reversal, and at no time does a success exterminate all those who intend to bring down the victors. Battle-scenes do not receive full endorsement because no heroic triumph or heroic death is a decisive resolution. What each victory requires is political wisdom, supported by power gained in battle, to assure the continuance of rule.

The structures created by heroic irony may now be summarized. The three parts of the trilogy are not identical in patterns of action. Each has a pivotal action near the center, and each ends with a choice or a resolve that proposes some new action that unsettles the resolution achieved in the last few scenes. In *I Henry VI,* Henry's choice of Margaret and the conclusion of a false peace with France clearly undo the strong alliance Gloucester has worked for and undo the military rule for which Talbot has fought. The pivotal action in *Part I,* as we have seen, prepares by an unheroic choice for Talbot's defeat. The choice of a woman for beauty alone may be censured as unheroic, like the peace, but both are also impolitic granting of concessions and trust for nothing in return. Neither may the concept of noble generosity be invoked to defend these actions, for they involve ungenerous, unjust, and dishonorable treatment of others. Henry's marriage to Margaret breaks arrangements made through Gloucester with the Duke of Armagnac. The peace with France dishonors all who have fought for nothing less than totally securing the English claims in France. Politics in this trilogy must be squared with the just demands of honor, if the political order is to endure.

The central scene of *II Henry VI* is likewise decisive in preparing for the last act, and is likewise an instance of ignoble behavior that is not balanced by a heroic triumph at the end of the play. Although a pitched battle occurs in Act V, and although that battle is fought by evenly-matched forces, the Yorkist victory is left inconclusive by the escape of the King and Queen and by York's decision to follow Henry to London and to negotiate with him there. The normal end of heroic encounter is, of course, decisive victory. Further, Clifford has left the battlefield vowing cruel revenge for the death of his father. It may be argued that Shakespeare is only following history: the historical York did not at first seek to kill Henry or to exterminate the Lancastrian party. But there is no need to end a play with a battle and then so carefully to signal its incomplete success, unless the dramatist desires not only fidelity of treatment but heroical irony. We are headed into *Part III* by the ending of *II Henry VI,* with a strong suggestion that military success at St. Albans is only temporary.

In *Part III,* Warwick's shift to the Lancastrian cause at a time when it seems defeated helps prepare for the renewal of civil war, but helps also to prepare for the scene of Warwick's death in defeat. His renunciation, as we have seen, is not a heroic gesture. The scene of Edward's wooing of Lady Grey (*III Henry VI,* III.ii) also reverses relationships and prepares for the closing scenes. At the end of III.ii, we find that Edward's success in wooing has provoked Richard of Gloucester to begin conspiring, out of sexual envy, against his royal brother. At the end of *Part III,* while Edward rejoices in having a male heir by Lady Grey, Richard in asides renews his cruel resolve to kill his brothers and their posterity if murder is necessary to win the crown. Here again, lapses from heroic loyalty and firmness lead to an inconclusive resolution at the end, rather than the heroic triumphs that the characters' ambitions would require. It is true, however, that the respective conclusions of the three parts of the trilogy are not similar in situation, just as the pivotal scenes are not closely similar in kind. Shakespeare was accommodating his plots to varied historical material, and so did not follow one structural pattern in every part of the trilogy.

Indeed English chronicle-history plays had no form of their own, and their purposes did not require a distinctive generic structure. F. P. Wilson's recent consideration of this matter showed that, although there are various types of history plays, they do not, as a group distinct from comedy and tragedy, have an identifying generic feature.[17] Neither would it be quite satisfactory to say, with Lily B. Campbell, that Elizabethan historical plays, especially those that are too serious to be comedies and yet not clearly tragic, all have the single purpose of accomplishing the moral ends of history;[18] for as plays rather than historical narratives they must also have accomplished some purposes peculiar to drama. One type of chronicle-history, the contention-play, represented by *The Wounds of Civil War,* seems to have grown structurally from the device in moral plays of alternating scenes featuring one group of characters with scenes featuring another group.[19] But unlike moral dramas, contention-plays pitted characters and factions that were not necessarily moral opposites; Sulla and Marius are equally irascible, equally able in war and politics, and Lodge's play dramatizes their terrible struggle and the eventual success of Sulla's faction. At least *Parts II* and *III* were also perceived as contention-plays with interest focused upon the struggle of antagonists rather than the fortunes of a single hero, for the titles of the bad quartos of these two plays include not only "contention" but also subtitle reference to various persons both primary and secondary in the struggle. If we take moral drama and *The Wounds of Civil War* as models, we may say that contention plays showed the triumphs of first one party and then those of the other. Yet the three parts of *Henry VI* do not respectively follow this model in the same way. Not only does Shakespeare provide more rivalries in *Parts I* and *II* than the contentions between the principal antagonists; he also distributes the clashes differently in *Part II,* say, than he does in *Part III.* In *II Henry VI,* verbal clashes between Gloucester and Winchester punctuate their political rivalry until Gloucester's fall and death; then begins the open struggle between Lancaster and York—first with a Lancastrian victory over the pseudo-Mortimer, Jack Cade, and then immediately after with York's closing (but not decisive) victory over Henry's forces. In *III Henry VI,* however, the action is largely a series of battles separated by interludes of political intrigue, and the Yorkist triumphs alternate with Yorkist defeats throughout the play.[20] *I Henry VI,* as we have already remarked, has manifold rivalries, and may also be considered a contention-play. Here the primary contention of French against English (or Joan against Talbot), continues throughout the play against a background of secondary struggles—some political and some military—among the English. Unlike *Part II,* the first play is organized by a heroic contention continuing throughout the action; unlike *Part III,* it contrasts the main heroic contention with less worthy domestic clashes. But Shakespeare's varied handling of the contention-pattern is not controlled by the facts of history. He has been found here to compress and rearrange historical facts, such as Joan's and Burgundy's careers, York's relationship to Gloucester, and Warwick's reaction to King Edward's marriage, in order to heighten and even to create antagonisms contrary to fact. Likewise he brought Talbot and Joan together at Bordeaux, conflated two battles at St. Albans, and conferred on Richard of Gloucester the double motive of sexual envy and Machiavellism—all for the sake of emphasizing contention despite the facts of the chronicle sources. He may well have thought the contention-pattern most natural for the plot of plays dealing with civil and foreign war, but he did not let the facts control the shaping of the action. And he may well have found the contention-pattern the readiest framework to support his heroical irony, for the very nature of such plotting allowed the contenders, especially in the field, to be tacitly measured against the stature of Tamburlaine, Sulla, and other heroes of drama. Further, he introduced scenes and situations that were conventional in heroic drama of the time, with the result that lapses from heroic conduct might be more clearly perceived. Far from writing simply a kind of moral-historical drama in which the right line of conduct might have led to the salvation of England,[21] Shakespeare has written a trilogy in which the right and effective course, embracing a heroic code as well as political wisdom, occurs to almost no one but Talbot and is not practicable by anyone but he. Finally, Shakespeare introduced into each of his varied contention-plots a pivotal scene or scenes that emphasized his heroical irony by showing the noble or the great undermined by the mean, the ignoble, and unheroic.

Notes

1. The main sources of the trilogy were probably the accounts of the reigns of Henry VI and Edward IV in Edward Hall's *The Union of the Two Noble and Illustre Famelies of Lancastre and Yorke* (1548-52) and Raphael Holinshed's *The Chronicles of England, Scotlande, and Irelande* (1587). Shakespeare may have used Grafton's *Chronicle at Large* in place of or in supplement to Hall. But because Grafton closely follows Hall, it is not necessary for my purposes to include him in comparing sources with Shakespeare's scenes. See: Geoffrey Bullough, *Narrative and Dramatic Sources of Shakespeare* (London: Routledge and Kegan Paul; New York: Columbia University Press, 1960), III, 25, 90-91, 158.

2. See Bullough's rejoinder in *Narrative and Dramatic Sources* (III, 36-37) to Tillyard. Virgil K. Whitaker shows that Shakespeare, though aware of Providence in historical causation, was also conventionally alert to the effects of Fortune and human character; see *Shakespeare's Use of Learning* (San Marino, Calif.: Huntington Library, 1953), pp. 57-59.

3. Thomas Lodge, *The Wounds of Civil War,* ed. John Dover Wilson and W. W. Greg, Malone Society Reprint (Oxford: Oxford University Press, 1910); George Peele, *The Battle of Alcazar,* ed. John Yoklavich, *The Life and Works,* Vol. II (New Haven: Yale University Press, 1961); *The Troublesome raigne of John, King of England,* ed. Charles Praetorius (London: C. Praetorius, 1888); Christopher Marlowe, *Tamburlaine the Great,* ed. Una Ellis-Fermor (London: Methuen and Co., Ltd., 1930).

4. *Tragedy of Locrine,* in *The Shakespeare Aprocrypha,* ed. C. F. Tucker Brooke (Oxford: Clarendon Press, 1918). Evidence that the author of *Selimus* revised and borrowed from *Locrine* has been presented by Baldwin Maxwell, *Studies in the Shakespeare Apocrypha* (New York: King's Crown Press, Columbia

University, 1956), pp. 47-51, 61-62. Maxwell also suggests that this reviser may have added two scenes, IV.ii and iv; I would further suggest that the two scenes replaced scenes in which Corineus discovers Locrine's adultery and Locrine kills Corineus.

5. Eugene Waith, *The Herculean Hero in Marlowe, Chapman, Shakespeare, and Dryden* (London: Chatto & Windus, 1962), chs. 1 and 2. On the code of martial honor, see Curtis B. Watson, *Shakespeare and the Renaissance Concept of Honor* (Princeton: Princeton University Press, 1960), pp. 102-35. Castiglione's disputants were unable to decide whether conquest or peaceable, just rule were more honorable (*The Book of the Courtier,* trans. Thomas Hoby, 1561, Book IV). For discussion of the Herculean type in drama as exemplar in humanist historiography and in plays of the late 1580's and early 1590's, see David Riggs, *Shakespeare's Heroical Histories: "Henry VI" and Its Literary Tradition* (Cambridge, Mass.: Harvard University Press, 1971), ch. 1, esp. pp. 9-10, and ch. 3, esp. pp. 72-74.

6. Watson, *Shakespeare and the Renaissance Concept of Honor,* pp. 91-93.

7. The phrase, of course, is J. P. Brockbank's; see his "The Frame of Disorder: 'Henry VI'" in *Early Shakespeare,* Stratford-upon-Avon Studies 3, ed. John Russell Brown and Bernard Harris (London: Edward Arnold, 1961), pp. 73-99. For explication of various motifs in the trilogy see Ernest W. Talbert, *Elizabethan Drama and Shakespeare's Early Plays* (Chapel Hill: University of North Carolina Press, 1963). For a claim that the trilogy is thematically unified but not constructed on any single conventional pattern of play see Hereward Price, *Construction in Shakespeare,* University of Michigan Contributions in Modern Philology, No. 17 (Ann Arbor: The University of Michigan Press, 1961).

8. Appian, *Civil Wars,* trans. Horace White (London: W. Heinemann; New York: The Macmillan Co., 1913), I, xii, 6; Plutarch, *Lives,* trans. Thomas North (London: D. Nutt, 1895), III, 298. Evidence for Lodge's use of Appian is given by Nathaniel B. Paradise, *Thomas Lodge* (New Haven: Yale University Press, 1931), pp. 137-39. Some details, however, such as Scipio's prophecy about Marius (*The Wounds of Civil War,* 137-40), the names of the Asian heroes vanquished by Sulla (1070-76), and Sulla's rally speech to his men (341-62) are not in Appian but in Plutarch's *Lives* (III, 165, 287-300, 298).

9. See John Dover Wilson, ed., "Introduction," *I Henry VI* (Cambridge, England: Cambridge University Press, 1952), pp. xi-xii, xxi-1; "Introduction," *II Henry VI* (Cambridge, England: Cambridge University Press, 1952), pp. xix-lii. Wilson's belief that Shakespeare revised other men's work and brought it to completion amounts to a belief that Shakespeare revised almost as carelessly as the others had written.

10. One cannot consider Robert Wilson, credited with at least partial authorship of sixteen plays on English history, for none of these has survived.

11. Hall, *Union,* pp. 173 f., 176-77. Holinshed, *Chronicles,* III, 181, 183. Holinshed simply adapts Hall's phrasings here.

12. Hall, *Union,* pp. 176-77.

13. Editions of *I, II, and III Henry VI,* ed. Andrew S. Cairncross, New Arden Edition (London: Methuen & Co., Ltd., 1957-62). All quotations are from this edition.

14. Hall, *Union,* pp. 208-11, 213-16. Holinshed, *Chronicles,* III, 210-12, 215-17. Neither writer names York among the peers who accused Gloucester.

15. Riggs, *Shakespeare's Heroical Histories,* pp. 115, 119 f., likewise finds this role imposed upon Gloucester.

16. Quotation from Hall, *Union,* p. 264. Hall further says that Queen Carlotta, wife to King Lewis, promoted the match between Edward and Bona, and refused overtures from Margaret; Margaret was not at court at this time. For Holinshed's version, see *Chronicles,* III, 283-85, 288-94.

17. Frank P. Wilson, "The English History Play," in *Shakespearian and Other Studies,* ed. Helen Gardner (Oxford: Clarendon Press, 1969), pp. 1-53.

18. Lily B. Campbell, *Shakespeare's "Histories": Mirrors of Elizabethan Policy* (San Marino, Calif.: The Huntington Library, 1947), pp. 15-17. This view was followed by Irving Ribner in *The English History Play in the Age of Shakespeare* (Princeton: Princeton University Press, 1957), esp. ch. 2.

19. David M. Bevington, *From "Mankind" to Marlowe: Growth of Structure in the Popular Drama of Tudor England* (Cambridge, Mass.: Harvard University Press, 1962).

20. Cairncross, "Introduction," *III Henry VI,* pp. lix-li.

21. Ribner, *The English History Play in the Age of Shakespeare,* p. 101; E. M. W. Tillyard, *Shakespeare's History Plays* (New York: The Macmillan Company, 1945), pp. 160-63.

Gwyn Williams (essay date 1974)

SOURCE: "Suffolk and Margaret: A Study of Some Sections of Shakespeare's *Henry VI,*" in *Shakespeare Quarterly,* Vol. 25, No. 3, Summer, 1974, pp. 310-22.

[*In the essay below, Williams probes Shakespeare's presentation of an unhistorical love affair between Queen Margaret of Anjou and the Earl of Suffolk as the drama-*

tist's first attempt at staging romantic relationships with tragic consequences.]

The illicit love affair which Shakespeare gave to Queen Margaret and the Earl (afterward Duke) of Suffolk in *1* and *2 Henry VI* is unhistorical. At a time when Shakespeare for his dramatic purposes was ruthlessly simplifying and trimming history, he chose to invent this tragic and, to most people, disagreeable love story, basing his invention only on some hints in Hall's *Chronicle*. There appears to have been no demanding reason, dramatically, for this invention, even though it does link together *Parts 1* and *2* to a degree which makes them seem one play. Some other situation, vouched for by history, could have done this equally well. When Shakespeare omitted or cut material from a source he was using, the dramatic purpose of the omission or cutting down is usually clear to us. But when he enlarged or invented on the basis of a hint and if there is no conspicuous dramatic need for the innovation, then one may be allowed to suspect a particular interest on Shakespeare's part in this addition to the story.

Let us look closely at the relationship between Princess Margaret, later Queen of England, and Suffolk as given by Shakespeare. In *1 Henry VI*, V. iii., the French are defeated and Joan la Pucelle is taken prisoner by the Duke of York. Margaret becomes, unhistorically, Suffolk's prisoner. Before he knows who she is, he is impressed by her beauty. He enters, dragging her by the hand, "Be what thou wilt, thou art my prisoner" (l. 45).[1] She has clearly been protesting her importance. He pauses to look at her:

> O fairest beauty, do not fear, nor fly,
> For I will touch thee but with reverent hands:
> I kiss these fingers for eternal peace
> And lay them gently on thy tender side.
> Who art thou? Say, that I may honour thee.
>
> (ll. 46-50)

She gives him her name and rank and he replies with his. Then follows a curious Wooing Scene in which Suffolk fights a delaying action while he works a plan to win her for himself:

> Be not offended, nature's miracle,
> Thou art allotted to be ta'en by me.
>
> (ll. 54-55)

Then, seeing a disdainful look on her face (we must remember that this is the future "she-wolf of France"), he says, "Go, and be free again, as Suffolk's friend" (l. 59). As she turns to go he stops her:

> O stay. . . . I have no power to let her pass;
> My hand would free her but my heart says no.
>
> (ll. 60-61)

He is daunted by her "gorgeous beauty" and dares not speak. He thinks of calling for pen and paper and putting his love in writing, but is ashamed of his weakness. She now offers a ransom but he turns aside, muttering his perplexity and trying to find a way out of his difficulty. The difficulty is, of course, that he is already married.

> Fond man, remember that thou hast a wife;
> Then how can Margaret be thy paramour?
>
> (ll. 81-82)

He continues these asides for nine consecutive speeches, which are interspersed with her comments which express a growing puzzlement and the thought that he must be mad. Losing patience she shouts at him:

> Hear ye, Captain—are you not at leisure?
>
> (l. 97)

He has now conceived the idea of marrying her to his king, and he turns to speak directly to her. But she now speaks aside, giving him what she calls "*quid* for *quo*." He makes the offer and almost a serious and revealing gaffe:

> I'll undertake to make thee Henry's queen,
> To put a golden sceptre in thy hand
> And set a precious crown upon thy head,
> If thou wilt condescend to be my—
> *Mar.* What?
> *Suf.* His love.
>
> (ll. 117-21)

He has retrieved the situation superficially, but his speech continues to reveal the confusion in his mind. When she protests her unworthiness to be Henry's wife he replies,

> No, gentle madam, I unworthy am
> To woo so fair a dame to be his wife
> And have no portion in the choice myself.
>
> (ll. 123-25)

She is content with this ambiguous offer. Up to this point everything is unhistorical except the fact that Suffolk is married, that he did suggest the marriage of Henry and Margaret, and that Margaret was impressive in beauty and personality. Hall said, "This woman excelled all other, as well in beautie and favor, as in wit and pollicie, and was of stomack and corage, more like to a man, then a woman."[2] One gets the impression that she understands what Suffolk hopes to gain by the arrangement and there is no sign of confusion in her mind. Her father, Reignier, quickly agrees and makes a hard bargain which Suffolk undertakes will be accepted. As they part, Reignier embraces Suffolk and Margaret says,

> Farewell, my lord. Good wishes, praise and prayers
> Shall Suffolk ever have of Margaret.
>
> (ll. 173-74)

He does not want to let her go and asks whether she has any message for the King. She answers modestly but he presses her: "No loving token for his majesty?" (l. 181). She answers,

> Yes, my good lord, a pure unspotted heart,
> Never yet taint of love, I send the king.
> *Suf.* And this withal. [*Kisses her*]
> *Mar.* That for thyself. I will not so presume
> To send such peevish token to a king.
>
> (ll. 182-86)

All this is done and said in the presence of her father. They understand each other already. When Margaret and Reignier have gone out, Suffolk soliloquizes. He wants her for himself but he is horrified at what this may involve:

> O wert thou for myself! But Suffolk, stay;
> Thou mayst not wander in that labyrinth;
> There minotaurs and ugly treasons lurk.
>
> (ll. 187-89)

Even if he is able to avoid the dangers, she may be Ariadne to his Theseus, a not entirely happy story. He decides to praise her virtues and natural graces to Henry in such a manner as will "bereave him of his wits with wonder." We do not hear Suffolk praising Margaret to the King, for when Act V, scene v, begins Suffolk has ended his account of Margaret's charms and Henry is suitably impressed. He is easily induced by Suffolk to break off his betrothal to the Earl of Armagnac's daughter, in spite of the protests of Gloucester and Exeter. Henry asks Suffolk to return at once to France to bring back Margaret. *Part 1* ends with Suffolk's comment:

> Thus Suffolk hath prevail'd; and thus he goes
> As did the youthful Paris once to Greece,
> With hope to find the like event in love,
> But prosper better than the Trojan did.
> Margaret shall now be queen, and rule the king:
> But I will rule both her, the king and realm.
>
> (V. v. 103-8)

The comparison with Paris is apt, for he intends to steal a king's wife. He realizes the dangers implied in the comparison but hopes to be luckier in the end than Paris was. We remember the disasters brought upon Troy by Paris's exploit, and we are prepared for similar results in England. The last line of the soliloquy is an echo of Hall: Suffolk "by the meanes of the Quene, was shortely erected to the estate and degree of a Duke, and ruled the Kyng at his pleasure."[3] Again, before dying, Suffolk will compare himself to heroes of antiquity (*2 Henry VI,* IV.i.), with no sign of irony on Shakespeare's part but rather the hint that we should take him seriously. Similarly, Margaret compares herself to Dido (III.ii.115-18), and Suffolk's farewell speech (end of III.ii.) has echoes of the exiled Ovid's complaint to his wife.[4] Shakespeare put this pair of lovers in famous company.

2 Henry VI begins with Suffolk presenting Margaret to the King. It appears that he has actually married her on Henry's behalf, and this is historical. History also records that Suffolk's wife went with him to France, and she would have kept a watchful eye on the proceedings, but in Shakespeare Suffolk goes untrammeled. What is unhistorical and invented by Shakespeare is for Margaret to praise Suffolk as her champion in the lists during these preliminary wedding celebrations (see below). All that Hall had to say is, "There wer triumphaunt Justes, costly feastes, and delicate banquettes."[5] The King is overwhelmed by Margaret's beauty and "her grace in speech." He creates Suffolk Duke and leaves the stage with him and Margaret, leaving Gloucester to fulminate against the alliance.

In Act I, scene iii, the Queen and Suffolk are walking in the palace grounds—clearly confirmed now in their intimacy—when they meet some petitioners, one of whom takes Suffolk to be Gloucester, the Lord Protector. The petitions anger both the Queen and Suffolk, and Margaret complains about her treatment at Court. She is annoyed that her husband is "a pupil still," and she compares him unfavorably with Suffolk:

> I tell thee, Pole, when in the city Tours
> Thou ran'st a tilt in honour of my love,
> And stol'st away the ladies' hearts of France,
> I thought King Henry had resembled thee
> In courage, courtship and proportion;
> But all his mind is bent to holiness,
> To number Ave-Maries on his beads . . .
>
> (ll. 50-56)

Suffolk tries to content her with a promise:

> Madam, be patient: as I was the cause
> Your Highness came to England, so will I
> In England work your Grace's full content.
>
> (ll. 65-67)

Their association is partly one of political ambition, but it is important to remember that he fell in love with her before he knew who she was and certainly before he conceived the plan of marrying her to his king.

Suffolk is already setting traps for Margaret's enemies, notably the Gloucesters. The spirit's answers in the séance contrived by Suffolk are Shakespeare's inventions and the unhistorical prophecy, "By water shall he die and take his end" (I.iv.32), is remembered by Suffolk on the day of his death. In the play Margaret's great rival is Eleanor, duchess of Gloucester, and this again is unhistorical for Eleanor's humiliation took place four years before Margaret came to England. Shakespeare brought it forward so that the struggle for control of the King and of England should fall chiefly between Suffolk and Margaret on the one hand and Gloucester and his wife on the other. A brilliant invention on Shakespeare's part is the dropping of the fan by Margaret and the box she administers to Eleanor's ear in the pretense that she took her for a servant. Eleanor's answer sends shivers down one's back:

> . . . proud Frenchwoman,
> Could I come near your beauty with my nails,
> I'd set my ten commandments in your face.
>
> (I.iii.140-42)

In Act II, scene i, Suffolk, in close attendance on Henry and Margaret, feels confident enough to taunt Gloucester, and in Act III, scene i, he arrests Gloucester on a trumped-up charge of treason. Beaufort, York, and Suffolk decide on Gloucester's death in the presence of Margaret and by the next scene Gloucester is dead, strangled by Suffolk's murderers. He has been laid in a bed to counterfeit a natural death. The King knows that it is murder, but Margaret defends Suffolk and puts on an act of ill-treated martyrdom. Warwick enters to announce that the commons have heard a report that Gloucester has been murdered by Suffolk and Beaufort and that they demand to know the truth. Warwick indicates the evidence of murder in the dead Gloucester's appearance, and a shouting match between Warwick and Suffolk leads to the drawing of weapons.

At the demand of the commons, Henry banishes Suffolk. Margaret pleads for him in vain, and they are left alone on the stage to curse their enemies and bewail their coming separation. She weeps over his clutched hand and then kisses it:

> O, could this kiss be printed in thy hand,
> That thou might'st think upon these by the seal
> Through whom a thousand sighs are breath'd for thee.
>
> (III.ii.342-44)

(This is the first occurrence of the seal-mouth image which runs through Shakespeare's work.) They embrace and kiss, "Loather a hundred times to part than die" (l. 354). For Suffolk the banishment is from her, not from England:

> 'Tis not the land I care for, wert thou thence:
> A wilderness is populous enough
> So Suffolk had thy heavenly company.
>
> (ll. 358-60)

He asks her to let him stay with her, even at the risk of death:

> If I depart from thee I cannot live;
> And in thy sight to die, what were it else
> But like a pleasant slumber in thy lap?
> Here could I breathe my soul into the air,
> As mild and gentle as the cradle-babe
> Dying with mother's dug between its lips;
> Where, from thy sight, I should be raging mad,
> And cry out for thee to close up mine eyes,
> To have thee with thy lips to stop my mouth.
> So shouldst thou either turn my flying soul
> Or I should breathe it so into thy body
> And then it liv'd in sweet Elysium . . .
>
> (ll. 387-98)

But they must part; she in the hope of meeting again, he full of foreboding of death:

> *Mar.* Though parting be a fretful corrosive,
> It is applied to a deathful wound.
> To France, sweet Suffolk! Let me hear from thee,
> For whereso'er thou art in this world's globe
> I'll have an Iris that shall find thee out.
> Away!
> *Suf.* I go.
> *Mar.* And take my heart with thee. [*She kisses him.*]
> *Suf.* A jewel lock'd into the woefull'st cask
> That ever did contain a thing of worth.
> Even as a splitted bark so sunder we:
> This way fall I to death.
> *Mar.* This way for me.
>
> (ll. 402-12)

So ends Act III, scene ii. Almost immediately, in Act IV, scene i, comes Suffolk's end. In a sea battle on his way to France, Suffolk has been taken prisoner with two other gentlemen. Hall tells us that his head was struck off on the side of a cock boat; head and body were left on the shore to be picked up by Suffolk's chaplain, who took the body to Wingfield College for burial. Shakespeare's invented version is very different. According to him, the two gentlemen promise to pay for their freedom but Suffolk has been allotted to Walter Whitmore—a character unknown to history but invented by Shakespeare to carry out the similarly invented prophecy that Suffolk will die by water, Walter being pronounced as water. Whitmore has lost an eye in the affray and is determined to kill Suffolk in dogged retribution. Suffolk recognizes the Captain[6] as one who has served at Court, and he trusts that this will save him. But the proud and contemptuous way in which he reminds the Captain of his former servile state hardens the latter's heart against him. In return, the Captain bitterly and offensively recounts the memory of what he has observed at Court. He lays the losses in France, the troubles at home, and the death of Gloucester squarely at Suffolk's door. Punning on Suffolk's family name, Pole (pronounced pool), he cries out,

> Poole! Sir Poole! Lord!
> Ay, kennel, puddle, sink, whose filth and dirt[7]
> Troubles the silver spring where England drinks.
> Now will I dam up this thy yawning mouth,
> For swallowing the treasure of the realm.
> Thy lips that kiss'd the Queen shall sweep the ground.
> . . .
>
> (IV.i.69-74)

To Shakespeare's mind, the physical degree to which the love of Margaret and Suffolk had gone must have been common knowledge at Court. Whitmore has mockingly referred to Suffolk as the "forlorn swain" (l. 65), the abandoned lover of the Queen, for that is surely the intention of this cruel joke. Suffolk at first pleads the Queen's commission, but then his pride supervenes and he decides to die bravely, without any further attempt to soften his captors:

> Come soldiers, show what cruelty you can,
> That this my death may never be forgot.
> Great men oft die by vile besonians:
> A Roman soldier and banditto slave
> Murder'd sweet Tully; Brutus' bastard hand
> Stabb'd Julius Caesar; savage islanders
> Pompey the Great; and Suffolk dies by pirates.
>
> (ll. 132-38)

He is removed for execution and a moment later Whitmore carries the severed head and body onto the stage, saying,

> There let his head and lifeless body lie,
> Until the Queen his mistress bury it.
>
> (ll. 142-43)

The horrified Gentleman cries out,

> O barbarous and bloody spectacle!
> His body will I bear unto the King:
> If he revenge it not, yet will his friends;
> So will the Queen, that living held him dear.
>
> (ll. 144-47)

But we are not told who took the head to the Queen. A little later, in Act IV, scene iv, we see Margaret in King Henry's presence, holding Suffolk's head to her breast. Grief has made her reckless in shamelessly acknowledging her love.

> Oft have I heard that grief softens the mind,
> And makes it fearful and degenerate;
> Think therefore on revenge, and cease to weep.
> But who can cease to weep and look on this?
> Here may his head lie on my throbbing breast,
> But where's the body that I should embrace?
>
> (ll. 1-6)

It is not long since she held the living head of her departing lover to her breast. While the King discusses the Jack Cade rebellion with his lords, Margaret continues her lament:

> Ah! barbarous villains, hath this lovely face
> Rul'd like a wandering planet over me,
> And could it not enforce them to relent
> That were unworthy to behold the same?
>
> (ll. 15-18)

The King turns to her:

> How now, madam?
> Still lamenting and mourning for Suffolk's death?
> I fear me, love, if that I had been dead,
> Thou wouldst not have mourn'd so much for me.

Even in this situation she is quick-witted enough to reply, with ready and triumphant hypocrisy, "My love, I should not mourn but die for thee" (ll. 21-24). The rebels are reported to be drawing near and Margaret says that if Suffolk were alive, "the Kentish rebels would be soon appeased." The King calls to her, "Come, Margaret; God, our hope, will succour us." As she goes out, still nursing the head, she replies, "My hope is gone, now Suffolk is deceas'd" (ll. 54-55).

So ends the story of Suffolk and Margaret, but there is yet another, more oblique reference to this love in the suggestion, in *3 Henry VI* (II.ii.131ff.), that the Prince of Wales is its fruit. The spirited young prince stands up to Warwick:

> If that be right which Warwick says is right,
> There is no wrong, but everything is right.

Warwick comments,

> Whoever got thee, there thy mother stands.

Ten lines later Edward, soon to be Edward IV, attacks Margaret as a "shameless callet."

> Helen of Greece was fairer far than thou,
> Although thy husband may be Menelaus;
> And ne'er was Agamemnon's brother wrong'd
> By that false woman as this king by thee.

We remember Suffolk's description of himself going to France to bring Margaret to England, "As did the youthful Paris once to Greece" (*1 Henry VI,* V.v.104). Critics and commentators appear to have ignored the paternity of Edward, Prince of Wales, as implied by these speeches and therefore as it appeared to Shakespeare.

This then is the tragic tale of adulterous love which Shakespeare based upon the merest hints in history. Hall once referred to Suffolk as "the Quenes dearlynge" and stated that the Queen "entierly loved the Duke,"[8] but even here darling could mean favorite (there is a reference to the Queen's "minions") and the entire love is not necessarily sexual. Holinshed, whose *Chronicle* Shakespeare closely followed, omitted these hints of an affection but stressed the close association of Suffolk and Margaret in the control of the country. In tracing the disruption of England under Henry VI, Holinshed wrote, "Richard, duke of Yorke, . . . perceiving the king to be no ruler, but the whole burthen of the realme to rest in direction of the queene, & the duke of Suffolke, began secretile to allure his friends of the nobilitie."[9] When the commons began openly to accuse Suffolk of being the cause of the many ills afflicting England, Holinshed said, "The queene hereat, doubting not onelie the dukes destruction, but also hir owne confusion, caused the parlement, before begun at the Blackfriers, to be adjourned to Leicester; thinking there, by force and rigor of law, to suppresse and subdue all the malice and evill will conceived against the duke & hir."[10] Shakespeare is justified by the Chronicles for holding this disastrous association of Suffolk and Margaret, as much as the weakness of the King, responsible for the fearful events which the tetralogy relates. He went yet further. But for this love, to Shakespeare's mind, the French provinces would not have been lost, the good Duke of Gloucester would not have been murdered, the crown would not have passed to the house of York, and Richard, Duke of Gloucester, might never have had the opportunities for the slaughter which brought him to the throne as Richard III. When later, in *Richard III,* we watch the aging Margaret lurking in the background to observe the terrible consequences of her association with Suffolk and of her husband's holy weakness, we should remember this, her only love. It is Shakespeare's first essay in tragic, destructive love, and there is something grand in this shameless affection between two passionate, ruthless, and physically splendid lovers. That it is neither historically nor dramatically called for may be the reason why Shakespeare partly concealed it by dividing it between two plays. Of course, it does tie *Parts 1* and *2* together in the most exciting way, since we see Suffolk's statement of his intentions in the last lines of *Part 1* being put into operation at the very beginning of *Part 2.* Put wholly into one play, however, this stated purpose and its carrying out could steal the show and make a mock of history. But spoken in their entirety, as they probably were in the original productions, the Suffolk-Margaret scenes would hold their own against the historical material, and the more intimate and continuous association of the lovers on the stage, even in the presence of other characters, would give flesh to Shakespeare's view of this segment of English history.

Recent productions of *Henry VI,* concentrating on the Wars of the Roses rather than on the human interest and relationships of Shakespeare's play and making the weakness of the King and the ruthless covetousness of the barons the cause of all, have cut the three great scenes—the courtship, the farewell, and the death of Suffolk—so that the love story almost disappears from the play and the nursing of Suffolk's severed head by Margaret almost becomes a shocking irrelevance. Critics and commentators too have played it down, embarrassed perhaps that a queen of England should have behaved thus and that Shakespeare should have invented such a tasteless story. Other meaningless excisions in recent productions—the omission of the Countess-Talbot and Pucelle-Burgundy scenes in *1 Henry VI* at Stratford—have robbed that play of passages of high and complex human interest and made such productions heavy with history, shorn of those parts of these plays which perhaps most interested their author, partly because he invented them.

Suffolk's brave death and the effects his deeds had, in Shakespeare's view, on English history, raise him to tragic level. His comparison of his own death with those of Tully, Julius Caesar, and Pompey is not there to be laughed at; neither is his own likening of himself to Paris and of Margaret to Helen, nor the associations with Dido and Aeneas and Ovid and his wife. And one is inevitably reminded of Lancelot and Guinevere.[11] The disastrous consequences of this love were made by Shakespeare to seem similar to those of the other adulterous love upon Troy, which Shakespeare was to set forth in *Troilus and Cressida.* It is a love as splendidly physical but as morally and politically reprehensible as that of Antony and Cleopatra, while Margaret in her ferocity is an earlier Lady Macbeth. For Margaret, Suffolk is the only love, the rest is bitterness. For Suffolk, the world was well lost in her service and its memory enables him to die nobly and proudly. Margaret's nursing of the hewn-off head is a tribute unique in love stories. His loss and the fuller realization of the unheroic qualities of her husband turn her into the doomed and desperate warrior queen, not to be released by death but to live on into *Richard III*—a malevolent ghost haunting Richard, commenting on the fateful developments, and cursing her enemies. The attitude of conventional morality to this love is expressed not in Henry's peevish comments but in the Lieutenant's condemnation,[12] and here the rough English view triumphs in dooming Suffolk unceremoniously to death. So respectable Romans must have thought of Antony and Cleopatra. But Margaret's exit with the head could be almost as strange and awe-inspiring as the madness of Lady Macbeth if the full text were performed to sustain it.

The historical part of the Suffolk story, as it was presented by the Tudor historians,[13] was sufficiently well known to be used as a moral example in *A Myrroure for Magistrates* (1559), "How Lorde William Delapole Duke of Suffolke was worthily punyshed for abusing his Kyng and causing the destruction of good Duke Humfrey." But there is no mention of love here either. How effective Shakespeare's distortions of and additions to history were may be judged from Drayton's *Englands Heroicall Epistles* (1598). Drayton pretended to depend upon "Chronicle Historie" in compiling these imaginary verse letters between famous English lovers, and on the title page he directed his readers to observe his pertinent annotations. But he had only Shakespeare's authority for a famous love between Queen Margaret and Suffolk, and much of what Drayton gave as historical fact is Shakespearean invention. In the Epistle from "Elinor Cobham to Duke Humphrey," we are told, "Poole needs must have his Darling made a Queene" (l. 80).[14] (Does the use of the word darling here suggest that Drayton too had read Hall before writing these Epistles?) "The Argument" of the exchange of letters between Suffolk and Margaret begins:

> This Duke of Suffolke, William, to advance
> A Lady, long belov'd of him in France,
> His Mistris, Margaret, that Duke Rayners Child,
> Himselfe who of Jerusalem instyl'd
> The King: this Poole, his Darling to preferre,
> Betwixt young Henry, nam'd the sixt, and her,
> Concludes a Marriage. . . .
>
> (p. 230)

Margaret's letter is written after Suffolk's banishment, and she expresses her sense of personal and political deprivation. She warns Suffolk of the dangers of the sea:

> I pray thee, Poole, have care how thou do'st passe,
> Never the Sea yet halfe so dang'rous was;
> And one fore-told, by Water thou should'st die. . . .
>
> (p. 242; ll. 139-41)

Drayton solemnly annotated this as though it came from the Chronicles. "The Witch of Eye received answere from her Spirit, That the Duke of Suffolke should take heed of Water: Which the Queene fore-warnes him of, as remembring the Witches Prophesie; which afterwards came to passe" (p. 246). We know, of course, that Shakespeare was the only source of this prophecy.

But if the Chronicles are silent, apart from the merest hints, in the matter of the love of Margaret and Suffolk, there is another source to suggest an authentic love affair between them. Suffolk has been revealed as a courtly poet, and poems previously attributed to Charles D'Orléans are now generally accepted as by Suffolk.[15] One of these at least, "Praise of a Flower," is taken as having been addressed to Queen Margaret (Marguerite). It begins,

> Myn hert ys set, and all myn hole entent,
> To serve this flour in my most humble wyse
> As faythfully as can be thought or ment,
> Wyth-out feynyng or slouthe in my servyse;
> For wytt the wele, yt ys a paradyse
> To se this floure when yt begyn to sprede,
> Wyth colours fressh ennewyd, white and rede.[16]

Another poem is a conventional complaint against fortune, but yet another (p. 189) is entitled "Lettyr" and begins,

> Myn hertys Ioy, and all myn hole plesaunce,
> Whom that I serve and shall do faythfully.

In spite of the "wyth-out feynyng," "Praise of a Flower" might be dismissed as a courtly exercise in the manner of medieval gallantry, but this last little poem has a ring of sincerity which might well have come from Suffolk's banishment:

> I wryte to yow no more for lak of space,
> But I beseche the only trinite
> Yow kepe and save be support of hys grace,
> And be your sheld from all adversyte.
> Go lytill byll, and say thou were wyth me
> Of verey trouth, as thou canst wele remembre,
> At myn upryst, the fyft day of Decembre.[17]

Had Drayton actually seen any of Suffolk's poems? I almost think he had when I read in Margaret's Epistle,

> My Daisie flower, which erst perfum'd the ayre,
> Which for my favour Princes dayn'd to weare . . .
>
> (p. 241; ll. 89-90)

But the play on Daisy-Marguerite-Margaret is perhaps too obvious to require knowledge of Suffolk's poem. Drayton noted, "The Daisie in French is called Margarite, which was Queene Margarets Badge; wherewithall the Nobilitie and Chivalrie of the Land, at her first Arrivall, were so delighted, that they wore it in their Hats, in token of Honour" (pp. 244-45).

It may be equally idle to speculate whether Shakespeare might have read or heard of Suffolk's poems for, even if he had, this would not lessen the range and significance of his inventions in setting forth this story and in linking it with the struggle for power. In Suffolk and Margaret, Shakespeare was already reaching out toward his great tragic relationships, not with full confidence yet but with astonishing boldness for an early play with which he was hoping to establish himself in the world of the theater. And he did this with more poetry, insight, and power than his *Henry VI* is usually credited with.

Notes

1. *The First Part of King Henry VI,* Arden edition, ed. A. S. Cairncross (London, 1962). All quotations are from this edition unless otherwise noted.
2. Edward Hall, *The Union of the Two Noble and Illustre Famelies of Lancastre and Yorke* (London, 1550), fol. cxlviii^{v}.
3. Hall, fol. cxlix-cl. The last line of Suffolk's speech resembles the younger Mortimer's plea to Queen Isabella in Marlowe's *Edward II,* "Be ruled by me, and we will rule the realme . . ." (*Edward II,* V. ii. 5, ed. W. M. Merchant, New Mermaid, Benn, London, 1967, l. 2147). But both these lines are traceable to the Chronicles, and the relationship between Queen Isabella and Mortimer is similar to that between Margaret and Suffolk. Both women become warrior queens; Isabella before, Margaret after her lover's death. Mortimer's severed head is brought onto the stage, but immediately after Isabella's exit at the end of the play. Shakespeare went much further in intensifying the passion between the lovers and in the invention of the prolonged farewell and the pathetic and grotesque hugging of Suffolk's head by Margaret. The adulterous affair is more dramatically justifiable but less interesting in Marlowe's play than in Shakespeare's, but the question of influence awaits agreement on the relative dating of the two plays.
4. *The Second Part of King Henry VI,* Arden edition, ed. A. S. Cairncross (London, 1957), p. 96. Further quotations from the play are from this edition unless otherwise noted.
5. Hall, fol. cxlviii.
6. Referred to as "Lieutenant" in FF.
7. There have been several attempts to clear up some confusion in these two lines. This is substantially the First Folio version. For others, see Arden edition, ed. Cairncross, p. 104.
8. Hall, fol. clviii.
9. Raphael Holinshed, . . . *The Chronicles of England, Scotlande, and Irelande* (London, 1587), III, 627.
10. Holinshed, III, 631.
11. Arden edition, ed. Cairncross, p. liv.
12. IV. i. 69-102.
13. Modern historians have found him a worthier person.
14. Michael Drayton, *Works,* ed. William Hebel (Oxford, 1931-41), II, 217. All quotations are taken from this edition.
15. See H. N. MacCracken, "An English Friend of Charles of Orléans," *PMLA,* XXVI, new ser., XIX (1911), 142-80.

16. Quotations from R. H. Robbins, *Secular Lyrics of the XIVth and XVth Centuries* (Oxford, 1952), p. 186.

17. Robbins, p. 190.

Thomas Cartelli (essay date 1994)

SOURCE: "Jack Cade in the Garden: Class Consciousness and Class Conflict in *2 Henry VI,*" in *Enclosure Acts: Sexuality, Property, and Culture in Early Modern England,* edited by Richard Burt and John Michael Archer, Cornell University Press, 1994, pp. 48-67.

[*In the essay below, Cartelli views Jack Cade as an embodiment of modern-style class distinctions and social transgression.*]

I

In Shakespeare's *2 Henry VI* the notorious career of Jack Cade concludes with the starving rebel's defeat at the hands of Alexander Iden, a self-styled "poor esquire of Kent" whom Cade formally terms "the lord of the soil" that provides the setting for their notably unequal combat. The end of Cade's career ironically becomes the occasion for a sudden turn in Iden's fortunes when Iden is "created knight for his good service," given a reward of a thousand marks, and effectively transformed into a courtier.[1] I say "ironically" because what may be termed the "garden scene" of *2 Henry VI* is initially framed in the manner of a pastoral interlude as Iden enters and criticizes the lust for worldly advancement which has made Cade a desperate fugitive and encouraged many of Iden's social superiors to turn the "garden of England" into a site of fraternal bloodletting. The pastoral note is first sounded by Cade himself, whose representation of Iden's garden is, however, decidedly more utilitarian than conventional versions of pastoral:

> Fie on ambitions! fie on myself, that have a sword, and yet am ready to famish! These five days have I hid me in these woods and durst not peep out, for all the country is laid for me; but now am I so hungry, that if I might have a lease of my life for a thousand years, I could stay no longer. Wherefore, on a brick wall have I clim'b into this garden, to see if I can eat grass, or pick a sallet another while, which is not amiss to cool a man's stomach in this hot weather.
>
> (4.10.1-9)

Cade proceeds in a casually self-deprecating vein to play on the word "sallet" in a manner that suggests a crucial difference between his version of pastoral and Iden's. While he curses the ambitions that have brought him there, Iden's garden offers Cade merely the possibility of refreshment and a temporary respite from his flight from a "country" that is "laid for me," not an Arden-like retreat from the stresses of life.

Iden's construction of his garden state is notably more idyllic and mines the same conventions as Thomas Wyatt's anticourt pastoral, "Mine Own Join Poins."[2] Like the disaffected speaker in Wyatt's poem, Iden is "in Kent and Christendom" where "in lusty leas at liberty" he may walk. Unlike Wyatt's speaker, Iden enjoys a liberty that is unenforced, apart, that is, from the constraint of "this small inheritance my father left me," out of which Iden makes a virtue of necessity:

> Lord! who would live turmoiled in the court,
> And may enjoy such quiet walks as these?
> This small inheritance my father left me
> Contenteth me, and worth a monarchy.
> I seek not to wax great by others' waning,
> Or gather wealth I care not with what envy:
> Sufficeth, that I have maintains my state,
> And sends the poor well pleased from my gate.
>
> (4.10.16-23)

As William Empson has taught us, pastoral effusions of this variety are seldom free of contextual qualification. In this instance we may observe that the self-congratulatory note Iden sounds harbors a discernible compensatory component, as if Iden were cheering himself up for his small inheritance by disparaging the profane pleasures the court offers those who can afford them and by overstating the worth of what the court would sneer at. Two additional qualifications are noteworthy. The first concerns Cade's altogether more material appraisal of Iden's "quiet walks" and "small inheritance." To Cade, Iden is less a poor esquire grazing on the pastoral margins of political life than the walking embodiment of established authority. Whereas Iden conceives of his walk in the garden as one in a series of daily demonstrations of an unturmoiled life neatly balanced between private pleasure and social obligation, Cade believes that "the lord of the soil" has walked forth expressly "to seize me for a stray, for entering his fee-simple without leave" (4.10.24-25).

Cade's legalistic and oppositional estimate of his imminent encounter with Iden demonstrates both his incapacity to appreciate Iden's version of pastoral and his complete exclusion from the privileged position that enables it. Unlike the poor who are sent "well pleased" from Iden's gate, Cade appears to be a complete stranger to the custom of feudal hospitality, of the mutual obligations that obtain, or are supposed to obtain, between prosperous giver and impoverished receiver. As befits the leader of a popular rebellion, Cade approaches his encounter with Iden from a thoroughly class-conscious and class-stratified position. For Cade, all possible relations between himself and Iden are construed in terms of the normative positioning of "stray" and "lord," hence in terms of mutual suspicion and hostility. From his perspective as a threatened stray, Iden's garden is "*enclosed private property,* not in any sense . . . a public or common domain."[3] And anyone in Cade's position would know that "a poacher could be . . . hanged for invading a park in search of what previously could be had for the taking in open countryside."[4] Cade's estimate of his position thus reveals the extent to which Iden's version of pastoral operates as a deeply privileged ideological construction.

Iden's effusion is further qualified by his own behavior during and after his encounter with Cade. Although Cade's aggressive challenge—"Ah, villain, thou wilt betray me, and get a thousand crowns of the King by carrying my head to him; but I'll make thee eat iron like an ostrich, and swallow my sword like a great pin, ere thou and I part" (4.10.26-29)—understandably discourages Iden from sending this particular poor man well pleased from his gate, the speed with which Iden confirms Cade's legalistic estimate of their relationship profoundly qualifies Iden's more placid conception of relations between rich and poor:

> Why, rude companion, whatsoe'er thou be,
> I know thee not; why then should I betray thee?
> Is't not enough to break into my garden,
> And like a thief to come to rob my grounds,
> Climbing my walls in spite of me the owner,
> But thou wilt brave me with these saucy terms?
>
> (4.10.30-35)

Iden's initial effort to allay Cade's anxieties suggests that Iden may be a more complex figure than Cade imagines, as does his subsequent reluctance to engage "a poor famish'd man" in combat. But as the passage moves—without further provocation from Cade—into a more magisterial restatement of Cade's own estimate of his transgression, Cade is summarily cast in the unvarying likeness of a "thief" who has "come to rob my grounds." Stephen Greenblatt notes, with respect to this encounter, that "status relations . . . are being transformed before our eyes into property relations, and the concern . . . for maintaining social and even cosmic boundaries is reconceived as a concern for maintaining freehold boundaries."[5] Although Greenblatt is certainly right to notice the crucial role that property plays in this transaction, Cade's braving of Iden with "saucy terms" seems to arouse Iden more than does his mere transgression of freehold boundaries. I would submit that it is primarily Cade's obstreperousness—his offensive refusal to maintain the habit of servility Iden expects both from "strays" who break into his fee-simple and from the poor who leave his gate well pleased—that motivates the violent turn in this encounter and consequently transforms Iden's pastoralized estimate of his garden state into a spirited defense of property rights.

Cade brings to Iden's garden a fully developed habit of resistance to even the most liberal ministrations of those who tower over him in the social order. His defiance rests partly on an overestimation of his notoriety, but largely on a conviction in his self-worth which has been fueled by his leadership of a rebellion that has already successfully leveled competing claims to distinction: "Brave thee! ay, by the best blood that ever was broach'd, and beard thee too. Look on me well: I have eat no meat these five days; yet, come thou and thy five men, and if I do not leave you all as dead as a door-nail, I pray God I may never eat grass more" (4.10.36-40). It is this that finally forces the issue between Cade and Iden, while Iden's response and the brief combat that follows ironically reveal the "true" nature of the relationship between social unequals:

> Nay, it shall ne'er be said, while England stands,
> That Alexander Iden, esquire of Kent,
> Took odds to combat a poor famish'd man.
> Oppose thy steadfast-gazing eyes to mine,
> See if thou canst outface me with thy looks:
> Set limb to limb, and thou art far the lesser;
> Thy hand is but a finger to my fist;
> Thy leg a stick compared with this truncheon;
> My foot shall fight with all the strength thou hast;
> And if mine arm be heaved in the air
> Thy grave is digg'd already in the earth.
> As for words, whose greatness answers words,
> Let this my sword report what speech forbears.
>
> (4.10.41-53)

Iden's speech fully appreciates and elaborates on the social disparity between the combatants by rendering it physical. Its comparative inventory of body parts casts Iden in the likeness of a giant and reduces Cade to the proportions of a dwarf. Although Iden's defeat of Cade may be accounted for—as Cade asserts—by the latter's current status as a starving fugitive, the text suggests that Cade is undone "naturally" in daring to contend with someone whose social superiority also makes him his superior in strength and skill. Iden's conscientiously degrading treatment of Cade's body—which Iden says he will drag "headlong by the heels / Unto a dunghill," leaving Cade's "trunk for crows to feed upon" after cutting off his head (4.10.75-83)—offers a last ironic gloss on the futility of Cade's defiance and on the curse that Cade lays on Iden's garden: "Wither, garden; and be henceforth a burying-place to all that do dwell in this house, because the unconquer'd soul of Cade is fled" (4.10.62-64).

This culminating act of enclosure also radically reorients Iden's attitude toward his own, previously celebrated, social position. Iden will "cut off [Cade's] most ungracious head" and "bear [it] in triumph to the King," thereby exchanging his garden state as a "poor esquire of Kent" for the status of a knight, having clearly "waxed great" by another's "waning," despite his earlier admonitory remarks. Cade's misadventure in Iden's garden thus becomes the medium through which Iden exercises his own desire for social advancement, one that may be said to be modeled on Cade's status as a very different kind of stray than Iden initially imagines. As Iden leaves his garden behind for what he has earlier appraised as the "turmoiled" life of a courtier, the notion of the garden itself as an unturmoiled place apart, untouched by the social strife that reigns elsewhere, also becomes radically qualified. In bringing to his encounter with Iden a deeply rooted, polarized, and polarizing consciousness of class, Cade elicits from Iden a response premised on the same which effectively demystifies Iden's conception of a private space where rich and poor can meet on common ground. Cade's violation of Iden's pastoral does not summarily transform Iden's garden into a site of social contestation; rather, it reveals the extent to which its unbreached walls had previously functioned as a facade of the imaginary, both for Iden himself and for the poor who came as supplicants to its gates. In contesting the ideological hold that the garden has heretofore maintained over all concerned parties, Cade effectively unlocks its actual status as a space intersected by mutually exclusive and competing class interests.

II

By assigning to a dramatic character a consciousness of something as problematic as our modern notion of class, I run the risk of being discredited on both interpretive and historical grounds. But I believe that a politically motivated class consciousness was capable of being both experienced and represented in early modern England, and that Jack Cade constitutes the most realized example in Shakespeare's work of a character who is able to transform his political subjection into something amounting to our modern sense of class-based resistance.[6] The few historians daring or reckless enough to use the word *class* in their representations of the period are usually careful to distance themselves from the implication that its use indicates "either the existence of a class society in the period or of class conflict."[7] Most seem content to accept Peter Laslett's argument that in early modern England "there were a large number of status groups but only one body of persons capable of concerted action over the whole area of society, only one class in fact."[8] Where Laslett's argument falls flat is in its determination that a social class must possess power commensurate with that of a ruling party in society. Class conflict, for Laslett, requires the capacity or potential of an oppositional party to contest successfully the ruling party's privileges or prerogatives: a formulation that—given the alleged lack of a duly qualified opposition—appears always and ever to guarantee the presence and predominance of a single class. R. S. Neale, by contrast, subscribes to E. P. Thompson's view "that class struggle precedes class"; in Thompson's words, "Class defines itself as, in fact, it eventuates."[9] Neale concludes that "the absence of a contemporary language which would enable men to express such relationships [as class] should not prevent historians from categorizing the past in ways unknown or only vaguely understood by men in the past."[10]

In her own recent essay on *2 Henry VI,* Annabel Patterson demonstrates that "there *was* a cultural tradition of popular protest" in early modern England, "a tradition in the sense of something handed down from the past, cultural in the sense that what was transmitted were symbolic forms and signifying practices, a history from below encoded in names and occasions, a memorial vocabulary and even a formal rhetoric."[11] In so doing, Patterson incisively redresses the traditional neglect of the incipiently class-based ideologies of oppositional movements without, however, specifically nominating class as a discursive focus of her own.[12] Nonetheless, *2 Henry VI* is sufficiently abundant in examples of a contemporary language expressive of class relationships to satisfy the evidential demands of the majority of critics. Most of this language is spoken by or through Jack Cade and his confederates, who supply a variety of statements expressive of a deep and divisive consciousness of class. Although Shakespeare draws from these statements no explicitly class-interested conclusions of his own, his characters frequently do, as, for example, Jack Cade does in this exchange with Lord Say:

> *Cade.* . . . Thou dost ride in a foot-cloth, dost thou not?
> *Say.* What of that?
> *Cade.* Marry, thou ought'st not to let thy horse wear a cloak, when honester men than thou go in their hose and doublets.
>
> (4.7.44-49)

I choose this early moment in what soon becomes a notoriously violent encounter to demonstrate how commonplace signs of social distinction can be made to appear symptomatic of social inequity in *2 Henry VI.* In this instance a seemingly negligible privilege enjoyed by a representative of the ruling class is subjected to the sharp-tongued scrutiny of a representative of the class that both suffers and provides for it. By being placed in direct relation to the impoverishment of workingmen, the previously freestanding and therefore "innocent" social distinction is transformed into a corrupt social practice.

Although it could be argued that Cade's subsequent execution of a character who pleads "so well for his life" retrospectively cancels any incursion Cade may make against the ruling order's mystification of social injustice, such an objection would be hard to sustain in the context of a play that is largely devoted to dramatizing the predatory behavior of England's ruling establishment.[13] In 4.2., the first scene in which Cade's rebellion is represented, the ruling order is arraigned in a particularly resonant manner by two of Cade's confederates, one of whom proclaims, "Well, I say it was never merry world in England since gentlemen came up" (4.2.7-9). The wording of this statement notably anticipates a presentment made several years after this play's initial production by a participant in the 1596 Oxfordshire rising. According to Buchanan Sharp, "The miller Richard Bradshawe was reported to have declared 'that he hoped that before yt were long to see some of the ditches throwne downe, and that yt wold never be merye till some of the gentlemen were knocked downe,'" a sentiment, Sharp notes, "which recurred frequently in the examinations of the principal suspects."[14] Rather than claim that Bradshaw and his fellow suspects got their language from Shakespeare, one may more reliably assume that Shakespeare was appropriating an expression that would have been familiar to many well before the Oxfordshire rising and the initial performances of *2 Henry VI.*

By having his character rehearse a rallying cry that may well have been a contemporary commonplace, Shakespeare was bringing the successive histories of past risings and rebellions (beginning with accounts of the Peasants' Revolt of 1381, which he deploys throughout his dramatization of Jack Cade's rising) into direct contact with latterday representations of class conflict, thereby giving added currency to an apparently old complaint.[15] As Sharp observes: "Popular feeling in the Tudor-Stuart period reserved its most intense outbursts for . . . 'the rich.' As expressed in anonymous libels, seditious utterances reported from alehouses, and the few surviving examinations of rioters and insurrectionaries, the opinions of common folk reveal a deep hatred of the people possessed of the power, social standing, and landed wealth denied to them."[16] Shakespeare, of course, balances his representation of the poor's complaints against the rich by emphasizing the rashness and brutality of the rebels in his play. But in also choosing to emphasize the derisive manner in which characters such as Suffolk speak of "the rascal people"—for example, he calls his pirate captors "paltry, servile, abject drudges" (4.1.104)—and the indifference with which they hear and address the common people's seemingly modest petitions (see, e.g., 1.3.), Shakespeare demonstrates that the hatred of poor for rich is but "the mirror image of the contempt and fear with which their superiors regarded the poor."[17]

The predictability of the terms that rich and poor employ to speak of each other in *2 Henry VI* has a contemporary Elizabethan analogue in the development of a "language of sorts," which, according to Keith Wrightson, "appears to have been used primarily to express a dichotomous perception of society." As Wrightson notes:

> Such language clearly reveals a world of social meanings untapped by the formal social classifications of the period—and arguably it was so widely used because it was of greater practical significance. Its utility lay above all in the fact that it was a terminology of social simplification, sweeping aside the fine-grained (and highly contested) distinctions of the hierarchy of degrees and regrouping the English into two broad camps which were clearly held to reflect the fundamental realities of the social and economic structure and the basic alignments of social relations. . . . It was a language of radical differentiation, cleaving society into the haves and have nots, the respected and the contemned. It was a language pregnant with conflict, aligning the "richer" over against the "poorer," the "better" over against the "meaner," "vulgar," "common," "ruder" or "inferior" sorts. It was also a language of radical dissociation, usually found in the mouths of those who identified themselves with the "better" sort and stigmatised those whom they excluded from that company with a barrage of pejorative adjectives.[18]

In *2 Henry VI* the "better sort" variously refer to the commons as "the abject people" (Duke Humphrey, 2.4.11); "an angry hive of bees / That want their leader, [who] scatter up and down, / And care not who they sting" (Warwick, 3.2.124-26); and as "rude unpolish'd hinds" (Suffolk, 3.2.270). But what is perhaps more notable is the extent to which the rising commons themselves appropriate the stigmatizing function of the language of sorts to "align" themselves in prosecuting their rebellion.

Their initial, generalized animus against gentlemen is, for example, soon extended to include "all scholars, lawyers, [and] courtiers," other "false caterpillars" such as magistrates, those who "can write and read and / cast accompt" (4.2.81-82), and anyone who speaks Latin (4.7.55). Reacting against the "scorn" the nobility reserve for those who "go in leather aprons" and the lack of regard shown to "virtue in handicraftsmen," the rebels invert the criteria by which honor is measured by contending that "there's no better sign of a brave / mind than a hard hand (4.2.10-20). For his part, Jack Cade brings this tendency to its logical conclusion when he calls the Staffords "silken-coated slaves" (4.2.122), traces his artisanal nobility back to Adam, who "was a gardener" (4.2.128), and identifies "such as go in clouted shoon" as "thrifty honest men":

> And you that love the commons, follow me.
> Now show yourselves men; 'tis for liberty.
> We will not leave one lord, one gentleman:
> Spare none but such as go in clouted shoon,
> For they are thrifty honest men, and such
> As would, but that they dare not, take our parts.
>
> (4.2.175-80)

What is especially revealing about Cade's call to arms is that its direct challenge to the very people Cade presumes to represent—namely, "the commons"—expresses a tolerance for (and expectation of) their failure to respond to it. Cade attempts to claim here a representative political character for his rebellion by presuming to speak on behalf of those who "dare not" join in it but are joined *to* it both by their status as workers and by their unvoiced allegiance to its aims. Although Cade's confident assumption that he speaks on behalf of those who dare not speak for themselves may well be mistaken, it *be*speaks a consciousness of collective interests and shared goals that is, for all rights and purposes, a consciousness of class. And it also demarcates that pivotal moment when "a class 'in itself' become[s] a class for 'itself.'"[19]

It is, of course, commonly held that Cade is represented as "a cruel, barbaric lout, whose slogan is 'kill and knock down,' and whose story as 'the archetype of disorder' is one long orgy of clownish arson and homicide fuelled by an infantile hatred of literacy and law." Shakespeare's decision to degrade the figure "whom [even the historian Edward] Hall respects as 'a youngman of godely stature and pregnaunt wit' . . . whose advisers were 'scholemasters' and 'teachers'" may well reflect his own negative appraisal of Cade.[20] But it does nothing to diminish the delegation to his character of an acute consciousness of class. Indeed, by separating *his* radically disorderly Cade from Hall's more respectable figure, Shakespeare may be said to have foregrounded class distinctions which a more accurate (or less prejudicial) estimate of the historical Cade would have occluded.[21]

The class distinctions Shakespeare foregrounds are almost exclusively those that distinguish the "better sort" from the "meaner sort," those who are socially and culturally privileged from those who privilege their own social and

KING HENRY THE SIXTH.

First Part. Act II. Scene V.

Act II, scene v. Mortimer and Richard in the Tower of London in Henry VI, Part 1.

cultural dispossession. The "middling sort" play a much more negligible role in the physical conflict represented onstage, as the following example suggests. After announcing that "Jack Cade hath almost gotten London Bridge," a messenger to the king reports that "the citizens fly and forsake their houses," while "the rascal people, thirsting after prey, / Join with the traitor; and . . . jointly swear / To spoil the city and your royal court" (4.4.48-52). In addition to distinguishing the (victimized) citizens of London from the (victimizing) people, this passage implicitly draws a connection between the interests of "the city" and those of the "royal court." This connection is elaborated in the brief scene (4.5.) that ensues, in which a textually identified "citizen" (apparently speaking at the behest of the Lord Mayor) exchanges information with Lord Scales, who urges the Londoners to "fight for your king, your country, and your lives" (4.5.11). This they apparently do under the leadership of Matthew Goffe. But apart from the evidence provided by a stage direction that reads "Alarums. Matthew Goffe is slain, and all the rest" (4.7.), Shakespeare appears to have chosen not to stage at any length the bloody battle between citizens and rebels for London Bridge which Hall represents in graphically lurid detail:

> The multitude of the rebelles drave the citezens from the stoulpes at the bridge foote, to the drawe bridge, and began to set fyre in divers houses. Alas what sorow it was to beholde that miserable chaunce: for some desyrynge to eschew the fyre, lept on his enemies weapon, and so died: fearfull women with chyldren in their armes, amased and appalled, lept into the river: other doubtinge how to save them self betwene fyre, water, and swourd, were in their houses suffocat and smoldered.[22]

Shakespeare not only fails to include a single dramatic reference to Hall's account in the text of *2 Henry VI;* he also fails to provide the kind of detailed commentary on undramatized action that would have lent a great deal more judgmental fervor to his representation of the episode in question. Conjoined with Cade's subsequent (and wildly anachronistic) order for "some" to go "and pull down the Savoy" (4.7.1) and "others" to do likewise to the Inns of Court—both references to actions undertaken during the rising of 1381—Shakespeare's deviations from Hall appear to repress the role played by citizens of "the middling sort" as opponents and victims of Jack Cade and as allies of the royal party. Rather than emerging as an "enemy of the people," whose conception of class warfare pits the commons against the citizens of London, Cade is consequently represented in a manner that more closely approximates his own self-estimate as protector or defender of "the people" against the depredations of the high and mighty.

The negligible role played by the citizen class or "middling sort" in Shakespeare's dramatization of Cade's rebellion does not, however, entirely mystify the position Shakespeare adopted in staging a conflict that primarily pits rich against poor. In largely choosing to remove citizens from the scene of Cade's rebellion and, for that matter, from the far more numerous scenes that portray the struggles between royalty and aristocracy which eventuate in civil war, Shakespeare may well be representing, as well as promoting, the point of view of the one component of English society that presumably remained both stable and reliable in the face of wholesale social disorder: namely, the literate, industrious, law-abiding citizen class. In identifying the point of view of *2 Henry VI* with the interests of what we today would term the "middle class," I am attempting to give some ideological basis to this play's author function while at the same time avoiding the facile equation of biography and ideology which makes Shakespeare a reactionary mouthpiece for the historically inevitable triumph of what Richard Wilson calls "the literate bourgeois."[23] Wilson detects nothing but "animus" in those episodes of the play that record "the people's garbled testimony or laboured puns" and that dramatize their "long orgy of clownish arson and homicide fuelled by an infantile hatred of literacy and law."[24] I detect, on the contrary, a politically astute reckoning with a long list of social grievances whose inarticulate and violent expression does not invalidate their demand for resolution. And I attribute the astuteness of that reckoning to a playwright whose manifest literacy and identification with citizen values may actually have made possible his sympathetic appraisal of the people's claims.

Garbled though they may be, the people's grievances are not, in any event, first expressed in the context of Cade's rebellion. They are, in fact, repeatedly addressed in the long series of events that lead up to it in the life of this particular play, beginning with the abortive presentation of the petition against the enclosure of Long Melford (1.3.) and with Simpcox's wife's testimony that she and her husband pursued their fraud "for pure need" (2.1.250). Even within the context of Cade's rebellion, powerful appraisals of social injustice are attached to ostensibly more intemperate diatribes against schooling and literacy, as is the case, for example, in Cade's rambling indictment of Lord Say:

> It will be prov'd to thy face that thou hast men about thee that usually talk of a noun, and a verb, and such abominable words as no Christian ear can endure to hear. Thou hast appointed justices of peace, to call poor men before them about matters they were not able to answer. Moreover, thou hast put them in prison; and because they could not read, thou hast hang'd them; when, indeed, only for that cause they have been most worthy to live.
>
> (4.7.36-44)

Whereas Wilson employs such examples to demonstrate Shakespeare's revulsion toward those members of his audience and his society who, like his own father, lacked the capacity to write, we would do better to view such passages as symptomatic of Shakespeare's representation of literacy as a crucial bridge between powerlessness and empowerment. Cade and his cohorts repeatedly revile the practices of reading, writing, and printing, and the collateral institution of grammar schools and printing mills, less out of ignorance than out of an assured belief in the role they play in dividing society into haves and have-nots. They read into such practices and institutions their own marginal status as dispossessed subjects ("because they could not read") of all-possessing masters ("thou hast hang'd them").

Illiteracy was surely not a capital offense in Shakespeare's England, but it would be disingenuous to contend that Cade radically misrepresents the legal implications of a social structure in which illiteracy could, indeed, have mortal consequences. As late as 1663 George Swinnock noted that "some for want of reading their neck-verse have lost their lives."[25] And as David Cressy notes with respect to more fortunate participants in the customary reading of the neck-verse, "the opportunity remained in Tudor and Stuart England for the literate felon to claim 'benefit of clergy' and escape the full severity of the law."[26] Cressy also reminds us of the social consequences of membership in that class of subjects Jack Cade claims to represent—a grouping that closely resembles what Thomas Smith identified as that "fourth sort or class" that had "no voice nor authoritie in our common wealth," which comprised "day labourers, poore husbandmen, yea, marchantes or retailers which have no free land, copiholders, and all artificers, as Taylers, Shoomakers, Carpenters, Brickemakers, Bricklayers, Masons, & c."[27] The evidence assembled by Cressy suggests a close correlation between illiteracy and the lack of "voice or authoritie" of the majority of subjects in this class. In a ranking of trades by illiteracy, Cressy's samples indicate that approximately half the tailors, blacksmiths, joiners, wrights, and butchers in rural England in the period 1580-1700 were functionally illiterate. Between 60 and 75 percent of the carpenters, glovers, shoemakers, masons, and bricklayers fall into this category as well (pp. 132-33). In virtually all the samples assembled "labourers" and "husbandmen" vie with women of every class for the claim to complete illiteracy.

Cressy also supplies evidence that helps explain the connection between Jack Cade's animosity toward literacy and its enabling institutions and his specific singling out of "all scholars, lawyers, courtiers, [and] gentlemen" as enemies of the people. A division of early modern English society into discrete classes on the basis of literacy would, for example, directly link members of the clergy, the professions, and the gentry in ways that other measurements—say, on the basis of property, wealth, or political power—would not (pp. 119-21). According to Cressy: "The gentry, clergy and members of the professions were so similar in their literacy that they can be regarded as inhabiting a single cluster at the accomplished end of the literacy scale. Thirty percentage points or more usually separated them from the next most literate cluster, the yeoman and tradesman" (p. 124). Cressy's findings offer a possible rationale for what is often construed to be Jack Cade's irrational and indiscriminate attack on citizens who would initially appear to operate at some remove from the most obvious structures of power. If, as Cressy's evidence suggests, Cade and his followers are correct in perceiving a connection between those who appear to be only culturally privileged and those who are socially and economically privileged as well, then conventional estimates of Cade's demagoguery and his followers' barbarity may themselves be in need of correction. Indeed, Shakespeare may be attributing to Cade and his rebels what is at once a critically acute and an ideologically predictable piece of social analysis, grounded in a consciousness of class differences and opposing class interests similar to that which appears to have characterized the attitude of the Elizabethan poor toward the rich.

In commenting on the nature of the connections between the educationally and socially privileged, Cressy would appear to confirm this possibility: "The social standing of priests and professionals depended on their training and function as well as on their connections and wealth. They were essentially skilled literate specialists, agents and associates of the ruling class. By virtue of their profession alone they were accorded a kind of honorary gentle status and were grouped with the gentry in most contemporary social classifications" (p. 122). Instead of engaging in a complicated bout of self-hatred in representing Cade's attack on literacy and the literate, Shakespeare instead provides Cade with an argument consistent with convictions that not only may have been shared by contemporary working men, but continue to characterize the struggle for control of the "means of communication" in societies similarly divided between literate haves and illiterate have-nots.[28] In its effort to root out such "false caterpillars" as "scholars and lawyers," Cade's "ragged multitude" of illiterate "hinds and peasants" effectively identifies these "skilled literate specialists" as "agents and associates of the ruling class." Although the attendant scorn directed at literacy itself may constitute a displaced (and arguably self-defeating) symptom of political dispossession, the indictment of its beneficiaries could not be more apt.

Like other positions taken by Cade and his followers, the animus toward literacy is rooted in a collective valorization of prevailing differences, a nostalgia for a simpler time of undistinction, and a correspondingly defensive anxiety regarding change which has at least some basis in contemporary events. At the beginning of his encounter with Lord Say, for example, Cade identifies Say's educational philanthropy as one of the chief sins he has committed against the commonwealth: "Thou hast most traitourously corrupted the youth of the realm in erecting a grammar-school; and whereas, before our forefathers had no other books but the score and the tally, thou hast caus'd printing to be us'd" (4.7.30-34).

The terms of Cade's indictment initially seem to subordinate willful ignorance to a conscious cultivation of comic effect, as Cade appears to relish his exaggeration of the threat posed to civil society by Say. But if we choose to take Cade at his word, his indictment may instead express the same nostalgia for a "bookless" existence presided over by satisfied forefathers, which Nicholas Breton describes in his representation of the semiliterate countryman's pastimes: "We can learne to plough and harrow, sow and reape, plant and prune, thrash and fanne, winnow and grinde, brue and bake, and all without booke. These are our chiefe businesse in the Country, except we be Jury-men to hang a theefe, or speake truth in a mans right, which conscience and experience wil teach us with a little learning."[29] Cade's claim that the heritage of this simpler state of affairs is jeopardized by the unsettling changes wrought by grammar schools may also be more broadly placed in the context of the "educational revolution" that took place in the first half of the Elizabethan period and that reached its peak in 1580. According to Cressy, "The reign of Elizabeth saw a solid improvement in literacy among tradesmen and craftsmen in all parts of England," with tailors and weavers in particular making considerable gains (p. 153). This "revolution" witnessed the dissemination of schoolmasters throughout the countryside and may have been directly responsible for making Shakespeare's own generation more literate than that of either his ancestors or his descendants. Of course, such a revolution may also have worked to create divisions between generations, to arouse anxiety among those incapable of benefiting from it, or to exacerbate already prevailing tensions and differences between the latter and those who could employ their newly acquired literacy in the interests of social mobility.

Rather than speculate further in this vein, I would prefer to explore the connection between Cade's scorn for literacy and valorization of illiteracy with the positions he and his followers take toward property, power, and status relations. In the course of the play we get from them an inventory of claims, principles, and resolves that identifies the "fall" of the "merry world" that was England with the institution of a system of distinctions whose beneficiaries are gentlemen, magistrates, lawyers, and scholars, among others. England's redemption is premised on a series of utopian proposals that variously call for the termination of distinction ("All the realm shall be in common" [4.2.65]); the extermination of those privileged by distinction ("The first thing we do, let's kill all the lawyers" [4.2.65]); and the absorption of those privileged by distinction into the great mass of the undistinguished ("Let the magistrates be laboring men" [4.2.16-17]. Having leveled distinction, Cade would apparel all "in one livery, that they may agree like brothers, and worship me their lord" (4.2.70-72). Cade's determination to reserve this pivotal distinction for himself is expressed with a good deal more consistency than are his other positions. Calling for the burning of "all the records of the realm," Cade claims that "my mouth shall be the parliament of England" (4.7.12-14). And in the same scene he asserts, "The proudest peer in the realm shall not wear a head on his shoulders, unless he pay me tribute" (4.7.114-15).

It is commonplace for commentators on the play to emphasize the many contradictions in Cade's positions, the most notable one involving Cade's demagogic claim to absolute power in a society in which all things are to be held "in common." But it is Cade's *impulse* to change radically the system by which goods and offices are distributed that might better occupy our attention. We learn from the examples the play gives us that what motivates Cade and his confederates most insistently is the wholesale destruction of a system of privileges which renders them visibly and permanently powerless. Gentlemen, magistrates, lawyers, and scholars are portrayed as accomplices in a ruling class conspiracy to cheat working men out of their "ancient rights." This conspiracy has been institutionalized in a rule of law, permanently housed in "the records of the realm," and handed down in incomprehensible Latin tags by magistrates who will excuse only those who are as literate as they are. Enclosures, price-fixing, coining, and the control of surpluses, and the delegation of easily distinguished vocational liveries, are all represented as activities that advance the interests of the ruling order at the expense of those who suffer them. Cade's communistic alternative is an oppositional dream of simplification and uniformity—of *undistinction*—of an equity born out of an intolerance with inequity, though, given its genocidal and demagogic components, hardly identifiable with what we today would call social justice. The root of the dream, in an apparent but fully explicable reversion to mystification, is Adam in the Garden, the common father of common men, who, as in the passage from Breton, can do "all without book."

III

As others have noted, one may trace the communistic dream in *2 Henry VI* to a common ideological source which helped define a succession of other popular uprisings and rebellions, succinctly summarized in John Ball's catchphrase, "When Adam delv'd and Eve span / Who was then the gentleman?"[30] Shakespeare's familiarity with Grafton's and Holinshed's representations of John Ball and the Peasant's Revolt of 1381 has long been recognized and acknowledged. It is especially obvious in his anachronistic decision to have Cade and his followers destroy the Savoy and attack the Inns of Court, and in Cade's response to Stafford's attempt to belittle him:

> *Staf.* Villian! thy father was a plasterer;
> And thou thyself a shearman, art thou not?
> *Cade.* And Adam was a gardener.
> *Bro.* What of that?
>
> (4.2.126-28)

But the question asked by Stafford's brother, to which Cade gives a characteristically arch and contradictory reply, is one that John Ball answered more incisively in the sermons reproduced by Grafton and Holinshed.

Richard Grafton offers a reconstruction of the commonplace address Ball would give his parishioners after Sunday services:

> Ah good people, matters go not wel to passe in England in these days, nor shall not do untill every thing be common, and that there be no Villeynes for gentlemen but that we be all as one, and that the Lordes be no greater than we be. What have we deserved, or why should we be thus kept in servitude and bondage? We be all come from one father and one mother, Adam and Eve. Wherefore can they saye or shewe that they are greater Lordes then we be? savying in that which we get and labour for, that doe they spend.[31]

Tracing the human family back to its presumptive source in Adam and Eve, Ball effectively declares that the oppressive divisions of the contemporary social order constitute an unauthorized deviation from a divinely ordained equality. He further identifies the distinctions that currently obtain between lords and commons in terms that would be familiar to any latter-day cultural materialist. According to Ball, social dominance is now delegated to those who consume but do not produce, while those who produce but do not consume are "kept in servitude and bondage." Given this state of affairs, the return he envisions to an originary condition in which "there be no Villeynes nor gentlemen but that we be all as one" would appear to require either the dissolution of differences among men or the elimination of one of the contending social classes.

In his famous speech to the rebels at Blackheath, Ball offered his auditors a solution to this dilemma based, like Cade's, on an inverted valorization of workers. Ball addressed his audience as "good husbands" who must set about to transform the decaying garden of England in a thoroughly class-conscious manner, and not merely restore it to an Edenic state that has its human counterpart in an all-inclusive equality. According to Holinshed:

> He counselled them . . . that after the manner of a good husband that tilleth his ground, and riddeth out thereof such evill weeds as choke and destroie the good corne, they might destroie first the great lords of the realme, and after the judges and lawiers, questmoongers, and all other whom they undertooke to be against the commons, for so might they produce peace and suertie to themselves in time to come, if dispatching out of the waie the great men, there should be an equalitie in libertie, no difference in degrees of nobilitie, but a like dignitie and equall authoritie in all things brought in among them.[32]

Ball's emphasis on the destruction of judges and lawyers provides another basis for understanding Shakespeare's delegation to Cade of an emphasis on the same and on the destruction of the "records of the realm." It may be traced to the same rationale that motivated "the common uplandish people" during the Peasants' Revolt "to burne and destroie all records, evidences, court-rolles, and other muniments," the rationale being "that the remembrance of ancient matters being remooved out of mind, their landlords might not have whereby to chalenge anie right at their hands."[33] What Ball, Cade, and the "uplandish people" want, in the end, is less the return to a garden state that antedates the history of their disenfranchisement than the recovery of an "ancient freedom" that will supersede the memory of their servitude and dispossession. That Cade ultimately meets his end at the hands of a powerfully endowed "lord of the soil" while hunting up a salad in that man's garden graphically demonstrates the nostalgic basis of this shared dream of undistinction at the same time as it validates its construction of prevailing class differences.

Notes

1. *2 Henry VI* 5.1.64-82. All quotations from *2 Henry VI* are from the Arden edition, ed. Andrew S. Cairncross (London: Methuen, 1969); subsequent citations appear in the text.

2. In his own commentary on this scene, William Carroll calls Iden "an Horatian figure" and offers an illuminating comparison of the language delegated to him in the Folio version—from which my quotations are drawn—and in *The First Part of the Contention.* Although I agree with Carroll that the evidence for viewing the *Contention's* Iden as "a potential encloser" becomes flimsier in the Folio, I find other reasons to question his alleged standing as "an

emblematic version of the happy rural man," as I suggest later in this chapter.

3. Stephen Greenblatt, "Murdering Peasants: Status, Genre, and the Representation of Rebellion," *Representations* 1 (1983), 24.

4. Simon Pugh, *Garden—Nature—Language* (Manchester: Manchester University Press, 1988), p. 11.

5. Greenblatt, "Murdering Peasants," p. 25.

6. As Michael Hattaway writes in "Rebellion, Class Consciousness, and Shakespeare's *2 Henry VI,*" *Cahiers Elisabethans* 33 (1988), 13-22: "What Cade proclaims constitutes a cause, . . . a cause that emerges from class oppression" (p. 13). Hattaway also claims that the nobility in the *Henry VI* plays "constitute a class—or if we prefer, an elite—defined by the conflict between individual aspirations of its members and everything that constitutes the culture or cultures of the plebeians" (p. 16).

7. Susan Amussen, "Gender, Family, and the Social Order, 1560-1725," in *Order and Disorder in Early Modern England,* ed. Anthony Fletcher and John Stevenson (Cambridge: Cambridge University Press, 1985), p. 206, n. 33. Michael Hattaway offers this commentary on the similar conclusion reached by the editors of the volume in which Amussen's essay appears: "Working from an analysis of cultural models, patterns of behaviour and local community, Anthony Fletcher and John Stevenson conclude that 'a class society had not in our period yet arrived' [ibid., p. 4]. I cannot dispute their conclusion if I work from the same material and the same premises. But it seems that yet again literary critics have something to offer the cultural historians" ("Rebellion, Class Consciousness," p. 16). On this subject, see note 12.

8. Peter Laslett, *The World We Have Lost* (New York: Scribner's, 1965), p. 23. A possible exception is David Underdown, who notes that "a heightened polarization of society . . . makes this period [1540-1640] an important stage in the long process of class formation. England was still very far from being a class society, but the lines were beginning to sharpen, the horizontal ties linking the 'respectable' and dividing them from the poor to cut across the vertical ones of local identity." David Underdown, *Revel, Riot, and Rebellion: Popular Politics and Culture in England, 1603-1660* (Oxford: Oxford University Press, 1985), p. 20.

9. R. S. Neale, *Class in English History: 1680-1850* (New York: Barnes & Noble, 1981), pp. 97-98.

10. Ibid., p. 99.

11. Annabel Patterson, *Shakespeare and the Popular Voice* (Oxford: Basil Blackwell, 1989), p. 38.

12. In her editor's note to *Shakespeare Quarterly* 42, 2 (1991), Gail Kern Paster calls attention to the lack of reciprocity of social historians to the work of literary scholars, who have been greatly influenced by their findings and methodologies. Paster notes that not even avowedly revisionist historians "seem as prepared as most literary practitioners to investigate the ideological or material consequences of dramatic representation, either on lived practices or on the social formation of consciousness" (p. vi). Although I do not claim that "literary evidence, the evidence of imaginative texts," should "be allowed a referential function, a power to give material and concrete evidence about the past" (p.iii)—a possibility that Paster poses without actually endorsing—I *do* think historians should attend more closely to the representational claims of what is imagined in such eminently social texts as *2 Henry VI.*

13. As Michael Hattaway writes, "The *Henry VI* plays offer a searing indictment of aristocratic factionalism and the haughtiness of prelates" ("Rebellion, Class Consciousness," p. 16).

14. Buchanan Sharp, *In Contempt of All Authority: Artisans and Riot in the West of England, 1586-1640* (Berkeley: University of California Press, 1980), pp. 38-39. See also Keith Wrightson, *English Society: 1580-1680* (New Brunswick, N.J.: Rutgers University Press, 1982), p. 150.

15. In *Shakespeare and the Popular Voice,* Annabel Patterson notes that in appropriating "the chronicle accounts of the Peasants' Revolt to thicken his description of Jack Cade's rebellion," Shakespeare "was clearly participating in an Elizabethan cultural practice, that of collating the popular protests of the past, both with each other and with the issues of the day" (pp. 38-39).

16. Sharp, *In Contempt,* p. 36.

17. Ibid.

18. Keith Wrightson, "Estates, Degrees & Sorts in Tudor and Stuart England," *History Today* 37 (1987), 21.

19. Anthony Giddens, *The Class Structure of the Advanced Societies* (New York: Barnes & Noble, 1973), p. 30.

20. Richard Wilson, "'A Mingled Yarn': Shakespeare and the Cloth Workers," *Literature & History* 12, 2 (1986), 167.

21. In her discussion of Kett's rebellion, Annabel Patterson remarks the "self-conscious acceptance, by the rebels themselves, of a 'peasant' ideology of the primitive," and concludes that "it is no accident that Shakespeare's Cade makes [the 'clouted shoon'] his distinguishing mark of class" (*Shakespeare and the Popular Voice,* p. 40).

22. Edward Hall, *The Union of the Two Noble and Illustre Famelies of Lancastre and Yorke* (London, 1548), f. 160^{v}.

23. Wilson, "A Mingled Yarn," p. 168. As Wilson writes: "Son of a provincial glover whose only testimony is the mark he left beside his name in borough records, Shakespeare used his professional debut to signal scorn of popular culture and identification with an establishment in whose eyes authority would henceforth belong exclusively to writers" (ibid., p. 169).
24. Ibid., pp. 168, 167-68.
25. George Swinnock, *The Christian mans calling . . . the second part* (London, 1663), pp. 22-23. Quoted in David Cressy, *Literacy and the Social Order: Reading and Writing in Tudor and Stuart England* (Cambridge: Cambridge University Press, 1980), p. 3. According to Cressy, "In medieval England, when literacy was virtually a clerical monopoly and criminous clerks were judged more leniently than lay felons, the ability to read a set text of the Bible was regarded as a competent proof of clerkship. The criminal had only to ask for the book and read the standard verse, the 'neck-verse,' to escape the gallows" (p. 16).
26. Cressy, *Literacy,* pp. 16-17; subsequent citations appear in the text.
27. Sir Thomas Smith, *De Republica Anglorum* (London, 1583; rpt. Cambridge: Cambridge University Press, 1906), p. 46.
28. See Bill Ashcroft, Gareth Griffiths, and Helen Tiffin, *The Empire Writes Back: Theory and Practice in Post-Colonial Literatures* (London: Routledge, 1989), pp. 78-85.
29. Nicholas Breton, *The Court and Country* (1618), rpt. in *The Works of Nicholas Breton,* ed. Ursula Kentish-Wright (London: Cressett Press, 1929), 1:203.
30. See, e.g., Hattaway, "Rebellion, Class Consciousness, pp. 18-20, and Patterson, *Shakespeare and the Popular Voice,* pp. 38-40.
31. Richard Grafton, *A Chronicle at Large and meere History of the affayres of Englande and Kings of the same* (London, 1569), p. 330.
32. Raphael Holinshed, *Holinshed's Chronicles* (London, 1589, rpt. 1807), 2:749.
33. Ibid., p. 737. See also Hattaway's treatment of the same passage in "Rebellion, Class Consciousness," pp. 19-20.

UNITY AND DESIGN

Sigurd Burckhardt (essay date 1968)

SOURCE: "'I Am But Shadow of Myself': Ceremony and Design in *1 Henry VI,*" in *Shakespearean Meanings,* Princeton University Press, 1968, pp. 47-77.

[*In the essay below, Burckhardt addresses the problems of integrity and episodic design in* Henry VI, Part 1, *finding an aesthetic unity in the ceremonial qualities of the narrative as well as in the play's thematic analogy between dramatist and God.*]

It is difficult, perhaps impossible, to say anything about *1 Henry VI* without raising the still vexed question of authorship. I too shall have to raise it, but I do not want to attack it frontally. I would rather state my position as a *working* assumption and hope that what follows will prove sound enough to bear me out. Here, then, is what I shall assume: *1 Henry VI* was written or thoroughly reworked—possibly both—by Shakespeare himself. As we have it in the Folio, it represents his effort to shape the chronicle accounts—whether directly from Hall, Holinshed, and Fabyan, or mediately from a play now lost—into a coherent dramatic whole within the still larger whole of the first tetralogy. In short, in the following interpretation I shall treat *1 Henry VI* as the Folio editors treated it: as part of the Shakespeare canon.

The scholars who have argued for this assumption have properly made it one of their tasks to show that most of the incidents in the play are by no means simply episodes but have a clear dramatic function.[1] In this they have, I think, been generally successful—especially where the incidents are not traceable to any source and so are likely to be Shakespeare's own, considered additions. The rose-plucking scene in the temple garden, the Mortimer-Richard scene right afterward, and the final scenes between Suffolk and Margaret of Anjou are all manifestly intended to knit the play more tightly into the larger design. Similarly, the great theme of dissension as the cause of English misfortunes—and of the disturbed succession as a cause of dissension—is more fully worked out in the play than it is in the sources. The hand of the dramatic strategist disposing events according to a master plan is clearly discernible.

Still it seems to me that the "integralists" have not given due weight to one obvious fact: that their arguments were needed. What Samuel Johnson said about the supposed benefits of poverty is not altogether inapplicable here; no one labors to persuade us that, say, *Richard II* is of one cast, just as no one labors to convince us that it is possible to live happily upon a plentiful fortune. Can the disintegrationist heresy—if such it is—be accounted for by no more than the obstinate longevity of Malone's error? Doesn't it feed upon some qualities in the play itself? That is the question to which, in a very indirect manner, I mean to address myself.

I

I shall do so by looking closely at the scene between Talbot and the Countess of Auvergne (II, iii). The scene is brief: right after the conquest of Orleans, Talbot is invited to visit the Countess at her castle. When he presents himself, she first taunts him with his smallness of stature;

when he turns to leave, she reveals that she has lured him into a trap and means to hold him prisoner. But Talbot has anticipated her plot; he has placed soldiers in readiness to occupy the castle. The scene ends amicably, with apologies offered and accepted and a joint feast.

For an integralist, the scene presents a difficult problem; it seems irretrievably episodic. It grows out of no prior event, leads to no subsequent one; the Countess appears in no other scene and is never again heard of. No major theme seems to be illustrated, no moral pointed. Moreover, there is no hint of the incident in any of the play's sources. Oddly, Shakespeare appears to have composed, with full deliberation, a scene that is purely episodic. The very oddity demands attention.

Here is the opening exchange between the Countess and Talbot:

> Countess: Is this the scourge of France?
> Is this the Talbot, so much feared abroad
> That with his name the mothers still their babes?
> I see report is fabulous and false.
> I thought I should have seen some Hercules,
> A second Hector, for his grim aspect,
> And large proportion of his strong-knit limbs.
> Alas, this is a child, a silly dwarf!
> It cannot be this weak and writhled shrimp
> Should strike such terror to his enemies.
> Talbot: Madam, I have been bold to trouble you;
> But since your ladyship is not at leisure,
> I'll sort some other time to visit you
>
> (15-27)

What happens here is that a *ceremony* is startlingly interrupted. The ceremony is that of the taunt, and the Countess' language is properly ceremonial, in the true Marlovian cadence: "Is this the face that launched a thousand ships?" Her lines call for a counter-taunt or defiance, a reply in the manner at least of Gloucester defying Winchester:

> Presumptuous priest! this place commands my patience,
> Or thou shouldst find thou hast dishonored me.
>
> (III, i, 8-9)

Substitute "lady" for "priest" and "thy sex" for "this place," and the reply should serve quite nicely. Talbot himself knows, elsewhere in the play, what the ceremony calls for:

> Foul fiend of France, and hag of all despite,
> Encompassed with thy lustful paramours!
> Becomes it thee to taunt his [Bedford's] valiant age,
> And twit with cowardice a man half dead?
>
> (III, ii, 52-55)

But here he refuses to play his part, to pick up the verbal gauntlet. With ironic urbanity, he implies that he has broken in upon the Countess as she was rehearsing a set-piece; his apology leaves her in the silly posture of someone striking a mighty blow at a vanished target.

It is the Countess, not Talbot, who in this scene speaks the language of the play. About *her* style there is nothing unusual; it is of a piece with the play's world. That world is one of vaunt and taunt, of "high terms" ceremonially put forward and ceremonially responded to—usually with the explicit or implicit invocation of force as the final arbiter:

> Thou hast astonished me with thy high terms.
> Only this proof I'll of thy valour make,
> In single combat thou shalt buckle with me,
> And if thou vanquishest, thy words are true;
> Otherwise I renounce all confidence.
>
> (I, ii, 93-97)

"Single combat" or multiple—the sword is always at least half unsheathed to make good the words. Gloucester or Winchester, Red Rose or White, England or France, it is all the same; as the Mayor of London says: "Good God, these nobles should such stomachs bear!"

My point is not that the language is appropriate to the world, but rather that it allows of no other. Every major actor is compelled—not necessarily by pride and pugnacity but by the language available to him—to step onto the stage, assume the proper posture, and rehearse his piece. The burden of the piece need not always be self-assertion or defiance, though most often it is. The mode lends itself equally well to grief:

> Hung be the heavens with black, yield day to night!
>
> (I, i, 1)

or to praise:

> And all the priests and friars in my realm
> Shall in procession sing her endless praise.
> A statelier pyramis to her I'll rear
> Than Rhodope's of Memphis ever was
>
> (I, vi, 19-22)

or even to submission:

> In sign whereof, this arm, that hath reclaimed
> To your obedience fifty fortresses,
> Twelve cities, and seven wallèd towns of strength,
> Beside five hundred prisoners of esteem,
> Lets fall his sword before your Highness' feet,
> And with submissive loyalty of heart
> Ascribes the glory of his conquest got
> First to my God and next unto your Grace.
>
> (III, iv, 5-12)

Self-assertion and praise (or submission) are difficult to tell apart. The ceremonial mode lends itself to every occasion, but what matters is that it makes an "occasion" of whatever it lends itself to. It is like Concord grapes: no matter what it is made into, the residual taste is always the same.

Prosodically, the mode engenders the end-stopped line. The lines of verse behave like the characters, each striving to stand in self-sufficient and self-assertive orotundity. A speech is like a recital of titles and honors (or dishonors, it makes no real difference):

> But where's the great Alcides of the field,
> Valiant Lord Talbot, Earl of Shrewsbury,
> Created, for his rare success in arms,
> Great Earl of Washford, Waterford and Valence;
> Lord Talbot of Goodrig and Urchinfield,
> Lord Strange of Blackmore, Lord Verdun of Alton
> . . .

etc., etc., for six more lines. Joan's response is predictable:

> Here's a silly stately style indeed! . . .
> Him that thou magnifi'st with all these titles
> Stinking and fly-blown lies here at our feet.
>
> (IV, vii, 60-76)

But even in ridiculing the stately style, Joan pays unwilling homage to it by obediently falling into the vaunt-taunt pattern. The speakers may think they master and use the style, but in fact it masters and uses them. Margaret of Anjou becomes a kind of embodiment of it:

> Henry: Your wondrous rare description, noble earl,
> Of beauteous Margaret hath astonished me.
> Her virtues graced with external gifts
> Do breed love's settled passions in my heart;
> And like as rigour of tempestuous gusts
> Provokes the mightiest hulk against the tide,
> So am I driven by breath of her renown
> Either to suffer shipwreck or arrive
> Where I may have fruition of her love.
> Suffolk: Tush, my good lord, this superficial tale
> Is but a preface to her worthy praise.
> The chief perfections of that lovely dame,
> Had I sufficient skill to utter them,
> Would make a volume of enticing lines,
> Able to ravish any dull conceit;
> And, which is more, she is not so divine,
> So full-replete with choice of all delights,
> But with as humble lowliness of mind
> She is content to be at your command.
>
> (V, v, 1-19)

Is she indeed? This "volume of enticing lines" will presently become Queen of England: contentious rather than content, overbearing rather than humble. She will have a major share in the ensuing shipwreck. As she is here talked about, she furnishes as neat an illustration as we can hope for of a style which, seeming to do its master's bidding, drives him toward a disastrous conclusion.

Rhetorically, the mode engenders hyperbole—a relentless reaching for the superlative which, in the effort to outdo what has gone before, is sure to end in collapse. We are warned at the outset:

> England ne'er had a king until his [Henry V's] time.
> Virtue he had, deserving to command.
> His brandished sword did blind men with his beams;
> His arms spread wider than a dragon's wings;
> His sparkling eyes, replete with wrathful fire,
> More dazzled and drove back his enemies
> Than mid-day sun fierce bent against their faces.
> What should I say? his deeds exceed all speech.
>
> (I, i, 8-15)

Here the mortal contention, closing with a feeble gasp, is between the similes of one speaker; elsewhere it is between those of two. In either case it is a "jarring discord of nobility":

> But howsoe'er, no simple man that sees
> This jarring discord of nobility,
> This should'ring of each other in the court . . .
> But that [he] doth presage some ill event.
>
> (IV, i, 187-191)

Where every line, every trope, every man strives for preeminence, what can come of it but "intestine broils"?

The mode of *1 Henry VI* seeks, in fact compels the seeking of, the fullest self-assertion at every moment; it is impatient of indirection, refuses to sacrifice immediate effects for long-range gains. It permits strategic retreats as little as litotes, genuine negotiation as little as genuine dialogue; it always "goes for broke." It has no sense of the implicit; whatever is not asserted does not exist. Its "order," except where it is kept in check by external, higher authority, is that of combat; by inner necessity it escalates toward more and more violent confrontations. The duel, single or multiple, is its most adequate metaphor, until finally it drives even duelling into "mere oppugnancy," sheer, vengeful slaughter (as it has in *3 Henry VI*).

My intention has not been to point up once again the obvious faults of Shakespeare's "immature" style, but rather to suggest that he *himself* was fully aware of them. Even in this supposedly early play he has mastered the trick of making the style he employs comment upon itself; is a better description of it imaginable than "rigour of tempestuous gusts," a phrase which catches precisely both its rigid compulsiveness and its destructive, blowhard yet short-winded unrestraint? But more important: Shakespeare has discovered that there is a perfect analogy between the verbal and the social order—an analogy that is almost an identity. Both the *modus loquendi* and the *modus agendi* of a society are governed by the same inner law or laws. For the dramatist who grasps this law, the stage *is* the world.

II

At this point I should like to construct a speculative little playlet of my own. I do not intend to claim historical validity for it, though I shall try to show that it is plausible, congruent with what we know. The playlet will serve me, I hope, to explain more easily and clearly the nature and implications of Shakespeare's discovery; but it is meant to be no more than a model, an interpretive device.

What little we do know about the textual history of the Henry VI plays indicates that they were involved in, were very possible the object of, a "war of the playwrights." There is, first of all, Greene's famous attack on Shakespeare in *A Groats-worth of Wit,* with its allusion to *3 Henry VI.* There is Chettle's subsequent apology, apparently at the instance of "diverse of worship," for having published the attack. There is the fact that the theatre in question was the *Rose;* Shakespeare would hardly have been Shakespeare if he had not been aware of the strangely significant coincidence that the *Rose* should furnish the stage for a "War of the Roses" which at the same time figured importantly in a war of playwrights. (Witness his later awareness of the dramatic significance of the *Globe.*) There is, finally, the fact that plays often were written in collaboration—a practice which must have encouraged each playwright to try to be the best "Shake-scene," to outdo his colleagues and competitors in the writing of theatrically effective scenes and let the play as a whole shift for itself.

Greene's attack has been variously interpreted and endlessly debated. The disintegrationists have naturally made the most of it, while the integralists have tended to explain it as the spiteful outburst of a bitter and destitute writer who saw himself neglected for a highly successful young rival. The integralist argument has been that where *Henry VI* sounds more like Greene or Nashe or Marlowe than like Shakespeare, we have evidence of a young poet's inevitable and natural tendency to imitate his elders, and that Greene's charge of plagiarism refers to this kind of imitation. But that can hardly be a correct reading of the passage. For Greene distinguishes explicitly between "past excellence" ("Let those apes imitate your past excellence") and "inventions" ("and never more acquaint them with your admired inventions").[2] *He* at least believed that the "feathers" with which Shakespeare had "beautified" himself were something a good deal more substantial than the imitation of past excellence; and his belief must have had sufficient basis in fact for his fellow playwrights to understand the allusion.

The question to ask, therefore, is: What did Greene mean by "admired inventions"? Let us imagine that several collaborating playwrights, Shakespeare and Greene among them, have met to block out a play or sequence of plays they have undertaken to do. Ideas are pooled, a division of labor is arranged. It becomes evident that each collaborator means to out-bombast the others as best he can; whereupon one of them, unwilling to see the whole torn apart by this contentious striving for short-range effects and personal glory, withdraws from the partnership and writes his own version of the play.

How are the others likely to react? Greene's attack, not only in general but in its actual wording, would be a very natural reaction. The others are almost certain to believe that their "admired inventions" were stolen by the defector, who, having picked their brains, then arrogantly set himself up as the "*only* Shake-scene" (i.e., demanding to write *all* the scenes), as an "absolute *Iohannes fac totum.*" And they are almost certain to have some plausible grounds for this belief; for, with the basic story given by the chronicles and the natural give-and-take of a planning session, there is bound to be considerable overlap between the ideas proposed and the defector's final product.

Greene's admonition to his fellow playwrights is most naturally read, I think, as a warning against any future collaboration with players, more especially with Shakespeare. Never, he enjoins, let the players see anything but your finished (and paid-for) products. Those they will imitate; let them. But beware of sitting down with them to plan a new play, for they will first steal your ideas and then (with a fine show of artistic integrity yet!) your credit. This reading would also explain the next sentence: "For it is pity men of such rare wits should be subject to the pleasures of such rude grooms." Is not Greene here alluding to attempts by Shakespeare to curb the self-seeking and self-will of the other writers, or (as naturally Greene saw it) to lord it (a mere player!) over these rare University Wits?

The scene, then, of my model shows Shakespeare sitting with other playwrights, arguing for a coherent and organic scheme for the Henry VI plays and more and more unhappily watching his collaborators tear the whole apart in a compulsive contention for the "finest" scenes and "noblest" speeches—in a "jarring discord of nobility." And suddenly the thought strikes him: Why shouldn't they? How could it be otherwise? Is not this exactly what the whole story is about? Are we not here *enacting* what we mean to represent? Would my idea of an integral dramatic whole not falsify the essence of the story we are supposed to tell? Is not the play we are here cutting into segments a perfect analogue of its true subject—England torn by civil war—and am I not in the position of Henry VI, a child, a mere beginner in the art of governing this play-world, surrounded by powerful and headstrong nobles, pleading helplessly for peace and amity, for subordination to the common purpose?

And then a further thought strikes him: Do we not also enact, act in, the very style in which, as dramatists, we speak? Is not this scene the inevitable result of the concept of ceremonial "order" implicit in that style, and is that concept of order not exactly analogous to the larger image of order, the "world picture" we have been taught to accept? Is there not a grim and self-destructive necessity governing a world, a kingdom, a body of playwrights, a play, or a speech which is constructed on this model? And if so, where is the remedy? Exit Shakespeare, pursued by troublesome doubts.

III

Where was the remedy? The first need would seem to be the discovery of what was wrong with the "picture." What were its essential qualities? One was that it was static; it existed in space but not in time. It allowed for a limited amount of internal motion (though even that seemed rather an unhappy violation of its spirit, commotion rather than motion); but it did not allow for general progressive change. It valued stability to the point of rigidity; what occurred in it was not so much an ordered sequence of events leading from the past into a different future as a succession of *exempla,* episodes meant to point the same permanent morals. Enthroned at its apex sat God, the fount of honor, the source of all authority, more unmoved than mover, more substance than energy, a figure encrusted with the symbols of macrocosmic sovereignty. Below Him, step by step, stood the hierarchical "orders": the angels in their various "degrees," and then men: kings, nobles, burghers, peasants, and, near the very bottom, even vagrant comedians.

A second essential quality of the picture was that it was rigorously analogical. Differences were of degree; unity was assured by analogical identity. A king was "God in little," while God was the "King of kings." A kingdom was to Christendom what a dukedom was to the kingdom. There were also, of course, innumerable "collateral" analogies, whose force was symbolic rather than legal: to the animal kingdom, the vegetable kingdom, the "little kingdom" man, the kingdom of the heavens. For the explaining of actual events, these analogies were heavily drawn upon: "distempers" or "perturbations" at one level were mirrored by disturbances at other levels; a king who did not control his subjects was like a man who did not control his appetites. Everything was like everything else; beneath the diversity in degree there was a remarkable likeness in kind.

Third, harmony at any level depended on both the acknowledgment and the effective exercise of the authority vested in the next higher level. Order was not implicit but always external to what was being "kept in order"—and consequently explicit. Of course, the picture as a whole was supposed, ideally, to rest in beautiful and total harmony; if every inferior acted in unfailing obedience and every superior in unfailing wisdom and justice, there was no reason why authority had to become explicit. But obviously this was a mere ideal, not the observable reality; and since the picture was in fact used as a tool of government, as a means to inculcate obedience and to discourage "rebellion," what was emphasized was the danger and wickedness of conflict and the duty, whenever conflict did arise, to submit to authority. The picture militated against any distinction between political and religious duty, between unlawful acts and sinful acts. Disobedience was the root and prototype of all evil, private as well as public; to it all sins were reducible. God was the King of kings much more than the Father, while the father was a "king in little," as the king was "God in little." At every level—since every level had *some* authority, i.e., some beings inferior to it over which it was appointed to rule—there was need for constant and explicit assertion of that authority. (I am speaking, of course, not of sociological realities in Elizabethan England, but of its world picture and what it implied.) The very logic which demanded submission in one direction demanded self-assertion, jealous insistence on one's place, titles, and prerogatives, in all others. Answerability was always vertical, never horizontal; always public, never private. When a man spoke on matters of importance, he spoke ceremonially, as belonging to a certain order, occupying a certain degree in the picture.

These, then, were the essential qualities of the picture; how well did it explain the actual events to be accounted for, the Wars of the Roses? At first glance, all seemed easy: England, under the rule of an ineffectual king, had fallen into dissension; her nobles had become rebellious and self-willed; and God had grievously punished her for these sins and failings. First she had lost her French possessions and then she had turned upon herself, falling into chaos and tyranny, until finally God had mercifully sent a redeemer, Henry VII.

But upon a closer look the picture proved to have some very disturbing consequences. Its structure of analogies contained the equation king=God; Tudor doctrine never tired of making that equation emphatically explicit, seemed in fact designed for no other purpose. But if under a king's ineffectual rule England suffered the horrors of the Barons' War, what followed about the King of kings and the horrors of, say, the Hundred Years' War?

A question not to be asked; and scholars and critics are virtually unanimous that Shakespeare, at least the Shakespeare of the histories, did not ask it. He would never have thought of drawing the analogy between the civil wars in England and the English wars against the "arch-enemy" France, however imperatively the God-king/Christendom-kingdom analogy seemed to demand it; his patriotism was logic-proof. But was it? Let us listen:

> See, see the pining malady of———!
> Behold the wounds, the most unnatural wounds,
> Which thou thyself hast given her woeful breast.
> O, turn thy edgéd sword another way;
> Strike those that hurt, and hurt not those that help.
> One drop of blood drawn from thy country's bosom
> Should grieve thee more than streams of foreign gore.
>
> (III, iii, 49-55)

This is not Henry or good Duke Humphrey pleading with one of the English barons; it is the witch Joan persuading Burgundy to break off his English alliance and return to his true allegiance. To be sure, as soon as Burgundy yields, she comments cynically: "Done like a Frenchman! Turn and turn again!" But that is precisely the point: this fine patriotic rhetoric is as available to her as to the sincerest Englishman—and more effective. The rhetoric is quite independent of the speaker's motives; it belongs to the nation. Which nation? We are at liberty to fill in the blank. Shakespeare gives it to France; and it strains credulity to believe that he did not know what he was doing. If Elizabethan attitudes argue otherwise, what—apart from the picture's logic, apart from Shakespeare's composing such a speech and then giving it to Joan—about medieval attitudes? The time lay not so far back when Christian kingdoms were considered provinces of Christendom and wars between Christian kings civil wars (so that the only pious war a king could wage was a crusade against the infidel). But if they were, what kind of sovereign was the King of kings?

There is, in *1 Henry VI,* at least one clear sign that Shakespeare did ask this forbidden question. At the end of IV.i, Henry, claiming to "be umpire in this doubtful strife" between Lancaster and York, puts on a red rose and explains this gesture, seemingly so contrary to the impartiality he has just professed, by saying:

> I see no reason, if I wear this rose,
> That anyone should therefore be suspicious
> I more incline to Somerset [Lancaster] than York.
> Both are my kinsmen, and I love them both.
> As well they may upbraid me with my crown,
> Because, forsooth, the King of Scots is crowned.
>
> (IV, i, 152-157)

I have not seen the last two lines glossed, though surely they are puzzling. Henry's argument makes sense only on the assumption that he happens to be King of England (and of France; he has just been crowned in Paris) *in exactly the same sense* as he happens to be of the house of Lancaster. Both are accidents of birth; they have no bearing on his function as umpire, which thus must rest on another quality altogether. That quality can only be his pious and loving Christian spirit, which is independent of his royal degree and both commands and entitles him to "instruct and teach" men to "continue peace and love." This view of himself is perfectly in keeping with his bearing throughout the trilogy; but of course it is this same view which makes him so disastrously ineffectual as a king. Christian precept and example are not enough to keep the ceremonial world in order; what is required is the full exercise of higher *authority.* His claim to impartiality even while putting on the symbol of partisanship can mean only that he refuses to exercise that authority.

An impartiality truly divine; how many divisions has God? Suppose there is a war between England and Scotland (there had been so many that Scotland was almost as much an "arch-enemy" as France, was in fact usually in league with France against England); what then? Is not Henry here saying that a king of England warring against a king of Scotland or any other Christian king is, from the divine purview, doing exactly the same thing as Somerset quarreling with York? And in saying this, is he not faithfully obeying the "ana-logic" of the Elizabethan world picture? If, therefore, Christendom is continually ravaged by wars—

> Henry: I always thought
> It was both impious and unnatural
> That such immanity and bloody strife
> Should reign among professors of one faith
>
> (V, i, 11-14)—

what blasphemous inference inescapably arises about the governance of the world and the fitness of its supreme head? Given the manifest facts of history, does not the world picture that is devised to give them meaning positively compel an impious conclusion?

IV

At this point—if I may briefly resume my little dramatic fancy—it may well have occurred to Shakespeare that there was a mode of ruling other than the picture provided for, a form of authority other than that of ceremony backed by force. He did not even have to invent it; it was embedded in the story itself but so overlaid with the ceremonial pomp of the picture that it was easily overlooked. As told by Hall and others, the story was, after all, *not* just one of discord, a succession of more and more savage spectacles; it did have a unifying design: beginning, middle, and end. It began with Richard II and ended with Henry VII; it told how the English monarchy, once having fallen from the happy state of unbroken succession and unquestioned legitimacy, sank into ever deeper confusion (except for one brief and glorious reign) and had to suffer all the horrors of civil war and tyranny before order was restored through the happy "Union of the two noble and illustre famelies of Lancastre and Yorke" in the persons of Henry Tudor and Elizabeth of York. That was the overall plot within which the events of the story had meaning; that was the design which created order out of the apparent chaos.

"Plot"? "Design"? What words were these? The effort to grasp the unity of the story seemed to call forth the vocabulary of sedition. In the picture designs and plots were proscribed; they were the work of "designing, crafty knaves," sinister and ill-meaning men whose "policy" (another word of evil) could not stand the light of the sun. The world, unless it was disordered, was a "goodly frame," essentially stationary, a palace that was like a statuesque body, or a body that was like a palace:

> And all her body, like a palace fair,
> Ascending up with many a stately stair.
>
> (Spenser)

Men who had grievances expected, and men who had done evil were summoned, to appear before the throne of justice to have their cases adjudicated—openly, explicitly, in due form. Sovereign decrees were solemnly promulgated and proclaimed by heralds or angels; every occasion was an occasion "of state," provided with the appropriate ceremony. Even war and combat, though temporary breaches of order, were ritualized; "stratagems" were wicked and dishonorable, devil's work. Indeed, all that was indirect and hidden belonged to the ignoble sphere of Satan; God's world had no room for it.

Strange: the God of Tudor history turned out to be a being altogether different from what the picture called for. The range and complexity of His plots—not to mention of the Master Plot from Fall to Resurrection—were the envy and despair of any merely human plotter. History, more particularly English history from Richard II to Henry VII, was anything but an orderly succession of events in the ceremonial mode of Henry VI's pastoral dreaming:

> So many hours must I tend my flock,
> So many hours must I take my rest.
> So many hours must I contemplate,
> So many hours must I sport myself.
>
> (*3 Henry VI,* II, v, 31)

"How sweet! how lovely" the world would be in which the Lord could be our shepherd. Evidently He couldn't; at least He wasn't. But neither was He the stern and prepotent judge and lord who in the fulness of His power and glory summoned evildoers directly and openly before His seat to receive their punishment and correction, or in righteous anger led His hosts against the rebellious. If He had heavenly hosts at His command, they must be committed elsewhere; at least they were not deployed in Christendom to check the wicked. The King of kings, it appeared, was altogether unlike His ideal earthly image, altogether unlike what the analogy to Henry V would lead one to expect.

What *was* He like, then? Surprisingly, He was like a dramatist. He planned, designed, plotted, employed stratagems; He worked by indirection and implication. Unable or unwilling to exert open authority and force, He nevertheless did not retreat into the pastoral mode, writing wistful Third, Fourth, and Fifth Shepherds' Plays and appealing to the still, small voice in men's hearts to do the rest. He wrote *histories* which, though on the surface they might look like savage spectacles, moved in truth by careful plotting toward an ordered conclusion. His purposes were hidden, wholly implicit in the design; while the action was still in progress, they could at most be guessed at. To the careless spectator as to the vain actor they were invisible: the actor would imagine that the play existed only to give him a chance to strut and rant and upstage his rivals, while the spectator would see it as a string of exciting episodes intended to entertain him, to confirm his nationalist self-esteem, and here and there (no pleasure is unalloyed) to point an obvious moral. But the divine dramatist knew better; in the end, and only then, His design would be manifest. And it might well be that the seemingly most episodic would, in retrospect, prove the most calculated and revealing.

With respect to kings and men of power, God evidently resembled the bad more than the good. Poor Henry VI, bullied by ambitious subjects, spoke his pitiful pieces and was discarded; but Richard III had an almost divine talent for long-range plotting. Generally, the more a king relied on the ceremonial mode and on the "picture" behind it, the surer was he to come to grief; witness Richard II. True, in the end even the plotters were only actors; the prouder they were of their subtle designs, the more harshly were they shown that they themselves had only played parts in a master plot. Their self-seeking vanity betrayed them; they could never resist the temptation to become explicit, to brag at least to the audience of their clever schemes. They fell short of the master dramatist's ultimate achievement: total self-effacement, complete immersion in the design. They wanted the glory as well as the power; even when, like Warwick, they were satisfied with being king-makers rather than kings, they wanted the world and the kings to *know* them as such. By their soliloquies they reimbursed themselves for the self-denial of plotting; they had not grasped the secret of divine dramaturgy: never to speak in the first person. Still, they had grasped enough of it to be temporarily successful. It was as though God, like men, judged less by virtue than by likeness to Himself and by pleasure received—as though He were bored by the arrangers of ritual and ceremonial tableaus and inclined to reward even wicked plotters for pleasing Him with genuine drama.

V

I seem to have moved far away from the Talbot-Countess episode, to have plunged headlong into the Intentional Fallacy, and constructed a playlet of my own under the presumptuous title "Shakespeare Thinking about *Henry VI.*" Let me repeat, therefore, that I claim no factuality for my drama, either in the setting or in the thought. I have tried to construct a model to account for observable facts, and I have chosen the narrative form simply because that seemed the best expository strategy. Like any other model, mine must be judged by the problems it solves—which brings me back to Talbot and the Countess, whom I hope I have kept in mind throughout.

Briefly to recapitulate: I began by pointing out that the scene shows every sign of being *deliberately* episodic and called attention to the programmatic contrast between the Countess' mode of speech and that of Talbot's reply. I identified the Countess' mode—which is that of the play as a whole—as ceremonial and argued that it is inherently combative and episodic. I then presented my model and tried to show not only that it satisfied the details of Greene's attack but, more importantly that it suggests how Shakespeare may have discovered some disquieting analogies between the problems he encountered in writing the play and problems at the heart of the Elizabethan world picture. The solution to these problems I described in terms of plotting.

Both Talbot and the Countess are plotters; but their plots are as different in quality as they are in final success. The Countess cannot resist telling us about hers:

> The plot is laid: if all things fall out right,
> I shall as famous be by this exploit
> As Scythian Tomyris by Cyrus' death. . . .
>
> (II, iii, 4-6)

Contrast Talbot upon accepting the Countess' invitation:

> Come hither, captain. [*whispers*] You perceive my mind?
>
> (II, ii, 59)

It is a contrast between a design announced, made explicit, and a design barely hinted at. It is at the same time a contrast between a less and a more encompassing plot, as well as between one that aims at personal glory and one that has no such aim. The parallel to, respectively, the Countess' mode of speech and Talbot's is evident.

What does the parallel signify? This question leads to the second part of the scene, in which the reason for the Countess' ill success is explained:

> Countess: Long time thy shadow hath been thrall to me,
> For in my gallery thy picture hangs;
> But now the substance shall endure the like. . . .
> Talbot: Ha, ha, ha! . . .
> I laugh to see your ladyship so fond
> To think that you have aught but Talbot's shadow. . . .
> No, no, I am but shadow of myself.
> You are deceived, my substance is not here;
> For what you see is but the smallest part
> And least proportion of humanity. . . .
> Countess: How can these contrarieties agree?
> Talbot: That will I show you presently.
> [*winds his horn: drums strike up: a peal of ordnance: enter soldiers*]
> How say you, madam? are you now persuaded
> That Talbot is but shadow of himself?
> These are his substance, sinews, arms and strength.
>
> (II, iii, 36-63)

Talbot is the more successful plotter because he does not naively and vainly assert himself as a "first person," a substantial being in and of himself. He is not what he is—to cite Shakespeare's favorite paradox for describing effective plotters. His strength lies precisely in his "negative capability," his having learned the secret of self-effacement, of assertion only through the larger design.

We must be clear that this is the Talbot of the episode, not that of the rest of the play. The "character" Talbot does not essentially differ from the other characters. He is, to be sure, loyal to his king and country; he puts the common cause above personal gain if not always above glory. But his *style* is ceremonial, and it is style that determines likeness. The first time we see Talbot, he shows himself as concerned about his dignity as the proudest baron. When he was a prisoner of the French:

> With a baser man of arms by far
> Once in contempt they would have bartered me;
> Which I disdaining scorned and cravéd death
> Rather than I would be so vile esteemed.
> In fine, redeemed I was as I desired.
>
> (I, iv, 30-34)

The French offer a remarkable bargain: the foremost English general for some nondescript soldier of their own. But ceremony is so much more important than function that Talbot refuses the bargain and, at risk of total loss, insists on a much worse one.

Talbot's notion of warfare is literally medieval, strictly ceremonial. When Joan takes Rouen by stratagem, he shouts "treason" and "hellish mischief" and challenges the French to come out and fight "like soldiers":

> Talbot: Dare ye come forth and meet us in the field?
> Joan: Belike your lordship takes us then for fools,
> To try if that our own be ours or no.
> Talbot: I speak not to that railing Hecate,
> But unto thee, Alençon, and the rest.
> Will ye, like soldiers, come and fight it out?
> Alençon: Signior, no.
> Talbot: Signior, hang! base muleteers of France!
> Like peasant foot-boys do they keep the walls
> And dare not take up arms like gentlemen.
>
> (III, ii, 61-70)

Railing Hecate! There is no need to multiply instances; Talbot never opens his mouth but to pay tribute to ceremony. In the end it is not he who captures Joan, but the wily plotter Richard of York. Talbot, unsuccoured by his contentious countrymen, is "tangled" in French "snares" and dies in glorious rhymed combat with his son over who should flee to fight again and who should die for the honor of the Talbot name. He makes a splendid exit:

> Then follow thou thy desperate sire of Crete,
> Thou Icarus; thy life to me is sweet.
> If thou wilt fight, fight by thy father's side;
> And, commendable proved, let's die in pride.
>
> (IV, vi, 54-57)

Just as a reminder of what he sounded like when he did *not* get tangled in French snares, here is his reply to the Countess once more:

> Madam, I have been bold to trouble you;
> But since your ladyship is not at leisure,
> I'll sort some other time to visit you.

Which of these two men, so strangely yoked by one name, is the "real" Talbot? It is the Countess' question. Relying on "great rumour" and "rare report" as well as on his picture in her gallery, she thinks to trap the man's substance, "writhled shrimp" though he suddenly turns out to be. His laughter makes her ask: "Why, art not thou the man?" It develops that where before she had but the shadow of his shadow, she still has no more than his shadow; substantiality is inversely proportional to illustriousness and "presence." The substance escapes her; but in that one little scene she and we come as close as we ever shall to actually *seeing* the real Talbot. For only in that scene is he gifted, for a moment, with the style of speech and action which must be learned if his true purpose, the cause of England, is to be served. Sincerity of intention is not enough; valor and nobility do not ensure success—rather the contrary. His one brief moment, not of glory—of those he has only too many—but of genuinely dramatic effectiveness comes when he realizes that his substance is in the "sinews, arms and strength" of common, anonymous Englishmen *and* in the plot, the design in which they are made to act.

I believe that we can and must expand the question: "Who is the real Talbot?" into the broader one, "What is the real play, the real *1 Henry VI*?" Some critics, usually disintegrationists, have called it a "Talbot-play," taking their lead from Nashe's *Pierce Penniless:*

> How would it have joyed brave Talbot (the terror of the French) to think that after he had lain two hundred years in his tomb, he should triumph again on the stage, and have his bones new embalmed with the tears of ten thousand spectators at least (at several times), who, in the tragedian that represents his person, imagine they behold him fresh bleeding.[3]

(There is the Countess' "picture" again!) The integralists, on the other hand, have argued that the real heroine of this as of the other histories is England, and that even Talbot is no more than a servant in her cause. I should say that the integralists are *demonstrably* in the right—but mostly on the strength of the Auvergne episode. For it is there, and there only, that Talbot clearly eliminates himself as "hero"; everywhere else he plays the part to the hilt.

This suggests that this most episodic of episodes is the "real" play, just as the Talbot in it is the "real" Talbot. How can that be? I am afraid the explanation will sound rather paradoxical, because in answer to the question: "How can these contrarieties agree?" I am unhappily not in the position to "wind my horn" and enact the answer physically. I shall try, however, to find help in my model. I suggested that Shakespeare saw the Wars of the Roses as a function and necessary product of the ceremonial style. This meant that, on the one hand, his immediate subject, if it was to be truly represented, required that style; while on the other hand his larger subject—the divine plot in which all the disorders and episodic contentions were but steps toward a new kind of unity and order—required a style altogether different. His way out of this dilemma was this: he *plotted,* on the whole, according to the new, functional style: looking ahead, condensing, eliminating episodic matter, adding and elaborating anticipatory scenes, strengthening the themes most important to the general design. But he *wrote* according to the old, ceremonial style—in part, quite possibly, because it was still the only style he fully controlled. But being Shakespeare, he could hardly be happy with these unresolved "contrarieties"—even though they were implicit in Tudor doctrine. So he plotted a scene which, looked at casually, seems purely episodic. But into the scene he wrote an utterly unexpected speech of three lines, which should startle us into looking closely. If we do, we discover that here the contrarieties, *both* in speech *and* in plotting, are made to confront each other, and that the victory goes to the new style—again both in speech and plotting. Drama wins over ceremony, self-effacement over self-assertion, the implicit over the explicit.

The expression "wins over" contains an ambiguity useful for my purpose; it can be read with the stress either on the first word or on the second. This brings me to the last part of the scene, which contains a final surprise. Of the "brave" Talbot, the "terror of the French," we would surely expect that he would take the Countess' treachery in very ill part. How is a man who is outraged by a ruse of war (employed by a declared enemy) likely to react to the discovery that he was to be trapped by feigned hospitality? Given the general level of rage and vengefulness in the play, a clean killing—after fearful verbal abuse—would seem a mild form of retaliation. But no; apology is sufficient to win grace:

> Countess: For I am sorry that with reverence
> I did not entertain thee as thou art.
> Talbot: Be not dismayed, fair lady; nor misconster
> The mind of Talbot, as you did mistake
> The outward composition of his body.
> What you have done hath not offended me;
> No other satisfaction do I crave,
> But only, with your patience, that we may
> Taste of your wine and see what cates you have;
> For soldiers' stomachs always serve them well.
> Countess: With all my heart, and think me honourèd
> To feast so great a warrior in my house.
>
> (II, iii, 71-82)

End of our scene. Having *won* over the Countess, Talbot now wins her over. Not with words or postures of ceremonial forgiveness; there is no kneeling and lifting up, no begging for mercy and magnanimous, magniloquent granting of it. The reconciliation is managed with unassertive kindness and wholly implicit generosity: "What you have done hath not offended me." It has not offended him because this is the real Talbot, whose mind we misconstrue if we interpret it by his "outward composition" in the rest of the play. This is the sovereign plotter, who has learned from his divine counterpart both the style and the responsibilities that go with such plotting and such sovereignty.

Shakespeare's *ultimate* purpose is not to unite the English by whipping and stirring them with self-assertive nationalist bombast into once again being "the terror of the French," by directing their vainglory and ceremonial combativeness outward. That style is outdated, undramatic; worse, it is self-defeating. Not only do the French master the same style (in fact, *Henry V* suggests that originally it *was* a French style, which the English adopted to their sorrow); the style is too readily importable for domestic use. Having learned to employ it against the French, the Yorks and Lancasters, the Suffolks and Cliffords (as well as the Raleighs and Essexes?) are only too ready to use it upon each other. The disorder in the world of *Henry VI* is not so much a rupture, a break in the chain of ordered being; it is a disease, an infection endemic in the all-too-pure, all-too-ceremonial lily that makes the noble flower smell far worse than weeds.

Shakespeare's ultimate purpose is greater, more encompassing, dictated by the new analogy (God-dramatist) he has discovered and by the old analogy (Christendom-Kingdom) he has rediscovered beneath the rhetoric of nationalism. His immediate responsibility is to his nation;

he does speak English, he is not God. But that responsibility is to teach his nation a *new style:* of grace, of easy self-confidence, of implicit courtesy and generosity, of function rather than ceremony. United by and in this style, England would deserve to "win over" other nations and to play a leading part in the divine masterplot. After the "Union of the two noble and illustre famelies of Lancastre and Yorke" there is promise of a still greater union, no longer "noble and illustre" but for that very reason likely to prove finer and truer, more lasting and closer to men's real needs:

> No other satisfaction do I crave,
> But only, with your patience, that we may
> Taste of your wine and see what cates you have.

But that final feast is still far off—many wars off. The action is still in progress; the design can only be guessed at. Meanwhile—a brief interlude of ease and grace in a spectacle of bloody stridency—the glimpse of it must suffice to keep up the soldier's energy and spirit:

> For soldiers' stomachs always serve them well.

A concluding comment on the textual question seems in order. If the foregoing interpretation is valid—by which I mean, necessary to solve the problems posed by *1 Henry VI* as a *work of literature*—it is a plausible guess that the play as we have it was reworked by Shakespeare. The shape of the original version, and hence the degree of Shakespeare's revisions, we can only surmise. It may be that the original play was indeed a "Talbot-play," a collaborative effort; that might account for Nashe's suspiciously generous praise of it. In that case my "model" would have to be adjusted—for instance, by assuming that it was Greene who bitterly withdrew (because he had been overruled by Shakespeare and his colleagues had failed to support him?), while the others stayed and did the job. Greene's attack would then be a plea for solidarity among playwrights against players—a very possible reading of it. Shakespeare's experiences would still be essentially what I suppose them to have been; in fact, the necessity of taking a hand in the making of an unsatisfactory play may have made them still more pointed. If so, it would be this play which he reworked, rather than a version that he could call fully his own. As for the date of the revision, I would propose one close to *King John* (1595?), which Shakespeare reworked from *The Troublesome Reign of King John* in a spirit and manner quite similar to that of *1 Henry VI.*[4] But these are all surmises; they are secondary, to be accommodated to what I am convinced is the primary evidence: the Folio play as an integral whole and the meanings implicit in its design and style.

Notes

1. For the most complete and thorough statement of the "integralist" case, literary as well as textual, see A. S. Cairncross' introduction to his edition of *1 Henry VI* (Arden Shakespeare, London, 1962), which refers abundantly to other recent criticism. For the "disintegrationist" position, see J. D. Wilson's introduction to the play, Cambridge edition (Cambridge, 1952).
2. A. B. Grossart, *Life and Complete Works in Prose and Verse of Robert Greene* (New York, 1964), vol. xii, p. 144.
3. R. B. McKerrow, *Works of Thomas Nashe* (London, 1910), vol. i, p. 212.
4. Cf. the following essay on *King John.*

Faye L. Kelly (essay date 1973)

SOURCE: "Oaths in Shakespeare's *Henry VI* Plays," in *Shakespeare Quarterly,* Vol. 24, No. 4, Autumn, 1973, pp. 357-71.

[*In the essay below, Kelly explores the structural, thematic, and unifying significance of oaths—kept and broken—in* Henry VI, Parts 1, 2, and 3.]

When Pistol said to Bardolph, "A sword is an oath, and oaths must have their course" (*Henry V*), he was stating not only a common Elizabethan belief, but also a principle of Shakespearean dramatic construction. In drama as in life, an oath calls for action. In drama, whenever a character swears to do something or not to do something, plot takes form as a direct result of his regard for his word. If the swearer honors his oath, the action takes one course; if he breaks his oath, the action veers in a different direction. The oaths in Shakespeare's *Henry VI* plays, set against the background of Elizabethan belief, gain considerable dramatic relevance. In these histories, concerned as they are with rebellion, usurpation, conspiracy, and war, great significance rests on the contractual relationships between king and subject, man and man, and man and woman. The oath, if honored, provides a lawful means of sustaining such contracts and contributes to an ordered society ordained by God, ideally upheld by king and supported by subject. If all persons concerned honored their oaths of allegiance, order would prevail in society, and in drama there would be no conflict and consequently no drama. We are concerned here only with formal oaths such as the oath of allegiance, the legal swearing before a magistrate, and the equally serious calling on God to witness and stand as guarantor that the swearer intends to execute his oath. Swearing by some sacred object serves the same purpose. The vow which often accompanies and strengthens the oath is a special application in which a personal condition or imprecation is contingent upon fulfillment of the vow.[1]

But whatever Shakespeare meant when he used an oath might differ from what we make of it unless we focus our attention on what the oath meant to Elizabethans. No doubt they were influenced by the Oath of Supremacy of 1558 required of archbishops, bishops, judges, clergymen as well as all persons taking orders or degrees from universities.[2] Failure to take the oath resulted in degrees of punishment varying from loss of promotion for first offenders to indictment for high treason for anyone so imprudent as to be guilty of a third offense. A look at some of the Elizabethan writings about oaths will give the modern reader a better understanding of the impact of the dramatic oath, particularly the broken oath, on the Elizabethan audience and lead to a deeper appreciation of the young Shakespeare's art of construction.

In Elizabethan society an oath was a serious matter, considered a "part of God's divine service and commanded by him."[3] Because Christ in the New Testament forbade swearing (Matt. 5:34-37), writers about oaths felt constrained to justify swearing by the Christian man. The dilemma was supposedly solved by the thirty-ninth article of the Church of England which declared an oath legal, "When the Magistrate requireth, in a cause of faith and charitie, so it be done accordyng to the prophetes teaching in justice, judgement, and trueth."[4] But justifications for swearing continued to appear in print. One of the most influential publications, and one which Shakespeare doubtless knew, was the "VII Official Homilie against Swearing and Perjury." This sermon expounds the nature and importance of a lawful oath, the sin of irreverent abuse, and God's punishment for perjury. An oath was considered lawful when

> Judges require othes of the people, for declaracion of the truth, or for execucion of justice; . . . [or] when men make faithefull promises with attestacion of the name of God, to observe covenauntes, honest promises, statutes, lawes, and good customes, . . . for due ordre to be had and continued emong men: when subjectes do sweare to bee true and faithefull to their kyng and sovereigne Lorde. . . . Therefore Christian people muste thynke lawful othes, both godly and necessarye. For by lawfull promises and covenauntes confirmed by othes, princes and their countreis are confirmed in common tranquillitie and peace.[5]

This statement, read regularly from the pulpits in Tudor England, leaves little doubt that oaths were considered a means of maintaining order and of ferreting out potential disorder.

> And by lawful othes, malefactors are searched out, wrong doers are punished, and thei whiche sustein wrong, are restored to their right. . . . Every Christian mannes worde . . . should be so true, that it should be regarded as an oth.[6]

The sanctity of the oath acts as a binder which holds all men together for the good of the land. Made under the watchful eye of God, oaths should promote harmonious relationships among all people.

In society the oath serves another important function in that through an oath God's searching eye can determine the truth of any matter.

> Because he oftentimes revealeth and bringeth foorth the verie trueth of a matter (untruely delivered by any man) either by inward inspiration of some other person, or else by bringing it to the open light . . . which afore was kept close and secret.[7]

The oath carries with it punishment for perjury, a grievous offense against God, for "whosoever wilfully forsweareth hymself . . . thei utterly forsake Gods mercy, goodnes, and truth." By terrible punishments "doth God shewe playnly, how muche he abhoreth breakers of honest promises, confirmed by an othe made in his name."[8] For God "is a lover of trueth and a revenger of perjurie."[9] Even though the perjurer might conceal his guilt in this life, he could not expect to escape punishment, for his guilt will be revealed "at the last daye, when the secretes of all mennes hartes, shalbe manifest to al the worlde. And then the truth shal appere, and accuse them and their owne conscience. . . . And Christ the righteous judge, shal then justly condempne them to everlastyng shame and death."[10]

Another possible influence on Shakespeare was the chronicler Edward Hall, who included the complete text of the oath required of all authorities, spiritual and temporal, in which they promised "upon their faith, dutie, and allegeaunce . . . truly to assist in kepyng of the kynges peace."[11] All concontemporary statements about oaths stress the ethical significance of personal responsibility. Thus the value of a man's word was at the very foundation of reliability in human affairs.

Aware of the frame of meaning surrounding the oath, Shakespeare utilized this background as he employed the oath in his dramatic construction to throw light on the character who makes an oath, his relationship to the other characters, and to his God. When made, an oath adumbrates plot; when later recalled by the maker of the oath or the character against whom it is made, the oath becomes structural as it links and tightens the elements of the plot. The complete disregard for the sanctity of an oath by many of the characters in the *Henry VI* plays illuminates the dramatic situation of chaos revealed. Examined against the milieu of Elizabethan thought, the oaths provide an added dimension to some of the usually accepted interpretations of these plays.[12]

1 Henry VI

In *1 Henry VI,* Shakespeare employs the oath with little subtlety. In mechanical fashion he has Exeter remind the nobles of their oaths to Henry V, and immediately they scurry off stage to fight the French. Talbot utters a vow of vengeance as Salisbury is shot and, "with God as his fortress," he and his English soldiers rout the French with brilliant stage effects as the French leap over the walls in disarray.

In the Temple Garden Scene, where Shakespeare symbolically sets up the factions which later result in civil war, the oaths by Somerset and York strengthen their determination to pursue their quarrel. The participants choose sides in ritualistic fashion as Somerset asks Warwick to choose between them. Plantagenet, later York, argues that

> The truth appears so naked on my side
> That any purblind eye may find it out.
>
> (II.iv.20-21)[13]

Somerset counters with

> And on my side it is so well appareled,
> So clear, so shining, and so evident
> That it will glimmer through a blind man's eye.
>
> (II.iv.22-24)

Somerset's oath provokes an equally determined one from Plantagenet:

> And, by my soul, this pale and angry rose,
> As cognizance of my blood-drinking hate,
> Will I forever and my faction wear
> Until it wither with me to my grave
> Or flourish to the height of my degree.
>
> (II.iv.107-10)

The ritualistic portion of the scene ends on this determined note. Shakespeare has created a tension out of which most of the remaining action of the *Henry VI* trilogy flows. Here he has demonstrated the technique of flinging speech against speech noted some years ago by Price.[14] What Price did not take into account is that a sworn statement carries much more power than ordinary speech, will generate more impact of character on character, and is more likely to elicit immediate response. In this instance the use of the oath becomes more subtle and looks forward to its still more intricate employment in *Parts 2* and *3*.

Shakespeare's most skillful use of the oath in *Part 1* involves the oath of allegiance in all of its ramifications. In Act IV, scene one, Henry is not permitted to take the actual oath at his own coronation, which was ordinarily a stage ceremony of pomp and splendor. The entire ceremony is perfunctorily accomplished in two lines, because as soon as the bishop deposits the crown on Henry's head, York demands an oath of allegiance from the French, only to have the second ceremony interrupted. During the interruption, Shakespeare shifts to a close-up as he demonstrates for the audience the complete lack of allegiance among the English: first, among the high-level military as Talbot rushes on stage accusing Fastolfe of cowardice and makes good his vow to "Tear the garter from his craven leg"; next, among the nobles as Gloucester reads a letter from Burgundy who has switched his loyalty back to the French. Gloucester laments

> Oh, monstrous treachery! Can this be so,
> That in alliance, amity, and oaths
> There should be found such false dissembling guile?
>
> (IV.i.61-63)

He has struck the keynote that echoes down the play, "false dissembling." Henry's vain attempt to reconcile the opposing English factions, so as to present a united front to the French, succeeds only in making things worse. The scene winds up with Exeter alone on stage to sum up the action and look forward to later events:

> 'Tis much when scepters are in children's hands,
> But more when envy breeds unkind division;
> There comes the ruin, there begins confusion.
>
> (IV.i.192-94)

Shakespeare now makes visual the confusion which had up to this point been mostly verbal. Talbot drives off the French only to have Joan return and drive off the English, a feat that could not have happened had either York or Somerset shown the allegiance of Talbot and rescued him with their armies. York blames Somerset, but admits to Lucy, who pleads for Talbot's rescue, "He dies, we lose; I break my warlike word." The ironic juxtaposition of York and Talbot delineates the character of York in complete contrast to the splendid Talbot. York does not keep his word; he admits it. To demonstrate to us the effect of York's broken word, Shakespeare throws the two Talbots into mortal combat and has Talbot remind the audience why he is in desperate circumstances:

> The Regent hath with Talbot broke his word
> And left us to the rage of France his sword.
>
> (IV.vi.2-3)

The act ends with each side predicting victory, and Shakespeare turns his attention to setting the stage for the broken oath which causes the downfall of the English.

The scene (V.i.) begins in a low key as Henry agrees disinterestedly to his betrothal to the wealthy daughter of the Earl of Armagnac. This seemingly insignificant detail actually furnishes the key to Henry's character. He agrees to marry any woman who "Tends to God's glory and my country's weal." A complexity of hints alerts us that this action has overtones of wide import. Henry binds the "contract" by sending the young lady a jewel in proof of the "contract" and "pledge" of his affection. The care with which Henry's language is formulated leaves no room for doubt that he considers the betrothal binding, and Shakespeare is signaling the audience to anticipate the outcome of his deed. At this point Shakespeare leaves the betrothal.

But not until Act V, scene four, does Shakespeare return to the interrupted oath of allegiance of Act IV, scene one. The situation is that after losing many nobles, including Talbot, the English have finally won a shaky peace with France; York demands that the French leaders swear an oath of allegiance to Henry. When Charles demands to know the terms of the peace, his nobles advise him not to cavil about the "contract." Winchester tells him that he must "pay tribute and submit" to Henry. It is York who articulates the oath for Charles:

> Then swear allegiance to His Majesty,
> As thou art knight, never to disobey
> Nor be rebellious to the Crown of England—
> Thou, nor thy nobles, to the Crown of England.
>
> (V.iv.169-72)

An intriguing irony emerges in the play because what we see and hear contradicts what we know about York. His word is false, yet he berates the French for the same fault. A still more subtle irony is that York can be reassured by Warwick that the French can be bound with such strict and severe "covenants" that they will gain little from the truce.

Another layer of irony comes from the words of the oath, which specify allegiance to the crown of England and not the man, a point to be explored in some detail in later plays.

Having set up his warring factions among the English and concluded an "effeminate" peace with the French, Shakespeare moves to pick up the theme of Henry's marriage. Henry's previous oath of betrothal now becomes the pivotal point of the dramatic action. If Henry is to marry Margaret, Suffolk must see to it that he breaks his oath. The wily Suffolk speaks glowingly of Margaret's charms and influences Henry to seek Gloucester's consent even though it does mean breaking his oath. Gloucester establishes the seriousness of the situation:

> How shall we then dispense with that contract,
> And not deface your honour with reproach?
>
> (V.v.28-29)

As plot develops, Henry's honor is repeatedly defaced because of this evil match, but at this moment Suffolk with elaborate casuistry offers a solution:

> As doth a ruler with unlawful oaths,
> Or one that, at a triumph having vowed
> To try his strength, forsaketh yet the lists
> By reason of his adversary's odds.
> A poor Earl's daughter is unequal odds,
> And therefore may be broke without offense.
>
> (V.v.30-35)

Almost too readily Henry agrees and sends Suffolk to France with these instructions:

> Agree to any covenants, and procure
> That Lady Margaret do vouchsafe to come
> To cross the seas to England, and be crowned
> King Henry's faithful and anointed Queen.
>
> (V.v.88-90)

Suffolk's reasoning is completely contrary to the Elizabethan concept of the sanctity of an oath and leads us to see him as devious, disloyal, and treacherous. But what about Henry? He has unwittingly revealed to the audience that the sovereign, the highest, most revered person in the land, cannot be trusted and is really no better than his jarring nobles.

By demonstrating to us the gravity associated with an oath and the consequences of broken oaths, Shakespeare has created and explored an atmosphere charged with suspicion, falseness, duplicity, and evil. He is yet to magnify and intensify this impression in *Parts 2* and *3*.

2 Henry VI

In *2 Henry VI,* the sanctity of a man's word, the truth and reliability of what he says, forms the crux of the dramatic argument and provides a strong force for unity. Without overt reference to oaths or breaking of oaths, the theme of reliability of a man's word undergirds the action of the play and carries out the implications of betrayal begun in *1 Henry VI.* Each instance that subjects the word of a character to the cold light of truth prepares a steppingstone to the final act in which the sworn oath of allegiance to the King dominates the action.

In the first scene Shakespeare creates an aura of falseness, suspicion, and distrust as Suffolk presents Henry with his Queen. The audience is informed that as a result of the "contracted peace" with France, Suffolk has signed away to the French the English claim to the duchy of Anjou and the county of Maine. Gloucester, the one truly honest and loyal person, later recalls the shameful marriage and prophesies the ruin of all England as a result. Each subsequent scene relates in some manner to the theme of duplicity and broken oaths and advances the complex intentions of the play.

Even the seemingly irrelevant Peter-Horner Scene (I.iii.) gains dramatic relevance as it introduces the theme of rightful succession to the crown and implicates York. The multiple crosscurrents of animosity between the Queen and the Duchess of Gloucester and the concerted efforts of York, Margaret, and Suffolk to discredit Gloucester all begin to converge. Act II, scene one, which has been called a mirror-scene, intensifies our sensitivity to the falsity which forms the core problem of the play.[15] The trumped-up arrest of the Duchess, the false accusation of Gloucester, the bogus miracle—all reflect the duplicity and unreliability of people throughout the Court and society. The pervading deception prepares the climate for York's recital in the next scene of his claim to the throne and the seemingly unmotivated support of Warwick and Salisbury.

As the snare tightens around Gloucester, accused of treason and embezzlement and deprived of the Nevils' support, he can strengthen his claim of innocence only with a solemn oath calling God to witness the truth of his words before the King:

> So help me God, as I have watched the night—
> Ay, night by night, in studying good for England!—
> That doit that e'er I wrested from the King,
> Or any groat I hoarded to my use,
> Be brought against me at my trial day!
>
> . . . . .
>
> I say no more than truth, so help me God!
>
> (III. i. 110-14, 120)

To Gloucester and the characters hearing the oath no stronger emphasis could be placed on his words than the solemn appeal to God to support his statement, the implication always being that perjury automatically brings with it the wrath of God. Shakespeare drives home the impression of mendacity abroad as he has Gloucester, in his next speech, further attempt to prove his innocence. Recurrent phrases suggesting falseness abound: "foul subornation," "false accuse," "false witness," "suborned to swear," "false allegations," "play me false." The truth of Gloucester's innocence becomes a dramatic reality when his dead body is brought on stage and Warwick swears a "dreadful oath with solemn tongue" that Gloucester has suffered foul play:

> As surely as my soul intends to live
> With that dread King, that took our state upon him
> To free us from his Father's wrathful curse,
> I do believe that violent hands were laid
> Upon the life of this thrice-famed duke.
>
> (III. ii. 153-57)

This oath, sworn by the gift of Christ to mankind, lends a tone of solemnity and foreboding to the entire scene and dramatizes a typically human reaction to a horrible crime. The phrases suggesting treachery, inconstancy, and hollow friends thicken and mingle with images of birds of prey and reptiles symbolic of the evil and chaos abroad in the land.

As a result of Gloucester's murder, the commoners rise up and demand retribution against Suffolk. Henry, finally shocked into decisive action, banishes Suffolk. His manner of doing so further dramatically illuminates his own character. He swears,

> For, sure, my thoughts do hourly prophesy
> Mischance unto my state by Suffolk's means.
> And therefore, by His majesty I swear,
> Whose far unworthy deputy I am,
> He shall not breathe infection in this air
> But three days longer, on the pain of death.
>
> (III. ii. 283-88)

In reply to Margaret's plea for Suffolk, Henry unwittingly reveals his innermost nature:

> Had I but said, I would have kept my word,
> But when I swear, it is irrevocable.
>
> (III. ii. 293-94)

Though his words follow the conventional pattern, they are in the light of his actions ironical, for had he not broken his oath of betrothal he would not be in his present situation.

Shakespeare now sets about to demonstrate the chaos spawned by a broken oath of allegiance. Although Suffolk gets his just due, the rebel Cade and his gang, goaded by York, try to take power into their hands. Cade vows to crown himself king, to make learning a sin, to put to death all scholars, lawyers, courtiers, and gentlemen. In this portrayal of treachery and revolution all the accepted values are overturned. But this is on the level of parody; next we see real usurpation. The whole of Act V deals with the problem of allegiance to the King.

York, returning from Ireland accompanied by many troops, is interrogated by Buckingham as to whether his intentions are honorable and why he has raised troops without the King's permission, "Against thy oath and true allegiance sworn." When York is informed that Somerset has been sent to the Tower, he dismisses his soldiers only to regret it when Somerset and Margaret appear. Henry issues orders that Margaret "hide him [Somerset] from the Duke." Once again Henry's capability for deceit is consummately demonstrated. York, all submission and humility a few moments earlier, now has an excuse to upbraid Henry:

> False King! Why hast thou broken faith with me,
> Knowing how hardly I can brook abuse?
> King did I call thee? No, thou art not King,
> Not fit to govern and rule multitudes,
> Which darest not, no, nor canst not rule a traitor.
> That head of thine doth not become a crown.
>
> . . . . .
>
> By heaven, thou shalt rule no more
> O'er him whom Heaven created for thy ruler.
>
> (V. i. 91-96, 104-5)

Now York's intentions are in the open, and the prominence of the themes of allegiance and rightful possession of the throne firmly establish them as a frame of meaning to circumscribe the subsequent action of the play.

When the business of allegiance needed to be dramatized visually on stage, Shakespeare frequently used the ceremony of kneeling, a commonplace on the Elizabethan stage. But in the *Henry VI* plays this gesture of respect does more than reinforce the dramatic meaning of a scene. Kneeling assumes a wider symbolic meaning, which reverberates throughout the last two parts of the trilogy. The crosscurrents of loyalties and disloyalties are focused on the willingness of a character to kneel to Henry: Iden enters with Cade's head and as he kneels to Henry is made Knight; Clifford kneels to Henry, but refuses to honor York's claim; York refuses to bow to anyone. His refusal to kneel carries with it an implication wider than the deed itself. His act epitomizes the significance of the oath of allegiance. With the entrance of support for both factions, the stage is set for the showdown. When Henry sees that York has more support than he, he laments, "Where is faith? Where is loyalty?"

Central to the structure projected in this portion of the play is the growing doubt of Henry's rightful possession of the crown. Shakespeare symbolizes the idea as Salisbury refuses to kneel. Unable to control the situation, Henry falls back on the oath of allegiance to him in an attempt to prevent open revolt, to maintain order, and to keep his crown. He asks Salisbury, "Canst thou dispense with heaven for such an oath?" (V. i. 181). Salisbury replies with elaborate casuistry in words which are often a loose paraphrase of the statements of Tudor nondramatic writers about oaths:

> It is great sin to swear unto a sin,
> But greater sin to keep a sinful oath.
> Who can be bound by any solemn vow
> To do a murderous deed, to rob a man,
> To force a spotless virgin's chastity,
> To reave the orphan of his patrimony,
> To wring the widow from her customed right,

And have no other reason for this wrong
But that he was bound by a solemn oath?

(V. i. 182-90)[16]

Here the Elizabethan concept of an oath is clearly stated: it is not merely a formal promise to a king, but a promise to which God stands witness for human truthfulness. It is a sin to swear to a sinful act, but also a sin to keep a sinful oath. The Queen replies, "A subtle traitor needs no sophister" (V. i. 191). Salisbury twists traditional thinking to suit his own purposes. His words support the philosophy of the day, but the point he refuses to establish is whether or not his oath of allegiance to Henry was, in fact, unlawful. He is engaging in the political tactic of equivocation. As a result, Henry flees and the frame of disorder becomes real, not because a vindictive God has punished evildoers but because men would not honor their word.

At this point Shakespeare leaves the problem of rightful succession, but the fact that he brings Henry's title into question prepares the groundwork for the alacrity with which Henry eventually yields to York's claim. Henry's realization that his claim is weak lends credence to his readiness to adopt York as heir, but in so doing he repudiates his rightful duty to his son, abrogates his oath as king, and paves the way for violence. For Henry as king, as deputy of God, had taken an oath to uphold the crown. He is subject only to God, but responsible to God to act as pastor to his subjects.

3 Henry VI

Permeating the entire structure of *3 Henry VI* are broken oaths, broken vows, and perjury. They serve as vehicles for dramatizing the themes of degree, allegiance, and lawful succession and the resulting chaos when any one of these is disregarded. Like a musician, Shakespeare states each theme, accompanies it with appropriate imagery, enlarges, embellishes, and enriches it as he interweaves all together. The first two scenes of *Part 3* explore one theme after another and build up a complexity of general dissension and vacillating, disloyal characters. In scene one, the Parliament House in London, Warwick goads York into committing dramatically his act of usurpation by actually seating himself on the throne. Warwick gives York his support:

Victorious Prince of York,
Before I see thee seated in that throne
Which now the House of Lancaster usurps,
I vow by Heaven these eyes shall never close.
This is the palace of the fearful King,
And this the regal seat. Possess it, York,
For this is thine, and not King Henry's heirs'.

(I.i.21-27)

Reminiscent of Lucifer of the mystery drama, York, like the first rebel of English drama, goads his antagonist. Henry retorts: "My Lords, look where the sturdy rebel sits, / Even in the chair of state" (I. i. 50-51). Momentum builds as Henry, intent on defeating York, incites Northumberland and Clifford by reminding them of their fathers' deaths at the hands of York and of their vowed revenge "On him, his sons, his favorites, his friends." Northumberland answers with a vow and a self-imprecation, "If I be not, Heavens be revenged on me!" Clifford adds his vow and the pattern of revenge emerges.

The ceremony of kneeling, notably extended and enriched throughout *Part 3,* now assumes the symbolic burden of all the broken oaths in the play. Henry now demands of York:

Thou factious Duke of York, descend my throne,
And kneel for grace and mercy at my feet.
I am thy sovereign.

(I.i.74-76)

York refuses, and they bicker back and forth as Shakespeare with tireless iteration has Warwick incite Northumberland and Clifford by reminding them once more that they had sworn revenge for the death of their fathers. Warwick's goad evokes another oath from Northumberland and the tempo increases. A note of irony enriches the texture of the play when Henry extracts from York a "solemn oath" that he cease civil war and allow Henry to reign in peace on the condition that the crown pass to York at Henry's death. York swears, "This oath I take and will perform." York's attitude toward his oath dispels any hope of lasting reconciliation. The structure of meaning here is closely connected with recurring and interrelated broken oaths by and to Henry.

The entire architecture of Act I, scene two, turns on York's attitude toward his oath. Edward first broaches the subject of perjury as he suggests to his father, "Now you are heir, therefore enjoy it now." York counters with, "I took an oath that he should quietly reign." Edward maintains that the end justifies the means and says,

But for a kingdom any oath may be broken,
I would break a thousand oaths to reign one year.

(I.ii.16-17)

Clever Richard mollifies York with, "No, God forbid your Grace should be forsworn," and promises to prove that York can have the crown without perjuring himself. Richard argues:

An oath is of no moment, being not took
Before a true and lawful magistrate
That hath authority over him that swears.
Henry had none, but did usurp the place.
Then, seeing 'twas he that made you to depose,
Your oath, my lord, is vain and frivolous.
Therefore to arms!

(II.ii.22-28)

York readily agrees to a course of action he already desires, but the important point is that even he hesitates, if only momentarily, to break an oath. To understand the probable impact of this scene on an Elizabethan audience, one has only to recall the punishment for perjury. Once convinced that he might escape punishment for perjury, York becomes adamant, and with utmost irony says, "Richard, enough, I will be king or die." York, who breaks his oath, expects all other people to do the same and says of Henry, "Trust not simple Henry nor his oaths." The attitudes of Richard and Edward toward their oaths anticipate dramatically their own disloyalty and revolt. York's broken oath provides Clifford and Margaret with the excuse they need to seize him, crown him ingnominiously with a paper crown, and kill him. As Margaret crowns York, she taunts him:

> But how is it that great Plantagenet
> Is crowned so soon and broke his solemn oath?
>
> . . . . .
>
> O, 'tis a fault too too unpardonable!
>
> (I.iv.99-100, 106)

Margaret's taunt elicits from York a vehement curse against her. He ends his curse with a cry of vengeance for Rutland's death. Not deterred by the curse, Clifford and Margaret stab him. Clifford gets revenge with, "here's for my oath, here's for my father's death."

Shakespeare now shifts the scene back to his weak anti-hero who, led by the Queen, has broken his vow to York. True to his nature, Henry disclaims responsibility and appeals to God to withhold revenge: "Withhold revenge, dear God! 'Tis not my fault, / Nor wittingly have I infringed my vow" (II.ii.7-8). Even though Henry professes innocence, Shakespeare places the responsibility squarely on his shoulders. The passage from Hall dealing with this incident indicates that Shakespeare was following his source.[17] Dramatically he is reminding the audience that before the sons of York can, as they suggest they will, "overshine the earth," they must do something about Henry who still wears the crown, but has vowed to pass it to York or his heirs.

Warwick takes up the thread of broken oaths as he reports that Queen Margaret is marching toward London with the intent to dash the decree of Parliament "touching Henry's oath" and Edward's succession. Warwick recalls for the audience Henry's oath:

> He swore consent to your succession,
> His oath enrollèd in the Parliament;
> And now to London all the crew are gone
> To frustrate both his oath and what beside
> May make against the House of Lancaster.
>
> (II.i.172-76)

From the point of view of his enemies, Henry has broken another oath.

To stage the fluctuations and complexities of allegiance, reversed allegiance, and the sanctity of oaths, Shakespeare repeats with subtle variations the ceremony of kneeling which epitomizes the meaning of the last half of the play. In ordinary circumstances on the Elizabethan stage, one kneels to the duly constituted authority. But that is just the point Shakespeare has been working up to and is now exploring more fully. Who is the duly constituted authority? To underscore this point Shakespeare repeats with almost complete inversion an earlier scene. In Act I, scene two, he explores the oath of allegiance of York to Henry; now in Act II, scene two, he probes Henry's oath to York and his heirs. Edward enters with his brothers and attendants; he immediately demands that Henry kneel to him—that is, acknowledge him as the duly constituted King. He says to Henry:

> Now perjur'd Henry! Wilt thou kneel for grace
> And set thy diadem upon my head,
> Or bide the mortal fortune of the field?
>
> (II.ii.80-83)

To Margaret's vehement refusal, Edward insists,

> I am his King, and he should bow his knee.
> I was adopted heir by his consent;
> Since when, his oath is broke, for, as I hear,
> You, that are King, though he do wear the crown,
> Have caused him, by new Act of Parliament,
> To blot out me and put his own son in.
>
> (II.ii.88-92)

Edward's cause gains additional support when Warwick learns of his brother's death and swears an oath of revenge:

> Here on my knee I vow to God above,
> I'll never pause again, never stand still,
> Till either death hath closed these eyes of mine,
> Or fortune given my measure of revenge.
>
> (II.ii.29-32)

Edward drops to his knees beside Warwick and vows to chain his soul to that of the "setter up and plucker down" of kings. The reverse of this scene appears when Edward, as King, demands that Warwick

> Speak gentle words, and humbly bend thy knee,
> Call Edward king, and at his hands beg mercy?
>
> (V.i.22-23)

Warwick refuses, reminds Edward who had made him king, and demands that Edward call him patron or he'll find himself Duke of York again. Yet another variation of this theme in a minor key and highly ironic tone occurs when Henry's son encounters the sons of York. The Prince demands that Edward resign his chair and kneel to him. Thus the oath of allegiance made visual by the ceremony of kneeling thrusts in many ways into the dramatic construction. The oath or vow usually has its course as the utterer endeavors to make it come to pass; the action of the play alters as the course of the oath does: many oaths carry the irony of the play.

In one of the subtlest scenes in early Shakespeare (III.i.), King Henry explores the sanctity of the oath of allegiance which has already been broken repeatedly on stage. Henry has of his own volition and in the face of great peril returned to England "even of pure love" for his homeland. As the keepers appear they tell the disguised Henry that they, the subjects of King Edward, are "sworn in all allegiance," and will apprehend Henry, the enemy of the King. Henry asks them, "But did you never swear and break an oath?" The second keeper replies, "No never such an oath nor will not now." Henry timidly suggests that he is the rightful King:

> And you were sworn true subjects unto me.
> And tell me, then, have you not broke your oaths?
>
> (III.i.78-79)

The keeper replies negatively, "For we were subjects but while you were king." Henry's answer probes the vacillating allegiance of the common man and recalls the same observation made by Cade in *Part 2:*

> Ah, simple men, you know not what you swear!
> Look, as I blow this feather from my face,
> And as the air blows it to me again,
> Obeying with my wind when I do blow
> And yielding to another when it blows,
> Commanded always by the greater gust,
> Such is the lightness of you commen men.
> But do not break your oaths, for of that sin
> My mild entreaty shall not make you guilty.
>
> (III.i.83-91)

Succinctly in this speech Shakespeare reveals the common people as a vacillating horde unable to think for themselves and interested only in self-preservation. Henry expresses poetically what Pistol describes more earthily in *Henry V:* the oaths of common people "are but wafer cakes" easily broken. Henry realizes that had his subjects valued their oaths to him, he would not now be on his way to prison and ultimately to death, but what Henry does not realize is that he is no better than those he criticizes: had he honored his own oath he would not be facing the extreme penalties of loss of freedom and loss of life.

Shakespeare relentlessly drives home the theme of broken oaths, deceit, and treachery. He has already established Edward as a perjurer once when he broke his oath to the Mayor of York (IV.vii.23-24). He makes him a second-time perjurer when he repeats with only slight variation the broken marriage vow as Edward marries Lady Grey after having sent Warwick to seek the hand of the sister of the French King, an alliance that might have brought peace and order. Ironically at the exact moment that Warwick is swearing to the French King that Edward's love for Lady Bona is "the eternal plant" whereof the root was "fixed in Virtue!" a messenger from Edward enters with the news that Edward has broken his word and has married Lady Grey. Again, with the iteration of a schoolmaster, Shakespeare demonstrates that war results from a king's broken oath: Margaret, supported by the King of France, and Warwick, irked by Edward's broken word, prepare for war. Clarence, too, switches to Warwick's side against his brother-king, an abrogation of two loyalties, only to revert later to Edward with the vow to be "no more unconstant." Warwick tags him "traitor, perjured, and unjust," a tag which sticks to him. When Warwick by a gesture recalls the oath of allegiance that Clarence had taken to King Henry, Clarence responds that

> To keep that oath were more impiety
> Than Jephthah's when he sacrific'd his daughter.
>
> (V.i.89-91)

When Clarence's perjury is recalled by the three sons of York as they stab Prince Edward, the theme of perjury assumes structural significance.[18] The layers of irony coalesce as Edward, committing his third perjury, labels the twice-perjured Clarence "perjured George," and, as Clarence in his turn stabs the Prince, he does so with his words: "And there's for twitting me with perjury" (V.v.40). Only moments later Clarence's regards for his oath is subjected to ironical scrutiny. The distraught Margaret, forced to witness the murder of her son, begs Clarence to stab her. He swears by heaven that he will do her no such favor. At her insistence, he replies that he cannot because he has sworn. Margaret chides:

> Aye, but thou usest to forswear thyself.
> 'Twas sin before, but now 'tis charity.
>
> (V.v.75-76)

The confirmation of Clarence as a perjurer supports the structural value of the theme, which carries over and becomes one of the dominant features of *Richard III.* Shakespeare has now held up for the audience to judge the word of every major and minor character and has only to complete the pattern of deceit and disloyalty with the murder of Henry, the ultimate act of treachery and disorder, and the development of Richard, the self-styled "Judas," who will become in his own play the prime example of all the duplicity which has only begun in the *Henry VI* plays.

Notes

1. A. E. Crawley, "Oath," *Encyclopedia of Religion and Ethics,* ed. James Hastings (Edinburgh, 1917), IX, 43.

2. *Statutes of the Realm,* (London, 1819), I Eliz. Chap. 1.

3. James Morice, *A Briefe Treatise of Oathes* (London, n.d.), sig. A2.

4. *Articles Whereupon It Was Agreed by the Archbishoppes and Bishoppes* (London, 1571), sig. D1.

5. *Certayne Sermons, or Homilies* (London, 1547), sig. L3, M1.

6. *Ibid.,* sig. M1[v].

7. R. Cosin, *An Apologie for Sundrie Proceedings by Jurisdiction Ecclesiasticall Treating of Oaths* (London, 1593), Part 3, p. 9.

8. *Certayne Sermons,* sig. M3[v], M2[v].

9. Morice, sig. A2. John Bale, *A Christen Exhortacion Unto Customable Swearers* (London, 1547?), painted a vivid picture of what happens to perjurers: "He shal eyther lose a fyngar, an eare, or els his tonge. For perjury was the noble city of Troy lost" (fol. 26). In the Folger Shakespeare Library a unique poem of 1600, written to be sung to the tune of "Airne Not Too High," describes the tortures of a Maid servant who forswore herself and, "lies rotting in Hospital unable to die, where many resort daily to see her."
10. *Certayne Sermons,* sig. M4.
11. Edward Hall, *The Union of the Two Noble and Illustrate Famelies of Lancastre & York* (London, 1548), "King Henry the VI" fol. xxvii^{v}.
12. E. M. W. Tillyard, *Shakespeare's History Plays* (London, 1948), sees these plays as the demonstration of the vengeance of God on a sinful people; J. P. Brockbank, "Frame of Disorder," *Stratford-upon-Avon Studies 3,* (London, 1961) concurs. A. S. Cairncross in the Arden edition mentions that the oath breach is vital and that in *Part 3* broken oaths and perjury abound. A. C. Hamilton, *The Early Shakespeare* (San Marino, 1967) states that Edward's remark that "for a kingdom any oath may be broken," guides all men's actions.
13. Quotations are taken from Shakespeare, *The Complete Works,* ed. G. B. Harrison (New York, 1948).
14. Hereward T. Price, *Construction in Shakespeare* (Ann Arbor, 1951), p. 21.
15. Hereward T. Price, "Mirror-Scenes in Shakespeare," *Adams Memorial Studies,* ed. James G. McManaway (Washington, 1948), p. 102.
16. The delicate question of whether or not it was worse to perjure oneself or to keep a sinful oath posed a problem for writers about oaths. The homilist in the sermon on "Swearing and Perjury" cited examples from the scriptures of universal famine sent upon the whole country of the Israelites during the days of Saul because he broke his oath of friendship with the Gabonites and murdered many of them: "And God would not withdraw hys punishment, until the saied offence was revenged, by the death of seven sonnes, or next kinsmen, of King Saule. . . . But if a man at any tyme shall, either of ignorance, or of malice, promise and sweare, to do any thyng, whiche is either against the lawe of almightye God, or not in hys power to perfourme: let hym take it, for an unlawfull and ungodly othe" (*Certayne Sermons,* sigs. M2^{v}, M3^{r}). Thomas Becon, quoting from the holy Beda said, "If it shall chance at any time we sweare or promise anything unadvisedly, which being kept should turn unto an evil end, . . . we ought rather to forswear ourselves than, for the eschewing of perjury, we should fall into any other more grievous sin" ("The Invective against Swearing," *Early Works,* ed. John Ayre for the Parker Society [Cambridge, 1843], p. 374).
17. Hall, "For as much as Kyng Henry, contrary to his othe, honor and agrement, had violated and infringed, the order taken and enacted in the last Parliament . . . he was therefore . . . deprived & dejected of all kyngly honor and regall sovereigntie" (fol. Clxxxv).
18. The sermon on "Swearing and Perjury" cites this unadvised oath of Jephthah's. Clarence is concerned only with achieving his own ends.

Raymond V. Utterback (essay date 1978)

SOURCE: "Public Men, Private Wills, and Kingship in *Henry VI, Part III,*" in *Renaissance Papers,* 1978, pp. 47-54.

[*In the essay below, Utterback considers the topics of political instability and the legitimate inheritance of the English crown in* Henry VI, Part 3.]

In the opening scene of *Henry VI, Part III,* Shakespeare faced a difficult expository problem. In solving it he devised a beginning powerful enough to epitomize the prior historical situation and to lead credibly to the play's subsequent involved actions. Further, and perhaps more important, he introduced the fundamental inconsistencies exhibited in the characters' motivations and actions throughout the play. These inconsistencies are displayed succinctly in the stances characters take toward the legal arguments over legitimate possession of the crown that the contrary factions put forward. As Robert Ornstein has observed, Shakespeare recognized that neither side in the Wars of the Roses had a consistent ideological position and that both shifted their positions "as circumstances required."[1] The way Shakespeare exploited his knowledge in shaping the themes of this drama of a disintegrating kingdom deserves careful consideration.

Numerous issues about kingship are raised in the play. Who is truly entitled to be King? What is required to be a good King? How shall the King order the realm? What is the worth of kingship to its possessor? The opening scene incorporates a debate over the first question in which each faction naturally supports the principles favorable to its leader. These arguments and principles are, by nature, claims upon public assent; around them the order of society is established and maintained. That the different principles issue in opposite conclusions as to who may properly wear the crown indicates the seriousness of the social crisis. Only one idea seems shared by all, the unstated assumption that there shall be one King over the realm. When self-contradictions in principles or their application appear, both Yorkists and Lancastrians act blind to them or simply refuse to be inhibited by them. The conflict of public principles is matched in the debate by equally significant conflicts between principles and private attitudes, and some characters, such as Clifford, exalt their private attitudes to the level of fundamental principles of state. The opening scene's interaction of characters, arguments, and positions thus produces complications, shifts, and alterations characteristic of the whole drama. In this society the public principles lack logical coherence, the factions cannot agree on what the principles of public order truly are, and the wilfulness of individuals abruptly overrules commitments to principles.

In molding the historical record into drama Shakespeare shaped the conflicts he wanted to develop, for he altered characterization, motivation, and causation, even as he oversimplified the Parliament of 1460, which Act I scene i represents. The Yorkists take over the stage at once, military victors literally securing the possession of Parliament, palace, and throne. Warwick enunciates York's position as "victorious Prince" (I.i.21)[2] and his evidently superior hereditary claim to the throne. York's own directness contrasts with Warwick's civility, for he announces bluntly that they have "broken in by force" (l. 29). It is implicitly acknowledged that Parliament must ratify any attempt to alter the possession of the throne, but in the very act of mentioning Parliament Warwick contradicts any such Parliamentary principle with an appeal to force:

> The bloody parliament shall this be call'd
> Unless Plantagenet, Duke of York, be king,
> And bashful Henry depos'd. . . .
>
> (ll. 39-41)

Clearly the Yorkists have sufficient military power to enforce their will on any Parliament bold enough to be recalcitrant. Warwick supplies a new principle, however, in referring to "bashful Henry," "whose cowardice / Hath made us by-words to our enemies" (41-42). The necessity of heroic *virtù* in kingship is indicated; this is the first of many references to Henry's lack of military disposition and to the loss of territory and prestige in France. Nearly everybody in the play agrees on at least one point, that York exhibits this form of kingly merit and King Henry does not. Applied to the Crown in general terms this becomes the principle that a King who fails to maintain the country's military success fails to maintain his right to the throne. While Warwick never presses this idea to its logical conclusion, he enlists it as a good supporting reason justifying what he says should be done about York's hereditary right. Shakespeare pursued the point about kingly *virtù* in *King John* and *Richard II.* The institution of kingship rests not merely on its divinely sanctioned dignity but also on its efficacy in society. As Ernest W. Talbert asserts about *Richard II,* "The sacred name of 'king' was not only inherited but also merited, and the problem of order became intense and perilous when those two attributes were not united in one person."[3]

The Yorkists actually argue that Henry has neither an inherited nor a merited right; thus York declares his determination to take possession of his right. Interestingly, Warwick thereupon takes the credit for establishing York (ll. 45-49) in a personal vaunt, an indulgence of his power[4] to gratify his private will. From this point of view, the King is hardly a public figure with publicly verifiable rights and duties. He is a figure Warwick creates by virtue of his armed might and the strength of his will. There is obviously no public principle in this; Warwick makes no claim to be the voice of the nation, the agent of a consensus among the noblemen, or the spokesman of any cause other than his own pleasure. He is simply doing what his power makes possible about the occupancy of the throne, a basis of action potentially threatening to any person placed on the throne.

When he enters, King Henry at once labels York a rebel, then reminds his retainers of their fathers' deaths at Yorkist hands and their vows of revenge. York had declared he would use words or blows as necessary against his enemies, but Henry limits himself to "frowns, words and threats" (l. 72). Henry thus initiates the contention in words that first approaches a Marlovian slanging match before it becomes rational argument. It does then, however, become a comprehensive debate. York introduces the principle of hereditary legitimacy; when Westmoreland offers to maintain Henry's title (presumably in chivalric combat), Warwick reminds him that the Yorkists have just defeated his party in battle (presumably a greater and thus more decisive chivalric combat). York asserts his title, though the audience is not given York's exposition of his ancestry—there had been enough of that, perhaps, in *II Henry VI.* Instead, King Henry, invoking the principle of hereditary legitimacy for himself, supplies a brief analysis covering three generations:

> What title hast thou, traitor, to the crown?
> Thy father was, as thou art, Duke of York;
> Thy grandfather, Roger Mortimer, Earl of March:
> I am the son of Henry the Fifth,
> Who made the Dauphin and the French to stoop. . . .
>
> (ll. 104-8)

The Yorkists, of course, pounce on this open opportunity to denounce Henry's own failure in France, and Henry, thus put on the defensive, moves back a generation to his grandfather's title: "Henry the Fourth by conquest got the crown" (l. 132). This also proves unfortunate, for the assumption that hereditary legitimacy may derive from Henry IV's action is exactly what York disputes. York avoids committing himself on what rights may derive from conquest—indeed it could well be to his advantage, having the upper hand militarily, to declare that right may accrue therefrom. What he does, however, is to deny that Henry IV's action is properly a conquest: "'Twas by *rebellion* against his king" (l. 133; italics added). The challenge defeats this line of defense for Henry's title, and Henry shifts ground to offer a new argument about the succession: "Tell me, may not a king adopt an heir?" (l. 135). York cautiously wants to know where this argument would lead, and Henry obligingly puts together all the deductive steps of his hypothetical syllogism:

> An if he may, then am I lawful king;
> For Richard, in the view of many lords,
> Resign'd the crown to Henry the Fourth,
> Whose heir my father was, and I am his.
>
> (ll. 137-40)

But nothing is so simple to the Yorkists. The allegation of rebellion is repeated, and a new allegation is made that Richard II resigned under compulsion and thus did not freely adopt an heir. A third argument then appears, that even a voluntary renunciation of the crown could not prejudice the rights of the next heir. When Exeter admits the justice of York's argument, Henry fears mass defection. The other Lancastrian loyalists, however, refuse to settle for this, and shift the ground of argument from right back to power. Clifford simply declares his personal loyalty to King Henry and his absolute refusal to acknowledge York whatever the arguments:

> King Henry, be thy title right or wrong,
> Lord Clifford vows to fight in thy defense. . . .
>
> (ll. 159-69)

Clifford sanctifies this assertion of will by making it a vow, but his bald statement of personal commitment seems an anachronistic, Anglo-Saxon declaration of faithfulness to a war-lord. There is no public principle in it, for it means that personal will and force are the final arbiters of conflicting claims.

Warwick breaks the impasse by asserting York's right and summoning troops. In this crisis Henry suddenly sends the situation in a new direction with a new application of the adopted heir argument. He proposes to entail the crown to York on the conditions of remaining King for life and receiving York's loyalty. York accepts the arrangement with alacrity, but obviously he does not reflect on the positions implicitly admitted. If York can become Henry VI's heir by "adoptive" process (and with Henry under military duress), then Henry IV was Richard II's legal heir, and his descendant Henry VI has the superior right. Further, the mere acceptance of the position of heir presupposes the validity of Henry's title, since no man can bequeath to an heir what he does not possess. The abuse Henry instantly receives from the Lancastrian lords is ironic, for Henry's compromise is what keeps him King when their power to maintain him has become clearly deficient. The alternative to Henry's solution would seem to be assassination of the Lancastrian party. Yet the Lancastrians desert Henry with ill grace, the erstwhile arch-loyalist Clifford uttering these intriguing maledictions:

> In dreadful war mayst thou be overcome,
> Or live in peace abandon'd and despis'd!
>
> (ll. 187-88)

Henceforth their official cause is with Queen Margaret, fighting for the principle of hereditary legitimacy in Henry's son's right to inherit the kingdom, though it seems an embarrassment that they must logically maintain Henry's legitimacy as well. Ironically, the Lancastrian Prince Edward shortly appears, declaring the previously Yorkist argument that the succession is inalienable and the immediate heir cannot be displaced (ll. 226-7; cf. ll. 143-6).

The historical situation differed considerably from Shakespeare's presentation. When York claimed the throne in October, 1460, Henry VI was his prisoner. "Public opinion was outraged by York's treatment of the gentle king, and the compromise was forced on him by the Lords," Geoffrey Bullough summarizes.[4] Edward Hall's account of the events even suggests a principle of kingship based on "received opinion," Henry having reigned so long already:

> After long argumentes made, & deliberate consultacion had emong the peeres, prelates, and commons of the realme: upon the vigile of all sainctes, it was condescended and agreed by the three estates, for so much as Kyng Henry had been taken as kyng by the space of xxxviii. yeres and more, that he should injoye the name and title of Kyng, and have possession of the realme, duryng his life naturall. . . . and that the duke [of York] from thensefurth, should be Protector and Regent of the lande.
>
> . . . These articles with many other, were not onely written, sealed, and sworne by the twoo parties: but also wer enacted, in the high court of Parliament.[5]

Parliament's role in imposing the compromise is omitted by Shakespeare and it becomes instead a personal arrangement of the two contending leaders.

What is satisfactory to them, however, is not acceptable to their followers. In I.ii. Edward urges York simply to violate his oath, while Richard subtly argues the oath is invalid, not having been sworn before "a true and lawful magistrate" (I.ii.23). Again a public principle, the sacredness of an oath, is denied as the validity of York's oath is made dependent upon the validity of Henry's title. Such a sophisticated route to oath-breaking is followed later by sheer wilful refusals to be found by oath. Warwick angrily renounces his oath of allegiance to King Edward, Edward perjures himself in swearing he comes to York only to claim his dukedom, and Clarence violates an oath sworn on the sacrament, changing sides for the second time to support Edward at Tewkesbury. Even King Henry feels caught up in this oath-breaking when he sees York's impaled head and declares he has not knowingly infringed his vow (II.ii.6-8). In response Clifford lectures the King about such conscientiousness, appealing to self-defense and a father's obligation to his son (II.ii.19-25), treating such motives as justifying oath-breaking.

King Henry considers more deeply than Clifford the heritage he should leave:

> didst thou never hear
> That things ill-got had ever bad success?
> And happy always was it for that son
> Whose father for his hoarding went to hell?
> I'll leave my son my virtuous deeds behind;
> And would my father had left me no more!
> For all the rest is held at such a rate
> As brings a thousand-fold more care to keep
> Than in possession any jot of pleasure.
>
> (II. ii. 45-53)

By introducing these reflections Shakespeare enhances the drier arguments over lawful inheritance. Another theme has begun to run across that of the King's official right—the King's personal feelings about his office—as one is reminded that the King is a private person as well as a public figure. To those who do not possess the crown, as Richard of Gloucester manifests, it seems a supremely desirable possession. But to King Henry it is a burden and a sorrow, the occasion for lament rather than celebration of power. The sense of the burden of kingship partly explains Henry's mild acceptance of both vicissitude and victory. The Yorkist King Edward, a younger and more vigorous man, also dislikes the responsibility of kingship. He seems to regard his public duties as a nuisance and even before his coronation virtually gives over the government to Warwick (II.vi.99-102). He sees kingship simply as the opportunity for unchecked self-indulgence, for he regards the King as the man whose will shall prevail and whose pleasure constitutes his policy. Thus the very man who lectured Henry about how unsuitable for the kingdom was his choice of Margaret as a bride (II.ii.144-62) ignores governmental and political considerations altogether in marrying Lady Grey. Neither the conscientious King Henry nor the irresponsible King Edward finds personal fulfillment in kingship itself or any satisfaction in the exercise of the King's public responsibilities.

The characters' lack of agreement on public principles, their wilful shifts of principle to indulge private feelings, loyalties, or advantages, and the personal attitudes which lead Henry VI and Edward IV to incapacity or neglect in asserting control of the kingdom and its government all demonstrate the impossibility of resolving the conflicts within a framework of public principles grounded in society's values, even those values not undermined or denied. There is no faithfulness to oath, title, right, or justice, but an aggressive assertion of private wills that accept no discipline from public principle or order. It is this England which the historian J. W. Allen succinctly described:

> It is not true that [the Tudor monarchy] superseded an ancient and established constitution. What it superseded was anarchy. The constitution of the late fourteenth or early fifteenth century had broken down long before [the battle of] Tewkesbury.[6]

It is also this England that Shakespeare saw in *III Henry VI.* The victories go first to one side, then the other, and no stability is achieved in the kingdom. The Yorkist victory at Tewkesbury at the end of the play is accompanied by wilful atrocities answering similar ones at the beginning, and Prince Edward is murdered not as a threat to the Yorkist dynasty nor even in revenge, but in a sudden angry expression of personal resentment and annoyance. In such a fashion Shakespeare dramatized a social world falling into a chaos where no public principle has any meaning.

Notes

1. *A Kingdom for a Stage: The Achievement of Shakespeare's History Plays* (Cambridge, Mass.: Harvard University Press, 1972), p. 53.
2. Citations are from *The Complete Works of Shakespeare,* rev. ed., ed. Hardin Craig and David Bevington (Glenview, Ill.: Scott, Foresman and Co., 1974).
3. *The Problem of Order: Elizabethan Political Commonplaces and an Example of Shakespeare's Art* (Chapel Hill, N.C.: University of North Carolina Press, 1962), p. 199.
4. *Narrative and Dramatic Sources of Shakespeare* (London: Routledge and Kegan Paul, 1960), III, 159.
5. *Union of the Two Noble Houses of Lancaster and York,* as quoted in Bullough, III, 175-6.
6. *English Political Thought, 1603-1644* (Hamden, Conn.: Archon Books; first pub. 1938), p. 15.

Maurice Hunt (essay date 1999)

SOURCE: "Unnaturalness in Shakespeare's *3 Henry VI,*" in *English Studies,* Vol. 80, No. 2, April, 1999, pp. 146-67.

[*In the essay below, Hunt locates in* Henry VI, Part 3 *a unity of design based upon the motif of unnaturalness, particularly in the unnatural disinheritance of Henry's son, which becomes a driving force in subsequent incidents in the drama.*]

While popular during Shakespeare's lifetime, *3 Henry VI* became relatively unpopular with audiences and readers alike in later centuries, partly because this chronicle history play has appeared loosely episodic rather than unified and rendered coherent by a principle informing history.[1] That is not to say that claims have not been made for its structural integrity. A. L. French, following the suggestion of R. G. Moulton, has argued that 'it is perfectly possible to read *Henry VI* and *Richard III* as being organized on the principle of Crime and Punishment or Hubris and Nemesis: the relevant sins being, not ones committed before the plays begin, but ones committed after they start. Men (it may be argued) sin grievously within the plays, and they are punished for their misdeeds, if not swiftly, at least surely.'[2] Having made this claim, French nevertheless proceeds to demonstrate that many deaths in the Henry VI plays are the result of often fortuitous events unconnected with a pattern such as Hubris and Nemesis.[3] Generally, when drama critics write of structure with regard to *3 Henry VI* (or for that matter either of the other two Henry VI plays), they concentrate upon schematic relationships between the plays of the First Tetralogy (or between them and the plays of the Second Tetralogy).[4] Rarely does one come across an analysis of a potential design internal within *3 Henry VI.*[5]

Commentators' difficulty in defining a complex dramatic structure in this pronouncedly episodic chronicle play has perhaps resulted in the large number of articles that argue that the design of *3 Henry VI* consists either of character revolutions on Fortune's Wheel or of simple repeated oppositions. M. M. Reese has remained the principal advocate for the Fortune's-Wheel schematic in *3 Henry VI.*[6] After remarking the play's especially episodic nature, Wayne L. Billings finds a pattern of oppositions in a series of contentions between changing antagonists, a strategy derived from the schemes of narrative chronicles. This organizational principle supposedly created a new dramatic subgenre: the contention play.[7] On the other hand, Faye L. Kelly locates the oppositional pattern in a sequence of oaths made and then broken, while Carol McGinnis Kay and Joseph Candido find it in the relationships of trapper and entrapped and of symbolic tempestuous winds and floods.[8] Despite these often useful and illuminating analyses, many of the play's episodes remain outside the pale of each critic's construction of dramatic design. My contribution to the critical debate surrounding *3 Henry VI* consists of the claim that the motif of unnaturalness unifies *3 Henry VI* to a degree greater than any scheme previously proposed for the play. A radical unnatural act by Henry VI—his disinheritance (and essential divorce) of his son Prince Edward—provides the dramatic rationale for consequent successive unnatural behavior between fathers and sons and among the members of English society of the Wars of the Roses. In fact, Shakespeare stresses that spreading unnaturalness, especially within families such as that of the Duke of York, both intensifies and prolongs this notorious fifteenth-century series of armed conflicts. Sackville and Norton in their influential historic tragedy *Gorboduc* (c. 1562, publ. 1565) set the English precedent for this dramaturgy, a fact that makes this mid-Tudor play more relevant for understanding *3 Henry VI* than critics have suggested.[9] The dramaturgy of unnaturalness in *3 Henry VI* resembles not only that of *Gorboduc* but also that of the later *King Lear.* Placing *3 Henry VI* in relation to two of the most important plays of early modern English drama helps us grasp at least one reason for this chronicle history's sixteenth- and seventeenth-century popularity.

Confronting a hostile Duke of York demanding the throne for himself, threatened by Warwick's armed soldiers, timid, pious King Henry VI at the beginning of the last play in the dramatic trilogy bearing his name strikes a deal with York that sets a fatally unnatural precedent for fifteenth-century English history. He agrees to give the crown to York and his heirs if they will let him reign quietly during his life-time (I.i.170-75).[10] He thus unnaturally denies the pull of a basic law—a father's love and care for his son. By his rash decision,[11] Henry VI essentially divorces his son Prince Edward, depriving him of legal rights and making him mortally vulnerable for the remainder of the boy's (short) life. Bystanders onstage immediately recognize the dreadful consequences of Henry's act. 'What wrong is this unto the Prince your son!' (I.i.176), Clifford exclaims. Henry's allies, disgusted by his 'unmanly deed' (I.i.186), straightaway abandon him for his wife Queen Margaret, who promises to fight for the Lancastrian right to rule. Surprisingly, King Henry realizes that his dispossession of his son Edward is unnatural: when Warwick asks him why he sighs, Henry replies,

> Not for myself, Lord Warwick, but my son,
> Whom I unnaturally shall disinherit.
> But be it as it may.
>
> (I.i.192-94)

With this knowledge, Henry nevertheless proceeds by oath to relinquish the throne to York upon his own death. Angry Queen Margaret's first concern when she enters to berate her husband is not the entailed loss of Lancastrian rule but Henry's unnatural divorce of his child. 'Would I had died a maid / And never seen thee', she tells the startled monarch,

> never borne thee son,
> Seeing thou hast proved so unnatural a father!
> Hath he deserved to lose his birthright thus?
> Hadst thou but loved him half so well as I,
> Or felt that pain which I did for him once,
> Or nourished him as I did with my blood,
> Thou wouldst have left thy dearest heart-blood there,
> Rather than have made that savage duke thine heir
> And disinherited thine only son.
>
> (I.i.216-25)

Through Margaret's speech, Shakespeare focuses Henry's unnaturalness as a failure to feel a blood bond with kin forged by pain endured for that kin. Basically she tells him that he does not understand how or why he and Edward are one flesh, sharing the same blood.[12]

The preferential argument of maternal love echoes later in *3 Henry VI,* serving in retrospect to underscore the unnaturalness of the king's deed.[13] In act IV, newly crowned Queen Elizabeth implicitly amplifies Queen Margaret's earlier sentiments. Threatened with the defeat of the York cause, the pregnant queen resolves to behave so as to protect the child in her womb. 'And I the rather wean me from despair,' she announces,

> For love of Edward's offspring in my womb.
> This is it that makes me bridle passion
> And bear with mildness my misfortune's cross.
> Ay, ay, for this I draw in many a tear
> And stop the rising of bloodsucking sighs,
> Lest with my sighs or tears I blast or drown
> King Edward's fruit, true heir to th' English crown.
>
> (IV.iv.17-24)

Thus she determines to proceed 'hence forthwith unto the sanctuary, / To save at least the heir of Edward's right' (IV.iv.31-32). One might object that, because Henry is not a mother, he could be excused for not feeling a natural bond experienced most intensely in the play by women. But it was a man, Warwick, who first told Henry that he wronged his son, and Henry himself called his deed unnatural. Furthermore, the intensity and poignant depth of a father's expression of grief over having unknowingly killed his own son during the Battle of Towton (II.v.82-93, 105-6, 110, 114-22) confirm in the play's world the assumption that men feel a natural bond for their child as strongly as women like Margaret and Elizabeth do. This father's heartrending plaint indirectly operates to, once again, make auditors upon reflection question Henry's disorder-causing disinheritance.

Henry's deed begins a cataclysmic chain-reaction of similarly unnatural acts in *3 Henry VI.* Enraged, Queen Margaret divorces herself from Henry's table and bed 'until that act of Parliament be repealed / Whereby [her] son is disinherited' (I.i.249-50).[14] This action, while perhaps not unnatural in itself, leads to another which certainly could be judged so by sixteenth-century playgoers: her 'mannish' assumption of the generalship of the Lancastrian troops (I.i.251-56). While Shakespeare's Queen Elizabeth apparently donned body armor in order to inspire the English army awaiting a 1588 Spanish invasion at Tilbury, she seemed to have provoked as much bewilderment as valor among her men.[15] In the eyes of some of her troops, Elizabeth almost certainly resembled an Amazon, an early modern masculinist archetype who had appropriated to herself the supposedly exclusive male traits of martial valor and ferocity. Leah Marcus has persuasively demonstrated that, as Amazon, Shakespeare's Joan la Pucelle in *1 Henry VI* represents an implicit criticism of Queen Elizabeth's 'Amazonian' characteristics.[16] When Richard of York, hearing that Margaret approaches leading five thousand men, asserts that five thousand will amount to five hundred because 'a woman's general' (I.ii.68), he voices the early modern male stereotype of natural order disordered by a woman usurping man's prerogative. But by becoming in male minds an Amazon,[17] Margaret develops into a fearful prodigy rather than a Venus-figure (wearing Mars's armor) whose prowess might be lightly dismissed.

Once her army has captured the Duke of York, Margaret's 'mannish' cruelty, regarded as unnatural in a woman, materializes. She taunts York with a napkin stained with the blood of his slaughtered child Rutland, telling him to weep and wipe his eyes with it. Sadistically she delays killing York so that she might see him pitiably cry over his loss. Her baiting draws this rebuke from grieving York:

> How ill-beseeming is it in thy sex
> To triumph, like an Amazonian trull
> Upon their woes whom fortune captivates!
>
> (I.iv.113-15)

'How couldst thou drain the lifeblood of the child', York asks,

> To bid the father wipe his eyes withal,
> And yet be seen to bear a woman's face?
> Women are soft, mild, pitiful, and flexible;
> Thou stern, obdurate, flinty, rough, remorseless.
>
> (I.iv.138-42)

Margaret herself has said that her experience of mothering a son has made her naturally responsive to the loving bond between parent and child. York's words imply that she has had to override this predisposition in order to dip her handkerchief in the blood of a slaughtered child so as terribly to taunt the father; in his despairing mind, she is no longer a woman or even an Amazon but an animal. 'O tiger's heart wrapped in a woman's hide!' (I.iv.137), he judges in the play's most notorious line of blank verse.

One may grant that York's notion of women's naturalness could be labeled a self-serving masculinist cliché of early modern patriarchy and that women can be just as aggressively hostile as men and still argue that the depth of Margaret's cruelty appears unnatural. Shakespeare invokes a Christian context that acts as a foil accentuating Margaret's bizarre sadism when playgoers realize that her bloody napkin is a blasphemous veronica and the paper crown she places on her victim's head a reminiscence of the callous crowning of the King of the Jews pinioned not on a molehill (as in the play) but on Calvary.[18] The alternative values latent in this implied Christian context coalesce in Northumberland's tears shed over Margaret's horrific treatment of York (I.iv.150-51). 'Had he been slaughterman to all my kin', remorseful Northumberland judges, 'I should not for my life but weep with him, / To see how inly sorrow gripes his soul' (I.iv.169-71).

If a rough man of war weeps over Margaret's sadism and if York, concerning the countenance of the slain child says, 'that face of his the hungry cannibals / Would not have touched, would not have stained with blood' (I.iv.152-53), one wonders what thing Margaret has become. Shakespeare gives Northumberland and York speeches designed to emphasize Margaret's unnatural metamorphosis from woman through Amazon to tiger.[19] King Henry indirectly bears some blame for this transformation. By divorcing his son and refusing to play traditional masculine roles within the royal family, Henry has created therein a male vacuum (or defect of masculinity).[20] This vacuum draws Margaret and later Prince Edward to overdevelop unnaturally compensatory mannish temperaments. In Margaret's case this phenomenon accelerates to push her past the persona of an army's general into the realm of beastly behavior. This will not be the only time that compensatory dynamics within the family *manqué* appear unnatural in *3 Henry VI.*

By analogy, Clifford's murder of the child Rutland additionally develops early in the play the dire meaning of Henry VI's divorce of his son. One day Prince Edward will be killed just as brutally as Rutland is in act I, scene iii. In one sense, Rutland's death grotesquely accentuates and literalizes the figurative destruction involved in Henry's oath of dispossession. Through certain speeches of Rutland, Shakespeare stresses the unnaturalness of Clifford's killing of a boy, even as he has the king's legalistic 'murder' of his heir. Clifford seeks blood revenge on York for the duke's killing Old Clifford. Rutland thus desperately argues that the adult Clifford ought to seek out York himself, not his defenseless and innocent small son. 'I am too mean a subject for thy wrath,' Rutland pleads; 'be thou revenged on men, and let me live' (I.iii.19-20). When Clifford snarls, 'My father's blood / Hath stopped the passage where thy words should enter' (I.iii.21-22), Rutland

Scene from Henry VI, Part 3, *engraving.*

repeats, 'Then let my father's blood open it again. He is a man, and, Clifford, cope with him' (I.iii.23-24). The next utterance of Clifford's characterizes the unnaturalness of his implacable desire for revenge, which concentrates on a harmless child rather than its adult catalyst. Clifford perversely proclaims,

> . . . if I digged up thy forefathers' graves
> And hung their rotten coffins up in chains,
> It could not slake mine ire nor ease my heart.
>
> (I.iii.27-29)

A question of Paris's in the later tragedy *Romeo and Juliet* serves to focus the unnaturalness of Clifford's sentiment. Believing that he sees Romeo opening the Capulet tomb in order to physically desecrate Tybalt's and Juliet's corpses, shocked Paris asks his adversary, 'Can vengeance be pursued further than death?' (V.iii.55). The spontaneous rational negative reply to this rhetorical question suggests the unnaturalness of Clifford's vengeful desire.

At this point, I must address an obvious counter-argument to my claims. Frightened Rutland represents the sight of grim Clifford thusly: 'So looks the pent-up lion o'er the wretch / That trembles under his devouring paws' (I.iii.12-13). Shakespeare has filled *3 Henry VI* with the imagery of strong beasts pursuing or killing their naturally weaker prey. During the initial battle of the play, the Duke of York likens his fleeing troops to 'lambs pursued by hunger-starvèd wolves' (I.iv.5). Furthermore, when Clifford hears the vaguely threatening words of cornered York, he asserts, 'So doves do [futilely] peck the falcon's piercing talons' (I.iv.41). These passages can stand for the many depictions in the play of the timeless ballet of natural predator and victim. Such imagery emphasizes the savage beasts into which hatred can transfigure its agents. In the iron age portrayed in *3 Henry VI,* vicious Margaret becomes a tiger at one moment and a 'She-wolf' at another (I.iv.111); and Clifford, we have seen, becomes a lion slaughtering a lamb. King Henry memorably characterizes these bloody relationships during the Battle of Towton:

> O piteous spectacle! O bloody times!
> Whiles lions war and battle for their dens,
> Poor harmless lambs abide their enmity.
>
> (II.v.73-75)

Clearly what I have been calling unnatural behavior can, when viewed from another perspective within the play, be called natural. If Clifford is lionish, his killing lamb-like Rutland illustrates a law of nature. Also running throughout *3 Henry VI* is imagery of irresistible natural forces. York compares his routed troops to swans 'with bootless labor' swimming against the tide and spending their strength against 'overmatching waves' (I.iv.18-21). 'Look, as I blow this feather from my face', captured King Henry tells his Keepers,

> And as the air blows it to me again,
> Obeying with my wind when I do blow,
> And yielding to another when it blows,
> Commanded always by the greater gust—
> Such is the lightness of you common men.
>
> (III.i.83-88)

'What fates impose, that men must needs abide', King Edward concludes later in the play; 'It boots not to resist both wind and tide' (IV.iii.58-59). The effect of these and other poetic renderings of irresistible natural forces carries over to the many associated representations of beasts naturally preying upon other animals. The result is the suggestion that bestial predator and victim can no more deviate from a powerful natural law coursing through them than the tide can from the moon's pull. And since this animal imagery always figures the conduct of the play's men and women, Shakespeare pushes playgoers' response to this symbolic logic toward the conclusion that certain nasty behavior of characters may not only be natural rather than unnatural but essentially blameless in specific circumstances as well. Watching the Battle of Towton from a distance, King Henry ruminates:

> Now sways it this way, like a mighty sea
> Forced by the tide to combat with the wind;

Now sways it that way, like the selfsame sea
Forced to retire by fury of the wind.
Sometimes the flood prevails, and then the wind;
Now one the better, then another best;
Both tugging to be victors, breast to breast,
Yet neither conqueror nor conquerèd.
So is the equal poise of this fell war.

(II.v.5-13)

The passion of blood revenge and the desperate physical violence of self preservation in battle amount to the human forces signified by this natural imagery of contending flood and wind. The fathers and sons who become mutual victims during the Battle of Towton could not resist feeling the above-described natural forces and acting upon their compulsion. Judged by this poetic logic, they—who excruciatingly blame themselves—are blameless. As blameless as the tide and wind. What seems so terribly unnatural to them and to King Henry is simply natural, when considered from a more removed viewpoint.

It is exclusively within the context of civilized values that characters onstage and members of the theater audience judge behavior in *3 Henry VI* as unnatural. Long before the writing of *King Lear,* Shakespeare in this early history play demonstrates that humankind's life, considered solely within the realm of nature, is as cheap as beasts' and that this realization urges people to want to civilize themselves and others, partly through the articulation of codes like Christian doctrine. The natural laws governing the creatures mainly involve birth, copulation, preying, and death. Frequently abandoning the ideal values of Christianity and European civilization, the combatants of *3 Henry VI* graphically illustrate the latter sadistic and thanatotic two of these four natural instincts. Shakespeare in this play forces into playgoers' consciousness the great paradox of Christianity and of the civilizing process generally—that to escape (perhaps the word should be transcend) the short, brutal life of the natural world and the spiritual despair attending its bloody laws, humankind must in one sense become unnatural. Men and women must learn to forbear their natural instinct to prey upon the weak (lest a stronger prey upon oneself), to savagely return hatred for hatred when injured. Shakespeare reveals in the character of Henry VI the familiar effort to break out of the self-destructive, depressing cycle of natural retribution and victimization by practicing the values of forgiveness, peace-making, and turning the other cheek.[21] Judged by the laws of nature, turning the other cheek, however, amounts to a highly unnatural act. In this early history play, Shakespeare boldly interrogates Christianity's solution to the deadly laws of nature by stressing how unnatural and equally self-destructive it can be for certain individuals in certain circumstances. Represented or inferred Christian values in *3 Henry VI* often appear attractive but only when they are considered as ideals abstracted from their local dramatic contexts of presentation. (Northumberland's previously noted tears, for example, acquire value once one ignores the fact that they neither soften Margaret's sadistic heart nor mitigate York's terrible suffering, once one forgets, in short, that they are part of a context of foil). Evaluated within the political contexts of their expression, Henry VI's Christian sentiments seem suicidally unnatural, for himself, for members of the royal family, and for English citizens deserving a society made relatively stable and peaceful by a monarch capable of practicing a necessary benign Machiavellianism.

Thus the sense of tragedy in *3 Henry VI* partly consists of playgoers' impression of a dilemma posed by these alternatives: unnatural human instincts (e.g., concerning paternal bonds, concerning retribution) versus an unnatural Christian piety (as locally expressed and practiced). Throughout *3 Henry VI* Shakespeare takes pains to stress the unnaturalness of Henry VI's practice of Christian principles. When bloodthirsty Margaret asks Henry whether York's head impaled upon the gates of the town of York cheers his heart, he replies horrified: 'Withhold revenge, dear God! 'Tis not my fault, / Nor wittingly have I infringed my vow' (II.ii.7-8). Clifford then provides the most developed account of the unnaturalness of Henry's piety and forgiveness:

My gracious liege, this too much lenity
And harmful pity must be laid aside.
To whom do lions cast their gentle looks?
Not to the beast that would usurp their den.
Whose hand is that the forest bear doth lick?
Not his that spoils her young before her face.
Who scapes the lurking serpent's mortal sting?
Not he that sets his foot upon her back.
The smallest worm will turn, being trodden on,
And doves will peck in safeguard of their brood.
Ambitious York did level at thy crown,
Thou smiling while he knit his angry brows.
He, but a duke, would have his son a king
And raise his issue, like a loving sire;
Thou, being a king, blest with a goodly son,
Didst yield consent to disinherit him,
Which argued thee a most unloving father.
Unreasonable creatures feed their young;
And though man's face be fearful to their eyes,
Yet, in protection of their tender ones,
Who hath not seen them, even with those wings
Which sometimes they have used with fearful flight,
Make war with him that climbed unto their nest,
Offering their own lives in their young's defense?
For shame, my liege, make them your precedent!
Were it not pity that this goodly boy
Should lose his birthright by his father's fault,
And long hereafter say unto his child,
'What my great-grandfather and grandsire got,
My careless father fondly gave away'?
Ah, what a shame were this! Look on the boy,
And let his manly face, which promiseth
Successful fortune, steel thy melting heart
To hold thine own and leave thine own with him.

(II.ii.9-42)

Clifford's appeal to the boy Edward's 'manly' face reminds playgoers that Henry VI's defects as a husband and father somehow have driven other members of the royal family to make unnatural personal compensations. Clifford in the above-quoted speech reveals another—a more positive—side to the operation of natural law. York partly seeks the throne because he loves his sons. Clifford appears right in suggesting that there is something unnatural in Henry's not loving his own son enough to even defend his boy's right (and life) against a hostile father promoting his beloved offsprings' cause. Strangely, Henry does not seem to feel the promptings of the laws of nature common to humankind. Here Clifford convincingly presents that likelihood as a defect rather than as a Christian advantage.

Responding to Clifford's plea, Henry finally offers an explanation for his stripping of his son Prince Edward's rights:

> Full well hath Clifford played the orator,
> Inferring arguments of mighty force.
> But, Clifford, tell me, didst thou never hear
> That things ill got had ever bad success?
> And happy always was it for that son
> Whose father for his hoarding went to hell?
> I'll leave my son my virtuous deeds behind;
> And would my father had left me no more!
> For all the rest is held at such a rate
> As brings a thousandfold more care to keep
> Than in possession any jot of pleasure.
>
> (II.ii.43-53)

This logic is specious. If—in Henry's words—'things ill got had ever bad success,' then successful rule indicates rightful succession (a thing well got). Chronicle accounts of Henry V's glorious consolidation of the English nation reveal his crown as well rather than ill got. At least they do so according to Henry VI's pragmatic terms. And if his crown was well got, his legitimate heirs Henry VI and Prince Edward might solidly claim and defend their monarchy.[22] Edward Berry concludes that 'Henry VI is a de facto king, in the direct line of succession of a house that has ruled for roughly fifty years; although weak, he is neither tyrant nor usurper'.[23] In fact, Henry's judgment about things ill-got always having bad success may not refer to his inheritance of his royal father's and grandfather's possessions. Henry A. Kelly has argued that Henry is *not* 'suggesting that the kingdoms he inherited from his father were ill-gotten. For the context clearly shows that he is simply speaking in generic terms concerning all the troubles his possessions have cost him, without specifying any cause for the troubles beyond his proprietorship. It could hardly be maintained that Shakespeare is giving an ironic expression to the Yorkist theme of hereditary punishment on the house of Lancaster.'[24]

And whose father for hoarding is bound for hell? Certainly not Henry V or Henry VI. Thus why should Prince Edward IV be divorced from the line of succession of a virtuous father and successful grandfather?[25] Cutting through Henry's 'reasoning', auditors detect in his utterances a *contemptus mundi* message consonant with the speaker's otherworldliness, with his conviction that earthly life inevitably consists of a 'thousandfold' pain and that only by the performance (if possible) of virtuous deeds does humankind leave a real legacy in this world or gain salvation in the next. This ethereal attitude, while praiseworthy from one point of view, essentially leaves Henry's little son naked before his enemies; the king's political naivete graphically reveals itself in his assumption that an inheritance of only his father's virtuous deeds would give Edward the resources to live either a long or full life in late medieval England.[26]

Mistakenly the unnatural father King Henry believes that he can be happiest living the natural life of a shepherd. Pastoral nature, in his opinion, offers escape from England's iron age with all its crimes. Physically removed from the carnage of the Battle of Towton, watching its bloody ebb and flow while sitting upon a molehill, Henry meditates:

> O God! Methinks it were a happy life
> To be no better than a homely swain,
> To sit upon a hill, as I do now,
> To carve out dials quaintly, point by point,
> Thereby to see the minutes how they run:
> How many makes the hour full complete,
> How many hours brings about the day,
> How many days will finish up the year,
> How many years a mortal man may live.
> When this is known, then to divide the times:
> So many hours must I tend my flock,
> So many hours must I take my rest,
> So many hours must I contemplate,
> So many hours must I sport myself,
> So many days my ewes have been with young,
> So many weeks ere the poor fools will ean,
> So many years ere I shall shear the fleece.
> So minutes, hours, days, months, and years,
> Passed over to the end they were created,
> Would bring white hairs unto a quiet grave.
> Ah, what a life were this, how sweet, how lovely!
> Gives not the hawthorn bush a sweeter shade
> To shepherds looking on their silly sheep
> Than doth a rich embroidered canopy
> To kings that fear their subjects' treachery?
> O, yes, it doth, a thousandfold it doth.
> And to conclude, the shepherd's homely curds,
> His cold thin drink out of his leather bottle,
> His wonted sleep under a fresh tree's shade,
> All which secure and sweetly he enjoys,
> Is far beyond a prince's delicates—
> His viands sparkling in a golden cup,
> His body couchèd in a curious bed—
> When care, mistrust, and treason waits on him.
>
> (II.v.21-54)

Upon initial consideration, Henry's word-picture of the wholesome simplicity of the natural life amounts to a standard sixteenth-century pastoral conceit praising the country life at the expense of the corrupt court. But Henry's poetic style of expression, reconsidered, implicitly (and ironically) devalues his tribute to the natural life. Shakespeare makes Henry's catalogue of the shepherd's minutes, hours, days, and years and the pastoral activities that fill them monotonously regular, mechanical in compilation, and thus seemingly tedious and empty of sophisticated value. The essentially lifeless, tick-tock rhythm of Henry's language suggests ironically that in fact the simply natural life that Henry covets would be void of meaning, especially for anyone nurtured by the arts and learning of civilization.[27] Even the iron age of the Wars of the Roses civilizes (or educates) humankind to the degree that the unadulterated natural life, spent away from cities and courts, would find daily existence reduced to biological processes and a few endlessly repeated tasks—until the shepherd's unremarkable death. Felt this way, the natural life would be unnatural, as Henry—oblivious to the satiric implications of his style of speech—never realizes.[28]

The son who unwittingly slays his father and the father who mistakenly kills his son reinforce the notion that pastoral nature offers no secure home for humankind; for the Battle of Towton takes place in a natural setting, and the Son's and Father's heartrending plaints shatter Henry's quiet, suggesting that pastoral includes neither walls to exclude human cruelty and misery nor remedies for them. The natural idyll is not exempt from humankind's destruction of its own kin. This unnatural destruction proceeds not from any natural law but from social injustice. Henry, hearing the Son's horrific complaint, explains the tragedy by saying 'whiles lions war and battle for their dens, / Poor harmless lambs abide their enmity' (II.v.74-75). As this son makes very clear, he has killed his father because he was involuntarily impressed by the king's agents while his father was by those of the Earl of Warwick (II.v.64-66).[29] Less directly than he would later do through the character of Falstaff (*2 Henry IV* III.ii.82-300), Shakespeare depicts the evil sometimes resulting from the Elizabethan practice of martial impressment.

Having witnessed unintended filial and paternal killings at the Battle of Towton, Henry, feeling excruciating guilt for being a primary catalyst of the Wars of the Roses, yearns to atone for bloody deeds by his own sacrificial death.[30] 'O, that my death would stay these ruthful deeds!' (II.v.95), he exclaims. Unable to live a benign natural life in either court or country, apparently the two inclusive realms of mortal existence, Henry seeks relief in a self-obliterating act of martyrdom. For the great mass of men and women, martyrdom amounts to an unnatural act—the deliberate extinction of the natural instinct to preserve one's life at any cost. One might say that Christ's martyrdom authorized this unnatural act for the ages by becoming its archetype. But Henry's many flaws, including his cowardly equivocations, demonstrate that he is not Christ. His sudden death at Richard of Gloucester's hands possesses no personally redemptive purpose, and his corpse serves only as a rallying point for future strife. In *3 Henry VI,* Shakespeare ironically underscores the absence of salvific martyrdom among the many deaths reported and portrayed onstage. When Clifford enters wounded with a fatal arrow sticking in his neck, the grisly tableau invites comparison with the widespread late medieval and early modern pictorial tradition of rendering the Christian martyr St. Sebastian dying from such an arrow wound.[31] But bloodthirsty Clifford is no martyr, a fact thrust deeper into the playgoer's mind by the irony of the iconic allusion. Thus without the possibility of redemptive martyrdom, the unnaturalness of the iron world of *3 Henry VI* continues to spread.

In fact, the harsh God of this history play appears to propel this dissemination of unnaturalness. 'Thou hast one son', Rutland, pleading for his life, tells homicidal Clifford:

> For his sake pity me,
> Lest in revenge thereof, sith God is just,
> He be as miserably slain as I.
>
> (I.iii.40-42)

But pitiless Clifford slays Rutland, thus by the logic of the above-quoted passage marking out young Clifford for death. But young Clifford never dies in *3 Henry VI* (in fact, he never appears in the play), thereby calling into question the reading of those critics who posit a God in the drama punishing, as Isaiah foretold, guilty fathers through the deaths of relatively blameless sons.[32] God's presence in this play cannot be said to form a coherent, sustained pattern; His manifestation is fitful, unorthodox. York, for example, never receives punishment through the deaths of three relatively blameless sons. In his case, the grown children match—indeed may be said to exceed—their father in unnaturalness and deceit. In the York instance, an unnatural sign from God precipitates an unusual dynamic of retribution.

Shakespeare partly devotes act II, scene i of the play to a representation of the unnatural working of the heavens. There, the three York brothers have a vision of three suns blazing in the same sky, three suns that 'join, embrace, and seem to kiss' (II.i.29) by soon merging into one familiar sun again. 'In this the heaven figures some event' (II.i.32), Richard concludes. It is Edward who applies the vision of the three sons to himself and his two brothers, judging that they should cooperatively merge to 'overshine the earth' (II.i.38), that is to say, rule it through their leagued political and military power. But this prophecy and the vision prompting it mislead the York brothers; in fact, they lead to the relationships that will destroy two of the three brothers. While the brothers temporarily succeed by bonding together, Edward, once king, prefers his wife's relatives in lucrative marriages before he does his bachelor brothers (alienating Richard and Clarence), Clarence deserts Edward to marry Warwick's daughter and join with him against the Yorkist troops, and Richard plots to gain the crown by fatally setting Edward against Clarence, exacerbating their enmity. The ultimate falseness of the prophecy based on the vision of the three suns reflects the unnaturalness of the heavenly phenomenon. Apparently the God of this dark play providentially mirrors characters' unnaturalness back at them, in certain cases actualizing their latent paternal, motherly, or (as in the case of the York brothers) filial unnaturalness through unnatural mystical signs. The God of *3 Henry VI* never retards or attempts to redeem the unnatural behavior of the characters of this play but instead seems to accelerate that spiritless unnaturalness, sometimes to work eventually poetically just punishments.

Apparently incapable of real martyrhood, King Henry continues to act unnaturally during the remainder of the play. He persists in disregarding his son, resigning the government of England after being freed from imprisonment to Warwick and Clarence rather than to his own flesh and blood (IV.vi.16-52). Late-play imagery emphasizes Henry's unnaturalness. Cataloguing the troops that he can muster to protect Henry from Edward of York's invasion, Warwick compares his shielded subject

> . . . to his island girt in with the ocean,
> Or modest Dian circled with her nymphs . . .
>
> (IV.viii.20-21)

The comparison of Henry to the goddess Diana foregrounds his unnatural effeminacy, a trait compelling the development of a premature and thus unnatural masculinity in both Queen Margaret and the boy-prince Edward (V.iv.39-49, V.v.17-24). Baffled and frightened by Edward of York's likely seduction of his countrymen to Edward's cause, Henry finally resolves that his own pious virtues will keep English men and woman true to him:

> No, Exeter, these graces challenge grace;
> And when the lion fawns upon the lamb,
> The lamb will never cease to follow him.
>
> (IV.viii.48-50)

The confused imagery of the last two verses of this speech reflects Henry's misunderstanding of natural law and indirectly his own unnaturalness. Henry by his metaphor seemingly implies that he (the royal lion) will have the citizenry (lambs) following himself rather than Edward of York because he has fawned on them (treated them well rather than oppressed them with taxes). Pusillanimous Henry however has never been capable of being the royal lion. If the metaphor has any meaning, it is ironic: Edward of York, capable of becoming the lion, *will* fawn upon the citizenry so that they will follow him rather than Henry. But in the natural world lions never fawn upon lambs; they quickly kill and eat them. And lambs never follow lions; they futilely flee from them instinctively. The biblical precedent Henry invokes of the lamb and lion peacefully lying down together is a utopian dream, one that underscores the unnaturalness of Christian ideals contextualized within the overpowering predatory natural instincts (or laws) motivating warriors in the last two acts of *3 Henry VI*.

The unnaturalness of Henry's son's death poetically reflects Henry's unnatural divorce of Prince Edward at the beginning of the play. Captured along with his mother by the Yorkist troops, Prince Edward taunts Edward, Clarence, and Richard of York:

> Lascivious Edward, and thou perjured George,
> And thou misshapen Dick, I tell ye all
> I am your better, traitors as ye are,
> And thou usurp'st my father's right and mine.
>
> (V.v.34-37)

Enraged by the boy's audacious naming of their individual flaws, the brothers successively stab him (V.v.38-40). Edward tragically taunts his captors chiefly because he believes the crown belongs to his father and himself—not them. But their knowledge of Henry's earlier divorce of his son, the King's oath to give the throne to their father and them after his own death, and—most important—their awareness that Henry resigned the crown to Clarence (and Warwick) makes Edward's claim seem especially outrageous and insulting. These feelings largely prompt their spontaneous murder. The unnaturalness of Henry's divorce of Prince Edward haunts the boy to its fatal end.

A horrified witness to the death of her child, Margaret articulates the unnaturalness of the York brothers' deed:

> O traitors, murderers!
> They that stabbed Caesar shed no blood at all,
> Did not offend, nor were not worthy blame,
> If this foul deed were by to equal it.
> He was a man; this, in respect, a child,
> And men ne'er spend their fury on a child.
>
> (V.v.52-56)

Even though Henry's unmanliness has caused his son unnaturally to play the role of a man, Edward remains a boy. By emphasizing the fact that Edward, Clarence, and Richard have killed a child, Margaret questions their manhood, implicitly redefining her own earlier idea of bloody masculinity. The York brothers join Clifford by performing an unnatural act—child murder. In one sense, of course, Margaret is getting her own due. She cruelly baited York before his death by gloating over Clifford's killing of York's child Rutland, and now she must endure the spectacle of her own flesh and blood's murder. The unexpected feelings of motherly love within this hard, masculinist woman amount to nature's long-delayed retribution for her unnatural savagery. 'You have no children', she tearfully tells her tormentors:

> if you had,
> The thought of them would have stirred up remorse.
> But if you ever chance to have a child,
> Look in his youth to have him so cut off
> As, deathsmen, you have rid this sweet young prince!
>
> (V.v.63-67)

Robert Y. Turner has argued that 'the major figures of the Henry VI plays undergo no moral change of character.'[33] While such a claim remains debatable, a realization like Margaret's approximates an anagnorisis in auditors' minds.[34]

Richard of Gloucester has killed young Edward because the boy called him 'misshapen Dick' (V.v.35). In other words, the stinging reminder of his unnaturally grotesque body prompts his participation in an unnatural killing. Regarded from one perspective, Richard's unnatural shape inscribes the unnatural behavior of many of the play's characters. It is as though their unnaturalness condenses graphically in Richard, who then on a few memorable occasions becomes the terrifying counter-agent of it. By killing their son, Richard especially proves so not only for Margaret and Henry but eventually in the final play of the First Tetralogy for his brother Clarence as well. Margaret first taunted Richard with being 'a foul misshapen stigmatic, / Marked by the destinies to be avoided, / As venom toads or lizards' dreadful stings' (II.ii.136-38). In his first soliloquy in the play, Richard characterizes himself as a 'chaos' that bears no resemblance to his mother (III.ii.161). Robert G. Hunter has persuasively argued that Richard's utterance in this soliloquy—'Why, love forswore me in my mother's womb' (III.ii.153)—should be taken in conjunction with his word 'chaos' to signify that Shakespeare's dramaturgy in *3 Henry VI* and *King Richard III* is Empedoclean.[35]

Assuming that love creatively shapes chaos and gives form and purpose to the world, Shakespeare shows in these plays that 'characters' failure or inability to love others reduces their world through intrigue and warfare to something resembling original chaos. This dramatic method implies that the absence of love is a primary source of unnaturalness in *3 Henry VI.* The conflation of two speeches from different parts of the play makes this point. Richard, in his final soliloquy, pronounces, 'I have no brother, I am like no brother';

> And this word 'love,' which graybeards call divine,
> Be resident in men like one another
> And not in me. I am myself alone.
>
> (V.vi.80-83)

Earlier, Clarence asks his father-in-law Warwick if he believes

> That Clarence is so harsh, so blunt, unnatural,
> To bend the fatal instruments of war
> Against his brother and his lawful king?
>
> (V.i.86-88)

When loveless Richard plots his brother Clarence's death, he ironically does not know that Clarence once declared such an act unnatural. Henry's strange indifference to his own, his family's, and his country's welfare may reflect not so much his focus on a heavenly crown as it does his lack of natural feeling, especially natural love. Perhaps not feeling the natural pull of fatherly love for a son to any significant degree, Henry thus appears unnatural in his seeming indifference to Prince Edward's welfare. And one could say that inner feelings of love attempt too late to order Margaret's world.

In the play's penultimate scene, Henry, restricted in the Tower of London, finally confronts Richard, a man not so much the bloody opposite of a Christian king as Henry's familiar—the grossly distorted but nevertheless punitive image of his own relatively loveless, unnatural self. Feeling a premonition of death, Henry prophesizes that 'Men for their sons', wives for their husbands', / Orphans for their parents' timeless death' shall lament the hour during which lumpen Richard was born (V.vi.41-42). Unnatural in his birth, Richard will go on through the widespread social ruin he forments later to in truth blight the wholesomely natural births and filial, paternal, and maternal loves of many citizens. Because Henry seems to taunt him with his unnatural birth and body (V.vi.35-56), Richard kills him in a sudden fit of rage. The circumstances of Henry's death exactly resemble those of his son. If he had acted naturally as husband, father, king, Henry might have won the hearts necessary to checkmate the York clan. But his unnatural behavior gave the clan's members the opportunity to defeat the Lancastrians and their allies. Like his son before him, Henry pays the ultimate price for mirroring the unnaturalness of his slayer, the unnaturalness that in a fainter image has been his all along.

The play ends with King Edward IV showing the protective love for a son that Henry VI ought to have demonstrated for Prince Edward. 'Come, hither, Bess, and let me kiss my boy', he affectionately states concerning his son:

> Young Ned, for thee, thine uncles and myself
> Have in our armors watched the winter's night,
> Went all afoot in summer's scalding heat,
> That thou mightst repossess the crown in peace;
> And of our labors thou shalt reap the gain.
>
> (V.vii.15-20)

Shakespeare appears to have placed these sentiments in the play's final lines to remind playgoers of the paternal love that might have preserved the Lancastrian monarchy, if only the king could have felt and acted upon it. Yet Richard is there at play's end, also, promising in an aside to kill the boy (as he in fact will do) once the disease-prone epicure King Edward dies, and kissing the child with a Judas kiss (V.vii.21-34). The redemption of the English monarchy lies decades in the future in the epiphany at Bosworth Field of Christ's champion Henry Tudor, Earl of Richmond. Thus Richard's unnaturally loveless plots darken the ascension of the sun of York at the close of *3 Henry VI.*

In conclusion, my reading of *3 Henry VI* suggests the importance of a major motif and dramatic method of Sackville and Norton's *Gorboduc* for an appreciation of Shakespeare's last Henry VI play. Like Shakespeare's Henry VI with regard to his son Prince Edward, Gorboduc foolishly but effectively divorces his elder son Ferrex of his 'birthright and heritage' (I.i.26),[36] guaranteed by the law of primogeniture, by giving before the king's death half of the kingdom to Porrex, the younger son. Immediately Videna and Philander term this deed unnatural. Gorboduc's wife complains that her husband's decision runs 'against all course of kind' (I.i.11) and that he is 'in kind a father, not in kindliness' (I.i.18). Gorboduc's counselor Philander then at length describes the unnaturalness of Gorboduc's act:

> . . . an unkindly wrong it seems to be
> To throw the brother subject under feet
> Of him whose peer he is by course of kind.

And nature, that did make this egalness,
Oft so repineth at so great a wrong
That oft she raiseth up a grudging grief
In younger brethren at the elder's state,
Whereby both towns and kingdoms have been razed.

(I.ii.183-90)

In his brave advice to the rash king, Philander enlarges upon the potential disaster entailed in a ruler's unnatural disinheritance of a son:

And oft it hath been seen where nature's course
Hath been perverted in disordered wise,
When fathers cease to know that they should rule,
And children cease to know they should obey.

. . . . .

Only I mean to show, by certain rules
Which kind hath graft within the mind of man,
That nature hath her order and her course,
Which, being broken, doth corrupt the state
Of minds and things, even in the best of all.

(I.i.205-8, 218-22)

Philander's grim predictions of course come true. Sackville and Norton anticipate Shakespeare's dramatic method in *3 Henry VI* of showing how the effects of a king's unnatural disinheritance of a son radiate into society, either precipitating or giving the occasion for related unnatural deeds that proliferate into civil war and chaos. Gorboduc's unnatural treatment of Ferrex breaks the bond of natural affection between elder and younger brother and leads to Porrex's killing of Ferrex, a crime that prompts the mother Videna's unnatural murder of her son Porrex. Sackville and Norton stress that the people then kill Gorboduc and Videna out of outrage over the unnaturalness of the queen's deed (V.i.1-17).[37] The playwrights (in the text of the play at least) project this linkage in the written commentary on the dumb show of act IV when Alecto, Megaera, and Tisiphone drive across the stage 'a king and a queen, which, moved by Furies, *unnaturally* had slain their children . . . Hereby was signified the *unnatural* murders to follow; that is to say, Porrex slain by his own mother, and of King Gorboduc and Queen Videna, killed by their own subjects' (92, my italics).

At one point before his death, Videna calls Porrex '[r]uthless, unkind, monster of nature's work' (IV.i.71). Yet the authors of this early Elizabethan historical tragedy emphasize that these appellations could equally apply to the speaker, to the mob that takes her life, and—by symbolic logic—in a milder but nevertheless profoundly grave sense to the royal father who indirectly catalyzed this carnage by unnaturally disinheriting his son. Like Shakespeare in *3 Henry VI,* Sackville and Norton suggest that the destruction of a society mirrors, in fact replicates, the self destruction of the primary royal family considered as a single organism. The people, according to Eubulus, Gorboduc's Secretary, may not kill their monarch 'No more than may the hand cut off the head' (V.i.45). But they do so, even as Gorboduc separates Ferrex from himself and Ferrex and Porrex from each other. Eubulus laments that from Britain's 'womb should spring / . . . those that will needs destroy / And ruin thee and eke themselves in fine' (V.ii.20-22). But this happens because Ferrex and Porrex once sprang from the womb of Videna and one unnaturally killed the other and the mother slew the survivor. As in Shakespeare's play, auditors have the sense of the family nuclear and then writ large cannibalistically feeding upon itself.

Even in some finer details *Gorboduc* becomes a worthy analogue of *3 Henry VI.* Philander prefaces the first long speech of his previously quoted advice to Gorboduc by saying that 'such an egalness hath nature made / Between the brethren of one father's seed / As an unkindly wrong it seems to be / To throw the brother subject under feet . . .' (I.ii.181-84). Throughout *Gorboduc* Sackville and Norton usually regard primogeniture as a natural rather than social law. But in the first two verses of Philander's utterance, they complicate this judgment by implying that primogeniture is unnatural, that nature strives for equality among siblings. This complication resembles the Shakespearean ambiguity of *3 Henry VI* regarding the possible unnaturalness of a social code (doctrinal Christianity) felt against the strain of instinctual natural urgings. This repeated ambiguity in each play makes more credible characters' mistaken or wavering opinion about what is natural and unnatural in their own and others' behavior.

Concerning the civil war that commences near the end of *Gorboduc* and that, like the Wars of the Roses, would last for fifty years, Eubulus sadly prophesizes that

One kinsman shall bereave another's life;
The father shall unwitting slay the son;
The son shall slay the sire and know it not.

(V.ii.212-15)

These lines not only exactly describe the family tragedy that Shakespeare depicts during the Battle of Towton, but they also may have constituted an influential scenario for act II, scene v of *3 Henry VI.* Whatever the case, this relatively neglected play of Shakespeare's occupies an important place in the development of early modern English drama between *Gorboduc* and *King Lear,* a tragedy whose many affinities with *Gorboduc* commentators have noted, one which consummately finds and traces the relationships between naturalness and unnaturalness, demonstrating in a terrifying way the chaos following a royal father's unnatural disinheritance of a child.[38] Placing *3 Henry VI* in this line of development may help modern playgoers appreciate the popularity that this chronicle history play once enjoyed.

Notes

1. According to Andrew S. Cairncross, editor of *The Second Part of King Henry VI* (London, 1957), the episodic nature of Shakespeare's Henry VI plays can be attributed to these facts: '[t]he critical and imaginative interpretation of historical trends was not yet, and the chronicles had in general little more

unity than was imposed by a king, a hero, or a conflict. The reign of Henry VI, in any case was too long, its events too rambling and fortuitous, to be easily digested into drama' (i). E. M. W. Tillyard, in *Shakespeare's History Plays* (New York, 1946), judges that in *3 Henry VI* 'formlessness of a sort was as necessary to his purposes . . . as the wide scattered geography of *Antony and Cleopatra* was to the imperial setting of that play. . . . Shakespeare had a great mass of chronicle matter to deal with and he failed to control it; or rather in paring it to manageable length he fails to make it significant' (190). 'The plot of *Part III* [of *Henry VI*] seems even more episodic and long-winded than that of *Part II*', Robert Ornstein concludes, 'although the plays are approximately the same length, because *Part III* does not have the central core of action provided in *Part II* by the unfolding of York's conspiracy' (*A Kingdom for a Stage: The Achievement of Shakespeare's History Plays* [Cambridge, MA, 1972] 52). Edward I. Berry, in *Patterns of Decay: Shakespeare's Early Histories* (Charlottesville, 1975), asserts that '[t]he structure of [*3 Henry VI*] is . . . indistinct. Unlike Part II, Part III does not move toward a central emotional climax, nor does it embody a unified action' (53). Finally, John W. Blanpied, in *Time and the Artist in Shakespeare's English Histories* (Newark, 1983) 64-76, esp. 66, finds *3 Henry VI* to be essentially formless.

2. A. L. French, 'The Mills of God and Shakespeare's Early History Plays', *English Studies* 55 (1974): 313-24, esp. 313.

3. French effectively questions 'whether the text of the First Tetralogy does, in fact, support any . . . notions of order, justice, and moral equity' (314).

4. See, for example, Tillyard and especially Sherman Hawkins, 'Structural Pattern in Shakespeare's Histories', *Studies in Philology* 88 (1991): 16-45. Tillyard was instrumental in establishing the notion that the working out of a divine curse on the House of Lancaster, prosecuted mainly on the sons and grandsons of sinning fathers and grandfathers, creates a pattern both within individual plays of the First Tetralogy and among them. Henry A. Kelly, however, in *Divine Providence in the England of Shakespeare's Histories* (Cambridge, MA, 1970), is skeptical of Tillyard's thesis, maintaining instead that *3 Henry VI* does not reveal a clear scheme of divine retribution operating through curses and broken oaths (262-76). Kelly concludes that, as for this play, 'it seems best . . . to regard opinions concerning the providential outcome of solitary events as characterizing only the sentiments of the speakers at the time they speak them, and not Shakespeare's own view' (272). Moody E. Prior, in *The Drama of Power: Studies in Shakespeare's History Plays* (Evanston, Illinois, 1973), also argues that Hall's pattern of God's vengeance does not organize *1, 2,* and/or *3 Henry VI* (39-41).

5. The best account of a dramatic design in *3 Henry VI* appears in Emrys Jones, *The Origins of Shakespeare* (Oxford, 1977), 179-92. Jones asserts that, like *Tamburlaine, Part One, 3 Henry VI* divides into two sections, breaking after act II. The first section is a brief two-act tragedy stressing the barbarousness of civil war, with revenge for a father the prime motif of this mini-play. Jones posits many structural and thematic symmetries within this section. The second section consisting of the play's final three acts is governed by Fortune, a goddess who demonstrates that the result of English rule by two essentially concurrent kings is giddy instability (181-89). Larry S. Champion admits that in *3 Henry VI* Shakespeare develops 'multiple plot strands' in which 'no single figure is predominant in lines spoken or time spent on the stage, and [that] the devices of internalization are spread among a wide range of characters' ('Developmental Structure in Shakespeare's Early Histories: The Perspective of *3 Henry VI*', *Studies in Philology* 76 (1979): 218-38, esp. 236). Granted this lack of focus, Champion asserts that the detection of structure depends upon associating 'elements of detachment and breadth with those of emotional engagement through depth of characterization' (236), chiefly as playgoers' affective engagement and detachment apply to their reactions to Shakespeare's complementary depictions of a pious but progressively tragic Henry VI and an evil but progressively fascinating Richard of Gloucester. Such a technique, however, hardly amounts to dramatic structure.

6. M. M. Reese, *The Cease of Majesty: A Study of Shakespeare's History Plays* (London, 1961), 196-98. Reese concedes that in *3 Henry VI* the Fortune's-Wheel 'pattern was largely artificial; in his insistence upon it Shakespeare was deliberately organising a crude, episodic story to an artistic purpose' (197).

7. Wayne L. Billings, 'Ironic Lapses: Plotting in *Henry VI*', *Studies in the Literary Imagination* 5 (1972): 27-49, esp. 48-49. Billings notes that in *3 Henry VI* Shakespeare 'uses a more schematic method' than he does in *1* and *2 Henry VI:* 'promise-breaking repeatedly breaks an uneasy peace and alters the military situation; there being no absolute loyalties, there can be no solidarity in any heroic triumph' (31). By arguing that *3 Henry VI* is designed along the lines of Senecan blood-revenge tragedy, David Riggs, in *Shakespeare's Heroical Histories: 'Henry VI' and Its Literary Tradition* (Cambridge, MA, 1971), 127-39, unintentionally conflates the idea of the drama as a contention play with the notion that it enacts a pattern of retribution for crimes. Riggs concludes that within the 'broad framework [of Senecan tragedy of blood revenge] Clifford and Margaret [in *3 Henry VI*] would resemble the paragons of Senecan cruelty, Atreus and Medea, each of whom satisfies a passion for revenge by tormenting an afflicted father with the death of his only child' (134).

8. Faye L. Kelly, 'Oaths in Shakespeare's *Henry VI* Plays', *Shakespeare Quarterly* 24 (1973): 357-71, esp. 366-71. Kelly's notion of the relationship between her motif and dramatic structure takes this form: 'In drama, whenever a character swears to do something or not to do something, plot takes form as a direct result of his regard for his word. If the swearer honors the oath, the action takes one course; if he breaks his oath, the action veers in a different direction' (357). 'When made, an oath adumbrates plot; when later recalled by the maker of the oath or the character against whom it is made, the oath becomes structural as it links and tightens the elements of the plot' (359). Carol McGinnis Kay, 'Traps, Slaughter, and Chaos: A Study of Shakespeare's *Henry VI* Plays', *Studies in the Literary Imagination* 5 (1972): 1-26, esp. 17-23; Joseph Candido, 'Getting Loose in the *Henry VI* Plays', *Shakespeare Quarterly* 35 (1984): 392-406, esp. 402.

9. Though his assertion may be a bit overstated, Eric Sams, in *The Real Shakespeare: Retrieving the Early Years, 1564-1594* (New Haven, 1995), has maintained that *Gorboduc* 'is the manifest source of Shakespeare's lifelong style and idiom' (20).

10. All references to *3 Henry VI* and other Shakespeare plays are to the texts in *The Complete Works of Shakespeare,* ed. David Bevington (New York, 1997).

11. A. L. French comments that Henry VI's swearing 'that, if he is allowed to remain king for his lifetime, the Duke of York will inherit the throne after his death' is 'a silly thing to swear . . . because it turns Henry into a permanent public temptation' (318).

12. The censurable element in King Henry VI's divorce of his son early in *3 Henry VI* qualifies playgoers' later inclination to pity the idealistic ruler or wholeheartedly admire him along the lines suggested by commentators such as Mattie Swayne, 'Shakespeare's *King Henry VI* as a Pacifist', *College English* 3 (1941-42): 143-49; and Larry S. Champion 220, 227-31. For criticism of King Henry's flaws of character, see H. M. Richmond, *Shakespeare's Political Plays* (New York, 1967) 57, 65-66.

13. Ronald S. Berman, in 'Fathers and Sons in the Henry VI Plays', *Shakespeare Quarterly* 13 (1962): 487-97, also notes the importance of King Henry's disenfranchisement of his son (494), regarding it as the first of several explorations in *3 Henry VI* of the tragic relationship of fathers and sons (494-97). The most complete explorations of father-son relationships and their severing in the playwright's historical drama appear in Robert B. Pierce, *Shakespeare's History Plays: The Family and the State* (Columbus, 1971) 76-84; and Berry 53-74. Berry notes that, 'at the core of [I.i. of *3 Henry VI*] is a question concerning the nature of parental and filial obligation—a question put to all parties, here and throughout the play, with corrosive irony' (56).

14. Of Queen Margaret, the chronicle historian Edward Hall wrote that she '"was a woman . . . of haute stomacke, desirous of glory, and covetous of honor, and of reason, pollicye, counsaill, and other giftes and talentes of nature belonging to a man . . ."' (*Narrative and Dramatic Sources of Shakespeare,* ed. Geoffrey Bullough [London, 1960] 3:105-6). Nevertheless, Robert Y. Turner, in 'Characterization in Shakespeare's Early History Plays', *ELH* 31 (1964): 241-58, claims that women as well as men in the noncomic drama of the later 1580s, women like Zenocrate, Zabina, Locrine's Queen Estrild, and Constance and Queen Elinor of *The Troublesome Reign of King John,* all 'share [a] masculine vigor of speech' (251).

15. See Leah S. Marcus, *Puzzling Shakespeare: Local Reading and Its Discontents* (Berkeley, 1988) 54-56. Marcus documents the impression that 'the queen's martial self-presentation at Tilbury was a glorious moment of patriotic triumph, but also . . . a spectacle that aroused distinct uneasiness among Englishmen' (54). See pages 62-66 of her study.

16. Marcus 51-96.

17. Margaret's Amazonian nature has been fully described by David M. Bevington, 'The Domineering Female in *1 Henry VI*', *Shakespeare Studies* 2 (1966): 51-58, esp. 56-57; and by Marilyn L. Williamson, '"When Men Are Rul'd by Women": Shakespeare's First Tetralogy', *Shakespeare Studies* 19 (1991): 41-59, esp. 44, 51-52. Barbara Hodgdon, in *The End Crowns All: Closure and Contradiction in Shakespeare's History* (Princeton, NJ, 1991), calls the Margaret of *3 Henry VI* the 'Amazonian apotheosis' of the Joan of Arc of *1 Henry VI* (69). The historical evolution of Margaret's 'mannish' character has been recounted by Patricia-Ann Lee, 'Reflections of Power: Margaret of Anjou and the Dark Side of Queenship', *Renaissance Quarterly* 39 (1986): 183-217, esp. 193 ff.

18. David M. Bergeron, in 'The Play-Within-the-Play in *3 Henry VI*', *Tennessee Studies in Literature* 22 (1977): 37-45, esp. 39, fully describes parallels to the Crucifixion. He notes that Margaret gives York a bloody napkin '"to dry [his] cheeks withal" (83), just as the dying Jesus was offered a sop of vinegar' (39). Richmond concludes that this 'blood-soaked cloth is grotesquely analogous to the one offered by St. Veronica to Christ' (61). Berman, however, states that 'the napkin stained with Rutland's blood', rather than provoking recollection of the veronica, is 'an ingredient in the symbolic counterpart of the feast of Thyestes . . .' (495).

19. In this respect, see Jonathan Bate, *Shakespeare and Ovid* (Oxford, 1993) 115, 181.

20. See Coppélia Kahn, *Man's Estate: Masculine Identity in Shakespeare* (Berkeley, 1981) 51-52, 60-61.

21. David L. Frey, in *The First Tetralogy: Shakespeare's Scrutiny of the Tudor Myth* (The Hague, 1976), has

also noted that 'growing constantly more evident as the play unfolds is the development of two opposing value systems: one based on a peace-oriented religious-moral law, the other based on a war-oriented natural law' (55).

22. Pierce remarks that Henry's above-quoted speech (II.ii.43-53) 'might seem to express the highest piety and wisdom. . . . Yet his father has left him not just the English crown but a tradition of glorious rule and conquest. He is losing the moral heritage of Agincourt just as surely as his reign has lost the territorial gains' (78).

23. Berry, *Patterns of Decay* 44.

24. Henry A. Kelly, *Divine Providence* 267.

25. Contrary to my reading of King Henry's act II justification for his son's material disinheritance, Berman interprets it as an 'intensely noble expression', which 'is dismissed [by onstage auditors] with typical obtuseness as "soft courage"'. In this critic's opinion, 'the piety of Henry has not been perverted enough to command respect in the [degenerate] world of the play' (495-96).

26. Sharply critical of Henry in his II.ii.43-53 speech is Robert C. Jones, *These Valiant Dead: Renewing the Past in Shakespeare's Histories* (Iowa City, 1991) 25.

27. Extended analyses of King Henry's pastoral soliloquy appear in Pierce 69-71 and in Ornstein 56-57.

28. For the possible literary sources of this episode, see D. J. Womersley, '*3 Henry VI:* Shakespeare, Tacitus, and Parricide', *Notes and Queries* 32 (1985): 468-73.

29. Berman asserts that kindred killing in this episode 'signif[ies] a national rather than a personal degeneracy, for it is the conflicting parties who are ultimately responsible for inflicting this particular form of parricide on the nation. As Henry states of the grieving father, "the red rose and the white are on his face" (496). In this vein, Elihu Pearlman, in *William Shakespeare: The History Plays* (New York, 1992), stresses that Henry VI himself must share some of the blame for the Father's and Son's deaths, a fact that the king understands as evidenced by his judgment that 'whiles lions war and battle for their dens, / Poor harmless lambs abide their enmity' (43).

30. Michael Manheim, in 'Duke Humphrey and the Machiavels', *American Benedictine Review* 23 (1972): 249-57, judges that, '[b]y the Machiavellian standards which govern just about everyone else [in the Henry VI plays], Henry is surely the wretchedest king in "Christendom"' (252).

31. See, for example, the *Martyrium des hl. Sebastian* (1516) by Hans Holbein the Elder, in which the shaft and feathers of an arrow protrude from the hollow of St. Sebastian's neck (*Alte Pinakothek München* [München: Hirmer Verlag München, 1957] pl. 58).

32. See also Exodus 20:5; cf. Numbers 14:18.

33. Turner 241.

34. Wayne L. Billings concludes that 'Queen Margaret, who had seemed unheroic as well as unwomanly in taunting the captive York with the blood of his son, comes later to seem, by contrast with King Edward IV and Richard of Gloucester, a genuinely heroic figure inspired by resolution and loyalty to her own son' (32).

35. Robert G. Hunter, *Shakespeare and the Mystery of God's Judgments* (Athens, 1976) 67-100, esp. 93 ff.

36. All references to *Gorboduc* are to the text appearing in *Drama of the English Renaissance: I The Tudor Period,* ed. Russell A. Fraser and Norman Rabkin (New York, 1976) 81-100.

37. Marcella, Videna's lady in waiting, makes this association when she exclaims, 'Should nature yet consent to slay her son? / O mother, thou to murder thus thy child!' (IV.ii.244-45).

38. The classic analysis of nature and unnaturalness in *King Lear* remains John F. Danby, *Shakespeare's Doctrine of Nature: A Study of 'King Lear'* (1948; rpt. London, 1961) esp. 15-53.

FURTHER READING

Criticism

Bernthal, Craig A. "Treason in the Family: The Trial of Thumpe v. Horner." *Shakespeare Quarterly* 42, No. 1 (Spring 1991): 44-54.

Considers Peter Thumpe's act of informing on his master for treason in *Henry VI, Part 2* within the cultural contexts of Tudor England.

Berryman, John. "*2 Henry VI*" and "*3 Henry VI.*" In *Berryman's Shakespeare,* edited by John Haffenden, pp. 308-13. New York: Farrar, Straus and Giroux, 1999.

Two essays, originally published in 1958, that contribute to the debate concerning the authorship controversy of the *Henry VI* plays and examine Shakespeare's stylistic touches in the second and third parts of the plays.

Blanpied, John W. "'Art and Baleful Sorcery': The Counterconsciousness of *Henry VI, Part 1.*" *Studies in English Literature 1500 to 1900* 15, No. 2 (Spring 1975): 213-27.

Discusses Shakespeare's dramatic subversion of history in *Henry VI, Part 1.*

Brockbank, Philip. "The Frame of Disorder—*Henry VI.*" In *On Shakespeare: Jesus, Shakespeare and Karl Marx, and Other Essays,* pp. 79-103. Oxford: Basil Blackwell, 1989.

Presents an overview of *Henry VI, Parts 1, 2, and 3*, discussing themes of dissension leading to degradation and anarchy, and analyzing Shakespeare's historical method in these plays.

Caldwell, Ellen C. "Jack Cade and Shakespeare's *Henry VI, Part 2*." *Studies in Philology* 92, No. 1 (1995): 18-52.
Evaluates Shakespeare's portrayal of the Cade rebellion in light of historical sources and previous critical analyses, concluding that the representation of Cade in *Henry VI, Part 2* may be viewed as evidence of Shakespeare's reaction against populism.

Carr, Virginia M. "Animal Imagery in *2 Henry VI*." *English Studies* 53, No. 5 (October 1972): 408-12.
Argues that the frequent allusions to animals in *Henry VI, Part 2* serve an organic function in the play by reinforcing its thematic texture.

Champion, Larry S. "The Search for Dramatic Form: *1, 2, 3 Henry VI*." In *Perspective in Shakespeare's English Histories*, pp. 12-53. Athens: University of Georgia Press, 1980.
Presents an overview and structural analysis of *Henry VI, Parts 1, 2* and *3* that focuses on developments in theme, character, and style in the plays.

Cox, John D. "Local References in *3 Henry VI*." *Shakespeare Quarterly* 51, No. 3 (Fall 2000): 340-52.
Enumerates topical allusions to Warwickshire and the figure of Somerville in *Henry VI, Part 3*.

Hattaway, Michael. Introduction to *The Second Part of King Henry VI*, by William Shakespeare, edited by Michael Hattaway, pp. 1-69. Cambridge: Cambridge University Press, 1991.
Extensive introductory commentary on *Henry VI*, including discussion of historical and political contexts, dramatic structure, stage history, composition, and sources.

Heberle, Mark. "Shakespeare's Boy King." *Durham University Journal* 51, No. 2 (July 1990): 177-79.
Comments on the thematic implications of Shakespeare's use of a child actor to portray Henry in *Henry VI, Part 1*.

Howard, Jean E. and Phyllis Rackin. *Engendering A Nation: A Feminist Account of Shakespeare's English Histories*. London: Routledge, 1997, 248 p.
Feminist analysis of gender representation in early modern England that includes sizeable chapters on the three parts of *Henry VI*.

Lee, Patricia-Ann. "Reflections of Power: Margaret of Anjou and the Dark Side of Queenship." *Renaissance Quarterly* 39, No. 2 (Summer 1986): 183-217.
Remarks on Shakespeare's depiction of Margaret as a villainous female ruler in *Henry VI, Parts 2* and *3* and comments on prevailing assumptions about feminine nature during the Tudor period.

Levine, Nina. "Lawful Symmetry: The Politics of Treason in *2 Henry VI*." *Renaissance Drama* 25 (1994): 197-218.
Highlights the subversive potential of Shakespeare's staging of treason cases in *Henry VI, Part 2*.

Martin, Randall. "Rehabilitating John Somerville in *3 Henry VI*." *Shakespeare Quarterly* 51, No. 3 (Fall 2000): 332-40.
Centers on autobiographical references to Catholicism associated with the character Somerville in *Henry VI, Part 3*.

Pearlman, E. "Shakespeare at Work: The Two Talbots." *Philological Quarterly* 75, No. 1 (Winter 1996): 1-22.
Offers evidence that Act 4, scene 5 of *Henry VI, Part 1* is a revised version of the play's subsequent scene and indicates substantial developments in Shakespeare's technique of characterization.

———. "The Duke and the Beggar in Shakespeare's *2 Henry VI*." *Criticism* 41, No. 3 (Summer 1999): 309-21.
Examines the sources, as well as thematic and theological significance, of the scene between the Duke of Gloucester and Saunder Simpcox in *Henry VI, Part 2*.

Rackin, Phyllis. "Anti-Historians: Women's Roles in Shakespeare's Histories." *Theatre Journal* 37, No. 3 (October 1985): 329-44.
Studies female characters as "the opponents and subverters of the historical and historiographic enterprise" in *Henry VI, Part 1* and *King John*.

Williams, George Walton. "Fastolf or Falstaff." *English Literary Renaissance* 5, No. 2 (Spring 1975): 308-12.
Claims that the Sir John Falstaff of *Henry VI, Part 1* should correctly be 'Fastolf'—the name of a historical personage found in Shakespeare's principal sources for the play.

Julius Caesar

For further information on the critical and stage history of *Julius Caesar,* see *SC,* Volumes 7, 17, 30, and 50.

INTRODUCTION

Likely written and first performed in 1599 between Shakespeare's *Henry V* and *Hamlet, Julius Caesar* occupies a transitional space between the genres of history and tragedy. Set in Julian Rome in 44 B.C., the play describes a senatorial conspiracy to murder the emperor Caesar and the political turmoil that ensues in the aftermath of the assassination. The play's two tragic figures—the slain emperor and Marcus Brutus, Caesar's close friend and the head of the conspirators—have steadily attracted the attention of critics. Many late twentieth-century scholars have continued the tradition of analyzing the motivations and ambiguities inherent in Shakespeare's dramatization of these historical personages, particularly Brutus, and studying the play's powerful and complex evocation of early Imperial Rome. Recent criticism has additionally concentrated on the work's dramaturgical qualities and its metadramatic status as a play about theater and performance. Contemporary scholars have also engaged numerous other topics, particularly focusing on varied linguistic and ideological issues in the play, including its philosophical content and its depiction of rhetoric as an influential force in manipulating human behavior, destabilizing meaning, and reflecting the vagaries of history.

Late twentieth-century emphasis on the dramaturgy of *Julius Caesar* combines a number of perspectives, including the study of explicit, internal references to the work as drama, and of Shakespeare's manipulation of his audience. Robert F. Willson, Jr. (1990) examines the metadramatic nature of the conspirators, who see themselves "as actors in a precedent-setting, historical drama." Enumerating theatrical metaphors presented during the murder, Willson calls attention to the Forum scene as a play-within-a-play that amplifies the drama's theme of passion as destroyer. Jean-Pierre Maquerlot (1995) highlights the formal ambiguities of the play, analyzing the work as a "Mannerist" drama in which Shakespeare controls audience expectations by coyly shifting their allegiances between Brutus, Caesar, and Antony. Dennis Kezar (1998) discusses Shakespeare's self-conscious use of dramatic spectacle and metadramatic irony in *Julius Caesar,* basing his observations around the play's motif of dismemberment.

Modern interpretations of character, informed to varying degrees by linguistic and psychoanalytic theory, have been consistently applied to *Julius Caesar,* resulting in ambivalent and ironic readings of Brutus, Caesar, and the other principal figures in the drama. Focusing on Brutus's attempt to disguise the brutal murder of the emperor beneath the language of ritual sacrifice, Lynn de Gerenday (1974) studies the thematic and psychological ambiguities with which the senator is depicted. Jan H. Blits (1982) offers a more traditional analysis, in which Brutus's idealized goals are thwarted by the political exigencies that arise in the power vacuum created after Caesar's death. Dennis Bathory (1996) follows a similar line, concentrating on Brutus's noble, yet futile, self-delusion as the chief cause of the conspiracy's failure to reinvigorate the republican ideals of Rome. James C. Bulman (1985) describes Shakespeare's deflation of heroic conventions as they are ironically applied to Caesar, Brutus, and Antony. Cynthia Marshall (1994) invokes poststructuralist theory in examining the destabilized historical identities of the female characters of the drama, Portia and Calphurnia.

Many critics are also interested in the play's ideological issues and philosophical content. Maynard Mack (1981) sees *Julius Caesar* as decidedly modern in its historical outlook, featuring a theory of history as an irrational process that exists beyond the influence of human reason or of individualized intentions. James Howe (1994) further comments on the broad ideological framework of the drama by noting its affinities to the Buddhist conception of a ceaseless cycle of worldly suffering that can only be overcome by unlimited compassion. Probing more concrete philosophical elements in the drama, Stephen M. Buhler (1996) regards the Epicurean skepticism of Cassius in *Julius Caesar* as it illustrates the play's concern with political materialism. Günter Walch (1989) explores Shakespeare's dramatization of discursive oppositions, such as that between republican freedom and tyrannical authority, in the work. Highlighting the significant focus on rhetoric in the play, Norman Nathan (see Further Reading) analyzes Brutus's frequently neglected funeral oration to Caesar, while John W. Velz (1982) considers the importance of Caesar's commanding rhetoric and the tumultuous effects of Brutus's and Antony's public orations on the course of Roman history.

OVERVIEWS AND GENERAL STUDIES

Maynard Mack (essay date 1981)

SOURCE: "The Modernity of *Julius Caesar,*" in *Everybody's Shakespeare: Reflections Chiefly on the Tragedies,* University of Nebraska Press, 1993, pp. 91-106.

[*In the following essay, originally published in 1981, Mack concentrates on the modern view of history presented in* Julius Caesar—*a conception of history as a process guided principally by nonrational forces rather than by reason, idealism, or conscious human influence.*]

1

In a tribute composed to introduce the collection of plays that we now call the *First Folio,* Shakespeare's fellow playwright Ben Jonson spoke of his colleague's works as not of an age but for all time. Though the compliment was something of a commonplace in Renaissance funerary rhetoric, it has proved to be remarkably clairvoyant, at least up to the present hour. And of no play, perhaps, has the continuing relevance been more striking than that of *Julius Caesar,* which again and again twentieth-century directors and producers have successfully presented as a parable for our days.

Among the many aspects of the play that contribute to its modernity, one in particular, to my mind, stands out, and it is to this exclusively, leaving out much, that I want to call attention here. The place to begin is the second scene.

We have just learned from scene I of Caesar's return in triumph from warring on Pompey's sons. We have seen the warm though fickle adulation of the crowd and the apprehension of the tribunes. Now we are to see the great man himself. The procession enters to triumphal music; with hubbub of a great press of people; with young men stripped for the ceremonial races, among them Antony; with statesmen in their togas: Decius, Cicero, Brutus, Cassius, Casca; with the two wives Calphurnia and Portia; and, in the lead, for not even Calphurnia is permitted at his side, the great man. As he starts to speak, an expectant hush settles over the gathering. What does the great man have on his mind?

> CAESAR: Calphurnia.
> CASCA: Peace, ho! Caesar speaks.
> CAESAR: Calphurnia.
> CALPHURNIA: Here, my lord.
> CAESAR: Stand you directly in Antonius' way
> When he doth run his course. Antonius.
> ANTONY: Caesar, my lord?
> CAESAR: Forget not in your speed, Antonius,
> To touch Calphurnia; for our elders say,
> The barren, touched in this holy chase,
> Shake off their sterile curse.
> ANTONY: I shall remember.
> When Caesar says, "Do this," it is performed.
>
> (1.2.1)

What the great man had on his mind, it appears, was to remind his wife, in this public place, that she is sterile; that there is an old tradition about how sterility can be removed; and that while of course he is much too sophisticated to accept such a superstition himself—it is "our elders" who say it—still, Calphurnia had jolly well better get out there and get tagged!

Then the procession takes up again. The hubbub is resumed, but once more an expectant silence settles as a voice is heard.

> SOOTHSAYER: Caesar!
> CAESAR: Ha! Who calls?
> CASCA: Bid every noise be still. Peace yet again!
> CAESAR: Who is it in the press that calls on me?
> I hear a tongue shriller than all the music
> Cry "Caesar!" Speak. Caesar is turned to hear.
> SOOTHSAYER: Beware the ides of March.
> CAESAR: What man is that?
> BRUTUS: A soothsayer bids you beware the ides of March.
> CAESAR: Set him before me; let me see his face.
> CASSIUS: Fellow, come from the throng; look upon Caesar.
> CAESAR: What say'st thou to me now? Speak once again.
> SOOTHSAYER: Beware the ides of March.
> CAESAR: He is a dreamer. Let us leave him. Pass.
>
> (1.2.13)

It is easy to see from even these small instances, I think, how a first-rate dramatic imagination works. There is no hint of any procession in Plutarch, Shakespeare's source. "Caesar," says Plutarch, "*sat* to behold."[1] There is no mention of Calphurnia in Plutarch's account of the Lupercalian race, and there is no mention anywhere of her sterility. Shakespeare, in nine lines, has given us an unforgettable picture of a man who would like to be emperor, pathetically concerned that he lacks an heir, and determined, even at the cost of making his wife a public spectacle, to establish that this is owing to no lack of virility in him. The first episode thus dramatizes instantaneously what I take to be the oncoming theme of the play: that a man's will is not enough; that there are other matters to be reckoned with, like the infertility of one's wife, or one's own affliction of the falling sickness that spoils everything one hoped for just at the instant when one had it almost in one's hand. Brutus will be obliged to learn this lesson too.

In the second episode the theme develops. We see again the uneasy rationalism that everybody in this play affects; we hear it reverberate in the faint contempt—almost a challenge—of Brutus's words as he turns to Caesar: "A soothsayer bids you beware the ides of March." Yet underneath, in the soothsayer's quiet defiance as he refuses to quail under Caesar's imperious gaze, and in his soberly reiterated warning, Shakespeare allows us to catch a hint of something else, something far more primitive and mysterious, from which rationalism in this play keeps trying vainly to cut itself away: "He is a dreamer. Let us leave him. Pass." Only we in the audience are in a position to see that the dreamer has foretold the path down which all these reasoners will go to their fatal encounter at the Capitol.

Meantime, in these same two episodes, we have learned something about the character of Caesar. In the first, it was the Caesar of human frailties who spoke to us, the husband with his hopeful superstition. In the second, it was the marble superman of state, impassive, impervious, speaking of himself in the third person: "Speak! Caesar is turned to hear." He even has the soothsayer brought before his face to repeat the message, as if the thought that somehow, in awe of the marble presence, the message would falter and dissolve: how can a superman need to beware the ides of March?

We hardly have time to do more than glimpse here a man of divided selves, then he is gone. But in his absence, the words of Cassius confirm our glimpse. Cassius's description of him exhibits the same duality that we had noticed earlier. On the one hand, an extremely ordinary man whose stamina in the swimming match was soon exhausted; who, when he had a fever once in Spain, shook and groaned like a sick girl; who even now, as we soon learn, is falling down with epilepsy in the market place. On the other hand, a being who has somehow become a god, who "bears the palm alone," who "bestrides the narrow world Like a colossus" (1.2.135). When the procession returns, no longer festive but angry, tense, there is the same effect once more. Our one Caesar shows a normal man's suspicion of his enemies, voices some shrewd human observations about Cassius, says to Antony, "Come on my right hand, for this ear is deaf" (1.2.213). Our other Caesar says, as if he were suddenly reminded of something he had forgotten, "I rather tell thee what is to be feared Than what I fear, for always I am Caesar" (1.2.211).

Wherever Caesar appears hereafter, we shall find this distinctive division in him, and nowhere more so than in the scene in which he receives the conspirators at his house. Some aspects of this scene seem calculated for nothing other than to fix upon our minds the superman conception, the Big Brother of Orwell's *1984,* the great resonant name echoing down the halls of time. Thus at the beginning of the scene:

> The things that threatened me
> Ne'er looked but on my back. When they shall see
> The face of Caesar, they are vanishèd.
>
> (2.2.10)

And again later:

> Danger knows full well
> That Caesar is more dangerous than he.
> We are two lions littered in one day,
> And I the elder and more terrible.
>
> (2.2.44)

And again still later: "Shall Caesar send a lie?" (2.2.65). And again: "The cause is in my will: I will not come." (2.2.71)

Other aspects of this scene, including his concern about Calphurnia's dream, his vacillation about going to the senate house, his anxiety about the portents of the night, plainly mark out his human weaknesses. Finally, as is the habit in this Rome, he puts the irrational from him that his wife's intuitions and her dream embody; he accepts the rationalization of the irrational that Decius skillfully manufactures, and, as earlier at the Lupercalia, hides from himself his own vivid sense of forces that lie beyond the will's control by attributing it to her:

> How foolish do your fears seem now, Calphurnia!
> I am ashamèd I did yield to them.
> Give me my robe, for I will go.
>
> (2.2.105)

2

So far we have looked at Caesar, the title personage of the play and its historical center. It is time now to consider Brutus, the play's tragic center, whom we also find to be a divided man—"poor Brutus," to use his own phrase, "with himself at war" (1.2.46). That war, we realize as the scene progresses, is a conflict between a quiet, essentially domestic and loving nature, and a powerful integrity expressing itself in a sense of honorable duty to the commonweal. This duality is what Cassius probes in his long disquisition about the mirror. The Brutus looking into the glass that Cassius figuratively holds up to him, the Brutus of this moment, now, in Rome, is a grave studious private man, of a wonderfully gentle temper as we shall see again and again later on; very slow to passion, as Cassius's ill-concealed disappointment in having failed to kindle him to an immediate response reveals; a man whose sensitive nature recoils at the hint of violence lurking in some of Cassius's speeches, just as he has already recoiled at going with Caesar to the market place, to witness the mass hysteria of clapping hands, sweaty nightcaps, and stinking breath. This is the present self that looks into Cassius's mirror.

The image that looks back out, that Cassius wants him to see, the potential other Brutus, is the man of public spirit, worried already by his uncertainty about Caesar's intentions, lineal descendant of an earlier Brutus who drove a would-be monarch from the city, a republican whose body is visibly stiffening in our sight at each huzza from the Forum, and whose anxiety, though he makes no reply to Cassius's inflammatory language, keeps bursting to the surface: "What means this shouting? I do fear the people Choose Caesar for their king" (1.2.79). The problem at the tragic center of the play, we begin to sense, is the tug of private versus public, the individual versus a world he never made, any citizen anywhere versus the selective service greetings that history is always mailing out to each of us. And this problem is to be traversed by the other tug this scene presents, between the irrational and the rational, the destiny we imagine we can control and the destiny that sweeps all before it.

Through 1.2, Brutus's patriotic self, the self that responds to these selective service greetings, is no more than a reflection in a mirror, a mere anxiety in his own brain, about which he refuses to confide, even to Cassius. In 2.1, we see the public self making further headway. First, there is Brutus's argument with himself about the threat of Caesar, and in his conclusion that Caesar must be killed we note how far his private self—he is, after all, one of Caesar's closest friends—has been invaded by the self of public spirit. From here on, the course of the invasion accelerates. A letter comes, tossed from the public world into the private world, into Brutus's garden, addressing, as Cassius had, the patriot image reflected in the mirror: "Brutus, thou sleep'st. Awake, and see thyself!" (2.1.46). Then follows the well-known brief soliloquy (which Shakespeare was to expand into the whole play of *Macbeth*), showing us that Brutus's mind has moved on from the phase of decision to the inquietudes that follow decision:

> Between the acting of a dreadful thing
> And the first motion, all the interim is
> Like a phantasma, or a hideous dream.
>
> (2.1.63)

Brutus anticipates here the dreamlike mood and motion with which Macbeth moves to the murder of Duncan. What is important to observe, however, is that these lines again stress the gulf that separates motive from action, that which is interior in man and controllable by his will from that which, once acted, becomes independent of him and moves with a life of its own. This gulf is a no man's land, a phantasma, a hideous dream.

Finally, there arrives in such a form that no audience can miss it the actual visible invasion itself, as this peaceful garden-quiet is intruded on by knocking, like the knocking of fate in Beethoven's Fifth Symphony, and by men with faces hidden in their cloaks. Following this, a lovely interlude with Portia serves to emphasize how much the private self, the private world, has been shattered. There is something close to discord here—as much of a discord as these gentle people are capable of—and though there is a reconciliation at the end and Brutus's promise to confide in her soon, this division in the family is an omen. So is the knock of the latecomer, Caius Ligarius, which reminds us once again of the exactions of the public life. And when Ligarius throws off his sick man's kerchief on learning that there is an honorable exploit afoot, we may see in it an epitome of the whole scene, a graphic visible renunciation, like Brutus's (or like Prince Hal's at about the same time in Shakespeare's career) of the private good to the public; and we may see this also in Brutus's own exit a few lines later, not into the inner house where Portia waits for him, but out into the thunder and lightning of the public life of Rome. It is not without significance that at our final glimpse of Portia, two scenes later, she too stands outside the privacy of the house, her mind wholly occupied with thoughts of what is happening at the Capitol, trying to put on a public self for Brutus's sake: "Run, Lucius, and commend me to my lord; Say I am merry . . ." (2.4.44).

3

Meantime, at the Capitol, the tragic center and the historical center meet. The suspense is very great as Caesar, seeing the Soothsayer in the throng, reminds him that the ides of March are come, and receives in answer, "Ay, Caesar, but not gone" (3.1.2). More suspense is generated as Artemidorus presses forward with the paper that we know contains a full discovery of the plot. Decius, apprehensive, steps quickly into the breach with another paper, a petition from Trebonius. More suspense still as Popilius sidles past Cassius with the whisper, "I wish your enterprise today may thrive" (3.1.13), and then moves on to Caesar's side, where he engages him in animated talk. But they detect no tell-tale change in Caesar's countenance; Trebonius steps into his assignment and takes Antony aside; Metellus Cimber throws himself at Caesar's feet; Brutus gives the signal to "Press near and second him" (3.1.29), and Caesar's "Are we all ready?" (3.1.31) draws every eye to Caesar's chair. One by one they all kneel before this demigod—an effective tableau which gives a coloring of priest-like ritual to what they are about to do. Caesar is to bleed, but, as Brutus has said, they will sublimate the act into a sacrifice:

> Let's kill him boldly but not wrathfully;
> Let's carve him as a dish fit for the gods,
> Not hew him as a carcass fit for hounds.
>
> (2.1.172)

In performance, everything in the scene will reflect this ceremonial attitude to emphasize the almost fatuous cleavage between the spirit of the enterprise and its bloody result.

The Caesar we are permitted to see as all this ceremony is preparing will be almost entirely the superman, for obvious reasons. To give a color of justice to Brutus's act, even if we happen to think the assassination a mistake as many members of an Elizabethan audience emphatically would, Caesar must be seen in a mood of super-humanity at least as fatuous as the conspirators' mood of sacrifice. Hence Shakespeare makes him first of all insult Metellus Cimber: "If thou dost bend and pray and fawn for him, I spurn thee like a cur" (3.1.45), and then comment with intolerable pomposity—in fact, blasphemy—on his own iron resolution, which he alleges to be immovable even by prayer and thus superior to the very gods. Finally, Shakespeare puts into his mouth one of those supreme arrogances that can hardly fail to remind us of the ancient adage "Whom the gods would destroy they first make mad." "Hence!" Caesar cries, "Wilt thou lift up Olympus?" (3.1.74). It is at just this point, when the colossus Caesar drunk with self-importance is before us, that Casca strikes. Then they all strike, with a last blow that brings out for the final time the other, human side of this double Caesar: "*Et tu, Brute?*" (3.1.77).

And now this little group of men has altered history. The representative of the evil direction it was taking toward autocratic power lies dead before them. The direction to which it must be restored becomes emphatic in Cassius's cry of "Liberty, freedom, and enfranchisement!" (3.1.81). Solemnly, and again like priests who have just sacrificed a victim, they kneel together and bathe their hands and swords in Caesar's blood. Brutus exclaims:

> Then walk we forth, even to the market place,
> And waving our red weapons o'er our heads,
> Let's all cry, "Peace, freedom, and liberty!"
>
> (3.1.108)

If the conjunction of those red hands and weapons with this slogan is not enough to give an audience a start, the next passage will; for now the conspirators explicitly invoke the judgment of history on their deed. On the stages of theaters the world over, so they anticipate, this lofty incident will be re-enacted, and

> So oft as that shall be,
> So often shall the knot of us be called
> The men that gave their country liberty.
>
> (3.1.116)

We in the audience, recalling what actually did result in Rome—the civil wars, the long line of despotic emperors—cannot miss the irony of their prediction, an irony that insists on our recognizing that this effort to control the consequences of an act is doomed to fail. (It is a theme that Shakespeare will touch again in *Macbeth* and *Lear.*) Why does it fail?

One reason why is shown us in the next few moments. The leader of this assault on history, like many another reformer, is a man of high idealism, who devoutly believes that the rest of the world is like himself. It was just to kill Caesar—so he persuades himself—because he was a threat to freedom. It would not have been just to kill Antony, and he vetoes the idea. Even now, when the consequence of that decision has come back to face him in the shape of Antony's servant kneeling before him, he sees no reason to reconsider it. There are good grounds for what they have done, he says; Antony will hear them, and be satisfied. With Antony, who shortly arrives in person, he takes this line again:

> Our reasons are so full of good regard
> That were you, Antony, the son of Caesar
> You should be satisfied.
>
> (3.1.224)

With equal confidence in the reasonableness of human nature, he puts by Cassius's fears of what Antony will do if allowed to address the people: "By your pardon; I will myself into the pulpit first And show the reason of our Caesar's death" (3.1.236). Here is a man so much a friend of Caesar's that he is still speaking of him as "our Caesar," so capable of rising to what he takes to be his duty that he has taken on the leadership of those who killed him, so trusting of common decency that he expects the populace will respond to reason, and Antony to honor the obligation laid on him by their permitting him to speak. At such a man, one hardly knows whether to laugh or cry.

The same mixture of feelings is likely to be stirring in us as Brutus speaks to the people in 3.2. As everybody knows, this is a speech in what used to be called the great liberal tradition, which assumes that men in the mass are reasonable. It has therefore been made a prose oration, spare and terse in diction, tightly patterned in syntax so that it requires close attention, and founded, with respect to its argument, on three elements: the abstract sentiment of duty to the state (because he endangered Rome, Caesar had to be slain); the abstract sentiment of political justice (because he had delusions of grandeur, Caesar deserved his fall); and the moral authority of the man Brutus.

As long as that moral authority is concretely before them in Brutus's presence, the populace is impressed. But since even trained minds do not always respond well to abstractions, they quite misunderstand the content of his argument, as one of them indicates by shouting, "Let him be Caesar!" (3.2.41). What moves them is the obvious sincerity and the known integrity of the speaker; and when he finishes, they are ready to carry him off on their shoulders on that account alone, leaving Antony a vacant Forum. The fair-mindedness of Brutus is thrilling but painful to behold as he calms this triumphal surge in his favor, urges them to stay and hear Antony, and then, in a moment very impressive dramatically as well as symbolically, walks off the stage, alone. We see then, if we have not seen before, a possible first answer to the question why the effort to take control of history failed as it so often does, blinkered by its own idealism.

4

When Antony takes the rostrum, we sense a possible second answer. It has been remarked that in a school for demagogues this speech should be the whole curriculum. Antony himself describes its method when he observes in the preceding scene, apropos of the effect of Caesar's dead body on the messenger from Octavius, "Passion, I see, is catching" (3.1.283). A statement that cannot be made about reason, as many of us learn to our cost.

Antony's speech differs from Brutus's as night from day. Brutus formulates from the outset positive propositions about Caesar and about his own motives on no other authority than his own. Because of his known integrity, Brutus can do this. Antony takes the safer alternative of concealing propositions in questions, by which the audience's mind is then guided to conclusions which seem its own:

> He hath brought many captives home to Rome,
> Whose ransoms did the general coffers fill.
> Did this in Caesar seem ambitious?
>
> (3.2.88)

> You all did see that on the Lupercal
> I thrice presented him a kingly crown,

> Which he did thrice refuse: Was this ambition?
>
> (3.2.95)

How well Shakespeare knew crowds becomes clear in the replies to Antony. Brutus, appealing to reason, is greeted with wild outbursts of emotion: "Let him be Caesar!" Antony appeals only to emotion and pocketbooks, but now they say, "Methinks there is much reason in his sayings," and chew upon it seriously.

With equal skill, Antony stirs up impulses only to thwart them. He appeals to curiosity and greed in the matter of the will, but then withholds it teasingly. In the same manner, he stirs up rage against the conspirators while pretending to dampen it (3.2.151): "I fear I wrong the honorable men Whose daggers have stabbed Caesar; I do fear it." Finally, he rests his case, not, like Brutus, on abstractions centering in the state and political justice, but on emotions centering in the individual listener. The first great crescendo of the speech, which culminates in the passage on Caesar's wounds, appeals first to pity and then to indignation. The second, culminating in the reading of Caesar's will, appeals first to curiosity and greed, then to gratitude.

His management of the will is particularly cunning: it is an item more concrete than words, an actual tantalizing document that can be flashed before the eye, as in many a modern political TV sound byte. He describes it at first vaguely, as being of such a sort that they would honor Caesar for it. Then, closer home, as something which would show "how Caesar loved you" (3.2.141). Then, with an undisguised appeal to self-interest, as a testament that will make them his "heirs." The emotions aroused by this news enable him to make a final test of his ironical refrain about "honorable men," and finding the results all that he had hoped, he can come down now among the crowd as one of them, and appeal directly to their feelings by appealing to his own: "If you have tears, prepare to shed them now" (3.2.169).

The power of this direct appeal to passion can be seen at its close. Where formerly we had a populace, now we have a mob. As a mob, its mind can be sealed against later recoveries of rationality by the insinuation that all reasoning is simply a surface covering up private grudges, like the "reason" they have heard from Brutus; whereas from Antony himself, the plain, blunt friend of Caesar, they are getting the plain, blunt truth and (a favorite trick) only what they already know.

So they are called back to hear the will. Antony no longer needs this as an incentive to riot; the mingled rage and pity he has aroused will take care of that. But, after the lynching when the hangover comes, and you are remembering how that fellow looked, swaying a little on the rope's end, with his eyes bugging out and the veins knotted at his temples, then it is good to have something really reasonable to cling to, like seventy-five drachmas (or thirty pieces of silver) and some orchards along a river.

By this point, we can fully understand that a further ground for the failure of the effort to control history is what has been left out of account—what all these Romans from the beginning, except Antony, have been trying to leave out of account: the phenomenon of feeling, one of many nonrational factors in the life of men, in the life of the world, in the processes of history itself—of which this blind infuriated mob is one kind of exemplification. Too secure in his own fancied suppression of this influence, Brutus has failed altogether to reckon with its power. Thus he could seriously say to Antony in the passage quoted earlier: Antony, even if you were "the son of Caesar You should be satisfied," as if the feeling of a son for a murdered father could ever be "satisfied" by reasons. And thus, too, urging the crowd to hear Antony, he could walk off the stage alone, the very figure of embodied "reason," unaware that only the irrational is catching.

Meantime, the scene of the mob tearing Cinna the Poet to pieces simply for having the same name as one of the conspirators (3.3) confirms the victory of unreason and gives us our first taste of the chaos invoked by Antony when he stood alone over Caesar's corpse. Now, reconsidering that prediction and this mob, we recognize a third reason why attempts to direct the course of history have usually failed. We have seen already that history is only minimally responsive to noble motives, only minimally responsive to rationality. Now we see clearly what was hinted in the beginning by those two episodes with Calphurnia and the soothsayer—that it is only minimally responsive to conscious human influence of any sort. With all their reasons, the conspirators and Caesar only carried out what the soothsayer foreknew. There is, in short—at least as this play sees it—a degree of determinism in history, whether we call it cultural, fatal, or providential, which *helps* to shape our ends, "Roughhew them how we will" (*Hamlet,* 5.2.11). One of the alternative names of that factor in this play is Caesarism, cult of the ever regenerating Will to Power. Brutus puts the point, all unconsciously, when the conspirators are gathered at his house:

> We all stand up against the spirit of Caesar,
> And in the spirit of men there is no blood.
> O that we then could come by Caesar's spirit,
> And not dismember Caesar! But, alas,
> Caesar must bleed for it.
>
> (2.1.167)

Then Caesar does bleed for it; but his spirit, as Brutus's own remark might have told him, proves invulnerable. It is simply set free by his assassination, and now, as Antony says, "ranging for revenge, . . . Shall in these confines with a monarch's voice Cry 'Havoc' and let slip the dogs of war" (3.1.270).

5

The rest of the play is self-explanatory. It is clear all through Acts 4 and 5 that Brutus and Cassius are defeated before they begin to fight. Antony knows it and says so at

5.1. Cassius knows it too. Cassius, an Epicurean in philosophy and therefore one who has never heretofore believed in omens, now mistrusts his former rationalism: he suspects there may be something after all in those ravens, crows, and kites that wheel overhead. Brutus too mistrusts *his* rationalism. As a Stoic, his philosophy requires him to repudiate suicide, but he admits to Cassius that if the need comes he will repudiate philosophy instead. This, like Cassius' statement, is an unconscious admission of the force of the non-rational in human affairs, a non-rational influence that makes its presence felt again and again during the great battle. Cassius, for instance, fails to learn in time that Octavius "Is overthrown by noble Brutus' power" (5.3.52), becomes the victim of a mistaken report of Titinius's death, runs on his sword crying, "Caesar, thou art revenged" (5.3.45), and is greeted, dead, by Brutus, in words that make still clearer their defeat by a power unforeseen: "O Julius Caesar, thou art mighty yet! Thy spirit walks abroad and turns our swords In our own proper entrails" (5.3.94). In the same vein, when it is Brutus's turn to die, we learn that the ghost of Caesar has reappeared, and he thrusts the sword home, saying, "Caesar, now be still" (5.5.50).

Among the many topics on which Shakespeare casts a cold eye in this short play—among them the nature of heroism, the toll that public life exacts, the legitimacy of power, the danger of violent change (this last especially relevant in 1599 because of the growing concern for the succession after the aging Queen should die)—the aspect that seems to me to account best for its hold on audiences in our totalitarian century of putsches, coups, and assassinations is its stress on the always ambiguous relation between humankind and history. During the first half of the play, what we are chiefly conscious of is the human will as a force in history—men making choices, controlling events. Our typical scenes are 1.2, where a man is trying to make up his mind; or 2.1, where a man first reaches a decision and then, with his fellows, lays plans to implement it; or 2.2, where we have Decius Brutus persuading Caesar to decide to go to the senate house; or 3.1 and 3.2, where up through the assassination, and even up through Antony's speech, men are still, so to speak, impinging on history, moulding it to their conscious will.

But then comes a change. Though we still have men in action trying to mould their world (or else we would have no play at all), one senses a real shift in the direction of the impact. We begin to feel the insufficiency of noble aims, for history is also consequences; the insufficiency of reason and rational expectation, for the ultimate consequences of an act in history are unpredictable, and usually, by all human standards, illogical as well; and finally, the insufficiency of the human will itself, for there is always something to be reckoned with that is nonhuman and inscrutable—Nemesis, Moira, Fortuna, the Parcae, Providence, Determinism: men have had many names for it, but it is always there. Accordingly, in the second half of the play, our typical scenes are those like 3.3, where Antony has raised something that is no longer under his control or anyone's. Or like 4.1, where we see men acting as if, under the thumb of expediency or necessity or call it what you will, they no longer had wills of their own but prick down the names of nephews and brothers indiscriminately for slaughter. Or like 4.3 and all the scenes thereafter, where we are constantly made to feel that Cassius and Brutus are in the hands of something bigger than they know.

In this light, we can see readily enough why it is that Shakespeare gives Julius Caesar a double character. The dilemma in all violence is that the human Caesar who has human ailments and is a human friend is the Caesar who can be killed. Whereas the marmoreal Caesar, the everlasting Big Brother, must repeatedly be killed but never dies because he lurks in each of us and all together. Any political system is a potential Rome, and there is no reason for the citizen of any country, when he reads or watches a production of *Julius Caesar,* to imagine that this is ancient history.

Notes

1. *Shakespeare's Plutarch,* ed. C. F. Tucker Brooke, 2 vols. (Haskell House reprint, New York, 1966), 1:92.

DRAMATURGY AND METADRAMA

Robert F. Willson, Jr. (essay date 1990)

SOURCE: "*Julius Caesar:* The Forum Scene as Historic Play-within," in *Shakespeare Yearbook,* Vol. 1, Spring, 1990, pp. 14-27.

[*In the following essay, Willson analyzes Act 3, scene 1 of* Julius Caesar*—in which Brutus and Antony give their funeral orations to Caesar—and examines Shakespeare's use of metadramatic allusions to the theater and the play's theme of 'destructive passion.'*]

That Brutus, Cassius, and the other conspirators see themselves as actors in a precedent-setting, historical drama is revealed in Cassius' exclamation following the assassination:

> How many ages hence
> Shall this our lofty scene be acted over
> In states unborn and accents yet unknown.
>
> (3.1.111-3)[1]

To amplify Cassius' prophetic claim, Brutus echoes the sentiment in a characteristically philosophical observation:

> How many times shall Caesar bleed in sport,
> That now on Pompey's basis lies along
> No worthier than the dust!
>
> (114-6)[2]

Such theatrical metaphors are of course common to Shakespearean tragic poetry. Hamlet affirms his "motive and . . . cue for passion" by adapting a play to sting his uncle's conscience. Lear speaks of "this great stage of fools" onto which crying infants are ushered at their birth. Macbeth compares his Herod's role to that of a "poor player" uttering an hour's worth of bombast, then disappearing forever. And Cleopatra, like Cassius glimpsing the future, shrinks from the vision of "Some squeaking Cleopatra who will boy my greatness / I' th' posture of a whore."

These reflexive references to the world as stage are so numerous in the canon that they are generally regarded as commonplaces.[3] Yet such allusions often serve as essential guides to reading the significance of pivotal scenes in major plays. We quickly grasp the clue that Hamlet's mousetrap, for instance, reveals as much about the hero's inability to distinguish between reality and illusion as it does about Claudius' guilt. Obsessed with the moral impact of *Gonzago* on Claudius (and, lest we forget, on Gertrude), Hamlet dispels the theatrical vision by directing Lucianus to speak his lines and stop making "damnable faces" (3.2.253). This overmanaging of the actors by Hamlet exposes his uncontrollable impulse to force his uncle's confession—and Gertrude's conversion. (The God-playing syndrome is further revealed in his prayer-scene decision not to send Claudius' apparently repentant soul to hell.) During the play-within, moreover, the prompting of Lucianus, nephew to the king, signifies Hamlet's desire to "prompt" action by a created image of himself. His threats are Lucianus', yet they are empty without attendant action. Hamlet's inability to distinguish between the actor's art and real-world performance becomes the quicksand of inaction into which he sinks ever deeper. This reading of the play-within's function suggests that Shakespeare may have had in mind more than just a convenient poetic lexicon when he employed theatrical allusion.[4] We comprehend Hamlet's state of mind through terminology that places him in a staged or performed "life."

Shakespeare also employs the theatrical metaphor as a means of representing Macbeth's ambitious career. By killing Duncan and seizing the crown, the thane succeeds in usurping a king's role. But what Shakespeare clarifies through subsequent events (i.e., the murder of Banquo; of Lady Macduff and her children) is that this performer has degenerated into a "poor player," a common Elizabethan label for inept actor. His ineptitude—a term that carries both professional and moral significance—is dramatized in the banquet scene (3.4), where Macbeth's fear-inspired ranting parallels histrionic excess. (As Emrys Jones sees it, Banquo's appearance has caused Macbeth to behave like an actor unable to recall his lines.[5]) The hurried departure of the Scottish lords can be likened to the embarrassed escape of an audience no longer willing to tolerate this bombastic amateur. When Macbeth later characterizes himself as just such a failure, he stresses the briefness of his "stage" career, his departure for oblivion. Without an heir to succeed him, Macbeth cannot even console himself with the thought of lineal immortality. This cutting-off can likewise be appreciated with reference to playhouse practice: As an unsuccessful player, he cannot expect to have even an apprentice take his place.

The preeminence of the world-as-stage metaphor in creating a context for interpreting prominent sequences in Shakespeare's tragedies gives readers a useful decoding language. We can reasonably assume, for instance, that Shakespeare, like many of his contemporaries, recognized how successful politicians fashioned public roles which enhanced their ability to lead. This is not to say that he readily applauded histrionic talent without the stuff of character necessary to its legitimate use—in monarchs or actors, one might say. Richard Gloucester's pious impersonation (3.7), so energetically stage-managed by Buckingham, demonstrates that acting has its despotic, demonic side as well. It is the Thespian *and* Satanic art. Richard's appearance, "aloft, between two bishops," serves only as a disguise, not as a true representation of the Christian prince. We witness the apparently monkish Richard refusing to assume the yoke of worldly power, characterizing himself as unfit for the part:

> Yet so much is my poverty of spirit,
> So mighty and so many my defects,
> That I would rather hide me from my greatness—
>
> (159-61)

This poor player speaks truer than he knows, as Shakespeare ironically exposes the pretender's nature in the language of rehearsal. When the citizens-as-audience threaten to undertake violent steps to keep the "illegitimate" princes from the throne, Richard relents and agrees to

> . . . buckle Fortune on my back,
> To bear her burthen, whe'er I will or no,
> I must have patience to endure the load;
>
> (228-30)

The allusion to Hercules underscores Richard's claim that the world is about to be dropped on his shoulders. However, the vision of a hunchback so burdened undercuts Richard's assumed heroic identity, transforming the godlike image into a seriocomic one. Buckingham and Richard's power play becomes an afterpiece, a parody of the coronation ritual.[6]

By contrast Prince Hal proves highly skilled as an actor, one seasoned in the art of fitting the role to the occasion. In *1 Henry IV,* the impromptu tavern-house play-within starring Falstaff and Hal (2.4.376ff.) demonstrates the hero's knack for both assuming his father's identity (thus foreshadowing his ready assumption of the crown) and using the interlude as a means of moral instruction. On the other hand, Falstaff shows himself woefully unable to jettison his monstrous ego in taking on either the princely or kingly part. What starts as a playful, time-wasting game for fat Jack grows into a serious morality play in which his fate is sealed. Abruptly ending the scene in his guise as player-king, Hal, in answer to his "son's" plea not to banish him, declares "I do, I will." This chilling period closes the performance and allows us to see that Hal clearly perceives the distinction between counterfeiting and true action.

Later, in *Henry V*, Hal's public and private performances—the tennis ball episode, the outwitting and arrest of Cambridge, Grey, and Scroop—reveal his awareness of the value of decorous acting in the consolidating and exercising of power. The political and personal identities (see the doctrine of the king's two bodies) meet as one in him, a ruler without rival on the imperial stage. If Richard is all show, obliterating the monarch's spiritual body, Hal epitomizes the happy union of show and substance, of the illusionary and real. In Hamlet's words, he suits "the action to the word, the word to the action" and does not "o'erstep . . . the modesty of nature." Richard ends ranting in "King Cambyses' vein."

1

With these theatrical or stage-as-world guides in mind, we turn to the assassination and Forum scenes in *Julius Caesar* equipped to understand the characters and events in terms that are central to Shakespeare's political theme. That is, the "lofty scene" described by Cassius changed the course of history and thereby influenced the lives of Shakespeare and his contemporaries. We need only remember the Elizabethans' ancestral identification with Rome through the legend of Britain's founding by Brutus, great-grandson of Aeneas. On the world stage, moreover, the assassination of Julius Caesar deserved the title of tragedy—and so the playwright dubbed it—through association with the murder of Jesus Christ. That such blows against God should be acted over in succeeding ages demonstrates how imperfectly their lessons (about social and political disruption) have been learned. Thus to return to the event is to take up old material, "a moldy tale," and once again rehearse its meaning, grapple with its complexities. Whether Shakespeare's additional motive was to warn his contemporaries about the danger of popular rebellion or to present the case for republicanism can never be finally known.[7] But by evaluating the assassination and Forum scenes from the perspective of theatrical metaphor, we may better appreciate the playwright's habit of interpreting events and characters by employing familiar analogues from his and the audience's playhouse experience.[8]

What strikes one immediately in assessing the dynamics of the conspiracy is the parallel between this group of plotters and a company of actors—even "sharers," if one adopts the language of the profession. If indeed these men are actors of a "lofty scene," it is probable that Shakespeare invites us to compare them to a cry of players. The term "sharers" takes on even greater weight if we think of its professional connotation: All the "actors" are presumed to be "full adventurers" in the enterprise of assassination.[9] And while the conspirators appear to number no more than seven or eight, they could be said to approximate the size of a company of fellows.[10] These men appeal to Brutus (at Cassius' urging) to lead them in their scheme to rid Rome of its despot, regarding him as chief actor and manager of the enterprise. Given this analogue, we in the audience might well be inclined to judge Brutus' skill at both playing and managing in the company's behalf.

In this connection, we are given some early clues that Brutus is wanting. He must be persuaded by Cassius and the others that he is capable of performing the lead part. When the conspirators meet for rehearsal, moreover, Brutus refuses to allow the swearing of an oath, by which the company would have become incorporated:

> No, not an oath! If not the face of men,
> The sufferance of our souls, the time's abuse—
> If these be motives weak, break off betimes,
> So let high-sighted tyranny rage on,
> Till each man drop by lottery.
>
> (2.1.114-9)

Such bold defiance of convention sounds noble, but it fails to recognize the vital importance of—and the word is critical here—incorporating the plotters. Without such a bond, each man would then be free to choose his own course following the performance of their historic interlude. Just as the players must swear an oath to undertake the business of the company, so must the conspirator-actors agree to share equally the profit and expense of their deed.[11] By failing to secure such an oath, as well as refusing to kill Antony with Caesar, Brutus shows himself ill-equipped to lead the company. Even though he later invites the assassins to bathe their hands in Casesar's blood (3.1.105-10), Brutus fails to comprehend that this outward badge of unity means nothing without the bond of an oath. Indeed, so attired the actors do appear as the bloody butchers of "a savage spectacle" to the waiting audience of citizens.

Though he aspires to act out his philosophical beliefs, then, Brutus emerges from the assassination scene a poor player. To further reinforce this impression, Shakespeare has him agree to allow Antony to deliver the eulogy over fallen Caesar. He assents despite the wise prompting of Cassius:

> [*Aside to Brutus*] You know not what you do. Do not
> consent
> That Antony speak in his funeral.
> Know you how much the people may be mov'd
> By that which he will utter.
>
> (3.1.232-5)

Brutus here is the actor who must be reminded of his proper role by a stage manager aware of the whole plot and the rhetorical power of another actor.

So Antony, at least in Cassius' eyes, qualifies as an interloper, an outsider who because of his recognized loyalty to Caesar threatens the unity of the group. But

Shakespeare may have intended a more particularized identity for Antony, one related to the acting troupe analogue. He could be regarded as the hired man brought in by Brutus for a special production.[12] This analogue helps us to fully comprehend the significance of the coup Antony effects. Not a member of the company of sharers, he is engaged to perform a minor role; in the Forum scene, however, Antony usurps the central role—which Brutus intended to play—in the historical drama. Cassius senses the danger, but Brutus assures him that the citizens will believe him when he declares that Antony speaks only by their permission: "It shall advantage more than do us wrong." A key to successful performing (as the playwright knew) is gauging the reaction of one's audience, something Brutus lacks the insight to do.

Had Antony been invited to join the conspiracy in its early stages, his state of mind and behavior might have been different (though Shakespeare affords no evidence that he possessed the motive or intellectual capacity to bring about the fall of the tyrant). Had he been murdered with Caesar, the plotters could then have used the occasion of their deaths to characterize Antony and Casesar as equally ambitious. But by giving him a role in the upcoming ceremonial interlude, Brutus has made possible the transformation of the scene from solemn funeral to outraged revolt, of the kind we witness in *2 Henry VI.* The actor who leads this rebellion proves to be one who, in Hamlet's words, "out-herods Herod":

> Blood and destruction shall be so in use,
> And dreadful objects so familiar,
> That mothers shall but smile when they behold
> Their infants quartered with the hands of war.
>
> (265-8)

This ranting vow is delivered over the body of dead Caesar; on the Forum stage, Antony seeks to "Suit the action to the word, the word to the action."

With Antony's assurance to Caesar's spirit that he will prove an apt instrument of revenge (see Hamlet's promise to his father's spirit), our attention is directed to the public play about to be performed and away from the murder itself. Indeed, Shakespeare depicts the assassination as something of a backstage event. True, we have witnessed the butchery, experienced the horror of the bloody spectacle. Yet the characters of Brutus and Cassius have preoccupied us from the beginning. In reality, Caesar dead emerges as a more significant force than Caesar alive.[13] So the assassination per se might be described as a kind of rehearsal, the true tragedy—Rome's dislocation?—waiting to be played out before the populace. Act Three, scene two depicts events that determine the course of the rebellion, the fate of those republican ideals Brutus holds so dear. Given Antony's "private" eulogy in 3.1, especially his "Woe to the hand that shed this costly blood!," we are led to expect not a funeral rite but a revenge tragedy.

2

When that play begins, Brutus seems to arrest the plebeians' full attention. Yet he commences the ceremony by dividing the company, sending Cassius with a group of citizens to whom he will explain the meaning of their act. That this too is an unwise decision is later confirmed when Brutus chooses to leave the stage while Antony speaks. For the moment, however, he appears to be in control. Spoken in prose, Brutus' explanation affirms his noble motive, his love of Rome and freedom. The best skills of an academic rhetorician are here exhibited: parallelism ("As Caesar lov'd me, I weep for him; as he was fortunate, I rejoice at it"); antithesis ("Not that I lov'd Caesar less, but that I lov'd Rome more"); repetition ("Believe me for mine honor, and have respect to mine honor, that you may believe"); and the inevitable rhetorical question ("Who is here so base that he would be a bondman?"). There is even an artful pause while Brutus waits for those who are offended to accuse him: "None, Brutus, none." With this reply the self-confident speaker concludes that all is settled and that the murder has been duly justified.

But what we recognize and the plebeians seem to sense is that Brutus' speech, especially its artful structure and reasoned tone, suits better the ears of Senators than those of rude mechanicals. Rendered in dispassionate prose, the justification exposes the speaker's blindness to the reality of human emotion. He does not touch their hearts but is satisfied instead that he has lectured to them on the consequences of ambition. Thus Brutus demonstrates beyond doubt that his proper forum is the hall, not the public stage. Antony entering with Caesar's gashed body in his arms need not speak a word to begin eroding the foundation of Brutus' argument.

Yet when Brutus leaves the Forum, he is acclaimed the new Caesar, an irony that the naive conspirator appears not to discern. While he has acted to save the people from bondage, they respond by urging the kingly part on him. How ignorant he is of the motives of those he seeks to serve! And his departure from the stage at this critical point highlights yet another irony, this one recalling the theatrical analogue. Brutus believes he has spoken the crucial lines of the scene, leaving Antony to perform the simple elegaic rite of burying Caesar. We realize instead that Brutus has delivered only the prologue or chorus and is unaware that he merely prepares the way for the main action and actor, who is now free to speak his vengeful mind without prompting. The change of role from Caesar's successor to prologue-speaker underscores how ill-suited Brutus is to perform the public show necessary to the consolidation of power.

On the other hand, Antony exhibits a gift for playing that stirs his hearers to sudden, violent action. He uses the same rhetorical tools as Brutus, but he makes heavier use of repetition and personal reminiscence (see especially "You all did see that on Lupercal . . . ," 95-7) than did his rival. He repeats two words—"honorable" and "ambitious"—so adeptly that he soon has his audience wondering whether Caesar or Brutus was truly ambitious. More calculatingly, Antony employs a pun to register a shocking picture of the horrible deed in his audience's mind: "O judgment! thou [art] fled to brutish beasts." Now the conspirators are no longer honorable men but destructive animals, a transformation achieved solely by Antony's trenchant poetic art. Like Brutus, Antony also pauses, but not to hear an answer to his rhetorical question. *His* pause is dramatic, an opportunity to choke back tears while his words sink in (105-7). During this pause one of the hearers (*2 Pleb.*) delivers possibly the baldest understatement in the canon: "If thou consider rightly the matter, Caesar has had great wrong."

Thus aroused, the audience stands ready to change its mind about Caesar and the assassination.[14] Antony need only produce the will, an ideal actor/politician's prop, to win the plebeians utterly to his side. But before he will consent to read it (here he reminds us of Richard Gloucester or Iago in his gesture of calculated restraint), Antony descends from the pulpit with the body in his arms. This masterstroke takes our breath away, but it also breaks the imaginary plane between stage and audience. Antony joins the mechanicals as if he were one of them and not a player in the historical drama. More important, as the plebeians make a ring around him and the body, Antony succeeds in creating another stage, with victim and revenger at its center. Now he retells the tragedy of the assassination, pointing to the wounds and identifying the conspirators who made them. Brutus' "most unkindest cut" recalls the "brutish beasts" pun of his earlier remarks and reinforces the moral that in striking down Caesar, Brutus has murdered his own father. Beside pointing to the unnaturalness of such a deed, Antony reminds his auditors that Caesar's fall was theirs: "Then I, and you, and all of us fell down, / Whilst bloody treason flourished over us" (191-2). How vividly this statement echoes Brutus' earlier claim that he was forced to act for fear of tyranny pressing down the citizenry! Shakespeare's irony here intimates that both men embrace their own selfish or sophistic motives for acting, ignoring all the while the good of Rome.

But Antony's inspired touch of scene-painting—traitors covered with innocent blood—confirms his ingenuity as an actor and poet. He has won the audience to his cause in a *coup de théâtre* that blatantly violates the end of playing. Witnesses of a tragedy should leave the playhouse purged of their emotions; instead these hearers are roused to destructive fury by Antony's words. By further associating Caesar's fate with Pompey's—"Even at the base of Pompey's statue / (Which all the while ran blood) great Caesar fell"—Antony seems to justify the citizens' lust for revenge, chronicling the act of treachery as if it were part of a Fall of Princes interlude. The mantle and wounds are assigned choric identities, moreover; they are voices crying against the inhumanity and unnaturalness of the sacrifice. Antony remembers that Caesar first wore the mantle on the day he overcame the Nervii, a tribe renowned for *its* pagan fierceness. The implied comparison between the barbarous Nervii and the assassins is obvious. But Antony's anecdote also underscores his resourcefulness: How did he manage to dredge up such an apparently trivial detail? Had he in fact been waiting for just such a moment to spring this memory on unsuspecting ears? Similarly, his opportunism prompts him to catalogue the wounds made by each conspirator, even though he was not a witness to the killing. How can he or we be sure of these attributions? The question goes unasked and unanswered, of course, because the citizens have been trapped in the web of deep-seated emotion aroused by the speaker. Each rent in the robe qualifies as a piece of evidence of the conspirators' cruelty.

At just the right moment, Antony pulls off the mangled robe (196) to reveal the "marred" body of Caesar himself. While Brutus had represented this event as a funeral, the somber interring of their dead leader's bones, Antony seizes the occasion (as Richard did the funeral of Henry VI) to transform the ceremony into a trial. The body, uncovered and gory, issues as the main piece of evidence in that trial of "honorable" men. (Surely Shakespeare wants *his* audience to associate Caesar's murder with the sacrifice of Christ, whose savaged body revealed the extent of barbarous destructiveness.[15]) When the First Plebeian exclaims "O piteous spectacle!" we recognize that Antony has succeeded brilliantly in creating his play-within-the-play by concurrently exceeding the bounds of art. Shakespeare's playhouse audience's attitude toward him should be shifting—away from admiration toward suspicion—with the increasing hyperbole of his words and actions. Not Caesar's but his own cause motivates him now.

This suspicion of Antony's motives is further confirmed with his disclaimer of oratorical or histrionic powers of speech (210-30). He only speaks "right on," assuring all that he lacks the persuasive skills of Brutus. By now this claim is as hollow and ironic as his affirmation that all the conspirators are "honorable men." (We likewise suspect none of the ingenuousness that attends remarks about his "rude speech" by Othello.) In place of his ill-trained speech, Caesar's wounds have mouths to rouse Romans to mutiny. This corporeal allusion refocuses the citizens' eyes on the body; their immediate reaction is to seek out Brutus' house and burn it down. The wheel has turned suddenly and decisively, and Antony assumes the central role once reserved for Brutus. It is now "most noble Antony!" whom the plebeians urge one another to heed.

As the crowning achievement of his performance Antony once again reminds the citizens of Caesar's will. This prop, like Caesar's muffled body, arrests the hearers' attention, even though it too seems suspiciously like a sham. Such a document is cited by Plutarch, but Shakespeare introduces it at a time convenient to Antony's political purposes. By possessing it he substantiates his claim of being Caesar's successor, the executor of his will. Knowing as well that nothing can stop the mob from trampling Caesar's "private arbors, and newplanted orchards," Antony simply lends legal status to civil disobedience. Caesar's will has become the will of the people, a dangerous principle for the state to condone. But Antony too now holds the script of events in his hands, symbolizing his possession of rule. The actor and avenging prince have merged in one identity, a reality confirmed by Antony's *ubi sunt*-like question: "When comes such another?" As the auditors spill out from the Forum stage into the Roman streets, Ambition and Revenge assume the mantle of leadership.

3

To underscore the representation of the Forum scene as play-within on the theme of destructive passion, Shakespeare creates an after-piece or *coda* depicting the murder of Cinna the poet. The aroused mob ignores this victim's disclaimer that he is not a conspirator, electing instead to tear apart their prey for his bad verses. The scene's didactic purpose seems to be to illustrate the consequences of disorder, the threat to innocent citizens caught in the tide of fury. But the murder of a poet also symbolizes Antony's willful distortion of the end of art. Murdering poets, as Orpheus was dismembered by the Bacchic women, signals the destruction of those charged with chronicling, not making, history. Coming as it does after the Forum interlude, the episode reveals just how completely Antony's actions have perverted the stage/state function. Not only is the play broken, but so is the playwright. The motif is comparable to the beating-of-messengers device in *Antony and Cleopatra,* where such behavior reveals the same blindness.

What began as stately ritual—a noble funeral—in *Julius Caesar* has degenerated into rule by a headless mob killing innocents along with combatants. Antony has shown just how potentially threatening events in the public playhouse can be to the public safety, a point which seems to suit well the moral goal of *Julius Caesar.* By shaping the scene to his own purposes—which prove both vengeful and ambitious—Antony has ravaged the very setting in which historical tragedy carries meaning and purpose. Likewise, the poet/playwright's artistic voice has been stilled by men whose emotions have not been purged but roused to perform yet more horrible deeds.[16] Both Brutus and Antony have in the end failed as actors, one for his inability to understand his audience, the other for manipulating its psyche only too well. In judging both leaders and actors, Shakespeare seems to say, we must look to that Aristotelian balance or "mean" so vital to the proper ruler. (Antony will soon confront such a mediated personality in the figure of Octavius, true inheritor of Julius Caesar's spirit.) Failing such a leader, the state suffers the consequences; Rome falls as the central victim of the tragedy. That men are prone to ignore this dramatic and historical truth is then aptly confirmed by Cassius' memorable comment:

> How many ages hence
> Shall this our lofty scene be acted over
> In states unborn and accents yet unknown.

Notes

1. All quotations are from G. Blakemore Evans, ed., *The Riverside Shakespeare* (Boston, Mass.: Houghton Mifflin, 1974).

2. That theatrical reenactment of the murder was a commonplace Shakespeare and his audience readily recognized is hinted at in Polonius' self-satisfied pronouncement: "I did enact Julius Caesar: I was kill'd i' the Capitol; Brutus killed me" (*Ham.* 3.2.108). E. K. Chambers cites the performance of "a storie of Pompey" at Court on Twelfth Night of 1581 (*The Elizabethan Stage* 4:158). This play may have depicted Caesar as Pompey's nemesis. Henslowe indentifies a play called "seser and pompie" on November 8, 1594, as well 'as "the 2 pte of sesore" on 18 June 1595 (see *Henslowe's Diary,* ed. W. W. Greg, 1:20). These plays do not survive, however.

3. James L. Calderwood has written extensively on the subject of metadrama. See his *Metadrama in Shakespeare's Henriad* (Berkeley: U of California P, 1979) and *To Be and Not To Be: Negation and Metadrama in 'Hamlet'* (New York: Columbia UP, 1983). See as well Wendy Coppedge Sanford, *Theater as Metaphor in* Hamlet (Cambridge: Harvard UP, 1967).

4. Maynard Mack speaks directly to the linguistic and dramatic implications of the word "acting" in his "The World of *Hamlet,*" *Yale Review* 41 (1952): 502-23.

5. *Scenic Form in Shakespeare* (Oxford: Oxford UP, 1971), 226. I have suggested that *Macbeth*'s banquet scene fits the play-within formula as well, Macbeth failing to maintain his mask of kingship and the order of the state. See my "*Macbeth:* The Banquet Scene as Frustrated Play Within," *Shakespeare Jahrbuch* (Weimar) 114 (1978): 107-14. S. Viswanathan explores the related idea of clothing imagery and its relationship to the theatrical metaphor in "Macbeth in the Tiring House: The Clothes and Actor Motifs in the Play," *Anglia* 100 (1982): 18-35.

6. The concept of the citizens as reluctant audience is established earlier in this scene when Buckingham informs Richard of his failed attempt to coax from them a proclamation of kingship. In answer to Buckingham's "God save Richard, England's royal king!" they "spake not a word." (See *R3* 3.7.5-41.) J. L. Styan argues convincingly that this scene, along with others in which Richard assumes roles, "tests . . . the theatre's power of elasticity: how far can an audience be persuaded by mere convention to lend itself to villainy?" See *Drama, Stage and Audience* (Cambridge: Cambridge UP, 1975), 176-7.

7. One is inclined to believe that Shakespeare's consistent belief is that rebellion invites chaos, which can only result in blind destruction of existing order. Stephen Greenblatt's list of instances of self-fashioning includes a description of the "alien" (#4) which seems to apply to Shakespearean rioters. See *Renaissance Self-Fashioning: From More to Shakespeare* (Chicago: U of Chicago P, 1980), 9.

8. G. E. Bentley, *The Profession of Player in Shakespeare's Time, 1590-1642* (Princeton: Princeton UP, 1984), 25.

9. The term "adventurer" had a commercial connotation as early as the 1480s, when Henry VII established the Society of Merchant Adventurers. See *OED.*
10. Ten sharers signed the debt contract of the Lord Admiral's men in 1598. See Bentley, 27.
11. Bentley, 26.
12. Though hired men performed a variety of services useful to the company—players, musicians, book holders or prompters, gatherers—those who acted were given unassigned roles in most productions. See Bentley, 68-112.
13. Nicholas Brooke observes that "Caesar's arrogance and weakness are part of an insistent naturalism set against another order governed by storm and blood" (*Shakespeare's Early Tragedies* [London: Methuen, 1968], 145).
14. The assassination was referred to in the 1587 edition of the *Mirror for Magistrates,* a collection of tragedies dramatized in the manner of Lydgate's rendering of Boccaccio's *Falls of Princes.*
15. See T. S. Dorsch, ed. *The Arden Julius Caesar* (London: Methuen, 1961), xxxviii-xxxix.
16. That Shakespeare had a clear sense of the purging purpose of tragedy is exhibited in Hamlet's speech to the players, 3.2.1-45. Antony's performance might be called "overdone" (26), leading the "judicious" to "grieve" (27).

Jean-Pierre Maquerlot (essay date 1995)

SOURCE: "*Julius Caesar* and 'Dramatic Coquetry,'" in *Shakespeare and the Mannerist Tradition: A Reading of Five Problem Plays,* Cambridge University Press, 1995, pp. 72-86.

[*In the following essay, Maquerlot evaluates* Julius Caesar *as a Mannerist drama fraught with ambiguity, and contends that Shakespeare constantly altered audience sympathies toward Caesar.*]

In the second volume of his book on Shakespeare's histories, Professor Paul Bacquet rightly insists on the pedagogical function of the Chorus in *Henry V.* The role of the Chorus, he argues, is more systematically developed in this play than in any other of the same period, and serves to guide the spectators through the play's various episodes and also to encourage them to perform an act of 'collective imagination' without which there would be no dramatic illusion.[1]

It seems to me that the Chorus' repeated plea to the audience to compensate mentally for the material limitations of stage production serves another equally indispensable, if less obvious, purpose, which is to secure the audience's adherence to the play's ideological message. In Shakespeare's view, the people assembled in the playhouse would be all the more willing to accept that a few square metres of boards in the centre of that wooden 'O' might represent the battlefield of Agincourt if they could be made to feel party to the glorious national epic that was being played out before them, for them and, up to a point, thanks to them. Whatever their social rank, cultural origin and religious or political allegiance, the members of the audience—possibly viewed by the dramatist as the epitome of British society or perhaps a peace-time reflection of the King's army—were urged to unite in a shared feeling of patriotic fervour. The special theatrical strategy geared to such an uncommon goal was to enlist them in the actual making of the show so that this rare moment of dramatic experience might also be one of ideological consensus.[2]

1599 is also, in all probability, the year of *Julius Caesar,* another history play but one with no Chorus to sustain the audience. Here the spectators are left to themselves and it is up to them alone to construe the meaning of what they see and hear on stage, not such an easy task, as we shall see. British history is no longer at stake. However decisive the murder of Caesar may have been in changing the face of the planet, this momentous event still concerns the ancient world. Ideologically, the play does not require the same emotional commitment from the audience and its progress does not depend on the same type of dramaturgic collaboration. It is enough for the audience to behave 'normally'—to consent to the usual suspension of disbelief expected at the theatre—to preserve the chances of minimal dramatic illusion.

Like *Richard II, Julius Caesar* is the story of a conspiracy undertaken in the name of the common weal. But Richard was king, a sacred figure, and his deposition and murder were impious acts. Like Richard's, Caesar's power is legitimate, but, contrary to what he would have the citizens of Rome believe, it is not of divine origin. His murder, therefore, is not technically a sacrilege, except in the minds of those who made him into a god in his own lifetime. Richard was an unworthy ruler and his replacement by Bolingbroke could appear as a measure of public salvation, a morally reprehensible but politically desirable usurpation despite the civil disorder it was bound to kindle. The answer to the question of whether the kingdom gained or lost from this change in dynasty is long in coming: the problem of monarchical legitimacy in the face of reasons of State and the dilemma between the sacred and the political haunt the end of *Richard II,* the whole of *Henry IV* (*Parts 1* and *2*) and occasionally surface again in *Henry V.* It is only the latter play that turns the scales in favour of the house of Lancaster. As to whether the violent overthrow of Caesar proved beneficial or detrimental to Rome, neither *Julius Caesar* nor *Antony and Cleopatra*—the sequel to the former play inasmuch as it dramatizes events subsequent to Caesar's death—offers the least clue. Though the Elizabethans knew, as well as we do, that the fall of Caesar was to give rise to the empire heralded by Octavius' glorious principate, Shakespeare remains conspicuously silent about this, focusing instead upon the convulsions attendant

Robert Christie as Caesar and members of the Festival Company in Act I, scene ii of the 1955 Stratford Festival production of Julius Caesar.

upon the murder, iniquitous proscriptions, the rivalry within the triumvirate, the war against the conspirators and the discords between Brutus and Cassius. Neither in Octavius' final speech nor elsewhere in the play is there a hint that good may eventually come from evil. The crucial issue of whether Caesar's blood was shed for the good or the ill of Rome is deliberately left pending. In *Julius Caesar,* Shakespeare highlights the event and its immediate consequences, thus enclosing the action within the impassable boundaries of an intensely dramatized present. Thus isolated from past and future, the facts confronting us cannot be fitted into a long-range vision that would give them meaning and relevance in terms of a country's destiny. Ideologically, the spectators of the play are well and truly alone.

Following close upon *Henry V, Julius Caesar* is yet another exploration of the hero figure. That Shakespeare was turning to Plutarch (via Sir Thomas North) after he had just brought to an epic finale the cycle of plays devoted to national history shows clearly that the theme of the great man still interested him. If antiquity was to supply a hero as prestigious as Henry, the choice naturally lay between Alexander and Caesar.[3] The circumstances of Caesar's assassination, the ensuing civil war and the conspirators' defeat offered excellent material for yet another history play structured around three dramatic moments: the hatching of a conspiracy, the execution of a murder and the meting out of retribution to the guilty. Not only could Shakespeare once again furnish the stage with vivid tableaux such as Caesar amid his court, Brutus deliberating with his conscience, Caesar stabbed to death at the foot of Pompey's statue, Brutus' and Antony's celebrated speeches at the market-place or the conspirators' suicide at Philippi, but he could also easily work these spectacular scenes into a unified drama, patterned on the old, still successful formula of the revenge tragedy.

More decisively, perhaps, Shakespeare's preference for the story of Caesar's life accorded well with the direction he was working in after the completion of his two historical tetralogies, namely towards a more curious probing into the complexities of the human mind and soul and a more realistic rendering of the often chaotic life of consciousness together with a more critical appraisal of man's 'greatness and nobility', a trend that *Hamlet* and the dark comedies were soon to exemplify. Shakespeare knew how controversial and enigmatic Caesar had appeared, both to his contemporaries and to succeeding generations. Borrowing from Roman antiquity, he no doubt felt free from the ideological constraints that inevitably impinge on the representation of national history. Furthermore, the story of Julius Caesar offered the advantage of including not one but two heroes in whom greatness and weakness intermingle, thus providing the dramatist with the exciting possibility of counterpointing two forms of heroism, each one marred with its own shortcomings: in Caesar, the glory of the conqueror and statesman tarnished by excessive pride; in Brutus, the integrity of the true republican led astray by political blindness. This dualistic vision, sanctioned by Renaissance historiography, whereby assessment of both personages could only be a qualified one, fitted exactly with Shakespeare's project. In many respects, the subject of Caesar's downfall at the hands of patriots who were diversely (and some of whom were dubiously) motivated carried enough ambiguity to lend itself to Mannerist treatment.

There was yet another advantage which, from a non-Mannerist perspective, would have seemed more like a drawback: no episode of ancient history was better known and more loaded with moral and political glosses than Caesar's rise and fall. His destiny had long been food for thought on the vagaries of Fortune and the ironic proximity of the Capitol to the Tarpeian Rock, revealing the dark face of greatness and the often conflicting demands of civic duty and friendship. Reflecting upon his choice, Shakespeare may well have felt that he was coming too late and that all had been said on the subject. Telling the story of Julius Caesar and of Brutus and his associates could only be a retelling. Substantially altering the facts of history was out of the question, and therefore innovation had to be confined to matters of form. It was as if, from the start, Shakespeare found himself in the position of a composer having to write variations on a canonical theme, a situation of relative constraint or conditional freedom most favourable to a Mannerist approach. When an artist has no other choice but to reproduce what C. G. Dubois calls 'une thématique magistrale' (a set of themes sanctioned by the authority of masters) he or she must gear his or her inspiration to 'the multiplying of forms and proliferating of variations'.[4] This incidentally sheds light on the old concept of refurbishing erstwhile successes according to current fashion; what has perhaps too often been taken for sheer opportunism on the part of authors in need of popularity may well evince—in some cases at least—a Mannerist propensity for subversive allegiance. Is it by accident that *Hamlet* (which is regarded by many as a Mannerist play, if not the epitome of Mannerist dramatic art) proceeds from an *Ur-Hamlet*? If this theory holds true, *Hamlet* can be seen as Shakespeare's personal variation upon the traditional formula of the revenge tragedy. Whether *Julius Caesar* was inspired by an existing play or not is of little importance. Because of the exceptional popularity of the fable, it is History itself, as constituted by the gradual sedimentation of the commentaries, which serves as reference or model. Addressing a subject like this with its compulsory figures (almost in the choreographic sense of the term), Shakespeare was practically forced to seek originality of treatment. More specifically, it is in the Mannerist presentation of the characters that Shakespeare's art is most innovative.

What I designate here as a Mannerist trait, Ernest Schanzer calls 'dramatic coquetry'. This facetious and telling expression denotes the method whereby the dramatist manipulates our response to the main characters 'playing fast and loose with our affections for them, engaging and alienating them in turn'.[5] Though a similar technique is at work in several other plays, it is never more systematically used than in *Julius Caesar*. Schanzer has studied in great detail how a succession of images, in turn positive and negative, disconcerts the spectator to the extent that he or she can no longer situate the characters on a scale of moral values. Since Caesar and the conspirators can gain our sympathy or antipathy only transiently and incompletely, the murder itself appears in an ambiguous light. If it is true that Caesar's murder was indeed a political error, was it also a morally reprehensible act? According to Schanzer, this is the central question posed by the play, one that Shakespeare is careful *not* to answer.

The presence of Mannerism is indicated not by Caesar, Brutus, Cassius and Antony (to mention only the major characters) being alloys of good and evil: this ambivalence is supported by history and can be thought of as inherent to all credible portrayals of human nature. This might even be another example of rhetorical formalism with characteristic effects of binary opposition and symmetrical balancing. That each character should view himself and others from an angle entirely his own is not particularly relevant to Mannerism either. It is not surprising that Caesar as seen by Cassius should not be a faithful mirror image of Caesar as seen by Brutus, even less so by Antony, not to mention Caesar seen by himself or by the audience. All plays and novels containing several characters consist of such sets of mirrors in which images are thus reflected and interconnected. It is through such reverberations that identities are formed. But Mannerist art has the particularity of thwarting this image-making process by maintaining the characters on this side of a true identity. Mannerism discourages us from ever being able to organize into a viable entity—that is, a coherent and credible whole—the pieces of the puzzle scattered before our eyes. Mannerism strives hard to preclude the possibility of a global, unified perception.

Why, when looking at a Mannerist bronze by Giovanni Bologna, are we seized with a desire to inspect it from all angles? As we cannot turn it this way and that, why are we tempted to walk around it as if to discover yet another hitherto unsuspected angle? How is it that having to stand in front of Pontormo's *Deposition* or Michelangelo's *Last Judgement,* we commission our gaze, as it were vicariously, to wander over the composition? The answer is that in a Mannerist work where everything attracts the eye, nothing arrests it. No standpoint imposes itself as decisive in procuring the most satisfying vision, which hopefully might best reveal to us the work's 'truth'. What reasons are there to prefer confronting the statue frontally rather than obliquely? Each point of view appeals to our eye and momentarily frustrates it from the pleasure of discovering what the next point of view would disclose. Unlike classical characters, collected in almost all of their actions and speeches, at all times coextensive with themselves, their Mannerist counterparts are always presented incomplete; they sharpen our curiosity and direct it towards a hypothetical 'elsewhere', the hidden face of their being, in the illusory expectation of a revelation of the whole self.

Something analogous to this wandering gaze occurs in *Julius Caesar.* I shall not restate Schanzer's excellent analyses showing how the characters are split into successive images, either flattering or derogatory, but equally credible. Dramatic coquetry is a dynamics of ambiguity, in that it arouses excitement and disappointment in turn: we believe we grasp the 'truth' about a character (on which the meaning of his action depends), only to realize immediately afterwards that it was premature to stop at what was only an aspect, a facet among others. When Caesar dies, we still do not know what we should 'really' think about this immensely proud character who swings from the grotesque:

> Danger knows full well
> That Caesar is more dangerous than he.
> We are two lions litter'd in one day,
> And I the elder and more terrible.
>
> II, ii, 44-7

To the sublime:

> constant as the northern star,
> Of whose true-fix'd and resting quality
> There is no fellow in the firmament.
>
> III, i, 60-2

Caesar is warm with his friends:

> Good friends, go in, and taste some wine with me;
> And we, like friends, will straightway go together.
>
> II, ii, 126-7

His irresolution verges on caricature:

> Caesar shall forth. The things that threaten'd me
> Ne'er look'd but on my back.
>
> II, ii, 10-11

> Mark Antony shall say I am not well,
> And for thy humour I will stay at home.
>
> II, ii, 55-6

> Give me my robe, for I will go.
>
> II, ii, 107

But he is stoical at the thought of his own death:

> Cowards die many times before their deaths;
> The valiant never taste of death but once.
> Of all the wonders that I yet have heard,
> It seems to me most strange that men should fear,
> Seeing that death, a necessary end,
> Will come when it will come.
>
> II, ii, 32-7

His self-centredness is exorbitant:

> Decius, go tell them Caesar will not come.
> DEC. Most mighty Caesar, let me know some cause,
> Lest I be laugh'd at when I tell them so.
> CAES. The cause is in my will: I will not come;
> That is enough to satisfy the Senate.
>
> II, ii, 68-72

But it is matched by equally uncompromising self-abnegation:

> What touches us ourself shall be last serv'd.
>
> III, i, 8

Caesar is superstitious:

> Forget not, in your speed, Antonius,
> To touch Calphurnia; for our elders say,
> The barren, touched in this holy chase,
> Shake off their sterile curse.
>
> I, ii, 6-9

Except however when he himself is concerned:

> What say'st thou to me now? Speak once again.
> SOOTH. Beware the ides of March.
> CAES. He is a dreamer. Let us leave him. Pass.
>
> I, ii, 22-4

His grasp of human psychology is remarkable and likely, one would think, to caution him against 'dangerous' persons:

> I do not know the man I should avoid
> So soon as that spare Cassius. He reads much,
> He is a great observer, and he looks
> Quite through the deeds of men. He loves no plays,
> As thou dost, Antony; he hears no music.
> Seldom he smiles, and smiles in such a sort
> As if he mock'd himself, and scorn'd his spirit
> That could be mov'd to smile at any thing.
> Such men as he be never at heart's ease
> Whiles they behold a greater than themselves,
> And therefore are they very dangerous.
>
> I, ii, 197-207

Yet his superhuman stature—notwithstanding his physical disabilities—puts him above the fears of common mortals:

> I rather tell thee what is to be fear'd
> Than what I fear; for always I am Caesar.
> Come on my right hand, for this ear is deaf.
>
> I, ii, 208-10

In addition to the images Caesar projects of himself there are those given by the receivers, namely the characters who look at him and judge him. Brutus, like the Plebeian Tribunes, sees in Caesar a potential tyrant:

> a serpent's egg,
> Which, hatch'd, would, as his kind, grow mischievous.
>
> II, i, 32-3

The one difference is that Brutus loves Caesar ('I love him well', I, ii, 81). Though Brutus detects in Caesar a weakness for honours ('He would be crown'd', II, i, 12), he sees him above all as a reasonable man in control of his passions:

> I have not known when his affections sway'd
> More than his reason.
>
> II, i, 20-1

For Cassius, on the other hand, Caesar is a clay-footed giant:

> A man no mightier than thyself, or me,
> In personal action, yet prodigious grown,
> And fearful, as these strange eruptions are.
>
> I, iii, 76-8

A 'colossus' who destroys all hope of honour in his fellow citizens:

> Why, man, he doth bestride the narrow world
> Like a Colossus, and we petty men
> Walk under his huge legs, and peep about
> To find ourselves dishonourable graves.
>
> I, ii, 133-6

His tyranny, more moral than political, teaches the Romans servility in defiance of their ancestral values:

> our fathers' minds are dead,
> And we are govern'd with our mothers' spirits;
> Our yoke and sufferance show us womanish.
>
> I, iii, 82-4

The one fleeting image of Caesar given by Antony while the former is alive is that of an authoritarian father figure who knows how to be obeyed:

> When Caesar says, 'Do this', it is perform'd.
>
> I, ii, 10

Yet he is someone to whom Antony can freely express his disagreement:

> Fear him not, Caesar, he's not dangerous.
>
> I, ii, 193

After the death of Caesar, Antony's words depict him as a man who could inspire the strongest friendship:

> That I did love thee, Caesar, O, 'tis true!
> If then thy spirit look upon us now,
> Shall it not grieve thee dearer than thy death,
> To see thy Antony making his peace,
> Shaking the bloody fingers of thy foes.
>
> III, i, 194-8

He is one whose nobility was incomparable:

> Thou art the ruins of the noblest man
> That ever lived in the tide of times.
>
> III, i, 256-7

His loss is felt with pain:

> for mine eyes,
> Seeing those beads of sorrow stand in thine,
> Began to water.
>
> III, i, 283-5

Such effusiveness, the sincerity of which cannot be doubted (unlike Antony's carefully studied posturing during his speech to the citizens at the market-place), evokes the figure of a friend, an aspect authenticated by Brutus himself:

> I slew my best lover for the good of Rome.
>
> III, ii, 46

On the negative side of things, the toadying of Caesar's entourage corroborates Cassius' claim that the Romans are overshadowed by Caesar and have abdicated all republican pride. So even Cassius' discourse on Caesar, biased as it is, and dictated, as we know it to be, by hatred and envy, holds elements of truth.

Of all the images that Caesar reflects, and they are diverse and numerous since no one is exposed to the others' gaze as much as Caesar, none is conclusive. The 'truth' about Caesar cannot be obtained by sorting out the true and false images, those which apparently bring us closer to the 'real' Caesar and those which do not. The truth about Caesar is to be found in every single reflection from these multifaceted mirrors. This helps to understand why the Mannerist method renders obsolete the traditional and rhetorical opposition between appearance and reality, between the mask of the public figure and the face of the private person. As Raymond Willems has neatly written:

> It would be vain to look for the 'true' Caesar behind the mask of the mythical Caesar. Caesar is not an impostor. He plays a role, of course, but it is his own role. He simply tries to be himself, not to give an embellished image of himself. His play-acting does not therefore tend towards duplicity, but towards the unity of his self. When he proclaims 'I am Caesar', it is not vain boasting. The phrase is the expression of the ter-

> rible effort he must make to stick to his character. Hence his almost incantory repetition of his own name which has become like a talisman.[6]

Why introduce this notion of tending towards 'the unity of the self'? It is because the self is not of the order of the given, but the ever-receding horizon of a never-ending quest, the forever disappointed promise of an illusory cohesion between disparate images.

After this dizzying kaleidoscopic review of the most telling images relating to Caesar, I hesitate to extend it to other characters. Suffice it to say that dramatic coquetry is not confined to Caesar alone. It is a deliberate stand on dramaturgy, a departure in the art of drawing characters and bringing them to life on stage. Shakespeare is Mannerist in so far as he constantly eludes the spectator's expectation of characters clustered around a key image. Like Mannerist painters or sculptors, he repudiates all sense of hierarchy in viewpoints, thus holding up disparity and off-centredness as the structural principles underlying his treatment of characters.

The corollary of this is that the actions themselves are irremediably ambiguous, the best example being the murder of Caesar. Shakespeare does not choose between the two conflicting images of the murder: Brutus' image of murder as sacrifice and Antony's image of butchery. History chooses for him and gives Antony the advantage over Brutus in the contest between images. It is clear that Antony has carried the day when the sacrificial and emblematic blood in which the conspirators have ritually bathed their hands and swords becomes the blood of the massacre, which murderous envy has caused to flow:

> Look, in this place ran Cassius' dagger through:
> See what a rent the envious Cassius made:
> Through this the well-beloved Brutus stabb'd;
> And as he pluck'd his cursed steel away,
> Mark how the blood of Caesar follow'd it,
> As rushing out of doors, to be resolv'd
> If Brutus so unkindly knock'd or no.
>
> III, ii, 176-82

Henceforth Antony's image of Caesar's death has supplanted Brutus' in the eyes of the citizens. Shakespeare had no other choice but to ratify the verdict of history, but this does not mean he had to *justify* it. It is not because the image propagated by Antony proves more credible to 'the masses who make history' and more profitable to those who are its privileged actors that Brutus' contrary image is invalidated. In an attempt to make ethics coincide with politics, it has been argued that Brutus' staged ceremony following the assassination of Caesar is a murderer's contrivance, designed to shelter his sensitivity from the unbearable horror of the collective crime, a ritual seen as the dressing up of bad faith.[7] I do not share this view. Here Willems is worth quoting again:

> To take appearances in hand is not necessarily to use them to deceive. Brutus is concerned about controlling them because he knows they are misleading. He wants to prevent his act from being misunderstood. From this perspective 'this shall make / Our purpose necessary' is only apparently paradoxical. According to Brutus' logic, it is the manner of killing Caesar which will give his act its true meaning. If he can convince the other conspirators to consider the murder as a sacrifice, then it will indeed be a sacrifice.[8]

In the ontological world of Mannerism, truth is a useless hypothesis, only representation matters. The Mannerist artist does not conceive of his or her work differently from the way Brutus looks upon his act: only the manner carries meaning.

If truth is reducible to a vertiginous parade of images which correct, contradict and complement but in no way *cancel* each other out, what is more tempting than to give oneself over to the impressions of the moment, since each moment expresses a truth? Mildred E. Hartsock thinks that the play is constructed in such a way as to place the spectator in a situation analogous to that of the Roman crowd at the market-place: 'We are fully committed at every point in the play to *someone.* Ironically, we have something in common with the Roman mob: we believe what we hear as we hear it, only to be involved in one emotional or intellectual partisanship after another.'[9] This opinion should be qualified, or the Mannerist game of dramatic coquetry will be over-simplified. Shakespeare is more subtle, more authentically Mannerist, less of a crude hoaxer than Hartsock supposes. We know that he is careful to ensure that no image can be purely and simply accepted or rejected. Coquetry or flirtatiousness is the art of not taking advances or rebuffs too far, lest the game come to a halt. This is why no character in the play inspires either love or hatred. The Mannerist artist takes care not to play on extremes of emotion, his or her range is voluntarily limited. He or she expects connivance more than participation from the audience, an attitude that is more playful than sentimental, more intellectual than emotional. Baroque characters—say Othello, Lear or Macbeth—violently catch hold of us for better or worse: Mannerist characters intrigue the audience more than inflame them. Even when the Mannerist hero is endowed with a strong presence both textually and scenically (as is the case with Caesar and Hamlet), he is always held at a distance, like an object of curiosity meant to be considered with a careful and critical eye. This is why the pleasure obtained from a Mannerist work always has a streak of narcissism about it, as if much of the enjoyment comes from detecting the irony of the message.

At two decisive moments—before his departure to the Senate and before the murder—Caesar indulges in a fit of self-aggrandizement, almost disowning his human nature, first through an animal metaphor (the image of the two lions already mentioned), and then through a cosmic simile which develops into a whole tirade:

> But I am constant as the northern star,
> Of whose true-fix'd and resting quality
> There is no fellow in the firmament.
> The skies are painted with unnumber'd sparks,

They are all fire, and every one doth shine;
But there's but one in all doth hold his place.
So in the world: 'tis furnis'd well with men,
And men are flesh and blood, and apprehensive;
Yet in the number I do know but one
That unassailable holds on his rank,
Unshak'd of motion; and that I am he,
Let me a little show it, even in this,
That I was constant Cimber should be banish'd,
And constant do remain to keep him so.

III, i, 60-73

T. S. Dorsch rightly sees in this speech an outburst of pride caused by the servility of Metellus and Cassius, come to plead the cause of Publius Cimber. But such arrogance, he claims, triggers so much antipathy among Caesar's entourage and the audience that the forthcoming murder appears almost justifiable.[10] I do not find this psychological interpretation of causes and effects entirely convincing. If this be pride, it is the legitimate pride of a monarch, something that an Elizabethan audience would not consider as grossly 'extravagant' as we do today. Shakespeare is not trying to justify the murder beforehand by making Caesar especially odious. A more plausible explanation that does justice to Caesar's self-coined image of superhuman infallibility is that Shakespeare is here presenting the murder as a truly political option rather than the outcome of accumulated personal grudges or resentments. Richard Marienstras' comment on this episode is very much to the point: 'this political murder, this sacrifice, the fall of this star, for one moment appears as an attempt to replace an inhuman cosmic order by an order of another nature, governed by the will of men and by social ethics founded purely on contract'.[11] The irony, therefore, is not exactly where Dorsch believes it to be found. It stems from the fact that it is Caesar *himself,* in his use of cosmic imagery to illustrate his 'constancy', who confirms the need for the conspirators to rid themselves of that inhuman authority of superterrestrial nature. In a pagan context, where the monarch's power does not proceed from God (meaning the Judaeo-Christian God), it is by no means impious to prefer a contract to an order founded on transcendence, which, in any case, is not of divine essence. By comparing himself to the pole star, the fixed point *par excellence* and keystone of the cosmos, Caesar had no notion of the extent to which he was playing into the conspirators' hands: this concept was precisely what they wanted to destroy.

As for the mini-parable of the two lions, through which Caesar expresses his contempt of danger, it shows almost in caricature how arrogance can sink into ridicule; danger is first the object of an unspecified personification ('Danger knows full well . . .'), then what might pass as a fairly bad flash of wit ('Caesar is more dangerous than' Danger itself) becomes a grotesque metaphor—Caesar and Danger are two lions 'litter'd in one day', but Caesar is 'the elder and more terrible' of the two. Calphurnia is right: excessive self-confidence causes her husband to rave. When Caesar presents himself as a fierce, invulnerable being, he only succeeds in prefiguring what could appear as a form of senility. When he proclaims himself as 'constant' as the pole star, he unveils the inanity of such pretensions when they are embodied in a mortal being. A few stabs will suffice—and what conspirator does not think of this when listening to Caesar—to turn this figure of immortality into a 'bleeding piece of earth'. Similarly, it is when Brutus professes honesty most vehemently that he is the least convincing:

There is no terror, Cassius, in your threats;
For I am arm'd so strong in honesty
That they pass by me as the idle wind,
Which I respect not.

IV, iii, 66-9

Such Caesar-like grandiloquence sounds strained and suggests that Brutus, like Caesar, has to struggle to live up to his own legend. These characters are engaged in the construction of their own myths. In everything they say and do, in the day-after-day management of the images they wish to convey of themselves, they have to take into account what history and legend have already made of them.

But in this play that is fraught with ambiguity, are there any moments when we are tempted to commit ourselves unreservedly to a character, if only for the time he speaks? At the market-place, before the crowd, Brutus expounds his reasons for having killed Caesar, with the vigorous clarity of his Lacedaemonian style. We might almost be convinced, thus imitating the citizens, as Hartsock would have it. Unlike Antony's succeeding oration, Brutus' speech strikes us as being basically honest, the opposite of manipulation. Yet one sentence at the end throws everything into doubt:

The question of his death is enroll'd in the Capitol; his glory not extenuated, wherein he was worthy; nor his offences enforc'd, for which he suffered death.

III, ii, 38-41

Brutus blames Caesar for errors *already* committed and turns the murder into a punishment, in blatant contradiction to the preventive murder theory he had developed in Act II:

And since the quarrel
Will bear no colour for the thing he is,
Fashion it thus: that what he is, augmented,
Would run to these and these extremities.

II, i, 28-31

What can justify this double language? Why does Brutus change from sacrificer to avenger or righter of wrongs? Is there a version of the murder for private use, his own and his associates', and another for public use, that of the Plebeians, whom the first version had no chance of convincing? What spectators would want to identify with this credulous, changeable and over-emotional crowd who is debarred from knowing the ins and outs of the affair?

The market scene is placed right in the middle of the play; it does indeed have an emblematic value, though not perhaps the one suggested by Hartsock. My hypothesis is that Brutus' and Antony's orations are theatrical pieces; the tribune is their stage and the Roman citizens are their spectators, a feverish, fascinated and easily manipulated audience, the very opposite of the sort of audience that Shakespeare would have wished for his own play. Through an act of negative symbolization strategically performed at the very core of *Julius Caesar,* Shakespeare treats his own audience to a show of irony aimed at a category of spectators he esteems incapable of reacting suitably to the subtleties of Mannerist theatre, and this brings me back to my starting-point which was the playwright's attitude to his audience. In *Henry V,* Shakespeare expected from them a sustained collaboration in the drama; he asked them to provide thought-out and voluntary support from the heart and mind, unlike the irrational, inconstant, follow-the-leader attitude of the Plebeians enslaved to their urges of the moment. Conversely, it is a totally receptive, totally free, totally critical audience that is needed for *Julius Caesar,* where ambiguity reigns, where dramatic coquetry feeds theatrical pleasure. But what use is to be made of such liberty and lucidity? To indulge without illusion in the Mannerist game of engagement and disengagement and to eschew the trap of images no further than the game requires, Shakespeare wants his audience to be astute enough to appreciate the ambivalence of words and situations, civilized enough both to understand the value of poetry and, unlike the Roman frenzied mob, not to kill the poet.

Notes

1. Paul Bacquet, *Les pièces historiques de Shakespeare,* 2 vols., Paris, 1979, vol. II, p. 156.
2. I do not find anything in the text to substantiate the view held by Bacquet and some other critics that the Epilogue spoken by the Chorus invites the audience to look back upon the King as an ultimately ineffectual warmonger, because France came to be lost under the next king. It seems to me that Henry remains 'this star of England' to the very end of the play, though Shakespeare's portrayal of him throughout the play is often touched with irony. The Chorus insists that Henry's valour is not to be ascribed to his personal merits only, but also to Fortune ('Fortune made his sword'), and as expected Fortune turns her wheel against Henry VI, his successor. In fact, the Chorus' last speech serves to put the glorious reign of Henry V in a double perspective: the unfolding of history, which is pre-eminently the site of Fortune's whimsical doings, and the sequence of the Histories 'which oft our stage hath shown'. It is part of the Chorus' pedagogical function to conclude the play on such a relativistic note.
3. See the Prologue to Act v in *Henry V,* in which the Chorus likens Henry's return to London from his wars in France to Caesar's return to Rome from his wars in Gaul. In Act v, scene vii, Fluellen and Gower compare Henry with Alexander the Great.
4. C. G. Dubois, *Le maniérisme,* Paris, 1979, p. 38.
5. E. Schanzer, *The Problem Plays of Shakespeare,* London, 1951, p. 70.
6. R. Willems, 'Ambiguïté et identité dans *Julius Caesar*', in *Aspects du théâtre anglosaxon,* Publication de l'Université de Rouen, 1981, p. 79.
7. This is the opinion notably of Brents Sterling in *Unity in Shakespearean Tragedy,* New York, 1956.
8. Willems, 'Ambiguïté et identité dans *Julius Caesar*', p. 82.
9. Mildred E. Hartsock, 'The Complexity of *Julius Caesar*', *PMLA,* 81, March 1966, p. 61.
10. T. S. Dorsch (ed.), *Julius Caesar* (Arden edn), London, 1955; 1977 edn, pp. xix-xx.
11. R. Marienstras, *Le proche et le lointain,* Paris, 1981, p. 92 (my translation). The book has been published in English under the title *New Perspectives on the Shakespearean World,* Cambridge, 1985; the passage quoted is p. 60.

Dennis Kezar (essay date 1998)

SOURCE: "*Julius Caesar* and the Properties of Shakespeare's Globe," in *English Literary Renaissance,* Vol. 28, No. 1, Winter, 1998, pp. 18-46.

[*In the following essay, Kezar maintains that in* Julius Caesar *Shakespeare explored the potential 'irresponsibility' of theater as it appropriates history, subverts audience response, and dismembers self-presentation.*]

> "The World makes many vntrue Constructions of these Speaches."[1]

For an antitheatricalist such as Stephen Gosson, the Renaissance stage travesties the courtroom, leaving the defendant with no voice and replacing a single judge with an injudicious jury: "At stage plays it is ridiculous, for the parties accused to reply, no indifference of judgment can be had, because the worst sort of people have the hearing of it, which in respect of their ignorance, of their fickleness, and of their fury, are not to be admitted in place of judgment. A judge must be grave, sober, discreet, wise, well exercised in cases of government, which qualities are never found in the baser sort."[2] In his indictment of drama Gosson charges poets and players with reducing the accused to a lifeless and common text, "openly blown into the ears of many and made a byword" (p. 167); and he charges the audience, "carried away with every rumor," with blind injustice: "they run together by heaps, they know not whither; and lay about with their clubs, they see not why. Which thing the ancient Philosophers considering called them a monster of many heads" (p. 164).

Conspicuously, few apologists for Renaissance theater directly engage Gosson's assertion that the stage is a law court perverted, that it submits false evidence to a biased, bacchant audience. Indeed, Thomas Heywood admits the malleability of this audience only when insisting upon the virtues of fictionalized exempla: "Lively and well spirited action . . . hath power to new mold the hearts of the spectators and fashion them to the shape of any noble and notable attempt."[3] Philip Sidney may obliquely concede the contingency of such modeling upon the audience's judgment when, for instance, he claims for the poet power "to bestow a Cyrus upon the world to make many Cyruses, *if they will learn aright why and how that maker made him.*"[4] But Sidney and the protheatricalists celebrate the bloodless "sweet violence"[5] of an exemplary and embellished drama that moves the spectator to virtuous and prescribed behavior; Gosson argues not only that this same transaction can promulgate vice—both intentionally and unintentionally[6]—but also that it commits felonious violence against the object of representation itself. Far from a "glass of behavior," Gosson's theater presents men as silent exteriors before a dangerously subjective audience, an inversion of the ideal courtroom: "For the place, no private man's life ought to be brought in question or accused, but where he may plead in his own defense and have indifferent judges to determine the case" (p. 163). Thus he approves of Roman theatrical censorship for restoring the judiciary to its rightful place: "[the Roman censors] would not have the life and behavior of the citizens, subject either to a poet's inkhorn, or a player's tongue, but to the seat of justice" (p. 165). In contrast to this fixed institution of judgment, he finds the Renaissance "common" stage an interpretively open-ended venue, where the inwardness of a "private man's life" becomes the property of a public both ductile and unpredictable.[7] At its most penetrating, Gosson's criticism of drama reveals the violence of what we might call "other-fashioning"—the coercion involved when a playwright silences a subject, appropriates that subject as spectacle, and displays it before the dubious construction of numberless judges.

Ironically, we find the most unflinching response to this definition of theatrical violence not in the prose of Gosson's opponents, but in the very public drama he seeks to censor. In my reading of *The Tragedy of Julius Caesar,* I claim that Shakespeare explores this same violence with acute self-consciousness; and that, more specifically, the dismemberment of Cinna the poet at the center of the dramatic action emblemizes the potentially ruinous energies of other-fashioning—focuses the anxieties about theatrical appropriation and audience response—that preside with thematic centrality over the play. Such a reading will involve an inversion of the paradigm typically imposed on the Renaissance stage when "self-fashioning" is the issue: rather than a cultural space that enables but ultimately contains a potentially subversive auto-poesis.[8] I argue that Shakespeare represents in this play a stage subversive for its incontinence, a theater in which self-presentation dissolves before the alternative gaze and indeterminate interpretation of the spectator. *Julius Caesar* will have a doubled part in this essay, however. While I seek to demonstrate that in his play Shakespeare metatheatrically considers the relation—as conceived by the antitheatricalists—between the playwright, his matter, and his audience, I also attempt to historicize this self-consciousness, arguing that the play appears in a time (1599) and a place (the Globe) at which the nature of this relation is being energetically redefined and debated. This reading of *Julius Caesar,* then, tries to present the play as a dramatic reading of a contentious contemporary issue, a critical representation of the public theater's epistemological economy. For it is through this critique that Shakespeare defines both the dramatist and his customers as rough-handlers of the representations they fashion and watch; it is through this critique that Shakespeare considers public drama's potential for irresponsibility. In so doing, he defines the playwright as implicated in a process of which many apologists for theater would absolve him: guilty by association with an untrustworthy audience, a corrupt jury, Shakespeare's dramatist knowingly violates the subjects he stages.

II "Fashion it Thus"

It might be objected that Gosson's view of theater as mistrial arises merely from his concern with a topical stage's potential for libel, a concern in fact shared by the state censors in Renaissance England.[9] But Gosson conceives the injury of theatrical misrepresentation much more broadly, so that even Roman history can be victimized by Elizabethan dramatic adaptations:

> If a true history be taken in hand . . . the poets drive it most commonly unto such points, as may best show the majesty of their pen . . . or wring in a show, to furnish the stage, when it is too bare; when the matter of itself comes short of this, they follow the practice of the cobbler, and set their teeth to the leather to pull it out.
>
> So was the history of Caesar and Pompey . . . when the history swelled, and ran too high for the number of the persons that should play it, the poet with Procrustes cut the same fit to his own measure; when it afforded no pomp at all, he brought it to the rack, to make it serve.
>
> (*Plays Confuted in Five Actions,* pp. 168-69)

Sidney's alchemy, whereby the brazen world of nature and history becomes golden, is here described as a violent and opportunistic craft. For Gosson does not seem to share Sidney's view of the inutile specificity of history; nor does he justify poetic fiction as the conversion of mundane fact into neoplatonic Truth. Rather, Gosson's "true history" exists as a prior authenticity endangered by subsequent authors who take it "in hand" and "make it serve" their own artistic designs—by playwrights who falsify historical evidence and "wring in" shows in order to construct compelling theatrical cases.

Something of this rhetoric of coercive and manipulative representation distinguishes Shakespeare's own metadramatic reflections upon the act of staging history. In the Prologue to *The Life of Henry the Fifth,* for instance, the

Chorus admits the difficulty of dramatizing epic, and concedes the impossibility if not the impropriety of "cram-[ming]" the play's historical subject "Within this wooden O"; and as the audience, we become accomplices to this constrictive, farcical force when we are invited to "Suppose within the girdle of these walls / Are now confined two mighty monarchies."[10] While Shakespeare's "Chorus to this history" grapples with the presentational problem of daring "to bring forth / So great an object . . . On this unworthy scaffold," however, it also introduces the interpretive consequences of treating an historical subject as a spectacular "object." By invoking the audience's "imaginary forces," this Chorus indicates that dramatist and spectator must collaborate in fashioning and evaluating the evidence before them, and implies that the ultimate meaning of dramatic representation resides in the subjective and constitutive response of the audience: "Linger your patience on, and we'll digest / Th' abuse of distance, force a play" (2.Chorus.31-32). If one subscribes to Gosson's dark view of the playwright and his "worst sort of" audience, moreover, this collaboration not only misrepresents "true history" through the dramatist's self-interested manipulation of the record, but also subjects the characters of that history to the equally suspect reception of spectators who—like an autonomous jury—follow their own ends in arriving at their verdict.

Julius Caesar dramatizes both sides of this exchange, demonstrating the potential violation of history and its subjects by theatrical representation and audience response. Replying skeptically to Casca's reading of the wonders and prodigies that herald the fifteenth of March, in fact, Cicero might be said to epigrammatize the open-ended process of other-fashioning: "Indeed it is a strange-disposed time. / But men may construe things after their fashion, / Clean from the purpose of the things themselves" (1.3.33-35). Primarily, of course, these lines warn against the inadvertent misprision central to tragedy—the defiance of augury, omens, and prophecy that generically signals Caesar's fall; the "hateful Error" that ruins Cassius, who dies having "misconstrued everything" (5.3.84). But in Shakespeare's history play Cicero's words resonate with a significance beyond the tragic myopia that can doom such interpreters. For the hermeneutic he describes—the subjective speculation and objectified spectacle that, for Gosson, corrupt the courtroom and reduce history to histrionics—also describes the theatrical mode by which men knowingly victimize others in *Julius Caesar*. Like the word "theater" itself (at once a place where one goes "to view" and a place where scenes are staged "to the view"), his verb "construe" blurs the distinction between the act of interpretation and the act of representation. Indeed, Cicero's insight becomes the conspirators' strategy as they construct their plot. Like the portents and soothsaying Caesar must ignore if this plot is to succeed, for instance, Calphurnia's dream has an internal validity and "purpose" that the conspirators must construe "after their fashion" if the show is to go on. Thus Decius claims that she has "all amiss interpreted" her vision (2.2.83), and he provides an alternative reading that effectively leads Caesar to his slaughter. Similarly, although Brutus regrets "That every like is not the same" (2.2.128), he realizes the republicans must represent Caesar as a simulacrum of himself in order to alienate him in the people's eyes. In a soliloquy that rehearses the apology for tyrannicide he will soon deliver to the plebeians, he admits the expediency of construing Caesar after his own fashion, clean from the purpose of the thing himself:

> And since the quarrel
> Will bear no color for the thing he is,
> Fashion it thus: that what he is, augmented,
> Would run to these and these extremities.
>
> (2.1.28-31)

For Brutus, as for Gosson's violator of "true history," "the matter of itself comes short"; and the solution to the troublesome limitations of fact threatening to impede his plot and obstruct his case lies in theatricalized fiction, in fashioning the audience's perspective on the scene he is to perform by altering the evidence and ascribing to Caesar a new *telos*. Refusing the passive role of Sidney's historian—a pedant "so tied not to what should be but to what is, to the particular truth of things and not to the general reason of things"[11]—Brutus instead plays the poet and forces the awkwardly sui generis Caesar into the generic catastrophe of the de casibus tradition. He forces a play by "wringing in" a show.

This scene, however, draws blood, and herein lies the play's specific self-consciousness: men die in *Julius Caesar* not only from accidental misreading, not only from accepting the intentional misreadings of others, but also—much more unusually—from being consciously misread. As we shall see, Cinna the poet, dismembered for his name by an audience that has become actors, falls as the superlative victim of this last category, the archetypal sacrifice of a "private man's life" to the mistrial of public theater. For Cicero's words apply as much to the plebeian audience of this theater as they do to those who attempt to control their perspective on the evidence put before them. If representations can be manipulated after the politicians' fashion, so can they be misconstrued by the people's reception; if men can be appropriated by the political theater, so can they become the property of those who observe them.

And if men can be subjected to this estranging process, so can "true history"; if Cicero's observation pertains to those who inhabit Shakespeare's play, it also pertains to the playwright himself. On this metadramatic level, in fact, Cicero's acknowledgment of the construction to which omens and prognostications are susceptible attains further significance and irony. For by the late sixteenth century, a great deal of skepticism had arisen in England over an illusionistic strategy that *Julius Caesar*, like many Renaissance history plays, employs dramaturgically: the temporal sleight of hand whereby history is given a compelling predictive force and narrative shape.[12] The strong rhetoric with which such manipulations of omens and prophecy were attacked, moreover, suggestively resembles that of the antitheatricalists. Most shrill, perhaps, is Raphael Holinshed's condemnation of Peter of Pomfret, "a man in great reputation with the common people" whom Holinshed brands a "pseudo-prophet or false foreteller of afterclaps . . . a deluder of the people."[13] Francis Bacon likewise regrets that "the nature of Man . . . coveteth divination." He approves of the "many severe laws made to suppress" such prophecies, "for they have done much mischief," and he claims "that almost all of them, being infinite in number, have been impostures, and by idle and crafty brains, merely contrived and feigned, after the event passed."[14] Holinshed and Bacon object to these anachronistic predictions for much the same reason that Gosson objects to the dramatization of history: in facilitating the "emplotment"[15] of history's chaos into an orderly story, they are the instruments of deceivers rather than decipherers.

There are obvious reasons for the author of *Julius Caesar* to consider his use of history so self-consciously. Shakespeare's principal source for the play—North's translation of Amyot's French version of a Latin translation of Plutarch's *Lives of the Noble Grecians and Romans*—already suggests the transformation of historical fact by collaborative human manufacture; as Sidney remarks, moreover, this poeticizing of history began with the first chronicler: "And who reads Plutarch's either history or philosophy, shall find he trimmeth both their garments with guards of poetry."[16] Shakespeare fashions his play, then, from a text already read and fashioned, moralized and translated. Significantly, the short scene of Cinna's apprehension occasions a disproportionate degree of poetic departure from this text. Shakespeare chooses to specify that this Cinna is "the poet"; chooses to subject this poet to a crowd that, realizing he is not Cinna the conspirator, nevertheless kills him because "his name's Cinna"; and chooses to suggest that Cinna's offstage fate will be dismemberment. In contrast, only one of the two accounts of "the murther of Cinna" in North's Plutarch describes the victim, in passing, as "a Poet." In this account, moreover, the crowd that kills Cinna genuinely confuses him with the conspirator, and tells us only that the plebeians "presently dispatched him" and "slue him outright."[17] In his first dramatic adaptation of a Plutarchan narrative the playwright thus freely alters his historical source.

Focusing on such authorial decisions, Gary Taylor has recently concluded the most extended discussion of Cinna's death with a judgment that would have pleased Gosson: "To tell the truth boldly, the more I think about Shakespeare's scene, the less I like it. It is wrong historically, it is wrong morally; it was wrong then, it is still wrong now."[18] Taylor does not, however, share Gosson's conception of the dramatist as an unabashed panderer to "the worst sort of people." Instead he indicts Shakespeare for both exaggerating the historical rabble's indiscriminate violence in this scene and depicting an apolitical poet's victimization at their hands, thereby creating a false opposition "between poet and plebeians, between poet and conspirator" (p. 338). The playwright, charges Taylor, creates a defense of poetry at the expense of truth. If we accept this argument, then Cinna's murder by the mob in 3.3 involves a program—a program extending to the camp poet's encounter with Cassius and Brutus in 4.3—whereby Shakespeare erects a false distinction between the poetic and political spheres. Far from a self-conscious exploration of the potential violence of the public theater, the scene appears on this reading a façade of false consciousness, a nefarious attempt to deny art's implication in the chaotic social world around it.

Is this the case? Taylor marshals strong evidence for his assertion that Shakespeare goes out of his way to enhance the fickleness of the rabble in this play. In North's Plutarch, for example, the funeral orations that precede Cinna's murder are separated by a day, and the crowd is constant in its disapproval of Caesar's assassination.[19] In Shakespeare's version, by contrast, the orations are juxtaposed, and "the popular voice" becomes a rhetorical barometer. Taylor also seems justified in arguing that the poets in this play conspicuously make nothing happen. Whereas in Plutarch it is a philosopher who intervenes in the quarrel between Brutus and Cassius, successfully reconciling them, in Shakespeare a poet enters after the reconciliation has already occurred, and his well-intended but untimely doggerel is subsequently ridiculed (4.2.187-91). But the distinction between the men of the word and the men of the world in *Julius Caesar* may not be as clear as this reading suggests. And if the nominal poets in this play seem to emphasize the division between art and politics, the politicians bridge this gulf in their representation as dramatists playing to an audience.

Taylor foists upon the author of *Julius Caesar* (1599) the conception of poetry expressed by the author of *Venus and Adonis* (1592-1593)—"a publicly intimate relationship between poet and patron" above history, ideology, and the *vulgus.*[20] A skeptic might object, of course, that intimacy is always a fictive pose for poets operating in a print culture, and that by submitting their words to fame's court such poets consciously (if surreptitiously) offer them as public property.[21] Whether or not this was Shakespeare's awareness when he composed his non-dramatic poetry for individual patrons, however, it must have become so in 1599, when a pirate divulged two of "his sugred Sonnets"—previously circulated only "among his priuate friends"—to the world.[22] Thus by 1599, if not before, there was irony, intentional or imposed, in the patronage poet's *occupatio,* as in Sonnet 102: "That love is merchandized whose rich esteeming / The owner's tongue doth publish everywhere." But the proto-romantic view of the poet Taylor ascribes to the author of *Julius Caesar* ignores more than the complex status of patronage poetry in the late sixteenth-century (and the significant body of recent criticism that has demonstrated this complexity).[23] It also ignores Shakespeare's awareness of the altogether different socioeconomic mise en scène that produced the play itself. Indeed, *Julius Caesar* dramatizes the irrelevance and obsolescence of the very mode of poetry Taylor accuses Shakespeare of perpetuating under false pretenses.

III "A Strange-disposed Time"

Although *poet* remained both the popular and technical term for the play-wright during Shakespeare's lifetime,[24] there are reasons both historical and textual to suppose that dramatists working in England's increasingly public theaters had occasion to reevaluate and revalue this term. As Elizabeth's court blurred the distinction between private courtship and public courtiership, so her elaborately theatricalized self-presentation erased the boundaries between stagecraft and statecraft. When political power can be dramatized, power itself devolves to a public where interpretive possibilities proliferate. On the Renaissance public stage, sovereign self-presentation is necessarily subjected to representation; the autonomous production of ideology (like selfhood) is rendered an object of the contingencies of reproduction. It was less theatrical self-assertion, therefore, than a complaint of theatrical vulnerability that underlay Elizabeth's remark to a deputation of Lords and Commons: "We princes are set upon stages in the sight and view of all the world."[25] Like Elizabeth, Hamlet realizes the danger of playing to the world. The collaborative social act of public theater, however, demands this economy, and Hamlet must finally submit to theatrical appropriation: "High on a stage . . . placed to the view"; reduced, like the court jester he has elegized, to a silent and portable synecdoche of the self; he becomes an erased mouth, a silence inviting spectators' glosses, the quietus ultimately required of the observed of all observers. For Hamlet and Elizabeth, the stage inexorably transforms the self into a passive spectacle fashioned for and by "the sight and view" of others.

In 1601 the Queen of England identified herself as the property of a public beyond her control: "I am Richard II. Know ye not that? . . . He that will forget God, will also forget his benefactors; this tragedy was played 40tie times in open streets and houses."[26] Stephen Greenblatt has observed that Elizabeth responds here to the potential for iteration and indeterminacy[27] of a play construed after a subversive fashion, a play that seems to have broken the boundaries of its house and emerged into a world of limitless audience and multiple factions. To this we should add that her response is concomitant with a perceived disintegration of patronage assumptions ("He that will forget God, will also forget his benefactors"), and with her recognition that she has become a victim of other-fashioning. Whether referring to Shakespeare's play or to Hayward's tract, the anger and anxiety of Elizabeth's self-identification with Richard responds to the fact that it is an identification thrust upon her, an identification that threatens her identity. Like the commissioning viewer of an anamorphic painting, she looks to the story of Henry of Lancaster and Richard of Bordeaux for a familiar reflection of her self-image and finds instead—from another's perspective—a radically subversive alterity, a subrogated persona that troubles the semiotics of the whole composition.[28]

Two years before this dramatic alteration challenged Elizabeth's "Semper Eadem," the Chamberlain's Men had completed a metaphoric transition—from The Theatre, through The Curtain, to The Globe—[29] that seems appropriately responsive to a self-conscious shift, in England's public drama, from the aesthetically insulated to the politically fraught. It was on the Globe's stage, in 1599, that an actor playing the Chorus in *Henry V* anticipated a Caesar-like "general of our gracious Empress" returning triumphantly from Ireland (5.30-34); and it was earlier in this same year, many scholars agree, that *Julius Caesar* was first produced as the inaugural play in "this wooden O."[30] 1599, the year the "newly built" Globe became "the possession of William Shakespeare and others,"[31] would have been particularly unaccommodating for the vision of playwrighting "as a publicly intimate relationship between poet and patron." For the preceding year, the Privy Council responded to the annual letter of complaint from the Lord Mayor and the Court of Aldermen with a resolution that was unprecedented: it declared that all public playhouses were to be "plucked down" due to the "lewd matters that are handled on the stages" and the "very great disorders" resulting from the "resort and confluence of bad people." This order of the Privy Council (July 28, 1598), which might have given specific topical resonance to the antitheatrical and anti-congregational Tribunes in the first scene of *Julius Caesar,* was of course never executed, but it marked the beginning of an intense period of legislation against London's public theaters. To gain "possession" of the Globe near the end of the sixteenth century was to enter a theater of contest in which private enterprise and state power were frequently at odds.

Indeed, the Globe itself was constructed of contested property. On December 28, 1598, James and Richard Burbage, together with a master carpenter and a dozen tradesmen, dismantled the deserted Theatre and transported its valuable timber to the Bankside, where it was erected as the new home of the Chamberlain's Men. Giles Allen, the increasingly antitheatrical landlord of the Theatre who had requested the departure of his thespian tenants earlier that year, seems to have desired to "convert the wood and timber thereof to some better use." In the subsequent lawsuit Allen's plaint is remarkable for its representation of the defendants as a mob run amok, threatening city and crown. The Burbages and their accessories, he charged,

> then and there armed themselves with divers and many unlawful and offensive weapons, as, namely, swords, daggers, bills, axes, and such like, and so armed did then repair unto the said Theatre. And then and there, armed as aforesaid, in very riotous, outrageous, and forcible manner, and contrary to the laws of your Highness' realm, attempted to pull down the said Theatre, whereupon divers of your subjects, servants, and farmers, then going about in peaceable manner to procure them to desist from that their unlawful enterprise, they (the said riotous persons aforesaid) notwithstanding procured then therein with great violence, not only then and there forcibly and riotously resisting your subjects, servants, and farmers, but also then and there pulling, breaking, and throwing down the said Theatre in very outrageous, violent, and riotous sort, to the great

> disturbance and terrifying not only of your subjects, said servants, and farmers, but of diverse others of your Majesty's loving subjects there near inhabiting.[32]

It is tempting to compare this riotous representation to the plebeians, "moved"—by Antony's promise of a new recreational park "On this side Tiber," fit for "common pleasures" (3.2.249-50)—to "Pluck down benches! Pluck down forms, windows, anything!" (3.2.258-59). Less conjecturally, we can observe that Allen's no doubt embellished account comes very near the energies that Shakespeare represents in the Globe's inaugural play. An intriguing insight into Shakespeare's complex response to this moment of artistic reassessment appears in Andrew Gurr's demonstration that, around the year 1600, he began to reconceive his customers as spectators rather than auditors.[33] Some of the epistemological and political implications of this transformation appear most clearly when we consider the altogether different response of a rival playwright to this same period of change.

For Ben Jonson, the recurrent metaphor of the "Poetomachia" is that of the trial or arraignment, so that the warring dramatists present, in Tibullus' phrase, competing "Law-cases in verse."[34] But Jonson's problem, even as he goes about defining the role of the socially relevant public poet, lies in determining that court in which he wishes to appeal his case. In *Poetaster* (1601), for instance, he legitimizes his ideal, politically and morally salutary poets (Horace and Vergil), by banishing the socially marginal (Ovid), and by purging the civically deleterious (Crispinus and Fannius). Jonson's poetic ideal proves less than efficacious on the public stage, however, where cases are tried not in Augustus' court, but by a corrupt jury. Jonson sends "An armed Prologue" to defend his play from rooms filled with "base detractors, and illiterate apes";[35] and in his "apologeticall Dialogue," addressing not a multitudinous spectatorship but an individual reader, he declares the world a "baud" and promises his next dramatic effort will seek a fit audience, however few: "Where, if I prove the pleasure but of one / So he judicious be; He shall b'alone / A Theatre unto me" (213-15). But in the public theater, such retreats into Stoic self-sufficiency are as impossible as imposing a fixed, textual meaning on a script intended for common consumption. In the Globe, to turn one's back on the world is inevitably to invite backstabbing. Thomas Dekker therefore prefaces his theatrical response to Jonson in terms perfectly pitched to elicit the latter's anxiety: "Horace hal'd his Poetasters to the barre, the Poetasters untruss'd Horace: how worthily eyther, or how wrongfully, (World) leave it to the jurie."[36] Before this jury, Dekker in *Satiro-Mastix* (1601) does with Horace much what the Essex party does with the story of Richard II in the same year: as a deposition scene appears subversive when placed in the contemporary political context, so does Horace look ridiculous when dropped "into the middle of a flamboyantly romantic tragi-comedy."[37] For Jonson, as for his Queen, the public theater submits one to an audience composed of *both* predatory rival playwrights and an injudicious tribunal.

Finding his case altered by 1603, then, Jonson replaces the Augustan court with the Tiberian to reflect the willful misreading and evidentiary misconstruction to which the public poet is vulnerable. In his dedicatory epistle to Lord Aubigny, he at once identifies *Sejanus*' reception with that of its dismembered "subject," and seeks to appeal the Globe's unjust verdict to a single patron: "It is a poem that—if I well remember—in your Lordship's sight, suffered no less violence from our people here than the subject of it did from the rage of the people of Rome, but with a different fate, as (I hope) merit."[38] Here, perhaps, is a case for Taylor's criticism of the dramatist disingenuously posing as an apolitical creature victimized by a world he claims the right to ignore, a playwright for whom "our people here" are indeed "vulgar interlopers" mangling the intimate artistic utterance of a play that has silently become "a poem."[39] For the Jonson of 1603, theatrical values ultimately prove corrosive to his conception of artistic integrity; the Globe, engaged in a bacchanalia of epistemological and evaluative indiscrimination, must either consume the Orphic poet or exile him to a private, meritocratic world elsewhere. What would later in Jonson's dramatic career become an effort to prevent this indiscrimination by seeking a poetic audience, not a theatrical spectatorship,[40] takes an early shape in his desire to place his literary evidence before homogeneous judges, not a heterogeneous jury. As late as 1611, in fact, he intermittently appeals to a higher evaluative court; his epistle to the Earl of Pembroke, published prefatorily to *Catiline,* reveals an attempt to convert drama into patronage poetry: "Now, it approcheth your censure cheerefully, and with the same assurance, that innocency would appeare before a magistrate." Like Milton after him, Jonson inhabits a "solitude" threatened by "evil tongues," a fragile kingdom of intentionality "with dangers compassed round," and he seeks to define his hermeneutically "fit audience" by insulating it from "the barbarous dissonance" of those inimical to his poetic meaning.

But this defiant, embattled stance must not be confused with Shakespeare's in the same period. If any Shakespearean dramatic text seems to invite such confusion, it is *Troilus and Cressida* (1601-03?), with its appended preface addressing an "eternal" reader in an ideal act of literary communication independent of history, the staling stage, and "the palmes of the vulger."[41] More substantially, however, the play represents a self-conscious departure from Jonson's conception of the theater poet; it may even be Shakespeare's fullest acknowledgment that the public playwright is not an innocent victim of the interpretive energies of a place such as The Globe.

Troilus and Cressida's chiastic mock of *Poetaster*'s "armed Prologue," for instance, recognizes the permeability of authorial prophylactics against promiscuous interpretation. Rather than guarding his play from the audience's subjective misconstruction, Shakespeare's "prologue arm'd" (Prologue, 23) invites the audience to participate in this martial drama as autonomous, potentially combative judges: "Like or find fault, do as your pleasures are, / Now good or bad, 'tis but the chance of war" (30-31). If the preface contemptuously dismisses the clapper-clawing hands of the multitude, this prologue submits the play's reception to the multiple "pleasures" of a similarly arbitrary jury. And in his epilogue Pandarus suggests that all those who have participated in this sullying "performance" are not only infected by a venereal clap, but also equipped with a rapacious claw. The "traders in the flesh" (5.10.45) who fill "Pandar's hall" (47) figure a collaborative spectatorship that would hypocritically distance itself from the prurient and purveyant drama it has employed. In a rebuke that reminds us his name means nothing but "to go between," however, Pandarus refuses his customers such a voyeuristic withdrawal:

> O world, world, world! thus is the poor agent despis'd!
> O traders and bawds, how earnestly are you set a-work,
> and how ill requited! Why should our endeavor be so
> lov'd and the performance so loath'd?
>
> (36-39)

Pandarus' diction here, if not his sense, is that of the antitheatricalist excoriation of a Babylonian stage endeavoring to satisfy a devouring world—a pandering playwright vending his diseased images to an easily infected audience in the "market of bawdrie." His almost post-coital regret and eruptive self-aversion, in fact, seem to anticipate the contrition, as described in *A Refutation of the Apology for Actors,* of playgoers who "know the Histories before they see them acted [and] are very ashamed when they have heard what lyes the Players insert among them, and how greatly they deprave them."[42] Far from a defense of poetry, this epilogue incorporates the antitheatrical position in an unrepentant admission of dramatic guilt that finally indicts the audience as an accessory. To show, claims Pandarus, is to violate; to watch is to participate.

Such a conclusion is the caustic culmination of a play that metatheatrically considers its own role in the deflation and perversion of classical heroic characterology. The "strange fellow" whose argument Ulysses reiterates to lure Achilles to battle seems to articulate a benign version of this role when he claims that "[N]o man is the lord of any thing . . . Till he communicate his parts to others; / Nor doth he of himself know them for aught, / Till he behold them formed in th' applause / Where th' are extended" (3.3.115, 117-20). But James Calderwood's description of this communicative theory as involving "a generative intercourse between bearer and observer"[43] plays down Shakespeare's emphasis on the degenerative potentiality of such intercourse. In a drama that itself refracts the epics of Homer and Vergil through several different "recuyells" of the histories of Troy,[44] the fate of history and its subjects ultimately rests in the hands of the dramatist and his audience. Like Pandarus, the playwright can commodify the "parts" of historical subjects by assembling a textual pastiche for a predatory public; like Thersites, who is himself addresed as a "fragment,"[45] the playgoer can reduce all such representations to scabrous objects through dissective evaluation. The same hands that manufacture constitutive applause can serve as claws of misconstruction. By dramatizing such a transaction and transformation, *Troilus and Cressida* explores the darker possibilities of a theater that defines the dramatist not as a victim but as a conspirator. We can trace this exploration back to the Globe's inaugural play.

IV "Censuring Rome"

Julius Caesar seems to know no other medium than the public stage, as critics have long demonstrated by pointing out its preference for the rhetorical mode over the lyrical, for public declamation and customary proverbs over private reflection and soliloquy.[46] As Brutus responds when asked if one can ever properly know one's self: "No, Cassius, for the eye sees not itself / But by reflection, by some other thing" (1.2.52-53). Frequently, this "other thing" proves to be the speculum of theater itself. In a marketplace reeking of the commoners' breath, Caesar is clapped and hissed for his political dumbshow "according as he pleas'd and displeas'd" his plebeian audience, "as they use to do the players in the theatre" (1.3.259-61). Brutus urges his fellow conspirators to dissemble their purpose by bearing the staid countenance of "our Roman actors" (2.1.226). And Antony, the lover of plays who most successfully exploits political theater, drops a telling term as he urges Octavius to reevaluate Lepidus, the least consequential and most easily manipulated member of the triumvirate: "Do not talk of him / But as a property" (4.1.39-40). One of *Julius Caesar*'s central dramas is the appropriation of the private by the public, the denotation of "that within which passeth show" by "actions that a man might play," and the reduction of autonomous men to communicable parts and transferable stage properties. The play concedes the potential violence of this drama in the central, emblematic scene of Cinna's dismemberment. In *Julius Caesar*'s earlier consumption of its eponym, however, the play suggests that such physical violence can serve as a metaphor for the injury of theatrical other-fashioning.

Shakespeare's later Roman tragedies pluck out the heart of mystery with the ceremony of sacrifice and the savage coolness of an anatomy.[47] Cleopatra would prefer to be a "stark-nak'd" corpse rather than face her audience as a conscious property in the figurative dismemberment she imagines Octavius staging in his theatrical triumph, "pinion'd," "hoist," and displayed "to the shouting varlotry / Of censuring Rome." She ruins her mortal house unwilling to witness the "Mechanic slaves" who will expose Antony and herself "to the view," distorting their biographies through mannered theatricalism (5.2.49-62, 208-21). But while Cleopatra may resist theatrical appropriation by playing the Roman, the irony of this refuge is as inescapable as the theater that subsumes her. For the theater imagined in Shakespeare's Roman tragedies is populated by an intrusive public and exploitative actors; it tolerates no inscrutable inwardness, no self-sufficient independence from the theatrical economy; it sheds blood and breaks bodies to render the private public, to sacrifice individual subjectivity to theatrical viability and spectacle.

Coriolanus may refuse to play to such a crowd, "turn[ing]" his "back" in a consummately antitheatrical gesture of introversion, standing instead "As if a man were author of himself," seeking to be "every man himself" and "not . . . other than one thing." But he is stabbed to death as the people shout "Tear him to pieces!"[48] And what is the public theater but the people? What are these people but Gosson's Hydra-like "monster"? As a proleptic and definitive answer to such questions, *Julius Caesar* digests its subject (who has proclaimed "always I am Caesar" [1.2.212] with the same self-consciousness, the same ironic untenability, and perhaps the same anxiety toward protean theatricality that underlies Elizabeth's "*Semper Eadem*") early in the third act, when the conspirators decide that Caesar must die to be seen. Brutus tries and condemns his friend not for what he is, but for what he might be, for the undetermined and undisclosed subjunctive mood of his spirit:

> He would be crown'd
> How that might change his nature, there's the question.
>
> (2.1.12-13)
>
> . . . . .
>
> O that we then could come by Caesar's spirit,
> And not dismember Caesar! But, alas,
> Caesar must bleed for it!
>
> (2.1.168-70)

Caesar must bleed because the conspiracy of *Caesar* can have no unscrutinized spirits. Caesar must bleed because the conspirators—no less than the plebeians who come to his funeral shouting "We will be satisfied! Let us be satisfied! (3.2.1)—wish to see his body opened before them like a text. Caesar must bleed for a theater whose liturgy is haruspication,[49] whose medium is synecdoche, and whose privileged jury is invariably comprised of multiple observers of a silenced object.

The constituents of this jury, however, proliferate wildly the moment the courtroom is confused with theater, the moment the accused is converted into evidentiary spectacle. A number of critics have demonstrated that Caesar's death coincides with his historicization and textualization.[50] His famous (*paene*) *ultima verba,* in fact, seem to function antithetically to the infamous anachronism that strikes in 2.1: as Sigurd Burckhardt has argued, the clock that punctuates the conspirators' plot resonates with the timelessness and interpretive indeterminacy of their action.[51] In an English stage-play, however, Caesar's marmoreal Latin appears to italicize the difference of history and its distance from the drama that relates it. Yet his last words are themselves the product of theatrical appropriation: although they live in the popular memory in Shakespeare's translation, they were originally delivered in Greek.[52] Caesar may die in his native tongue, but his speech is rendered alien by his maker. It is a fundamental irony of *Julius Caesar* that its most self-conscious presentation of the autonomous past of history proves inextricably bound to the eternal present of dramatic reenactment and reinterpretation.

While Caesar's blood is still warm, this metadramatic irony operates at the conspirators' expense as they celebrate the conclusion of their case and their authorship of a history play:

> *Cassius:* Stoop then, and wash. How many ages hence
> Shall this our lofty scene be acted over
> In states unborn and accents yet unknown.
> *Brutus:* How many times shall Caesar bleed in sport;
> That now on Pompey's basis lies along
> No worthier than the dust!
>
> (3.1.111-16)

Cassius and Brutus assert the historical primacy of their action while anticipating the future stage history of this "lofty scene." They attempt to distinguish between a gory event and its aestheticized dramatization as "sport." But in *Julius Caesar* history is conceived a priori in theatrical terms, by actors who recognize its perspectival malleability. It is Brutus' presumed dramatic control over the action and evaluation of the history in which he participates that signals his hybris. Just as Brutus seeks to mold Caesar into a figure of deservingly punished *pleonexia,* for instance, so does he attempt to direct the roles of his fellow conspirators. Calling for Caius Ligarius, he prepares to convert a man with undetermined political allegiances into a character with an unambiguous part to play: "Send him but hither, and I'll fashion him" (2.1.220). And after assuming direction of an assassination rehearsed in "Pompey's Theatre" (1.3.152), Brutus insists on the conspirators' billing as sacrificers, not butchers, as purgers, not murderers. *Julius Caesar,* however, proves to be beyond Brutus' management; and his reversal from conspirator to conspired against coincides with the deposition of his self-presentation and an authorial usurpation of the play for which it was intended. Restaging the scene of tyrannicide around the property of Caesar's corpse, Antony in 3.2 assigns to the conspirators the very parts they had eschewed. Cassius and Brutus condemn themselves when they draw a false distinction between bloody history and bloodless drama, declaring the case closed while the jury is still out, and abandoning the public stage to Antony's constructions. Having reduced Caesar's body to a text with wounds that gape "like dumb mouths" (3.1.260), they forget the instability of this text. They fail to recognize that the ambiguous body of the condemned "may signify equally well the truth of the crime or the error of the judges, the goodness or evil of the criminal."[53] Thus, like their victim, the conspirators become objects of other-fashioning.

Shakespeare reveals his awareness that his own plotting of history is subject to the same interpretive energies it employs. Critics such as Taylor would deny this consciousness of contingency, reading Shakespeare's public drama as the literary "work" of an entrenched patronage poet rather than the "play" of an author willingly de-centered by the common theater.[54] An instructive corrective to this anachronism, however, appears in Samuel Johnson's editorial complaint:

> But of the works of Shakespeare the condition has been far different [from that of works published under the direct supervision of their authors]: he sold them, not to be printed, but to be played. They were immediately copied for the actors, and multiplied by transcript, vitiated by the blunders of the penmen, or changed by the affectation of the player; perhaps enlarged to introduce a jest, or mutilated to shorten the representation; and printed at last without the concurrence of the author, without the consent of the proprietor, from compilations made by chance or by stealth out of the separate parts written for the theatre.[55]

The original "condition" of Shakespeare's dramatic texts resembles Gosson's description of history adapted to the theater, a description that applies equally well to Caesar's body: "mutilated" as occasion demands; deconstructed into, and reconstituted from, the "separate parts" of different participatory perspectives; they exist less as intrinsic meaning than as material to be recreated in performance.

If this metaphor of a corporeal text subject to the unkindest cuts of all implies a distinction between victimhood and aggression, it is clear that Shakespeare identifies with the latter. To insist like a Jonsonian prologue upon a fixed, hermeneutically determined textualism is almost invariably to be a victim or a fool on Shakespeare's stage. Calling for a judgment consonant with his inflexible reading of a bond he has authored, Shylock becomes a victim of alternative interpretations; fashioning himself in a letter that seems to reflect the greatness of his own self-image, Malvolio becomes a "propertied" fool when he realizes his ridiculous part and cross-gartered fashion have been assigned by unseen witnesses.[56] Nobody's fool and never a self-proclaimed victim outside of the sonnets, Shakespeare recognizes the terms of the theatrical economy in which he operates. While the theater is open, no case is closed; when the jury is "the common eyes," a moment can transform plaintiff into defendant, text into pretext, the carefully wrought self into an appropriated other; when the price of admission buys the audience something as insubstantial as a play, the theater compensates by procuring all that it represents as the interpretive property of this audience.

There is evidence suggesting the special inevitability of this economy for the Renaissance author of *Julius Caesar.* By imagining "states unborn" and "accents yet unknown," Cassius prophesies the linguistic and cultural differences Shakespeare encounters as he recovers this "lofty scene" from history; simultaneously, then, this play looks back to an anterior future when the English state and language were "yet unknown" and forward to a present when those restaging the scene might have "Small Latine and Lesse Greek," a time when Cicero's linguistic inaccessibility to Casca might reflect Plutarch's to Shakespeare: it was Greek to both of them. But like the playwright's history, Cassius' prophecy is construed after a dramatic fashion: on a level we have already considered, this prophecy becomes for Shakespeare an opportunity for dramatic irony. We know what for Casca is tragically "unknown" and "unborn"—that the conspirators' "lofty scene" will be first "acted over" by Antony's accent, and that the play will conclude with the conspirators' deaths and the birth of the Second Triumvirate. From Shakespeare's literary and historical moment, however, the irony goes further. For by the end of the sixteenth century, Cassius' and Brutus' first performance had long been the stock of artists and the debated exemplum of moralists and political theorists, receiving different "accents" or evaluative emphases as monarchy and republic, tyrants and traitors, were viewed from different perspectives.[57] For a playwright capable of imagining an audience of "eyes not yet created,"[58] though, the shortest path to obsolescence and revisionary victimization is to deny the contingency of such emphasis upon the historical moment, to assume a unanimous and monological interpretive community, and to forget that his play is the property of the very history it represents—that his text (before the posthumous First Folio) has no status, only unforeseen "states." The political ambiguity of *Julius Caesar* is therefore the design of a survivor, not a victim. With Aufidius, Shakespeare acknowledges a truth fatally denied by Coriolanus: that in both history plays and history, "virtues / Lie in th' interpretation of the time" (4.7.49-50). Accordingly, if *Julius Caesar* has a central reference point, it is an audience at once constitutive and prone to metamorphosis.

The plebeians who comprise this audience, however, also embody the misconstructive jury, the bacchanalian rout, posited by the antitheatricalists in their indictment of the public stage as a courtroom travestied. In the central scene of Cinna's apprehension by this audience Shakespeare seems to concede many of the terms of the antitheatrical position as he looks critically at the economy in which he is implicated. This scene presents a mock treason trial, made disturbingly absurd by the fact that the accused withholds no interior allegiances to be revealed. If Caesar represented for the conspirators a mysterious "serpent's egg" of potentiality (2.1.32), Cinna discloses his innocence in direct, brief, wise, and true replies to his interrogators. The plebeians' response is to collapse the distinction between body and spirit that Brutus himself honored in the breach his dagger made; and the result is a savage farce, a brutal simplification of the theatrical appropriation that pervades the play.

As Cinna speaks his last vain words, he becomes what the plebeians wish him to be, a silent stage property to be fashioned as an insistent audience likes it:

> *Cinna:* I am not Cinna the conspirator.
> *4. Plebeian:* It is no matter, his name's Cinna. Pluck but his name out of his heart, and turn him going.
> *3. Plebeian:* Tear him, tear him!
> *Exeunt all the Plebeians dragging off Cinna.*
>
> (3.3.32-35)

We might follow Taylor's "Bardicide" in reading this passage as a self-conscious reference to Orpheus' dismemberment (pp. 334-38). But we must make a crucial distinction between Shakespeare's apparent allusion to the archetypal poet-victim here and the similarly oblique suggestion of Orpheus' fate we have seen in Jonson's dedication to *Sejanus.* Unlike Jonson, Shakespeare does not represent this figure—and the violence inflicted upon him by "the rage of the people of Rome"—in a moment of injured self-identification. Rather, Shakespeare seems to conjure the specter of Orpheus' *sparagmos* to demonstrate the fate of a *kind* of poet, a *kind* of voice, when subjected to the abattoir of public theater. Such a generic application, in fact, had precedent in the Renaissance: "the euhemeristic reading of the Orpheus myth as the displacement of Greek lyric poetry by Dionysiac ritual drama" might, for instance, have presented itself to the playwright in Golding's Ovid.[59] If Cinna serves as a figure for Orpheus, moreover, then we have in *Julius Caesar* an important early example of what Kenneth Gros Louis has described as a seventeenth-century poetic and iconographic development: the shift from representations of Orpheus triumphant to representations of Orpheus dismembered, reflecting an emergent skepticism toward poetry's ability to communicate clearly and to achieve its desired humanistic effects on its audience.[60] In the world of *Julius Caesar,* at any rate, to treat the nominal poets as Shakespeare's self-representations is to confuse the purpose of the play's conscious differentiation between victims and victimizers, between an obsolescent mode of poetic subjectivity and the drama that consumes it. Far from an insidious defense of drama's innocence and inconsequence, *Julius Caesar* enacts a farsighted, metatheatrical critique of the dramatist and his diverse clientele.

Cinna is no more Shakespeare than is the officious camp poet dismissed later in the play for his inutility and for his decidedly unheroic couplet:

> *Poet:* For shame, you generals! what do you mean?
> Love, and be friends, as two such men should be,
> For I have seen more years, I'm sure, than ye.
> *Cassius:* Ha, ha! how vildly does this cynic rhyme!
> *Brutus:* Get you hence, sirrah; saucy fellow, hence!
> *Cassius:* Bear with him, Brutus, 'tis his fashion.
> *Brutus:* I'll know his humor, when he knows his time.
> What should the wars do with these jigging fools?
> Companion, hence!
>
> (4.3.130-38)

Like Cinna, although by verbal rather than physical violence, this poet is removed from the stage because he is an anachronism, a "fashion" in the wrong place at the wrong time. Nearly ten years before *Julius Caesar* first appeared, Christopher Marlowe had introduced a revolutionary play with a prologue defining his theater in negative terms remarkably similar to Brutus':

> From jigging veins of rhyming mother wits,
> And such conceits as clownage keeps in pay,
> We'll lead you to the stately tent of war,
> Where you shall hear the Scythian Tamburlaine
> Threatening the world with his high astounding terms,
> And scourging kingdoms with his conquering sword.
> View but his picture in this tragic glass,
> And then applaud his fortunes as you please.[61]

For Shakespeare as for Marlowe, "the stately tent of war" offers little shelter for poets who do not know their time, exposing them instead to ridicule and to the ruinous energies of a theater that has overtaken them. For Shakespeare as for Marlowe, moreover, the "tragic glass" of this public theater confines mighty men in little room, represents historical figures through dramatic spectacle, and proffers this dramatized exterior to an uncertain reception. In such an economy, authorial intention can claim no more control over a text's consequences than Antony claims over the people he has "moved" through a carefully staged scene:

> Now let it work. Mischief, thou art afoot,
> Take thou what course thou wilt!
>
> (3.2.259-60)

In such an economy, a text's consequentiality consists in part of this predictability.

V

Significantly, every act of writing in *Julius Caesar* draws blood. In the broadsheets Cassius writes "in several hands," "wherein obscurely Caesar's ambition shall be glanced at" (1.2.316, 319-20); in the anonymous notes Cinna the conspirator throws in Brutus' way (1.3.145); and in the proscription list on which Antony damns lives with spots of ink (4.1.6), the injury textually inflicted seems to correspond with the author's intention. And yet the conspirators, as we have seen, involuntarily involve themselves in their own plot the moment they script it and declare it finished. Antony in turn loses sole authorship of his counterplot as it becomes the collaborative product of the other triumvirs. Having judged the proscription list complete, he is forced by Octavius to add the name of Lepidus' brother, a revision Lepidus makes contingent upon the inclusion of Antony's nephew. Similarly, once a text is composed in this play, it is subject to politicized readings beyond the author's control, and of this pervasive process the poet's death once again provides a central, emblematic image. Culminating a scene in which he amplifies the plebeians' outrage by gradually undressing Caesar's torn corpse, Antony publicly reads the dead man's will as a last incitement to riot (3.2.240-52). Just two scenes later, however, Caesar's will is figuratively dismembered as Antony determines "How to cut off some charge in legacies" (4.1.9). The intervening scene of Cinna's murder presents the literal dismemberment of an author whose will counts for nothing and whose audience chooses to misread him. In this scene Shakespeare schematizes the fate of all communication in the play. When the audience is both mobile and prone to action, when spectators become collaborators, when the jury arrogates the dual privilege of constituting meaning and executing its sentence, a speech-act's illocutionary intention dissolves into its perlocutionary effect. From the vantage point of 1601, such an awareness can only appear prophetic, for two years earlier Shakespeare claims for his drama the dangerous power to bestow an Exton on the world to make many Extons.[62]

But what justification have we for treating *Julius Caesar*'s plebeians as an unflattering, unmitigated representation of the Globe audience's potential? To what extent is Shakespeare's metadramatic antitheatricalism contained by Rome and the play that concerns it? A limited answer lies in recognizing the diachronic transformation of the crowd in *Julius Caesar.* The plebeians who make their final exit bearing Cinna at the end of Act 3 first took the stage preparing for Caesar's triumph at the beginning of Act 1 and we must include the facts of this metamorphosis in our assessment of Shakespeare's representation of the audience in this play. Instead of a pack of marauding plebeians pursuing a poet, we find in 1.1 "certain commoners" (*s.d.*) set upon by inquisitorial tribunes; instead of an indistinct rabble seeking blood we find a remarkably individuated cobbler able to pun with the best of Shakespeare's English tradesmen. The line distinguishing sixteenth-century England and ancient Rome in *Julius Caesar* is never more blurred than in this scene. The Tribunes alternately seem like London aldermen policing sumptuary laws and Puritan antitheatricalists censuring the license, social confusion, and spectacle of the public theater: Flavius and Murellus chastise the keepers of this shoemaker's holiday for doffing "the sign" of their profession and donning their "best attire" (4, 48); and having dispersed the crowd, they set out to "Disrobe the images" decked with Caesar's "ceremonies" (64-65). The "certain Commoners" who cross the stage in 1.1 would appear to have no more objectionable motive than the desire for spectacle, the wish "to see Caesar and rejoice in his triumph" (31). And yet the Tribunes' antitheatrical anxiety in this scene is justified (and, significantly, left unchallenged by a play that does not make them the conventional object of protheatrical satire). Not only do the masquerading commoners range about the liberties dislocated from their social station; they are also interpretive individuals, each capable of construing the meaning of words after his fashion, as the cobbler's relentless punning reveals. When the vulgar can divest themselves of their social signifiers, when the vernacular can be invested with paronomasial significance, the theatrical audience acquires interpretive agency and the theater itself thereby becomes epistemologically open-ended and politically consequential. In 1.1 the plebeians enter as political innocents, and Murellus reproves them for failing to realize that the triumph they yearn to watch "comes . . . over Pompey's blood" (51). In 3.3 the plebeians exit bloodied with the experience of political theater, having demonstrated that to watch in this play is also to act. While in 1.1 they observe a social carnival, in 3.3 they effect political carnage. In 1.1, the cobbler's playfulness with language, his witty misreading of the Tribunes' sense, appears innocuous, whereas in 3.3, the fourth plebeian's wordplay is fatal, his misreading of Cinna a literal pun that tears name from thing. In 1.1, finally, Shakespeare's audience might have recognized itself in the protheatrical image of a harmless, recreational spectatorship; in 3.3 this audience would have seen itself transformed into (or revealed as?) the misconstruing miscreation that elicited Roman theatrical censorship.

Such is the plebeians' metamorphosis from "stones" (1.1.36) to "men" (3.2.142),[63] from theatrical naïfs to initiates in the political theater. Like all metamorphoses, it involves less a break than a continuum: the difference between culling out a holiday and killing a man depends only on the degree of the spectators' participation. And like many initiations, it involves a ceremonial rite. If Caesar dies at the hands of republican fellow players unwilling to cede the theater to a single monarchical actor, Cinna dies as a sacrifice to an audience that has taken the stage. It may seem strange for Shakespeare to inaugurate his Globe in these terms, to baptize his audience with the blood of a poet, to figure its interpretive autonomy in a literal act of dismemberment. But dismemberment is his metaphor when, less than a year after *Julius Caesar*'s first performance, he invokes his audience's imaginative collaboration in *Henry V:* "Piece out our imperfections with your thoughts; / Into a thousand parts divide one man" (Prol. 24-25). In the theater of the world every character is subject to synecdochic reading, every act and representation imperfect and unfinished, every text submitted to the cutting room, the deceptively "little room" where spectators, no less than actors, conspire to "force a play." It is as an emblem of this theater's censurable energies and properties that Cinna is dragged offstage.[64]

Notes

1. Rowland Whyte, describing the interpretive frenzy provoked by a device displayed by Essex at an entertainment for the Queen in 1595, in *Letters and Memorials of State . . . Written and Collected by Sir Henry Sidney, Sir Philip Sidney, Robert Earl of Leicester, and Viscount Lisle,* ed. Arthur Collins (1746), 1:362.

2. Stephen Gosson, *Playes Confuted in Five Actions* (1582), sig. C8v. All references to Gosson's works in this essay appear in Arthur F. Kinney's edition (*Markets of Bawdrie: The Dramatic Criticism of Stephen Gosson* [Salzburg, 1974]). I have modernized the spelling but retained the punctuation of this edition. Unless otherwise noted, all references to Gosson appear in *Playes Confuted in Five Actions.*

3. Thomas Heywood, *An Apology for Actors,* ed. Arthur Freeman (New York and London, 1973), sig. B4.

4. Philip Sidney, *An Apology for Poetry,* in *Prose Works,* ed. Albert Feuillerat (Cambridge, Eng., 1963), p. 12 (my italics).

5. *An Apology for Poetry,* p. 24.

6. See *Playes Confuted in Five Actions,* p. 161.

7. Gosson specifically objected to the recent arrival of the public stage, noting that even "modest" and "good" plays are "not fit for every man's diet: neither ought they commonly to be shown" (*The Schoole of Abuse,* p. 97).

8. A (now besieged) formulation of Michel Foucault's subversion-containment model appearing most

influentially in Stephen Greenblatt's *Shakespearean Negotiations: The Circulation of Social Energy in Renaissance England* (Berkeley, 1988), esp. pp. 21-65.

9. For an excellent discussion of the state's attempts to control topical references on the Renaissance stage, see Paul Yachnin, "The Powerless Theater," *English Literary Renaissance,* 21.1 (Winter, 1991), 49-74.

10. *The Life of Henry the Fifth,* Pro., 12, 19-20. References are to *The Riverside Shakespeare,* gen. ed. G. Blakemore Evans (Boston, 1974).

11. *An Apology for Poetry,* p. 45.

12. See Marjorie Garber, "'What's Past Is Prologue': Temporality and Prophecy in Shakespeare's History Plays," in *Renaissance Genres,* ed. Barbara Kiefer Lewalski (Cambridge, 1986), pp. 301-31. See also Sharon L. Jansen Jaech, "Political Prophecy and Macbeth's 'Sweet Bodements,'" *Shakespeare Quarterly,* 34 (1983), esp. p. 291.

13. *Shakespeare's Holinshed,* ed. Richard Hosley (New York, 1968), p. 48 (*Chronicles,* 1587 ed., p. 180).

14. Francis Bacon, "Of Prophecies," in *Essays,* ed. Edwin A. Abbott, 2 vols. (London, 1881), 2:20-21.

15. Following Garber (p. 311, *n.* 15), I borrow this term from Hayden White's *Metahistory* (Baltimore, 1973), pp. 6-7.

16. *An Apology for Poetry,* p. 68. Plutarch himself refused the title of "historian," choosing instead to relate and *evaluate* the "lives" and "minds" of his subjects.

17. Plutarch's *Liues of the Noble Grecians and Romans,* trans. Sir Thomas North (1579), intro. George Wyndham, 6 vols. (New York, 1967), 6:69-70, 201.

18. Gary Taylor, "Bardicide," in *Shakespeare and Cultural Traditions: The Selected Proceedings of the International Shakespeare Association World Congress, Tokyo, 1991,* ed. Tetsuo Kishi, Roger Pringle, and Stanley Wells (Newark, Del., 1991), p. 343. We must dismiss as specious Taylor's assertion that the scene also presents "a theatrically impossible dismemberment" (p. 334). The stage directions indicate Cinna is to be dragged offstage for his fate. Moreover, false limbs for such scenes appear in the few extant lists of Elizabethan stage properties, and the illusion of onstage dismemberment seems not to have been impossible in such plays as *Doctor Faustus* and *Titus Andronicus* (see Philip Henslowe's inventory of March, 1598, in C. Walter Hodges, *The Globe Restored* [New York, 1953], pp. 71-72. On pp. 73-74, Hodges demonstrates Elizabethan "stage machinery to produce the illusion of a beheading").

19. See North's Plutarch, 6:15. In *The Life of Brutus* no mention is made of Brutus' oration; in *The Life of Caesar* no mention made of Antony's.

20. Such is at least the ostensible authorial stance in *Venus and Adonis,* the epigram of which exhorts, "*Vilia miretur vulgus: mihi flavus Apollo / Pocula Castalia plena ministret aqua*" (from Ovid's *Amores,* 1.15.35-36). The subsequent dedicatory epistle to Henry Wriothesley also distinguishes between the unimportant censure of "the world" and the all-important pleasure of Shakespeare's patron.

21. Arthur F. Marotti remains one of the more vocal proponents of this view. See his "Patronage, Poetry, and Print," *Yearbook of English Studies,* 21 (1991), pp. 1-26; and his "Shakespeare's Sonnets as Literary Property," in *Soliciting Interpretation: Literary Theory and Seventeenth-Century English Poetry,* ed. Elizabeth D. Harvey and Katharine Eisaman Maus (Chicago, 1990), pp. 143-73.

22. Francis Meres, *Palladis Tamia, Wits Treasury* (1598), ed. D. C. Allen (Urbana, 1933), p. 283. William Jaggard printed the two sonnets (138 and 144) in *The Passionate Pilgrim* (1599).

23. In "The Politics of *Astrophil and Stella,*" Ann Rosalind Jones and Peter Stallybrass reveal that the distinction between literary courtship and public courtiership was often blurred in late sixteenth-century England's "publicly intimate" poetry (*Studies in English Literature,* 24.1 [Winter, 1984], 53-68). For further demonstrations of the difficulty of maintaining privacy in the Elizabethan and Jacobean patronage systems, see Annabel M. Patterson, *Censorship and Interpretation: the Conditions of Writing and Reading in Early Modern England* (Madison, 1984); and David Norbrook, *Poetry and Politics in the English Renaissance* (London and Boston, 1984), esp. pp. 109-56, 195-234.

24. Taylor observes this fact only to conflate what I am suggesting are the increasingly divergent roles of the patronage poet and the "theatre-poet" in late sixteenth-century England ("Bardicide," p. 345 *n.*8).

25. Quoted in J. E. Neale, *Elizabeth I and her Parliaments, 1584-1601,* 2 vols. (London, 1965), 2:119.

26. The Queen's comments were recorded by William Lambarde. See the Arden edition of Shakespeare's *King Richard II,* ed. Peter Ure (Cambridge, 1956), pp. lvii-lxii.

27. *The Power of Forms in the English Renaissance,* ed. Stephen Greenblatt (Norman, Ok., 1982), p. 3.

28. In one of the best recent readings of Hans Holbein's *The Ambassadors,* Charles Harrison describes its anamorphic effect as an intrusion of historicity upon essentiality: "the carefully achieved illusion of its instantaneity, its 'presentness,' damaged beyond repair by the representation of its contingency" ("On the Surface of Painting," *Critical Inquiry,* 15:2 [Winter, 1989], 324).

29. Between 1597 and 1599 the Chamberlain's Men probably performed at The Curtain while The Theatre

at Shoreditch was being razed and its timber used to build The Globe at Bankside. See Glynne Wickham, *Early English Stages, 1300-1660,* 2 vols. (Oxford 1972).

30. See Gary Taylor, "Canon and Chronology," in *William Shakespeare: A Textual Companion* (Oxford, 1987), p. 121; and *Julius Caesar,* in *The New Cambridge Shakespeare,* ed. Marvin Spevack (Cambridge, Eng., 1988), pp. 1-5.

31. From the postmortem inventory of Sir Thomas Brend (May 16, 1599). Cited by S. Schoenbaum, *Shakespeare: A Compact Documentary Life* (Oxford, 1977), p. 209.

32. This and the preceding quotation of Allen appear in C. W. Wallace, *The First London Theatre: Materials for a History* (Lincoln, 1913), pp. 278-79.

33. Andrew Gurr, *Playgoing in Shakespeare's London* (Cambridge, Eng., 1987), p. 93.

34. *Poetaster,* 1.3.7. Citations are to *Ben Jonson,* ed. C. H. Herford, Percy and Evelyn Simpson, 11 vols. (Oxford, 1925-1952).

35. *Poetaster,* "The Third Sounding," 6, 9. Like other playwrights in the War of the Theaters, Jonson imagines an audience that includes antagonistic playwrights and actors bent upon adulterating his text (see "The Third Sounding," 18-20, and Envy's speech, "After the Second Sounding"). John Michael Archer has shown that "the paranoid construction of Jonsonian authorship" was also a response to his fear of spies among his own actors and audience (*Sovereignty and Intelligence: Spying and Court Culture in the English Renaissance* [Stanford, 1993], pp. 94-120). One effect of the theatrical war, then, is to literalize the subjective and deliberately misconstruing audience—the audience-turned-actors—that I argue is a source of concern in *Julius Caesar.*

36. Thomas Dekker, *Satiro-Mastix,* ed. Josiah H. Penniman (Boston and London, 1962), "To the World," 15-17.

37. Katharine Maus, *Ben Jonson and The Roman Frame of Mind* (Princeton, 1984), p. 92.

38. Jonson, "To The No Less Noble, By Virtue Than Blood: Esme, Lord Aubigny," 7-10.

39. *Sejanus* provides many targets for Taylor's program of exposure. The indictment of Cremutius Cordus in Act 3, for instance, presents an untenable claim for the disinterestedness of historiography, a disingenuous denial of contemporary relevance, in a history play judged treasonously topical by the Privy Council in 1603.

40. For Jonson's fully articulated desire for a "blind audience," see the Prologue to *The Staple of News.* For a discussion of the antagonism between spectacle and word that developed with some continuity throughout Jonson's career, see D. J. Gordon, "Poet and Architect: The Intellectual Setting of the Quarrel Between Ben Jonson and Inigo Jones," in *The Renaissance Imagination,* ed. Stephen Orgel (Berkeley 1975), pp. 77-101.

41. Just as the play's genre is an early topic of debate, so its earliest stage history is contested by the 1609 preface, which advertises *Troilus and Cressida* as "a new play, neuer stal'd with the stage, neuer clapper-clawd with the palmes of the vulger"; by the Stationers' Register, which records its existence in February, 1603; and by the quarto title-page (first state), which advertises the play "As it was acted by the Kings Maiesties seruants at the Globe."

42. *A Refutation of the Apology for Actors,* by I. G. (1605). Quoted in Herschel Baker, *The Race of Time: Three Lectures on Renaissance Historiography* (Toronto, 1967), p. 80. For similar statements, see *The Schoole of Abuse,* pp. 92-93, and *Playes Confuted in Five Actions,* pp. 194-95.

43. James L. Calderwood, *Shakespearean Metadrama* (Minneapolis, 1971), p. 136. See also his "Appalling Property in *Othello,*" *University of Toronto Quarterly,* 57:3 (Spring, 1988), 357.

44. William Caxton's *Recuyell of the Histories of Troye* was just one of Shakespeare's available sources. See also Geoffrey Bullough, *Narrative and Dramatic Sources of Shakespeare* (London, 1966), 6:83-111.

45. Carol Cook considers this same issue, though from a Lacanian perspective, in "Unbodied Figures of Desire," *Theatre Journal,* 38 (March, 1986), 44-46.

46. See esp. Paul Cantor, *Shakespeare's Rome: Republic and Empire* (Ithaca, 1974), pp. 108-10.

47. A similar claim has been made for the earlier *Titus Andronicus* (1593-1594), in which rape and dismemberment render Lavinia's body an annotated text, a silent emblem submitted to others' reconstructive reading. See Douglas E. Green, "Interpreting 'her martyr'd signs': Gender and Tragedy in *Titus Andronicus,*" *Shakespeare Quarterly,* 40 (1989), 317-26.

48. *Coriolanus,* 3.3.134; 5.3.36; 4.7.42; 5.6.120; 5.2.65-66. Earlier Coriolanus seems to recognize that it is death that submits one to other-fashioning, life that grants the temporary privilege of maintaining one's self-conception: "While I remain above the ground you shall / Hear from me still, and never of me aught / But what is like me formerly" (4.1.51-53).

49. David Kaula has found a pattern of eucharistic allusions in the ritual attending Caesar's murder in "'Let Us Be Sacrificers': Religious Motifs in *Julius Caesar,*" *Shakespeare Studies,* 14 (1981), 197-214.

50. See Mark Rose, "Conjuring Caesar: Ceremony, History, and Authority in 1599," in *True Rites and*

Maimed Rites: Ritual and Anti-Ritual in Shakespeare and His Age, ed. Linda Woodbridge and Edward Berry (Urbana and Chicago, 1992), p. 264.

51. Sigurd Burckhardt, *Shakespearean Meanings* (Princeton, 1968), pp. 3-21.

52. See Richard Macksey, "Last Words: The *Artes Moriendi* and a Transtextual Genre," *Genre,* 16 (Winter, 1983), 508. "*Et tu Brute?*" appears to have been a not uncommon theatrical tag before Shakespeare's play, and in *Every Man Out of His Humour* (5.6.79) Jonson would parody it as a cliché.

53. Michel Foucault, *Discipline and Punish: The Birth of the Prison,* trans. Alan Sheridan (New York, 1979), p. 46.

54. See Alvin Kernan's *Shakespeare, The King's Playwright in the Stuart Court, 1603-1613* (New Haven, 1995). While Kernan demonstrates aspects of the patronage system in Shakespeare's Stuart drama, his case seems to me overstated and to ignore some of the performative issues considered here.

55. Samuel Johnson, *Johnson on Shakespeare,* in *The Yale Edition of the Works of Samuel Johnson,* ed. Arthur Sherbo (New Haven, 1968), 7:51-52. Alexander Pope also speaks of Shakespeare's original manuscripts being "cut" and "divided" into the "*Piecemeal Parts*" of the "*Prompter's Book*" ("Preface to 'The Works of Shakespear'," in *Eighteenth-Century Essays on Shakespeare,* ed. D. Nichol Smith [Oxford, 1963], p. 54).

56. See *Twelfth Night,* 4.2.89. Like Shylock, Malvolio leaves his play less assimilated than "propertied" by the comedy's reestablished social order. Such coercion certainly appears elsewhere in Shakespeare's comedies and romances; but the appropriation of individuals as stage spectacle—as James Calderwood has argued—is essentially a tragic device, a problematic ethos that comedy and romance must finally transcend or absorb. See his "Appalling Property in *Othello,*" pp. 353-75.

57. One need only consider the different assessments of Caesar's death in Plutarch, Appian, Dante, Michelangelo, Fulbecke, Sidney, and Milton for a sense of its interpretive possibilities. For a history of political interpretations of *Julius Caesar,* see John Ripley, "*Julius Caesar*" *on Stage in England and America, 1599-1973* (Cambridge, Eng., 1980).

58. Sonnet 81, line 10. In the case of *Julius Caesar,* Shakespeare's prophecy of literary survival was especially appropriate: the committee established to erect his monument in Westminster Abbey initiated this canonization with a commissioned performance of the play at Drury Lane, April 28, 1738 (see David Piper, *The Image of the Poet: British Poets and their Portraits* [Oxford, 1982], pp. 78-82).

59. James Calderwood comes very close to ascribing such a reading to Shakespeare elsewhere, arguing that in *Titus Andronicus* Shakespeare explores a tension between lyric and dramatic genres suggested in the eleventh book of Golding's Ovid (*Shakespearean Metadrama,* pp. 28-30).

60. Kenneth R. R. Gros Louis, "The Triumph and Death of Orpheus in the English Renaissance," *Studies in English Literature,* 9.1 (Winter, 1969), 63-80. Elizabeth Sewell has claimed that Shakespeare "trusts poetry, if Orpheus is undivided, if poetry and dreams and shadows and the theater are taken as a means toward learning and even toward science." See *The Orphic Voice: Poetry and Natural History* (New Haven, 1960), p. 110.

61. *Tamburlaine the Great, Part I* (Prologue, 1-8), in *The Complete Works of Christopher Marlowe,* ed. Roma Gill (Oxford, 1987).

62. In his reading of *Richard II* as a dramatization of "the interpretive efforts of the listener," Keir Elam considers Sir Pierce of Exton's construction of Bolingbroke's ambiguous utterance (5.4.1-2, 7-9) as the nexus between an undetermined illocutionary speech-act and perlocutionary action (*The Semiotics of Theatre and Drama* [London and New York, 1980], pp. 164-65).

63. The plebeians' transformation from passive spectators to furious actors seems to evoke Ovid's account of the death of Orpheus (though, it should be noted, without tidy correspondence). Murellus calls them "blocks," "stones," "worse than senseless things" for their unreflective devotion to Caesar (1.1.34). In Ovid's account, Orpheus draws the trees, beasts, and stones to follow him, but these same stones become involuntarily "reddened with the blood of the singer" only when the Maenads hurl them at the poet (*Ovid's Metamorphoses,* trans. Rolfe Humphries [Bloomington, 1955], p. 259). Antony seems to contrast the plebeians to such passivity, however, when he declares in his funeral oration, "You are not wood, you are not stones" (3.2.142). Here the semi-autonomous plebeians resemble the bloodthirsty Maenads rather than their inanimate instruments. Nor does *Julius Caesar* clearly designate one particular character as a figure of Orpheus' victimization. The ominous "bird of night" that sits "Even at noon-day upon the market-place / Howting and shrieking" (1.3.26-28), for instance, may recall Ovid's description of the Maenads' attack on Orpheus: "they came thronging / Like birds who see an owl, wandering in daylight" (p. 260); thus the owl in 1.3 may represent an Orphic Caesar, soon to be set upon by the Furious conspirators. But if the conspirators are likened to the Maenads here, then reading the plebeians as "stones" turned against the conspirators by Antony's oration, or as Maenads themselves in the dismemberment of Cinna the poet, seems dubious. Nevertheless, both Caesar and Cinna die like Orpheus, "who stretched out / His hands in supplication, and whose voice / For the first time, moved no one" (p. 260). I

would argue that Shakespeare's allusions to the death of Orpheus are in fact overdetermined in *Julius Caesar,* and that this reflects the play's bifurcation of the tragic victim (Orpheus) into Caesar and Brutus. This bifurcation pivots on the death of Cinna. Thus Antony, the conspirators, and the plebeians are described with reference to the Maenads.

64. A version of this paper was presented at the 1996 International Shakespeare Association World Congress. I am grateful to Gordon Braden, Paul Cantor, James Nohrnberg, Herbert Tucker, and especially Katharine Maus for their help.

PHILOSOPHY AND THEOLOGY

William O. Scott (essay date 1988)

SOURCE: "The Speculative Eye: Problematic Self-Knowledge in *Julius Caesar,*" in *Shakespeare Survey,* Vol. 40, 1988, pp. 77-89.

[*In the following essay, Scott considers Shakespeare's ironic treatment of self-knowledge in* Julius Caesar.]

Terry Eagleton began his early book on *Shakespeare and Society* by quoting from Ulysses' effort to draw Achilles into action in act 3, scene 3 of *Troilus and Cressida;* at Ulysses' urging, Achilles remarked on the notion that we see ourselves only by reflection:

> The beauty that is borne here in the face
> The bearer knows not, but commends itself
> To others' eyes . . .
> For speculation turns not to itself
> Till it hath travel'd and is mirror'd there
> Where it may see itself

and Ulysses continued,

> no man is the lord of anything,
> Though in and of him there be much consisting,
> Till he communicate his parts to others
>
> (3.3.103-11, 115-17)[1]

Eagleton read these words as saying that 'uncommunicated qualities don't have any real existence at all; a man is not simply known to others through communication, he can only know his own experience by putting it in a communicable form' and that 'a man who contracts out of public life is contracting out of reality'. He did not discuss the parallel and in some ways more challenging exchange when Cassius tries to recruit Brutus for his conspiracy in act I, scene 2 of *Julius Caesar:* Tell me, good Brutus, can you see your face?

> *Cassius.* Tell me, good Brutus, can you see your face?
> *Brutus.* No, Cassius, for the eye sees not itself
> But by reflection, by some other things.
> *Cassius.* 'Tis just.
> And it is very much lamented, Brutus,
> That you have no such mirrors as will turn
> Your hidden worthiness into your eye,
> That you might see your shadow. I have heard
> Where many of the best respect in Rome,
> Except immortal Caesar, speaking of Brutus
> And groaning underneath this age's yoke,
> Have wish'd that noble Brutus had his eyes.
>
> (1.2.51-62)

Though Ulysses certainly has his own purposes in his scene, Cassius is even more obvious in pursuing self-interested objectives, and these call in doubt his claim to speak for society in interpreting Brutus. Thus Cassius' questioning is in turn questionable though it is not cancelled. In the development of modern literary theory too, critiques of both individual experience and social authority have made each seem increasingly complex and unstable; in a revisionary spirit one might now reread into Eagleton's early views something like Mikhail Bakhtin's proclamation of an open-ended polyphony of voices in the novel.[2] But there were doubts too in Shakespeare's own time about the individual's access to private experience of selfhood that have been overlooked, and in some sort post-modernism may actually stimulate a recovery of the past.

First, though, it is helpful to clarify the occasion of Brutus' and Cassius' dialogue. Brutus has reported the Soothsayer's warning to Caesar about the ides of March and has expressed a desire to withdraw from Caesar's ceremony; Cassius next complains of Brutus' recent pensiveness. The prophecy may be as powerful a stimulus as the witches' greetings to Macbeth, though it is addressed to neither of them and though for the moment Brutus may resemble a Banquo more than a Macbeth. Its eventual impact on Brutus is shown when, having decided on Caesar's death, he checks the calendar (2.1.40). Along with the potentially related question whether to join Caesar in the ritual by which he seeks an heir, the prophecy creates a good moment for Cassius to sound out Brutus.

These are political matters, and Brutus too is doubtless aware of their public nature, which probably underlies the verbal sparring on both sides. But he chooses to define his response as a solely personal one:

> If I have veil'd my look,
> I turn the trouble of my countenance
> Merely upon myself. Vexed I am
> Of late with passions of some difference,
> Conceptions only proper to myself,
> Which give some soil, perhaps, to my behaviors.
> But let not therefore my good friends be griev'd—
> Among which number, Cassius, be you one—
> Nor construe any further my neglect,
> Than that poor Brutus, with himself at war,
> Forgets the shows of love to other men.
>
> (1.2.37-47)[3]

Cassius' reply, which depends on the analogy with the eye's inability to see the face in response to Brutus' claim to turn inward, does not so much question the basis of personal qualities in the individual (as Ulysses' and Achilles' discussion does) as it denies the privileged status of Brutus' assertion of self-knowledge. The power to determine what Brutus may become (ironically a similar issue to Brutus' later deliberations about Caesar) resolves first into the power to perceive what he is now.

The claim of a uniquely privileged self-knowledge was by no means secure in Shakespeare's time, despite the impressions we are likely to form from popular moral tags. Evidence lies at hand in some of the most widely read authors, including sources or parallels that have been named for the passages in *Julius Caesar* and *Troilus and Cressida*.[4] Perhaps the simplest is Cicero's raising of a doubt in his *Tusculan Disputations;* he interprets the command of Apollo's oracle at Delphi, 'Know thyself', to mean 'Know thy soul' (l. 52), and reasons as follows:

> the soule is not able in this bodye to see him selfe. No more is the eye whyche although he seeth all other thinges, yet (that whiche is one of the leaste) can not discerne his owne shape. But admit that the soule can not consider him selfe: howebeit perhaps he may. His operacions, as quyckenes of inuention, sure remembraunce, continuance and swiftnes of motion, it doth wel ynoughe perceyue. And these be greate, yea heauenlye, yea euerlastinge thinges.
>
> (1.67)[5]

There is a gap here, however Cicero may try to reduce it, between knowledge of the soul directly and knowledge merely through its actions. Human self-knowledge also suffers from comparison with divine self-intuition, as in the Neoplatonic meditations (with citations from Plotinus) of Philippe de Mornay's *Woorke concerning the trewnesse of the Christian Religion:* the discursively-reasoning human subject has a hard time knowing 'his owne Soule by the power of his Soule . . . For the maner of his discourse is but to proceede from kynd to kynd, and to passe from one reason to another. But on the contrary part, his mynd seeth not it selfe, but onely turneth into it selfe. . . .' In contrast, God's self-intuition yields 'a reflexion backe againe to it self, as a face doth in a Lookingglasse. . . . And whereas wee comprehend not our selves; that commeth of the darknesse and lumpishnesse of our flesh, which maketh us unlike our selves.'[6] Several difficulties are raised by Marcantonio Zimara, whose *Problemata* appeared in British editions of the pseudo-Aristotelian work of that name; he questions whether self-knowledge can be attained only by 'a reflexed action': 'to reflect and looke vnto himselfe, is a token that we are separated from the flesh. For he who would know himselfe, should be drawne from sensible affections, and how hard this is, no man is ignorant. Or is it because a man liueth by vnderstanding? But the vnderstanding of a man cannot conceiue himselfe, but after the vnderstanding of another, and this is very hard.'[7] Showing through the precise philosophical content of these difficulties is the notion that for a variety of reasons the discrepancies between knower and known hinder full self-knowledge; but if self-knowledge is merely of externals, it is only as certain as other knowledge. In Brutus' case an interested party directs the other knowledge and tries to weaken the status of self-knowledge.

The instabilities in *Julius Caesar* find closer analogues among critiques of self-knowledge that invoke a radical scepticism (even with a fideistic aim) towards all human knowledge. These involve a turning of statements that restrict knowledge back on their own origins to show that the mind is trapped in its own self-limitations and self-descriptions; though the play does not go so far in general statement, we may wish, for a start, to turn Cassius' words back on him and ask what mirror shows him himself, and how accurately. A world made up of selves each determined by all the others would not be simple or stable. Though he does not raise questions of this last sort, Sir John Davies gives a sharp critique in *Nosce Teipsum* of the problems of reflexive knowledge (however necessary it may be). The stanzas that are usually cited to parallel Shakespeare are these:

> Is it because the minde is like the eye,
> (Through which it gathers knowledge by degrees)
> Whose rayes reflect not, but spread outwardly,
> Not seeing it selfe, when other things it sees?
> No doubtlesse: for the minde can backward cast
> Upon her selfe her understanding light;
> But she is so corrupt, and so defac't,
> As her owne image doth her selfe affright.[8]
>
> (lines 105-12)

This corruption of the mind is explained better by Davies's retelling of the fall of Adam and Eve: the 'Spirit of lies' tempted them by suggesting 'That they were blind, because they saw not Ill', and their first act of self-knowledge was of the evil they had just learned to do (lines 13-24) in order to know. Self-knowledge was tainted from the start, and even now we are mocked by Socrates, Democritus, and the Delphic oracle (the devil's continuing triumph):

> For this, the wisest of all Moral men,
> Said *he knew nought, but that he nought did know;*
> And the great mocking Maister, mockt not then,
> When he said, *Truth was buried deepe below.*
> For how may we to other things attaine?
> When none of us his owne soule understands?
> For which the Divell mockes our curious braine,
> When *know thy selfe,* his oracle commands.
>
> (lines 77-84)

The powers of human and diabolic knowledge combine only to show us how little we know of ourselves and to taunt us with the impossible. In a related passage Du Bartas (who says in another place that 'as the Eye perceaves / All but it selfe, even so our Soule conceaves / All save her owne selfes Essence') tells that before the Fall,

> Mankind was then a thousand fold more wise
> Then now, blind error had not bleard his eyes,

With mists which make th'*Athenian Sage* suppose
That *nought he knows, save this, that nought he knowes.*
That even light *Pirrhons* wavering fantasies
Reave him the skill his unskill to agnize.
And th'*Abderite,* within a well obscure
As deep as darke, the truth of things immure.[9]

Socrates and Democritus are here joined as critics of the limits of knowledge by Pyrrho, spokesman for a radically sceptical school: he would disallow as being dogmatic even the one point of knowledge claimed by Socrates. But then he would have to refrain from actually asserting universal doubt, because that assertion, too, being a positive statement, would contradict its own principle; thus it is that his 'fantasies / Reave him the skill his unskill to agnize' ('la fantasque inconstance / Luy oste le sçavoir de sçavoir l'ignorance').[10] The weakened human reason strikes at itself by the very power of language through which it must operate. In the form of a single statement rather than a general philosophical position, a model for such self-undermining would be the liar paradox, 'This very sentence is false', which refers to itself so as to seem false if true, and true if false. There is good reason to think that Shakespeare knew this paradox from Thomas Wilson's *The Rule of Reason* (1553 or later edition).[11] Though there is nothing in *Julius Caesar* like the content of this paradox or these sceptical views, there are major occasions when the text is at war with itself in this fashion (even if the war is undeclared as in Cassius' mirror concept which simply invites other applications). Self-reference generates highly productive conflicts, especially when the reference is to the action as itself a play.

In a play which throws so much open to interpretation—the meaning of dreams, comparison of rhetorical skills to motivate political reactions—it is fitting that Cicero complains that 'men may construe things after their fashion, / Clean from the purpose of the things themselves' (1.3.34-5). But it may still be questioned whether things do have a purpose that can be specified as Cicero seems to assume. Though he did not use it in the play, Shakespeare had before him in Plutarch's *Life of Brutus* a view, propounded by Cassius as Epicurean philosophy, which gives a broad scope to subjectivity:

> In our secte, Brutus, we have an opinion, that we doe not alwayes feele, or see, that which we suppose we doe both see and feele: but that our senses beeing credulous, and therefore easily abused (when they are idle and unoccupied in their owne objects) are induced to imagine they see and conjecture that, which they in truth doe not. For, our minde is quicke and cunning to worke (without eyther cause or matter) any thinge in the imagination whatsoever.
>
> But yet there is a further cause of this in you. For you being by nature given to melancholick discoursing, and of late continually occupied: your wittes and sences having bene overlabored, doe easilier yeelde to such imaginations.[12]

If Brutus is as melancholic as Cassius says here, there is another basis for considering that 'cause or matter' is absent. Timothy Bright finds absence of an object characteristic of melancholy:

> The reason is because, they measure all outward accidents, by that they finde of discontentment within: not that the humor that discontenteth is any instrument of passion, or carieth with it faculty to be displeased: but because it disquieteth the body, and giueth discontentment to nature, it is occasion why displeasures are made great: and where there is no cause, nature troubled within, faireth as greatly displeased with that which outwardly should not displease. . . .[13]

The melancholic's self-perception would be especially problematic and circular, for the perceptions on which it depends would be themselves conditioned strongly by the self as perceiver. All these circumstances invite manipulation of appearances by Cassius, Caesar, and in remarkable ways Brutus. The situation has a notable effect on the individualistic politics of the play, well described by A. W. Bellringer: 'The cross-assessments and counter-estimates, the generalisations on men and their worth, are not mere constructions of ambiguous "characters" on Shakespeare's part, but fall essentially into a dialectic of suspicion.'[14] Suspicion is doubtless a more honest fulfilment of Cassius' proposal that persons evaluate each other than the portrayal of it that he gives to Brutus.

For these several reasons given or implied by the various writers, self-knowledge, either direct or reflected, is problematic: the otherness of the soul as object of knowledge from the consciousness-in-a-body that is to do the knowing, the imperfectness of reflection in an imperfect being, the difficulty of modelling knowledge to oneself after knowledge of others, the tendency of self-limiting descriptions of oneself to reflect back on the means and degree to which they are known, and the relativity of the perceptions by which one might judge oneself (including especially their dependence on that very same self). To these can be added a comment by Elizabeth Freund on the passage in *Troilus and Cressida* which lays open the connection with paradoxical self-reference:

> The drift of the text Ulysses is so 'rapt in' concerns a perennial philosophical and literary critical topos: we cannot step outside our own minds and must rely on reflection, echo, and mirroring otherness to constitute us. The 'eye', organ of sight, cannot see itself but by reflection; the 'I' cannot know itself with any immediacy, but must loop along strange courses of speculative mirroring which prohibit it from ever coinciding with itself. Achilles remains unperturbed by the prospect of a strange loop which puts in question the very existence of himself as subject, and he persists in believing that 'speculation' (eyesight, insight, consciousness, the self) does eventually—even if indirectly—rise into view. But Ulysses pursues the more radical conclusion, that no man can ever be in full possession of himself, and continues to attack and undercut Achilles' confident self-possession until, by the end of the scene, Achilles is no longer so sure that he can see himself.[15]

Self-knowledge involves self-reference, and in both processes the subject and object fail to coincide. To introduce another person as mediator of self-knowledge is to compound the discrepancy, especially if that person is duplicitous as, for instance, Cassius is. Yet (to continue the application to Brutus and Cassius) after Cassius had shown Brutus a reflection, the situation might not be as much in his control as he thought or wished, if Brutus could in turn adjust his self-image to his own perceptions of Cassius. (Mirrors can reflect reciprocally, though Cassius takes care not to say so.) Trusting though Brutus is, something of the dialectic of suspicion might operate. But Brutus would not be in control either, for self-knowledge would presumably change him, especially to the degree that it involved something alien introduced by Cassius. For this reason, even if he could perceive a good deal about particular strategies of his own and Cassius' at particular moments, Brutus would really never be able to coincide fully with himself in self-knowledge, view himself from an 'absolute' or unchanging position outside his interaction with Cassius. He could never make an absolute, accurate statement of self-knowledge that would be definitive, even for that moment.

Thus, although in a large sense self-knowledge and its relation to knowledge of others must be questioned, Brutus may well have a keen eye for Cassius' immediate strategies.[16] In the second scene he responds not directly to Cassius' offer to be a mirror but rather to the obvious political implications in his report of 'many of the best respect in Rome, / Except immortal Caesar, speaking of Brutus / And groaning underneath this age's yoke'; Brutus replies, 'Into what dangers would you lead me, Cassius' (1.2.59-61, 63). Anyone who can then discuss whether Caesar's crowning is to be feared (a slip of the tongue that may be calculated) and can desire that Cassius might impart to him 'aught toward the general good' has a fair idea of what he expects to hear. He keeps his counsel about what he does hear, the obvious envy by Cassius of the Caesar whom Brutus professes to love well, yet he shows not only awareness of Cassius' purpose but some acceptance: 'What you would work me to, I have some aim' (1.2.163). Brutus is thus a willing collaborator in being manipulated; but if self-knowledge alone is problematic, compounded with self-management and collusion it is doubly or trebly so.

Brutus' soliloquy in the orchard sounds most natural not as isolated self-reflection but as meditation conditioned by an internal dialogue with an imagined other, someone like Cassius:

> It *must be* by his death. And, for *my* part,
> I know no personal cause to spurn at him,
> But for the general. He would be crown'd.
> How that might change his nature, there's the question.
> It is the bright day that brings forth the adder,
> And that craves wary walking. Crown him that,
> And then I *grant* we put a sting in him
> That at his will he may do danger with.
> Th' abuse of greatness is when it disjoins
> Remorse from power. And, to *speak truth* of Caesar,
> I have not known when his affections sway'd
> More than his reason. But 'tis a common proof
> That lowliness is young ambition's ladder,
> Whereto the climber-upward turns his face;
> But when he once attains the upmost round,
> He then unto the ladder turns his back,
> Looks in the clouds, scorning the base degrees
> By which he did ascend. So Caesar may.
> Then, lest he may, prevent.
>
> (2.1.10-28)

My italics mark the clearest signs of dialogic response. Brutus begins with what seems like a conclusion;[17] but he would have been brought to that point as if by an unheard voice letting him reach the decision himself. Death is no new concept to him in these deliberations, and the word needs no emphasis; the change is rather in the assertion of will signalled by the verbs. Brutus next defines himself in contrast to the unheard other by his lack of personal animus and his ability to speak truly of Caesar, yet he must concede decisively that Caesar would be crowned and that crowning puts a sting in him. Brutus carries on this persuasion by the imagined other-in-himself through flagrantly rhetorical means: by application of abstract principles to individual cases, and by argument from analogy.[18] Although these arts are ultimately directed against himself, they are at first weapons in a constant mental skirmish with the idea of Cassius' influence.

Brutus' final direction in this speech seems all the more an artful self-manipulation:

> And, since the quarrel
> Will bear no color for the thing he is,
> Fashion it thus: that what he is, augmented,
> Would run to these and these extremities.
> And therefore think him as a serpent's egg
> Which, hatch'd, would, as his kind, grow mischievous,
> And kill him in the shell.
>
> (lines 28-34)

But A. D. Nuttall rightly puts the emphasis instead on the abstract argument Brutus is pursuing (again, one might add, a more understandable activity if it serves an internal polemic): Nuttall paraphrases 'Fashion it thus' as 'Let's try the argument this way.'[19] His final point, though, is that even if the argument is not itself an attempt by Brutus to dictate a motive to himself, it eventually may become that: 'the proper corruption of moral abstraction is diabolical cynicism'. Surely it is here that self-delusion takes place: though Brutus has consciously cultivated an imagined debate, the dispute does not really establish by rational inquiry what would be sufficient motive for killing Caesar, but rather it becomes itself that motive. Process usurps over substance, and mental staging impinges on overt action. The rhetorical quality of Roman culture (reproduced in Elizabethan education) projects itself into dramatic imagining, and this dramatic pre-enactment in turn governs the act of assassination that will be staged for us. Brutus' self-consciousness thus generates its own self-altering self-reference, a metadrama that rewrites his internal drama and thereby shapes the overt one that we see.

Brutus acknowledges the decisiveness of his commitment though he feels its cost:

> Since Cassius first did whet me against Caesar,
> I have not slept.
> Between the acting of a dreadful thing
> And the first motion, all the interim is
> Like a phantasma, or a hideous dream.
> The Genius and the mortal instruments
> Are then in council; and the state of man,
> Like to a little kingdom, suffers then
> The nature of an insurrection.
>
> (lines 61-9)

In this he is like Macbeth, but he himself is the dagger of the mind, to be held by another. He well knows and accepts that he has been whetted by Cassius.[20] He seems to view his suffering not as a warning to turn back but quite the contrary, as a goading to take relief in action. By the end of the scene images of sickness are being converted to frenzied activity through an effort of will: Portia's wound to Brutus' prayer that he may be worthy of her in conspiracy, and Ligarius' probably feigned sickness to companionship in the exploit.

If Brutus' attitude seems strangely self-detached, it befits not only the knowing paradox of self-imaging through others but an ironic distancing from the shows of Caesar's politics. The tone is set by Casca as he describes the display that incited the rebels, Caesar's refusal of a crown:

> I can as well be hang'd as tell the manner of it. It was mere foolery; I did not mark it. I saw Mark Antony offer him a crown—yet 'twas not a crown neither, 'twas one of these coronets—and, as I told you, he put it by once; but, for all that, to my thinking, he would fain have had it. Then he offer'd it to him again; then he put it by again; but, to my thinking, he was very loath to lay his fingers off it.
>
> If the tag-rag people did not clap him and hiss him, according as he pleas'd and displeas'd them, as they use to do the players in the theatre, I am no true man.
>
> . . . when he perceiv'd the common herd was glad he refus'd the crown, he pluck'd me ope his doublet and offer'd them his throat to cut. An I had been a man of any occupation, if I would not have taken him at a word, I would I might go to hell among the rogues.
>
> (1.2.235-42, 258-61, 263-8)

Caesar, like Richard III appearing between two bishops to reject an offer of the throne (*Richard III,* 3.7), has mastered the art of the political feeler, which allows him to claim credit now for refusing what he most wants but which also prepares for eventual acceptance. For the more knowing, the performance is, if need be, a transparent ruse that coerces with the force of political prophecy; its effect is to be like the Scrivener's response to another of Richard's stratagems, 'Who is so gross / That cannot see this palpable device? / Yet who so bold but says he sees it not?' (3.6.10-12). As if displaying humility, Caesar also makes an offer to the crowd (like Richard reversing the hostility of Lady Anne) of his undefended body: but again he tries to intimidate possible rebels by showing how safe he is. Almost to foreshadow the assassination, Casca thinks of taking literally this offer that was not meant so; the cynical display is an occasion for a cynical reaction. He looks on Caesar's show with an unwilling suspension of disbelief. Brutus' response too is jaded: where public life is lie and show, and is at least half meant to be known as such, it is paradoxically likely (and not unknown in our own time) that he should willingly connive at distorting his image of himself to prepare for action. And as audience we are yet more directly touched by Casca's gibe at playgoers: powerless to alter a famous event of history and wanting the fictive-historical show to go on however bloody, we anticipate with the eagerness of tragic audiences for dramatic irony a more literal enactment of Caesar's open-doublet gesture.

The conspiracy can rise to an acceptable claim of nobility only by an effort of will, and Brutus at once sets out to achieve it. As if to ennoble the deed by style and theatricality he sets high standards for the conspirators:

> do not stain
> The even virtue of our enterprise,
> Nor th' insuppressive mettle of our spirits,
> To think that or our cause or our performance
> Did need an oath . . .
> O, that we then could come by Caesar's spirit,
> And not dismember Caesar! But, alas,
> Caesar must bleed for it. And, gentle friends,
> Let's kill him boldly, but not wrathfully;
> Let's carve him as a dish fit for the gods,
> Not hew him as a carcass fit for hounds.
> Let not our looks put on our purposes,
> But bear it as our Roman actors do,
> With untir'd spirits and formal constancy.
>
> (2.1.132-6, 169-74, 225-7)

As critics have said, he tries himself to write a tragedy in which the act of killing Caesar is purified.[21] The artifice of such writing, evidenced by the resistance of fact and eventually by the course of the play, is as clear in its self-undermining as a liar paradox.

As the conspirators finally enact their sanctified bloody deed, they at once look forward to future performances which already for us carry their own belying:

> *Brutus.* Stoop, Romans, stoop,
> And let us bathe our hands in Caesar's blood
> Up to the elbows, and besmear our swords.
> Then walk we forth, even to the market-place,
> And, waving our red weapons o'er our heads,
> Let's all cry, 'Peace, freedom, and liberty!'
> *Cassius.* Stoop, then, and wash. [*They bathe their hands and weapons.*] How many ages hence
> Shall this our lofty scene be acted over
> In states unborn and accents yet unknown!
> *Brutus.* How many times shall Caesar bleed in sport,
> That now on Pompey's basis lies along
> No worthier than the dust!

Cassius. So oft as that shall be,
So often shall the knot of us be call'd
The men that gave their country liberty.

(3.1.105-19)

The spectacle of stage blood, so popular in Shakespeare's time, reinforces the word-picturing,[22] but at the same time it both corrupts the verbal purification that Brutus sought and reminds us, the tragic spectators, of our thirst for gore. Moreover, in the contrast between the play that the characters thought they were staging for posterity and the way we actually judge the outcome we see how 'history denies their dreams'.[23] Here is a truer action of the mirror than in Cassius' pretensions to represent Brutus: all the characters on stage have their being only as we the audience judge them, but they are in turn a mirror held up to disclose and determine for us our own nature. We see that Caesar bleeds in the sport now played by his jubilant killers, but we know that they themselves will bleed. And are those future tragedies, which are called sport by an actor in the present tragedy, any more or less sportive as entertainment than what we see at the moment? There is moreover no reassuring distinction between reality and its enactment either present or future, since all that we see is staged and our own existence is paradoxically drawn into that staging by the metadramatic mirror. And what is our own sportive nature if we behold in the mirror the expected and desired tragic bloodbath?

More positively, the mental force exerted by Brutus to make his deed other than it is can be viewed as poetic. Probably the word 'sport' is only coincidence, but a comment by Plutarch as he prepares to discuss Alexander the Great puts importance on the smallest mental activity and, somewhat like Cassius, compares the image of the face:

> the noblest deedes doe not alwayes shew mens vertues and vices, but oftentimes a light occasion, a word, or some sporte makes mens naturall dispositions and maners appeare more plaine, then the famous battells wonne, wherein are slaine tenne thowsande men, or the great armies, or cities wonne by siege or assault. For like as painters or drawers of pictures, which make no accompt of other partes of the bodie, do take the resemblaunces of the face and favor of the countenance, in the which consisteth the judgement of their maners and disposition: even so they must geve us leave to seeke out the signes and tokens of the minde only, and thereby shewe the life of either of them, referring you unto others to wryte the warres, battells, and other great thinges they did.[24]

Here is almost a challenge to the dramatist to project an internal life into history imaginatively. The imaginative poetic power or 'phantasie' is to George Puttenham a mirror, though there are both false and true glasses: 'And this phantasie may be resembled to a glasse as hath bene sayd, whereof there be many tempers and manner of makinges, as the *perspectiues* doe acknowledge, for some be false glasses and shew thinges otherwise than they be in deede, and others right as they be in deede. . . .'[25] These ambivalent notions are put to their hardest test in tragedy where the images are hard to distinguish and where the characters make their choices knowing the difficulties.

The outcome of the deed is foreshadowed almost as soon as Antony comes upon the bloody scene. At once he seems overcome with grief, but he does not lose control of himself:

O mighty Caesar! Dost thou lie so low?
Are all thy conquests, glories, triumphs, spoils,
Shrunk to this little measure? Fare thee well.—
I know not, gentlemen, what you intend,
Who else must be let blood, who else is rank;
If I myself, there is no hour so fit
As Caesar's death's hour, nor no instrument
Of half that worth as those your swords, made rich
With the most noble blood of all this world.
I do beseech ye, if you bear me hard,
Now, whilst your purpled hands do reek and smoke,
Fulfill your pleasure.

(3.1.149-60)

His feelings may well be sincere, but if they are they also serve a politic purpose by making him seem trustworthy in any possible deal with the conspirators.[26] He actually repeats Caesar's gesture in the coronation episode of putting himself at the others' mercy, though not as a show of strength; yet the conspirators are in fact in a weak position, for they must treat him gently if they are to prove themselves in their own minds (or at least in Brutus' mind) not to be butchers. He places an important proviso on any compact he might make with them:

Antony. Friends am I with you all, and love you all,
Upon this hope, that you shall give me reasons
Why and wherein Caesar was dangerous.
Brutus. Or else were this a savage spectacle.
Our reasons are so full of good regard
That were you, Antony, the son of Caesar,
You should be satisfied.

(lines 221-7)

He thus manages to reduce Brutus' project of justifying the death to a condition for a political bargain (an empty one, since Antony has already privately made up his mind). Of course it will also become a public rhetorical contest in the Forum, and that major concession Antony arranges at once, while a show of fairness is still uppermost in Brutus' mind. The old cynical politics of Caesar still live in Antony's somewhat calculated emotional shows and in his purposes which are meant to be partly divined. Antony also knows something like the craftiness of Cassius' mirror tactics: the image of himself he shows to Brutus, or allows him to discover in half-hidden purposes, will minister to the image that Brutus wants to have of himself as sanctified killer.

The triumph of Antony's funeral oration is even more the triumph of the Caesarian politics of show, along with the rhetoric that mirrors and serves them. Again he trots out the display of Caesar's refusing the crown to establish what was always its crudest meaning, and he is obvious in his use of irony and rhetorical question, and also of litotes or perhaps occupatio:[27]

> You all did see that on the Lupercal
> I thrice presented him a kingly crown,
> Which he did thrice refuse. Was this ambition?
> Yet Brutus says he was ambitious,
> And, sure, he is an honorable man.
> I speak not to disprove what Brutus spoke,
> But here I am to speak what I do know.
>
> (3.2.97-103)

The heavy-handedness of his rhetoric and its contrast with our subtler assessments of character produce opposite effects on us and on the plebeians (though they have been, and remain, parodies of the theatre audience). The result is well described by Nicholas Brooke:

> His repulsive 'Friends, Romans, countrymen' speech is an exhibition of the destruction of reason by rhetoric; the continuous play on 'Brutus is an honourable man' becomes unbearable in its insistence—to us—on its truth, at the same time that it is used to enforce—on the crowd—the belief that it is not true.
>
> (p. 157)

Almost the same divergence occurs in the beginning of his speech:

> I come to bury Caesar, not to praise him.
> The evil that men do lives after them;
> The good is oft interred with their bones.
> So let it be with Caesar.
>
> (lines 76-9)

Though his statement of intention seems straightforward to his hearers in the Forum at the time, he means them to discover gradually his purpose of actually praising Caesar and to congratulate themselves on their sagacity in sharing in his rhetoric (his tactics of flattery might parody Cassius' initial handling of Brutus). Thus too the crowd would come to perceive a 'good' that ought to live after Caesar, first when his will is read and then when they resolve to avenge his death. For us, who know Antony's resolve that 'Caesar's spirit, ranging for revenge, / With Ate by his side come hot from hell, / Shall in these confines with a monarch's voice / Cry "Havoc!" and let slip the dogs of war' (3.1.271-4), the intended effect of his speech sounds more like one of the evils living after Caesar. Somewhat like Cassius, Antony projects to his auditors the images he desires them to have of Caesar and themselves (and of course Brutus and the rest), partly by their planned divining of his not-so-hidden meaning. Behind all this there is another art hidden from them in his deeper purposes; if they knew of it, they might not be moved as they are, but one cynically suspects that they would nonetheless. Meanwhile, on the less consoling metadramatic level, the plebeians who execute and partly mirror Antony's intention are parodic versions of us.

In the abstract, as well as in the practical examples displayed by Antony, verbal irony is an especially paradoxical intertwining of notions of truth and falsity. Irony is transparent dissimulation, and its transparency is what distinguishes it from lying; the irony must at once be apparent to the initiated reader. Yet it could be said that a text must be always already understood by the reader in order to be comprehended at all, and this oddity would seem to be especially the case with ironic texts. Further, to the extent that a text contains a signal of its irony, that signal destroys in literalism the irony it displays, so that an ideal irony would dispense altogether with signals.[28] From this viewpoint, irony almost makes the liar paradox, with its overt statement that undoes itself by self-reference, seem unproblematic by comparison. In this play, though, there are multiple levels of paradox which are latent as irony is, and they are all the more hidden when they seem to have disclosed something of themselves. The half-open political moves and the staged disclosures of character (one's own or someone else's) are reversed by what remains for the time hidden; yet events become overt enough in the end for Brutus and Cassius, and therefore us.

Metadramatically too we would like to see and refer to or mirror ourselves in the best qualities of Brutus, especially his self-description, which seems to be our way into his character and into the whole play. But Brutus all but self-consciously turns his best into a great mistake; and apart from that the play continually forces us to compare ourselves and the world we know with characters and situations that are less than perceptive and ideal. Whether through Renaissance puzzlings about the limits and difficulty of self-knowledge, the traditional liar paradox, Cassius' disingenuous notions about mirrors, the metadramatic vision of tragedy as a blood sport, or some more modern problematics, we may have to concede that like Brutus we did not always already know and therefore never will, can never complete the task without paradox, nor indeed begin. Yet these statements themselves claim that *Julius Caesar* has shown Brutus and us a great deal.

Notes

1. *Shakespeare and Society* (1967), pp. 13-14. I have quoted more from *Troilus* than Eagleton did and have used, as throughout, the *Complete Works,* ed. David Bevington, 3rd edn (Glenview, 1980). I gratefully acknowledge the assistance of the University of Kansas General Research Fund grant 3439-0038.

2. The example of Bakhtin is not casual: the view quoted from Eagleton resembles the thesis in *Marxism and the Philosophy of Language,* published under the name of V. N. Volosinov but argued to be Bakhtin's by Katerina Clark and Michael Holquist, *Mikhail Bakhtin* (Cambridge, Mass., 1984), pp. 160, 166. Without naming titles, Eagleton describes Raymond Williams, to whom his early book is dedicated, as a long-time enthusiast of Volosinov—*The Function of Criticism* (1984), p. 109. Bakhtin's views on the novel are expressed in *Problems of Dostoevsky's Poetics* and *The Dialogic Imagination.* Eagleton cites

both the *Marxism* book and Bakhtin's book on Rabelais in *William Shakespeare* (Oxford, 1986), p. 106.

3. His flight into privacy is well discussed by Jonathan Goldberg, *James I and the Politics of Literature* (Baltimore, 1983), pp. 170-1.

4. There are discussions in the Oxford, Arden, and Cambridge editions of *Julius Caesar,* and the New Variorum edition of *Troilus and Cressida.* Sources for wording and ideas are discussed by Gary Taylor, '*Musophilus, Nosce Teipsum,* and *Julius Caesar*', *Notes and Queries,* NS 31 (June, 1984), 191-5. The ideas about eyes and reflections are treated as proverbial in Morris Palmer Tilley, *A Dictionary of the Proverbs in England in the Sixteenth and Seventeenth Centuries* (Ann Arbor, 1950), and R. W. Dent, *Shakespeare's Proverbial Language* (Berkeley, 1981), E231a and 232. There is much information on writings about self-knowledge in Rolf Soellner, *Shakespeare's Patterns of Self-Knowledge* (Columbus, 1972).

5. *Those fyue qvestions, which Marke Tullye Cicero, disputed in his manor of Tuscalanum,* trans. John Dolman (1561), E6v-E7. Perhaps Cicero is influenced by Plato's distinction in *1 Alcibiades* (another source which has been claimed for Shakespeare), 132E-133E, between the soul itself and qualities or things which merely belong to the person.

6. Trans. Sir Philip Sidney, *Prose Works of Sir Philip Sidney,* ed. Albert Feuillerat (1912; repr. Cambridge, 1962), vol. 3, 252, 264-5; other references include 266, 270-1, and 296 (Plotinus).

7. *Problemes,* in *The Problemes of Aristotle* (Edinburgh, 1595), G5-G5v. Zimara's work appeared with Aristotle in at least the Latin edition of 1583 and the English ones of 1595 and 1597. He is mentioned as raising problems about self-knowledge in the oft-printed annotations by Claudius Minoes on Andrea Alciati's *Emblemata* (Emblem CLXXXVII, 'Submouendam ignorantiam'). He was very well known as a commentator on Aristotle and Averroës.

8. *Poems,* ed. Robert Krueger (Oxford, 1975), p. 9 (ll. 105-12). Other pertinent passages include ll. 185-8 and 761-4. J. L. Simmons says that this first-quoted passage 'shows the incoherence of the image when pursued too far on the literal level'—*Shakespeare's Pagan World* (Charlottesville, 1973), p. 96.

9. Guillaume de Saluste, Sieur du Bartas, *The Divine Weeks and Works,* trans. Josuah Sylvester, ed. Susan Snyder (Oxford, 1979), vol. I, 283, 323-4 (I.vi.773-5; II.i. 'Eden' 261-8). His knowledge of Greek philosophy is evident in 'Le Triomfe de la foi', Chant Second.

10. The French is quoted from *Works,* ed. Urban Tigner Holmes, Jr, John Coriden Lyons, and Robert White Linker (Chapel Hill, 1940), vol. III, 8 (ll. 229-30). Pyrrhonian scepticism is described by Diogenes Laertius (IX.61f.) and by Sextus Empiricus, *Outlines of Pyrrhonism.* In I. 14 Sextus discusses the statements such as 'All things are false' which cancel themselves out in the manner of the liar paradox, my next topic.

11. The relevant passage from Wilson is in the edition by Richard S. Sprague (Northridge, 1972), pp. 216-17, where Epimenides the Cretan, describing Cretans as liars, self-referentially undercuts his own statement. I have given reasons for Wilson's pertinence and have applied the paradox critically to Shakespeare's plays in two articles in *Shakespeare Quarterly:* 'The Paradox of Timon's Self-Cursing', 35 (1984), 290-304; and 'Macbeth's—And Our—Self-Equivocations', 37 (1986), 160-74.

12. *Narrative and Dramatic Sources of Shakespeare,* ed. Geoffrey Bullough (1964), vol. 5, p. 116. This, along with the speech by Cicero, is cited by D. J. Palmer, 'The Self-Awareness of the Tragic Hero', in *Shakespearian Tragedy,* ed. David Palmer and Malcolm Bradbury, Stratford-upon-Avon Studies 20 (1984), p. 138.

13. *A Treatise of Melancholie* (1586), facsimile ed. Hardin Craig (New York, 1940), p. 96. Brutus is discussed as melancholic by W. Nicholas Knight, 'Brutus' Motivation and Melancholy', *Upstart Crow,* 5 (Fall 1984), 108-24. Though the description is just, Brutus seems, for reasons which will appear, to be more self-conscious and perhaps therefore less pathological than Knight describes.

14. A. W. Bellringer, '*Julius Caesar:* Room Enough', *Critical Quarterly,* 12 (1970), 31-48; rpr. in *Shakespeare's Wide and Universal Stage,* ed. C. B. Cox and D. J. Palmer (Manchester, 1984), pp. 146-163; p. 152.

15. '"Ariachne's Broken Woof": the Rhetoric of Citation in *Troilus and Cressida*', in *Shakespeare and the Question of Theory,* ed. Patricia Parker and Geoffrey Hartman (New York, 1985), pp. 28-9. 'Strange loops' are discussed in relation to the self-reference of the liar paradox by Douglas Hofstadter, *Gödel, Escher, Bach* (New York, 1979). In *Gadamer's Hermeneutics* (New Haven, 1985), Joel C. Weinsheimer applies Gödel's reasoning about self-reference in mathematical axioms to the claims of Hegelian self-knowledge (as an explanation of Gadamer's views): self-knowledge, though it may be true, must be incomplete (as it is, given the nature of language) or else potentially paradoxical (pp. 37-59). William R. Brashear discusses the implications for tragedy of non-correspondence of knower and known according to Schopenhauer, Nietzsche, and Spengler in *The Gorgon's Head* (Athens, Georgia, 1977), pp. 1-26.

16. His awareness of Cassius' doings is discussed by Camille Wells Slights, *The Casuistical Tradition* (Princeton, 1981), p. 83.

17. Palmer, p. 136. He also says of Brutus that 'The sequence of his speeches progresses inwards, reveal-

ing a disordered judgement'—and perhaps, one might add, a strange loop.

18. Slights, pp. 82-91 (with emphasis, however, on a casuistical rather than rhetorical tradition); Gayle Greene, 'The Language of Brutus' Soliloquy: Similitude and Self-Deception in Shakespeare's *Julius Caesar*', in *Humanitas: Essays in Honor of Ralph Ross,* ed. Quincy Howe, Jr (Claremont, 1977), pp. 74-86. The rhetorical emphasis in the play is justly described by Anne Barton, '*Julius Caesar* and *Coriolanus:* Shakespeare's Roman World of Words', in *Shakespeare's Craft,* ed. Philip H. Highfill, Jr (Carbondale, 1982), pp. 24-47, and by James R. Siemon, *Shakespearean Iconoclasm* (Berkeley, 1985), pp. 153-66. Constitution of an individual through the words of another is a subject of Pierre Spriet, 'Amour et politique: le discours de l'autre dans *Julius Caesar*', *Coriolan* (Travaux de l'Université de Toulouse-Le Mirail, Série B, Tome 5, 1984), pp. 227-39.

19. *A New Mimesis* (1983), p. 108. Perhaps Brutus' mind is almost running ahead to a justifying speech he would make in the Forum; the outline has a heading 'Extremities', though the subtopics are as yet unspecified.

20. The note on l. 61 by the Oxford editor, Arthur Humphreys, partially agrees with this interpretation; but I do not think the implications of 'whet' are unconscious for Brutus.

21. Sigurd Burkhardt, *Shakespearean Meanings* (Princeton, 1968), pp. 7-8; Nicholas Brooke, *Shakespeare's Early Tragedies* (1968), pp. 152-3; Lawrence Danson, *Tragic Alphabet* (New Haven, 1974), pp. 56-67 (the latter two critics with emphasis on the failure of purification). An earlier treatment of ritual and counter-ritual is Brents Stirling, *Unity in Shakespearian Tragedy* (New York, 1956), pp. 44-53.

22. Maurice Charney, *Shakespeare's Roman Plays* (Cambridge, Mass., 1961), p. 51.

23. Thomas F. Van Laan, *Role-Playing in Shakespeare* (Toronto, 1978), p. 160.

24. *Plutarch's Lives,* trans. Sir Thomas North, ed. George Wyndham, Tudor Translations (1895), vol. 4, p. 298. Reuben A. Brower, *Hero & Saint* (Oxford, 1971), p. 207, remarks on Plutarch's failure to follow his precept.

25. *The Arte of English Poesie,* ed. Gladys Doidge Willcock and Alice Walker (Cambridge, 1936), p. 19. This passage is cited by Palmer, p. 139. The element of deceit in figurative language according to Puttenham is discussed by Inga-Stina Ewbank, 'Shakespeare's Liars' (British Academy Shakespeare Lecture, 1983), *Proceedings of the British Academy,* 69 (1983), p. 166.

26. Alessandro Serpieri, 'Reading the Signs: towards a Semiotics of Shakespearean Drama', in *Alternative Shakespeares,* ed. John Drakakis (1985), p. 129. He also notices (p. 134) that Antony's soliloquy revealing his stratagem (ll. 255-76) parallels one by Cassius after he has worked on Brutus (1.2.308-22).

27. Serpieri discusses litotes, paralepsis (occupatio), and negation among Antony's techniques (p. 133).

28. These points about irony are made by Beda Allemann, 'De l'ironie en tant que principe littéraire', *Poétique,* 36 (November, 1978), 388-96. He does not draw a comparison to the liar paradox.

James Howe (essay date 1994)

SOURCE: "The Cause of Suffering and the Birth of Compassion in *Julius Caesar,*" in *A Buddhist's Shakespeare: Affirming Self-Deconstructions,* Associated University Presses, 1994, pp. 96-113.

[*In the following essay, Howe interprets* Julius Caesar *in terms of Buddhist conceptions of samsara (the endless cycle of worldly life and death) and compassion arising from the acceptance of life as suffering.*]

In several subsequent plays, Shakespeare enlarged his exploration of both the frightening and the fortunate implications of this awareness of our confusion about the self and the world. Indeed, as he began more and more to emphasize the tragic mode of perception, his shift may seem natural. Tragedy (and history, as we have seen with *Richard III*) is specifically the discourse of the empowered. Linking themselves to the inexorable turning of the wheel of fortune, its principal characters place the ebb and flow of political power in the foreground. As a result, from the Buddhist point of view, they also enact in this foreground the first two of the Buddha's Four Noble Truths, perceptions that by now may seem familiar: first, that suffering is a constant in human life; and second, that the cause of this suffering is our mistaken belief in a solid self and our consequent endless self-entrapment in the vicious cycle of hope and fear—our constant striving to achieve happiness by satisfying our desires and, once they are satisfied, our fear of losing this needed self-confirmation.[1]

The play *Julius Caesar* presents this confusion differently than *Merchant.* Instead of closing interpretive options down, it opens its major events and characters to ambiguous, even contradictory, possibilities. At the same time, it presents one character of extremely noble intentions who is driven to face his impasse-situation more directly than any character we have so far examined. Thus this play dramatizes an alternative version of confusion, as well as a fuller representation of how it works within us to create an impasse situation, and of how impossible such situations are to escape. Awareness of the cycle of samsara is in this way shown to be the frightening yet necessary ground of nirvana.

The play's political foreground introduces us to the openness of our interpretive options at once, with the ambiguous phenomenon of the rising Caesar. The humor of his supporters the plebeians, their plays on "sole" and "soul," on "with awl" and "withal," their ambiguous use of "conscience," "mend," and "out" (1.1.13-26), are too obvious to seem clever. This wit has a further political agenda, however, for it shows the plebeians' deliberate defiance of the tribunes' authority. When with greater eloquence and, apparently, reason, these tribunes chastise them as a changeable mob (1.1.32-62), the criticism therefore seems just and Caesar's cause suspect. However, we might also hear self-righteousness in the tribunes' rebukes, and we might remember that the discourse of authority often cloaks itself in the language of reason. When in addition we remember that these tribunes are elected to represent the interests of these very plebeians, it becomes clear that they have a vested interest in opposing their own constituency's support of Caesar: if he becomes emperor, the tribunes will be out of a job. Further, it is the tribune Murellus's unaccountable failure to understand the cobbler's trade (1.1.12) which makes the circumstances of the plebeians' puns seem contrived, and this in turn undercuts what cleverness they may have. The first scene, then, introduces the fact of social discord in Rome, torn by two antagonistic political attitudes between which we cannot choose.[2] This political ambiguity intensifies in the second scene. Despite Cassius's egoism and his admission that he is trying to manipulate Brutus (1.1.308-15), his cause has great appeal. His distrust of unnatural ambition; his idea of the republic's senate as a group of noble equals; and, in general, his appeal to the idea of freedom—all have power. On the other hand, in act 2 we see the private side of things more fully, and this does not give us confidence in the conspirators. At 2.1.10-34, Brutus makes it clear that he will kill Caesar because Caesar "may" forget his human limitations and the general good. Brutus concedes that he has never known Caesar's "affections sway'd / More than his reason," but because he "might change" he must die. Under such reasoning, which of us is safe?

This discomfort with the conspirators is shortly generalized. Act 2, scene 2 fills us to satiation with their deceit. The plotters crowd into Caesar's house, permeating his private world with manipulative deceivers so that his death seems inescapable. At the same time, Calphurnia's concern for Caesar, and his for her, humanizes him. This domestic scene that precedes the murder makes it difficult to see Caesar as the monster pictured in the conspirators' rhetoric. By the end of this second act, we are watching the inexorable progression of events with a kind of helpless horror.

The larger dimensions of existence that stand behind the political foreground and occasionally penetrate it (the dimensions of prodigy, prophecy, dream, and ghost) are even more intensely mysterious, both to the characters and to us, though in different ways. Casca summarizes the characters' general insecurity in an inscrutable universe with a literal description of its behavior: "all the sway of earth / Shakes like a thing unfirm" (1.1.3-4). However, to us in the audience there is another level of uncertainty. The unnatural events described at 1.3.3-28 and 63-68 (and again at 2.2.17-24), as well as Calphurnia's dream in act 2, scene 2, each have equally plausible yet contradictory interpretations, and in each case both of these interpretations are "true." In the case of the prodigies and unnatural events, only one interpretation is given onstage, by Cassius: that Caesar has grown larger than any man should, and is about to create an imbalance in the universe by becoming emperor. The prodigies of nature reflect the unnaturally "prodigious" growth of Caesar (1.3.77-78), such

> that heaven hath infus'd them with these spirits,
> To make them instruments of fear and warning
> Unto some monstrous state.
>
> (1.3.69-71)

From this perspective, the prodigies are signs that Caesar should not be crowned. However, there is an unspoken but well-known Elizabethan alternative. These prodigies come immediately after the scene in which the conspiracy plan is broached to Brutus. They can therefore be "read" as a cosmic reflection of the horror of the thing planned (and to be accomplished, as we in the audience know from our history books): the murder of Caesar. If he is not in fact crowned, he is certainly viewed by the general populace as their leader; he is all but emperor; he is certainly the order-figure.[3] One conventional response for an Elizabethan audience would be to see the prodigies as reflections of the chaos that will inevitably attend the murder of authority. *Both these possibilites are proven "true" in the play.* In act 3, scene 1, we will see that Caesar is indeed ripe for dying, yet the rest of the play will present the universal chaos that results from his death.

The same contradiction applies to Calphurnia's dream of Caesar's bleeding statue (2.2.76-79). She herself interprets the dream as a portent that Caesar will die if he goes to the senate on the Ides of March. Decius deliberately tries to mislead Caesar into the opposite interpretation, that "great Rome shall suck / Reviving blood" from Caesar's leadership (2.2.87-88). Despite Decius's deceitful motive, it is again clear that *both* interpretations are "true." Caesar *does* die, as Calphurnia fears. But also, his spirit lives and nourishes the empire. Antony's swearing vengeance is accomplished in Caesar's name, and Cassius and Brutus both die with his name on their lips.[4]

This is a universe, then, all of whose dimensions—the individual, the political, and the cosmic; the human, the animal, and the heavenly; the dead and the living—are ambiguous and yet interpenetrate one another. This is a play world which is not only opaque and unreadable, but inescapable as well. Brutus is placed at the center of this pressurized world's gravity, its microcosm. The division within his mind that he vents in 2.1.10-34 parallels the political division in society and is a microcosm of the uncertain cosmos. The shift from the public places of act 1 to the private homes of act 2, which are then themselves penetrated by the group of conspirators, suggests a similar interpenetration of public and private life. Jonathan Goldberg, in a different context, and focusing on act 1 alone, has made a similar observation about the "continuity of inner life and outer life, private and public" (Goldberg 1983, 168).

The claustrophobic nature of this situation for Brutus is intensified by our awareness in the audience that he is trapped in a double-bind situation, partly self-created. On the one hand, his soliloquy opening act 2, scene 1, shows Brutus to have the noblest and most unselfish of motives: he will be his nation's savior, even though it means sacrificing the man he loves. He creates for himself an imperative for action even though certainty is impossible. Given his public conscience and his personal identification with his own integrity, he has no choice but to kill Caesar. However, things are never so simple. The Elizabethan audience might recognize a second moral imperative: to avoid the risk of civil war, general misery, and universal discord.[5] Although Brutus himself does not state this view, we cannot miss it. Calphurnia reminds us of it at 2.2.30-31:

> When beggars die there are no comets seen;
> The heavens themselves blaze forth the death of princes.

If there were further doubt, of course the events subsequent to the assassination would be enough to resolve them. Caesar must not be killed.

Nor are we merely passive observers of Brutus's no-win situation. We too have seen Caesar's blind pride. We have heard him say, in assessing Cassius,

> I rather tell thee what is to be fear'd
> Than what I fear; for always I am Caesar.
>
> (1.2.211-12)

And we have watched him find a way to keep his image of greatness while justifying his decision not to go to the Capitol:

> Cannot, is false; and that I dare not, falser:
> I will not come today.
>
> (2.2.63-64)

Although we may see the weakness in Brutus's argument, we have information of our own. We too are pulled in two directions at once about Caesar, and this uncertainty allows us to appreciate the double-sidedness of Brutus's position. Yet it is his position, not ours; it is his insistence on nobility, on taking action and making things right when he cannot know what "right" is, that most fully entraps him.

Caesar, though ambiguous, seems less complicated. He is ignorant from the start. Uniquely, he thinks he knows who he is and what he wants. Like Richard of Gloucester, he resorts to the stage to get the crown, opening the play with a formal procession, a show of power and majesty for the city ("Set on, and leave no ceremony out," 1.2.11). As part

Henry Marston as Marc Antony in Act II, scene ii of Julius Caesar, *engraving.*

of this show, he enacts "appropriate" humility (offstage) by refusing the offer of the crown three times (1.2.221-47). But although Caesar knows the pageant he performs to be a pretense, the role he plays in it is of the great man he actually believes himself to be. It is because of this belief in the role he plays (in defiance of his knowledge that it is a role) that the script he writes for himself is so easily incorporated into that written by the conspirators. He, not the soothsayer, is a dreamer.

Despite his inner conflict, Brutus is not radically different. It is his belief in his own nobility that shows his blindness. His discomfort with the secrecy and deceit needed to kill a great leader (2.1.77-85), and his discomfort in general with widespread killing, not to mention chaos, indicates not only his moral values, but his naïveté. He still believes in the world's stability and clarity. He believes in himself and his ability to save Rome, and so he joins the conspiracy. It is, ironically, these naïvely self-serving beliefs that make him the prime architect of just that instability and chaos from which he meant to save his beloved country.

It is also this naïveté that moves him to ritualize the murder.[6] Brutus wishes to transform the assassination into a pure and cleansing act: "Let's be sacrificers, but not butchers," "purgers, not murderers" (2.1.166, 180). He wishes to enact a tragedy with Aristotelian effects. The audience, Rome, will be purged of its impurity. He is therefore scrupulous about the form of the act. Every move must reflect those high principles that alone can justify the deed. Thus he refuses to swear an oath:

> . . . unto bad causes swear
> Such creatures as men doubt; but do not stain
> The even virtue of our enterprise,
> Nor th' insuppressive mettle of our spirits.
>
> (2.1.131-32)

And thus he leads a carefully selected cast of Roman aristocrats to Caesar, that they may first display the nature of the victim to be sacrificed, then perform the ritual murder itself. They begin by asking him to be "moved," to change his mind in human sympathy for another, and his reaction shows that Brutus's guess was right. Caesar delivers a showpiece of tragic *hybris* (3.1.58-73). He compares himself to the one star perfect enough to be constant—the "northern star," the pole star about whose central position the heavens revolve. He cannot even "pray to move" (3.1.59). He believes in his role of righteous power, a role that the circling conspirators provide him the occasion to play out to its ultimate self-apotheosis when Cinna renews the request for mercy, and Caesar again refuses: "Hence! wilt thou lift up Olympus?" (3.1.74). Caesar is revealed as the appropriate victim. He deserves to be sacrificed.

Caesar has risen to great heights, and is on the brink of being crowned emperor. The wheel of fortune turns. From the tragic perspective—from the perspective of Brutus's ritual pattern of action—Caesar *should fall now.* We cannot fail to see this. When, in his funeral oration, Brutus emphasizes that he killed Caesar "as he was / ambitious" (3.2.26- 27), that he gave him "death for his / ambition" (28-29), Brutus explains not only his own motives, but also the relationship between the wheel of fortune, *hybris,* and the fall of the tragic hero. He appeals, that is, to our sense of theatrical genre as well as to our political understanding. If there is uncertainty about the political efficacy of killing an order-figure, the act is further justified by appealing to the rules of tragedy. It is mystified by its ritual/aesthetic form.

As part of this ritual, each conspirator stabs the victim. Then, the sacrifice done, the circle opens again to show the victim's corpse to the populace, and to complete the ritual:

> Stoop, Romans, stoop,
> And let us bathe our hands in Caesar's blood
> Up to the elbows, and besmear our swords;
> Then walk we forth, even to the market-place,
> And waving our red weapons o'er our heads,
> Let's all cry, "Peace, freedom, and liberty!"
>
> (3.1.105-10)

With their arms and swords splashed with blood, Brutus's cry of "Peace" may seem too obvious a mystification to succeed. Yet we do not question Brutus's noble sincerity about Rome. Rather, we question his wisdom, for it is this very sincerity that empowers his belief in the righteousness of his ritual, and in the truthfulness to himself of his role in it. Ironically, the sacrificer at last seems as naïve, as blind, as ignorant, as does his victim. They both believe equally in their self-created and grandiose roles: Caesar as emperor, Brutus as savior.

This grandiose view and its exposure is made virtually explicit in the next exchange:

> *Cas.* . . . How many ages hence
> Shall this our lofty scene be acted over
> In states unborn and accents yet unknown!
> *Bru.* How many times shall Caesar bleed in sport,
> That now on Pompey's basis lies along
> No worthier than the dust!
> *Cas.* . . . So oft as that shall be,
> So often shall the knot of us be call'd
> The men that gave their country liberty.
>
> (3.1.111-18)

From the self-glorifying point of view of the conspirators, this is such a great deed that it will be remembered through reenactment in "many ages hence," "in states unborn and accents yet unknown." From the point of view of the theater audience, however, the speech is self-referential: this present representation of *Julius Caesar* is obviously the ready example of such a reenactment, of such a remystification of the murder. And, this metadramatic dimension of the play opened, we may see that Caesar played to the cue that the conspirators offered him because it was perfectly designed for his own script; he was perfectly prepared to glorify himself. He fits himself precisely into the tragic script prepared for him by Brutus by playing his own role, his own self-image. Caesar, that is, is perfectly cast in two plays at once, the second (Brutus's) enclosing the first (his own). He is self-entrapped. Shakespeare makes this fact evident by representing it in transparently theatrical form.

Seen from Brutus's perspective, this tragic play within the play has a different effect, one very like that of illusionism in the visual arts. (For a fuller discussion of this issue, see the analyses of Masaccio, Mantegna, Romano, and Carracci in Appendix A.) It enacts a "real" event, the murder of Caesar, the effect of which depends on viewer recognition that it is not what it seems to be (not a murder). Thus the artist, Brutus, gives it a ritualized tragic form, and it is this form of ritual sacifice, this artwork, which is in fact the "reality" Brutus intends. He makes the manufactured nature of its form transparent so that he himself will be seen to be inscribed within it, so that his motives will become more important to the viewer than the deed itself, so that his motives will determine how the deed is received. Brutus gives a carefully crafted construction that contains himself as gift to the people of Rome. In both self-glorification and selfless idealism, he tries to make himself rather than Caesar the central issue of his tragedy.

This self-ennoblement may work briefly: we see the murder from the tragic (rather than the political) perspective that Brutus gives it, and see that from this perspective blind Caesar needed to die. However, like Caesar, Brutus plays his role out to its ultimate extension, insisting on enacting a conclusion to his tragedy, a funeral ritual in which he will explain the meaning of his tragic act, will spell out his motive. Like Caesar too, Brutus plays his role perfectly. And, as in the case of Caesar, this perfectly played role destroys him; he is blind to its danger because he believes in its "truth"—that he is indeed his country's savior and that this will be evident to everyone, once explained. He has the naïveté of the idealist: his motives are pure, and so his acts must be efficacious.

Therefore he lets Antony live, he lets Antony speak, and he lets Antony speak last. Brutus is scrupulously fair, and thereby he plays into Antony's still more all-enclosing script.[7]

A funeral ceremony seems a fitting conclusion to a tragedy. The deceased will be memorialized and mourned. His death will somehow be rationalized. The participants will be emotionally purged. The whole community will come together to contemplate their common mortality, exemplified by Caesar, the great man who fell. The *memento mori* theme is implicit: along with personal feeling there is a distancing, philosophical view of human life and its transience. Human life is filtered through an aesthetic lens.

Brutus plans to shape the image this lens projects, but so does Antony. We see him commit himself to avenge Caesar's death almost as soon as he learns of it (3.1.259-75). There is therefore dramatic irony in our recognition of the difference between what the Romans hear and what we hear. This irony seems to distance us comfortably from the mob, his audience onstage. We are uniquely in a position to appreciate his cleverness in manipulation, without ourselves being manipulated. This cleverness extends even to Antony's ability to seem to follow Brutus's rules not to say anything against the murderers (3.1.245), yet get the opposite of the effect Brutus intends. He insinuates suspicion; his art defamiliarizes the tragedy made by Brutus. Caesar's death is demystified.

Once Antony crystalizes our uncertainties about the assassination, he establishes our common ground: "Then I, and you, and all of us fell down" (3.2.191). This is true for us in the theater as well as for the mob onstage. Brutus's tragedy has raised us from the political to the philosophical view of Caesar. As Antony returns us again and again to the fact of Caesar's death, we are reminded again and again of human frailty, of our own mortality. Pacified by our conviction of our own superiority to the mob, we too allow ourselves to be leveled. We too will die. Our distance from the Roman funeral audience diminishes in spite of the dramatic irony of the situation. Despite our awareness that Antony is deliberately being manipulative, he engages us in the theater audience as directly as he does the audience onstage. Not only does the so-called "mob" change its sympathies from Brutus to Caesar, but so do we.

Then he lifts the mantle from Caesar's corpse and shows "us all" the naked, bleeding body covered with wounds, Caesar's "dumb mouths" (3.2.225). The illusionist Antony displays the truth behind his funereal enactment, which is also the truth behind the ritual of purification staged by Brutus, as well as the implication of Caesar's own pursuit of power. This revelation affects us as do the changed vantage points we take when faced with Holbein's *Ambassadors.* Never again will we see Brutus, or the action of the play generally, outside of the context of death, outside of our sense of both their and our mortality. The funeral is not merely a turning point for the plot and for our feelings about the characters. It is also a turning point for our consciousness of ourselves. What we have been led to know, we cannot unknow. Whether we think by analogy of illusionist art, or of Holbein's forcing us to change our vantage point, the effect is the same. We are now, by the very things we see, in collusion with the artist whose artistry caused these shifts. We are aware of seeing as Antony would have us see.[8] Brutus for a moment caused us to suspend judgment about his murder of Caesar by concentrating our attention on its aesthetic form, on the murder as tragedy. Antony's ceremony has carried us a step further. We see the transparently constructed form of the funeral; we also see the gap between this perception and the mob's blindness to it. This second level of awareness shifts our attention from the form of the funeral to the more elemental fact of its transparency. Antony, that is, deepens the illusionism begun by Brutus. Seeing through the funeral, we are consumed (as the mob is) by the "reality" underlying it. The political influence desired by Brutus is exposed as essentially theatrical, just as Caesar's was.[9] In its expression of universal uncertainty, of death, and of actual personal loss, Antony's art opens to the full dimensions of the terrifying world in which we now find ourselves implicated. There is no welcoming refuge, no orderly status quo, either with an emperor or with a republic.

It is as if during the funeral we gradually become aware of a deepening vanishing point in this play, and even of multiple systems of perspective. Its ironies and contradictions begin to cluster together. The second play within the play, Brutus's, ends the tragedy of Caesar while at the same time being the act of self-assertion that begins his own. It is the culmination of the anti-Caesar side of the meanings of the prodigies and of Calphurnia's dream, and at the same time the beginning of a chain reaction that will fulfill their second meanings: that Caesar should not be killed and that Rome will be nourished by his blood. The full implications of Brutus's double bind will now be enacted.

This second movement is underlined in subsequent scenes by the aftermath to Caesar's now-demystified assassination. The many-leveled uncertainty of the first two acts intensifies into human chaos: Cinna the poet's dismemberment, the senatorial bloodbath, civil war. Smaller reflections of this discord make it seem directionless, as if in a moral and political void, yet nonetheless universal and inescapable. The avengers decide whom to purge, even to trading off their own relatives with one another (4.1.1-6). Antony schemes to reduce Caesar's legacy to Rome, even though it was one of the foundations of his funeral eloquence (7-9); and he turns against Lepidus in the rest of act 4, scene 1, without any clear need to do so. In this scene, indeed, Shakespeare seems to demystify an Antony who has himself been the agent of Brutus's demystification. Antony's image as agent of justified chaos is balanced against an image of Antony as self-seeking gangster/terrorist.[10] As the disagreements between Antony and Octavius are renewed (5.1.16-20), and as the more prolonged one between Cassius and Brutus is added to it (scenes 2 and 3 in act 4), there seems to be no corner of the play's world which is free of blind destructiveness. There is savagery and chaos and betrayal on all sides.

The full irony of Brutus's predicament is now clear. The man who would be noble must follow the implications of his noble convictions to their end. He does so, and achieves the opposite of his intentions. Because of his nobility he, more than any of the other characters, must face the world's ambiguity and mystery at their most intense.

At the same time that our vantage point is distanced from the play to see this large context, however, we are also drawn into the depths of its mystery, as the lines of perspective that issue from a painting's vanishing point enclose its viewers. Our distance allows a panoramic awareness of the play's full chaotic canvas; in this awareness, Antony and Brutus and Julius Caesar are merely the figures it contains. This awareness, in turn, intensifies our sympathy for these figures as they become victims. Antony's funeral teaches us to see far more than he, and thus even to feel sympathetic toward his enemy Brutus.

This mystery, and the split awareness with which we experience it, is well illustrated in the second half of the play by Caesar's ghost (in act 4, scene 3). From one point of view this ghost, whether hallucinatory or "real," seems a penetration into the mundane from another dimension. We have already seen the prophetic truth of dreams, as well as the prophetic prodigies of nature. Whether objective or subjective, the ghost exists as a similar mystery in Brutus's consciousness. This mystery is further deepened, and made to seem inescapable, however, by the fact that we experience it as both objective and subjective at the same time.

It comes to Brutus when he is restless from his long wrangle with Cassius; he has called for music, a book, anything to distract him. We know that he killed Caesar in spite of loving him, and that Brutus's sense of morality is meticulous. One natural assumption, therefore, is that the ghost is a hallucination, a representation of his divided, perhaps guilty, mind. He alone sees it, and he alone hears those nearby crying out in their sleep.[11]

However, we have also heard Antony invoke "Caesar's spirit" in alliance with the goddess of discord (3.1.270), and we have seen the objectively real chaos which has become ubiquitous, in private as well as in Rome generally, and in the animal and human as well as the heavenly dimensions. In this play's world, Caesar's spirit can with equal plausibility be seen as an objective presence, as another "real" representation of discord, just as indeed can Antony himself. Even the play's title seems to suggest this continuing presence.

The discussion by Leonard Tennenhouse of the queen's two bodies is suggestive of this duality (although Tennenhouse argues with reference to the history plays and, at greater length, to *Hamlet;* see Tennenhouse 1986, 79-93). He points out the distinction between the natural body of Elizabeth the individual person and the symbolic body of Elizabeth the icon of the state. This double dimension applies equally to Caesar, and therefore to his ghost. On the one hand it exists objectively as the spirit of Caesar and of the empire that Caesar would have brought about. On the other hand, it represents Brutus's personal feelings of loss and guilt from the killing of the individual who was his friend.

Here, then, Brutus begins the process of facing the full horror of the double bind in which his own nobility placed him. Since the first act he has been "with himself at war" (1.2.46). Now he begins to feel the pain of the vicious cycle of samsara, of the self-destructive nature of desire, even more acutely. He has tried to break out of this cycle by denying the fact of Caesar's natural body, obscuring the fact that he murdered a private person whom he loved. He tried to kill the spirit of Caesar, to divorce his iconic boy from his personal one, to transform Caesar's body and blood into ceremonial symbols. The ghost's integration of its objective and subjective existence represents the impossibility of Brutus divorcing the two. In seeing Brutus with this ghost, we see him exposed to the inevitability of his failure.

From this point of view, then, it is also inevitable that he will kill himself, for there seem no other options so long as he clings to his sense of honor and nobility. With Cassius dead, Brutus seems accurate in his assessment that he has lost the war. He will therefore kill himself not "to prevent / The time of life" (5.1.104-5), but because he believes that it is all but over anyway. He will do it himself rather than have an enemy do it. He can at least keep the independent self-mastery that his noble self-image requires.

He does not do it from a failure of nerve, as Messala says Cassius did: "Mistrust of good success hath done this deed" (5.3.66). Nor does he turn his face away as Cassius did, nor have another person plunge the sword into him. In these respects Brutus seems more right, more noble. He lives up to his own high standards.

However, he does not see beyond those standards, as we have been taught to do. He seems merely to believe that he has miscalculated in political and military terms:

> Our enemies have beat us to the pit.
> It is more worthy to leap in ourselves
> Than tarry till they push us.
>
> (5.5.23-25)

He demonstrates his self-mastery by ending himself as he did Caesar, with an impeccably enacted ritual. Perhaps this self-mastery, indeed, implies an acceptance of fate that might exemplify a kind of Stoic heroism. However, just before killing himself, Brutus shows the egoism of such acceptance:

> I shall have glory by this losing day
> More than Octavius and Mark Antony
> By this vile conquest shall attain unto.
>
> (5.5.36-38)[12]

He is still wedded to his nobility; he kills himself not in wise renunciation, but for a greater reputation in the world than he could otherwise achieve. As in his ritual murder of Caesar, so in his own ritual suicide Brutus means to mystify a real death, this time in the self-interested pursuit of fame. He makes a display of his nobility for future generations to admire. In this context his final words, "Caesar, now be still, / I kill'd not thee with half so good a will" (5.5.50-51), suggests that his suicide is also an escape from guilt, an erasure of the only stain on his honor.

Thus the root issue remains untouched by Brutus. The self-destructiveness inherent in desire was clear to us in Caesar's death, but not to Brutus. Even more obviously here at the end, then, Brutus reenacts this truth, that to keep the noble identity in which he believes, he must obliterate himself. The pain of the dilemma of ego is taken to its ultimate implication, to the self's final recourse in escaping pain. At last, it is not the world, but the self, which is inescapable.[13]

Dead, Brutus is proclaimed by his enemy to be "the noblest Roman of them all," the type against which the concept of humanity is measured and defined:

> . . . the elements
> So mix'd in him that Nature might stand up
> And say to all the world, "This was a man!"
>
> (5.5.68, 73-75)

There is no certain reason to doubt Antony's sincerity. Although the victor often rewrites history to his own advantage, he is not always conscious of what he does. However, we must be suspicious, for it is the kind of thing we have seen him do before, quite consciously, when in the funeral scene he rewrote Brutus's version of Caesar's death in order to open his own terrorist campaign. Having demystified Brutus's ritual in the third act, he now tries to remystify Brutus in the play's final ritual. But here too, of course, the attempt is self-serving. Antony the victor is at once glorified by beating a glorified opponent, and ennobled by his gracious show of noble magnanimity.

In fact, though, whether this closing speech is sincere or consciously self-serving does not matter. Either way, it cannot ennoble Brutus in our eyes. We already know too much. Instead, it shows that Antony too has failed to learn the lesson of Brutus's failure—failed to learn the very lesson that, by distancing us from the action, he himself has taught us to see. Antony is as blind as Brutus and Caesar.[14] Not a new stability, then, but a renewal of the flux of the endless struggle for power is placed squarely in the foreground of the play's conclusion. The Roman ideal, "glories," remains on Octavius's lips in the final line.

We can now see, thanks to Antony, the blindness that always motivates this struggle—that of Antony and Octavius, that of Brutus, that of Caesar. Antony implicated us in the play's action during the funeral by swaying us with the mob, defamiliarizing tragedy, exposing Brutus, and reminding us that we, like the characters in the play, will die. We can see our common humanity with Julius Caesar. We can see that it is Brutus's noble self-image that blinds him and that makes his fall inevitable. Yet by the end we can also sympathize with Brutus, for he sees at last what we have seen since the funeral, that there is no escape. At the same time, because the subsequent action of this tragedy has purged us of the false view of the world held by Antony and Caesar as well as Brutus, we are distanced into a new self-awareness. Tragedy has done its work of renewal on its audience. In this awareness we see through the values taught by Roman society. We see through these values' confirmation of the solid self on which ego depends, but without losing our fellow feeling for the characters who suffer in this delusion. We find ourselves in a Derridean gap where society's conventions of meaning are dissolved—and, therefore, where the space necessary for the beginning of Buddhist wisdom has been cleared.

However, this space is very frightening. Although it is an emptiness that to the awakened mind displays itself as fullness, it is at the same time a lonely place "of desolation" (Trungpa 1976a, 151):

> The attainment of enlightenment from ego's point of view is extreme death, the death of self, the death of me and mine, the death of the watcher. It is the ultimate and final disappointment.
>
> (Trungpa 1976a, 6)

Brutus demonstrates in literal terms the truth of this assertion. Faced with the possibility that he might be less noble than he had thought, Brutus chooses to kill himself. He illustrates the startling fact that the loss of our idea of ourselves as solid beings with stable identities, the loss of the idea of what one calls "I," and the reciprocal recognition that the place we habitually think "we" fill in the world is actually a void, is in fact more frightening to us than the loss of life itself. From ego's point of view, that is, enlightenment is a threat, quite the reverse of what is "normally" desired. Therefore, Brutus retreats.

Yet as we have been taught by Brutus to see through this desire for the self, so the play leaves us with the alternative that he rejects. In this desolate landscape, it is true, we will be frighteningly alone, without the reference points of a solid world or self. "But," Trungpa encourages us,

> it is possible to make friends with the desolation and appreciate its beauty. Great sages . . . marry themselves to desolation, to the fundamental psychological aloneness . . . , the marriage of shunyata and wisdom in which your perception of aloneness suggests the needlessness of dualistic occupation. . . . We discover how samsaric occupations feed and entertain us. Once we see samsaric occupations as games, then that in itself is the absence of dualistic fixation, nirvana. Searching for nirvana becomes redundant at that point.
>
> (Trungpa 1976a, 151).

Precisely by facing the fact of our samsaric "occupations" fully, we can come to feel free in them. We need not stop our normal activities, but simply see them differently. Trungpa says that "the phenomenal world is an outfit, it is a show, a self-existing show. It is a performance, living theater" (1975, 160) in which

> you do not regard the situation outside as separate from you because you are so involved with the dance and play of life. . . . You experience no warfare of any kind, neither trying to defeat an enemy nor trying to achieve a goal.
>
> (1973, 100)

We are wrong to think that we are our egos. They are merely our *idea* of what we are, an idea that Shakespeare teaches us through *Julius Caesar* to unlearn. We must get used to the idea of going to our own funeral every moment, rather than, like Brutus in *Julius Caesar,* staging someone else's. Thus this play positions us on the brink of a void which, when fully realized, becomes the ground of our fulfillment. It pushes us toward the perception that "we are just a speck of dust in the midst of the universe." With such a recognition we can see that

> at the same time our situation is very spacious, very beautiful and workable. In fact, it is very inviting, inspiring. If you are a grain of sand, the rest of the universe, all the space, all the room is yours, because you obstruct nothing, overcrowd nothing, possess nothing. There is tremendous openness. You are the emperor of the universe because you are a grain of sand.
>
> (1976a, 6-7)

In this state we come to realize

> that space contains matter, that matter makes no demands on space and that space makes no demands on matter. It is a reciprocal and open situation. . . . The Buddha had no ground, no sense of territory.
>
> (1976a, 58-59)

And in such spaciousness we approach the Buddha's Third Noble Truth: that the constant pain created by hope and fear and desire is not to be evaded, as Brutus tried to do in his suicide; rather, it ends when it is so fully experienced that a state of nonstriving and nonopposition is achieved. For indeed it is this samsara that is in fact "the origin of the path" (1975, 56), the very basis of our liberation:

> Generally, when the idea of ego is presented, the immediate reaction on the part of the audience is to regard it as a villain, an enemy. . . . But having seen the emotions as they are, we have more material with which to work creatively. This makes it quite clear that the notion of samsara is dependent upon the notion of nirvana, and the notion of nirvana is dependent upon the notion of samsara; they are interdependent. If there were no confusion, there would be no wisdom.
>
> (1976a, 68)

This open situation, without a sense of territory, is not only personal in its implications, however. Like Shakespeare's play, it can radiate outward; its emptiness provides the space where Buddhist compassion can arise, a state of being quite different from normal pity. Trungpa explains the Buddhist stance toward ending the suffering of others:

> . . . true compassion is ruthless, from ego's point of view, because it does not consider ego's drive to maintain itself. It is "crazy wisdom." It is totally wise, but it is crazy as well, because it does not relate to ego's literal and simple-minded attempts to secure its own comfort.
>
> (1973, 210)

In this state, we do not assume that what the sufferer thinks he wants is necessarily what is best for him. However, because we do not need to maintain "our territory," we do not impose our own sense of what is right or good or helpful on him, either. Instead, we try to provide a situation in which there are no externally imposed demands or even expectations, in which the sufferer can be free from striving for a moment, become still, see himself more clearly than usual, perhaps experience his own emptiness and see for himself what is truly needed—whatever that may be for the particular individual. Thus,

> . . . compassion is environmental generosity, without direction, without "for me" and without "for them." . . . It implies larger scale thinking, a freer and more expansive way of relating to yourself and the world. . . . [It] is . . . not a matter of giving something to someone else, but it means giving up your demand and the basic criteria of the demand.
>
> (1973, 99)

If we now look back at *Julius Caesar* from this large perspective which it has opened for us, Antony's tragedy in a later play may already seem implicit in his failure to learn the lesson Brutus teaches us here. And that of Brutus himself seems merely a more detailed reenactment of Caesar's; Brutus's tragedy clarifies—is *about*—Caesar's.

Indeed, from this view the two character's tragedies are reciprocal. As we see the tragic form of the death of Julius Caesar defamiliarized, and as we see Caesar's essential similarity to Brutus, the tragic form of Brutus's death is also defamiliarized. The action of the play as a whole becomes self-reflexive. Antony's exposure of Brutus's ritual, the killing of Julius Caesar, becomes the exposure of the full play's epitome. Shakespeare's tragedy is defamiliarized as well.

From this point of view, the title may refer to a specific act: Brutus's tragedy of Julius Caesar in act 3, scene 1. As Brutus's play is an attempt to mystify Caesar, so does Shakespeare's *seem* an attempt to mystify *his* Caesar, the sitting English monarch. It is a tragedy: it seems to heroicize the fallen by seeming to show the fall to be both unmerited and unfortunate. It gives full voice to the noble-sounding egalitarian rhetoric of the rebels Brutus and Cassius in order to show the chaos to which it leads. Set in Rome, the play seems at once to defend monarchy, and to posit this defense in universal rather than local terms. There seems no harm in it.

But if there *is* harm in Brutus's tragedy of Julius Caesar, there is also harm in Shakespeare's. Its self-reflexiveness subverts its seemings. Shakespeare has used an approved discourse, the tragic play, to subvert that discourse, to subvert the vehicle on which the self-justifying ideas of established social authority depend.[15] By showing us that the cause of Brutus's impasse in the world is ours, is within ourselves, Shakespeare implies that it is avoidable. One *need* not be tragic, whether one is Roman or Elizabethan. Another life, one in which we feel Buddhist-style compassion for other beings in the "real" world as well as in a play, is possible.

At the end of *The Merchant of Venice* we imagined ourselves in the process of free fall, without tenable options, all positions having been rendered both threatening and self-contradictory. By the end of *Julius Caesar* we have progressed one step farther. The cause of this destructive impasse has been shown to be the need to solidify the self in a self-image, and then to live up to that image. This desire has been given the form of ambition, the will to nobility and power. If, in our fall after the dissolution of our secure self-belief in *Merchant,* we felt tempted to look for something solid to hold onto, something to cling to for security, a tree perhaps on the edge of a cliff, in *Caesar* we learn that nothing is solid. The tree will fall away when touched. Possibly there is no tree. Certainly, hoping for such a tree has caused our fall in the first place.

We have learned the Buddha's Second Noble Truth, that this desire to cling perpetuates and intensifies our pain in the world. We have also learned the Third, its antidote: the teaching not to escape, but to allow ourselves to be in the process of falling. Our compassion for Brutus is reciprocal: it has prepared us to allow this possibility for ourselves. Unlike Brutus, we must give ourselves up, not pursue an image of ourselves, no matter what the source: the Buddha, society, even the queen. And our example may clear a space in which others can do the same.

This, it may be, is precisely the subversive act to which Shakespeare leads us at the end of this play—not by precept, to be sure (that would be impossible, from both the Derridean and the Buddhist perspectives), but by guiding us to see through the transparent artwork that he entitles *Julius Caesar.* Seeing through it, we glimpse the now unmasked artist inscribed within. His project, unlike that of his characters, is not to mystify himself, but to reveal himself, to use the power of his art to undermine his authority as artist. In doing so, he laughs at the king's game he pretends to play; in teaching us to see his laughter, he beckons us to join him.

Notes

1. This was discussed at the end of the last chapter. For an exposition of the Four Noble Truths, see Trungpa 1973, 151-57. For a brief indication of the Third and Fourth, see the Glossary.

2. Robert S. Miola has argued the ambivalence of our perception of the character Julius Caesar from the perspective of the sixteenth-century tyrannicide debate. James Siemon argues to a similar conclusion from the point of view of the Protestant reformers' attack on images and metaphors which might be mistaken for truth (1985, 125-82). See also David Daiches 1976, 9; Lawrence Danson 1974, 51-53; Ernest Schanzer 1963, 70; and D. A. Traversi 1963, 12. For a diametrical opposition, see for example D. S. Brewer 1952 and J. Dover Wilson 1949, xxiii-xxv.

3. See Northrop Frye 1967, 83. In a similar vein, J. Leeds Barroll (1958) argues that the play is a statement against civil war, and that it takes a Christian view of Roman history.

4. 5.3.41-46 and 5.5.50-51. Kenneth Burke argues that Antony embodies the "Caesar-principle" for the rest of the play (1941, 333-34).

5. Thus Irving Ribner, for example, explains the nature of the full tragedy in these moral terms, and sees an analogy between it and a morality play; both Caesar and Brutus are tragic because each, confronted with a moral choice, chooses wrongly. In his view, the tragedy's emphasis is mainly on "the exact process by which the hero is led to commit his error" (1960, 53). These conventions of private and public morality operate, however, despite the fact that the element of sacredness accorded medieval and Renaissance monarchs is lacking with Caesar, for of course he is neither crowned nor divinely anointed.

6. This is true regardless of whether we see his enactment as Jonathan Goldberg does, i.e., as a deliberate pretense in the service of a good deed (1983, 165), or as Ralph Berry does, as "the priestly slaying of a victim" (1985, 75). However, Berry's argument that these Romans all play roles of "identity," roles in which they believe they truly show and express themselves (1985, 79-83), leads more directly toward the relations between a character's self-image and the specific theatrical form he chooses for his action.

   The idea that Brutus ritualizes the murder of Caesar has often been observed. See for example Ralph

Berry 1985, 75; Lawrence Danson 1974, 52-63; Leo Kirschbaum 1949, 520-24; and Peter Ure 1974, 24.

7. Because these script manipulations involve both the order figure and the noble rebel, they represent a politically interesting shift in application from Jonathan Goldberg's description of a *king:* "Destiny is what is spoken. The king was subjected, shaped, imposed upon, by the language in which, and with which, he attempted to impose himself on others" (1983, 20). This observation leads Goldberg to the conclusion that the common metaphor of king as actor often "leads us to see the doubleness in performance in the royal view," such that we see the paradox of "subversiveness in absolutist rhetoric" (1983, 120). Shakespeare's Caesar and Brutus, as I see their enactments, complicate their play's political ambiguity by playing out this paradox in the persons of both the àuthority figure and his challenger.

8. Kenneth Burke calls particular attention to the metadramatic nature of Antony's speech, albeit to a different purpose: "Instead of being a dramatic character *within* the play, he is here made to speak as a critical commentator *upon* the play" (1941, 329-30).

9. Some aspects of this complex metadramatic situation have been used by others to serve other argumentative ends. For instance, Jonathan Goldberg refers to the "inherent theatricalization" to which this play's "images of the nature of political power" call our attention (1983, 185). Leonard Tennenhouse argues more generally that aesthetics are *always* political (1986, 14-16). Antony Dawson believes that the metadramatic emphasis, without reference to its political implications, leads to "a deeper penetration of reality as we know it" (1978, xiv). Sidney Homan feels that the murder's self-reflexiveness calls our attention to it as the reenactment of a historical event, a reenactment that binds us to the stage audience (1981, 11-12). Ralph Berry, arguing from different premises, also believes that "the roots of the tragic action" in this play "lie in communal identity" (1985, 87).

10. For a related interpretation of Antony, see Rosalie L. Colie (1974, 175) and Northrop Frye (1967, 26-27). R. A. Foakes suggests the pessimistic interpretation to which this view can lead: the "various themes in language and action all suggest a full circle of events in the play, civil war leading to civil war, blood to blood . . ." (1954, 263).

11. Thus G. Wilson Knight sees Brutus as a kind of first draft for the character Macbeth ([1930] 1970, 120). However, Kenneth Burke argues that the ghost represents a version of "the Caesar-persona" ([1941] 1973, 343).

12. Gordon Braden discusses Seneca's stoic ideal in precisely these terms. In it, "the classical drive for esteem is not being suppressed but only redirected toward a more secure and elite kind of self-esteem" (1985, 18). Again, "the philosophically virtuous life becomes a new version of the martial hero's traditional struggle with contingency" (1985, 19). The self is still involved in a power game, but the battlefield is now internalized; it becomes the individual will whose "operative values are, time and again, power and control" (1985, 20).

    Brutus's stature in his suicide is a bone of contention among scholars. Hugh M. Richmond asserts that his "complacent equanimity" and "pride" do not make him "a tragic hero" (1968, 103). Norman Council argues that by the last act Brutus's unorthodox view of honor (as guide rather than reward) "has become merely self-protective, isolated from any concern but its own preservation" (1973, 69). On the other side, Richard G. Moulton speaks for several generations: "In his fall he is glorious" (1966, 183). Matthew N. Proser goes so far as to write, "In his death Brutus achieves pure freedom" (1965, 59).

13. Chögyam Trungpa refers in a similar context to the "suicidal approach to reality" (1976, 58).

14. Thomas F. Van Laan argues that all the major characters have inflated self-images, into which they try unsuccessfully to fit themselves—which they try to "play," and that the audience is extremely aware of this fact (1978, 152-53). Peter Ure makes related observations about Brutus (1974, 24).

15. This is a point argued at some length above with reference to the *Pyramus and Thisby* play within *A Midsummer Night's Dream.* With *Julius Caesar,* Shakespeare has moved from subverting the characters in the stage audience by subverting a play within a play, to subverting the theater audience by subverting the whole play.

Stephen M. Buhler (essay date 1996)

SOURCE: "No Spectre, No Sceptre: The Agon of Materialist Thought in Shakespeare's *Julius Caesar,*" in *English Literary Renaissance,* Vol. 26, No. 2, Spring, 1996, pp. 313-32.

[*In the following essay, Buhler regards the Epicurean skepticism of Cassius in* Julius Caesar *as it illustrates the play's concern with political materialism.*]

> Postremo cur sancta deum delubra suasque discutit infesto praeclaras fulmine sedes, et bene facta deum frangit simulacra suisque demit imaginibus violento volnere honorem?
>
> (Lucretius, *De rerum natura* 6.417-20: Lastly, why does he shatter holy shrines of the gods, and even his own illustrious habitations, with the fatal thunderbolt, why smash finely-wrought images of the gods and rob his own statues of their grandeur with a violent wound?)[1]

In *Julius Caesar,* Shakespeare depicts a cosmological as well as a political struggle. The correspondential order of things is manipulated on all sides of an increasingly bloody conflict, and the downfall of one faction occurs when its members stop manipulating that order and begin, partly and then thoroughly, to credit it. For that reason alone the play lends itself well to criticism of what might be called "naive Tillyardism."[2] A workable argument along such lines would be similar to the one offered in the above passage. Lucretius asks why, if Jove desires to command reverence and to reinforce pious practices, he would so often destroy the sites associated with that piety with his own thunderbolts; a cultural materialist might ask why, if Shakespeare indeed wanted to affirm the validity of the cultural edifices reinforcing the dominant ideology, he would so often leave major components of these constructs in ruins.[3]

Without becoming the dominant discourse of our time, critical approaches such as those advanced by Jonathan Dollimore in *Radical Tragedy* have themselves now come under nearly as strong an attack as Tillyard's once had. In a recent study of the skeptical in Shakespeare, Graham Bradshaw distinguishes between "dogmatic" and—in something of a pre-emptive strike aimed at Dollimore's work—"radical" modes of skepticism. He equates the former with "the terminal, materialistic nihilism of a Thersites, Iago, or Edmund"; this list could also include Cassius, whose skepticism is grounded in Epicurean philosophy. "Radical" skepticism is described as self-reflexive: it "turns on itself—weighing the human need to affirm values against the inherently problematic nature of all acts of valuing."[4] The radical nature of this skepticism further problematizes belief as well, for in the examples of Edmund and of Cassius we see skeptics repenting. Bradshaw, though, does not account for the disturbing hollowness that marks these returns to more conventional values and beliefs. The unsettling effect does not stem from any lack of sincerity or even dramatic credibility, but rather from the impotence and ineffectuality that accompany the characters' penitence. Edmund's remorse comes too late to save Cordelia or ultimately Lear himself. In his return to what Lucretius terms the *antiquae religiones* (5.86), the old superstitions, Cassius has emulated his Stoic friend too well. He has not "tried to be better" than his professed philosophy would permit, as some critics have alleged, but has rather abandoned its principles, acting upon erroneous judgments of events as a result. In his own suicide Brutus repays Cassius' tribute in kind.

The correspondential order receives less than simple affirmation in *Julius Caesar* and the play consequently participates in what has been described as anti-essentialist strains at work in Renaissance culture. I cannot agree with the accusation that critics such as Dollimore are guilty of anachronism when they attach the term *materialism* to such strains of thought. John D. Cox has suggested that in the intervening centuries "philosophical materialism" has been identified with critiques of political culture: to apply the term with all its modern associations to the Renaissance is anachronistic and misleading.[5] But while the term itself may not have had wide currency in the period, the ideas the term represents and their "modern" associations are not as inappropriate as Cox contends. Materialist philosophies were openly considered in the Renaissance and were judged both upon their supposed and actual political ramifications and upon the kind of challenges they presented to established social orders.[6]

Julius Caesar engages fully with the classical and Renaissance debates over philosophical materialism and its political import. It does so not only through its depiction of Cassius, the play's professed materialist, but also through its portrayal of Brutus, his political ally and philosophical adversary whose idealism contributes to the failure of the tyrannicides' cause. The classical heritage of political philosophy is a powerful presence in *Julius Caesar,* and the tension and friendship which exist between the Stoic Brutus and the Epicurean Cassius provide both sources of that power and bases for the play's analysis of power. Two important studies of the play, by David C. Green and Robert S. Miola, neglect to point out fully the political importance of these philosophical allegiances. What results in Green's case is a Tillyardian assurance that "Shakespeare respects the monarchical authority which Caesar for him represents." Miola provides the more sophisticated view that "no trustworthy source of sovereignty arises" in the play, but he still hears the political debate as only "a confusing cacophony of claims and counterclaims."[7] The choice, however, is not merely one between naive order and problematic chaos, or between dominant ideology and polyvocal, heteroglossic subversion: there are strictly discernible voices in the political culture of Shakespeare's age and the historical period depicted in the play. *Julius Caesar* permits us to hear their counsel and to see the possible results of following or rejecting those policies.

James R. Siemon has noted that the play "fosters analysis and interpretation," most notably of the macrocosmic portents, "to a degree far beyond that encouraged in any other of the early plays,"[8] and he points to Cassius' shifting reinterpretations of the storm in 1.3 as a crucial if "disconcerting" instance of the play's intellectual provocation. Siemon, though, sees Cassius as wavering between different readings which nevertheless are similarly grounded in a faith that these prodigies can "clearly reveal their 'true cause'" and show themselves to be "not arbitrary events but iconic signs" (p. 127). In this reading the play focuses upon an inconstancy and arbitrariness in such icons of which Cassius himself is unaware. But as an Epicurean, Cassius would be very mindful of precisely this question of the arbitrary nature of cosmological correspondences, and Shakespeare—following his Plutarchan sources—highlights Cassius' philosophical affiliations. Much of the play's success in placing correspondential schemes under scrutiny is due both to this character's initial insistence on such questioning and to his ultimate abandonment of the interrogative project.

II

Shakespeare and his contemporaries learned about the Epicurean analysis and rejection of the *polis* and its claims to validation through both natural and supernatural arguments from a variety of sources, both sympathetic and critical. In the former camp one finds Lucretius' *De rerum natura,* which explores not only Epicurus' scientific theories but their foundation in the sage's efforts to keep aloof from the state and from state religion, and the *Lives of the Eminent Philosophers* compiled by Diogenes Laertius, who concludes his survey with a dogged defense of the much-maligned philosopher. Critics who nonetheless provide a wealth of often-accurate detail about Epicureanism include Cicero, himself a player in the events depicted by Shakespeare, and Plutarch, who constantly reminds his readers of the philosophical affiliations of the principal conspirators, Cassius and Brutus. Along with these widely available—and widely read—classical sources, Shakespeare had more contemporary reasons to be interested in the skeptical analysis of religion and its relation to political power. The playwright alludes to these reasons at the end of Act 2, scene 1 of *Julius Caesar,* after Brutus has agreed to join and to lead the conspiracy.

All the other self-declared tyrannicides have left, when the aged and ailing Caius Ligarius visits the resolved Marcus Brutus. In paying tribute to his newly-acknowledged leader, Ligarius directs the following simile at Brutus: "Thou, like an exorcist, hast conjured up/My mortified spirit" (2.1.323-24).[9] The precise terms of the compliment here are Shakespeare's alone, and do not appear in the Plutarchan original, *Brutus* 11. In the witty praise of Ligarius there is more than a hint of problematization and outright criticism of Brutus' character and of the political scene in Rome. As Stephen Greenblatt has reminded us in connection with *King Lear,* exorcism was not only a highly suspect practice to a great many of Shakespeare's contemporaries, but a profoundly unsettling one as well. Commentators such as Samuel Harsnett, in his *Declaration of Egregious Popish Impostures,* as he justified Protestant suspicion and skepticism, may have been operating on the tactical assumption that "[t]o glimpse the designing clerical playwright behind the performance [that is exorcism] is to transform terrifying supernatural events into a human strategy."[10] Greenblatt further argues that "acknowledging theatricality kills the credibility of the supernatural" in ways beyond the polemicist's control, in ways that often "unsettle all official lines" of denominational and factional authority (pp. 109, 128). A crucial point of contention in *Julius Caesar* is control over the systems of interpretation which recognize what is and is not supernatural validation. While the polemicist might paradoxically lose control in trying to insist on making such distinctions, the dramatist gains power by examining the struggle over interpretive control. Central to this struggle is the intellectual rivalry between friends and allies: Cassius, the Epicurean scoffer at portents, and Brutus, the Stoic believer in the organic integrity of the cosmos, and therefore in divination.[11]

Mark Rose has discussed the epithet *exorcist* in the context of the play, and deftly traces its impact on the rest of the passage with Ligarius: all the imagery involving decrepitude and disease follows as a consequence of the term. Can Brutus, as exorcist, heal the body politic by casting out the spirit of Caesar or will he invoke—indeed reinscribe—that spirit? With his now impolitic sympathies for the last strong man, Ligarius seems to be thinking as much of the spirit of Pompey as his own spirit being revived, and might therefore intend fully his use of the term *conjured.* As Rose succinctly states this aspect of the problem: "'exorcise' can mean to raise a spirit as well as to expel one. . . . Is Brutus an exorcist or a conjurer?"[12] In many ways, however, the distinction is an artificial one in Shakespeare's time as well as in the play: all exorcisms and conjurations were subject to empirical and moral skepticism. One consequence of the epithet "exorcist" is to call into question Brutus' desirability and suitability as a leader. Throughout Shakespeare's plays as well as in the "official" Protestant religio-political view, the term suggests self-deception at best and charlatanism at the worst.[13] One may wonder, then, what kind of legitimacy could possibly accrue to a regime taking its direction from Brutus. Yet another consequence is more expansive: the term contributes to the play's questioning of all authoritative structures and personalities in the late Republic.

This is, after all, a play in which Cassius very deliberately endeavors to show how both the powerful and those who challenge that power can "transform terrifying supernatural events" into political strategies. It is also a play in which the title character himself comments on the frailty of human bodies and minds, "Men are flesh and blood, and apprehensive" (3.1.67), using the later term much as Theseus does in *A Midsummer Night's Dream* when he distinguishes between what Imagination may "apprehend" and what Reason "comprehends" (5.1.6-7).[14] Caesar's words glance here at the very foundations of the Epicurean critique of political culture: the *polis* is supported by the cult of the gods, which is in turn sustained by humankind's apprehensive dread of its own mortality. The Epicurean solution recommends cultivating a detached and skeptical stance toward the *polis.* The Shakespearean program enables us to investigate the interrelations between philosophical allegiances, political *praxis,* and the skeptical detachment which, paradoxically, can link the first two most effectively.

The *De rerum natura* is a prime source here, and Shakespeare's use of Lucretius in Cassius' disquisition on thunder should come as no surprise. In borrowing from this work the playwright strengthens his character's involvement with Epicurean thought by incorporating elements from the classical world's most famous surviving work on Epicureanism, a work which is itself a product of the time that *Julius Caesar* depicts. Lucretius' skepticism toward the supernatural origin of thunder is connected with his sense that from the outset the cult of the gods was a justification for political society. The gods not only help to explain mysterious natural events, but also extend the long arm of punitive law into the next world, into the supernatural realm: this is, Lucretius suggests, the reason why religion has spread over great nations—*"causa deum per magnas numina gentis / pervulgarit"* (5.1161-62).[15] So Lucretius does more than urge his readers to distinguish between the true attributes of divinity and those attributes which are the products of what in another context Epicurus calls "vain imaginings."[16] He also cautions his readers against believing in the civic ramifications of the cult of the gods. By their very nature ataraxic and impassive, the gods cannot possibly be angry at supposed violations of the natural and civic order; one may reject, then, any claim (or curse) that such anger will follow such a disturbance.

Cassius acts out Epicurus' defiance of the cult of the gods, as described by Lucretius. The *De rerum natura* proclaims that nothing could keep Epicurus from opposing Superstition: *"quem neque fama deum nec fulmina nec minitanti / murmure compressit caelum"* (1.68-69: neither fables of the gods could quell him, nor thunderbolts, nor heaven with menacing roar). Cassius continues in this vein, as he informs Casca:

> For my part, I have walk'd about the streets,
> Submitting me unto the perilous night;
> And thus unbraced, Casca, as you see,
> Have bar'd my bosom to the thunder-stone;
> And when the cross blue lightning seem'd to open
> The breast of heaven, I did present myself
> Even in the aim and very flash of it.
>
> (1.3.46-52)

Casca is understandably shocked, having earlier confessed to Cicero his fear that the thunder indicates that humankind—including his own droll self—has been "too saucy with the gods" (1.3.11). He believes it to be the role and even the duty of humankind "to fear and tremble / When the most mighty gods by tokens send / Such dreadful heralds to astonish us." In response to Casca's pious dismay at his behavior, Cassius announces that such heralds need not be interpreted along the lines of Caesarian *pietas.* He demonstrates this by reading these signs as "instruments of fear and warning / Unto some *monstrous state*" (70-71). I emphasize the last two words to call attention to Cassius' insistence on linking politics with ways of viewing and reading the spectacular. *Monstrous* here retains its full Latinate associations with "showing" and with the wondrous and portentous, along with its obvious utility for expressing Cassius' moral indignation; *state* in this context refers to Rome as a political entity.

After revising the customary and corresponding reading of celestial events, Cassius can then attribute all interpretations of the night's prodigies to the exigencies of human polity. Caesar himself is, in Cassius' estimation,

> a man
> Most like this dreadful night
> That thunders, lightens, opens graves, and roars
> As doth the lion in the Capitol—
> A man no mightier than thyself, or me,
> In personal action, yet prodigious grown,
> And fearful, as these strange eruptions are.
>
> (1.3.72-77)

There is, Cassius implies, nothing inherently meaningful or ominous in these events, nothing which should inspire divine awe; no supernatural agency is needed to explain them. Similarly, Caesar's remarkable successes do not betoken divine favor since all-too-human factors suffice as explanation. Cassius suggests that an understanding of how nature truly operates, and of how human nature is prevailed upon, can keep one from being mystified by even the most dramatic of celestial or political phenomena. He thus provides a clearer philosophical rationale for his earlier sneer at "*immortal* Caesar" and his dismay that "this man / Is now become a *God*" (1.2.60 and 115-16).[17] Already seeing the cult of the gods and absolute forms of authority as sharing a common origin, Cassius readily perceives Caesar engaged in a latter-day application of the same principles. While this might strike us as unlikely, since Caesar's credulity rivals that of Gloucester in *Lear,* one should note that Caesar (like Gloucester) is very selective in his superstitions: those that are most aggrandizing are the ones he comes to hold most tenaciously.

III

At this point Cassius functions not only as an Epicurean scoffer, but also as a kind of proto-Harsnett, debunking Roman superstition and pointing out the political consequences of credulous belief.[18] Another conspirator, Decius Brutus, uses his own insight into the interworkings of religious and political authority in persuading Caesar to come to the Capitol. In an argument remarkable for its mediation between ancient beliefs and contemporary controversies, he interprets Calphurnia's dream in terms strongly reminiscent of the "old religion" in England before promising an imminent offer of royal power. Toward the blood issuing from Caesar's statue in the dream, Decius advises, "great men shall press / For tinctures, stains, relics, and cognizance" (2.2.88-89). Caesar responds favorably to this ceremonial language and transfers credence from Calphurnia's alarmist response to the complaisance Decius Brutus advises. Cassius, though, loses the interpretive control that his co-conspirator practices upon Caesar and that he himself displays with Casca: he eventually comes to believe in the involvement of the supernatural in both physical and human events. This is suggested even by the context in which Cassius' rejection of the supernatural appears: before Cassius arrives on the scene, Cicero laconically observes that "men may construe things after their fashion, / Clean from the purpose of the things themselves" (1.3.34-35). Cicero's words imply that there is a determined and determinable purpose at work in these prodigies, although his composure in the face of these wonders can suggest as much the wryly skeptical observer as the man of firm faith.

Later on, as Cassius looks ahead to the battle at Philippi, he tells Messala of his newfound respect for divination:

"You know that I held Epicurus strong, / And his opinion; now I change my mind, / And partly credit things that do presage" (5.1.76-78). After describing the departure of the auspicious eagles and the arrival of dire birds of ill omen at his camp, Cassius concludes that his army is "ready to give up the ghost" (88). Even his repeated insistence that he believes in all this but *partly* is undercut by the dramatic irony of his haunted language, which increasingly hints at the supernatural as well as the natural. He describes himself as "fresh of *spirit,* and resolv'd / To meet all perils very constantly" (90-91). In his address to Brutus before battle, he goes so far as to assert that "The gods to-day stand friendly" (93) to their cause. In short, Cassius is undergoing a reversion to the *antiquae religiones.* He is haunted not only by the oracular birds and the shifting language of transcendence, but also by his sense that he has come full circle upon the date of his birth, that his "life is run his compass" (5.2.25).

IV

In the dramatic logic of *Julius Caesar,* Cassius' newly superstitious turn of mind leads him directly to credit Pindarus' misinterpretation of the evidence, to believe that Titinius has been captured. One of the most important ways in which Shakespeare departs from Plutarch is in suggesting that Cassius' apostasy from Epicureanism leads to his fall into error and subsequent destruction. Cassius forgoes the philosophy's emphases on natural explanations and on direct observation. Plutarch, less attuned to the philosophy, enjoys something of a grim joke at Cassius' and Epicureanism's expense when Cassius, the persistent believer in empirical knowledge, suffers from weak vision and misinterprets what occurs.[19] But Shakespeare ascribes the misinterpretation directly to Pindarus, thereby showing Cassius' mistake to be *not* relying on his own perceptions, *not* observing the tenets of his erstwhile philosophy. Despite his grief-stricken cry, Cassius has not lived to see his best friend taken before his face (5.2.35); deviating from his initial principles, he acts in accordance with what he has been told, rather than what he himself has observed. As Messala subsequently puts it in the same scene, such an error "show[s] to the apt thoughts of men / The things that are not" (68-69). Cassius' acceptance of the supernatural order initiates the credulity that culminates in his suicide. That death turns the tide of battle against the originally anti-superstitious defenders of the Republic.

Nearly two decades ago Jean Auffret noted some of the discrepancies between Plutarch's presentation of Cassius and his philosophy and Shakespeare's own portrayals.[20] Commenting on the character's defiance of the thunderous omens, Auffret saw the connection between this scene and Lucretius' discussion of thunder and its psychological effects. While Auffret takes the philosophic background seriously, he does not consider fully the politics of that background. He takes the Lucretian passage out of its strongly political context and allows the old tradition that Lucretius fought and finally succumbed to melancholic madness to color his reading both of the passage and of Cassius' character. In Auffret's reading of the scene, "Cassius gets infected with the terror he describes—and so does Lucretius—, but his hysteria prepares us for his breakdown at 4.3.92-106 [where Cassius admits to Brutus how deeply pained he is that they are at odds] and his suicide" (p. 71). The "breakdown" Auffret detects in Act 4 is, rather, a demonstration of the strong friendship Cassius feels toward Brutus, and of the strong devotion with which Cassius accepts the Epicurean privileging of friendship. As we have seen, Cassius is far from "hysterical" in the scene with Casca; he effectively uses Epicurean skepticism to undermine political orders that claim legitimacy on supernatural grounds. Shakespeare's attribution of this rhetorical strategy to an Epicurean character has more contemporary precedents as well, and these precedents often take advantage of the parallels between the Renaissance conception of the Epicure and of the Machiavel.

At first this seems a patently risible connection when one considers both Epicurus' and Lucretius' resolve to avoid the corridors of power, termed the *angustum iter ambitionis* (the narrow—petty and constricting—road of ambition) in the *De rerum natura* (5.1132). But the association between Epicure and Machiavel can be justified partly by the historical phenomenon of Epicureanism's popularity among the well-to-do and the powerful during the era which spanned the passing of the Republic and the foundation of the Empire.[21] Men of letters seemed particularly vulnerable. In addition to Lucretius' proselytizing, the Epicurean leanings (or at least training of Vergil and Horace) announce the philosophy's appeal. We can also see, in reaction, Cicero's tireless campaign against Epicureanism in works such as *De finibus* and *De natura deorum.* J. D. Minyard's comments in connection with Caesar and Epicureanism may also indicate Renaissance suspicions toward the philosophy: "Acceptance of Epicurean mechanical materialism and disregard of Epicurean moral conclusions would give someone a great field for action in the world, freeing him from fear and laying on him no obligations except to his own rationalizing sophistication" (p. 18). Such a suspicious attitude provides the rationale for Cicero's references to Epicureanism throughout the oration *In Pisonem.*[22]

V

It was often thought in the Renaissance that those who embraced Epicurean skepticism toward divine and political orders did so for their own selfish ends. Such characters were regularly depicted on the English stage: the name of the Machiavel, at this time, was Legion. So Cassius might be dismissed as philosophically and dramatically suspect, as he draws upon a marginalized body of thought to further his own ends. He freely translates the signs which seem to warn against Caesar's death as calling for Caesar's murder, and in a move which presages Iago's confidences to the audience in *Othello,* he freely admits that he is "inventing" the public call for Brutus to take action against Caesar. In Plutarch the letters which appeal to Brutus are authentic (*Brutus* 9.3-4); in the play Cassius not only pens the appeals himself but has one planted upon the iconic statue of "old Brutus," the founder of the Republic. Shakespeare's Cassius comes close to Iago in his stage-management of perception and most closely reminds us of the ensign in the lines, "If I were Brutus now and he were Cassius, / He should not humor me" (1.2.314-15). But we also find in the Renaissance—such as with the exposure of fraudulent exorcisms—a sense that anyone who believes in supernatural explanations for purely natural events joins the lunatic, the lover, and the poet in being of imagination all compact. So Cassius' rigorous debunking of the burgeoning Caesarian cult and his turning its tactics upon itself need not have been viewed with horror. The rich ambivalence of the character and his philosophy can be found in these famous lines: "The fault, dear Brutus, is not in our stars, / But in ourselves, that we are underlings" (1.2.140-41). While the final clause suggests personal ambition and a personal *animus* against Caesar, the rest of the sentence not only conforms to Epicurean resistance toward astral determinism but also accords nicely with Christian—especially Reformed Christian—dismissals of astrology. At least where political and religious values other than one's own are concerned, philosophical skepticism is acceptable, and its historical bases can often be explored with impunity.[23]

In addition, Cassius' suicide in response to the supposed capture of his friend is philosophically as well as psychologically consistent. After his heartfelt expressions (in 4.3) of pain at Brutus' criticisms of him, and of joyful relief when he and Brutus are reconciled, it comes as no surprise that Cassius considers friendship such a life-and-death issue. In fact the importance of Brutus' friendship to Cassius personally as well as politically leads Cassius to defer to Brutus' oft-mistaken judgments and misperceptions. But the bond between friends is also of prime value in Epicurus' ethics: what replaces the political relationship that exists between and among human beings in the wake of the Epicurean renunciation of the *polis* is exactly friendship. Admirers of Epicurus point to this as evidence that the philosophy is not solipsistic or hedonistic; critics make similar concessions or point out the apparent inconsistency between a commitment to one's own personal pleasure and a concern for that of others.[24] Failure to recognize the centrality of friendship in the Epicurean scheme of things has not only led Auffret to judge Cassius as psychologically unstable in his devotion to Brutus, but has also led Allan Bloom to see Cassius in these scenes as being in open conflict with Epicureanism:

> The man whose doctrine insisted that all action is selfish turns out to be the truest and most sentimental of friends. He even dies for friendship. . . . This is no true Epicurean; it is rather a man who has schooled himself in a teaching which ran counter to a fund of common goodness and ordinary political weakness within him. In Cassius, we see the case of a man who thinks worse of himself than he ought to and does so because he has accepted a philosophy which depreciates, discourages, and explains away what is good in him. In the final crisis, this arbitrary shell breaks, and the true man emerges. But it is too late.[25]

Such pronouncements reflect both an unshakable prejudice toward Epicurean philosophy and a determined unwillingness to consider it either on its own terms or in the terms set out in Shakespeare and his sources. Despite Bloom's own training in philosophy, there is little sense here of the complexity at work in the classical philosophical traditions. Instead we have a reductive, even monolithic model of that tradition in which the moral and political significance of a philosophy is determined and held in stasis by its adversaries. Certainly a glance at Diogenes Laertius' definition of the Epicurean sage—"And he will on occasion die for a friend"[26]—should restrain any surprise at Cassius' responses and any conclusion that the philosophy suppresses human good. Cassius is, after all, confronted by the impending loss of men for whom he cares deeply; he faces emotional estrangement from Brutus and responsibility for Titinius' capture. What has been described in these scenes as "Cassius' generosity of spirit"[27] is not only a matter of personality but also of philosophical principle. Shakespeare shows that what is most admirable in Cassius is sustained by his philosophy; what results in his and his compatriots' destruction is precipitated by a fall from the Epicurean "faith."

VI

Brutus attributes Cassius' death to Caesar's spirit, which "walks abroad, and turns our swords / In our own proper entrails" (5.3.95-96). It is not only Ligarius' "mortified spirit" which Brutus conjures up. While "Caesar's spirit, ranging for revenge" is first invoked by Antony (3.1.270), Brutus himself invokes the preconditions for the eventual triumph of both "Caesar" and the entire correspondential construct:

> Between the acting of a dreadful thing
> And the first motion, all the interim is
> Like a phantasma, or a hideous dream.
> The genius and the mortal instruments
> Are then in council, and the state of man,
> Like to a little kingdom, suffers then
> The nature of an insurrection
>
> (2.1.63-69)

And Brutus is the one who eventually calls the apparition he had seen before at the battle at Philippi by Caesar's name. Despite the stage direction of the First Folio—"*Enter the Ghost of Caesar*"—the play leaves open to question the identity and ontology of the apparition which Brutus sees. While Plutarch judges both that the apparition was the responsibility of Caesar's "great guardian-spirit [daimon]" and that "the phantom that appeared to Brutus showed that the murder of Caesar was not pleasing to the gods," he also has the image describe itself as Brutus' own "evil genius."[28] Shakespeare follows this account ("Thy evil spirit") and suggests something of a physiological explanation by having Brutus share in the bad eyesight Plutarch assigns to Cassius. Brutus, the only one to see the spectre, identifies the apparition only in the final scene, after blaming Cassius' suicide on that mighty spirit and before ordering Strato to help him in taking his own life.

Despite Cassius' skeptical opinion expressed earlier, that in conjuration the name of "Brutus will start a spirit as soon as Caesar" (1.2.147)—that is, never—Brutus carries out his early wish to "come by Caesar's spirit" (2.1.169) even though he must "dismember Caesar" and dismember his own faction and cause in the process. We should qualify David Bevington's understanding that Brutus is here "victimized by the unshakable flaw of rebellion [which] must force aside the very institutions of legitimate power that it had hoped to preserve"[29] with a realization that in Shakespeare's play neither Brutus nor Cassius can shake off their rivals' claims to supernatural bases for power. They fall victim to the politically-grounded cult of the gods Lucretius militates against in the passages Cassius echoes and enacts.

Perhaps the most crucial deviation from Plutarch's account is the deletion of any hint of Cassius' skeptical reading of Brutus' apparition. In the *Brutus,* just before he comments upon "the superstitious fears which were gradually carrying even Cassius himself away from his Epicurean doctrines," Plutarch describes how Cassius tries to assuage his friend's fears that they have transgressed the limits of the political, natural, and supernatural orders:

> "In our sect, Brutus, we have an opinion that we do not always feel or see that which we suppose we do both see and feel. . . . For the mind of man is ever occupied; and that continual moving is nothing but an imagination."[30]

This attitude, too, has an analogue in the *De rerum natura.* Working from the super-subtle images it received from the distant, detached, ataraxic gods, the human mind was able to embellish and intensify the impressions, through the power of the imagination:

> Quippe etenim iam tum divom mortalia saecla egregias animo facies vigilante videbant, et magis in somnis mirando corporis auctu. his igitur sensum tribuebant propterea quod membra movere videbantur vocesque superbas mittere pro facie praeclara et viribus amplis.
>
> (5.1169-74: The truth is that even in those days the generations of men used to see with waking mind, and still more in sleep, gods conspicuous in beauty and of marvellous bodily stature. To these therefore they attributed sensation, because they appeared to move their limbs and to utter proud speech in keeping with their splendid beauty and vast strength.)[31]

Lucretius suggests, moreover, that anxiety over a shakily established order gave strong impetus for these attributions, since this explanation is prefaced by his account of the earliest foundations of political society.

While Plutarch permits Cassius to retain no small measure of Epicurean skepticism toward transcendent orders even at this juncture, Shakespeare's compression of events allows for little in the way of recusancy. The only signs of resistance are his claims to place only partial credence in the omens and his sharing with Brutus a farewell "for ever, and for ever" (5.1.116, 119), still confident, perhaps, in his philosophy's belief that death is the cessation of consciousness and existence. While Brutus here may be flirting with his friend's philosophy, his earlier encounters with Epicurean materials show his distance from its principles. Brutus' insistence that by making Caesar the conspirators' sole target they will "carve him as a dish fit for the gods" (2.1.179) hints at the crimes of Tantalus. Epicurean philosophy interprets both the crime and punishment of Tantalus in ways which make him the type of the superstitious individual. In one version of the myth he serves his son Pelops as a meal to the gods out of desperation at not having enough (or anything special enough) to entertain them properly.[32] In another version, much noted by Epicureans, Tantalus is eternally threatened by a rock hanging over him—that is what prevents him from satisfying either hunger or thirst.[33] Brutus argues that the manner and singularity of Caesar's death must be pleasing to the gods, and he is more than ready to perceive supernatural expressions of their apparent disfavor. He and Cassius slip into superstitious belief, dragging their friends and allies down with them. Skepticism seems to have passed out of Cassius altogether and to have possessed—at least in part—the playwright and the audience. In this "spirit" we may even read Brutus' Stoicism as the source for his Senecan taste in bloody-minded, vengeful, and psychologically-driven ghosts;[34] in the same spirit we may raise serious questions about the philosophical orientations of other characters as well.

It is Antony, we recall, who first invokes Caesar's spirit directly in his soliloquy after the death of Caesar. We can relate this invocation to similar ones in Shakespeare's Henriad: Richard's and Carlisle's incantatory "hauntings" of Bollingbroke and his descendents with the spectre of the deposed rightful king.[35] Antony is able to recall Caesar's ceremonial rejection of the crown—with advantages—and use it against Caesar's supplanters. This tactical skill parallels Richard's ability to use the relinquishing of the crown against his enemies and Cassius' previous ability to manipulate appearances to politic ends. Interestingly, Caesar opines early on that "Cassius has a lean and hungry look," and suggests that we associate Antony with the "fat / Sleek-headed" men who sleep (well into the morning) the sleep of the sensually indulgent. Cassius is here identified with the asceticism of authentic Epicurean teaching and Antony with the Epicure of popular imagination.

While adapting his Plutarchan source, Shakespeare may well be echoing Horace's assessment of himself as a fat, sleek pig of Epicurus' herd.[36] Antony, we soon learn, is no mere sensualist. It is Antony who, with Octavius, shows chillingly ataraxic detachment in negotiating which rivals and allies are to be executed and which spared; the two strongest pillars of the triumvirate partake aggressively in the role of Machiavel. We might also note the "friendship" Antony invokes in this scene is far removed from the depth of personal feeling for which Cassius ultimately dies. Yet Cassius does recognize Antony as a kindred spirit, if an enemy: he judges Antony to be a "shrewd contriver" (2.1.158), an estimation grandly fulfilled in Antony's manipulation of the crowd—using relics, significantly, to maximum effect. "Let it work" is Antony's own laconic, Iago-like comment on the mob violence he has unleashed (3.2.260) while triumphantly overshadowing Cassius' own machinations. This aspect of Antony's Epicureanism should be added to our understanding of the Epicurean elements at work in *Antony and Cleopatra* that have been observed by both Barbara Bono and Hilary Gatti.[37]

VII

Shakespeare shares in his age's widespread mistrust of what motivates those who reject a correspondential relation between the cosmic and political orders. Through the drama of both personality and philosophy, however, he repeatedly ponders the validity of that relation: *Julius Caesar* does not echo Plutarch's belief that in these events we can clearly see that "Heaven wish[ed] to remove from the scene the only man who stood in the way"[38] of change from republican to imperial governance. A similar complexity informs *King Lear.* Edmund may pay the price for sneering at all bonds of sympathy and then repent, albeit ineffectually. But Edgar, like the exorcists Harsnett wishes to expose, still has to invent proofs of such bonds for the benefit of his disillusioned father. Through its encounters with Plutarch and Lucretius, *Julius Caesar* shows "Caesar's spirit" extending the religious *realpolitik* reportedly expressed by James I as "no bishop, no king" to the genuinely radical skepticism of "no spectre, no sceptre." Decius Brutus' ability to link in Caesar's mind the "tinctures, stains, relics, and cognizance" of Calphurnia's dream with the promise of a kingly crown—and all as a ploy to lure Caesar to his death—is but one instance of Shakespeare pondering these political and metaphysical equations.

We can detect Renaissance versions and analogues of what our age calls cultural materialism not only in fissures in the correspondential facade. They can be found clearly in the ideas considered, debated, and dramatized in texts written and read during the period. The history of ideas, then, can lead us to a better grasp of historicized ideas, of the shifting social and political significances invested in intellectual and philosophical systems. The political materialist strain of Epicurean thought, which held a sometimes horrified fascination for readers and writers in the Renaissance, demands that some discrimination be made between Bradshaw's "materialistic nihilism" and skeptical inquiries into the grand scheme of correspondences that Tillyard thought was the age's World Picture. That same philosophical strain also indicates that *materialism,* with much of the term's more recent meaning, was part of the age's political consciousness as well as its unconscious.

Notes

1. All quotations from Lucretius are taken from the Loeb Classical Library edition, translated by W. H. D. Rouse and revised by Martin Ferguson Smith (Cambridge, Mass., 1982).
2. E. M. W. Tillyard, *The Elizabethan World Picture* (London, 1943), has been a prime *locus* of debate as well as a target. Even student guides written by traditional scholars have questioned Tillyard's contentions, as in Isabel Rivers, *Classical and Christian Ideas in English Renaissance Poetry* (London, 1979), p. 2: "the blending of these elements did not create one uniform world picture."
3. See, for example, Jonathan Dollimore, *Radical Tragedy: Religion, Ideology, and Power in the Drama of Shakespeare and his Contemporaries* (Chicago, 1984), esp. pp. 189-217. Alan Sinfield addresses the political significances at work in stagings as well as interpretations of *Julius Caesar* in *Faultlines: Cultural Materialism and the Politics of Dissident Reading* (Oxford, 1992), pp. 10-21.
4. Graham Bradshaw, *Shakespeare's Scepticism* (Brighton, 1987), p. 39. Similar—but far less nuanced—criticisms of cultural materialist readings have been offered by Robin Headlam Wells, *Elizabethan Mythologies: Studies in Poetry, Drama, Music* (Cambridge, 1994), pp. 12-15.
5. John D. Cox, *Shakespeare and the Dramaturgy of Power* (Princeton, 1989), pp. x-xi. David Cressy has detected other kinds of "anachronism and dislocation" in *Radical Tragedy* stemming from its theoretical foundations in Foucault's often ahistorical work; see "Foucault, Stone, and Social History," *English Literary Renaissance* 21 (1991), 125.
6. Cox observes that Augustinian Christianity often resisted claims of transcendentally-sanctioned political authority. Yet he is not always attuned to the problematics of Augustine's views on political authority, since what Cox calls "Christian political realism" often translates into quietism. Epicureanism's original strictures against involvement with political culture are themselves profoundly quietist.
7. David C. Green, *"Julius Caesar" and Its Source,* Salzburg Studies in English Literature 86 (Salzburg, 1979), p. 20. Robert S. Miola, *"Julius Caesar* and the Tyrannicide Debate," *Renaissance Quarterly* 39 (1985), 288.
8. James R. Siemon, *Shakespearean Iconoclasm* (Berkeley, 1985), p. 125.
9. All references to Shakespeare's plays are taken from *The Riverside Shakespeare,* ed. G. Blakemore Evans *et al.* (Boston, 1974).
10. Stephen Greenblatt, *Shakespearean Negotiations* (Berkeley, 1988), p. 107. John L. Murphy considers some of the more pragmatic political ramifications of the events Harsnett chronicles in *Darkness and Devils: Exorcism and "King Lear"* (Athens, Ohio, 1984), pp. 153-70.

11. For classical applications of the principle, see Thomas G. Rosenmeyer, *Senecan Drama and Stoic Cosmology* (Berkeley, 1989), p. 79: Seneca's interest in divination is related to Stoicism's conservative view that "the world is full of signs guaranteed by the benevolence of the gods."

12. Mark Rose, "Conjuring Caesar: Ceremony, History, and Authority in 1599," *English Literary Renaissance* 19 (1989), 297.

13. Greenblatt, pp. 114-16, briefly discusses exorcism in *The Comedy of Errors, Twelfth Night,* and *All's Well That Ends Well.* While Harsnett's *Declaration* was not published until 1603, the cases which he describes date from 1585-1586.

14. The connection between Caesar's and Theseus' language has been drawn by Bradshaw, p. 41. Since his study avoids considerations of philosophical backgrounds, it touches on skepticism or materialism in *Julius Caesar* only briefly.

15. This assertion that punishment can only curb and channel violent ambition—not extirpate it—provides another possible link between Epicurean and Augustinian political theories.

16. From Epicurus' Principal Doctrine 30; see Diogenes Laertius, *Lives of the Eminent Philosophers,* 10:149. In the translation by R. D. Hicks for the Loeb Classical Library edition (Cambridge, Mass., 1925), the phrase is rendered as "illusory opinion."

17. Miola, p. 275, argues that "Shakespeare takes pains to corroborate Cassius' opinion of Caesar's unnatural usurpation." I would suggest, though, that Cassius reacts not so much to Caesar's "unnaturalness," but rather to Caesar's claims to supernatural power and significance.

18. Rose, pp. 292 and 295, suggests striking analogies between the militant republicans in Shakespeare's Rome and the militant reformers in Shakespeare's London: virtually all of Caesar's political opponents, most notably Cassius and Casca, express themselves in anti-ritualistic terms. Siemon, p. 143, also sees the Reformist "desire to reveal certain cultural and social patterns as both historically real and yet ultimately arbitrary in nature" reflected in *Julius Caesar.* He does not, however, observe similar desires motivating characters *within* the play or appearing as part of the philosophic temper of the age the play represents.

19. See the excerpts from Sir Thomas North in *Shakespeare's Plutarch,* ed. T. J. B. Spencer (Baltimore, 1964), p. 159; in the Loeb edition of Plutarch's *Parallel Lives,* vol. 6, trans. Bernadotte Perrin (Cambridge, Mass., 1918) the passage is found in *Brutus* 43.3. Green, p. 106, also notes this difference between Shakespeare and Plutarch.

20. Jean Auffret, "The Philosophical Background of *Julius Caesar,*" *Cahiers Élisabéthains* 5 (1974), 69-71.

21. This popularity has been examined by J. D. Minyard in his monograph, *Lucretius and the Late Republic* (Leiden, 1985), esp. pp. 18-20 and 33-70.

22. Cicero, *In Pisonem* 28: "Audistis profecto dici philosophos Epicureos omnis res, quae sint homini expetendae, voluptate metiri; rectene an secus, nihil ad nos aut, si ad nos, nihil ad hoc tempus; sed tamen lubricum genus orationis adulescenti non acriter intellegenti et saepe praeceps." (You surely have heard it said that the Epicurean philosophers evaluate by pleasure all the things for which men strive. Whether that is truly said is nothing to us, or if it be anything to us, it is nothing to the present matter. But for all that it is a slippery kind of message for a youth of no sharp wit and always a dangerous one.) I have used the C. F. W. Mueller edition of Cicero's *Scripta,* (Leipzig, 1893-1908), vol. 3, part 2, 189. For the polemical function of "Epicureanism" in this oration, see Phillip DeLacy, "Cicero's Invective against Piso," *Transactions and Proceedings of the American Philological Association* 72 (1941), 49-58.

23. I am reminded of how Greenblatt, p. 65, formulates both Elizabethan and twentieth-century attitudes: "There is subversion, no end of subversion, only not for us." But I am more skeptical than he is of both the will-to-containment (in Shakespeare, his contemporaries, and ourselves) and its supposed effectiveness in squelching analyses of one's own culture and political structure.

24. Phillip Mitsis, *Epicurus' Ethical Theory: The Pleasures of Invulnerability* (Ithaca, 1988), pp. 98-101; source texts include Diogenes Laertius 10.118 and 120, and Cicero, *De finibus* 1.20.65-69. Charles Wells has connected Cassius' fierce devotion to friendship with Epicurean precepts; see *The Wide Arch: Roman Values in Shakespeare* (New York, 1992), p. 81.

25. Allan Bloom, with Harry V. Jaffa, *Shakespeare's Politics* (New York, 1964), pp. 103-04. As Darryl J. Gless sharply challenges Bloom's reading of the play, he also notes that, in spite of "relentless invocations of the classics, Bloom's convictions receive neither documentation nor specific argument"; see "*Julius Caesar,* Allan Bloom, and the Value of Pedagogical Pluralism," in *Shakespeare Left and Right,* ed. Ivo Kamps (New York, 1991), p. 187.

26. Diogenes Laertius, 10.120; translation by Hicks.

27. Vivian Thomas, *Shakespeare's Roman Worlds* (London, 1989), p. 57.

28. These passages appear in Plutarch, *Caesar* 69.2 and 69.5 in vol. 7 of the Loeb *Parallel Lives* (London, 1919). North, generally following Amyot, describes *genius* as "great prosperity and good fortune" in Caesar's case, and as "ghost" and "ill angel" in the case of Brutus' apparition. See *Shakespeare's Plutarch,* pp. 99-100; and Plutarch, *Les vies des hommes*

illustres, trans. Jacques Amyot, ed. Gérard Walter 2 vols. (Paris, 1951), 2:485-86.

29. David Bevington, *Tudor Drama and Politics* (Cambridge, Mass., 1968), p. 249.

30. In this case, I have quoted the clearer rendering in Perrin's translation of *Brutus* 39.3; but see also *Shakespeare's Plutarch,* p. 152.

31. *Shakespeare's Plutarch,* pp. 149-50; *Brutus* 37.1-3.

32. Servius Grammaticus, *Commentarius in Aeneidos* 6.603. Miola, p. 285, argues that the "dish fit for the gods" passage in *Julius Caesar* is an expression not only of piety but ultimately of fear, since it continues the play's descent "into a strange, unfathomable universe, wherein characters continually misconstrue and misunderstand [the gods'] wishes."

33. Lucretius, *De rerum natura* 3.978-83:

> Atque ea nimirum quaecumque Acherunte profundo prodita sunt esse, in vita sunt omnia nobis. nec miser inpendens magnum timet aere saxum Tantalus, ut famast, cassa formidine torpens; sed magis in vita divom metus urget inanis mortalis
>
> (And assuredly whatsoever things are fabled to exist in deep Acheron, these all exist for us in this life. There is no wretched Tantalus, as the story goes, fearing the great rock that hangs over him in the air and frozen in vain terror; rather it is in this life that the fear of gods oppresses mortals without cause).

See also Cicero, *De finibus* 1.18.62, where Cicero's Epicurean interloculor, Torquatus, alludes to Tantalus and his fearful stone.

34. Marjorie Garber has suggested that the "Ghost of Caesar" has both a generic source in Senecan tragedy and an intradramatic basis in Brutus' psychological state; see *Dream in Shakespeare: From Metaphor to Metamorphosis* (New Haven, 1974), p. 50. A further connection might be made with the Ghost of Tantalus in *Thyestes* 107-21: his very presence, prompted by a Fury, "infects" his descendents' house; that infection is signalled by omens. Thyestes recalls these signs, especially the late, hesitant dawn, when he discovers how Atreus has taken vengeance upon him (1035-36). See Rosenmeyer, pp. 136-59, on "Sickness, Portents, and Catastrophe" in Senecan drama, especially pp. 140-42.

35. As in the persuasive reading by Harry Berger, Jr., in *Imaginary Audition* (Berkeley, 1989), pp. 66-73.

36. Horace, *Epistolae* 1.4.16.

37. Barbara Bono, *Literary Transvaluation: From Vergilian Epic to Shakespearean Tragicomedy* (Berkeley, 1984), esp. pp. 173-83. Hilary Gatti, "Epicurean Elements in Elizabethan Drama," a paper given at the Sixteenth Century Studies Conference in Tempe, Arizona, October 1987.

38. *Brutus* 47.4. North, convinced that Rome "could no more abide to be governed by many lords" (that is, could no longer stand republicanism), declares that divine intervention was meant to keep Brutus from becoming the "only absolute governor" in the wake of the Republic's fall; see *Shakespeare's Plutarch,* p. 165.

RHETORIC AND MEANING

John W. Velz (essay date 1982)

SOURCE: "*Orator* and *Imperator* in *Julius Caesar:* Style and the Process of Roman History," in *Shakespeare Studies,* Vol. XV, 1982, pp. 55-75.

[*In the following essay, Velz delineates the combined influence of oratory and command on Roman history in* Julius Caesar.]

Among the sigla of Roman life in *Julius Caesar,* two, oratory and the role of the *imperator,* have been seen by commentators only fractionally.[1] Discussion of oratory has focused on the Forum speeches of Act III, Scene ii without cognizance of the numerous other formal discourses, primarily deliberative, that dominate the first half of the play and are distantly echoed in the epideictic oratory of Act V.[2] Discussion of "Caesarism" has focused on Caesar himself—pompous, fallible, illeistic[3]—without recognition that his imperiousness is conveyed by his grammatical mood as well as by his references to himself, and that others in the play, especially Octavius in Act V, also speak his imperial-imperious style.

It is important to see oratory and the imperial mode as and where they are in *Julius Caesar* because oratory is the energizing force behind the process of history in the play, while the *Imperium* is the *telos* of that process. The roles of *orator* and *imperator* are linked at the moral core of *Julius Caesar;* it may be that Shakespeare thought of them as near the center of *Romanitas* itself. In any case, the movement toward the *Imperium* begins in *Julius Caesar* in the turbulence that oratory creates. An analysis of the play can show that in Shakespeare's conception the fall of the Republic is very much a matter of style.

I

In his oration, Antony denigrates Brutus with the label "orator." The *orator,* he implies, is the moral opposite of the "plain blunt man" that speaks "right on," spontaneously, without assistance from the devious art of rhetoric (III.ii.219-32).[4] That Antony is manifesting the putative deviousness of the *orator* in denying that he has it, and that his claims for his own character and that of Brutus are both nearly exactly the opposite of the truth as the audience sees it—these are among the finest ironies in the play.[5] Antony, the "Asiatic" stylist, lays claim to the "Attic" style that Brutus has just spoken[6] and accuses Brutus of having spoken as he himself is now speaking, Asiatically. Antony's prototypical *orator* manipulates his audience with calculated sophistry to "ruffle up" their spirits (230); the phrase is an apt, if colloquial, translation of Cicero's *permoveo* (*De Oratore* II.185 et passim). The "Asiatik" style of the historical Marcus Antonius' speeches, florid and emotive, was calculated to make "uprore among the people," as Sir Thomas North put it;[7] Shakespeare conveys this style admirably in Antony's vivid blank verse. Brutus' prose speech which precedes is regularly contrasted by critics with Antony's, and its Attic style—the result of Shakespeare's mistaken inference from Plutarch that Marcus Brutus spoke as he wrote[8]—is indeed quite different from Antony's. But Brutus' oration is no less artificial, no less contrived to move the hearer.[9] Aristotle would have termed Brutus' oration a failure in that it produces results contrary to those intended.[10] Brutus means his speech as a forensic defense of the conspirators, but the Plebeians take it as a deliberative political speech—and as it were the speech forms the hearers into a Brutan political party. As a forensic speaker, then, Brutus is a failure, but there is no doubt about the power of his rhetoric—the many critics who have said that Brutus' oration is flat compared to Antony's have ignored the extent to which it stirs the Plebeians: they offer him a triumphal procession, a statue with his ancestors, and the role of Caesar (III.ii.50-54). Antony's superiority over Brutus lies as much in his place in the sequence of speakers as in his oratorical method.[11]

Brutus adopts what Shakespeare regularly portrays in the play as the *orator*'s stance: sophistic *ad hominem* argument and equally sophistic rhetorical questions:

> Who is here so base, that would be a bondman? If any, speak; for him have I offended.
>
> (*III.ii.30-31*)

The rhetorical device is what Aristotle calls a spurious enthymeme, a fallacious syllogism in which the listener is to infer one of the premises.[12] Brutus iterates the formula to make a compelling tricolon:

> Who is here so rude, that would not be a Roman? If any, speak; for him have I offended. Who is here so vile, that will not love his country? If any, speak; for him have I offended. I pause for a reply.
>
> (*III.ii.31-35*)

Antony is right to see the sophistry of the *orator* in Brutus. But he himself uses exactly this technique, the combination of *ad hominem* innuendo with rhetorical questions:

> You all did love him once, not without cause;
> What cause withholds you then to mourn for him?
> O judgment, thou art fled to brutish beasts,
> And men have lost their reason.
>
> (*III.ii.104-07*)

Antony is persistent with emotionally charged questions: "Did this in Caesar seem ambitious?" (92); "Was this ambition?" (99); "'Tis good you know not that you are his heirs; / For if you should, O, what would come of it?" (147-48); "You will compel me then to read the will?" (159). The differences, then—and they are real enough—between Antony's oration and Brutus' bespeak the persons involved; the underlying similarities, equally real, evoke the role these two men play successively.[13]

Others in *Julius Caesar* assume the *orator*'s role as well; Brutus and Antony are, in fact, anticipated by several speakers. The play is scarcely under way when we encounter the first of them, Marullus, whose harangue to the Plebeians in the street attacks their new affection for Caesar by juxtaposing it with their old affection for his adversary Pompey—exactly as Antony will later attack the crowd's new loyalty to Brutus by juxtaposing it with their old loyalty to his adversary Caesar. Marullus speaks only for twenty-five lines, but he stirs his hearers deeply as Brutus and Antony will later stir theirs. After Flavius has added a second brief *peroratio* to Marullus', he exclaims at their success, providing as he does so another translation of Cicero's *permoveo:* "See where their basest mettle be not mov'd" (I.i.61). This *permotio,* the moving of mettle, has been achieved by just the techniques Brutus and Antony will use in Act III, *ad hominem* argument and rhetorical questions. Marullus implies quite unsubtly that the Plebeians are blocks and stones, worse than senseless things, if they do not reject Caesar in their grief for Pompey and his just-defeated sons. And of the twelve sentences in the speech, eight are rhetorical questions:

> And do you now put on your best attire?
> And do you now cull out a holiday?
> And do you now strew flowers in his way,
> That comes in triumph over Pompey's blood?
>
> (*I.i.48-51*)

Though its impassioned verse foreshadows the style of Antony's Forum speech, Marullus' oration is more like Brutus' in the elaborate formulaic balance it works from, for example the isocolon quoted just above. Marullus' oration also anticipates Brutus' in its merely temporary effectiveness, for the Plebeians, who "vanish tongue-tied in their guiltiness" (62) when Marullus has "mov'd" them, regroup only a few lines later to follow Caesar to the marketplace, ready to be moved by the next *orator* they hear.

In the marketplace they hear Cicero (in Greek), and possibly Antony, certainly Caesar (but not with oratorical polish); we have only Casca's jaundiced account. But the crowd is excited, to judge from the offstage noise; and Antony, at least, is formulaic, as we hear in the tricolon of shouts[14] in response to his ritualized three offers of the crown to Caesar and Caesar's ritualized charade of "put[ting] it by with the back of his hand, thus" (I.ii.218-19). Even this early in *Julius Caesar* we may feel that Rome is a world of speeches to crowds and that the course of Rome's history is a record of what effect speeches had.

While this oratory is in progress offstage,[15] we hear another oration, Cassius' effective monologue which persuades Brutus toward the conspiracy.[16] Cassius asks Brutus, his audience of one, the sort of highly charged rhetorical questions we have heard from Marullus and will later hear from Brutus and Antony:

> Brutus and Caesar: what should be in that "Caesar"?
> Why should that name be sounded more than yours?
>
> . . . . .
>
> Now in the names of all the gods at once,
> Upon what meat doth this our Caesar feed,
> That he is grown so great?
>
> . . . . .
>
> When went there by an age, since the great flood,
> But it was fam'd with more than with one man?
> When could they say, till now, that talk'd of Rome,
> That her wide walks encompass'd but one man?
>
> (*I.ii.140-53*)

The iteration is powerful; just after Cassius asks these climactic questions in his *argumentatio* Brutus, as it were, capitulates. Though Brutus "For this present, / . . . would not . . . / Be any further mov'd," he promises to "find a time / Both meet to hear and answer such high things" (163-68). Cassius uses the other identifying device of the *orator* as well: he makes a marked *ad hominem* appeal. The argument takes two forms. First there is flattery combined with *non sequitur:* if you could see yourself as I see you, he suggests, you would see "hidden worthiness" (56) and "honour" (85-90); because you now with my help see these virtues in yourself, you will join me against Caesar. The second prong of the *ad hominem* attack is directed against Caesar in the well-known *narratio* which has earned for Cassius the epithet "envious" among modern interpreters. Actually it is Casca whom Mark Antony calls "envious" (III.ii.177), and later Antony speaks of all the conspirators but Brutus as equally tainted with envy (V.v.69-70). Cassius may envy Caesar when he seeks to make the colossus a weak swimmer and petulant bed patient,[17] but it seems obvious that he speaks more from the sophist's head than from the angry man's heart in undercutting Caesar's divinity for Brutus. He himself later speaks of the methods he has employed with Brutus as specious and contrived, methods by which he himself would not be moved if Brutus were to employ them with him:

> Well, Brutus, thou art noble; yet I see
> Thy honourable mettle may be wrought
> From that it is dispos'd: therefore 'tis meet
> That noble minds keep ever with their likes;
> For who so firm that cannot be seduc'd?
> Caesar doth bear me hard; but he loves Brutus.
> If I were Brutus now, and he were Cassius,
> He should not humour me.
>
> (*I.ii.305-12*)

Cassius follows this shrewd use of the *orator*'s arts to seduce a firm man with an analogous approach to Casca. He begins the attack in I.ii with a skillful brief application of *orator*'s rhetoric when Casca describes Caesar's seizure in the marketplace.

> *Brutus.* 'Tis very like; he hath the falling-sickness.
> *Cassius.* No, Caesar hath it not; but you, and I,
> And honest Casca, we have the falling-sickness.
>
> (*I.ii.251-53*)

Here the unexpected antanaclasis shocks the two listeners, and the tricolon places both Brutus and Casca where Cassius is politically and morally; that Shakespeare thought of this forced political allegory as an *orator*'s device becomes plain when we find Antony echoing it precisely in his funeral oration:

> . . . great Caesar fell.
> O, what a fall was there, my countrymen!
> Then I, and you, and all of us fell down,
> Whilst bloody treason flourish'd over us.
>
> (*III.ii.191-94*)

That Cassius and Antony use the same antanaclasis, the same tricolon, and analogous moralizing of physical falls by Caesar to precisely opposite political ends says a great deal about the levelling effect of the *orator*'s role in *Julius Caesar;* the role seemingly subsumes both partisan politics and individual character (Cassius and Antony are not only political opponents; they are utterly unlike temperamentally, according to Caesar in his famous characterization of Cassius). We must not, of course, make too simple an assumption about the levelling effect of oratory in the play: the energies of *Julius Caesar* allow for utterance that springs spontaneously from the character it reflects—one need only think of the language of the quarrel scene in Act IV. But from the podium speech reflects the type as much as it does the individual. The possibilities for irony are correspondingly great.

Cassius renews his approach to Casca in the storm of I.iii., delivering what amounts to a deliberative oration to an audience of one as in I.ii.,[18] though his method is slightly different, as he has a different audience. The rhetorical questions we have heard before and will hear again are here, though not in comparable numbers:

> And why should Caesar be a tyrant then?
>
> (*I.iii.103*)

> But, O grief,
> Where hast thou led me?
>
> (*I.iii.111-12*)

The second of these is as much an apostrophe as a rhetorical question, Cassius' affectation of allowing Casca to overhear language he addresses to another;[19] we may compare Antony's apostrophe to judgment in his oration (III.ii.106-07), and more immediately we may compare Cassius' other formulaic apostrophes in this same oration:

Therein [in suicide], ye gods, you make the weak
most strong;
Therein, ye gods, you tyrants do defeat.

(I.iii.91-92)

The formulaic repetition here will recall Marullus' anaphoristic "And do you now . . ." and Brutus' "If any, speak. . . ." Cassius goes on in a solemn tetracolon as if musing, or perhaps continuing his address to the gods—in any case treating his audience as if it were not an audience:

Nor stony tower, nor walls of beaten brass,
Nor airless dungeon nor strong links of iron,
Can be retentive to the strength of spirit;
But life, being weary of these worldly bars,
Never lacks power to dismiss itself.
If I know this, know all the world besides,
That part of tyranny that I do bear
I can shake off at pleasure.

(I.iii.93-100)

And cynical Casca, who has been shaken by the hyperbolic storm, is now *permotus,* hastening to join an audience from which he has as it were been excluded. He completes Cassius' last line with an impulsive "So can I." But Cassius strategically ignores this interruption as he has ignored Brutus' interruption earlier,[20] forging on, as if Casca were not there, in exclamations about Caesar as wolf and lion and Romans as sheep and hinds and about Rome as straw and trash, rubbish, offal, and base matter, until, pretending to recall that he has an audience, he uses the same *ad hominem* innuendo that Brutus will use later in his oration in the Forum:

I, perhaps, speak this
Before a willing bondman . . .

(I.iii.112-13)

(Compare "Who is here so base, that would be a bondman?" [III.ii.30].) The effect of this *orator*'s device on Casca is precisely the one that Brutus will obtain with the Plebeians, impulsive commitment.

You speak to Casca, and to such a man
That is no fleering tell-tale. Hold, my hand:
Be factious for redress of all these griefs,
And I will set this foot of mine as far
As who goes furthest.

(I.iii.116-20)

The commitment won, Cassius instantly drops his oratorical mode and falls into an informative, conversational style:

There's a bargain made.
Now know you, Casca, I have mov'd already
Some certain of the noblest-minded Romans
To undergo with me an enterprise. . . .

(I.iii.120-23)

Casca has been enrolled in the conspiracy, added to the list of men Cassius has "mov'd" in a fashion Shakespeare thought quintessentially Roman.

We have heard one short oration and two long ones in the three scenes of Act I; in his usual fashion Shakespeare has crowded the early scenes of a play with the motif he is interested in. This motif, the role of the *orator* and its special style, recurs throughout the first three acts of the play, though not all instances need be analyzed in the detail devoted to Act I.

Brutus, who has been persuaded into the conspiracy by oratorical means, ironically enough speaks a miniature oration as he seizes control of that conspiracy from Cassius in the orchard scene; in the "No, not an oath" speech in Act II, Scene i, Brutus employs the insistent formal repetition, the rhetorical questions, and the *ad hominem* argument we have come to recognize as peculiar to oratory in this play:

But if these, [their motives]
As I am sure they do, bear fire enough
To kindle cowards and to steel with valour
The melting spirits of women, then, countrymen,
What need we any spur but our own cause
To prick us to redress? what other bond
Than secret Romans, that have spoke the word,
And will not palter? and what other oath
Than honesty to honesty engag'd,
That this shall be, or we will fall for it?

(II.i.119-28)

Brutus' audience of conspirators moves swiftly to his position about this and the other questions at issue in the orchard.

Then the tables are turned, so to speak, when Portia addresses her husband persuasively. She plays a role like the one Cassius had played in Act I—but this time the speaker pleads to be admitted, not to admit. To win Brutus, Portia uses the devices of an *orator,* including anecdotal *narratio* ("yesternight at supper . . ." II.i.238 ff.), *ad hominem* argument ("If it be no more, / Portia is Brutus' harlot, not his wife" 286-87), and rhetorical questions arranged in a climactic tricolon:

Within the bond of marriage, tell me, Brutus,
Is it excepted I should know no secrets
That appertain to you? Am I your self
But, as it were, in sort or limitation,
To keep with you at meals, comfort your bed,
And talk to you sometimes? Dwell I but in the suburbs
Of your good pleasure?

(II.i.280-86)

Portia understands the arts of the *orator* perfectly, and she succeeds admirably as she employs them in an entirely nonpublic context: much moved, Brutus admits her to the conspiracy. A mark of the centrality of oratory in Shakespeare's Rome is this adaptation of its devices to private discourse. We have already seen Cassius use them in confidential conversations with two Romans and we have seen Brutus use them in the most private of gatherings; now Portia in nightdress uses the rhetoric of the Forum to address her husband about their domestic life. The *orator* and his linguistic world have power to enter even the *penetralia* of a Roman household. Oratory is very nearly conterminous with *Romanitas* at this point in the play. Portia, in pleading to be regarded as a high-minded Roman, falls into the stance of an *orator.*

Ironically enough, Act II, Scene ii, in which Caesar is twice persuaded against his will, first by Calphurnia and then by Decius Brutus, is less oratorical than several other scenes of persuasion. Calphurnia is too distraught to contrive her utterance in the *orator*'s formalities, and Decius Brutus adopts the stance of the confidential advisor rather than that of the public pleader, though at one point he indulges in a rhetorical question of strong *ad hominem* thrust:

> If Caesar hide himself, shall they not whisper,
> "Lo, Caesar is afraid"?
>
> (*II.ii.100-01*)

The hypothetical whisper, with its blatant *ad hominem* appeal, is couched in an emphatic half line in mid speech.

The next occasion on which oratory persuades is after the assassination when Antony's servant sways Brutus with carefully rehearsed formulaic rhetoric:

> Thus, Brutus, did my master bid me kneel;
> Thus did Mark Antony bid me fall down;
>
> Say I love Brutus, and I honour him;
> Say I fear'd Caesar, honour'd him, and lov'd him.
>
> (*III.i.123-24, 128-29*)[21]

Antony follows the subdued eloquence of this prologue with an epideictic performance that in its contrived flamboyance prepares us for the theatrics of his funeral oration in the next scene. Apostrophe serves Antony's purpose here with the conspirators as it served Cassius' purpose with Casca in Act I, Scene iii. Ignoring his audience, he addresses Caesar's corpse in rhetorical questions:

> O mighty Caesar! dost thou lie so low?
> Are all thy conquests, glories, triumphs, spoils,
> Shrunk to this little measure? Fare thee well.
>
> (*III.i.148-50*)

Then he abruptly acknowledges that he has an audience and just as promptly offers them his life, as Brutus will do to the Plebeians somewhat less theatrically at the end of his oration in the Forum. After a ritual handclasp with each of the conspirators, he returns to his "private" communion with Caesar's body, pouring out apostrophe after apostrophe until Cassius is forced to interrupt with questions that decidedly are not rhetorical:

> I blame you not for praising Caesar so;
> But what compact mean you to have with us?
> Will you be prick'd in number of our friends,
> Or shall we on, and not depend on you?
>
> (*III.i.214-17*)

Antony suavely claims to have been distracted from the public occasion by his private grief, "sway'd from the point by looking down on Caesar" (219). In this pretense he anticipates the pretense in his ostensibly artless funeral oration that he must pause to recover his composure:

> Bear with me.
> My heart is in the coffin there with Caesar,
> And I must pause till it come back to me.
>
> (*III.ii.107-09*)

It may seem ironically involuted to us that Antony is using oratorical manipulation in Act III, Scene i to gain the right to practice more oratorical manipulation in Act III, Scene ii. But this is the sort of play *Julius Caesar* is, a play in which oratory opens doors. The great orations of Act III, Scene ii follow, a climax to the motif of *permotio* in the play. The power of oratory to move people, the basest mettle and the most exalted alike, has been shown repeatedly. The terms *mov'd* and *move* appear a total of thirteen times in the play; in all cases but one the sense is "stirred emotionally"; in nine cases the sense is of oratorical *permotio.* Now, late in the third act, we see the potency of oratory hyperbolized as Antony's Plebeians make their violent exeunt from the Forum and, their spirits still ruffled up, impulsively and frantically murder a passerby moments later.[22]

II

Oratory is nearly everywhere in the first half of *Julius Caesar,* but for all practical purposes Caesar himself is absent from the list of characters who play the *orator*'s role in the action; we do not actually see him persuading others, and we may well ask what this means in the moral symbolism of the play. It is true that Caesar asks rhetorical questions in Act II, Scene ii:

> What can be avoided
> Whose end is purpos'd by the mighty gods?
>
> (*II.ii.26-27*)

> Shall Caesar send a lie?
> Have I in conquest stretch'd mine arm so far,
> To be afeard to tell greybeards the truth?
>
> (*II.ii.65-67*)

His stance, however, here and elsewhere, is not persuasive but declarative, not manipulative but pontifical. Of the eighteen sentences Caesar speaks in his first appearance in Act I, Scene ii, eleven (including all of the first six) are imperatives.

> Speak. Caesar is turn'd to hear.
>
> Set on, and leave no ceremony out.
>
> Set him before me; let me see his face.
>
> He is a dreamer. Let us leave him. Pass.

Antony's response to one of Caesar's earliest imperatives is to define the role of *imperator:*

> I shall remember:
> When Caesar says, "Do this," it is perform'd.
>
> (*I.ii.9-10*)

Caesar speaks a dozen more imperatives in Act II, Scene ii.

Shakespeare chose an appropriate style for a man whose authority stemmed from a military career.[23] Julius Caesar had been given the honorific "*Imperator*" by his legions in Spain.[24] In a real sense the play is about Caesar's attempt to convert this unofficial military title into an official political one.[25] He is, as it were, bringing a military mode of speech into a political world, where oratory is a more normative mode than command: we can virtually hear the tone of the commanding officer in his speeches. When Caesar is not being imperative, he is likely to be declarative, even emphatically so:

> . . . I was constant Cimber should be banish'd,
> And constant do remain to keep him so.
>
> (*III.i.72-73*)

> The cause is in my will: I will not come;
> That is enough to satisfy the Senate.
>
> (*II.ii.71-72*)

Caesar may place himself outside the world of the *orator* linguistically, but he is more closely linked to that world than he realizes, because it is oratory and resulting *permotio* that makes and unmakes the *imperator* in Shakespeare's Rome. We need only hear the crowd with ruffled-up spirits shouting after Brutus' oration, "Let him be Caesar" (III.ii.52) to see that this is so. We hear and see that ruffled-up crowd throughout the first three acts of the play, endorsing once a Pompey, now a Caesar, next a Brutus, finally an Antony. Had Caesar been less the *imperator* and more the *orator* he might have profited. He makes the mistake of adopting the imperative mood, the imperative cast of mind, before he has the *Imperium* in his grasp; and he falls when oratory gathers the conspiracy against him. It is indicative that just before his death Caesar expresses contempt for those who can be moved by the pleader's art; he boasts hubristically that he lies beyond its power and beyond the need to practice it:

> I could be well mov'd, if I were as you;
> If I could pray to move, prayers would move me;[26]
> But I am constant as the northern star. . . .
>
> (*III.i.58-60*)

This is a rhetoric of power already attained, not a rhetoric of power in the making—Caesar's very syntax suggests his hubris. Caesar is not a star, of course,[27] but a man vulnerable like all others, and in a sense he can be said to die at the hands of rhetoric. His first assailant, Casca, and his last, Brutus, both have before our eyes been moved by the *orator*'s arts to kill him. It is therefore sadly ironic, as it is entirely characteristic, that he should die with an imperative on his lips: "Then fall Caesar!" (III.i.77). This last imperative is directed inward, but the dying voice is recognizably the voice Caesar has lived by.[28]

Though Caesar is a striking figure, he does not stand entirely alone in his imperiousness any more than Brutus and Antony stand alone in their oratorical sophistry. No one replicates his style identically—Caesar's voice is finally inimitable—but others echo his imperative mode, significantly when they are feeling delight in their power.

Near the end of Act I, Scene iii, Cassius is fully in command of the nascent conspiracy; he has successfully wooed both Brutus and Casca with persuasive oratory and is feeling his power as he orders Cinna (and Casca) about in an imperious manner and an imperative style:

> Am I not stay'd for? Tell me.
> *Cinna.* Yes, you are.
> O Cassius, if you could
> But win the noble Brutus to our party—
> *Cass.* Be you content. Good Cinna, take this paper,
> And look you lay it in the praetor's chair,
> Where Brutus may but find it; and throw this
> In at his window; set this up with wax
> Upon old Brutus' statue: all this done,
> Repair to Pompey's porch, where you shall find us.
> . . . . .
> That done, repair to Pompey's theatre. [*Exit Cinna.*]
> Come, Casca. . . .
>
> (*I.iii.139-53*)

Caesar would not have asserted himself so breathlessly, so officiously; but we may nevertheless feel here that Shakespeare is replicating at a lesser level (and therefore intensifying) Caesar's characteristic style.[29] The difference between Cassius and Caesar stylistically is the difference between the leader of an ad hoc conspiracy and the commander of legions.

Much later Antony, feeling the power that has accrued to him from his funeral oration, orders Lepidus about in Act IV, Scene i in a way that reminds us of Cassius in the storm:

> . . . Lepidus, go you to Caesar's house;
> Fetch the will hither, and we shall determine
> How to cut off some charge in legacies.
>
> (*IV.i.7-9*)

In this scene Antony also asserts himself over a more substantial colleague in Octavius. We feel the imperiousness in his patronizing dismissal of Octavius' defense of Lepidus and in his authoritative tone:

Do not talk of him [Lepidus]
But as a property. And now, Octavius,
Listen great things. Brutus and Cassius
Are levying powers; we must straight make head.
Therefore let our alliance be combin'd,
Our best friends made, our means stretch'd;
And let us presently go sit in council,
How covert matters may be best disclos'd,
And open perils surest answered.

(*IV.i.39-47*)

Something of the busy officiousness that appeared in Cassius' bustle in Act I, Scene iii is conveyed by Antony's shift here from one subject to another in mid speech: "And now, Octavius. . . ." Antony will attempt an imperious manner with Octavius again in Act V, but—significantly—to much lesser effect, as will appear.

To make servants of one's peers, ordering them to fetch and carry, is to shadow the role of *imperator*. In Cassius' and Antony's commands to Cinna and Lepidus we hear an approximation of the tone of Caesar's voice on his first entrance; everyone around him must be at his orders:

Caesar. Calphurnia.
Calphurnia. Here, my lord.
Caesar. Stand you directly in Antonius' way
When he doth run his course. Antonius.
Antony. Caesar, my lord?
Caesar. Forget not, in your speed, Antonius,
To touch Calphurnia . . .

(*I.ii.1-7*)

In light of such imperiousness and its reflection in a Cassius or an Antony, we may find special meaning in Brutus' gentle benevolence to his servant, Lucius—for example at II.i.229-30 and at IV.iii.258-71. Lucius is not in Plutarch; Shakespeare may have created him to show the contrast between Brutus and those around him who would be *imperator*, if they could.

It is Octavius, of course, who will become "*Imperator*" in fact as well as in intention, and we might expect to hear Caesar's style in his speeches. It is there, indeed, especially in Act V, Scene i, when he first asserts his authority over Antony. Antony tries ordering him about as he has ordered Lepidus about:

Octavius, lead your battle softly on
Upon the left hand of the even field.

(*V.i.16-17*)

But Octavius responds with an even more imperious tone, abruptly Caesarian:

Upon the right hand I. Keep thou[30] the left.

(*V.i.18*)

Antony's response is almost plaintive, while Octavius presses his advantage with a most Caesarian assertion:

Ant. Why do you cross me in this exigent?
Oct. I do not cross you; but I will do so.[31]

We may compare Caesar's

The cause is in my will: I will not come.

(*II.ii.71*)

Something of Caesar's tone is also discernible in the assurance of "I was not born to die on Brutus' sword" (V.i.58) and of "If you dare fight today, come to the field; / If not, when you have stomachs" (65-66).

Octavius is the mediate beneficiary of Antony's oration in the Forum, and he knows how to guard his benefice; he promptly incorporates Brutus' army in his own after the Battle of Philippi and is making plans as the play ends to divide up the spoils of victory. Not blind, as Caesar was, to his situation, Octavius woos support even as he is asserting his authority. In a brief but morally significant ritual, Strato, a synecdoche for "All that serv'd Brutus" (V.v.60) is enlisted[32] and Octavius becomes the inheritor of all that has preceded him. If he asserts himself in the closing lines of the play—and he does—it is with a voice less the harsh soldier's and more the confident politician's than Caesar's was:

According to his virtue let us use him [Brutus],
With all respect and rites of burial.
Within my tent his bones to-night shall lie,
Most like a soldier, order'd honourably.
So call the field to rest, and let's away,
To part the glories of this happy day.

(*V.v.76-81*)

We can imagine this *imperator* as Augustus, however far off the *Imperium* still is at the end of *Julius Caesar*.

III

As the *imperator*'s role is not suppressed after the assassination, though it is in some ways altered, the *orator*'s role does not quite disappear after the Forum scene either. The brief funeral speeches of Titinius and Brutus over fallen Cassius are solemn and resonant with *Romanitas:*

. . . this was he, Messala,
But Cassius is no more. O setting sun,
As in thy red rays thou dost sink to night,
So in his red blood Cassius' day is set.
The sun of Rome is set. Our day is gone;
Clouds, dews, and dangers come; our deeds are done.

(*V.iii.59-64*)

The last of all the Romans, fare thee well!
It is impossible that ever Rome
Should breed thy fellow. Friends, I owe moe tears
To this dead man than you shall see me pay.
I shall find time, Cassius, I shall find time.

(*V.iii.99-103*)

The distant analogy to the funeral orations for Caesar in Act III is obvious. But the differences are even more obvious. The reverberations from Act III are mild to just the extent that the epideictic oration differs from the deliberative. Here is formality without contrivance, rhetoric without ulterior purpose. Titinius and Brutus both use apostrophes that we may place beside those of Cassius with Casca in the storm and those of Antony with the conspirators over Caesar's body. The difference between grief-stricken direct address and sophistic manipulation of hearers is apparent.

The more famous *laudatio funebris* which Antony delivers over fallen Brutus follows two scenes later, with the same emphasis on *Romanitas,* the same ungrudging respect, the same quiet dignity:

> This was the noblest Roman of them all.
> All the conspirators save only he
> Did that they did in envy of great Caesar;
> He only, in a general honest thought
> And common good to all, made one of them.
> His life was gentle, and the elements
> So mix'd in him, that Nature might stand up
> And say to all the world, "This was a man!"
>
> (*V.v.68-75*)

Antony's magnanimity here is the more remarkable when one recalls that his funeral oration for Caesar was a cloak for an indictment of Brutus. The Roman world has changed greatly in the interim between the assassination and Philippi: as the battle ends, the turbulence which oratory aroused in the dying Republic subsides, and the *Imperium* draws inexorably nearer. At such a time exhortation yields to panegyric and manipulation to sincerity. One sees the difference in the contrast between "For Brutus is an honourable man" (III.ii.84 etc.) and "This was the noblest Roman of them all" (V.v.68).[33] The contrast is analogous to the difference between Caesar's strident imperatives and Octavius' confident assertions in the closing lines of the play.

Without the *orator* as Antony has described him in his oration—clever, ulterior, calculating, nearly sinister—the mass *permotio* that impels history would not be stirred. But once events have carried the world beyond change into new stasis, one speaks over a dead friend's (or enemy's) body with a different purpose, a different voice.

Notes

1. By comparison, others, for example, patriotism and Stoicism, have been perceived repeatedly and synoptically. The interpretation of *Julius Caesar* proposed here was first made in the colloquium "Classical Traditions in Shakespeare and the Renaissance" sponsored by the Classical Civilization Program at the University of Minnesota, April 7, 1982; I offer my thanks to Thomas Clayton, Director of the Program and organizer of the colloquium, for many courtesies. It is also a privilege to acknowledge the suggestions made by Frau Margret Popp when we were colleagues at Universität Würzburg in 1981.
2. Milton B. Kennedy's *The Oration in Shakespeare* (Chapel Hill: Univ. of North Carolina Press, 1942) is typical of scholarship before the 1970s: he discusses only the two orations in Act III, Scene ii (*passim*), although he does tabulate Marullus' harangue in Act I, Scene i, under "Demonstrative [that is, epideictic] Orations." More recently a number of scholars such as Reuben Brower (*Hero and Saint: Shakespeare and the Graeco-Roman Heroic Tradition* [Oxford: Clarendon Press, 1971], p. 217) and Paul Cantor (*Shakespeare's Rome: Republic and Empire* [Ithaca, N.Y.: Cornell Univ. Press, 1976], pp. 112-13) have pointed out that persuasive rhetoric pervades the play, but until 1979 there was no comprehensive analysis of the oratory in *Julius Caesar* outside the Forum scene. Wolfgang Müller's *Die Politische Rede bei Shakespeare* (Tübingen: Gunter Narr Verlag, 1979) does something substantial to fill that lacuna, although Müller's emphasis is as much political as rhetorical. With erudition and sensibility he discusses (pp. 89-156) speeches by Marullus, Cassius (I.ii), and Brutus (the soliloquy in the orchard), as well as the Forum speeches. (See also note 16 below.) My somewhat different approach (worked out before I encountered *Die Politische Rede bei Shakespeare*) should be seen as a complement, not an alternative, to Müller's.
3. See Dorsch's Arden Edition (1955-58), pp. xxvii-xxviii, for an account of the pejorative criticism of Caesar's character since Hazlitt. Dorsch's own more moderate view (xxviii-xxxix) has been followed by a number of balanced interpretations, but none from the vantage taken here.
4. T. S. Dorsch's edition is the authority for all *JC* quotations here. The inspiration for Antony's device is to be found in Plutarch's "Life of Julius Caesar": "In a booke [Caesar] wrote against that which Cicero made in the praise of Cato, he prayeth the readers not to compare the stile of a souldier, with the eloquence of an excellent Orator, that had followed it the most part of his life." See Geoffrey Bullough, *Narrative and Dramatic Sources of Shakespeare,* V (London: Routledge & Kegan Paul; New York: Columbia Univ. Press, 1964), p. 60. "The stile of a souldier" is, of course, the unadorned prose of Caesar's *Commentarii;* Shakespeare here characterizes it as speaking "right on." Like Shakespeare's Antony, the historical Caesar was more clever than honest; he had, Plutarch reports, "an excellent naturall gift to speake well before the people . . . so that doubtlesse he was counted the second man for eloquence in his time" (ibid.).
5. Curiously, Shakespeare puts the same sophistic disclaimer of sophistic arts in the mouth of Othello, a character we are to think of as otherwise of a "free and open nature" (I.iii.397-Arden *Oth.*): "Rude am I

in my speech,. . . . / And therefore little shall I grace my cause, / In speaking for myself: yet (by your gracious patience) / I will a round unvarnish'd tale deliver" (I.iii.81-90).

6. "Atticism" was an unadorned oratorical style popular in Rome in the first century B.C.; it purported to be an imitation of Athenian oratory of the fifth and fourth centuries B.C. See George A. Kennedy, *Classical Rhetoric and Its Christian and Secular Tradition from Ancient to Modern Times* (Chapel Hill: Univ. of North Carolina Press, 1980), pp. 117-18.

7. See Plutarch's "Life of Marcus Antonius" (Bullough, V, 255): "He used a manner of phrase in his speeche, called Asiatik, which caried the best grace and estimation at that time, and was much like to his manners and life: for it was full of ostentation, foolishe braverie, and vaine ambition." As Bullough notes, Shakespeare made nothing of Plutarch's disapproval. North's marginal note, "Antonius maketh uprore among the people, for the murther of Caesar," appears opposite the account of the oration (p. 265).

8. Plutarch says that in his letters Brutus "counterfeated that briefe compendious maner of speach of the *Lacedaemonians*" (Bullough, V, 91). As M. L. Clarke recently noted, however, the evidence from Cicero's *Orator, Brutus,* and *Tusculans* is that Brutus was not an Atticist in oratory; Brutus' Greek epistolary style and his Latin oratorical style were apparently not analogues. Shakespeare's erroneous inference is one that scholars since have made repeatedly, down to our own day. (*The Noblest Roman: Marcus Brutus and His Reputation* [Aspects of Greek and Roman Life, gen. ed. H. H. Scullard] Ithaca: Cornell Univ. Press, 1981, p. 26).

9. Cf. "counterfeated" in Plutarch's description of Brutus' letters (note 8 above). Rhetorical contrivance does not, of course, make one a hypocrite by definition. For an excellent brief comment on the tenuous and largely unexplored relation between rhetoric and moral intention in Shakespeare, see L. C. Knights, "Rhetoric and Insincerity," *Shakespeare's Styles: Essays in Honour of Kenneth Muir,* ed. Philip Edwards et al. (Cambridge, U.K.: Cambridge Univ. Press, 1980), pp. 1-8.

10. My colleague John Ruszkiewicz kindly pointed this out to me.

11. Cicero shows someone in Antony's position how to counter an opponent's earlier arguments, if necessary by emotional appeal, "ut odio benevolentia, misericordia invidia tollatur" (*De Oratore* II.215-16). Cf. Aristotle, *Rhetorica* II.2.

12. *Rhetorica* II.24; see especially the fourth kind of false enthymeme.

13. Jean Fuzier makes an admirably detailed analysis of both orations in rhetorical terms, enumerating and discussing sixty-six different figures in them and tabulating the similarities and differences between the two speeches; see "Rhetoric versus Rhetoric: A Study of Shakespeare's *Julius Caesar,* Act III, Scene 2," *Cahiers Elisabéthains,* No. 5 (April 1974), 25-65.

14. Only two of these are in the Folio stage directions, though Cassius says he heard three (I.ii.222). Charles Jennens (ed. of 1774) argued that the third should precede I.ii.146, serving as the precipitant of Cassius' angry outburst in that line; the nineteenth-century editors followed Jennens, though the twentieth-century editors have not done so. Cf. Müller's full perceptive rhetorical analysis of both speeches, op. cit., pp. 118-49.

15. There is another offstage oration in the play about which we know even less; Cassius addresses a crowd in "the other street" in III.ii. while Brutus is holding the center of the stage in his own oration.

16. In a detailed analysis of this monologue, Wolfgang G. Müller has shown convincingly that it is a classical oration in form, proceeding from *exordium* through *narratio* and *propositio* to *argumentatio:* only a full *conclusio* (*peroratio*) lacks. See "A Hidden Oration in Shakespeare's 'Julius Caesar,'" *Sprachkunst,* 6 (1975), 104-14.

17. It has often been observed that Cassius' two anecdotes are slanderous; Plutarch's "Life" portrays Caesar as an exceptionally strong swimmer (Bullough, V, 74-75), and so far from crying for drink "as a sick girl" (I.ii.126-27), Caesar in Spain "yeelded not to the disease of his bodie, to make it a cloke to cherishe him withall, but contrarilie, tooke the paines of warre, as a medicine to cure his sicke bodie fighting alwayes with his disease, travelling continually, living soberly, and commonly lying abroade in the field" (V, 66). The substance of this interpretation is subsumed in Müller's later book (see n. 2 above).

18. Müller hints that this part of Act I, Scene iii, can be analyzed as an oration, but he does not perform the analysis; see n. 16, above.

19. Müller quotes *Ad Herennium* in his article, on the effect of turning away from one's audience in this fashion: "If we use apostrophe in its proper place . . . we shall instil in the hearer as much indignation as we desire" (p. 112).

20. At I.ii.65, Cassius' "Therefore, good Brutus, be prepar'd to hear" is not a response to Brutus' question about what dangers lie ahead but the completion of Cassius' own earlier statement that "many of the best respect in Rome / . . . Have wish'd that noble Brutus had his eyes."

21. In *Shakespeare's Dramatic Language* (Madison: Univ. of Wisconsin Press, 1976), Madeleine Doran comments cogently on the formulaic rhetoric of the servant's speech which she sees as serving the purpose of balancing Brutus against Caesar (pp. 146-47 and note).

22. Cicero's *De Oratore* II. 178 can be taken as a revealing gloss on the passions oratory has aroused in the first half of *Julius Caesar* and on the emotional appeals of its rhetoric, apostrophe and *ad hominem* implication especially: most men make up their minds on emotional, not rational, grounds. "Plura enim multo homines iudicant odio aut amore aut cupiditate aut iracundia aut dolore aut laetitia aut spe aut timore aut errore aut aliqua permotione mentis, quam veritate aut praescriptio aut iuris norma aliqua aut iudicii formula aut legibus."

23. The phenomenon is the more notable as it contravenes Plutarch's observation that as an orator Caesar was second only to Cicero in his time. See n. 4 above. Cicero (*Brutus, Ad Atticum*) repeatedly speaks admiringly of Caesar's eloquence.

24. Plutarch, after detailing Caesar's conquests and administrative innovations in the Iberian peninsula, records that "He having wonne great estimacion by this good order taken, returned from his government very riche, and his souldiers also full of rich spoyles, who called him Imperator, to say soveraine Captaine" ("Life of Caesar," Bullough, V, 63). The marginal notation in North's translation calls attention to the anecdote.

25. Julius Caesar was the first Roman commander to retain the military honorific beyond the point when it would customarily lapse (with his triumph or with the end of his magistracy); see Donald McFayden, *The History of the Title Imperator Under the Roman Empire* (Chicago: Univ. of Chicago Press, 1920), pp. 15-27. Caesar also intruded military power into the political process, as Pompey and Sulla had done before him: both had made efforts to maneuver politically with the backing of their legions. Such intrusion of the military into the political world was made possible by the conversion in Marius' time of a militia loyal to the State into a standing army loyal to its general; see Moses Hadas, *A History of Rome from its Origins to 529 A.D. as Told by the Roman Historians* (Garden City, N.Y.: Doubleday, 1956), pp. 54-55, 61. Eventually the military honorific became a *de facto* political term, though it retained its military flavor: the emperors adopted it as a specious means of claiming credit for the battles their generals had won.

26. We may recall that prayer and oratory are linked in the Latin etymon *oro.*

27. Ovid stellifies his Caesar in Book XV of *The Metamorphoses* in a passage Shakespeare alludes to in the first scene of *Henry VI Part I* (see Bedford's lines at I.i.55-56). A measure of Caesar's hubris in *JC* is this posthumous apotheosis in Ovid: Shakespeare's character confers it on *himself.*

28. A second style Caesar affects, the illeistic, has often been regarded as a mark of his pompousness. Shakespeare may indeed have thought it a voice of the *imperator,* because it is the style that Julius Caesar employed in his *Commentarii,* the account of the wars that earned him that title. I have discussed this style elsewhere (*ShakS,* 4 [1968], 153; *ShS,* 31 [1978], 9-10).

29. In a similar manner Shakespeare has other characters use Caesar's illeistic style also, again less obtrusively than the primary speaker. See the *ShakS* article referred to in n. 28, above.

30. Editors have sometimes emended Octavius' *thou* to *you;* but the Folio reading makes excellent sense: in his Caesarian imperiousness, Octavius lets slip a most patronizing pronoun, then recovers and speaks more courteously afterward.

31. V.i. 19-20. In *Die Politische Rede . . . ,* p. 155, Müller comments similarly on the passage.

32. If Strato were played by an actor who had been a Plebeian in the first half of the play, the doubling could make a moral point at this moment in the action.

33. Madeleine Doran (op. cit., p. 152) emphasizes the reconciliation in Antony's magnanimous eulogy: "In separating Brutus from his fellow conspirators by the purity of his motives . . . Antony ends the disjunction between Brutus and Caesar which Cassius began in setting their names against one another" at I.ii.140-45.

Günter Walch (essay date 1989)

SOURCE: "The Historical Subject as Roman Actor and Agent of History: Interrogative Dramatic Structure in *Julius Caesar,*" in *Shakespearean Illuminations: Essays in Honor of Marvin Rosenberg,* edited by Jay L. Halio and Hugh Richmond, Associated University Presses, 1998, pp. 220-36.

[*In the following excerpt, originally published in 1989, Walch comments on the volatility of historical and linguistic meaning in* Julius Caesar, *concentrating on the oppositional discursive structure of the drama.*]

Our time is characterized by rapid social and political changes, growing concern about the future, and an increasing awareness of the individual's precarious situation. This has been made clear by the pivotal role of power relations in scholarship and the arts from such contemporary theoretical discourses as structuralism, post-structuralism, the New Historicism, some forms of psychoanalysis, and Marxism. The GDR's current lively interest in the anniversary of the French Revolution, for instance, has not been limited to a handful of specialized historians, but involves artists and musicians and, above all, the general public. History is traditionally a strong component of this country's intellectual and cultural life and seems now to be acquiring a new significance. Methodologically this calls for an open approach and for a richer understanding of history. Humankind will not survive the onslaught of the scourges of armament, hunger, and environmental destruction, so the argument goes, if a world different from the one we now live in is no longer imaginable. History along with the theater and the arts are thus important sources for the (necessary) social imagination. And Marxists should, for these reasons, turn to history for a study without illusions about its real contradictions, and try to comprehend it as a complex sequence of decision-taking situations rather than looking at it primarily as an affirmation of political ideology.[1]

The fortunes of the historical subject in the throes of fundamental historical change is a concern shared by scholars, readers, directors, actors, and theater audiences. But *Julius Caesar,* even though it has been referred to as a play about revolution, has yet to play a major role in any recent national or international discussion of the stage or in literary criticism. This point is underlined by reference to the choice of plays by Shakespeare critics interested in power relations, social contradictions, and resulting political conflicts. At the center of the canon that has developed in recent years are *Hamlet, Coriolanus, Henry IV, Measure for Measure,* and *The Tempest.* Other plays include *Henry V, King Lear,* and *Troilus and Cressida* as well as a few of the comedies. The latter are especially evident within various trends in feminist Shakespeare criticism. Some other plays are occasionally referred to or at least mentioned, but very rarely *Julius Caesar.*[2]

One reason for this is that *Julius Caesar* is Shakespeare's apparently most pronouncedly neoclassical play. Ever since the later seventeenth century the theatrical and critical reception of *Julius Caesar* has tended toward the neoclassical representation of rounded characters and, above all, of a closed narration of events that are largely of a public nature. This does not necessarily mean that internal contradictions in the characters have been consistently ignored. But there has been a marked tendency to consider these prerequisite for lifelike characters. People harbor internal contradictions. So do characters. Characters are like people. Depending on the critics' or directors' political, philosophical, and aesthetic views, either Brutus or Caesar has been extolled as the tragic protagonist, and embarrassing passages have been faded out. As a result, the play's characters have seemed highly stable. As seemingly true-to-life personages they have developed a degree of persuasive pressure that has led to an urge to rid them of traits marring their seemingly "natural" character.

Thus Granville-Barker, to give just one example, like Pope and others before him, attributed Brutus' important speech accompanying the blood ritual, "Stoop, Romans, stoop, / And let us bathe our hands in Caesar's blood, / Up to the elbows, and besmear our swords" (3.1.105-9) to Cassius as unfitting to Brutus' noble character.[3] In the same spirit, all T. S. Dorsch can find to say about this particular theatrical scene is that it "merely disgusts us." Also, Brutus' association of Caesar with pillage in his quarrel with Cassius—Caesar, he says, was slain "but for supporting robbers" (4.3.23)—is, to Dorsch in the introduction to his influential Arden edition (1975), simply an "inexplicable statement," a "careless" mistake on the part of Shakespeare, who happened to be following Plutarch very closely but was deplorably lacking in consistency at this point (xxxvi).

The impression of exceptionally stable meaning consolidated by such moves seems to have been aided by the remarkable stability of the printed text itself. Unlike, notoriously, *King Lear* or (considering the texts chronologically closest to *Julius Caesar) Hamlet* and even *Henry V, Julius Caesar* raises few exciting textual problems. There is, of course, no Quarto, let alone several. The only authoritative text is in the First Folio. This does contain what seem to be a few absurdities that most probably result from doubling at least one actor's part (Cassius/Ligarius) and from a few contradictory stage directions. Or there is the famous illogicality (if it is an illogicality) of the two passages telling us about Portia's death (4.3.143-61; 4.3.180-94), probably the result of different stages of work with the text. Such traces of theatrical textual activity as these have been, it appears, too faint to inspire fresh readings of a play exceptionally well printed from a well ordered and legible copy text.[4] Or again, if we look at *Coriolanus* for a comparison with a Roman play favored by modern critics and writers interested in problems of power and authority, we find that to Bertolt Brecht, for example, this play appeared significant because of the fundamental class conflict at its base. He was interested in staging, in a new and topical way, the political and economic strategies of the patricians defending the profits accruing from their usury, and the resistance by the plebeians in which we can surmise echoes of the first stirrings in 1607 of the Levellers and Diggers.[5] Leaping forward to the most recent critical work, *Coriolanus* is analyzed in terms of a political legitimation crisis,[6] or of the failure of entrenched authority,[7] or, as part of an examination of the dialogic-mimetic speech act structure of Shakespeare's oeuvre; attention is also drawn to *Coriolanus*' open form of representation in which the dramatist, after previous experiments in breaking up firmly established significations of authority in his textual work, from the turn of the century makes that approach a compositional principle.[8]

In all of these instances, the angry plebeians, and the political, linguistic, and aesthetic issues that have been raised in connection with them, then as now, are at the center of interest. But compared with the active plebeians in *Coriolanus,* those in *Julius Caesar,* almost prototypically dirigible objects of political manipulation, and, no doubt largely for that reason, generally have not been attractive to recent critics endeavoring to understand more carefully the complex causes and consequences of historical and textual contradictions in the terms just indicated. Yet, as I propose to demonstrate, *Julius Caesar,* written in 1599, is as much part of Shakespeare's turn of the century theatrical exploration of power as *Henry V* and *Hamlet,* its closest chronological neighbors to which the same historical, political, and aesthetic conditions of theatrical signification apply. In these plays particularly, as on the Shakespearean stage as an emerging mode generally, authority is both a represented object of, and a representing agency in, theatrical production. An historically new type of theater, a commercially funded, secular, professional, shareholding enterprise represents the established authorizing types of political, ecclesiastical, and juridical discourse dominant in Elizabethan England within its texts and productions. But at the same time, generating and sustained by, and helping to generate, a modern type of authority, itself unrepresented, and now openly embracing "as authoritative the provision of pleasure, the efficacy of communication, the distribution of information and news-value, and the functions of social release and collective memory,"[9] this theater in its synthesis of textual and theatrical signification breaks with the fixed correlation of signs of officially sanctioned ideological meanings. It thus engenders "a new discursive paradigm" contributing to "the project of modernity . . . for which new modes of negotiating and appropriating authority were indispensible and, indeed, constitutive."[10] Considering the prominence of the English Renaissance theater as a medium of communication, its contribution to that project, which is of undiminished relevance to this time, is of considerable significance.

All of this is emerging more clearly in our own time. As we begin to penetrate post-Enlightenment appropriations and adjustments of Shakespearean drama and its wealth of theatrical means and devices that undermine the authorized representation of power, we can also appreciate that drama's affinity to indeterminate interrogative textual structures. This certainly applies to *Henry V* and *Hamlet* that are chronologically closest to *Julius Caesar,* written and performed at a time of sharpening crisis during the last years of the aging Queen's reign. In *Henry V* Shakespeare uses the natural analogy of the honeybee along with its rich Renaissance intertextuality. It is one of several time-honored contemporary topoi drawing on *natural* phenomena for their *ideologically* stabilizing effect. This makes it particularly hard to de-essentialize Canterbury's imperative discourse of power. Furthermore, Shakespeare's handling of the Chorus character makes evident the difference between what is said and what is shown on the stage, between the officially sanctioned patriotic ideology and the actual political situation. In *Hamlet,* first performed between 1599 and 1601 but probably composed after *Julius Caesar,* Shakespeare employs a variety of approaches and devices contributing to the degree of intensity to which the problem of the historical individual caught between the necessary and the possible, obedience and desire, is dramatically explored. The popular characters of the philosophical gravediggers illustrate this, as does at the level of official culture, neoclassical poetic theory itself, that the Prince, while prescribing it in his advice to the actors, contradicts in his own actions.[11]

My point of departure for the subsequent reading of *Julius Caesar* is that, through this text, Shakespeare unfolds on the public stage a political alternative to imperial *tyranny.* This feudal term, along with *tyrant(s)* (and accompanied by the relevant register generally), appears seven times in key positions and is used very much through Marcus Antonius' apologetic language to associate absolutist ancient regime thinking and practice on- and off-stage. However, although the play possibly sympathizes with republicanism, it does not seem able or willing to take sides in the struggle of constitutional systems as early as 1599. Shakespeare keeps his distance from both systems and their ideologies. Yet to allow the comparison to unfold dramatically meant, and still means, moving it into the sphere of what is becoming thinkable, this being always specified by meaning in circulation; and, possibly, to suggest by implication a third alternative: instead of the rule by one (Caesar) or a privileged elite (Brutus' republicanism), the determination of public affairs by the many or even by all. In this way the play excels in raising questions rather than in being able to answer them. Catherine Belsey asks two such questions: "Perhaps the play condemns usurpation rather than tyranny? Or tyranny but not absolutism?"[12] Since the play, sustained by the self-authorization of the new theater for which it was written, foregrounds this process of questioning, it is here discussed in terms of an interrogative text.[13] As an interrogative text, *Julius Caesar* urges the reader or auditor to venture answers to questions that are raised or, more typically, suggested. Furthermore, it operates as an interrogative text by drawing attention to its own textuality, for instance, the appropriation of classical material, and by inviting questions concerning itself, that can undermine dramatic illusion where it emerges. At crucial points the audience is distanced from stage events. And it is an interrogative text since, on the strength of its distancing interrogative structure, it does not permit any single and privileged discourse to contain and situate the others.[14] Shakespeare develops a specific interrogative structure in which several discourses work together and against each other. This undermines the control of any of them by a single discourse—primarily the imperative discourse of established authority. The dramatist works toward an altogether new discourse the object of which involves a problem of representation, the problem of representing something as yet undeveloped, something historically new just then emerging, and something without precedent.

Why does Shakespeare turn from writing English history plays to writing Roman tragedy? What explains this radical generic break? The classical material and mode were of course anything but new to him. But *Julius Caesar* was a far cry from *Titus Andronicus* (1589-90) and, in a different genre, from *The Rape of Lucrece* (1594). Above all, for the first time Shakespeare turned to Plutarch, a highly political writer, in his search for suitable material. If we think of the dramatist's writing process in terms of historical activity and thus as an integral part of history itself (rather than as an act of inspiration passively outside history and at best merely reflecting some of its aspects) to ask, for example, what might possibly explain that generic change is not only legitimate but becomes indeed indispensable. A connection may be presumed with *Julius Caesar* as one of the first plays, if not the very first, opening the Globe. The superior new building and its favorable position on the Bankside may also have attracted more refined people with more elevated classical tastes.[15] It seems possible that the Lord Chamberlain's Men were worried by the bishop's order of 1599 which, although it did not ban English history from the stage, subjected it to prior licensing by the Privy Council. However, other companies went on performing history plays for at least another half dozen years. If abandoning national history as a subject for its stage by Shakespeare's company signals extreme caution and the wish to avoid clashes with the censor, this stands in curious contrast to their willingness to perform *Richard II* on the eve of the Essex Rebellion. That example, including Elizabeth's much quoted remark—"I am Richard II, know ye not that"—tells us how sensitively the authorities did, and could be expected to, react to any suspected form of subversive activity. (The stumbling block in this case, however, may not have been Shakespeare's play at all but—as Barroll (1988) has tried to show—John Hayward's *The first part of the life and raigne of King Henrie the III* of 1599.)[16] Whatever the external reasons may have been, it now appears fairly certain that the history play, which in the late sixteenth century had given to the theater such an excellent opportunity to communicate Tudor historiography with its audience about the need for national unity both at home and abroad, was around the turn of the century becoming more and more of a liability since, as Shakespeare had consistently done, political issues were raised through the agency of the genre.

The ideological boundaries of plays representing English history, a discourse always already interpreted by establishment historiography, were now being more and more jealously guarded. Compared with the growing constraints imposed by writing and staging English histories, the new historical, philosophical, linguistic, gestic, and visual material provided by the classical discourse offered a number of creative advantages. Above all, the exploration of contemporary reality[17] could be continued with stage characters less encumbered by domestic accretions, with great figures that could display what appeared to be exemplary civic virtues in a spirit of free humanity, and whose pathos communicated a concentrated historical experience and bestowed on stage events a dimension of universal history. In political terms highly topical at that point in English history and for the "project of modernity" generally, Shakespeare, in Harry Levin's words, "[i]n transferring his venue from the English monarchy to the Roman republic . . . shifted his emphasis from kingship to citizenship, and from the duties of the subject to the rights of the citizen."[18] In turning to Rome and *Romanitas,* Shakespeare was, however, dealing with a thoroughly ambiguous discourse. Its potential for self-representation had long since been appropriated by Renaissance monarchies, the Tudors among them. Public displays of the representatives of authority and their insignia became an indispensable method of wielding power. Classical mythology was central to public spectacles, court celebrations, and royal progresses. King James's style of government and representation was conceived wholly in terms of *Romanitas,* his court theater as well as his (and Elizabeth's) understanding of the royal personage as an actor always on public display, setting his own standard right up to the construction of a royal pedigree, invariably including Hercules as the ancestor of all European monarchs.

The ambivalence of the Roman discourse allows associations with both republican civic virtues and free humanity on the one hand, and with absolute power on the other; its differences and contradictory functions constitute the tragedy and particularly the dramatically decisive scene, 3.2, in which first Brutus, then Antony carry on their rhetorical struggle for power. Antony presents Caesar, who had kept "the general coffers" (91) filled, as the people's benefactor. He has left the citizens seventy-five drachmas each and his "private arbours, and new-planted orchards, / . . . To walk about and recreate yourselves" (250, 252-53). Above all, Antony identifies Caesar with Rome. The common weal is identical with Caesar's welfare, and now with that of his party. Therefore the conspirators' crime was not merely directed against Caesar, but against Rome. Their reasons can only have been personal:

> What private griefs they have, alas, I know not,
> That made them do it.
>
> (215-16)

Since realm and ruler are identical, opposition against the regime is opposition against the realm itself. Consequently the conspirators are "traitors" (199, 203, 207, 257; Antony first skillfully elicits the word from the Fourth Plebeian at 155). This is the language and the strategy of absolute power[19] as we also find them in Shakespeare's other dramatic genres, from the early histories to the late romances. The native discourse of absolute power merges easily with the Roman discourse. On the other hand, Brutus' discourse, because of his republicanism, is more narrowly associated with *Romanitas.* Among Brutus' civic virtues his honor is most prominent, clearly no longer a discredited feudal concept of honor but that of a free and proud citizen. This is a significant conceptual change pointing toward, perhaps, the ultimate causes for Shakespeare's decision respecting genre. Brutus' honor safeguards his credibility, certainly to the conspirators and to his own thinking. In accordance with dramatic requirements his speech relies on logical, although finally tautological, arguments. Its conspicuous lack of manipulative intent is indicated by its prose form, and it foregoes all concrete detail. There is nothing in this speech to answer the will, the drachmas, or the gardens. He, too, speaks on behalf of Rome. As republican Rome it is a Rome of liberty that has to ward off the absolutism of the individual tyrant.

But this speech, so thoroughly informed by an emancipatory program shockingly opposed to any kind of absolute power, contains a significantly empty space. It originates in Brutus' silence about the particularity of the claim to power by these republican patricians, themselves a small privileged elite. Historically, democratic rule can hardly become a forthright subject of drama in 1599. Yet the possibility that it is suggested even at that point by the play of differences within the dialogues cannot altogether be excluded. The actual republican particularity, which in Shakespeare's play does not contradict the facts from ancient history, is veiled in this text by the subjective honesty of Brutus' ideas as submitted in his speech and then by the conspirators' assertive slogans proclaiming their own understanding of their cause:

> Liberty! Freedom! Tyranny is dead!
>
> (Cinna, 3.1.78)

> Liberty, freedom, and enfranchisement!
>
> (Cassius, 81)

> Peace, freedom, and liberty!
>
> (Brutus, 110)

Accompanying the blood ritual immediately after the killing, these slogans are pragmatically adequate. But neither here nor anywhere else in the play, in a situation of less excitement, are they filled with any kind of programmatic content. What the liberty threatened by Caesar was like politically, what republican liberty is meant to be like, even the assessment of Caesar as a tyrant, and of absolutist rule itself, all remains entirely unresolved and is (as I shall demonstrate) deliberately opened up for questioning.

The language of *Romanitas,* particularly close, but by no means limited, to Brutus, seems to favor a tendency toward rhetorical abstractness. At the same time Shakespeare uses this very discourse to break up a closed dramatic representation of traditional material. In other words, he does this to achieve something similar to that achieved by the use of, say, an anachronistic chorus or natural analogies in *Henry V.* In *Julius Caesar,* as at roughly the same time in *Hamlet,* he avails himself of the metaphors of his profession, the theater, to literally dramatize, and thus direct attention to at a most prominent point in the play the sense-generating function of the discourse of *Romanitas.* The crucial moment comes in the second scene of act 2 when the great conspirators' conference has been concluded and the necessary arrangements made. Speaking last, Brutus dismisses the others by admonishing them to dissemble—a piece of advice entirely out of character by conventional standards and justifiable only by the noble aim they aspire to:

> Good Gentlemen, look fresh and merrily.
> Let not our looks put on our purposes,
> But bear it as our Roman actors do,
> With untir'd spirits and formal constancy.
> And so good morrow to you every one.
> [*Exeunt. Manet Brutus.*]
>
> (2.1.224-28)

This is much more than a piece of indirect characterization. Shakespeare, to use Homann's term in making "the theater turn to itself"[20] as he so often does, is quite specific. Brutus refers to Roman actors as conceived by an Elizabethan, with stylistic characteristics of the histrionic representation of *Romanitas.* Their style of performance is determined by a "formal constancy" that elevates it beyond all common human weakness, by a rigidly formal and ceremonial regularity, unity, and immutability. *Romanitas* has endowed these actors with the timeless constancy and grand harmonious stance of a classical statue.

There is a fascinating aspect to these surreally statuesque Roman actors, whom the dramatist here evokes on the stage for his agents of history, as the standard of demeanor adequate to a most crucial situation. Brutus refers to them to conceal from himself that empty space in his long speech. To quote Marx on the needs of the French revolutionaries, they have been summoned by the "world-historical necromancy . . . in order to conceal from themselves the bourgeois limitations of the content of their struggles and to maintain their passion on the high plane of great historical tragedy."[21] The ghosts from the days of Rome already haunted the Renaissance stage and because of the ambivalence of classical discourse, served aristocratic as well as bourgeois interests.

Although the historical situations, the earlier English prerevolutionary and the later French revolutionary situation, are quite different from each other, the representational coincidence is not accidental as long as we do not limit our concept of revolution just to the change of political hegemony, but conceive of it in the far more comprehensive terms of a change in historical formation.[22] As a site where, in one dimension, illusions are produced, the public stage is a most adequate place for classical actors in their Roman robes and once—again in Marx's words about the agents of history—"their dramatic effects."[23] In the play, Cassius, standing by Caesar's dead body, reminds his fellow conspirators and the audience of the theatrical nature of the "lofty scene" that has just taken place by his famous anticipation of future revivals as theater shows:

> *Cassius.* Stoop then, and wash. How many ages hence
> Shall this our lofty scene be acted over.
> In states unborn, and accents yet unknown!
> *Brutus.* How many times shall Caesar bleed in sport,
> That now on Pompey's basis lies along,
> No worthier than the dust.
> *Cassius.* So oft as that shall be,
> So often shall the knot of us be call'd
> The men that gave their country liberty.
>
> (3.1.111-18)

The dramatic ironies involved in the dramatic characters' assessments of themselves have been commented on so often that there is no need for repetition. What concerns us here is that at this moment they have reached the climax of their historical action. As late as at 2.1.101-11 the conspirators were shown to be unable to agree even on the direction in which the Sun rises, a point on which an argument would seem to hold little promise in any situation. Now, after having been admonished to emulate the perfect actors of antiquity, the "lofty scene" just then performed can be celebrated as exalted and perfectly achieved. The historical act of the liberators can now be reviewed like a premiere: a huge success. Cassius and Brutus quite unambiguously associate the historical act represented with its representational form as a theatrical performance during the blood ritual. Brutus had earlier defined the murder itself as a sacral scenic event: "Let's be sacrificers, but not butchers, Caius" (2.1.166). What has thus been achieved is that, at the climax of their historical act, for a brief passing moment, "the most boldest and best hearts of Rome" (3.1.121) are shown, during the ritualized sacrifice and now during the blood ritual, to live up to the high demands made by the classical discourse. Such agreement of classical norm and dignified "lofty" action will only be reached again by Cassius, Titinius, and Brutus after Philippi by their classically heroic suicides. But even then a high price has to be paid. It consists in the relinquishment by Cassius of his Epicurean philosophy (5.1.77-79), and by Brutus of his Stoic philosophy (101-8).

Yet even in act 3 Shakespeare's use of the classical discourse as theatrical language at the moment of that climax contains the implication of the element of illusion that is inherent in the events shown. At that moment, at the height of the task, the characters are simultaneously agents of world history and "Roman actors." But from now on they will be measured against the standard raised by *Romanitas.* The discourse of *Romanitas* has helped to bring together in one great moment both history and human endeavor as authorized by universal history, but has not eliminated their difference. On the contrary, after the production and performance of "our lofty scene" by these Roman actors, that very difference breaks open and begins to take command of the action. And this is precisely the function of the theatrically marshaled discourse of *Romanitas* in *Julius Caesar:* to make visible the difference between expectations and their fulfillment, between what is said and what is done, between theory and practice, between the normative "formal constancy" of the "Roman actor" and the actual activity of historical subjects under the conditions and constraints of social crisis. *Romanitas* informs and provides orientation for this dramatic text. It enables strategy to be organized as a process.

In conclusion, let me indicate at least some of the problems, and consequences for *Julius Caesar* as a whole, of Shakespeare's dramatic use of the discourse of *Romanitas.* Setting up, for emulation on the stage of the theater and on the stage of history, the ideal type of the "Roman actor" in acts 2 and 3 entails the consequences of raising, through both declaration and the stage events, a classicist expectation among the audience. But his expectation is fulfilled only incompletely. The fact that the reason is a critical distance from Roman values on the part of Shakespeare, increasing from *Titus Andronicus* to *Julius Caesar,* is substantiated by Robert Miola's analysis in *Shakespeare's Rome* (1983) of Shakespeare's representation of misogyny from which female characters suffer in this and other works. All Romans, women as well as men, are expected to behave heroically according to "our fathers' minds," as Cassius insists, and definitely not according to "our mothers' spirits" (1.3.82-83). Miola comments: "Any civilization founded on principles such as these, Shakespeare suggests, is strange, unnatural, inhuman, and doomed" (96-97). From a different point of view, Shakespeare's critical distance from *Romanitas* is thus corroborated. It allowed Shakespeare to use the discourse of *Romanitas* not only as a representing discourse, which was after all dominant in Renaissance culture, but also as a discourse critically represented for dramatically functional purposes.

But that makes the play much less stable than has commonly been assumed. Instability is indeed, as such, one of its central motifs, a fact that has, however, more often than not been interpreted in terms of formal dramatic irony rather than as a result of different discourses working against each other. One further consequence of that function of discourses is that the aesthetic determination of the "Roman actors" is inscribed in the text of Caesar himself, of the man nourishing the plain belief, "for always I am Caesar" (1.2.209):

> But I am constant as the northern star,
> Of whose true-fix'd and resting quality
> There is no fellow in the firmament. . . .
>   I do know but one
> That unassailable holds on his rank
> Unshak'd of motion; and that I am he,
> Let me a little show it, even in this,
> That I was constant Cimber should be banish'd,
> And constant do remain to keep him so.
>
> (3.1.60-62, 68-73)

The "constancy" Caesar claims for himself at this point appears eight times in the play, as "constancy" / "constant(ly)." He is made to lay claim to the "constancy" of the "Roman actors" so highly commended by Brutus as their essential formal characteristic in his last words, a few lines before his fall. The many apparent disparities or breaks in the other characters can also be interpreted in the light of this sort of textual activity. If, for instance, the noble Brutus keeps rejecting, with a kind of stubborn constancy, the politically and strategically reasonable alternative suggestions submitted by Cassius, a character with a low measure of "formal constancy," the audience's attention is very deliberately directed toward the contradictions of the political process unfolded by the activity of historical subjects. Furthermore, from a different perspective, the famous line, "Caesar did never wrong, but with just cause," ridiculed by Ben Jonson and obviously changed in the First Folio (3.1.47-48), might be considered as a signal of textual activity rather than dismissed as sheer nonsense. To the classicist ear this line must needs be devoid of all ethical consistency and, as an allegation mentioned nowhere else in the play, seems to infer logical instability of the worst order, which can only sound aesthetically ludicrous. But as a form of utterance originating in a representational crisis of absolutist power, it generates political sense. It disrupts the tendency toward closure instinctively seized upon and made essential by critics who can only explain the line by seeing it as a leftover from Plutarch and something Shakespeare neglected to tidy up. That political sense is generated by making the crisis of legitimation appear in a paradox. After all, attempts to justify an exercise of power that has become doubtful with arguments meant to sound just, reasonable, and natural are common practice among representatives of established authority. What makes the example of Caesar never doing wrong "but with just cause" stand out is its paradoxical directness. We should be wary of dismissing it too lightly; all the evidence, chiefly the attacks on it by Ben Jonson, himself a member of that company, repeated over many years, indicates that the actors went on using the original version of that line apparently unperturbed.

There is yet another indication that *Julius Caesar* is less stable than has been assumed. Caroline Spurgeon demonstrated many years ago that the imagery in *Julius Caesar* is peculiar in that it does not come from any one single dominant area, even though images of civil strife are prominent in the first half and animal imagery has contributed with some consistency to building the main characters.[24] Such relatively open audience response guidance, which can encourage auditors to increase their efforts of making sense of what they hear and see, has been corroborated by E. A. J. Honigmann's analysis generally of "a steady move away from the notion that character is fixed, defined, an object, a formula, an ascertainable humour, a ruling passion" so that the result is a strategy of "mixed" audience response guidance reaching a climax in *Julius Caesar.*[25] For Honigmann, as for Dr. Johnson before him, who was uncomfortable with the play's relatively cool atmosphere, Shakespeare's mixture of the tactical means guiding audience response is "very slightly wrong." If illusion is impeded by that coolness, it is of course the result of a procedure creating distance to the stage events by which Shakespeare "wished the audience to respond in an entirely new way to his hero."[26] This, I suggest, is one of the principal reasons why Shakespeare should have abruptly, as it may appear, resorted to classical discourse. Only in the context that this makes possible can attention be wholly directed, in Honigmann's words, to "Brutus' muddles."

Placed at the center of attention, along with their activity, are the intellectual and emotional problems of historical subjects in a situation that, contrasting with the traditional story of antiquity, can be discerned as historically new; it is a situation involving unprecedented tasks for the solution of which the previously acquired, traditionally authorized patterns of thinking and behavior suddenly no longer provide adequate orientation. Thus they are subjected to inquiry. In *Hamlet* this will happen most obviously in the monologues, from which their essential instability derives. In *Julius Caesar* the text's interrogative strategy becomes thematic through the work of interpretation that is performed—in the double sense of the word—by the characters: "During the fearsome night many men try to construe events according to their own ends and desires. Brutus interprets murder as a sacrifice; many try to interpret Caesar's dream."[27] Cicero is given only nine lines in the whole play, most of them actually of a phatic nature. He seems to have been put in the play specifically to dramatize that emphasis on interpretation:

> Indeed, it is a strange-disposed time:
> But men may construe things, after their fashion,
> Clean from the purpose of the things themselves.
>
> (1.3.33-35)

Cicero's reading of "portentous things" is by no means the only example. Passages probing the differences between "seeming," "appearing," "acting," "fashioning," "construing," and the world of reality occur thirty-five times in the text.[28] They are part of an exploration that is directed, not at the subjectivity generally of human perception and the limits of all human understanding,[29] but at a specific historical situation. The various devices used by Shakespeare for the purpose are too numerous to be accidental. From a distance, Cicero puts the gnoseological problem as such in words but remains even more passive and ineffective than the many other intellectuals in the play—the soothsayer, Artemidorous, Cinna.[30] This may reflect the way in which Elizabethan intellectuals felt in the face of the breakdown of the traditional alliance between intellectuals and the crown, forged during the Reformation. *Julius Caesar*'s activity as interrogative text is in search of the aesthetic object to be appropriated, that is, the historical subject working at historical change. Text is generated accordingly. Brutus has 720 lines. We are being continually reminded of Caesar even when he does not himself speak, but 150 lines are sufficient for all he has to say in the play. He represents what is equally well-known to Romans and Elizabethans, absolutist authority. What the text directs attention to is the process of countering Caesar's power along with its consequences, and hence to the character of Brutus. Leaving the programmatic details of the political struggle as vague as they are helps audiences to concentrate on the underlying process.

The plebeian scenes, so often discussed primarily in terms of timeless psychology, can also be read as part of the exploration of the historical activities involved in that process. In 3.2., little is left of the intelligently aggressive wordplay of the citizens, especially of the cobbler, right at the beginning of the play. In the end, law and order are restored, but initially the plebeian wit of Shakespeare's carpenters and cobblers (and, elsewhere, gravediggers) clearly triumphs. As can be shown by dialogue analysis, a considerable though ultimately illusory power base is built for the cobbler by the calculated granting or withholding of information. But why does Shakespeare introduce such self-assured plebeians at all if at their reappearance all their self-assurance has evaporated, and they are shown to be such easy prey to rhetorical manipulation? The answer is implicit in the question: the first scene on "A Street" is needed not merely to open up right at the beginning a representation signaled to the audience as closed by the very genre of the play, but also as a precondition for the later ones. Such guided audience response is aimed less at representing changes in the psychology of the masses than at the process they inevitably help to constitute. Another problem is thus raised, new certainly as far as the way and context of posing it is concerned. In this theatrical situation unprecedented in Elizabethan England, in which the republican revolutionaries become active, it is shown, over and above what the masses may actually be like, that there is no choice but to mobilize them if the political power struggle is to be won. This part of a new dramatic discourse is emerging slowly under the conditions of the Elizabethan popular theater where patricians have to share the stage with plebeians and where closed forms of representation can be opened at significant moments by a host of theatrical signs.

It was characteristic of Samuel Johnson that he should have been affected by Shakespeare's opposition of discourses, but only as a disturbance causing him deep anxiety. "A quibble was the golden apple," he wrote in his *Preface to Shakespeare* "for which he would always turn aside from his career, or stoop from his elevation."[31]

Notes

1. See Wolfgang Klein, "Ungebundene Menschlichkeit," *Sinn und Form* 41 (1989): 463 concerning our study of history without illusions; and Thomas Metscher, "Geschichte, Humanität, Utopie," in *Gulliver 6: Shakespeare inmitten der Revolution* (Berlin, 1979), 26, for *JC* as a play about revolution.
2. My tentative description of the new canon is based on the following publications: J. Drakakis, ed., *Alternative Shakespeare,* (1985); J. Dollimore and A. Sinfield, eds., *Political Shakespeare: New Essays in Cultural Materialism* (Manchester, 1985); T. Hawkes, *That Shakespearian Rag. Essays of a Critical Process* (London, 1986); P. Parker and G. Hartman, eds., *Shakespeare and the Question of Theory* (N.Y.: Methuen, 1985); J. Howard and M. F. O'Connor, eds., *Shakespeare Reproduced: The Text in History and Ideology* (N.Y., 1987); and L. Tennenhouse, *Power on Display: The Politics of Shakespeare's Genres* (N.Y., 1986).
3. See Ernst Th. Sehrt, "*Julius Caesar:* Brutus," in *Sympathielenkung in den Dramen Shakespeares,* eds., W. Habicht and I. Schabert (Munich: Fink, 1979), 65-71, esp. 65, who correctly criticizes the previous critical neglect of the blood ritual as stage spectacle—All references are to The Arden edition, ed. T. S. Dorsch (London: Methuen, 1975).
4. See Stanley Wells and Gary Taylor with John Jowett and William Montgomery, *William Shakespeare. A Textual Companion* (Oxford: Clarendon Press, 1987), 386-91.
5. See Christopher Hill, "The Many-Headed Monster," in *Change and Continuity in Seventeenth Century England* (Cambridge: Harvard University Press, 1975), 182.
6. Michael Bristol, "'Lenten Butchery': Legitimation Crisis in *Coriolanus,*" in *Shakespeare Reproduced,* 207-24.
7. See Thomas Sorge, "The Failure of Orthodoxy in *Coriolanus,*" in ibid., 225-41.
8. Robert Weimann, "Bifold Authority in Shakespeare's Theatre," *Shakespeare Quarterly* 39 (1988): 403-4, esp. 402.
9. Ibid., 402-3.
10. Ibid., 402.
11. See Robert Weimann, "Mimesis in *Hamlet:* Spiegel und Wirklichkeit," in *Shakespeare und die Macht der Mimesis* (Berlin: Aufbau, 1988), 219-55.
12. Catherine Belsey, *The Subject of Tragedy* (London: Methuen, 1985), 90.
13. Our approach draws on Emile Benveniste's linguistic distinction between declarative, imperative, and interrogative statements in *Problems in General Linguistics* (Coral Gables, FL: University of Miami Press, 1971).
14. Belsey, *Critical Practice* (London: Methuen, 1986), 92.
15. Walter Cohen, *Drama of a Nation. Public Theater in Renaissance England and Spain* (Ithaca: Cornell University Press, 1985), 302-3.
16. Leeds Barroll, "A New History for Shakespeare and His Time," *Shakespeare Quarterly* 39 (1988): 441-64.
17. The continuity of the project is emphasized, for example, by Paul N. Siegel, *Shakespeare's English and Roman History Plays. A Marxist Approach* (London: Associated University Presses, 1986).
18. Harry Levin, "General Introduction," in The Riverside Shakespeare (Boston: Houghton-Mifflin, 1974), 20.
19. See Belsey, *Subject of Tragedy,* 101-3 for a similar interpretation.
20. Sidney Homann, *When the Theater Turns to Itself: The Aesthetic Metaphor in Shakespeare* (London: Associated University Presses, 1981).
21. Cf. Karl Marx, "The Eighteenth Brumaire of Louis Bonaparte," in *Collected Works,* vol. 11 (Moscow: Progress Publishers, 1979), 104-5.
22. See Wilfried Schröder, "War die französische Revolution auch eine Epochenzäsur in der kulturellen, künstlerischen und literarischen Entwicklung? Probleme und Problemfelder," *Weimarer Beiträge* 34 (1988): 37.
23. Marx, "Eighteenth Brumaire," 104, 106.
24. Caroline Spurgeon, *Shakespeare's Imagery and What It Tells Us* (Cambridge: Cambridge University Press, 1935), 346-47.

25. E. A. J. Honigmann, *Seven Tragedies* (New York: Barnes & Noble, 1976), 12.
26. Ibid., 30.
27. Jean Howard, *Shakespeare's Art of Orchestration. Stage Technique and Audience Response* (Urbana: University of Illinois Press, 1982), 145.
28. Robert Miola, *Shakespeare's Rome* (Cambridge: Cambridge University Press, 1983), 79-80.
29. That is the approach of René E. Fortin in "Julius Caesar: An Experiment in Point of View," *Shakespeare Quarterly* 19 (1968): 341-47.
30. Honigmann, *Seven Tragedies,* 38.
31. "Preface to Shakespeare," in *Criticism: The Major Texts,* ed., W. J. Bate (New York: Harcourt, 1970), 213.

THE ROMAN HERO: INTERPRETING CHARACTER

Lynn de Gerenday (essay date 1974)

SOURCE: "Play, Ritualization, and Ambivalence in *Julius Caesar,*" in *Literature and Psychology,* Vol. 1, November, 1974, pp. 24-33.

[In the following essay, de Gerenday explores the psychological and thematic significance of Brutus's ritualization of Caesar's murder, and the resulting ambiguity this produces in Julius Caesar.*]*

> Indeed, it is a strange-disposed time:
> But men may construe things after their fashions,
> Clean from the purpose of the things themselves.
>
> Cicero, Act I, scene iii

One of the frustrations of reading criticism on *Julius Caesar* is the extent to which we may be caught up in the critic's attempt to determine what attitude we should assume toward the play as a whole, and toward the character of Brutus in particular. This propensity for either/or interpretations; this need for a norm of heroism and villainy; this insistence that, in the words of one graduate student, lamenting the ambiguity of the main characters, "there's got to be a good guy, there's got to be," violates the psychological insights of a "problem play" in which ambivalence *is* the norm, the meaning and the motivation. The way out of endless partisan speculation, which ignores L. C. Knight's observation that "human actuality is more important than *any* political abstraction,"[1] is suggested by the central significance the drama of Brutus and Caesar held for Freud.

In Chapter VI of *Interpretation of Dreams,* Freud discovers, in the antithetical structure and meaning of Brutus' speech at the Forum, a model for his hostile and affectionate dream-thought, "As he had deserved well of science I built him a memorial; but as he was guilty of an evil wish . . . I annihilated him." He concludes that he has been "playing the part of Brutus in the dream," and goes on to recall that he "really did once play the part of Brutus" to the "Caesar" of his nephew whom he calls, "my tyrant."[2] It was this nephew who, according to Freud in a letter to his friend Fliess, March 10, 1897, "Determined, not only the neurotic side of all my friendships, but also their depth;" who was, Freud writes in *Interpretation of Dreams,* both his superior, against whom he had to learn to defend himself, *and* his inseparable friend, setting the pattern for Freud's future relationships:

> My emotional life, has always insisted that I should have an intimate friend and a hated enemy. I have always been able to provide myself afresh with both, and it has not infrequently happened that the ideal situation of childhood has been so completely reproduced that friend and enemy have come together in a single individual—though not, of course, both at once or with constant oscillations, as may have been the case in my early childhood.[3]

Brutus' most rhetorical speech became a model for, and a clarification of, Freud's own dream-thought; the drama of Brutus and Caesar, a symbolic means to enact Freud's own conflicting emotions towards his nephew. What the play illuminated for Freud, and illuminates for now for us, is the nature of ambivalence, the way such formal devices as rhetoric and ceremony (reinforced by an emphasis on play-acting) bind and distance intense love and hostility from conscious expression.

Perhaps Brutus' most revealing speech is his soliloquy at the opening of the orchard scene, Act II, scene i. Brutus is alone, meditating; unable to sleep, unaware of the time of day, his precision of thought and energy is directed toward one resolution: the death of Caesar. In Act I, he has seemed a figure of indecision and distraction, "with himself at war, / Forget[ting] the *shows of love* to other men." (italics mine) (I.ii.46-7) lacking "that quick spirit that is in Antony." (29) He has withdrawn his "gentleness and show of love" (33-4) from Portia as he has from Cassius,

> Y' have urgently, Brutus,
> Stole from my bed: and yesternight, at supper,
> You suddenly arose, and walk'd about.
> Musing and sighing, with your arms across;
> You stared upon me with ungentle looks:
> I urg'd you further; then you scatched your head,
> And too impatiently stamp'd with your foot:
> Yet I insisted, yet you answer'd not;
> But with an angry wafture of your hand,
> Gave sign for me to leave you . . .
>
> (II.i.237-47)

She begs to know the cause of his grief, which "will not let you eat, nor talk, nor sleep;" (252) this "sick offence within [his] mind," as Portia perceives, has led to his rejection of the "wholesome bed" of married love. It is this same "sick offence," which Brutus has tried to deny before Cassius,

> Into what dangers would you lead me, Cassius,
> That you would have me seek into myself
> For that which is not in me?
>
> (I.ii.63-5)

—after Cassius has "lamented" Brutus' lack of mirrors to turn his "hidden worthiness into your eye, / That you might see your shadow." (57-8) In this image of the mirror and the shadow, and in Cassius' comparison of himself to a glass which will reveal to Brutus "That of yourself which you yet know not of," (70) Shakespeare suggests the Elizabethan dramatic conception of the play as *speculum,* a mirror up to nature, a mirror which can reflect "false unreal shadows" as well as penetrate the "false appearance of things," and "uncover deceit."[4] Cassius does not "whet" Brutus against Caesar, nor does he manipulate him (by clever words, appeals to heritage and forged letters) into an action which is totally alien to Brutus; although Cassius believes that these devices will "yield him ours," (156) the first line of Brutus' soliloquy emphasizes that he has *already* determined that Caesar must die,

> It must be by his death: and, for my part,
> I know no personal cause to spurn at him,
> But for the general. He would be crown'd:
> How that might change his nature, there's the question:
> It is the bright day that brings forth the adder;
> And that craves wary walking. Crown him?—that;—
> And then, I grant, we put a sting in him,
> That at his will he may do danger with . . .
>
> (II.i.10-17)

"It must be by his death": a powerful resolution placed before all the "justifications," suggesting the *wish* for Caesar's death existed before and beyond the intellectualized *need* for his death; Brutus must speculate on what Caesar might become in order to justify the killing, the fulfillment of his shadowy wish, to himself. As he continues, he attributes to Caesar what is true of his own flawed nobility: "Th' abuse of greatness is, when it disjoins / Remorse from power . . .". (19) Mercy isolated from power—as Brutus assumes greater control and emerges as recognized leader of the conspiracy, as he stabs the man who once showed him the mercy of pardon, this "abuse" becomes central to the tragedy of his self-deception, central to the alienation from his own repressed emotion which thwarts his potentially integrative ideals.

Brutus cannot find this abuse true of Caesar in past or present action, and so he retreats into speculation once again in order to build his "reasons . . . full of good regard," (III.i.224)

> . . . to speak true of Caesar,
> I have not known when his affections sway'd
> More than his reason. But 'tis a common proof,
> That lowliness is young ambition's ladder,
> Whereto the climber-upward turns his face;
> But when he once attains the upmost round,
> He then unto the ladder turns his back,
> Looks into the clouds, scorning the base degrees
> By which he did ascend: so Caesar may;
> Then, lest he may, prevent . . .
>
> (II.i.19-28)

So, Caesar is not to be killed for specific acts of injustice and oppression, but for a projected image of what he might become.[5] As the soliloquy ends, Brutus' use of language to create a private reality, isolated from existing reality, is dramatically revealed,

> . . . *And, since the quarrel*
> *Will bear no colour for the thing he is,*
> *Fashion it thus:* that what he is, augmented,
> Would run to these and these extremities:
> And therefore, think him as a serpent's egg,
> Which, hatch'd, would, as his kind, grow mischievous;
> And kill him in the shell.
>
> (italics mine) (28-34)

Since the cause of rebellion has no excuse in "the thing he is," Brutus must "Fashion it," construct it, *compose* it: the mold is there in "these and these extremities"—blanks to be filled in later. Here is Brutus telling Brutus *how* he must think ("And therefore think him . . .") in order to kill, in order to prevent his emotional knowledge of Caesar from interfering with an act he wishes to envision as impersonal, "for the general." Here also, it might be added, is a scene of Shakespearean self-consciousness, an awareness of the playwright creating a reality through his words, composing a play, an action, potentially as ambiguous as that of Brutus.

As the scene progresses, Brutus continues to "compose," and emerges in control of the action. His rhetorical appeal to the "virtue of our enterprise," his attribution of honesty and virtue to "our cause," dismisses Cassius' call for an oath; "do not stain / The even virtue of our enterprise . . . To think that or our cause or our performance / Did need an oath." (132-6) The metaphor of drama, "our performance", for the conspiracy is continued in his dismissal of Cassius' next suggestion, that the shrewd Antony be killed with Caesar,

> Our course will seem too bloody, Caius Cassius,
> To cut the head off, and then hack the limbs,—
> Like wrath in death, and envy afterwards;
> For Antony is but a limb of Caesar:
> Let's be sacrificers but not butchers, Caius.
> We all stand up against the spirit of Caesar;
> And in the spirit of men there is no blood;
> O, that we, then, could come by Caesar's spirit,
> And not dismember Caesar! But, alas,
> Caesar must bleed for it! And, gentle friends,
> Let's kill him boldly, but not wrathfully;
> Let's carve him as a dish fit for the gods,
> Not hew him as a carcass for the hounds:
> And let our hearts, as subtle masters do,
> Stir up their servants to an act of rage,
> And after seem to chide 'em. This shall make

William Hutt as Brutus and members of the Festival Company in Act III, scene ii of the 1965 Stratford Festival production of Julius Caesar.

> Our purpose necessary, and not envious:
> Which so appearing to the common eyes,
> We shall be call'd purgers, not murderers.
> And for Marc Antony, think not of him;
> For he can do no more than Cassius' arm
> When Caesar's head is off.
>
> (162-183)

Images of fragmentation and dismemberment, repeated throughout, are concentrated in this speech as Caesar's body is separated from his spirit and broken in "necessary" sacrifice; thus, under Brutus' leadership, the planning becomes a question of style.[6] We have experienced Brutus' creation of a reality to fit his resolution, his composition of a basic outline for action, his mastery of rhetoric which will reach its climax in the speech at the Forum; now, his drive to *ritualize* action becomes apparent. What the conspirators must kill is the bloodless spirit of Caesar, the Caesar who would be king and worshipped as a deity; the killing is to be a ritual, a formal sacrifice, the "tragedy of Julius Caesar," enacted in classical style (noble, impersonal, inevitable, purgative).[7] It is to be "A piece of work that will make sick men whole," but which must be accomplished by making some that are whole, sick. (327-8) The irony is, that even within the structural device of the full circle, nothing, no one, is made whole; Rome is not redeemed. The images of fragmentation, as Holland observes, suggest the split within the conspirators in their attempt to isolate the connotations of their act.[8] We are made conscious of this act as "act" through Brutus' attention to seeming and appearance; his direction,

> Good gentlemen, look fresh and merrily;
> Let not our looks put on our purposes;
> But bear it as our Roman actors do,
> With untired spirits and formal constancy . . .
>
> (244-7)

is far removed from the disorder within, which he earlier compared to "The nature of an insurrection." (69)

When Brutus directs the conspiracy to sacrifice, not butchery, when his language stylizes the murder into a dish carved for the gods, he is inhibiting any awareness of aggression; or, rather, he is attempting to consciously prohibit the element of aggression—"Or else were this a savage spectable." (III.i.223) "Hostility is not admitted as such, but masquerades as ceremonial."[9] The mind must trick itself in disassociation from action: "hearts, as subtle masters do, / Stir up their servants to an act of rage, / And after seem to chide 'em." So Bolingbroke with Exton after Richard II's death:

> *Exton.* From your own mouth, my lord, did I this deed.
> *Bolingbroke.* They love not poison what do poison need,
> Nor do I thee: though I did wish him dead,
> I hate the murderer, love him murdered.
>
> (*Richard II.* V.vi.38-41)

Bolingbroke's emotional ambivalence toward Richard (his mingled distrust and admiration) is separated from action in order that his death wish against his king might be fulfilled, and rejoined after the murder in a manifestation of remorse. Brutus' remorse has anticipated the murder in the melancholic dejection (loss of capacity to love, inhibition of energy, refusal of nourishment, sleeplessness) which Cassius and Portia have observed.[10] Now, the energy he has withdrawn into himself must strike out again, at Caesar; loving the man, as he tells Antony, even as he strikes down the spirit Caesar em-bodies.

In his examination of ritual in *Julius Caesar,* Brents Stirling suggests that, "as the impersonal member of a conspiracy motivated largely by personal ends, [Brutus] sought in a complex way to resolve his contradiction by depersonalizing, ritualizing, the means."[11] Although my thesis would maintain that Brutus' "impersonality" is itself a formal device to ward off the anxiety of his ambivalent attachment to Caesar,[12] Stirling's discussion of Antony's function as master of counter-ritual is illuminating. "Given / To sports, to wildness, and much company," (II.i.188-9) a lover of plays, (I.ii.203) Antony bears a firmly rooted love for Caesar; Caesar, in turn, has chosen Antony to take his place, in a ritualized action, with Calphurnia: he is to "leave no ceremony out" of the "holy chase" which Caesar hopes will turn barrenness to fertility. (I.ii.6-11) In Act III, Antony uses *language* to effect transformation: to turn Brutus' creation of a dish carved for the gods back into the bloody carcass hewn for hounds.

After the assassination, Brutus' aggression betrays itself through ritual; he instructs his fellow actors to stoop and bathe their hands in Caesar's blood, the blood he has usually denied in his imagery. The act unifies the conspiracy: each has stabbed Caesar, each has washed himself in Caesar's blood. Brutus insists on their mutual recognition of each other in their responsibility for their action, ("let no man abide this deed, / But we the doers,") (III.i.94-5) but he is clearly the "lead," the "Soul of Rome," the inheritor of the republican tradition. He stands, blood dripping from his arms, envisioning with Cassius the great theatricality of what they have just done,

> *Cassius* . . . How many ages hence
> Shall this our lofty scene be acted over
> In states unborn and accents yet unknown!
> *Brutus.* How many times shall Caesar bleed in sport,
> That now on Pompey's basis lies along
> No worthier than the dust!
>
> (111-116)

but Antony enters to undercut this metaphor of play, to counter and break their potential community-in-ritual; their arms, which were to be seen as a symbolic bond become, through Antony's language, "purpled" as they "do reek and smoke" with the blood of a victim. (158) Brutus continues to split act from emotion through language as he argues that it is only the conspirators' appearance, their *hands* (servants stirred to an act of rage) which are bloody; their hearts are full of pity for "the general wrong of Rome— / As fire drives out fire, so pity pity—." (170-1) Antony insists upon another sense of what has happened, repeatedly bringing the conceptualized, overformalized ritual of Brutus back to the bloody reality of the butchered Caesar. The unity in conspiracy which Brutus' language and ritual have created is systematically broken by Antony as he shakes hands with, and names, the members of the "knot" individually; in his speech at the Forum, he names each stroke, each wound of Caesar.[13] The conspirators are "hunters," "Sign'd in [Caesar's] spoil, and crimson'd in his lethe" (206). Rather than a sacrificial offering, as he is in Brutus' words, Caesar is transformed into a deer struck down, a benevolent, martyred ruler who loved his people, loved Brutus above all; "the men that gave their country liberty" in Cassius' vision, become traitors through the vision Antony presents to the people.

This theme of double interpretation is recurrent; summarized in the words of Cicero which I have used as an epigraph, the possibility of misinterpretation, of fashioning things according to an individual reality is present for the characters, the audience and the critic. The soothsayer is both prophet and "dreamer." (I.i.24) The omens are "instruments of fear and warning / Unto some monstrous state" which may be the inflated role of Caesar, as Cassius believes, (I.iii.70-8) or the "domestic fury and fierce civil strife . . . blood and destruction . . . Caesar's spirit, ranging for revenge, / With Ate by his side come hot from hell," which Antony chillingly invokes (III.i.263, 5;270-1). The augury of the beast without a heart warns Caesar not to go forth, but in his own interpretation, warns him that would be cowardice. The image of a heartless beast also suggests remorse disjoined from power: words, ideas, conceptions isolated from emotion. Calpurnia's dream is given alternate interpretations, both of which prove true: the murderers so press for tinctures to take on the power of Caesar, but through the assassination ironically establish Caesarism, thus empowering the spirit they sought to destroy. Brutus' underestimation of Antony, which causes him to dismiss Cassius' clear-sighted misgivings, conspires with his guilt and desire for punishment to doom the conspiracy; assuming his role as "composer" too confidently, Brutus gives Antony lines ("You shall not . . . And say you . . . and you shall speak") which are twisted back against him. (III.i.244)[14]

The themes of "doubleness" of interpretation, of the splitting of name from person, idea from emotion, are unified in the elusive figure of Caesar. We glimpse him through various images as a god and a colossus, a raging lion and a serpent's egg, "the noblest man / That ever lived in the tide of times" (III.i.255-6) and a "vile . . . thing" illuminated by a Rome which has become "trash . . . rubbish . . . offal." (I.iii.108-11) His absolute power is magnified by Cassius and Brutus in order that he may be made responsible for the turmoil within themselves;[15] he exists in created images within his own mind and the minds of others.[16] He deifies himself, but even Cassius comments that "he would not be a wolf, / But that he sees the Romans are but sheep. / He were no lion, were not Romans hinds." (I.iii.104-6) Paradoxically, we glimpse his humanity at the moments he labors to act in accordance with his name as public office,

> I rather tell thee what it is to be fear'd
> Than what I fear,—*for always I am Caesar.*
> Come in on my right hand, for this ear is deaf . . .
>
> (I.ii.211-3; italics mine)

> I fear him not.
> Yet if my name were liable to fear,
> I do not know the man I should avoid
> So soon as that spare Cassius.
>
> (199-201)

When Calpurnia seeks to persuade him to stay home, she allows him to project his own fear and say it is hers, "call it my fear / That keeps you in the house, and not your own." (II.ii.50-1) Caesar's name does not permit Caesar to fear; his actions are a process of ritualizing a social role. When Casca describes Caesar's refusal of the crown, the play-metaphor is used to catch the tone of the performance, "If the rag-tag people did not clap him and hiss him, according as he pleased and displeased them, as they used to do the players in the theatre, I am no true man." (I.ii.257-61) Caesar refusing the crown three times, Caesar plucking open his doublet and offering his throat to the crowd—this is Caesar the play-actor, exploiting the passions of the mob[17] just as Antony and, in another sense, Brutus, play-act after the assassination.

In his sense of his name as both part of his personality, a portion of his soul,[18] *and* as disembodied spirit allied with a rich heritage, Brutus may be identified with Caesar. In the second half of the play, he uses the third person with increasing frequency; his speech at the Forum is characterized by a rhetorical aristocracy equal to Caesar's. Brutus shares a love for words with Antony, the ardent lover of plays, but their use and style of language differ radically, as revealed in their exchange in Act V,

> *Brutus.* Words before blows:—is it so, countrymen?
> *Octavius.* Not that we love words better, as you do.
> *Brutus.* Good words are better than bad strokes, Octavius.
> *Antony.* In your bad strokes, Brutus, you give good words;
> Witness the hole you made in Caesar's heart,
> Crying "Long live! hail, Caesar!"
> *Cassius.* Antony,
> The posture of your blows are yet unknown;
> But for your words, they rob the Hybla bees,
> And leave them honeyless.
> *Antony.* Not stingless too.
> *Brutus.* O, yes, and soundless, too;
> For you have stolen their buzzing, Antony,
> And very wisely threat before you sting.
> *Antony.* Villains, you did not so, when your vile daggers
> Hack'd one another in the sides of Caesar . . .
>
> (i.28-40)

Antony uses words to manipulate the crowd, to get nearer, to descend into their midst; Brutus uses words to ritualize, to distance, to create a private reality isolated from that of the crowd—and isolate from Cassius and the other characters as well. The danger of isolating names from the individual, personal identity is demonstrated in the death of the poet Cinna, torn to pieces for his bad verses because he bears the same name as a conspirator (Cinna's death also dramatizes the uselessness of trying to disassociate oneself from "conspiracies" in a world which judges by appearances); the danger of isolating ambivalence from consciousness is the dramatic and psychological center of Brutus' tragedy.

Caesar becomes more powerful after his death, even as "the dead father becomes stronger than the living one had been."[19] By the law of talion, his murder can be expiated only by the deaths of his murderers, just as Pompey was revenged by Caesar's death at the foot of his statue, within his "theatre." Caesar lives on in the guilt of the conspirators, projected into an expectation of, and desire for punishment which is present through much of the play in Brutus self-destructive course of action. Erikson's comments on the preparations of ritual in the child at "the play age" seem illuminating here: Erikson observes that,

> [the child's] themes . . . are often dominated by usurpation and impersonation of adult roles; and I would nominate for the principal *inner estrangement* which finds expression, aggravation or resolution in play, the *sense of guilt* . . . an inescapable sense of self-condemnation which does not even wait for the phantasied deed to be actually committed; or if committed, to be known to others; or if known to others, to be punished by them.[20]

The analogy with Erikson's description recalls both the complexity of Brutus' ambivalence, grounded not only in love and hostility but also in ambition and identification, and my earlier reference to the melancholia which precedes the assassination. After the murder of a figure of primal authority, certain ceremonies involving appeasement of the victim and acts of expiation and purification, are observed by the murderer. Freud concluded from these observances that "the impulses which they express toward an enemy are not solely hostile ones. They are also manifestations of remorse, of admiration for the enemy, and of a bad conscience for having killed him."[21]—observances derive from an emotional ambivalence. This "bad conscience" takes the form of the ghost of Caesar, ambiguous and elusive of definition as the living Caesar, part of the images in the minds of others; but, the ghost also suggests the unwanted, repudiated parts of Brutus which have broken through his attempts to deny them.

Brutus' identification with Caesar has been implied through their formal rhetoric and use of the third person; their confusion of *name* with identity defined by abstract conceptions of kingship and honor; the lack of generativity in their marriages (Calphurnia is barren; Portia stabs herself in the thigh and swallows coals in a perverted parody of sexuality); their sense of drama and ceremony. Like Caesar, Brutus' "wisdom seems consumed in confidence" (II.ii.49) as his emphasis on his own honor, honesty, purity of action and intent increases in the last acts. Impersonal moral virtues, isolated from ambivalent emotions, have become attached to the intense sense of anxiety surrounding those emotions. Brutus' insistence on purity, as a defense against an awareness of his impurity, distances him from the reality outside of himself. This is painfully apparent in his scene with Cassius in Act IV: he reveals his own inner contradictions even as he accuses Cassius, "When love begins to sicken and decay, / It useth an enforcéd ceremony." (IV.ii.20-1) He demands of Cassius what cannot be given except through the "corruption" of which he accuses him; Brutus compulsively attempts to resist any ambivalent interpretation of Caesar's murder by excessive condemnation of Cassius,

> Remember March, the ides of March remember:
> Did not great Julius bleed for justice' sake?
> What villain touch'd his body, that did stab,
> And not for justice? What, shall one of us,
> That struck the foremost man of all this world
> But for supporting robbers, shall be now
> Contaminate our fingers with base bribes . . .
>
> (iii.18-24)

Both his repressed love and admiration for Caesar, and his ideal of impersonal action are balanced in this speech, but the balance is momentary and threatening; retreating into self-righteousness, he continues to bait Cassius.

Caesar feared Cassius partly because "He is a great observer, and he looks / Quite through the deeds of men: he loves no plays." (I.ii.202-3) Cassius' energetic directness perceives the split between outward appearance and shows, and the inner man. Even at the height of passion, he achieves emotional insight; when he bares his breast and challenges Brutus to enact with his dagger what he has already done with his words, he penetrates to the Brutus beneath "enforcéd ceremony,"

> Strike, as thou didst at Caesar; for, I know,
> When thou didst hate him worst, thou lovedst him better
> Than ever thou lovedst Cassius.
>
> (104-6)

Earlier, when Brutus responds to his direct statement, "Most noble brother, you have done me wrong" with the evasive outburst, "Judge me, you gods! wrong I mine enemies? / And if not so, how should I wrong a brother?", Cassius sees through his use of rhetoric and formality: "Brutus, this sober form of yours hides wrongs." (IV.ii.37-40) In one line, Cassius has expressed what Brutus has feared to acknowledge throughout the play.

Brutus' reaction to the poet may imply a reaction to himself; while Cassius laughs at the old man's command to "Love, and be friends, as two such men should be," and reasons with Brutus to "Bear with him . . . 'tis his fashion," Brutus angrily responds, "I'll know his humour, when he knows his time. / What should the wars do with these jigging fools?' (130:134-6) This is ironic, for Brutus is "out of time" with all around him, from the citizens of Rome to his fellow conspirator. In contrast to Cassius' observation of the realities of war and practical knowledge of appropriate action, Brutus may seem a "jigging fool" caught in his own rhetoric. War, for him, is a ritualization of his need to be defeated and punished, his need to fail as a reparation for his aggression against Caesar. When Cassius suggests what would have undoubtably proven successful strategy, Brutus twice dismisses him and brushes him aside with his famous speech, "There is a tide in the affairs of men . . ." (IV.iii.217) But this is neither the time, nor the tide; Brutus' speech is placed against the direct emotions of the scene with Cassius, whose clear, pragmatic vision must be overruled in order that the tragedy of Brutus be completed as he hastens toward his own destruction. Isolated in his own composition of reality, Brutus cannot understand another.

Like Macbeth upon hearing of his Lady's suicide, Brutus must deny his painful feeling of loss, as he must later postpone his grief for Cassius, for reasons other than the "morale" of his troops; in order to act, he must prevent emotion from breaking loose. This is in contrast to Cassius, whose pragmatism is balanced by emotional directness, part of "that rash humor which my mother gave me;" (118) he has changed from the would-be manipulator of Brutus in Act I to a friend subservient to Brutus in his dependence on his recognition and love. Cassius can mourn Portia and cry out at Cicero's death; Brutus must caution him twice to "Speak no more of her . . . No more, I pray you." (157;165) *His* haste is not toward practical action,[22] but toward death,

> . . . Brutus' tongue
> Hath almost ended his life's history:
> Night hangs upon mine eyes; my bones would rest.
> That have but labour'd to attain this hour.
> . . . Caesar, now be still:
> I kill'd not thee with half so good a will.
>
> (V.v.39-42; 50-1)

—the final, unambiguous resolution of a painful ambivalence.

"True ritualization represents," according to Erikson, "a *creative formalization* which avoids both impulsive excess and overly compulsive self-restriction."[23] This formalization involves an "*order perceived* and yet also *participated in;*" but there is always the danger, he warns, of "over-formalization, perfectionism, and empty ceremonialism, not to speak of the neurotic 'ritual' marked by total isolation. . . ."[24] The tragedy of Brutus, then, is a tragedy of failed ritual: a potentially integrative, adaptive, creative ego prevented from realization through the use of ritualistic elements as defense against ambivalence.

. . . . .

Toward the end of his report to Cassius and Brutus in Act I, scene ii, Casca adds the news that "Marullus and Flavius, for pulling scarfs off Caesar's images, are put to silence;" (285-6) scene one had closed with this extremely resonant instruction, "disrobe the images / If you do find them deck's with ceremonies." (67-8) The stripping away of images may in one sense uncover latent meaning, buried emotion; in another sense, it may "kill" the play. In order to prevent the latter possibility, image must be sounded for what lies beneath, not stripped away as surface meaning. Our consciousness must rejoin that which has been separated (action and emotion, ritual and primitive aggression, spirit and person, ideal and impulse) while at the same time admitting that *our* resolutions are at best ambiguous; the warning of Cicero a comment upon our attempt.

Notes

1. Leonard Dean, "'Julius Caesar' and Modern Criticism" in *Julius Caesar,* Signet ed. (New York, 1963), p. 191.

2. Sigmund Freud, *Interpretation of Dreams* (New York, 1966) pp. 549-50.

3. *Ibid.* pp. 520-21.

4. Kathleen Williams, *Spenser's Faerie Queene: The World of Glass* (London, 1966), p. 94.

5. Gordon Ross Smith, "Brutus, Virtue, and Will," in *Shakespeare Quarterly,* X (1959).

   Smith has suggested that anxiety about the loss of Caesar's love in the process of ascent might be informing this image.

6. Sigurd Burckhardt, *Shakespearean Meanings* (Princeton, 1968), p. 7.

   Burckhardt points this out in his seductive essay, "How Not to Murder Caesar."

7. *Ibid.* p. 8.

8. Norman Holland, *Psychoanalysis and Shakespeare,* p. 340.

9. Freud, *Totem and Taboo* (New York, 1950), p. 49.

10. Freud, "Mourning and Melancholia," in *General Psychological Theory* (New York, 1963), 1. 165.

11. Brents Stirling, "'Or Else were This a Savage Spectacle,'" in *Shakespeare: The Tragedies* (Englewood Cliffs, 1964), p. 43.

12. See Seimon O. Lesser, *Fiction and the Unconscious* (New York, 1957) on the function of form as devices managing expressive content ready to break loose and cause anxiety if not ordered.

13. Stirling, *passim.*

14. Plutarch, selection from *The Lives of the Noble Grecians and Romans* in Signet Shakespeare.

15. Freud, *Totem and Taboo,* p. 50.

16. Ernest Schanzer, "The Problem of 'Julius Caesar'" in Signet Shakespeare.

17. *Ibid.* p. 220.

18. Freud, *Totem and Taboo,* p. 112.

19. *Ibid.* p. 143.

20. Erik Erikson. "The Ontogeny of Ritualization in Man:" presented to the Royal Society in June, 1965 for the symposium "Ritualization in Animals and Man," *Proceedings of the Royal Society.*

21. Freud, *Totem and Taboo,* p. 143.

22. Stirling suggests "practical action" as Brutus' goal in "Brutus and the Death of Portia," *Shakespeare Quarterly,* X (1959).

23. Erikson, "The Ontogeny of Ritualization," p. 341.

24. *Ibid.* p. 345.

Jan H. Blits (essay date 1982)

SOURCE: "Politics and the Ethics of Intention: Brutus' Glorious Failure," in *The End of the Ancient Republic: Essays on 'Julius Caesar,'* Carolina Academic Press, 1982, pp. 39-61.

[*In the following essay, Blits studies the motivations of Brutus, and finds that in his inability to reconcile virtue and political action, Brutus ultimately fails to realize his idealized intentions for Rome.*]

Edward Gibbon, the historian of Rome, begins his study of Brutus by drawing attention to the wide discrepancy between his illustrious reputation for patriotic virtue and his actual contribution to his country:

> The memory of Caesar, celebrated as it is, has not been transmitted down to posterity with such uniform and encreasing applause as that of his Patriot Assassin. Marc Antony acknowledged the rectitude of his Inten-

> tions. Augustus refused to violate his Statues. All the great Writers of the succeeding Age, enlarged on his Praises, and more than two hundred Years after the Establishment of the Imperial Government the Character of Brutus was studied as the Perfect Idea of Roman Virtue. In England as in France, in modern Italy as in ancient Rome, his name has always been mentioned with Respect by the Adherents of Monarchy, and pronounced with Enthusiasm by the Friends of Freedom. It may seem rash and invidious to appeal from the Sentence of Ages; yet surely I may be permitted to enquire, in what consisted THE DIVINE VIRTUE OF BRUTUS?
>
> The few Patriots, who by a bold and well concerted Enterprize, have delivered their Country from foreign or domestic Slavery, [among whom Gibbon includes "the elder Brutus"] . . . excite the warmest Sensations of Esteem and Gratitude in those breasts which feel for the interest of Mankind. But the Design of the younger Brutus was vast and perhaps impracticable, the Execution feeble and unfortunate. Neither as a Statesman nor as a General did Brutus ever approve himself equal to the arduous task he had so rashly undertaken, of restoring the Commonwealth; instead of restoring it, the Death of a mild and generous Usurper produced only a series of Civil Wars, and the Reign of three Tyrants whose union and whose discord were alike fatal to the Roman People.
>
> The sagacious Tully often laments that he could be pleased with nothing in the Ides of March, except the Ides themselves; that the Deed was executed with a manly Courage, but supported by childish counsels; that the Tyranny survived the Tyrant; as the Conspirators, satisfied with Fame and Revenge, had neglected every Measure that might have restored public Liberty. Whilst Brutus and Cassius contemplated their own Heroism with the most happy Complacency, Marc Antony who had preserved his Life, and the first Magistracy of the State by their injudicious clemency, seized the Papers and Treasure of the Dictator, inflamed the People and the Veterans, and drove them out of Rome and Italy, without any other Opposition than some grave Remonstrances which the Patriots vainly addressed to the Consul.[1]

Gibbon is of course speaking of the "historical" Brutus, but everything he says applies with at least equal force to Shakespeare's Brutus. Shakespeare has Brutus make all the mistakes Gibbon lists, and others. Moreover, just as Gibbon in answer to his own question says Brutus' virtue consisted in his disinterested intention,[2] so Shakespeare reworks his source materials so that Brutus' concern for pure intentions becomes the decisive cause of the conspirators' major errors and defeat. Yet Shakespeare's Brutus, like his historical model, enjoys the highest esteem and respect for his virtue. Nearly everyone in the play loves or admires him:[3]

> O, he sits high in all the people's hearts;
> And that which would appear offence in us
> His countenance, like richest alchemy,
> Will change to virtue and to worthiness.
>
> (I.iii.157-160)

Cassius bows to his judgment out of love and respect for his "noble mind" (I.ii.308). Portia loves him dearly and looks up to him as the model Roman. Caius Ligarius considers him the "Soul of Rome" and pledges to do anything, even "things impossible," if only Brutus leads him (II.i.321-325). Lucilius gladly risks life and honor for him, and Brutus' defeated soldiers finally measure their own worth by how devotedly they served him. Even his enemies honor him highly. Octavius pays his virtue last respects, and Antony's final words laud his disinterested motives:

> This was the noblest Roman of them all.
> All the conspirators save only he
> Did that they did in envy of great Caesar;
> He only,[4] in a general honest thought
> And common good to all, made one of them.
> His life was gentle, and the elements
> So mix'd in him, that Nature might stand up
> And say to all the world, "This was a man!"
>
> (V.v.68-75)

To most Shakespearean critics, too, Brutus seems the perfect idea of Roman virtue. Mungo MacCallum, perhaps the play's most respected and influential 20th Century critic, expresses a conclusion shared by many. While stressing that Shakespeare actually "heightens the folly" of Brutus' mistakes by altering Plutarch's account so as to point up his Stoic intentions, MacCallum nevertheless argues that the playwright "screens from view whatever in the career of Brutus might prejudice his claims to our affection and respect." Indeed, while "to Plutarch Brutus is, so to speak, the model republican, the paragon of private and civic virtue," to Shakespeare, MacCallum believes, he is even more. Plutarch reports that

> Brutus in a contrary manner [to Cassius], for his virtue and valiantness, was well-beloved of the people and his own, esteemed of noble men, and hated of no man, not so much as of his enemies, because he was a marvelous lowly and gentle person, noble minded, and would never be in any rage, nor carried away with pleasure and covetousness, but had ever an upright mind with him, and would never yield to any wrong or injustice, the which was the chiefest cause of his fame, of his rising, and of the good will that every man bore him; for they were all persuaded that his intent was good.[5]

Shakespeare, "adopt[ing] and purif[ying]" this conception of Brutus, "carries much further [the] process of idealization that Plutarch had already begun."[6] In MacCallum's eyes, neither Rome's defeat, nor Brutus' heightened folly in contributing to that defeat, detracts from his stature as the paragon of civic as well as private virtue.[7]

Impressed by his Stoic principles, even the best critics have taken Brutus' republicanism for granted. Although recognizing something ambiguous about his virtue, Allan Bloom's interpretation of *Caesar* rests squarely on the traditional view that "virtue, to [Brutus], is incorporated in the life of a good citizen."[8]

> The motivation of both Brutus and Cassius are truly republican, with the difference that, according to the formula of the time, the one hated tyranny, and the

> other, tyrants. . . . Both positions reflect elements in the republican character; the one presents the principles, the other, the passions which must be combined for a republican regime to endure. . . . Both Brutus and Cassius are noble Romans, the sort of men who made republican Rome the glory of political history.[9]

Yet Brutus' patriotism is not so unproblematical. His Stoic ethics of intention, depending on an opposition between self-interest and duty, proves to contain an antirepublican disdain for the success of his own political cause and even for the welfare of his country. Far from representing the principles of republican Rome, Brutus' celebrated virtue is, on the contrary, at once a reflection of and a reaction to the rise of imperial Rome.[10]

The first three sections of this essay will concentrate on the meeting at Brutus' house shortly before Caesar's assassination, when the conspiracy's intended moral figurehead becomes its political brains, as Brutus makes three important decisions against Cassius' better judgment: 1) not to swear an oath of resolution, 2) not to include Cicero in the plot, and 3) not to kill Antony along with Caesar. The last two sections will then consider Brutus' notion of the general good and the specific connection between his virtue and the rise of imperial Rome.[11]

1

The conspirators arrive at Brutus' house with "their hats . . . pluck'd about their ears, / And half their faces buried in their cloaks" (II.i.73-74). Although the night is so unusually bright that he can read without a candle (44-45), Brutus immediately assumes the conspirators' concealment is a sign of shame. His strong aversion to stealth, which seems of a piece with his devotion to the common good, leads him to believe they are ashamed to show their faces even "by night, / When evils are most free" (78-79). He regards their concealment not as a reasonable precaution in the pursuit of an honorable cause, but as a tacit confession that their cause is unjust. Justice, he believes, is public in every respect, and thus he considers the cloaked conspirators merely a "faction" (77). Their partial appearance betokens a partisan purpose. This moral revulsion to their covert activity is emblematic of his political decisions.

Brutus asks the other conspirators to give him their "hands over all, one by one." But when Cassius then proposes they "swear [their] resolution," Brutus immediately objects.

> No, not an oath. If not the face of men,
> The sufferance of our souls, the time's abuse—
> If these be motives weak, break off betimes,
> And every man hence to his idle bed.
> So let high-sighted tyranny range on,
> Till each man drop by lottery. But if these,
> As I am sure they do, bear fire enough
> To kindle cowards and to steel with valour
> The melting spirits of women, then, countrymen,
> What need we any spur but our own cause
> To prick us to redress? what other bond
> Than secret Romans, that have spoke the word,
> And will not palter? and what other oath
> Than honesty to honesty engag'd,
> That this shall be, or we will fall for it?
> Swear priests and cowards, and men cautelous,
> Old feeble carrions, and such suffering souls
> That welcome wrongs; unto bad causes swear
> Such creatures as men doubt; but do not stain
> The even virtue of our enterprise,
> Nor th' insuppressive mettle of our spirits,
> To think that or our cause or our performance
> Did need an oath; when every drop of blood,
> That every Roman bears, and nobly bears,
> Is guilty of a several bastardy,
> If he do break the smallest particle
> Of any promise that hath pass'd from him.
>
> (114-140)

Brutus' spirited objection presents a manly challenge: those needing to swear their resolution lack even the strength of women. His first decision is thus often praised for expressing republican sentiments. For example, Norman Rabkin, calling him "the ardent republican, the ideal Roman," argues that

> Brutus is right. What good is an oath which merely ornaments an action conceived in honor and love of country? Moreover, he is right practically. Any member of the band so inclined could break the oath to his own advantage and warn Caesar, but none does so in the absence of an oath. Oaths then are meaningless.[12]

Rabkin may have a point, but it is not Brutus'. Brutus objects not because a sworn oath would be superfluous, but for the opposite reason. He objects because swearing would be meaningful. Because it compels obedience, swearing an oath would "stain" the conspirators' "motives" and give the assassination the wrong meaning. The conspirators must do nothing that would belie virtue as their only concern.

Brutus' veto rests on a crucial distinction between a sworn oath, i.e., one sworn to the gods, and an oath exchanged among the conspirators, which, witnessed by no one save the "secret Romans" themselves, consists entirely in the integrity of their word. He objects to the former in the name of the latter because he considers swearing a sign of "need" (cp. 123 and 137). Brutus believes that virtuous men practice virtue for its own sake and not for the sake of its extrinsic consequences. Such men therefore need nothing but their virtue to spur their action. Since their virtue is unconditional, they do their duty because it is right, not because it is compulsory. Swearing an oath, however, suggests just the opposite, that the actors' resolution depends on outside compulsion or supports. By calling upon the powerful gods to witness our oaths, swearing enforces our promises through fear of divine punishment for perjury. A sworn oath is thus a sign of moral weakness, for, rather than pledging the strength we have, it provides the strength we need. To suggest that the conspirators swear an oath is, then, to "think" that they "did need" one. It is to "stain" their "virtue" by doubting their "motives."[13]

2

The second decision enlarges upon the rationale of the first.[14] Cassius asks whether they should sound out Cicero, adding that he thinks he will stand very strong with them. Several others agree, including Metellus Cimber:

> O, let us have him, for his silver hairs
> Will purchase us a good opinion,
> And buy men's voices to commend our deeds.
> It shall be said his judgment rul'd our hands;
> Our youths and wildness shall no whit appear,
> But all be buried in his gravity.
>
> (144-149)

But Brutus quickly vetoes the proposal:

> O, name him not; let us not break with him;
> For he will never follow any thing
> That other men begin.
>
> (150-152)

One important effect of this decision is to deprive the conspiracy of Cicero's vast rhetorical abilities. As Bloom remarks, it is hard to believe that the man universally acknowledged the greatest orator in Roman history would not have presented the reasons for the assassination at Caesar's funeral better than Brutus did.[15] However, the issue of Cicero's rhetoric is subordinate to the issue of his "judgment." Brutus rejects including Cicero because he objects to prudence on principle.

For Brutus, his rivalry with Cicero involves not only who will be the conspiracy's acknowledged leader, but also, and especially, what "shall be said" to have "rul'd [the assassins'] hands." Brutus knows that both would add respectability to the plot, but each for opposite virtues: Brutus for the purity of his intentions, Cicero for the prudence of his judgment.[16]

According to Brutus' conception of virtue, since virtue is voluntary, an action possesses no moral significance except insofar as it is voluntary. Its moral element therefore lies wholly within its initial inception or inward prompting—what Brutus calls "the first motion" (64)—and not in its ultimate outcome or outward consequence. It rests in the actor's will or intention, not the action's results. The actor's motives are thus the sole standard for judging the justice of an action. Standing above its outcome, virtue consists in choosing the right end rather than in achieving it, in aiming straight rather than in hitting the target. Moreover, since virtue is a disposition or attitude of the mind, it does not require knowledge. Exclusive regard for intention makes judgment superfluous while making justice inherently good.[17]

Prudence, on the other hand, is essentially instrumental. While presupposing a moral purpose, it deals directly with means rather than with ends. As Metellus Cimber's unfortunate metaphor of commerce signifies, it is always exercised for the sake of an end outside its own activity and not simply for its own sake.[18] Cassius is correct when he reminds Brutus:

> Of your philosophy you make no use,
> If you give place to accidental evils.
>
> (IV.iii.144-145)

But whereas Stoic wisdom patiently endures such evils,[19] prudence is concerned with carefully avoiding them. To follow its counsels is therefore tantamount to conceding that virtue is not the only good or perhaps even the highest good and that happiness is indeed affected by things independent of one's will. It amounts to acknowledging that virtue is neither selfless nor self-sufficient, that its practice includes a consideration of extrinsic consequences and depends on the support of external goods.

Brutus rejects Cicero, then, for essentially the same reason he rejected swearing an oath. To be ruled by Cicero's "judgment" is to "make no use" of his own "philosophy."[20] The second decision goes beyond the first, however, in pointing up how concerned Brutus is with what others will say or think about his motives. An honorable reputation is as important to him as to any other Roman. But whereas a more traditional Roman would seek honor for his beneficial actions, Brutus seeks fame and glory for his honorable motives. Brutus, whose character in part combines personal ambition and selfless principles, fears that the reputation "the sagacious Tully" would lend the conspiracy would compromise the one he seeks for himself.[21] The third decision will show how far he is prepared to go to avoid the compromising appearance of prudence.

3

Decius next raises the question of whether only Caesar should be killed, and Cassius, thinking to events beyond the assassination, urges that Antony should also fall lest in sparing him the conspirators in effect save Caesar. But Brutus objects. His objection, however, has almost nothing to do with Antony. It is concerned instead with how the conspirators' motives for killing Caesar will appear. "Our course will seem too bloody, Caius Cassius," he explains,

> To cut the head off and then hack the limbs,
> Like wrath in death and envy afterwards;
> For Antony is but a limb of Caesar.
> Let's be sacrificers, but not butchers, Caius.
> We all stand up against the spirit of Caesar,
> And in the spirit of men there is no blood.
> O, that we then could come by Caesar's spirit,
> And not dismember Caesar! But, alas,
> Caesar must bleed for it. And, gentle friends,
> Let's kill him boldly, but not wrathfully;
> Let's carve him as a dish fit for the gods,
> Not hew him as a carcass fit for hounds.
> And let our hearts, as subtle masters do,
> Stir up their servants to an act of rage,
> And after seem to chide 'em. This shall make

> Our purpose necessary, and not envious;
> Which so appearing to the common eyes,
> We shall be call'd purgers, not murderers.
> And for Mark Antony, think not of him;
> For he can do no more than Caesar's arm
> When Caesar's head is off.
>
> (162-183)

Brutus' opposition springs from a paramount concern for the conspirators' reputation, not their eventual success. Killing Antony, he fears, would cause them to be "call'd" the wrong thing because the additional violence would give the wrong impression of their "purpose" for killing Caesar.

Critics often point out that Brutus, unable to permit himself full consciousness of what he is doing, tries to transform Caesar's assassination into something it is not. He tries to purify the deed of any taint of butchery by raising it to the level of pious sacrifice.[22] He attempts this, however, not to cloak the deed with false appearances, but so the truth can be seen. The assassination must seem to be exactly what it is. Insisting on moral transparency, he demands that the assassination be performed in such a way as will show that the killers' "purpose" was "necessary, and not envious." Their actions must assure "the common eyes" that their intention was free from any interested or passionate motive.

Imitating the indirect ways of "subtle masters," the conspirators must show that their hearts were not in their action, that Caesar's death was nothing but a reluctant concession to justice. They must therefore not only act dispassionately and limit the violence by sparing Antony; they must also seem reluctant to kill Caesar, for reluctance, even more than dispassion, attests to disinterestedness. Reluctance to do their duty will show that their action was prompted by nothing but their duty—a paradox that helps explain why Brutus, although very careful to conceal his internal torments after deciding to kill Caesar, is willing, even eager, to let others see how painful it was for him to choose public duty over personal friendship.

But Brutus knows that protests of reluctance, while important, are not enough. "Though now we must appear bloody and cruel," he explains to Antony after Caesar's death,

> As by our hands and this our present act
> You see we do, yet see you but our hands
> And this the bleeding business they have done.
> Our hearts you see not; they are pitiful;
> And pity to the general wrong of Rome—
> As fire drives out fire, so pity pity—
> Hath done this deed on Caesar.
>
> (III.i.165-172)

Because men tend to judge intentions by results, it is most important to Brutus that Caesar's death promise the assassins no personal gain. Others, including Caesar's partisans, may benefit, but not the assassins (III.ii.42-48). Their action, in fact, must entail a deep and conspicuous personal loss. The sacrifice of his "best lover" shows that Brutus acted "for the good of Rome" (III.ii.46). "Not that I loved Caesar less, but that I loved Rome more." (III.ii.22-23) What men give up, not what they gain, shows their disinterestedness. Accordingly, when Cassius says he still fears Antony "For the ingrafted love he bears to Caesar," Brutus replies,

> Alas, good Cassius, do not think of him:
> If he love Caesar, all that he can do
> Is to himself: take thought, and die for Caesar.
>
> (II.i.184-187)

Men's loves are measured by their losses. The purity of a man's intentions is best shown by the sacrifice of what he holds most dear. As the purity of an act is best revealed by its imprudence, the ethics of intention, disdaining prudence, ultimately courts political defeat.[23]

4

Brutus' conception of the general good lacks a public or republican spirit. Before the conspirators arrive at his house, Brutus, having deliberated alone all night, reviews the considerations that led him to conclude Caesar must be killed. His speech begins,

> It must be by his death: and for my part,
> I know no personal cause to spurn at him,
> But for the general.
>
> (II.i.10-12)

Brutus affirms (as any republican might) that he will act for the sake of the general good. But what he means by "the general" is unrelated to republicanism.[24] His Stoic soliloquy is devoid of considerations of republican freedom, honor, and tradition. In it, he never equates monarchy and tyranny; he shows no shame at living in awe of an equal; and while ignoring the sacred oath his ancestor made the Romans swear never to tolerate another king in Rome, he expresses readiness to accept Rome's return to monarchy providing only that reason continue to rule the king monarchically. Perhaps most telling, he never even mentions Rome.

What Brutus means by "the general good" is indicated by the way in which he begins the speech. Focusing on his own "part," he denies any "personal cause" against Caesar. He sees dedication to the general good in terms of the motives for, not the results of, his actions. Brutus thus confuses impartiality with public-spiritedness. His failure to recognize a middle ground between base self-interest and noble self-sacrifice leads him to believe that sacrificing his own private satisfaction is the same as serving the public good. Brutus is thus dedicated to the general good chiefly in the negative sense of being willing to accept self-sacrifice, but not in the positive sense of actually benefiting his country. As is true of Stoicism in general, his virtue is related principally to enduring evils, not to bestowing goods.

To be sure, Brutus also wishes to live up to his illustrious name and emulate his revered ancestor, Junius Brutus, the founder of Rome's liberties. This is the side of him that Cassius appeals to when trying to arouse his republicanism to overcome his Stoic patience:

> O, you and I have heard our fathers say,
> There was a Brutus once that would have brook'd
> Th' eternal devil to keep his state in Rome
> As easily as a king.
>
> (I.ii.156-159)

And Cassius' efforts have an effect best seen in Brutus' patriotic response to his anonymous note:

> Shall Rome stand under one man's awe? What, Rome?
> My ancestors did from the streets of Rome
> The Tarquin drive, when he was call'd a king.
> "Speak, strike, redress!" Am I entreated
> To speak, and strike? O Rome, I make thee promise,
> If the redress will follow, thou receivest
> Thy full petition at the hand of Brutus.
>
> (II.i.52-58)

All the republican considerations missing from his Stoic deliberations are present here. Far from tolerating a king in Rome providing the king could remain virtuous, Brutus is now unwilling to endure Rome's standing under "one man's awe" under any conditions. The issue is no longer the overthrow of monarchy in Caesar, but of republicanism in Rome. Accordingly, Brutus does not present himself as Rome's disinterested arbiter, standing dispassionately over his country's fate. Instead, imagining himself petitioned by Rome, he pledges himself to an apostrophized Rome and, in further contrast to his Stoic soliloquy, emphasizes his own hand in the promised action. Whereas in the other speech he never mentions Rome, in this one (II.i.46-58) he mentions Rome as many times as in the rest of his lines combined.[25] What matters to him now is Rome's redress, not his own motives. Concern for his country's well-being replaces concern for the purity of his own intentions.[26] Cassius' republican instigations, however, have only a short-lived effect. The conspirators soon arrive, and Brutus' civic virtue gives way again to his Stoicism.[27] Without constant prodding, his virtue lacks a genuine public dimension. Nowhere is this more apparent than at the end of his life.

Although he seems willing to sacrifice every personal good to the common good, what Brutus finally sacrifices is not so much himself as his country. Brutus says he knows "no personal cause" to act against Caesar. And at Caesar's funeral, just as he argues that the sacrifice of a dear friend shows that he killed Caesar for the good of Rome, so he also declares his willingness to kill himself for that cause: "as I slew my best lover for the good of Rome, I have the same dagger for myself, when it shall please my country to need my death." (III.ii.26-28) But Brutus does not die for his country, or even thinking of his country. His thoughts center on himself as he prepares to die, and he judges his life by a standard wholly unconnected with "the good of Rome."

> Countrymen,
> My heart doth joy that yet in all my life
> I found no man but he was true to me.
> I shall have glory by this losing day
> More than Octavius and Mark Antony
> By this vile conquest shall attain unto.
> So fare you well at once; for Brutus' tongue
> Hath almost ended his life's history.
> Night hangs upon mine eyes; my bones would rest,
> That have but labour'd to attain this hour.
>
> (V.v.33-42)

Brutus says he has labored his whole life only "to attain this hour." But his hour of triumphant "glory" is also his country's "losing day." What he has striven his entire life to attain stands apart from, or above, the downfall of his country. His personal moral victory shines through and eclipses the "vile conquest" of Rome herself. Similarly, just as his decisions as the conspiracy's leader are made not with a view to the political results of the conspirators' actions but with a view to the rectitude of their intentions, so too, running upon his sword, his dying thought is not of Rome or of the effects of his actions but of the goodness of his will:

> Caesar, now be still;
> I kill'd not thee with half so good a will.
>
> (V.v.50f.)

In the end, Brutus' ethics of intention, rather than extending his view to the whole community, narrows his vision to a purely personal concern. He ultimately values the purity of his soul above the welfare of his country.

5

Brutus heralds the rise of a postrepublican, apolitical or antipolitical moral virtue. His ethics of intention, reflecting the transition to or the emergence of imperial Rome, is essentially a sign of deep disenchantment. It marks a world in which political action and victory have lost their noble quality because political causes have lost their public character.

In the earlier days of the Republic, Romans strove for Rome's highest honors by competing with one another against her foreign enemies. In winning conquests for Rome, they also won honor and glory for themselves. Their private ambitions were at once served and ennobled by their public service. The public realm, linking together self-interest and duty, allowed men to rise above their merely private concerns while at the same time devoting themselves to something they could love as their own. By the time of *Caesar,* however, Rome's vast expansion had seriously diminished her public realm.

> When could they say, till now, that talk'd of Rome,
> That her wide walks encompass'd but one man?

> Now is it Rome indeed, and room enough,
> When there is in it but one only man.
>
> (I.ii.152-155)

Since actions derive their meaning chiefly from the causes they serve, Rome's "universal" empire (I.i.44) robs her political life of its ennobling spirit by reducing political causes to private causes. Only one man in *Caesar*—Young Cato—dies in battle for his country. And just as his appearance is largely unexpected, so, too, the standard others use for measuring his nobility is the action of a man who kills himself to show personal loyalty to a friend (V.iv.9-11).[28] With this single exception, the Romans serve their various leaders rather than their country under their leaders and measure their own worth by what amounts to private "service to [their] master[s]" (see esp. V.v.53-67).

Brutus' ethics of intention is a reaction to this degradation of political life.[29] It attempts to show or to find nobility in a world in which political victories become "vile" because no political action or cause is any longer truly public. As opportunities for public action and hence noble victories diminish, nobility does not so much disappear as it comes to be viewed in a radically new light. The dignity of intention rises as the dignity of action falls. Rather than seen chiefly in terms of action, nobility becomes internalized and, thought to dwell wholly within the actor himself, is understood in separation from or opposition to political action.[30]

Brutus' conception of honor reflects this new light. Honor was traditionally thought to be primarily an external reward for virtuous actions. Volumnia can speak of Coriolanus' "deed-achieving honour" (*Cor.* II.i.161), i.e., the honor he achieved for his deeds. No one would describe Brutus' honor in that way, least of all Brutus himself. Brutus begins his funeral oration by reminding the crowd of his honor:

> Romans, countrymen, and lovers, hear me for my cause, and be silent, that you may hear. Believe me for mine honour, and have respect to mine honour, that you may believe.
>
> (III.ii.13-16)

"Honour" here signifies a virtuous disposition, not a noble reward. It is the standard for judging rather than the recognition for performing a certain action. Like "honesty" (which is even more closely associated with Brutus), it is a virtue or virtuous motive rather than virtue's noblest effect; and, again like "honesty," it has the sense rather of abstaining from wrongdoing than of actually conferring benefits. Characteristically, Brutus believes that, if the people keep in mind that he is honorable, they will be convinced that Caesar's killing was just. Honorable motives by themselves make for an honorable deed. Since intentions are everything, the actions of an honorable man are just simply because he is honorable. They are and remain honorable whatever their consequences or success.[31]

Brutus' virtue also reflects Rome's emerging regime insofar as imperial Rome has no public life. It is especially fitting that Antony eulogizes Brutus for his disinterestedness, for even though Brutus considers him his moral opposite, Antony proves to epitomize the postrepublican notion that one can gain more by losing politically than by winning.[32] Brutus' virtuous self-denial is of a piece with Antony's sensual self-indulgence. They are the twin representatives of the new Rome. The one is duty, the other desire, separated from public concerns; and in imperial Rome, as we find in *Antony and Cleopatra,* there is "no midway / 'Twixt these extremes at all." (*A & C* III.iv.19-20) Characterized by a middle void, imperial Rome has nothing that can mediate between desire and duty.

Whereas citizen virtue, combining elements of "realism" and "idealism," adds nobility to self-interest and friendship or fraternity to justice, and in so doing both ennobles and moderates these two extremes, Brutus' virtue, recognizing only the noble and not the necessary as just, lacks moderation and ultimately even more. In the end it lacks humanity. If man is somehow connected to both what is above and what is below him, his humanity depends on recognizing these two aspects of his nature and giving each its due. It may even be that man is man by virtue of that middle ground or part of the soul that mediates between these extremes, for neither extreme is distinctly human; one is bestial, the other divine. Brutus shows he recognizes this, at least in some sense, when he fears that Caesar would sink to the level of the lowest beast if, upon reaching the highest rung of ambition's ladder, he thought himself a god (II.i.10-34). To remember one's humanity means to remember one's place "in between." But this is just what Brutus forgets in practicing a moral virtue that disdains political results.

There is something brutish about Brutus or his "idealism." As Caesar's last words to him suggest (III.i.77), in killing Caesar he does indeed manage to live up to his name, but in a way he never meant. When Antony demands to be told why Caesar was dangerous, Brutus answers,

> Or else were this a savage spectacle.
> Our reasons are so full of good regard,
> That were you, Antony, the son of Caesar,
> You should be satisfied.
>
> (III.i.223-226)

The assasssins' deed would be savage, he says, unless their reasons could overcome the natural love of one's own.[33] Yet it is in trying to demonstrate just such disinterestedness that Brutus proves to be truly brutish.

Moments after the assassination, he exhorts the killers:

> Stoop, Romans, stoop,
> And let us bathe our hands in Caesar's blood
> Up to the elbows, and besmear our swords:
> Then walk we forth, even to the market-place,

> And waving our red weapons o'ver our heads,
> Let's all cry, "Peace, freedom, and liberty!"
>
> (III.i.105-110)

This speech and the bloody ritual it ushers in remind us of Brutus' vain hope to kill Caesar without spilling his blood so that the conspirators' impersonal motives will be apparent to everyone. The speech and ritual are the solemn fulfillment of his wish to convert the assassination into a religious sacrifice. But what exactly does Brutus sacrifice? Unwilling to swear an oath to the gods lest it stain the conspirators' motives, he is willing to make the assassination a human sacrifice to the gods in order to demonstrate those motives. His moral idealism requires the barbaric sacrifice of human blood. Brutus expresses manly contempt for "such suffering souls / That welcome wrongs." Yet, unable to reconcile virtue and prudence, he ultimately pursues defeat. The defeat, however, is not his but Rome's. Unlike a soldier who sacrifices his own life for his country's victory, Brutus sacrifices the prospect of his country's victory for something entirely his own. Some Shakespearean critics, in important respects the spiritual heirs of postrepublican Rome, consider Brutus "the noblest Roman of them all" and admire him for prizing his ideals more than his country:

> The life of Brutus, as the lives of such men must be, was a good life, in spite of its disastrous fortunes. He had found no man who was not true to him. And he had known Portia. The idealist was predestined to failure in the positive world. But for him true failure would have been disloyalty to his ideals. Of such failure he suffered none. Octavius and Mark Antony remained victors at Philippi. Yet the purest wreath of victory rests on the forehead of the defeated conspirator.[34]

But Shakespeare finds such idealism a degenerate form of nobility. Brutus' moral purity is his central moral as well as political defect. Rather than raise him to man's highest moral levels, his desire to place pure duty or justice over every ordinary human attachment finally degrades his humanity.

> O judgment, thou art fled to brutish beasts,
> And men have lost their reason.
>
> (III.ii.106-107)

The idealistic attempt to rise above every attachment to one's own proves in the end not to be a divine willingness to sacrifice one's own well-being for the sake of a higher good, but an inhuman willingness to sacrifice the welfare and happiness of those one seems selflessly to serve. Deprecating political results, Brutus ultimately disdains humanity.

Notes

1. "Digression on the Character of Brutus," in *The English Essays of Edward Gibbon,* ed. Patricia B. Craddock (Oxford: Clarendon Press, 1972), 96f.

2. *Ibid.,* 98.

3. E. A. J. Honigmann, *Shakespeare: Seven Tragedies* (New York: Harper and Row, 1976), 42f.

4. The Arden edn., like most recent edns., follows the Quarto (1691). The usually authoritative First Folio reads, "He, onely . . ." In a sense both are right. Properly speaking, "only" does double duty here, modifying what precedes and what follows it.

5. *Brutus,* 29.2-3; *Shakespeare's Plutarch,* ed. W. W. Skeat (London: Macmillan and Co., 1875), 129.

6. *Shakespeare's Roman Plays and Their Background* (London: Macmillan and Co., 1967), 249, 234, 233.

7. Edward Dowden (*Shakespeare: His Mind and Art* [3rd edn.] [New York: Harper and Brothers, n.d.] 249), an important 19th Century critic, goes further:

   > In *Julius Caesar* Shakespeare makes a complete imaginative study of the case of a man predestined to failure, who, nevertheless retains to the end the moral integrity which he prized as his highest possession, and who with each new error advances a fresh claim upon our admiration and our love.

   Consider also Nietzsche, *Joyful Wisdom,* 98.

8. *Shakespeare's Politics,* 92. Bloom sees the problem of Brutus' virtue not in terms of its antirepublicanism but rather in terms of his hypocritical refusal to acknowledge the necessary conditions of his high-minded virtue; see *ibid.,* 96ff.

9. *Ibid.,* 94.

10. Paul A. Cantor (*Shakespeare's Rome* [Ithaca: Cornell Univ. Press, 1976]), while offering an excellent discussion of the connection between imperial Rome and the ethics of intention (145-154), follows Bloom in taking for granted that Brutus' virtue is essentially republican or public spirited (37f.). Cantor, in other words, fails to see the basic similarity between the apparent moral opposites, Brutus and Antony.

11. Recent studies of Brutus' Stoicism include Marvin L. Vawter, "'Division 'tween Our Souls': Shakespeare's Stoic Brutus," *Shakespeare Studies,* Vol. 7 (1974), 173-195, and Ruth M. Levitsky, "'The Elements Were So Mix'd . . .'" *PMLA,* Vol. 88, No. 2 (March 1973), 240-245.

12. *Shakespeare and the Common Understanding* (New York: Free Press, 1967), 108f.

13. Ernest Schanzer to the contrary notwithstanding (*The Problem Plays of Shakespeare* [New York: Schocken Books, 1965] 46), Shakespeare alters Plutarch's account of Brutus to give central importance to his ethics of intention and its political effects. In Plutarch nothing is said about Brutus' role in the first decision (or even that a decision, strictly speaking, was taken); the issue is not the conspirators' ability to maintain their "resolution" but to keep their "secret"; furthermore, "having never taken oaths together, nor taken

or given any caution or assurance, nor binding themselves one to another by any religious oaths," they do not forswear a religious oath in the interests of another, purer sort of oath (*Brutus,* 12.6; Skeat, *Shakespeare's Plutarch,* 114). Note that the conspirators' meeting as a whole is Shakespeare's invention.

14. Critics have failed to see the relation between the first decision and those that follow, or even that they are related. Either approving or simply ignoring the first decision while generally criticizing the others, they misjudge its significance because, like Rabkin, they look to the wrong sort of evidence. The question is not whether the conspirators need to swear an oath, but why Brutus insists they prove they do not. His insistence, not their resolution, is the real issue. By recognizing this, we can see that the three decisions are in fact a concatenation.

15. *Shakespeare's Politics,* 98; also MacCallum, *Shakespeare's Roman Plays,* 249.

16. Here I borrow from Bloom (*Shakespeare's Politics,* 98) where a similar formulation is used. Bloom, however, sees Brutus' imprudence not as a matter of principle but as the unwitting result of his rashness and hypocrisy; see *ibid.,* 92-101.

17. See esp. Cicero, *De Finibus,* III.

18. Aristotle, *Nicomachean Ethics,* 1112b12ff.

19. I.ii.137-139; IV.iii.66-69, 189-191; V.i.101-108.

20. Stoicism differs from Aristotle's teaching in regarding moral virtue as the highest good and consequently in making moral choice the final as well as the efficient cause of action. It differs from Kant's teaching, on the other hand, in considering the moral life to be the life according to nature and in holding that the virtuous man is always happy.

21. In Plutarch (*Brutus,* 12.1-2; *Cicero,* 42.1) the conspirators as a group, not Brutus alone in opposition to their collective judgment, decide to exclude Cicero, and not because of his unwillingness to follow another's lead but because they fear his natural timidity, increased by age, would blunt the edge of their ardor at a crisis demanding speed.

22. E.g., Bloom, *Shakespeare's Politics,* 96; Brents Stirling, *Unity in Shakespearean Tragedy* (New York: Columbia Univ. Press, 1956), 46.

23. In Plutarch Brutus does not spare Antony for the sake of how the assassins' motives will appear. Moreover, his naivete has a different quality there from what it has in Shakespeare. Plutarch reports that all the conspirators except Brutus thought Antony should be killed because he was wicked and naturally favored monarchy, was held in high esteem by the soldiers, and, particularly, because in addition to a mind bent to great actions he also had the great authority of the consulship, being then consul with Caesar.

> But Brutus would not agree to it. First, for he said it was not honest; secondly, because he told them there was hope of change in him. For he did not mistrust but that Antonius, being a noble-minded and courageous man (when he should know that Caesar was dead) would willingly help his country to recover her liberty, having them as an example to him, to follow their courage and virtue.
>
> (*Brutus,* 18.2-3; Skeat, *Shakespeare's Plutarch,* 119f.)

Whereas in Plutarch Brutus expects a virtuous example to have a virtuous effect on the "noble-minded" Antony, in Shakespeare he dismisses him as politically harmless because he considers him morally despicable (II.i.185-190). In Plutarch he expects too much; in Shakespeare, too little. In both accounts he believes that strength comes from virtue, but in Shakespeare he believes that vice renders a man negligible in every respect while in Plutarch he believes that even a man like Antony can be "noble-minded and courageous." In sparing Antony, Shakespeare's Brutus seems at once more naive and less generous than his historical model.

We should also note that Shakespeare makes Brutus' most notorious blunder—agreeing to arrange Caesar's funeral as Antony would have it—merely the culmination of his previous decisions. Brutus agrees to Antony's proposal so he can "show the reason of our Caesar's death" (III.i.237). By "show," however, he means to demonstrate by action as well as to tell. He offers Antony the last word at the funeral (III.i.226-252) and then begs the crowd to stay and listen (III.ii.57-63), not so much because he thinks he will give unanswerable reasons for Caesar's death, but because he wants to demonstrate his disinterestedness by allowing Caesar's loyal partisan to speak. As least as important to him as what he will say is that both he and Antony will announce that Antony speaks by the assassins' permission (III.i.235-251; III.ii.56-63, 83-85). Antony does indeed speak "For Brutus' sake" (III.ii.58, 67). By allowing Antony to praise their victim's glories, the conspirators will show their honorable motives. See the text at n. 33 below.

For an excellent discussion of how Shakespeare modifies Plutarch's account both to make Brutus' "responsibility" for the error "undivided" and to remove "all the explanatory circumstances" for the decision, see MacCallum, *Shakespeare's Roman Plays,* 249f. Note also that Shakespeare even takes from Plutarch Antony's cunning reason to bury Caesar honorably and gives it to Brutus (Algeron de Vivier, "Julius Caesar," in *Shakespearean Studies,* ed. Matthews and Thorndike [New York, 1916; rpt. New York: Russell and Russell, 1962], 261).

24. Saying he does not see "in what point of view [Shakespeare] meant Brutus' character to appear" in

this soliloquy, Coleridge (*Lectures and Notes on Shakespeare* [London: George Bell and Sons, 1908], 313) remarks that "surely nothing can seem more discordant with our historical preconceptions of Brutus, or more lowering to the intellect of the Stoico-Platonic tyrannicide, than the tenets here attributed to him—to him, the stern republican." Note that the soliloquy is Shakespeare's invention.

25. Brutus mentions Rome twelve times altogether, six in these thirteen lines. This soliloquy is also the only speech in the play to begin and end with the speaker's name.

26. In *Lucrece,* Junius Brutus is so contemptuous of the wish to show pure intentions that he criticizes not only Lucrece's soft husband, Collatine, for not revenging her rape, but Lucrece as well for killing herself to prove her "mind" was "pure" (1. 1704): "Why Collatine, is woe the cure for woe? / Do wounds help wounds, or grief help grievous deeds? / Is it revenge to give thyself a blow / For his foul act by whom thy fair wife bleeds? / Such childish humour from weak minds proceeds; / Thy wretched wife mistook the matter so, / To slay herself that should have slain her foe." (11. 1821-1827) Republican Rome might be said to combine the qualities of Junius Brutus and Lucrece.

27. Note that Brutus' three decisions are decreasingly republican. The first contains his only mention of tyranny (II.i.118).

28. Young Cato dies declaring himself "A foe to tyrants, and my country's friend" (V.iv.5), but it is unclear whether he is honored for his action or for "being Cato's son" (V.iv.9-11).

29. Consider Caius Ligarius, who regards Brutus as the "Soul of Rome" (II.i.321) and is the only character to look to him from the start to lead the conspiracy. Ligarius, a "mortified spirit" (II.i.324) who almost literally embodies the ethics of intention, suffers an unjust fate which shows what his limited actions could not show—that he is too noble to live at Caesar's continued sufferance. While accompanying Brutus to Caesar's house, he does not proceed to the Senate and so has no hand in the deed for which the mob punishes him; II.i.215-220, 310-334; II.ii.111-113; III.iii.35-38.

30. For the difference between the pagan hero and the Christian hero or martyr ("witness"), see Augustine, *The City of God,* X.21. Among many allusions throughout *Caesar* to the coming of Christianity with its new sort of hero are the conversation immediately preceding Brutus' first decision in which "the high east" is said to stand directly beyond the Capitol (II.i.101-111); Decius' interpretation of Calphurnia's purported dream concerning Caesar's death, in which, as Samuel Johnson (1765) says, "There are two allusions: one to coats armorial . . . ; the other to martyrs. . . . The Romans, says Decius, all come to you, as to a saint, for reliques; as to a prince, for honours." (quoted by Dorsch, *Julius Caesar,* 55f.); and the number of Caesar's wounds, which in Plutarch, Suetonius and Appian are twenty-three but in Shakespeare thirty-three (V.i.53). (For the symbolic significance of this number in Shakespeare, see Howard B. White, *Copp'd Hills Toward Heaven: Shakespeare and the Classical Polity* [The Hague: Nijhoff, 1970], 75.) For other allusions, see Roy W. Battenhouse, *Shakespearean Tragedy* (Bloomington: Indiana Univ. Press, 1969), 92f.

31. See Norman Council, *When Honour's at the Stake* (New York: Harper and Row, 1973), 60-74, and note esp. his remarks on Casca's alchemical metaphor at I.iii.157-160 (63).

    The difference between the spirit of Brutus' virtue and republicanism is further indicated by the following Shakespearean revision. According to Plutarch, when Portia disclosed to Brutus that she had gashed herself in the thigh to prove herself worthy of his trust, "Brutus was amazed to hear what she said unto him, and lifting up his hands to heaven, he besought the goddess to give him the grace he might bring his enterprize to so good pass that he might be found a husband worthy of so noble a wife as Portia." (*Brutus,* 13.6; Skeat, *Shakespeare's Plutarch,* 116) In Shakespeare, Brutus, hearing of her proof, also prays to the gods to "Render me worthy of this noble wife!" but is silent about the success of the republican cause (II.i.302f.).

32. See Cantor, *Shakespeare's Rome,* 148ff.

33. Hence Caesar's last words to Brutus in Suetonius, "And thou, my son?" (*Divus Julius,* 82) become "*Et tu, Brute?*" (III.i.77) in Shakespeare.

34. Dowden, *Shakespeare,* 272.

James C. Bulman (essay date 1985)

SOURCE: "Ironic Heroism in *Julius Caesar:* A Repudiation of the Past," in *Modern Critical Interpretations: William Shakespeare's Julius Caesar,* edited by Harold Bloom, Chelsea House Publishers, 1988, pp. 121-32.

[In the following essay, originally published in 1985, Bulman investigates Shakespeare's manipulation of heroic conventions in his depiction of Brutus, Antony, and Caesar.]

The idioms Shakespeare employed to delineate heroism in his early plays were too restrictive to allow him a personal signature. It is not by chance that these plays for years were thought to be the work, or at least to contain the work, of other dramatists: they fully partake of the conventions that were the stock-in-trade of stage heroism. But together they constitute only Shakespeare's apprenticeship to already-established writers. Within a few years, he was forging a mimesis more sophisticated than any that had yet been tried and, as a consequence, was recutting the heroic patterns that only yesterday he had found fashionable enough. His new heroes were characterized by their awareness of conventional expectations, and their tragedies arose from their failure to live up to them—from their inability to wear hand-me-down roles with any comfort or conviction. The authenticity of the plays themselves sprang likewise from their simultaneous employment and repudiation of the conventions that had bodied forth a heroic reality in the "old plays."

The death of Caesar illustrates how Shakespeare had come to use conventions with detachment, even irony. *Julius Caesar* is often labeled a sort of revenge play, harking back to various Senecan plays on the theme of Caesar's hubris and perhaps directly to an academic play called *Caesar's Revenge.* Certainly it has the ethical confrontations and at times the rhetorical style of Senecan offshoots; and the trappings of portentous storms, daggers, ritual murder, and a vengeful ghost cast it in the mold of the more popular *Spanish Tragedie* and *Locrine.* Caesar himself bestrides the stage like a conquering colossus. He has an egotistical self-assurance to rival Tamburlaine's—"for always I am Caesar" (1.2.212)—and an imperious will that bends to no external persuasion—"The cause is in my will. I will not come" (2.2.71). His epic hubris, the insolent pride that dares fate to match him in a test of strength, finds apt expression in the conventional outdoing topos:

> Danger knows full well
> That Caesar is more dangerous than he.
> We are two lions litter'd in one day,
> And I the elder and more terrible.
>
> (2.2.44-47)

And his passionate assertion of heroic selfhood is supremely embodied in the rhetorical set-piece he delivers just prior to his murder. The epic simile, with enough Ovidian fire to make the gods blush, is strongly reminiscent of Tamburlaine:

> I am constant as the northern star,
> Of whose true-fix'd and resting quality
> There is no fellow in the firmament.
> The skies are painted with unnumb'red sparks,
> They are all fire and every one doth shine,
> But there's but one in all doth hold his place.
> So in the world: 'tis furnish'd well with men,
> And men are flesh and blood, and apprehensive;
> Yet in the number I do know but one
> That unassailable holds on his rank,
> Unshak'd of motion. And . . . I am he.
>
> (3.1.60-70)

With the hyperbole that has characterized all conqueror heroes, Caesar ingenuously identifies in himself an absolute integrity of self and self-image. Like Talbot, he is what he says he is—a godlike hero of mythic proportions. The language defines him as such; and public acclaim, heard offstage each time he refuses the crown, affirms it. But Shakespeare does not let this assertion stand unchallenged. Against that offstage acclaim, he gives us an antiphonal voice *on*stage that relentlessly, right up to the time of the murder, points out Caesar's naked frailties: he is deaf in one ear; he has epilepsy; Cassius once had to save him from drowning. Even his wife Calpurnia qualifies our admiration by gently mocking his vaunt as unwise boasting: "Alas, my lord, / Your wisdom is consum'd in confidence" (2.2.48-49). In the judgment of various Renaissance historians, such hubris provided ample justification for Caesar's murder; and so Brutus characterizes it: "People and senators, be not affrighted. / Fly not; stand still. *Ambition's debt is paid*" (3.1.82-83, my italics).

But much as Brutus would like to conceive of Caesar's death as a moral exemplum, a just retribution in the tradition of the *Fall of Princes,* he cannot: he is too circumspect to believe in the public construction he puts on it. Like a chivalric defender of national honor in the early histories, or even more like Titus who takes great risks to preserve Rome's honor, Brutus would define his role in Caesar's death as that of heroic justicer. He would prefer to regard the murder as consonant with public rather than private honor—

> If it be aught toward the general good,
> Set honor in one eye and death i' th' other,
> And I will look on both indifferently;
>
> (1.2.85-87)

—but he senses more deeply that his role likens him to a revenger who calls wrongs to a private accounting without recourse to law.

Brutus is aware that he has insufficient evidence of those "wrongs" to justify the murder. "To speak truth of Caesar, / I have not known when his affections sway'd / More than his reason" (2.1.19-21). Thus, in order to persuade himself, he must conjecture some future cause and proceed to act on that conjecture as if it were proof:

> And, since the quarrel
> Will bear no color for the thing he is,
> Fashion it thus.
>
> (2.1.28-30)

The vocabulary of his internal debate, "Fashion it thus," reveals in him an active will to dissemble. He will seek no "cavern" to mask the "monstrous visage" of conspiracy, but rather will "hide it in smiles and affability" (ll. 80-82, passim). Beyond the mask of smiles, he advocates a grander imposture that would disguise blood revenge in the cloak of ceremony. "Let's be sacrificers, but not butchers," he urges his fellow conspirators (l. 166):

> And let our hearts, as subtle masters do,
> Stir up their servants to an act of rage,
> And after seem to chide 'em. This shall make
> Our purpose necessary, and not envious;

> Which so appearing to the common eyes,
> We shall be call'd purgers, not murderers.
>
> (2.1.175-80)

Brutus's advice to his coconspirators is remarkably like Volumnia's to Coriolanus: as the public eye alone will determine the legitimacy of your heroic fame, act the part nobly, even if you do not believe in it. The pretense to heroism, reflected in the "seem" and the "so appearing," is ironic because Brutus would include his own among the "common eyes" he is trying to deceive. With a duplicity of which the more conventionally drawn heroes of Shakespeare's earlier plays were incapable, Brutus teaches his fellows to play a role to convince the audience of their integrity, and at the same time he would convince himself that the role is perfectly consistent with his ethical selfhood. He would be as absolute as Caesar in believing himself a hero. The traditional heroic vocabulary he uses conveys that wish: "our hearts," seats of the will, must stir "their servants," the passions, to "an act of rage," an essential component of heroes from Achilles onward. And why? Because murder resulting from a noble wrath will always be condoned as a heroic deed. So strong is Brutus's wish, in fact, that it almost fathers self-delusion.

His wish is undermined by the self-consciousness with which he uses the heroic idiom, however. In his attempt to use the idiom to effect only an *appearance* of heroic purpose, its credibility as a means of representing reality suffers. Brutus tries hard to convince us otherwise. To reinforce the legitimacy of his purpose, he resorts to a form of traditional oath-taking; but he metamorphoses it into a fellowship of honesty, suggesting that the reality of the oath transcends mere words: "What need we any spur but our own cause. . . . And what other oath / Than honesty to honesty engag'd?" (ll. 123, 126-27). Shakespeare recalls for us the moment when the Andronici, with no discrepancy between a heroic sign and its significance, took vows against Saturninus, and the even earlier episode when York's family vowed revenge against Clifford. Brutus adopts the ritual—"Give me your hands all over, one by one" (l. 112)—only to try to outdo it in high-minded pretense: "No, not an oath. If not the face of men, / The sufference of our souls, the time's abuse" (ll. 114-15). But in declining the oath itself, in reaching instead for something more universal, he fails to engage himself with the form and with the power of its accumulated meaning that generations of heroes had counted on for sustenance. The self-consciousness with which he manipulates the form betrays his detachment from the ethos it signifies.

Brutus's failure to be engaged with the forms he enacts is dramatized even more explicitly in the murder of Caesar. Ritual murder scenes were a popular part of the revenge tradition. Shakespeare had played them to the hilt in his *Henry VI* plays, especially when Edward, Richard, and Clarence one by one stab young Prince Edward before his mother's eyes (*3 Henry VI* 5.5) and again, even more sensationally, in the Thyestian banquet of blood that concludes the festivities in *Titus Andronicus.* Caesar himself had been ritually murdered in the academic *Caesar's Revenge,* falling to the music of Cassius's couplet, "Stab on, stab on, thus should your Poniards play, / Aloud deepe note upon this trembling Kay" (ll. 1699-1700), and confronted at the last by Brutus's stern rebuke:

> But lives hee still, yet doth the Tyrant breath?
> Chalinging Heavens with his blasphemies,
>
> . . . . .
>
> I bloody *Caesar, Caesar, Brutus* too,
> Doth geeve thee this, and this to quite *Romes* wrongs.
>
> (ll. 1723-24, 1729-30)

Shakespeare's Brutus, unlike his earlier counterpart, is not content simply to do the deed out of moral conviction. Rather, he arranges Caesar's murder as a theatrical event. He directs his accomplices to play their parts "as our Roman actors do, / With untir'd spirits and formal constancy" (2.1.226-27)—an admission that constancy is no more to him than outward form—and bestows legitimacy on the murder by bidding them to bathe their hands in Caesar's blood, besmear their swords, then walk with him to the market-place,

> And, waving our red weapons o'er our heads,
> Let's all cry, "Peace, freedom, and liberty!"
>
> (3.1.109-10)

Through these conventional signs of ritual sacrifice, Brutus hopes to persuade his audience of Romans that Caesar's murder was a heroic act—a purge of tyranny, as in the old play—and that he and his accomplices are liberators, Rome's saviors, not butchers. He and Cassius even speculate that players in "ages hence" will reenact this "lofty scene" to the glory of their memory. "How many times shall Caesar bleed in sport," Brutus ponders (l. 114); and in so pondering, he "places" the event in a theatrical context and attempts to convince us, as well as himself, that outward shows may *create* a substantial reality.

Allusion to the theater was not new to a Shakespearean hero. As far back as *3 Henry VI,* Warwick, in his scene of oath-taking, had asked in agitation,

> Why stand we like soft-hearted women here,
> Wailing our losses, whiles the foe doth rage,
> And look upon, as if the tragedy
> Were play'd in jest by counterfeiting actors?
>
> (2.3.25-28)

Warwick's rejection of jest and counterfeit, however, affirms the reality of himself, his friends, and their cause: they must not act, but *be,* revengers. Brutus's use of theatrical imagery is far more complex. He tries to make acting and being inseparable. He instructs his friends to counterfeit like actors; he embraces the ritual shows by which he will win public approval; he conceives of the murder throughout as a scene played for posterity. Reality, for him, may be no deeper than the stage. But if the audience sees that Brutus can manipulate conventions to give a false appearance of heroism, then one's faith in conventional criteria for judging the reality of heroism on the stage cannot rest secure. The nature of dramatic illusion shifts. We do not trust, as Brutus hopes the Romans will trust, in the absolute correspondence of sign and significance. We may see more heroism in Brutus's struggle to come to terms with the heroic idiom than we see in the idiom itself. His self-consciousness becomes more compelling than his actual deeds. And the tension he feels between aping heroic forms and knowing that those forms are, for him, counterfeit, *makes* him real in a way that no conventionally drawn hero, not even Caesar himself, could ever be.

Shakespeare treats the heroic idiom with more irony in the various voices Antony adopts following Caesar's death. Most famous of these is the voice of heroic revenger. Left alone, after the conspirators have departed, Antony addresses Caesar's corpse in a lament that harks back to Clifford's lament over the corpse of his father, in which he vows to dry up all tears of pity in a "flaming wrath" and to find solace in cruelty. But Antony's prophecy is more universal:

> A curse shall light upon the limbs of men;
> Domestic fury and fierce civil strife
> Shall cumber all the parts of Italy;
> Blood and destruction shall be so in use
> And dreadful objects so familiar
> That mothers shall but smile when they behold
> Their infants quartered with the hands of war,
> All pity chok'd with custom of fell deeds.
>
> (3.1.263-70)

It stems from a long tradition of curse and threat of the sort that Shakespeare sprinkled liberally through his histories. Tamburlaine had called on it, "threatening a death and famine to this land," at the death of Zenocrate. Talbot had threatened to "conquer, sack, and utterly consume" Bordeaux; and Henry V, to shut up the gates of mercy and mow "like grass" the "fresh-fair virgins" and "flow'ring infants" of Harfleur. Behind these manifestations lie imprecations in earlier English tragedies that invoke both biblical sources, such as this in *Gorboduc:* "But dearth and famine shall possesse the land! / The townes shall be consumed and burnt with fire"; and classical sources, such as this in *Jocasta:* "And angry *Mars* shall ouercome it all / With famine, flame, rape, murther, dole and death." But Antony does not forget the more Senecan elements of revenge tragedy either. The ghost that appeared three times in *Caesar's Revenge,* once in the company of Discord, who comes from hell to ring down civil war, may be on his mind when he says,

> And Caesar's spirit, ranging for revenge,
> With Ate by his side come hot from hell,
> Shall in these confines with a monarch's voice
> Cry "Havoc!" and let slip the dogs of war.
>
> (3.1.271-74)

Antony's speech thus fuses rhetorical traditions with remarkable originality by sounding the voices of prophecy, curse, and threat all at once. Ironically, the warning of impending horrors, usually spoken by a choric observer such as Carlisle who, in *Richard II,* prophesies another Golgotha, here is spoken by the man who will bring those horrors about. The prophecy is thus self-fulfilling: not Caesar's spirit, but Antony himself, will let slip the dogs of war. Antony's language, on reflection, seems to be spoken with a self-conscious passion; and one may grow more suspicious that he is employing the heroic idiom to disguise his motives when, in the Forum scene that immediately follows, he turns revenge to political advantage and manipulates the throng with rhetorical artifice. His method is well known, so I shall cite just one overlooked allusion to revenge tradition to prove my point. Claiming that he is not disposed to "stir" the "hearts and minds" of the people "to mutiny and rage" against the "honorable men" who killed Caesar (3.2.123-26)—a disclaimer that echoes the language Brutus uses to stir the conspirators to do the deed—Antony produces Caesar's will, which, he says, "I do not mean to read":

> Let but the commons hear this testament—
>
> . . . . .
>
> And they would go and kiss dead Caesar's wounds
> And dip their napkins in his sacred blood.
>
> (3.2.132-35)

Antony's lines poignantly recall the by-then-famous scenes in which Hieronimo dipped his napkin in Horatio's blood as a token of revenge and in which Margaret tormented York with the napkin dipped in the blood of his son Rutland. It is important to recognize the power of Antony's allusion. He says, in effect, that if the people knew the will of Caesar, they would all turn into Hieronimos ranging for revenge against the "honorable" assassins. He adopts, for the moment, a diction that had served him in his earlier lament and to which, after this, he need not return. The arch control of his Forum speech, in fact, employs little of such emotive language. He has no need for it. The allusion to *The Spanish Tragedie* simply is a reminder of an idiom Antony had milked and then cast off. In his shift of rhetorical gears, Shakespeare marks Antony's emergence from the role of antique revenger to the role of Machiavellian leader who recognizes, like the later Ulysses and Aufidius, that virtue lies in the interpretation of the times.

Antony's manipulation of the revenge idiom should not come as a revelation in the Forum scene. Even before his lament, he tries out different voices that serve his immediate purposes. Entering the conspirators, uncertain of what they have in store for him, he at once adopts the conventional language of *de casibus* tragedy, moralizing in best *ubi sunt* tradition the ephemeral nature of man's greatness:

> O mighty Caesar! Dost thou lie so low?
> Are all thy conquests, glories, triumphs, spoils,
> Shrunk to this little measure? Fare thee well.
>
> (3.1.149-51)

In this are the seeds of Hamlet's "Imperious Caesar, dead and turn'd to clay, / Might stop a hold to keep the wind away" (5.1.213-14). But Antony is canny. Recognizing that Brutus will most respect a noble response to the murder of a friend, Antony turns to the lurid vocabulary of blood tragedy to *dare* the conspirators to butcher him too:

> I do beseech ye, if you bear me hard,
> Now, whilst your purpled hands do reek and smoke,
> Fulfill your pleasure.
>
> (3.1.158-60)

The dare works: it forces Brutus to defend his deed against Antony's characterization of it as a crime and, in the process, to offer Antony an honorable love. Antony seizes the opportunity to insure his safety by ceremonially shaking hands with the conspirators—

> Let each man render me his bloody hand.
> First, Marcus Brutus, will I shake with you;
> Next, Caius Cassius, do I take your hand;
> Now, Decius Brutus, yours; now yours, Metellus;
>
> (3.1.185-88)

—and adopts thereby a traditional heroic form that Brutus had tried to surpass in claiming that inner honesty, not outward show, determined the honor of his course. Outward show stands Antony in good stead here.

Yet he fears that his credit may stand on slippery ground. By too easily embracing a heroic alliance with the enemies of Caesar, he thinks they may have cause to suspect his honesty. Cunningly, he puts the question to them: "what shall I say?" (l. 191). What he decides to say is politically shrewd: first, to beg Caesar's forgiveness for his apparent betrayal, then to lapse back into lament for greatness gone:

> Pardon me, Julius! Here wast thou bay'd, brave hart,
> Here didst thou fall, and here thy hunters stand,
> Sign'd in thy spoil, and crimson'd in thy lethe.
> O world, thou wast the forest to this hart,
> And this, indeed, O world, the heart of thee!
> How like a deer, strucken by many princes,
> Dost thou here lie!
>
> (3.1.205-11)

To the conspirators, this sounds convincing enough to be interrupted. To us, it ought to sound like "art." The style—one Antony has not used before—is Ovidian. The pun on "heart" anticipates that of Orsino who, some one or two years later, laments that he is another Acteon hounded by his desires: this romantic context tells us something about the artifice of such verse. But Antony's pretty conceit about the hunted hart bears a more striking resemblance to Shakespeare's early narrative poetry and to the pastoral similes and crimson conceits by which Titus and Marcus prettified Lavinia's mutilation:

> Marcus: O, thus I found her, straying in the park,
> Seeking to hide herself, as doth the deer
> That hath receiv'd some unrecuring wound.
> Titus: It was my deer, and he that wounded her
> Hath hurt me more than had he kill'd me dead.
>
> (3.1.88-92)

Even earlier, Talbot had rallied his English forces against the French "curs" by calling them "timorous deer" who ought to transform themselves into "desperate stags" and "turn on the bloody hounds with heads of steel" (*1 Henry VI* 4.2.45-52). But by the time of *Julius Caesar,* such Ovidian metamorphosing of violence was a thing of the past, an idiom Shakespeare had experimented with, found wanting, and discarded. Antony, in reverting to it, deliberately sets Caesar's murder in an outmoded context: the language is showy enough to persuade the conspirators that he is a man of noble feeling but artificial enough to indicate that Antony is speaking from the mind, not from the heart.

The dispassionate ease with which Antony adopts expedient voices allows him inevitably to get the better of Brutus. Brutus tries manfully to identify himself by the heroic forms he enacts; he denies that there is any disparity between idiom and selfhood. Antony admits the disparity and thus is free to play on it as he sees fit. The divorce between acting and being causes no dilemma in Antony as it does in Brutus. A particular idiom does not define his character; the self-consciousness to play roles defined by the idiom does. Lest I be thought to mean that Antony is no more than an impostor, however, let me issue a caveat. The audience's awareness that Antony has a selfhood deeper than his idiom dawns only gradually. When he laments over Caesar, offers his breast to the conspirators' swords, shakes their hands, mourns the hunting of a noble hart, and swears to avenge the murder and appease Caesar's ghost, the audience may believe in the rhetorical reality of his character. Only in retrospect—and the moment of discovery will differ for each of us—will the audience appreciate that rhetoric and character are distinct from one another. Antony's idiom shifts, not for the reason York's shifts between the second and third parts of *Henry VI*—that is, to satisfy Shakespeare's rhetorical design, but because by those shifts, Shakespeare can dramatize in Antony a dynamic process of thought that psychologically justifies the choice of idiom. Motivated by political self-interest, Antony himself has both the reason and the autonomy, lacking in Shakespeare's early heroes, to manipulate rhetorical conventions: Shakespeare allows him to usurp his own prerogative to determine character by rhetorical means. As one moves chronologically through the scene of Caesar's death, therefore, Shakespeare preserves conventional modes of speech as momentarily adequate to define traditional attitudes and types of heroism, as if he, in a manner of old, has applied character with rhetorical brushstrokes; but in a retrospective analysis of all such moments, we realize that he has been forging new criteria for determining heroic character. Antony *is* the roles he plays in sequence, but the reality of his character is more than the sum of his parts.

As with Antony, so with the play. In a sense, Shakespeare satisfies conventional expectations of blood tragedy in the cosmic unrest, the ritual slaughter, the scenes of civil discord, the appearance of the ghost. He also satisfies expectations of heroic tragedy in Caesar's de casibus fall, the noble reconciliation of Brutus and Cassius, the stoicism of Brutus's suicide, even in the conventional elegies spoken over Cassius—"The sun of Rome is set. Our day is gone" (5.3.63)—and over Brutus—"This was the noblest Roman of them all" (5.5.68). But he does so only after exposing the conventions of heroism to ironic scrutiny, occasionally (as in Caesar's bombast) to parody, and finding them inadequate to represent a heroic reality. Heroism in *Julius Caesar* becomes real when Shakespeare holds conventions at arm's length—cuts traditional heroic patterns out of well-worn cloth only so that characters, scenes, the play itself, may try them on and complain, "These don't fit. They're yesterday's fashion. Fustian! We have outgrown them."

Cynthia Marshall (essay date 1994)

SOURCE: "Portia's Wound, Calphurnia's Dream: Reading Character in *Julius Caesar,*" in *English Literary Renaissance,* Vol. 24, No. 2, Spring, 1994, pp. 471-88.

[*In the following essay, Marshall discusses Portia's self-wounding and Calphurnia's dream of Caesar's death as they represent the linguistic instability of character in* Julius Caesar.]

> "If the body had been easier to understand, nobody would have thought that we had a mind."[1]

Roland Barthes sardonically described the Mankiewicz film of *Julius Caesar* as portraying "a universe without duplicity, where Romans are Romans thanks to the most legible of signs: hair on the forehead."[2] The film's use of hair fringes to signify Roman identity and its use of sweat to signify thought were to Barthes examples of "degraded spectacle," for according to his professed "ethic of signs," "it is both reprehensible and deceitful to confuse the sign with what is signified" (p. 28). Barthes approves those signs which are "openly intellectual and so remote that they are reduced to an algebra" and those which are "deeply rooted, invented, so to speak, on each occasion, revealing an internal, a hidden facet, and indicative of a moment in time, no longer of a concept." He objects to "hybrid" (p. 28) forms—those which are intentionally presented as naturalistic.

Barthes's characteristically pregnant remarks suggest some of the difficulties of reading character. It seems that inevitably there is slippage between "the sign" of character—textual, gestural, or otherwise—and "what is signified"—the assumption or production of a coherent subject. Barthes's two realms of allowable signs—"the intellectual and the visceral" (p. 28)—might serve as the poles between which knowledge of character moves. We know that character is an intellectual construct conveyed in literature through words. Yet we generally assume, in literature, in the theater, and in our own lives, that character can be revealed through actions, occasional responses, "visceral signs." I want eventually to return to this matter of the semiotics of character, but I will do so by way of a meditation on *Julius Caesar* and its own "ethic of signs." My effort to rethink the epistemic relation of body to dramatic character, and ultimately of body to identity itself, begins with consideration of the theories of character enfolded in the episode in which Portia wounds her thigh. After that I will go on to suggest how Calphurnia's dream of Caesar's bleeding statue exemplifies a more tentative sense of how characters are comprehensible to each other and to us.

II

By Barthes's criteria, one could consider the text of *Julius Caesar,* rather than merely Mankiewicz's film, to be "reprehensible and deceitful," haunted as it is by ambiguous symbols, what Barthes might call illegitimate signs—physical events and bodily images drafted into the service of symbolism. The stabbing of Caesar presents the most notorious example of this virtually obsessive symbol-making. Laden with tags of historical importance, Caesar's death can (and does) signify murder, betrayal, assassination, an allegory of civic disruption, an Oedipal crime, or the inauguration of "liberty, freedom, and enfranchisement" (3.1.81);[3] only very rarely does the event receive attention as an act of physical suffering and bodily death. Calphurnia's dream of Caesar's statue spouting blood and Portia's wounding her thigh as "proof" (2.1.299) of her constancy, along with the augurs' discovery of a beast without a heart, are also odd juxtapositions of sign and signified. Each of these images aspires to be what Barthes calls a "visceral" sign, for each reveals, like sweating, a literally hidden facet, evidence of a bodily interior. Yet they lack the spontaneity of properly "visceral" signs, since their meaning is forced, even gratuitous. Calphurnia's dream and the augury are assigned contradictory meanings within the play itself; each occasions an interpretive dispute. Portia's wound, however, occurs without such mediation. Offered at once to Brutus and to the audience as "strong proof of [her] constancy" (2.1.299), the wound receives by way of interpretation within the play only Brutus' response: "O ye gods, / Render me worthy of this noble wife!" (2.1.302-03). I think that it is no longer possible (if it ever was) for audiences simply to accept this Stoic formulation. So in considering several responses to Portia's wound, I will be concerned with the challenge theatrical violence presents to our systems for ordering knowledge of the world and more particularly of other people—the sort of knowledge we debate when we consider the notion of character.

As the first act of violence in a work centering on assassination and the first knife wound in a dramatic action in which five more characters will be stabbed, Portia's "voluntary wound" formally establishes a certain brutal pattern.[4] It is scarcely surprising that images of fractured bodily forms should figure in a play about assassination, and traditional approaches order the image cluster initiated with Portia's wound around the central motif of Caesar's body pierced by wounds. My concern here is not with formal order, however, but with the ways of knowing represented in the play. Portia uses her body to establish the validity of her claim on Brutus. When she appeals to Brutus on his own Stoic terms, Portia's proffered "proof" that she will not "disclose" her husband's "counsels" appears to be highly successful. Brutus quickly promises that her "bosom shall partake / The secrets of my heart" (2.1.305-06). Adopting her metaphor of the body as a container for truth, he locates his secrets within his heart and images her bosom as opening to receive or "partake" them. Seeking to be "worthy of this noble wife," Brutus emulates her action when he stabs Caesar and later when he stabs himself. Brutus sees the assassination as proof of his dedication to the Roman state ("Not that I loved Caesar less, but that I / loved Rome more" [3.2.21-22]). Later, his suicide at once demonstrates and obliterates Brutus' guilt: "Caesar, now be still. / I killed not thee with half so good a will" (5.5.50-51). The pattern Portia's wound establishes, then, is that of Stoic exaltation of the will and abnegation of the body.

Critical responses to this episode have often been marked by a commitment to reading historically that covers an implicit identification with Brutus. The Arden editor, T. S. Dorsch, for instance, saw Portia as "a wife of whom any man would wish to prove himself worthy," one who "has proved her fortitude in bearing physical pain" and thereby demonstrated her "moral courage."[5] Reuben Brower praised "her grand Stoic gesture" without detectable irony.[6] G. Wilson Knight effaced Portia's nascent subjectivity even more completely by reading the action as a reflection of Brutus' honor, which is "so strong . . . that Portia knows she must play up to it, show herself courageous, possessing a sense of 'honour' like his."[7] These critics have in common an investment in a brand of Stoicism, with its value-laden opposition of spirit and body. When character is regarded as a matter of mind and spirit, Portia's verbal ascription of meaning to her action is unproblematically endorsed; the brokenness of her body figures in the service of an abstract, if personal, goal. The wounding, from this perspective is granted no signification as an event on stage, but is regarded as symbolic only within the conceptual system through which Portia presents it and Brutus receives it.

Yet the theatrical presentation of this episode suggests the inadequacy of such a reading. Because the medium of drama to a certain extent privileges the physical realm over the linguistic, Portia's wound—whether staged or not, but especially if staged—will signify independently of her own words about it. Certainly for a modern, Western audience, deep assumptions about the value to the individual of bodily integrity will strain the purported meaning of this masochistic action. Rather than demonstrating Portia's strength of character, the act of wounding herself suggests to such an audience desperation, hysteria, perhaps derangement. The historical and philosophical slippage between the purported meaning of the wound and the understanding that "naturally" presents itself to a post-Freudian audience suggests the need for further scrutiny of the relation between violence and validity.

III

When Portia wounds her thigh, she directs attention inward, toward the vulnerable interior of her bodily self. As with any theatrical wound, the surface of spectacle is pierced. The character's body is presented as something that bleeds, feels pain, may die—something more "real" than mere spectacle. One obvious place to turn in theorizing about this interior dimension is toward psychoanalysis, which will see the wound and the dagger as, in various ways, symbolic. While psychoanalysis typically subsumes body to symbol, it will grant to Portia, in contrast to historicist criticism, an active (if unhealthy) inner life.

Perhaps because the action of a woman plunging a dagger into her thigh is so heavily loaded with Freudian sexual symbolism, critics have tended to proceed from noting the wound's sexual suggestiveness to endorsing Portia's stated claim that fortitude is a masculine attribute ("Think you I am no stronger than my sex, / Being so fathered and so husbanded?" [2.1.296-97]). Clifford Ronan constructs a symbolic pregnancy for Portia: "The penetration she has made upon her thigh results in the unwelcome rebirth of her femininity, not an affirmation of her manliness."[8] Robert Miola implicitly compares Portia to Lady Macbeth—"she denies her sex and changes from wife to comrade-in-arms"[9]—thus also equating the female sex with passivity. While such readings acknowledge symbolic conflicts within Portia, the difficulty of mediating between the literal action and a contextualized meaning remains.

Madelon Sprengnether points in such a direction with the remark that "it is a woman who, oddly enough, articulates the fundamental masculine ethic of the play."[10] David Kranz sees the "knife trick" as Portia's calculated move in a gamble to out-Roman the Romans by appropriating their "masculine ethic."[11] Displaying her ability to perform by Stoic standards and explicitly offering to define herself according to masculine expectations ("so fathered, and so husbanded" [2.1.297]), Portia momentarily destabilizes the masculine code by claiming it as her own. As Gail Kern Paster observes, Portia is "seeking to efface the physical difference that separates her from her husband."[12] In Paster's reading, "Portia calls attention to this bodily site not to remind Brutus of her femaleness, her lack of the phallus, but rather to offer the wound as substitute phallus" (p. 294). While I agree that Portia attempts to erase difference, I see her as attempting to do so by embodying it, by playing a double role. The action of wounding herself, explicitly presentational, requires self-division: the will (tropologically masculine) attacks and conquers the body (correspondingly feminine). As both wielder and victim of the knife/phallus, Portia momentarily brings gender opposition into equilibrium—but at the cost of violence to herself. Her performance of this double role impresses Brutus, even inspires him to carry out the conspiratorial plan, partially because his own personality includes sensitive and nurturing attributes marked as feminine. Thus he must prove himself more manly, more Roman—and inevitably, more violent—than Portia.

Oppositional constructions of gender are of course far too deeply engrained in Roman culture for Portia to neutralize them. In 2.4, Portia retreats from her fierce challenge and declares, even insists upon, gendered difference: "I have a man's mind, but a woman's might. / How hard it is for women to keep counsel!" (2.4.8-9); "Ay me, how weak a thing / The heart of woman is!" (2.4.39-40) Later, her suicide—"she fell distract, / And (her attendants absent) swallowed fire" (4.3.155-56)—while in one sense repeating the topos of the knife wound, is presented as an act of "distract[ion]" rather than of nobility.

In M. D. Faber's view, Portia's behavior is consistent with modern constructions of the pathologically "self-destructive" personality.[13] Faber sees Portia's "anger and frustration" as "rooted in an exaggerated dependence upon her spouse" (p. 111). Here, as so often, the psychoanalytic perspective serves to bolster a male order. Although Portia's behavior may be pathological, it has identifiable social and cultural causes. She rebels against a social contract that relegates her to the private sphere of inaction, and that breaks the emotional bonds between her and Brutus. While Brutus meditates on the grounds for action, consults with other conspirators, and takes part in recognizably significant events, Portia is left "in the suburbs / Of [his] good pleasure" (2.1.285-86). Wounding herself, she converts psychic suffering into physical. Her situation and response resemble the female terrorists Julia Kristeva explains as so "brutally excluded from [the] sociosymbolic stratum" as to feel their "affective life" or "condition as a social being" to be "ignored by existing discourse or power."[14] Like Kristeva's terrorists, Portia "counterinvest[s] the violence she has endured, mak[ing] of herself a 'possessed' agent of this violence in order to combat what was experienced as frustration" (p. 28). She rebels against a social contract that relegates her to the private sphere of inaction by becoming wielder of the knife. Portia's suicide, as well as her "voluntary wound," manifest the unacknowledged violence with which she has been thrust aside by Brutus personally and the male order more generally. Staging herself as both agent and victim of violence, she attempts to close the circle of a significant violence within herself. These two acts of personal violence indicate an apparently obsessive need to literalize, to embody, conflict and suffering.

Julius Caesar, establishing a dramatic myth of political origins, encodes violence in the tissue of language. The ongoing process of textualizing the body determines the play's treatment of Caesar's assassination; it also shapes the account of Portia's death. Her suicide figures as a text with which Brutus can (twice) demonstrate his philosophical equanimity (4.3.146-56; 180-94). The manner of her suicide itself links Portia with linguistic violence. Her body, which previously had contained Brutus's words ("partake[n] / The secrets of [his] heart" [2.1.305-6]), becomes the container of fiery coals. "Swallow[ing] fire," she kills herself by obliterating the organs of speech. And of course the thigh wound also occurs because of words; it is delivered in quest of Brutus's "secret." Her two acts of violence suggest that Portia is in revolt against the symbolic order, against language as a structure of power. In this sense she resembles an hysteric.

Existing in a culture that grants her few emotional outlets, Portia channels repressed aggression and desire into symbolic violence, as an hysteric would convert these drives into the bodily language of symptoms. Freud understood hysterical symptoms as a language, the body speaking the encoded desires of the unconscious mind. But his own failures, particularly with Dora, led Freud eventually to admit that a reading of this language is uncertain, bivalent, as unstable as gender itself, for "the hysterical symptom is the expression of both a masculine and a feminine unconscious phantasy."[15] Freud also refers to "hysterical attacks in which the patient acts at one and the same time both parts of the underlying sexual phantasy" (p. 151). So too in *Julius Caesar,* Portia expresses and performs doubleness. Her self-wounding looks from one perspective like the appropriative gesture of a frustrated masculine desire; from another, the thigh wound seems to draw attention to her already-castrated feminine weakness, and thus to emblematize Portia as passive object. Using her own body as a theater, Portia sets numerous and conflicting meanings into play. Thus her performance of violence can be differentiated from that of the other suicides in the play, whose action is primarily directed to the goal of eliminating the self, and only secondarily to the demonstration of Stoicism.

But considering Portia as hysteric leads back to the epistemic question of understanding the internal dimensions of another person, since psychoanalysis postulates hysteria as what Charles Bernheimer calls "pathological interiority."[16] Foucault points to moral and ethical connotations in the conception of internal density; hysteria is associated with a less "solidly dense and firmly organized . . . internal space of body."[17] Whereas a traditional historicist approach produces a strong, unified Portia, psychoanalysis would see her wound as symptomatic of a character marked by fragmentation, brokenness, neurosis. As Bernheimer writes, "the psychological understanding of hysteria was born in complicity with a moral condemnation of its victims" (pp. 4-5). Despite attempts like that of Hélène Cixous to reclaim hysteria for feminism ("those wonderful hysterics, who subjected Freud to so many voluptuous moments too shameful to mention . . . they were dazzling"[18]), the concept of hysteria remains less descriptive than normative in our culture, and it warns of the diagnostician's appropriating role. As the performances of Charcot's patients made so clear, hysteria labels a spectacle that depends in large part on an attentive audience. Hysteria comes to look like a species of characterology, a "linguistic sign" in Harold Fisch's sense,[19] ascribing meaning to symptom in order to render the suspect interior of another person knowable, much as a decision as to character type allows comfortably summary conclusions about literature. While Portia's resemblance to an hysteric is instructive in accounting for the unstable meanings her self-wounding sets into motion, the charged significance of the discourse on hysteria serves as an alert to the psychoanalytic (and critical) predilection to stigmatize the deviant (other) woman.

IV

Reading Portia as Stoic or hysteric lends coherence and shape to her self-destructive actions. Her wounding and her suicide become comprehensible; they fall into accordance with the dictates of a symbol system. Both these diagnoses also preserve the separate domains of sign and signified. When the voluntary wound is considered the sign of Stoicism, or the symptom of an hysterical "acting out," the significant reality of character is posited as prior to the gesture of taking knife to flesh. The wound can thus be regarded as linguistic sign, as an intertextual stage direction, and indeed, to the extent that Shakespeare's plays are treated as poetic texts, this would be the limit of the wound's phenomenal reality. But when we attend to what Alessandro Serpieri calls "the theatrical destiny of textual meaning,"[20] the wound can be seen to offer compelling surplus meanings; it may even become significant in its own right. To read Portia's wound—or, by extension, any act of onstage violence—as independently significant may, in Barthes's terms, "confuse the sign with what is signified" (p. 28). Yet I would argue that such confusion is inevitable if a notion of dramatic character encompasses the body's fate, as represented on stage, as well as the character's more purely linguistic presentation.

I think we need to set the theatrical moment of physical violence against an exaggerated poststructuralist dictum that we have only language, and not each other, or even ourselves, in any preverbal way. An audience's response to physical violence will certainly be conditioned, even largely determined, by the prior experiences of the individual viewer and by the group experiences of the audience as a whole, including most saliently the immediate theatrical production—both the play text and its particular enactment. Obviously an audience treats farce differently from tragedy, views Macbeth's death differently from Cordelia's. Blood is crucial to the staging of a violent wounding, and as Leo Kirschbaum recognized long ago, the presence of stage blood "will always excite horror in the audience."[21] Stage blood, as Kirschbaum indicates, has significance that surpasses the symbolic or imagistic. It marks a certain represented experience, one of bodily suffering, that has great relevance to the notion of character. Because pain fractures language, the phenomenon of onstage violence can, and often does, powerfully alter the semiotics of drama.

Elaine Scarry has written eloquently of pain's inexpressibility: "Physical pain does not simply resist language but actively destroys it, bringing about an immediate reversion to a state anterior to language, to the sounds and cries a human being makes before language is learned."[22] This insight holds true with lower forms of drama, such as Pyramus' "Tongue, lose thy light, / Moon, take thy flight. / Now die, die, die, die, die" (*MND* 5.1.297-99), where not only does the repeated syllable drain itself of meaning, but reference is made (however nonsensically) to the abandonment of powers of speech ("Tongue, lose thy light"), as well as sight ("Moon, take thy flight"). Gloucester's blinding offers a more compelling example—"O cruel! O you gods!" (*KL,* 3.7.70)—especially as it is followed by the slain servant's "O, I am slain! My lord, you have one eye left / To see some mischief on him. O!" (*KL,* 3.7.81-82). The speech is bracketed with the pre-verbal "O," whose second occurrence, especially, rings hollowly as the servant dies. The eloquent death speeches of the major characters in *Julius Caesar*—Caesar's, at the play's center, binding his fate to Brutus' betrayal, and Brutus' final speech reiterating the psychic bond with Caesar—might seem to obviate any sense that the moment of death is one of extremity. But in general tragedy's "project," as Sheila Murnaghan puts it, is that of "replacing the body's adventures with forms of speech."[23] Aiming as it does to express the inexpressible, tragedy's encoding of pain and death in language succeeds not simply through mimetic realism but through the creation in the reader's or viewer's mind of the represented phenomena of suffering and loss.

Moments of onstage violence such as that of Portia's voluntary wound offer a distinctive variation on models of theatrical involvement that are based on the concept of spectacle. The pain occasioned by Portia's wound can be said to occur not in Portia's body (as it is represented by the actor's) and not in Portia's mind (to which the audience has no access). Rather the represented (that is fake) wound might best be said to occasion pain in the mind of the members of the audience. The question of where pain occurs has long been a test case for philosophers probing the epistemic relation of mind and body. I would suggest that represented violence has an affect that is powerful or cathartic largely because it breaks down the barriers of self and other that shape ordinary human interaction. Portia's wound directs attention inward, asserts an interior dimension to her character. But since the pain from the wound occurs in the audience's imagination, and not only in the actor's, Portia's interior dimension becomes coterminous with that of the individual viewer. While pain may be inexpressible, and pain's victim can in certain situations be relegated to a status of abjection, the representation of pain in the theater has the potential to offer a different sort of dynamic. Such a representation presents the peculiar possibility of feeling the pain of another—albeit an imagined or represented other.

What does this mean for the concept of character? For one thing, just as we have always known, those characters seem most compellingly real whom we, for one reason or another, take into ourselves. When this happens we experience a character just as we do ourselves—as discontinuous, partial, at once present and absent, known and unknown. When we feel a character's pain we do not experience him or her in the way Freud (would say he) experienced a patient, as something of a mystery to be deciphered. Still less does a model of historical alterity describe such an interaction. Focusing on the theatrical dynamic as activated by physical violence onstage suggests linkage between Barthes's categories of intellectual and visceral signs. A moment of wounding or suffering onstage, while evidently revelatory of "an internal, a hidden facet, and indicative of a moment in time," is also "openly intellectual" and "remote," in the sense that an audience recognizes the represented pain as fictional, at the same time that it is felt as real.

Responding to a character in this way may seem to erase difference, to evoke what Cixous calls "the you-as-I relationship,"[24] a fundamental refusal (which she sees as inherent in the notion of character itself) to admit the indecipherable otherness of the represented subject. Scarry's insight into the incommunicability of pain would also seem to point toward the futility or presumption of an empathic response. Indeed, Scarry suggests that pain emblematizes the skeptical dilemma: "'hearing about pain' may exist as the primary model of what it is 'to have doubt'" (p. 4). Theater, however, is uniquely suited to break the impasse of skepticism, providing as it does a simultaneous awareness of the character's presence and absence. The character and her pain are located in the text, on the stage, and in the minds of the audience. Thus the enactment of violence or pain onstage can force an audience to "stay in the presence of the Other." This is Johannes Fabian's goal for ethnography, but one that applies also to theater, which allows an audience "recognition of the Other that is not limited to representations."[25] Whereas representation requires the power to fix and signify, recognition of the "presence of the Other" preserves the strangeness and instability of a knowledge gained, lost, and regained.[26] This epistemological model of recognition, born in a sympathy with primary, bodily modes of expression, is exemplified within *Julius Caesar* by Calphurnia's dream.

V

Plutarch reports two versions of Calphurnia's dream: first, "that Caesar was slain, and that she had him in her arms"; and second, that "the Senate having set upon the top of Caesar's house, for an ornament and setting forth of the same, a certain pinnacle, Calphurnia dreamed that she saw it broken down, and that she thought she lamented and wept for it."[27] Shakespeare erases the types of bodily intimacy—the first maternal, the second phallic—represented by these dreams, and creates in their stead the dream in which Calphurnia sees Caesar's statue "with an hundred spouts / . . . run pure blood" (2.2.77-78). The dream foreshadows Caesar's fate at the hands of the conspirators, and it lends coherence to a play about assassination. It also comprehends Caesar's problematic identity and thereby reveals Calphurnia's capacity as dreaming subject. In an unusual reversal of an established gender dynamic, Calphurnia functions as the subject to whose knowledge the audience receives (mediated) access, while Caesar is the object of scrutiny.

That she is denied even the articulation of her dream, which is narrated by the appropriating Caesar, demonstrates an effacement of her linguistic presence; Calphurnia is largely without the power of words in the play. But her relative muteness also confers on Calphurnia the paradoxical freedom of one unconfined by limiting verbal structures. In a world where words have grown false, where a term such as "honorable" has been emptied of its established meaning, the dream employs a sensory form of knowledge, a literal envisioning of Caesar's fate. In its opposition to linguistic codes and in its emphasis on an experiential base of knowledge, the dream suggests the Kristevan semiotic and the corresponding "rejection of the symbolic" (p. 24).

The dream discovers an image that condenses two opposite conceptions of Caesar, monumental and vulnerable. In terms of plot and symbol, *Julius Caesar* proceeds on a developed contrast between the idea or reputation of Caesar—what Brutus calls his "spirit" (2.1.169), what is represented on stage by the ghost, what the conspirators fear but fail to destroy—and the mortal man to whom this created, mythic identity is attached, whose physical weaknesses Shakespeare underscores. Considered in these dualistic terms, the power Caesar retains after his death—imaged in the ghost and in the growing similarity Brutus and Octavius bear to him—appears a triumph of spirit over body, an affirmation that the concept of Caesarism is indeed detachable from the mortal man who is Caesar. But the attention given to Caesar's dead body, which "dominates the scene for almost 450 lines after his death,"[28] contradicts the relatively simple vision of Stoic triumph. With Brutus' command, "Stoop, Romans, stoop, / And let us bathe our hands in Caesar's blood / Up to the elbows" (3.1.105-07), the body becomes the central prop in the highly self-conscious series of political dramas through which the conspirators and triumvirs attempt to grasp power. Antony vows to Caesar's body ("O, pardon me, thou bleeding piece of earth" [3.1.254]) his curse of vengeance. And whereas Brutus' dispassionate funeral oration discusses Caesar in terms of typically Roman abstractions (love, fortune, valor, ambition), Antony combines his simple and provocative irony with repeated reference to Caesar's body.[29]

Yet Antony's focus on the body betrays nothing of what could be called visceral sympathy. His attentions are strictly purposive and performative. When he asks the crowd to "Bear with me. / My heart is in the coffin there with Caesar" (3.2.105-06), Antony draws attention squarely to himself, not to Caesar or Caesar's body. The corpse demonstrates the conspirators' "bloody treason" (3.2.192) and occasions Antony's own show of nobility. Antony introduces to the plebeians the iconic dimension of Caesar's corpse:

> Let but the commons hear this testament,
> Which (pardon me) I do not mean to read,
> And they would go and kiss dead Caesar's wounds
> And dip their napkins in his sacred blood;
> Yea, beg a hair of him for memory.
>
> (3.2.130-34)

After rousing the crowd to a frenzy by enumerating the separate holes in Caesar's mantle and graphically locating the scene of the murder "at the base of Pompey's statue" (188), Antony displays the "piteous spectacle" (198) of the body itself. His use of the corpse contributes importantly to his successful manipulation of the crowd. Caesar's body, a prop used to demonstrate Antony's purposeful interpretation of the assassination, becomes the equivalent of the augurs' beast, a sign capable of demonstrating multiple, conflicting meanings. Antony's detailed account of the murder has doubtful veracity, since he himself fled from the scene of the crime.[30] But with a genius for the theatrical, he realizes the capacity of the graphically wounded body to verify ideas—here, his reading of the assassination as "bloody treason"—placed in conjunction with it.[31] To solidify his audience's own part in this visceral process, Antony attributes to them a capacity for emotion, figured as possession of a physical interior, and hence a reality corresponding to Caesar's wounded corpse. Prohibiting them from responding unemotionally, he says, "You are not wood, you are not stones, but men; / And being men, hearing the will of Caesar, / It will inflame you, it will make you mad" (3.2.142-44). His references to their "tears" (169), their "spirits" (228), and his own ability "To stir men's blood" (223) likewise attribute to the plebeians a visceral source of authentic response.

As a result of Antony's attentions, Caesar's body is freighted with enormous significance by the end of the second funeral oration. This accretion of meaning to the body compounds the question of Caesar's identity: as Hamlet might put it, is Caesar "with the body"? Theatrical presentation erases some degree of body-soul dualism, since the same actor will ordinarily portray the living Caesar and his ghost. But how completely does the theatrical condition, in which Caesar's spirit is embodied and the actor's body spiritualized, destory the initial conception of Caesar's body and soul as separate? The difficulty is not simply presentational, and not limited to knowing Caesar; rather, as Fisch puts it, "the real question is whether we can speak of identities at all" (p. 601). In *Julius Caesar,* the general inability of central characters to acknowledge the separate reality of others renders identity an opaque and illusive concept. William O. Scott, writing on the play's current of philosophical skepticism, observes: "Self-knowledge involves self-reference, and in both processes the subject and object fail to coincide."[32] In the midst of such a crisis of knowledge, Calphurnia's dream presents a decided contrast with other impressions of Caesar, for the dream image spans the contested notions of Caesar as myth and Caesar as mortal man.

In its concern with the ritualized production of political authority, *Julius Caesar* questions the notion of stable historical identity, and emblematizes its doubts in the image of the bleeding statue.[33] The fixity of monumental art is betrayed by blood, by the body's separateness from the symbolic order (Thus the bleeding statue bears a certain analogy to the theatrical presentation of the "monumental" text.) Statues provide "a metaphor for identity,"[34] and the bleeding statue precisely figures constructed, contingent, and vulnerable identity. Within the play, Shakespeare gives this awareness to Calphurnia alone. Calphurnia dreams of Caesar as statue because she fears for the public, monumental Caesar; yet she realizes the private Caesar's inseparability from that role, as Brutus had, at least momentarily, when he acknowledged how "Caesar must bleed for it" (2.1.171). The conspirators forget or disregard Caesar's vulnerability, granting him, with the act of assassination, the very power they fear he will seize.[35] Ultimately the world of physical consequences belies the goals and ambitions of the conspirators; their monumental aspirations are revealed as ideologies of power that can disregard human identity and human life. Dreaming of the body, Calphurnia foresees such an outcome.

By attributing this dream to Calphurnia, Shakespeare suggests her independence from the linguistic order. The dream image, positing a vital interior to the public monument, uses graphic (rather than linguistic) terms to undo the opposition between Caesar and "Caesarism." Immediately upon the translation of the dream image into words, conflicting theories of its meaning cloud the response she proposes. Decius Brutus' cunning interpretation, in which "blood" becomes a reviving substance and the wounded body a source of "tinctures, stains, relics" (2.2.88-89), illustrates the instability and danger inherent in language. Calphurnia's dream offers a model of an intuitive understanding, one presented as epistemologically prior to language, one able to acknowledge the differences that manifest another person. Validated within the play by the realization of her prophecy, Calphurnia's dream stands in essential contrast to the play's dubiously realized constructions of character as myth or political authority.

I may well be one of the first ever to suggest Calphurnia as a role model of any sort, but at least in terms of the issue of knowing other people, she seems preferable to the other Romans in Shakespeare's play. Theories of character are compromised by the poor fit between mind and body, yet *Julius Caesar* teaches us to eschew Brutus' lofty goal with its tragic consequence: "O that we then could come by Caesar's spirit / And not dismember Caesar! But, alas, / Caesar must bleed for it" (2.1.169-71). The play shows violence to be the inevitable if unintentional result of an attempt, like Brutus', to grasp another's spirit, or to subordinate another to one's own political vision. Attending to the theater's physical dynamic, in effect we join Calphurnia in dreaming of the body. Character, viewed as an other that is partially coextensive with the otherness within the self, is rendered a more contradictory and vulnerable proposition, since however real our dreams may be, we can never be entirely certain what they mean.

Notes

1. Richard Rorty, *Philosophy and the Mirror of Nature* (Princeton, 1979), p. 239. This essay originated as a seminar paper at the Shakespeare Association of America meeting in Vancouver, March 1992, and was presented at the South Atlantic Modern Language

Association meeting in Atlanta, November, 1992. An earlier related paper was presented at the Patristic, Medieval, and Renaissance convention in Villanova, September 1990. Thanks to various audience members for helpful suggestions, and to Wendy Clein, David Kranz, and John Traverse for their comments on the manuscript.

2. Roland Barthes, "The Romans in Films" in *Mythologies,* trans. Annette Lavers (New York, 1972), p. 26.

3. Quotations from Shakespeare's plays refer to Alfred Harbage's *Complete Works* (Baltimore, 1969).

4. In Plutarch's account Portia wounds herself and falls into a resulting fever before confronting Brutus, who is "amazed to hear" what she has done (See *Shakespeare's Plutarch,* ed. C. F. Tucker Brooke [New York, 1909], vol. 1, p. 127). In Shakespeare's text, Brutus' shocked response ("O ye gods") may indicate that Portia actually wounds herself onstage, although my interpretation does not turn on this production decision. Even if Portia refrains from showing the wound (showing it would have raised interesting problems of staging in the Elizabethan theater) and simply gestures toward the site of a previous injury, she uses her body as a crucial signifier, thus setting its meanings into action on stage.

5. *Julius Caesar,* by William Shakespeare, ed. T. S. Dorsch (London, 1955), p. lix.

6. Reuben A. Brower, *Hero and Saint: Shakespeare and the Graeco-Roman Heroic Tradition* (Oxford, 1971), p. 212.

7. G. Wilson Knight, *The Imperial Theme: Further Interpretations of Shakespeare's Tragedies Including the Roman Plays,* 1931 (London, 1951), p. 72.

8. Clifford Ronan, "Lucan and the Self-Incised Voids of *Julius Caesar,*" *Comparative Drama* 22:3 (1988), 222.

9. Robert Miola, *Shakespeare's Rome* (New York, 1983), p. 95.

10. Madelon Sprengnether, "Annihilating Intimacy in *Coriolanus,*" in *Women in the Middle Ages and the Renaissance: Literary and Historical Perspectives,* ed. Mary Beth Rose (Syracuse, 1986), p. 96.

11. David Kranz, private correspondence.

12. Gail Kern Paster, "'In the spirit of men there is no blood': Blood as Trope of Gender in *Julius Caesar,*" *Shakespeare Quarterly* 40:3 (1989), 292.

13. M. D. Faber, "Lord Brutus' Wife: A Modern View," *Psychoanalytic Review* 52 (1965-66), 109.

14. Julia Kristeva, "Women's Time," trans. Alice Jardine and Harry Blake, *Signs: Journal of Women in Culture and Society* 7:1 (1981), 28.

15. Sigmund Freud, "Hysterical Phantasies and Their Relation to Bisexuality," in *Dora: An Analysis of a Case of Hysteria* (New York, 1963), p. 151; quoted by Clare Kahane, "Hysteria, Feminism, and the Case of *The Bostonians,*" in *Feminism and Psychoanalysis,* ed. Richard Feldstein and Judith Roof (Ithaca, 1989), p. 284.

16. Charles Bernheimer, "Introduction: Part 1," in *In Dora's Case: Freud—Hysteria—Feminism,* ed. Bernheimer and Kahane (New York, 1985), p. 1.

17. Quoted by Bernheimer, p. 4.

18. Hélène Cixous and Catherine Clément, *The Newly Born Woman,* trans. Betsy Wing (Minneapolis, 1986), p. 95.

19. Harold Fisch, "Character as Linguistic Sign," *New Literary History* 21:3 (1990), 593-606.

20. Alessandro Serpieri, "Reading the Signs: Towards a Semiotics of Shakespearean Drama," trans. Keir Elam, in *Alternative Shakespeares,* ed. John Drakakis (New York, 1985), p. 122.

21. Leo Kirschbaum, "Shakespeare's Stage Blood and Its Critical Significance," *PMLA* 64 (1949), 528.

22. Elaine Scarry, *The Body in Pain: The Making and Unmaking of the World* (New York, 1985), p. 4.

23. Sheila Murnaghan, "Body and Voice in Greek Tragedy," *The Yale Journal of Criticism* 1:2 (1988), 23.

24. Hélène Cixous, "The Character of 'Character,'" *New Literary History* 5:2 (1974), 396.

25. Johannes Fabian, "Presence and Representation: The Other and Anthropological Writing," *Critical Inquiry* 16:4 (1990), 770, 771.

26. Herbert Blau makes a similar point in his *The Audience* (Baltimore, 1990). Blau objects to sympathy as that which "draws things toward each other in an affinity that wants to intensify until it is nothing but the Same, so that likeness loses its difference through an assimilative power" (p. 301), but concludes that "there is more to be said for empathy than might be deduced from the critique of psychological realism or the values of bourgeois humanism that it represents" (p. 374). He suggests that theater be considered "an extension of the body's capacity *to perceive*" (p. 377).

27. Brooke, vol. 1, p. 97.

28. Maurice Charney, *Shakespeare's Roman Plays: The Function of Imagery in the Drama* (Cambridge, Mass., 1961), p. 52.

29. Charney observes that "the body plays a conspicuous role during Antony's funeral oration" (p. 52). Gayle Greene notes Antony's use of "techniques and props to supplement the verbal: the will, the bloody mantle, and the body" ("'The Power of Speech / To Stir Men's Blood': The Language of Tragedy in Shakespeare's *Julius Caesar,*" *Renaissance Drama* 11 [1980], 86).

30. Much here depends on staging, of course—the point at which Antony flees will determine the reliability of his account in the funeral oration.

31. Repeatedly the play illustrates Scarry's point that the body is used "to confirm the truth of [a] verbal assertion . . . when there is a crisis of substantiation" (p. 127).

32. William O. Scott, "The Speculative Eye: Problematic Self-Knowledge in 'Julius Caesar,'" *Shakespeare Survey* 40 (1988), 82.

33. In a compelling reading of *Julius Caesar,* James R. Siemon sees Shakespeare's treatment of the assassination as fundamentally iconoclastic in destabilizing established views of the Roman hero (*Shakespearean Iconoclasm* [Berkeley, 1985]). It is iconoclasm's task "to drive home the merely arbitrary status of specific symbolism" (p. 143). Siemon's argument has important ramifications for Shakespeare's treatment of historical myth, although I would argue that drama cannot in the final (theatrical) analysis be iconoclastic, since it continually offers images and dignifies them by their stage presence. Dramatic presence—the conjunction in the actor of the signified (the role) and signifier (the body)—anchors meaning inextricably to the physical realm.

34. Ralph Berry, *Shakespeare and the Awareness of the Audience* (New York, 1985), p. 78.

35. As Lynn de Gerenday puts it, "Through the assassination [the conspirators] ironically establish Caesarism, thus empowering the spirit they sought to destroy" ("Play, Ritualization, and Ambivalence in *Julius Caesar,*" *Literature and Psychology* 24 [1974], 29).

Dennis Bathory (essay date 1996)

SOURCE: "'With Himself at War': Shakespeare's Roman Hero and the Republican Tradition," in *Shakespeare's Political Pageant: Essays in Literature and Politics,* edited by Joseph Alulis and Vickie Sullivan, Rowman & Littlefield, 1996, pp. 237-61.

[*In the following essay, Bathory examines the relationship between self-knowledge and politics in* Julius Caesar *and* Coriolanus, *and elucidates the affinity between Brutus's self-delusion and the collapse of the Roman Republic.*]

> "We make out of the quarrel with others, rhetoric, but of the quarrel with ourselves, poetry."
>
> —William Butler Yeats

Shakespeare's challenge to Roman republicanism suggests that the political virtue upon which Rome rested was well suited to Rome's imperial foreign policy but was less well suited to its domestic politics. Honor not justice provides the political foundation of the Roman Republic. The Roman tradition had led time and again to the forging of internal peace in time of domestic crisis by going to war with a foreign enemy. This strategy, Shakespeare suggests, failed to educate either Roman leaders or citizens in the most important lessons of politics—the arts of sustaining a regime while simultaneously sustaining the virtue of its citizens. Shakespeare knew that Rome was touted as a model worthy of emulation, and he was clearly skeptical. His examination of the virtues and vices of the Roman Republic is most clear in two plays, one set at the very beginning of the Republic and one set near its demise—*Coriolanus* and *Julius Caesar.*

Julius Caesar was written first, near the end of the Elizabethan era; *Coriolanus* was written a decade later, at the dawn of the Jacobean era. Thus Shakespeare, not, I think, coincidentally, writes of dramatic Roman transitions in the midst of transitions equally dramatic in his own world.[1] Shakespeare's sophisticated skepticism reaches to the heart of the Roman Republic as he describes the central character in Julius Caesar. "Brutus, with himself at war" (1.2.46) provides us with a remarkably contemporary look at the dilemmas of the political reformer/revolutionary.[2] Shakespeare in his development first of Brutus and later of Coriolanus tells us of the danger of such internal, psychic warfare, not simply to frame the tragedy that befalls each, but to introduce as well the problems that all republican leaders have to face in times of rapid change and crisis. They have need (always, but especially in such times) of resources that Rome could not provide.

The need for solace and strength, and even more, for self-examination and self-evaluation on the part of leaders of republics in the midst of change and crisis is profoundly central to Shakespeare's stories. Confronted with the problem of republican virtue, many, including Niccolò Machiavelli, would attempt to substitute institutional arrangements for virtue as a support for the republic. For Shakespeare, Rome's lesson led to a call for a better political virtue, one based on self-reflection. Self-reflection permits a public language that introduces the possibility of accommodation among the various conflicting parts of the city. The danger in Rome, Shakespeare understood, was that, having defeated all foreign enemies, Caesar would, and Augustus did, forge Roman unity by denying Roman freedom. For Shakespeare, the person and the torment of Brutus frames the discussion. Brutus fails in his efforts to save the Republic because he does not understand the need to educate Rome to a better political virtue. Rome had offered little instruction in such education and for all his republican spirit, Brutus had little alternative save to exercise the sound but limited and ultimately self-defeating strategy of joining the conspiracy to assassinate Caesar. These powerful lessons, important for Shakespeare's audience, are no less important for contemporary audiences.

Shakespeare offers us a "mirror of republics" to replace the medieval "mirror of princes." What is needed, he suggests, is not only a place for reflection removed from the chaos of rapidly changing public opinion, but also the means to engage in that reflection consistent with obligations to the common good. If the problem of the leader's ability to get good advice is ancient and common to all cultures, so is the problem of the leader finding time to himself to reflect. The need for self-examination even, or especially, in the face of extreme pressure, deadlines, and crises has never been more obvious. The need for leaders to confront public opinion and to offer wise counsel to those whom they lead seems to be ever more difficult. These plays address such problems and offer wisdom to our age as well as Shakespeare's. They suggest that poets and storytellers may have much to offer us as well. Western political science has always known this, but it has not always acted on what it knows. We need stories about politics, but we need to tell them to one another in ways that facilitate understanding across times and cultures.

Political Knowledge and Knowledge of the Self

Shakespeare's teaching about Roman politics in *Julius Caesar* and *Coriolanus* addresses the relationship between self-knowledge and political knowledge. The inability of major characters in each play to come to terms with their *selves* leads them to make critical, self-defeating, ultimately tragic political errors. This is particularly true of Marcus Brutus, whose role in the conspiracy against Julius Caesar masks a fundamental lack of self-knowledge, and of Coriolanus, whose lack of self-reflection leads to unthinking action that destroys his political opportunity. In each case, the Roman hero,[3] as portrayed by Shakespeare, "confronts" inner turmoil or self-doubt by turning to decisive external action that masks internal tension and uncertainty.

Shakespeare thus develops in these and other characters a parallel between their personal crises and Rome's centuries-old tradition (habit) of turning to foreign warfare—both conquest and defense—to mask domestic faction. In this pattern, domestic politics was continually challenged by disorder, and order was reclaimed by the discipline required in time of war or by an emerging Roman legalism. The relationship between domestic and foreign politics was thus dominated by the foreign and external; domestic politics was left on unsure footing for the Republic and for its leaders. Shakespeare asks us to reflect on the relationship between the internal and the external through his portrayal of individual characters, who turn to the "outside" to solve their individual, internal problems. The inability of individuals to recognize the important link between self-knowledge and political knowledge leaves internal strife unaddressed and makes political life sometimes difficult, sometimes tragic, and always confused. The relationship between the internal and external—both for the individual and the state—is thus dramatized in these plays and presented as a central political problem.

Marcus Brutus, leader of the conspiracy against Julius Caesar, the "noblest Roman of them all" (5.5.68)—Brutus, "with himself at war,"—is the central political figure in Shakespeare's Roman plays.[4] Well respected by Romans of all classes, Brutus reveals both the politics of Rome in crisis and Shakespeare's understanding of that politics. Yet, if this is so—and if as some have suggested, the Romans were the "greatest political people who ever lived"[5]—what is Shakespeare's teaching about politics, Roman and otherwise? Brutus—"with himself at war"—makes a number of critical errors of judgment and surely fails in his stated goal of saving the Republic. If "the noblest Roman of them all" could not save the Republic, then who or what could have? Had Roman republican politics run its course? Is this simple and obvious teaching the core of Shakespeare's tragedy, and, thus, of his understanding of Roman politics?[6]

Brutus *is* central to Shakespeare's teaching, but he must not be judged, simply, through Mark Antony's praise, words that must, after all, be filtered through Antony's own prism.[7] Brutus's speeches provide a more apt point of departure. But, Brutus's "war" with himself is complex. To be sure, Shakespeare invites us to consider the obvious source of this psychological "war." Torn *between his* loves for Caesar and Rome, Brutus reports that the reason he conspired against Caesar was "not that [he] loved Caesar less, but that [he] loved Rome more" (3.2.21-22). Resolved to overcome his personal, internal civil war, Brutus takes the lead in planning the assassination. His *words* frame the *deed.* The conspirators must be "sacrificers, but not butchers," he counsels, so that it will be the "spirit of Caesar" that is assaulted, not his body (2.1.166-67). His self-deception will haunt him throughout the play. To save Rome he must change Rome, not just Caesar's power over Rome. His war with himself as a Roman requires a change of Rome that would, as well, require a change in Brutus. Before he can change Rome he must change himself, and before he can change himself he must "see" himself.

Shakespeare's teaching of Roman politics begins with Brutus because he understands that Brutus's confusion is Rome's. To a great extent Rome was always (at least in times of peace) with *itself* at war. Roman politics—both external warfare and party politics at home—depended on an understanding of conflict, latent and manifest. The failure of Shakespeare's Roman heroes to understand the subtlety of that conflict is common to both the beginning and the end of the Republic, to his portrayal of Roman politics in both *Julius Caesar* and *Coriolanus.* Coriolanus, at war with the "many-headed multitude" (2.3.15) of Rome, was equally "with himself at war." The Roman world, in which he sought honor, had changed. Like Brutus he failed to understand the extent of the change and the need to change himself in the face of these changes. Political judgment requires, Shakespeare teaches, self-awareness. Complex and difficult under any circumstances, the Roman world made the process of self-examination even more difficult.

From its origin, recorded in myth and history, Rome's was a heterogeneous and syncretic culture.[8] Incorporating different language and cultures and conflicting religious

William Macready as Cassius and Edward Loomis Davenport as Brutus in Act IV, scene iii of Julius Caesar, *engraving.*

practices, Rome was from the very beginning a centrifugal society, threatening always to fly apart from the center. A turn inward—to Rome's origins, to its original disorder—was always difficult, potentially fragmenting. Roman conquest exacerbated the centrifugal tendencies making self-examination at once more difficult and more dangerous—difficult because Rome constantly changed, dangerous because it highlighted the tenuous connection any one individual had to *romanitas.*[9] The temptation to look outward for "solace" was powerful and almost always overwhelmed an invitation to self-examination.[10] The republican transitions emphasized in each play exacerbate the problem from Shakespeare's vantage point.

Through the intervention of family and friends, fellow patricians and soldiers, Shakespeare seems to urge the protagonists to look more carefully at their politics and themselves.[11] All lessons about the relation of the self to the community, the noble individual to the broader *res publica,* fail. In part this is the result of life in the city, which must be plural, conflicting, faction ridden. The "conquest" of this disorder may be beyond human capacity. An acceptance of its limitations *and* an ability to work within those limits are, however, necessary. Politics is of the city, and being of the city, Brutus and Coriolanus are, willy nilly, political and must confront conflict. However, they must also understand the internal implications and reflections of that conflict.

The self in Shakespeare's Roman construction is ridden with "faction." But how does Shakespeare suggest confronting that factional division? The alternatives are three: 1) Attempt to overcome "war" with the self by turning one's attention away from internal conflict and artificially "unifying" the self through confrontation with an external enemy. This solution, Shakespeare implies, involves the self-delusion that haunted not only Brutus and Coriolanus but Caesar, Antony, and others as well. 2) Escape internal conflict by escaping politics. That alternative—one Thomas Hobbes would promote in England later in the seventeenth century—was one that Octavius, become Caesar Augustus, would embrace in Rome. Shakespeare's coolness toward Octavius is clear in both *Julius Caesar* and in *Antony and Cleopatra* so that he seems to have rejected the Augustan alternative.[12] 3) Accept the enduring reality of conflict, both external and internal, and fashion an accommodation to it. This last, which Shakespeare seems to recommend, requires careful instruction and the creation of a perspective that his Roman heroes lack.

While instruction in "policy" and "process," in rhetoric and political tactics is, of course, found within the plays, the perspective required for self-examination is that of the poet. Shakespeare addresses the problem of faction, internal and external, not to offer a solution to the Roman republican dilemma but to make his audience aware of issues that the Roman ear could not, or would not hear.

Brutus and Cassius: At War with Rome

"[P]oor Brutus, with himself at war, / Forgets the shows of love to other men," says Brutus to Cassius (1.2.46-47). He has been with Julius Caesar. Now, alone with Cassius, he is distracted. This is not, he says, due to anything that Cassius has done, but "I turn the trouble of my countenance / Merely upon myself" (1.2.38-39). The problem, as Cassius makes him understand, is that he cannot see himself, "for the eye sees not itself, / But by reflection, by some other things" (1.2.52-53). But, who or what will reveal Brutus to himself? Cassius "modestly" offers to be his "glass," to "discover . . . / That of [himself] which [he] yet know[s] not of" (1.2.68-70). But Cassius's needs and those of Brutus are different and Cassius's instruction will prove wanting.

Cassius's "Epicurean" opinion offers little thoughtful "policy" to Brutus's "Stoicism" (5.1.77-106).[13] Brutus steadfastly defends "honor" and the "general good," but he wonders at Cassius: "wherefore do you hold me here so long? / What is it that you would impart to me?" (1.2.83-84). He would not, it appears, impart anything about Brutus. Cassius's "glass" reflects himself (Cassius), *not Brutus.* Brutus learns something of the case that Cassius puts before him. He is moved by Cassius's summary report of Caesar's ingratitude and injustice. Politically, Brutus is challenged; indeed, he says:

> Brutus had rather be a villager
> Than to repute himself a son of Rome
> Under these hard conditions as this time
> Is like to lay upon us.
>
> (1.2.172-75)

But, of himself, he has learned little. The war raging inside needs a weighing of the "hard conditions" that is more thoughtful than that to which he is led by Cassius's "mirror."

"Noble Brutus" is needed by Cassius and his words are meant to pull the "warring" parts of Brutus together in the service of the conspiracy, not to bring "peace" to Brutus's internal war, certainly not to make him "well in health" (1.3.141 and 2.1.257). Cassius is, of course, successful and Brutus's resolve delivers him "wholly" to the conspirators, though it does not make him whole. Cassius notes that "three parts of him / Is ours already," his search for "the man entire" (1.3.154-55) is a search for an accomplice, one whose nobility will legitimate their cause; he is not concerned for Brutus's inner well-being. Brutus's malaise, all the while, grows. He compares the "state of a man" to "a little kingdom" that suffers "the nature of an insurrection" and describes his waking hours as a "hideous dream" (2.1.65, 67-69). Aware of the task that awaits he urges "smiles and affability" lest his inner turmoil betray a "monstrous visage" (2.1.81-82). But he *appears* focused as he directs the conspiracy and defines its spirit. There is no need to include Cicero he insists, nor to punish Mark Antony (2.1.150-61). The conspirators need not swear an "oath" among themselves, given the strength of what he calls the "even virtue of our enterprise" (2.1.114, 133). Again, they will be "sacrificers," not "butchers." Ironically, his recently expressed fear of Caesar—that "Th' abuse of greatness is, when it disjoins / Remorse from power"—is lost, masked in his carefully chosen, but self-deceptive words (2.1.166, 18-19).[14]

Theirs is a "purely" ordained enterprise, though it must be undertaken with the skills of "Roman actors." The dilemma, as Shakespeare conveys it, is still apparent: Caesar has become Rome and Rome must be saved from itself, but will Rome consent to be "saved"? Brutus wars *with* Rome and *against* Rome as he leads the conspiracy and, so, as a noble Roman is still "with himself at war." It is Portia who recognizes the "actor" and his "act" and "some sick offense within [his] mind" (2.1.268). She is his "glass," the mirror he needs to reflect his discontent, to anticipate and appreciate the consequences, still unrecognized and clearly unanticipated. Portia sees what Brutus cannot or will not. Unlike Cassius who seeks to manipulate his discontent, Portia seeks the source of his "sickness." The "right and virtue of [her] place" requires that she know his secret. Though "I am a woman," she persists, I am "well reputed" and presumably well able to help (2.1.269, 294-95). Brutus has, however, turned his attention away from the "domestic." Like Rome in time of crisis, this "little kingdom," suffering from "insurrection," turns its attention to the outside. The answer to his enduring illness, he says to Ligarius after Portia has left, is "A piece of work that will make sick men whole" (2.1.327). But, like Rome's centuries-old politics, the turn to external warfare leaves internal conflict unresolved. Brutus's anxiety reemerges as he meets with Caesar and the final pieces of the conspiracy are assembled. Caesar compels Brutus to consider the full scope of his role as a "Roman actor." "We (like friends) will straightway go together," says Caesar to the conspirators (2.2.126). Brutus, uneasy with his deception, replies in an aside: "That every like is not the same, O Caesar, / The heart of Brutus yearns to think upon" (2.2.128-29). But little thought is given. Shakespeare makes it clear that Brutus's only true "mirror," Portia, with "a man's mind, but a woman's might," is unable to encourage Brutus's self-examination (2.4.8).

The result is self-delusion as Shakespeare reveals in act 3, scene 2. The assassination plot accomplished, Brutus turns to the plebeians gathered in the forum. Restless, they await explanation of the murder of the man to whom they would, so recently, have given a crown. Brutus's eloquence marks both his position and his naiveté (as well as Shakespeare's poetic genius as he sets up Antony's speech to follow). It is "not that I loved Caesar less," he says, "but that I loved Rome more" (3.2.21-22). For a moment the crowd is appeased, but Brutus has sorely overestimated them. They do not share his "nobility," as Antony's ironic defense of Caesar's "ambitions" makes clear. He cleverly appeals to the greedy "ambitions" of an audience he knows far better than Brutus does. Whipped into a frenzy with promises of a "rich legacy" bequeathed to them by Caesar, the crowd is quickly turned against Brutus. The task of Brutus and the conspirators was far greater than the "mere" assassination of Caesar.

Caesar's "spirit" had a monetary value far greater to this Roman audience than Brutus's noble sentiments about Rome and Roman freedom. It was this "spirit," which Brutus obviously did not anticipate and apparently did not understand, that threatened Rome as surely as Caesar's impending dictatorship. The question for the conspirators, for Rome, for Shakespeare and for Shakespeare's audience was the same: How to conquer that "spirit"? Brutus was right to say that it was the "spirit" of Caesar that had to be conquered (2.1.167), but the "spirit" of the people in the streets of Rome was as well a product of Caesar's "spirit." The task of the Roman republican patriot was to educate or reeducate the people of Rome. Brutus's internal warfare blinded him to the most important challenge to his Roman nobility—the education of the Roman citizenry in the face of the changes that were, indeed, threatening the Republic that he loved. Whether or not such education was possible in the Rome of his day is less the issue than his blindness to the need for it. In a world in which foreign war could less easily provide either a common enemy around which warring domestic factions could coalesce or the booty with which to bribe the audience of Brutus and Antony, such education was necessary for the continuation of the Republic. Brutus's story is the story of Rome. Brutus is at war with himself because he fails to understand the proper nature of the relation between the parts of the community—both the community of the soul and the community of the city. He requires an understanding of both, if he is to be an effective republican leader.

Shakespeare urges us to consider the parallel between Brutus's internal war and Rome's—both turn to the outside but leave the sources of internal conflict unresolved. The result, as Jan Blits points out, is a "conception of the common good [of Rome which] lacks a public or republican spirit."[15] Shakespeare invites us to pass judgment on this shortsightedness both in *Julius Caesar,* and ten years later, when he turned to the beginning of the Republic in *Coriolanus.*

Coriolanus: At War with Himself and Rome

In turning to the beginning of the Republic in the *Tragedy of Coriolanus* Shakespeare continues his examination of Roman politics with a study of another major transition. The Republic is in its infancy, the tribunate only recently created. Caius Martius (Coriolanus), a heroic figure in the overthrow of Tarquin's tyranny, confronts the transition, as Brutus did his, with confusion and uncertainty. Again this is a world *with itself at war.* Most obviously, the plebeians are upset with the patricians. A shortage of corn has exposed class distinctions, differences that for the plebs are most clearly represented by the arrogance of Caius Martius (Coriolanus) (1.1). Yet, Caius Martius's role in the overthrow of tyranny has made the Republic possible in the first place, and the citizens know this. More, they understand the gratitude they owe him. He has only to recognize the changes in Rome and the "honor" that he craves will be granted, for, they understand, "there was never a worthier man" (2.3.36-37).

As with Brutus,[16] the problem for Coriolanus lies not only with understanding Rome's transformations but also how those changes affect him. As Rome's upheavals in the reign of Julius Caesar required Brutus to reexamine his very "self," so Rome's changes in the early days of the Republic required the same of Coriolanus.

A "worthy" man whose "chiefest virtue" is "valor," Coriolanus is a hero "by his rare example," even a man of generous spirit (2.2.35, 81-85, 102; 1.9.82-86).[17] He shuns flattery—both as flattered and flatterer. He resists the new "custom" that requires that he "speak to the people" (2.2.133), if he would be consul. He asks that he might "o'erleap that custom" (2.2.134) rightly fearing, as Shakespeare plays it out, that the public is fickle and easily manipulated. More, he articulates a suspicion of custom itself, which left unexamined can, like "the dust on antique time," lie "unswept" and leave a "mountainous error . . . too highly heaped / For truth t' o'erpeer" (2.3.114-16). Ironically though, it is the very dust of an older custom, patrician custom, that Coriolanus cannot himself "o'erpeer."

Rome has changed; it will not do to return to still older customs, especially, if he "would be consul" (2.3.126). He recognizes the danger of a political order without "purpose" (3.1.148-49), an order manipulated by the winds of public opinion that "With every minute . . . do change a mind" (1.1.177). Yet, if he would lead the new Rome, he must look inside himself and discover new resources required for a new political order. To do so, however, he, like Brutus, will need assistance.[18]

Shakespeare gives Coriolanus three "mirrors": Menenius, patrician and friend to Coriolanus; his wife, Virgilia; and, most crucially, his mother, Volumnia. None of these, however, is able to bring him face to face with himself. Menenius's teasing (and sometimes effective) rhetoric preaches "patience" to both plebeians and tribunes. His "fable," a variation on the medieval organic analogy, cleverly sets the plebeians to consider the difficulty the Senate has in meeting the needs of the "weal o' th' common" (1.1.146). His tale is at least in part successful. With words carefully crafted for their ears, he convinces the plebeians that the Senate, the "belly" in his unusual account, looks out for their interests, distributing goods even to "the great toe of this assembly" (1.1.150). It is the tribunes, however, that are his real concern. Again, his use of words is important both for *his* audience and Shakespeare's. He confronts the two tribunes, Sicinius and Junius Brutus, directly. Their power, though derivative, is great. Their "pride," however, masks "infant-like" behavior. In fact, he says, "you know neither me, yourselves, nor anything" (2.1.34-37, 62-63), and this is precisely why they are dangerous.

Menenius himself knows a great deal. Through his rhetoric he conveys and uses his knowledge to significant effect. His effectiveness is, however, limited by his position. Though his audiences respect him, he is not destined for leadership. Coriolanus's "valor," his "chiefest virtue," has made him ripe for "honor" and so for the position of leadership the Senate seeks to convey. Menenius is a shrewd analyst and has the tools, as Coriolanus's friend, to be an excellent counselor, but Coriolanus must first learn to listen. This, for all Menenius's skill, he apparently cannot teach. Menenius is direct in his counsel: ". . . go fit you to the custom and / Take to you, as your predecessors have, / Your honor with your form" (2.2.140-42).

Coriolanus will not or cannot hear him. Incapable of a "gentler spirit" Coriolanus rages at the tribunes. "Not now, not now," Menenius urges, but Coriolanus does not listen (3.1.55, 63). Failing at directly influencing him, Menenius will turn his rhetorical skills back directly against Coriolanus's antagonists. He pleads with the tribunes to "proceed by process" (3.1.313), lest they threaten the very Rome they claim to serve:

> Lo, citizens, he says he is content.
> The warlike service he has done, consider; think
> Upon the wounds his body bears, which show
> Like graves i' th' holy churchyard.
>
> (3.3.48-51)

Coriolanus's petulance continues and so prompts Menenius:

> Consider further,
> That when he speaks not like a citizen,
> You find him like a soldier. Do not take
> His rougher accents for malicious sounds,
> But, as I say, such as become a soldier,
> Rather than envy you.
>
> (3.3.52-57)

But the game is lost, for it is Coriolanus whom Menenius must engage. He cannot overpower Coriolanus's antagonists without Coriolanus's assistance, and that assistance cannot be forthcoming until Coriolanus confronts himself. But Coriolanus's pride will not permit him. Rather, his own flagrant, violent use of words deafens Coriolanus to his friend's plea. Instead, the self-destructive nature of his language ironically leads a senator to beseech: "No more words" (3.1.75).

In need of words to claim his honor, in need of words to know Rome, and in need of words to know himself, Coriolanus is instead conquered by his own "deeds." Words "debase / The nature of our seats," he says, when "deeds" should "speak" for themselves. (3.1.135-36). His understanding of the Roman world is based on "deeds." The plebeians and their tribunes are portrayed as incapable of such "deeds" and thus must have recourse to words—words that, for Coriolanus, merely flatter and deceive. To be sure, words *can* flatter and deceive and Shakespeare gives us many examples in this play. But words can also instruct and reveal. Coriolanus has not been taught this wiser use of words. In the Roman fashion he lets action speak for itself.

Rome defines itself in large part externally. Roman heroes like Brutus's "little kingdoms" define themselves externally as well.[19] The domestic "mirrors" of Caius Martius Coriolanus, like those of Brutus, are unsuccessful in their attempts to bring him face to face with himself. His wife and mother are no more able to instruct Coriolanus than was Menenius. Virgilia's traditional support of her husband reinforces all of his intransigence. Her role is to "support" him. She tells Volumnia that she will "not over the threshold till my lord return from the wars" (1.2.71-72). Her "affection" will never turn him in on himself. Her "lord and husband" is distant. She supports him but primarily "to keep [his] *name* / Living to time" through the son she bore him (5.3.37, 126-27).[20] His mother is another story.

In some ways Coriolanus is as much Volumnia's creation as he is Rome's. She taught him to "seek danger where he was like to find fame" (1.3.12-13). When he returns from battle with the Volscians, she proudly asserts: "O, he is wounded; I thank the gods for't" (2.1.113). She wants him to have fame, honor and power, but she has done her work too well. His pride in all of its excess is, in part, her creation as well. His anger, uncontrolled, lacks her "brain that leads [her] use of anger / To better vantage" (3.2.30-31). She rebukes him for being "too absolute" and counsels a combination of "honor and policy" (39, 42). He has understood that deception is necessary in time of war; she says to him:

> If it be honor in your wars *to seem*
> The same you are not . . .
> how is it less or worse,
> That it shall hold companionship in peace
> With honor, as in war. . . .
>
> (3.2.46-50)[21]

How indeed? If those he addresses in peacetime in Rome are, like his enemies in war, deceived, then they are like his enemies. Yet, they are by the *new* "custom" a part of Rome and so to war with them is to war with Rome and for Coriolanus to war with himself. However debased they may be, however contemptible, they cannot be deceived as one would deceive an enemy in war.[22]

Volumnia's advice to combine "honor and policy" is, in general, not dissimilar from that of Menenius. In its particulars, however, it is quite different. Menenius's fable creates a space for discussion of the Senate's concern for the common good. Volumnia's analogy implies civil war. Shakespeare quickly helps us to understand the source of her problem. She too prefers "deeds" over words. "Action is eloquence," she proclaims, "and the eyes of th' ignorant / More learned than the ears . . ." (3.2.76-77). Hers is not an effort to return to the organic analogy of Menenius's fable, but rather to describe a pestilence to be overcome. They are his "enemy," these common people of Rome. The only difference between them and Aufidius is that they must be flattered.[23] None of this counsel will Coriolanus hear, however, perhaps because he is too proud, perhaps because her words have been preceded by action that render them meaningless. Of the latter we can only guess, though we are later shown his reaction to his mother's action as she kneels to her now traitorous son. That she finally reaches him is clear:

> What is this?
> Your knees to me? to your corrected son?
> Then let the pebbles on the hungry beach
> Fillip the stars! Then let the mutinous winds
> Strike the proud cedars 'gainst the fiery sun,
> Murd'ring impossibility, to make
> What cannot be, slight work.
>
> (5.3.56-62)

She responds: "Thou art my warrior; / I holp to frame thee" (5.3.62-63). She has helped create a "warrior" but not a consul of Rome. Volumnia's Coriolanus lacks "purpose" save that which demands enemies and this, Shakespeare teaches, is a long-standing Roman dilemma that makes domestic politics and peace difficult.

Republican Rome can be governed neither by Coriolanus's arrogance nor by the people's "multitudinous tongue." When they stand in opposition to one another, their mutual impotence is apparent and, more, the manipulative tribunate is empowered. How then is that manipulation to be quelled? In the first place, given the fact that Rome is changing, Rome's past has to be accommodated to the new reality of the Republic and so there must be a new foundation for public authority. In this story Coriolanus becomes a representative of that past and stories of his exploits and ancestors are central to the political story that Shakespeare tells. First, Cominius, his commanding general who has named him in honor of his conquest of Corioli, speaks of Coriolanus's "deeds," of his "rare example" in fighting the tyranny of Tarquin (2.2.102). Praised as someone who in defeating Tarquin helped give rise to the Republic, his action at Corioli only confirms prior deeds and makes him clearly worthy of the consulship. In the very next scene, his recent exploits now ignored, the tribunes portray him in contrast to his illustrious ancestors (2.3.233-40). As Shakespeare plays the scene, arrogance is pitted against ignorance, and the tribunes, at least for the moment, emerge victorious.

Sicinius and Junius Brutus at once commend Coriolanus's heritage and condemn the pride that is "descended" from that very same lineage.[24] Still, their audience is beguiled, the tribunes' message has been artfully delivered. They have at once praised the past[25] (of which their Roman clients are proud) and attacked its progeny. Coriolanus is attacked as a representative of the patrician class even as that class is apparently, implicitly praised. The result for Rome is confusion, the very coin of the tribunate in this play, and the perpetuation of the world without "purpose" that Coriolanus will soon criticize.[26] But the tribunes' words have hit their mark. The citizens change their mind again, confirming both Coriolanus's analysis and the tribunes' power.

Coriolanus's republican successors will have to find their way among these portrayals of Rome's past, holding on to that which still defines Rome, while still learning to "o'erpeer" the past and the "antique dust" that clings to it. The purpose of Rome is not as easily identified as it might seem to be. It is surely beyond Virgilia's domestic support for her warrior, and Volumnia's apparent move beyond Virgilia's traditionalism does not offer the "foundation" that is needed. Moreover, republican institutions, Shakespeare insinuates, require more than Cominius's love of "valor." The question that must be asked is *the* republican question: What is the city? The tribunes respond too easily, "the people," but that begs the question, for the people are clearly muddled, in need of leadership and education (1.1. and 2.3). The tribunes manipulate and in turn risk being outmanipulated, for they manipulate without "purpose." Coriolanus cannot learn from any of these "teachers," but his successors must, if they are to be the definers of the broad "public weal" Rome requires.[27]

The dilemma is that the "public weal" will continue to be founded in part on the virtue of men like Coriolanus. The heroic ideal is still critical.[28] The hero stands for Roman honor and represents *romanitas;* but heroic action is by definition rare and exceptional, distant from ordinary citizens, whose participation in the "spirit" of Rome is generally vicarious, distant, and indirect. The problem for the Republic then is always to find leaders whose stature helps redefine *romanitas* while still making contact with the people whose greater good and glory they must represent. Such leaders must, Shakespeare seems to suggest, confront warfare—not simply warfare with external enemies, not simply the "warfare" among Roman factions in time of peace, but also the "warfare" within.[29] Rome's republicanism dictates that each of these battles continues.[30]

Rome artfully used external warfare to forge internal unity throughout the republican era. Shakespeare frames this practice from the earliest scenes of *Coriolanus* to the end of the Republic and *Julius Caesar.* Caius Martius applauds the Volscian threat to Rome: "I am glad on 't. / Then we shall ha' means to vent / Our musty superfluity" (1.1.220-21). Julius Caesar's Rome, on the other hand, has nearly used up this strategy.[31] The factional politics of the age of Caesar were not overcome by Caesar's military victories; quite the contrary.[32] Caesar's conquering majesty makes recourse to external war superfluous and unavailable; his subjection of the external "world" eliminates the "vent," which Coriolanus and many of those who followed used with great success. Lacking that vent, the "superfluities" of Roman internal politics explode. The dilemma for Marcus Brutus, Cassius, and their fellow conspirators is on one level not unlike that which Volumnia describes to her son. They, too, must combine "honor and policy." "Process" and "policy" are required, Menenius says, "lest parties . . . break out / And sack great Rome with Romans" (3.1.313-14). And from the very beginning of *Julius Caesar,* it is clear that this very problem is infecting Julius Caesar's Rome.

Several questions remain unaddressed by the Romans whether early or late in the Republic: Is shrewd political calculation enough? If it is, where will it come from, who will offer it? Of what does this calculation and advice consist? Menenius attempts to persuade his friend, but Coriolanus remains "untaught."[33] Coriolanus knows himself only in the "Senate House" (2.3.143). His mother's advice would, he says, have him be "false to [his] nature" (3.2.15). Similarly, Brutus cannot hear Portia. "Honor and policy" do not easily combine in domestic politics. Brutus's lack of "policy" is in its way, as glaring as Coriolanus's, though again Shakespeare points to a more basic dilemma. Perhaps, having killed Antony in the plot would have aided the conspirators' "purpose"[34] (3.2.147); perhaps, Cicero's oratory would have helped their cause. Shakespeare hints at both possibilities, but the fundamental problem lies elsewhere: The city requires more than "honor and policy." The pride that both accompanies honor and leads to it makes the proud and honorable reluctant to engage in "policy" and disdainful of "process." Indeed, the proud and honorable are not predisposed by "nature," Shakespeare suggests, to "policy" and "process" within the city. The justness of their common cause leads time and again to honorable victory over external enemies. Justice, within the city and in the soul of the Roman hero, is, however, more difficult to discover.

Times of crisis such as those portrayed in both plays merely emphasize problems endemic to the Roman republican world. With themselves at war, Shakespeare's Roman heroes find tragic ends. Merely to adapt, cunningly, to the times is inadequate. As Aufidius ironically notes, "Our virtues lie / In th' interpretation of the time" (4.7.49-50). The virtue of Shakespeare's Roman hero is not well suited to peacetime. Honor, not justice, is the hallmark of Rome. Coriolanus's crudeness would be cosmetically hidden; Roman leaders would learn to flatter and be flattered, but they would not come to know themselves as leaders of the Roman public in peacetime. Rome could not teach these lessons; Shakespeare could and did.

The citizens of Rome, both at the beginning and at the end of the Republic, required more than flattery. Republican virtue could be manipulated, even subverted, by rhetoric's flattery. Coriolanus was right to be suspicious.[35] It is, however, one thing to be aware of the limits, and even the corrupting dangers, of rhetoric and another to dismiss the Roman public because of its need to flatter and be flattered. Shakespeare understands that rhetoric is needed to make contact with that public—to educate it as well as to manipulate it. He knew of the temptation to misuse rhetoric and explored the narrow line between education and manipulation. He suggested that the leader must proceed with great caution or risk his own undoing. Neither Brutus nor Coriolanus understood the self-defeating consequences of their "deeds." At war with themselves they were unable to establish a relationship with Rome that successful leadership required. Neither flatterers nor educators, their political efforts were destined to fail.

The Roman military-political strategy was a brilliant one, enduring for centuries; but Roman politics was, as Shakespeare's Roman plays invite us to consider, radically incomplete. The Roman hero at once contributed to that incompleteness, was a victim of it, and was symptomatic of a broader Roman political dilemma. With deeds that turned attention away from internal strains, the hero unwittingly lets those strains fester, offering a powerful palliative—but a palliative nonetheless. Also victimized by his very distance, the Roman hero had both to be an exceptional individual and to subordinate himself to the greater good of the Republic, which included, throughout the Republic's long history, an appeal to those intimidated by and often jealous of his "deeds." In the end Shakespeare insinuates a tragedy beyond that of his hero. Rome itself is the victim, for republican Rome, defined by the hero, is defeated by the hero's success—the success of Julius Caesar. The problem is constant: the force of the "lion's" honor can only be masked, cosmetically hidden, by the "fox-like" cunning of "policy." The combination of the lion and the fox is, for Shakespeare, incomplete. It is not enough for Coriolanus to learn to be cunning, nor for Brutus to learn political tactics. The greatness of the Romans reveals lessons that only the philosopher or the poet can complete. The Romans lacked both philosophic and poetic spirit. There was little room for either in their public world.

Shakespeare offers to his England, and perforce to us, what seemingly could not be offered to Rome. What Portia could not accomplish with Brutus, what Menenius and Volumnia lacked the capacity to convey to Coriolanus, Shakespeare introduced to his English audiences. Shakespeare thus becomes a mirror for an audience he hopes will look into its own "eye" as it learns to listen to words that counsel self-examination.

Conclusion: Shakespeare's "Mirror of Republics"

Shakespeare's language is in some ways an antidote to republican Rome's self-destructive words. Stephen Coote argues that in *Coriolanus* "language—which should be the bond of civil community—has been used as an instrument to tear it apart."[36] Shakespeare's brief is for more than "policy" and "process" and the rhetoric they require. The people, whose corruption is the key to these plays, require more than the palliative of Menenius's fable. Still in need of education at the close of the Republic, the Romans are unable to hear either their tribunes or Marcus Brutus. They listen to Mark Antony's artful deception, but his rhetoric lacks the requisite nobility, at least insofar as that "nobility" is meant to create "the bond of the civil community."[37]

The modern state, following Machiavelli's lead, lowered the stakes of honor and raised "policy" to new heights. Shakespeare resists the shift even as he criticized the excesses of "honor." It was never enough simply to temper the "lion's" honor with the "fox's" cunning. Shakespeare does not applaud Octavius's Roman solution. Shakespeare presents Caesar Augustus, Bloom writes, as a man who was "no hero [but] a dry opportunist with the capacity for neither loving nor fighting."[38] Whatever his success in Rome, Octavius gets no commendation from Shakespeare. It is, of course, Octavius who puts Brutus's nobility in perspective when, immediately following Antony's praise of the "noblest Roman of them all," Octavius closes the play by replying: "According to his virtue let us use him . . ." (5.5.76). New modes and orders were introduced by Caesar Augustus, but they are not endorsed by Shakespeare. As the "stillness of the Augustan peace" approaches, Shakespeare reveals, as Michael Platt has argued, a world "as stale and motionless as a 'gilded puddle.'"[39]

For Shakespeare's own more positive message, we must return to Aufidius's reminder that "our virtues / Lie in th' interpretation of the time . . ." (4.7.49-50). Shakespeare would have his audience reexamine Roman republicanism in order to reevaluate it on its own terms and theirs. Rome's was a great politics, but it was a politics that absorbed itself. Fatally limited, its example taught lessons crucial to late Elizabethan and early Jacobean audiences. *Coriolanus,* Shakespeare's last tragedy, addresses an audience well aware of the advantages and of the difficulties of "mixed government."[40] This was, however, an audience undergoing profound social changes, and Shakespeare's teaching reminds them subtly of the way in which they might evaluate the "virtues" appropriate to their "time."

Shakespeare's use of Roman history for this purpose is in sharp contrast to that of his Renaissance predecessor, Niccolò Machiavelli. Shakespeare offers a searching treatment of "antique Rome," but his "purpose" was quite different from that of Machiavelli. Though confronted with republican ideas, Shakespeare is not an uncritical republican enthusiast.[41] By the time he wrote *Coriolanus* he had begun to hear of James I's unflattering descriptions of puritans as "Tribunes of the people."[42] Yet Shakespeare's Roman plays cannot be labeled defenses of monarchy—Roman, "divine right," or otherwise. Not a "modern" in the sense that he believed that significant progress in the human condition was either immanent or for that matter possible, not a republican after the fashion of Rome or Machiavelli, Shakespeare nonetheless offers counsel to an audience for whom republican images would be increasingly important. Bloom has argued that, "Shakespeare indicates that he himself possesses a spirit of acceptance. That is the way things are, and there is no hope of reforming humanity."[43] Still, his treatment of Roman republicanism is critical for the education of his audience and for others to follow.

If, as Bloom further suggests, Shakespeare's Roman hero stands out as a "public example of virtue . . . necessary for civil society,"[44] that example must convey its "virtue" to the "public." For Shakespeare the vehicle for the conveyance of public honor in Rome was complex and ambiguous, an uncertain model for his world (and so it remains). Still, for all his skepticism, his is not a Hobbesian rejection of politics. Though his audience and that of Thomas Hobbes nearly overlap, Shakespeare's analyses both of human nature and politics are far less dire. To be sure, violence is everywhere apparent in Shakespeare's republican Rome. Indeed, one might argue that the rise of Octavius is in part the result of the very exhaustion that Hobbes postulates as the result of the "fear of (violent) death."[45] A ruler, like Octavius, who in many ways relieves Romans of their *political* obligations and imposed a dry but effective Roman peace[46] on their heretofore chaotic and violent existence does, in fact, have a strikingly Hobbesian "countenance." Shakespeare seems, however, unwilling to settle for, let alone to advocate, such an undignified end to political virtue. Roman virtue created problems for Shakespeare's Roman hero not so much because political virtue and politics generally are dangerous but because they revealed particular weaknesses that Rome could not overcome. And Roman failure, Shakespeare hoped, might provide for English political education.[47]

In his way, Shakespeare is as devious in his teaching about Rome as Machiavelli but his "purpose" is quite different. Unlike Shakespeare's, Machiavelli's lessons were not, in the first instance, directed at the soul of the audience. On the contrary, Machiavelli seeks to promote "policy" and "process" in ways that avoid self-examination. He develops, as a recent commentator has suggested, a politics based on the "calculating deference and sensational performance of the elected official who relishes the opportunity to advance his ambitions. . . ."[48] Machiavelli's politics is in the end an "institutional politics," which "relies on institutions rather than virtue."[49] This offers a sharp contrast indeed with the renewal afforded Rome by the virtuous actions of its exceptional individuals.[50]

This was a more subversive "policy" than Shakespeare could accept. For Shakespeare, the inadequacy of Roman virtue rightly learned, pointed to a better understanding of political virtue and its limits, and especially, to the necessity of self-reflection. In Shakespeare's teaching, the soul remains at the center of politics. He invites us to reconsider the relationship between self-knowledge and political knowledge in at least three ways. In the simplest sense internal conflict can fog political judgment and lead to rash, self-defeating, even tragic decisions. In a second, and more complex case, when internal conflicts are directly related to political conflicts as is the case with both Brutus and Coriolanus, the possibilities for confusion and imprudence are greater. Finally, if internal conflicts are symptomatic of broader political problems (as again seems to be the case in these plays) the danger is even greater. In this situation one finds a repression of the internal and domestic. The internal is private and secondary in this more extreme rendering, and so is all the more difficult to confront; soulful reflection is a sign of "weakness" and, therefore, rejected out of hand, no matter how necessary and therapeutic it may be. Shakespeare's message is clear. Look at yourself and see what your "external" actions reflect of that self. Avoid, thereby, some of the unseen, unanticipated, and unintended consequences of action carried out for its own sake or action carried out to avoid other more painful, more private reflection.[51] Not as optimistic as Machiavelli, Shakespeare had no new science, but his poetry offered an enduring way of examining the challenges and changes of political life.

William Butler Yeats said that "We make out of the quarrel with others, rhetoric, but of the quarrel with ourselves, poetry." Unable to fathom the quarrel within themselves, poetry was unavailable to most Romans of the republican era.[52] Rome's alternative—rhetoric—was obvious, for Rome's quarrels were defined externally, they were with "others." Not of themselves aware, they were destined to be "with [themselves] at war." Shakespeare provided a "mirror" to his audience with his Roman plays, a "mirror of republics" that was in its way a successor to the "mirror of princes."[53]

Notes

1. Paul Cantor stresses the importance of these transitions in *Shakespeare's Rome: Republic and Empire* (Ithaca: Cornell University Press, 1976), 12.

2. Quotations to the plays are drawn from Alfred Harbage, ed., *William Shakespeare: The Complete Works* (New York: The Viking Press, 1977).

3. See, for example, Jan H. Blits, *The End of the Ancient Republic* (Lanham, Md.: Rowman & Littlefield, 1993), 73 for a discussion of Shakespeare's concern with Roman heroes and heroism.

4. Michael Platt, *Rome and Romans According to Shakespeare* (Lanham, Md.: University Press of America, 1983), 204-5.

5. Allan Bloom makes this point in "The Morality of the Pagan Hero," in *Shakespeare's Politics* (New York: Basic Books, 1964), 78.

6. The self-consuming nature of Roman republican politics has been the subject of many commentaries on this play: both Bloom and Platt make a strong case in this regard. J. G. A. Pocock finds a civic virtue in Rome that is strikingly different from that which Shakespeare discusses (*The Machiavellian Moment: Florentine Political Thought and the Republican Tradition* [Princeton: Princeton University Press, 1975]).

7. Antony's rhetoric is dominating but his motives are mixed at best. His manipulation of the people of Rome, far from "noble," his manipulation of the Roman political scene in the months and years that follow suggest a person whose judgment is often faulty. This is not to say that Brutus's nobility is called into question, but that its full scope is not revealed by Antony.

8. See, for example, Fustel de Coulanges, *The Ancient City* (Garden City, N.Y.: Doubleday Anchor, 1956).

9. Roman culture, of course, demanded that the self and Rome be closely identified. See, for example, Stephen Coote, *Coriolanus* (London: Penguin Books, 1992). For Shakespeare, the problem was that the "self" revealed in Rome was far too limited.

10. The failures of Portia, Calpurnia, and Volumnia to counsel Brutus, Caesar, and Coriolanus are indicative.

11. Shakespeare does not use these interventions to counsel either noble Roman to be at "peace" with himself. He understood that service to the city necessitated uncertainty, even turmoil. Indeed, to be utterly at peace would, for Shakespeare, seem to require separation from the city and so would in a sense be seditious. Shakespeare's counsel is not seditious. On the contrary, he seeks sound political judgment. Such judgment requires, for Shakespeare, knowledge of both political circumstances and of the self. Brutus's failure to examine more fully his internal conflict leads him to a series of poor political judgments. Most significantly, he misjudges the Roman people and so fails them as a leader and a patriot.

    A more careful self-examination would surely not have brought him peace, but might have permitted him to understand better than he did the complex interaction between political knowledge and knowledge of the self. This would be a problem not only for Brutus but for Coriolanus, Caesar, and Mark Antony as well. Indeed, it may be a problem endemic to Rome, symptomatic of Rome's internal crises. Shakespeare warns that self-knowledge must precede political knowledge, and so, effective political leadership.

12. See Cantor, *Shakespeare's Rome,* 204.

13. See David Lowenthal, "Shakespeare's Caesar's Plan," *Interpretation* 10 (1982) for a discussion of the Epicureanism and Stoicism of Brutus and Cassius.

14. Brutus is unaware of his own great power in these circumstances and so "disjoins" power from remorse, though in a manner quite different from Caesar's.

15. See Blits, *Ancient Republic,* 51ff.

16. Of course, the worlds of Brutus and Coriolanus are dramatically different. The tribunate, for example, greedy and self-serving in *Coriolanus,* are thoughtful and public spirited in the beginning of *Julius Caesar* (see Bloom, "Pagan Hero," 82). But, for all of the differences, Shakespeare still draws our attention to a set of common underlying themes.

17. His generosity, however, is limited. He forgets the name of the man of Corioli whom he would save.

18. See Blits, *Ancient Republic,* 3-20. See also Wilson Carey McWilliams, "Lyndon Johnson and the Politics of Mass Society," in *Leadership in America: Consensus, Corruption and Charisma,* ed. P. D. Bathory (New York: Longman, 1978), 190-91. McWilliams discusses friendship and the lack of friendship as a central component in the understanding of American political leadership, especially in the presidency of Lyndon Johnson.

19. Indeed, in the very scene in which Coriolanus rages about "deeds" and "words" he receives news of Aufidius. "Spoke he of me," asks Coriolanus (3.1.127). He apparently defines himself not only by his martial actions but also, ironically, through and by his opponents' words. A turn inside, a meeting with himself may be unnecessary in such a situation; perhaps it is even dangerous.

20. There is none of the support of the sort that Portia gives, or attempts to give, Brutus. Emphasis supplied.

21. Emphasis supplied.

22. The danger here is crucial and that Volumnia does not recognize it any more clearly than her son is telling in Shakespeare's political story.

    On the relation between "war" and domestic politics see Arlene Saxonhouse, "An Unspoken Theme in

Plato's *Gorgias:* War," *Interpretation* 11 (May 1983): 139-69. Saxonhouse argues that in this dialogue Callicles looks outside the city to relations between cities and the inclination to war among states as a model that he will use to justify the actions he would like to take within the city. That action is based on a "law of nature," which justifies inequality. In some ways the Roman "way" is similar to that of Callicles, though it is clothed in rhetoric that masks its true intention.

23. Coriolanus will soon flatter Aufidius, however, as his treachery begins. Ironically, this comes more easily than flattery of his own Romans. The *Gorgias,* again, provides an important point of reference, as Socrates' discussion of rhetoric and its reliance on flattery serves as an interesting complement to Shakespeare's analysis of Coriolanus.
24. As a descendant of Numa, however, Coriolanus can hardly be expected to bow to the plebeians with abject flattery.
25. This is presumably important to the Roman identity of these people whom Coriolanus earlier describes as liking neither "war nor peace," the one making them afraid, the other proud (1.1.175).
26. The people had forgotten the advice of the tribunes—the lessons they had been taught about Coriolanus's insolence—and have accepted Coriolanus as consul. The tribunes here try, successfully, to undo the "damage." Again the difference between the tribunate here and in *Julius Caesar* is considerable.
27. The danger here is much like that discussed by Plato in the *Gorgias.* Relying solely on rhetorical manipulation and "flattery," the tribunes risk being outmanipulated by a better rhetorician. Compare, for example, *Julius Caesar,* act 3, scene 2, and Antony's speech to the people of Rome.
28. Coote commenting on Coriolanus's conquest of Corioli suggests: "The stature of the hero and his worth to the community could hardly be made more nobly clear. The reappearance of the living Martius, covered in blood and fighting the enemy, is thereby made all the more amazing and welcome. Communal joy raises new energies and we are presented with a . . . vivid military encounter: 'They fight, and all enter the city.' Rome and *romanitas* have triumphed."
29. Of course, such warfare is defining of Roman republican history, however, and continues throughout to be the setting for Roman honor and heroism. See also Cantor, *Shakespeare's Rome,* 72-98 for a fascinating discussion of Coriolanus's understanding of republican politics and his reluctance to participate in it.
30. Compare Platt, *Rome and Romans,* 53, for a slightly different take on this issue.
31. Bloom, "Pagan Hero," 79.
32. See, for example, Lily Ross Taylor, *Party Politics in the Age of Caesar* (Berkeley: University of California Press, 1961).
33. Quoted in Coote, *Coriolanus,* 18.
34. The lack of "purpose" is as important in *Julius Caesar* as it is in *Coriolanus,* at least insofar as unanticipated and unintended consequences occur in each, consequences that could have been planned for.
35. See Antony's speech in *Julius Caesar,* act 3, scene 2 and Plato's *Gorgias.*
36. Coote argues that it is only Coriolanus whose "native language" preserves "the ideal of a speech in which language and intention are one" (*Coriolanus,* 55). The problem is, of course, with Coriolanus's intention, and that problem, Shakespeare wants us to understand, is not simply a matter of the lack of "temperance" of the early Republic. Though the price of "civil survival" may have been "compromise, dishonesty and deceitful language," as Coote says, Shakespeare sees another problem.
37. Coote, *Coriolanus,* 55.
38. Bloom, "Pagan Hero," 79.
39. Platt, *Rome and Romans,* 313.
40. C. C. Huffman charts the course of these plays and understands *Coriolanus* to represent a return by Shakespeare "to an overtly political concern" last raised a decade earlier in *Julius Caesar* (C. C. Huffman, *Coriolanus in Context* [Lewisburg, Penn.: Bucknell University Press], 170). As before, he asserts: "Shakespeare relied on the more cultivated to use their knowledge of a wide range of political opinion, made possible by contact with the classics and with Italy, to consider the dramatized situation and the normative standards for civic virtue which the play proposes. If honored, they would yield continued honorable political and moral existence."
41. Platt, *Rome and Romans,* 313.
42. Huffman, *Coriolanus in Context,* 74.
43. Bloom, "Pagan Hero," 84.
44. Bloom, "Pagan Hero," 103.
45. Thomas Hobbes, *Leviathan* (Oxford: Basil Blackwell, 1960), 83ff.
46. Hobbes, *Leviathan,* 112.
47. The standpoint of the poet was unavailable to the Roman hero because he could not look inside. The poet might, however, make the lessons of his virtue and his vices available to Elizabethan England and to us.
48. Harvey Mansfield, Jr., *Machiavelli's New Modes and Orders* (Ithaca: Cornell University Press, 1979), 301.
49. Mansfield, *New Modes and Orders,* 301. See Niccolò Machiavelli, *The Discourses on the First Ten Books of Livy* (New York: The Modern Library, 1950), 297-302. In the process Machiavelli solves the problem that would nag Hobbes. Machiavelli moves beyond

the need of the fear of violent death by reintroducing, via sensational punishments "every ten years," a memory of that anxiety that made the Leviathan state possible and attractive in the first place.

50. My colleague Carey McWilliams reminds me that for Machiavelli the prince's only real concern should be war and that Machiavelli's doctrine suggests that foreign policy is a matter of external conflicts, at least in the first instance. Shakespeare, in my account, returns to the classical view that domestic politics and the soul have at least equal primacy.

51. If, like Plato, Shakespeare is investigating the self and politics as "mirrors" for one another, if justice in the city is related to justice in the self, then it is crucial to permit an inward-looking musing of the sort that Shakespeare finds lacking in his Roman heroes. It may be that Rome's inability to look inside makes justice difficult for Rome. But, if such a standard of judgment is unavailable to Romans themselves, it is surely not unavailable to those commenting on Rome (see, for example, St. Augustine, *The City of God Against the Pagans,* and Montesquieu, *The Greatness of the Romans and Their Decline,* for two very different examples). Shakespeare's use of Rome and Roman history employs such a standard of judgment, one available *to* and *for* his audience.

52. Of course, rhetoric is crucial to politics, and these "quarrels" with others are inescapable, but it is possible to imagine a politics for which rhetoric is a means to a broader public good.

53. The suggestion is not that Shakespeare, advocating republican government, held a "mirror" of ideal republics to England which would permit them to perfect their putative republicanism. Rather it suggests that there are republican sentiments in late Elizabethan and early Jacobean England and that Shakespeare wanted his audience to examine those sentiments with great care.

Shakespeare was not, it has been argued, willing to give up "political virtue." He educates his audience about the limits of Roman heroic nobility, which seemed so profoundly and deeply associated with Roman republicanism, in order to expose and explore what he understood to be the complex, sometimes paradoxical nature of republican government.

FURTHER READING

Criticism

Berry, Ralph. "Communal Identity and the Rituals of *Julius Caesar.*" In *Shakespeare and the Awareness of the Audience,* pp. 75-87. London: Macmillan, 1985.

Maintains that the struggle to define the meaning of 'Roman' is the principal subject of *Julius Caesar.*

Blits, Jan H. "Manliness and Friendship in Shakespeare's *Julius Caesar.*" *Interpretation* 9, Nos. 2-3 (September 1981): 155-67.

Examines the manly virtues and masculine relationships that inform Shakespeare's portrayal of Rome in *Julius Caesar.*

Bono, Barbara J. "The Birth of Tragedy: Tragic Action in *Julius Caesar.*" *English Literary Renaissance* 24, No. 2 (Spring 1994): 449-70.

Evaluation of *Julius Caesar* that comments on the play's sources and deconstructive nuances, as well as its motifs of subverted authority and feminine reproductive power appropriated for political ends.

Brockbank, Philip. "Julius Caesar and the Catastrophes of History." In *On Shakespeare: Jesus, Shakespeare and Karl Marx, and Other Essays,* pp. 122-39. Oxford: Basil Blackwell, 1989.

Approaches *Julius Caesar* from the perspective of tragic finalities—the deaths of Caesar and Brutus—mediated by historical continuity.

Burt, Richard A. "'A Dangerous Rome': Shakespeare's *Julius Caesar* and the Discursive Determinism of Cultural Politics." In *Contending Kingdoms: Historical, Psychological, and Feminist Approaches to the Literature of Sixteenth-Century England and France,* edited by Marie-Rose Logan and Peter L. Rudnytsky, pp. 109-27. Detroit: Wayne State University Press, 1991.

Uses *Julius Caesar* as part of a theoretical critique of contemporary, political assessments of Shakespearean texts.

Charney, Maurice. "The Imagery of *Julius Caesar.*" In *Shakespeare's Roman Plays: The Function of Imagery in the Drama,* pp. 41-65. Cambridge, Mass.: Harvard University Press, 1961.

Focuses on the stylistic and thematic function of storm, blood, and fire imagery in *Julius Caesar.*

Daniell, David. Introduction to *Julius Caesar,* by William Shakespeare, edited by David Daniell, pp. 1-147. Walton-on-Thames: Thomas Nelson and Sons, 1998.

Extensive introduction to *Julius Caesar* that examines the drama's language, structure, sources, and critical and stage history.

Hamer, Mary. *William Shakespeare: 'Julius Caesar.'* Plymouth, U.K.: Northcote House, 1998, 96 p.

Study of *Julius Caesar* that principally concentrates on the roles of Portia and Calphurnia.

Kaula, David. "'Let Us Be Sacrificers': Religious Motifs in *Julius Caesar.*" *Shakespeare Studies* XIV (1981): 197-214.

Interprets Shakespeare's application of sixteenth-century religious ideas, attitudes, and language to the pre-Christian subject of *Julius Caesar.*

Miola, Robert S. "*Julius Caesar* and the Tyrannicide Debate." *Renaissance Quarterly* 38, No. 2 (Summer 1985): 271-89.

Employs Renaissance texts concerning tyrannicide to illustrate Shakespeare's depiction of Caesar as a tyrant and to weigh evidence in the play for the justifiability of his assassination.

Nathan, Norman. "Brutus' Oratory." *San Jose Studies* 8, No. 1 (February 1982): 82-90.

Assesses the rhetorical power of Brutus's funeral oration to Caesar.

Parker, Barbara L. "The Whore of Babylon and Shakespeare's *Julius Caesar.*" *Studies in English Literature, 1500-1900* 35, No. 2 (Spring 1995): 251-69.

Draws comparisons between the Rome of *Julius Caesar* and the biblical representation of Babylon, seeing in Shakespeare's play an implied critique of the Catholic Church.

Pughe, Thomas. "'What Should the Wars Do with these Jigging Fools?': The Poets in Shakespeare's *Julius Caesar.*" *English Studies* 69, No. 4 (August 1988): 313-22.

Highlights the minor theme of imagination suppressed by political power in *Julius Caesar* as embodied by the abused poets Cinna and the camp-poet of Act 4, scene 3.

Sandison, Alan G. *Julius Caesar and Friends: The Idea of Rome in Shakespeare's 'Julius Caesar.'* Armidale, N.S.W.: University of New England, Armidale, 1987, 20 p.

Contemplates the intertwined issues of problematic language and the question of what it means to be Roman addressed in *Julius Caesar.*

Sohmer, Steve. "Endemic Time Confusion in *Julius Caesar.*" In *Shakespeare's Mystery Play: The Opening of the Globe Theatre 1599,* pp. 77-102. Manchester: Manchester University Press, 1999.

Investigates references to uncertainties of time and date associated with Julian calendar reform in *Julius Caesar.*

Thomas, Vivian. "Images and Self-Images in *Julius Caesar.*" In *Shakespeare's Roman Worlds,* pp. 40-92. London: Routledge, 1989.

Discusses the relationship of *Julius Caesar* to its source material—particularly Sir Thomas North's translation of Plutarch's *Lives of the Noble Grecians and Romans*—and Shakespeare's evocation of early Imperial Rome in the work.

Tice, Terrence N. "Calphurnia's Dream and Communication with the Audience in Shakespeare's *Julius Caesar.*" *Shakespeare Yearbook* 1 (Spring 1990): 37-49.

Comments on interpretations and misinterpretations of Calphurnia's dream portending Caesar's murder and on the "depressive" mood of *Julius Caesar.*

Wilson, Richard. "'Is This a Holiday?': Shakespeare's Roman Carnival." *ELH* 54, No. 1 (Spring 1987): 31-44.

Describes carnivalesque elements of the "world turned upside down" in *Julius Caesar.*

———. "A Brute Part: *Julius Caesar* and the Rites of Violence." *Cahiers Élisabéthains* 50 (October 1996): 19-32.

Enumerates instances of bloody imagery and iconography in *Julius Caesar* and other Shakespearean dramas.

The Two Gentlemen of Verona

For further information on the critical and stage history of *The Two Gentlemen of Verona,* see *SC,* Volumes 6, 12, 40, and 54.

INTRODUCTION

One of Shakespeare's early comedies (written circa 1590-91), *The Two Gentlemen of Verona* has never been as highly acclaimed as his later romantic and comic works. Considered by most as an apprentice-like romantic comedy, critics perceive the play to be marred by problematic plot development, uneven verse, and an awkward ending. These shortcomings have led many scholars to question both the circumstances of its composition and the authenticity of Shakespeare as its author. Some critics view *The Two Gentlemen of Verona* as an example of the playwright's early work and point to the flaws in the play as evidence that it was composed when Shakespeare was still a young playwright who had not yet perfected his craft. Other critics contend that the problematic fifth act and ending are proof that the play was hastily completed by Shakespeare to fill a gap in his theater company's repertory schedule. However, there is little evidence that *The Two Gentlemen of Verona* was ever performed during Shakespeare's lifetime. The main source of the play is Jorge de Montemayor's Spanish romance *Diana Enamorada* (1559; English translation 1598), a tale of an unfaithful lover and his mistress. Shakespeare followed this and other sources closely, molding the action of the play to explore the themes of love and friendship. While many issues and themes have been addressed in the critical appraisals of *The Two Gentlemen of Verona,* most commentaries on the play address both the flaws of the play as well as its influence on Shakespeare's later comedies.

As is typical of most Shakespearean comedies, there is a contrast between the idyllic setting of the forest or country versus the worldly and sophisticated environment of the court where Proteus and Valentine begin their educational journey. In contrast to the main characters of Proteus and Valentine, note Marvin Felheim and Philip Traci (1980), the characters of Speed and Launce comment on, as well as parody, the situations in which the main characters find themselves. In the course of the play, Proteus and Valentine must finally learn that the well-mannered court of Milan is not an appropriate place for an education, but that true love and real life only exist outside this arena. Settings such as the forest offer reform, a refuge, and a place where innate virtue is recognized and rewarded. According to Felheim and Traci, all these themes, though not as skillfully explored in *The Two Gentlemen of Verona* as in Shakespeare's later plays, provide the groundwork for many of his later, more successful, romantic comedies.

Since the early twentieth century, study of *The Two Gentlemen of Verona* has focused heavily on Shakespeare's treatment of the romantic material in the play. Muriel C. Bradbrook (1989) states that the play is built on the conventions of love and friendship, and that Shakespeare used these to explore the moods embodied in the comedy. In her discussion of the setting, Bradbrook calls the play an evocative drama that is more closely related to Shakespeare's final romances, such as *The Tempest,* rather than to later comedies, despite the fact that *The Two Gentlemen of Verona* shares its Italian setting with the later comedies. The critic also proposes that the play, which includes a great deal of parody, is founded upon the courtly assumptions of the "game" of love. Frederick Kiefer (1986) examines the role of love letters in the play, characterizing them as experimental theatrical props that serve multiple functions. According to Kiefer, love is connected with reading and writing throughout the play, and the letters are integral to the advancement of the plot, to the revelation of character, and to the evocation of emotions. In fact, Kiefer feels that contrary to the generally held opinion that this play is an apprentice piece, the use of letters in *The Two Gentlemen of Verona* reveals it as a skillfully composed and thoughtful effort. Kiefer points to the letters in the play as a highly effective plot device, serving to move the action forward both for comic purpose and tragicomic direction.

Like most other Shakespearean comedies, the main action of *The Two Gentlemen of Verona* focuses on the contrast and interaction of male and female characters. Jonathan Hall (1995) characterizes this type of involvement in the play as a study of the contrast between male inconstancy and female constancy. According to Hall, the evil of inconstancy is a male failing, and this male changeability is seen by the critic as more than just an unfortunate inclination of the sex. Instead, Hall calls it the source of cultural dislocation in the play, in which the foundations of the patriarchal order are dishonored. The resistance of the female characters to male rhetoric, says Hall, allows the women the power to help restore the men to the truth, just as the women in *Love's Labour's Lost* do. The female characters in *The Two Gentlemen of Verona,* like Shakespeare's other redeeming heroines, combat the threats to the patriarchal order.

A study of contemporary records indicates that *The Two Gentlemen of Verona* was not successful in performance during Shakespeare's lifetime. In fact, the first record of its performance occurs a century and a half after Shakespeare's death, when David Garrick, a noted eighteenth-century actor and manager, directed an altered version of the play. In their essay detailing the major productions of the play, Carol J. Carlisle and Patty S. Derrick (1997) note that *The Two Gentlemen of Verona* has seen more productions in British provincial and American regional theaters than it has on major stages in England or the United States. According to Carlisle and Derrick, although *The Two Gentlemen of Verona* is a charming play, a production needs to overcome its weaknesses, somehow turning these to advantages in order to stage it effectively. The play's major flaws, note the critics, include a formulaic plot, thinly-drawn characters, and an "absurd" conclusion. The critics point to Shakespeare's method, so notable in later comedies, of balancing romance and humor and note that it has been employed much less skillfully in this early attempt, thus making it difficult to translate the text into theatrical terms. Regardless of the obstacles inherent to the staging of the play, Carlisle and Derrick contend that *The Two Gentlemen of Verona* is becoming better known in the theater and that it will continue to present a challenge because it demands a significant collaboration between the author and the theater.

OVERVIEWS AND GENERAL STUDIES

Marvin Felheim and Philip Traci (essay date 1980)

SOURCE: "*The Two Gentlemen of Verona,*" in *Realism in Shakespeare's Romantic Comedies: "O Heavenly Mingle,"* University Press of America, 1980, pp. 51-65.

[*In the following essay, Felheim and Traci discuss* The Two Gentlemen of Verona *as a comedy based on realism, characterizing it as a play about change and growth.*]

> Proteus: Yet writers say: as in the sweetest bud
> The eating canker dwells, so eating Love
> Inhabits in the finest wits of all
>
> (I. i. 42-44).

I

The theme of *The Two Gentlemen of Verona* centers in the idea of change, a concept embodied in the very name, Proteus, of one of the two gentlemen. When we first meet the young men, they are provincials, ". . . living dully sluggardiz'd at home" (I. i. 7), in Verona. And, as Valentine asserts, "Home-keeping youth have ever homely wits" (l. 2). His thesis is almost immediately demonstrated in the scene between Proteus and Speed (ll. 70ff.) where the lugubrious wit of gentlemen and clown alike is amply shown in a discussion about sheep and shepherds.

Valentine is not alone in his view that "shapeless idleness" (l. 8) tends to demoralize the young. A bit later, Proteus' uncle requests Panthino "to importune" Proteus' father, Antonio, "to let him [Proteus] spend his time no more at home" (I. iii. 13-14). Antonio agrees that a youth "cannot be a perfect man,"

> Not being tried and tutor'd in the world:
> Experience is by industry achiev'd,
> And perfected by the swift course of time
>
> (ll. 20-23).

Consequently, by the end of Act I, both young gentlemen are headed for the Court of the Emperor at Milan. Their exposure to "experience" and to "travel" will be their education. And so the comedy has as its base a very realistic situation:[1] the need for young gentlemen to be educated in the ways of the world. The play follows its chief characters to Milan. Indeed, only six short scenes of *The Two Gentlemen of Verona* are set in the city mentioned in the title; three of these scenes make up Act I; three others are in Act II. After that, we are either in Milan (a total of eleven scenes) or in a forest on the frontiers of Mantua (three scenes). In these latter two settings the real education of Valentine and Proteus takes place.

At the beginning of Act II, we find Valentine at the Court. Curiously, from this point on there are no further reference to the "Emperor" who, according to Proteus, once "daily graced" (I. iii. 58) the life of Valentine. In this very much love-centered Court, Valentine has a more interesting instructor: Silvia, the daughter of the Duke. His training with her has already begun: at her command, he has been engaged in writing love letters for her. She, lazy but clever (at least more agile-minded than he), simply sends the letters back to him, a device which he fails utterly to understand. Fortunately, Speed prompts him: ". . . she hath made you write to yourself" (II. i. 144), and queries: ". . . do you not perceive the jest?" Valentine's education, alas, has not progressed as quickly as Speed's. He is blinded by love. Speed, whose name ordinarily belies his condition but who is generally on hand to parody the situation, has, after all, had experience of this kind before: in Verona, he delivered letters for Proteus to his love, Julia. Letters, then, represent no new educational experience for Speed. Valentine has so far learned little, but he is in no condition to apprehend much; he is in love. Thus the initial situation in Milan repeats that in Verona: a young gentleman in love. He has "learned," as Speed points out,

> (like Sir Proteus) to wreath your arms like a malcontent; to relish a love-song, like a robin redbreast; to walk alone, like one that had the pestilence; to sigh, like a schoolboy that had lost his ABC; to weep, like a young wench that had buried her grandam; to fast, like one that takes diet; to watch, like one that fears robbing; to speak puling, like a beggar at Hallowmas
>
> (ll. 18-25)

The practice of writing letters, a task imposed upon him by Silvia, provides in truth an apt but difficult lesson for the schoolboy, Valentine.

By the end of Act II, both the young gentlemen of Verona are in Milan and both are in love with Silvia. Further, Proteus has admitted that in his new love he is both "forsworn" and "threefold" (II. vi. 3-5) perjured (he has left Julia, he loves Siliva, he wrongs his friend Valentine). So much for the "experience" provided by the Court in Milan: sophisticated and worldly, it is also, at least for Valentine and Proteus, exclusively love-oriented. Only the servants, Speed and Launce, perceive the absurdity of the situation; their actions provide a continual comment and parody.

If neither of the young gentlemen learns much (except perfidy on the part of Proteus) in Milan, that failure may be a revealing truth on Shakespeare's part. The corrupted, excessively mannered Court is no place for real education. The lesson will be repeated in *A Midsummer Night's Dream,* where, again, the Court at Athens threatens the young lovers. At a court, especially one in a city, the best things that can be learned are likely to be manners and rhetoric. Love letters become a substitute for love itself; the game of love—wooing—becomes an end in itself. This is indeed Shakespeare's point; as always, he makes it directly in terms of action; and here, as elsewhere in the comedies, clowns and servants are on hand to demonstrate the reality and truth of the dramatist's position. By parody—accomplished both in actions and in words—the central comic situation is reinforced and intensified.

But real love is possible, of course. So, too, young people can learn. Shakespeare's comedies are essentially optimistic documents. The learning and the loving, however, must take place in an appropriate setting—in nature. Hence the scenes on the frontiers of Mantua, where both men and the physical world exist in a state of nature. As in both *A Midsummer Night's Dream* and *As You Like It,* the forest is a haunt for free men and true. Valentine is immediately welcomed there "for he is a proper man" (IV. i. 10). After a bit of preliminary braggadocio, "I kill'd a man, whose death I much repent" (l. 27), he is invited to ". . . be the captain of us all" (l. 65). His acceptance is conditional:

> Provided that you do no outrages
> On silly women or poor passengers
>
> (ll. 71-72).

As expected, these followers of the doctrine of Robin Hood are men who "detest such vile base practices" (l. 73). Thus the world of the outlaws is presented as a refuge of justice and good deeds, away from the disorders of the city and the court.

To this retreat come the principal characters, one and all to be reformed or rewarded in the natural setting. Proteus, Thurio and the Duke will change from baseness to goodness here; Valentine, Silvia and Julia (her "grace" is more obvious than her disguise) will have their innate virtue recognized and rewarded. And, finally, the outlaws who, after all, "Are men endu'd with worthy qualities" (V. iv. 151), will be pardoned and reintegrated into civil society.

In this manner, the education of the young gentlemen is completed. In the process, Valentine has acquired a knowledge of languages (interestingly enough, this attribute is the crowning achievement which renders him fit to be "king" of the outlaws):

> My youthful travel therein made me happy [he is a "linguist"
>
> (l. 57)]
>
> Or else I often had been miserable
>
> (ll. 34-35),

of nature:

> This shadowy desert, unfrequented woods,
> I better brook than flourishing peopled towns
>
> (V. iv. 2-3),

and of men: once Proteus admits his "shame and guilt" (l. 73) and asks for forgiveness, Valentine can with equanimity offer him "All that was mine in Silvia . . ." (l. 83), knowing full well that Proteus can but match his own open heartedness (especially since Julia is on hand to provide Proteus "my wish for ever" [l. 118]). In addition, Valentine has learned to recognize the goodness of his fellow outlaws, so he is able to persuade the Duke to rescind their banishment. Finally, of course, he possesses the knowledge of the constant love he shares with Silvia. Proteus also has learned his lesson: "O heaven, were man But constant, he were perfect!" (ll. 109-110) And on the basis of this pious hope, he reverts to his former love.

Thurio, too, has undergone a natural change. His experiences in the forest have led him to the realistic discovery that a man is "but a fool that will endanger / His body for a girl that loves him not" (ll. 131-132).

Finally, the hot-headed Duke of Milan has cooled off in the forest. First, he must recognize Valentine's worth, to which he subscribes:

> Sir Valentine
> Thou art a gentleman . . .
> Take thou thy Siliva, for thou hast deserv'd her
>
> (ll. 143-145).

Next he pardons the outlaws and joins with the others in a general recapitulation of all that has transpired: "The story of your loves discovered" (l. 169). It is altogether fitting (and realistic), then, that the conclusion of this tale of two city gentlemen should take place in the forest, for only after a series of disquieting experiences have they learned the truth about the human condition. Now, at least, are they fit for a "day of marriage / One feast, one house, one mutual happiness" (ll. 170-171). The rewards are great, but the trials have been sufficient and the play has demonstrated the profound truth at its heart that love can be earned by wisdom and faith.

II

The comic subplot of *The Two Gentlemen of Verona* revolves realistically around the words and antics of two servants, Speed and Launce. They are the typical lower-class clowns of Shakespearean drama, drawn probably from the Elizabethan world in the midst of which Shakespeare lived. Insofar as they can be isolated from the main plot their actions and their statements provide both a parody of and a comment on the principal doings. As such theirs is an extension of the main action. Generally speaking, however, they are intricately involved in the main plot: they go from Verona to Milan with their masters, Speed with Valentine, Launce with Proteus; when Valentine is captured by the outlaws in the forest, Speed is with him and is also taken prisoner. On the other hand, they can see their masters with some objectivity and they inform the audience of their masters' states. So Speed observes Valentine to be in love, just as later Launce notes the perfidious behavior of Proteus. Both comics generally speak in prose; and, on most occasions, they are the cause for the use of prose on the part of other characters who converse with them.

In all, the comics appear in seven scenes, out of the twenty in the play. Their actions are neatly spaced through the first four acts. Needless to say, neither appears in the final act, for in Act V the young gentlemen and their ladies, the Duke and Thurio are at last undergoing the real experience of education and neither parody nor comment is necessary. The final act of *The Two Gentlemen of Verona* is, indeed, quite serious; the absence of Speed and Launce testifies to that condition.

The two clowns have quite markedly different natures. Speed is a punster; he is continually involved in making witty comments either to or about other characters in the play. Launce is more elemental. He has three soliloquies in the course of the action; two are with his dog, and although they are extremely funny, both in terms of action and words, he is not a deliberate word manipulator; he succeeds accidentally or unconsciously, whereas Speed uses words with his quick sense of meaning fully at work. Launce's third soliloquy occurs in Act III, scene i, when he explains to the audience that despite his own foolishness he can see through the knavery of his master, Proteus. Launce's first soliloquy (II. iii) consists of his farewell to his indifferent dog, Crab; the episode follows immediately upon the scene of parting between Proteus and Julia and thus serves as a parody of sentimentality. The other soliloquy with Crab (IV. iv) relates the misbehavior of the dog in polite society and in this way pokes fun at all the stereotyped love and wooing at the Court. These two soliloquies are immensely funny, not only because they expose Launce's very low origins and concepts but because Crab, too, is a comic figure, indifferent to the parting from his master in the first instance and having behaved in a shameless unhousebroken fashion in the second.

Speed's scenes involve him in repartee with Proteus (I. i), with Valentine (II. i) and with Launce (II. v and III. i). In the opening scene of the play, he jests with Proteus about the sheep-like behavior of human beings; then they discuss the payment which Speed wangles out of Proteus in return for delivering a love letter to Julia. In the next act, we find Speed noting Valentine's state (love); he then points out that love is blind. Later in the scene, he explains to Valentine how Silvia is using him to write letters for her. In the first of his two scenes with Launce, Speed puns on words such as "stand" and "understand." Their second scene together finds Speed again involved with a "love" letter: this one is simply a list of the qualities, virtues and vices both, of Launce's girl. The comedy here consists of the unexpected: the nature both of the young woman described and of Launce's reactions to her characteristics.

III

The soliloquy is, certainly, one of the most interesting as well as most typical of Shakespearean dramatic devices. Ordinarily, we are inclined to associate the dramatic monologue with the more serious tragic characters, with Hamlet especially and with Macbeth.

Generally speaking, Shakespeare uses the soliloquy infrequently in his early plays; the best known examples are in the early histories, particularly in *Richard II* and *Richard III*. The *Two Gentlemen of Verona* is an interesting minor exception to Shakespeare's usual practice. Launce's three comic prose soliloquies have already been mentioned. More provocative are four soliloquies of Julia and seven of Proteus.

Julia's monologues occur in pairs. The first two (in. I. ii) deal with a letter from Proteus, which has been delivered by Speed to Julia's waiting-woman, Lucetta. In her first soliloquy Julia expresses her dilemma: she is caught between her desire to see the letter and the need she feels to appear indifferent to love. Her second soliloquy (40 lines later in the same scene; Lucetta has three entrances and three exits in the scene, thus providing Julia with opportunities to be alone in order to soliloquize) finds her picking up pieces of the torn-up letter in an effort to find meaningful phrases. This letter scene is delightful. It shows us a young, aristocratic girl in love, being coy and forward by starts. The soliloquies provide a means for her to utter her thought aloud. As such, they are of course conventional stage devices. But they also allow for a kind of psychological realism; we are enabled thereby to understand the character and situation of Julia; soliloquies used in this manner are a short cut, for they supply information directly and quickly which would otherwise require a longer scene and several characters.

Julia's second brace of soliloquies occurs in Act IV. She is now in Milan, in disguise as a young man named Sebastian, in the service of her lover, Proteus. Her "master" has just requested that she take a ring to his new love, Silvia. She soliloquizes: in the course of some eighteen lines, she tells us that the ring is the same she herself gave to Proteus in Verona; and she explains further that she is

Richard Moore as Launce and Irish wolfhound Wolly as Crab in the 1991 Royal Shakespeare Company production of The Two Gentlemen of Verona.

prompted to do Proteus' wooing—although somewhat "coldly"—out of pity, for being in love she can pity another lover. Some lines later, she concludes the scene (iv) with a second soliloquy (of 27 lines). She has just had a long interview with Silvia, during which she has learned that that lady does not return Proteus' affection. Further, she has posed as a former intimate of Julia. Now, alone, she compares Silvia's picture to herself, not to her own discredit (Love, however, is blind; or, if not, he certainly does not at the moment see with Julia's eyes). Again, in these lines, Julia seems to be offering the audience a realistic explanation for her behavior: knowing now that Silvia does not love Proteus, Julia can pursue her course of pretending to be Proteus' go-between. Thus, again, the monologue enables Shakespeare easily to present a complex dramatic situation; at the same time, we are allowed a true insight into a young woman's heart.

Julia's soliloquies arise directly from the action and/or the situation in which she finds herself. The soliloquies of Proteus, on the other hand, are consequent upon his character. Thus, we find at the very beginning of his career that Shakespeare demonstrates a varied dramaturgy, even in the use of such a conventional device as the soliloquy.

Two of Proteus' soliloquies are very short (3 lines); they are merely tags to end a scene. Such are his lines at the end of Act I, scene i, when he indicates that he cannot trust Speed to deliver his letters or, again, when in Act II, scene ii, he exchanges rings with Julia before parting; she is obviously too overcome to speak and so exits. His three lines simply acknowledge that "true love . . . cannot speak." (And we must acknowledge that the fact that Shakespeare puts words into Proteus' mouth at this moment gives us a hint that his love may not be "true.")

Proteus' first soliloquy occurs in the opening scene of the play, following his farewell to Valentine. He tells us frankly that whereas his friend "after honour hunts," he, Proteus, seeks only "love" (l. 63). At the moment, it is

> . . . Julia, thou hast metamorphos'd me;
> Made me neglect my studies, lose my time,
> War with good counsel, set the world at nought
>
> (ll. 66-68).

But, like the young Romeo, he will soon enough change his allegiance. As a matter of fact, in his ten-line soliloquy in scene iii of Act I, he acknowledges the fickleness of young love.

> O, how this spring of love resembleth
> The uncertain glory of an April day
>
> (ll. 84-85),

is his lament; the careful listener is thus prepared for change à la Proteus.

And change is not long in coming. By scenes iv and vi of Act II, Proteus, in two lengthy soliloquies (23 lines and 43 lines respectively), admits his nature. He relationalizes, of course, and excuses himself by analogy:

> Even as one heat another heat expels
> Or as one nail by strength drives out another
>
> (II. iv. 188-189).

All this, yet he has seen only Silvia's picture and heard her praised by Valentine. Impressionable young man, indeed! A veritable votary of the love goddess. Speed and Launce in scene v provide the substance between Proteus' two soliloquies, one at the end of scene iv, the other at the beginning of scene vi. The meeting of the two servants in Milan (Launce has his dog with him) raises the question, will Proteus marry Julia, and allows Speed to inform Launce that Valentine has become "a notable lover" (l. 37). Perhaps their somewhat silly punning of the words, "stand" and "understand" is intended to be a reflection on Proteus' position. At any event, Proteus' soliloquy in scene vi is his longest speech in the play. He tells us frankly that although he is forsworn for it, he no longer loves Julia but loves his friend's lover, Silvia. To all this he adds a disarmingly candid statement about self-love which prompts him to his present state. For should he retain the love of Julia and Valentine, then he loses himself (i.e., his new identity as lover of Silvia. "I to myself am dearer than a friend" (l. 23), is his creed. On this basis he will inform the Duke of Valentine's plans to abduct Silvia; then, the Duke having banished Valentine as a consequence, Proteus has no doubt of his own capacity to win Silvia's love for himself, away from the potential rival, Thurio. He concludes by putting himself completely under the power of the God of Love:

> Love, lend me wings to make my purpose swift
> As thou has lent me wit to plot this drift
>
> (ll. 42-43).

Thus Shakespeare carefully and realistically presents the youthful deceiver, explaining as clearly as possible, the basis of his character and actions.

Proteus has one more soliloquy, in Act IV. He begins scene ii (in scene i, Valentine has been captured by the outlaws) with a short recapitulation of his perfidy:

> Already have I been false to Valentine
> And now I must be as unjust to Thurio

To this he adds the information that Silvia rejects his love, chastising him for his unfaithfulness to friend and former beloved.

> Yet, spaniel-like, the more she spurns my love,
> The more it grows, and fawneth on her still
>
> (ll. 14-15).

(His "dog-like" devotion differs in character and style from the "indifference" of the real dog, Crab.) This is the last insight we have into Proteus' thinking via the soliloquy. In Act V, he will reform, both in deed and word; hence, there will be no need for the kind of rationalizing which has characterized his soliloquies in the preceding four acts.

Act V of *The Two Gentlemen of Verona,* as has been pointed out above, is different from the other four acts, in terms of setting, action, theme. There is a shift, too, in the character of the soliloquy as it is used here. Proteus has been the most consistent user of this convention; his seven soliloquies total 105 lines. Julia, in turn, has spoken 87 lines of verse in four soliloquies. Launce, in three comic prose monologues has accounted for 87 lines. In Act V, there are two soliloquizers: Eglamour and Valentine. The former opens the first scene of the act with a 6-line statement, necessary for establishing time, place and action. He tells us it is dusk, he is at "An Abbey" to meet Silvia to conduct her to Valentine. The practical dramatic nature of these lines is obvious.

Valentine's soliloquy (V. iv. 1-18) is his second in the play. Previously, in Act III, scene i, he uttered some 18 lines of verse in which he lamented his banishment from Silvia: "What joy is joy, if Silvia be not by?" (l. 175). Now he opens the final scene of the play with a statement about the beauties of the Arcadian world:

> This shadowy desert, unfrequented woods
> I better brook than flourishing peopled towns
>
> (ll. 2-3).

These haunts charm because they allow him to think about his missing love. Such reveries are soon interrupted, however, by the "stir" of the outlaws and the arrival of the other principal characters. Again, this soliloquy is significant primarily because it sets the scene and the mood, an atmosphere which, on the other hand, will all too soon be changed and left behind. For all its loveliness, the Arcadian setting, where human conflicts can be resolved, does not in Shakespeare ever provide the ultimate home of men. Purified and restored by nature, Shakespeare's characters inevitably return to the cities, there presumably to lead their lives amid pressing, realistic but civilized conditions. So *The Two Gentlemen of Verona* ends with complete acceptance of the way of life of the city state. The Duke forgives those who need his benevolence; he will return to Milan to rule. The others, after their forest "exile," will reenter civil life as his subjects. The ending, while it celebrates marriage, forgiveness and reconciliations also emphasizes the social aspect of existence and thus suggests the basic realism of Shakespearean comedy.

Notes

1. Although we join with Clifford Leech in his assertion prefaced to his New Arden edition of the play that "no one is likely to claim that *The Two Gentlemen of Verona* is a masterpiece" (p. lxxi), we would hardly adhere to the standard view that "in some ways *The Two Gentlemen* appears to take its place among his most artificial plays, as a play on the débat-theme of lover versus friendship" (p. xxv), or that it is "not a play where detailed comment on the characters is a worthwhile occupation" (p. lxxiii).

LOVE AND COURTESY

Frederick Kiefer (essay date 1986)

SOURCE: "Love Letters in *The Two Gentlemen of Verona*," in *Shakespeare Studies,* Vol. 18, 1986, pp. 65-85.

[*In the following essay, Kiefer asserts that in* The Two Gentlemen of Verona *love is linked to reading and writing, and characterizes the play's love letters as effective theatrical props used to propel the action forward and to display character.*]

The two gentlemen of Verona are what their youth and courtly upbringing predispose them to be—bookish. Appropriately, the word *book* appears in their opening conversation when Proteus, contemplating the dangers his friend may encounter on a journey, pledges, "I will be thy beadsman," and Valentine replies, "And on a love-book pray for my success?" (I.i.18-19).[1] The expression *love-book* anticipates the conjunction of love with reading and writing that characterizes the entire play. This conjunction is apparent in the first scene when, the conversation having turned to love, both Proteus and Valentine solemnly cite what "writers say." It is also apparent when the two gentlemen, each having fallen in love, become writers themselves. Their writing takes the form of letters to their ladies, and those letters in turn beget additional letters as the initial talk about what writers say gives way to a blizzard of paper. No other Shakespearean comedy contains so many letters; no other devotes so many scenes to the composition, delivery, and reception of love letters.

The very number of these letters suggests the dramaturgical importance they have in *Two Gentlemen,* where they fulfill a variety of functions. They advance the plot, reveal character, generate laughter, and evoke emotions in the audience ranging from shock to pathos. Whatever their particular purpose in particular scenes, though, the letters have this in common: even if their inspiration is to be found ultimately in prose romance, the letters are eminently theatrical. As hand properties, they command attention: in full view of the audience, the characters give and receive, hide and destroy, write and read those letters.

The letters, moreover, have a significance that transcends the obviously theatrical. For Shakespeare uses them to explore a paradox: that people seek to express the most intense emotion by the most conventional of literary modes, the epistolary. Because the act of writing involves some deliberation, there is no necessary congruence between written expression and heartfelt sentiment. In fact, the stylistic patterns of love letters are at variance with the turbulent nature of lovers' passions. Therefore, although reading and writing may have the most profound significance for lovers, the letters that pass between them may lead to misunderstanding and even permit deception. In the world of the play characters learn to distrust amatory declarations, no matter how artful or affecting.

Because Shakespeare wrote *Two Gentlemen* early in his career and because he would employ such devices as love letters again in later plays, *Two Gentlemen* has come to be thought of chiefly as an apprentice piece. It is, however, a better comedy than is implied by its status as precursor to other comedies. By examining Shakespeare's handling of the letters, we shall see that *Two Gentlemen* is at once a more theatrically adroit and a more thoughtful play than is usually supposed.

Letter-writing begins early in *Two Gentlemen.* In fact, when the play opens, Proteus has already written of his love to Julia, and he has entrusted his letter to the servant Speed.[2] Concerned that she may deem the messenger unsuitable, Proteus frets, "I fear my Julia would not deign my lines, / Receiving them from such a worthless post" (I.i.152-53). But he has at least put his feelings into words, and his words into writing. And that, in *Two Gentlemen,* is the first step in encouraging love. For Proteus, as for Valentine later, the written word is an essential ingredient of wooing.

Proteus' letter becomes the focus of the following scene, where, from the moment the letter appears onstage, it claims the attention of its recipient—and of the audience. In assigning the letter so much importance, Shakespeare purposefully departs from what he found in his chief source, the Spanish romance *Diana Enamorada* by the Portuguese author Jorge de Montemayor. For the playwright, with an eye to the stage, adds to and subtracts from *Diana.*[3] In comparing the first episode involving a letter in the play with the corresponding episode in the romance, we can appreciate Shakespeare's capacity for exploiting the theatrical possibilities he found in the prose narrative.

The letter writers in *Diana* are Felismena and Don Felix. Having fallen in love with her, Don Felix seeks to convince

Felismena of his affection, though to little effect at first. One day he decides to express his feelings in a letter, which he gives to Rosina, Felismena's maid. The letter will prove the turning point in their relationship, though its importance is difficult to gauge by Felismena's frosty demeanor when Rosina produces the letter. Instead of accepting it graciously, Felismena strikes a haughty, even reproachful, pose. Taken aback by her mistress's vehemence, Rosina apologizes, saying defensively and a little disingenuously, "I gave it you, bicause you might laugh at it, and not to moove your pacience with it in this sort."[4] The maid then leaves the room, taking the letter with her. Felismena, despite her cool exterior, is interested in Don Felix's attentions but does not wish to appear improperly eager. That night when Rosina returns to help her mistress to bed, Felismena hopes that Rosina will offer the letter again, but the maid, having been rebuffed earlier, says no more about the matter. Then in frustration Felismena broaches the subject, again feigning indignation in order to conceal her true feelings: "And is it so *Rosina,* that *Don Felix* without any regard to mine honour dares write unto me?" The ploy fails. Rosina says only that "These are things Mistresse . . . that are commonly incident to love, wherfore I beseech you pardon me." She leaves the room without presenting the letter, and so a disconsolate Felismena spends a sleepless night. The next morning, however, when Rosina reappears, "she let the letter closely fall." Felismena demands to see it, and the maid explains that it is the same letter proffered the day before. Pretending skepticism, Felismena denies Rosina's claim: "Nay that it is not . . . wherefore shew it me, that I may see if you lie or no." At last Rosina puts the letter into her mistress's hands.

When the corresponding characters in *Two Gentlemen* make their first appearance, Julia asks her maid Lucetta,

> Of all the fair resort of gentlemen
> That every day with parle encounter me,
> In thy opinion which is worthiest love?
>
> (*I.ii.4-6*)

The two women discuss the merits of various suitors, and when Lucetta praises Proteus, Julia says wistfully, "I would I knew his mind" (l. 33). Seizing this auspicious moment, Lucetta produces his letter: "Peruse this paper, madam" (l. 34). The letter, a hand property for Shakespeare, enables the playwright to dramatize the internal conflict between propriety and passion, as well as the tension between mistress and confidante.[5]

Like Felismena, Julia professes irritation so as to conceal a depth of feeling that others might regard as unseemly: "Dare you presume to harbor wanton lines? / To whisper and conspire against my youth?" (I.ii.42-43). She peremptorily orders her maid, "There! take the paper; see it be return'd." Like Montemayor's heroine, however, Julia is less hostile in her heart (or less affected) than she appears. In fact, no sooner does Lucetta exit than Julia reflects, "And yet I would I had o'erlook'd the letter" (l. 50). With more boldness than Felismena, Julia immediately calls back her maid, who proceeds just as quickly to drop the letter deliberately and then pick it up. Her attention caught by this byplay, Julia makes a trumped-up, if not wholly serious, charge: "Some love of yours hath writ to you in rhyme" (l. 76). After some witty badinage Julia says, "Let's see your song" (l. 85), and takes the letter. Then, with exaggerated scorn she tears it to pieces, unread.[6]

Shakespeare has deftly dramatized the incident in Montemayor, displaying in this early comedy a gift for converting a slowly moving narrative into a lively entertainment suited for the stage. He makes a number of changes, each of which enhances the physicality of the situation. For example, he creates stage action when Julia accepts the letter, then hands it back; when she seizes the letter, then tears it to pieces; and when, after Lucetta exits, Julia scurries about the stage, frantically gathering together the scraps of paper, and reads aloud parts of what Proteus has written. By introducing the destruction and then reconstruction of the letter (neither of which occurs in Montemayor), Shakespeare not only satisfies the audience's desire to see some engaging incident but also makes that incident comically surprising. By telescoping time, moreover, Shakespeare accelerates the pace of the action. Between Lucetta's dismissal and return, there is no intervening night, only a soliloquy in which Julia reflects, "What fool is she, that knows I am a maid, / And would not force the letter to my view!" (I.ii.53-54). And although, in *Diana,* Rosina waits until the next day to produce the letter again, Lucetta drops it at once upon her immediate return. By giving Julia something to do as well as to say, and by quickening the sequence of events, Shakespeare effectively engages the interest of the audience.

Proteus' letter provides the basis not only for the dialogue between Julia and Lucetta but also for the soliloquies spoken by Julia in this scene. In composing those two speeches, Shakespeare is mindful of both the resources and the limitations of his stage. He knows that a dramatist cannot present the contents of Proteus' letter to the audience as easily as Montemayor presents Don Felix's letter to the reader of *Diana.* What Shakespeare can effectively convey is Julia's state of mind, as the audience eavesdrops on her thoughts. Consequently, he shifts the focus of the episode from the words of the letter itself (furnished by Montemayor) to the psyche of the letter's recipient. We hear of Julia's frustration and anger in her first soliloquy: "How angerly I taught my brow to frown, / When inward joy enforc'd my heart to smile!" (I.ii.62-63). In the second soliloquy, after she has torn up the letter, we hear of her affection for Proteus and her self-reproach: "O hateful hands, to tear such loving words!" (l. 102); "I'll kiss each several paper for amends. / Look, here is writ 'kind Julia.' Unkind Julia . . ." (ll. 105-06). Exuberant at discovering Proteus' profession of love, she even hints at her sexuality. Suggestively handling the pieces of paper, she says:

> Lo, here in one line is his name twice writ,
> "Poor forlorn Proteus, passionate Proteus:
> To the sweet Julia"—that I'll tear away—
> And yet I will not, sith so prettily

He couples it to his complaining names.
Thus will I fold them one upon another;
Now kiss, embrace, contend, do what you will.

(*I.ii.120-26*)

As she speaks these lines, Julia presses together the pieces of paper, folds them, and perhaps holds them close to her heart. Through this action and the soliloquies, Shakespeare dramatizes the vitality of the character. What he may have sacrificed of Proteus' words, he more than compensates for in the presentation of Julia's feelings as she responds to the letter.

In the scene following Julia's receipt of the letter, Shakespeare again embellishes what he found in Montemayor. Shaping his material for the theater, the playwright employs another letter, this one without precedent in *Diana.* It is as though, having discovered how useful a letter could be, Shakespeare decided to construct a second scene around the same prop. In Montemayor's romance he had read of parental intrusion when Don Felix's father, learning of his son's love for Felismena, sends him away to court. Shakespeare exploits the theatrical possibilities by creating between father and son a confrontation triggered by the father spotting a letter in Proteus' hands.

The young man comes onstage with Julia's letter, saying, "Sweet love, sweet lines, sweet life! / Here is her hand, the agent of her heart" (I.iii.45-46). The mood changes abruptly when Antonio enters, sees the paper, and inquires, "what letter are you reading there?" (l. 51). Unwilling to disclose his love for Julia (just as she in the preceding scene was unwilling, albeit with a difference, to disclose to Lucetta her love for him), Proteus dissembles. He pretends to be reading a letter from Valentine. When Antonio asks to see it, his son demurs, saying only that Valentine wishes Proteus would join him in Milan. Seizing on this news, Antonio, as he has already determined to do, instructs his son to leave Verona: "I am resolv'd that thou shalt spend some time / With Valentinus in the Emperor's court" (ll. 66-67). Like many another parent in the world of comedy, Antonio, even if unwittingly, by his stubbornness frustrates his son's love affair: "Muse not that I thus suddenly proceed; / For what I will, I will, and there an end" (ll. 64-65). A despondent Proteus is left to ruminate on the role Julia's letter has played (or so he thinks) in their imminent separation:

I fear'd to show my father Julia's letter,
Lest he should take exceptions to my love,
And with the vantage of mine own excuse
Hath he excepted most against my love.

(*ll. 80-83*)

The image of the forlorn Proteus, the letter in his hands, contrasts vividly with our fresh memory of the buoyant Julia, the letter from Proteus in hers. In each of these juxtaposed scenes, a letter moves the plot swiftly forward, first drawing Proteus and Julia together, then apart.

Not only does Shakespeare invent letters that have no counterpart in *Diana,* he also extends the reading and writing to characters who themselves have no source in Montemayor's romance. Hence the letter-writing of Valentine, whose origin apparently lies in a Continental story of friendship told by Boccaccio in the *Decameron* (10.8) and by Sir Thomas Elyot in *The Boke named the Governour* (2.12).[7] Elyot's version tells of two friends, one of whom (Gisippus) generously offers his bride to his friend (Titus), much as Valentine offers Silvia to Proteus in the play's final scene. There is no letter-writing on the part of the friends in Elyot, whereas Shakespeare creates a scene in which Valentine (the counterpart of Gisippus) writes a letter at the behest of his beloved.

If earlier letters in the play advance the plot, Valentine's letter-writing is primarily to amuse the audience while the plot stands still. Silvia, in Milan, asks him for a letter, telling Valentine that she means to send it to a suitor of hers, as though she herself were its author. Valentine diligently applies himself to the work, for he tells her, "As you enjoin'd me, I have writ your letter / Unto the secret, nameless friend of yours" (II.i.104-05). Alas, the result fails to please Silvia, who remarks, "'tis very clerkly done" (l. 108). Sensing her disapproval, Valentine begins to make excuses: "I writ at random, very doubtfully" (l. 111). Seemingly unmoved, Silvia claims to detect a lack of enthusiasm in Valentine's words, and so, while conceding that "the lines are very quaintly writ," she adds, "(since unwillingly) take them again" (ll. 122-23). When an anguished Valentine protests, she says, "I would have had them writ more movingly" (l. 128).

Valentine is the very embodiment of naiveté. Ignorant of Silvia's true purpose, he fails to realize that the letter requested is really intended for his benefit—she has no other suitor to whom she means to write. The playwright, however, is not here concerned to explore Valentine's character, for that is manifest from the outset. Shakespeare's purpose in this scene is rather to create a comic effect: he generates laughter by the absurdity of Valentine's situation. In an aside Speed points the way for the audience's response: "O excellent device, was there ever heard a better, / That my master being scribe, to himself should write the letter?" (II.i.139-40). Servant must laboriously explain to master the significance of what has happened:

Speed. Why, do you not perceive the jest?
Valentine. No, believe me.
Speed. No believing you indeed, sir: but did you perceive her earnest?
Valentine. She gave me none, except an angry word.
Speed. Why, she hath given you a letter.
Valentine. That's the letter I writ to her friend.
Speed. And that letter hath she deliver'd, and there an end.

(*ll. 153-62*)

In their conversation Speed invites us to relish the contrast between the compliant Valentine's grave demeanor and the ridiculousness of his plight, a contrast heightened by the physical presence of the letter.

If a letter can form the basis of a comic scene, one in which nothing very important happens, a letter can also provide the focus of a theatrically big scene, in which the plot moves rapidly forward in a tragicomic direction. The letter that accomplishes this is written by Valentine on the brink of his elopement with the Duke's daughter, Silvia. It comes to light after Proteus, having joined his friend in Milan and having fallen in love with Silvia himself, betrays Valentine's plans to the Duke. The angry Duke finds Valentine in a great hurry: the young man explains, "there is a messenger / That stays to bear my letters to my friends, / And I am going to deliver them" (III.i.52-54). Sensing a lie, the Duke seeks to delay Valentine. On the pretext of seeking advice, the Duke claims to have fallen in love and says he needs to know how best to reach and woo his lady. Valentine, perhaps unconsciously, proceeds to counsel the very methods he means to employ with Silvia. Interpreting this as confirmation of what Proteus had told him, the Duke throws open Valentine's cloak to find the incriminating evidence—a rope ladder and a love letter addressed to Silvia.

This letter of Valentine's (actually a fusion of letter and poem) has a distinction denied other letters in the play: it receives a word-for-word recitation. Until now, we have not been given the text of anyone's letter—neither Proteus' letter to Julia (except for snippets), nor Julia's to Proteus, nor Valentine's for Silvia. In each instance Shakespeare prefers the revelation of the reader's character to the recitation of the writer's words. The playwright treats the words themselves as theatrically unimportant: the dramatic context and the response of the reader within the play suggest the gist of the letters. By omitting the actual text, Shakespeare demonstrates his instinct for what works onstage. Realizing that there is nothing particularly stageworthy about reading a letter, either silently or aloud, he dispenses with the contents altogether.

The Duke's reading of Valentine's letter, one without precedent in *Diana Enamorada* or in Elyot's *Governour,* manages to be at once complete and dramatically effective:

> "My thoughts do harbor with my Silvia nightly,
> And slaves they are to me that send them flying:
> O, could their master come and go as lightly,
> Himself would lodge where, senseless, they are lying!
> My herald thoughts in thy pure bosom rest them,
> While I, their king, that thither them importune,
> Do curse the grace that with such grace hath blest them,
> Because myself do want my servants' fortune.
> I curse myself, for they are sent by me,
> That they should harbor where their lord should be."
>
> (*III.i.140-49*)

It is easy to see why it would have been theatrically inappropriate for either Valentine or Silvia to have recited these lines. They are conventional thoughts expressed conventionally.[8] The opposition of "slave" and "king," of "curse" and "blest"—this is the familiar stuff of Elizabethan love poetry. And the rhymes—"nightly" and "lightly," "flying" and "lying"—are comically grotesque. Spoken by one of the lovers, the poem might well seem treacly or tiresome. Spoken by the Duke, however, the words create dramatic tension: the Duke's public reading is utterly out of keeping with Valentine's sentiments. Spluttering with rage, the Duke (if the actor does his work properly) invests the public reading—and thus the scene—with an energy and impact that it never would have had otherwise.

If a letter can help to raise the energy level of a scene, a letter can also contribute to the denouement, relaxing through laughter the tension created by the Duke's outburst. Thus Shakespeare employs, later in the same scene, a second "letter." Actually, this is not so much a proper letter as it is a compilation of the virtues and vices that make a certain woman a suitable, or unsuitable, match for Launce.[9] He shows the paper to Speed, who proceeds to read it aloud, beginning, "*Inprimis,* She can milk" (III.i.301). After the recitation of each item, Launce provides a commentary. For example:

> *Speed.* "*Item,* She is slow in words."
> *Launce.* O villain, that set this down among her vices! To be slow in words is a woman's only virtue. I pray thee out with't, and place it for her chief virtue.
>
> (*III.i.332-36*)

Although what the servant reads is, strictly speaking, scarcely more than an inventory, Speed treats it as though it were a letter. In fact, when he discovers that he is late in meeting his master, he tells Launce, "Pox of your love-letters!" (ll. 380-81). Of course, this letter (in prose) is nothing like Valentine's paean to Silvia (in verse). The one is romantic and fanciful, the other literal-minded and pragmatic. In mood and style there is a complete contrast, one that Shakespeare uses to spoof the conventions which Valentine and, presumably, Proteus observe in their writing. The send-up of epistolary conventions allows us to catch our breath after the Duke's tirade, and it prevents the play from veering too closely toward tragicomedy.

The use of two letters in a single scene may appear to some playgoers excessive. M. C. Bradbrook contends that "whenever Shakespeare can think of nothing else to do, he puts in a misdirected letter, of which there are a record number in this play."[10] A "record number" there may be, but it does not necessarily bespeak a flagging imagination. The plenitude of letters may just as well be interpreted as an expression of Shakespeare's ingenuity. Indeed, there is an exuberance about their use that betokens creative energy. In tracing the handling of the love letters, we appreciate how many variations Shakespeare could work on a motif: a letter torn to shreds; a letter read with delight; a letter rebuffed; a letter read aloud by the hostile parent of its intended recipient; a letter read aloud by an amused and condescending friend. No other comic dramatist devised so many theatrical applications for love letters or used them to better effect.

Despite their quantity in *Two Gentlemen,* love letters paradoxically frustrate love as well as foster it. Julia's letter to Proteus becomes the agent of their separation when he fears to reveal its contents to his father. Similarly, Valentine's letter to Silvia, falling into the hands of the Duke, helps to precipitate his banishment. If letters as physical instruments can foil lovers, letters can present problems of another and more subtle kind, too. For such letters are not always what they appear to be. Although they may contain pledges of enduring love, those oaths may not stand the test of time. It is Proteus who brings this matter to issue.

When he joins Valentine in Milan, sees his friend's beloved, and promptly falls in love with her himself, Proteus demonstrates the fragility of words as guarantors of emotional commitment. Thinking back on all that he had vowed to Julia, he sets about rationalizing his change of affections:

> Unheedful vows may heedfully be broken,
> And he wants wit that wants resolved will
> To learn his wit t' exchange the bad for better.
> Fie, fie, unreverend tongue, to call her bad,
> Whose sovereignty so oft thou hast preferr'd
> With twenty thousand soul-confirming oaths.
>
> *(II.vi.11-16)*

True to his name, Proteus changes abruptly, in this instance altering allegiance from one woman to another. Unfortunately, Julia, not knowing of the transformation, continues to think of him as he was only a short while ago. In fact, she remains so much in love that she determines to follow him to Milan. Before setting out she affirms the congruence of Proteus' words and feelings:

> His words are bonds, his oaths are oracles,
> His love sincere, his thoughts immaculate,
> His tears pure messengers sent from his heart,
> His heart as far from fraud as heaven from earth.
>
> *(II.vii.75-78)*

Syntactically, the language of the first line ("words" and "oaths") is paired with that of the second ("love" and "thoughts"). Julia has complete confidence in this equivalence. But by the time she speaks these lines Proteus has already violated his oaths to her. His words, so lovingly recollected, are worthless. As Julia is shortly to discover, oaths need not signify permanence, and they may be broken with little or no remorse.

Full of self-righteousness, Proteus sets out to displace Valentine in Silvia's affections: first he will engineer his friend's banishment, then dislodge Thurio, whom the Duke intends as a husband for Silvia. Feigning solicitude, Proteus tells the Duke of Valentine's plan to elope with Silvia, and the Duke nabs Valentine.

Proteus succeeds in large measure because of hypocrisy: he manages to conceal his selfishness beneath the guise of good will. He tells the Duke that his motive for revealing Valentine's plan is noble: "For love of you, not hate unto my friend, / Hath made me publisher of this pretense" (III.i.46-47). Similarly, Proteus convinces Valentine of his solicitude, even after the betrayal. And the reprobate actually offers to act as intermediary between his absent friend and Silvia:

> Thy letters may be here, though thou art hence,
> Which, being writ to me, shall be deliver'd
> Even in the milk white bosom of thy love.
>
> *(III.i.250-52)*

The prospect of aid is, of course, delusory, a sham designed to hasten the removal of a rival in love. But Valentine never guesses how improbable it is that Proteus should forward to Silvia any letters sent from exile.

Proteus' ability to convince others of his benevolence owes a great deal to his verbal fluency, apparent near the beginning of the play when Julia reads his first letter. It is apparent too when he betrays Valentine to the Duke and then suggests how Silvia may be made to forget her love: "The best way is to slander Valentine" (III.ii.31). Pointing out that his daughter may be skeptical of anything said against Valentine, the Duke thinks to have Proteus perpetrate the slander; a friend's knowledge of the accused man's character will presumably lend credence to the charges. It is not only the betrayal itself that is disturbing but also the connection between the ability to praise (so useful and appropriate in a speech or letter of love) and the ability to damn (so useful to the Duke and Proteus in besmirching Valentine's character). Thurio makes explicit the connection between the two actions when he asks that Proteus help him "by praising me as much / As you in worth dispraise Sir Valentine" (ll. 54-55). Even though Thurio is something of a buffoon, his request raises a troubling question. For if verbal fluency may be perverted, if a man's word is not his bond, and if there is no necessary connection between eloquence of expression and nobility of feeling, then what significance can a profession of love have? It may be artful and clever, affecting and even compelling—without being true.

As if to underscore the untrustworthiness of words, Shakespeare portrays the schemers exulting in their skill with language. To woo Silvia, Proteus tells Thurio,

> You must lay lime to tangle her desires
> By wailful sonnets, whose composed rhymes
> Should be full-fraught with serviceable vows.
>
> *(III.ii.68-70)*

Listening closely, the Duke endorses the advice: "Ay, much is the force of heaven-bred poesy" (l. 71). But as the audience recognizes, there is nothing "heaven-bred" either in Thurio's suit or in the notion of "tangling" one's beloved in lime. Indeed, Proteus' image of entrapment conveys a sinister suggestion. But, indifferent to such implications, Proteus becomes increasingly carried away with the prospect of what the written word can accomplish. He tells Thurio:

Write till your ink be dry, and with your tears
Moist it again, and frame some feeling line
That may discover such integrity.

(*ll.* 74-76)

We might regard Proteus' injunction with more equanimity if we felt that Thurio were a suitable match for Silvia or if Proteus' affection for her were likely to be more lasting than that for Julia. But Thurio is bumbling and Proteus callow. So all the talk of "dire-lamenting elegies" and "sweet-complaining grievance" is offensive as advice proffered by a slanderer to a fool.

Of that advice the Duke says approvingly, "This discipline shows thou hast been in love" (III.ii.87). But the audience, at least, has grown skeptical of equating depth of feeling with force of expression. Although the Duke's notion may have seemed valid earlier in the play, it seems so no longer, for we cannot forget that Proteus has violated his oaths to Julia and betrayed his friend. We shudder at the thought of what Thurio may write and at what Proteus may accomplish. From this point on, we view with suspicion both praise and dispraise. Words have come to seem, at best, like coins that have lost their value. At worst, they are no better than counterfeits, employed by the unscrupulous for nefarious ends.

Paradoxically, Proteus' very glibness hastens the erosion of his credibility. Silvia instinctively distrusts his slander against Valentine, and she upbraids him for wooing her when he is supposed to be aiding the hapless Thurio. When she learns of Proteus' former love for another woman, he loses the last of whatever stature remains to him. He reflects,

When I protest true loyalty to her,
She twits me with my falsehood to my friend;
When to her beauty I commend my vows,
She bids me think how I have been forsworn
In breaking faith with Julia whom I lov'd.

(*IV.ii.7-11*)

With some relief we listen as Silvia sees through his designs and dismisses his eloquence:

Thou subtile, perjur'd, false, disloyal man,
Think'st thou I am so shallow, so conceitless,
To be seduced by thy flattery,
That hast deceiv'd so many with thy vows?

(*ll.* 95-98)

She recognizes that the power to praise may also be the power to feign; the power to vow may be the power to lie. Armed with this knowledge, Silvia brushes aside Proteus' entreaties.

Even in the face of her rejection, Proteus doggedly persists. Maintaining faith in what words can achieve, he turns from speech to writing, and he has a servant deliver his letters to Silvia. In dramatizing the courtship, Shakespeare draws closely on Montemayor's *Diana.* Just as Felismena disguises herself as a page to follow Don Felix, so does Julia disguise herself in order to follow Proteus to Milan. Just as Felismena overhears Don Felix serenading Celia one evening, so does Julia overhear Proteus serenading Silvia. And just as Felismena in disguise enters Don Felix's service as a page (named Valerius), so too Julia enters Proteus' service as a page (named Sebastian). In his employ she functions, like Felismena, as an intermediary, carrying his letters to Silvia and her rebuffs back to him. Shakespeare's indebtedness to Montemayor here is strong and clear. He departs from *Diana* in a small but significant detail, however, and in so doing dramatizes the debasement that language has suffered during the dramatic action.

When Julia delivers Proteus' letter to Silvia, she finds that she has made a mistake, quickly takes back the letter, then replaces it with another:

Madam, please you peruse this letter—
Pardon me, madam, I have unadvis'd
Deliver'd you a paper that I should not:
This is the letter to your ladyship.

(*IV.iv.121-24*)

Almost certainly the first letter is one that Proteus had written earlier to Julia, perhaps even the letter destroyed and then reconstructed in the play's second scene.[11] Seeing this letter together with the letter to Silvia, we cannot help reflecting on what they contain: equally ardent professions of love written by the same man to different women. Even though Julia obviously still treasures her original letter, we know that Proteus' words are no longer to be taken at face value. They lack the intrinsic worth which they seemed to possess in the opening scenes of the play. Thus we feel that Silvia's treatment of her letter is justified. She tells the page,

I will not look upon your master's lines;
I know they are stuff'd with protestations,
And full of new-found oaths, which he will break
As easily as I do tear his paper.

(*ll.* 128-31)

Then, as the last line indicates, Silvia does something without precedent in *Diana.* Whereas her counterpart, Celia, accepts the letter of Don Felix and peruses it carefully, Silvia tears her letter to pieces. The dramatic action recalls Julia's similar tearing of Proteus' letter early in the play, and the repetition creates an obvious parallel—but with a difference. Proteus' letter to Julia (in I.ii) conveyed sincere feeling; and there was presumably nothing ignoble then about either the man or his letter. Therefore, when Julia destroyed that letter, we felt the disjunction between the contents and the letter's fate. The letter to Silvia (in IV.iv) is another matter altogether, for it is the creation of a slanderer and philanderer. And although Proteus' feelings may seem outwardly sincere, his profession of love for Silvia will soon be revealed as sham by his behavior in the forest. The second letter, then, deserves to be torn up;

Proteus' words are now as valueless as the scraps of paper that fall to the stage.

If words seem diminished in Silvia's view, they no longer enjoy the same importance in Proteus' view either. Although he may continue to revel in what he imagines that language, written or spoken, can accomplish, Silvia correctly perceives that his attitude is essentially manipulative. He employs words not out of any respect for them, but out of selfishness. Words are useful to him only so long as they seem likely to win over Silvia. When importuning proves ineffectual, he abandons words, substituting brute force. He follows Silvia into the forest and, claiming that "the gentle spirit of moving words" has failed him, attempts to rape her. This demonstrates as nothing else could the essential falsity of his devotion to her. And with his perfidy revealed for all to see, Julia at last drops her disguise and rails at him:

> Behold her that gave aim to all thy oaths,
> And entertain'd 'em deeply in her heart.
> How oft hast thou with perjury cleft the root?
>
> (*V.iv.101-03*)

Here outrage vies with pain as Julia excoriates a history of betrayed oaths.

Ironically, she herself has participated in the misuse of language. As Sebastian she has had to diverge from the truth. "And now am I (unhappy messenger)," Julia said earlier, "To praise his faith which I would have disprais'd" (IV.iv.99, 102). And so in her conversation with Silvia she fell into equivocation not altogether different in kind from that of Proteus when he concealed the truth about Julia. Awkward in her role as go-between, she affected a certain detachment in manner: "Yet will I woo for him, but yet so coldly / As, heaven it knows, I would not have him speed" (ll. 106-07). This strategy, however, does not entirely absolve Julia of responsibility for manipulating language so as to obscure her own feelings and purpose. Only our knowledge of her suffering at Proteus' hands and of Silvia's determination to resist Proteus' blandishments tempers our judgment of what Julia does.

Even Valentine, who expresses shock at the disjunction between Proteus' past words and present deeds in the forest, has himself participated in the devaluation of language. Earlier, advising the Duke on how to win his lady, Valentine espoused an attitude that sounded uncomfortably like Proteus':

> Flatter and praise, commend, extol their graces;
> Though ne'er so black, say they have angels' faces.
> That man that hath a tongue, I say is no man,
> If with his tongue he cannot win a woman.
>
> (*III.i.102-05*)

Even if we posit a distracted state of mind on Valentine's part—this is the day of his planned elopement—there remains something distinctly unpleasant about these lines. In their calculation they are not so very different from Proteus' advice to the Duke and Thurio in the next scene (III.ii).[12]

That even Valentine should have become a little cynical is perhaps the inevitable corollary of a society that attaches inordinate importance to convention. The courtly world of Verona and Milan is one in which the "right" speech, writing, and behavior are expected. There may be nothing intrinsically unreasonable in deferring to social norms. But the more that language is used to serve the expectations of society, the less reliably does it express an individual's feelings. The fine line between observing and manipulating convention can easily be crossed by the unscrupulous or even the careless. A profession of love, then, may leave the recipient wondering where convention leaves off and genuine feeling begins.

Love letters become a repository of conventions for a variety of reasons: they allow a writer to express an otherwise ineffable state of mind; they give attractive form to passions that are by nature unruly and turbulent; and by their durability they obscure the fact that passion may subside as quickly as it surges. Of course, lovers would deny such inconstancy. They want—perhaps need—to believe that the beloved will remain steadfast; and they themselves want to be perceived in the same way. Whether consciously or unconsciously, they seek the illusion of permanence. To this end epistolary conventions prove useful: in a world of shifting emotion, conventions by virtue of their stability provide psychological reassurance.

In *Two Gentlemen,* the impermanence of passion, however intense, is most acutely revealed in Proteus, the most indefatigable letter-writer in the play. His language captures the vicissitudes of his nature. In a speech describing, successively, Silvia, Julia, and himself, he says:

> She is fair; and so is Julia that I love
> (That I did love, for now my love is thaw'd,
> Which like a waxen image 'gainst a fire
> Bears no impression of the thing it was).
> Methinks my zeal to Valentine is cold,
> And that I love him not as I was wont.
>
> (*II.iv.199-204*)

The imagery of warmth and cold conveys his notion that love is a fleeting disposition, destined to perish just as surely as a "waxen image."[13] This attitude issues in his concern with the conventions governing the expression of love. He imparts his concern to Thurio, who proves an enthusiastic pupil: "I have a sonnet that will serve the turn / To give the onset to thy good advice" (III.ii.92-93). Sonnets of this kind, apparently already prepared and awaiting a suitable occasion for deployment, are meant to lend dignity to an emotional state which the sonneteer knows is evanescent.

The Duke applauds Proteus' advice to Thurio and sends the two men forth to pursue Silvia: "About it, gentlemen!" This approval arises out of a concept of love virtually identical to Proteus'. Indeed, when he assures Thurio that Silvia will forget Valentine, the Duke uses terminology similar to Proteus':

> This weak impress of love is as a figure
> Trenched in ice, which with an hour's heat
> Dissolves to water, and doth lose his form.
> A little time will melt her frozen thoughts,
> And worthless Valentine shall be forgot.
>
> *(III.ii.6-10)*

Although Proteus' speech cited above concerns his own volatile temperament, and the Duke here is speaking of his daughter, both men share the notion that "love" is mercurial and its effect on personality slight. They even use the same term: the Duke speaks of love as a "weak impress"; Proteus speaks of an "impression" that no longer exists.

Proteus and the Duke may find encouragement in one another's views, but this does not prevent them from misunderstanding the nature of love. Hence they misconstrue Silvia's relationship to Valentine. If her father and her relentless wooer confuse love with infatuation, Silvia experiences love as an altogether stronger and more enduring force. When Proteus tells her, "I . . . hear that Valentine is dead," she replies, "And so suppose am I; for in his grave / Assure thyself my love is buried" (IV.ii.112-14). Just as their attitude toward love is reflected in their attitude toward love letters, so is hers. She judges the letter that Valentine writes for her to be "very clerkly" and tells him that it is "very quaintly writ" (II.i.108, 122). Her criticism suggests that it is a tissue of conventional figures. What she finds missing, evidently, is language that by its vitality conveys the depth of love that she feels, for of Valentine's lines she says, "I would have had them writ more movingly" (l. 128). If writing comes easily to Proteus and Thurio, it does not to Silvia. Or at least she chooses not to entrust her thoughts to paper. Alone among the lovers in the play, she fails to write a single letter. Nor does the audience see her accept any proffered letter. Her reticence is the antithesis of Proteus' easy eloquence.

This does not mean that true love is necessarily antithetical to written expression: the one can and does accompany the other—witness Julia's letter to Proteus. But writing that reflects genuine love (as opposed to a fit of passion) is more than a matter of words on paper. Love involves a compelling interaction of one's words and one's innermost being. Julia alludes to this in her speech to Lucetta before embarking on the journey to Milan. Deeply in love with Proteus, Julia seeks her maid's advice:

> Counsel, Lucetta; gentle girl, assist me;
> And ev'n in kind love I do conjure thee,
> Who art the table wherein all my thoughts
> Are visibly character'd and engrav'd. . . .
>
> *(II.vii.1-4)*

Asking her confidante to articulate the impression that she (Julia) has created, mistress imagines that maid is a writing tablet or notebook on which her thoughts take visible shape in the form of words. Julia's speech concerns the relationship of two women, but her words "kind love" suggest that the imagery may have a wider application, that other relationships, including those between men and women, may be similarly imagined.

Much the same image that Julia uses in *Two Gentlemen* is employed in *Diana Enamorada* to express romantic love. There, literal and figurative writing coalesce when Felismena, the counterpart of Julia, ponders the effect of Don Felix's first letter:

> When I had now seene my *Don Felix* his letter, whether it was for reading it at such a time, when by the same he shewed, that he loved me more then himselfe, or whether he had disposition and regiment over part of this wearied soule, to imprint that love in it, whereof he wrote unto me, I began to love him too well. . . .
>
> *(p. 85)*

The word "imprint" need not refer to the activities of a printing house, but the context here points to the importance of actual reading and writing for Felismena. It is not until she reads the letter that she is brought to a recognition of her love for Don Felix; his words are inextricably connected with her experience of love. For her, the act of reading seems to release an emotion already present within. Of course, this is not simply a matter of epistolary conventions having their desired effect. She responds to the genuineness of Don Felix's sentiments, and they, rather than the conventions *per se,* "imprint" his love. In short, the literal writing is but the means to a more important "writing." The most profound imprinting, after all, is not that which occurs on paper but in Felismena's "soule."

In *Two Gentlemen,* as in *Diana,* love is virtually inseparable from the written word. This, at least, is suggested by Silvia's reproof of Proteus in the play's final scene:

> Read over Julia's heart (thy first best love),
> For whose dear sake thou didst then rend thy faith
> Into a thousand oaths; and all those oaths
> Descended into perjury, to love me.
>
> *(V.iv.46-49)*

The word "read" has a variety of possible meanings, including look over, see, discern, study, and apprehend. But it can also, of course, specifically mean "comprehend the written word." If it has that meaning here, then it underscores the importance of reading and writing that transcend ink and paper. Silvia implies that Proteus' original words are registered in Julia's heart where they remain as vivid as on the day first formulated. They remain there because Julia's love is undiminished. Since the words remain unaltered, they represent a potential source of stability, a steady point in a world of emotional flux, for if Proteus recollects the words he wrote to Julia, and if he recollects the effect of his words upon her, then perhaps her love for him will evoke the memory of his love for her. His present feelings may become congruent with his past words.

By its presence in the play's final scene, Silvia's injunction to read Julia's heart prevents *Two Gentlemen* from concluding with a repudiation of words. Her speech affirms the value of language, especially the language of love. Despite Proteus' broken oaths, Julia's equivocation as go-between, Valentine's cynicism when he advises the Duke on wooing, and Thurio's literary contrivance, words have not lost their significance entirely. They retain the capacity not only to express a writer's love but also to shape the amorphous feelings of a reader. This does not mean that, in *Two Gentlemen,* words actually create love; if they could, love letters would be even more numerous than they are. But love and letters can have the most profound relationship.

Notes

1. *The Riverside Shakespeare,* ed. G. Blakemore Evans, et al. (Boston: Houghton Mifflin, 1974).

2. Proteus' employment of Valentine's servant to deliver the letter is one of numerous anomalies listed by Clifford Leech in the New Arden *Two Gentlemen of Verona* (London: Methuen, 1969), pp. xviii-xxi.

3. Although it is generally accepted that *Diana* is Shakespeare's chief source, it remains unclear exactly how he came to know the romance. An English translation by Bartholomew Yong was published in 1598, but *Two Gentlemen* was probably written some years earlier. Shakespeare may have seen Yong's translation in manuscript; according to the translator, the work was completed sixteen years before publication. Shakespeare may have known *Diana* in a French translation by Nicholas Collin (1578 and 1587). It is also possible that Shakespeare was indebted to a lost play entitled *The History of Felix and Philiomena,* performed at court in 1585. Geoffrey Bullough, in *Narrative and Dramatic Sources of Shakespeare,* I (New York: Columbia Univ. Press, 1957), suggests that the lost play "was probably a pastoral based on Montemayor" (p. 206).

4. *A Critical Edition of Yong's Translation of George of Montemayor's Diana and Gil Polo's Enamoured Diana,* ed. Judith M. Kennedy (Oxford: Clarendon Press, 1968), p. 84.

5. The relationship of this scene to the incident in *Diana* is the subject of much commentary. See T. P. Harrison, Jr., "Shakespeare and Montemayor's *Diana,*" *University of Texas Studies in English,* 6 (1926), 76-78; John A. Guinn, "The Letter Device in the First Act of *The Two Gentlemen of Verona,*" *University of Texas Studies in English,* 20 (1940), 72-81; Bertrand Evans, Introduction to the Signet Classic *Two Gentlemen of Verona* (New York: New American Library, 1964), pp. xxvii-xxviii; Judith M. Kennedy, ed. *A Critical Edition of Yong's Translation,* pp. xliv-xlv.

6. John A. Guinn, in "The Letter Device," suggests that Julia's tearing of Proteus' letter is indebted to *De Duobus Amantibus* by Aeneas Sylvius Piccolomini. However, William Leigh Godshalk, in *Patterning in Shakespearean Drama: Essays in Criticism* (The Hague: Mouton, 1973), finds Guinn's argument "inconclusive" (p. 45, note 6). Julia's tearing of the letter may be related to an incident in a German play, published in Germany in 1620, entitled *Julio und Hyppolita.* Clifford Leech, in the New Arden *Two Gentlemen,* observes, "we cannot determine the priority between this play and Shakespeare's, but that a connection exists seems likely" (p. xxxix). Geoffrey Bullough, who describes the German play as an analogue, notes that the letter torn by Hyppolita (Julia's counterpart) is forged (I, 208-09).

7. Ralph M. Sargent, in "Sir Thomas Elyot and the Integrity of *The Two Gentlemen of Verona,*" *PMLA* [*Publications of the Modern Language Association*], 65 (1950), 1166-80, contends, "There can now be little doubt that it was exactly this story of Titus and Gisippus which Shakespeare used as the second of his major sources for the action of *Two Gentlemen*" (p. 1173). Elyot's narrative may have influenced Shakespeare not only directly but also indirectly through John Lyly, who, according to Sargent, "used elements of Elyot's story of Titus and Gisippus, in a sort of reverse way, in *Euphues*" (p. 1173). The extent of Lyly's influence on *Two Gentlemen* remains unclear. G. K. Hunter, in *John Lyly: The Humanist as Courtier* (London: Routledge and Kegan Paul, 1962), enumerates certain resemblances between *Euphues* and the play, concluding, "one may justly suspect that *Euphues* has helped to shape Shakespeare's handling of his story" (p. 326). R. Warwick Bond, himself an editor of Lyly's works, in the Old Arden edition of *Two Gentlemen* (London: Methuen, 1906), suggests specifically that the letter writing of the play may have an inspiration in Lyly: "The six (or seven) letters that figure in the play remind us of Lyly's novel" (p. xxx). But Geoffrey Bullough, in *Narrative and Dramatic Sources,* sees a greater influence exerted by Lyly's plays than by his novel: "Shakespeare's debt to Lyly was probably more one of technique than of matter, and he worked out any suggestions got from *Euphues* in accordance with the symmetrical balance of character found more in Lyly's plays than in his moral romance" (I, 204).

8. R. Warwick Bond, in the Old Arden edition, observes of Valentine's verse letter: "The lines form a regular Shakespearean sonnet lacking the first quatrain, like the ten lines spoken by Orlando, *As You Like It,* III.ii., and the ten spoken by Beatrice, *Much Ado,* III.i.107-116" (p. 55). Inga-Stina Ewbank, in "'Were man but constant, he were perfect': Constancy and Consistency in 'The Two Gentlemen of Verona,'" *Shakespearian Comedy* (London: Edward Arnold, 1972), pp. 31-57, points to a connection between this play and Shakespeare's sonnets: "the really important relationship between *The Two Gentlemen of Verona* and the sonnets seems to me to have to do with

Shakespeare's attitude to his own poetry and to the traditions of love poetry in which he finds himself writing" (p. 35).

9. R. Warwick Bond notes: "This catalogue, read by one page with comments by the other, is adapted from the very similar scene in Lyly's *Midas* (printed 1592), I.ii.20-87, where the page Licio rehearses, to his fellow Petulus' comment, the properties of Caelia, his mistress (in domestic service)" (p. 64).

10. M. C. Bradbrook, *Shakespeare and Elizabethan Poetry* (London: Chatto & Windus, 1951), p. 153. It is worth noting that Shakespeare did not employ all the letters he found in *Diana.* For instance, Montemayor provides the song and the sonnet of Don Felix to Celia; in *Two Gentlemen* we hear a song but no sonnet to Silvia (IV.ii). In *Diana* Don Felix reads the text of Celia's letter to the disguised Felismena; Proteus recites no letter from Silvia because she has not written to him. And although Don Felix's letter to Celia is given in full, there is no corresponding text from Proteus to Silvia provided in the play.

11. In Kristoffer Tabori's production of *Two Gentlemen* at the Grove Shakespeare Festival (Garden Grove, California) in 1983, the first letter Julia presented to Silvia was lavender, and when she took it back she held it close to her heart, suggesting that it was a love letter received from Proteus.

12. Geoffrey Bullough, in *Narrative and Dramatic Sources,* notes that Valentine's advice to the Duke on wooing (III.i) recalls a scene in Lyly's *Sapho and Phao* (II.iv), where one character says to another: "Chuse such words as may (as many may) melt her mind . . . Write, and persist in writing; they reade more than is written to them, and write lesse than they thinke" (I, 204-05). Proteus' advice to Thurio in III.ii may have had the same inspiration.

13. Clifford Leech, in the New Arden edition, cites the explanation of George Steevens: "Alluding to the figures made by witches, as representatives of those whom they designed to torment or destroy" (p. 44).

Muriel C. Bradbrook (essay date 1989)

SOURCE: "Love and Courtesy in *The Two Gentlemen of Verona,*" in *Shakespeare in his Context: The Constellated Globe, The Collected Papers of Muriel Bradbrook,* Vol. IV, Harvester Wheatsheaf, 1989, pp. 44-57.

[*In the following essay, Bradbrook explores the play as a comedy of manners, suggesting that it is more closely affiliated with Shakespeare's last romances than his later comedies of love.*]

It is a great honour to be invited in this ancient city to celebrate a poet who wrote of this region with varying degrees of knowledge but always with reverence, as of a visionary country, a country of the heart. On the stage of his day, Italy was depicted either as very beautiful or very, very wicked. There was nothing in between a country full of lovers and a country full of murderous ducal feuds. No ordinary lives at all; the moonlight of the summer garden was heavenly or else the 'smiler with the knife beneath the cloak', Iago or Iachimo, trapped the unpractised alien. From the beginning to end of his career Shakespeare turned to Italy, and his last play celebrated a unification which had happened between parts of the British Isles; he shows the heiress of Milan betrothed to the heir of Naples.

Today I wish to look at his comedy of courtly love, named from this city—*The Two Gentlemen of Verona,* for him *par excellence* the City of Lovers. I would place it in 1593, the year when plague closed London theatres and the young writer (he was 29) retired to the country to write *Venus and Adonis.* It has not received as much attention as later comedies, but it is a beautiful and delicate piece of *sprezzatura,* that links it not with the later comedies of love, several of which are also set in Italy, such as *Much Ado about Nothing,* but rather with last romances, *The Tempest* particularly in which Shakespeare turned back to memories of earlier traditions. But Shakespeare's work, though so full of variety, is also deeply unified. The element of fantasy in his art struck his contemporaries.

The early morning freshness of *The Two Gentlemen of Verona* was very well caught visually in the BBC's television production. Many plays were given an Italian flavour—*Antony and Cleopatra,* in Renaissance style, was heavily flavoured with the opulence of Titian. *The Two Gentlemen of Verona* was based on Fra Angelico and the early Botticelli of *Primavera.* Lightness, innocence, delicacy and grace were embodied in the heroine, with her transparent draperies, her garden setting; her wooers also reminded me of Botticelli's young men.

The Two Gentlemen of Verona is built on a tale of love and friendship, not for the sake of developing characters, but for exploring moods embodied in manners; for displaying sentiments, not conflicts—sentiments in the psychological sense of habitual sets of feelings emerging from implanted disposition, not innate. This is the Italy of Petrarch and Castiglione, perhaps of Ariosto.

No supernatural beings hover in the summer air, but something like the music of Ariel is heard in the aubade procured by the two unworthiest of her suitors to be sung at Silvia's window—in Schubert's setting, the best known words of this play:

> Who is Silvia? what is she
> That all our swains commend her?
> Holy, fair and wise is she:
> The heaven such grace did lend her
> That she might admired be.
>
> (IV.ii.38-42)

'Admired'—a wonder, like the 'most admired' Miranda; not a mortal but to her lover 'the goddess on whom these airs attend'. Silvia indeed radiates the grace of heaven; she is 'excelling', sent from on high. Her father's courtiers are her servants in the sense of professing to love her, without daring to aspire to her hand, rendering the service of '*fin amours*' like the trouvères.

England indeed knew such a divinity; although no longer either young or fair, Elizabeth now enjoyed the height of her literary cult among poets, all vying to assert her eternal beauty in terms often borrowed from the cult of the Virgin Mary. In Spenser, presented as Belphoebe

> Her face so fair as flesh it seemed not,
> But heavenly portrait of bright angel's hue . . .

to Ben Jonson she is a heavenly being from an older religion, Cynthia, still excelling.

> Queen and huntress chaste and fair,
> Now the sun is laid to sleep,
> Seated in thy silver chair,
> State in wonted manner keep.
> Hesperus entreats thy light,
> Goddess excellently bright.

John Lyly wrote plays in her praise, as he also wrote wittily to provide models of conversation for the Court. His plays were given by the choristers of her chapel and these have the most powerful and refining influence on Shakespeare's court comedies of love, although he outgrew Lyly. Here is the praise of Cynthia by Endimion in a play upon which Shakespeare closely depended:

> Such a difference hath the gods set between our states that all must be duty, loyalty, reverence; nothing (without it please your highness) be termed love. My spotted thoughts, my languishing body, my discontented life, let them obtain by princely favour that which to challenge they must not presume, only wishing of impossibilities; with imagination of which, I will spend my spirits, and softly to myself, that no creature may hear, call it love. And if any urge to utter what I whisper, then I will term it honour.

Shakespeare's first sixteen sonnets exhort marriage on the model of the early pleas to the Queen; but in this comedy wooing instruction, whether the First Gentleman's to the Duke or the Second's to his rival, are farcical and lead to entrapment.

The first of the two Gentlemen to be sent from Verona to Milan is a professed mocker of his lovelorn friend but his role as true lover is proclaimed in his name, Valentine, named for the patron saint of lovers, on whose feast not only men but birds chose their mates. He falls instantly into worship of the heiress of Milan, the divine Silvia, but does not aspire to woo her; she instead asks him to write a love letter for her to one she loves, which she then tells him to keep. His witty page has to enlighten him that this modest device is to make him aware of her favour. For the little love god blinds his votaries; the engagingly silly infatuation of first love was to receive affectionate banter and very clear demonstration in Shakespeare's later comedy, *A Midsummer Night's Dream,* where the Duke describes the lover's frenzy that can

> see Helen's beauty in a brow of Egypt.

The Duke of Milan, with his own blindness, is encouraging the rich but stupid Thurio to court his daughter, and Valentine engages in a sharp duel of wits with him. But when the second Gentleman arrives and is generously introduced by Valentine with the request that he be enrolled [as] Silvia's courtly servant, Proteus, though now betrothed by a ring to Julia, keeps neither friendship nor vows, although he has not been given any magic love juice by a fairy; but he has already termed himself metamorphosed by love, and now proves his name from the great shape-changer Proteus to be fitting. He debates quite sharply within himself: for he has been told by Valentine that his own love for Silvia is of the heart.

> To leave my Julia, shall I be forsworn:
> To love fair Silvia, shall I be forsworn:
> To wrong my friend I shall be much forsworn.
> And e'en that power which gave me first my oath
> Provokes me to this threefold perjury:
> Love bade me swear and love bids me forswear.
> O sweet-suggesting love, if thou hast sinn'd,
> Teach me, thy tempted subject, to excuse it.
>
> (II.vi.1-8)

Wronging his friend is the worst sin. But prompted by love, he puts the counterplea, as in a later play, 'some salve for perjury' had to be found at another court.

> At first I did adore a twinkling star,
> But now I worship a celestial sun.
>
> (9-10)

With the same wit that earlier he had defended himself against Valentine's mocks he crowns his sophistry:

> Julia I lose and Valentine I lose.
> If I keep them I needs must lose myself:
> If I lose them, thus find I by their loss:
> For Valentine, myself; for Julia, Silvia.
>
> (19-22)

This is but wordplay; in the last scene, when Valentine discovers the depths to which Proteus has been brought, *he* feels a loss which is not that of self-sufficiency but of the vulnerable self that is invested in honourable trust. Valentine, like a later hero, is 'most generous and free from all contriving'; in fact his contriving to elope with Silvia had been deftly uncovered by the Duke, prompted by Proteus. Finally, he witnesses Proteus' threat of force towards his lady

> Treacherous man,
> Thou hast beguil'd my hopes; naught but mine eye
> Could have persuaded me. Now I dare not say
> I have one friend alive; thou wouldst disprove me.
> Who should be trusted now, when one's right hand

Is perjured to the bosom? . . .
The private wound is deepest. O most accurst!
'Mongst all foes that a friend should be the worst!

(V.iv.63-72)

Confronted with depth of grief, Proteus is immediately struck into deep remorse; and then comes the turn of events which is universally misunderstood, universally considered to destroy the play. I think the lines are misconstrued and they do not destroy it at all, but depend on the contrast between private and courtly status.

What has happened is that after betraying the lovers to the Duke, Proteus follows Silvia in her flight to the banished Valentine. Meeting her in a wood, where Valentine had earlier been turned into the captain of a band of outlaws, he begins to woo her, and on repulse, attempts to rape her. Valentine who has overheard it all, has heard his lady declare her love of himself:

O heaven be judge how I love Valentine
Whose life's as tender to me as my soul

(V.iv.36-7)

and the words with which he delivers her are those of courtly decorum, very restrained (but presumably he has drawn his sword):

Ruffian, let go that rude, uncivil touch,
Thou friend of an ill fashion.

(60-1)

After Proteus' repentance, his 'forgive me', he proceeds:

Then I am paid;
And once again I do receive thee honest.
Who by repentance is not satisfied
Is not of heaven nor earth, for these are pleased.
By penitence th'Eternal's wrath's appeased.
And that my love may appear plain and free,
All that was mine in Silvia I give thee.

(77-83)

The outcry is all but universal. 'By this time, there are *no* gentlemen in Verona!' exclaimed Sir Arthur Quiller-Couch. But the verb is all important: 'was' is not 'is', as another wise character was to remark. (See above p. 35.) Proteus, who is on his knees before Valentine, may be invited, kneeling, to kiss the lady's other hand. What is offered to Proteus is public reinstatement to the position they had formerly shared and Valentine had procured; what had been theirs was the position of courtly servant to the lady but Valentine is now speaking as Silvia's betrothed lover (II.iv.176) and protector—a generous but not preposterous act. Valentine in the wood assumes an authority which enables him, when the Duke arrives as captive to the outlaws, to defy Thurio with a physical directness which comes from the new relation that his rescue and Silvia's declaration of love had conferred:

I dare thee but to breathe upon my love!

(V.iv.132)

He ends with great assurance, though in the Duke's presence, by inviting Proteus and his restored Julia to be married on the day he marries Silvia. Proteus never addresses Silvia. And Silvia says nothing at all. Outside the charmed circle of the court, she does not now speak to Proteus, or to her father. In the opening scenes Julia had nothing to say by way of farewell to Proteus. And now, at this point, present in disguise as Proteus' page, she swoons. It may be thought that this confirms the modern idea that Valentine is relinquishing Silvia to Proteus, but is it not the hand-in-hand postures of the lovers that recalls to her betrothal-ring (and Proteus' ring) both now in her keeping?

Valentine had first, after entreating Proteus' admission as 'fellow servant to your ladyship', exalted her to Proteus 'a heavenly saint' to which Proteus replies 'No, but she is an earthly paragon'; and in his new feelings, the grosser level is stressed ''Tis but her picture I have yet beheld' (II.iv.207). His stupid servant Launce presents the divine Silvia instead of Proteus' toy dog with a rough cur of his own, who befouls her farthingale; and the animal level of Proteus comes out in the wood. Valentine is re-educating him, using that line of the Paternoster that echoes down to the epilogue of *The Tempest*: Forgive us our sins as we forgive those who sin against us.

Julia's first acts are Protean; she tears up the letter that her lover sends her, then picks up the torn pieces and puts them together. Her maid is well versed in the feminine perversity that 'says nay and takes it': her resolution to follow her lover in disguise is a familiar romance complication. He employs her as a page. It is not necessary to stress on the stage the very intimate attendance this implies, helping her master to dress and undress. In *Love's Labour's Lost* Don Armado's page knows him in this way. This it is which makes her apologise not to, but on behalf of Proteus when she recovers from her swoon:

O Proteus, let this habit make thee blush!
Be thou asham'd that I have took upon me
Such an immodest raiment, if shame live
In a disguise of love.
It is the lesser blot, modesty finds,
Women to change their shapes, than men their minds.

(V.iv.105-10)

The shock for Proteus, as in *Twelfth Night* for Orsino, is to discover that it is a woman who enjoyed such intimacy 'so far beneath your soft and tender breeding'.

Julia and Proteus are the more interesting couple to modern readers since they seem, because more changeable and more physically expressive, to be individuals. The difference between the two levels may be illustrated from the life and poetry of Sir Walter Ralegh, who at this time (1592) had incurred the Queen's displeasure and imprisonment for first seducing and afterwards secretly marrying one of her maids of honour. (Shakespeare's patron was to do the same.) He wrote an ingenious poem in which he

Clare Holman as Julia and Barry Lynch as Proteus in the 1992 Royal Shakespeare Company production of The Two Gentlemen of Verona.

adopted one of the regular defences of a courtly lover (one which appears in the discussion of love between Julia and her maid, (I.ii.29-30) as well as in the opening discussions in Castiglione *Il Cortegiano,* that the truest lover does not declare his love). In the lyric 'Wrong not, dear Empress of my heart' Ralegh writes

> For knowing that I sue to serve
> A saint of such perfection
> As all desire, but none deserve
> A place in her affection . . .

He anticipates that kind of humility which adopts a disguise of poverty, which Castiglione thinks may enhance the nobility of a knight, and which in Silvia's aubade describes her wooers as 'swains' and their offering a pastoral 'garland'.

The sentiments, tone and mood of Castiglione are to my mind more relevant and more illuminating than the narrative sources which are so carefully collected in such works as Geoffrey Bullough's eight learned volumes. The narrative lines are all of romance commonplaces, even the story of Julia's disguise which is the closest and comes from the Spanish *Diana Enamorada* of Jorge de Montemayor, a work beloved of Sir Philip Sidney's Mistress, the heroine of his beautiful sonnet sequence *Astrophil and Stella,* first printed in 1591, the most powerful set of love sonnets before Shakespeare's own. But I think the mood, sentiments and tone are more important than the narrative line, and these come from Castiglione through Sidney—who stole away to the wars, where he met his untimely death in October 1586, with a copy of Castiglione. The chivalrous treatment of wars as jousting, forbade him to put on his thigh pieces because a friend had ridden out without them. He received his death wound and England mourned one who was a model of chivalry.

Il Cortegiano had first appeared in print in 1527, two years before Castiglione's death at the court of Spain where the Emperor Charles V exclaimed 'I tell you that one of the best *caballeros* of the world is dead'. Sir Thomas Hoby's translation, *The Courtyer* was published in 1561.

In this book the courtly games played at Urbino in the presence of the Duchess are moderated by her deputy, the Lady Emilia Pia. The Duchess herself is Surrogate for her lord, the highly judicious and watchful though crippled Duke. In the preliminary choice of the game, questions of love like those of ancient Provençal Courts of Love, are proposed and laid aside; such as which are the greater, the joys of love or its sorrows? Which lover shall a lady take, one who confesses his love or one who does not dare to do so? A question as we have seen posed between Julia and her maid in *The Two Gentlemen of Verona* (I.ii.29-30) and the basis of Ralegh's plea to his Queen. However, the game chosen at Urbino, the definition of the perfect Courtier, is not of this kind; it leads to deeper self-examination. Every barbed and searching point is made with 'laughter'. The most realistic and even shameless opportunism is concealed under exquisite refinement; and the facts of history are dexterously rearranged for the most favourable construction. When the Duchess asks Ottaviano what he would do if he won the Prince's favour so completely that he could tell him anything, he laughs and replies that if he were able to tell the Prince what he thinks 'I fear I should soon lose that favour' (IV.26). The final hymn to Platonic love from Pietro Bembo stuns the company into silence, because it goes beyond the game into the realm of Petrarch's Laura and Dante's Beatrice, and the Lady Emilia Pia, taking Bembo gently by the sleeve, says 'Takes care, Messer Pietro' (IV.71).

The limitations of the charmed circle are well understood; *grace* and *sprezzatura*—those key words of the definition—were absorbed by Sidney; Beauty can be attained only by ease and cannot be reached by directly taking pains; it emanates from the graceful negligence that conceals art after long practice, the irony and self-depreciation that Sidney practised with such wit. He ridiculed false Petrarchism: so later did Shakespeare: 'My mistress' eyes are nothing like the sun' (*Sonnet* 130).

The Two Gentlemen of Verona is founded upon the courtly assumptions of the 'game', which includes a good deal of parody. Valentine and Proteus open with a sharp bout of wit about the folly of love; later Valentine and Thurio attack each other with unbaited rapiers of wit and are separated by Silvia. Of course the assumptions are tested and parodied, this gives a frame to the romance. The true lover is given the malicious and witty page Speed; the dissembling Proteus is given the clown Launce, a character of immense vigour whose parting from his family to accompany Proteus is a parody of the previous scene, the parting of Proteus and Julia. Launce's dog is theatrically a winner, and often steals the show as outrageously as ever he stole a pudding. Animals are utterly natural and do not play a game with the audience as the actors do. Launce's catalogue of his mistress's charms parodies those of the divine Silvia. She is black as ink, but 'she hath more hair than wit, more faults than hairs, and more wealth than faults' (III.i.343-4). He is the Sancho Panza to Valentine's Quixote; while Speed explains to Valentine the riddle of Silvia's letter and advises joining the outlaws 'Master, be one of them; it's an honourable kind of thievery' (IV.i.39). Launce, having lost the toy dog Proteus was sending to Sylvia, gives her Crab; and just such an ill-mannered animal does Proteus himself become. For throughout the play we are conscious of that freedom of man to ascend and become a god or descend to a beast which was the theme of Pico della Mirandola's oration on the Dignity of Man.

Of course the story is comic, in the way that in Ariosto the knights are comic, when two mounting one horse in pursuit of their lady, urge the horse by the pricking of four spurs instead of two, to an unwonted pace. But in the last Act the clown and the page both disappear, for the final scene must maintain the courtly game against the counterpoint of the outlaws and the wood, and the important servant is the page, Julia in disguise—other servants must fade. This use of the wild wood was to be much further worked into the action in *A Midsummer Night's Dream*.

The comedies of Lyly included pages, and sometimes clowns; early wit combats do not give much more skill to courtiers than to their pages.

> *Silvia*: Servant, you are sad.
> *Val.*: Indeed, madam, I seem so.
> *Thurio*: Seem you that you are not?
> *Val.*: Haply I do.
> *Thurio*: So do counterfeits.
> *Val.*: So do you.
> *Thurio*: What seem I that I am not?
> *Val.*: Wise.
>
> (II.iv.8-15)

The deeper feelings are given in soliloquy and when called for in the dialogue, they simply are not there. Courtship is always in another's presence; so much is obliquely done by letters, tokens, gifts. Unlike other great ladies, Silvia has not even a waiting gentlewoman for confidante; moving only among courtiers or priests. The most poignant and self-revelatory of her scenes is when Julia, disguised as a page, brings Silvia as a love token the very ring she had given Proteus. Silvia knows its history and returns it; Julia, speaking out of part, gives her thanks.

> *Silvia*: She is beholding to thee, gentle youth.
> Alas, poor lady, desolate and left!
> I weep myself to think upon thy words.
> Here, youth; there is my purse; I give this thee
> For thy sweet mistress' sake, because thou lov'st her
>
> (IV.iv.170-4)

'Pity runneth soon in gentle heart', as Chaucer said more than once. If this were an allegory, Silvia would stand for the Divine Imagination and she appeals to the highest level of the *audience's* response. In this, she anticipates again the divine Miranda of Shakespeare's last play, *The Tempest,* who wept to see the shipwreck, suffered with those she saw suffer; 'O, the cry did knock against my very heart'. To which her father replies:

> tell your piteous heart
> There's no harm done.
>
> (I.ii.15-16)

Silvia and Julia's mutual sympathy delicately balances the friendship of the two gentlemen. Julia has been sent to get

Silvia's picture, but this decorous mode of worship is not what Proteus has in mind; for he said before ''Tis but her picture I have yet beheld' (II.iv.207)—he hopes to look on her 'perfections' later. Valentine uses this word in his poignant soliloquy upon his own banishment, engineered by Proteus.

> What light is light if Silvia be not seen?
> What joy is joy, if Silvia be not by?
> Unless it be to think that she is by
> And feed upon the shadow of perfection?
> Except I be by Silvia in the night,
> There is no music in the nightingale;
> Unless I look on Silvia in the day,
> There is no day for me to look upon.
> She is my essence, and I leave to be,
> If I be not by her fair influence
> Foster'd, illumin'd, cherish'd, kept alive.
>
> (III.i.174-84)

This is almost in that realm of high constancy which Pietro Bembo celebrated; the most beautiful lines given to Proteus celebrate, again, the world as mirrored in the beloved.

> O how this spring of love resembleth
> The uncertain glory of an April day,
> Which now shows all the beauty of the sun,
> And by and by a cloud takes all away
>
> (I.iii.84-87)

The Two Gentlemen of Verona belongs (one might say) to the State of Innocence. The delicate acquarelle tints cannot be fully appreciated if Launce and his dog are taken for the more real, the more developed characters, although in the present culture they appear more 'rounded'. Nothing could well be further removed from the Court of Urbino than the sentimental animal lovers of today, but they would welcome the self-sacrifice of Launce. The first great clown, Richard Tarlton, had a man-and-dog act; he fought a combat with Queen Elizabeth's lap dog. Launce's dog represents all that is excluded from Royal Courts; as the horse and jennet, the little hunted hare in *Venus and Adonis* represent in animal shapes the love-making of Venus, the hunt that destroys Adonis; the monstrous animal form of the boar appears only in vision. Here is Crab:

> He thrusts me himself into the company of three or four gentlemen-like dogs under the Duke's table; but he had not been there, bless the mark, a pissing while but all the chamber smelt him. 'Out with the dog!' says one; 'What cur is that?' saith another; 'Whip him out' says a third: 'Hang him up' says the Duke. I having been acquainted with the smell before, knew it was Crab, and goes me to the fellow that whips the dogs. 'Friend', quoth I 'you mean to whip the dog?' 'Ay, marry do I' quoth he. 'You do the more wrong' quoth I; ''Twas I did the thing you wot of.' He makes me no more ado but whips me out of the chamber. How many masters would do this for his servant?
>
> (IV.iv.15-28)

This breaks right out of the frame and addresses the audience directly, like an epilogue, and marks the grand exit of Launce (and Crab) immediately preceding the scene between Silvia and Julia, the high note in selflessness and sympathy. I do not think the collocation is an accident. But one of the most experienced editors, Clifford Leech, thinks that the play was rewritten and that Launce belongs to a later stage than the rest of the play.

The text that has come down to us is a bad one—it seems to have been torn in pieces like Proteus' love letter and put together by the playhouse scribe, Ralph Crane, from Shakespeare's rough papers. Yet his old friends, who collected his plays seven years after his death, put it second in the volume, immediately after *The Tempest,* his last play, given at Court as a wedding play. A lifetime of experience lay between these two. I shall end by trying to suggest something about its place of Courtesy in the context of its time.

I have already mentioned that I would place it in 1593, the time of plague, when London theatres were closed and the actors disappeared; many companies broke up. The best refuge was in some noble household in the country. At this time Shakespeare published his first poem with a dedication to the Earl of Southampton, whom most people identify with the fair youth of the Sonnets that circulated privately and which are most probably belonging to the years 1594-6.

As the courtly figures of the opening to the *Decameron* retreated into an enclosed garden in the time of plague, Shakespeare took to the rich woodland scene of *Venus and Adonis*; its country sports, the deep woodlands of Hampshire and a frank eroticism which is fleshly enough. Venus sweats, pants almost overpowers the boy. Love is 'deaf and cruel when he means to prey' as the poet who was probably Shakespeare's rival, Christopher Marlowe had commented in his own erotic masterpiece of *Hero and Leander,* the very poem Proteus is reading at the opening of *The Two Gentlemen of Verona* (I.i.21-2).

In this Court, however, we are in the realm not of Venus but of Cupid, the innocent world—well, very nearly innocent—of Lyly's courtly elegance. Our poet's epigraph to *Venus and Adonis* would better fit the comedy:

> *Vilia miretur vulgus: mihi flavus Apollo*
> *Pocula Castalia plena ministret acqua.*

which Marlowe translated

> Let base-conceited wits admire vile things,
> Fair Phoebus lead me to the Muses' springs
>
> (*Elegy* XV.35-36)

To live within a noble household would give a unique opportunity for a sensitive receptive poet to absorb the finer nuances of courtly life, as they could never be learnt from outside. The young Earl was nineteen years of age, handsome and self-willed, decidedly a Proteus in matters of love and frustrated of his wish to visit Italy by the Queen's refusal to allow it. Perhaps she feared the influence of the

Roman church, for the family were Catholics, and so the young man had been first brought up. Among his retinue was John Florio, the most famous Italian teacher in England. Shakespeare showed himself acquainted with Florio's works before he published the translation of Montaigne which so pervasively influenced the writing of *Hamlet.*

Here, then, if he were in the Earl's country house, Shakespeare would be under new and excellent literary influences. He would find a library. But he would also find a household and a patron to whom he might modestly hope to show the ideal courtly life. The growth of Shakespeare's art was phenomenal, under any consideration; he was famous as a writer already, with the plays on King Henry VI. But *The Two Gentlemen of Verona,* I think, was written for boy players, with one part for a professional actor, that of Launce; a regular clown's role, as Tarlton and Kempe had created it on the public stage. In a noble household the children of the private chapel, or of a local school, or the household pages might be recruited; in this same plague time Thomas Nashe wrote such a play for the Archbishop of Canterbury's country house, with a part for one mature actor as jester.

The air of modest but lofty exclusiveness implies an audience who savoured the cult of fine manners. Boys can be sharply satiric, mimicking absurdity and affectation, and they can sing with piercing purity of tone impossible to the adult voice. Their range however is limited. There are no duels and no ensemble scenes; as Stanley Wells noted, the dialogue consists of duets, solos, soliloquies; even if more than two people are together on stage they do not engage as a group.[1] This is surely not incapacity in the writer but in the actors; they are amateurs, and cannot manage anything complicated—technically complicated. Apart from its perfect song, the play has achieved no great fame. The vision of an enchanted enclosure, a world whose reticences and limitations define its beauty, the fragility of first love, a violet in the youth of primy nature, the perfume and suppliance of a minute are found in the first tentative Sonnets of Shakespeare's sequence (1-17)

> Music to hear, why hear'st thou music sadly?
> Sweets with sweets war not, joy delights in joy
>
> (8.1-2)

or

> Thou art thy mother's glass and she in thee
> Calls back the lovely April of her prime
>
> (3.9-10)

or

> Shall I compare thee to a summer's day?
> Thou art more lovely and more temperate
>
> (18.1-2)

Valentine's admission of idolatry (II.iv.142) is rebutted later with words that chime with the praises of Silvia, who is kind as she is fair:

> Let not my love be call'd idolatry . . .
> Fair, kind and true is all my argument
>
> (105.1.9)

That very perceptive critic, Inga-Stina Ewbank, comparing this play with the Sonnets, thinks its dependence on verbal techniques fails to reach the fully dramatic terms, the truth to complex human relationships that is achieved in the Sonnets—for perhaps the contribution of the Veneto to Shakespeare's work, represented by the advent of the Dark Lady, had not yet appeared.[2] Was she Emilia Bassano? I am not so sure as A. L. Rowse.

Roger Prior has made out a strong case for identifying the whole group of the Bassano family with this region; they were Jewish musicians who came to the royal court in the reign of Henry VIII, where they formed a compact little enclave. By tracing their wills, he has unravelled their history.[3] If Emilia Bassano, the mistress of the Lord Chamberlain, whom Shakespeare would have encountered in that household when he joined the Lord Chamberlain's company in 1594, is indeed the dark lady, as Rowse and others have considered her, the deeper knowledge of *The Merchant of Venice,* the distancing of the magic garden of Belmont, would be explained. The tragic notes of *Romeo and Juliet* followed *The Two Gentlemen of Verona* very quickly, indeed Shakespeare may already have read the English poem from which he took this story; but its form and the depth of its passion belong to the public theatres, to which he returned. *The Two Gentlemen of Verona,* with the bloom of dawning that is not quite full day, has its own particular magic—a magic which Wordsworth echoes in his line on first love:

> Earth moved in one great presence of the spring.

In the future lie the passions of Venice, but in the garden of Belmont the arrival of Bassanio's messenger brings hope of what is to come:

> Yet I have not seen
> So likely an Ambassador of love,
> A day in April never came so sweet
> To show how costly summer was at hand,
> Than his forespurrer comes before his lord.
>
> (*Merchant of Venice* II.ix.91-5)

Such a forespurrer is this comedy, which I do not think was ever clapper clawed with the palms of the vulgar.[4]

Notes

1. *Shakespeare Jahrbuch* XCIX, 1963.

2. *Shakespearean Comedy* (London, Stratford upon Avon Studies, 14, 1972).

3. His article appeared in *The Literary Supplement of The Jewish Chronicle* for June 1979; see also 'Jewish musicians at the Tudor Court' *The Musical Quarterly* Spring 1983, 258-65.

4. In a later study I suggested that the modern reading might have been that of the popular stages, where ordeals in the last minutes were the custom. ('Castiglione, Lyly and Shakespeare's *Two Gentlemen of Verona*', listed p. 211).

PATRIARCHY

Jonathan Hall (essay date 1995)

SOURCE: "Patriarchy Rescued in *The Two Gentlemen of Verona,*" in *Anxious Pleasures: Shakespearean Comedy and the Nation-State,* Fairleigh Dickinson University Press, 1995, pp. 116-26.

[*In the following essay, Hall contends that the female characters in* The Two Gentlemen of Verona *have a redemptive role, in that they help their male counterparts to restore patriarchal order by the play's end.*]

A remarkable number of Shakespeare's comedies focus on the contrast between male inconstancy and female constancy. Indeed, with the single exception of *Troilus and Cressida,* it seems possible to assert that there are no inconstant heroines, although the comedies which feature the lovers' debates (*The Taming of the Shrew* and the Beatrice-Benedick plot in *Much Ado about Nothing*), might be said to make the constant/inconstant opposition irrelevant. Still, the generalization seems valid. In the comedies, the evil of inconstancy to the given word is a male failing. It does not affect the heroines except insofar as they may be bewildered by the changeability of the men (e.g., *The Comedy of Errors, The Two Gentlemen of Verona,* and *A Midsummer Night's Dream*).

The romances frequently make the constant heroine a redemptive figure in the fallen male world, and this enables us to grasp what is at stake. In this drama, male changeability is not just an unfortunate proclivity of the sex. It is a source of cultural dislocation, for the order that is betrayed is patriarchal, and therefore has a strong investment in reasserting male self-possession. I have argued earlier how the resistance of the heroines to male rhetoric in *Love's Labour's Lost* enables them to restore the lords to their "truth." The ladies are the defenders of the patriarchal order and agents of its restabilization. The romances, like *The Two Gentlemen of Verona, All's Well That Ends Well, The Winter's Tale,* and *Pericles,* take this further. They all pick up this redemptive role of the heroine, and endow her with a physical mobility, in addition to a verbal one, to combat the mobility of signs threatening the patriarchal order. The paradox is that it is the women who rescue the patriarchy.

Studies of influence easily place the Proteus-Valentine relationship in *The Two Gentlemen of Verona* firmly within the tradition of "friendship literature," particularly Boccaccio's story of Titus and Gisippus in the *Decameron,* and Sir Thomas Elyot's retelling of it in *The Governour* (1531). Boccaccio's story is a celebration of competitive male generosity. It tells of one friend (Gisippus) yielding his betrothed to the other (Titus), who loves her more passionately. Then Titus returns to Rome with his bride, while Gisippus remains in Athens. Gisippus is then bankrupted and goes to Rome to seek his friend. In Rome, he witnesses a crime, and makes a false confession to it, as a way of ending his wretched life. At the moment of execution, Titus, who is in secure possession of both fortune and wife, steps forward and also makes a false confession. In other words, he generously attempts to pay all debts of friendship. Such a display of generosity makes the real criminal volunteer a confession. And the agents of the law are so impressed that they are all pardoned. Thus, an idealized competitive male generosity replaces the law as the basis of social harmony.[1] The story elaborates an aristocratic topos that exalts male friendship above heterosexual love. The transferable wife is a highly valued but alienable possession. She functions like the valued "gift" in Mauss's account of the potlatch, which is a means of establishing male bonding within a clan structure through competitive generosity.[2] One can easily understand why the "cult of friendship," when it is affirmed through such male "generosity," would come into conflict with the Petrarchan "cult of love" which enjoins a posture of male subordination to the mistress, to whom it grants sovereign sway. For the gift of a person is the most emphatic assertion of sovereign ownership. From this point of view, the "cult of friendship" must be seen as a discursive defense of aristocratic patriarchy, and the "cult of love" as a disruptive challenge to male sovereignty, and even self-possession.

Shakespeare's play makes a mockery of the topos of "the two friends," but there are serious issues at stake too. At first the constant Valentine mocks Proteus for being susceptible to love for Julia, but then, having moved from Verona to Padua, he falls in love himself with Silvia. Proteus, true to his name, changes and also falls in love with Silvia, who rejects him. The betrayal of Julia is doubled by a betrayal of his friend to Silvia's father, who intends to marry her to the ridiculous suitor, Sir Thurio. Thus, under pressure of his love for Silvia, Proteus has betrayed his former love, his friend, and importantly, his former self. This culminates in his intention to rape the unyielding Silvia in a desolate spot. At this moment Valentine appears on the scene and, after the most perfunctory of apologies from Proteus, he dumbfounds everybody (including generations of critics and, it seems, Silvia too, since she never speaks for the rest of the play), by the transformation of the adored lady into the transferable potlach gift of the traditional story:

> *Valentine.* And that my love may appear plain and free,
> All that was mine in Silvia I give thee.
>
> (*The Two Gentlemen of Verona,* 5.4.82 ff.)

Critics who find this merely ludicrous, or crude on Shakespeare's part (as Tillyard does), tend to ignore Valentine's extreme concern, expressed a few lines earlier, with a general historical crisis in values, which he sees in the disappearance of the bond of aristocratic male friendship. When Valentine moralizes Proteus's betrayal in terms of the "o tempora, o mores" theme, he prepares the ground for his own heroic generosity as a means to mend both a psychological and a historical rift:

> *Valentine.* Thou common friend, that's without faith or love,
> *For such is a friend now.* Treacherous man,
> Thou hast beguiled my hopes. Naught but mine eye
> Could have persuaded me. Now I dare not say
> I have one friend alive. Thou wouldst disprove me.
> Who should be trusted, when one's right hand
> Is perjured to the bosom? Proteus,
> I am sorry but I must never trust thee more,
> But count the world a stranger for thy sake.
> *The private wound is deepest. O time most accursed,*
> *'Mongst all the foes that a friend should be the worst*
>
> [emphases added] (*5.4.62*ff.)

It does *not* follow that Shakespeare's dramatic discourse endorses the role of restorative culture hero that Valentine constructs for himself here. On the contrary, there is a monstrous narcissistic theatricality, which continues even in his very "generous" refusal to question Proteus's quick repentance. For Proteus's confession of guilt gives to Valentine the gratifying role of an earthly God:

> *Valentine.* Then I am paid,
> And once again I do receive thee honest.
> Who by repentance is not satisfied
> Is nor of heaven nor earth. For these are pleased;
> By penitence th'Eternal's wrath's appeased.
>
> (*5.4.77*ff.)

What could be more gratifying to a patriarchal culture hero than this assumption of divinity? If an audience identifies with its triumphant note, it could never be without embarrassment or mocking reservations. But, however crude the psychological construction of character may appear now, the issues within this comic posturing are serious enough. What is at stake within the attempt to live by the standards of the literature of "friendship" is a newly intensified regressive desire to restore a purely male world. And Valentine is a little absolute monarch of that world.

The narrative of *The Two Gentlemen of Verona* is in some respects similar to that of *Love's Labour's Lost.* There the lords move from an initial oath to maintain a strongly narcissistic male bonding into heterosexual involvements which entail betrayal of their former "selves." Yet this loss of self remains unacceptable, engendering a nostalgia channeled into reinvented feudal rituals where the male warrior can prove his truth. In these courtly plays, a new nostalgia for a male-centered order arises within (and against) the pleasures of a discourse given over to wit and the seductive power of signs. This nostalgia, which is sometimes grotesque and sometimes violent, takes the form of what Eve Kosofsky Sedgwick has called "homosocial" bonding, which overlaps with homosexuality but is not always exactly coterminous with it.[3]

The imperviousness of the women to the seductive strategies of language also links this play with *Love's Labour's Lost,* for it does not imply an absence of sexual desire. On the contrary, the heroines are active in the pursuit of their desires. The issue concerns resistance to the rhetoric of intended mastery mobilized by the males, and hidden within the postures of Petrarchan subordination. In this play, all the males (including Silvia's father) are seen to be totally deluded in their belief that "wailful sonnets" and the "force of heaven-bred poesy" can be strategically deployed to sway or construct the desires of women. Indeed, in the requisite attempt at seduction by love letter, Silvia actually composes the letter to herself on Valentine's behalf (*2.1*), and Julia, while pretending to reject Proteus by tearing up his letter, actually recomposes it in accordance with her desires:

> *Julia.* Lo here in one line is his name twice writ;
> "Poor forlorn Proteus", "passionate Proteus",
> "To the sweet Julia": that I'll tear away.
> And yet I will not, sith so prettily
> He couples it to his complaining names.
> Thus I will fold them, one upon another;
> Now kiss, embrace, contend, do what you will.
>
> (*1.2.124*ff.)

Julia is not a passive or manipulated reader. She physically rends Proteus's written text, and undoes its claims to control. But then, she becomes another author and rewrites it as a scene of copulating signs! Clearly she responds to the text, but equally clearly her active desires effect a transformation. Similarly, Valentine's foolish and misdirected lesson in seduction to Silvia's father, the duke, is a satire on overconfident male investment in the phallic power of speech, particularly when it concludes with the wooden and indecent lines:

> *Valentine.* That man that hath a tongue I say is no man
> If with his tongue he cannot win a woman.
>
> (*3.1.104*ff.)

In this respect, the play might be said to satirize courtly Petrarchanism. But in another much more far reaching sense, it relies on the Petrarchan, and very Elizabethan, concept of the sovereign lady, unmoved by the strategems of the poet, to bring about the closure and the restoration of male identities lost in the decentering language of erotic desire. Here the constancy of Julia to Proteus is even more important than Silvia's constancy to Valentine, since it is through Julia's active search that Proteus is restored to "the truth" of his former self. Thus she is a redemptive figure, as powerful in her way as the more conventionally Petrarchan, inaccessible Silvia.

It is essential to the resolution of the crisis of this plot, which allegorizes an underlying historical crisis of values, that the erring Proteus has an "original" loved one to whom he can be restored. The restoration of Proteus to Julia is represented as identical with a restoration to his former self and to friendship with Valentine. In this perspective, his numerous monologues, in which he claims to be pursuing the true interests of his self by betraying his friend and his word, are finally to be construed as casuistical products of "error."

Julia's active pursuit of Proteus in male guise assumes great importance here. Her story is a romance quest through the world of male aberrations. (Silvia learns to imitate her, because of the total, and always ridiculous, failure of Valentine's initiatives.) Now, this romance plot of female initiative is potentially shocking, as Julia herself is very aware. Its impropriety is underlined in a series of jokes, in which her maid, Lucetta asks her about her trousers and advises her that she must wear a fashionable codpiece. Similar jokes occur in virtually identical situations in *The Merchant of Venice, All's Well That Ends Well, As You Like It,* and *Twelfth Night.* One cannot maintain that the romance plot of active female desire was simply acceptable at the time. It requires a strategy of legitimation to make it acceptable.

Shakespeare's solution in this play is to fall back on the very poetic myths that in a certain sense are also being demystified. Petrarchan conventions allow a conflation of human love and divine adoration, in an endless series of metaphoric transformations. Accordingly, in this play, passionate self-abandonment by the heroine is *unlike* the male loss of self-hood. Her defiance of formal propriety, through her potentially dishonoring flight from the paternal home in pursuit of her erotic goal, are rewritten via dramatic metaphors as Christian devotion and scorn of worldly goods. Metaphorically, the erotic flight becomes the quest of the pilgrim:

> *Julia.* A true devoted pilgrim is not weary
> To measure kingdoms with his feeble steps.
> Much less shall she that hath love's wings to fly,
> And when the flight is made to one so dear,
> Of such divine perfection as Sir Proteus.
>
> (*2.7.9*ff.)

Although Julia's faith in the constancy of Proteus is misplaced, to say the least, it is the constancy of *her* passion that guarantees the (nonetheless precarious) validity of the religious metaphor. Lucetta, who has earlier displayed a worldly knowingness about sexual desire in contrast to Julia's modest resistance, now maintains an equally worldly posture, but in an opposite sense. She is now the worldly-wise, even cynical, opponent of Julia's pilgrim-like wholeheartedness. Against her words enjoining restraint, Julia argues that the fury of frustrated desire can become the sweet journey of the pilgrim, by being permitted to seek its goal:

> *Julia.* The more thou damm'st it up, the more it burns.
> The current that with gentle murmur glides,
> Thou know'st, being stopped, impatiently doth rage.
> But when his fair course is not hindered
> He makes sweet music with th'enamelled stones,
> Giving a gentle kiss to every sedge
> He overtaketh in his pilgrimage.
>
> (*2.7.24*ff.)

This metaphorical pilgrimage, however, is also legitimized by a traditionally virtuous abandonment of worldly goods and status, as she gives up all she has to follow her lord. (It is also worth noting that, whether it is violent in its rebellion or harmonious in its pilgrimage, Julia ascribes the active river of her passion to the masculine gender.) Thus, the rebellious overthrowing of maidenly restraint becomes musical and harmonious as it is equated with a supreme act of faith in Proteus:

> *Julia.* Now, as thou lov'st me, do him not that wrong
> To bear a hard opinion of his truth.
> Only deserve my love by loving him,
> And presently go with me to my chamber
> To take a note of what I stand in need of
> To furnish me upon my longing journey.
> All that is mine I leave at thy dispose,
> My goods, my lands, my reputation,
> Only in lieu thereof dispatch me hence.
>
> (*2.7.80*ff.)

Since the two previous scenes have dealt with Proteus's abandonment of Julia and his faithlessness to his friend, Julia's self-abandonment and passionate "pilgrimage" acquire connotations of active spiritual rescue, no matter how far Proteus sinks. The disciple redeems the lord when she sets out to rescue "his truth." There could be no more powerful legitimation of active and mobile female desire than this plot, but its gratifications are nonetheless permissible only because they lead to the restoration of the male self to its supposedly preexisting essential "truth."

But we should also ask: what is it that divided Proteus from his "truth" in the first place? The obvious answer would be the invasion of heterosexuality into a purely "homosocial" relationship, on the pattern of *Love's Labour's Lost.* But, while this is correct, it requires careful discrimination. A common sense view of the play, which is not incorrect but merely insensitive to the submerged side of the overt dialogue between the two heroes, has it that the mutable Proteus betrays the constant Valentine. And yet, it is the constant Valentine, in his absorption in thoughts of Silvia, who first announces to Proteus that heterosexual love breaks the bonds of male friendship:

> *Valentine.* Pardon me, Proteus, all I can is nothing
> To her whose worth makes other worthies nothing.
> She is alone.
> *Proteus.* Then let her alone.
> *Valentine.* Not for the world. Why man, she is mine own,
> And I as rich in having such a jewel
> As twenty seas, if all their sand were pearl,
> The water nectar, and the rocks pure gold.
> *Forgive me that I do not dream on thee*
> *Because thou seest me dote upon my love.*
>
> [Emphasis added] (*2.4.163*ff.)

The treason to male bonding, therefore, starts with Valentine and his overvaluation of Silvia as possessable riches. And it is this very exclusivity that takes the ritual joking combat of boasting about the qualities of their respective mistresses (in itself an established topos, cf. *Love's Labour's Lost 4.3*), beyond its normal bounds and into a competitive aggression of rival owners:

> *Proteus.* Have I not reason to prefer mine own?
> *Valentine.* And I will help thee to prefer her, too.
> She shall be dignified with this high honour,
> To bear my lady's train, lest the base earth
> Should from her vesture chance to steal a kiss
> And, of so great a favour growing proud,
> Disdain to root the summer-swelling flower,
> And make rough winter everlastingly.
> *Proteus.* Why, Valentine, what braggartism is this?
>
> (*2.4.154*ff.)

Here Valentine's rhetorical "braggartism" *produces* a rivalry for possession of the same object, even where that is obviously not his conscious intention. His utterance is a provocation, of which only he seems to be truly oblivious. It is contrary to common sense that he should actually want Proteus to recognize that Silvia is preferable to Julia. And yet that desire, that Proteus too should desire Silvia, is present and active, however much it is formally contradicted by Valentine's statements of exclusive possession, which in this context become provocative. It is as though Silvia's desirability for Valentine depends upon her being desired by others. So that her triumph in the little beauty contest being constructed here is in a covert way the triumph of her owner over his rival. It is no accident that Proteus is the cleverer of the two. His mutability is inseparable from his interpretive sensitivity to the nuances of Valentine's utterance, so that in a very real sense he is correct to wonder whether his passion for Silvia is not in fact produced by Valentine. But he is unable to say *how much* his new position is constructed by Valentine or how much by Silvia as a desirable object in herself. He becomes a spectator of himself, caught guilty and bewildered in the power of signs:

> *Proteus.* Even as one heat another expels,
> Or as one nail by strength drives out another,
> So the remembrance of my former love
> Is by a newer object quite forgotten. [*sic*]
> Is it mine eye, or Valentine's praise,
> Her true perfection, or my false transgression
> That makes me, reasonless, to reason thus?
>
> (*2.4.190*ff.)

Valentine's very success in constructing his friend's desires on the pattern of his own is the cause of all the trouble. But it is an unconscious success, inseparable from his own impenetrable confidence and stupid blindness to the meanings of his own words and gestures.

I have borrowed the term "homosocial" from Eve Kosofsky Sedgwick, who introduces it precisely because it permits a space of possible difference between "homosocial" bonding and homosexual attachments. It may be that homosocial and homosexual sometimes coincide or overlap, but they may also be violently opposed. For example, modern patriarchal discourse is homosocial in seeking to preserve male solidarity in dominance, whereas it is also violently homophobic, probably negating its homosexual tendencies in its desire to be completely non-feminized. But this relationship is historically variable, and is moreover gender specific. Looking at Shakespeare's sonnets in this light, she is able to say that the modern projection of "homosexuality," as that which excludes the heterosexual, is anachronistic, for in fact we are dealing with a continuum comparable to Greek attitudes. Thus, the "fair youth" sonnets, though obviously homosexual to many modern readers, are also heterosexual, for it is through the woman that males relate to each other:

> My point is . . . not that we are here in the presence of homosexuality (which would be anachronistic) but rather (risking anachronism) that we are in the presence of male heterosexual desire, in the form of a desire to consolidate partnership with authoritative males in and through the bodies of females.[4]

Sedgwick cites René Girard's structure of mediated or "triangular" desire and Lévi-Strauss' "traffic in women," where I have preferred to cite Mauss's potlach gift for its inherent competitiveness and its assertion of direct ownership of the mediating "other." But the arguments are similar.[5] She argues from this position, that in the early sonnets, where the woman functions as a medium for a mutual relationship between the poet and the fair youth, there is no sense of crisis. Crisis only emerges when the relationship with a woman threatens male identity:

> The heterosexuality that succeeded in eclipsing women [in the earlier poems—J. H.] was also, as we have seen, relatively unthreatened by the feminization of one man in relation to another. To be feminized or suffer gender confusion within a framework that includes a woman is, however, dire; and, as we shall see, *any* erotic involvement with an actual woman threatens to be unmanning. Lust itself (meaning, in this context, desire for women) is a machine for depriving males of self-identity (Sonnet 129).[6]

The notion of "an actual woman" is perhaps a weak point here, but the argument is clear and persuasive enough. Insofar as the woman, even as discursive construct, resists the role of mere structural medium within patriarchal relations, she is dangerous. But we have noted already how the dangerous woman, mobile and not subject to male discursive strategies, becomes the source of salvation through Shakespeare's miraculous comic plot.

There is another aspect to Sedgwick's reading of the sonnets which casts light on the comic strategies of this play. As long as criticism treats Proteus and Valentine as opposed but morally distinct "characters," it cannot really address the nature of the polarization which produces them and the hidden matrix which links them. But Sedgwick, writing of the demonization of the "dark lady" in the sonnets, observes that the poetic voice attributes doubleness and deceit to her in order to preserve some undivided masculine purity of image in the beloved male. And she adds:

> In the sonnets addressed to the fair youth, there is plenty of dissonance, doubleness, and self-division, but it is all described as located outside the youth himself, and wherever possible, *within the speaker.* [emphasis added][7]

In contrast to the inwardly divided speaker, there is something of the "dumb blonde" in the fair youth:

> Like Marilyn Monroe, the youth makes the man viewing him feel old, vitiated, and responsible, even as the man luxuriates in the presence (the almost promise) of youth and self-possession.[8]

The construction of a unified, ideal self in the representation of the male beloved is not simply a feminization of the fair youth but almost the opposite:

> If anything, the fair youth, "woman's face" and all, is presented as exaggeratedly phallic—unitary, straightforward, unreflective, pink, and dense.[9]

The polarization here means that the older speaker assumes all the duplicity and deviousness of language, of which the desired and ideal alter-ego is free. Sedgwick summarizes this polarization as follows:

> I am sense; you are animal ease and sweetness and authenticity, I am guilt and self-subversion and ambivalence.

These qualities, she says, are what makes the older man somewhat "feminine" in this discourse (p. 44). To this I would only add that it is this self-divided decentered "femininity" that also makes him the poet.

This division of homosocial roles, through the invasion of heterosexual rivalry, is exactly what characterizes the Proteus-Valentine relationship. Valentine is the male "dumb blonde" who is also the unified phallic ideal from which Proteus falls guiltily away. Valentine's unreflecting impenetrability (his "stupidity" is undeniable, but that commonly used term is inadequate), is part of that superior ideal. Proteus, on the other hand, is the one who is afflicted by a linguistic consciousness so alert to duplicity that he even detects it in what Valentine fails to know about himself.

Valentine is not the only male "dumb blonde" in Shakespeare's comedy. Claudio, in *Much Ado About Nothing,* is another; "unitary, straightforward, unreflective, pink, and dense" all seem fitting terms for him. But, as we will see in chapter 10, things have changed by then. Claudio is a potential murderer in his *pursuit* of unitary truth, because, unlike Valentine, he is penetrated with anxiety. Instead of being the ideal image of regressive male desire, he is displaced and caught up in the desire himself.

Notes

1. Giovanni Boccaccio, *The Decameron, X, 8,* [c. 1350], translated by Mark Musa and Peter Bondanella (New York and London: Norton, 1982), 640-655; Sir Thomas Elyot, *The Governour, II. 12* [1531], in *The Narrative and Dramatic Sources of Shakespeare,* volume 1, Geoffrey Bullough ed. (London and New York: Routledge and Kegan Paul, 1961), 212-217. For the Arabic sources, and the Latin and vernacular versions of this tale, see Juan Bautista Avalle-Arce, *Deslindes Cervantinos* (Madrid: Edhigar, 1961), 121ff.
2. Marcel Mauss, *The Gift: Forms and Functions of Exchange in Archaic Societies* (London: Cohen and West, 1954).
3. Eve Kosofsky Sedgwick, *Between Men: English Literature and Male Homosocial Desire* (New York: Columbia University Press, 1985).
4. Eve Kosofsky Sedgwick, *Between Men,* 38.
5. However, I feel that Sedgwick's recourse to Girard's structure of mimetic desire does not fully serve her argument. Girard's view of the competitive mutual conditioning of the desires of the two friends is certainly based on a structure which resembles what Sedgwick calls homosociality, but Girard is not concerned with either gender positioning or historical shifts in discourse. Thus he emphatically denies that the *Two Gentlemen of Verona* has anything to do with the conflict of "friendship" and "love": *A Theatre of Envy* (Oxford: Oxford University Press. 1991), 17. But, after explaining that two men brought up together unconsciously imitate each other in everything, he adds: "All of a sudden, with no advance warning, the attitude that has always nourished friendship tears it apart. Thus imitation is a double-edged sword." (*A Theatre of Envy,* 9) For Girard, it is not heterosexuality but mutual male imitation that "suddenly" (Girard's untheorized moment) produces rivalry out of bonding. And yet, the effect is still a conflict of "friendship" and "love." Girard's own narrative goes beyond his structural explanation.
6. Eve Kosofsky Sedgwick, *Between Men,* 36.
7. Eve Kosofsky Sedgwick, *Between Men,* 41.
8. Eve Kosofsky Sedgwick, *Between Men,* 43.
9. Eve Kosofsky Sedgwick, *Between Men,* 44.

STAGING AND PRODUCTION

Carol J. Carlisle and Patty S. Derrick (essay date 1997)

SOURCE: "*The Two Gentlemen of Verona* on Stage: Protean Problems and Protean Solutions," in *Shakespeare's*

Sweet Thunder: Essays on the Early Comedies, edited by Michael J. Collins, 1997, pp. 126-54.

[*In the following essay, Carlisle and Derrick provide an overview of the major theatrical productions of* The Two Gentlemen of Verona, *noting the importance of collaboration between all members of the theater—including directors, actors, and designers—and the author in order to produce a successful staging of the play.*]

In the theater, as in the study, *The Two Gentlemen of Verona,* possibly Shakespeare's earliest comedy, has traditionally been one of his least popular plays. By our present count, there have been just twenty-four productions of it on the London stage since Shakespeare's time, and seven of these were first seen elsewhere.[1] At Stratford-upon-Avon there have been only ten since the annual Festivals began there in 1879. Most of the productions in these two major centers have been in the twentieth century, the greater number in the second half. The play has also been produced three times by the BBC, twice on radio and once on television. In New York, as one would expect, *Two Gentlemen* has had a much slighter stage history than in London,[2] and at the "other Stratford" in Ontario it has had just four productions in a forty-year history. Curiously enough, however, a surprising number of British provincial theaters and American regional or festival companies have been willing, at least once or twice, to tackle the problems of this "flawed but endearing play."[3]

Two Gentlemen does have its charms, but they are largely offset by its peculiar weaknesses. To evoke its magic, a production must overcome these weaknesses or somehow turn them to advantage. Although the same basic problems have confronted producers of the play in all post-Shakespearean periods, some have loomed larger at one time than at another because of differing social and theatrical conventions, and the solutions that actors and directors have found for them have therefore varied considerably. Since such solutions (or attempted solutions) have influenced interpretation of the play, not singly but in varying combinations, it is best to consider them within the contexts of particular productions. Accordingly, we shall discuss here some salient productions from each period *in toto,* giving our fullest attention to seminal ones and occasionally mentioning others to illustrate trends.

First, the problems. For the average reader, *Two Gentlemen,* with its formula-ridden plot, outdated conventions, sketchily drawn characters, and absurd conclusion, is probably too simplistic and too incredible to be very interesting; at the same time, it may have an oddly disturbing effect since the apparent simplicities prove, on examination, too slippery to catch hold of with assurance. This combination of characteristics is not a hopeful one for effective stage production.

The dramatic action of *Two Gentlemen* is largely illustrative of either faithfulness or disloyalty to the potentially conflicting ideals of heroic friendship and courtly love—impossibly rarefied ideals for everyday human life, as the action demonstrates, yet far better than none at all.[4] The concept of ideal friendship, grounded in a medieval blend of classical and scholastic ideas with the lore of blood brotherhood, was prominent in Elizabethan retellings and dramatizations of old tales like *Titus and Gisippus,* glorifying two men of equal endowments and mutual interests who were so united in love that each became the other's *alter ego*—a relation that could transcend love between the sexes.[5] The ideals and conventions of courtly love, a Renaissance descendant of medieval literature portraying love as an all-consuming power and the lover as humble "servant" to a religiously worshipped lady, were found in the Petrarchan lyrics and the romances of the Renaissance, including Jorge de Montemayor's *Diana,* the source (direct or indirect) of Shakespeare's Julia-Proteus plot.[6] Although love and friendship are ageless, these particular concepts had lost their familiarity before any post-Shakespearean revival of *Two Gentlemen;* thus, the heroes' language and actions might well seem a little strange to later audiences. But, even within the context of their own world, Valentine and Proteus are hard to take seriously as romantic heroes.

The naive Valentine is (or becomes) a devotee of both ideals. He exalts Proteus's merits (2.4.62-74), identifies his friend with himself (2.4.62), and feels Proteus's treachery as if his own right hand had turned against his heart (5.4.67-68). Originally he scorns love as an underminer of manly accomplishments, but, once he meets Silvia, he becomes the conventional courtly lover: he recounts the sufferings inflicted by the "mighty lord" Love (2.4.128-42); he resorts to outrageous hyperbole in praising Silvia (2.4.151-53, 156-63) and shows his veneration of her in terms like "heavenly saint," "divine," and "sacred" (2.4.145, 147; 3.1.212); he calls her "myself" and says that without her, his "essence," he will "cease to be" (3.1.172, 182-84). In the courtly game of Milan's aristocratic society, a lady may have publicly acknowledged "servants," whose chivalrous devotion need not be—though it can be—erotically inspired. Valentine becomes Silvia's "servant" in both senses. Though fleetingly aware that Silvia has usurped Proteus in his thoughts (2.4.172-73), he never questions that each of them is his very "self" or wonders what would happen if love and friendship should collide. He persuades Silvia to accept his friend as a "servant" socially, never suspecting that he will make an amorous claim as well.

Proteus, though less idealistic than his friend, is obviously attached to Valentine at first, and he is passionately in love with Julia. He knows all along, however, that his emotions are in conflict: thus he simultaneously approves and rejects his father's command to join Valentine in Milan, since he must leave Julia to do so (1.3.90-91). When he falls in love with Silvia, Valentine's lady, he notes the loss of "zeal" toward his friend as well as toward Julia; he adopts an amusingly pragmatic attitude, promising to master his new passion if he can, but vowing to win Silvia for himself if he cannot (2.4.192-214). His sophistry in rationalizing infidelity to both friend and love (2.6.1-32) is almost disarmingly juvenile, but with self-love as guide, he plunges into ever-increasing treachery. His villainy causes little concern, however. He cuts a poor figure in wooing "holy" Silvia, and he is plainly enmeshing himself in a tightening net.

The crux of the play occurs when the demands of love and friendship finally clash, and Valentine, after his long absorption in love, chooses friendship without the blink of an eye—without, in fact, showing any recognition that he is making a choice. Faced with the shocking evidence of Proteus's treachery, quickly followed by a brief speech of repentance, he instantly pardons his friend, and to demonstrate the restoration of his affection, surrenders to Proteus his own claim to Silvia's love (5.4.77-83). The only response to this astonishing offer is Julia's swoon, and the disclosure of her real identity is sufficient to restore the heroes to their abandoned true-loves. Conflict has not been resolved, just ignored.

Some scholars defend Valentine's offer by associating it with the noble self-sacrifices of the friendship tradition or the "courtly virtue of Magnanimity."[7] But if Shakespeare means the audience to sympathize and admire, he does little to elicit this reaction. He hints at no motive for Valentine, no sense of regret over losing his "essence," no sign of consideration for Silvia herself. Even worse, dramatically speaking, he gives Silvia no response when her ideally constant lover proposes to turn her over to her would-be ravisher (indeed no speech at all for the rest of the play). To treat her as a passive "prize," aside from giving the actress a thankless task and (in modern times) offending feminist sensibilities, would contradict the effect of her previous speeches and actions—defying her father's will about Thurio, going after Valentine, denouncing Proteus. Muriel Bradbrook, once a "prize" adherent, later suggested a different interpretation: Valentine, holding Silvia by one hand, "invites" the kneeling Proteus to kiss the other, as he offers him "all that *was* [not is] mine in Silvia." What he offers is not Silvia herself, but reinstatement as her courtly servant, a position which he and Proteus had formerly shared but from which he has now risen to be Silvia's betrothed.[8] Although the interpretation of Valentine's words seems too subtle for the theater, the suggestion is appealing. Another "Elizabethan" interpretation—one which has actually been tried on the stage—construes Valentine's offer as a "courteous gesture that will give Proteus a chance to be his best self" by declining it. To implement this, Valentine must signal his real purpose somehow, most easily by exchanging meaningful looks with an approving Silvia.[9]

Read and played without sophistication, however, the climactic scene seems to cast ridicule on all three members of the love triangle: on Valentine, whose mechanical adherence to one code makes him an unwitting traitor to another or (for spectators unacquainted with these codes) whose sudden shift in attitude suggests a more-than-Protean instability; on Proteus, whose clever scheming has led only to disgraceful exposure; and even on Silvia, the paragon for whom three men have striven, who finds herself forsaken by the winner. Only Julia, who loves not an ideal but a particular man, who loves him steadfastly, if foolishly, despite his well-known flaws, escapes absurdity.

These effects are partly the result of unskillful plot development, but there are hints that the two gentlemen at least—idealist as much as villain—were meant to appear comic. One hint is the comic exposure of Valentine himself in an earlier scene, caught by the Duke with a rope ladder under his cloak. Another is the incongruous behavior of that other idealist, Sir Eglamour, whose valor, wisdom, and compassion are praised by Silvia (4.3.11-13), but who takes to his heels when confronted by the outlaws, leaving Silvia unprotected (5.3.6-7). Most notable is Shakespeare's use of the comic servants to comment on or reflect their masters' behavior: Speed satirizes Valentine's romantic excesses (2.1.18-32, 42-78), and Launce unwittingly parodies the aristocrats' behavior in several passages—for example, his account of the family farewell (2.3.1-32), which exaggerates to absurdity the pathos of Proteus and Julia's parting.

It has been suggested that *Two Gentlemen,* which presents many problems as romantic comedy, makes perfect sense when considered as burlesque.[10] There are burlesque elements, certainly; but, although Shakespeare sometimes ridicules his young friends and lovers, he does not ridicule friendship or love. To turn the whole romance into burlesque is to lose some of the play's qualities that can be particularly attractive in performance: the lyricism, the passion (often moving, despite the exaggeration), and the youthful spirit, which makes the adolescent lovers appealing without obscuring their follies and vices. Shakespeare's method, so notable in later comedies, of balancing romance with deflating humor yet without destroying its charm, seems to have been attempted in this early play, though less firmly and skillfully: it is hence more puzzling in its effect and more difficult to translate into theatrical terms.

In addition to major problems in interpretation and tone, there are minor ones in simple "factual" matters due to confusing or inconsistent references: to "Verona" and "Padua" in passages seemingly related to Milan: to an Emperor who turns out to be a Duke; to two different Sir Eglamours, only one of whom actually appears on the stage; and so on. These are comparatively easy to deal with, but the mere listing of an Eglamour among Julia's suitors has occasionally colored the representation of the one we see, a sworn celibate who befriends Silvia. There are also failures in dramatic technique, such as an undue reliance on monologue and duologue, the latter even when a number of characters are on the stage.[11] Casual readers may overlook such lapses until the end, when they are suddenly shocked by Silvia's silence; in the theater, however, even the minor awkwardnesses must be dealt with in some way.

The three earliest productions of *Two Gentlemen* that can be described with any confidence tried to cure the play's

Jordan Pettle as Speed, Graham Abbey as Valentine, David W. Smith as an Outlaw, Steve Ross as an Outlaw, Rory Feore as an Outlaw, David Kirby as an Outlaw, and Mark Harapiak as an Outlaw in Act IV, scene i of the 1998 Stratford Festival production of The Two Gentlemen of Verona.

ills by radical textual revisions; the third used, in addition, a more potent medicine. Being closely related, they can be discussed together: (1) David Garrick's production at Drury Lane, using an adapted text by Benjamin Victor, introduced on 22 December 1762—the first production of the play now known, though there had probably been one in the 1590s; (2) John Philip Kemble's production at Covent Garden, using his own version (based on Victor's but with alterations), first seen on 20 April 1808; and (3) an "operatic" production at Covent Garden, opening on 21 November 1821, with libretto by Frederick Reynolds and music by Henry Bishop—the text evidently based on Kemble's but with extensive cuts to make way for the interpolated songs and for new passages of dialogue to justify them.[12] (Two other London productions of this period, seen just four times in all, may have had texts closer to Shakespeare's, but the evidence is sparse.)[13]

Some of the changes that Victor made and Kemble adopted were typical of that period's theatrical editing of Shakespeare: cuts (mainly in out-of-date wordplay and some indecorous references) and rearrangement of scenes to tighten structure and suit the convenience of the scenic stage. But their other alterations were more drastic. In addition to numerous verbal substitutions, there were many new passages, some to clarify motives left obscure by Shakespeare, others to fill gaps in his action, to strengthen or modernize characterization, to give greater prominence to the comic roles, or to bolster a new interpretation. The rearrangements and amplifications of scenes did give the play a greater sense of coherence and drive, but at the sacrifice of Shakespeare's subtler dramatic effects: for instance Launce's monologue about his family's farewell was no longer paired with Julia and Proteus's parting, and Julia's decision to follow Proteus, now placed immediately after his departure, was no longer in ironic juxtaposition with Proteus's determination to win Silvia. Among Victor's additions were two scenes for the comic players; Kemble retained (with a softening touch) the first one, in which a badly frightened Launce and a phlegmatic Crab are captured by outlaws, but not the second, in which a disguised Speed plays a callous joke on Launce. Reynolds evidently followed Kemble's lead.

The characters most affected by Victor's additions were Lucetta and Thurio, each of which was economically but effectively remodeled into a contemporary stage type. Shakespeare's Lucetta, a lively but sketchily drawn waiting woman of the Nerissa type, became a pert, intriguing chambermaid, who vowed that Julia shouldn't "think . . . to carry on even an honourable intrigue" without her (Victor, 9); Jane Pope, known for her saucy and hoydenish roles, was Garrick's Lucetta. Kemble returned to the original version of this character, but he followed Victor in giving a new personality to Thurio—that of an affected devotee of the arts, absurdly vain of his ability to write sonnets, set them to music, and sing them himself. In one passage, Thurio, instead of joining the search for Silvia, lingers to practice his new song; when he hears that Proteus has already galloped off, he promises to "gallop after him—fal, fal, fal": he exits singing and, one imagines, "galloping" mincingly (48). On the stage this character may have become progressively more ridiculous: Garrick's Thurio, Joseph Vernon, a gifted singer as well as an actor of some comic parts, is depicted in a contemporary engraving as an elegant figure gracefully posing with a lute (he sang "Who is Silvia?" himself); in Kemble's production, John Liston, famous for his "vain, rich, cowardly, stupid" characters, probably repeated his parodies of the *corps de ballet*'s dancing, which he had recently used successfully as Caper in a farce by J. T. Allingham; William Farren, in the Reynolds-Bishop production, reportedly made Thurio a "sportive coxcomb," and a drawing of him in the character, wearing an elaborate, finicky costume and holding a looking-glass, suggests that he did heavily emphasize Thurio's vanity and foppishness.[14] One character that Victor left as he found it was Eglamour. Kemble, however, smoothed out the Shakespearean wrinkles: to avoid confusion, he substituted "Altamont" for "Eglamour" in Julia's list of suitors, and to redeem Silvia's friend Eglamour from the ironic inconsistency between reputation and deed, he had him fight manfully and, after being struck down and left for dead, revive in time for the denouement.

The most important changes, however, affected the interpretation of the whole play. Evidently the adaptors saw nothing comic in Valentine's worship of Silvia but found his climactic offer to Proteus incredible; accordingly they concentrated upon the love story, elaborating the relationship of Valentine and Silvia by additional passages (for example, mutual declarations of love in Act 2 and a tender reunion after Silvia's rescue from Proteus). They completely reformed the climactic scene: Valentine, instead of forgiving Proteus immediately, threatened him with death; this precipitated Julia's swoon and, ultimately, the revelation of her identity; Silvia, not Valentine, joined the hands of Proteus and Julia, then persuaded Valentine to be reconciled to his friend. Victor ended the play by having the reformed Proteus speak a moralizing couplet, which Kemble expanded into seven lines, ending with "A lover must be constant to be bless'd." The love interest must have suffered when stately, fifty-year-old Kemble played Valentine: he was heroic and, in his best scene (the last) very energetic, but, according to the *Morning Chronicle* (22 April 1808), "cold and unimpressive" where love was the "immediate impulse."

The operatic production went well beyond its predecessors in expedients for popularizing *Two Gentlemen*: its revised and much-cut text was embellished with a great deal of music and spectacle. In addition to a newly-set "Who Is Silvia?", there were an overture and eleven elaborately-arranged vocal pieces—solos, duets, glees, choruses, and a grand finale. The words for the new songs were based, with considerable freedom, on passages from other Shakespearean works, mostly sonnets and other poems, but also four plays. The music was obviously more important than the drama, though Maria Tree, a good Shakespearean actress as well as a fine mezzo-soprano, seems to have given an effective portrayal of Julia despite the slender text. None of the male characters except the outlaws had singing parts, and none except John Liston as Launce got much attention from reviewers. Most of the praise went to the two heroines and a young singer who played the interpolated role of Julia's page. The staging was extravagant, with "wonders of scenery and machinery." Especially "gorgeous" was the final scene of Act 4, set in the Great Square of Milan, with grotesque groups of dancers and merrymakers celebrating Carnival. It featured a series of spectacles, notably a huge model of Cleopatra's galley and "an artificial mountain transformed into the Temple of Apollo, by the singular process of conflagration." This "noble pageant," half an hour long, would seem irrelevant to the play, but apparently the distractions of Carnival enabled Silvia and Eglamour to leave Milan unnoticed.[15]

This was the first popular production of *Two Gentlemen*: Garrick's had been seen only six times, Kemble's only three, but the operatic version had twenty-nine performances in its first season and six in its second—an excellent record at that time. Audiences obviously preferred less of the play (even in revised form) and more of the embellishments. As the *Examiner* explained, the passages omitted for the sake of music and spectacle were not "*dramatically* beautiful," and there was nothing a modern audience appreciated less than mere blank-verse recitation.

The first documented production of *Two Gentlemen* that restored Shakespeare's text was William Charles Macready's, which premiered at Drury Lane on 29 December 1841.[16] "Restoring," of course, did not mean returning to Shakespeare's complete text or strictly adhering to his arrangement of scenes. Macready took the usual liberties in both respects. In fact, he cut more lines than either Victor or Kemble, his most noticeable omissions being the whole of 3.2, in which Proteus hypocritically advises Thurio how to woo Silvia (though he transferred seven of its lines, with some verbal changes, to 4.2), and the most vulgar passages of Launce's monologue about Crab's misbehavior. In making structural changes, however, he was more sensitive to the dramatic consequences than the adaptors had been. For example, he preserved the ironic relationship between Julia's plan to join Proteus and the latter's defection to Silvia.

Textual restoration, as Macready understood it, consisted of purifying the original text from "the gross interpolations that disfigure it": in this case, ridding it of all the adaptor's additions and refraining from making any new ones.[17] In preparing his version of *Two Gentlemen,* he came close to this ideal: he cut out all previous accretions to Shakespeare's text; he made far fewer verbal changes within the lines than his predecessors had done; and he added only one full line of his own. But he not only purged the text, he also restored the long-abandoned lines in which Valentine forgives Proteus and offers him "all that was mine in Silvia" (5.4.83). This revived emphasis on friendship reflected a current interest of Macready's: later in the same season he produced Gerald Griffin's *Titus and Gisippus,* a blank-verse dramatization of the old story.

Macready's comparatively slight changes in characterization were made through cuts rather than additions: for example, he made Eglamour seem more consistent by omitting Silvia's praise of his valor rather than by making his behavior conform to it. Several cuts made the two heroes appear in a somewhat better light, but performance, more than textual changes, revealed his interpretation of these roles.

As Valentine, Macready was a noble hero—frank, kindly, warm-hearted. (At forty-eight he was too old for Shakespeare's inexperienced, slightly ridiculous idealist, but he would have rejected that interpretation anyway.) He and James R. Anderson, a "gallant" Proteus, "more picturesque than villainous," played well together; they were better, according to one critic, in their "manly cordiality" as friends than in their "boisterous ardor" as lovers. Another critic found fault with Macready, however, for his "overly-fervid" demonstration of friendship when bidding farewell to Proteus; his "perilous sighs" seemed too emotional for male friends in England's "'cauld clime.'" Young Miss Fortescue, as Julia, was the center of the audience's sympathetic attention, charming them with her warmth, passion, and pathos. Robert Keeley, a fine comedian, played Launce effectively despite his missing vulgarities. Thurio, though now deprived of a chance to sing and caper, was by tradition a fop; Compton created a new identity by combining "foppishness" with "surliness."[18]

The difficult climactic scene was played like this: As Proteus advanced on Silvia, theatening rape, Valentine rushed forward, sword in hand, commanding him to "let go." Proteus drew his own sword and was about to attack, but when he recognized his opponent, he dropped it and staggered back in horror. The actors froze in their positions, creating the effect of a "fixed group" by an artist or sculptor, before Proteus fell to his knees and begged for forgiveness. The applause was "tumultuous." Proteus's horror-struck attitude, which epitomized his shocked self-conviction, seemed to one critic "worth a life's repentance." Idealizing the encounter as a work of art gave the moment of first remorse a symbolic importance, countering, as much as possible, the commonplace demands of probability. Valentine's rebuke was "delivered with manly grace, which was enhanced by the generosity of his forgiveness." Not everyone was reconciled to his offer of Silvia, but critics made surprisingly little objection—perhaps because Miss Ellis's dignified but cold Silvia aroused little sympathy. What did she *do*? We have only a negative clue: the remark that she had not yet mastered "the mystery of by-play."[19]

Among the most effective features of this production were the artistic scenes of characters in Renaissance dress moving against carefully-detailed, authentic-looking Italian backgrounds. Macready had chosen the year 1500 as the approximate time of the story and had consulted the antiquarian authority Colonel Hamilton Smith about the costumes. He had new scenery painted (less common for legitimate plays than for opera at that time) with emphasis on specific, identifiable places. For example, the opening scene, in which Valentine parts from Proteus, was located not simply on "A Street in Verona" (as in Kemble's promptbook), but before the "Tombs of the Scaligeri," and there were several views of the Duke's palace, with differing Milanese landmarks in the distance—the Duomo in one, the City Gate in another, and so on.[20] Reviewers approved the "attention to the local scenery and uses of the period," and they praised the "succession of beautiful and animated pictures," noting that the decor, rather than "overlay[ing] the drama," was "in fine keeping with [its] effects."[21]

Audiences and critics were enthusiastic. The latter praised not only the production but (equally complimentary to it) the play itself. The *Argus,* which called *Two Gentlemen* "charming," said that it was "so admirably got up and so deliciously acted" that it produced "a quiet and continual succession of pleasurable sensations." For the *Times* critic, the atmosphere of "Southern warmth" evidently turned what were usually-considered flaws into part of the play's charm: excessive use of conceits became the "freshness and recklessness" with which *concetti* are "sprinkle[d]" over everything, and the lack of strong characterization hardly mattered with this "company of graceful sonneteers." Such reviews were a pleasant change from some earlier ones, which had condemned the play as dull and not worth reviving.[22] The new appreciation seemingly reflected not only the appeal of the Italian Renaissance decor and the fine acting, but also—for the *Morning Chronicle*'s critic, at least—the liberating effect of the rediscovered Shakespearean text. Macready's revival, he wrote, was "in the simple form" intended by Shakespeare, something that had been previously misunderstood by adaptors and managers. Neither an elaborate work of art nor "a collection of . . . stage effects," it is a "careless, graceful, romantic piece" from Shakespeare's earliest years. Treated that way, "what beauty, what inimitable grace, what freshness and buoyancy" it had! The audience could laugh, sigh, and sympathize with the characters without bothering very much about "character": they need not even feel unhappy about Proteus's perfidy, for it was "clear from the first that everything must come right in the end."

Macready's production had thirteen performances—as many as all preceding ones put together, except for those of the "opera." Unimpressive as the number sounds, it was a very good showing for a minor Shakespearean play at that time. For *Two Gentlemen* without textual or musical embellishments it was remarkable. This production, whose promptbook was used again by Charles Kean (New York, 1846; London, 1848), established the theatrical use of Shakespeare's text with few, if any, additions and often, though not always, with Valentine's offer intact. Stage versions of later years would vary in the amount of liberty taken with the original text (Augustin Daly's in 1895, for example, was heavily edited), but they would, on the whole, conform more closely to it, not less so, than Macready's did.

The next productions of particular interest were William Poel's, important for radical innovations in staging. Unlike the other directors in this study, Poel gave his attention not to making the play more stageworthy, but to revealing its own qualities, which were currently obscured by elaborate sets, artificial breaks in the action, and slow, overly-emphatic speech. His search for "some means of acting Shakespeare naturally and appealingly from a full text"[23] led him back to the original staging as he envisioned it—continuous action on a thrust platform and rapid speech accented only on key words. His involvement with the New Shakespeare Society was an early example of cooperation between stage and study. Although Poel was at first ridiculed, his influence and that of more flexible followers revolutionized Shakespearean production.

Not counting a dramatic reading in 1892, Poel directed two London productions of *Two Gentlemen,* both for the Elizabethan Stage Society: at the Merchant Taylors Hall on 28 November 1896 and at His Majesty's Theatre on 20 April 1910 during Beerbohm-Tree's annual Shakespeare Festival. (Each was repeated at other locations.) For both he used a conservative text, with no changes except occasional cuts (the only notable ones being the references to Eglamour's running away), and he tried to create the theatrical conditions of Shakespeare's day.[24] The costumes were authentically Elizabethan, if not always appropriate to character and situation: the women wore ruffs and farthingales, the gentlemen's clothes were based on some sixteenth-century frescoes in the Hall of the Carpenters' Company, and the outlaws' on a costume design for a halberdier in the Fishmongers' Pageant of 1609. (A semi-military group, the outlaws marched with banner and trumpeter.)

The first production was not successful, largely because the "stage," an open space at the upper end of a large hall, was too flat to allow good visibility and the amateur actors had difficulty making themselves heard. The second one, however, though seen only once in London, was, in Robert Speaight's opinion, one of Poel's "most important contributions to the Elizabethan Revival." Poel had an apron built out over the orchestra pit of Tree's theater, thus gaining something like a platform stage. The acting seems to have been generally good. Critics approved the distinct enunciation and the use of the old pronunciation when the verse required it; they also noticed some "Elizabethan" gesture. One of Poel's eccentricities, occasionally casting women in men's parts (a reverse reminder of the boy-actress), was used successfully in this production: Valentine and Panthino were reportedly played well by actresses, though Valentine (Winifred Rae) was chided by her director for lack of "virility." Individual performances were less impressive, however, than the mood or atmosphere created by the whole group. Thus Speaight recalled the "innkeeper nodding over his lantern," not as an example of the actor's art, but as one of the production's "beauties which lingered in the memory," and the *Times* mentioned the "'right' Shakespearian" fooling of the "two clowns" without naming the actors or noting any details of performance. In this production, declared the latter, the "puerile complications and improbabilities" of the plot, which would have been "more glaring" in a realistic setting, "became of little account," and the play's best qualities were clearly brought out—the "verve of its dialogue, the lyric beauty of many of its passages," and "the atmosphere of warm, romantic amorism."

During virtually the next half-century, productions of *Two Gentlemen,* in both London and Stratford, generally used Elizabethan costumes, or something like them, though at least one used medieval Italian decor; the settings varied from pictorial to simplified and suggestive. But on 22 January 1957 Michael Langham broke the trend with a production at the Old Vic set in the early nineteenth century, the first *Two Gentlemen* at either major center in a period later than Shakespeare's.[25] The acting text was Shakespearean except for a good many cuts, occasional brief changes in wording, and some (not many) additional lines. Valentine's famous offer in the last act was retained. Changes in interpretation were effected mainly through innovative decor and greatly amplified stage business.[26]

A vaguely Italian permanent set, suggestive of a garden in neo-Gothic style, had flower-entwined pillars, an ivy-covered ruin, and, in the foreground, a small, ornate structure, from whose high window Silvia looked down in the serenade scene; different backcloths indicated changes of location. The "mock-Regency" costumes pleased both eye and fancy with their romantic flair—the gentlemen in brightly-colored jackets, close-fitting trousers, caped coats, and velour top hats, the ladies in full-skirted dresses with lace parasols. Valentine and Proteus, "attractively posturing juveniles," looked like Byron and Shelley. The outlaws (stretching chronology) resembled the Pirates of Penzance.[27] The Romantic period, closer to the present than the Renaissance, yet remote enough to evoke a "make-believe" atmosphere, seemed to most critics an inspired choice: it sorted well with the play's sighings and swoonings, its poetic fervor and idealism, and its Byronic philandering. Turning the two gentlemen into "a couple of bucks" heightened the absurdities of the plot and, at the same time, "almost conjured away" one's impatience with them. Reviewers disagreed about the amount of burlesque Langham used, but most thought he managed it delicately (at least, until the climax): as one of them remarked, his production succeeded because the play's "naively young but passionate poetry . . . survive[d] the drastic treatment."[28]

The acting created the effect of irony balanced with sympathy. Robert Gale, a Valentine of "dashing 'true-blue' simplicity," was both lovelorn and valorously spirited. Keith Michell as the Byronic Proteus was "so fiercely driven by passion" as to be "unaware that he was turning into a knave"; at times he seemed "astonished at his own behavior," his attitude varying from humorous ruefulness to "Keatsian melancholy." Barbara Jefford's "shiningly sincere" Julia was praised for "genuine fire and eloquence." Ingrid Hafner's Silvia, though comparatively colorless, was a lovely-looking, nobly-bred heroine. Dudley Jones gave a "brisk" performance of the word-mongering Speed. Robert Helpmann, with comic precision and "ingratiating audience-contact," portrayed Launce as a squeaky-voiced, vacant-looking, but likable Cockney, "funny with pathos." A clever yellow Labrador named Duff was "engagingly miscast" as that dirty dog Crab: he "shook hands," carried parcels, and behaved so decorously as to belie his master's vulgar account of him (all its vulgarities intact).[29]

The most notable aspect of Langham's production was its constant and ingenious use of stage business which, though not implied by Shakespeare's text, seemed to grow naturally out of it. It endowed the most archaic verbal conceits with a modern spirit, and it often won laughs with the ironic touches it gave to the speaker's words. Since the actors rarely said anything without doing something too, they gave the illusion of a fuller, faster-moving plot than the play actually has. Among other embellishments were an artist painting Silvia's portrait, archery practice, and dancing in the candlelit palace garden. Stage business, combined with distinctive costumes, was also used to "develop" minor characters: Antonio, apparently a country squire, came in with bag and gun, fresh from hunting; Thurio, vain as ever but now a "superannuated rake," was shown being shaved; the Duke, wearing a splendid uniform with epaulettes, strode about, smoking cigars and seeming "always on the edge of sending a gunboat to subdue rebellious tribesmen." Eglamour was uniquely reinterpreted: the "two Eglamours" were combined into one, an ineffectual but dapper old beau, who first courted Julia in Verona, then turned up at Milan, paying his addresses to Silvia. (Chaste devotion to a dead lady was not mentioned.) Stage business, added to scenes where Eglamour did not originally appear, carried out the new interpretation; at one point he was visually paired with Thurio—two silly old fops together.[30] The portrayal, as the *Guardian* suavely remarked, was "not quite perhaps what Shakespeare meant," but it "fitted well in this 'Vanity Fair' treatment of the tale."

The most striking use of stage business, however, was in the climactic scene, where it gave a new explanation of Valentine's notorious offer. Proteus's rescue of Silvia was heard offstage (not merely referred to, as in Shakespeare), with Proteus demanding Silvia's release and, when an outlaw refused, threatening force. The outlaws having fled, Silvia hurried on stage, closely pursued by Proteus, armed with a pistol and followed in turn by Julia-as-Sebastian. Silvia, trying to escape from Proteus, who had gained hold of her, succeeded in taking the pistol from his pocket and, presumably pointing it at him, broke loose and backed away from him, down the shallow steps. He wheeled down after her, took the pistol away, and threatened to force her; he then swung her to him, laying the pistol down for freer action. When Valentine advanced from behind a rock, ordering, "Villain, let go . . . ," Proteus released her, exclaiming, "Valentine!" Silvia fell in a faint, and Valentine and Julia knelt to help her. Julia stayed with her as Valentine confronted Proteus and denounced him. At one point Proteus put his hand on his old friend's shoulder, but Valentine ignored this overture. Proteus, after begging forgiveness, picked up the pistol; Silvia, who had revived, took cover behind a pillar, Julia (drawn toward Proteus?) behind Valentine. Proteus, however, was bent on suicide, not murder. Valentine hastily forgave him, then, taking the pistol from him, made his offer of Silvia "on the spur of an emotional moment."

Critics joined in the audience's merriment over the transformation of Shakespeare's puzzling finale into nineteenth-century melodrama—"a sort of abridged version of . . . 'The Corsican Brothers.'" Nothing could "finally disguise" Valentine's lunatic forbearance, wrote one, "but the players' confidence survived the inevitable laughter"; another said that the mask of light romance, which had been kept in place until now, dropped under the strain of this scene, and "the repressed burlesque [burst] out." The tongue-in-cheek response was, no doubt, exactly what Langham wished. His "brilliant" solution to the problem of Valentine's offer was praised as the best example of his inventive talent.[31]

Langham's successful treatment of the play influenced both critical attitudes and some later productions. Its springlike gaiety was remembered and favorably contrasted with the autumnal mood of Peter Hall's production (Stratford-upon-Avon, 1960), with its decor in the deep, rich tones of an Italian Old Master. And its long-lived influence was felt in Richard Digby Day's productions (Open Air Theatre, Regent's Park, London, summers of 1968 and 1969) with their nineteenth-century costumes, their light-hearted lyricism, and their sharply-defined minor characters (including some anachronistic ones—outlaws in Robin Hood suits and Sir Eglamour in cobwebbed armor like an ancient Quixote).[32]

Among the most interesting of other productions with latter-day settings was Robin Phillips's contemporary *Two Gentlemen* at the Royal Shakespeare Theatre, Stratford-upon-Avon, 23 July 1970 (revived in December for a brief run at the Aldwych in London). Its permanent set, which served for both Verona and Milan (and for the forest, with the help of dangling ropes and dappled light), depicted a scene at an Italian resort, featuring a miniature swimming pool with real water; the lovers were wealthy, golden-tanned adolescents, wearing trendy leisure clothes and huge sunglasses. Antonio, a cigar-smoking tycoon, or perhaps a Mafia boss, doffed his monogrammed beachrobe for a quick swim; the Duke, who sometimes appeared in an academic gown, looked like a vice chancellor of a university. The outlaws were hippies, and Eglamour was an aging scout-master, dressed in bare-kneed uniform, who arrived on a bicycle, brought along his camping gear and ordnance map, and laid a bridge across the pool for Silvia to escape on. Launce (Patrick Stewart) was a dour, North-Country workman, dressed in black, who stood apart, a grave, unmoved observer of the others' follies.

The production reflected the current emphasis on a search for identity—it began and ended with an echo-song "Who is Silvia? Who is Valentine? Who is Proteus? Who is Julia?"—and also a modern concern with psychological motivation. Proteus, more cerebral than the handsome, athletic Valentine but relatively puny physically, seemed to be moved to treachery by envious admiration and a sense of his own inadequacy. Simply as interesting characters, the lovers were well played: Peter Egan's Valentine, sincere and naive, a little conceited but maturing under the influence of love and its troubles; Ian Richardson's Proteus, "coldly impassioned," subtle, and self-aware; Helen Mirren's Julia, "delightfully spirited and endearing," at times a "tigress" or "whirlwind," at times an agonized adolescent, sucking her thumb for comfort; Estelle Kohler's Silvia, a graceful socialite, but capable of taking the initiative and acting with spirit. The reconciliation scene was effectively played: as he wound up his expression of forgiveness, Valentine kissed Silvia; then, crossing to Proteus, he ended "And that my love may appear plain and free" (5.4.82) by kissing him. The crucial line that followed ("All that was mine in Silvia I give thee") evidently meant, "The love I have given to Silvia I also give to you." Even so, the play ended on an uncertain note, as Valentine spoke its final line with a doubtful pause before the last word, "One feast, one house, one mutual—happiness." The sound of a cuckoo underlined the ambiguity.

Some critics deplored the effects of the modernization: "incongruities," substitution of irony for lyricism, loss of the lovers' innocence, sacrifice of serious Shakespearean themes. (Once again the Langham production of 1957 was wistfully recalled as the contrasting ideal.) Others insisted that the play had gained by the contemporary treatment of timeless truths. Most reviewers, however, like most audiences, simply enjoyed the production.[33]

An unusual amount of experimentation with *Two Gentlemen* has taken place in North American regional and festival theaters: the play has had settings, for example, in Little Italy of 1900; on a 1920s campus of "Millen University," where Valentine had an athletic scholarship; and in a farcical Wild West, with Silvia doubling as a teasing Mae West and the disguised Julia wearing a ten-gallon hat over her enormous beehive hairdo. It has been given in the style of circus, *commedia dell'arte,* vaudeville, and a combination of all these.[34] In 1984 the American Repertory in New York even revived Kemble's 1808 adaptation.

Among other experiments have been several musical ones. The most famous was the award-winning "rock musical" (which also used other popular rhythms like jazz and Latin American dance), directed by Mel Shapiro from his and John Guare's text, Guare's lyrics and Galt MacDermot's music. It was produced in the summer of 1971 for Joseph Papp's New York Shakespeare Festival in Central Park, had a successful run at the St. James, Broadway, in 1971-72, and was revived (with a different cast) at the Phoenix, London, in 1973. This *Two Gentlemen* was much more, and much less, than an adaptation. Fewer than 450 Shakespearean lines survived, some of them from sonnets and other plays, and a good many new lines were added, besides those of the numerous songs (nearly forty, finally). Some striking character changes produced a pregnant Julia, a lusty Silvia who hated to be idealized, a tough-looking Duke in dark glasses who was a sleazy politician as well as a tyrant, an Eglamour (Silvia's old boyfriend) who had been drafted into the army, a Lucetta who paired off with Thurio, and metadramatic servants (Launce and Speed) who bemoaned the plight of the working man with no time for love and wished to be a "hot lover . . . like the kids in the play." There were references to contemporary concerns—war, abortion, the environment. A racially mixed cast made the point of brotherhood. But the chief emphasis was on the songs, the dances, the mood of lively abandon—and the theme of love, love, love. It was a long way from Shakespeare, but it had some of the same youthfulness, vitality, and, in its own way, innocence.[35]

Some modern directors have attacked the problem of anti-feminism in *Two Gentlemen,* usually by reinterpreting Valentine's offer so as to remove its callousness toward Silvia. As we have seen, Robin Phillips tried this solution, yet a critic of his production remarked that this play could "provoke a demonstration by the Women's Liberation Movement." Some North American productions have simply made the offer ridiculous, for example by using double-takes or having the men walk off together and then turn to see with comic dismay the women leaving in the other direction. The most effective expedient, however, has been to involve Silvia in the forgiveness of Proteus.[36]

The *Two Gentlemen* that best illustrates this method—the Royal Shakespeare Company's latest production of the play—also offers examples of other strategies for bringing audience and play together. Directed by David Thacker, it opened at the Swan Theatre in Stratford-upon-Avon on 6 April 1991, transferred to the Pit at the Barbican in October 1992, and later went on tour with a largely different cast, finally closing at the Haymarket Theatre in London in January 1994.[37] Its most obvious features, the choice of period and the related use of music, proved interpretive as well as entertaining. The play was set in the 1930s, when "Coward dressing gowns . . . Lonsdale evening dress and Wodehouse tennis gear" were fashionable—a period whose combination of elegance and shallowness revealingly reflected the same qualities in the play's characters. The atmosphere was established during the quarter-hour before the play began: a palm-court orchestra, ensconced in a bandstand, played hit-parade songs by George Gershwin, Cole Porter, Irving Berlin, and others, while couples in evening wear danced downstage. Between the scenes of the play, a blonde *chanteuse* crooned songs like "Blue Moon," "Night and Day," and "Love Is the Sweetest Thing"—all "cunningly chosen to point and counter-point the action." The evocation of a past distinctly different from today, yet familiar as Bertie Wooster on TV, brought the audience into tune with the play. As Benedict Nightingale explained in the *Times*: "When lovers appear in doublet and hose, we expect them to behave in conventionally romantic ways. Transpose them to places we more easily associate with youthful skittishness and folly, and they can seem perfectly plausible." The actors never mocked or patronized their characters, but their innocent yet artificial world was one whose adolescent passions might well be the subject of fun. The tone was close to Shakespeare's own. Interestingly, a critic who disapproved of the chosen setting—an unusual response—admitted that a post-Shakespearean period makes sense but preferred the early nineteenth century, with a Byronic Proteus. Langham's production and its imitators were hard to forget.[38]

Another notable feature of the production was its success in giving Shakespeare's sketchilly drawn characters some sense of development or depth. Valentine (Richard Bonneville), though never profound, progressed from "an awkwardly ingratiating lover" to "an impressively bold one." Even Thurio (Henry Guy) was no mere fop or "silly-ass wooer," but "a stilted prig desperately trying to hide his intellectual and emotional limitations"; unlike the Thurios with literary pretensions, he was depressed by Proteus's suggestions that he woo Silvia with poetry. As usual in modern productions, however, the chief interest was in Proteus (Barry Lynch) and the motivation for his treachery. Here the use of potentially symbolic stage business was striking, though the interpretation depended on the spectator's own bent. The introductory scene showed the two friends in adolescent horseplay, wrestling on the floor, which, for some viewers, would inevitably connote latent sexuality. Paul Nelsen, who was struck by the strange mixture of devotion and rivalry he saw here, has described Lynch's Proteus in some detail, emphasizing the actor's "subtext." For Nelsen, this Proteus was "sullen . . . and Iago-like," and his treacherous actions stemmed from ambiguous feelings toward Valentine rather than erotic desire for Silvia. This dark interpretation was not widely shared, however. Some critics, indeed, saw a boyish charm in Lynch's Proteus: they found him "likeable and inexperienced," even "more naive and impressionable" than Valentine, before he became obsessed with Silvia. And one critic noticed a "curious sense of baffled innocence" (much in line, we think, with Shakespeare's text) even as he argued his way into treachery. Yet there was also something in the actor's manner—a "nervous intensity," a slight instability, a "disturbing little flicker of a smile"—that suggested, even to sympathetic viewers, introversion and suppressed emotion. Lynch's psychological suggestiveness obviously did not clarify Proteus's motivation, but it did result in an intriguing portrayal.

The other roles were acted well, but there was nothing unusual about them psychologically. Julia (Clare Holman) had a "jaunty boyishness" as Sebastian but also a touching pathos; Silvia (Saskia Reeves) was cool, elegant, but determined. Richard Moore's shuffling, bowler-hatted Launce, with his "hangdog dignity" and deftly executed "takes," was, with his lugubrious-looking lurcher, Woolly, among the memorable pleasures of the production. Small parts were given sharp or colorful touches: the wisecracking Speed (Sean Murray) in his cheap suit had the personality of a traveling salesman; the Duke (Terence Wilton), an amateur cook, zestfully dismembered a lobster.[39]

The use of symbolic stage pictures was most effective in the climactic scene of the final act: Valentine stopped Proteus from raping Silvia by wrestling him to the ground, "echoing, now in desperate earnest, the playful roughhousing of act one." The parallel visually marked the change that had occurred in the relationship, with perhaps a suggestion that the comradely closeness had always included some potential hostility.[40] The actual violence might be interpreted as cathartic. When the change from conflict to reconciliation occurred, the pictorial elements remained strong. After Valentine's denunciation, spoken with "a moving sense of heartfelt grief," there was a lengthy pause before Proteus bowed his head, knelt, and made his short speech of confession. Critics were generally impressed by the poignancy of Lynch's acting here: he "[caught] very well the conflicting emotions of Proteus's final onset of guilt," "flesh[ing] out the character's woefully underscripted moment of shame most realistically." (Nelsen, however, questioned Proteus's sincerity, and indeed, as Smallwood has explained, Lynch's interpretation varied from one performance to another, according to whether he let "that enigmatic flicker of a smile" appear.) The most difficult part of the scene—and the most illuminating example of pictorial acting—followed. As Proteus begged forgiveness, Silvia stood beside him, facing Valentine, and silently but eloquently seconded the plea by her attitude and expression; as Valentine pardoned his friend, she crossed over and stood with him while he offered Proteus "all that was mine in Silvia"—meaning, perhaps, a share in "the mutual love and trust" between himself and Silvia. The exact interpretation of the words was not important; what mattered was Silvia's participation in the forgiveness and the gift of restored love.

Response to this production was joyously enthusiastic. A number of critics, both journalists and scholars, praised Thacker's handling of the difficult climax: his approach made "such perfect sense" that the "'crux' was not evident," and the "near-impossible" scene became both "riveting" and "plausible." But even critics who still found the ending either "risible" or "outrageous" applauded the production. As for the audiences, in Smallwood's euphoric words, "Shakespeare's so-called failure, his apprentice work, his unplayable flop, became the hit of the season."[41]

Reviewing these theatrical attempts to popularize *Two Gentlemen,* one sees some salient trends. Rewriting the text to improve it, never successful, has long since been abandoned, though using it as a framework for new creations has occasionally resulted in popular productions (opera, rock musical). In every age nonverbal elements have been determining factors in making the play's simplicities attractive or, alternatively, in creating the impression of additional depth and development. Extra music has been used, not just in outright musicals, but in a good many regular productions. Decor and style of performance have often been important, especially when a new look has revealed certain aspects of the play more clearly than before—for example, Macready's meticulous Italian sets at a time when stock scenery often sufficed for Shakespeare, Poel's return to simple Elizabethan staging for an audience accustomed to visual illusion, and Langham's evocation of the Byronic period when Elizabethan productions had become the norm. The search for novelty has led to a variety of unusual and inventive treatments. It seems, indeed, that some directors have been willing to undertake this play largely because its reputation for unpopularity serves as a license to experiment without giving much offense. Other things being equal, however, the most effective productions have been those whose staging had some special affinity with the youthful mixture of passion, artifice, lyricism, and folly in the play itself.

In all periods there has been a noticeable attempt to give life and color to Shakespeare's minor characters. In early productions certain roles were transformed into contemporary stage types by textual additions, and even after the adaptations had been discarded, some influence from the memory of previous portrayals probably remained, at least for Thurio. About the middle of the present century, directors began, through inventive use of decor and stage business, to give more distinctive personalities to other mainly functional characters. The types of roles assigned to them have, of course, been suitable to the chosen setting, but they have also reflected the interests and concerns of the period when the production occurred. Eglamour's transformations are particularly interesting in this respect: he has moved from Kemble's perfect knight, to Macready's coward, to Poel's representative of spiritualized love, to modern portrayals as a figure of fun—an elderly beau, an anachronistic Don Quixote, a childish do-gooder. Directors have never quite known what to do with Eglamour, but their different ways of dealing with this absurd but poignant figure reveal him as a touchstone for a production and its time.

Some interesting analogies are found in the climactic scene as staged in otherwise dissimilar productions, widely separated in time. In the earliest ones, using adapted texts with a heavily revised climax, Silvia persuaded a formidably reluctant Valentine to forgive her would-be ravisher; in the latest one (Thacker's), using Shakespeare's version with a more amenable Valentine, she silently did the same. A closer parallel links Macready's production, using a restored text, with Thacker's: in both, Proteus froze for a long moment after Valentine's denunciation, his attitude and facial expression suggesting the emotions he felt at the sudden disclosure of his treachery; in both, the stage picture helped to fill in what was lacking in the short repentance speech.

Sarah-Jane Holm and Alison Reid perform in the 1993 Royal Shakespeare Company production of The Two Gentlemen of Verona.

One aspect of the play noticed by modern scholars, the satirical and parodic function of Launce and Speed, has often been overlooked in the theater. Indeed, some reviewers have remarked that Launce, entertaining as he is, has nothing to do with the main part of the play.[42] The Phillips production called attention to his metadramatic function with a Launce silently brooding over the antics of his social superiors, but although one critic was impressed by this conception of the play's "dark angel," another thought it was merely pretentious. Less blatant was the extra stage business in Thacker's production that showed Launce making clownish use of facilities designed for more elegant purposes (like putting dogfood in the Duke's fruitbowl); thus, as Robert Smallwood observed, "mov[ing] in the hinterland between the audience and the fiction."[43] While less scholarly reviewers, writing to deadlines, did not notice the implications, that hardly matters. Provided Launce is not allowed to overwhelm the romance completely, it is just as well simply to laugh at him, responding unconsciously to his subversive ironies and leaving anything more to afterthoughts.

A notable recent change is the increasing interest in the two gentlemen themselves. In 1808, Leigh Hunt wrote that they came and went, talked or were silent, without exciting sympathy for the one or contempt for the other; in 1842, reviewers commended Macready for taking such a slight role as Valentine in the interests of art.[44] Proteus has always been condemned, of course, though he has frequently seemed less villainous on the stage than in the study; in more recent times Valentine, too, has been denigrated. But some stage productions, in dealing with the problems of Proteus's motivation and Valentine's callousness, have so developed these characters that their central importance in the play goes unquestioned. While the friends' relationship has not reflected the *alter ego* conception (indeed, quite the opposite), Shakespeare himself shows a reality that does not conform to Valentine's ideal.

Again and again over the years some reviewer of a successful production has asked why *Two Gentlemen* has been so neglected; then it has been neglected again for awhile. Today, however, the play is becoming better known in the theater. With Thacker's production to brighten its reputation, with revivals by regional companies to test its wilder possibilities, and with the BBC's stylized work of television art to be viewed on demand, this trend will probably continue. *Two Gentlemen* will always be a special challenge, though. All dramatic productions are collaborations between author and theater—director, actors, designers, and so on. In productions of this play, Shakespeare's collaborators are more than usually responsible for a significant part of the "text."

Notes

1. This does not include any with amateur actors, except for William Poel's—too important to leave out.
2. Even counting a rock musical, we know of only five full-length productions (one of which had a single performance) in New York; three of these were later seen in London. Short entertainments based on *Two Gentlemen* included two skits (one with black minstrels) and a farce. See George C. D. Odell, *Annals of the New York Stage,* 15 vols. (New York: Columbia University Press, 1927-49), 8:219; 11:549; 12:104, 312.
3. Charles Spencer's phrase, in his review of David Thacker's production, *The Daily Telegraph,* 19 April 1991.
4. Other concerns (education, the courtly code of behavior, the qualities essential to a gentlemen), though important, do not impress a spectator as driving impulses of speech and action for the major characters. Kurt Schlueter, in the introduction to his edition, *The Two Gentlemen of Verona,* The New Cambridge Shakespeare (Cambridge: Cambridge University Press, 1990), 2-6, gives a good, condensed discussion of the play's themes. In addition to the scholarly articles he cites, see Ann Jennalie Cook, "Shakespeare's Gentlemen," *Shakespeare Jahrbuch* (West) (1985): 9-27.
5. Gervase Mathew, "Ideals of Friendship," *Patterns of Love and Courtesy: Essays in Memory of C. S. Lewis,* ed. John Lawlor (Evanston: Northwestern University Press, 1966), 46-50; Laurens J. Mills, *One Soul in Bodies Twain: Friendship in Tudor Literature and Stuart Drama* (Bloomington, Indiana: Principia Press, 1937), 259 et passim; Geoffrey Bullough, ed. *Narrative and Dramatic Sources of Shakespeare,* 8 vols. (London: Routledge and Kegan Paul, 1957-75), 1: 204.
6. Bernard O'Donoghue gives a good review of courtly love's various features and its influence on English Renaissance literature, in *The Courtly Love Tradition,* Literature in Context (Manchester: Manchester University Press; Totowa, New Jersey: Barnes and Noble, 1982), 5-6, 15. He defends the term "courtly love" against modern attacks (14).
7. See Mills, 258; Muriel C. Bradbrook, *Shakespeare and Elizabethan Poetry: A Study of His Earlier Work in Relation to the Poetry of the Time* (New York: Oxford University Press, 1952), 151.
8. Bradbrook speculates that the play was written for a private performance by boy actors. See "Love and Constancy in *The Two Gentlemen of Verona,*" *Shakespeare in His Context: The Constellated Globe.* The Collected Papers of Muriel Bradbrook, vol. 4 (Totowa, N.J.: Barnes and Noble, 1989), 47-49, 55. In *Shakespeare and Elizabethan Poetry* (152) she had declared that Silvia "should not react at all. She is the prize, for the purpose of argument, and must not call attention to herself. . . ."
9. Camille Wells Slights, "*The Two Gentlemen of Verona* and the Courtesy Book Tradition," *Shakespeare Studies* 16 (1983): 27. A 1974 production had already used a similar interpretation. See note 36.
10. See, for example, William Rossky, "*The Two Gentlemen of Verona* as Burlesque," *English Literary Renaissance* 12 (1982): 210-19.
11. For the "minor oddities" in the play, see Clifford Leech's introduction to his edition, *The Two Gentlemen of Verona,* The Arden Edition of the Works of William Shakespeare (London: Methuen, 1969; University Paperback, 1986), xv-xxi. For a discussion of its technical failures, see Stanley Wells, "The

Failure of *The Two Gentlemen of Verona,*" *Shakespeare Jahrbuch* 99 (1963): 162-66.

12. Discussion of the Victor and Kemble versions will be based on these published texts: (1) [Benjamin Victor, adaptor], *The Two Gentlemen of Verona. A Comedy Written by William Shakespeare. With Alterations and Additions. As it is performed at the Theatre-Royal in Drury Lane* (1763; London: Cornmarket, 1969); and (2) John Philip Kemble, *John Philip Kemble's Promptbook of William Shakespeare's* Two Gentlemen of Verona. *Revised by J. P. Kemble.* In Vol. 9 of *John Philip Kemble's Promptbooks,* ed. Charles H. Shattuck, 11 vols. (Charlottesville: University Press of Virginia, for the Folger Shakespeare Library, 1974). Reynolds's dramatic text has not been preserved, but words of the interpolated songs, along with Bishop's music, are available in a rare volume: Henry R. Bishop, *The Overture, Songs, Duetts, Glees & Chorusses. In Shakespeare's Play of the* The Two Gentlemen of Verona. *as Performed at the Theatre Royal, Covent Garden. The Words Selected entirely from Shakespeare's Plays, Poems & Sonnets. The Music Composed (with exception of Two Melodies) . . . by Henry R. Bishop . . .* (London, [1821]). The songs, together with reviews, give a good idea of the operatic production. For Reynolds's probable use of Kemble, see Schlueter, 31-33.

13. These were a single performance at Covent Garden, 1784, and a first attempt by Kemble, at Drury Lane, 1790. Although stage historians have said that these used the original text, or the original with slight alterations, Schlueter argues persuasively (22, 24, 25) that the alterations were probably more substantial than previously supposed.

14. Vernon: Engraving by J. Roberts, published for Bell's Edition of Shakespeare, 7 March 1776 (copy in the Folger Shakespeare Library; also reproduced by Schlueter, 20). Liston: Jim Davis, *John Liston, Comedian* (London: Society for Theatre Research, 1985), 104; 16-18. Leigh Hunt, in *Examiner,* 24 April 1808: 266-67, accused Liston of turning Thurio into Caper. Farren: *Morning Herald* 30 November 1821; contemporary drawing published by J. Smart, London, 29 January 1822 (copy in the Folger Shakespeare Library).

15. Reviews used in discussing music and spectacle: *Times,* 30 November 1821 ("noble pageant"); *Morning Post,* 30 November; *Morning Herald,* 30 November ("artificial mountain"); *Examiner,* 2 December. Relevance of spectacle: Kemble's version, the basis for Reynolds's, ended Act 4 with Silvia and Eglamour preparing to flee.

16. Discussion of Macready's production is based on his promptbook (Folger Shakespeare Library PROMPT Two Gent. 11) and the following reviews: *Morning Chronicle,* 30 December 1841; *Morning Herald,* 30 December; *Morning Post,* 30 December; *Theatrical Observer,* 30 December; *Times,* 30 December; *Spectator,* 1 January 1842: 9-10; *Argus,* 1 January; *Athenaeum,* 1 January: 19; *Theatrical Journal,* 8 January: [9]-10; *The Age,* 9 January: 5-6.

17. *The Diaries of William Charles Macready,* ed. William Toynbee, 2 vols. (London: Chapman and Hall, 1912) 2: 18-19.

18. *Athenaeum* ("gallant"); *Morning Chronicle* ("more picturesque"); *Spectator* ("manly cordiality"); *Morning Herald* ("overly fervid"); *Times* ("foppishness and surliness").

19. CONFRONTATION: Promptbook, 254 and opp.; *Times* ("fixed group" and applause); *Morning Chronicle* ("a life's repentance"); *Theatrical Observer* (rebuke and forgiveness). NOT RECONCILED: *Times.* SILVIA: *Spectator* (dignified); *Times* and *Theatrical Journal* (cold); *Morning Herald* (lack of byplay).

20. Details of scenery are based on a printed flyer that was handed out at the theater, a copy of which is bound with Macready's promptbook in the Folger Library. Apparently the Reynolds-Bishop production had also used some localized Italian scenes, but with less correctness in both place and detail. See Schlueter, 33.

21. Quoted phrases are, in sequential order, from *Theatrical Observer, Athenaeum, Times,* and *Morning Chronicle.* The only dissenting voice, as far as we know, was from *John Bull,* 10 January 1842, which praised the scenery but said the costumes were "in some particulars almost grotesque, and as a whole apparently hardly in unison." "Historically accurate" costumes did sometimes strike viewers as strange, but the appropriateness and harmony attributed to Macready's decor by other critics were characteristics generally associated with his productions. See Alan Downer, *The Eminent Tragedian* (Cambridge, Massachusetts: Harvard University Press, 1966), 225-26; 252.

22. See, for example, *Morning Chronicle* 22 April 1808 and *Examiner* 24 April 1808: 266-67.

23. Quoted by Robert Speaight, in *William Poel and the Elizabethan Revival* (Cambridge, Massachusetts: Harvard University Press, 1954), 90.

24. See Poel's promptbook for *The Two Gentlemen of Verona,* now in the Theatre Museum, London. Though obviously made for the 1896 production, it was almost certainly used for both. For descriptions of the first production see reviews in the *Times,* 30 November 1896, and *Sunday Times,* 29 November; also George Bernard Shaw, *Our Theatres in the Nineties,* 3 vols. (1932: London: Constable, 1948), 2: 284; and Speaight, 119-20 (note his quotation from a favorable article by the French director Lugné-Poe). Our description of the second production is based

mainly on Speaight, 120-22, and *Times,* 21 April 1910: 12, but see also *Sunday Times,* 24 April 1910: 6.

25. A production using modern dress had been seen much earlier in the provinces, at the People's Theatre, Newcastle, on 17 May 1930. See *Observer* (London), 18 May, and *Shields Daily News,* 19 May 1930.

26. Discussion of Langham's production is based on his promptbook, now in the University of Bristol Theatre Collection, and the following reviews, clippings of which are found in the Shakespeare Library, Birmingham Reference Library: Stephen Williams, *Evening News,* 23 January 1957; *Times* 23 January; J. C. T. [Trewin], *Birmingham Post,* 23 January; Anthony Carthew, *Daily Herald,* 23 January; Alan Dent, *News Chronicle,* 23 January; Patrick Gibbs, *Daily Telegraph,* 24 January; D. H., *Bristol Evening Post,* 24 January; Philip Hope-Wallace, *Manchester Guardian,* 24 January; A. M., *Stage,* 24 January; Patrick Keatley, *Montreal Star,* 26 January; *Western Independent,* 27 January; W. G. McS., *Scotsman,* 28 January; *Daily Worker,* 29 January; *Punch,* 30 January; Derek Grainger, *Financial Times,* 23 January; George Scott, *Truth,* 1 February; P. R., *Kensington News,* 1 February. See also Richard David, "Actors and Scholars: A View of Shakespeare in the Modern Theatre," *Shakespeare Survey* 12 (1959): 76-87.

27. SETTING: *Times, Punch, Western Independent, Daily Telegraph.* COSTUMES: Men—*Montreal Star, Times, Western Independent;* Women—*Financial Times;* Byron and Shelley—*News Chronicle.* Outlaws: *Birmingham Post.*

28. QUOTED PHRASES: *News Chronicle* ("make-believe"); *Scotsman* ("bucks," etc.); *Daily Worker* (the rest). AMOUNT OF BURLESQUE: *Daily Herald* (much); *Birmingham Post* ("shiver[ed] on the knife edge"); *Stage* (resisted the temptation); *Daily Worker* (just the right touch). RESERVATIONS ABOUT THE REGENCY TREATMENT: *Stage*; Richard David, 85.

29. VALENTINE: *Kensington News.* See also *Times* and *Punch.* PROTEUS: *Times, Punch, Financial Times, Kensington News.* JULIA: *Times, Evening News.* (*Kensington News* deplored her boisterousness, but *Financial Times* said she later muted it.) SILVIA: *Stage, Truth* (colorless); *Bristol Evening Post* (lovely); *Kensington News* (nobly-bred). SPEED: *Times*; see also *Kensington News.* LAUNCE: *Financial Times* ("comic precision," "squeaky"), *Stage* ("audience-contact," vacant expression), *Evening News* (Cockney), *Punch* ("funny with pathos"). CRAB: *Bristol Evening Post* ("engagingly miscast"), *Daily Herald* ("shook hands").

30. EXTRA STAGE BUSINESS: *Daily Worker* (reinterprets archaic conceits, passion survives treatment); *Times* (ironic touches); *Financial Times* (action always accompanies speech; archery, artist, dancing); *Stage* (many realistic touches). ANTONIO: promptbook, 14, 16. THURIO: quoted phrase from *Daily Telegraph*; shaving scene, promptbook, 92. DUKE: *Punch.* See also *Kensington News* and *Daily Telegraph.* EGLAMOUR: see descriptive phrases in *Daily Worker* and *Manchester Guardian*; stage directions in promptbook, especially in 1.2 (8) and in 2.4 (30, 32, 34—Eglamour and Thurio retire upstage together when Proteus arrives).

31. ACTING OF CLIMAX: See stage directions in the promptbook, pp. 95-100. One vital stage direction is lacking—Proteus' actually pointing the pistol at himself,—but the implications of the stage directions, together with Patrick Gibbs's reference to Proteus's suicide attempt (*Daily Telegraph* review), leave no doubt about the performance. The quoted phrase is from Gibbs. CRITICS' RESPONSE: *Manchester Guardian*; *Financial Times*; *Bristol Evening Post*; *Daily Telegraph*; *Truth.*

32. HALL: *Education,* 15 April 1960. DIGBY DAY: *Times,* 18 July 1968; *Daily Mail,* 18 July 1968; *Birmingham Post,* 20 July 1968 and 4 June 1969 (Eglamour). Putting Eglamour in armor might have been inspired by the bearded and helmeted Eglamour of Hall's production.

33. This discussion is based on the promptbook, in the Shakespeare Centre Library, Stratford-upon-Avon (see stage directions, opp. 123 for climactic scene), and on the following reviews, many from the *Two Gentlemen* clippings, Birmingham (see note 26): Irving Wardle, *Times,* 24 July 1970 (decor, Antonio, Eglamour, Proteus, some disapproval), but see more positive review in *Times,* 25 December 1970; B. A. Young, *Financial Times,* 24 July (Julia, Silvia); Pearson Phillips, *Daily Mail,* 24 July (Julia, Valentine); *Evening Standard,* 24 July (Julia); J. C. Trewin, *Birmingham Post,* 24 July (decor, deplores Eglamour); Harold Hobson, *Sunday Times,* 26 July (Launce [enthusiastic], Proteus, production shows ancient truths); Wendy Monk, *Stage and Television,* 30 July 1970 (decor, Eglamour, Silvia, loss of innocence, preference for Langham): J. A. P., *Warwick Advertiser,* 31 July (Eglamour, Julia, approves modern treatment); W. T., *Nottingham Evening Post,* 24 July (Eglamour, outlaws, loss of innocence); *Oxford Mail,* 25 July (incongruities, Launce [negative]); Neville Miller, *South Wales Evening Argus,* 25-26 July (Valentine, Silvia, approves "fable on the uncertainties of adolescence"); Eric Shorter, *Daily Telegraph,* 23 December 1970 (serious content "jettisoned") *Glasgow Herald,* 28 December 1970 (theme subtly underlined); Peter Thomson, "A Necessary Theatre: The Royal Shakespeare Season 1970," *Shakespeare Survey* 24 (1971): 120-21 (decor, Antonio, Eglamour, Launce [dubious], psychological analysis, Proteus, Silvia).

34. These settings were, in the order of their mention, for productions at the Champlain Shakespeare

Festival, 1977, at the Pittsburgh Public Theater, 1981, and by the Acting Company on tour, 1990-91. A circus setting and style were combined with Byronic romanticism by the San Diego National Shakespeare Repertory in 1980; the *commedia* style was used at the Odessa Globe Shakespeare Festival (Texas) in 1977, the Utah Shakespeare Festival in 1983 (for some scenes and characters), and the Kentucky Shakespeare Festival in 1988 (in adapted and modernized form); a combination of vaudeville with other styles was used for the heavily burlesqued production of the Acting Company in 1990-91.

35. John Guare and Mel Shapiro, *The Two Gentlemen of Verona. Adapted from the Shakespeare Play . . . Lyrics by John Guare, Music by Galt MacDermot* (New York: Holt, Rinehart and Winston, 1973). For details of both American and British productions, see reviews by Walter Kerr in *New York Times,* 12 December 1971, Foster Hirsch in *Educational Theatre Journal* 24 (1971): 194, and Irving Wardle in *Times,* 27 April 1973.

36. PHILLIPS: Milton Shulman, *Evening Standard,* 23 December 1970. DOUBLE TAKES: Alabama Shakespeare Festival, 1991. MEN GOING OFF TOGETHER: started to do so, Folger Theatre Group, 1977; did so, Great Lakes Shakespeare Festival, 1978. SILVIA'S APPROVAL: At the Oregon Shakespeare Festival, 1974, the offer was made as a ruse, conceived by Valentine and Silvia. In the BBC television production, 1983-84, although the camera focused solely on Valentine and Proteus during the offer, Silvia had silently shown approval of forgiveness before that. For varying interpretations of the BBC scene, see Patty S. Derrick, "*Two Gents*: A Critical Moment," *Shakespeare on Film Newsletter* (December 1991): 1, 4.

37. The promptbook for this production was lost after the provincial tour had ended; if it is found, it will be housed in the Shakespeare Centre Library, Stratford-upon-Avon. Reviews used in discussing the production are: Benedict Nightingale, *Times,* 19 April 1991 and 15 October 1992; John Peter, *Sunday Times,* 21 April; Michael Billington, *Guardian* 19 April; Rex Gibson, *Times Educational Supplement,* 3 May: 25; Paul Nelsen, *Shakespeare Bulletin* 9, no. 4 (Fall 1991): 15-17; Thomas Clayton, "The Climax of *The Two Gentlemen of Verona*: Text and performance at the Swan Theatre, Stratford-upon-Avon, 1991," *Shakespeare Bulletin* 9, no. 4 (Fall 1991): 17-19; Robert Smallwood, "Shakespeare at Stratford-upon-Avon, 1991," *Shakespeare Quarterly* 43 (1992): 350-53. Also passages from the following, as quoted by Clayton from the *London Theatre Record,* 9-22 April 1991: Paul Taylor, *Independent,* 19 April; Claire Armistead, *Financial Times,* 19 April; Carole Waddis, *What's On,* 19 April; Charles Spencer, *Daily Telegraph,* 19 April; Rod Dungate, *Tribune* 3 May.

38. SETTING AND MUSIC: *Times,* 19 Apr. ("Coward dressing gowns," "cunningly chosen,"); Smallwood, 351, and *Sunday Times* (appositeness of period to play); Nelsen, 15 (prelude of music, etc., reference to Masterpiece Theatre); *Times Educational Supplement* (musical interludes); *Guardian* (dislikes interludes, prefers nineteenth-century setting).

39. VALENTINE: *Times,* 1992. Thurio: *Times,* 1992; Smallwood, 351-52. PROTEUS: Clayton ("likeable"); *Financial Times* ("naive"); Smallwood, 351 ("puzzled innocence," "disturbing . . . smile"); *Times,* 1991 and 1992 (intensity, secrecy, passion); *Independent* ("nervous intensity"); *Sunday Times* (slightly unstable). JULIA AND SILVIA: Smallwood, 351; *Guardian* (Julia, "jaunty"); *Sunday Times* (considers both women warm, lively); Nelsen, 16 (emphasizes "deconstruction"). LAUNCE: Smallwood, 352 (detailed description); *Sunday Times* ("hangdog dignity"). SPEED: Smallwood, 352. DUKE: *Sunday Times*; *Times,* 1991; Nelsen, 17. Note that the second *Times* review was for the revival at the Barbican; descriptions of Valentine, Proteus, and Thurio are similar to those in the original review but fuller, possibly reflecting further development in the acting.

40. A similar parallel had been used the previous year in the Acting Company's touring production (U.S.A.), but, in our opinion, the unrestrained burlesque of the production as a whole canceled out (at least for the average spectator) any serious effect beyond a momentary shock. See, however, Jean Peterson's interesting review in *Shakespeare Bulletin,* 9, no. 1 (Winter, 1991): 33-34.

41. CLIMAX AND ENDING: Nelsen, 16 ("echoing . . . act one," "outrageous"—he still considered the women victims); *What's On* ("great poignancy"); *Guardian* ("conflicting emotions"); *Independent* ("flesh[ing] out"); Clayton, 18 (description of Silvia's actions, abstruse interpretation of Valentine's offer, "crux" not evident); Smallwood, 352-53 (description of scene, Lynch's smile, simple interpretation of offer—the one we accept); *Tribune* ("near-impossible," "riveting," "plausible"); *Sunday Times* (previous skeptic persuaded by actors); *Daily Telegraph* ("risible"); HIT OF THE SEASON: The popularity continued next season at the Barbican in London. By the end of the tour, however, the production had evidently lost its sparkle. See Jeremy Kingston, *Times,* 16 December 1993.

42. *Manchester Evening News,* 20 April 1938; *Times,* 3 April 1958; Peter Lewis, *Daily Mail,* 18 July 1968.

43. PHILLIPS: Harold Hobson, *Sunday Times,* 26 July 1970 (approves "dark angel"); *Oxford Mail,* 25 July 1970 (pretentious). THACKER: Smallwood, *Shakespeare Quarterly* 43 (1992): 352.

44. HUNT: *Examiner,* 24 April 1808: 266. ABOUT MACREADY: *Argus,* 1 January 1842: 10; *Theatrical Journal,* 8 January 1842: [9].

FURTHER READING

Criticism

Beadle, Richard. "Crab's Pedigree." In *English Comedy,* edited by Michael Cordner, Peter Holland, and John Kerrigan, pp. 12-35. Cambridge: Cambridge University Press, 1994.

Examines the role of the dog, Crab, in *The Two Gentlemen of Verona,* and discusses the influence of the "clown-and-dog" tradition on Shakespeare's use of Crab in the play.

Berryman, John. "*The Two Gentlemen of Verona.*" In *Berryman's Shakespeare,* edited by John Haffenden, pp. 314-17. New York: Farrar, Straus, and Giroux, 1999.

A brief overview of *The Two Gentlemen of Verona,* including comments on the sources and dating of the play.

Brooks, Harold F. "Two Clowns in a Comedy (to say nothing of the Dog): Speed and Launce (and Crab) in *The Two Gentlemen of Verona.*" *Essays and Studies,* n.s. 16 (1963): 91-100.

Suggests that the comic characters in the play are paralleled in the major themes.

Jaarsma, Richard J. "The 'Lear Complex' in *The Two Gentlemen of Verona.*" *Literature and Psychology* 22, No. 4 (1972): 199-202.

Explores the similarities between the way father-daughter relationships are portrayed in *King Lear* and *The Two Gentlemen of Verona.*

Rossky, William. "*The Two Gentlemen of Verona* as Burlesque." *English Literary Renaissance* 12, No. 2 (Spring 1982): 210-19.

Suggests that the play is actually a satirical study of love and romance, especially in regards to its controversial ending.

Schleiner, Louise. "Voice, Ideology, and Gendered Subjects: The Case of *As You Like It* and *Two Gentlemen.*" *Shakespeare Quarterly* 50, No. 3 (Fall 1999): 285-309.

A comparative analysis of the ideology and subjects addressed in *As You Like It* and *The Two Gentlemen of Verona.*

Slights, Camille Wells. "Common Courtesy in *The Two Gentlemen of Verona.*" In *Shakespeare's Comic Commonwealths,* pp. 57-73. Toronto: University of Toronto Press, 1993.

Examines the play as a study of the manners of courtly society, and studies the way in which that society valued both love and friendship.

Weimann, Robert. "Laughing with the Audience: *The Two Gentlemen of Verona* and the Popular Tradition of Comedy." *Shakespeare Survey* 22 (1969): 35-42.

Maintains that audience participation serves a central dramatic function, structuring and controlling the play's comic vision.

Wells, Stanley. "The Failure of *The Two Gentlemen of Verona.*" *Shakespeare Jahrbuch* 99 (1963): 161-73.

Interpretation of *The Two Gentlemen of Verona* informed by H. B. Charlton's reading of the play, which contends that Shakespeare failed to make successful use of the conventions of romantic love in this work.

Cumulative Character Index

The Cumulative Character Index identifies the principal characters of discussion in the criticism of each play and non-dramatic poem. The characters are arranged alphabetically. Page references indicate the beginning page number of each essay containing substantial commentary on that character.

Aaron
Titus Andronicus **4:** 632, 637, 650, 651, 653, 668, 672, 675; **27:** 255; **28:** 249, 330; **43:** 176; **53:** 86, 92

Achilles and Patroclus
Troilus and Cressida **60:** 105

Adonis
Venus and Adonis **10:** 411, 420, 424, 427, 429, 434, 439, 442, 451, 454, 459, 466, 473, 489; **25:** 305, 328; **28:** 355; **33:** 309, 321, 330, 347, 352, 357, 363, 370, 377; **51:** 345, 377

Adriana
The Comedy of Errors **16:** 3; **34:** 211, 220, 238; **54:** 189

Albany
King Lear **32:** 308

Alcibiades
Timon of Athens **25:** 198; **27:** 191

Angelo
Measure for Measure
anxiety **16:** 114
authoritarian portrayal of **23:** 307; **49:** 274
characterization **2:** 388, 390, 397, 402, 418, 427, 432, 434, 463, 484, 495, 503, 511; **13:** 84; **23:** 297; **32:** 81; **33:** 77; **49:** 274, 293, 379
hypocrisy **2:** 396, 399, 402, 406, 414, 421; **23:** 345, 358, 362
repentance or pardon **2:** 388, 390, 397, 402, 434, 463, 511, 524; **60:** 12

Anne (Anne Boleyn)
Henry VIII See **Boleyn**

Anne (Anne Page)
The Merry Wives of Windsor See **Page**

Anne (Lady Anne)
Richard III **52:** 223, 227, 239, 249, 280

Antigonus
The Winter's Tale
characterization **7:** 394, 451, 464
death (Act III, scene iii) **7:** 377, 414, 464, 483; **15:** 518, 532; **19:** 366

Antonio
The Merchant of Venice
excessive or destructive love **4:** 279, 284, 336, 344; **12:** 54; **37:** 86
love for Bassanio **40:** 156
melancholy **4:** 221, 238, 279, 284, 300, 321, 328; **22:** 69; **25:** 22
pitiless **4:** 254
as pivotal figure **12:** 25, 129;
versus Shylock **53:** 187
Twelfth Night **22:** 69; **60:** 115

Antonio and Sebastian
The Tempest **8:** 295, 299, 304, 328, 370, 396, 429, 454; **13:** 440; **29:** 278, 297, 343, 362, 368, 377; **45:** 200; **60:** 129; **61:** 338

Antony
Antony and Cleopatra
characterization **6:** 22, 23, 24, 31, 38, 41, 172, 181, 211; **16:** 342; **19:** 270; **22:** 217; **27:** 117; **47:** 77, 124, 142; **58:** 2, 41, 118, 134
Caesar, relationship with **48:** 206
Cleopatra, relationship with **6:** 25, 27, 37, 39, 48, 52, 53, 62, 67, 71, 76, 85, 100, 125, 131, 133, 136, 142, 151, 161, 163, 165, 180, 192; **27:** 82; **47:** 107, 124, 165, 174
death scene **25:** 245; **47:** 142; **58:** 41; **60:** 46
dotage **6:** 22, 23, 38, 41, 48, 52, 62, 107, 136, 146, 175; **17:** 28
nobility **6:** 22, 24, 33, 48, 94, 103, 136, 142, 159, 172, 202; **25:** 245
political conduct **6:** 33, 38, 53, 107, 111, 146, 181
public vs. private personae **6:** 165; **47:** 107; **58:** 41
self-knowledge **6:** 120, 131, 175, 181, 192; **47:** 77
as superhuman figure **6:** 37, 51, 71, 92, 94, 178, 192; **27:** 110; **47:** 71
as tragic hero **6:** 38, 39, 52, 53, 60, 104, 120, 151, 155, 165, 178, 192, 202, 211; **22:** 217; **27:** 90
Julius Caesar
characterization **7:** 160, 179, 189, 221, 233, 284, 320, 333; **17:** 269, 271, 272, 284, 298, 306, 313, 315, 358, 398; **25:** 272; **30:** 316; **63:** 310
funeral oration **7:** 148, 154, 159, 204, 210, 221, 238, 259, 350; **25:** 280; **30:** 316, 333, 362; **63:** 219, 225, 278

Apemantus
Timon of Athens **1:** 453, 467, 483; **20:** 476, 493; **25:** 198; **27:** 166, 223, 235

Arcite
The Two Noble Kinsmen See **Palamon and Arcite**

Ariel
The Tempest **8:** 289, 293, 294, 295, 297, 304, 307, 315, 320, 326, 328, 336, 340, 345,

356, 364, 420, 458; **22:** 302; **29:** 278, 297, 362, 368, 377

Armado
Love's Labour's Lost **23:** 207

Arthur
King John **9:** 215, 216, 218, 219, 229, 240, 267, 275; **22:** 120; **25:** 98; **41:** 251, 277; **56:** 345, 357

Arviragus
Cymbeline See **Guiderius and Arviragus**

Audrey
As You Like It **46:** 122

Aufidius
Coriolanus **9:** 9, 12, 17, 19, 53, 121, 148, 153, 157, 169, 180, 193; **19:** 287; **25:** 263, 296; **30:** 58, 67, 89, 96, 133; **50:** 99

Autolycus
The Winter's Tale **7:** 375, 380, 382, 387, 389, 395, 396, 414; **15:** 524; **22:** 302; **37:** 31; **45:** 333; **46:** 14, 33; **50:** 45

Banquo
Macbeth **3:** 183, 199, 208, 213, 278, 289; **20:** 279, 283, 406, 413; **25:** 235; **28:** 339

Baptista
The Taming of the Shrew **9:** 325, 344, 345, 375, 386, 393, 413; **55:** 334

Barnardine
Measure for Measure **13:** 112

Bassanio
The Merchant of Venice **25:** 257; **37:** 86; **40:** 156

the Bastard
King John See **Faulconbridge (Philip) the Bastard**

Beatrice and Benedick
Much Ado about Nothing
Beatrice's femininity **8:** 14, 16, 17, 24, 29, 38, 41, 91; **31:** 222, 245; **55:** 221
Beatrice's request to "kill Claudio" (Act IV, scene i) **8:** 14, 17, 33, 41, 55, 63, 75, 79, 91, 108, 115; **18:** 119, 120, 136, 161, 245, 257; **55:** 268
Benedick's challenge of Claudio (Act V, scene i) **8:** 48, 63, 79, 91; **31:** 231
Claudio and Hero, compared with **8:** 19, 28, 29, 75, 82, 115; **31:** 171, 216; **55:** 189
marriage and the opposite sex, attitudes toward **8:** 9, 13, 14, 16, 19, 29, 36, 48, 63, 77, 91, 95, 115, 121; **16:** 45; **31:** 216; **48:** 14
mutual attraction **8:** 13, 14, 19, 24, 29, 33, 41, 75; **48:** 14
nobility **8:** 13, 19, 24, 29, 36, 39, 41, 47, 82, 91, 108
popularity **8:** 13, 38, 41, 53, 79
transformed by love **8:** 19, 29, 36, 48, 75, 91, 95, 115; **31:** 209, 216; **55:** 236
unconventionality **8:** 48, 91, 95, 108, 115, 121; **55:** 221, 249, 268
vulgarity **8:** 11, 12, 33, 38, 41, 47
wit and charm **8:** 9, 12, 13, 14, 19, 24, 27, 28, 29, 33, 36, 38, 41, 47, 55, 69, 95, 108, 115; **31:** 241; **55:** 199

Belarius
Cymbeline **4:** 48, 89, 141

Benedick
Much Ado about Nothing See **Beatrice and Benedick**

Berowne
Love's Labour's Lost **2:** 308, 324, 327; **22:** 12; **23:** 184, 187; **38:** 194; **47:** 35

Bertram
All's Well That Ends Well
characterization **7:** 15, 27, 29, 32, 39, 41, 43, 98, 113; **26:** 48; **26:** 117; **48:** 65; **55:** 90; **63:** 60, 99
conduct **7:** 9, 10, 12, 16, 19, 21, 51, 62, 104; **50:** 59; **55:** 143, 154; **63:** 99
identity **63:** 89
masculinity **63:** 60
physical desire **22:** 78
transformation or redemption **7:** 10, 19, 21, 26, 29, 32, 54, 62, 81, 90, 93, 98, 109, 113, 116, 126; **13:** 84

Bianca
The Taming of the Shrew **9:** 325, 342, 344, 345, 360, 362, 370, 375
Bianca-Lucentio subplot **9:** 365, 370, 375, 390, 393, 401, 407, 413, 430; **16:** 13; **31:** 339

the boar
Venus and Adonis **10:** 416, 451, 454, 466, 473; **33:** 339, 347, 370

Boleyn (Anne Boleyn)
Henry VIII **2:** 21, 24, 31; **41:** 180; **61:** 119, 129

Bolingbroke
Richard II See **Henry (King Henry IV, previously known as Bolingbroke)**

Borachio and Conrade
Much Ado about Nothing **8:** 24, 69, 82, 88, 111, 115

Bottom
A Midsummer Night's Dream
awakening speech (Act IV, scene i) **3:** 406, 412, 450, 457, 486, 516; **16:** 34; **58:** 181
folly of **46:** 1, 14, 29, 60
his dream **60:** 142
imagination **3:** 376, 393, 406, 432, 486; **29:** 175, 190; **45:** 147
self-possession **3:** 365, 376, 395, 402, 406, 480; **45:** 158
Titania, relationship with **3:** 377, 406, 441, 445, 450, 457, 491, 497; **16:** 34; **19:** 21; **22:** 93; **29:** 216; **45:** 160; **58:** 203, 215
transformation **3:** 365, 377, 432; **13:** 27; **22:** 93; **29:** 216; **45:** 147, 160

Brabantio
Othello **25:** 189

Brutus
Coriolanus See **the tribunes**
Julius Caesar **50:** 194, 258
arrogance **7:** 160, 169, 204, 207, 264, 277, 292, 350; **25:** 280; **30:** 351
as chief protagonist or tragic hero **7:** 152, 159, 189, 191, 200, 204, 242, 250, 253, 264, 268, 279, 284, 298, 333; **17:** 272, 372, 387; **63:** 260, 295, 310
citizenship **25:** 272
funeral oration **7:** 154, 155, 204, 210, 350; **63:** 219, 225, 278
motives **7:** 150, 156, 161, 179, 191, 200, 221, 227, 233, 245, 292, 303, 310, 320, 333, 350; **25:** 272; **30:** 321, 358; **63:** 295, 301
nobility or idealism **7:** 150, 152, 156, 159, 161, 179, 189, 191, 200, 221, 242, 250, 253, 259, 264, 277, 303, 320; **17:** 269, 271, 273, 279, 280, 284, 306, 308, 321, 323, 324, 345, 358; **25:** 272, 280; **30:** 351, 362; **63:** 219, 301
political ineptitude or lack of judgment **7:** 169, 188, 200, 205, 221, 245, 252, 264, 277, 282, 310, 316, 331, 333, 343; **17:** 323, 358, 375, 380; **50:** 13; **63:** 322
self-knowledge or self-deception **7:** 191, 200, 221, 242, 259, 264, 268, 279, 310, 333, 336, 350; **25:** 272; **30:** 316; **60:** 46; **63:** 252, 295, 322
soliloquy (Act II, scene i) **7:** 156, 160, 161, 191, 221, 245, 250, 253, 264, 268, 279, 282, 292, 303, 343, 350; **25:** 280; **30:** 333
The Rape of Lucrece **10:** 96, 106, 109, 116, 121, 125, 128, 135

Buckingham
Henry VIII **22:** 182; **24:** 129, 140; **37:** 109

Bushy, Bagot, and Greene
Richard II **58:** 259

Cade (Jack Cade)
Henry VI, Parts 1, 2, and 3 **3:** 35, 67, 92, 97, 109; **16:** 183; **22:** 156; **25:** 102; **28:** 112; **37:** 97; **39:** 160, 196, 205

Caesar
Antony and Cleopatra
Antony, relationship with as leader **48:** 206
Julius Caesar **50:** 189, 230, 234
ambiguous nature **7:** 191, 233, 242, 250, 272, 298, 316, 320; **63:** 219, 231
ambitious nature **50:** 234
arrogance **7:** 160, 207, 218, 253, 272, 279, 298; **25:** 280; **63:** 219, 231, 310
idolatry **22:** 137
leadership qualities **7:** 161, 179, 189, 191, 200, 207, 233, 245, 253, 257, 264,

272, 279, 284, 298, 310, 333; **17:** 317, 358; **22:** 280; **30:** 316, 326; **50:** 234; **63:** 278
as tragic hero **7:** 152, 200, 221, 279; **17:** 321, 377, 384
weakness **7:** 161, 167, 169, 179, 187, 188, 191, 207, 218, 221, 233, 250, 253, 298; **17:** 358; **25:** 280; **63:** 219, 231

Caius, Doctor
The Merry Wives of Windsor **47:** 354

Caliban
The Tempest **8:** 286, 287, 289, 292, 294, 295, 297, 302, 304, 307, 309, 315, 326, 328, 336, 353, 364, 370, 380, 390, 396, 401, 414, 420, 423, 429, 435, 454; **13:** 424, 440; **15:** 189, 312, 322, 374, 379; **22:** 302; **25:** 382; **28:** 249; **29:** 278, 292, 297, 343, 368, 377, 396; **32:** 367; **45:** 211, 219, 226, 259; **53:** 45, 64; **61:** 307, 356, 362

Calphurnia
Julius Caesar
Calphurnia's dream **45:** 10; **63:** 315

Cambridge
Henry V See **traitors**

Canterbury and the churchmen
Henry V **5:** 193, 203, 205, 213, 219, 225, 252, 260; **22:** 137; **30:** 215, 262

Cardinal Wolsey
Henry VIII See **Wolsey**

Casca
Julius Caesar
as Cynic **50:** 249
as proto-Christian **50:** 249

Cassio
Othello **25:** 189

Cassius
Julius Caesar **7:** 156, 159, 160, 161, 169, 179, 189, 221, 233, 303, 310, 320, 333, 343; **17:** 272, 282, 284, 344, 345, 358; **25:** 272, 280; **30:** 351; **37:** 203; **60:** 46; **63:** 315

Celia
As You Like It **46:** 94

the changeling
A Midsummer's Night Dream **58:** 162, 167

Chorus
Henry V
role of **5:** 186, 192, 226, 228, 230, 252, 264, 269, 281, 293; **14:** 301, 319, 336; **19:** 133; **25:** 116, 131; **30:** 163, 202, 220

the churchmen
Henry V See **Canterbury and the churchmen**

Cinna
Julius Caesar
as poet **48:** 240

Claudio
Much Ado about Nothing
boorish behavior **8:** 9, 24, 33, 36, 39, 44, 48, 63, 79, 82, 95, 100, 111, 115; **31:** 209
credulity **8:** 9, 17, 19, 24, 29, 36, 41, 47, 58, 63, 75, 77, 82, 95, 100, 104, 111, 115, 121; **31:** 241; **47:** 25
mercenary traits **8:** 24, 44, 58, 82, 91, 95
noble qualities **8:** 17, 19, 29, 41, 44, 58, 75; **55:** 232
reconciliation with Hero **8:** 33, 36, 39, 44, 47, 82, 95, 100, 111, 115, 121; **55:** 236
repentance **8:** 33, 63, 82, 95, 100, 111, 115, 121; **31:** 245
sexual insecurities **8:** 75, 100, 111, 115, 121
Measure for Measure **60:** 12

Claudius
Hamlet **13:** 502; **16 246; 21:** 259, 347, 361, 371; **28:** 232, 290; **35:** 104, 182; **44:** 119, 241; **59:** 62

Cleopatra
Antony and Cleopatra
Antony, relationship with **6:** 25, 27, 37, 39, 48, 52, 53, 62, 67, 71, 76, 85, 100, 125, 131, 133, 136, 142, 151, 161, 163, 165, 180, 192; **25:** 257; **27:** 82; **47:** 107, 124, 165, 174
characterization **47:** 77, 96, 113, 124; **58:** 24, 33, 59, 118, 134
contradictory or inconsistent nature **6:** 23, 24, 27, 67, 76, 100, 104, 115, 136, 151, 159, 202; **17:** 94, 113; **27:** 135
costume **17:** 94
creativity **6:** 197; **47:** 96, 113
death **6:** 23, 25, 27, 41, 43, 52, 60, 64, 76, 94, 100, 103, 120, 131, 133, 136, 140, 146, 161, 165, 180, 181, 192, 197, 208; **13:** 383; **17:** 48, 94; **25:** 245; **27:** 135; **47:** 71; **60:** 46
personal attraction of **6:** 24, 38, 40, 43, 48, 53, 76, 104, 115, 155; **17:** 113
self-knowledge **47:** 77, 96
staging issues **17:** 94, 113
as subverter of social order **6:** 146, 165; **47:** 113
suicide **58:** 33
as superhuman figure **6:** 37, 51, 71, 92, 94, 178, 192; **27:** 110; **47:** 71, 174, 192; **58:** 24
as tragic heroine **6:** 53, 120, 151, 192, 208; **27:** 144
as voluptuary or courtesan **6:** 21, 22, 25, 41, 43, 52, 53, 62, 64, 67, 76, 146, 161; **47:** 107, 174; **58:** 24

Cloten
Cymbeline **4:** 20, 116, 127, 155; **22:** 302, 365; **25:** 245; **36:** 99, 125, 142, 155; **47:** 228

Collatine
The Rape of Lucrece **10:** 98, 131; **43:** 102; **48:** 291 **59:** 180

Cominius
Coriolanus **25:** 245

Conrade
Much Ado about Nothing See **Borachio and Conrade**

Constance
King John **9:** 208, 210, 211, 215, 219, 220, 224, 229, 240, 251, 254; **16:** 161; **24:** 177, 184, 196

Cordelia
King Lear
attack on Britain **25:** 202
characterization **2:** 110, 116, 125, 170; **16:** 311; **25:** 218; **28:** 223, 325; **31:** 117, 149, 155, 162; **46:** 218, 225, 231, 242; **61:** 220, 230
as Christ figure **2:** 116, 170, 179, 188, 222, 286
death of **60:** 2
gender identity **48:** 222
rebelliousness **13:** 352; **25:** 202; **61:** 194
on stage **11:** 158
transcendent power **2:** 137, 207, 218, 265, 269, 273
women, the Christian ideal of **48:** 222

Corin
As You Like It See **pastoral characters**

Coriolanus
Coriolanus
anger or passion **9:** 19, 26, 45, 80, 92, 157, 164, 177, 189; **30:** 79, 96
as complementary figure to Aufidius **19:** 287
death scene (Act V, scene vi) **9:** 12, 80, 100, 117, 125, 144, 164, 198; **25:** 245, 263; **50:** 110; **60:** 46
as epic hero **9:** 130, 164, 177; **25:** 245; **50:** 119
immaturity **9:** 62, 80, 84, 110, 117, 142; **30:** 140
inhuman attributes **9:** 65, 73, 139, 157, 164, 169, 189, 198; **25:** 263
internal struggle **9:** 31, 43, 45, 53, 72, 117, 121, 130; **44:** 93
introspection or self-knowledge, lack of **9:** 53, 80, 84, 112, 117, 130; **25:** 296; **30:** 133
isolation or autonomy **9:** 53, 65, 142, 144, 153, 157, 164, 180, 183, 189, 198; **30:** 58, 89, 111;50: 128
manipulation by others **9:** 33, 45, 62, 80; **25:** 296
as military leader **48:** 230
modesty **9:** 8, 12, 19, 26, 53, 78, 92, 117, 121, 144, 183; **25:** 296; **30:** 79, 96, 129, 133, 149
narcissism **30:** 111
noble or aristocratic attributes **9:** 15, 18, 19, 26, 31, 33, 52, 53, 62, 65, 84, 92, 100, 121, 148, 157, 169; **25:** 263; **30:** 67, 74, 96; **50:** 13
pride or arrogance **9:** 8, 11, 12, 19, 26, 31, 33, 43, 45, 65, 78, 92, 121, 148, 153, 177; **30:** 58, 67, 74, 89, 96, 129
punishment of **48:** 230
reconciliation with society **9:** 33, 43, 45, 65, 139, 169; **25:** 296

as socially destructive force **9:** 62, 65, 73, 78, 110, 142, 144, 153; **25:** 296
soliloquy (Act IV, scene iv) **9:** 84, 112, 117, 130
as tragic figure **9:** 8, 12, 13, 18, 25, 45, 52, 53, 72, 80, 92, 106, 112, 117, 130, 148, 164, 169, 177; **25:** 296; **30:** 67, 74, 79, 96, 111, 129; **37:** 283; **50:** 99
traitorous actions **9:** 9, 12, 19, 45, 84, 92, 148; **25:** 296; **30:** 133
as unsympathetic character **9:** 12, 13, 62, 78, 80, 84, 112, 130, 157

the courser and the jennet
Venus and Adonis **10:** 418, 439, 466; **33:** 309, 339, 347, 352

Cranmer
Henry VIII
prophesy of **2:** 25, 31, 46, 56, 64, 68, 72; **24:** 146; **32:** 148; **41:** 120, 190; **56:** 196, 230, 248, 273

Cressida
Troilus and Cressida
as ambiguous figure **43:** 305
inconsistency **3:** 538; **13:** 53; **16:** 70; **22:** 339; **27:** 362
individual will vs. social values **3:** 549, 561, 571, 590, 604, 617, 626; **13:** 53; **27:** 396; **59:** 234, 272
infidelity **3:** 536, 537, 544, 554, 555; **18:** 277, 284, 286; **22:** 58, 339; **27:** 400; **43:** 298
lack of punishment **3:** 536, 537
as mother figure **22:** 339
objectification of **43:** 329; **59:** 323
as sympathetic figure **3:** 557, 560, 604, 609; **18:** 284, 423; **22:** 58; **27:** 396, 400; **43:** 305; **59:** 234, 245
as a Trojan **59:** 257

Cymbeline
Cymbeline
characterization **61:** 54

Dark Lady
Sonnets **10:** 161, 167, 176, 216, 217, 218, 226, 240, 302, 342, 377, 394; **25:** 374; **37:** 374; **40:** 273; **48:** 346; **51:** 284, 288, 292, 321; **62:** 121

the Dauphin
Henry V See **French aristocrats and the Dauphin**

Desdemona
Othello
as Christ figure **4:** 506, 525, 573; **35:** 360
culpability **4:** 408, 415, 422, 427; **13:** 313; **19:** 253, 276; **35:** 265, 352, 380
innocence **35:** 360; **43:** 32; **47:** 25; **53:** 310, 333
as mother figure **22:** 339; **35:** 282; **53:** 324
passivity **4:** 402, 406, 421, 440, 457, 470, 582, 587; **25:** 189; **35:** 380
spiritual nature of her love **4:** 462, 530, 559
staging issues **11:** 350, 354, 359; **13:** 327; **32:** 201

Diana
Pericles
as symbol of nature **22:** 315; **36:** 233; **51:** 71

Dogberry and the Watch
Much Ado about Nothing **8:** 9, 12, 13, 17, 24, 28, 29, 33, 39, 48, 55, 69, 79, 82, 88, 95, 104, 108, 115; **18:** 138, 152, 205, 208, 210, 213, 231; **22:** 85; **31:** 171, 229; **46:** 60; **55:** 189, 241

Don John
Much Ado about Nothing See **John (Don John)**

Don Pedro
Much Ado about Nothing See **Pedro (Don Pedro)**

Dromio Brothers
Comedy of Errors **42:** 80; **54:** 136, 152

Duke
Measure for Measure
as authoritarian figure **23:** 314, 317, 347; **33:** 85; **49:** 274, 300, 358
characterization **2:** 388, 395, 402, 406, 411, 421, 429, 456, 466, 470, 498, 511; **13:** 84, 94, 104; **23:** 363, 416; **32:** 81; **42:** 1; **44:** 89; **49:** 274, 293, 300, 358; **60:** 12
as dramatic failure **2:** 420, 429, 441, 479, 495, 505, 514, 522
godlike portrayal of **23:** 320
noble portrayal of **23:** 301
speech on death (Act III, scene i) **2:** 390, 391, 395
Othello **25:** 189

Duncan
Macbeth **57:** 194, 236

Edgar
King Lear **28:** 223; **32:** 212; **32:** 308; **37:** 295; **47:** 9; **50:** 24, 45
Edgar-Edmund duel **22:** 365

Edmund
King Lear **25:** 218; **28:** 223
Edmund's forged letter **16:** 372

Edmund of Langley, Duke of York
Richard II See **York**

Elbow
Measure for Measure **22:** 85; **25:** 12

Elbow (Mistress Elbow)
Measure for Measure **33:** 90

elder characters
All's Well That Ends Well **7:** 9, 37, 39, 43, 45, 54, 62, 104

Elizabeth I
Love's Labour's Lost **38:** 239

Emilia
Othello **4:** 386, 391, 392, 415, 587; **35:** 352, 380; **43:** 32
The Two Noble Kinsmen **9:** 460, 470, 471, 479, 481; **19:** 394; **41:** 372, 385; **42:** 361; **58:** 322, 338, 345, 356, 361

Enobarbus
Antony and Cleopatra **6:** 22, 23, 27, 43, 94, 120, 142; **16:** 342; **17:** 36; **22:** 217; **27:** 135

Evans, Sir Hugh
The Merry Wives of Windsor **47:** 354

fairies
A Midsummer Night's Dream **3:** 361, 362, 372, 377, 395, 400, 423, 450, 459, 486; **12:** 287, 291, 294, 295; **19:** 21; **29:** 183, 190; **45:** 147

Falstaff
Henry IV, Parts 1 and 2
characterization **1:** 287, 298, 312, 333; **25:** 245; **28:** 203; **39:** 72, 134, 137, 143; **48:** 117, 151; **57:** 120, 156
as comic figure **1:** 287, 311, 327, 344, 351, 354, 357, 410, 434; **39:** 89; **46:** 1, 48, 52; **57:** 120
as comic versus tragic figure **49:** 178
as coward or rogue **1:** 285, 290, 296, 298, 306, 307, 313, 317, 323, 336, 337, 338, 342, 354, 366, 374, 391, 396, 401, 433; **14:** 7, 111, 125, 130, 133; **32:** 166
as deceiver deceived **47:** 308
diminishing powers of **47:** 363
dual personality **1:** 397, 401, 406, 434; **49:** 162
female attributes **13:** 183; **44:** 44; **47:** 325; **60:** 154
Iago, compared with **1:** 341, 351
as Jack-a-Lent **47:** 363
Marxist interpretation **1:** 358, 361
moral reformation **60:** 26
as outlaw **49:** 133
as parody of the historical plot **1:** 314, 354, 359; **39:** 143
as positive character **1:** 286, 287, 290, 296, 298, 311, 312, 321, 325, 333, 344, 355, 357, 389, 401, 408, 434
rejection by Hal **1:** 286, 287, 290, 312, 314, 317, 324, 333, 338, 344, 357, 366, 372, 374, 379, 380, 389, 414; **13:** 183; **25:** 109; **39:** 72, 89; **48:** 95; **57:** 147
as satire of feudal society **1:** 314, 328, 361; **32:** 103
as scapegoat **1:** 389, 414; **47:** 358, 363, 375; **57:** 156
stage interpretations **14:** 4, 6, 7, 9, 15, 116, 130, 146; **47:** 1
as subversive figure **16:** 183; **25:** 109
Henry V **5:** 185, 186, 187, 189, 192, 195, 198, 210, 226, 257, 269, 271, 276, 293, 299; **28:** 146; **46:** 48; **60:** 26
The Merry Wives of Windsor
characterization in 1 and 2 Henry IV, compared with **5:** 333, 335, 336, 337, 339, 346, 347, 348, 350, 373, 400 **18:** 5, 7, 75, 86; **22:** 93

diminishing powers **5:** 337, 339, 343, 347, 350, 351, 392
as Herne the Hunter **38:** 256, 286; **47:** 358
incapability of love **5:** 335, 336, 339, 346, 348; **22:** 93
personification of comic principle or as Vice figure **1:** 342, 361, 366, 374; **5:** 332, 338, 369, 400; **38:** 273
recognition and repentance of follies **5:** 338, 341, 343, 348, 369, 374, 376, 397
sensuality **5:** 339, 343, 353, 369, 392
shrewdness **5:** 332, 336, 346, 355
threat to community **5:** 343, 369, 379, 392, 395, 400; **38:** 297
as unifying force **47:** 358
vanity **5:** 332, 339
victimization **5:** 336, 338, 341, 347, 348, 353, 355, 360, 369, 373, 374, 376, 392, 397, 400; **59:** 144
as villain **47:** 358

Faulconbridge, (Philip) the Bastard
King John **41:** 205, 228, 251, 260, 277; **48:** 132; **56:** 306
as chorus or commentator **9:** 212, 218, 229, 248, 251, 260, 271, 284, 297, 300; **22:** 120
as comic figure **9:** 219, 271, 297; **56:** 365
development **9:** 216, 224, 229, 248, 263, 271, 275, 280, 297; **13:** 158, 163; **56:** 335
as embodiment of England **9:** 222, 224, 240, 244, 248, 271
heroic qualities **9:** 208, 245, 248, 254, 263, 271, 275; **25:** 98; **56:** 348
political conduct **9:** 224, 240, 250, 260, 280, 297; **13:** 147, 158; **22:** 120; **56:** 314

Fenton
The Merry Wives of Windsor
Anne Page-Fenton plot **5:** 334, 336, 343, 353, 376, 390, 395, 402; **22:** 93

Ferdinand
The Tempest **8:** 328, 336, 359, 454; **19:** 357; **22:** 302; **29:** 362, 339, 377

Feste
Twelfth Night
characterization **1:** 558, 655, 658; **26:** 233, 364; **46:** 1, 14, 18, 33, 52, 60, 303, 310
role in play **1:** 546, 551, 553, 566, 570, 571, 579, 635, 658; **46:** 297, 303, 310
song **1:** 543, 548, 561, 563, 566, 570, 572, 603, 620, 642; **46:** 297
gender issues **19:** 78; **34:** 344; **37:** 59

Flavius and Murellus
Julius Caesar **50:** 64

Fluellen
Henry V **30:** 278; **37:** 105

Fool
King Lear **2:** 108, 112, 125, 156, 162, 245, 278, 284; **11:** 17, 158, 169; **22:** 227; **25:** 202; **28:** 223; **46:** 1, 14, 18, 24, 33, 52, 191, 205, 210, 218, 225; **61:** 176

Ford, Francis
The Merry Wives of Windsor **5:** 332, 334, 343, 355, 363, 374, 379, 390; **38:** 273; **47:** 321

Ford, Mistress Alice
The Merry Wives of Windsor **47:** 321

Fortinbras
Hamlet **21:** 136, 347; **28:** 290

French aristocrats and the Dauphin
Henry V **5:** 188, 191, 199, 205, 213, 281; **22:** 137; **28:** 121

Friar
Much Ado about Nothing **8:** 24, 29, 41, 55, 63, 79, 111; **55:** 249

Friar John
Romeo and Juliet See **John (Friar John)**

Friar Lawrence
Romeo and Juliet See **Lawrence (Friar Lawrence)**

the Friend
Sonnets **10:** 279, 302, 309, 379, 385, 391, 394; **51:** 284, 292, 300, 304, 316, 321; **62:** 121

Ganymede
The Winter's Tale **48:** 309

Gardiner (Stephen Gardiner)
Henry VIII **24:** 129

Gaunt
Richard II **6:** 255, 287, 374, 388, 402, 414; **24:** 274, 322, 325, 414, 423; **37:** 222; **52:** 174, 183

Gertrude
Hamlet **21:** 259, 347, 392; **28:** 311; **32:** 238; **35:** 182, 204, 229; **43:** 12; **44:** 119, 160, 189, 195, 237, 247; **59:** 39, 62, 74
death monologue **48:** 255

Ghost
Hamlet **1:** 75, 76, 84, 85, 128, 134, 138, 154, 171, 218, 231, 254; **16:** 246; **21:** 17, 44, 112, 151, 334, 371, 377, 392; **25:** 288; **35:** 152, 157, 174, 237; **44:** 119; **59:** 2, 10

Gloucester
King Lear **46:** 254

Gobbo, Launcelot
The Merchant of Venice **46:** 24, 60; **53:** 187, 214

Goneril
King Lear **31:** 151; **46:** 231, 242; **61:** 160

Gonzalo
The Tempest **22:** 302; **29:** 278, 343, 362, 368; **45:** 280

Gower chorus
Pericles **2:** 548, 575; **15:** 134, 141, 143, 145, 149, 152, 177; **36:** 279; **42:** 352

Grey
Henry V See **traitors**

Guiderius and Arviragus
Cymbeline **4:** 21, 22, 89, 129, 141, 148; **25:** 319; **36:** 125, 158

Hal
See **Henry (King Henry V, formerly known as Prince Henry of Wales)**

Hamlet
Hamlet
as a fool **46:** 1, 29, 52, 74
compared to Vindice **59:** 10
death of **60:** 96
delay **1:** 76, 83, 88, 90, 94, 98, 102, 103, 106, 114, 115, 116, 119, 120, 148, 151, 166, 171, 179, 188, 191, 194, 198, 221, 268; **13:** 296, 502; **21:** 81; **25:** 209, 288; **28:** 223; **35:** 82, 174, 212, 215, 237; **44:** 180, 209, 219, 229; **59:** 10
divided nature **16:** 246; **28:** 223; **32:** 288; **35:** 182, 215; **37:** 241; **59:** 2
elocution of the character's speeches **21:** 96, 104, 112, 127, 132, 172, 177, 179, 194, 245, 254, 257
and identity (nature of) **59:** 18
madness **1:** 76, 81, 83, 95, 102, 106, 128, 144, 154, 160, 234; **21:** 35, 50, 72, 81, 99, 112, 311, 339, 355, 361, 371, 377, 384; **35:** 117, 132, 134, 140, 144, 212; **44:** 107, 119, 152, 209, 219, 229
meeting with the pirates (Act IV, scene vi) **59:** 56
melancholy **21:** 99, 112, 177, 194; **35:** 82, 95, 117; **44:** 209, 219
as negative character **1:** 86, 92, 111, 171, 218; **21:** 386; **25:** 209; **35:** 167; **59:** 10
reaction to his father's death **22:** 339; **35:** 104, 174; **44:** 133, 160, 180, 189
reaction to Gertrude's marriage **1:** 74, 120, 154, 179; **16:** 259; **21:** 371; **22:** 339; **35:** 104, 117; **44:** 133, 160, 189, 195
religion **48:** 195
romantic aspects of the character **21:** 96; **44:** 198; **59:** 47
as scourge or purifying figure **1:** 144, 209, 242; **25:** 288; **35:** 157; **59:** 26, 62, 79
sentimentality vs. intellectuality **1:** 75, 83, 88, 91, 93, 94, 96, 102, 103, 115, 116, 120, 166, 191; **13:** 296; **21:** 35, 41, 44, 72, 81, 89, 99, 129, 132, 136, 172, 213, 225, 339, 355, 361, 371, 377, 379, 381, 386; **25:** 209; **44:** 198
soliloquies **1:** 76, 82, 83, 148, 166, 169, 176, 191; **21:** 17, 31, 44, 53, 89, 112, 268, 311, 334, 347, 361, 384, 392; **25:** 209; **28:** 223; **44:** 107, 119, 229
as a stoic at the end **54:** 96
theatrical interpretations **21:** 11, 31, 78, 101, 104, 107, 160, 177, 179, 182, 183, 192, 194, 197, 202, 203, 208, 213, 225, 232, 237, 249, 253, 254, 257, 259, 274,

Character Index

311, 339, 347, 355, 361, 371, 377, 380; **44:** 198
virility **21:** 213, 301, 355

Hector
Troilus and Cressida
combat with Ajax **59:** 251
as a Trojan **59:** 257

Helena
All's Well That Ends Well
as agent of reconciliation, renewal, or grace **7:** 67, 76, 81, 90, 93, 98, 109, 116; **55:** 176; **63:** 21
as dualistic or enigmatic character **7:** 15, 27, 29, 39, 54, 58, 62, 67, 76, 81, 98, 113, 126; **13:** 66; **22:** 78; **26:** 117; **48:** 65; **54:** 30; **55:** 90, 170, 176; **63:** 50
desire **38:** 96; **44:** 35; **55:** 109, 170; **63:** 36, 41, 60
as "female achiever" **19:** 113; **38:** 89; **55:** 90, 101, 109, 122, 164; **63:** 36, 41, 50
pursuit of Bertram **7:** 9, 12, 15, 16, 19, 21, 26, 27, 29, 32, 43, 54, 76, 116; **13:** 77; **22:** 78; **49:** 46; **55:** 90; **63:** 36, 41, 50, 60, 99
virginity **38:** 65; **55:** 131, 176
virtue and nobility **7:** 9, 10, 12, 16, 19, 21, 27, 32, 41, 51, 58, 67, 76, 86, 126; **13:** 77; **50:** 59; **55:** 122
A Midsummer Night's Dream **29:** 269; **58:** 194;
relationship with Hermia **60:** 142

Henry (King Henry IV, previously known as Bolingbroke)
Henry IV, Parts 1 and 2 **39:** 123, 137
effectiveness as ruler **49:** 116
guilt **49:** 112
historical context **49:** 139
illegitimacy of rule **49:** 112, 133, 137
power **49:** 139
as tragic figure **49:** 186
as usurper **49:** 116, 137
Richard II
Bolingbroke and Richard as opposites **24:** 423
Bolingbroke-Mowbray dispute **22:** 137
comic elements **28:** 134
guilt **24:** 423; **39:** 279
language and imagery **6:** 310, 315, 331, 347, 374, 381, 397; **32:** 189; **58:** 301
as Machiavellian figure **6:** 305, 307, 315, 331, 347, 388, 393, 397; **24:** 428
as politician **6:** 255, 263, 264, 272, 277, 294, 364, 368, 391; **24:** 330, 333, 405, 414, 423, 428; **39:** 256; **52:** 124
Richard, compared with **6:** 307, 315, 347, 374, 391, 393, 409; **24:** 346, 349, 351, 352, 356, 395, 419, 423, 428; **52:** 108, 124; **58:** 241
seizure of Gaunt's estate **49:** 60
his silence **24:** 423
structure, compared with **39:** 235
usurpation of crown, nature of **6:** 255, 272, 289, 307, 310, 347, 354, 359, 381, 385, 393; **13:** 172; **24:** 322, 356, 383, 419; **28:** 178; **52:** 108, 124

Henry (King Henry V, formerly known as Prince Henry of Wales)
Henry IV, Parts 1 and 2
and betrayal **49:** 123
as the central character **1:** 286, 290, 314, 317, 326, 338, 354, 366, 374, 396; **39:** 72, 100
compared with the fair friend of the sonnets **60:** 154
dual personality **1:** 397, 406; **25:** 109, 151; **48:** 95; **49:** 112, 139, 153, 162; **57:** 130
as Everyman **1:** 342, 366, 374
from audience's perspective **49:** 153; **57:** 116
from Henry's perspective **49:** 153
fall from humanity **1:** 379, 380, 383
general assessment **1:** 286, 287, 289, 290, 314, 317, 326, 327, 332, 357, 397; **25:** 245; **32:** 212; **39:** 134; **48:** 151; **57:** 116, 130
as ideal ruler **1:** 289, 309, 317, 321, 326, 337, 342, 344, 374, 389, 391, 434; **25:** 109; **39:** 123; **47:** 60; **60:** 154
as Machiavellian ruler **47:** 60
as negative character **1:** 312, 332, 333, 357; **32:** 212
as outlaw **49:** 112
preparation for rule **49:** 112; **57:** 116, 130
reformation **57:** 160
as restorer of law **49:** 133
Richard II, compared with **1:** 332, 337; **39:** 72
Henry V
brutality and cunning **5:** 193, 203, 209, 210, 213, 219, 233, 239, 252, 260, 271, 287, 293, 302, 304; **30:** 159; **43:** 24
characterization in 1 and 2 Henry IV contrasted **5:** 189, 190, 241, 304, 310; **19:** 133; **25:** 131; **32:** 157
chivalry **37:** 187
courage **5:** 191, 195, 210, 213, 228, 246, 257, 267
disguise **30:** 169, 259
education **5:** 246, 267, 271, 289; **14:** 297, 328, 342; **30:** 259
emotion, lack of **5:** 209, 212, 233, 244, 264, 267, 287, 293, 310
as heroic figure **5:** 192, 205, 209, 223, 244, 252, 257, 260, 269, 271, 299, 304; **28:** 121, 146; **30:** 237, 244, 252; **37:** 187; **49:** 194, 200, 236, 247
humor **5:** 189, 191, 212, 217, 239, 240, 276
intellectual and social limitations **5:** 189, 191, 203, 209, 210, 225, 226, 230, 293; **30:** 220
interpersonal relations **5:** 209, 233, 267, 269, 276, 287, 293, 302, 318; **19:** 133; **28:** 146
mercy **5:** 213, 267, 289, 293
mixture of good and bad qualities **5:** 199, 205, 209, 210, 213, 244, 260, 304, 314; **30:** 262, 273; **49:** 211
piety **5:** 191, 199, 209, 217, 223, 239, 257, 260, 271, 289, 310, 318; **30:** 244; **32:** 126
public vs. private selves **22:** 137; **30:** 169, 207
self-doubt **5:** 281, 310
slaughter of prisoners **5:** 189, 205, 246, 293, 318; **28:** 146
speech **5:** 212, 230, 233, 246, 264, 276, 287, 302; **28:** 146; **30:** 163, 227

Henry (King Henry VI)
Henry VI, Parts 1, 2, and 3
characterization **3:** 64, 77, 151; **39:** 160, 177; **47:** 32; **63:** 114, 144, 205
source of social disorder **3:** 25, 31, 41, 115; **39:** 154, 187; **63:** 205
as sympathetic figure **3:** 73, 143, 154; **24:** 32

Henry (King Henry VIII)
Henry VIII
as agent of divine retribution **2:** 49
characterization **2:** 23, 39, 51, 58, 60, 65, 66, 75; **28:** 184; **37:** 109; **56:** 242; **61:** 119, 136
incomplete portrait **2:** 15, 16, 19, 35; **41:** 120; **56:** 209
as realistic figure **2:** 21, 22, 23, 25, 32

Henry (Prince Henry)
King John **41:** 277; **56:** 348

Hermia
A Midsummer Night's Dream **29:** 225, 269; **45:** 117; **58:** 194
relationship with Helena **60:** 142

Hermione
The Winter's Tale
characterization **7:** 385, 395, 402, 412, 414, 506; **15:** 495, 532; **22:** 302, 324; **25:** 347; **32:** 388; **36:** 311; **47:** 25; **49:** 18; **57:** 319
restoration (Act V, scene iii) **7:** 377, 379, 384, 385, 387, 389, 394, 396, 412, 425, 436, 451, 452, 456, 464, 483, 501; **15:** 411, 412, 413, 518, 528, 532; **49:** 18; **57:** 294, 367; **60:** 2, 40
sex as identity **48:** 309
supposed death **25:** 339; **47:** 25
trial of **49:** 18

Hero
Much Ado about Nothing **8:** 13, 14, 16, 19, 28, 29, 44, 48, 53, 55, 82, 95, 104, 111, 115, 121; **31:** 231, 245; **47:** 25; **55:** 209

Hippolyta
A Midsummer Night's Dream **48:** 23

Holofernes
Love's Labour's Lost **23:** 207

Horatio
Hamlet **44:** 189
stoic perfection, example of **48:** 195

Hostess
Henry IV, Parts 1 and 2 **60:** 26

Hotspur
Henry IV, Parts 1 and 2 **25:** 151; **28:** 101; **39:** 72, 134, 137; **42:** 99; **60:** 154
and prisoners of war **49:** 137

versus Henry **49:** 137
Henry V **5:** 189, 199, 228, 271, 302

Humphrey
Henry VI, Parts 1, 2, and 3 **13:** 131; **56:** 187

Iachimo
Cymbeline **25:** 245, 319; **36:** 166; **47:** 274

Iago
Othello
affinity with Othello **4:** 400, 427, 468, 470, 477, 500, 506; **25:** 189; **44:** 57
as conventional dramatic villain **4:** 440, 527, 545, 582; **53:** 238
as homosexual **4:** 503; **53:** 275
Machiavellian elements **4:** 440, 455, 457, 517, 545; **35:** 336, 347
motives **4:** 389, 390, 397, 399, 402, 409, 423, 424, 427, 434, 451, 462, 545, 564; **13:** 304; **25:** 189; **28:** 344; **32:** 201; **35:** 265, 276, 310, 336, 347; **42:** 273; **53:** 246, 275, 324
revenge scheme **4:** 392, 409, 424, 451
as scapegoat **4:** 506
as victim **4:** 402, 409, 434, 451, 457, 470

Imogen
Cymbeline **4:** 21, 22, 24, 29, 37, 45, 46, 52, 56, 78, 89, 108; **15:** 23, 32, 105, 121; **19:** 411; **25:** 245, 319; **28:** 398; **32:** 373; **36:** 129, 142, 148; **47:** 25, 205, 228, 245, 274, 277; **61:** 34, 45, 76
reawakening of (Act IV, scene ii) **4:** 37, 56, 89, 103, 108, 116, 150; **15:** 23; **25:** 245; **47:** 252

Isabella
Measure for Measure **2:** 388, 390, 395, 396, 397, 401, 402, 406, 409, 410, 411, 418, 420, 421, 432, 437, 441, 466, 475, 491, 495, 524; **16:** 114; **23:** 278, 279, 280, 281, 282, 296, 344, 357, 363, 405; **28:** 102; **33:** 77, 85; **60:** 12

Jack Cade
Henry VI, Parts 1, 2, and 3 See **Cade**

the jailer's daughter
The Two Noble Kinsmen **9:** 457, 460, 479, 481, 486, 502; **41:** 340; **50:** 295, 305, 310, 348, 361; **58:** 338, 371

Jaques
As You Like It
love-theme, relation to **5:** 103; **23:** 7, 37, 118, 128
as malcontent **5:** 59, 70, 84
melancholy **5:** 20, 28, 32, 36, 39, 43, 50, 59, 63, 68, 77, 82, 86, 135; **23:** 20, 26, 103, 104, 107, 109; **34:** 85; **46:** 88, 94; **57:** 31
pastoral convention, relation to **5:** 61, 63, 65, 79, 93, 98, 114, 118
Seven Ages of Man speech (Act II, scene vii) **5:** 28, 52, 156; **23:** 48, 103, 105, 126, 138, 152; **46:** 88, 156, 164, 169
Shakespeare, relation to **5:** 35, 50, 154; **48:** 42
as superficial critic **5:** 28, 30, 43, 54, 55, 63, 65, 68, 75, 77, 82, 86, 88, 98, 138; **34:** 85

the jennet
Venus and Adonis See **the courser and the jennet**

Jessica
The Merchant of Venice **4:** 196, 200, 228, 293, 342; **48:** 54, 77; **53:** 159, 211

Joan of Arc
Henry VI, Parts 1, 2, and 3 **16:** 131; **32:** 212; **60:** 33; **63:** 124, 131, 149

John (Don John)
Much Ado about Nothing **8:** 9, 12, 16, 17, 19, 28, 29, 36, 39, 41, 47, 48, 55, 58, 63, 82, 104, 108, 111, 121

John (Friar John)
Romeo and Juliet
detention of **5:** 448, 467, 470

John (King John)
King John **41:** 205, 260
death **9:** 212, 215, 216, 240; **56:** 345
decline **9:** 224, 235, 240, 263, 275
Hubert, scene with (Act III, scene iii) **9:** 210, 212, 216, 218, 219, 280
moral insensibility **13:** 147, 163
negative qualities **9:** 209, 212, 218, 219, 229, 234, 235, 244, 245, 246, 250, 254, 275, 280, 297; **56:** 325
positive qualities **9:** 209, 224, 235, 240, 244, 245, 263

John of Lancaster, Prince
Henry IV **49:** 123
and betrayal **49:** 123

Julia
The Two Gentlemen of Verona **6:** 450, 453, 458, 476, 494, 499, 516, 519, 549, 564; **40:** 312, 327, 374; **54:** 325, 332; **63:** 336

Juliet
Romeo and Juliet See **Romeo and Juliet**

Launcelot Gobbo
The Merchant of Venice See **Gobbo**

Kate
The Taming of the Shrew
characterization **32:** 1; **43:** 61
final speech (Act V, scene ii) **9:** 318, 319, 329, 330, 338, 340, 341, 345, 347, 353, 355, 360, 365, 381, 386, 401, 404, 413, 426, 430; **19:** 3; **22:** 48; **54:** 65; **55:** 299, 331
love for Petruchio **9:** 338, 340, 353, 430; **12:** 435; **55:** 294
portrayals of **31:** 282
shrewishness **9:** 322, 323, 325, 332, 344, 345, 360, 365, 370, 375, 386, 393, 398, 404, 413
transformation **9:** 323, 341, 355, 370, 386, 393, 401, 404, 407, 419, 424, 426, 430; **16:** 13; **19:** 34; **22:** 48; **31:** 288, 295, 339, 351; **55:** 294, 315

Katherine
Henry V **5:** 186, 188, 189, 190, 192, 260, 269, 299, 302; **13:** 183; **19:** 217; **30:** 278; **44:** 44
Henry VIII
characterization **2:** 18, 19, 23, 24, 38; **24:** 129; **37:** 109; **41:** 180; **61:** 119, 136
Hermione, compared with **2:** 24, 51, 58, 76
politeness strategies **22:** 182; **56:** 262
religious discourse **22:** 182
as tragic figure **2:** 16, 18

Kent
King Lear **25:** 202; **28:** 223; **32:** 212; **47:** 9

King
All's Well That Ends Well **38:** 150; **55:** 148

King Richard II
Richard II See **Richard**

King Richard III, formerly Richard, Duke of Gloucester
Richard III See **Richard**

Lady Macbeth
Macbeth See **Macbeth (Lady Macbeth)**

Laertes
Hamlet **21:** 347, 386; **28:** 290; **35:** 182; **59:** 26

Launce and Speed
The Two Gentlemen of Verona
comic function of **6:** 438, 439, 442, 456, 458, 460, 462, 472, 476, 478, 484, 502, 504, 507, 509, 516, 519, 549; **40:** 312, 320; **63:** 336

Lavatch
All's Well That Ends Well **26:** 64; **46:** 33, 52, 68; **55:** 143; **63:** 28

Lavinia
Titus Andronicus **27:** 266; **28:** 249; **32:** 212; **43:** 1, 170, 239, 247, 255, 262; **62:** 225, 233, 242

Lawrence (Friar Lawrence)
Romeo and Juliet
contribution to catastrophe **5:** 437, 444, 470; **33:** 300; **51:** 253; **60:** 96
philosophy of moderation **5:** 427, 431, 437, 438, 443, 444, 445, 458, 467, 479, 505, 538
as Shakespeare's spokesman **5:** 427, 431, 437, 458, 467

Lear
King Lear **61:** 176
curse on Goneril **11:** 5, 7, 12, 114, 116
death of **60:** 2
love-test and division of kingdom **2:** 100, 106, 111, 124, 131, 137, 147, 149, 151, 168, 186, 208, 216, 281; **16:** 351; **25:** 202; **31:** 84, 92, 107, 117, 149, 155; **46:** 231, 242; **61:** 194
madness **2:** 94, 95, 98, 99, 100, 101, 102, 103, 111, 116, 120, 124, 125, 149, 156,

191, 208, 216, 281; **46:** 264
as scapegoat **2:** 241, 253
self-knowledge **2:** 103, 151, 188, 191, 213, 218, 222, 241, 249, 262; **25:** 218; **37:** 213; **46:** 191, 205, 225, 254, 264; **54:** 103; **60:** 65, 75; **61:** 215, 220, 250
spiritual regeneration **54:** 103; **60:** 65, 75

Leontes
The Winter's Tale
characterization **19:** 431; **43:** 39; **45:** 366
jealousy **7:** 377, 379, 382, 383, 384, 387, 389, 394, 395, 402, 407, 412, 414, 425, 429, 432, 436, 464, 480, 483, 497; **15:** 514, 518, 532; **22:** 324; **25:** 339; **36:** 334, 344, 349; **44:** 66; **45:** 295, 297, 344, 358; **47:** 25; **57:** 294
Othello, compared with **7:** 383, 390, 412; **15:** 514; **36:** 334; **44:** 66; **47:** 25
repentance **7:** 381, 389, 394, 396, 402, 414, 497; **36:** 318, 362; **44:** 66; **57:** 294

Lord Chief Justice
Henry IV
as keeper of law and justice **49:** 133

the lovers
A Midsummer's Night Dream **58:** 151, 169

Lucentio
The Taming of the Shrew **9:** 325, 342, 362, 375, 393

Lucio
Measure for Measure **13:** 104; **49:** 379

Lucrece
The Rape of Lucrece
chastity **33:** 131, 138; **43:** 92
as example of Renaissance virtù **22:** 289; **43:** 148
heroic **10:** 84, 93, 109, 121, 128; **59:** 175, 193
patriarchal woman, model of **10:** 109, 131; **33:** 169, 200
Philomela **59:** 193
self-perception **48:** 291
self-responsibility **10:** 89, 96, 98, 106, 125; **33:** 195; **43:** 85, 92, 158; **59:** 206
unrealistic **10:** 64, 65, 66, 121
verbose **10:** 64, 81, 116; **25:** 305; **33:** 169
as victim **22:** 294; **25:** 305; **32:** 321; **33:** 131, 195; **43:** 102, 158; **59:** 175, 180, 189, 193, 206

Macbeth
Macbeth
ambition **44:** 284, 324; **57:** 256
characterization **20:** 20, 42, 73, 107, 113, 130, 146, 151, 279, 283, 312, 338, 343, 379, 406, 413; **29:** 139, 152, 155, 165; **44:** 289; **57:** 189, 194, 236, 263, 267
courage **3:** 172, 177, 181, 182, 183, 186, 234, 312, 333; **20:** 107; **44:** 315
disposition **3:** 173, 175, 177, 182, 186; **20:** 245, 376
imagination **3:** 196, 208, 213, 250, 312, 345; **20:** 245, 376; **44:** 351
as "inauthentic" king **3:** 245, 302, 321, 345
inconsistencies **3:** 202
as Machiavellian villain **3:** 280; **57:** 236
manliness **20:** 113; **29:** 127, 133; **44:** 315; **57:** 256
psychoanalytic interpretations **20:** 42, 73, 238, 376; **44:** 284, 289, 297, 324; **45:** 48, 58; **57:** 267
Richard III, compared with **3:** 177, 182, 186, 345; **20:** 86, 92; **22:** 365; **44:** 269
as Satan figure **3:** 229, 269, 275, 289, 318
self-awareness **3:** 312, 329, 338; **16:** 317; **44:** 361; **57:** 256; **60:** 46
as sympathetic figure **3:** 229, 306, 314, 338; **29:** 139, 152; **44:** 269, 306, 337
as tragic hero **44:** 269, 306, 315, 324, 337; **57:** 267

Macbeth (Lady Macbeth)
Macbeth
ambition **3:** 185, 219; **20:** 279, 345
characterization **20:** 56, 60, 65, 73, 140, 148, 151, 241, 279, 283, 338, 350, 406, 413; **29:** 109, 146; **57:** 256, 263
childlessness **3:** 219, 223; **48:** 214
good and evil, combined traits of **3:** 173, 191, 213; **20:** 60, 107
inconsistencies **3:** 202; **20:** 54, 137
influence on Macbeth **3:** 171, 185, 191, 193, 199, 262, 289, 312, 318; **13:** 502; **20:** 345; **25:** 235; **29:** 133; **57:** 263
psychoanalytic interpretations **20:** 345; **44:** 289, 297; **45:** 58
sleepwalking scene **44:** 261
as sympathetic figure **3:** 191, 193, 203

Macduff
Macbeth **3:** 226, 231, 253, 262; **25:** 235; **29:** 127, 133, 155; **57:** 194

MacMorris
Henry V **22:** 103; **28:** 159; **30:** 278

Malcolm
Macbeth **25:** 235
fatherhood **48:** 214

Malvolio
Twelfth Night
characterization **1:** 540, 544, 545, 548, 550, 554, 558, 567, 575, 577, 615; **26:** 207, 233, 273; **46:** 286; **62:** 339, 348
forged letter **16:** 372; **28:** 1
punishment **1:** 539, 544, 548, 549, 554, 555, 558, 563, 577, 590, 632, 645; **46:** 291, 297, 338
as Puritan **1:** 549, 551, 555, 558, 561, 563; **25:** 47
role in play **1:** 545, 548, 549, 553, 555, 563, 567, 575, 577, 588, 610, 615, 632, 645; **26:** 337, 374; **46:** 347; **62:** 339

Mamillius
The Winter's Tale **7:** 394, 396, 451; **22:** 324

Margaret
Henry VI, Parts 1, 2, and 3
characterization **3:** 18, 26, 35, 51, 103, 109, 140, 157; **24:** 48; **63:** 114, 131, 205
Suffolk, relationship with **3:** 18, 24, 26, 157; **39:** 213; **63:** 131, 169
Richard III **8:** 153, 154, 159, 162, 163, 170, 193, 201, 206, 210, 218, 223, 228, 243, 248, 262; **39:** 345; **62:** 2, 14, 18, 31, 52, 78

Marina
Pericles **37:** 361; **51:** 118

Menenius
Coriolanus **9:** 8, 9, 11, 14, 19, 26, 78, 80, 106, 148, 157; **25:** 263, 296; **30:** 67, 79, 89, 96, 111, 133

Mercutio
Romeo and Juliet
bawdy **5:** 463, 525, 550, 575
death **5:** 415, 418, 419, 547; **33:** 290
as worldly counterpart to Romeo **5:** 425, 464, 542; **33:** 290; **51:** 195

minor characters
Richard III **8:** 154, 159, 162, 163, 168, 170, 177, 184, 186, 201, 206, 210, 218, 223, 228, 232, 239, 248, 262, 267

Miranda
The Tempest **8:** 289, 301, 304, 328, 336, 370, 454; **19:** 357; **22:** 302; **28:** 249; **29:** 278, 297, 362, 368, 377, 396; **53:** 64

Mistress Elbow
Measure for Measure See **Elbow (Mistress Elbow)**

Mistress Quickly
Henry V See **Quickly**

Mortimer
Henry IV, Parts 1 and 2 **25:** 151

Norfolk
Henry VIII **22:** 182

Northumberland
Richard II **24:** 423

Nurse
Romeo and Juliet **5:** 419, 425, 463, 464, 575; **33:** 294

Oberon
A Midsummer Night's Dream **58:** 151, 162, 167, 203
as controlling force **3:** 434, 459, 477, 502; **29:** 175; **60:** 142

Octavius
Antony and Cleopatra **6:** 22, 24, 31, 38, 43, 53, 62, 107, 125, 146, 178, 181, 219; **25:** 257; **58:** 33
Julius Caesar **30:** 316; **63:** 278

Olivia
Twelfth Night **1:** 540, 543, 545; **46:** 286, 324, 369; **47:** 45; **62:** 325, 343

Ophelia
Hamlet **1:** 73, 76, 81, 82, 91, 96, 97, 154, 166, 169, 171, 218, 270; **13:** 268; **16:** 246; **19:** 330; **21:** 17, 41, 44, 72, 81, 101, 104, 107, 112, 136, 203, 259, 347, 381, 386, 392, 416; **28:** 232, 325; **35:** 104, 126, 140, 144, 182, 238; **44:** 189, 195, 248; **59:** 31, 39
in art **48:** 255
death **48:** 255
as icon **48:** 255
influence on popular culture **48:** 255
as Mary Magdalen **59:** 68

Orlando
As You Like It
as ideal man **5:** 32, 36, 39, 162; **34:** 161; **46:** 94
relationship with Rosalind/Ganymede **60:** 115
as younger brother **5:** 66, 158; **46:** 94

Orsino
Twelfth Night **46:** 286, 333; **47:** 45; **62:** 343

Othello
Othello
affinity with Iago **4:** 400, 427, 468, 470, 477, 500, 506; **25:** 189; **35:** 276, 320, 327
as conventional "blameless hero" **4:** 445, 486, 500; **53:** 233, 238, 298, 304
credulity **4:** 384, 385, 388, 390, 396, 402, 434, 440, 455; **13:** 327; **32:** 302; **47:** 25, 51
Desdemona, relationship with **22:** 339; **35:** 301, 317; **37:** 269; **43:** 32; **53:** 315
divided nature **4:** 400, 412, 462, 470, 477, 493, 500, 582, 592; **16:** 293; **19:** 276; **25:** 189; **35:** 320; **53:** 268, 289, 343
egotism **4:** 427, 470, 477, 493, 522, 536, 541, 573, 597; **13:** 304; **35:** 247, 253
self-destructive anger **16:** 283; **53:** 324
self-dramatizing or self-deluding **4:** 454, 457, 477, 592; **13:** 313; **16:** 293; **35:** 317; **60:** 46
self-knowledge **4:** 462, 470, 477, 483, 508, 522, 530, 564, 580, 591, 596; **13:** 304, 313; **16:** 283; **28:** 243; **35:** 253, 317; **53:** 233, 343
spiritual state **4:** 483, 488, 517, 525, 527, 544, 559, 564, 573; **28:** 243; **35:** 253; **54:** 119; **60:** 46

Page, Anne
The Merry Wives of Windsor **47:** 321
Anne Page-Fenton plot **5:** 334, 336, 343, 353, 376, 390, 395, 402; **22:** 93; **47:** 308

Page, Mistess Margaret
The Merry Wives of Windsor **47:** 321

Painter
Timon of Athens See **Poet and Painter**

Palamon and Arcite
The Two Noble Kinsmen **9:** 474, 481, 490, 492, 502; **50:** 295, 305, 348, 361; **58:** 322, 338, 345, 356, 361

Pandarus
Troilus and Cressida **59:** 245

Parolles
All's Well That Ends Well
characterization **7:** 8, 9, 43, 76, 81, 98, 109, 113, 116, 126; **22:** 78; **26:** 48, 73, 97; **26:** 117; **46:** 68; **55:** 90, 154
exposure **7:** 9, 27, 81, 98, 109, 113, 116, 121, 126
Falstaff, compared with **7:** 8, 9, 16

pastoral characters (Silvius, Phebe, and Corin)
As You Like It **23:** 37, 97, 98, 99, 108, 110, 118, 122, 138; **34:** 147; **60:** 115

Paulina
The Winter's Tale **7:** 385, 412, 506; **15:** 528; **22:** 324; **25:** 339; **36:** 311; **57:** 319

Pedro (Don Pedro)
Much Ado about Nothing **8:** 17, 19, 48, 58, 63, 82, 111, 121

Perdita
The Winter's Tale
characterization **7:** 395, 412, 414, 419, 429, 432, 452, 506; **22:** 324; **25:** 339; **36:** 328; **43:** 39
reunion with Leontes (Act V, scene ii) **7:** 377, 379, 381, 390, 432, 464, 480

Pericles
Pericles
characterization **36:** 251; **37:** 361
patience **2:** 572, 573, 578, 579
suit of Antiochus's daughter **2:** 547, 565, 578, 579; **51:** 126
Ulysses, compared with **2:** 551

Petruchio
The Taming of the Shrew
admirable qualities **9:** 320, 332, 341, 344, 345, 370, 375, 386; **55:** 294
audacity or vigor **9:** 325, 337, 355, 375, 386, 404
characterization **32:** 1
coarseness or brutality **9:** 325, 329, 365, 390, 393, 398, 407; **19:** 122; **43:** 61
as lord of misrule **9:** 393; **50:** 64; **55:** 322
love for Kate **9:** 338, 340, 343, 344, 386; **12:** 435
portrayals of **31:** 282
pragmatism **9:** 329, 334, 375, 398, 424; **13:** 3; **31:** 345, 351
taming method **9:** 320, 323, 329, 340, 341, 343, 345, 355, 369, 370, 375, 390, 398, 407, 413, 419, 424; **19:** 3, 12, 21 **31:** 269, 295, 326, 335, 339; **55:** 334

Phebe
As You Like It See **pastoral characters**

Pistol
Henry V **28:** 146

plebeians
Coriolanus **9:** 8, 9, 11, 12, 15, 18, 19, 26, 33, 39, 53, 92, 125, 153, 183, 189; **25:** 296; **30:** 58, 79, 96, 111

Poet and Painter
Timon of Athens **25:** 198

the poets
Julius Caesar **7:** 179, 320, 350

Polixenes
The Winter's Tale
Leontes, relationship with **48:** 309

Polonius
Hamlet **21:** 259, 334, 347, 386, 416; **35:** 182

Porter
Henry VIII **24:** 155
Macbeth **3:** 173, 175, 184, 190, 196, 203, 205, 225, 260, 271, 297, 300; **20:** 283; **60:** 89

Portia
The Merchant of Venice **4:** 194, 195, 196, 215, 254, 263, 336, 356; **12:** 104, 107, 114; **13:** 37; **22:** 3, 69; **25:** 22; **32:** 294; **37:** 86; **40:** 142, 156, 197, 208; **49:** 27

Posthumus
Cymbeline **4:** 24, 30, 53, 78, 116, 127, 141, 155, 159, 167; **15:** 89; **19:** 411; **25:** 245, 319; **36:** 142; **44:** 28; **45:** 67, 75; **47:** 25, 205, 228 **61:** 34, 45, 76

Prince Henry
King John See **Henry (Prince Henry)**

Prospero
The Tempest
characterization **8:** 312, 348, 370, 458; **16:** 442; **22:** 302; **45:** 188, 272; **61:** 307
as God or Providence **8:** 311, 328, 364, 380, 429, 435
magic, nature of **8:** 301, 340, 356, 396, 414, 423, 458; **25:** 382; **28:** 391; **29:** 278, 292, 368, 377, 396; **32:** 338, 343; **61:** 272
psychoanalytic interpretation **45:** 259
redemptive powers **8:** 302, 320, 353, 370, 390, 429, 439, 447; **29:** 297; **61:** 326, 338
as ruler **8:** 304, 308, 309, 420, 423; **13:** 424; **22:** 302; **29:** 278, 362, 377, 396; **61:** 315
self-control **8:** 312, 414, 420; **22:** 302; **44:** 11
self-knowledge **16:** 442; **22:** 302; **29:** 278, 292, 362, 377, 396
as Shakespeare or creative artist **8:** 299, 302, 308, 312, 320, 324, 353, 364, 435, 447; **61:** 280, 288
as tragic hero **8:** 359, 370, 464; **29:** 292

Proteus
The Two Gentlemen of Verona **6:** 439, 450, 458, 480, 490, 511; **40:** 312, 327, 330, 335, 359; **42:** 18; **54:** 325, 332

Puck
A Midsummer Night's Dream **45:** 96, 158

Quickly (Mistress Quickly)
Henry V **5:** 186, 187, 210, 276, 293; **30:** 278

Regan
King Lear **31:** 151; **46:** 231, 242; **61:** 160

Richard (King Richard II)
Richard II
artistic temperament **6:** 264, 267, 270, 272, 277, 292, 294, 298, 315, 331, 334, 347, 368, 374, 393, 409; **24:** 298, 301, 304, 315, 322, 390, 405, 408, 411, 414, 419; **39:** 289
Bolingbroke, compared with **24:** 346, 349, 351, 352, 356, 419; **39:** 256; **52:** 108, 124; **58:** 275
characterization **6:** 250, 252, 253, 254, 255, 258, 262, 263, 267, 270, 272, 282, 283, 304, 343, 347, 364, 368; **24:** 262, 263, 267, 269, 270, 271, 272, 273, 274, 278, 280, 315, 322, 325, 330, 333, 390, 395, 402, 405, 423; **28:** 134; **39:** 279, 289; **52:** 169; **58:** 229, 241, 253, 259, 267, 307
dangerous aspects **24:** 405; **58:** 253
death of **60:** 21
delusion **6:** 267, 298, 334, 368, 409; **24:** 329, 336, 405
homosexuality **24:** 405
kingship **6:** 253, 254, 263, 272, 327, 331, 334, 338, 364, 402, 414; **24:** 278, 295, 336, 337, 339, 356, 419; **28:** 134, 178; **39:** 256, 263; **52:** 169; **58:** 241, 275
language and imagery **58:** 301
loss of identity **6:** 267, 338, 368, 374, 381, 388, 391, 409; **24:** 298, 414, 428
as martyr-king **6:** 289, 307, 321; **19:** 209; **24:** 289, 291; **28:** 134
nobility **6:** 255, 258, 259, 262, 263, 391; **24:** 260, 263, 274, 280, 289, 291, 402, 408, 411
political acumen **6:** 263, 264, 272, 292, 310, 327, 334, 364, 368, 374, 388, 391, 397, 402, 409; **24:** 405; **39:** 256
private vs. public persona **6:** 317, 327, 364, 368, 391, 409; **24:** 428
role in Gloucester's death **52:** 108, 124
role-playing **24:** 419, 423; **28:** 178
seizure of Gaunt's estate **6:** 250, 338, 388
self-dramatization **6:** 264, 267, 307, 310, 315, 317, 331, 334, 368, 393, 409; **24:** 339; **28:** 178; **60:** 21
self-hatred **13:** 172; **24:** 383; **39:** 289
self-knowledge **6:** 255, 267, 331, 334, 338, 352, 354, 368, 388, 391; **24:** 273, 289, 411, 414; **39:** 263, 289; **60:** 21, 46
spiritual redemption **6:** 255, 267, 331, 334, 338, 352, 354, 368, 388, 391; **24:** 273, 289, 411, 414; **52:** 124; **60:** 21, 46

Richard (King Richard III, formerly Richard, Duke of Gloucester)
Henry VI, Parts 1, 2, and 3
characterization **3:** 35, 48, 57, 64, 77, 143, 151; **22:** 193; **39:** 160, 177; **63:** 114
as revenger **22:** 193
soliloquy (3 Henry VI, Act III, scene ii) **3:** 17, 48
Richard III
ambition **8:** 148, 154, 165, 168, 170, 177, 182, 213, 218, 228, 232, 239, 252, 258, 267; **39:** 308, 341, 360, 370, 383; **52:** 201, 223
attractive qualities **8:** 145, 148, 152, 154, 159, 161, 162, 165, 168, 170, 181, 182, 184, 185, 197, 201, 206, 213, 228, 243, 252, 258; **16:** 150; **39:** 370, 383; **52:** 272, 280; **62:** 104
credibility, question of **8:** 145, 147, 154, 159, 165, 193; **13:** 142
death **8:** 145, 148, 154, 159, 165, 168, 170, 177, 182, 197, 210, 223, 228, 232, 243, 248, 252, 258, 267
deformity as symbol **8:** 146, 147, 148, 152, 154, 159, 161, 165, 170, 177, 184, 185, 193, 218, 248, 252, 267; **19:** 164; **62:** 110
inversion of moral order **8:** 159, 168, 177, 182, 184, 185, 197, 201, 213, 218, 223, 232, 239, 243, 248, 252, 258, 262, 267; **39:** 360; **52:** 205, 214
as Machiavellian villain **8:** 165, 182, 190, 201, 218, 232, 239, 243, 248; **39:** 308, 326, 360, 387; **52:** 201, 205, 257, 280, 285; **62:** 2, 60, 78, 110
as monster or symbol of diabolic **8:** 145, 147, 159, 162, 168, 170, 177, 182, 193, 197, 201, 228, 239, 248, 258; **13:** 142; **37:** 144; **39:** 326, 349; **52:** 227, 272
other literary villains, compared with **8:** 148, 161, 162, 165, 181, 182, 206, 213, 239, 267
role-playing, hypocrisy, and dissimulation **8:** 145, 148, 154, 159, 162, 165, 168, 170, 182, 190, 206, 213, 218, 228, 239, 243, 252, 258, 267; **25:** 141, 164, 245; **39:** 335, 341, 387 **52:** 257, 267; **62:** 78
as scourge or instrument of God **8:** 163, 177, 193, 201, 218, 228, 248, 267; **39:** 308; **62:** 60
as seducer **52:** 223, 227; **62:** 91, 104
self-esteem **52:** 196; **62:** 78
as Vice figure **8:** 190, 201, 213, 228, 243, 248, 252; **16:** 150; **39:** 383, 387; **52:** 223, 267; **62:** 78

Richard Plantagenet, Duke of York
Henry VI, Parts 1, 2, and 3 See **York**

Richmond
Richard III **8:** 154, 158, 163, 168, 177, 182, 193, 210, 218, 223, 228, 243, 248, 252; **13:** 142; **25:** 141; **39:** 349; **52:** 214, 257, 285

the Rival Poet
Sonnets **10:** 169, 233, 334, 337, 385; **48:** 352

Roman citizenry
Julius Caesar
portrayal of **7:** 169, 179, 210, 221, 245, 279, 282, 310, 320, 333; **17:** 271, 279, 288, 291, 292, 298, 323, 334, 351, 367, 374, 375, 378; **22:** 280; **30:** 285, 297, 316, 321, 374, 379; **37:** 229

Romeo and Juliet
Romeo and Juliet
death-wish **5:** 431, 489, 505, 528, 530, 538, 542, 550, 566, 571, 575; **32:** 212
first meeting (Act I scene v) **51:** 212
immortality **5:** 536
Juliet's epithalamium speech (Act III, scene ii) **5:** 431, 477, 492
Juliet's innocence **5:** 421, 423, 450, 454; **33:** 257
maturation **5:** 437, 454, 467, 493, 498, 509, 520, 565; **33:** 249, 257
rebellion **25:** 257
reckless passion **5:** 419, 427, 431, 438, 443, 444, 448, 467, 479, 485, 505, 533, 538, 542; **33:** 241
Romeo's dream (Act V, scene i) **5:** 513, 536, 556; **45:** 40; **51:** 203
Rosaline, Romeo's relationship with **5:** 419, 423, 425, 427, 438, 498, 542, 575

Rosalind
As You Like It **46:** 94, 122
Beatrice, compared with **5:** 26, 36, 50, 75
charm **5:** 55, 75; **23:** 17, 18, 20, 41, 89, 111
disguise, role of **5:** 75, 107, 118, 122, 128, 130, 133, 138, 141, 146, 148, 164, 168; **13:** 502; **23:** 35, 42, 106, 119, 123, 146; **34:** 130; **46:** 127, 134, 142; **57:** 23, 40
femininity **5:** 26, 36, 52, 75; **23:** 24, 29, 46, 54, 103, 108, 121, 146
as Ganymede **60:** 115
love-theme, relation to **5:** 79, 88, 103, 116, 122, 138, 141; **23:** 114, 115; **34:** 85, 177

rustic characters
As You Like It **5:** 24, 60, 72, 84; **23:** 127; **34:** 78, 161
A Midsummer Night's Dream **3:** 376, 397, 432; **12:** 291, 293; **45:** 147, 160

Scroop
Henry V See **traitors**

Sebastian
The Tempest See **Antonio and Sebastian**

Shylock
The Merchant of Venice
alienation **4:** 279, 312; **40:** 175; **48:** 77; **49:** 23, 37
ambiguity **4:** 247, 254, 315, 319, 331; **12:** 31, 35, 36, 50, 51, 52, 56, 81, 124; **40:** 175; **53:** 111
ghettoization of **53:** 127
forced conversion **4:** 209, 252, 268, 282, 289, 321

Jewishness **4:** 193, 194, 195, 200, 201, 213, 214, 279; **22:** 69; **25:** 257; **40:** 142, 175, 181; **48:** 65, 77
master-slave relationship **53:** 136
motives in making the bond **4:** 252, 263, 266, 268; **22:** 69; **25:** 22
as outsider **53:** 127, 224
as Puritan **40:** 127, 166
as scapegoat figure **4:** 254, 300; **40:** 166; **49:** 27
as traditional comic villain **4:** 230, 243, 261, 263, 315; **12:** 40, 62, 124; **40:** 175
as tragic figure **12:** 6, 9, 10, 16, 21, 23, 25, 40, 44, 66, 67, 81, 97; **40:** 175

Sicinius
Coriolanus See **the tribunes**

Silvia
The Two Gentlemen of Verona **6:** 450, 453, 458, 476, 494, 499, 516, 519, 549, 564; **40:** 312, 327, 374; **54:** 325, 332; **63:** 336

Silvius
As You Like It See **pastoral characters**

Sly
The Taming of the Shrew **9:** 320, 322, 350, 370, 381, 390, 398, 430; **12:** 316, 335, 416, 427, 441; **16:** 13; **19:** 34, 122; **22:** 48; **37:** 31; **50:** 74

soldiers
Henry V **5:** 203, 239, 267, 276, 281, 287, 293, 318; **28:** 146; **30:** 169

Speed
The Two Gentlemen of Verona See **Launce and Speed**

Stephano and Trinculo
The Tempest
comic subplot of **8:** 292, 297, 299, 304, 309, 324, 328, 353, 370; **25:** 382; **29:** 377; **46:** 14, 33

Stephen Gardiner
Henry VIII See **Gardiner**

Talbot
Henry VI, Parts 1, 2, and 3 **39:** 160, 213, 222; **56:** 85, 145; **60:** 33; **63:** 114, 185

Tamora
Titus Andronicus **4:** 632, 662, 672, 675; **27:** 266; **43:** 170; **62:** 233

Tarquin
The Rape of Lucrece **10:** 80, 93, 98, 116, 125; **22:** 294; **25:** 305; **32:** 321; **33:** 190; **43:** 102; **59:** 180
Petrarchan lover **48:** 291
platonic tyrant **48:** 291
Satan role **48:** 291

Thersites
Troilus and Cressida **13:** 53; **25:** 56; **27:** 381; **59:** 265

Theseus
A Midsummer Night's Dream
characterization **3:** 363; **58:** 151, 220
Hippolyta, relationship with **3:** 381, 412, 421, 423, 450, 468, 520; **29:** 175, 216, 243, 256; **45:** 84
as ideal **3:** 379, 391
"lovers, lunatics, and poets" speech (Act V, scene i) **3:** 365, 371, 379, 381, 391, 402, 411, 412, 421, 423, 441, 498, 506; **29:** 175
as representative of institutional life **3:** 381, 403; **51:** 1

Time-Chorus
The Winter's Tale **7:** 377, 380, 412, 464, 476, 501; **15:** 518

Timon
Timon of Athens
comic traits **25:** 198
as flawed hero **1:** 456, 459, 462, 472, 495, 503, 507, 515; **16:** 351; **20:** 429, 433, 476; **25:** 198; **27:** 157, 161
death of **60:** 46
misanthropy **13:** 392; **20:** 431, 464, 476, 481, 491, 492, 493; **27:** 161, 175, 184, 196; **37:** 222; **52:** 296, 301
as noble figure **1:** 467, 473, 483, 499; **20:** 493; **27:** 212

Titania
A Midsummer Night's Dream **29:** 243; **58:** 151, 162, 167, 203

Titus
Titus Andronicus **4:** 632, 637, 640, 644, 647, 653, 656, 662; **25:** 245; **27:** 255; **62:** 258

Touchstone
As You Like It
callousness **5:** 88
comic and farcical elements **46:** 117
as philosopher-fool **5:** 24, 28, 30, 32, 36, 63, 75, 98; **23:** 152; **34:** 85; **46:** 1, 14, 18, 24, 33, 52, 60, 88, 105
relation to pastoral convention **5:** 54, 61, 63, 72, 75, 77, 79, 84, 86, 93, 98, 114, 118, 135, 138, 166; **34:** 72, 147, 161
satire or parody of pastoral conventions **46:** 122
selflessness **5:** 30, 36, 39, 76

traitors (Scroop, Grey, and Cambridge)
Henry V **16:** 202; **30:** 220, 278

the tribunes (Brutus and Sicinius)
Coriolanus **9:** 9, 11, 14, 19, 33, 169, 180

Trinculo
The Tempest See **Stephano and Trinculo**

Troilus
Troilus and Cressida
contradictory behavior **3:** 596, 602, 635; **27:** 362
Cressida, relationship with **3:** 594, 596, 606; **22:** 58; **59:** 245, 261
integrity **3:** 617
opposition to Ulysses **3:** 561, 584, 590
as a Trojan **59:** 257
as unsympathetic figure **18:** 423; **22:** 58, 339; **43:** 317; **59:** 261
as warrior **3:** 596; **22:** 339

Ulysses
Troilus and Cressida **59:** 245
speech on degree (Act I, scene iii) **3:** 549, 599, 609, 642; **27:** 396

Valentine
The Two Gentlemen of Verona **54:** 325, 332

Venetians
The Merchant of Venice **4:** 195, 200, 228, 254, 273, 300, 321, 331

Venus
Venus and Adonis **10:** 427, 429, 434, 439, 442, 448, 449, 451, 454, 466, 473, 480, 486, 489; **16:** 452; **25:** 305, 328; **28:** 355; **33:** 309, 321, 330, 347, 352, 357, 363, 370, 377; **51:** 335, 352, 377, 388

Viola
Twelfth Night **26:** 308; **46:** 286, 324, 347, 369; **60:** 115, 129; **62:** 308, 319, 325

Virgilia
Coriolanus **9:** 11, 19, 26, 33, 58, 100, 121, 125; **25:** 263; **30:** 79, 96, 133; **50:** 99

Volumnia
Coriolanus
Coriolanus's subservience to **9:** 16, 26, 33, 53, 62, 80, 92, 100, 117, 125, 142, 177, 183; **30:** 140, 149; **44:** 79
influence on Coriolanus **9:** 45, 62, 65, 78, 92, 100, 110, 117, 121, 125, 130, 148, 157, 183, 189, 193; **25:** 263, 296; **30:** 79, 96, 125, 133, 140, 142, 149; **44:** 93
as noble Roman matron **9:** 16, 19, 26, 31, 33
personification of Rome **9:** 125, 183; **50:** 119

Wat the hare
Venus and Adonis **10:** 424, 451

the Watch
Much Ado about Nothing See **Dogberry and the Watch**

Williams
Henry V **13:** 502; **16:** 183; **28:** 146; **30:** 169, 259, 278

witches
Macbeth
and supernaturalism **3:** 171, 172, 173, 175, 177, 182, 183, 184, 185, 194, 196, 198, 202, 207, 208, 213, 219, 229, 239; **16:** 317; **19:** 245; **20:** 92, 175, 213, 279, 283, 374, 387, 406, 413; **25:** 235; **28:** 339; **29:** 91, 101, 109, 120

Wolsey (Cardinal Wolsey)
Henry VIII **2:** 15, 18, 19, 23, 24, 38; **22:** 182; **24:** 80, 91, 112, 113, 129, 140; **37:** 109; **41:** 129; **56:** 248, 262; **61:** 44

York (Edmund of Langley, Duke of York)
Richard II **6:** 287, 364, 368, 388, 402, 414; **24:** 263, 320, 322, 364, 395, 414; **39:** 243, 279; **58:** 241

York (Richard Plantagenet, Duke of York)
Henry VI, Parts 1, 2, and 3
death of **13:** 131; **60:** 33

Cumulative Topic Index

The Cumulative Topic Index indentifies the principal topics of discussion in the criticism of each play and non-dramatic poem. The topics are arranged alphabetically. Page references indicate the beginning page number of each essay containing substantial commentary on that topic. A parenthetical reference after a topic indicates that the topic is extensively discussed in that volume.

absurdities, inconsistencies, and shortcomings
The Two Gentlemen of Verona **6:** 435, 436, 437, 439, 464, 507, 541, 560; **54:** 295, 311

accident or chance
Romeo and Juliet **5:** 418, 444, 448, 467, 470, 487, 573

acting and dissimulation
Richard II **6:** 264, 267, 307, 310, 315, 368, 393, 409; **24:** 339, 345, 346, 349, 352, 356

adolescence
Romeo and Juliet **33:** 249, 255, 257

adultery
The Comedy of Errors **34:** 215

aggression
Coriolanus **9:** 112, 142, 174, 183, 189, 198; **30:** 79, 111, 125, 142; **44:** 11, 79

alienation
Timon of Athens **1:** 523; **27:** 161

allegorical elements
Antony and Cleopatra **52:** 5
King Lear **16:** 311; **61:** 215
Measure for Measure **52:** 69
The Merchant of Venice **4:** 224, 250, 261, 268, 270, 273, 282, 289, 324, 336, 344, 350
The Phoenix and Turtle **10:** 7, 8, 9, 16, 17, 48; **38:** 334, 378; **51:** 138, 188
The Rape of Lucrece **10:** 89, 93
Richard II **6:** 264, 283, 323, 385
Richard III **52:** 5; **62:** 60
The Tempest **8:** 294, 295, 302, 307, 308, 312, 326, 328, 336, 345, 364; **42:** 320; **61:** 326
Troilus and Cressida **52:** 5
Venus and Adonis **10:** 427, 434, 439, 449, 454, 462, 480; **28:** 355; **33:** 309, 330

ambiguity
Antony and Cleopatra **6:** 53, 111, 161, 163, 180, 189, 208, 211, 228; **13:** 368
Hamlet **1:** 92, 160, 198, 227, 230, 234, 247, 249; **21:** 72; **35:** 241
King John **13:** 152; **41:** 243
Measure for Measure **2:** 417, 420, 432, 446, 449, 452, 474, 479, 482, 486, 495, 505
A Midsummer Night's Dream **3:** 401, 459, 486; **45:** 169
Richard III **44:** 11; **47:** 15
Sonnets **10:** 251, 256; **28:** 385; **40:** 221, 228, 268
Troilus and Cressida **3:** 544, 568, 583, 587, 589, 599, 611, 621; **27:** 400; **43:** 305
Twelfth Night **1:** 554, 639; **34:** 287, 316
Venus and Adonis **10:** 434, 454, 459, 462, 466, 473, 480, 486, 489; **33:** 352; **51:** 368, 377, 388

ambition or pride
Henry IV, Parts 1 and 2 **57:** 94
Henry VIII **2:** 15, 38, 67
Macbeth **44:** 284, 324;
Richard III **52:** 201, 223

ambivalent or ironic elements
Henry VI, Parts 1, 2, and 3 **3:** 69, 151, 154; **39:** 160; **56:** 131; **63:** 131, 149, 158
Richard III **44:** 11
Troilus and Cressida **43:** 340; **59:** 287

amorality, question of
The Two Noble Kinsmen **9:** 447, 460, 492

amour-passion or Liebestod myth
Romeo and Juliet **5:** 484, 489, 528, 530, 542, 550, 575; **32:** 256; **51:** 195, 219, 236

amputations, significance of
Titus Andronicus **48:** 264

anachronisms
Julius Caesar **7:** 331

androgyny
Antony and Cleopatra **13:** 530
As You Like It **23:** 98, 100, 122, 138, 143, 144; **34:** 172, 177; **46:** 134; **57:** 13
Romeo and Juliet **13:** 530
Twelfth Night **60:** 129

anti-Catholic rhetoric
King John **22:** 120; **25:** 98

anti-romantic elements
As You Like It **34:** 72

antithetical or contradictory elements
Macbeth **3:** 185, 213, 271, 302; **25:** 235; **29:** 76, 127; **47:** 41

anxiety
Romeo and Juliet **13:** 235; **60:** 96

appearance, perception, and illusion
A Midsummer Night's Dream **3:** 368, 411, 425, 427, 434, 447, 459, 466, 474, 477, 486, 497, 516; **19:** 21; **22:** 39; **28:** 15; **29:** 175,190; **45:** 136

Appearance versus Reality (Volume 34: 1, 5, 12, 23, 45, 54)
All's Well That Ends Well **7:** 37, 76, 93; **26:** 117
As You Like It **34:** 130, 131; **46:** 105; **57:** 35, 40
The Comedy of Errors **34:** 194, 201
Coriolanus **30:** 142
Cymbeline **4:** 87, 93, 103, 162; **36:** 99; **47:** 228, 286
Hamlet **1:** 95, 116, 166, 169, 198; **35:** 82, 126, 132, 144, 238; **44:** 248; **45:** 28
Macbeth **3:** 241, 248; **25:** 235
The Merchant of Venice **4:** 209, 261, 344; **12:** 65; **22:** 69
Much Ado about Nothing **8:** 17, 18, 48, 63, 69, 73, 75, 79, 88, 95, 115; **31:** 198, 209; **55:** 259, 268
The Taming of the Shrew **9:** 343, 350, 353, 365, 369, 370, 381, 390, 430; **12:** 416; **31:** 326; **55:** 278, 299, 334
Timon of Athens **1:** 495, 500, 515, 523; **52:** 311, 329
The Two Gentlemen of Verona **6:** 494, 502, 511, 519, 529, 532, 549, 560
Twelfth Night **34:** 293, 301, 311, 316
The Winter's Tale **7:** 429, 446, 479; **57:** 336

appetite
Twelfth Night **1:** 563, 596, 609, 615; **52:** 57

archetypal or mythic elements
Macbeth **16:** 317

archetypal structure
Pericles **2:** 570, 580, 582, 584, 588; **25:** 365; **51:** 71, 79

aristocracy and aristocratic values
As You Like It **34:** 120
Hamlet **42:** 212
Julius Caesar **16:** 231; **22:** 280; **30:** 379; **50:** 194, 196, 211

art and nature
See also **nature**
Pericles **22:** 315; **36:** 233
The Phoenix and Turtle **10:** 7, 42

art versus nature
See also **nature**
As You Like It **5:** 128, 130, 148; **34:** 147; **57:** 35, 75
The Tempest **8:** 396, 404; **29:** 278, 297, 362; **61:** 356
The Winter's Tale **7:** 377, 381, 397, 419, 452; **36:** 289, 318; **45:** 329; **57:** 278

artificial nature
Love's Labour's Lost **2:** 315, 317, 324, 330; **23:** 207, 233; **54:** 234, 248, 257, 263

Athens
Timon of Athens **27:** 223, 230

Athens and the forest, contrast between
A Midsummer Night's Dream **3:** 381, 427, 459, 466, 497, 502; **29:** 175

assassination
Julius Caesar **7:** 156, 161, 179, 191, 200, 221, 264, 272, 279, 284, 350; **25:** 272; **30:** 326

audience interpretation
Julius Caesar **48:** 240

audience perception
The Comedy of Errors **1:** 37, 50, 56; **19:** 54; **34:** 258; **54:** 136, 144
King Lear **19:** 295; **28:** 325; **61:** 176
Richard II **24:** 414, 423; **39:** 295
Pericles **42:** 352; **48:** 364

audience perception, Shakespeare's manipulation of
The Winter's Tale **7:** 394, 429, 456, 483, 501; **13:** 417; **19:** 401, 431, 441; **25:** 339; **45:** 374

audience perspective
All's Well That Ends Well **7:** 81, 104, 109, 116, 121

audience response
Antony and Cleopatra **48:** 206; **58:** 88
Hamlet **28:** 325; **32:** 238; **35:** 167; **44:** 107
Julius Caesar **7:** 179, 238, 253, 255, 272, 316, 320, 336, 350; **19:** 321; **48:** 240; **63:** 231
Macbeth **20:** 17, 400, 406; **29:** 139, 146, 155, 165; **44:** 306
Measure for Measure **48:** 1
Richard II **58:** 293
The Two Noble Kinsmen **58:** 330

audience versus character perceptions
The Two Gentlemen of Verona **6:** 499, 519, 524

authenticity
The Phoenix and Turtle **10:** 7, 8, 16
Sonnets **10:** 153, 154, 230, 243; **48:** 325; **62:** 128

Authorship Controversy (Volume 41: 2, 5, 18, 32, 42, 48, 57, 61, 63, 66, 76, 81, 85, 98, 110)
Cymbeline **4:** 17, 21, 35, 48, 56, 78
Henry VI, Parts 1, 2, and 3 **3:** 16, 18, 19, 20, 21, 26, 27, 29, 31, 35, 39, 41, 55, 66; **24:** 51; **56:** 77
Henry VIII **2:** 16, 18, 19, 22, 23, 27, 28, 31, 35, 36, 42, 43, 44, 46, 48, 51, 58, 64, 68; **41:** 129, 146, 158, 171
Love's Labour's Lost **2:** 299, 300; **32:** 308
Pericles **2:** 538, 540, 543, 544, 545, 546, 548, 550, 551, 553, 556, 558, 564, 565, 568, 576, 586; **15:** 132, 141, 148, 152; **16:** 391, 399; **25:** 365; **36:** 198, 244
Timon of Athens **1:** 464, 466, 467, 469, 474, 477, 478, 480, 490, 499, 507, 518; **16:** 351; **20:** 433
Titus Andronicus **4:** 613, 614, 615, 616, 617, 619, 623, 624, 625, 626, 628, 631, 632, 635, 642; **62:** 208, 254
The Two Gentlemen of Verona **6:** 435, 436, 437, 438, 439, 449, 466, 476
The Two Noble Kinsmen **58:** 330; **63:** 361
Shakespeare not a co-author **9:** 445, 447, 455, 461
Shakespearean portions of the text **9:** 446, 447, 448, 455, 456, 457, 460, 462, 463, 471, 479, 486; **41:** 308, 317, 355; **58:** 330
Shakespeare's part in the overall conception or design **9:** 444, 446, 448, 456, 457, 460, 480, 481, 486, 490; **37:** 313; **41:** 326; **50:** 326

autobiographical elements
As You Like It **5:** 25, 35, 43, 50, 55, 61
The Comedy of Errors **1:** 16, 18
Cymbeline **4:** 43, 46; **36:** 134
Hamlet **1:** 98, 115, 119; **13:** 487
Henry VI, Parts 1, 2, and 3 **3:** 41, 55
King John **9:** 209, 218, 245, 248, 260, 292
King Lear **2:** 131, 136, 149, 165
Measure for Measure **2:** 406, 410, 414, 431, 434, 437
A Midsummer Night's Dream **3:** 365, 371, 379, 381, 389, 391, 396, 402, 432
Othello **4:** 440, 444
Pericles **2:** 551, 554, 555, 563, 581
The Phoenix and Turtle **10:** 14, 18, 42, 48; **51:** 155
Sonnets **10:** 159, 160, 166, 167, 175, 176, 182, 196, 205, 213, 215, 226, 233, 238, 240, 251, 279, 283, 302, 309, 325, 337, 377; **13:** 487; **16:** 461; **28:** 363, 385; **42:** 296; **48:** 325
The Tempest **8:** 302, 308, 312, 324, 326, 345, 348, 353, 364, 380; **61:** 272
Timon of Athens **1:** 462, 467, 470, 473, 474, 478, 480; **27:** 166, 175
Titus Andronicus **4:** 619, 624, 625, 664
Troilus and Cressida **3:** 548, 554, 557, 558, 574, 606, 630; **59:** 225
Twelfth Night **1:** 557, 561, 599; **34:** 338
The Winter's Tale **7:** 395, 397, 410, 419

avarice
The Merry Wives of Windsor **5:** 335, 353, 369, 376, 390, 395, 402

battle of Agincourt
Henry V **5:** 197, 199, 213, 246, 257, 281, 287, 289, 293, 310, 318; **19:** 217; **30:** 181

battle of the sexes
Much Ado about Nothing **8:** 14, 16, 19, 48, 91, 95, 111, 121, 125; **31:** 231, 245; **55:** 199

bawdy elements
As You Like It **46:** 122
Cymbeline **36:** 155

bear-baiting
Twelfth Night **19:** 42

beauty
Sonnets **10:** 247; **51:** 288
Venus and Adonis **10:** 420, 423, 427, 434, 454, 480; **33:** 330, 352

bed-trick
All's Well That Ends Well **7:** 8, 26, 27, 29, 32, 41, 86, 93, 98, 113, 116, 126; **13:** 84; **26:** 117; **28:** 38; **38:** 65, 118; **49:** 46; **54:** 52; **55:** 109, 131, 176; **63:** 50, 60
Measure for Measure **13:** 84; **49:** 313; **54:** 52

Beginnings and Endings in Shakespeare's Works (Volume 54: 2, 6, 19, 24, 30, 35, 39, 43, 52, 58, 65, 75, 84, 96, 103, 110, 114, 119, 125)
All's Well That Ends Well **54:** 30, 52
Antony and Cleopatra **54:** 6
Coriolanus **54:** 6
Hamlet **54:** 2, 6, 19, 96; **59:** 18, 74
Henry VIII **54:** 35
Julius Caesar **54:** 6
King Lear **54:** 2, 6, 103, 110, 114; **60:** 46, 65, 75; **61:** 262
Love's Labour's Lost **54:** 58
Macbeth **54:** 2, 6, 84
Measure for Measure **54:** 52, 65
The Merchant of Venice **54:** 52, 65
Othello **54:** 2, 6, 119; **60:** 2, 91
Pericles **54:** 35
Romeo and Juliet **54:** 6, 125
Richard III **54:** 84
The Taming of the Shrew **54:** 58, 65
The Tempest **54:** 19
Troilus and Cressida **54:** 84
Twelfh Night **54:** 19
The Two Gentlemen of Verona **54:**
The Two Noble Kinsmen **54:** 35

betrothal
All's Well That Ends Well **63:** 84

Biblical references
Henry IV, Parts 1 and 2 **57:** 147

bird imagery
The Phoenix and Turtle **10:** 21, 27; **38:** 329, 350, 367; **51:** 145, 181, 184

body, role of
Troilus and Cressida **42:** 66; **59:** 287, 306

body politic, metaphor of
Coriolanus **22:** 248; **30:** 67, 96, 105, 125; **50:** 105, 110, 119, 140, 145, 152

bonding
The Merchant of Venice **4:** 293, 317, 336; **13:** 37

British nationalism
See also **nationalism and patriotism**
Cymbeline **4:** 19, 78, 89, 93, 129, 141, 159, 167; **32:** 373; **36:** 129; **45:** 6; **47:** 219, 265; **61:** 54
Henry VIII **61:** 92, 111

brutal elements
A Midsummer Night's Dream **3:** 445, 491, 497, 511; **12:** 259, 262, 298; **16:** 34; **19:** 21; **29:** 183, 225, 263, 269; **45:** 169

Cade scenes
Henry VI, Parts 1, 2, and 3 **50:** 45, 51; **56:** 117, 122, 131, 180; **63:** 149, 176

Caesarism
Julius Caesar **7:** 159, 160, 161, 167, 169, 174, 191, 205, 218, 253, 310; **30:** 316, 321; **50:** 196, 234

Calvinist implications
Hamlet **48:** 195

capriciousness of the young lovers
A Midsummer Night's Dream **3:** 372, 395, 402, 411, 423, 437, 441, 450, 497, 498; **29:** 175, 269; **45:** 107

caricature
The Merry Wives of Windsor **5:** 343, 347, 348, 350, 385, 397

carnival elements
Henry IV, Parts 1 and 2 **28:** 203; **32:** 103
Henry VI, Parts 1, 2, and 3 **22:** 156; **63:** 149
Richard II **19:** 151; **39:** 273

casket scenes
The Merchant of Venice **49:** 27

Catholic components
Henry IV, Parts 1 and 2 **57:** 167

censorship
Richard II **24:** 260, 261, 262, 263, 386; **42:** 118; **52:** 141, 144

ceremonies, rites, and rituals, importance of
See also **pageantry**
Coriolanus **9:** 139, 148, 169
Hamlet **13:** 268; **28:** 232
Henry VI, Parts 1, 2, and 3 **63:** 185
Julius Caesar **7:** 150, 210, 255, 259, 268, 284, 316, 331, 339, 356; **13:** 260; **22:** 137; **30:** 374; **50:** 258, 269; **63:** 295
A Midsummer Night's Dream **58:** 189
Richard II **6:** 270, 294, 315, 368, 381, 397, 409, 414; **24:** 274, 356, 411, 414, 419
Titus Andronicus **27:** 261; **32:** 265; **48:** 264; **62:** 254
The Two Noble Kinsmen **9:** 492, 498

change
Henry VIII **2:** 27, 65, 72, 81

characterization
As You Like It **5:** 19, 24, 25, 36, 39, 54, 82, 86, 116, 148; **34:** 72; **48:** 42
The Comedy of Errors **1:** 13, 21, 31, 34, 46, 49, 50, 55, 56; **19:** 54; **25:** 63; **34:** 194, 201, 208, 245; **54:** 144, 176
Henry IV, Parts 1 and 2 **1:** 321, 328, 332, 333, 336, 344, 365, 383, 385, 389, 391, 397, 401; **19:** 195; **39:** 123, 137; **42:** 99, 162; **49:** 93; **57:** 88, 120, 156, 167, 181
Henry V **5:** 186, 189, 192, 193, 199, 219, 230, 233, 252, 276, 293; **30:** 227, 278; **42:** 162
Henry VI, Parts 1, 2, and 3 **3:** 18, 20, 24, 25, 31, 57, 64, 73, 77, 109, 119, 151; **24:** 22, 28, 38, 42, 45, 47; **39:** 160; **47:** 32; **63:** 114
Henry VIII **2:** 17, 23, 25, 32, 35, 39; **24:** 106
King John **9:** 222, 224, 229, 240, 250, 292; **41:** 205, 215; **56:** 365
King Lear **2:** 108, 125, 145, 162, 191; **16:** 311; **28:** 223; **46:** 177, 210
Love's Labour's Lost **2:** 303, 310, 317, 322, 328, 342; **23:** 237, 250, 252; **38:** 232; **47:** 35
Macbeth **20:** 12, 318, 324, 329, 353, 363, 367, 374, 387; **28:** 339; **29:** 101, 109, 146, 155, 165; **45:** 67; **47:** 41; **57:** 189, 194, 236, 256, 263, 267
Measure for Measure **2:** 388, 390, 391, 396, 406, 420, 421, 446, 466, 475, 484, 505, 516, 524; **23:** 299, 405; **33:**
The Merry Wives of Windsor **5:** 332, 334, 335, 337, 338, 351, 360, 363, 366, 374, 379, 392; **18:** 74, 75; **38:** 264, 273, 313, 319
The Tempest **8:** 287, 289, 292, 294, 295, 308, 326, 334, 336; **28:** 415; **42:** 332; **45:** 219
Titus Andronicus **4:** 613, 628, 632, 635, 640, 644, 647, 650, 675; **27:** 293; **43:** 170, 176,;
Troilus and Cressida **3:** 538, 539, 540, 541, 548, 566, 571, 604, 611, 621; **27:** 381, 391; **59:** 234, 245, 251, 257, 261, 265, 272
Twelfth Night **1:** 539, 540, 543, 545, 550, 554, 581, 594; **26:** 257, 337, 342, 346, 364, 366, 371, 374; **34:** 281, 293, 311, 338; **46:** 286, 324
The Two Gentlemen of Verona **6:** 438, 442, 445, 447, 449, 458, 462, 560; **12:** 458; **40:** 312, 327, 330, 365; **54:** 338; **63:** 336
The Two Noble Kinsmen **9:** 457, 461, 471, 474; **41:** 340, 385; **50:** 305, 326
The Winter's Tale **47:** 25

chastity
A Midsummer Night's Dream **45:** 143

Chaucer's Criseyde, compared with
Troilus and Cressida **43:** 305

chivalry
Troilus and Cressida **16:** 84; **27:** 370, 374
The Two Noble Kinsmen **50:** 305, 348

Christian elements
See also **religious, mythic, or spiritual content**
As You Like It **5:** 39, 98, 162; **57:** 31
Coriolanus **30:** 111
King Lear **2:** 137, 170, 179, 188, 191, 197, 207, 218, 222, 226, 229, 238, 249, 265, 286; **22:** 233, 271; **25:** 218; **46:** 276; **52:** 95; **60:** 75; **61:** 194, 262
Macbeth **3:** 194, 239, 260, 269, 275, 286, 293, 297, 318; **20:** 203, 206, 210, 256, 262, 289, 291, 294; **44:** 341, 366; **47:** 41; **57:** 236
Measure for Measure **2:** 391, 394, 399, 421, 437, 449, 466, 479, 491, 511, 522; **48:** 1; **49:** 325; **60:** 12
The Merchant of Venice **52:** 89
Much Ado about Nothing **8:** 17, 19, 29, 55, 95, 104, 111, 115; **31:** 209; **55:** 228
The Phoenix and Turtle **10:** 21, 24, 31; **38:** 326; **51:** 162, 171, 181
The Rape of Lucrece **10:** 77, 80, 89, 96, 98, 109; **59:** 165

Topic Index

Sonnets **10:** 191, 256
Titus Andronicus **4:** 656, 680
Twelfth Night **46:** 338
The Two Gentlemen of Verona **6:** 438, 494, 514, 532, 555, 564; **63:** 357
The Winter's Tale **7:** 381, 387, 402, 410, 417, 419, 425, 429, 436, 452, 460, 501; **36:** 318; **60:** 40

as Christian play
King Lear **48:** 222

Chorus, role of
Henry V **49:** 194, 200, 211, 219, 260

church versus state
King John **9:** 209, 212, 222, 235, 240; **22:** 120

civilization versus barbarism
Titus Andronicus **4:** 653; **27:** 293; **28:** 249; **32:** 265; **62:** 265, 270

Clarissa, (Samuel Richardson), compared with
King Lear **48:** 277
Measure for Measure **48:** 277
Othello **48:** 277
Titus Andronicus **48:** 277

class distinctions, conflict, and relations
General Commentary **50:** 1, 34
Henry V **28:** 146
Henry VI, Parts 1, 2, and 3 **37:** 97; **39:** 187; **50:** 45, 51; **56:** 117, 131; **63:** 114, 176
The Merry Wives of Windsor **5:** 338, 343, 346, 347, 366, 390, 395, 400, 402; **22:** 93; **28:** 69
A Midsummer Night's Dream **22:** 23; **25:** 36; **45:** 160; **50:** 74, 86
The Taming of the Shrew **31:** 300, 351; **50:** 64, 74; **55:** 342
The Two Noble Kinsmen **50:** 295, 305, 310

classical influence and sources
The Comedy of Errors **1:** 13, 14, 16, 31, 32, 43, 61; **54:** 169
The Tempest **29:** 278, 343, 362, 368; **61:** 362

Clowns and Fools in Shakespeare's Works (Volume 46: 1, 14, 18, 24, 29, 33, 48, 52, 60)
As You Like It **5:** 24, 28, 30, 32, 36, 39, 54, 61, 63, 72, 75, 76, 77, 79, 84, 86, 93, 98, 114, 118, 135, 138, 166; **23:; 152; 34:** 72, 85, 147, 161; **46:** 88, 105, 117, 122
King Lear **2:** 108, 112, 125, 156, 162, 245, 278, 284; **11:** 17, 158, 169; **22:** 227; **25:** 202; **28:** 223; **46:** 191, 205, 210, 218, 225
Twelfth Night **1:** 543, 548, 558, 561, 563, 566, 570, 572, 603, 620, 642, 655, 658; **26:** 233, 364; **46:** 297, 303, 310

colonialism
Henry V **22:** 103
A Midsummer Night's Dream **53:** 32
The Tempest **13:** 424, 440; **15:** 228, 268, 269, 270, 271, 272, 273; **19:** 421; **25:** 357, 382; **28:** 249; **29:** 343, 368; **32:** 338, 367, 400; **42:** 320; **45:** 200, 280; **53:** 11, 21, 45, 67; **61:** 297, 307
Titus Andronicus **62:** 270

combat
King Lear **22:** 365
Macbeth **22:** 365

comedy of affectation
Love's Labour's Lost **2:** 302, 303, 304; **23:** 191, 224, 226, 228, 233

comic and tragic elements, combination of
King Lear **2:** 108, 110, 112, 125, 156, 162, 245, 278, 284; **46:** 191
Measure for Measure **16:** 102
Romeo and Juliet **5:** 496, 524, 528, 547, 559; **46:** 78
Troilus and Cressida **43:** 351

comic and farcical elements
All's Well That Ends Well **26:** 97, 114; **48:** 65; **55:** 148, 154, 164; **63:** 10
Antony and Cleopatra **6:** 52, 85, 104, 125, 131, 151, 192, 202, 219; **47:** 77, 124, 149, 165; **58:** 41
The Comedy of Errors **1:** 14, 16, 19, 23, 30, 34, 35, 43, 46, 50, 55, 56, 59, 61; **19:** 54; **26:** 183, 186, 188, 190; **34:** 190, 245; **54:** 136, 144, 189
Coriolanus **9:** 8, 9, 14, 53, 80, 106
Cymbeline **4:** 35, 56, 113, 141; **15:** 111, 122; **47:** 296
Henry IV, Parts 1 and 2 **1:** 286, 290, 314, 327, 328, 336, 353; **19:** 195; **25:** 109; **39:** 72; **57:** 120
Henry V **5:** 185, 188, 191, 192, 217, 230, 233, 241, 252, 260, 276; **19:** 217; **28:** 121; **30:** 193, 202
Henry VI, Parts 1, 2, and 3 **63:** 144, 149
The Merry Wives of Windsor **5:** 336, 338, 346, 350, 360, 369, 373; **18:** 74, 75, 84; **59:** 105
A Midsummer Night's Dream **58:** 169
Richard II **24:** 262, 263, 395; **39:** 243
Twelfth Night **26:** 233, 257, 337, 342, 371; **51:** 1; **52:** 57
Venus and Adonis **10:** 429, 434, 439, 442, 459, 462, 489; **33:** 352; **51:** 377

comic form
As You Like It **46:** 105; **51:** 1; **57:** 2
Love's Labour' Lost **54:** 257, 263
Measure for Measure **2:** 456, 460, 479, 482, 491, 514, 516; **13:** 94, 104; **23:** 309, 326, 327; **49:** 349

comic resolution
As You Like It **52:** 63
Love's Labour's Lost **2:** 335, 340; **16:** 17; **19:** 92; **38:** 209; **51:** 1; **54:** 240, 248, 274

comic, tragic, and romantic elements, fusion of
The Winter's Tale **7:** 390, 394, 396, 399, 410, 412, 414, 429, 436, 479, 483, 490, 501; **13:** 417; **15:** 514, 524, 532; **25:** 339; **36:** 295, 380; **57:** 347

commodity
King John **9:** 224, 229, 245, 260, 275, 280, 297; **19:** 182; **25:** 98; **41:** 228, 269; **56:** 335

communication, failure of
Troilus and Cressida **43:** 277

compassion, theme of
The Tempest **42:** 339

complex or enigmatic nature
The Phoenix and Turtle **10:** 7, 14, 35, 42; **38:** 326, 357; **51:** 145, 162

composition date
The Comedy of Errors **1:** 18, 23, 34, 55
Henry VIII **2:** 19, 22, 35; **24:** 129
Pericles **2:** 537, 544
Sonnets **10:** 153, 154, 161, 166, 196, 217, 226, 270, 277; **28:** 363, 385
Twelfth Night **37:** 78

conclusion
All's Well That Ends Well **38:** 123, 132, 142; **55:** 148, 154, 170
Love's Labour's Lost **38:** 172; **54:** 240, 248, 274
Troilus and Cressida **3:** 538, 549, 558, 566, 574, 583, 594
comedy vs. tragedy **43:** 351; **59:** 278

conflict between Christianity and Judaism
The Merchant of Venice **4:** 224, 250, 268, 289, 324, 344; **12:** 67, 70, 72, 76; **22:** 69; **25:** 257; **40:** 117, 127, 166, 181; **48:** 54, 77; **53:** 105, 159, 214

conflict between idealism and pragmatism
Hamlet **60:** 71

conscience
Cymbeline **61:** 136
Macbeth **52:** 15
Richard III **8:** 148, 152, 162, 165, 190, 197, 201, 206, 210, 228, 232, 239, 243, 252, 258; **39:** 341; **52:** 5, 196, 205

as consciously philosophical
The Phoenix and Turtle **10:** 7, 21, 24, 31, 48; **38:** 342, 378

conspiracy or treason
The Tempest **16:** 426; **19:** 357; **25:** 382; **29:** 377
Henry V **49:** 223

constancy and faithfulness
The Phoenix and Turtle **10:** 18, 20, 21, 48; **38:** 329

construing the truth
Julius Caesar **7:** 320, 336, 343, 350; **37:** 229; **63:** 287, 295

consummation of marriage
Othello **22:** 207

contemptus mundi
Antony and Cleopatra **6:** 85, 133

contractual and economic relations
Henry IV, Parts 1 and 2 **13:** 213
Richard II **13:** 213; **49:** 602

contradiction, paradox, and opposition
As You Like It **46:** 105
Romeo and Juliet **5:** 421, 427, 431, 496, 509, 513, 516, 520, 525, 528, 538; **33:** 287; **44:** 11
Troilus and Cressida **43:** 377; **59:** 318

contrasting dramatic worlds
Henry IV, Parts 1 and 2 **14:** 56, 60, 61, 84, 105; **48:** 95; **49:** 162; **57:** 183
The Merchant of Venice **44:** 11

contrasts and oppositions
Othello **4:** 421, 455, 457, 462, 508; **25:** 189

corruption in society
As You Like It **46:** 94; **57:** 35
King John **9:** 222, 234, 280, 297

costume
As You Like It **46:** 117
Hamlet **21:** 81
Henry VIII **24:** 82, 87; **28:** 184
Richard II **24:** 274, 278, 291, 304, 325, 356, 364, 423
Romeo and Juliet **11:** 505, 509
Troilus and Cressida **18:** 289, 371, 406, 419; **59:** 323

counsel
The Winter's Tale **19:** 401

Court of Love
The Phoenix and Turtle **10:** 9, 24, 50

court society
The Winter's Tale **16:** 410; **57:** 305, 336

courtly love
Troilus and Cressida **22:** 58; **59:** 349

courtly love tradition, influence of
Romeo and Juliet **5:** 505, 542, 575; **33:** 233

courtship and marriage
See also **marriage**
As You Like It **34:** 109, 177; **48:** 32; **51:** 44
Much Ado about Nothing **8:** 29, 44, 48, 95, 115, 121, 125; **31:** 191, 231; **51:** 33, 44; **55:** 209

credibility
Twelfth Night **1:** 540, 542, 543, 554, 562, 581, 587

critical history
Henry IV, Parts 1 and 2 **42:** 185; **48:** 167

cross-dressing
Twelfth Night **62:** 297, 319

cynicism
Troilus and Cressida **43:** 298

dance
Henry VI, Parts 1, 2, and 3 **22:** 156

dance and patterned action
Love's Labour's Lost **2:** 308, 342; **23:** 191, 237

dark elements
All's Well That Ends Well **7:** 27, 37, 39, 43, 54, 109, 113, 116; **26:** 85; **48:** 65; **50:** 59; **54:** 30; **55:** 164, 170
Twelfth Night **46:** 310

Death (**Volume 60:** 2, 12, 21, 26, 33, 46, 71, 91)
Antony and Cleopatra **60:** 46
Coriolanus **60:** 46
Hamlet **60:** 46
Henry IV, Parts 1 and 2 **60:** 26
Henry V **60:** 26
Henry VI, Parts 1, 2, and 3 **60:** 33
Julius Caesar **60:** 46
King Lear **60:** 2, 46, 65, 75
Macbeth **60:** 46, 84
Measure for Measure **60:** 12
Othello **60:** 2, 46, 91
Richard II **60:** 21, 46
Romeo and Juliet **60:** 96
Timon of Athens **60:** 46
The Winter's Tale **60:** 2, 40

death, decay, nature's destructiveness
Antony and Cleopatra **47:** 71
As You Like It **46:** 169
Hamlet **1:** 144, 153, 188, 198, 221, 242; **13:** 502; **28:** 280, 311; **35:** 241; **42:** 279; **60:** 71, 91, 194
King Lear **2:** 93, 94, 101, 104, 106, 109, 112, 116, 129, 131, 137, 143, 147, 149, 156, 160, 170, 179, 188, 197, 207, 218, 222, 226, 231, 238, 241, 245, 249, 253, 265, 269, 273; **16:** 301; **25:** 202, 218; **31:** 77, 117, 137, 142; **46:** 264
Love's Labour's Lost **2:** 305, 331, 344, 348
Measure for Measure **2:** 394, 452, 516; **25:** 12; **49:** 370
Venus and Adonis **10:** 419, 427, 434, 451, 454, 462, 466, 473, 480, 489; **25:** 305; **33:** 309, 321, 347, 352, 363, 370

decay of heroic ideals
Henry VI, Parts 1, 2, and 3 **3:** 119, 126; **56:** 95; **63:** 158

deception, disguise, and duplicity
As You Like It **46:** 134; **57:** 40, 45
Henry IV, Parts 1 and 2 **1:** 397, 406, 425; **42:** 99; **47:** 1, 60; **48:** 95
The Merry Wives of Windsor **5:** 332, 334, 336, 354, 355, 379; **22:** 93; **47:** 308, 314, 321, 325, 344
Much Ado about Nothing **8:** 29, 55, 63, 69, 79, 82, 88, 108, 115; **31:** 191, 198; **55:** 236
Sonnets **25:** 374; **40:** 221
The Taming of the Shrew **12:** 416

Deconstructionist interpretation of
Pericles **48:** 364

deposition scene
Richard II **42:** 118

Desire (**Volume 38:** 1, 19, 31, 40, 48, 56)
All's Well That Ends Well **38:** 96, 99, 109, 118; **55:** 122
As You Like It **37:** 43; **52:** 63; **60:** 115
Henry IV, Parts 1 and 2 **60:** 129
Love's Labour's Lost **38:** 185, 194, 200, 209
The Merchant of Venice **22:** 3; **40:** 142; **45:** 17
The Merry Wives of Windsor **38:** 286, 297, 300
Romeo and Juliet **51:** 227, 236
Troilus and Cressida **43:** 317, 329, 340; **59:** 337
Twelfth Night **60:** 115

disappointment, theme of
The Merchant of Venice **53:** 211

discrepancy between prophetic ending and preceding action
Henry VIII **2:** 22, 25, 31, 46, 49, 56, 60, 65, 68, 75, 81; **32:** 148; **41:** 190; **56:** 273

disillusioned or cynical tone
Troilus and Cressida **3:** 544, 548, 554, 557, 558, 571, 574, 630, 642; **18:** 284, 332, 403, 406, 423; **27:** 376; **59:** 234

disorder
Troilus and Cressida **3:** 578, 589, 599, 604, 609; **18:** 332, 406, 412, 423; **27:** 366; **54:** 84; **55:** 48; **59:** 251

disorder and civil dissension
Henry VI, Parts 1, 2, and 3 **3:** 59, 67, 76, 92, 103, 126; **13:** 131; **16:** 183; **24:** 11, 17, 28, 31, 47; **25:** 102; **28:** 112; **39:** 154, 177, 187, 196, 205; **56:** 80, 110; **63:** 114, 185, 202

displacement
All's Well That Ends Well **22:** 78
Measure for Measure **22:** 78

divine providence
Cymbeline **61:** 144

divine right versus justice
Henry IV **49:** 116; **57:** 88, 130

divine vs. worldly
King Lear **49:** 1

divine will, role of
Romeo and Juliet **5:** 485, 493, 505, 533, 573

divorce
All's Well That Ends Well **63:** 96

domestic elements
As You Like It **46:** 142
Coriolanus **42:** 218; **50:** 145
Venus and Adonis **51:** 359

double-plot
King Lear **2:** 94, 95, 100, 101, 104, 112, 116, 124, 131, 133, 156, 253, 257; **46:** 254
Troilus and Cressida **3:** 569, 613

doubling of roles
Pericles **15:** 150, 152, 167, 173, 180

dramatic elements
Sonnets **10:** 155, 182, 240, 251, 283, 367
Venus and Adonis **10:** 459, 462, 486

dramatic shortcomings or failure
As You Like It **5:** 19, 42, 52, 61, 65
Love's Labour's Lost **2:** 299, 301, 303, 322; **54:** 240, 248
Romeo and Juliet **5:** 416, 418, 420, 426, 436, 437, 448, 464, 467, 469, 480, 487, 524, 562

dramatic structure
The Comedy of Errors **1:** 19, 27, 40, 43, 46, 50; **26:** 186, 190; **34:** 190, 229, 233; **37:** 12 **54:** 136, 155, 189
Cymbeline **4:** 17, 18, 19, 20, 21, 22, 24, 38, 43, 48, 53, 64, 68, 89, 116, 129, 141; **22:** 302, 365; **25:** 319; **36:** 115, 125; **60:** 240; **61:** 2
Othello **4:** 370, 390, 399, 427, 488, 506, 517, 569; **22:** 207; **28:** 243; **53:** 261
The Winter's Tale **7:** 382, 390, 396, 399, 402, 407, 414, 429, 432, 473, 479, 493, 497, 501; **15:** 528; **25:** 339; **36:** 289, 295, 362, 380; **45:** 297, 344, 358, 366; **57:** 278, 285, 347

as dream-play
A Midsummer Night's Dream **3:** 365, 370, 372, 377, 389, 391; **29:** 190; **45:** 117; **58:** 181

Dreams in Shakespeare (Volume 45: 1, 10, 17, 28, 40, 48, 58, 67, 75)
Antony and Cleopatra **45:** 28
Cymbeline **4:** 162, 167; **44:** 28; **45:** 67, 75
Hamlet **45:** 28
Julius Caesar **45:** 10
A Midsummer Night's Dream **45:** 96, 107, 117
Richard III **62:** 14, 18
Romeo and Juliet **45:** 40
The Tempest **45:** 236, 247, 259

dualisms
Antony and Cleopatra **19:** 304; **27:** 82; **58:** 2, 71, 79, 105
Cymbeline **4:** 29, 64, 73

duration of time
As You Like It **5:** 44, 45
A Midsummer Night's Dream **3:** 362, 370, 380, 386, 494; **45:** 175

economic relations
Henry V **13:** 213

economics and exchange
Coriolanus **50:** 152
The Merchant of Venice **40:** 197, 208; **53:** 116

editorial and textual issues
Sonnets **28:** 363; **40:** 273; **42:** 296

education
All's Well That Ends Well **7:** 62, 86, 90, 93, 98, 104, 116, 126
The Two Gentlemen of Verona **6:** 490, 494, 504, 526, 532, 555, 568; **63:** 336

education or nurturing
The Tempest **8:** 353, 370, 384, 396; **29:** 292, 368, 377

egotism or narcissism
Much Ado about Nothing **8:** 19, 24, 28, 29, 55, 69, 95, 115; **55:** 209
Twelfth Night **60:** 265, 270, 287

Elizabeth, audience of
Sonnets **48:** 325

Elizabeth's influence
The Merry Wives of Windsor **5:** 333, 334, 335, 336, 339, 346, 355, 366, 402; **18:** 5, 86; **38:** 278; **47:** 344

Elizabethan and Jacobean politics, relation to
Cymbeline **61:** 54, 76
Hamlet **28:** 232; **28:** 290, 311; **35:** 140; **58:** 79, 134

Elizabethan attitudes, influence of
Richard II **6:** 287, 292, 294, 305, 321, 327, 364, 402, 414; **13:** 494; **24:** 325; **28:** 188; **39:** 273; **42:** 118; **52:** 141, 144; **58:** 283, 293

Elizabethan betrothal and marriage customs
Measure for Measure **2:** 429, 437, 443, 503; **49:** 286

Elizabethan commerce
Cymbeline **61:** 76

Elizabethan culture, relation to
General Commentary **50:** 34; **53:** 169; **56:** 2, 3, 15, 47
Antony and Cleopatra **47:** 103; **58:** 118
As You Like It **5:** 21, 59, 66, 68, 70, 158; **16:** 53; **28:** 46; **34:** 120; **37:** 1; **46:** 142; **57:** 23, 31, 64, 75
The Comedy of Errors **26:** 138, 142; **34:** 201, 215, 233, 238, 258; **42:** 80; **54:** 169, 200
Hamlet **1:** 76, 148, 151, 154, 160, 166, 169, 171, 176, 184, 202, 209, 254; **13:** 282, 494; **19:** 330; **21:** 407, 416; **22:** 258; **59:** 74
Henry IV, Parts 1 and 2 **19:** 195; **48:** 117, 143, 151, 175
Henry V **5:** 210, 213, 217, 223, 257, 299, 310; **16:** 202; **19:** 133, 233; **28:** 121, 159; **30:** 215, 262; **37:** 187; **49:** 260
Julius Caesar **16:** 231; **30:** 342, 379; **50:** 13, 211, 269, 280
King Lear **2:** 168, 174, 177, 183, 226, 241; **19:** 330; **22:** 227, 233, 365; **25:** 218; **46:** 276; **47:** 9; **49:** 67; **61:** 172, 176, 187, 194
Measure for Measure **2:** 394, 418, 429, 432, 437, 460, 470, 482, 503
The Merchant of Venice **32:** 66; **40:** 117, 127, 142, 166, 181, 197, 208; **48:** 54, 77; **49:** 37; **53:** 105, 111, 116, 127, 159
A Midsummer Night's Dream **50:** 86; **58:** 220
Much Ado about Nothing **8:** 23, 33, 44, 55, 58, 79, 88, 104, 111, 115; **51:** 15; **55:** 209, 241, 259
The Rape of Lucrece **33:** 195; **43:** 77
Richard II **58:** 267, 275
Richard III **62:** 66
The Taming of the Shrew **31:** 288, 295, 300, 315, 326, 345, 351; **55:** 315, 322, 334
Timon of Athens **1:** 487, 489, 495, 500; **20:** 433; **27:** 203, 212, 230; **50:** 13; **52:** 320, 354
Titus Andronicus **27:** 282; **62:** 233, 270
Troilus and Cressida **3:** 560, 574, 606; **25:** 56; **59:** 225, 295, 306
Twelfth Night **1:** 549, 553, 555, 563, 581, 587, 620; **16:** 53; **19:** 42, 78; **26:** 357; **28:** 1; **34:** 323, 330; **46:** 291; **51:** 15; **62:** 319, 348

Elizabethan dramatic conventions
Cymbeline **4:** 53, 124
Henry VIII **24:** 155; **56:** 196, 248

Elizabethan literary influences
Henry VI, Parts 1, 2, and 3 **3:** 75, 97, 100, 119, 143; **22:** 156; **28:** 112; **37:** 97; **56:** 162, 180; **63:** 194

Elizabethan love poetry
Love's Labour's Lost **38:** 232

Elizabethan poetics, influence of
Romeo and Juliet **5:** 416, 520, 522, 528, 550, 559, 575

Elizabethan politics, relation to
Hamlet **60:** 346
Henry IV, Parts 1 and 2 **22:** 395; **28:** 203; **47:** 60; **48:** 117, 143, 167, 175; **57:** 88, 94
Henry VIII **22:** 395; **24:** 115, 129, 140; **32:** 148; **56:** 201, 248
King John **48:** 132; **56:** 306, 314, 325; **60:** 295, 329
Macbeth **60:** 357
Richard III **22:** 395; **25:** 141; **37:** 144; **39:** 345, 349; **42:** 130; **52:** 201, 214, 257; **62:** 2

Elizabethan setting
The Two Gentlemen of Verona **12:** 463, 485

Elizabethan society
The Merry Wives of Windsor **47:** 331

Epicureanism
Julius Caesar **50:** 249; **63:** 269

emulation or rivalry
Julius Caesar **16:** 231; **50:** 211

England and Rome, parallels between
Coriolanus **9:** 39, 43, 106, 148, 180, 193; **25:** 296; **30:** 67, 105

English language and colonialism
Henry V **22:** 103; **28:** 159

English Reformation, influence of
Henry VIII **2:** 25, 35, 39, 51, 67; **24:** 89; **56:** 201; **61:** 92

epic elements
Henry V **5:** 192, 197, 246, 257, 314; **30:** 181, 220, 237, 252

erotic elements
A Midsummer Night's Dream **3:** 445, 491, 497, 511; **12:** 259, 262, 298; **16:** 34; **19:** 21; **29:** 183, 225, 269; **58:** 194
Venus and Adonis **10:** 410, 411, 418, 419, 427, 428, 429, 442, 448, 454, 459, 466, 473; **25:** 305, 328; **28:** 355; **33:** 321, 339, 347, 352, 363, 370; **51:** 345, 352, 359, 368

as experimental play
Romeo and Juliet **5:** 464, 509, 528

Essex Rebellion, relation to
Richard II **6:** 249, 250; **24:** 356; **58:** 293

ethical or moral issues
King John **9:** 212, 222, 224, 229, 235, 240, 263, 275, 280; **56:** 335
King Lear **52:** 1, 95;
Measure for Measure **52:** 69
Twelfth Night **52:** 57

ethnicity
The Winter's Tale **37:** 306

Euripides, influence of
Titus Andronicus **27:** 285

evil
See also **good versus evil**
Macbeth **3:** 194, 208, 231, 234, 239, 241, 267, 289; **20:** 203, 206, 210, 374; **52:** 23; **57:** 267
Othello **52:** 78
Richard III **52:** 78
Romeo and Juliet **5:** 485, 493, 505
Titus Andronicus **53:** 86, 92

excess
King John **9:** 251

fable of the belly
Coriolanus **50:** 13, 110, 140

fame
Coriolanus **30:** 58

family honor, structure, and inheritance
Richard II **6:** 338, 368, 388, 397, 414; **39:** 263, 279
Richard III **8:** 177, 248, 252, 263, 267; **25:** 141; **39:** 335, 341, 349, 370

family relations
All's Well That Ends Well **63:** 89

family, theme of
Cymbeline **44:** 28

fancy
Twelfth Night **1:** 543, 546

as farce
The Taming of the Shrew **9:** 330, 337, 338, 341, 342, 365, 381, 386, 413, 426; **55:** 357

farcical elements
See **comic and farcical elements**

fate
Richard II **6:** 289, 294, 304, 352, 354, 385
Romeo and Juliet **5:** 431, 444, 464, 469, 470, 479, 480, 485, 487, 493, 509, 530, 533, 562, 565, 571, 573; **33:** 249; **54:** 125

Fathers and Daughters (**Volume 36:** 1, 12, 25, 32, 37, 45, 70, 78)
As You Like It **46:** 94
Cymbeline **34:** 134
King Lear **34:** 51, 54, 60
cruelty of daughters **2:** 101, 102, 106; **31:** 84, 123, 137, 142
Pericles **34:** 226, 233
The Winter's Tale **34:** 311, 318, 328

Feast of the Lupercal
Julius Caesar **50:** 269

female identity
See also **Gender Identity and Issues**
Macbeth **57:** 256

feminine power, role of
Macbeth **57:** 242

Feminist Criticism (**Volume 55:** 1, 16, 27, 37, 48, 56, 68, 78)
General Commentary **55:** 1, 16, 27, 56, 68, 78
As You Like It **23:** 107, 108;
Comedy of Errors **42:** 93
Hamlet **55:** 56; **59:** 31, 39
King Lear **55:** 68
Love's Labour's Lost **42:** 93
Measure for Measure **23:** 320; **55:** 16, 68
Merchant of Venice **55:** 27
A Midsummer Night's Dream **48:** 23
The Rape of Lucrece **59:** 165, 189, 193
Troilus and Cressida **55:** 37, 48; **59:** 337

feminism
As You Like It **57:** 2, 13

festive or folklore elements
Twelfth Night **46:** 338; **51:** 15

feud
Romeo and Juliet **5:** 415, 419, 425, 447, 458, 464, 469, 479, 480, 493, 509, 522, 556, 565, 566, 571, 575; **25:** 181; **51:** 245

fire and water
Coriolanus **25:** 263

flattery
Coriolanus **9:** 26, 45, 92, 100, 110, 121, 130, 144, 157, 183, 193; **25:** 296
Henry IV, Parts 1 and 2 **22:** 395
Henry VIII **22:** 395
Richard III **22:** 395

folk drama, relation to
The Winter's Tale **7:** 420, 451; **57:** 356

folk elements
The Taming of the Shrew **9:** 381, 393, 404, 426

folk rituals, elements and influence of
Henry VI, Parts 1, 2, and 3 **39:** 205
The Merry Wives of Windsor **5:** 353, 369, 376, 392, 397, 400; **38:** 256, 300

food, meaning of
The Comedy of Errors **34:** 220
Troilus and Cressida **43:** 298; **59:** 306

forest
The Two Gentlemen of Verona **6:** 450, 456, 492, 514, 547, 555, 564, 568

Forest of Arden
As You Like It
as "bitter" Arcadia **5:** 98, 118, 162; **23:** 97, 98, 99, 100, 122, 139
Duke Frederick's court, contrast with **5:** 46, 102, 103, 112, 130, 156; **16:** 53; **23:** 126, 128, 129, 131, 134; **34:** 78, 102, 131; **46:** 164; **57:** 64
pastoral elements **5:** 18, 20, 24, 32, 35, 47, 50, 54, 55, 57, 60, 77, 128, 135, 156; **23:** 17, 20, 27, 46, 137; **34:** 78, 147; **46:** 88
as patriarchal society **5:** 168; **23:** 150; **34:** 177; **57:** 2
as source of self-knowledge **5:** 98, 102, 103, 128, 130, 135, 148, 158, 162; **23:** 17; **34:** 102; **57:** 35
as timeless, mythical world **5:** 112, 130, 141; **23:** 132; **34:** 78; **37:** 43; **46:** 88
theme of play **46:** 88

forgiveness or redemption
Henry IV, Parts 1 and 2 **57:** 116
Venus and Adonis **51:** 377
The Winter's Tale **7:** 381, 389, 395, 402, 407, 436, 456, 460, 483; **36:** 318

free will versus fate
Macbeth **3:** 177, 183, 184, 190, 196, 198, 202, 207, 208, 213; **13:** 361; **44:** 351, 361, 366, 373; **54:** 6
The Two Noble Kinsmen **9:** 474, 481, 486, 492, 498

Topic Index

freedom and servitude
The Tempest **8:** 304, 307, 312, 429; **22:** 302; **29:** 278, 368, 377; **37:** 336

French language, Shakespeare's use of
Henry V **5:** 186, 188, 190; **25:** 131

Freudian analysis
A Midsummer Night's Dream **44:** 1

friendship
See also **love and friendship** *and* **love versus friendship**
Coriolanus **30:** 125, 142
Sonnets **10:** 185, 279; **28:** 380; **51:** 284, 288
The Two Noble Kinsmen **9:** 448, 463, 470, 474, 479, 481, 486, 490; **19:** 394; **41:** 363, 372; **42:** 361; **58:** 345, 356, 371

Gender Identity and Issues (Volume 40: 1, 9, 15, 27, 33, 51, 61, 65, 75, 90, 99)
All's Well That Ends Well **7:** 9, 10, 67, 126; **13:** 77, 84; **19:** 113; **26:** 128; **38:** 89, 99, 118; **44:** 35; **55:** 101, 109, 122, 164; **63:** 60
Antony and Cleopatra **13:** 368; **25:** 257; **27:** 144; **47:** 174, 192; **53:** 67, 77; **58:** 59
As You Like It **46:** 127, 134; **57:** 13, 23, 45
The Comedy of Errors **34:** 215, 220
Coriolanus **30:** 79, 125, 142; **44:** 93; **50:** 128
Hamlet **35:** 144; **44:** 189, 195, 198; **59:** 31, 39
Henry IV, Parts 1 and 2 **13:** 183; **25:** 151; **44:** 44; **48:** 175; **60:** 154
Henry V **13:** 183; **28:** 121, 146, 159; **44:** 44
Julius Caesar **13:** 260
Macbeth **57:** 256
The Merchant of Venice **40:** 142, 151, 156
Othello **32:** 294; **35:** 327 **53:** 255, 268, 310
A Midsummer Night's Dream **53:** 1; **58:** 215
The Rape of Lucrece **53:** 1; **59:** 189, 193, 206
Richard II **25:** 89; **39:** 295
Richard III **25:** 141; **37:** 144; **39:** 345; **52:** 223, 239; **62:** 41
Romeo and Juliet **32:** 256; **51:** 253
Sonnets **37:** 374; **40:** 238, 247, 254, 264, 268, 273; **53:** 1
The Taming of the Shrew **28:** 24; **31:** 261, 268, 276, 282, 288, 295, 300, 335, 351; **55:** 278, 299, 305, 315, 322, 357
Titus Andronicus **62:** 242
The Tempest **53:** 64, 67
Twelfth Night **19:** 78; **34:** 344; **37:** 59; **42:** 32; **46:** 347, 362, 369; **60:** 129; **62:** 297, 319, 325
The Two Gentlemen of Verona **40:** 374
The Two Noble Kinsmen **42:** 361

genre
All's Well That Ends Well **48:** 65; **63:** 10, 28
As You Like It **5:** 46, 55, 79
The Comedy of Errors **34:** 251, 258
Coriolanus **9:** 42, 43, 53, 80, 106, 112, 117, 130, 164, 177; **30:** 67, 74, 79, 89, 111, 125; **50:** 99
Cymbeline **61:** 2
Hamlet **1:** 176, 212, 237
Love's Labour's Lost **38:** 163
The Merchant of Venice **4:** 191, 200, 201, 209, 215, 221, 232, 238, 247; **12:** 48, 54, 62; **54:** 65
Merry Wives of Windsor **59:** 111
Much Ado about Nothing **8:** 9, 18, 19, 28, 29, 39, 41, 44, 53, 63, 69, 73, 79, 82, 95, 100, 104; **48:** 14; **55:** 232, 268
Richard III **8:** 181, 182, 197, 206, 218, 228, 239, 243, 252, 258; **13:** 142; **39:** 383; **52:** 239 **62:** 2, 41
The Taming of the Shrew **9:** 329, 334, 362, 375; **22:** 48; **31:** 261, 269, 276; **55:** 278
Timon of Athens **1:** 454, 456, 459, 460, 462, 483, 492, 499, 503, 509, 511, 512, 515, 518, 525, 531; **27:** 203
Troilus and Cressida **3:** 541, 542, 549, 558, 566, 571, 574, 587, 594, 604, 630, 642; **27:** 366; **59:** 278
The Two Gentlemen of Verona **6:** 460, 468, 472, 516; **40:** 320

genres, mixture of
Timon of Athens **16:** 351; **25:** 198

gift exchange
Love's Labour's Lost **25:** 1

good versus evil
See also **evil**
Measure for Measure **2:** 432, 452, 524; **33:** 52, 61; **52:** 69
The Tempest **8:** 302, 311, 315, 370, 423, 439; **29:** 278; 297; **61:** 338, 362

grace
The Winter's Tale **7:** 420, 425, 460, 493; **36:** 328

grace and civility
Love's Labour's Lost **2:** 351

Greece
Troilus and Cressida **43:** 287

grotesque or absurd elements
Hamlet **42:** 279
King Lear **2:** 136, 156, 245; **13:** 343; **52:** 1

handkerchief, significance of
Othello **4:** 370, 384, 385, 396, 503, 530, 562; **35:** 265, 282, 380

Hercules Furens (Seneca) as source
Othello **16:** 283

heroism
Henry V **49:** 194, 200, 211, 236

Hippolytus, myth of
A Midsummer Night's Dream **29:** 216; **45:** 84

historical accuracy
Henry VI, Parts 1, 2, and 3 **3:** 18, 21, 35, 46, 51; **16:** 217; **24:** 16, 18, 25, 31, 45, 48; **63:** 169
Richard III **8:** 144, 145, 153, 159, 163, 165, 168, 213, 223, 228, 232; **39:** 305, 308, 326, 383

historical allegory
The Winter's Tale **7:** 381; **15:** 528
The Merchant of Venice **53:** 179, 187

historical and dramatic elements
Henry IV **49:** 93

historical and romantic elements, combination of
Henry VIII **2:** 46, 49, 51, 75, 76, 78; **24:** 71, 80, 146; **41:** 129, 146, 180; **56:** 196, 201

historical content
Henry IV, Parts 1 and 2 **1:** 310, 328, 365, 366, 370, 374, 380, 387, 421, 424, 427, 431; **16:** 172; **19:** 157; **25:** 151; **32:** 136; **39:** 143; **48:** 143, 167; **57:** 137
Henry V **5:** 185, 188, 190, 192, 193, 198, 246, 314; **13:** 201; **19:** 133; **25:** 131; **30:** 193, 202, 207, 215, 252
King John **9:** 216, 219, 220, 222, 235, 240, 254, 284, 290, 292, 297, 300, 303; **13:** 163; **32:** 93, 114; **41:** 234, 243; **56:** 286, 296, 306, 357; **60:** 329
The Tempest **8:** 364, 408, 420; **16:** 426; **25:** 382; **29:** 278, 339, 343, 368; **45:** 226; **53:** 21, 53; **61:** 297

historical determinism versus free will
Julius Caesar **7:** 160, 298, 316, 333, 346, 356; **13:** 252; **63:** 219

historical elements
Cymbeline **47:** 260

historical epic, as epilogue to Shakespeare's
Henry VIII **2:** 22, 25, 27, 39, 51, 60, 65

historical epic, place in or relation to Shakespeare's
Henry IV, Parts 1 and 2 **1:** 309, 314, 328, 374, 379, 424, 427
Henry V **5:** 195, 198, 205, 212, 225, 241, 244, 287, 304, 310; **14:** 337, 342; **30:** 215
Henry VI, Parts 1, 2, and 3 **3:** 24, 59; **24:** 51; **48:** 167; **56:** 95

historical principles
Richard III **39:** 308, 326, 387

historical relativity, theme of 41: 146;
Henry VIII **56:** 220; **61:** 111

historical revisionism 56: 85, 110, 122, 131, 145

historical sources, compared with
Richard II **6:** 252, 279, 343; **28:** 134; **39:** 235; **49:** 60; **58:** 259, 275, 283

historiography
General Commentary **56:** 3, 15, 25, 47, 53, 60
Henry IV, Parts 1 and 2 **56:** 2, 15, 25
Henry V **56:** 2, 15
Henry VI, Parts 1, 2, and 3 **56:** 2, 25
Henry VIII **37:** 109, 201, 209, 230; **61:** 92, 101, 111

Richard II **56:** 2, 15
Richard III **56:** 2

homoerotic elements
As You Like It **46:** 127, 142; **57:** 23; **60:** 115
Henry V **16:** 202
Sonnets **10:** 155, 156, 159, 161, 175, 213, 391; **16:** 461; **28:** 363, 380; **37:** 347; **40:** 254, 264, 273; **51:** 270, 284; **62:** 128

Homosexuality (Volume 60: 105, 115, 129, 142, 154)
As You Like It **46:** 127, 142; **57:** 13; **60:** 115
Henry IV, Parts 1 and 2 **60:** 154
Measure for Measure **42:** 1
The Merchant of Venice **22:** 3, 69; **37:** 86; **40:** 142, 156, 197
A Midsummer Night's Dream **60:** 142
Sonnets **60:** 105
Troilus and Cressida **60:** 105
Twelfth Night **22:** 69; **42:** 32; **46:** 362; **60:** 115, 129
The Winter's Tale **48:** 309

honor or integrity
Coriolanus **9:** 43, 65, 73, 92, 106, 110, 121, 144, 153, 157, 164, 177, 183, 189; **30:** 89, 96, 133
Henry VIII **61:** 101

hospitality
The Winter's Tale **19:** 366

as humanistic play
Henry VI, Parts 1, 2, and 3 **3:** 83, 92, 109, 115, 119, 131, 136, 143

hunt motif
Venus and Adonis **10:** 434, 451, 466, 473; **33:** 357, 370

hypocrisy
Henry V **5:** 203, 213, 219, 223, 233, 260, 271, 302

ideal love
See also **love**
Cymbeline **61:** 34, 45
Romeo and Juliet **5:** 421, 427, 431, 436, 437, 450, 463, 469, 498, 505, 575; **25:** 257; **33:** 210, 225, 272; **51:** 25; **51:** 44, 195, 203, 219

idealism versus pragmatism
Hamlet **16:** 246; **28:** 325

idealism versus realism
See also **realism**
Love's Labour's Lost **38:** 163
Othello **4:** 457, 508, 517; **13:** 313; **25:** 189; **53:** 350

identities of persons
Sonnets **10:** 154, 155, 156, 161, 166, 167, 169, 173, 174, 175, 185, 190, 191, 196, 218, 226, 230, 233, 240; **40:** 238; **62:** 128

identity
The Comedy of Errors **34:** 201, 208, 211; **54:** 155, 169, 200
Coriolanus **42:** 243; **50:** 128
A Midsummer Night's Dream **29:** 269; **58:** 215
The Two Gentlemen of Verona **6:** 494, 511, 529, 532, 547, 560, 564, 568; **19:** 34

illusion
The Comedy of Errors **1:** 13, 14, 27, 37, 40, 45, 59, 63; **26:** 188; **34:** 194, 211; **54:** 169, 200

illusion versus reality
Love's Labour's Lost **2:** 303, 308, 331, 340, 344, 348, 356, 359, 367, 371, 375; **23:** 230, 231

imagery
Venus and Adonis **10:** 414, 415, 416, 420, 429, 434, 449, 459, 466, 473, 480; **25:** 328; **28:** 355; **33:** 321, 339, 352, 363, 370, 377; **42:** 347; **51:** 335, 388

imagination and art
A Midsummer Night's Dream **3:** 365, 371, 381, 402, 412, 417, 421, 423, 441, 459, 468, 506, 516, 520; **22:** 39; **45:** 96, 126, 136, 147

immortality
Measure for Measure **16:** 102

imperialism
Antony and Cleopatra **53:** 67, 77
Henry V **22:** 103; **28:** 159
The Merchant of Venice **53:** 116

implausibility of plot, characters, or events
All's Well That Ends Well **7:** 8, 45
King Lear **2:** 100, 136, 145, 278; **13:** 343
The Merchant of Venice **4:** 191, 192, 193; **12:** 52, 56, 76, 119
Much Ado about Nothing **8:** 9, 12, 16, 19, 33, 36, 39, 44, 53, 100, 104
Othello **4:** 370, 380, 391, 442, 444; **47:** 51

inaction
Troilus and Cressida **3:** 587, 621; **27:** 347

incest, motif of
Pericles **2:** 582, 588; **22:** 315; **36:** 257, 264; **51:** 97, 110

inconsistencies
Henry VIII **2:** 16, 27, 28, 31, 60

inconsistency between first and second halves
Measure for Measure **2:** 474, 475, 505, 514, 524; **49:** 349, 358

induction
The Taming of the Shrew **9:** 320, 322, 332, 337, 345, 350, 362, 365, 369, 370, 381, 390, 393, 407, 419, 424, 430; **12:** 416, 427, 430, 431, 441; **19:** 34, 122; **22:** 48; **31:** 269, 315, 351; **55:** 331, 357

as inferior or flawed play
Henry VI, Parts 1, 2, and 3 **3:** 20, 21, 25, 26, 35
Pericles **2:** 537, 546, 553, 563, 564; **15:** 139, 143, 156, 167, 176; **36:** 198; **51:** 79
Timon of Athens **1:** 476, 481, 489, 499, 520; **20:** 433, 439, 491; **25:** 198; **27:** 157, 175; **52:** 338, 349

infidelity
Troilus and Cressida **43:** 298; **55:** 37, 48; **59:** 251

innocence
Macbeth **3:** 234, 241, 327; **57:** 267
Othello **47:** 25
Pericles **36:** 226, 274

innocence to experience
The Two Noble Kinsmen **9:** 481, 502; **19:** 394

Ireland, William Henry, forgeries of
Sonnets **48:** 325

Irish affairs
Henry V **22:** 103; **28:** 159

ironic or parodic elements
The Two Gentlemen of Verona **6:** 447, 472, 478, 484, 502, 504, 509, 516, 529, 549; **13:** 12; **54:** 295, 307; **63:** 336
Henry VIII **41:** 129; **56:** 220

irony
All's Well That Ends Well **7:** 27, 32, 58, 62, 67, 81, 86, 109, 116
Antony and Cleopatra **6:** 53, 136, 146, 151, 159, 161, 189, 192, 211, 224
As You Like It **5:** 30, 32, 154
Coriolanus **9:** 65, 73, 80, 92, 106, 153, 157, 164, 193; **30:** 67, 89, 133
Cymbeline **4:** 64, 77, 103
Henry V **5:** 192, 210, 213, 219, 223, 226, 233, 252, 260, 269, 281, 299, 304; **14:** 336; **30:** 159, 193
Julius Caesar **7:** 167, 257, 259, 262, 268, 282, 316, 320, 333, 336, 346, 350; **63:** 231, 252, 295, 310, 315
The Merchant of Venice **4:** 254, 300, 321, 331, 350; **28:** 63
Much Ado about Nothing **8:** 14, 63, 79, 82; **28:** 63
The Rape of Lucrece **10:** 93, 98, 128
Richard II **6:** 270, 307, 364, 368, 391; **24:** 383; **28:** 188
Sonnets **10:** 256, 293, 334, 337, 346; **51:** 300
The Taming of the Shrew **9:** 340, 375, 398, 407, 413; **13:** 3; **19:** 122; **55:** 278, 299, 322
The Two Noble Kinsmen **9:** 463, 481, 486; **41:** 301; **50:** 348
The Winter's Tale **7:** 419, 420

the island
The Tempest **8:** 308, 315, 447; **25:** 357, 382; **29:** 278, 343

Italian influences
Sonnets **28:** 407; **62:** 121, 146

Jacobean culture, relation to
Antony and Cleopatra **58:** 79, 134
Coriolanus **22:** 248
Macbeth **19:** 330; **22:** 365; **57:** 218, 256; **60:** 340, 357
Pericles **37:** 361; **51:** 86, 110
The Winter's Tale **19:** 366, 401, 431; **25:** 347; **32:** 388; **37:** 306; **57:** 305, 336, 356

Jacobean court and politics
Henry VIII **61:** 92

jealousy
The Merry Wives of Windsor **5:** 334, 339, 343, 353, 355, 363; **22:** 93; **38:** 273, 307
Othello **4:** 384, 488, 527; **35:** 253, 265, 282, 301, 310; **44:** 57, 66; **51:** 30
The Winter's Tale **44:** 66; **47:** 25

Jonsonian humors comedy, influence of
The Merry Wives of Windsor **38:** 319; **59:** 105

judicial versus natural law
Measure for Measure **2:** 446, 507, 516, 519; **22:** 85; **33:** 58, 117; **49:** 1, 293

justice
As You Like It **46:** 94
Henry IV **49:** 112, 123; **57:** 137
King Lear **49:** 1
Othello **35:** 247

justice and mercy
Measure for Measure **2:** 391, 395, 399, 402, 406, 409, 411, 416, 421, 437, 443, 463, 466, 470, 491, 495, 522, 524; **22:** 85; **33:** 52, 61, 101; **49:** 1, 274, 293, 300
The Merchant of Venice **4:** 213, 214, 224, 250, 261, 273, 282, 289, 336; **12:** 80, 129; **40:** 127; **49:** 1, 23, 27, 37
Much Ado about Nothing **22:** 85

justice, divine vs. worldly
King Lear **49:** 67, 73; **60:** 185

juxtaposition of opposing perspectives
As You Like It **5:** 86, 93, 98, 141; **16:** 53; **23:** 119; **34:** 72, 78, 131

Kingship (Volume 39: 1, 16, 20, 34, 45, 62)
Henry IV, Parts 1 and 2 **1:** 314, 318, 337, 366, 370, 374, 379, 380, 383, 424; **16:** 172; **19:** 195; **28:** 101; **39:** 100, 116, 123, 130; **42:** 141; **48:** 143; **57:** 88, 94, 108, 137, 160
Henry V **5:** 205, 223, 225, 233, 239, 244, 257, 264, 267, 271, 287, 289, 299, 302, 304, 314, 318; **16:** 202; **22:** 137; **30:** 169, 202, 259, 273; **42:** 141; **49:** 200
Henry VI, Parts 1, 2, and 3 **3:** 69, 73, 77, 109, 115, 136, 143; **24:** 32; **39:** 154, 177, 187; **47:** 32; **63:** 202
Henry VIII **2:** 49, 58, 60, 65, 75, 78; **24:** 113; **41:** 129, 171; **56:** 242; **61:** 92, 119
King John **9:** 235, 254, 263, 275, 297; **13:** 158; **19:** 182; **22:** 120; **56:** 314
Richard II **6:** 263, 264, 272, 277, 289, 294, 327, 354, 364, 381, 388, 391, 402, 409, 414; **19:** 151, 209; **24:** 260, 289, 291, 322, 325, 333, 339, 345, 346, 349, 351, 352, 356, 395, 408, 419, 428; **28:** 134; **39:** 235, 243, 256, 263, 273, 279, 289; **42:** 173; **58:** 275, 301
Richard III **39:** 335, 341, 345, 349

knighthood
The Merry Wives of Windsor **5:** 338, 343, 390, 397, 402; **47:** 354

knowledge
Love's Labour's Lost **22:** 12; **47:** 35

language and imagery
All's Well That Ends Well **7:** 12, 29, 45, 104, 109, 121; **38:** 132, 65; **63:** 36
Antony and Cleopatra **6:** 21, 25, 39, 64, 80, 85, 92, 94, 100, 104, 142, 146, 155, 159, 161, 165, 189, 192, 202, 211; **13:** 374, 383; **25:** 245, 257; **27:** 96, 105, 135; **58:** 79, 88, 118
As You Like It **5:** 19, 21, 35, 52, 75, 82, 92, 138; **23:** 15, 21, 26; **28:** 9; **34:** 131; **37:** 43; **48:** 42; **57:** 35, 56
The Comedy of Errors **1:** 16, 25, 39, 40, 43, 57, 59; **34:** 233; **54:** 152, 162
Coriolanus **9:** 8, 9, 13, 53, 64, 65, 73, 78, 84, 100, 112, 121, 136, 139, 142, 144, 153, 157, 174, 183, 193, 198; **22:** 248; **25:** 245, 263; **30:** 111, 125, 142; **37:** 283; **44:** 79
Cymbeline **4:** 43, 48, 61, 64, 70, 73, 93, 108; **13:** 401; **25:** 245; **28:** 373, 398; **36:** 115, 158, 166, 186; **47:** 205, 286, 296; **60:** 240
Hamlet **1:** 95, 144, 153, 154, 160, 188, 198, 221, 227, 249, 259, 270; **22:** 258, 378; **28:** 311; **35:** 144, 152, 238, 241; **42:** 212; **44:** 248; **52:** 35; **59:** 42, 47, 56, 62, 74
Henry IV, Parts 1 and 2 **13:** 213; **16:** 172; **25:** 245; **28:** 101; **39:** 116, 130; **42:** 153; **47:** 1; **57:** 137
Henry V **5:** 188, 230, 233, 241, 264, 276; **9:** 203; **19:** 203; **25:** 131; **30:** 159, 181, 207, 234; **30:** 159, 181, 207, 234
Henry VI, Parts 1, 2, and 3 **3:** 21, 50, 52, 55, 57, 66, 67, 71, 75, 76, 97, 105, 109, 119, 126, 131; **24:** 28; **37:** 157; **39:** 213, 222; **56:** 154, 162, 172, 180
Henry VIII **41:** 180, 190; **56:** 262, 273
Julius Caesar **7:** 148, 155, 159, 188, 204, 207, 227, 242, 250, 277, 296, 303, 324, 346, 350; **13:** 260; **17:** 347, 348, 350, 356, 358; **19:** 321; **22:** 280; **25:** 280; **30:** 333, 342; **50:** 196, 258
King John **9:** 212, 215, 220, 246, 251, 254, 267, 280, 284, 292, 297, 300; **13:** 147, 158; **22:** 120; **37:** 132; **48:** 132; **56:** 286
King Lear **2:** 129, 137, 161, 191, 199, 237, 257, 271; **16:** 301; **19:** 344; **22:** 233; **46:** 177; **61:** 215, 230
Love's Labour's Lost **2:** 301, 302, 303, 306, 307, 308, 315, 319, 320, 330, 335, 344, 345, 348, 356, 359, 362, 365, 371, 374, 375; **19:** 92; **22:** 12, 378; **23:** 184, 187, 196, 197, 202, 207, 211, 221, 227, 231, 233, 237, 252; **28:** 9, 63; **38:** 219, 226; **54:** 225, 274
Macbeth **3:** 170, 193, 213, 231, 234, 241, 245, 250, 253, 256, 263, 271, 283, 300, 302, 306, 323, 327, 338, 340, 349; **13:** 476; **16:** 317; **20:** 241, 279, 283, 367, 379, 400; **25:** 235; **28:** 339; **29:** 76, 91; **42:** 258; **44:** 366; **45:** 58
Measure for Measure **2:** 394, 421, 431, 466, 486, 505; **13:** 112; **28:** 9; **33:** 69; **49:** 370
The Merry Wives of Windsor **5:** 335, 337, 343, 347, 351, 363, 374, 379; **19:** 101; **22:** 93, 378; **28:** 9, 69; **38:** 313, 319; **59:** 89
The Merchant of Venice **4:** 241, 267, 293; **22:** 3; **25:** 257; **28:** 9, 63; **32:** 41; **40:** 106; **53:** 169
A Midsummer Night's Dream **3:** 397, 401, 410, 412, 415, 432, 453, 459, 468, 494; **22:** 23, 39, 93, 378; **28:** 9; **29:** 263; **45:** 143, 169, 175; **48:** 23, 32; **58:** 181, 186, 194
Much Ado about Nothing **8:** 9, 38, 43, 46, 55, 69, 73, 88, 95, 100, 115, 125; **19:** 68; **25:** 77; **28:** 63; **31:** 178, 184, 222, 241, 245; **48:** 14; **55:** 199, 259
Othello **4:** 433, 442, 445, 462, 493, 508, 517, 552, 587, 596; **13:** 304; **16:** 272; **22:** 378; **25:** 189, 257; **28:** 243, 344; **42:** 273; **47:** 51; **53:** 261
Pericles **2:** 559, 560, 565, 583; **16:** 391; **19:** 387; **22:** 315; **36:** 198, 214, 233, 244, 251, 264; **51:** 86, 99
The Rape of Lucrece **10:** 64, 65, 66, 71, 78, 80, 89, 93, 116, 109, 125, 131; **22:** 289, 294; **25:** 305; **32:** 321; **33:** 144, 155, 179, 200; **43:** 102, 113, 141; **59:** 159, 175, 212
Richard II **6:** 252, 282, 283, 294, 298, 315, 323, 331, 347, 368, 374, 381, 385, 397, 409; **13:** 213, 494; **24:** 269, 270, 298, 301, 304, 315, 325, 329, 333, 339, 356, 364, 395, 405, 408, 411, 414, 419; **28:** 134, 188; **39:** 243, 273, 289, 295; **42:** 173; **52:** 154, 157, 169, 174, 183; **58:** 253, 267, 293, 301, 307; **60:** 21
Richard III **8:** 159, 161, 165, 167, 168, 170, 177, 182, 184, 186, 193, 197, 201, 206, 218, 223, 243, 248, 252, 258, 262, 267; **16:** 150; **25:** 141, 245; **39:** 360, 370, 383; **47:** 15; **52:** 285, 290; **62:** 14, 66, 71, 91, 104
Romeo and Juliet **5:** 420, 426, 431, 436, 437, 456, 477, 479, 489, 492, 496, 509, 520, 522, 528, 538, 542, 550, 559; **25:** 181, 245, 257; **32:** 276; **33:** 210, 272, 274, 287; **42:** 266; **51:** 203, 212, 227
Sonnets **10:** 247, 251, 255, 256, 290, 353, 372, 385; **13:** 445; **28:** 380, 385; **32:** 327, 352; **40:** 228, 247, 284, 292, 303; **51:** 270, 304; **62:** 153, 159, 170, 180, 196
The Taming of the Shrew **9:** 336, 338, 393, 401, 404, 407, 413; **22:** 378; **28:** 9; **31:** 261, 288, 300, 326, 335, 339; **32:** 56
The Tempest **8:** 324, 348, 384, 390, 404, 454; **19:** 421; **29:** 278; **29:** 297, 343, 368, 377; **61:** 280, 288
Timon of Athens **1:** 488; **13:** 392; **25:** 198; **27:** 166, 184, 235; **52:** 329, 345, 354
Titus Andronicus **4:** 617, 624, 635, 642, 644, 646, 659, 664, 668, 672, 675; **13:** 225; **16:** 225; **25:** 245; **27:** 246, 293, 313, 318, 325; **43:** 186, 222, 227, 239, 247, 262; **62:** 225, 254

Troilus and Cressida **3:** 561, 569, 596, 599, 606, 624, 630, 635; **22:** 58, 339; **27:** 332; 366; **42:** 66; **59:** 287, 295, 306, 318
Twelfth Night **1:** 570, 650, 664; **22:** 12; **28:** 9; **34:** 293; **37:** 59; **62:** 343
The Two Gentlemen of Verona **6:** 437, 438, 439, 445, 449, 490, 504, 519, 529, 541; **28:** 9; **40:** 343
The Two Noble Kinsmen **9:** 445, 446, 447, 448, 456, 461, 462, 463, 469, 471, 498, 502; **41:** 289, 301, 308, 317, 326; **50:** 310; **58:** 322, 330
The Winter's Tale **7:** 382, 384, 417, 418, 420, 425, 460, 506; **13:** 409; **19:** 431; **22:** 324; **25:** 347; **36:** 295; **42:** 301; **45:** 297, 344, 333; **50:** 45; **57:** 278, 285, 319, 347

language versus action
Titus Andronicus **4:** 642, 644, 647, 664, 668; **13:** 225; **27:** 293, 313, 325; **43:** 186; **62:** 225

Law and Justice (**Volume 49:** 1, 18, 23, 27, 37, 46, 60, 67, 73)
Henry IV **49:** 112,116,123,133,137
Henry V **49:** 223, 236, 260
Henry VIII **61:** 92
Measure for Measure **49:** 274, 286, 293
The Merchant of Venice **53:** 169
Othello **53:** 288, 350

law versus passion for freedom
Much Ado about Nothing **22:** 85

laws of nature, violation of
Macbeth **3:** 234, 241, 280, 323; **29:** 120; **57:** 242, 263

legal issues
King Lear **46:** 276

legitimacy
Henry VI, Parts 1, 2, and 3 **3:** 89, 157; **39:** 154; **63:** 194, 202
Henry VIII **37:** 109; **56:** 209, 220, 230
Macbeth **60:** 340

legitimacy or inheritance
King John **9:** 224, 235, 254, 303; **13:** 147; **19:** 182; **37:** 132; **41:** 215; **56:** 325, 335; **60:** 295, 329

letters, role of
The Two Gentlemen of Verona **63:** 341

letters, as theatrical device
The Two Gentlemen of Verona **63:** 341

liberty versus tyranny
Julius Caesar **7:** 158, 179, 189, 205, 221, 253; **25:** 272; **63:** 287

love
See also **ideal love**
All's Well That Ends Well **7:** 12, 15, 16, 51, 58, 67, 90, 93, 116; **38:** 80; **51:** 33, 44
As You Like It **5:** 24, 44, 46, 57, 79, 88, 103, 116, 122, 138, 141, 162; **28:** 46, 82; **34:** 85
King Lear **2:** 109, 112, 131, 160, 162, 170, 179, 188, 197, 218, 222, 238, 265; **25:** 202; **31:** 77, 149, 151, 155, 162; **61:** 220, 237
Love's Labour's Lost **2:** 312, 315, 340, 344; **22:** 12; **23:** 252; **38:** 194; **51:** 44
The Merchant of Venice **4:** 221, 226, 270, 284, 312, 344; **22:** 3, 69; **25:** 257; **40:** 156; **51:** 1, 44
sacrificial love **13:** 43; **22:** 69; **40:** 142
A Midsummer Night's Dream
passionate or romantic love **3:** 372, 389, 395, 396, 402, 408, 411, 423, 441, 450, 480, 497, 498, 511; **29:** 175, 225, 263, 269; **45:** 126, 136; **51:** 44; **58:** 175
Much Ado about Nothing **8:** 24, 55, 75, 95, 111, 115; **28:** 56; **51:** 30
Othello **4:** 412, 493, 506, 512, 530, 545, 552, 569, 570, 575, 580, 591; **19:** 253; **22:** 207; **25:** 257; **28:** 243, 344; **32:** 201; **35:** 261, 317; **51:** 25, 30; **53:** 315; **54:** 119
The Phoenix and Turtle **10:** 31, 37, 40, 50; **38:** 342, 345, 367; **51:** 145, 151, 155
Sonnets **10:** 173, 247, 287, 290, 293, 302, 309, 322, 325, 329, 394; **28:** 380; **37:** 347; **51:** 270, 284, 288, 292; **62:** 153, 170
The Tempest **8:** 435, 439; **29:** 297, 339, 377, 396
Twelfth Night **1:** 543, 546, 573, 580, 587, 595, 600, 603, 610, 660; **19:** 78; **26:** 257, 364; **34:** 270, 293, 323; **46:** 291, 333, 347, 362; **51:** 30; **52:** 57; **62:** 297
The Two Gentlemen of Verona **6:** 442, 445, 456, 479, 488, 492, 494, 502, 509, 516, 519, 549; **13:** 12; **40:** 327, 335, 343, 354, 365; **51:** 30, 44; **63:** 336, 350
The Two Noble Kinsmen **9:** 479, 481, 490, 498; **41:** 289, 301, 355, 363, 372, 385; **50:** 295, 361; **58:** 345, 356, 371
The Winter's Tale **7:** 417, 425, 469, 490; **51:** 30, 33, 44

love and friendship
See also **friendship**
Julius Caesar **7:** 233, 262, 268; **25:** 272

love and honor
Troilus and Cressida **3:** 555, 604; **27:** 370, 374; **59:** 251, 257, 337

love and passion
Antony and Cleopatra **6:** 51, 64, 71, 80, 85, 100, 115, 159, 165, 180; **25:** 257; **27:** 126; **47:** 71, 124,, 174, 192; **51:** 25, 33, 44; **58:** 2, 41, 105; **60:** 179, 222

love and reason
See also **reason**
Othello **4:** 512, 530, 580; **19:** 253

Love and Romance (**Volume 51:** 1, 15, 25, 30, 33, 44)
Pericles **51:** 71
The Phoenix and Turtle **51:** 145, 151, 155
Romeo and Juliet **51:** 195, 203, 212
Sonnets **51:** 284, 288, 292
Venus and Adonis
The Rhetoric of Desire **51:** 345, 352, 359, 368

love, lechery, or rape
Troilus and Cressida **43:** 357

love versus fate
Romeo and Juliet **5:** 421, 437, 438, 443, 445, 458; **33:** 249

love versus friendship
See also **friendship**
The Two Gentlemen of Verona **6:** 439, 449, 450, 458, 460, 465, 468, 471, 476, 480; **40:** 354, 365; **54:** 295, 307, 325, 344; **63:** 350

love versus lust
Venus and Adonis **10:** 418, 420, 427, 434, 439, 448, 449, 454, 462, 466, 473, 480, 489; **25:** 305; **28:** 355; **33:** 309, 330, 339, 347, 357, 363, 370; **51:** 359

love versus reason
See also **reason**
Love's Labour's Lost **54:** 225, 234
Sonnets **10:** 329

love versus war
Troilus and Cressida **18:** 332, 371, 406, 423; **22:** 339; **27:** 376; **59:** 234, 251, 257

Machiavellianism
Henry V **5:** 203, 225, 233, 252, 287, 304; **25:** 131; **30:** 273; **60:** 304
Henry VI, Parts 1, 2, and 3 **22:** 193; **60:** 304
King John **60:** 304
Macbeth **52:** 29; **57:** 236

Madness (**Volume 35:** 1, 7, 8, 24, 34, 49, 54, 62, 68)
Hamlet **19:** 330; **35:** 104, 117, 126, 132, 134, 140, 144; **59:** 31
King Lear **19:** 330
Macbeth **19:** 330
Othello **35:** 265, 276, 282
Twelfth Night **1:** 554, 639, 656; **26:** 371

Magic and the Supernatural (**Volume 29:** 1, 12, 28, 46, 53, 65)
The Comedy of Errors **1:** 27, 30; **54:** 215
Macbeth
supernatural grace versus evil or chaos **3:** 241, 286, 323
witchcraft and supernaturalism **3:** 171, 172, 173, 175, 177, 182, 183, 184, 185, 194, 196, 198, 202, 207, 208, 213, 219, 229, 239; **16:** 317; **19:** 245; **20:** 92, 175, 213, 279, 283, 374, 387, 406, 413; **25:** 235; **28:** 339; **29:** 91, 101, 109, 120; **44:** 351, 373; **57:** 194, 242
A Midsummer Night's Dream **29:** 190, 201, 210, 216
The Tempest **8:** 287, 293, 304, 315, 340, 356, 396, 401, 404, 408, 435, 458; **28:** 391, 415; **29:** 297, 343, 377; **45:** 272; **61:** 326356

Topic Index

Sonnets
occult **48:** 346
The Winter's Tale
witchcraft **22:** 324

male discontent
The Merry Wives of Windsor **5:** 392, 402

male domination
Love's Labour's Lost **22:** 12
A Midsummer Night's Dream **3:** 483, 520; **13:** 19; **25:** 36; **29:** 216, 225, 243, 256, 269; **42:** 46; **45:** 84; **58:** 203, 220; **60:** 142

male/female relationships
As You Like It **46:** 134
The Comedy of Errors **16:** 3
Love's Labour's Lost **54:** 284
The Rape of Lucrece **10:** 109, 121, 131; **22:** 289; **25:** 305; **43:** 113, 141; **59:** 180, 193
Troilus and Cressida **16:** 70; **22:** 339; **27:** 362; **59:** 349
The Two Gentlemen of Verona **63:** 357

male sexual anxiety
Love's Labour's Lost **16:** 17

manhood
Macbeth **3:** 262, 309, 333; **29:** 127, 133; **57:** 242, 256, 263

Marlowe's works, compared with
Richard II **42:** 173

marriage
See also **courtship and marriage**
All's Well That Ends Well **63:** 50, 84, 89, 96, 99
The Comedy of Errors **34:** 251
Cymbeline **61:** 34, 45
Hamlet **22:** 339; **51:** 44; **54:** 215
Love's Labour's Lost **2:** 335, 340; **19:** 92; **38:** 209, 232; **51:** 1, 44
Measure for Measure **2:** 443, 507, 516, 519, 524, 528; **25:** 12; **33:** 61, 90; **49:** 286; **51:** 44
The Merry Wives of Windsor **5:** 343, 369, 376, 390, 392, 400; **22:** 93; **38:** 297; **51:** 44; **59:** 95
A Midsummer Night's Dream **3:** 402, 423, 450, 483, 520; **29:** 243, 256; **45:** 136, 143; **48:** 32; **51:** 1, 30, 44; **58:** 175
Othello **35:** 369; **51:** 44;
The Taming of the Shrew **9:** 322, 325, 329, 332, 329, 332, 334, 341, 342, 343, 344, 345, 347, 353, 360, 362, 375, 381, 390, 398, 401, 404, 413, 426, 430; **13:** 3; **19:** 3; **28:** 24; **31:** 288; **51:** 44; **55:** 315, 331
Titus Andronicus
marriage as political tyranny **48:** 264
Troilus and Cressida **22:** 339; **51:** 44
The Two Gentlemen of Verona **48:** 32
The Two Noble Kinsmen **58:** 338, 345, 356

martial vs. civil law
Coriolanus **48:** 230

Marxist criticism
Hamlet **42:** 229
King Lear **42:** 229; **55:** 16
Macbeth **42:** 229; **55:** 16
Othello **42:** 229

masculine identity
Henry VIII **61:** 129

masque elements
The Two Noble Kinsmen **9:** 490
The Tempest **42:** 332

master-slave relationship
Troilus and Cressida **22:** 58; **59:** 265

mediation
The Merry Wives of Windsor **5:** 343, 392

as medieval allegory, drama, or morality play
Hamlet **59:** 68
Henry IV, Parts 1 and 2 **1:** 323, 324, 342, 361, 366, 373, 374; **32:** 166; **39:** 89; **47:** 60
Measure for Measure **2:** 409, 421, 443, 466, 475, 491, 505, 511, 522; **13:** 94; **60:** 12
Timon of Athens **1:** 492, 511, 518; **27:** 155

medieval chivalry
Richard II **6:** 258, 277, 294, 327, 338, 388, 397, 414; **24:** 274, 278, 279, 280, 283; **39:** 256
Troilus and Cressida **3:** 539, 543, 544, 555, 606; **27:** 376; **59:** 349

medieval dramatic influence
All's Well That Ends Well **7:** 29, 41, 51, 98, 113; **13:** 66
King Lear **2:** 177, 188, 201; **25:** 218
Othello **4:** 440, 527, 545, 559, 582

medieval homilies, influence of
The Merchant of Venice **4:** 224, 250, 289

medieval influence
Romeo and Juliet **5:** 480, 505, 509, 573

medieval literary influence
Henry VI, Parts 1, 2, and 3 **3:** 59, 67, 75, 100, 109, 136, 151; **13:** 131
Titus Andronicus **4:** 646, 650; **27:** 299

medieval mystery plays, relation to
Macbeth **44:** 341; **57:** 194

medieval physiology
Julius Caesar **13:** 260

mercantilism and feudalism
Richard II **13:** 213

merit versus rank
All's Well That Ends Well **7:** 9, 10, 19, 37, 51, 76; **38:** 155; **50:** 59

Messina
Much Ado about Nothing **8:** 19, 29, 48, 69, 82, 91, 95, 108, 111, 121, 125; **31:** 191, 209, 229, 241, 245

metadramatic elements
As You Like It **5:** 128, 130, 146; **34:** 130
Henry V **13:** 194; **30:** 181; **49:** 200, 211
Julius Caesar **63:** 225, 238
Love's Labour's Lost **2:** 356, 359, 362
Measure for Measure **13:** 104
A Midsummer Night's Dream **3:** 427, 468, 477, 516, 520; **29:** 190, 225, 243; **50:** 86
The Taming of the Shrew **9:** 350, 419, 424; **31:** 300, 315
The Winter's Tale **16:** 410

metamorphosis or transformation
The Merry Wives of Windsor **47:** 314
Much Ado about Nothing **8:** 88, 104, 111, 115; **55:** 209, 228
The Taming of the Shrew **9:** 370, 430

metaphysical poem
The Phoenix and Turtle **10:** 7, 8, 9, 20, 31, 35, 37, 40, 45, 50; **51:** 143, 171, 184

Midlands Revolt, influence of
Coriolanus **22:** 248; **30:** 79; **50:** 140, 172

military and sexual hierarchies
Othello **16:** 272

mimetic desire
A Midsummer Night's Dream **60:** 172, 245

mimetic rivalry
The Two Gentlemen of Verona **13:** 12; **40:** 335; **54:** 332
Troilus and Cressida **60:** 172

as "mingled yarn"
All's Well That Ends Well **7:** 62, 93, 109, 126; **38:** 65

Minotaur, myth of
A Midsummer Night's Dream **3:** 497, 498; **29:** 216

as miracle play
Pericles **2:** 569, 581; **36:** 205; **51:** 97

misgovernment
Measure for Measure **2:** 401, 432, 511; **22:** 85
Much Ado about Nothing **22:** 85; **55:** 241

misogyny
King Lear **31:** 123
Measure for Measure **23:** 358

misperception
Cymbeline **19:** 411; **36:** 99, 115; **47:** 228, 237, 252, 277, 286, 296

mistaken identity
The Comedy of Errors **1:** 13, 14, 27, 37, 40, 45, 49, 55, 57, 61, 63; **19:** 34, 54; **25:** 63; **34:** 194; **54:** 162, 176, 189, 215

modernization
Richard III **14:** 523

Montaigne's Essais, relation to
Sonnets **42:** 375
The Tempest **42:** 339

moral choice
Hamlet **52:** 35
Julius Caesar **7:** 179, 264, 279, 343

moral corruption
Macbeth **52:** 15, 23, 78
Othello **52:** 78
Troilus and Cressida **3:** 578, 589, 599, 604, 609; **18:** 332, 406, 412, 423; **27:** 366; **54:** 84; **59:** 261, 265

moral corruption of English society
Richard III **8:** 154, 163, 165, 177, 193, 201, 218, 228, 232, 243, 248, 252, 267; **39:** 308; **52:** 201

moral inheritance
Henry VI, Parts 1, 2, and 3 **3:** 89, 126

moral intent
Henry VIII **2:** 15, 19, 25; **24:** 140; **54:** 35; **61:** 92, 101, 144

moral lesson
Macbeth **20:** 23

moral relativism
Antony and Cleopatra **22:** 217; **27:** 121

moral seriousness, question of
Measure for Measure **2:** 387, 388, 396, 409, 417, 421, 452, 460, 495; **23:** 316, 321

Morality in Shakespeare's Works (Volume 52: 1, 5, 15, 23, 29, 35, 43, 57, 63, 69, 78, 89, 95)
Antony and Cleopatra **52:** 5
As You Like It **52:** 63; **57:** 13
Henry V **5:** 195, 203, 213, 223, 225, 239, 246, 260, 271, 293
Macbeth **52:** 29
The Merchant of Venice **52:** 89
The Merry Wives of Windsor **5:** 335, 339, 347, 349, 353, 397; **59:** 132
Richard III **52:** 5
The Tempest **52:** 43; **61:** 338
Troilus and Cressida **52:** 5; **59:** 251, 257
The Two Gentlemen of Verona **6:** 438, 492, 494, 514, 532, 555, 564; **63:** 336
Venus and Adonis **10:** 411, 412, 414, 416, 418, 419, 420, 423, 427, 428, 439, 442, 448, 449, 454, 459, 466; **33:** 330

multiple endings
Henry IV **49:** 102

multiple perspectives of characters
Henry VI, Parts 1, 2, and 3 **3:** 69, 154; **56:** 131

music
The Tempest **8:** 390, 404; **29:** 292; **37:** 321; **42:** 332; **61:** 315
Twelfth Night **1:** 543, 566, 596

music and dance
A Midsummer Night's Dream **3:** 397, 400, 418, 513; **12:** 287, 289; **25:** 36
Much Ado about Nothing **19:** 68; **31:** 222

mutability, theme of
Sonnets **42:** 375

Myth in Shakespeare's Works (Volume 60: 169, 172, 179, 185, 194, 205, 214, 222, 231, 240, 245, 254, 259, 265, 270, 276, 281, 287)
All's Well That Ends Well **60:** 169
Antony and Cleopatra **60:** 222
Coriolanus **60:** 205
Cymbeline **60:** 240
King Lear **60:** 185
Macbeth **60:** 169, 214
Measure for Measure **60:** 281
The Merchant of Venice **60:** 276
A Midsummer Night's Dream **60:** 172, 245, 259
Romeo and Juliet **60:** 96
The Taming of the Shrew **60:** 281
Titus Andronicus **60:** 276
Troilus and Cressida **60:** 172
Twelfth Night **60:** 265, 270, 287
The Winter's Tale **60:** 254, 281

mythic or mythological elements
See also **religious, mythic, or spiritual content**
All's Well That Ends Well **60:** 169
Antony and Cleopatra **60:** 222
Coriolanus **60:** 205
Cymbeline **60:** 240
King Lear **60:** 185
Macbeth **60:** 169, 214
Measure for Measure **60:** 281
The Merchant of Venice **60:** 276
A Midsummer Night's Dream **58:** 194; **60:** 172, 245, 259
Richard II **52:** 154, 157, 169
Romeo and Juliet **60:** 96
The Taming of the Shrew **60:** 281
Titus Andronicus **60:** 276
Troilus and Cressida **60:** 172
Twelfth Night **60:** 265, 270, 287
The Winter's Tale **60:** 254, 281

mythological allusions
As You Like It **46:** 142; **60:** 231
Antony and Cleopatra **16:** 342; **19:** 304; **27:** 110, 117; **47:** 71, 192 **60:** 179, 222

naming, significance of
Coriolanus **30:** 58, 96, 111, 125

narrative strategies
The Rape of Lucrece **22:** 294

nationalism and patriotism
See also **British nationalism**
Henry V **5:** 198, 205, 209, 210, 213, 219, 223, 233, 246, 252, 257, 269, 299; **19:** 133, 217; **30:** 227, 262; **49:** 219, 247
Henry VI, Parts 1, 2, and 3 **24:** 25, 45, 47; **56:** 80
King John **9:** 209, 218, 222, 224, 235, 240, 244, 275; **25:** 98; **37:** 132
The Merry Wives of Windsor **47:** 344
The Winter's Tale **32:** 388

naturalism
All's Well That Ends Well **60:** 169
Macbeth **60:** 169

nature
See also **art and nature** *and* **art versus nature**
As You Like It **46:** 94
The Tempest **8:** 315, 370, 390, 408, 414; **29:** 343, 362, 368, 377; **61:** 362
The Winter's Tale **7:** 397, 418, 419, 420, 425, 432, 436, 451, 452, 473, 479; **19:** 366; **45:** 329

nature as book
Pericles **22:** 315; **36:** 233

nature, philosophy of
Coriolanus **30:** 74

negative appraisals
Cymbeline **4:** 20, 35, 43, 45, 48, 53, 56, 68; **15:** 32, 105, 121
Richard II **6:** 250, 252, 253, 255, 282, 307, 317, 343, 359
Venus and Adonis **10:** 410, 411, 415, 418, 419, 424, 429

Neoclassical rules
As You Like It **5:** 19, 20
Henry IV, Parts 1 and 2 **1:** 286, 287, 290, 293
Henry VI, Parts 1, 2, and 3 **3:** 17, 18
King John **9:** 208, 209, 210, 212; **56:** 365
Love's Labour's Lost **2:** 299, 300
Macbeth **3:** 170, 171, 173, 175; **20:** 17
Measure for Measure **2:** 387, 388, 390, 394; **23:** 269
The Merry Wives of Windsor **5:** 332, 334
Romeo and Juliet **5:** 416, 418, 426
The Tempest **8:** 287, 292, 293, 334; **25:** 357; **29:** 292; **45:** 200
Troilus and Cressida **3:** 537, 538; **18:** 276, 278, 281
The Winter's Tale **7:** 376, 377, 379, 380, 383, 410; **15:** 397

Neoplatonism
The Phoenix and Turtle **10:** 7, 9, 21, 24, 40, 45, 50; **38:** 345, 350, 367; **51:** 184
Sonnets **10:** 191, 205

nightmarish quality
Macbeth **3:** 231, 309; **20:** 210, 242; **44:** 261

Topic Index

nihilistic elements
King Lear **2:** 130, 143, 149, 156, 165, 231, 238, 245, 253; **22:** 271; **25:** 218; **28:** 325
Timon of Athens **1:** 481, 513, 529; **13:** 392; **20:** 481
Troilus and Cressida **27:** 354

nihilistic or pessimistic vision
King Lear **49:** 67

"nothing," significance of
Much Ado about Nothing **8:** 17, 18, 23, 55, 73, 95; **19:** 68; **55:** 259

nurturing or feeding
Coriolanus **9:** 65, 73, 136, 183, 189; **30:** 111; **44:** 79; **50:** 110

oaths, importance of
Henry VI, Parts 1, 2, and 3 **63:** 194
Love's Labour's Lost **54:** 257, 284
Pericles **19:** 387

obscenity
Henry V **5:** 188, 190, 260

Oldcastle, references to
Henry IV, Parts 1 and 2 **48:** 117

omens
Julius Caesar **22:** 137; **45:** 10; **50:** 265, 280
Richard III **62:** 14, 18

oppositions or dualisms
King John **9:** 224, 240, 263, 275, 284, 290, 300

order
Henry V **5:** 205, 257, 264, 310, 314; **30:** 193
Twelfth Night **1:** 563, 596; **34:** 330; **46:** 291, 347

order versus disintegration
Titus Andronicus **4:** 618, 647; **43:** 186, 195

other sonnet writers, Shakespeare compared with
Sonnets **42:** 296

Ovid, compared with
Venus and Adonis **51:** 335, 352

Ovid, influence of
A Midsummer Night's Dream **3:** 362, 427, 497, 498; **22:** 23; **29:** 175, 190, 216
Titus Andronicus **4:** 647, 659, 664, 668; **13:** 225; **27:** 246, 275, 285, 293, 299, 306; **28:** 249; **43:** 195, 203, 206

Ovid's Metamorphoses, relation to
Measure for Measure **60:** 281
The Merchant of Venice **60:** 276
A Midsummer Night's Dream **60:** 172
The Taming of the Shrew **60:** 281
Titus Andronicus **60:** 276
Twelfth Night **60:** 265, 270, 287
The Winter's Tale **42:** 301; **57:** 319, 367 **60:** 281
Venus and Adonis **42:** 347

pagan elements
King Lear **25:** 218

pageantry
See also **ceremonies, rites, and rituals, importance of**
Henry VIII **2:** 14, 15, 18, 51, 58; **24:** 77, 83, 84, 85, 89, 91, 106, 113, 118, 120, 126, 127, 140, 146, 150; **41:** 120, 129, 190

paradoxical elements
Coriolanus **9:** 73, 92, 106, 121, 153, 157, 164, 169, 193
Hamlet **59:** 47

parent-child relations
Coriolanus **60:** 205
A Midsummer Night's Dream **13:** 19; **29:** 216, 225, 243

pastoral convention, parodies of
As You Like It **5:** 54, 57, 72

pastoral convention, relation to
As You Like It **5:** 72, 77, 122; **34:** 161; **37:** 1

pastoralism
Cymbeline **61:** 18

pastoral tradition, compared with
A Lover's Complaint **48:** 336

patience
Henry VIII **2:** 58, 76, 78
Pericles **2:** 572, 573, 578, 579; **36:** 251

patriarchal claims
Henry VI, Parts 1, 2, and 3 **16:** 131; **25:** 102; **63:** 124

patriarchal or monarchical order
King Lear **13:** 353, 457; **16:** 351; **22:** 227, 233; **25:** 218; **31:** 84, 92, 107, 117, 123, 137, 142; **46:** 269; **61:** 172, 237

patriarchy
General Commentary **55:** 78
Cymbeline **32:** 373; **36:** 134; **47:** 237; **51:** 25
Henry V **37:** 105; **44:** 44
Henry VIII **61:** 129
A Midsummer Night's Dream **60:** 259
The Rape of Lucrece **59:** 189, 206
Titus Andronicus **50:** 13
Troilus and Cressida **22:** 58; **59:** 272, 337, 349

patriotism
See **nationalism and patriotism**

Pattern of Painful Adventures (Lawrence Twine), compared with
Pericles **48:** 364

Pauline doctrine
A Midsummer Night's Dream **3:** 457, 486, 506

pedagogy
Sonnets **37:** 374
The Taming of the Shrew **19:** 122

perception
Othello **19:** 276; **25:** 189, 257; **53:** 246, 289

performance history
The Taming of the Shrew **31:** 282; **55:** 357

performance issues
See also **staging issues**
Julius Caesar **50:** 186
King Lear **2:** 106, 137, 154, 160; **11:** 10, 20, 27, 56, 57, 132, 136, 137, 145, 150, 154; **19:** 295, 344; **25:** 218; **61:** 187
Much Ado about Nothing **18:** 173, 174, 183, 184, 185, 186, 187, 188, 189, 190, 191, 192, 193, 195, 197, 199, 201, 204, 206, 207, 208, 209, 210, 254; **55:** 221
Sonnets **48:** 352
The Taming of the Shrew **12:** 313, 314, 316, 317, 337, 338; **31:** 315; **55:** 357
Sonnets **62:** 159

pessimistic elements
Timon of Athens **1:** 462, 467, 470, 473, 478, 480; **20:** 433, 481; **27:** 155, 191

Petrarchan poetics, influence of
Hamlet **59:** 47
Romeo and Juliet **5:** 416, 520, 522, 528, 550, 559, 575; **32:** 276; **51:** 212, 236

philosophical elements
Julius Caesar **7:** 310, 324; **37:** 203; **63:** 260, 269
Twelfth Night **1:** 560, 563, 596; **34:** 301, 316; **46:** 297

physical versus intellectual world
Love's Labour's Lost **2:** 331, 348, 367

pictorial elements
Venus and Adonis **10:** 414, 415, 419, 420, 423, 480; **33:** 339

Platonic elements
A Midsummer Night's Dream **3:** 368, 437, 450, 497; **45:** 126

play-within-the-play, convention of
Henry VI, Parts 1, 2, and 3 **3:** 75, 149
The Merry Wives of Windsor **5:** 354, 355, 369, 402
The Taming of the Shrew **12:** 416; **22:** 48

plebians
Coriolanus **50:** 13, 105, 189, 196, 230

plot
Love's Labur's Lost **54:** 225
Twelfth Night **62:** 297, 339, 343, 348

The Winter's Tale **7:** 376, 377, 379, 382, 387, 390, 396, 452; **13:** 417; **15:** 518; **45:** 374; **57:** 285

plot and incident
Richard III **8:** 146, 152, 159; **25:** 164

Plutarch and historical sources
Coriolanus **9:** 8, 9, 13, 14, 16, 26, 39, 92, 106, 130, 142, 164; **30:** 74, 79, 105; **50:** 99

poet-patron relationship
Sonnets **48:** 352; **62:** 128

poetic justice, question of
King Lear **2:** 92, 93, 94, 101, 129, 137, 231, 245; **49:** 73
Othello **4:** 370, 412, 415, 427

poetic style
Sonnets **10:** 153, 155, 156, 158, 159, 160, 161, 173, 175, 182, 214, 247, 251, 255, 260, 265, 283, 287, 296, 302, 315, 322, 325, 337, 346, 349, 360, 367, 385; **16:** 472; **40:** 221, 228; **51:** 270

political and social disintegration
Antony and Cleopatra **6:** 31, 43, 53, 60, 71, 80, 100, 107, 111, 146; 180, 197, 219; **22:** 217; **25:** 257; **27:** 121

political content
Titus Andronicus **43:** 262

Politics (Volume 30: 1, 4, 11, 22, 29, 39, 42, 46, 49)
General Commentary **56:** 3
All's Well That Ends Well **63:** 96
Coriolanus **9:** 15, 17, 18, 19, 26, 33, 43, 53, 62, 65, 73, 80, 92, 106, 110, 112, 121, 144, 153, 157, 164, 180; **22:** 248; **25:** 296; **30:** 58, 67, 79, 89, 96, 105, 111, 125; **37:** 283; **42:** 218; **48:** 230; **50:** 13, 140, 172
Cymbeline **61:** 54
Hamlet **44:** 241
Henry IV, Parts 1 and 2 **28:** 101; **39:** 130; **42:** 141; **48:** 143, 175; **57:** 108
Henry V **49:** 219, 247, 260
Henry VIII **2:** 39, 49, 51, 58, 60, 65, 67, 71, 72, 75, 78, 81; **24:** 74, 121, 124; **41:** 146; **56:** 242; **61:** 101
Julius Caesar **7:** 161, 169, 191, 205, 218, 221, 245, 262, 264, 279, 282, 310, 324, 333, 346; **17:** 317, 318, 321, 323, 334, 350, 351, 358, 378, 382, 394, 406; **22:** 137, 280; **25:** 272, 280; **30:** 285, 297, 316, 321, 342, 374, 379; **37:** 203; **50:** 13; **63:** 322
King John **9:** 218, 224, 260, 280; **13:** 163; **22:** 120; **37:** 132; **41:** 221, 228; **56:** 314, 325
King Lear **46:** 269; **50:** 45; **61:** 160, 172, 187, 237
Macbeth **52:** 29; **57:** 218, 228
Measure for Measure **23:** 379; **49:** 274
A Midsummer Night's Dream **29:** 243
Pericles **37:** 361
The Tempest **8:** 304, 307, 315, 353, 359, 364, 401, 408; **16:** 426; **19:** 421; **29:** 339; **37:** 336; **42:** 320; **45:** 272, 280; **52:** 43; **61:** 315
Timon of Athens **27:** 223, 230; **50:** 13
Titus Andronicus **27:** 282; **48:** 264
Troilus and Cressida **3:** 536, 560, 606; **16:** 84; **59:** 225, 318

popularity
Pericles **2:** 536, 538, 546; **37:** 361
Richard III **8:** 144, 146, 154, 158, 159, 162, 181, 228; **39:** 383
The Taming of the Shrew **9:** 318, 338, 404
Venus and Adonis **10:** 410, 412, 418, 427; **25:** 328

power
Henry IV **57:** 108
Henry V **37:** 175
Measure for Measure **13:** 112; **22:** 85; **23:** 327, 330, 339, 352; **33:** 85
The Merchant of Venice **53:** 136
A Midsummer Night's Dream **42:** 46; **45:** 84; **58:** 151
Much Ado about Nothing **22:** 85; **25:** 77; **31:** 231, 245

pride and rightful self-esteem
Othello **4:** 522, 536, 541; **35:** 352

primitivism
Macbeth **20:** 206, 213; **45:** 48

primogeniture
As You Like It **5:** 66, 158; **34:** 109, 120
Titus Andronicus **50:** 13

as "problem" plays
All's Well That Ends Well **63:** 10, 89
The Comedy of Errors **34:** 251
Julius Caesar **7:** 272, 320
Measure for Measure **2:** 416, 429, 434, 474, 475, 503, 514, 519; **16:** 102; **23:** 313, 328, 351; **49:** 358, 370
Troilus and Cressida **3:** 555, 566
lack of resolution **43:** 277; **59:** 278

procreation
Sonnets **10:** 379, 385; **16:** 461
Venus and Adonis **10:** 439, 449, 466; **33:** 321, 377

Protestant components
Henry IV, Parts 1 and 2 **57:** 167
Henry VIII **61:** 129

providential order
General Commentary **56:** 15, 25
Henry IV, Parts 1 and 2 **56:** 15
Henry V **56:** 15
King Lear **2:** 112, 116, 137, 168, 170, 174, 177, 218, 226, 241, 253; **22:** 271; **49:** 1, 73; **56:** 25
Macbeth **3:** 208, 289, 329, 336; **57:** 218
Measure for Measure **48:** 1;
Richard II **56:** 15;
Richard III **60:** 304, 322
Tempest **52:** 43

Psychoanalytic Interpretations of Shakespeare's Works (Volume 44: 1, 11, 18, 28, 35, 44, 57, 66, 79, 89, 93)
As You Like It **5:** 146, 158; **23:** 141, 142; **34:** 109; **48:** 42
Coriolanus **44:** 93
Cymbeline **45:** 67, 75
Hamlet **1:** 119, 148, 154, 179, 202; **21:** 197, 213, 361; **25:** 209; **28:** 223; **35:** 95, 104, 134, 237; **37:** 241; **44:** 133, 152, 160, 180, 209, 219
Henry IV, Parts 1 and 2 **13:** 457; **28:** 101; **42:** 185; **44:** 44
Henry V **13:** 457; **44:** 44
Julius Caesar **45:** 10
Macbeth **3:** 219, 223, 226; **44:** 11, 284, 289, 297; **45:** 48, 58; **63:** 315
Measure for Measure **23:** 331, 332, 333, 334, 335, 340, 355, 356, 359, 379, 395; **44:** 89
Merchant of Venice **45:** 17
A Midsummer Night's Dream **3:** 440, 483; **28:** 15; **29:** 225; **44:** 1; **45:** 107, 117; **58:** 167
Othello **4:** 468, 503; **35:** 265, 276, 282, 301, 317, 320, 347; **42:** 198; **44:** 57
Romeo and Juliet **5:** 513, 556; **51:** 253
The Tempest **45:** 259
Troilus and Cressida **43:** 287, 349
Twelfth Night **46:** 333; **62:** 348

psychological elements
Cymbeline **36:** 134; **44:** 28; **60:** 240; **61:** 18

public versus private principles
Julius Caesar **7:** 161, 179, 252, 262, 268, 284, 298; **13:** 252; **63:** 301, 322

public versus private speech
Love's Labour's Lost **2:** 356, 362, 371

public versus private worlds
As You Like It **46:** 164
Coriolanus **37:** 283; **42:** 218
Romeo and Juliet **5:** 520, 550; **25:** 181; **33:** 274

as "pure" poetry
The Phoenix and Turtle **10:** 14, 31, 35; **38:** 329

Puritanism
Measure for Measure **2:** 414, 418, 434; **49:** 325
Twelfth Night **1:** 549, 553, 555, 632; **16:** 53; **25:** 47; **46:** 338

Pyramus and Thisbe interlude
A Midsummer Night's Dream **50:** 74

Race (Volume 53: 1, 11, 21, 32, 45, 53, 64, 67, 77, 86, 92)
Antony and Cleopatra **53:** 67, 77
The Merchant of Venice **53:** 111, 116, 127, 136, 159, 169; **55:** 27
A Midsummer Night's Dream **53:** 1, 32
Othello **4:** 370, 380, 384, 385, 392, 399, 401, 402, 408, 427, 564; **13:** 327; **16:** 293; **25:** 189, 257; **28:** 249, 330; **35:** 369; **42:** 198; **53:** 1, 233, 238, 246, 255, 261, 268, 275, 289, 298, 304; **55:** 27

Topic Index

The Rape of Lucrece **53:** 1
Sonnets **53:** 1
The Tempest **53:** 1, 21, 45, 64, 67
Titus Andronicus **53:** 86, 92

rape
Titus Andronicus **43:** 227, 255; **48:** 277
The Rape of Lucrece **59:** 189, 193, 206, 212

realism
See also **idealism versus realism**
The Merry Wives of Windsor **38:** 313
The Tempest **8:** 340, 359, 464
Troilus and Cressida **43:** 357

reality and illusion
The Tempest **8:** 287, 315, 359, 401, 435, 439, 447, 454; **22:** 302; **45:** 236, 247

reason
See also **love and reason** ***and*** **love versus reason**
Venus and Adonis **10:** 427, 439, 449, 459, 462, 466; **28:** 355; **33:** 309, 330

reason versus imagination
Antony and Cleopatra **6:** 107, 115, 142, 197, 228; **45:** 28
A Midsummer Night's Dream **3:** 381, 389, 423, 441, 466, 506; **22:** 23; **29:** 190; **45:** 96

rebellion
See also **usurpation**
Henry IV, Parts 1 and 2 **22:** 395; **28:** 101
Henry VIII **22:** 395; **56:** 230
King John **9:** 218, 254, 263, 280, 297
Richard III **22:** 395

rebirth, regeneration, resurrection, or immortality
All's Well That Ends Well **7:** 90, 93, 98
Antony and Cleopatra **6:** 100, 103, 125, 131, 159, 181
Cymbeline **4:** 38, 64, 73, 93, 105, 113, 116, 129, 138, 141, 162, 170
Measure for Measure **13:** 84; **16:** 102, 114; **23:** 321, 327, 335, 340, 352; **25:** 12
Pericles **2:** 555, 564, 584, 586, 588; **36:** 205
The Tempest **8:** 302, 312, 320, 334, 348, 359, 370, 384, 401, 404, 414, 429, 439, 447, 454; **16:** 442; **22:** 302; **29:** 297; **37:** 336
The Winter's Tale **7:** 397, 414, 417, 419, 429, 436, 451, 452, 456, 480, 490, 497, 506; **25:** 339 452, 480, 490, 497, 506; **45:** 366; **60:** 40

reconciliation
As You Like It **46:** 156
All's Well That Ends Well **7:** 90, 93, 98; **51:** 33
Antony and Cleopatra **6:** 100, 103, 125, 131, 159, 181
Cymbeline **4:** 38, 64, 73, 93, 105, 113, 116, 129, 138, 141, 162, 170; **61:** 2
The Merry Wives of Windsor **5:** 343, 369, 374, 397, 402
A Midsummer Night's Dream **3:** 412, 418, 437, 459, 468, 491, 497, 502, 513; **13:** 27; **29:** 190
Romeo and Juliet **5:** 415, 419, 427, 439, 447, 480, 487, 493, 505, 533, 536, 562
The Tempest **8:** 302, 312, 320, 334, 348, 359, 370, 384, 401, 404, 414, 429, 439, 447, 454; **16:** 442; **22:** 302; **29:** 297; **37:** 336; **45:** 236

reconciliation of opposites
As You Like It **5:** 79, 88, 103, 116, 122, 138; **23:** 127, 143; **34:** 161, 172; **46:** 156

redemption
The Comedy of Errors **19:** 54; **26:** 188; **54:** 152, 189
Cymbeline **61:** 18

regicide
Macbeth **3:** 248, 275, 312; **16:** 317, 328

relation to tetralogy
Henry V **49:** 223

relationship to other Shakespearean plays
Twelfth Night **46:** 303
Henry IV, Parts 1 and 2 **42:** 99, 153; **48:** 167; **49:** 93, 186

relationship between Parts 1 and 2
Henry IV, Parts 1 and 2 **32:** 136; **39:** 100; **49:** 178

religious and theological issues
Macbeth **44:** 324, 341, 351, 361, 366, 373
Measure for Measure **48:** 1

religious, mythic, or spiritual content
See also **Christian elements**
All's Well That Ends Well **7:** 15, 45, 54, 67, 76, 98, 109, 116
Antony and Cleopatra **6:** 53, 94, 111, 115, 178, 192, 224; **47:** 71; **58:** 24, 41; **60:** 179
As You Like It **60:** 231
Cymbeline **4:** 22, 29, 78, 93, 105, 108, 115, 116, 127, 134, 138, 141, 159; **28:** 373; **36:** 142, 158, 186; **47:** 219, 260, 274
Hamlet **1:** 98, 102, 130, 184, 191, 209, 212, 231, 234, 254; **21:** 361; **22:** 258; **28:** 280; **32:** 238; **35:** 134; **59:** 2; **60:** 194
Henry IV, Parts 1 and 2 **1:** 314, 374, 414, 421, 429, 431, 434; **32:** 103; **48:** 151; **57:** 147, 156, 167; **60:** 26
Henry V **25:** 116; **32:** 126; **60:** 26
King Lear **49:** 67
Macbeth **3:** 208, 269, 275, 318; **29:** 109
Measure for Measure **48:** 1
Othello **4:** 483, 517, 522, 525, 559, 573; **22:** 207; **28:** 330
Pericles **2:** 559, 561, 565, 570, 580, 584, 588; **22;** **315;** **25:** 365; **51:** 97
Richard III **62:** 66, 71
The Tempest **8:** 328, 390, 423, 429, 435; **45:** 211, 247; **61:** 280
Timon of Athens **1:** 505, 512, 513, 523; **20:** 493

repentance and forgiveness
Much Ado about Nothing **8:** 24, 29, 111; **55:** 228
The Two Gentlemen of Verona **6:** 450, 514, 516, 555, 564
The Winter's Tale **44:** 66

resolution
Measure for Measure **2:** 449, 475, 495, 514, 516; **16:** 102, 114; **54:** 65
The Merchant of Venice **4:** 263, 266, 300, 319, 321; **13:** 37; **51:** 1
The Two Gentlemen of Verona **6:** 435, 436, 439, 445, 449, 453, 458, 460, 462, 465, 466, 468, 471, 476, 480, 486, 494, 509, 514, 516, 519, 529, 532, 541, 549; **19:** 34; **54:** 307, 311, 338

retribution
Henry VI, Parts 1, 2, and 3 **3:** 27, 42, 51, 59, 77, 83, 92, 100, 109, 115, 119, 131, 136, 151
Julius Caesar **7:** 160, 167, 200
Macbeth **3:** 194, 208, 318; **48:** 214
Richard III **8:** 163, 170, 177, 182, 184, 193, 197, 201, 206, 210, 218, 223, 228, 243, 248, 267

revenge
Hamlet **1:** 74, 194, 209, 224, 234, 254; **16:** 246; **22:** 258; **25:** 288; **28:** 280; **35:** 152, 157, 167, 174, 212; **44:** 180, 209, 219, 229; **54:** 96; **59:** 10, 79
The Merchant of Venice **60:** 276
The Merry Wives of Windsor **5:** 349, 350, 392; **38:** 264, 307
Othello **35:** 261
Titus Andronicus **60:** 276; **62:** 258

revenge tragedy elements
Julius Caesar **7:** 316; **63:** 310
Titus Andronicus **4:** 618, 627, 628, 636, 639, 644, 646, 664, 672, 680; **16:** 225; **27:** 275, 318

reversals
A Midsummer Night's Dream **29:** 225; **60:** 245
The Two Gentlemen of Verona **54:** 338

rhetoric
Julius Caesar **63:** 278
Romeo and Juliet **42:** 266
Venus and Adonis **33:** 377; **51:** 335, 345, 352

rhetoric of consolation
Sonnets **42:** 375

rhetoric of politeness
Henry VIII **22:** 182; **56:** 262

rhetorical style
King Lear **16:** 301; **47:** 9

riddle motif
Pericles **22:** 315; **36:** 205, 214

rings episode
The Merchant of Venice **22:** 3; **40:** 106, 151, 156

role-playing
Julius Caesar **7:** 356; **37:** 229
The Taming of the Shrew **9:** 322, 353, 355, 360, 369, 370, 398, 401, 407, 413, 419, 424; **13:** 3; **31:** 288, 295, 315

as romance play
As You Like It **5:** 55, 79; **23:** 27, 28, 40, 43

romance or chivalric tradition, influence of
Much Ado about Nothing **8:** 53, 125; **51:** 15

romance or folktale elements
All's Well That Ends Well **7:** 32, 41, 43, 45, 54, 76, 104, 116, 121; **26:** 117; **63:** 1

romance or pastoral tradition, influence of
The Tempest **8:** 336, 348, 396, 404; **37:** 336

romance versus history
Henry VIII **61:** 101

Roman citizenry, portrayal of
Julius Caesar **50:** 64, 230; **63:** 238

romantic and courtly conventions
The Two Gentlemen of Verona **6:** 438, 460, 472, 478, 484, 486, 488, 502, 507, 509, 529, 541, 549, 560, 568; **12:** 460, 462; **40:** 354, 374; **54:** 344; **63:** 341, 350

romantic elements
The Comedy of Errors **1:** 13, 16, 19, 23, 25, 30, 31, 36, 39, 53
Cymbeline **4:** 17, 20, 46, 68, 77, 141, 148, 172; **15:** 111; **25:** 319; **28:** 373; **61:** 34
King Lear **31:** 77, 84
The Taming of the Shrew **9:** 334, 342, 362, 375, 407

royalty
Antony and Cleopatra **6:** 94

sacrifice
Titus Andronicus **62:** 258, 265

Salic Law
Henry V **5:** 219, 252, 260; **28:** 121

as satire or parody
Love's Labour's Lost **2:** 300, 302, 303, 307, 308, 315, 321, 324, 327; **23:** 237, 252; **54:** 234
The Merry Wives of Windsor **5:** 338, 350, 360, 385; **38:** 278, 319; **47:** 354, 363

satire or parody of pastoral conventions
As You Like It **5:** 46, 55, 60, 72, 77, 79, 84, 114, 118, 128, 130, 154

satirical elements
Hamlet **59:** 79
The Phoenix and Turtle **10:** 8, 16, 17, 27, 35, 40, 45, 48
Timon of Athens **27:** 155, 235
Troilus and Cressida **3:** 539, 543, 544, 555, 558, 574; **27:** 341

Saturnalian elements
Twelfth Night **1:** 554, 571, 603, 620, 642; **16:** 53

schemes and intrigues
The Merry Wives of Windsor **5:** 334, 336, 339, 341, 343, 349, 355, 379

Scholasticism
Macbeth **52:** 23
The Phoenix and Turtle **10:** 21, 24, 31; **51:** 188

School of Night, allusions to
Love's Labour's Lost **2:** 321, 327, 328

self-conscious or artificial nature of play
Cymbeline **4:** 43, 52, 56, 68, 124, 134, 138; **36:** 99

self-deception
Twelfth Night **1:** 554, 561, 591, 625; **47:** 45

self-indulgence
Twelfth Night **1:** 563, 615, 635

self-interest or expediency
Henry V **5:** 189, 193, 205, 213, 217, 233, 260, 287, 302, 304; **30:** 273; **49:** 223

self-knowledge
As You Like It **5:** 32, 82, 102, 116, 122, 133, 164; **57:** 45
Much Ado about Nothing **8:** 69, 95, 100
Timon of Athens **1:** 456, 459, 462, 495, 503, 507, 515, 518, 526; **20:** 493; **27:** 166

self-love
Sonnets **10:** 372; **25:** 374; **51:** 270, 300, 304; **62:** 180
Twelfth Night **60:** 265, 270, 287

Senecan or revenge tragedy elements
Timon of Athens **27:** 235
Titus Andronicus **4:** 618, 627, 628, 636, 639, 644, 646, 664, 672, 680; **16:** 225; **27:** 275, 318; **43:** 170, 206, 227; **62:** 208

servitude
See also **freedom and servitude**
Comedy of Errors **42:** 80

setting
The Merry Wives of Windsor **47:** 375; **59:** 89, 139
Much Ado about Nothing **18:** 173, 174, 183, 184, 185, 186, 187, 188, 189, 190, 191, 192, 193, 195, 197, 199, 201, 204, 206, 207, 208, 209, 210, 254
Richard III **14:** 516, 528; **52:** 263; **62:** 104
The Two Gentlemen of Verona **12:** 463, 465, 485; **63:** 361

sexual ambiguity and sexual deception
As You Like It **46:** 134, 142; **57:** 23, 40, 45
Twelfth Night **1:** 540, 562, 620, 621, 639, 645; **22:** 69; **34:** 311, 344; **37:** 59; **42:** 32; **62:** 319, 325
Troilus and Cressida **43:** 365

sexual anxiety
Macbeth **16:** 328; **20:** 283

sexual politics
General Commentary **55:** 68
King Lear **55:** 68
Measure for Measure **55:** 68
The Merchant of Venice **22:** 3; **51:** 44
The Merry Wives of Windsor **19:** 101; **38:** 307; **59:** 95

Sexuality in Shakespeare (**Volume 33:** 1, 12, 18, 28, 39)
As You Like It **46:** 122, 127, 134, 142
All's Well That Ends Well **7:** 67, 86, 90, 93, 98, 126; **13:** 84; **19:** 113; **22:** 78; **28:** 38; **44:** 35; **49:** 46; **51:** 44; **55:** 109, 131, 143, 176; **63:** 41, 50, 60, 99
Coriolanus **9:** 112, 142, 174, 183, 189, 198; **30:** 79, 111, 125, 142
Cymbeline **4:** 170, 172; **25:** 319; **32:** 373; **47:** 245
Hamlet **55:** 56; **59:** 31, 68
King Lear **25:** 202; **31:** 133, 137, 142
Love's Labour's Lost **22:** 12; **51:** 44
Measure for Measure **13:** 84; **16:** 102, 114; **23:** 321, 327, 335, 340, 352; **25:** 12; **33:** 85, 90, 112; **49:** 286, 338; **51:** 44
A Midsummer Night's Dream **22:** 23, 93; **29:** 225, 243, 256, 269; **42:** 46; **45:** 107; **53:** 45; **58:** 203, 215, 220
Othello **22:** 339; **28:** 330, 344; **35:** 352, 360; **37:** 269; **44:** 57, 66; **51:** 44; **53:** 275, 310, 315
Romeo and Juliet **25:** 181; **33:** 225, 233, 241, 246, 274, 300; **51:** 227, 236
Sonnets **25:** 374; **48:** 325; **62:** 153
The Tempest **53:** 45; **61:** 288
Troilus and Cressida **22:** 58, 339; **25:** 56; **27:** 362; **43:** 365; **59:** 323, 337, 349
The Two Noble Kinsmen **58:** 338, 345, 356

Shakespeare and Classical Civilization (**Volume 27:** 1, 9, 15, 21, 30, 35, 39, 46, 56, 60, 67)
Antony and Cleopatra
Egyptian versus Roman values **6:** 31, 33, 43, 53, 104, 111, 115, 125, 142, 155, 159, 178, 181, 211, 219; **17:** 48; **19:** 270; **27:** 82, 121, 126; **28:** 249; **47:** 96, 103, 113, 149; **58:** 59, 71, 88, 105; **60:** 179
The Rape of Lucrece
Roman history, relation to **10:** 84, 89, 93, 96, 98, 109, 116, 125, 135; **22:** 289; **25:** 305; **33:** 155, 190; **59:** 175
Timon of Athens **27:** 223, 230, 325
Titus Andronicus **27:** 275, 282, 293, 299, 306
Roman elements **43:** 206, 222; **62:** 277, 284
Troilus and Cressida
Trojan versus Greek values **3:** 541, 561, 574, 584, 590, 596, 621, 638; **27:** 370

Shakespeare's artistic growth, Richard III's contribution to
Richard III **8:** 165, 167, 182, 193, 197, 206, 210, 228, 239, 267; **25:** 164; **39:** 305, 326, 370

Topic Index

Shakespeare's canon, place in
Titus Andronicus **4:** 614, 616, 618, 619, 637, 639, 646, 659, 664, 668; **43:** 195
Twelfth Night **1:** 543, 548, 557, 569, 575, 580, 621, 635, 638

Shakespeare's dramas, compared with
The Phoenix and Turtle **51:** 151, 155
The Rape of Lucrece **43:** 92; **59:** 159

Shakespeare's moral judgment
Antony and Cleopatra **6:** 33, 37, 38, 41, 48, 51, 64, 76, 111, 125, 136, 140, 146, 163, 175, 189, 202, 211, 228; **13:** 368, 523; **25:** 257

Shakespeare's other plays, compared with
King John **56:** 306, 348, 357
The Merchant of Venice **53:** 74
Much Ado about Nothing **55:** 189, 209, 232, 241, 249
The Taming of the Shrew **50:** 74; **55:** 331
Twelfth Night **62:** 297, 308

Shakespeare's political sympathies
Coriolanus **9:** 8, 11, 15, 17, 19, 26, 39, 52, 53, 62, 80, 92, 142; **25:** 296; **30:** 74, 79, 89, 96, 105, 133; **50:** 172
Richard II **6:** 277, 279, 287, 347, 359, 364, 391, 393, 402
Richard III **8:** 147, 163, 177, 193, 197, 201, 223, 228, 232, 243, 248, 267; **39:** 349; **42:** 130

Shakespeare's Representation of History (Volume 56: 2, 3, 15, 25, 47, 53, 60, 95, 196, 286)
Henry VI **56:** 95, 110, 122, 131, 145
Henry VIII **56:** 196, 201, 209, 220, 230
King John **56:** 286, 296, 306, 348, 357

Shakespeare's Representation of Women (Volume 31: 1, 3, 8, 12, 16, 21, 29, 34, 35, 41, 43, 48, 53, 60, 68)
Henry VI, Parts 1, 2, and 3 **3:** 103, 109, 126, 140, 157; **16:** 183; **39:** 196; **63:** 124, 131
King John **9:** 222, 303; **16:** 161; **19:** 182; **41:** 215, 221
King Lear **31:** 117, 123, 133
Love's Labour's Lost **19:** 92; **22:** 12; **23:** 215; **25:** 1
The Merry Wives of Windsor **5:** 335, 341, 343, 349, 369, 379, 390, 392, 402; **19:** 101; **38:** 307
Much Ado about Nothing **31:** 222, 231, 241, 245
Othello **19:** 253; **28:** 344
Richard III **62:** 31, 41, 52
The Taming of the Shrew **31:** 288, 300, 307, 315
The Winter's Tale **22:** 324; **36:** 311; **42:** 301; **51:** 30; **57:** 294, 305, 356; **60:** 254

Shakespeare's romances, compared with
Henry VIII **41:** 171; **54:** 35; **56:** 273
Pericles **54:** 35
The Two Noble Kinsmen **54:** 35

shame
Coriolanus **42:** 243

sibling rivalry
As You Like It **34:** 109
Henry VI, Parts 1, 2, and 3 **22:** 193

slander or hearsay, importance of
Coriolanus **48:** 230
Much Ado about Nothing **8:** 58, 69, 82, 95, 104; **55:** 249

social action
Sonnets **48:** 352; **62:** 159

social and moral corruption
King Lear **2:** 116, 133, 174, 177, 241, 271; **22:** 227; **31:** 84, 92; **46:** 269; **61:** 160

social and political context
All's Well That Ends Well **13:** 66; **22:** 78; **38:** 99, 109, 150, 155; **49:** 46

social aspects
Measure for Measure **23:** 316, 375, 379, 395
The Merchant of Venice **53:** 214

Social Class (Volume 50: 1, 13, 24, 34, 45, 51, 59, 64, 74, 86)
General Commentary **50:** 1, 34
Coriolanus **50:** 105, 110, 119
Julius Caesar **50:** 189, 194, 196, 211, 230
Timon of Athens **1:** 466, 487, 495; **25:** 198; **27:** 184, 196, 212
The Two Noble Kinsmen **50:** 295, 305, 310

social milieu
The Merry Wives of Windsor **18:** 75, 84; **38:** 297, 300; **59:** 132, 139, 144

social order
As You Like It **37:** 1; **46:** 94; **57:** 2
The Comedy of Errors **34:** 238; **54:** 155, 215
Richard III **60:** 322
Henry VIII **61:** 101
The Two Gentlemen of Verona **63:** 357

society
Coriolanus **9:** 15, 17, 18, 19, 26, 33, 43, 53, 62, 65, 73, 80, 92, 106, 110, 112, 121, 144, 153, 157, 164, 180; **22:** 248; **25:** 296; **30:** 58, 67, 79, 89, 96, 105, 111, 125; **50:** 13, 105, 119, 152
Troilus and Cressida **43:** 298

soldiers
Henry V **49:** 194

songs, role of
Love's Labour's Lost **2:** 303, 304, 316, 326, 335, 362, 367, 371, 375; **54:** 240

sonnet arrangement
Sonnets **10:** 174, 176, 182, 205, 226, 230, 236, 315, 353; **28:** 363; **40:** 238; **62:** 121, 128

sonnet form
Sonnets **10:** 255, 325, 367; **37:** 347; **40:** 284, 303; **51:** 270

sonnets, compared with
A Lover's Complaint **48:** 336

source of tragic catastrophe
Romeo and Juliet **5:** 418, 427, 431, 448, 458, 469, 479, 480, 485, 487, 493, 509, 522, 528, 530, 533, 542, 565, 571, 573; **33:** 210; **51:** 245

sources
General Commentary **56:** 25
Antony and Cleopatra **6:** 20, 39; **19:** 304; **27:** 96, 126; **28:** 249
As You Like It **5:** 18, 32, 54, 59, 66, 84; **34:** 155; **46:** 117 **60:** 231
The Comedy of Errors **1:** 13, 14, 16, 19, 31, 32, 39; **16:** 3; **34:** 190, 215, 258; **54:** 155, 176
Coriolanus **60:** 205
Cymbeline **4:** 17, 18; **13:** 401; **28:** 373; **47:** 245, 265, 277
Hamlet **1:** 76, 81, 113, 125, 128, 130, 151, 191, 202, 224, 259; **59:** 68
Henry IV, Parts 1and 2 **56:** 2
Henry V **56:** 2
Henry VI, Parts 1, 2, and 3 **3:** 18, 21, 29, 31, 35, 39, 46, 51; **13:** 131; **16:** 217; **39:** 196; **56:** 2, 122, 131, 187; **63:** 114, 158, 169
Henry VIII **2:** 16, 17; **24:** 71, 80; **61:** 111
Julius Caesar **7:** 149, 150, 156, 187, 200, 264, 272, 282, 284, 320; **30:** 285, 297, 326, 358; **63:** 269
King John **9:** 216, 222, 300; **32:** 93, 114; **41:** 234, 243, 251; **56:** 296, 357
King Lear **2:** 94, 100, 143, 145, 170, 186; **13:** 352; **16:** 351; **28:** 301 **60:** 185; **61:** 250
Love's Labour's Lost **16:** 17
Macbeth **60:** 214
Measure for Measure **2:** 388, 393, 427, 429, 437, 475; **13:** 94; **49:** 349 **60:** 281
The Merry Wives of Windsor **5:** 332, 350, 360, 366, 385; **32:** 31; **52:** 69; **59:** 123
A Midsummer Night's Dream **29:** 216; **60:** 259
Much Ado about Nothing **8:** 9, 19, 53, 58, 104
Othello **28:** 330
Pericles **2:** 538, 568, 572, 575; **25:** 365; **36:** 198, 205; **51:** 118, 126
The Phoenix and Turtle **10:** 7, 9, 18, 24, 45; **38:** 326, 334, 350, 367; **51:** 138
The Rape of Lucrece **10:** 63, 64, 65, 66, 68, 74, 77, 78, 89, 98, 109, 121, 125; **25:** 305; **33:** 155, 190; **43:** 77, 92, 148; **59:** 165
Richard II **56:** 2
Richard III **52:** 263, 290; **56:** 2; **62:** 2, 31, 60, 78
chronicles **8:** 145, 165, 193, 197, 201, 206, 210, 213, 228, 232
Marlowe, Christopher **8:** 167, 168, 182, 201, 206, 218
morality plays **8:** 182, 190, 201, 213, 239
Seneca, other classical writers **8:** 165, 190, 201, 206, 228, 248; **62:** 31, 60
Romeo and Juliet **5:** 416, 419, 423, 450; **32:** 222; **33:** 210; **45:** 40; **54:** 125
Sonnets **10:** 153, 154, 156, 158, 233, 251, 255, 293, 353; **16:** 472; **28:** 407; **42:** 375; **62:** 121, 128
The Taming of the Shrew **60:** 281

folk tales **9:** 332, 390, 393
Old and New Comedy **9:** 419
Ovid **9:** 318, 370, 430
Plautus **9:** 334, 341, 342
shrew tradition **9:** 355; **19:** 3; **32:** 1, 56; **55:** 342
text and sources **55:** 334, 357
The Tempest **45:** 226; **61:** 326
Timon of Athens **16:** 351; **27:** 191; **52:** 301
Titus Andronicus **62:** 208, 277, 284
Troilus and Cressida **3:** 537, 539, 540, 541, 544, 549, 558, 566, 574, 587; **27:** 376, 381, 391, 400
Twelfth Night **1:** 539, 540, 603; **34:** 301, 323, 344; **46:** 291 **60:** 265, 270, 287; **62:** 308
The Two Gentlemen of Verona **6:** 436, 460, 462, 468, 476, 480, 490, 511, 547; **19:** 34; **40:** 320; **54:** 295
The Two Noble Kinsmen **19:** 394; **41:** 289, 301, 363, 385; **50:** 326, 348; **58:** 361, 371
Venus and Adonis **10:** 410, 412, 420, 424, 429, 434, 439, 451, 454, 466, 473, 480, 486, 489; **16:** 452; **25:** 305; **28:** 355; **33:** 309, 321, 330, 339, 347, 352, 357, 370, 377; **42:** 347
The Winter's Tale **60:** 254, 281

spectacle
Love's Labour's Lost **38:** 226
Macbeth **42:** 258
Pericles **42:** 352
Titus Andronicus **62:** 277

spectacle versus simple staging
The Tempest **15:** 206, 207, 208, 210, 217, 219, 222, 223, 224, 225, 227, 228, 305, 352; **28:** 415

stage history
As You Like It **46:** 117; **57:** 56
Antony and Cleopatra **17:** 84, 94, 101
The Merry Wives of Windsor **18:** 66, 67, 68, 70, 71; **59:** 123

staging issues
See also **performance issues**
All's Well That Ends Well **19:** 113; **26:** 15, 19, 48, 52, 64, 73, 85, 92, 93, 94, 95, 97, 114, 117, 128; **54:** 30
Antony and Cleopatra **17:** 6, 12, 84, 94, 101, 104, 110; **27:** 90; **47:** 142
As You Like It **13:** 502; **23:** 7, 17, 19, 22, 58, 96, 97, 98, 99, 101, 110, 137; **28:** 82; **32:** 212; **57:** 56, 75
The Comedy of Errors **26:** 182, 183, 186, 188, 190; **54:** 136
Coriolanus **17:** 172, 242, 248
Cymbeline **15:** 6, 23, 75, 105, 111, 121, 122; **22:** 365
Hamlet **13:** 494, 502; **21:** 11, 17, 31, 35, 41, 44, 50, 53, 78, 81, 89, 101, 112, 127, 139, 142, 145, 148, 151, 157, 160, 172, 182, 183, 202, 203, 208, 225, 232, 237, 242, 245, 249, 251, 259, 268, 270, 274, 283, 284, 301, 311, 334, 347, 355, 361, 371, 377, 379, 380, 381, 384, 386, 392, 407, 410, 416; **44:** 198
Henry IV, Parts 1 and 2 **32:** 212; **47:** 1; **49:** 102
Henry V **5:** 186, 189, 192, 193, 198, 205, 226, 230, 241, 281, 314; **13:** 194, 502; **14:** 293, 295, 297, 301, 310, 319, 328, 334, 336, 342; **19:** 217; **32:** 185
Henry VI, Parts 1, 2, and 3 **24:** 21, 22, 27, 31, 32, 36, 38, 41, 45, 48, 55; **32:** 212; **56:** 154, 172, 180, 187
Henry VIII **24:** 67, 70, 71, 75, 77, 83, 84, 85, 87, 89, 91, 101, 106, 113, 120, 127, 129, 136, 140, 146, 150, 152, 155; **28:** 184; **56:** 220, 248
Julius Caesar **48:** 240; **50:** 186
King John **16:** 161; **19:** 182; **24:** 171, 187, 203, 206, 211, 225, 228, 241, 245, 249; **56:** 286, 365
King Lear **11:** 136, 137, 142, 145, 150, 151, 154, 158, 161, 165, 169; **32:** 212; **46:** 205, 218
Love's Labour's Lost **23:** 184, 187, 191, 196, 198, 200, 201, 202, 207, 212, 215, 216, 217, 229, 230, 232, 233, 237, 252
Macbeth **13:** 502; **20:** 12, 17, 32, 64, 65, 70, 73, 107, 113, 151, 175, 203, 206, 210, 213, 245, 279, 283, 312, 318, 324, 329, 343, 345, 350, 353, 363, 367, 374, 376, 379, 382, 387, 400, 406, 413; **22:** 365; **32:** 212
Measure for Measure **2:** 427, 429, 437, 441, 443, 456, 460, 482, 491, 519; **23:** 283, 284, 285, 286, 287, 291, 293, 294, 298, 299, 311, 315, 327, 338, 339, 340, 342, 344, 347, 363, 372, 375, 395, 400, 405, 406, 413; **32:** 16
The Merchant of Venice **12:** 111, 114, 115, 117, 119, 124, 129, 131
The Merry Wives of Windsor **18:** 74, 75, 84, 86, 90, 95
A Midsummer Night's Dream **3:** 364, 365, 371, 372, 377; **12:** 151, 152, 154, 158, 159, 280, 284, 291, 295; **16:** 34; **19:** 21; **29:** 183, 256; **48:** 23
Much Ado about Nothing **8:** 18, 33, 41, 75, 79, 82, 108; **16:** 45; **18:** 245, 247, 249, 252, 254, 257, 261, 264; **28:** 63; **55:** 221
Othello **11:** 273, 334, 335, 339, 342, 350,354, 359, 362
Pericles **16:** 399; **48:** 364; **51:** 99; **53:** 233, 304
Richard II **13:** 494; **24:** 273, 274, 278, 279, 280, 283, 291, 295, 296, 301, 303, 304, 310, 315, 317, 320, 325, 333, 338, 346, 351, 352, 356, 364, 383, 386, 395, 402, 405, 411, 414, 419, 423, 428; **25:** 89; **58:** 241
Richard III **14:** 515, 527, 528, 537; **16:** 137; **52:** 263, 272
Romeo and Juliet **11:** 499, 505, 507, 514, 517; **13:** 243; **25:** 181; **32:** 212
The Tempest **15:** 343, 346, 352, 361, 364, 366, 368, 371, 385; **28:** 391, 415; **29:** 339; **32:** 338, 343; **42:** 332; **45:** 200; **54:** 19; **61:** 297
Timon of Athens **20:** 445, 446, 481, 491, 492, 493
Titus Andronicus **17:** 449, 452, 456, 487; **25:** 245; **32:** 212, 249
Troilus and Cressida **16:** 70; **18:** 289, 332, 371, 395, 403, 406, 412, 419, 423, 442, 447, 451; **59:** 225, 323
Twelfth Night **26:** 219, 233, 257, 337, 342, 346, 357, 359, 360, 364, 366, 371, 374; **46:** 310, 369; **54:** 19
The Two Gentlemen of Verona **12:** 457, 464; **42:** 18; **63:** 361
The Winter's Tale **7:** 414, 425, 429, 446, 464, 480, 483, 497; **13:** 409; **15:** 518; **48:** 309

Stoicism
Hamlet **48:** 195
Julius Caesar **50:** 249; **63:** 301

strategic analysis
Antony and Cleopatra **48:** 206

structure
All's Well That Ends Well **7:** 21, 29, 32, 45, 51, 76, 81, 93, 98, 116; **22:** 78; **26:** 128; **38:** 72, 123, 142
Antony and Cleopatra **58:** 71, 88
As You Like It **5:** 19, 24, 25, 35, 44, 45, 46, 86, 93, 116, 138, 158; **23:** 7, 8, 9, 10, 11; **34:** 72, 78, 131, 147, 155
Coriolanus **9:** 8, 9, 11, 12, 13, 14, 16, 26, 33, 45, 53, 58, 72, 78, 80, 84, 92, 112, 139, 148; **25:** 263; **30:** 79, 96
Hamlet **22:** 378; **28:** 280, 325; **35:** 82, 104, 215; **44:** 152; **59:** 2, 42
Henry IV, Parts 1 and 2 **49:** 93 **56:** 53, 60; **57:** 181
Henry V **5:** 186, 189, 205, 213, 230, 241, 264, 289, 310, 314; **30:** 220, 227, 234, 244
Henry VI, Parts 1, 2, and 3 **3:** 31, 43, 46, 69, 83, 103, 109, 119, 136, 149, 154; **39:** 213; **56:** 77, 80, 85; **63:** 158, 185
Henry VIII **2:** 16, 25, 27, 28, 31, 36, 44, 46, 51, 56, 68, 75; **24:** 106, 112, 113, 120; **56:** 209
Julius Caesar **7:** 152, 155, 159, 160, 179, 200, 210, 238, 264, 284, 298, 316, 346; **13:** 252; **30:** 374; **63:** 287
King John **9:** 208, 212, 222, 224, 229, 240, 244, 245, 254, 260, 263, 275, 284, 290, 292, 300; **24:** 228, 241; **41:** 260, 269, 277
King Lear **28:** 325; **32:** 308; **46:** 177
Love's Labour's Lost **22:** 378; **23:** 191, 237, 252; **38:** 163, 172
Macbeth **16:** 317; **20:** 12, 245
Measure for Measure **2:** 390, 411, 449, 456, 466, 474, 482, 490, 491; **33:** 69; **49:** 379
The Merchant of Venice **4:** 201, 215, 230, 232, 243, 247, 254, 261, 263, 308, 321; **12:** 115; **28:** 63; **60:** 276
The Merry Wives of Windsor **5:** 332, 333, 334, 335, 343, 349, 355, 369, 374; **18:** 86; **22:** 378; **59:** 89, 111
A Midsummer Night's Dream **3:** 364, 368, 381, 402, 406, 427, 450, 513; **13:** 19; **22:** 378; **29:** 175; **45:** 126, 175; **58:** 186, 189
Much Ado about Nothing **8:** 9, 16, 17, 19, 28, 29, 33, 39, 48, 63, 69, 73, 75, 79, 82, 115; **31:** 178, 184, 198, 231; **55:** 189
Othello **22:** 378; **28:** 325
The Phoenix and Turtle **10:** 27, 31, 37, 45, 50; **38:** 342, 345, 357; **51:** 138, 143
The Rape of Lucrece **10:** 84, 89, 93, 98, 135; **22:** 294; **25:** 305; **43:** 102, 141; **59:** 159
Richard II **6:** 282, 304, 317, 343, 352, 359, 364, 39; **24:** 307, 322, 325, 356, 395; **58:** 229, 241

Richard III **8:** 154, 161, 163, 167, 168, 170, 177, 184, 193, 197, 201, 206, 210, 218, 223, 228, 232, 243, 252, 262, 267; **16:** 150; **62:** 14, 18, 91
Romeo and Juliet **5:** 438, 448, 464, 469, 470, 477, 480, 496, 518, 524, 525, 528, 547, 559; **33:** 210, 246
Sonnets **10:** 175, 176, 182, 205, 230, 260, 296, 302, 309, 315, 337, 349, 353; **40:** 238; **62:** 146
The Taming of the Shrew **9:** 318, 322, 325, 332, 334, 341, 362, 370, 390, 426; **22:** 48, 378; **31:** 269; **55:** 278, 342, 371
The Tempest **8:** 294, 295, 299, 320, 384, 439; **28:** 391, 415; **29:** 292, 297; **45:** 188
Timon of Athens **27:** 157, 175, 235; **52:** 338, 345, 349 375
Titus Andronicus **4:** 618, 619, 624, 631, 635, 640, 644, 646, 647, 653, 656, 659, 662, 664, 668, 672; **27:** 246, 285; **60:** 276
Troilus and Cressida **3:** 536, 538, 549, 568, 569, 578, 583, 589, 611, 613; **27:** 341, 347, 354, 391
Twelfth Night **1:** 539, 542, 543, 546, 551, 553, 563, 570, 571, 590, 600, 660; **26:** 374; **34:** 281, 287; **46:** 286; **62:** 308
The Two Gentlemen of Verona **6:** 445, 450, 460, 462, 504, 526; **63:** 361
The Two Noble Kinsmen **37:** 313; **50:** 326, 361; **58:** 322
Venus and Adonis **10:** 434, 442, 480, 486, 489; **33:** 357, 377

style
Henry VIII **41:** 158
The Phoenix and Turtle **10:** 8, 20, 24, 27, 31, 35, 45, 50; **38:** 334, 345, 357; **51:** 171, 188
The Rape of Lucrece **10:** 64, 65, 66, 68, 69, 70, 71, 73, 74, 77, 78, 81, 84, 98, 116, 131, 135; **43:** 113, 158;
Titus Andronicus **62:** 254
Venus and Adonis **10:** 411, 412, 414, 415, 416, 418, 419, 420, 423, 424, 428, 429, 439, 442, 480, 486, 489; **16:** 452

subjectivity
Hamlet **45:** 28; **59:** 42
Sonnets **37:** 374

subplot
Twelfth Night **62:** 297, 339, 343, 348

substitution of identities
Measure for Measure **2:** 507, 511, 519; **13:** 112; **49:** 313, 325

subversiveness
Cymbeline **22:** 302
The Tempest **22:** 302
The Winter's Tale **22:** 302

Succession (**Volume 60:** 295, 304, 322, 329, 340, 346, 357)
General Commentary **60:** 346, 357
Hamlet **60:** 346
Henry IV, Parts 1 and 2 **60:** 304
Henry V **60:** 304
Henry VI, Parts 1, 2, and 3 **60:** 304
King John **60:** 295, 304, 329
Macbeth **60:** 340, 357
Richard II **60:** 304
Richard III **60:** 304, 322
Titus Andronicus **4:** 638

supernatural grace versus evil or chaos
Measure for Measure **48:** 1

suffering
King Lear **2:** 137, 160, 188, 201, 218, 222, 226, 231, 238, 241, 249, 265; **13:** 343; **22:** 271; **25:** 218; **50:** 24
Pericles **2:** 546, 573, 578, 579; **25:** 365; **36:** 279

symbolism
The Winter's Tale **7:** 425, 429, 436, 452, 456, 469, 490, 493

textual arrangement
Henry VI, Parts 1, 2, and 3 **24:** 3, 4, 6, 12, 17, 18, 19, 20, 21, 24, 27, 42, 45; **37:** 165
Richard II **24:** 260, 261, 262, 263, 271, 273, 291, 296, 356, 390

textual issues
Henry IV, Parts 1 and 2 **22:** 114
King Lear **22:** 271; **37:** 295; **49:** 73; **61:** 262
A Midsummer Night's Dream **16:** 34; **29:** 216; **58:** 151
The Taming of the Shrew **22:** 48; **31:** 261, 276; **31:** 276; **55:** 342, 371
The Winter's Tale **19:** 441; **45:** 333; **57:** 278, 285, 356

textual problems
Henry V **5:** 187, 189, 190; **13:** 201

textual revisions
Pericles **15:** 129, 130, 132, 134, 135, 136, 138, 152, 155, 167, 181; **16:** 399; **25:** 365; **51:** 99

textual variants
Hamlet **13:** 282; **16:** 259; **21:** 11, 23, 72, 101, 127, 129, 139, 140, 142, 145, 202, 208, 259, 270, 284, 347, 361, 384; **22:** 258; **32:** 238

theatrical viability
Henry VI, Parts 1, 2, and 3 **24:** 31, 32, 34; **56:** 80, 172; **63:** 144

theatricality
Antony and Cleopatra **47:** 96, 103, 107, 113
Macbeth **16:** 328
Measure for Measure **23:** 285, 286, 294, 372, 406; **49:** 358
The Merry Wives of Windsor **47:** 325

thematic disparity
Henry VIII **2:** 25, 31, 56, 68, 75; **41:** 146

themes
Hamlet **59:** 74, 79

time
As You Like It **5:** 18, 82, 112, 141; **23:** 146, 150; **34:** 102; **46:** 88, 156, 164, 169
Macbeth **3:** 234, 246, 283, 293; **20:** 245; **57:** 218
Richard II **22:** 137
Sonnets **10:** 265, 302, 309, 322, 329, 337, 360, 379; **13:** 445; **40:** 292
The Tempest **8:** 401, 439, 464; **25:** 357; **29:** 278, 292; **45:** 236
Troilus and Cressida **3:** 561, 571, 583, 584, 613, 621, 626, 634
Twelfth Night **37:** 78; **46:** 297
The Winter's Tale **7:** 397, 425, 436, 476, 490; **19:** 366; **36:** 301, 349; **45:** 297, 329, 366, 374

time and change, motif of
Henry IV, Parts 1 and 2 **1:** 372, 393, 411; **39:** 89; **48:** 143
As You Like It **46:** 156, 164, 169

time scheme
Othello **4:** 370, 384, 390, 488; **22:** 207; **35:** 310; **47:** 51

topical allusions or content
Hamlet **13:** 282
Henry V **5:** 185, 186; **13:** 201
Love's Labour's Lost **2:** 300, 303, 307, 315, 316, 317, 319, 321, 327, 328; **23:** 187, 191, 197, 203, 221, 233, 237, 252; **25:** 1
Macbeth **13:** 361; **20:** 17, 350; **29:** 101

traditional values
Richard III **39:** 335

tragicomedy, as
Cymbeline **61:** 2, 18

tragedies of major characters
Henry VIII **2:** 16, 39, 46, 48, 49, 51, 56, 58, 68, 81; **41:** 120

tragic elements
The Comedy of Errors **1:** 16, 25, 27, 45, 50, 59; **34:** 229; **54:** 144
Cymbeline **25:** 319; **28:** 373; **36:** 129; **47:** 296
Hamlet **55:** 78
Henry V **5:** 228, 233, 267, 269, 271
Henry VI, Parts 1, 2, and 3 **60:** 33
Julius Caesar **50:** 258, 265
King John **9:** 208, 209, 244
King Lear **55:** 78; **61:** 250
Macbeth **52:** 15; **55:** 78; **57:** 189
A Midsummer Night's Dream **3:** 393, 400, 401, 410, 445, 474, 480, 491, 498, 511; **29:** 175; **45:** 169; **58:** 175, 186
Othello **55:** 78
The Rape of Lucrece **10:** 78, 80, 81, 84, 98, 109; **43:** 85, 148
Richard II **58:** 229
Romeo and Juliet **55:** 78
The Tempest **8:** 324, 348, 359, 370, 380, 408, 414, 439, 458, 464
Twelfth Night **1:** 557, 569, 572, 575, 580, 599, 621, 635, 638, 639, 645, 654, 656; **26:** 342

treachery
Coriolanus **30:** 89
King John **9:** 245

treason and punishment
Macbeth **13:** 361; **16:** 328
Richard II **58:** 307

trial scene
The Merchant of Venice **49:** 1, 23, 37

trickster, motif of
Cymbeline **22:** 302
The Tempest **22:** 302; **29:** 297
The Winter's Tale **22:** 302; **45:** 333

triumph over death or fate
Romeo and Juliet **5:** 421, 423, 427, 505, 509, 520, 530, 536, 565, 566; **51:** 219

Trojan War
Troilus and Cressida
as myth **43:** 293

The Troublesome Reign (anonymous), compared with
King John **41:** 205, 221, 260, 269; **48:** 132; **56:** 357

Troy
Troilus and Cressida **43:** 287

Troy passage
The Rape of Lucrece **43:** 77, 85; **59:** 206

Tudor doctrine
King John **9:** 254, 284, 297; **41:** 221; **56:** 345

Tudor myth
Henry VI, Parts 1, 2, and 3 **3:** 51, 59, 77, 92, 100, 109, 115, 119, 131; **39:** 222
Richard III **8:** 163, 165, 177, 184, 193, 201, 218, 228, 232, 243, 248, 252, 267; **39:** 305, 308, 326, 387; **42:** 130

Turkish elements
Henry IV, Parts 1 and 2 **19:** 170
Henry V **19:** 170

two fathers
Henry IV, Parts 1 and 2 **14:** 86, 101, 105, 108; **39:** 89, 100; **49:** 102

tyranny
King John **9:** 218

unity
Antony and Cleopatra **6:** 20, 21, 22, 24, 25, 32, 33, 39, 43, 53, 60, 67, 111, 125, 146, 151, 165, 208, 211, 219; **13:** 374; **27:** 82, 90, 135
Cymbeline **61:** 54
Hamlet **1:** 75, 76, 87, 103, 113, 125, 128, 142, 148, 160, 184, 188, 198, 264; **16:** 259; **35:** 82, 215
Henry VI, Parts 1, 2, and 3 **39:** 177, 222
A Midsummer Night's Dream **3:** 364, 368, 381, 402, 406, 427, 450, 513; **13:** 19; **22:** 378; **29:** 175, 263

unity of double plot
The Merchant of Venice **4:** 193, 194, 201, 232; **12:** 16, 67, 80, 115; **40:** 151

unnatural ordering
Hamlet **22:** 378
Love's Labour's Lost **22:** 378
The Merry Wives of Windsor **22:** 378
A Midsummer Night's Dream **22:** 378
Othello **22:** 378

as unsuccessful play
Measure for Measure **2:** 397, 441, 474, 482; **23:** 287

usurpation
See also **rebellion**
Richard II **6:** 263, 264, 272, 287, 289, 315, 323, 331, 343, 354, 364, 381, 388, 393, 397; **24:** 383; **52:** 108, 141, 154
The Tempest **8:** 304, 370, 408, 420; **25:** 357, 382; **29:** 278, 362, 377; **37:** 336

utopia
The Tempest **45:** 280

value systems
Troilus and Cressida **3:** 578, 583, 589, 602, 613, 617; **13:** 53; **27:** 370, 396, 400; **59:** 234, 245; **59:** 287, 295, 318

Venetian politics
Othello **32:** 294

Venice, Elizabethan perceptions of
The Merchant of Venice **28:** 249; **32:** 294; **40:** 127

Venus and Adonis
The Rape of Lucrece **43:** 148

Vergil, influence of
Titus Andronicus **27:** 306; **28:** 249

verisimilitude
As You Like It **5:** 18, 23, 28, 30, 32, 39, 125; **23:** 107

Verona society
Romeo and Juliet **5:** 556, 566; **13:** 235; **33:** 255; **51:** 245

Violence in Shakespeare's Works (Volume 43: 1, 12, 24, 32, 39, 61)
Hamlet **59:** 26
Henry IV, Parts 1 and 2 **25:** 109
Henry VI, Parts 1, 2, and 3 **24:** 25, 31; **37:** 157
Julius Caesar **48:** 240
Love's Labour's Lost **22:** 12
Macbeth **20:** 273, 279, 283; **45:** 58; **57:** 228, 267
Othello **22:** 12
The Rape of Lucrece **43:** 148, 158; **59:** 189, 193, 212
The Taming of the Shrew **55:** 322
Titus Andronicus **13:** 225; **25:** 245; **27:** 255; **28:** 249; **32:** 249, 265; **43:** 186, 203, 227, 239, 247, 255, 262; **62:** 208, , 225, 233, 242, 254, 258, 265
Troilus and Cressida **43:** 329, 340, 351, 357, 365, 377

virginity or chastity, importance of
Much Ado about Nothing **8:** 44, 75, 95, 111, 121, 125; **31:** 222; **55:** 268

Virgo vs. Virago
King Lear **48:** 222

visual arts, relation to
Sonnets **28:** 407

visual humor
Love's Labour's Lost **23:** 207, 217

virtue versus vice
Antony and Cleopatra **60:** 222
Macbeth **60:** 214

war
Coriolanus **25:** 263; **30:** 79, 96, 125, 149
Henry V **5:** 193, 195, 197, 198, 210, 213, 219, 230, 233, 246, 281, 293; **28:** 121, 146; **30:** 262; **32:** 126; **37:** 175, 187; **42:** 141; **49:** 194, 236, 247, 260

Wars of the Roses
Richard III **8:** 163, 165, 177, 184, 193, 201, 218, 228, 232, 243, 248, 252, 267; **39:** 308; **62:** 71

Watteau, influence on staging
Love's Labour's Lost **23:** 184, 186

wealth
The Merchant of Venice **4:** 209, 261, 270, 273, 317; **12:** 80, 117; **22:** 69; **25:** 22; **28:** 249; **40:** 117, 197, 208; **45:** 17; **49:** 1; **51:** 15

wealth and social class
Timon of Athens **1:** 466, 487, 495; **25:** 198; **27:** 184, 196, 212; **50:** 13

wheel of fortune, motif of
Antony and Cleopatra **6:** 25, 178; **19:** 304
Hamlet **52:** 35
Henry VIII **2:** 27, 65, 72, 81; **61:** 144

widowhood and remarriage, themes of
Hamlet **32:** 238

wisdom
King Lear **37:** 213; **46:** 210
Love's Labour's Lost **54:** 257

wit
The Merry Wives of Windsor **5:** 335, 336, 337, 339, 343, 351
Much Ado about Nothing **8:** 27, 29, 38, 69, 79, 91, 95; **31:** 178, 191; **55:** 228

witchcraft
See **Magic and the Supernatural**

women, role of
See **Shakespeare's Representation of Women**

wonder, dynamic of
The Comedy of Errors **37:** 12

wordplay
As You Like It **46:** 105
Romeo and Juliet **32:** 256

written versus oral communication
Love's Labour's Lost **2:** 359, 365; **28:** 63

youth
The Two Gentlemen of Verona **6:** 439, 450, 464, 514, 568; **63:** 336

youth versus age
All's Well That Ends Well **7:** 9, 45, 58, 62, 76, 81, 86, 93, 98, 104, 116, 126; **26:** 117; **38:** 109

Cumulative Topic Index, by Play

The Cumulative Topic Index, by Play identifies the principal topics of discussion in the criticism of each play and non-dramatic poem. The topics are arranged alphabetically by play. Page references indicate the beginning page number of each essay containing substantial commentary on that topic. A parenthetical reference after a play indicates which volumes discuss the play extensively.

All's Well That Ends Well **(Volumes 7, 26, 38, 55, 63)**

appearance versus reality **7:** 37, 76, 93; **26:** 117
audience perspective **7:** 81, 104, 109, 116, 121
bed-trick **7:** 8, 26, 27, 29, 32, 41, 86, 93, 98, 113, 116, 126; **13:** 84; **26:** 117; **28:** 38; **38:** 65, 118; **49:** 46; **54:** 52; **55:** 109, 131, 176; **63:** 50, 60
Bertram
characterization **7:** 15, 27, 29, 32, 39, 41, 43, 98, 113; **26:** 48; **26:** 117; **55:** 90; **63:** 60, 99
conduct **7:** 9, 10, 12, 16, 19, 21, 51, 62, 104; **50:** 59; **55:** 143, 154; **63:** 99
desire **22:** 78
identity **63:** 89
masculinity **63:** 60
transformation or redemption **7:** 10, 19, 21, 26, 29, 32, 54, 62, 81, 90, 93, 98, 109, 113, 116, 126; **13:** 84
betrothal **63:** 84
comic elements **26:** 97, 114; **48:** 65; **55:** 148, 154, 164; **63:** 10
conclusion **38:** 123, 132, 142; **54:** 52 **55:** 148, 154, 170
dark elements **7:** 27, 37, 39, 43, 54, 109, 113, 116; **26:** 85; **48:** 65; **50:** 59; **54:** 30; **55:** 164, 170
Decameron (Boccaccio), compared with **7:** 29, 43
desire **38:** 99, 109, 118; **55:** 122
displacement **22:** 78
divorce **63:** 96
education **7:** 62, 86, 90, 93, 98, 104, 116, 126
elder characters **7:** 9, 37, 39, 43, 45, 54, 62, 104
family relations **63:** 89
gender issues **7:** 9, 10, 67, 126; **13:** 77, 84; **19:** 113; **26:** 128; **38:** 89, 99, 118; **44:** 35; **55:** 101, 109, 122, 164; **63:** 60
genre **48:** 65; **63:** 10, 28
Helena
as agent of reconciliation, renewal, or grace **7:** 67, 76, 81, 90, 93, 98, 109, 116; **55:** 176; **63:** 21
desire **38:** 96; **44:** 35; **55:** 109, 170; **63:** 36, 41, 60
as dualistic or enigmatic character **7:** 15, 27, 29, 39, 54, 58, 62, 67, 76, 81, 98, 113, 126; **13:** 66; **22:** 78; **26:** 117; **54:** 30; **55:** 90, 170, 176; **63:** 50
as "female achiever" **19:** 113; **38:** 89; **55:** 90, 101, 109, 122, 164; **63:** 36, 41, 50
pursuit of Bertram **7:** 9, 12, 15, 16, 19, 21, 26, 27, 29, 32, 43, 54, 76, 116; **13:** 77; **22:** 78; **49:** 46; **55:** 90; **63:** 36, 41, 50, 60, 99
virginity **38:** 65; **55:** 131, 176
virtue and nobility **7:** 9, 10, 12, 16, 19, 21, 27, 32, 41, 51, 58, 67, 76, 86, 126; **13:** 77; **50:** 59; **55:** 122
implausibility of plot, characters, or events **7:** 8, 45
irony, paradox, and ambiguity **7:** 27, 32, 58, 62, 67, 81, 86, 109, 116
King **38:** 150; **55:** 148
language and imagery **7:** 12, 29, 45, 104, 109, 121; **38:** 132; **48:** 65; **63:** 36
Lavatch **26:** 64; **46:** 33, 52, 68; **55:** 143; **63:** 28
love **7:** 12, 15, 16, 51, 58, 67, 90, 93, 116; **38:** 80; **51:** 33, 44
marriage **63:** 50, 84, 89, 96, 99
merit versus rank **7:** 9, 10, 19, 37, 51, 76; **38:** 155; **50:** 59
"mingled yarn" **7:** 62, 93, 109, 126; **38:** 65
morality plays, influence of **7:** 29, 41, 51, 98, 113; **13:** 66
mythic or mythological elements **60:** 169
naturalism **60:** 169
opening scene **54:** 30
Parolles
characterization **7:** 8, 9, 43, 76, 81, 98, 109, 113, 116, 126; **22:** 78; **26:** 48, 73, 97; **26:** 117; **46:** 68; **55:** 90, 154
exposure **7:** 9, 27, 81, 98, 109, 113, 116, 121, 126
Falstaff, compared with **7:** 8, 9, 16
politics **63:** 96
as problem play **63:** 10, 89
reconciliation **7:** 90, 93, 98; **51:** 33
religious, mythic, or spiritual content **7:** 15, 45, 54, 67, 76, 98, 109, 116
romance or folktale elements **7:** 32, 41, 43, 45, 54, 76, 104, 116, 121; **26:** 117; **63:** 1
sexuality **7:** 67, 86, 90, 93, 98, 126; **13:** 84; **19:** 113; **22:** 78; **28:** 38; **44:** 35; **49:** 46; **51:** 44; **55:** 109, 131, 143, 176; **63:** 41, 50, 60, 99
social and political context **13:** 66; **22:** 78; **38:** 99, 109, 150, 155; **49:** 46
staging issues **19:** 113; **26:** 15, 19, 48, 52, 64, 73, 85, 92, 93, 94, 95, 97, 114, 117, 128; **54:** 30
structure **7:** 21, 29, 32, 45, 51, 76, 81, 93, 98, 116; **22:** 78; **26:** 128; **38:** 72, 123, 142
youth versus age **7:** 9, 45, 58, 62, 76, 81, 86, 93, 98, 104, 116, 126; **26:** 117; **38:** 109

Antony and Cleopatra **(Volumes 6, 17, 27, 47, 58)**

allegorical elements **52:** 5
All for Love (John Dryden), compared with **6:** 20, 21; **17:** 12, 94, 101
ambiguity **6:** 53, 111, 161, 163, 180, 189, 208, 211, 228; **13:** 368

androgyny **13:** 530
Antony
  characterization **6:** 22, 23, 24, 31, 38, 41, 172, 181, 211; **16:** 342; **19:** 270; **22:** 217; **27:** 117; **47:** 77, 124, 142; **58:** 2, 41, 118, 134
  Cleopatra, relationship with **6:** 25, 27, 37, 39, 48, 52, 53, 62, 67, 71, 76, 85, 100, 125, 131, 133, 136, 142, 151, 161, 163, 165, 180, 192; **27:** 82; **47:** 107, 124, 165, 174
  death scene **25:** 245; **47:** 142; **58:** 41; **60:** 46
  dotage **6:** 22, 23, 38, 41, 48, 52, 62, 107, 136, 146, 175; **17:** 28
  nobility **6:** 22, 24, 33, 48, 94, 103, 136, 142, 159, 172, 202; **25:** 245
  political conduct **6:** 33, 38, 53, 107, 111, 146, 181
  public versus private personae **6:** 165; **47:** 107; **58:** 41
  self-knowledge **6:** 120, 131, 175, 181, 192; **47:** 77
  as superhuman figure **6:** 37, 51, 71, 92, 94, 178, 192; **27:** 110; **47:** 71
  as tragic hero **6:** 38, 39, 52, 53, 60, 104, 120, 151, 155, 165, 178, 192, 202, 211; **22:** 217; **27:** 90
audience response **48:** 206; **58:** 88
Cleopatra
  Antony, relationship with **6:** 25, 27, 37, 39, 48, 52, 53, 62, 67, 71, 76, 85, 100, 125, 131, 133, 136, 142, 151, 161, 163, 165, 180, 192; **25:** 257; **27:** 82; **47:** 107, 124, 165, 174
  characterization **47:** 77, 96, 113, 124; **58:** 24, 33, 59, 118, 134
  contradictory or inconsistent nature **6:** 23, 24, 27, 67, 76, 100, 104, 115, 136, 151, 159, 202; **17:** 94, 113; **27:** 135
  costume **17:** 94
  creativity **6:** 197; **47:** 96, 113
  death, decay, and nature's destructiveness **6:** 23, 25, 27, 41, 43, 52, 60, 64, 76, 94, 100, 103, 120, 131, 133, 136, 140, 146, 161, 165, 180, 181, 192, 197, 208; **13:** 383; **17:** 48, 94; **25:** 245; **27:** 135; **47:** 71
  death scene **60:** 46
  personal attraction of **6:** 24, 38, 40, 43, 48, 53, 76, 104, 115, 155; **17:** 113
  self-knowledge **47:** 77, 96
  staging issues **17:** 94, 113
  as subverter of social order **6:** 146, 165; **47:** 113
  suicide **58:** 33
  as superhuman figure **6:** 37, 51, 71, 92, 94, 178, 192; **27:** 110; **47:** 71, 174, 192; **58:** 24
  as tragic heroine **6:** 53, 120, 151, 192, 208; **27:** 144
  as voluptuary or courtesan **6:** 21, 22, 25, 41, 43, 52, 53, 62, 64, 67, 76, 146, 161; **47:** 107, 174; **58:** 24
comic elements **6:** 52, 85, 104, 125, 131, 151, 192, 202, 219; **47:** 77, 124, 149, 165; **58:** 41
contemptus mundi **6:** 85, 133
dreams **45:** 28
dualisms **19:** 304; **27:** 82; **58:** 2, 71, 79, 105
Egyptian versus Roman values **6:** 31, 33, 43, 53, 104, 111, 115, 125, 142, 155, 159, 178, 181, 211, 219; **17:** 48; **19:** 270; **27:** 82, 121, 126; **28:** 249; **47:** 96, 103, 113, 149; **58:** 59, 71, 88, 105; **60:** 179
Elizabethan culture, relation to **47:** 103; **58:** 118
Enobarbus **6:** 22, 23, 27, 43, 94, 120, 142; **16:** 342; **17:** 36; **22:** 217; **27:** 135
gender issues **13:** 368; **25:** 257; **27:** 144; **47:** 174, 192; **53:** 67, 77; **58:** 59
imperialism **53:** 67, 77
irony or paradox **6:** 53, 136, 146, 151, 159, 161, 189, 192, 211, 224
Jacobean culture, relation to **58:** 79, 134
Jacobean politics, relation to **58:** 79, 134
language and imagery **6:** 21, 25, 39, 64, 80, 85, 92, 94, 100, 104, 142, 146, 155, 159, 161, 165, 189, 192, 202, 211; **13:** 374, 383; **25:** 245, 257; **27:** 96, 105, 135; **58:** 79, 88, 118
love and passion **6:** 51, 64, 71, 80, 85, 100, 115, 159, 165, 180; **25:** 257; **27:** 126; **47:** 71, 124, 174, 192; **51:** 25, 33, 44; **58:** 2, 41, 105; **60:** 179, 222
monument scene **13:** 374; **16:** 342; **17:** 104, 110; **22:** 217; **47:** 142, 165
morality **52:** 5
moral relativism **22:** 217; **27:** 121
mythic or mythological elements **60:** 222
mythological allusions **16:** 342; **19:** 304; **27:** 110, 117; **47:** 71, 192; **60:** 179, 222
Octavius **6:** 22, 24, 31, 38, 43, 53, 62, 107, 125, 146, 178, 181, 219; **25:** 257; **58:** 33
opening scene **54:** 6
political and social disintegration **6:** 31, 43, 53, 60, 71, 80, 100, 107, 111, 146; 180, 197, 219; **22:** 217; **25:** 257; **27:** 121
race **53:** 67, 77
reason versus imagination **6:** 107, 115, 142, 197, 228; **45:** 28
reconciliation **6:** 100, 103, 125, 131, 159, 181
religious, mythic, or spiritual content **6:** 53, 94, 111, 115, 178, 192, 224; **47:** 71; **58:** 24, 41; **60:** 179
royalty **6:** 94
Seleucus episode (Act V, scene ii) **6:** 39, 41, 62, 133, 140, 151; **27:** 135; **58:** 33
Shakespeare's major tragedies, compared with **6:** 25, 53, 60, 71, 120, 181, 189, 202; **22:** 217; **47:** 77
Shakespeare's moral judgment **6:** 33, 37, 38, 41, 48, 51, 64, 76, 111, 125, 136, 140, 146, 163, 175, 189, 202, 211, 228; **13:** 368, 523; **25:** 257
sources **6:** 20, 39; **19:** 304; **27:** 96, 126; **28:** 249
stage history **17:** 84, 94, 101
staging issues **17:** 6, 12, 84, 94, 101, 104, 110; **27:** 90; **47:** 142
strategic analysis **48:** 206
structure **58:** 71, 88
theatricality and role-playing **47:** 96, 103, 107, 113
unity **6:** 20, 21, 22, 24, 25, 32, 33, 39, 43, 53, 60, 67, 111, 125, 146, 151, 165, 208, 211, 219; **13:** 374; **27:** 82, 90, 135
virtue versus vice **60:** 222
wheel of fortune, motif of **6:** 25, 178; **19:** 304

***As You Like It* (Volumes 5, 23, 34, 46, 57)**

Appearance versus Reality **46:** 105 **57:** 35, 40
androgyny **23:** 98, 100, 122, 138, 143, 144; **34:** 172, 177; **46:** 134; **57:** 13
anti-romantic elements **34:** 72
aristocracy **34:** 120
art versus nature **5:** 128, 130, 148; **34:** 147; **57:** 35, 75
Audrey **46:** 122
autobiographical elements **5:** 25, 35, 43, 50, 55, 61
bawdy elements **46:** 122
Celia **46:** 94
characterization **5:** 19, 24, 25, 36, 39, 54, 82, 86, 116, 148; **34:** 72; **48:** 42
Christian elements **5:** 39, 98, 162; **57:** 31
contradiction, paradox, and opposition **46:** 105
comic form **46:** 105; **51:** 1; **57:** 2
comic resolution **52:** 63
corruption in society **46:** 94; **57:** 35
costume **46:** 117
courtship and marriage **34:** 109, 177; **48:** 32; **51:** 44
death, decay, nature's destructiveness **46:** 169
deception, disguise, and duplicity **46:** 134; **57:** 40
desire **37:** 43; **52:** 63 **60:** 115
domestic elements **46:** 142
dramatic shortcomings or failure **5:** 19, 42, 52, 61, 65
duration of time **5:** 44, 45
Elizabethan culture, relation to **5:** 21, 59, 66, 68, 70, 158; **16:** 53; **28:** 46; **34:** 120; **37:** 1; **46:** 142; **57:** 23, 31, 64, 75
Fathers and Daughters **46:** 94
feminism **23:** 107, 108; **57:** 2, 13
Forest of Arden
  as "bitter" Arcadia **5:** 98, 118, 162; **23:** 97, 98, 99, 100, 122, 139
  Duke Frederick's court, contrast with **5:** 46, 102, 103, 112, 130, 156; **16:** 53; **23:** 126, 128, 129, 131, 134; **34:** 78, 102, 131; **46:** 164; **57:** 64
  pastoral elements **5:** 18, 20, 24, 32, 35, 47, 50, 54, 55, 57, 60, 77, 128, 135, 156; **23:** 17, 20, 27, 46, 137; **34:** 78, 147; **46:** 88
  as patriarchal society **5:** 168; **23:** 150; **34:** 177; **57:** 2
  as source of self-knowledge **5:** 98, 102, 103, 128, 130, 135, 148, 158, 162; **23:** 17; **34:** 102; **57:** 35
  as timeless, mythical world **5:** 112, 130, 141; **23:** 132; **34:** 78; **37:** 43; **46:** 88
  theme of play **46:** 88
gender identity **46:** 127, 134; **57:** 13, 23, 45
genre **5:** 46, 55, 79
homoerotic elements **46:** 127, 142; **57:** 23; **60:** 115
homosexuality **46:** 127, 142; **57:** 13
Hymen episode **5:** 61, 116, 130; **23:** 22, 48, 54, 109, 111, 112, 113, 115, 146, 147; **57:** 40
irony **5:** 30, 32, 154
Jaques
  love-theme, relation to **5:** 103; **23:** 7, 37, 118, 128
  as malcontent **5:** 59, 70, 84

melancholy **5:** 20, 28, 32, 36, 39, 43, 50, 59, 63, 68, 77, 82, 86, 135; **23:** 20, 26, 103, 104, 107, 109; **34:** 85; **46:** 88, 94
pastoral convention, relation to **5:** 61, 63, 65, 79, 93, 98, 114, 118
Seven Ages of Man speech (Act II, scene vii) **5:** 28, 52, 156; **23:** 48, 103, 105, 126, 138, 152; **46:** 88, 156, 164, 169
Shakespeare, relation to **5:** 35, 50, 154
as superficial critic **5:** 28, 30, 43, 54, 55, 63, 65, 68, 75, 77, 82, 86, 88, 98, 138; **34:** 85
justice **46:** 94
juxtaposition of opposing perspectives **5:** 86, 93, 98, 141; **16:** 53; **23:** 119; **34:** 72, 78, 131
language and imagery **5:** 19, 21, 35, 52, 75, 82, 92, 138; **23:** 15, 21, 26; **28:** 9; **34:** 131; **37:** 43; **48:** 42; **57:** 35, 56
love **5:** 24, 44, 46, 57, 79, 88, 103, 116, 122, 138, 141, 162; **28:** 46, 82; **34:** 85
Love in a Forest (Charles Johnson adaptation) **23:** 7
metadramatic elements **5:** 128, 130, 146; **34:** 130
morality **52:** 63; **57:** 13
mythological allusions **46:** 142
nature **46:** 94; **60:** 231
Neoclassical rules **5:** 19, 20
Orlando
as ideal man **5:** 32, 36, 39, 162; **34:** 161; **46:** 94
relationship with Rosalind/Ganymede **60:** 115
as younger brother **5:** 66, 158; **46:** 94
pastoral characters (Silvius, Phebe, and Corin) **23:** 37, 97, 98, 99, 108, 110, 118, 122, 138; **34:** 147; **60:** 115
pastoral convention, parodies of **5:** 54, 57, 72
pastoral convention, relation to **5:** 72, 77, 122; **34:** 161; **37:** 1
primogeniture **5:** 66, 158; **34:** 109, 120
psychoanalytic interpretation **5:** 146, 158; **23:** 141, 142; **34:** 109; **48:** 42
public versus private worlds **46:** 164
reconciliation of opposites **5:** 79, 88, 103, 116, 122, 138; **23:** 127, 143; **34:** 161, 172; **46:** 156
religious, mythic, or spiritual content **60:** 231
as romance **5:** 55, 79; **23:** 27, 28, 40, 43
Rosalind **46:** 94, 122
Beatrice, compared with **5:** 26, 36, 50, 75
charm **5:** 55, 75; **23:** 17, 18, 20, 41, 89, 111
disguise, role of **5:** 75, 107, 118, 122, 128, 130, 133, 138, 141, 146, 148, 164, 168; **13:** 502; **23:** 35, 42, 106, 119, 123, 146; **34:** 130; **46:** 134
femininity **5:** 26, 36, 52, 75; **23:** 24, 29, 46, 54, 103, 108, 121, 146
as Ganymede **46:** 127, 142 **60:** 115
love-theme, relation to **5:** 79, 88, 103, 116, 122, 138, 141; **23:** 114, 115; **34:** 85, 177
rustic characters **5:** 24, 60, 72, 84; **23:** 127; **34:** 78, 161
sexual ambiguity and sexual deception **46:** 134, 142; **57:** 23, 40, 45
Sexuality in Shakespeare **46:** 122, 127, 134, 142
as satire or parody of pastoral conventions **5:** 46, 55, 60, 72, 77, 79, 84, 114, 118, 128, 130, 154
self-knowledge **5:** 32, 82, 102, 116, 122, 133, 164; **57:** 45
sibling rivalry **34:** 109
social order **37:** 1; **46:** 94; **57:** 2
sources **5:** 18, 32, 54, 59, 66, 84; **34:** 155; **46:** 117 **60:** 231
stage history **46:** 117; **57:** 56
staging issues **13:** 502; **23:** 7, 17, 19, 22, 58, 96, 97, 98, 99, 101, 110, 137; **28:** 82; **32:** 212; **57:** 56, 75
structure **5:** 19, 24, 25, 35, 44, 45, 46, 86, 93, 116, 138, 158; **23:** 7, 8, 9, 10, 11; **34:** 72, 78, 131, 147, 155
time **5:** 18, 82, 112, 141; **23:** 146, 150; **34:** 102; **46:** 88, 156, 164, 169
Touchstone
callousness **5:** 88
comic and farcical elements **46:** 117
as philosopher-fool **5:** 24, 28, 30, 32, 36, 63, 75, 98; **23:** 152; **34:** 85; **46:** 1, 14, 18, 24, 33, 52, 60, 88, 105
relation to pastoral convention **5:** 54, 61, 63, 72, 75, 77, 79, 84, 86, 93, 98, 114, 118, 135, 138, 166; **34:** 72, 147, 161
selflessness **5:** 30, 36, 39, 76
verisimilitude **5:** 18, 23, 28, 30, 32, 39, 125; **23:** 107
wordplay **46:** 105

***The Comedy of Errors* (Volumes 1, 26, 34, 54)**

Adriana **16:** 3; **34:** 211, 220, 238; **54:** 189
adultery **34:** 215
audience perception **1:** 37, 50, 56; **19:** 54; **34:** 258; **54:** 136, 144
autobiographical elements **1:** 16, 18
characterization **1:** 13, 21, 31, 34, 46, 49, 50, 55, 56; **19:** 54; **25:** 63; **34:** 194, 201, 208, 245 **54:** 144, 176
classical influence and sources **1:** 13, 14, 16, 31, 32, 43, 61; **54:** 169
comic elements **1:** 43, 46, 55, 56, 59; **26:** 183, 186, 188, 190; **34:** 190, 245
composition date **1:** 18, 23, 34, 55
dramatic structure **1:** 19, 27, 40, 43, 46, 50; **26:** 186, 190; **34:** 190, 229, 233; **37:** 12; **54:** 136, 155, 189
Dromio brothers **42:** 80; **54:** 136, 152
Elizabethan culture, relation to **26:** 138, 142; **34:** 201, 215, 233, 238, 258; **42:** 80; **54:** 169, 200
farcical elements **1:** 14, 16, 19, 23, 30, 34, 35, 46, 50, 59, 61; **19:** 54; **26:** 188, 190; **34:** 245; **54:** 136, 144, 189
feminist criticism **42:** 93
food, meaning of **34:** 220
gender issues **34:** 215, 220
genre **34:** 251, 258
identity **34:** 201, 208, 211; **54:** 155, 169, 200
illusion **1:** 13, 14, 27, 37, 40, 45, 59, 63; **26:** 188; **34:** 194, 211; **54:** 169, 200
language and imagery **1:** 16, 25, 39, 40, 43, 57, 59; **34:** 233; **54:** 152, 162
male/female relationships **16:** 3
marriage **34:** 251; **54:** 215
mistaken identity **1:** 13, 14, 27, 37, 40, 45, 49, 55, 57, 61, 63; **19:** 34, 54; **25:** 63; **34:** 194; **54:** 176, 162, 189, 215
Plautus's works, compared with **1:** 13, 14, 16, 53, 61; **16:** 3; **19:** 34; **54:** 162, 176
problem comedy **34:** 251
redemption **19:** 54; **26:** 188; **54:** 152, 189
romantic elements **1:** 13, 16, 19, 23, 25, 30, 31, 36, 39, 53
servitude **42:** 80
social order **34:** 238; **54:** 155, 215
sources **1:** 13, 14, 16, 19, 31, 32, 39; **16:** 3; **34:** 190, 215, 258; **54:** 155, 176
staging issues **26:** 182, 183, 186, 188, 190; **54:** 136
supernatural, role of **1:** 27, 30; **54:** 215
tragic elements **1:** 16, 25, 27, 45, 50, 59; **34:** 229; **54:** 144
wonder, dynamic of **37:** 12

***Coriolanus* (Volumes 9, 17, 30, 50)**

aggression **9:** 112, 142, 174, 183, 189, 198; **30:** 79, 111, 125, 142; **44:** 11, 79
Anthony and Cleopatra, compared with **30:** 79, 96; **50:** 105
appearance versus reality **30:** 142
Aufidius **9:** 9, 12, 17, 19, 53, 121, 148, 153, 157, 169, 180, 193; **19:** 287; **25:** 263, 296; **30:** 58, 67, 89, 96, 133; **50:** 99
body politic, metaphor of **22:** 248; **30:** 67, 96, 105, 125; **50:** 105, 110, 119, 140, 145, 152
butterfly episode (Act I, scene iii) **9:** 19, 45, 62, 65, 73, 100, 125, 153, 157
capitulation scene (Act V, scene iii) **9:** 19, 26, 53, 65, 100, 117, 125, 130, 157, 164, 183
ceremonies, rites, and rituals, importance of **9:** 139, 148, 169
Christian elements **30:** 111
comic elements **9:** 8, 9, 14, 53, 80, 106
Cominius **25:** 245
Cominius's tribute (Act II, scene ii) **9:** 80, 100. 117, 125, 144, 164, 198; **25:** 296
Coriolanus
anger or passion **9:** 19, 26, 45, 80, 92, 157, 164, 177, 189; **30:** 79, 96
as complementary figure to Aufidius **19:** 287
death scene (Act V, scene vi) **9:** 12, 80, 100, 117, 125, 144, 164, 198; **25:** 245, 263; **50:** 110; **60:** 46
as epic hero **9:** 130, 164, 177; **25:** 245; **50:** 119
immaturity **9:** 62, 80, 84, 110, 117, 142; **30:** 140
inhuman attributes **9:** 65, 73, 139, 157, 164, 169, 189, 198; **25:** 263
internal struggle **9:** 31, 43, 45, 53, 72, 117, 121, 130; **44:** 93
introspection or self-knowledge, lack of **9:** 53, 80, 84, 112, 117, 130; **25:** 296; **30:** 133
isolation or autonomy **9:** 53, 65, 142, 144, 153, 157, 164, 180, 183, 189, 198; **30:** 58, 89, 111; **50:** 128
manipulation by others **9:** 33, 45, 62, 80; **25:** 296
modesty **9:** 8, 12, 19, 26, 53, 78, 92, 117, 121, 144, 183; **25:** 296; **30:** 79, 96, 129, 133, 149
narcissism **30:** 111
noble or aristocratic attributes **9:** 15, 18, 19, 26, 31, 33, 52, 53, 62, 65, 84, 92, 100, 121, 148, 157, 169; **25:** 263; **30:** 67, 74, 96; **50:** 13

pride or arrogance **9:** 8, 11, 12, 19, 26, 31, 33, 43, 45, 65, 78, 92, 121, 148, 153, 177; **30:** 58, 67, 74, 89, 96, 129
reconciliation with society **9:** 33, 43, 45, 65, 139, 169; **25:** 296
as socially destructive force **9:** 62, 65, 73, 78, 110, 142, 144, 153; **25:** 296
soliloquy (Act IV, scene iv) **9:** 84, 112, 117, 130
as tragic figure **9:** 8, 12, 13, 18, 25, 45, 52, 53, 72, 80, 92, 106, 112, 117, 130, 148, 164, 169, 177; **25:** 296; **30:** 67, 74, 79, 96, 111, 129; **37:** 283; **50:** 99
traitorous actions **9:** 9, 12, 19, 45, 84, 92, 148; **25:** 296; **30:** 133
as unsympathetic character **9:** 12, 13, 62, 78, 80, 84, 112, 130, 157
domestic elements **42:** 223; **50:** 145
economics **50:** 152
England and Rome, parallels between **9:** 39, 43, 106, 148, 180, 193; **25:** 296; **30:** 67, 105; **50:** 172
fable of the belly (Act I, scene i) **9:** 8, 65, 73, 80, 136, 153, 157, 164, 180, 183, 189; **25:** 296; **30:** 79, 105, 111; **50:** 13, 110, 140
fame **30:** 58
fire and water **25:** 263
flattery or dissimulation **9:** 26, 45, 92, 100, 110, 121, 130, 144, 157, 183, 193; **25:** 296
friendship **30:** 125, 142
gender issues **30:** 79, 125, 142; **44:** 93; **50:** 128
genre **9:** 42, 43, 53, 80, 106, 112, 117, 130, 164, 177; **30:** 67, 74, 79, 89, 111, 125; **50:** 99
honor or integrity **9:** 43, 65, 73, 92, 106, 110, 121, 144, 153, 157, 164, 177, 183, 189; **30:** 89, 96, 133
identity **42:** 248; **50:** 128
irony or satire **9:** 65, 73, 80, 92, 106, 153, 157, 164, 193; **30:** 67, 89, 133
Jacobean culture, relation to **22:** 248
language and imagery **9:** 8, 9, 13, 53, 64, 65, 73, 78, 84, 100, 112, 121, 136, 139, 142, 144, 153, 157, 174, 183, 193, 198; **22:** 248; **25:** 245, 263; **30:** 111, 125, 142; **37:** 283; **44:** 79
Macbeth, compared with **30:** 79
martial vs. civil law **48:** 230
Menenius **9:** 8, 9, 11, 14, 19, 26, 78, 80, 106, 148, 157; **25:** 263, 296; **30:** 67, 79, 89, 96, 111, 133
Midlands Revolt, influence of **22:** 248; **30:** 79; **50:** 140, 172
naming, significance of **30:** 58, 96, 111, 125
nature, philosophy of **30:** 74
nurturing or feeding **9:** 65, 73, 136, 183, 189; **30:** 111; **44:** 79; **50:** 110
mythic or mythological elements **60:** 205
opening scene **54:** 6
paradoxical elements **9:** 73, 92, 106, 121, 153, 157, 164, 169, 193
parent-child relations **60:** 205
plebeians **9:** 8, 9, 11, 12, 15, 18, 19, 26, 33, 39, 53, 92, 125, 153, 183, 189; **25:** 296; **30:** 58, 79, 96, 111; **50:** 13, 105
Plutarch and historical sources **9:** 8, 9, 13, 14, 16, 26, 39, 92, 106, 130, 142, 164; **30:** 74, 79, 105; **50:** 99
politics **9:** 15, 17, 18, 19, 26, 33, 43, 53, 62, 65, 73, 80, 92, 106, 110, 112, 121, 144, 153, 157, 164, 180; **22:** 248; **25:** 296; **30:** 58, 67, 79, 89, 96, 105, 111, 125; **37:** 283; **42:** 223; **48:** 230; **50:** 13, 140, 172
psychoanalytic interpretations **44:** 93
public versus private worlds **37:** 283; **42:** 223
sexuality **9:** 112, 142, 174, 183, 189, 198; **30:** 79, 111, 125, 142
shame **42:** 248
Shakespeare's political sympathies **9:** 8, 11, 15, 17, 19, 26, 39, 52, 53, 62, 80, 92, 142; **25:** 296; **30:** 74, 79, 89, 96, 105, 133; **50:** 145, 172
slander **48:** 230
society **9:** 15, 17, 18, 19, 26, 33, 43, 53, 62, 65, 73, 80, 92, 106, 110, 112, 121, 144, 153, 157, 164, 180; **22:** 248; **25:** 296; **30:** 58, 67, 79, 89, 96, 105, 111, 125; **50:** 13, 105, 119, 152
sources **60:** 205
staging issues **17:** 172, 242, 248
structure **9:** 8, 9, 11, 12, 13, 14, 16, 26, 33, 45, 53, 58, 72, 78, 80, 84, 92, 112, 139, 148; **25:** 263; **30:** 79, 96
treachery **30:** 89
the tribunes (Brutus and Sicinius) **9:** 9, 11, 14, 19, 33, 169, 180
Virgilia **9:** 11, 19, 26, 33, 58, 100, 121, 125; **25:** 263; **30:** 79, 96, 133; **50:** 99
Volumnia
Coriolanus's subservience to **9:** 16, 26, 33, 53, 62, 80, 92, 100, 117, 125, 142, 177, 183; **30:** 140, 149; **44:** 79
influence on Coriolanus **9:** 45, 62, 65, 78, 92, 100, 110, 117, 121, 125, 130, 148, 157, 183, 189, 193; **25:** 263, 296; **30:** 79, 96, 125, 133, 140, 142, 149; **44:** 93
as noble Roman matron **9:** 16, 19, 26, 31, 33
personification of Rome **9:** 125, 183; **50:** 119
war **25:** 263; **30:** 79, 96, 125, 149

Cymbeline (Volumes 4, 15, 36, 47, 61)

appearance versus reality **4:** 87, 93, 103, 162; **36:** 99; **47:** 228, 286
authorship controversy **4:** 17, 21, 35, 48, 56, 78
autobiographical elements **4:** 43, 46; **36:** 134
bawdy elements **36:** 155
Beaumont and Fletcher's romances, compared with **4:** 46, 52, 138
Belarius **4:** 48, 89, 141
British nationalism **4:** 19, 78, 89, 93, 129, 141, 159, 167; **32:** 373; **36:** 129; **45:** 67; **47:** 219, 265; **61:** 54
Cloten **4:** 20, 116, 127, 155; **22:** 302, 365; **25:** 245; **36:** 99, 125, 142, 155; **47:** 228
combat scenes **22:** 365
comic elements **4:** 35, 56, 113, 141; **15:** 111, 122; **47:** 296
Cymbeline **61:** 54
dramatic structure **4:** 17, 18, 19, 20, 21, 22, 24, 38, 43, 48, 53, 64, 68, 89, 116, 129, 141; **22:** 302, 365; **25:** 319; **36:** 115, 125; **60:** 240; **61:** 2
dreams **4:** 162, 167; **44:** 28; **45:** 67, 75
dualisms **4:** 29, 64, 73
Elizabethan dramatic conventions **4:** 53, 124
family, theme of **44:** 28
genre controversy **61:** 2
Guiderius and Arviragus **4:** 21, 22, 89, 129, 141, 148; **25:** 319; **36:** 125, 158
historical elements **47:** 260
Iachimo **25:** 245, 319; **36:** 166
Imogen **4:** 21, 22, 24, 29, 37, 45, 46, 52, 56, 78, 89, 108; **15:** 23, 32, 105, 121; **19:** 411; **25:** 245, 319; **28:** 398; **32:** 373; **36:** 129, 142, 148; **47:** 25, 205, 228, 245, 274, 277; **61:** 34, 45, 76
Imogen's reawakening (Act IV, scene ii) **4:** 37, 56, 89, 103, 108, 116, 150; **15:** 23; **25:** 245; **47:** 252
irony **4:** 64, 77, 103
language and imagery **4:** 43, 48, 61, 64, 70, 73, 93, 108; **13:** 401; **25:** 245; **28:** 373, 398; **36:** 115, 158, 166, 186; **47:** 205, 286, 296; **60:** 240
Jacobean politics **61:** 54, 76
James I **61:** 54
love ideal **61:** 34, 45
Lucretia, analogies to **36:** 148
marriage **61:** 34, 45
misperception **19:** 411; **36:** 99, 115; **47:** 228, 237, 252, 277, 286, 296
mythic or mythological elements **60:** 240
negative appraisals **4:** 20, 35, 43, 45, 48, 53, 56, 68; **15:** 32, 105, 121
pastoralism **61:** 18
patriarchy **32:** 373; **36:** 134; **47:** 237; **51:** 30
peace **61:** 54
political allegory **61:** 76
politics **61:**
Posthumus **4:** 24, 30, 53, 78, 116, 127, 141, 155, 159, 167; **15:** 89; **19:** 411; **25:** 245, 319; **36:** 142; **44:** 28; **45:** 67, 75; **47:** 25, 205, 228; **61:** 34, 45, 76
psychological elements **36:** 134; **44:** 28; **45:** 67, 75; **60:** 240; **61:** 18
reconciliation **4:** 38, 64, 73, 93, 105, 113, 116, 129, 138, 141, 162, 170; **61:** 2
redemption **61:** 18
religious, mythical, or spiritual content **4:** 22, 29, 78, 93, 105, 108, 115, 116, 127, 134, 138, 141, 159; **28:** 373; 36: 142, 158, 186; **47:** 219, 260, 274
romantic elements **4:** 17, 20, 46, 68, 77, 141, 148, 172; **15:** 111; **25:** 319; **28:** 373; **61:** 34
self-conscious or artificial nature of play **4:** 43, 52, 56, 68, 124, 134, 138; **36:** 99
sexuality **4:** 170, 172; **25:** 319; **32:** 373; **47:** 245
Shakespeare's lyric poetry, compared with **13:** 401
sources **4:** 17, 18; **13:** 401; **28:** 373; **47:** 245, 265, 277
staging issues **15:** 6, 23, 75, 105, 111, 121, 122; **22:** 365
subversiveness **22:** 302
tragedy, as **61:** 2
tragicomedy, as **61:** 2, 18
tragic elements **25:** 319; **28:** 373; **36:** 129; **47:** 296
unity **61:** 54
trickster, motif of **22:** 302
vision scene (Act V, scene iv) **4:** 17, 21, 28, 29, 35, 38, 78, 105, 108, 134, 150, 167; **47:** 205
wager plot **4:** 18, 24, 29, 53, 78, 155; **22:** 365; **25:** 319; **47:** 205, 277

***Hamlet* (Volumes 1, 21, 35, 44, 59)**

ambiguity **1:** 92, 160, 198, 227, 230, 234, 247, 249; **21:** 72; **35:** 241
appearance versus reality **1:** 95, 116, 166, 169, 198; **35:** 82, 126, 132, 144, 238; **44:** 248; **45:** 28
aristocracy **42:** 217
audience response **28:** 325; **32:** 238; **35:** 167; **44:** 107
autobiographical elements **1:** 98, 115, 119; **13:** 487
beginning **54:** 19; **59:** 18
Calvinist implications **48:** 195
classical Greek tragedies, compared with **1:** 74, 75, 130, 184, 212; **13:** 296; **22:** 339
Claudius **13:** 502; **16 246; 21:** 259, 347, 361, 371; **28:** 232, 290; **35:** 104, 182; **44:** 119, 241; **59:** 62
closet scene (Act III, scene iv) **16:** 259; **21:** 151, 334, 392; **35:** 204, 229; **44:** 119, 237
conflict between idealism and pragmatism **60:** 71
costume **21:** 81
death, decay, and nature's destructiveness **1:** 144, 153, 188, 198, 221, 242; **13:** 502; **28:** 280, 311; **35:** 241; **42:** 284; **60:** 71, 91, 194
dreams **45:** 28
dumbshow and play scene (Act III, scene ii) **1:** 76, 86, 134, 138, 154, 160, 207; **13:** 502; **21:** 392; **35:** 82; **44:** 241; **46:** 74; **59:** 42, 62
Elizabethan culture, relation to **1:** 76, 148, 151, 154, 160, 166, 169, 171, 176, 184, 202, 209, 254; **13:** 282, 494; **19:** 330; **21:** 407, 416; **22:** 258; **59:** 74
Elizabethan and Jacobean politics, relation to **28:** 232; **28:** 290, 311; **35:** 140
ending **54:** 96; **59:** 74; **60:** 346
feminist criticism **55:** 56; **59:** 31, 39
fencing scene (Act V, scene ii) **21:** 392; **54:** 96; **59:** 26
Fortinbras **21:** 136, 347; **28:** 290
gender issues **35:** 144; **44:** 189, 195, 198; **59:** 31, 39
genre **1:** 176, 212, 237
Gertrude **21:** 259, 347, 392; **28:** 311; **32:** 238; **35:** 182, 204, 229; **44:** 119, 160, 189, 195, 237, 248; **59:** 39, 62, 74
Ghost **1:** 75, 76, 84, 85, 128, 134, 138, 154, 171, 218, 231, 254; **16:** 246; **21:** 17, 44, 112, 151, 334, 371, 377, 392; **25:** 288; **35:** 152, 157, 174, 237; **44:** 119; **59:** 2, 10
gravedigger scene (Act V, scene i) **21:** 392; **28:** 280; **46:** 74; **60:** 71
grotesque elements **42:** 284
Hamlet
  compared to Vindice **59:** 10
  death of **60:** 46
  delay **1:** 76, 83, 88, 90, 94, 98, 102, 103, 106, 114, 115, 116, 119, 120, 148, 151, 166, 171, 179, 188, 191, 194, 198, 221, 268; **13:** 296, 502; **21:** 81; **25:** 209, 288; **28:** 223; **35:** 82, 174, 212, 215, 237; **44:** 180, 209, 219, 229; **59:** 10
  divided nature **16:** 246; **28:** 223; **32:** 288; **35:** 182, 215; **37:** 241; **59:** 2
  elocution of the character's speeches **21:** 96, 104, 112, 127, 132, 172, 177, 179, 194, 245, 254, 257
  as a fool **46:** 1, 29, 52, 74
  and identity (nature of) **59:** 18
  madness **1:** 76, 81, 83, 95, 102, 106, 128, 144, 154, 160, 234; **21:** 35, 50, 72, 81, 99, 112, 311, 339, 355, 361, 371, 377, 384; **35:** 117, 132, 134, 140, 144, 212; **44:** 107, 119, 152, 209, 219, 229; **59:** 31
  meeting with the pirates (Act IV, scene vi) **59:** 56
  melancholy **21:** 99, 112, 177, 194; **35:** 82, 95, 117; **44:** 209, 219
  as negative character **1:** 86, 92, 111, 171, 218; **21:** 386; **25:** 209; **35:** 167; **59:** 10
  reaction to his father's death **22:** 339; **35:** 104, 174; **44:** 133, 160, 180, 189
  reaction to Gertrude's marriage **1:** 74, 120, 154, 179; **16:** 259; **21:** 371; **22:** 339; **35:** 104, 117; **44:** 133, 160, 189, 195
  romantic aspects of the character **21:** 96; **44:** 198; **59:** 47
  as scourge or purifying figure **1:** 144, 209, 242; **25:** 288; **35:** 157; **59:** 26, 62, 79
  sentimentality versus intellectuality **1:** 75, 83, 88, 91, 93, 94, 96, 102, 103, 115, 116, 120, 166, 191; **13:** 296; **21:** 35, 41, 44, 72, 81, 89, 99, 129, 132, 136, 172, 213, 225, 339, 355, 361, 371, 377, 379, 381, 386; **25:** 209; **44:** 198
  soliloquies **1:** 76, 82, 83, 148, 166, 169, 176, 191; **21:** 17, 31, 44, 53, 89, 112, 268, 311, 334, 347, 361, 384, 392; **25:** 209; **28:** 223; **44:** 107, 119, 229
  as a stoic at the end **54:** 96
  theatrical interpretations **21:** 11, 31, 78, 101, 104, 107, 160, 177, 179, 182, 183, 192, 194, 197, 202, 203, 208, 213, 225, 232, 237, 249, 253, 254, 257, 259, 274, 311, 339, 347, 355, 361, 371, 377, 380
  virility **21:** 213, 301, 355; **44:** 198
Hamlet with Alterations (David Garrick adaptation) **21:** 23, 334, 347
Horatio **44:** 189
idealism versus pragmatism **16 246; 28:** 325
Laertes **21:** 347, 386; **28:** 290; **35:** 182; **59:** 26
language and imagery **1:** 95, 144, 153, 154, 160, 188, 198, 221, 227, 249, 259, 270; **22:** 258, 378; **28:** 311; **35:** 144, 152, 238, 241; **42:** 217; **44:** 248; **52:** 35; **59:** 42, 47, 56, 62, 74
madness **19:** 330; **35:** 104, 126, 134, 140, 144; **44:** 107, 119, 152, 209, 219, 229
marriage **22:** 339; **51:** 44
Marxist criticism **42:** 234
medieval drama **59:** 68
moral choice **52:** 35
nunnery scene (Act III, scene i) **21:** 157, 381, 410
opening scene **54:** 2, 6, 19
Ophelia **1:** 73, 76, 81, 82, 91, 96, 97, 154, 166, 169, 171, 218, 270; **13:** 268; **16:** 246; **19:** 330; **21:** 17, 41, 44, 72, 81, 101, 104, 107, 112, 136, 203, 259, 347, 381, 386, 392, 416; **28:** 232, 325; **35:** 104, 126, 140, 144, 182, 238; **44:** 189, 195, 248; **59:** 31, 39, 68
paradoxical elements **59:** 47
Petrarchan love poetry **59:** 47
Polonius **21:** 259, 334, 347, 386, 416; **35:** 182
prayer scene (Act III, scene iii) **1:** 76, 106, 160, 212, 231; **44:** 119
psychoanalytic interpretations **1:** 119, 148, 154, 179, 202; **21:** 197, 213, 361; **25:** 209; **28:** 223; **35:** 95, 104, 134, 237; **37:** 241; **44:** 133, 152, 160, 180, 209, 219
religious, mythic, or spiritual content **1:** 98, 102, 130, 184, 191, 209, 212, 231, 234, 254; **21:** 361; **22:** 258; **28:** 280; **32:** 238; **35:** 134; **59:** 2; **60:** 194
revenge **1:** 74, 194, 209, 224, 234, 254; **16:** 246; **22:** 258; **25:** 288; **28:** 280; **35:** 152, 157, 167, 174, 212; **44:** 180, 209, 219, 229; **54:** 96; **59:** 10, 79
Richard II, compared with **1:** 264
rites, rituals, and ceremonies, importance of **13:** 268; **28:** 232
satire **59:** 79
sexuality **55:** 56; **59:** 31, 68
sources **1:** 76, 81, 113, 125, 128, 130, 151, 191, 202, 224, 259; **59:** 68
staging issues **13:** 494, 502; **21:** 11, 17, 31, 35, 41, 44, 50, 53, 78, 81, 89, 101, 112, 127, 139, 142, 145, 148, 151, 157, 160, 172, 182, 183, 202, 203, 208, 225, 232, 237, 242, 245, 249, 251, 259, 268, 270, 274, 283, 284, 301, 311, 334, 347, 355, 361, 371, 377, 379, 380, 381, 384, 386, 392, 407, 410, 416; **44:** 198; **54:** 19
Stoicism **48:** 195
structure **22:** 378; **28:** 280, 325; **35:** 82, 104, 215; **44:** 152; **59:** 2, 42
subjectivity **45:** 28; **59:** 42
succession **60:** 346
textual variants **13:** 282; **16:** 259; **21:** 11, 23, 72, 101, 127, 129, 139, 140, 142, 145, 202, 208, 259, 270, 284, 347, 361, 384; **22:** 258; **32:** 238
themes **59:** 74, 79
topical allusions or content **13:** 282
tragic elements **13:** 78
unity **1:** 75, 76, 87, 103, 113, 125, 128, 142, 148, 160, 184, 188, 198, 264; **16:** 259; **35:** 82, 215
unnatural ordering **22:** 378
violence **59:** 26
wheel of fortune, motif of **52:** 35
widowhood and remarriage, themes of **32:** 238

***Henry IV, Parts 1 and 2* (Volumes 1, 14, 39, 49, 57)**

adaptations of **60:** 154
ambition **57:** 94
Biblical references **57:** 147
carnival elements **28:** 203; **32:** 103
Catholic components **57:** 167
characterization **1:** 321, 328, 332, 333, 336, 344, 365, 383, 385, 389, 391, 397, 401; **19:** 195; **39:** 123, 137; **42:** 101, 164; **49:** 93; **57:** 88, 167, 181
comic elements **1:** 286, 290, 314, 327, 328, 336, 353; **19:** 195; **25:** 109; **39:** 72; **57:** 120
contractual and economic relations **13:** 213
contrasting dramatic worlds **14:** 56, 60, 61, 84, 105; **48:** 95; **49:** 162; **57:** 183
critical history **42:** 187; **48:** 167
deception, disguise, and duplicity **1:** 397, 406, 425; **42:** 101; **47:** 1, 60; **48:** 95
desire **60:** 154
divine right versus justice **49:** 116; **57:** 88, 130

Topic Index, by Play

Elizabethan culture, relation to **19:** 195; **48:** 117, 143, 151, 175
Elizabethan politics, relation to **22:** 395; **28:** 203; **47:** 60; **48:** 117, 143, 167, 175; **57:** 88, 94
Falstaff
- characterization **1:** 287, 298, 312, 333; **25:** 245; **28:** 203; **39:** 72, 134, 137, 143; **57:** 120, 156
- as comic figure **1:** 287, 311, 327, 344, 351, 354, 357, 410, 434; **39:** 89; **46:** 1, 48, 52; **49:** 178; **57:** 120
- as coward or rogue **1:** 285, 290, 296, 298, 306, 307, 313, 317, 323, 336, 337, 338, 342, 354, 366, 374, 391, 396, 401, 433; **14:** 7, 111, 125, 130, 133; **32:** 166
- dual personality **1:** 397, 401, 406, 434; **49:** 162
- female attributes **13:** 183; **44:** 44; **60:** 154
- Iago, compared with **1:** 341, 351
- Marxist interpretation **1:** 358, 361
- moral reformation **60:** 26
- as outlaw **49:** 133
- as parody of the historical plot **1:** 314, 354, 359; **39:** 143
- as positive character **1:** 286, 287, 290, 296, 298, 311, 312, 321, 325, 333, 344, 355, 357, 389, 401, 408, 434
- rejection by Hal **1:** 286, 287, 290, 312, 314, 317, 324, 333, 338, 344, 357, 366, 372, 374, 379, 380, 389, 414; **13:** 183; **25:** 109; **39:** 72, 89; **57:** 147
- as satire of feudal society **1:** 314, 328, 361; **32:** 103
- as scapegoat **1:** 389, 414; **57:** 156
- stage interpretations **14:** 4, 6, 7, 9, 15, 116, 130, 146; **47:** 1
- as subversive figure **16:** 183; **25:** 109
- as Vice figure **1:** 342, 361, 366, 374

flattery **22:** 395
gender issues **13:** 183; **25:** 151; **44:** 44; **48:** 175; **60:** 154
Hal
- audience's perspective of **49:** 153; **57:** 116
- and betrayal **49:** 123
- as the central character **1:** 286, 290, 314, 317, 326, 338, 354, 366, 374, 396; **39:** 72, 100
- compared with the fair friend of the sonnets **60:** 154
- dual personality **1:** 397, 406; **25:** 109, 151; **49:** 112, 139, 153, 162; **57:** 130
- as Everyman **1:** 342, 366, 374
- fall from humanity **1:** 379, 380, 383
- general assessment **1:** 286, 287, 289, 290, 314, 317, 326, 327, 332, 357, 397; **25:** 245; **32:** 212; **39:** 134; **57:** 116, 130
- Henry's perspective of **49:** 153
- as ideal ruler **1:** 289, 309, 317, 321, 326, 337, 342, 344, 374, 389, 391, 434; **25:** 109; **39:** 123; **47:** 60; **60:** 154
- as Machiavellian ruler **47:** 60
- as negative character **1:** 312, 332, 333, 357; **32:** 212
- as outlaw **49:** 112
- preparation for rule **49:** 112; **57:** 116, 130
- reformation **57:** 160
- Richard II, compared with **1:** 332, 337; **39:** 72
- as restorer of law **49:** 133

Henry **39:** 123, 137; **49:** 139
- effectiveness as ruler **49:** 116
- guilt **49:** 112
- illegitimacy of rule **49:** 112, 133, 137
- as tragic figure **49:** 186
- as usurper **49:** 116, 137

historical content **1:** 310, 328, 365, 366, 370, 374, 380, 387, 421, 424, 427, 431; **16:** 172; **19:** 157; **25:** 151; **32:** 136; **39:** 143; **48:** 143, 167; **49:** 139; **57:** 137
historical and dramatic elements **49:** 93
historical epic, place in or relation to Shakespeare's **1:** 309, 314, 328, 374, 379, 424, 427; **48:** 167
historiography **56:** 2, 15, 25
homosexuality **60:** 154
Hostess **60:** 26
Hotspur **25:** 151; **28:** 101; **39:** 72, 134, 137; **42:** 101; **49:** 137; **60:** 154
- and prisoners of war **49:** 137
- versus Henry **49:** 137

John of Lancaster, Prince
- and betrayal **49:** 123

justice **49:** 112, 123; **57:** 137
kingship **1:** 314, 318, 337, 366, 370, 374, 379, 380, 383, 424; **16:** 172; **19:** 195; **28:** 101; **39:** 100, 116, 123, 130; **42:** 143; **48:** 143; **57:** 88, 94, 108, 137, 160
language and imagery **13:** 213; **16:** 172; **25:** 245; **28:** 101; **39:** 116, 130; **42:** 155; **47:** 1; **57:** 137
Lord Chief Justice
- as keeper of law and justice **49:** 133

as medieval allegory or morality play **1:** 323, 324, 342, 361, 366, 373, 374; **32:** 166; **39:** 89; **47:** 60
Mortimer **25:** 151
multiple endings **49:** 102
Neoclassical rules **1:** 286, 287, 290, 29
politics **28:** 101; **39:** 130; **42:** 143; **48:** 143, 175; **57:** 108
power **49:** 139; **57:** 108
Protestant components **57:** 167
providential order **56:** 15
psychoanalytic interpretations **13:** 457; **28:** 101; **42:** 187; **44:** 44
rebellion **22:** 395; **28:** 101
redemption **57:** 116
references to **22:** 114; **32:** 166; **48:** 117
relationship to other Shakespearean plays **1:** 286, 290, 309, 329, 365, 396; **28:** 101; **42:** 101, 155; **48:** 167; **49:** 93, 186
relationship of Parts 1 and 2 **32:** 136; **39:** 100; **49:** 178; **57:** 160, 181
religious, mythic, or spiritual content **1:** 314, 374, 414, 421, 429, 431, 434; **32:** 103; **48:** 151; **57:** 147, 156, 167; **60:** 26
- as autonomous works **1:** 289, 337, 338, 347, 348, 373, 387, 393, 411, 418, 424
- comparison **1:** 290, 295, 329, 348, 358, 393, 411, 419, 429, 431, 441
- unity of both parts **1:** 286, 290, 309, 314, 317, 329, 365, 373, 374, 396, 402, 404, 419

sources **56:** 2
sovereignty **57:** 94
staging issues **32:** 212; **47:** 1; **49:** 102
structure **49:** 93; **56:** 53, 60; **57:** 181
succession **60:** 304
textual issues **22:** 114
time and change, motif of **1:** 372, 393, 411; **39:** 89; **48:** 143
Turkish elements **19:** 170
two fathers **14:** 86, 101, 105, 108; **39:** 89, 100; **49:** 102
violence **25:** 109

***Henry V* (Volumes 5, 14, 30, 49)**

battle of Agincourt **5:** 197, 199, 213, 246, 257, 281, 287, 289, 293, 310, 318; **19:** 217; **30:** 181
Canterbury and churchmen **5:** 193, 203, 205, 213, 219, 225, 252, 260; **22:** 137; **30:** 215, 262
characterization **5:** 186, 189, 192, 193, 199, 219, 230, 233, 252, 276, 293; **30:** 227, 278
Chorus, role of **5:** 186, 192, 226, 228, 230, 252, 264, 269, 281, 293; **14:** 301, 319, 336; **19:** 133; **25:** 116, 131; **30:** 163, 202, 220; **49:** 194, 200, 211, 219, 260
class distinctions, conflict, and relations **28:** 146
colonialism **22:** 103
comic elements **5:** 185, 188, 191, 192, 217, 230, 233, 241, 252, 260, 276; **19:** 217; **28:** 121; **30:** 193, 202
economic relations **13:** 213
Elizabethan culture, relation to **5:** 210, 213, 217, 223, 257, 299, 310; **16:** 202; **19:** 133, 233; **28:** 121, 159; **30:** 215, 262; **37:** 187; **49:** 260
English language and colonialism **22:** 103; **28:** 159
epic elements **5:** 192, 197, 246, 257, 314; **30:** 181, 220, 237, 252
Falstaff **5:** 185, 186, 187, 189, 192, 195, 198, 210, 226, 257, 269, 271, 276, 293, 299; **28:** 146; **46:** 48
- death of **60:** 26

Fluellen **30:** 278; **37:** 105
French aristocrats and the Dauphin **5:** 188, 191, 199, 205, 213, 281; **22:** 137; **28:** 121
French language, Shakespeare's use of **5:** 186, 188, 190; **25:** 131
gender issues **13:** 183; **28:** 121, 146, 159; **44:** 44
Henry
- brutality and cunning **5:** 193, 203, 209, 210, 213, 219, 233, 239, 252, 260, 271, 287, 293, 302, 304; **30:** 159
- characterization in 1 and 2 Henry IV contrasted **5:** 189, 190, 241, 304, 310; **19:** 133; **25:** 131; **32:** 157
- chivalry **37:** 187
- courage **5:** 191, 195, 210, 213, 228, 246, 257, 267
- disguise **30:** 169, 259
- education **5:** 246, 267, 271, 289; **14:** 297, 328, 342; **30:** 259
- emotion, lack of **5:** 209, 212, 233, 244, 264, 267, 287, 293, 310
- as heroic figure **5:** 192, 205, 209, 223, 244, 252, 257, 260, 269, 271, 299, 304; **28:** 121, 146; **30:** 237, 244, 252; **37:** 187; **49:** 194, 200, 236, 247
- humor **5:** 189, 191, 212, 217, 239, 240, 276
- intellectual and social limitations **5:** 189, 191, 203, 209, 210, 225, 226, 230, 293; **30:** 220
- interpersonal relations **5:** 209, 233, 267, 269, 276, 287, 293, 302, 318; **19:** 133; **28:** 146

mercy **5:** 213, 267, 289, 293
mixture of good and bad qualities **5:** 199, 205, 209, 210, 213, 244, 260, 304, 314; **30:** 262, 273; **49:** 211
piety **5:** 191, 199, 209, 217, 223, 239, 257, 260, 271, 289, 310, 318; **30:** 244; **32:** 126
public versus private selves **22:** 137; **30:** 169, 207
self-doubt **5:** 281, 310
slaughter of prisoners **5:** 189, 205, 246, 293, 318; **28:** 146
speech **5:** 212, 230, 233, 246, 264, 276, 287, 302; **28:** 146; **30:** 163, 227
heroism **49:** 194, 200, 211, 236
historical content **5:** 185, 188, 190, 192, 193, 198, 246, 314; **13:** 201; **19:** 133; **25:** 131; **30:** 193, 202, 207, 215, 252; **49:** 223
historical epic, place in or relation to Shakespeare's **5:** 195, 198, 205, 212, 225, 241, 244, 287, 304, 310; **14:** 337, 342; **30:** 215
historiography **56:** 2, 15
homoerotic elements **16:** 202
Hotspur **5:** 189, 199, 228, 271, 302
hypocrisy **5:** 203, 213, 219, 223, 233, 260, 271, 302
imperialism **22:** 103; **28:** 159
Irish affairs **22:** 103; **28:** 159
irony **5:** 192, 210, 213, 219, 223, 226, 233, 252, 260, 269, 281, 299, 304; **14:** 336; **30:** 159, 193
Katherine **5:** 186, 188, 189, 190, 192, 260, 269, 299, 302; **13:** 183; **19:** 217; **30:** 278; **44:** 44
kingship **5:** 205, 223, 225, 233, 239, 244, 257, 264, 267, 271, 287, 289, 299, 302, 304, 314, 318; **16:** 202; **22:** 137; **30:** 169, 202, 259, 273; **49:** 200
language and imagery **5:** 188, 230, 233, 241, 264, 276; **19:** 203; **25:** 131; **30:** 159, 181, 207, 234
law and justice **49:** 223, 226, 260
Machiavellianism **5:** 203, 225, 233, 252, 287, 304; **25:** 131; **30:** 273; **60:** 304
MacMorris **22:** 103; **28:** 159; **30:** 278
Marlowe's works, compared with **19:** 233
metadramatic elements **13:** 194; **30:** 181; **49:** 200, 211
Mistress Quickly **5:** 186, 187, 210, 276, 293; **30:** 278
morality **5:** 195, 203, 213, 223, 225, 239, 246, 260, 271, 293
obscenity **5:** 188, 190, 260
order **5:** 205, 257, 264, 310, 314; **30:** 193
patriarchy **37:** 105; **44:** 44
politics and ideology **49:** 219, 247, 260
providential order **56:** 15
nationalism and patriotism **5:** 198, 205, 209, 210, 213, 219, 223, 233, 246, 252, 257, 269, 299; **19:** 133, 217; **30:** 227, 262; **49:** 219, 247
Pistol **28:** 146
power **37:** 175
psychoanalytic interpretations **13:** 457; **44:** 44
religious, mythic, or religious content **25:** 116; **32:** 126; **60:** 26
Salic Law **5:** 219, 252, 260; **28:** 121
self-interest or expediency **5:** 189, 193, 205, 213, 217, 233, 260, 287, 302, 304; **30:** 273; **49:** 223
soldiers **5:** 203, 239, 267, 276, 281, 287, 293, 318; **28:** 146; **30:** 169; **49:** 194
sources **56:** 2
staging issues **5:** 186, 189, 192, 193, 198, 205, 226, 230, 241, 281, 314; **13:** 194, 502; **14:** 293, 295, 297, 301, 310, 319, 328, 334, 336, 342; **19:** 217; **32:** 185
structure **5:** 186, 189, 205, 213, 230, 241, 264, 289, 310, 314; **30:** 220, 227, 234, 244
succession **60:** 304
tetralogy, relation to **49:** 223
textual problems **5:** 187, 189, 190; **13:** 201
topical allusions or content **5:** 185, 186; **13:** 201
tragic elements **5:** 228, 233, 267, 269, 271
traitors (Scroop, Grey, and Cambridge) **16:** 202; **30:** 220, 278
Southampton conspiracy **49:** 223
Turkish elements **19:** 170
violence **43:** 24
war **5:** 193, 195, 197, 198, 210, 213, 219, 230, 233, 246, 281, 293; **28:** 121, 146; **30:** 262; **32:** 126; **37:** 175, 187; **42:** 143; **49:** 194, 236, 247, 260
Williams **13:** 502; **16:** 183; **28:** 146; **30:** 169, 259, 278
wooing scene (Act V, scene ii) **5:** 186, 188, 189, 191, 193, 195, 260, 276, 299, 302; **14:** 297; **28:** 121, 159; **30:** 163, 207

***Henry VI, Parts 1, 2, and 3* (Volumes 3, 24, 39, 56, 63)**

ambivalent or ironic elements **3:** 69, 151, 154; **39:** 160; **56:** 131; **63:** 131, 149, 158
authorship controversy **3:** 16, 18, 19, 20, 21, 26, 27, 29, 31, 35, 39, 41, 55, 66; **24:** 51; **56:** 77
autobiographical elements **3:** 41, 55
Bordeaux sequence **37:** 165
Cade scenes **3:** 35, 67, 92, 97, 109; **16:** 183; **22:** 156; **25:** 102; **28:** 112; **37:** 97; **39:** 160, 196, 205; **50:** 45, 51; **56:** 117, 122, 131, 180; **63:** 149, 176
carnival elements **22:** 156; **63:** 149
ceremony **63:** 185
characterization **3:** 18, 20, 24, 25, 31, 57, 64, 73, 77, 109, 119, 151; **24:** 22, 28, 38, 42, 45, 47; **39:** 160; **63:** 114
class distinctions, conflict, and relations **37:** 97; **39:** 187; **50:** 45, 51; **56:** 117, 131; **63:** 114, 176
comic elements **63:** 144, 149
dance **22:** 156
decay of heroic ideals **3:** 119, 126; **56:** 95; **63:** 158
disorder and civil dissension **3:** 59, 67, 76, 92, 103, 126; **13:** 131; **16:** 183; **24:** 11, 17, 28, 31, 47; **25:** 102; **28:** 112; **39:** 154, 177, 187, 196, 205; **56:** 80, 85, 110; **63:** 114, 185, 202
Elizabethan literary and cultural influences **3:** 75, 97, 100, 119, 143; **22:** 156; **28:** 112; **37:** 97; **56:** 162, 180; **63:** 194
Folk rituals, elements and influence of **39:** 205
Henry
characterization **3:** 64, 77, 151; **39:** 160, 177; **47:** 32; **63:** 114, 144, 205
source of social disorder **3:** 25, 31, 41, 115; **39:** 154, 187
as sympathetic figure **3:** 73, 143, 154; **24:** 32
historical accuracy or revisionism **3:** 18, 21, 35, 46, 51; **16:** 217; **24:** 16, 18, 25, 31, 45, 48; **56:** 85, 110, 122, 131, 145; **63:** 169
historical epic, place in or relation to Shakespeare's **3:** 24, 59; **24:** 51; **56:** 95
historiography **56:** 2, 25
as humanistic play **3:** 83, 92, 109, 115, 119, 131, 136, 143
Humphrey **13:** 131; **56:** 187
as inferior or flawed plays **3:** 20, 21, 25, 26, 35
Joan of Arc **16:** 131; **32:** 212; **60:** 33; **63:** 124, 131, 149
kingship **3:** 69, 73, 77, 109, 115, 136, 143; **24:** 32; **39:** 154, 177, 187; **47:** 32; **63:** 202
language and imagery **3:** 21, 50, 52, 55, 57, 66, 67, 71, 75, 76, 97, 105, 109, 119, 126, 131; **24:** 28; **37:** 157; **39:** 213, 222; **56:** 154, 162, 172, 180
legitimacy **3:** 89, 157; **39:** 154; **63:** 194, 202
Machiavellianism **22:** 193; **60:** 304
Margaret
characterization **3:** 18, 26, 35, 51, 103, 109, 140, 157; **24:** 48; **63:** 114, 131, 205
Suffolk, relationship with **3:** 18, 24, 26, 157; **39:** 213; **63:** 131, 169
Marlowe's works, compared with **19:** 233
medieval literary influence **3:** 59, 67, 75, 100, 109, 136, 151; **13:** 131
molehill scene (3 Henry VI, Act III, scene ii) **3:** 75, 97, 126, 149; **56:** 154; **60:** 33
moral inheritance **3:** 89, 126
multiple perspectives of characters **3:** 69, 154; **56:** 131
nationalism and patriotism **24:** 25, 45, 47; **56:** 80 25, 45, 47
Neoclassical rules **3:** 17, 18
oaths **63:** 194
patriarchal claims **16:** 131 **25:** 102; **63:** 124
play-within-the-play, convention of **3:** 75, 149
retribution **3:** 27, 42, 51, 59, 77, 83, 92, 100, 109, 115, 119, 131, 136, 151
Richard of Gloucester
characterization **3:** 35, 48, 57, 64, 77, 143, 151; **22:** 193; **39:** 160, 177; **63:** 114
as revenger **22:** 193
soliloquy (3 Henry VI, Act III, scene ii) **3:** 17, 48
sibling rivalry **22:** 193
sources **3:** 18, 21, 29, 31, 35, 39, 46, 51; **13:** 131; **16:** 217; **39:** 196; **56:** 2, 122, 131, 187; **63:** 114, 158, 169
staging issues **24:** 21, 22, 27, 31, 32, 36, 38, 41, 45, 48, 55; **32:** 212; **56:** 154, 172, 180, 187
structure **3:** 31, 43, 46, 69, 83, 103, 109, 119, 136, 149, 154; **39:** 213; **56:** 77, 80, 85; **63:** 158, 185
succession **60:** 304
Talbot **39:** 160, 213, 222; **56:** 85, 145; **60:** 33; **63:** 114, 185
textual arrangement **24:** 3, 4, 6, 12, 17, 18, 19, 20, 21, 24, 27, 42, 45; **37:** 165
theatrical viability **24:** 31, 32, 34; **56:** 80, 172; **63:** 144
tragic elements **60:** 33

Tudor myth **3:** 51, 59, 77, 92, 100, 109, 115, 119, 131; **39:** 222
Unity **39:** 177, 222
violence **24:** 25, 31; **37:** 157
women, role of **3:** 103, 109, 126, 140, 157; **16:** 183; **39:** 196; **63:** 124, 131
York's death **13:** 131; **60:** 33

***Henry VIII* (Volumes 2, 24, 41, 56, 61)**

ambition or pride **2:** 15, 38, 67
authorship controversy **2:** 16, 18, 19, 22, 23, 27, 28, 31, 35, 36, 42, 43, 44, 46, 48, 51, 58, 64, 68; **41:** 129, 146, 158, 171,
Anne Boleyn **2:** 21, 24, 31; **41:** 180; **61:** 129
Buckingham **22:** 182; **24:** 129, 140; **37:** 109
change **2:** 27, 65, 72, 81
characterization **2:** 17, 23, 25, 32, 35, 39; **24:** 106
composition date **2:** 19, 22, 35; **24:** 129
costumes **24:** 82, 87; **28:** 184
Cranmer's prophecy **2:** 25, 31, 46, 56, 64, 68, 72; **24:** 146; **32:** 148; **41:** 120, 190; **56:** 196, 230, 248, 273; **61:** 144
Chronicle sources **61:** 111
conscience **61:** 136
Cymbeline, compared with **2:** 67, 71
discrepancy between prophetic ending and preceding action **2:** 22, 25, 31, 46, 49, 56, 60, 65, 68, 75, 81; **32:** 148; **41:** 190; **56:** 273
divine providence **61:** 144
Elizabethan dramatic conventions **24:** 155; **56:** 196, 248
Elizabethan politics, relation to **22:** 395; **24:** 115, 129, 140; **32:** 148; **56:** 201, 248
English Reformation, influence of **2:** 25, 35, 39, 51, 67; **24:** 89; **56:** 201; **61:** 92
flattery **22:** 395
English nationalism **61:** 92, 111
historical and romantic elements, combination of **2:** 46, 49, 51, 75, 76, 78; **24:** 71, 80, 146; **41:** 129, 146, 180; **56:** 196, 201
historical epic, as epilogue to Shakespeare's **2:** 22, 25, 27, 39, 51, 60, 65
historical relativity, theme of **41:** 146; **56:** 220; **61:** 111
historiography **37:** 109 **56:** 201, 209, 230; **61:** 92, 101, 111
honor **61:** 101
inconsistencies **2:** 16, 27, 28, 31, 60
ironic aspects **41:** 129; **56:** 220
Jacobean court and politics **61:** 92
Katherine
characterization **2:** 18, 19, 23, 24, 38; **24:** 129; **37:** 109; **41:** 180; **61:** 119, 144
feminine power **61:119**
Hermione, compared with **2:** 24, 51, 58, 76
politeness strategies **22:** 182; **56:** 262
religious discourse **22:** 182
as tragic figure **2:** 16, 18
King Henry
as agent of divine retribution **2:** 49
characterization **2:** 23, 39, 51, 58, 60, 65, 66, 75; **28:** 184; **37:** 109; **56:** 242; **61:** 119, 136
incomplete portrait **2:** 15, 16, 19, 35; **41:** 120; **56:** 209
as realistic figure **2:** 21, 22, 23, 25, 32
patriarchy **61:** 119
kingship **2:** 49, 58, 60, 65, 75, 78; **24:** 113; **41:** 129, 171; **56:** 242; **61:** 92, 119
language and imagery **41:** 180, 190; **56:** 262, 273
law and justice **61:** 92
legitimacy **37:** 109; **56:** 209, 220, 230
masculine identity **61:** 129
moral intent **2:** 15, 19, 25; **24:** 140; **54:** 35 **61:** 92, 101, 144
Norfolk **22:** 182
pageantry **2:** 14, 15, 18, 51, 58; **24:** 77, 83, 84, 85, 89, 91, 106, 113, 118, 120, 126, 127, 140, 146, 150; **41:** 120, 129, 190
patience **2:** 58, 76, 78
patriarchy **61:** 129
personal motives **61:** 92
politics **2:** 39, 49, 51, 58, 60, 65, 67, 71, 72, 75, 78, 81; **24:** 74, 121, 124; **41:** 146; **56:** 242; **61:** 101
Porter **24:** 155
Prologue **54:** 35
Protestant philosophy **61:** 92, 129
romance versus history **61:** 101
rebellion **22:** 395; **56:** 230
rhetoric of politeness **22:** 182; **56:** 262
Shakespeare's romances, compared with **2:** 46, 51, 58, 66, 67, 71, 76; **41:** 171; **54:** 35; **56:** 273
social order **61:** 101
sources **2:** 16, 17; **24:** 71, 80
staging issues **24:** 67, 70, 71, 75, 77, 83, 84, 85, 87, 89, 91, 101, 106, 113, 120, 127, 129, 136, 140, 146, 150, 152, 155; **28:** 184; **56:** 220, 248
Stephen Gardiner **24:** 129
structure **2:** 16, 25, 27, 28, 31, 36, 44, 46, 51, 56, 68, 75; **24:** 106, 112, 113, 120; **56:** 209
style **41:** 158
thematic disparity **2:** 25, 31, 56, 68, 75; **41:** 146
tragedies of major characters **2:** 16, 39, 46, 48, 49, 51, 56, 58, 68, 81; **41:** 120
wheel of fortune, motif of **2:** 27, 65, 72, 81; **61:** 144
Wolsey (Cardinal Wolsey) **2:** 15, 18, 19, 23, 24, 38; **22:** 182; **24:** 80, 91, 112, 113, 129, 140; **37:** 109; **41:** 129; **56:** 248, 262; **61:** 144

***Julius Caesar* (Volumes 7, 17, 30, 50, 63)**

anachronisms **7:** 331
Antony
characterization **7:** 160, 179, 189, 221, 233, 284, 320, 333; **17:** 269, 271, 272, 284, 298, 306, 313, 315, 358, 398; **25:** 272; **30:** 316; **63:** 310
funeral oration **7:** 148, 154, 159, 204, 210, 221, 238, 259, 350; **25:** 280; **30:** 316, 333, 362; **63:** 219, 225, 278
aristocratic values **16:** 231; **22:** 280; **30:** 379; **50:** 194, 196, 211
the assassination **7:** 156, 161, 179, 191, 200, 221, 264, 272, 279, 284, 350; **25:** 272; **30:** 326
audience interpretation **48:** 240
audience response **7:** 179, 238, 253, 255, 272, 316, 320, 336, 350; **19:** 321; **48:** 240; **63:** 231, 238
Brutus **50:** 194, 258
arrogance **7:** 160, 169, 204, 207, 264, 277, 292, 350; **25:** 280; **30:** 351
as chief protagonist or tragic hero **7:** 152, 159, 189, 191, 200, 204, 242, 250, 253, 264, 268, 279, 284, 298, 333; **17:** 272, 372, 387; **63:** 260, 295, 310
citizenship **25:** 272
funeral oration **7:** 154, 155, 204, 210, 350; **63:** 219, 225, 278
motives **7:** 150, 156, 161, 179, 191, 200, 221, 227, 233, 245, 292, 303, 310, 320, 333, 350; **25:** 272; **30:** 321, 358; **63:** 295, 301
nobility or idealism **7:** 150, 152, 156, 159, 161, 179, 189, 191, 200, 221, 242, 250, 253, 259, 264, 277, 303, 320; **17:** 269, 271, 273, 279, 280, 284, 306, 308, 321, 323, 324, 345, 358; **25:** 272, 280; **30:** 351, 362; **50:** 194; **63:** 219, 301
political ineptitude or lack of judgment **7:** 169, 188, 200, 205, 221, 245, 252, 264, 277, 282, 310, 316, 331, 333, 343; **17:** 323, 358, 375, 380; **50:** 13; **63:** 322
self-knowledge or self-deception **7:** 191, 200, 221, 242, 259, 264, 268, 279, 310, 333, 336, 350; **25:** 272; **30:** 316; **60:** 46; **63:** 252, 295, 322
soliloquy (Act II, scene i) **7:** 156, 160, 161, 191, 221, 245, 250, 253, 264, 268, 279, 282, 292, 303, 343, 350; **25:** 280; **30:** 333
Caesar **50:** 189, 230, 234
ambiguous nature **7:** 191, 233, 242, 250, 272, 298, 316, 320; **63:** 219, 231
ambitious nature **50:** 234
arrogance **7:** 160, 207, 218, 253, 272, 279, 298; **25:** 280; **63:** 219, 231, 310
idolatry **22:** 137
leadership qualities **7:** 161, 179, 189, 191, 200, 207, 233, 245, 253, 257, 264, 272, 279, 284, 298, 310, 333; **17:** 317, 358; **22:** 280; **30:** 316, 326; **50:** 234; **63:** 278
as tragic hero **7:** 152, 200, 221, 279; **17:** 321, 377, 384
weakness **7:** 161, 167, 169, 179, 187, 188, 191, 207, 218, 221, 233, 250, 253, 298; **17:** 358; **25:** 280; **63:** 219, 231
Caesarism **7:** 159, 160, 161, 167, 169, 174, 191, 205, 218, 253, 310; **30:** 316, 321; **50:** 196, 234
Calphurnia
dream **45:** 10; **63:** 315
Casca
as Cynic **50:** 249
as proto-Christian **50:** 249
Cassius **7:** 156, 159, 160, 161, 169, 179, 189, 221, 233, 303, 310, 320, 333, 343; **17:** 272, 282, 284, 344, 345, 358; **25:** 272, 280; **30:** 351; **37:** 203; **60:** 46; **63:** 269
ceremonies, rites, and rituals, importance of **7:** 150, 210, 255, 259, 268, 284, 316, 331, 339, 356; **13:** 260; **22:** 137; **30:** 374; **50:** 258, 269; **63:** 295
construing the truth **7:** 320, 336, 343, 350; **37:** 229; **63:** 287, 295
Elizabethan culture, relation to **16:** 231; **30:** 342, 379; **50:** 13, 211, 269, 280
emulation or rivalry **16:** 231
Epicureanism **50:** 249; **63:** 269
Flavius and Murellus **50:** 64
gender issues **13:** 260
historical determinism versus free will **7:** 160, 298, 316, 333, 346, 356; **13:** 252; **63:** 219
irony or ambiguity **7:** 167, 257, 259, 262, 268, 282, 316, 320, 333, 336, 346, 350; **63:** 231, 252, 295, 310, 315

language and imagery **7:** 148, 155, 159, 188, 204, 207, 227, 242, 250, 277, 296, 303, 324, 346, 350; **13:** 260; **17:** 347, 348, 350, 356, 358; **19:** 321; **22:** 280; **25:** 280; **30:** 333, 342; **50:** 196, 258
liberty versus tyranny **7:** 158, 179, 189, 205, 221, 253; **25:** 272; **63:** 287
love and friendship **7:** 233, 262, 268; **25:** 272
medieval physiology **13:** 260
metadrama **63:** 225, 238
moral choice **7:** 179, 264, 279, 343
Octavius **30:** 316; **63:** 278
omens **22:** 137; **45:** 10; **50:** 265, 280
opening scene **54:** 6
patricians versus plebeians **50:** 189, 196
philosophical elements **7:** 310, 324; **37:** 203; **63:** 260, 269
plebeians versus tribunes **50:** 230
the poets **7:** 179, 320, 350
politics **7:** 161, 169, 191, 205, 218, 221, 245, 262, 264, 279, 282, 310, 324, 333, 346; **17:** 317, 318, 321, 323, 334, 350, 351, 358, 378, 382, 394, 406; **22:** 137, 280; **25:** 272, 280; **30:** 285, 297, 316, 321, 342, 374, 379; **37:** 203; **50:** 13; **63:** 322
as "problem play" **7:** 272, 320
psychoanalytic interpretation **45:** 10;; **63:** 315
public versus private principles **7:** 161, 179, 252, 262, 268, 284, 298; **13:** 252; **63:** 301, 322
quarrel scene (Act IV, scene iii) **7:** 149, 150, 152, 153, 155, 160, 169, 188, 191, 204, 268, 296, 303, 310
retribution **7:** 160, 167, 200
revenge tragedy elements **7:** 316; **63:** 310
rhetoric **63:** 278
role-playing **7:** 356; **37:** 229
Roman citizenry, portrayal of **7:** 169, 179, 210, 221, 245, 279, 282, 310, 320, 333; **17:** 271, 279, 288, 291, 292, 298, 323, 334, 351, 367, 374, 375, 378; **22:** 280; **30:** 285, 297, 316, 321, 374, 379; **37:** 229; **50:** 230; **63:** 238
Senecan elements **37:** 229
Shakespeare's English history plays, compared with **7:** 161, 189, 218, 221, 252; **22:** 137; **30:** 369
Shakespeare's major tragedies, compared with **7:** 161, 188, 227, 242, 264, 268
sources **7:** 149, 150, 156, 187, 200, 264, 272, 282, 284, 320; **30:** 285, 297, 326, 358; **63:** 269
staging **48:** 240; **50:** 186
Stoicism **50:** 249; **63:** 301
structure **7:** 152, 155, 159, 160, 179, 200, 210, 238, 264, 284, 298, 316, 346; **13:** 252; **30:** 374; **63:** 287
tragic elements **50:** 258, 265
violence **48:** 240

King John (Volumes 9, 24, 41, 56)

ambiguity **13:** 152; **41:** 243
anti-catholic rhetoric **22:** 120; **25:** 98
Arthur **9:** 215, 216, 218, 219, 229, 240, 267, 275; **22:** 120; **25:** 98; **41:** 251, 277; **56:** 345, 357
autobiographical elements **9:** 209, 218, 245, 248, 260, 292
characterization **9:** 222, 224, 229, 240, 250, 292; **41:** 205, 215; **56:** 365
church versus state **9:** 209, 212, 222, 235, 240; **22:** 120
commodity or self-interest **9:** 224, 229, 245, 260, 275, 280, 297; **19:** 182; **25:** 98; **41:** 228; **56:** 335
commodity versus honor **41:** 269
Constance **9:** 208, 210, 211, 215, 219, 220, 224, 229, 240, 251, 254; **16:** 161; **24:** 177, 184, 196
corruption in society **9:** 222, 234, 280, 297
Elizabethan politics, relation to **48:** 132; **56:** 306, 314, 325; **60:** 295, 329
ethical or moral issues **9:** 212, 222, 224, 229, 235, 240, 263, 275, 280 **56:** 335
excess **9:** 251
Faulconbridge, the Bastard **41:** 205, 228, 251, 260, 277; **56:** 306, 314, 335, 348, 365
  as chorus or commentator **9:** 212, 218, 229, 248, 251, 260, 271, 284, 297, 300; **22:** 120
  as comic figure **9:** 219, 271, 297; **56:** 365
  development **9:** 216, 224, 229, 248, 263, 271, 275, 280, 297; **13:** 158, 163; **56:** 335
  as embodiment of England **9:** 222, 224, 240, 244, 248, 271
  heroic qualities **9:** 208, 245, 248, 254, 263, 271, 275; **25:** 98; **56:** 348
  political conduct **9:** 224, 240, 250, 260, 280, 297; **13:** 147, 158; **22:** 120; **56:** 314
Henry **41:** 277; **56:** 348
historical content **9:** 216, 219, 220, 222, 235, 240, 254, 284, 290, 292, 297, 300, 303; **13:** 163; **32:** 93, 114; **41:** 234, 243; **56:** 286, 296, 357 **60:** 329
John **41:** 205, 260; **56:** 325, 345
  death, decay, and nature's destructiveness **9:** 212, 215, 216, 240; **56:** 345
  decline **9:** 224, 235, 240, 263, 275
  Hubert, scene with (Act III, scene iii) **9:** 210, 212, 216, 218, 219, 280
  moral insensibility **13:** 147, 163
  negative qualities **9:** 209, 212, 218, 219, 229, 234, 235, 244, 245, 246, 250, 254, 275, 280, 297; **56:** 325
  positive qualities **9:** 209, 224, 235, 240, 244, 245, 263
kingship **9:** 235, 254, 263, 275, 297; **13:** 158; **19:** 182; **22:** 120; **56:** 314
language and imagery **9:** 212, 215, 220, 246, 251, 254, 267, 280, 284, 292, 297, 300; **13:** 147, 158; **22:** 120; **37:** 132; **48:** 132; **56:** 286
legitimacy or inheritance **9:** 224, 235, 254, 303; **13:** 147; **19:** 182; **37:** 132; **41:** 215; **56:** 325, 335; **60:** 295, 329
Machiavellianism **60:** 304
nationalism and patriotism **9:** 209, 218, 222, 224, 235, 240, 244, 275; **25:** 98; **37:** 132
Neoclassical rules **9:** 208, 209, 210, 212; **56:** 365
oppositions or dualisms **9:** 224, 240, 263, 275, 284, 290, 300
Papal Tyranny in the Reign of King John (Colley Cibber adaptation) **24:** 162, 163, 165
politics **9:** 218, 224, 260, 280; **13:** 163; **22:** 120; **37:** 132; **41:** 221, 228; **56:** 314, 325
rebellion **9:** 218, 254, 263, 280, 297
Roman citizenry, portrayal of **50:** 64
Shakespeare's other history plays, compared with **9:** 218, 254; **13:** 152, 158; **25:** 98; **56:** 306, 348, 357
sources **9:** 216, 222, 300; **32:** 93, 114; **41:** 234, 243, 251; **56:** 296, 357
staging issues **16:** 161; **19:** 182; **24:** 171, 187, 203, 206, 211, 225, 228, 241, 245, 249; **56:** 286, 365
structure **9:** 208, 212, 222, 224, 229, 240, 244, 245, 254, 260, 263, 275, 284, 290, 292, 300; **24:** 228, 241; **41:** 260, 269, 277
succession **60:** 295, 304, 329
tragic elements **9:** 208, 209, 244
treachery **9:** 245
The Troublesome Reign (anonymous), compared with **9:** 216, 244, 260, 292; **22:** 120; **32:** 93; **41:** 205, 221, 260, 269; **48:** 132; **56:** 357
Tudor doctrine **9:** 254, 284, 297; **41:** 221; **56:** 345
tyranny **9:** 218
women, role of **9:** 222, 303; **16:** 161; **19:** 182; **41:** 205, 221

King Lear (Volumes 2, 11, 31, 46, 61)

Albany **32:** 308
allegorical elements **16:** 311; **61:** 215
audience perception **19:** 295; **28:** 325; **61:** 176
autobiographical elements **2:** 131, 136, 149, 165
characterization **2:** 108, 125, 145, 162, 191; **16:** 311; **28:** 223; **46:** 177, 210
Christian elements **2:** 137, 170, 179, 188, 191, 197, 207, 218, 222, 226, 229, 238, 249, 265, 286; **22:** 233, 271; **25:** 218; **46:** 276; **49:** 67; **52:** 95; **60:** 75; **61:** 194, 262
as Christian play **48:** 222
Clarissa (Samuel Richardson), compared with **48:** 277
combat scenes **22:** 365
comic and tragic elements, combination of **2:** 108, 110, 112, 125, 156, 162, 245, 278, 284; **46:** 191
Cordelia
  attack on Britain **25:** 202
  characterization **2:** 110, 116, 125, 170; **16:** 311; **25:** 218; **28:** 223, 325; **31:** 117, 149, 155, 162; **46:** 225, 231, 242; **61:** 220, 230
  as Christ figure **2:** 116, 170, 179, 188, 222, 286
  rebelliousness **13:** 352; **25:** 202; **61:** 194
  self-knowledge **46:** 218
  on stage **11:** 158
  transcendent power **2:** 137, 207, 218, 265, 269, 273
Cornwall's servants (III.vii) **54:** 114
cruelty of daughters **2:** 101, 102, 106; **31:** 84, 123, 137, 142
death, decay, and nature's destructiveness **2:** 93, 94, 101, 104, 106, 109, 112, 116, 129, 131, 137, 143, 147, 149, 156, 160, 170, 179, 188, 197, 207, 218, 222, 226, 231, 238, 241, 245, 249, 253, 265, 269, 273; **16:** 301; **25:** 202, 218; **31:** 77, 117, 137, 142; **46:** 264
deaths of Lear and Cordelia **54:** 103, 110, 114; **60:** 2

Topic Index, by Play

double-plot **2:** 94, 95, 100, 101, 104, 112, 116, 124, 131, 133, 156, 253, 257; **46:** 254
Dover Cliff scene **2:** 156, 229, 255, 269; **11:** 8, 151; **54:** 103
Edgar **28:** 223; **32:** 212; **32:** 308; **37:** 295; **47:** 9; **50:** 24, 45
Edgar-Edmund duel **22:** 365
Edmund **25:** 218; **28:** 223
Edmund's forged letter **16:** 372
Elizabethan culture, relation to **2:** 168, 174, 177, 183, 226, 241; **19:** 330; **22:** 227, 233, 365; **25:** 218; **46:** 276; **47:** 9; **49:** 67; **61:** 172, 176, 187, 194
ending **54:** 103, 110, 114; **60:** 46, 65, 75; **61:** 262
ethical and moral issues **52:** 1
feminist criticism **55:** 68
Fool **2:** 108, 112, 125, 156, 162, 245, 278, 284; **11:** 17, 158, 169; **22:** 227; **25:** 202; **28:** 223; **46:** 1, 14, 18, 24, 33, 52, 191, 205, 210, 218, 225; **61:** 176
Gloucester **46:** 254; **61:** 250
Goneril **31:** 151; **46:** 231, 242; **61:** 160
grotesque or absurd elements **2:** 136, 156, 245; **13:** 343; **52:** 1
implausibility or plot, characters, or events **2:** 100, 136, 145, 278; **13:** 343
Job, compared with **2:** 226, 241, 245; **25:** 218
justice, divine vs. worldly **49:** 1, 67, 73; **61:** 230
Kent **25:** 202; **28:** 223; **32:** 212; **47:** 9; **60:** 185
language and imagery **2:** 129, 137, 161, 191, 199, 237, 257, 271; **16:** 301; **19:** 344; **22:** 233; **46:** 177; **61:** 215, 230
Lear **61:** 176
  curse on Goneril **11:** 5, 7, 12, 114, 116
  love-test and division of kingdom **2:** 100, 106, 111, 124, 131, 137, 147, 149, 151, 168, 186, 208, 216, 281; **16:** 351; **25:** 202; **31:** 84, 92, 107, 117, 149, 155; **46:** 231, 242; **61:** 194
  madness **2:** 94, 95, 98, 99, 100, 101, 102, 103, 111, 116, 120, 124, 125, 149, 156, 191, 208, 216, 281; **46:** 264
  as scapegoat **2:** 241, 253
  self-knowledge **2:** 103, 151, 188, 191, 213, 218, 222, 241, 249, 262; **25:** 218; **37:** 213; **46:** 191, 205, 225, 254, 264, **54:** 103; **60:** 65, 75; **61:** 215, 220, 250
spiritual regeneration **60:** 65, 75
legal issues **46:** 276
love **2:** 109, 112, 131, 160, 162, 170, 179, 188, 197, 218, 222, 238, 265; **25:** 202; **31:** 77, 149, 151, 155, 162; **61:** 220, 237
madness **19:** 330
Marxist criticism **42:** 234; **55:** 16
medieval or morality drama, influence of **2:** 177, 188, 201; **25:** 218
misogyny **31:** 123
moral or ethical issues **52:** 95
mythic or mythological elements **60:** 185
nihilistic or pessimistic vision **2:** 130, 143, 149, 156, 165, 231, 238, 245, 253; **22:** 271; **25:** 218; **28:** 325; **49:** 67
opening scene **54:** 2, 6
order **56:** 25
pagan elements **25:** 218
patriarchal or monarchical order **13:** 353, 457; **16:** 351; **22:** 227, 233; **25:** 218; **31:** 84, 92, 107, 117, 123, 137, 142; **46:** 269; **61:** 172, 237
performance issues **2:** 106, 137, 154, 160; **11:** 10, 20, 27, 56, 57, 132, 136, 137, 145, **150, 154; 19:** 295, 344; **25:** 218; **61:** 187
poetic justice, question of **2:** 92, 93, 94, 101, 129, 137, 231, 245; **49:** 73
politics **46:** 269; **50:** 45; **61:** 160, 172, 187, 237
providential order **2:** 112, 116, 137, 168, 170, 174, 177, 218, 226, 241, 253; **22:** 271; **49:** 1, 73
Regan **31:** 151; **46:** 231, 242; **61:** 160
rhetorical style **16:** 301; **47:** 9
romantic elements **31:** 77, 84
sexuality **25:** 202; **31:** 133, 137, 142
sexual politics **55:** 68
social and moral corruption **2:** 116, 133, 174, 177, 241, 271; **22:** 227; **31:** 84, 92; **46:** 269; **61:** 160
sources **2:** 94, 100, 143, 145, 170, 186; **13:** 352; **16:** 351; **28:** 301 **60:** 185; **61:** 250
spiritual regeneration **54:** 103
staging issues **11:** 1-178; **32:** 212; **46:** 205, 218; **54:** 103
structure **28:** 325; **32:** 308; **46:** 177
suffering **2:** 137, 160, 188, 201, 218, 222, 226, 231, 238, 241, 249, 265; **13:** 343; **22:** 271; **25:** 218; **50:** 24
Tate's adaptation **2:** 92, 93, 94, 101, 102, 104, 106, 110, 112, 116, 137; **11:** 10, 136; **25:** 218; **31:** 162
textual issues **22:** 271; **37:** 295; **49:** 73; **61:** 262
Timon of Athens, relation to **16:** 351
tragic elements **55:** 78; **61:** 250
Virgo vs. Virago **48:** 222
wisdom **37:** 213; **46:** 210

***Love's Labour's Lost* (Volumes 2, 23, 38, 54)**

Armado **23:** 207
artificial nature **2:** 315, 317, 324, 330; **23:** 207, 233; **54:** 234, 248, 257, 263
authorship controversy **2:** 299, 300; **32:** 308
Berowne **2:** 308, 324, 327; **22:** 12; **23:** 184, 187; **38:** 194; **47:** 35
characterization **2:** 303, 310, 317, 322, 328, 342; **23:** 237, 250, 252; **38:** 232; **47:** 35
as comedy of affectation **2:** 302, 303, 304; **23:** 191, 224, 226, 228, 233
comic resolution **2:** 335, 340; **16:** 17; **19:** 92; **38:** 209; **51:** 1; **54:** 240, 248, 274
comic form **54:** 257, 263
conclusion **38:** 172; **54:** 240, 248, 274
dance and patterned action **2:** 308, 342; **23:** 191, 237
death, decay, and nature's destructiveness **2:** 305, 331, 344, 348
desire **38:** 185, 194, 200, 209
dramatic shortcomings or failure **2:** 299, 301, 303, 322; **54:** 240, 248
Elizabeth I **38:** 239
Elizabethan love poetry **38:** 232
ending **54:** 58
feminist criticism **42:** 93
genre **38:** 163
gift exchange **25:** 1
grace and civility **2:** 351
Holofernes **23:** 207
illusion versus reality **2:** 303, 308, 331, 340, 344, 348, 356, 359, 367, 371, 375; **23:** 230, 231
knowledge **22:** 12; **47:** 35
language and imagery **2:** 301, 302, 303, 306, 307, 308, 315, 319, 320, 330, 335, 344, 345, 348, 356, 359, 362, 365, 371, 374, 375; **19:** 92; **22:** 12, 378; **23:** 184, 187, 196, 197, 202, 207, 211, 221, 227, 231, 233, 237, 252; **28:** 9, 63; **38:** 219, 226; **54:** 225, 274
love **2:** 312, 315, 340, 344; **22:** 12; **23:** 252; **38:** 194; **51:** 44
love vs. reason **54:** 225, 234
male domination **22:** 12
male/female relationships **54:** 284
male sexual anxiety **16:** 17
marriage **2:** 335, 340; **19:** 92; **38:** 209, 232; **51:** 1, 44
metadramatic elements **2:** 356, 359, 362
Neoclassical rules **2:** 299, 300
oaths **54:** 257, 284
physical versus intellectual world **2:** 331, 348, 367
plot **54:** 225
public versus private speech **2:** 356, 362, 371
as satire or parody **2:** 300, 302, 303, 307, 308, 315, 321, 324, 327; **23:** 237, 252; **54:** 234
School of Night, allusions to **2:** 321, 327, 328
sexuality **22:** 12; **51:** 44
songs, role of **2:** 303, 304, 316, 326, 335, 362, 367, 371, 375; **54:** 240
sources **16:** 17
spectacle **38:** 226
staging issues **23:** 184, 187, 191, 196, 198, 200, 201, 202, 207, 212, 215, 216, 217, 229, 230, 232, 233, 237, 252
structure **22:** 378; **23:** 191, 237, 252; **38:** 163, 172
theme
  idealism versus realism **38:** 163
topical allusions or content **2:** 300, 303, 307, 315, 316, 317, 319, 321, 327, 328; **23:** 187, 191, 197, 203, 221, 233, 237, 252; **25:** 1
unnatural ordering **22:** 378
violence **22:** 12
visual humor **23:** 207, 217
Watteau, influence on staging **23:** 184, 186
women, role of **19:** 92; **22:** 12; **23:** 215; **25:** 1
wisdom and folly **54:** 257
written versus oral communication **2:** 359, 365; **28:** 63

***Macbeth* (Volumes 3, 20, 29, 44, 57)**

antithetical or contradictory elements **3:** 185, 213, 271, 302; **25:** 235; **29:** 76, 127; **47:** 41
appearance versus reality **3:** 241, 248; **25:** 235
archetypal or mythic elements **16:** 317
audience response **20:** 17, 400, 406; **29:** 139, 146, 155, 165; **44:** 306
banquet scene (Act III, scene iv) **20:** 22, 32, 175
Banquo **3:** 183, 199, 208, 213, 278, 289; **20:** 279, 283, 406, 413; **25:** 235; **28:** 339

characterization **20:** 12, 318, 324, 329, 353, 363, 367, 374, 387; **28:** 339; **29:** 101, 109, 146, 155, 165; **44:** 289; **47:** 41; **57:** 267
Christian elements **3:** 194, 239, 260, 269, 275, 286, 293, 297, 318; **20:** 203, 206, 210, 256, 262, 289, 291, 294; **44:** 341, 366; **47:** 41; **57:** 236
combat scenes **22:** 365
conscience **52:** 15
dagger scene (Act III, scene i), staging of **20:** 406
Duncan **57:** 194, 236
Elizabethan politics, relation to **54:** 357
ending **54:** 84
evil **3:** 194, 208, 231, 234, 239, 241, 267, 289; **20:** 203, 206, 210, 374; **52:** 23; **57:** 267
female identity **57:** 256
feminine power, role of **57:** 242
free will versus fate **3:** 177, 183, 184, 190, 196, 198, 202, 207, 208, 213; **13:** 361; **44:** 351, 361, 366, 373; **54:** 6
innocence **3:** 234, 241, 327; **57:** 267
Jacobean culture, relation to **19:** 330; **22:** 365; **57:** 218, 256; **60:** 340, 357
Lady Macbeth
  ambition **3:** 185, 219; **20:** 279, 345
  characterization **20:** 56, 60, 65, 73, 140, 148, 151, 241, 279, 283, 338, 350, 406, 413; **29:** 109, 146; **57:** 256, 263
  childlessness **3:** 219, 223
  good and evil, combined traits of **3:** 173, 191, 213; **20:** 60, 107
  inconsistencies **3:** 202; **20:** 54, 137
  influence on Macbeth **3:** 171, 185, 191, 193, 199, 262, 289, 312, 318; **13:** 502; **20:** 345; **25:** 235; **29:** 133; **57:** 263
  psychoanalytic interpretations **20:** 345; **44:** 289, 297, 324; **45:** 58
  as sympathetic figure **3:** 191, 193, 203
language and imagery **3:** 170, 193, 213, 231, 234, 241, 245, 250, 253, 256, 263, 271, 283, 300, 302, 306, 323, 327, 338, 340, 349; **13:** 476; **16:** 317; **20:** 241, 279, 283, 367, 379, 400; **25:** 235; **28:** 339; **29:** 76, 91; **42:** 263; **44:** 366; **45:** 58
laws of nature, violation of **3:** 234, 241, 280, 323; **29:** 120; **57:** 242, 263
legitimacy **60:** 340
letter to Lady Macbeth **16:** 372; **20:** 345; **25:** 235
Macbeth
  ambition **44:** 284, 324; **57:** 256
  characterization **20:** 20, 42, 73, 107, 113, 130, 146, 151, 279, 283, 312, 338, 343, 379, 406, 413; **29:** 139, 152, 155, 165; **44:** 289; **57:** 189, 194, 236, 263, 267
  courage **3:** 172, 177, 181, 182, 183, 186, 234, 312, 333; **20:** 107; **44:** 315
  disposition **3:** 173, 175, 177, 182, 186; **20:** 245, 376
  imagination **3:** 196, 208, 213, 250, 312, 345; **20:** 245, 376; **44:** 351
  as "inauthentic" king **3:** 245, 302, 321, 345
  inconsistencies **3:** 202
  as Machiavellian villain **3:** 280; **57:** 236
  manliness **20:** 113; **29:** 127, 133; **44:** 315; **57:** 256
  psychoanalytic interpretations **20:** 42, 73, 238, 376; **44:** 284, 289, 297, 324; **45:** 48, 58; **57:** 267
  Richard III, compared with **3:** 177, 182, 186, 345; **20:** 86, 92; **22:** 365; **44:** 269
  as Satan figure **3:** 229, 269, 275, 289, 318
  self-awareness **3:** 312, 329, 338; **16:** 317; **44:** 361; **57:** 256; **60:** 46
  as sympathetic figure **3:** 229, 306, 314, 338; **29:** 139, 152; **44:** 269, 306, 337
  as tragic hero **44:** 269, 306, 315, 324, 337; **57:** 267
Macduff **3:** 226, 231, 253, 262,; **25:** 235; **29:** 127, 133, 155; **57:** 194
Machiavellianism **52:** 29; **57:** 236
madness **19:** 330
major tragedies, relation to Shakespeare's other **3:** 171, 173, 213; **44:** 269; **57:** 189
Malcolm **25:** 235
manhood **3:** 262, 309, 333; **29:** 127, 133; **57:** 242, 263
Marxist criticism **42:** 234; **55:** 16
medieval mystery plays, relation to **44:** 341; **57:** 194
morality **52:** 15, 23, 29
moral lesson **20:** 23
murder scene (Act II, scene ii) **20:** 175
mythic or mythological elements **60:** 169, 214
naturalism **60:** 169
Neoclassical rules **3:** 170, 171, 173, 175; **20:** 17
nightmarish quality **3:** 231, 309; **20:** 210, 242; **44:** 261
opening scene **54:** 2, 6
politics **52:** 29; **57:** 218, 228
Porter scene (Act II, scene iii) **3:** 173, 175, 184, 190, 196, 203, 205, 225, 260, 271, 297, 300; **20:** 283; **44:** 261; **46:** 29, 78; **60:** 89
primitivism **20:** 206, 213; **45:** 48
providential order **3:** 208, 289, 329, 336; **57:** 218
psychoanalytic interpretations **3:** 219, 223, 226; **44:** 11, 284, 289, 297
regicide **16:** 317, 328; **45:** 48 248, 275, 312
religious and theological issues **44:** 324, 341, 351, 361, 366, 373
religious, mythic, or spiritual content **3:** 208, 269, 275, 318; **29:** 109
retribution **3:** 194, 208, 318; **48:** 214
Scholasticism **52:** 23
sexual anxiety **16:** 328; **20:** 283
sleepwalking scene (Act V, scene i) **3:** 191, 203, 219; **20:** 175; **44:** 261
sources **60:** 214
staging issues **13:** 502; **20:** 12, 17, 32, 64, 65, 70, 73, 107, 113, 151, 175, 203, 206, 210, 213, 245, 279, 283, 312, 318, 324, 329, 343, 345, 350, 353, 363, 367, 374, 376, 379, 382, 387, 400, 406, 413; **22:** 365; **32:** 212
structure **16:** 317; **20:** 12, 245
succession **60:** 340, 357
supernatural grace versus evil or chaos **3:** 241, 286, 323
theatricality **16:** 328
time **3:** 234, 246, 283, 293; **20:** 245; **57:** 218
topical allusions or content **13:** 361; **20:** 17, 350; **29:** 101
tragic elements **52:** 15; **55:** 78; **57:** 189
treason and punishment **13:** 361; **16:** 328
violence **20:** 273, 279, 283; **45:** 58; **57:** 228, 267
virtue versus vice **60:** 214
witches and supernaturalism **3:** 171, 172, 173, 175, 177, 182, 183, 184, 185, 194, 196, 198, 202, 207, 208, 213, 219, 229, 239; **16:** 317; **19:** 245; **20:** 92, 175, 213, 279, 283, 374, 387, 406, 413; **25:** 235; **28:** 339; **29:** 91, 101, 109, 120; **44:** 351, 373; **57:** 194, 242

***Measure for Measure* (Volumes 2, 23, 33, 49)**

allegorical elements **52:** 69
ambiguity **2:** 417, 420, 432, 446, 449, 452, 474, 479, 482, 486, 495, 505
Angelo
  anxiety **16:** 114
  authoritarian portrayal of **23:** 307; **49:** 274
  characterization **2:** 388, 390, 397, 402, 418, 427, 432, 434, 463, 484, 495, 503, 511; **13:** 84; **23:** 297; **32:** 81; **33:** 77; **49:** 274, 293, 379
  hypocrisy **2:** 396, 399, 402, 406, 414, 421; **23:** 345, 358, 362
  repentance or pardon **2:** 388, 390, 397, 402, 434, 463, 511, 524
audience response **48:** 1; **60:** 12
autobiographical elements **2:** 406, 410, 414, 431, 434, 437
Barnardine **13:** 112
bed-trick **13:** 84; **49:** 313; **54:** 52
characterization **2:** 388, 390, 391, 396, 406, 420, 421, 446, 466, 475, 484, 505, 516, 524; **23:** 299, 405; **33:** 77
Christian elements **2:** 391, 394, 399, 421, 437, 449, 466, 479, 491, 511, 522; **48:** 1; **49:** 325; **60:** 12
Clarissa (Samuel Richardson), compared with **48:** 277
Claudio **60:** 12
comic form **2:** 456, 460, 479, 482, 491, 514, 516; **13:** 94, 104; **23:** 309, 326, 327; **49:** 349
death, decay, and nature's destructiveness **2:** 394, 452, 516; **25:** 12; **49:** 370
death, motif of **60:** 12
displacement **22:** 78
Duke
  as authoritarian figure **23:** 314, 317, 347; **33:** 85; **49:** 274, 300, 358
  characterization **2:** 388, 395, 402, 406, 411, 421, 429, 456, 466, 470, 498, 511; **13:** 84, 94, 104; **23:** 363, 416; **32:** 81; **42:** 1; **44:** 89; **49:** 274, 293, 300, 358; **60:** 12
  dramatic shortcomings or failure **2:** 420, 429, 441, 479, 495, 505, 514, 522
  godlike portrayal of **23:** 320
  noble portrayal of **23:** 301
  speech on death (Act III, scene i) **2:** 390, 391, 395
Elbow **22:** 85; **25:** 12
Elbow, Mistress **33:** 90
Elizabethan betrothal and marriage customs **2:** 429, 437, 443, 503; **49:** 286
Elizabethan culture, relation to **2:** 394, 418, 429, 432, 437, 460, 470, 482, 503
ending **54:** 52, 65
ethical or moral issues **52:** 69
feminist criticism **55:** 16, 68
feminist interpretation **23:** 320
good and evil **2:** 432, 452, 524; **33:** 52, 61; **52:** 69
homosexuality **42:** 1

immortality **16:** 102
inconsistency between first and second halves **2:** 474, 475, 505, 514, 524; **49:** 349, 358
Isabella **2:** 388, 390, 395, 396, 397, 401, 402, 406, 409, 410, 411, 418, 420, 421, 432, 437, 441, 466, 475, 491, 495, 524; **16:** 114; **23:** 278, 279, 280, 281, 282, 296, 344, 357, 363, 405; **28:** 92; **33:** 77, 85; **60:** 12
judicial versus natural law **2:** 446, 507, 516, 519; **22:** 85; **33:** 58, 117; **49:** 293
justice and mercy **2:** 391, 395, 399, 402, 406, 409, 411, 416, 421, 437, 443, 463, 466, 470, 491, 495, 522, 524; **22:** 85; **33:** 52, 61, 101; **49:** 274, 293, 300
judicial vs. natural law **49:** 1
justice and mercy **49:** 1
language and imagery **2:** 394, 421, 431, 466, 486, 505; **13:** 112; **28:** 9; **33:** 69; **49:** 370
Lucio **13:** 104; **49:** 379
marriage **2:** 443, 507, 516, 519, 524, 528; **25:** 12; **33:** 61, 90; **49:** 286; **51:** 44
as medieval allegory or morality play **2:** 409, 421, 443, 466, 475, 491, 505, 511, 522; **13:** 94; **60:** 12
metadramatic elements **13:** 104
misgovernment **2:** 401, 432, 511; **22:** 85
misogyny **23:** 358;
moral seriousness, question of **2:** 387, 388, 396, 409, 417, 421, 452, 460, 495; **23:** 316, 321
mythic or mythological elements **60:** 281
Neoclassical rules **2:** 387, 388, 390, 394; **23:** 269
Ovid' Metamorphoses, relation to **60:** 281
politics **23:** 379; **49:** 274
power **13:** 112; **22:** 85; **23:** 327, 330, 339, 352; **33:** 85
as "problem play" **2:** 416, 429, 434, 474, 475, 503, 514, 519; **16:** 102; **23:** 313, 328, 351; **49:** 358, 370
providential order **48:** 1
psychoanalytic interpretations **23:** 331, 332, 333, 334, 335, 340, 355, 356, 359, 379, 395; **44:** 79
Puritanism **2:** 414, 418, 434; **49:** 325
rebirth, regeneration, resurrection, or immortality **13:** 84; **16:** 102, 114; **23:** 321, 327, 335, 340, 352; **25:** 12
religious and theological issues **48:** 1
religious, mythic, or spiritual content **48:** 1
resolution **2:** 449, 475, 495, 514, 516; **16:** 102, 114; **54:** 65
sexuality **13:** 84; **16:** 102, 114; **23:** 321, 327, 335, 340, 352; **25:** 12; **33:** 85, 90, 112; **49:** 286, 338; **51:** 44
sexual politics **55:** 68
social aspects **23:** 316, 375, 379, 395; **49:** 338
sources **2:** 388, 393, 427, 429, 437, 475; **13:** 94; **49:** 349; **52:** 69; **60:** 281
staging issues **2:** 427, 429, 437, 441, 443, 456, 460, 482, 491, 519; **23:** 283, 284, 285, 286, 287, 291, 293, 294, 298, 299, 311, 315, 327, 338, 339, 340, 342, 344, 347, 363, 372, 375, 395, 400, 405, 406, 413; **32:** 16
structure **2:** 390, 411, 449, 456, 466, 474, 482, 490, 491; **33:** 69; **49:** 379
substitution of identities **2:** 507, 511, 519; **13:** 112; **49:** 313, 325
supernatural grace vs. evil or chaos **48:** 1
theatricality **23:** 285, 286, 294, 372, 406; **49:** 358
comic and tragic elements, combination of **16:** 102
as unsuccessful play **2:** 397, 441, 474, 482; **23:** 287

The Merchant of Venice (Volumes 4, 12, 40, 53)

Act V, relation to Acts I through IV **4:** 193, 194, 195, 196, 204, 232, 270, 273, 289, 300, 319, 321, 326, 336, 356
allegorical elements **4:** 224, 250, 261, 268, 270, 273, 282, 289, 324, 336, 344, 350; **53:** 179, 187
Antonio
  excessive or destructive love **4:** 279, 284, 336, 344; **12:** 54; **37:** 86
  love for Bassanio **40:** 156
  melancholy **4:** 221, 238, 279, 284, 300, 321, 328; **22:** 69; **25:** 22
  pitiless **4:** 254
  as pivotal figure **12:** 25, 129
  versus Shylock **53:** 187
appearance versus reality **4:** 209, 261, 344; **12:** 65; **22:** 69
Bassanio **25:** 257; **37:** 86; **40:** 156
bonding **4:** 293, 317, 336; **13:** 37
casket scenes **4:** 226, 241, 308, 344; **12:** 23, 46, 47, 65, 117; **13:** 43; **22:** 3; **40:** 106; **49:** 27
Christian elements **52:** 89
comparison to other works of Shakespeare **53:** 105
contrasting dramatic worlds **44:** 11
conflict between Christianity and Judaism **4:** 224, 250, 268, 289, 324, 344; **12:** 67, 70, 72, 76; **22:** 69; **25:** 257; **40:** 117, 127, 166, 181; **48:** 54, 77; **53:** 105, 159, 214
desire **22:** 3; **40:** 142; **45:** 17
disappointment, theme of **53:** 211
Economics and exchange **40:** 197, 208; **53:** 116
Elizabethan culture, relation to **32:** 66; **40:** 117, 127, 142, 166, 181, 197, 208; **48:** 54, 77; **49:** 37; **53:** 105, 111, 127, 159, 169, 214, 224
ending **54:** 52, 65
feminist criticism **55:** 27
genre **4:** 191, 200, 201, 209, 215, 221, 232, 238, 247; **12:** 48, 54, 62; **54:** 65
homosexuality **22:** 3, 69; **37:** 86; **40:** 142, 156, 197
imperialism **53:** 116
implausibility of plot, characters, or events **4:** 191, 192, 193; **12:** 52, 56, 76, 119
irony **4:** 254, 300, 321, 331, 350; **28:** 63
Jessica **4:** 196, 200, 228, 293, 342; **53:** 159, 211
justice and mercy **4:** 213, 214, 224, 250, 261, 273, 282, 289, 336; **12:** 80, 129; **40:** 127; **49:** 1, 23, 27, 37
language and imagery **4:** 241, 267, 293; **22:** 3; **25:** 257; **28:** 9, 63; **32:** 41; **40:** 106; **53:** 169
Launcelot Gobbo **46:** 24, 60; **50:** 64; **53:** 187, 214
law and justice **53:** 169
love **4:** 221, 226, 270, 284, 312, 344; **22:** 3, 69; **25:** 257; **40:** 156; **51:** 1, 44
medieval homilies, influence of **4:** 224, 250, 289
morality **52:** 89
mythic or mythological elements **60:** 276
Ovid's Metamorphoses, relation to **60:** 276
Portia **4:** 194, 195, 196, 215, 254, 263, 336, 356; **12:** 104, 107, 114; **13:** 37; **22:** 3, 69; **25:** 22; **32:** 294; **37:** 86; **40:** 142, 156, 197, 208; **49:** 27
psychoanalytic interpretation **45:** 17
race **53:** 111, 116, 127, 136, 159, 169; **55:** 27
resolution **4:** 263, 266, 300, 319, 321; **13:** 37; **51:** 1
revenge **60:** 276
rings episode **22:** 3; **40:** 106, 151, 156
sacrificial love **13:** 43; **22:** 69; **40:** 142
sexual politics **22:** 3; **51:** 44
Shylock
  alienation **4:** 279, 312; **40:** 175; **49:** 23, 37
  ambiguity **4:** 247, 254, 315, 319, 331; **12:** 31, 35, 36, 50, 51, 52, 56, 81, 124; **40:** 175; **53:** 111
  forced conversion **4:** 209, 252, 268, 282, 289, 321
  ghettoization of **53:** 127
  Jewishness **4:** 193, 194, 195, 200, 201, 213, 214, 279; **22:** 69; **25:** 257; **40:** 142, 175, 181
  master-slave relationship **53:** 136
  motives in making the bond **4:** 252, 263, 266, 268; **22:** 69; **25:** 22
  as outsider **53:** 127, 224
  as Puritan **40:** 127, 166
  as scapegoat figure **4:** 254, 300; **40:** 166 **49:** 27
  as traditional comic villain **4:** 230, 243, 261, 263, 315; **12:** 40, 62, 124; **40:** 175
  as tragic figure **12:** 6, 9, 10, 16, 21, 23, 25, 40, 44, 66, 67, 81, 97; **40:** 175
social criticism **53:** 214
staging issues **12:** 111, 114, 115, 117, 119, 124, 129, 131
structure **4:** 201, 215, 230, 232, 243, 247, 254, 261, 263, 308, 321; **12:** 115; **28:** 63; **60:** 276
trial scene **13:** 43; **25:** 22; **40:** 106, 156; **49:** 1, 23, 27, 37
unity of double plot **4:** 193, 194, 201, 232; **12:** 16, 67, 80, 115, **40:** 151
Venetians **4:** 195, 200, 228, 254, 273, 300, 321, 331
Venice, Elizabethan perceptions of **28:** 249; **32:** 294; **40:** 127
wealth **4:** 209, 261, 270, 273, 317; **12:** 80, 117; **22:** 69; **25:** 22; **28:** 249; **40:** 117, 197, 208; **45:** 17; **49:** 1; **51:** 15

The Merry Wives of Windsor (Volumes 5, 18, 38, 47, 59)

Anne Page-Fenton plot **5:** 334, 336, 343, 353, 376, 390, 395, 402; **22:** 93; **47:** 308
avarice **5:** 335, 353, 369, 376, 390, 395, 402
Caius, Doctor **47:** 354
caricature **5:** 343, 347, 348, 350, 385, 397
characterization **5:** 332, 334, 335, 337, 338, 351, 360, 363, 366, 374, 379, 392; **18:** 74, 75; **38:** 264, 273, 313, 319
class distinctions, conflict, and relations **5:** 338, 343, 346, 347, 366, 390, 395, 400, 402; **22:** 93; **28:** 69

comic and farcical elements **5:** 336, 338, 346, 350, 360, 369, 373; **18:** 74, 75, 84; **59:** 105
The Comical Gallant (John Dennis adaptation) **18:** 5, 7, 8, 9, 10
deception, disguise, and duplicity **5:** 332, 334, 336, 354, 355, 379; **22:** 93; **47:** 308, 314, 321, 325, 344
desire **38:** 286, 297, 300
Elizabethan society **47:** 331
Elizabeth's influence **5:** 333, 334, 335, 336, 339, 346, 355, 366, 402; **18:** 5, 86; **38:** 278; **47:** 344
Evans, Sir Hugh **47:** 354
Falstaff
  characterization in 1 and 2 Henry IV, compared with **5:** 333, 335, 336, 337, 339, 346, 347, 348, 350, 373, 400, **18:** 5, 7, 75, 86; **22:** 93
  diminishing powers **5:** 337, 339, 343, 347, 350, 351, 392; **28:** 373; **47:** 363
  as Herne the Hunter **38:** 256, 286; **47:** 358
  incapability of love **5:** 335, 336, 339, 346, 348; **22:** 93
  as Jack-a-Lent **47:** 363
  personification of comic principle or Vice figure **5:** 332, 338, 369, 400; **38:** 273
  recognition and repentance of follies **5:** 338, 341, 343, 348, 369, 374, 376, 397
  as scapegoat **47:** 358, 363, 375
  sensuality **5:** 339, 343, 353, 369, 392
  shrewdness **5:** 332, 336, 346, 355
  threat to community **5:** 343, 369, 379, 392, 395, 400; **38:** 297
  as unifying force **47:** 358
  vanity **5:** 332, 339
  victimization **5:** 336, 338, 341, 347, 348, 353, 355, 360, 369, 373, 374, 376, 392, 397, 400; **59:** 144
  as villain **47:** 358
  as a woman **47:** 325
folk rituals, elements and influence of **5:** 353, 369, 376, 392, 397, 400; **38:** 256, 300
Ford, Francis **5:** 332, 334, 343, 355, 363, 374, 379, 390; **38:** 273; **47:** 321
Ford, Mistress Alice **47:** 321
genre, issues of **59:** 111
insults **47:** 331
Italian comedy, influence of **59:** 105
jealousy **5:** 334, 339, 343, 353, 355, 363; **22:** 93; **38:** 273, 307
Jonsonian humors comedy, influence of **38:** 319; **59:** 105
knighthood **5:** 338, 343, 390, 397, 402; **47:** 354
language and imagery **5:** 335, 337, 343, 347, 351, 363, 374, 379; **19:** 101; **22:** 93, 378; **28:** 9, 69; **38:** 313, 319; **59:** 89
male discontent **5:** 392, 402
marriage **5:** 343, 369, 376, 390, 392, 400; **22:** 93; **38:** 297; **51:** 44; **59:** 95
mediation **5:** 343, 392
morality **5:** 335, 339, 347, 349, 353, 397; **59:** 132
Neoclassical rules **5:** 332, 334
Page, Anne **47:** 321
Page, Mistress Margaret **47:** 321
pastoral elements **59:** 132
play and theatricality **47:** 325
play-within-the-play, convention of **5:** 354, 355, 369, 402
realism **38:** 313
reconciliation **5:** 343, 369, 374, 397, 402
revenge **5:** 349, 350, 392; **38:** 264, 307
as satire or parody **5:** 338, 350, 360, 385; **38:** 278, 319; **47:** 354, 363
schemes and intrigues **5:** 334, 336, 339, 341, 343, 349, 355, 379
setting **47:** 375 **59:** 89, 139
sexual politics **19:** 101; **38:** 307; **59:** 95
social milieu **18:** 75, 84; **38:** 297, 300; **59:** 132, 139, 144
sources **5:** 332, 350, 360, 366, 385; **32:** 31; **59:** 123
stage history **18:** 66, 67, 68, 70, 71; **59:** 123
staging issues **18:** 74, 75, 84, 86, 90, 95
structure **5:** 332, 333, 334, 335, 343, 349, 355, 369, 374; **18:** 86; **22:** 378; **59:** 89, 111
unnatural ordering **22:** 378
wit **5:** 335, 336, 337, 339, 343, 351
women, role of **5:** 335, 341, 343, 349, 369, 379, 390, 392, 402; **19:** 101; **38:** 307

***A Midsummer Night's Dream* (Volumes 3, 12, 29, 45, 58)**

adaptations **12:** 144, 146, 147, 153, 280, 282
ambiguity **3:** 401, 459, 486; **45:** 169
appearance, perception, and illusion **3:** 368, 411, 425, 427, 434, 447, 459, 466, 474, 477, 486, 497, 516; **19:** 21; **22:** 39; **28:** 15; **29:** 175,190; **45:** 136
Athens and the forest, contrast between **3:** 381, 427, 459, 466, 497, 502; **29:** 175
autobiographical elements **3:** 365, 371, 379, 381, 389, 391, 396, 402, 432
Bottom
  awakening speech (Act IV, scene i) **3:** 406, 412, 450, 457, 486, 516; **16:** 34; **58:** 181
  his dream **60:** 142
  folly of **46:** 1, 14, 29, 60
  imagination **3:** 376, 393, 406, 432, 486; **29:** 175, 190; **45:** 147
  self-possession **3:** 365, 376, 395, 402, 406, 480; **45:** 158
  Titania, relationship with **3:** 377, 406, 441, 445, 450, 457, 491, 497; **16:** 34; **19:** 21; **22:** 93; **29:** 216; **45:** 160; **58:** 203, 215
  transformation **3:** 365, 377, 432; **13:** 27; **22:** 93; **29:** 216; **45:** 147, 160
brutal elements **3:** 445, 491, 497, 511; **12:** 259, 262, 298; **16:** 34; **19:** 21; **29:** 183, 225, 263, 269; **45:** 169
capriciousness of the young lovers **3:** 372, 395, 402, 411, 423, 437, 441, 450, 497, 498; **29:** 175, 269; **45:** 107
ceremonies, rites, and rituals, importance of **58:** 189
the changeling **58:** 162, 167
chastity **45:** 143
class distinctions, conflict, and relations **22:** 23; **25:** 36; **45:** 160; **50:** 74, 86
colonialism **53:** 32
as dream-play **3:** 365, 370, 372, 377, 389, 391; **29:** 190; **45:** 117; **58:** 181
dreams **45:** 96, 107, 117
duration of time **3:** 362, 370, 380, 386, 494; **45:** 175
Elizabethan culture, relation to **50:** 86; **58:** 220
erotic elements **3:** 445, 491, 497, 511; **12:** 259, 262, 298; **16:** 34; **19:** 21; **29:** 183, 225, 269; **58:** 194
fairies **3:** 361, 362, 372, 377, 395, 400, 423, 450, 459, 486; **12:** 287, 291, 294, 295; **19:** 21; **29:** 183, 190; **45:** 147
farcical elements **58:** 169
feminist interpretation **48:** 23
gender **53:** 1; **58:** 215
Helena **29:** 269; **58:** 194
Helena and Hermia, relationship between **60:** 142
Hermia **29:** 225, 269; **45:** 117; **58:** 194
Hippolytus, myth of **29:** 216; **45:** 84
homosexuality **60:** 142
identity **29:** 269; **58:** 215
imagination and art **3:** 365, 371, 381, 402, 412, 417, 421, 423, 441, 459, 468, 506, 516, 520; **22:** 39
language and imagery **3:** 397, 401, 410, 412, 415, 432, 453, 459, 468, 494; **22:** 23, 39, 93, 378; **28:** 9; **29:** 263; **45:** 96, 126, 136, 143, 147, 169, 175; **48:** 23, 32; **58:** 181, 186, 194
the lovers **58:** 151, 169
male domination **3:** 483, 520; **13:** 19; **25:** 36; **29:** 216, 225, 243, 256, 269; **42:** 46; **45:** 84; **58:** 203, 220; **60:** 142
marriage **3:** 402, 423, 450, 483, 520; **29:** 243, 256; **45:** 136, 143; **48:** 32; **51:** 1, 30, 44; **58:** 175
metadramatic elements **3:** 427, 468, 477, 516, 520; **29:** 190, 225, 243; **50:** 86
Metamorphoses (Golding translation of Ovid) **16:** 25
mimetic desire **60:** 172, 245
Minotaur, myth of **3:** 497, 498; **29:** 216
music and dance **3:** 397, 400, 418, 513; **12:** 287, 289; **25:** 36
mythic or mythological elements **58:** 194 **60:** 172, 245, 259
Oberon **58:** 151, 162, 167, 203; **60:** 142
  as controlling force **3:** 434, 459, 477, 502; **29:** 175
Ovid, influence of **3:** 362, 427, 497, 498; **22:** 23; **29:** 175, 190, 216; **60:** 172
parent-child relations **13:** 19; **29:** 216, 225, 243
passionate or romantic love **3:** 372, 389, 395, 396, 402, 408, 411, 423, 441, 450, 480, 497, 498, 511; **29:** 175, 225, 263, 269; **45:** 126, 136; **51:** 44; **58:** 175
patriarchy **60:** 259
Pauline doctrine **3:** 457, 486, 506
Platonic elements **3:** 368, 437, 450, 497; **45:** 126
politics **29:** 243
power **42:** 46; **45:** 84; **58:** 151
psychoanalytic interpretations **3:** 440, 483; **28:** 15; **29:** 225; **44:** 1; **45:** 107, 117; **58:** 167
Puck **45:** 96, 158
Pyramus and Thisbe interlude **3:** 364, 368, 379, 381, 389, 391, 396, 408, 411, 412, 417, 425, 427, 433, 441, 447, 457, 468, 474, 511; **12:** 254; **13:** 27; **16:** 25; **22:** 23; **29:** 263; **45:** 107, 175; **50:** 74
race **53:** 1, 32
reason versus imagination **3:** 381, 389, 423, 441, 466, 506; **22:** 23; **29:** 190; **45:** 96
reconciliation **3:** 412, 418, 437, 459, 468, 491, 497, 502, 513; **13:** 27; **29:** 190
reversal **29:** 225; **60:** 245
Romeo and Juliet, compared with **3:** 396, 480
rustic characters **3:** 376, 397, 432; **12:** 291, 293; **45:** 147, 160

sexuality **22:** 23, 93; **29:** 225, 243, 256, 269; **42:** 46; **45:** 107 **53:** 32; **58:** 203, 215, 220
sources **29:** 216; **60:** 259
staging issues **3:** 364, 365, 371, 372, 377; **12:** 151, 152, 154, 158, 159, 280, 284, 291, 295; **16:** 34; **19:** 21; **29:** 183, 256; **48:** 23
structure **3:** 364, 368, 381, 402, 406, 427, 450, 513; **13:** 19; **22:** 378; **29:** 175; **45:** 126, 175; **58:** 186, 189
textual issues **16:** 34; **29:** 216; **58:** 151
Theseus **51:** 1
characterization **3:** 363; **58:** 151, 220
Hippolyta, relationship with **3:** 381, 412, 421, 423, 450, 468, 520; **29:** 175, 216, 243, 256; **45:** 84
as ideal **3:** 379, 391
"lovers, lunatics, and poets" speech (Act V, scene i) **3:** 365, 371, 379, 381, 391, 402, 411, 412, 421, 423, 441, 498, 506; **29:** 175
as representative of institutional life **3:** 381, 403
Titania **29:** 243; **58:** 151, 162, , 167, 203
tragic elements **3:** 393, 400, 401, 410, 445, 474, 480, 491, 498, 511; **29:** 175; **45:** 169; **58:** 175, 186
as a transgressive play **60:** 142
unity **3:** 364, 368, 381, 402, 406, 427, 450, 513; **13:** 19; **22:** 378; **29:** 175, 263
unnatural ordering **22:** 378

***Much Ado about Nothing* (Volumes 8, 18, 31, 55)**

appearance versus reality **8:** 17, 18, 48, 63, 69, 73, 75, 79, 88, 95, 115; **31:** 198, 209; **55:** 259, 268
battle of the sexes **8:** 14, 16, 19, 48, 91, 95, 111, 121, 125; **31:** 231, 245 **55:** 199
Beatrice and Benedick
Beatrice's femininity **8:** 14, 16, 17, 24, 29, 38, 41, 91; **31:** 222, 245; **55:** 221
Beatrice's request to "kill Claudio" (Act IV, scene i) **8:** 14, 17, 33, 41, 55, 63, 75, 79, 91, 108, 115; **18:** 119, 120, 136, 161, 245, 257; **55:** 268
Benedick's challenge of Claudio (Act V, scene i) **8:** 48, 63, 79, 91; **31:** 231
Claudio and Hero, compared with **8:** 19, 28, 29, 75, 82, 115; **31:** 171, 216; **55:** 189
marriage and the opposite sex, attitudes toward **8:** 9, 13, 14, 16, 19, 29, 36, 48, 63, 77, 91, 95, 115, 121; **16:** 45; **31:** 216
mutual attraction **8:** 13, 14, 19, 24, 29, 33, 41, 75
nobility **8:** 13, 19, 24, 29, 36, 39, 41, 47, 82, 91, 108
popularity **8:** 13, 38, 41, 53, 79
transformed by love **8:** 19, 29, 36, 48, 75, 91, 95, 115; **31:** 209, 216; **55:** 236
unconventionality **8:** 48, 91, 95, 108, 115, 121; **55:** 221, 249, 268
vulgarity **8:** 11, 12, 33, 38, 41, 47
wit and charm **8:** 9, 12, 13, 14, 19, 24, 27, 28, 29, 33, 36, 38, 41, 47, 55, 69, 95, 108, 115; **31:** 241; **55:** 199
Borachio and Conrade **8:** 24, 69, 82, 88, 111, 115
Christian elements **8:** 17, 19, 29, 55, 95, 104, 111, 115; **31:** 209 **55:** 228
church scene (Act IV, scene i) **8:** 13, 14, 16, 19, 33, 44, 47, 48, 58, 63, 69, 75, 79, 82, 91, 95, 100, 104, 111, 115; **18:** 120, 130, 138, 145, 146, 148, 192; **31:** 191, 198, 245; **55:** 236
Claudio
boorish behavior **8:** 9, 24, 33, 36, 39, 44, 48, 63, 79, 82, 95, 100, 111, 115; **31:** 209
credulity **8:** 9, 17, 19, 24, 29, 36, 41, 47, 58, 63, 75, 77, 82, 95, 100, 104, 111, 115, 121; **31:** 241; **47:** 25
mercenary traits **8:** 24, 44, 58, 82, 91, 95
noble qualities **8:** 17, 19, 29, 41, 44, 58, 75; **55:** 232
reconciliation with Hero **8:** 33, 36, 39, 44, 47, 82, 95, 100, 111, 115, 121; **55:** 236
repentance **8:** 33, 63, 82, 95, 100, 111, 115, 121; **31:** 245
sexual insecurities **8:** 75, 100, 111, 115, 121
courtship and marriage **8:** 29, 44, 48, 95, 115, 121, 125; **31:** 191, 231; **51:** 33, 44; **55:** 209
deception, disguise, and duplicity **8:** 29, 55, 63, 69, 79, 82, 88, 108, 115; **31:** 191, 198; **55:** 236
Dogberry and the Watch **8:** 9, 12, 13, 17, 24, 28, 29, 33, 39, 48, 55, 69, 79, 82, 88, 95, 104, 108, 115; **18:** 138, 152, 205, 208, 210, 213, 231; **22:** 85; **31:** 171, 229; **46:** 60; **55:** 189, 249
Don John **8:** 9, 12, 16, 17, 19, 28, 29, 36, 39, 41, 47, 48, 55, 58, 63, 82, 104, 108, 111, 121
Don Pedro **8:** 17, 19, 48, 58, 63, 82, 111, 121
eavesdropping scenes (Act II, scene iii and Act III, scene i) **8:** 12, 13, 17, 19, 28, 29, 33, 36, 48, 55, 63, 73, 75, 82, 121; **18:** 120, 138, 208, 215, 245, 264; **31:** 171, 184; **55:** 259
egotism or narcissism **8:** 19, 24, 28, 29, 55, 69, 95, 115; **55:** 209
Elizabethan culture, relation to **8:** 23, 33, 44, 55, 58, 79, 88, 104, 111, 115; **51:** 15; **55:** 209, 241, 259
Friar **8:** 24, 29, 41, 55, 63, 79, 111; **55:** 249
genre **8:** 9, 18, 19, 28, 29, 39, 41, 44, 53, 63, 69, 73, 79, 82, 95, 100, 104; **48:** 14; **55:** 232, 268
Hero **8:** 13, 14, 16, 19, 28, 29, 44, 48, 53, 55, 82, 95, 104, 111, 115, 121; **31:** 231, 245; **47:** 25; **55:** 209
implausibility of plot, characters, or events **8:** 9, 12, 16, 19, 33, 36, 39, 44, 53, 100, 104
irony **8:** 14, 63, 79, 82; **28:** 63
justice and mercy **22:** 85
language and imagery **8:** 9, 38, 43, 46, 55, 69, 73, 88, 95, 100, 115, 125; **19:** 68; **25:** 77; **28:** 63; **31:** 178, 184, 222, 241, 245; **48:** 14; **55:** 199, 259
law versus passion for freedom **22:** 85
love **8:** 24, 55, 75, 95, 111, 115; **28:** 56; **51:** 30
Messina **8:** 19, 29, 48, 69, 82, 91, 95, 108, 111, 121, 125; **31:** 191, 209, 229, 241, 245
misgovernment **22:** 85; **55:** 241
music and dance **19:** 68; **31:** 222
"nothing," significance of **8:** 17, 18, 23, 55, 73, 95; **19:** 68; **55:** 259
performance issues **18:** 173, 174, 183, 184, 185, 186, 187, 188, 189, 190, 191, 192, 193, 195, 197, 199, 201, 204, 206, 207, 208, 209, 210, 254; **55:** 221
power **22:** 85; **25:** 77; **31:** 231, 245
repentance or forgiveness **8:** 24, 29, 111; **55:** 228
resurrection, metamorphosis, or transformation **8:** 88, 104, 111, 115; **55:** 209
romance or chivalric tradition, influence of **8:** 53, 125; **51:** 15
self-knowledge **8:** 69, 95, 100
setting **18:** 173, 174, 183, 184, 185, 186, 187, 188, 189, 190, 191, 192, 193, 195, 197, 199, 201, 204, 206, 207, 208, 209, 210, 254
slander or hearsay, importance of **8:** 58, 69, 82, 95, 104; **55:** 249
sources **8:** 9, 19, 53, 58, 104
staging issues **8:** 18, 33, 41, 75, 79, 82, 108; **16:** 45; **18:** 245, 247, 249, 252, 254, 257, 261, 264; **28:** 63; **55:** 221
structure **8:** 9, 16, 17, 19, 28, 29, 33, 39, 48, 63, 69, 73, 75, 79, 82, 115; **31:** 178, 184, 198, 231; **55:** 189
virginity or chastity, importance of **8:** 44, 75, 95, 111, 121, 125; **31:** 222; **55:** 268
wit **8:** 27, 29, 38, 69, 79, 91, 95; **31:** 178, 191; **55:** 228
works by Shakespeare or other authors, compared with **8:** 16, 19, 27, 28, 33, 38, 39, 41, 53, 69, 79, 91, 104, 108; **31:** 231; **55:** 189, 209, 232, 241, 249

***Othello* (Volumes 4, 11, 35, 53)**

autobiographical elements **4:** 440, 444; **53:** 324
Brabantio **25:** 189
Cassio **25:** 189
Clarissa (Samuel Richardson), compared with **48:** 277
consummation of marriage **22:** 207; **53:** 246, 333
contrasts and oppositions **4:** 421, 455, 457, 462, 508; **25:** 189; **53:** 268
Desdemona
as Christ figure **4:** 506, 525, 573; **35:** 360
culpability **4:** 408, 415, 422, 427; **13:** 313; **19:** 253, 276; **35:** 265, 352, 380
innocence **35:** 360; **47:** 25; **53:** 310, 333
as mother figure **22:** 339; **35:** 282; **53:** 324
passivity **4:** 402, 406, 421, 440, 457, 470, 582, 587; **25:** 189; **35:** 380
spiritual nature of her love **4:** 462, 530, 559
staging issues **11:** 350, 354, 359; **13:** 327; **32:** 201
dramatic structure **4:** 370, 390, 399, 427, 488, 506, 517, 569; **22:** 207; **28:** 243; **53:** 261
Duke **25:** 189
Emilia **4:** 386, 391, 392, 415, 587; **35:** 352, 380
ending **54:** 119; **60:** 2
evil **52:** 78; **60:** 91
gender issues **32:** 294; **35:** 327; **53:** 255, 268, 310, 315, 324

handkerchief, significance of **4:** 370, 384, 385, 396, 503, 530, 562; **35:** 265, 282, 380; **53:** 333
Hercules Furens (Seneca) as source **16:** 283
Iago
affinity with Othello **4:** 400, 427, 468, 470, 477, 500, 506; **25:** 189; **44:** 57
as conventional dramatic villain **4:** 440, 527, 545, 582; **53:** 288
as homosexual **4:** 503; **53:** 275
Machiavellian elements **4:** 440, 455, 457, 517, 545; **35:** 336, 347
motives **4:** 389, 390, 397, 399, 402, 409, 423, 424, 427, 434, 451, 462, 545, 564; **13:** 304; **25:** 189; **28:** 344; **32:** 201; **35:** 265, 276, 310, 336, 347; **42:** 278; **53:** 246, 275, 324
revenge scheme **4:** 392, 409, 424, 451
as scapegoat **4:** 506
as victim **4:** 402, 409, 434, 451, 457, 470
idealism versus realism **4:** 457, 508, 517; **13:** 313; **25:** 189; **53:** 350
implausibility of plot, characters, or events **4:** 370, 380, 391, 442, 444; **47:** 51
jealousy **4:** 384, 488, 527; **35:** 253, 265, 282, 301, 310; **44:** 57, 66; **51:** 30
justice **35:** 247; **53:** 288, 350
language and imagery **4:** 433, 442, 445, 462, 493, 508, 517, 552, 587, 596; **13:** 304; **16:** 272; **22:** 378; **25:** 189, 257; **28:** 243, 344; **42:** 278; **47:** 51; **53:** 261
love **4:** 412, 493, 506, 512, 530, 545, 552, 569, 570, 575, 580, 591; **19:** 253; **22:** 207; **25:** 257; **28:** 243, 344; **32:** 201; **35:** 261, 317; **51:** 25, 30; **53:** 315; **54:** 119
love and reason **4:** 512, 530, 580; **19:** 253
madness **35:** 265, 276, 282
marriage **35:** 369; **51:** 44; **53:** 315
Marxist criticism **42:** 234
Measure for Measure, compared with **25:** 189
medieval dramatic conventions, influence of **4:** 440, 527, 545, 559, 582
Merchant of Venice, compared with **53:** 288, 255, 268, 298
military and sexual hierarchies **16:** 272; **53:** 324
moral corruption **52:** 78
opening scene **54:** 2, 6
Othello
affinity with Iago **4:** 400, 427, 468, 470, 477, 500, 506; **25:** 189; **35:** 276, 320, 327
as conventional "blameless hero" **4:** 445, 486, 500; **53:** 233, 288, 298, 304
credulity **4:** 384, 385, 388, 390, 396, 402, 434, 440, 455; **13:** 327; **32:** 302; **47:** 25, 51
Desdemona, relationship with **22:** 339; **35:** 301, 317; **37:** 269; **53:** 315
divided nature **4:** 400, 412, 462, 470, 477, 493, 500, 582, 592; **16:** 293; **19:** 276; **25:** 189; **35:** 320; **53:** 268, 289, 343
egotism **4:** 427, 470, 477, 493, 522, 536, 541, 573, 597; **13:** 304; **35:** 247, 253
self-destructive anger **16:** 283; **53:** 324
self-dramatizing or self-deluding **4:** 454, 457, 477, 592; **13:** 313; **16:** 293; **35:** 317; **60:** 46
self-knowledge **4:** 462, 470, 477, 483, 508, 522, 530, 564, 580, 591, 596; **13:** 304, 313; **16:** 283; **28:** 243; **35:** 253, 317; **53:** 233, 343
spiritual state **4:** 483, 488, 517, 525, 527, 544, 559, 564, 573; **28:** 243; **35:** 253; **53:** 298; **60:** 46
perception **19:** 276; **25:** 189, 257; **53:** 246, 289
poetic justice, question of **4:** 370, 412, 415, 427
pride and rightful self-esteem **4:** 522, 536, 541; **35:** 352
psychoanalytic interpretations **4:** 468, 503; **35:** 265, 276, 282, 301, 317, 320, 347; **42:** 203; **44:** 57; **53:** 275, 343
racial issues **4:** 370, 380, 384, 385, 392, 399, 401, 402, 408, 427, 564; **13:** 327; **16:** 293; **25:** 189, 257; **28:** 249, 330; **35:** 369; **42:** 203 **37:** 336; **53:** 1, 233, 238, 246, 255, 261, 268, 275, 289, 298, 304; **55:** 27
religious, mythic, or spiritual content **4:** 483, 517, 522, 525, 559, 573; **22:** 207; **28:** 330; **53:** 289
revenge **35:** 261
Romeo and Juliet, compared with **32:** 302
sexuality **22:** 339; **28:** 330, 344; **35:** 352, 360; **37:** 269; **44:** 57, 66; **51:** 44; **53:** 275, 310, 315
sources **28:** 330
staging issues **11:** 273, 334, 335, 339, 342, 350,354, 359, 362; **53:** 233, 304
structure **22:** 378; **28:** 325
time scheme **4:** 370, 384, 390, 488; **22:** 207; **35:** 310; **47:** 51; **53:** 333
tragic elements **55:** 78
unnatural ordering **22:** 378
Venetian politics **32:** 294; **53:** 350
violence **22:** 12; **43:** 32
The Winter's Tale, compared with **35:** 310
women, role of **19:** 253; **28:** 344; **53:** 310

Pericles (Volumes 2, 15, 36, 51)

archetypal structure **2:** 570, 580, 582, 584, 588; **25:** 365; **51:** 71, 79
art and nature **22:** 315; **36:** 233
audience perception **42:** 359; **48:** 364
authorship controversy **2:** 538, 540, 543, 544, 545, 546, 548, 550, 551, 553, 556, 558, 564, 565, 568, 576, 586; **15:** 132, 141, 148, 152; **16:** 391, 399; **25:** 365; **36:** 198, 244
autobiographical elements **2:** 551, 554, 555, 563, 581
brothel scenes (Act IV, scenes ii and vi) **2:** 548, 550, 551, 553, 554, 586, 590; **15:** 134, 145, 154, 166, 172, 177; **36:** 274; **51:** 118
composition date **2:** 537, 544
Deconstructionist interpretation of **48:** 364
Diana, as symbol of nature **22:** 315; **36:** 233; **51:** 71
doubling of roles **15:** 150, 152, 167, 173, 180
Gower chorus **2:** 548, 575; **15:** 134, 141, 143, 145, 149, 152, 177; **36:** 279; **42:** 359
incest, motif of **2:** 582, 588; **22:** 315; **36:** 257, 264; **51:** 110, 97
as inferior or flawed plays **2:** 537, 546, 553, 563, 564; **15:** 139, 143, 156, 167, 176; **36:** 198; **51:** 79
innocence **36:** 226, 274
Jacobean culture, relation to **37:** 361; **51:** 110, 86
language and imagery **2:** 559, 560, 565, 583; **16:** 391; **19:** 387; **22:** 315; **36:** 198, 214, 233, 244, 251, 264; **51:** 86, 99
Marina **37:** 361; **51:** 118
as miracle play **2:** 569, 581; **36:** 205; **51:** 97
nature as book **22:** 315; **36:** 233
oaths, importance of **19:** 387
patience **2:** 572, 573, 578, 579; **36:** 251
Pericles
characterization **36:** 251; **37:** 361
patience **2:** 572, 573, 578, 579
suit of Antiochus's daughter **2:** 547, 565, 578, 579; **51:** 126
Ulysses, compared with **2:** 551
politics **37:** 361
popularity **2:** 536, 538, 546; **37:** 361
Prologue **54:** 35
recognition scene (Act V, scene i) **15:** 138, 139, 141, 145, 161, 162, 167, 172, 175
reconciliation **2:** 555, 564, 584, 586, 588; **36:** 205
religious, mythic, or spiritual content **2:** 559, 561, 565, 570, 580, 584, 588; **22; 315; 25:** 365; **51:** 97
riddle motif **22:** 315; **36:** 205, 214
Shakespeare's other romances, relation to **2:** 547, 549, 551, 559, 564, 570, 571, 584, 585; **15:** 139; **16:** 391, 399; **36:** 226, 257; **51:** 71, 79 **54:** 35
spectacle **42:** 359
sources **2:** 538, 568, 572, 575; **25:** 365; **36:** 198, 205; **51:** 118, 126
staging issues **16:** 399; **48:** 364; **51:** 99
suffering **2:** 546, 573, 578, 579; **25:** 365; **36:** 279
textual revisions **15:** 129, 130, 132, 134, 135, 136, 138, 152, 155, 167, 181; **16:** 399; **25:** 365; **51:** 99

The Phoenix and Turtle (Volumes 10, 38, 51)

allegorical elements **10:** 7, 8, 9, 16, 17, 48; **38:** 334, 378; **51:** 138, 188
art and nature **10:** 7, 42
authenticity **10:** 7, 8, 16
autobiographical elements **10:** 14, 18, 42, 48; **51:** 155
bird imagery **10:** 21, 27; **38:** 329, 350, 367; **51:** 145, 181, 184
Christian elements **10:** 21, 24, 31; **38:** 326; **51:** 162, 171, 181
complex or enigmatic nature **10:** 7, 14, 35, 42; **38:** 326, 357; **51:** 145, 162
consciously philosophical **10:** 7, 21, 24, 31, 48; **38:** 342, 378
constancy and faithfulness **10:** 18, 20, 21, 48; **38:** 329
Court of Love **10:** 9, 24, 50
Donne, John, compared with **10:** 20, 31, 35, 37, 40; **51:** 143
satiric elements **10:** 8, 16, 17, 27, 35, 40, 45, 48
love **10:** 31, 37, 40, 50; **38:** 342, 345, 367; **51:** 145, 151, 155
as metaphysical poem **10:** 7, 8, 9, 20, 31, 35, 37, 40, 45, 50; **51:** 143, 171, 184
Neoplatonism **10:** 7, 9, 21, 24, 40, 45, 50; **38:** 345, 350, 367, 184
as "pure" poetry **10:** 14, 31, 35; **38:** 329
Scholasticism **10:** 21, 24, 31; **51:** 188

Topic Index, by Play

Shakespeare's dramas, compared with **10:** 9, 14, 17, 18, 20, 27, 37, 40, 42, 48; **38:** 342; **51:** 151, 155
sources **10:** 7, 9, 18, 24, 45; **38:** 326, 334, 350, 367; **51:** 138
structure **10:** 27, 31, 37, 45, 50; **38:** 342, 345, 357; **51:** 138, 143
style **10:** 8, 20, 24, 27, 31, 35, 45, 50; **38:** 334, 345, 357, 171; **51:** 188

***The Rape of Lucrece* (Volumes 10, 33, 43, 59)**

allegorical elements **10:** 89, 93
Brutus **10:** 96, 106, 109, 116, 121, 125, 128, 135
Christian elements **10:** 77, 80, 89, 96, 98, 109; **59:** 165,
Collatine **10:** 98, 131; **43:** 102; **59:** 180
Elizabethan culture, relation to **33:** 195; **43:** 77
feminist criticism **59:** 165, 189, 193
gender **53:** 1; **59:** 189, 193, 206
irony or paradox **10:** 93, 98, 128
language and imagery **10:** 64, 65, 66, 71, 78, 80, 89, 93, 116, 109, 125, 131; **22:** 289, 294; **25:** 305; **32:** 321; **33:** 144, 155, 179, 200; **43:** 102, 113, 141; **59:** 159,175,212
Lucrece
  chastity **33:** 131, 138; **43:** 92
  as example of Renaissance virtù **22:** 289; **43:** 148
  heroic **10:** 84, 93, 109, 121, 128; **59:** 175, 193
  patriarchal woman, model of **10:** 109, 131; **33:** 169, 200
  Philomela, compared with **59:** 193
  self-responsibility **10:** 89, 96, 98, 106, 125; **33:** 195; **43:** 85, 92, 158; **59:** 206
  unrealistic **10:** 64, 65, 66, 121
  verbose **10:** 64, 81, 116; **25:** 305; **33:** 169
  as victim **22:** 294; **25:** 305; **32:** 321; **33:** 131, 195; **43:** 102, 158; **59:** 175, 180, 189, 193, 206
male/female relationships **10:** 109, 121, 131; **22:** 289; **25:** 305; **43:** 113, 141; **59:** 180,193
narrative strategies **22:** 294
patriarchy **59:** 189, 206
Petrarchan lovers, parody of **59:** 180
race **53:** 1
rape **59:** 189, 193, 206, 212
Roman history, relation to **10:** 84, 89, 93, 96, 98, 109, 116, 125, 135; **22:** 289; **25:** 305; **33:** 155, 190; **59:** 175
Shakespeare's dramas, compared with **10:** 63, 64, 65, 66, 68, 71, 73, 74, 78, 80, 81, 84, 98, 116, 121, 125; **43:** 92; **59:** 159
sources **10:** 63, 64, 65, 66, 68, 74, 77, 78, 89, 98, 109, 121, 125; **25:** 305; **33:** 155, 190; **43:** 77, 92, 148; **59:** 165
Southampton, Earl of **59:** 165
structure **10:** 84, 89, 93, 98, 135; **22:** 294; **25:** 305 **43:** 102, 141; **59:** 159
style **10:** 64, 65, 66, 68, 69, 70, 71, 73, 74, 77, 78, 81, 84, 98, 116, 131, 135; **43:** 113, 158
Tarquin **10:** 80, 93, 98, 116, 125; **22:** 294; **25:** 305; **32:** 321; **33:** 190; **43:** 102
tragic elements **10:** 78, 80, 81, 84, 98, 109; **43:** 85, 148
the Troy passage **10:** 74, 89, 98, 116, 121, 128; **22:** 289; **32:** 321; **33:** 144, 179; **43:** 77, 85; **59:** 206
Venus and Adonis, compared with **10:** 63, 66, 68, 69, 70, 73, 81; **22:** 294; **43:** 148
violence **43:** 148, 158; **59:** 189, 193, 212

***Richard II* (Volumes 6, 24, 39, 52, 58)**

abdication scene (Act IV, scene i) **6:** 270, 307, 317, 327, 354, 359, 381, 393, 409; **13:** 172; **19:** 151; **24:** 274, 414; **52:** 141, 144
acting and dissimulation **6:** 264, 267, 307, 310, 315, 368, 393, 409; **24:** 339, 345, 346, 349, 352, 356
allegorical elements **6:** 264, 283, 323, 385
audience perception **24:** 414, 423; **39:** 295; **58:** 293
Bolingbroke
  comic elements **28:** 134
  guilt **24:** 423; **39:** 279
  language and imagery **6:** 310, 315, 331, 347, 374, 381, 397; **32:** 189; **58:** 301
  as Machiavellian figure **6:** 305, 307, 315, 331, 347, 388, 393, 397; **24:** 428
  as politician **6:** 255, 263, 264, 272, 277, 294, 364, 368, 391; **24:** 330, 333, 405, 414, 423, 428; **39:** 256; **52:** 124
  Richard, compared with **6:** 307, 315, 347, 374, 391, 393, 409; **24:** 346, 349, 351, 352, 356, 395, 419, 423, 428; **52:** 108, 124; **58:** 241
  his silence **24:** 423
  structure, compared with **39:** 235
  usurpation of crown, nature of **6:** 255, 272, 289, 307, 310, 347, 354, 359, 381, 385, 393; **13:** 172; **24:** 322, 356, 383, 419; **28:** 178; **52:** 108, 124
Bolingbroke and Richard as opposites **24:** 423
Bolingbroke-Mowbray dispute **22:** 137
Bushy, Bagot, and Greene **58:** 259
carnival elements **19:** 151; **39:** 273
censorship **24:** 260, 261, 262, 263, 386; **42:** 120; **52:** 141, 144
ceremonies, rites, and rituals, importance of **6:** 270, 294, 315, 368, 381, 397, 409, 414; **24:** 274, 356, 411, 414, 419
comic elements **24:** 262, 263, 395; **39:** 243
contractual and economic relations **13:** 213; **49:** 60
costumes **24:** 274, 278, 291, 304, 325, 356, 364, 423
deposition scene (Act III, scene iii) **24:** 298, 395, 423; **42:** 120
Elizabethan attitudes, influence of **6:** 287, 292, 294, 305, 321, 327, 364, 402, 414; **13:** 494; **24:** 325; **28:** 188; **39:** 273; **42:** 120; **52:** 141, 144; **58:** 283, 293
Elizabethan culture, relation to **58:** 267, 275
Essex Rebellion, relation to **6:** 249, 250; **24:** 356; **58:** 293
family honor, structure, and inheritance **6:** 338, 368, 388, 397, 414; **39:** 263, 279
fate **6:** 289, 294, 304, 352, 354, 385
garden scene (Act III, scene iv) **6:** 264, 283, 323, 385; **24:** 307, 356, 414
Gaunt **6:** 255, 287, 374, 388, 402, 414; **24:** 274, 322, 325, 414, 423; **39:** 263, 279
gender issues **25:** 89; **39:** 295
historical sources, compared with **6:** 252, 279, 343; **28:** 134; **39:** 235; **49:** 60; **58:** 259, 275, 283
historiography **56:** 2, 15
irony **6:** 270, 307, 364, 368, 391; **24:** 383; **28:** 188
King of Misrule **19:** 151; **39:** 273
kingship **6:** 263, 264, 272, 277, 289, 294, 327, 354, 364, 381, 388, 391, 402, 409, 414; **19:** 151, 209; **24:** 260, 289, 291, 322, 325, 333, 339, 345, 346, 349, 351, 352, 356, 395, 408, 419, 428; **28:** 134; **39:** 235, 243, 256, 273, 279, 289; **42:** 175; **58:** 275, 301
language and imagery **6:** 252, 282, 283, 294, 298, 315, 323, 331, 347, 368, 374, 381, 385, 397, 409; **13:** 213, 494; **24:** 269, 270, 298, 301, 304, 315, 325, 329, 333, 339, 356, 364, 395, 405, 408, 411, 414, 419; **28:** 134, 188; **39:** 243, 273, 289, 295; **42:** 175; **52:** 154, 157, 169, 174, 183; **58:** 253, 267, 293, 301, 307; **60:** 21
Marlowe's works, compared with **19:** 233; **24:** 307, 336; **42:** 175
medievalism and chivalry, presentation of **6:** 258, 277, 294, 327, 338, 388, 397, 414; **24:** 274, 278, 279, 280, 283; **39:** 256
mercantilism and feudalism **13:** 213
mirror scene (Act IV, scene i) **6:** 317, 327, 374, 381, 393, 409; **24:** 267, 356, 408, 414, 419, 423; **28:** 134, 178; **39:** 295
mythological elements **52:** 154, 157, 169
negative assessments **6:** 250, 252, 253, 255, 282, 307, 317, 343, 359
Northumberland **24:** 423
providential order **56:** 15
Richard
  artistic temperament **6:** 264, 267, 270, 272, 277, 292, 294, 298, 315, 331, 334, 347, 368, 374, 393, 409; **24:** 298, 301, 304, 315, 322, 390, 405, 408, 411, 414, 419; **39:** 289
  Bolingbroke, compared with **24:** 346, 349, 351, 352, 356, 419; **39:** 256; **52:** 108, 124; **58:** 275
  characterization **6:** 250, 252, 253, 254, 255, 258, 262, 263, 267, 270, 272, 282, 283, 304, 343, 347, 364, 368; **24:** 262, 263, 267, 269, 270, 271, 272, 273, 274, 278, 280, 315, 322, 325, 330, 333, 390, 395, 402,405, 423; **28:** 134; **39:** 279, 289; **52:** 169; **58:** 229, 241, 253, 259, 267, 307
  dangerous aspects **24:** 405; **58:** 253
  death of **60:** 21
  delusion **6:** 267, 298, 334, 368, 409; **24:** 329, 336, 405
  homosexuality **24:** 405
  kingship **6:** 253, 254, 263, 272, 327, 331, 334, 338, 364, 402, 414; **24:** 278, 295, 336, 337, 339, 356, 419; **28:** 134, 178; **39:** 256, 263; **52:** 169; **58:** 241, 275
  language and imagery **58:** 301
  loss of identity **6:** 267, 338, 368, 374, 381, 388, 391, 409; **24:** 298, 414, 428
  as martyr-king **6:** 289, 307, 321; **19:** 209; **24:** 289, 291; **28:** 134
  nobility **6:** 255, 258, 259, 262, 263, 391; **24:** 260, 263, 274, 280, 289, 291, 402, 408, 411
  political acumen **6:** 263, 264, 272, 292, 310, 327, 334, 364, 368, 374, 388, 391, 397, 402, 409; **24:** 405; **39:** 256

private versus public persona **6:** 317, 327, 364, 368, 391, 409; **24:** 428
role-playing **24:** 419, 423; **28:** 178
role in Gloucester's death **52:** 108, 124
seizure of Gaunt's estate **6:** 250, 338, 388; **49:** 60
self-dramatization **6:** 264, 267, 307, 310, 315, 317, 331, 334, 368, 393, 409; **24:** 339; **28:** 178; **60:** 21
self-hatred **13:** 172; **24:** 383; **39:** 289
self-knowledge **6:** 255, 267, 331, 334, 338, 352, 354, 368, 388, 391; **24:** 273, 289, 411, 414; **39:** 263, 289; **60:** 21, 46
spiritual redemption **6:** 255, 267, 331, 334, 338, 352, 354, 368, 388, 391; **24:** 273, 289, 411, 414; **52:** 124; **60:** 21, 46
Shakespeare's other histories, compared with **6:** 255, 264, 272, 294, 304, 310, 317, 343, 354, 359; **24:** 320, 325, 330, 331, 332, 333; **28:** 178
Shakespeare's sympathies, question of **6:** 277, 279, 287, 347, 359, 364, 391, 393, 402
Sicilian Usurper (Nahum Tate adaptation) **24:** 260, 261, 262, 263, 386, 390
sources **56:** 2
staging issues **13:** 494; **24:** 273, 274, 278, 279, 280, 283, 291, 295, 296, 301, 303, 304, 310, 315, 317, 320, 325, 333, 338, 346, 351, 352, 356, 364, 383, 386, 395, 402, 405, 411, 414, 419, 423, 428; **25:** 89; **58:** 241
structure **6:** 282, 304, 317, 343, 352, 359, 364, 39; **24:** 307, 322, 325, 356, 395; **58:** 229, 241
succession **60:** 304
textual arrangement **24:** 260, 261, 262, 263, 271, 273, 291, 296, 356, 390
time **22:** 137
treason and punishment **58:** 307
tragic elements **58:** 229
usurpation **6:** 263, 264, 272, 287, 289, 315, 323, 331, 343, 354, 364, 381, 388, 393, 397; **24:** 383; **52:** 108, 141, 154
York **6:** 287, 364, 368, 388, 402, 414; **24:** 263, 320, 322, 364, 395, 414; **39:** 243, 279; **58:** 241

Richard III **(Volumes 8, 14, 39, 52, 62)**

allegorical elements **52:** 5; **62:** 60
ambivalence and ambiguity **44:** 11; **47:** 15
conscience **8:** 148, 152, 162, 165, 190, 197, 201, 206, 210, 228, 232, 239, 243, 252, 258; **39:** 341; **52:** 5, 196, 205
Elizabethan culture, relation to **62:** 66
Elizabethan politics, relation to **22:** 395; **25:** 141; **37:** 144; **39:** 345, 349; **42:** 132 **52:** 201, 214, 257; **62:** 2
ending **54:** 84
evil **52:** 78
family honor, structure and inheritance **8:** 177, 248, 252, 263, 267; **25:** 141; **39:** 335, 341, 349, 370
flattery **22:** 395
gender issues **25:** 141; **37:** 144; **39:** 345; **52:** 223, 239; **62:** 41
genre **8:** 181, 182, 197, 206, 218, 228, 239, 243, 252, 258; **13:** 142; **39:** 383; **52:** 239; **62:** 2, 41
ghost scene (Act V, scene iii) **8:** 152, 154, 159, 162, 163, 165, 170, 177, 193, 197, 210, 228, 239, 243, 252, 258, 267
Henry VI, relation to **8:** 159, 165, 177, 182, 193, 201, 210, 213, 218, 228, 243, 248, 252, 267; **25:** 164; **39:** 370; **62:** 41
historical accuracy **8:** 144, 145, 153, 159, 163, 165, 168, 213, 223, 228, 232; **39:** 305, 308, 326, 383
historical principles **39:** 308, 326, 387
historiography **56:** 2
language and imagery **8:** 159, 161, 165, 167, 168, 170, 177, 182, 184, 186, 193, 197, 201, 206, 218, 223, 243, 248, 252, 258, 262, 267; **16:** 150; **25:** 141, 245; **39:** 360, 370, 383; **47:** 15; **52:** 285, 290; **62:** 14, 18, 66, 71, 91, 104
Margaret **8:** 153, 154, 159, 162, 163, 170, 193, 201, 206, 210, 218, 223, 228, 243, 248, 262; **39:** 345; **62:** 2, 14, 18, 31, 52, 78
Christopher Marlowe's works, compared with **19:** 233
minor characters **8:** 154, 159, 162, 163, 168, 170, 177, 184, 186, 201, 206, 210, 218, 223, 228, 232, 239, 248, 262, 267
modernization **14:** 523
moral corruption of English society **8:** 154, 163, 165, 177, 193, 201, 218, 228, 232, 243, 248, 252, 267; **39:** 308; **52:** 78, 201
morality **52:** 5, 78
omens **62:** 14, 18
plot and incident **8:** 146, 152, 159; **25:** 164
popularity **8:** 144, 146, 154, 158, 159, 162, 181, 228; **39:** 383
providential order **60:** 304, 322
rebellion **22:** 395
retribution **8:** 163, 170, 177, 182, 184, 193, 197, 201, 206, 210, 218, 223, 228, 243, 248, 267
Richard III
ambition **8:** 148, 154, 165, 168, 170, 177, 182, 213, 218, 228, 232, 239, 252, 258, 267; **39:** 308, 341, 360, 370, 383; **52:** 201, 223
attractive qualities **8:** 145, 148, 152, 154, 159, 161, 162, 165, 168, 170, 181, 182, 184, 185, 197, 201, 206, 213, 228, 243, 252, 258; **16:** 150; **39:** 370, 383; **52:** 272, 280, 285; **62:** 104
credibility, question of **8:** 145, 147, 154, 159, 165, 193; **13:** 142
death, decay, and nature's destructiveness **8:** 145, 148, 154, 159, 165, 168, 170, 177, 182, 197, 210, 223, 228, 232, 243, 248, 252, 258, 267
deformity as symbol **8:** 146, 147, 148, 152, 154, 159, 161, 165, 170, 177, 184, 185, 193, 218, 248, 252, 267; **19:** 164; **62:** 110
inversion of moral order **8:** 159, 168, 177, 182, 184, 185, 197, 201, 213, 218, 223, 232, 239, 243, 248, 252, 258, 262, 267; **39:** 360; **52:** 205, 214
as Machiavellian villain **8:** 165, 182, 190, 201, 218, 232, 239, 243, 248; **39:** 308, 326, 360, 387; **52:** 201, 205, 257, 285; **62:** 2, 60, 78, 110
as monster or symbol of diabolic **8:** 145, 147, 159, 162, 168, 170, 177, 182, 193, 197, 201, 228, 239, 248, 258; **13:** 142; **37:** 144; **39:** 326, 349; **52:** 227, 272
other literary villains, compared with **8:** 148, 161, 162, 165, 181, 182, 206, 213, 239, 267
role-playing, hypocrisy, and dissimulation **8:** 145, 148, 154, 159, 162, 165, 168, 170, 182, 190, 206, 213, 218, 228, 239, 243, 252, 258, 267; **25:** 141, 164, 245; **39:** 335, 341, 387; **52:** 257, 267; **62:** 78
as scourge or instrument of God **8:** 163, 177, 193, 201, 218, 228, 248, 267; **39:** 308; **62:** 60
as seducer **52:** 223; **62:** 91, 104
self-esteem **52:** 196; **62:** 78
shamelessness **52:** 196
as Vice figure **8:** 190, 201, 213, 228, 243, 248, 252; **16:** 150; **39:** 383, 387; **52:** 223, 267; **62:** 78
religious, myghic, or spiritual content **62:** 66, 71
Richmond **8:** 154, 158, 163, 168, 177, 182, 193, 210, 218, 223, 228, 243, 248, 252; **13:** 142; **25:** 141; **39:** 349; **52:** 214, 257, 285
settings **14:** 516, 528; **52:** 263; **62:** 104
Shakespeare's artistic growth, Richard III's contribution to **8:** 165, 167, 182, 193, 197, 206, 210, 228, 239, 267; **25:** 164; **39:** 305, 326, 370
Shakespeare's political sympathies **8:** 147, 163, 177, 193, 197, 201, 223, 228, 232, 243, 248, 267; **39:** 349; **42:** 132
social order **60:** 322
sources **52:** 263, 290; **56:** 2; **62:** 2, 31, 60, 78
chronicles **8:** 145, 165, 193, 197, 201, 206, 210, 213, 228, 232
Marlowe, Christopher **8:** 167, 168, 182, 201, 206, 218
morality plays **8:** 182, 190, 201, 213, 239
Seneca, other classical writers **8:** 165, 190, 201, 206, 228, 248; **62:** 31, 60
staging issues **14:** 515, 527, 528, 537; **16:** 137; **52:** 263, 272
structure **8:** 154, 161, 163, 167, 168, 170, 177, 184, 193, 197, 201, 206, 210, 218, 223, 228, 232, 243, 252, 262, 267; **16:** 150; **62:** 14, 18, 91
succession **60:** 304, 322
The Tragical History of King Richard III (Colley Cibber adaptation), compared with **8:** 159, 161, 243
traditional values **39:** 335
Tudor myth **8:** 163, 165, 177, 184, 193, 201, 218, 228, 232, 243, 248, 252, 267; **39:** 305, 308, 326, 387; **42:** 132
Wars of the Roses **8:** 163, 165, 177, 184, 193, 201, 218, 228, 232, 243, 248, 252, 267; **39:** 308; **62:** 71
wooing scenes (Act I, scene ii and Act IV, scene iv) **8:** 145, 147, 152, 153, 154, 159, 161, 164, 170, 190, 197, 206, 213, 218, 223, 232, 239, 243, 252, 258, 267; **16:** 150; **19:** 164; **25:** 141, 164; **39:** 308, 326, 360, 387; **52:** 227, 249, 280; **62:** 31, 78, 91, 110

Romeo and Juliet **(Volumes 5, 11, 33, 51)**

accident or chance **5:** 418, 444, 448, 467, 470, 487, 573
adolescence **33:** 249, 255, 257

amour-passion or Liebestod myth **5:** 484, 489, 528, 530, 542, 550, 575; **32:** 256; **51:** 195, 219, 236
androgyny **13:** 530
anxiety **13:** 235; **60:** 96
balcony scene **32:** 276; **51:** 219
Caius Marius (Thomas Otway adaptation) **11:** 377, 378, 488, 495
comic and tragic elements, combination of **5:** 496, 524, 528, 547, 559 **46:** 78
contradiction, paradox, and opposition **5:** 421, 427, 431, 496, 509, 513, 516, 520, 525, 528, 538; **33:** 287; **44:** 11; **54:** 125
costuming **11:** 505, 509
courtly love tradition, influence of **5:** 505, 542, 575; **33:**
death 233 **60:**
desire **51:** 227, 236
detention of Friar John **5:** 448, 467, 470
divine will, role of **5:** 485, 493, 505, 533, 573
double opening **54:** 6
dramatic shortcomings or failure **5:** 416, 418, 420, 426, 436, 437, 448, 464, 467, 469, 480, 487, 524, 562
Elizabethan poetics, influence of **5:** 416, 520, 522, 528, 550, 559, 575
ending **54:** 125
evil **5:** 485, 493, 505
as experimental play **5:** 464, 509, 528
fate **5:** 431, 444, 464, 469, 470, 479, 480, 485, 487, 493, 509, 530, 533, 562, 565, 571, 573; **33:** 249; **54:** 125
feud **5:** 415, 419, 425, 447, 458, 464, 469, 479, 480, 493, 509, 522, 556, 565, 566, 571, 575; **25:** 181; **51:** 245
Friar Lawrence
  contribution to catastrophe **5:** 437, 444, 470; **33:** 300; **51:** 253; **60:** 96
  philosophy of moderation **5:** 427, 431, 437, 438, 443, 444, 445, 458, 467, 479, 505, 538
  as Shakespeare's spokesman **5:** 427, 431, 437, 458, 467
ideal love **5:** 421, 427, 431, 436, 437, 450, 463, 469, 498, 505, 575; **25:** 257; **33:** 210, 225, 272; **51:** 25, 44, 195, 203, 219
gender issues **32:** 256; **51:** 253
lamentation scene (Act IV, scene v) **5:** 425, 492, 538
language and imagery **5:** 420, 426, 431, 436, 437, 456, 477, 479, 489, 492, 496, 509, 520, 522, 528, 538, 542, 550, 559; **25:** 181, 245, 257; **32:** 276; **33:** 210, 272, 274, 287; **42:** 271; **51:** 203, 212, 227
love versus fate **5:** 421, 437, 438, 443, 445, 458; **33:** 249; **54:** 125
medieval influence **5:** 480, 505, 509, 573
Mercutio
  bawdy **5:** 463, 525, 550, 575
  death, decay, and nature's destructiveness **5:** 415, 418, 419, 547; **33:** 290
  as worldly counterpoint to Romeo **5:** 425, 464, 542; **33:** 290; **51:** 195
  myth of Psyche and Cupid **60:** 96
Neoclassical rules **5:** 416, 418, 426
Nurse **5:** 419, 425, 463, 464, 575; **33:** 294
Othello, compared with **32:** 302
Petrarchian poetics, influence of **5:** 416, 520, 522, 528, 550, 559, 575; **32:** 276; **51:** 212, 236
prose adaptations of Juliet's character **19:** 261
psychoanalytic interpretation **5:** 513, 556; **51:** 253
public versus private worlds **5:** 520, 550; **25:** 181; **33:** 274
reconciliation **5:** 415, 419, 427, 439, 447, 480, 487, 493, 505, 533, 536, 562
rhetoric **42:** 271
rival productions **11:** 381, 382, 384, 385, 386, 487
Romeo and Juliet
  death-wish **5:** 431, 489, 505, 528, 530, 538, 542, 550, 566, 571, 575; **32:** 212
  first meeting (Act I, scene v) **51:** 212
  immortality **5:** 536
  Juliet's epithalamium speech (Act III, scene ii) **5:** 431, 477, 492
  Juliet's innocence **5:** 421, 423, 450, 454; **33:** 257
  maturation **5:** 437, 454, 467, 493, 498, 509, 520, 565; **33:** 249, 257
  rebellion **25:** 257
  reckless passion **5:** 419, 427, 431, 438, 443, 444, 448, 467, 479, 485, 505, 533, 538, 542; **33:** 241
  Romeo's dream (Act V, scene i) **5:** 513, 536, 556; **45:** 40; **51:** 203
  Rosaline, Romeo's relationship with **5:** 419, 423, 425, 427, 438, 498, 542, 575
sexuality **25:** 181; **33:** 225, 233, 241, 246, 274, 300; **51:** 227, 236
source of tragic catastrophe **5:** 418, 427, 431, 448, 458, 469, 479, 480, 485, 487, 493, 509, 522, 528, 530, 533, 542, 565, 571, 573; **33:** 210; **51:** 245
sources **5:** 416, 419, 423, 450; **32:** 222; **33:** 210; **45:** 40; **54:** 125
staging issues **11:** 499, 505, 507, 514, 517; **13:** 243; **25:** 181; **32:** 212
structure **5:** 438, 448, 464, 469, 470, 477, 480, 496, 518, 524, 525, 528, 547, 559; **33:** 210, 246
tomb scene (Act V, scene iii) **5:** 416, 419, 423; **13:** 243; **25:** 181, 245; **51:** 219; **54:** 125
triumph over death or fate **5:** 421, 423, 427, 505, 509, 520, 530, 536, 565, 566; **51:** 219
tragic elements **55:** 78
Verona society **5:** 556, 566; **13:** 235; **33:** 255; **51:** 245
wordplay **32:** 256

***Sonnets* (Volumes 10, 40, 51, 62)**

ambiguity **10:** 251, 256; **28:** 385; **40:** 221, 228, 268
audience **51:** 316
authenticity **10:** 153, 154, 230, 243; **48:** 325; **62:** 128
autobiographical elements **10:** 159, 160, 166, 167, 175, 176, 182, 196, 205, 213, 215, 226, 233, 238, 240, 251, 279, 283, 302, 309, 325, 337, 377; **13:** 487; **16:** 461; **28:** 363, 385; **42:** 303; **48:** 325
beauty **10:** 247; **51:** 288
Christian elements **10:** 191, 256
composition date **10:** 153, 154, 161, 166, 196, 217, 226, 270, 277; **28:** 363, 385
Dark Lady **10:** 161, 167, 176, 216, 217, 218, 226, 240, 302, 342, 377, 394; **25:** 374; **37:** 374; **40:** 273; **48:** 346; **51:** 284, 288, 292, 321; **62:** 121
deception, disguise, and duplicity **25:** 374; **40:** 221
dramatic elements **10:** 155, 182, 240, 251, 283, 367
editorial and textual issues **28:** 363; **40:** 273; **42:** 303
Elizabeth, audience of **48:** 325
the Friend **10:** 279, 302, 309, 379, 385, 391, 394; **51:** 284, 288, 292, 300, 304, 316, 321; **62:** 121
friendship **10:** 185, 279; **28:** 380; **51:** 284
gender issues **37:** 374; **40:** 238, 247, 254, 264, 268, 273; **53:** 1
homoerotic elements **10:** 155, 156, 159, 161, 175, 213, 391; **16:** 461; **28:** 363, 380; **37:** 347; **40:** 254, 264, 273; **51:** 270, 284; **62:** 128
homosexuality **60:** 105
identities of persons **10:** 154, 155, 156, 161, 166, 167, 169, 173, 174, 175, 185, 190, 191, 196, 218, 226, 230, 233, 240; **40:** 238; **62:** 128
Ireland, William Henry, forgeries of **48:** 325
irony or satire **10:** 256, 293, 334, 337, 346; **51:** 300
Italian influences **28:** 407; **62:** 121, 146
language and imagery **10:** 247, 251, 255, 256, 290, 353, 372, 385; **13:** 445; **28:** 380, 385; **32:** 327, 352; **40:** 228, 247, 284, 292, 303; **51:** 270, 304; **62:** 153, 159, 170, 180, 196
love **10:** 173, 247, 287, 290, 293, 302, 309, 322, 325, 329, 394; **28:** 380; **37:** 347; **51:** 270, 284, 288, 292; **62:** 153, 170
love versus reason **10:** 329
A Lover's Complaint (the Rival Poet) **10:** 243, 353
  gender issues **48:** 336
  pastoral tradition, compared with **48:** 336
  sonnets, compared with **48:** 336
lust **51:** 292
lust versus reason **51:** 288
magic **48:** 346
Mr. W. H. **10:** 153, 155, 161, 169, 174, 182, 190, 196, 217, 218, 377
Montaigne's Essais, relation to **42:** 382
mutability, theme of **42:** 382
Neoplatonism **10:** 191, 205
occult **48:** 346
other sonnet writers, Shakespeare compared with **10:** 247, 260, 265, 283, 290, 293, 309, 353, 367; **28:** 380, 385, 407; **37:** 374; **40:** 247, 264, 303; **42:** 303
pedagogy **37:** 374
performative issues **48:** 352; **62:** 159
poet-patron relationship **48:** 352; **62:** 128
poetic style **10:** 153, 155, 156, 158, 159, 160, 161, 173, 175, 182, 214, 247, 251, 255, 260, 265, 283, 287, 296, 302, 315, 322, 325, 337, 346, 349, 360, 367, 385; **16:** 472; **40:** 221, 228; **51:** 270
procreation **10:** 379, 385; **16:** 461
race **53:** 1
rhetoric of consolation **42:** 382
the Rival Poet **10:** 169, 233, 334, 337, 385; **48:** 352
self-love **10:** 372; **25:** 374; **51:** 270, 300, 304; **62:** 180
selfishness versus self-knowledge **51:** 292
sexuality **25:** 374; **62:** 153
as social action **48:** 352; **62:** 159
sonnet arrangement **10:** 174, 176, 182, 205, 226, 230, 236, 315, 353; **28:** 363; **40:** 238; **62:** 121, 128

sonnet form **10:** 255, 325, 367; **37:** 347; **40:** 284, 303; **51:** 270
sonnets (individual):
3 **10:** 346
12 **10:** 360
15 **40:** 292
18 **40:** 292
20 **10:** 391; **13:** 530; **60:** 105
21 **32:** 352
26 **10:** 161
30 **10:** 296
35 **10:** 251
49 **10:** 296
53 **10:** 349; **32:** 327, 352
54 **32:** 352
55 **13:** 445
57 **10:** 296
59 **16:** 472
60 **10:** 296; **16:** 472
64 **10:** 329, 360
65 **10:** 296; **40:** 292
66 **10:** 315
68 **32:** 327
71 **10:** 167
73 **10:** 315, 353, 360
76 **10:** 334
79 **32:** 352
82 **32:** 352
86 **32:** 352
87 **10:** 296; **40:** 303
93 **13:** 487
94 **10:** 256, 296; **32:** 327
95 **32:** 327
98 **32:** 352
99 **32:** 352
104 **10:** 360
105 **32:** 327
107 **10:** 270, 277
116 **10:** 329, 379; **13:** 445
117 **10:** 337
119 **10:** 337
121 **10:** 346
123 **10:** 270
124 **10:** 265, 270, 329
126 **10:** 161
129 **10:** 353, 394; **22:** 12
130 **10:** 346
138 **10:** 296
144 **10:** 394
145 **10:** 358; **40:** 254
146 **10:** 353
sonnets (groups):
1-17 **10:** 296, 315, 379, 385; **16:** 461; **40:** 228; **62:** 170
1-21 **10:** 176; **40:** 268
1-126 **10:** 161, 176, 185, 191, 196, 205, 213, 226, 236, 279, 309, 315, 372; **62:** 180, 196
18-22 **10:** 315
18-126 **10:** 379
23-40 **10:** 315
27-55 **10:** 176
33-9 **10:** 329
56-77 **10:** 176
76-86 **10:** 315
78-80 **10:** 334, 385
78-101 **10:** 176
82-6 **10:** 334
100-12 **10:** 337
102-26 **10:** 176
123-25 **10:** 385
127-52 **10:** 293, 385
127-54 **10:** 161, 176, 185, 190, 196, 213, 226, 236, 309, 315, 342, 394
151-52 **10:** 315
sources **10:** 153, 154, 156, 158, 233, 251, 255, 293, 353; **16:** 472; **28:** 407; **42:** 382; **62:** 121, 146
structure **10:** 175, 176, 182, 205, 230, 260, 296, 302, 309, 315, 337, 349, 353; **40:** 238; **62:** 146
subjectivity **37:** 374
time **10:** 265, 302, 309, 322, 329, 337, 360, 379; **13:** 445; **40:** 292
visual arts, relation to **28:** 407
voice **51:** 316
apparent inconsistencies in **51:** 321

***The Taming of the Shrew* (Volumes 9, 12, 31, 55)**

appearance versus reality **9:** 343, 350, 353, 365, 369, 370, 381, 390. 430; **12:** 416; **31:** 326; **55:** 278, 299, 334
Baptista **9:** 325, 344, 345, 375, 386, 393, 413; **55:** 334
Bianca **9:** 325, 342, 344, 345, 360, 362, 370, 375
Bianca-Lucentio subplot **9:** 365, 370, 375, 390, 393, 401, 407, 413, 430; **16:** 13; **31:** 339
Catherine and Petruchio (David Garrick adaptation) **12:** 309, 310, 311, 416
class distinctions, conflict, and relations **31:** 300, 351; **50:** 64, 74; **55:** 342
deception, disguise, and duplicity **12:** 416
Elizabethan culture, relation to **31:** 288, 295, 300, 315, 326, 345, 351; **55:** 315, 322, 334
ending **54:** 58, 65
as farce **9:** 330, 337, 338, 341, 342, 365, 381, 386, 413, 426; **55:** 357
folk elements **9:** 381, 393, 404, 426
gender issues **28:** 24 **31:** 261, 268, 276, 282, 288, 295, 300, 335, 351; **55:** 278, 299, 305, 315, 322, 357
genre **9:** 329, 334, 362, 375; **22:** 48; **31:** 261, 269, 276; **55:** 278
induction **9:** 320, 322, 332, 337, 345, 350, 362, 365, 369, 370, 381, 390, 393, 407, 419, 424, 430; **12:** 416, 427, 430, 431, 441; **19:** 34, 122; **22:** 48; **31:** 269, 315, 351; **55:** 331, 357
irony or satire **9:** 340, 375, 398, 407, 413; **13:** 3; **19:** 122; **55:** 278, 299, 322
Kate
characterization **32:** 1
final speech (Act V, scene ii) **9:** 318, 319, 329, 330, 338, 340, 341, 345, 347, 353, 355, 360, 365, 381, 386, 401, 404, 413, 426, 430; **19:** 3; **22:** 48; **55:** 299, 331
love for Petruchio **9:** 338, 340, 353, 430; **12:** 435; **55:** 294
portrayals of **31:** 282
shrewishness **9:** 322, 323, 325, 332, 344, 345, 360, 365, 370, 375, 386, 393, 398, 404, 413
transformation **9:** 323, 341, 355, 370, 386, 393, 401, 404, 407, 419, 424, 426, 430; **16:** 13; **19:** 34; **22:** 48; **31:** 288, 295, 339, 351 **55:** 294, 315
Kiss Me, Kate (Cole Porter adaptation) **31:** 282
language and imagery **9:** 336, 338, 393, 401, 404, 407, 413; **22:** 378; **28:** 9; **31:** 261, 288, 300, 326, 335, 339; **32:** 56
Lucentio **9:** 325, 342, 362, 375, 393
marriage **9:** 322, 325, 329, 332, 329, 332, 334, 341, 342, 343, 344, 345, 347, 353, 360, 362, 375, 381, 390, 398, 401, 404, 413, 426, 430; **13:** 3; **19:** 3; **28:** 24; **31:** 288; **51:** 44; **55:** 315, 331
metadramatic elements **9:** 350, 419, 424; **31:** 300, 315
metamorphosis or transformation **9:** 370, 430
mythic or mythological elements **60:** 281
Ovid' Metamorphoses, relation to **60:** 281
pedagogy **19:** 122
performance history **31:** 282; **55:** 357
performance issues **12:** 313, 314, 316, 317, 337, 338; **31:** 315; **55:** 357
Petruchio
admirable qualities **9:** 320, 332, 341, 344, 345, 370, 375, 386; **55:** 294
audacity or vigor **9:** 325, 337, 355, 375, 386, 404
characterization **32:** 1
coarseness or brutality **9:** 325, 329, 365, 390, 393, 398, 407; **19:** 122
as lord of misrule **9:** 393; **50:** 64; **55:** 322
love for Kate **9:** 338, 340, 343, 344, 386; **12:** 435
portrayals of **31:** 282
pragmatism **9:** 329, 334, 375, 398, 424; **13:** 3; **31:** 345, 351
taming method **9:** 320, 323, 329, 340, 341, 343, 345, 355, 369, 370, 375, 390, 398, 407, 413, 419, 424; **19:** 3, 12, 21 **31:** 269, 295, 326, 335, 339; **55:** 334
popularity **9:** 318, 338, 404
role-playing **9:** 322, 353, 355, 360, 369, 370, 398, 401, 407, 413, 419, 424; **13:** 3; **31:** 288, 295, 315
romantic elements **9:** 334, 342, 362, 375, 407
Shakespeare's other plays, compared with **9:** 334, 342, 360, 393, 426, 430; **31:** 261; **50:** 74; **55:** 331
Sly **9:** 320, 322, 350, 370, 381, 390, 398, 430; **12:** 316, 335, 416, 427, 441; **16:** 13; **19:** 34, 122; **22:** 48; **37:** 31; **50:** 74
sources **60:** 281
Ariosto **9:** 320, 334, 341, 342, 370
folk tales **9:** 332, 390, 393
Gascoigne **9:** 370, 390
Old and New Comedy **9:** 419
Ovid **9:** 318, 370, 430
Plautus **9:** 334, 341, 342
shrew tradition **9:** 355; **19:** 3; **32:** 1, 56; **55:** 342
structure **9:** 318, 322, 325, 332, 334, 341, 362, 370, 390, 426; **22:** 48, 378; **31:** 269; **55:** 278, 342, 371
play-within-a-play **12:** 416; **22:** 48
The Taming of a Shrew (anonymous), compared with **9:** 334, 350, 426; **12:** 312; **22:** 48; **31:** 261, 276, 339; **55:** 305, 371
text and sources **55:** 334, 357
textual issues **22:** 48; **31:** 261, 276; **31:** 276; **55:** 342, 371
violence **43:** 61; **55:** 322

***The Tempest* (Volumes 8, 15, 29, 45, 61)**

allegorical elements **8:** 294, 295, 302, 307, 308, 312, 326, 328, 336, 345, 364; **42:** 327; **61:** 326
Antonio and Sebastian **8:** 295, 299, 304, 328, 370, 396, 429, 454; **13:** 440; **29:** 278, 297, 343, 362, 368, 377; **61:** 338
Ariel **8:** 289, 293, 294, 295, 297, 304, 307, 315, 320, 326, 328, 336, 340, 345, 356, 364, 420, 458; **22:** 302; **29:** 278, 297, 362, 368, 377
art versus nature **8:** 396, 404; **29:** 278, 297, 362; **61:** 356
autobiographical elements **8:** 302, 308, 312, 324, 326, 345, 348, 353, 364, 380; **61:** 272
beginning **54:** 19
Caliban **8:** 286, 287, 289, 292, 294, 295, 297, 302, 304, 307, 309, 315, 326, 328, 336, 353, 364, 370, 380, 390, 396, 401, 414, 420, 423, 429, 435, 454; **13:** 424, 440; **15:** 189, 312, 322, 374, 379; **22:** 302; **25:** 382; **28:** 249; **29:** 278, 292, 297, 343, 368, 377, 396; **32:** 367; **45:** 211, 219, 226, 259; **53:** 45, 64; **61:** 307, 356, 362
characterization **8:** 287, 289, 292, 294, 295, 308, 326, 334, 336; **28:** 415; **42:** 339; **45:** 219
classical influence and sources **29:** 278, 343, 362, 368; **61:** 362
colonialism **13:** 424, 440; **15:** 228, 268, 269, 270, 271, 272, 273; **19:** 421; **25:** 357, 382; **28:** 249; **29:** 343, 368; **32:** 338, 367, 400; **42:** 327; **45:** 200, 280; **53:** 11, 21, 45, 67; **61:** 297, 307
compassion, theme of **42:** 346
conspiracy or treason **16:** 426; **19:** 357; **25:** 382; **29:** 377
dreams **45:** 236, 247, 259
education or nurturing **8:** 353, 370, 384, 396; **29:** 292, 368, 377
exposition scene (Act I, scene ii) **8:** 287, 289, 293, 299, 334
Ferdinand **8:** 328, 336, 359, 454; **19:** 357; **22:** 302; **29:** 362, 339, 377
freedom and servitude **8:** 304, 307, 312, 429; **22:** 302; **29:** 278, 368, 377; **37:** 336
gender **53:** 64, 67
Gonzalo **22:** 302; **29:** 278, 343, 362, 368
Gonzalo's commonwealth **8:** 312, 336, 370, 390, 396, 404; **19:** 357; **29:** 368; **45:** 280
good versus evil **8:** 302, 311, 315, 370, 423, 439; **29:** 278; 297; **61:** 338, 362
historical content **8:** 364, 408, 420; **16:** 426; **25:** 382; **29:** 278, 339, 343, 368; **45:** 226; **53:** 21, 53; **61:** 297
the island **8:** 308, 315, 447; **25:** 357, 382; **29:** 278, 343
language and imagery **8:** 324, 348, 384, 390, 404, 454; **19:** 421; **29:** 278; **29:** 297, 343, 368, 377; **61:** 280, 288
love **8:** 435, 439; **29:** 297, 339, 377, 396
magic or supernatural elements **8:** 287, 293, 304, 315, 340, 356, 396, 401, 404, 408, 435, 458; **28:** 391, 415; **29:** 297, 343, 377; **45:** 272; **61:** 272, 356
the masque (Act IV, scene i) **8:** 404, 414, 423, 435, 439; **25:** 357; **28:** 391, 415; **29:** 278, 292, 339, 343, 368; **42:** 339; **45:** 188
Miranda **8:** 289, 301, 304, 328, 336, 370, 454; **19:** 357; **22:** 302; **28:** 249; **29:** 278, 297, 362, 368, 377, 396; **53:** 64
Montaigne's Essais, relation to **42:** 346
morality **52:** 43; **61:** 338
music **8:** 390, 404; **29:** 292; **37:** 321; **42:** 339; **61:** 315
nature **8:** 315, 370, 390, 408, 414; **29:** 343, 362, 368, 377; **61:** 362
Neoclassical rules **8:** 287, 292, 293, 334; **25:** 357; **29:** 292; **45:** 200
politics **8:** 304, 307, 315, 353, 359, 364, 401, 408; **16:** 426; **19:** 421; **29:** 339; **37:** 336; **42:** 327; **45:** 272, 280; **52:** 43; **61:** 315
Prospero
characterization **8:** 312, 348, 370, 458; **16:** 442; **22:** 302; **45:** 188, 272; **61:** 307
as God or Providence **8:** 311, 328, 364, 380, 429, 435
magic, nature of **8:** 301, 340, 356, 396, 414, 423, 458; **25:** 382; **28:** 391; **29:** 278, 292, 368, 377, 396; **32:** 338, 343; **61:** 272
psychoanalytic interpretation **45:** 259
redemptive powers **8:** 302, 320, 353, 370, 390, 429, 439, 447; **29:** 297; **61:** 326, 338
as ruler **8:** 304, 308, 309, 420, 423; **13:** 424; **22:** 302; **29:** 278, 362, 377, 396; **61:** 315
self-control **8:** 312, 414, 420; **22:** 302; **44:** 11
self-knowledge **16:** 442; **22:** 302; **29:** 278, 292, 362, 377, 396
as Shakespeare or creative artist **8:** 299, 302, 308, 312, 320, 324, 353, 364, 435, 447; **61:** 280, 288
as tragic hero **8:** 359, 370, 464; **29:** 292
providential order **52:** 43
race **53:** 11, 21, 45, 53, 64, 67
realism **8:** 340, 359, 464
reality and illusion **8:** 287, 315, 359, 401, 435, 439, 447, 454; **22:** 302; **45:** 236, 247
reconciliation **8:** 302, 312, 320, 334, 348, 359, 370, 384, 401, 404, 414, 429, 439, 447, 454; **16:** 442; **22:** 302; **29:** 297; **37:** 336; **45:** 236
religious, mythic, or spiritual content **8:** 328, 390, 423, 429, 435; **45:** 211, 247; **61:** 280
romance or pastoral tradition, influence of **8:** 336, 348, 396, 404; **37:** 336
sexuality **53:** 45; **61:** 288
Shakespeare's other plays, compared with **8:** 294, 302, 324, 326, 348, 353, 380, 401, 464; **13:** 424
spectacle versus simple staging **15:** 206, 207, 208, 210, 217, 219, 222, 223, 224, 225, 227, 228, 305, 352; **28:** 415
sources **45:** 226; **61:** 326
staging issues **15:** 343, 346, 352, 361, 364, 366, 368, 371, 385; **28:** 391, 415; **29:** 339; **32:** 338, 343; **42:** 339; **45:** 200; **54:** 19; **61:** 297
Stephano and Trinculo, comic subplot of **8:** 292, 297, 299, 304, 309, 324, 328, 353, 370; **25:** 382; **29:** 377; **46:** 14, 33
structure **8:** 294, 295, 299, 320, 384, 439; **28:** 391, 415; **29:** 292, 297; **45:** 188
subversiveness **22:** 302
The Tempest; or, The Enchanted Island (William Davenant/John Dryden adaptation) **15:** 189, 190, 192, 193
The Tempest; or, The Enchanted Island (Thomas Shadwell adaptation) **15:** 195, 196, 199
time **8:** 401, 439, 464; **25:** 357; **29:** 278, 292; **45:** 236
tragic elements **8:** 324, 348, 359, 370, 380, 408, 414, 439, 458, 464
trickster, motif of **22:** 302; **29:** 297
usurpation or rebellion **8:** 304, 370, 408, 420; **25:** 357, 382; **29:** 278, 362, 377; **37:** 336
utopia **45:** 280

***Timon of Athens* (Volumes 1, 20, 27, 52)**

Alcibiades **25:** 198; **27:** 191
alienation **1:** 523; **27:** 161
Apemantus **1:** 453, 467, 483; **20:** 476, 493; **25:** 198; **27:** 166, 223, 235
appearance versus reality **1:** 495, 500, 515, 523; **52:** 311, 329
Athens **27:** 223, 230
authorship controversy **1:** 464, 466, 467, 469, 474, 477, 478, 480, 490, 499, 507, 518; **16:** 351; **20:** 433
autobiographical elements **1:** 462, 467, 470, 473, 474, 478, 480; **27:** 166, 175
Elizabethan culture, relation to **1:** 487, 489, 495, 500; **20:** 433; **27:** 203, 212, 230; **50:** 13; **52:** 320, 354
as inferior or flawed plays **1:** 476, 481, 489, 499, 520; **20:** 433, 439, 491; **25:** 198; **27:** 157, 175; **52:** 338, 349
genre **1:** 454, 456, 459, 460, 462, 483, 492, 499, 503, 509, 511, 512, 515, 518, 525, 531; **27:** 203
King Lear, relation to **1:** 453, 459, 511; **16:** 351; **27:** 161; **37:** 222
language and imagery **1:** 488; **13:** 392; **25:** 198; **27:** 166, 184, 235; **52:** 329, 345, 354
language and philosophy **52:** 311
as medieval allegory or morality play **1:** 492, 511, 518; **27:** 155
mixture of genres **16:** 351; **25:** 198
nihilistic elements **1:** 481, 513, 529; **13:** 392; **20:** 481
pessimistic elements **1:** 462, 467, 470, 473, 478, 480; **20:** 433, 481; **27:** 155, 191
Poet and Painter **25:** 198; **52:** 320
politics **27:** 223, 230; **50:** 13
religious, mythic, or spiritual content **1:** 505, 512, 513, 523; **20:** 493
satirical elements **27:** 155, 235
self-knowledge **1:** 456, 459, 462, 495, 503, 507, 515, 518, 526; **20:** 493; **27:** 166
Senecan elements **27:** 235
Shakespeare's other tragedies, compared with **27:** 166; **52:** 296
sources **16:** 351; **27:** 191; **52:** 301
staging issues **20:** 445, 446, 481, 491, 492, 493
structure **27:** 191; **52:** 338, 345, 349
Timon
comic traits **25:** 198
death of **60:** 46
as flawed hero **1:** 456, 459, 462, 472, 495, 503, 507, 515; **16:** 351; **20:** 429, 433, 476; **25:** 198; **27:** 157, 161

misanthropy **13:** 392; **20:** 431, 464, 476, 481, 491, 492, 493; **27:** 161, 175, 184, 196; **37:** 222; **52:** 296, 301
as noble figure **1:** 467, 473, 483, 499; **20:** 493; **27:** 212
wealth and social class **1:** 466, 487, 495; **25:** 198; **27:** 184, 196, 212; **50:** 13

Titus Andronicus **(Volumes 4, 17, 27, 43, 62)**

Aaron **4:** 632, 637, 650, 651, 653, 668, 672, 675; **27:** 255; **28:** 249, 330; **43:** 176; **53:** 86, 92
amputations, significance of **48:** 264
authorship controversy **4:** 613, 614, 615, 616, 617, 619, 623, 624, 625, 626, 628, 631, 632, 635, 642; **62:** 208, 254
autobiographical elements **4:** 619, 624, 625, 664
banquet scene **25:** 245; **27:** 255; **32:** 212
ceremonies, rites, and rituals, importance of **27:** 261; **32:** 265; **48:** 264; **62:** 254
characterization **4:** 613, 628, 632, 635, 640, 644, 647, 650, 675; **27:** 293; **43:** 170, 176
Christian elements **4:** 656, 680
civilization versus barbarism **4:** 653; **27:** 293; **28:** 249; **32:** 265; **62:** 265, 270
colonialism **62:** 270
Clarissa (Samuel Richardson), compared with **48:** 277
Elizabethan culture, relation to **27:** 282; **62:** 233, 270
Euripides, influence of **27:** 285
evil **53:** 86, 92
gender issues **62:** 242
language and imagery **4:** 617, 624, 635, 642, 644, 646, 659, 664, 668, 672, 675; **13:** 225; **16:** 225; **25:** 245; **27:** 246, 293, 313, 318, 325; **43:** 186, 222, 227, 239, 247, 262; **62:** 225, 254
language versus action **4:** 642, 644, 647, 664, 668; **13:** 225; **27:** 293, 313, 325; **43:** 186; **62:** 225
Lavinia **27:** 266; **28:** 249; **32:** 212; **43:** 170, 239, 247, 255, 262; **62:** 225, 233, 242
marriage as political tyranny **48:** 264
medieval literary influence **4:** 646, 650; **27:** 299
mythic or mythological elements **60:** 276
order versus disintegration **4:** 618, 647; **43:** 186, 195
Ovid, influence of **4:** 647, 659, 664, 668; **13:** 225; **27:** 246, 275, 285, 293, 299, 306; **28:** 249; **43:** 195, 203, 206
Ovid' Metamorphoses, relation to **60:** 276
partiarchy **50:** 13
political content **43:** 262
politics **27:** 282; **48:** 264
primogeniture **50:** 13
race **53:** 86, 92
rape **43:** 227, 255; **48:** 277
revenge **60:** 276
rightful succession **4:** 638
Roman elements **43:** 206, 222; **62:** 277, 284
Romans versus Goths **27:** 282; **62:** 265, 270
sacrifice **62:** 258, 265
Senecan or revenge tragedy elements **4:** 618, 627, 628, 636, 639, 644, 646, 664, 672, 680; **16:** 225; **27:** 275, 318; **43:** 170, 206, 227; **62:** 208, 258
Shakespeare's canon, place in **4:** 614, 616, 618, 619, 637, 639, 646, 659, 664, 668; **43:** 195
Shakespeare's other tragedies, compared with **16:** 225; **27:** 275, 325
sources **62:** 208, 277, 284
spectacle **62:** 277
staging issues **17:** 449, 452, 456, 487; **25:** 245; **32:** 212, 249
structure **4:** 618, 619, 624, 631, 635, 640, 644, 646, 647, 653, 656, 659, 662, 664, 668, 672; **27:** 246, 285; **60:** 276
style **62:** 254
Tamora **4:** 632, 662, 672, 675; **27:** 266; **43:** 170; **62:** 233
Titus **4:** 632, 637, 640, 644, 647, 653, 656, 662; **25:** 245; **27:** 255; **62:** 258
Vergil, influence of **27:** 306; **28:** 249
violence **13:** 225; **25:** 245; **27:** 255; **28:** 249; **32:** 249, 265; **43:** 1, 186, 203, 227, 239, 247, 255, 262; **62:** 208, 225, 233, 242, 254, 258, 265

Troilus and Cressida **(Volumes 3, 18, 27, 43, 59)**

Achilles and Patroclus, relationship between **60:** 105
allegorical elements **52:** 5
ambiguity **3:** 544, 568, 583, 587, 589, 599, 611, 621; **27:** 400; **43:** 365
ambivalence **43:** 340; **59:** 287
assignation scene (Act V, scene ii) **18:** 442, 451
autobiographical elements **3:** 548, 554, 557, 558, 574, 606, 630
body, role of **42:** 66; **59:** 225, 287, 306
characterization **3:** 538, 539, 540, 541, 548, 566, 571, 604, 611, 621; **27:** 381, 391; **59:** 234, 245, 251, 257, 261, 265, 272
Chaucer's Criseyde, compared with **43:** 305
chivalry, decline of **16:** 84; **27:** 370, 374
communication, failure of **43:** 277
conclusion **3:** 538, 549, 558, 566, 574, 583, 594
comedy vs. tragedy **43:** 351; **59:** 278
contradictions **43:** 377; **59:** 318
costumes **18:** 289, 371, 406, 419; **59:** 323
courtly love **22:** 58; **59:** 349
Cressida
as ambiguous figure **43:** 305
inconsistency **3:** 538; **13:** 53; **16:** 70; **22:** 339; **27:** 362
individual will versus social values **3:** 549, 561, 571, 590, 604, 617, 626; **13:** 53; **27:** 396; **59:** 234, 272
infidelity **3:** 536, 537, 544, 554, 555; **18:** 277, 284, 286; **22:** 58, 339; **27:** 400; **43:** 298
lack of punishment **3:** 536, 537
as mother figure **22:** 339
objectification of **43:** 329; **59:** 323
as sympathetic figure **3:** 557, 560, 604, 609; **18:** 284, 423; **22:** 58; **27:** 396, 400; **43:** 305; **:59** 234, 245
as a Trojan **59:** 257
cynicism **43:** 298
desire **43:** 317, 329, 340; **59:** 337
disillusioned or cynical tone **3:** 544, 548, 554, 557, 558, 571, 574, 630, 642; **18:** 284, 332, 403, 406, 423; **27:** 376; **59:** 234
disorder **3:** 578, 589, 599, 604, 609; **18:** 332, 406, 412, 423; **27:** 366; **54:** 84; **55:** 48; **59:** 251
double plot **3:** 569, 613
Elizabeth I
waning power **43:** 365
Elizabethan culture, relation to **3:** 560, 574, 606; **25:** 56
ending **54:** 84; **59:** 225, 295, 306
feminist criticism **55:** 37, 48; **59:** 337
food imagery **43:** 298; **59:** 306
genre **3:** 541, 542, 549, 558, 566, 571, 574, 587, 594, 604, 630, 642; **27:** 366; **59:** 278
Greece **43:** 287
Hector
combat with Ajax **59:** 251
as a Trojan **59:** 257
homosexuality **60:** 105
inaction **3:** 587, 621; **27:** 347
infidelity **55:** 37, 48; **59:** 251
language and imagery **3:** 561, 569, 596, 599, 606, 624, 630, 635; **22:** 58, 339; **27:** 332; 366; **42:** 66; **59:** 287, 295, 306, 318
love and honor **3:** 555, 604; **27:** 370, 374; **59:** 251, 257, 337
love versus war **18:** 332, 371, 406, 423; **22:** 339; **27:** 376; **43:** 377; **59:** 234, 251, 257
male/female relationships **16:** 70; **22:** 339; **27:** 362; **59:** 349
marriage **22:** 339; **51:** 44
master-slave relationship **22:** 58; **59:** 265
medieval chivalry **3:** 539, 543, 544, 555, 606; **27:** 376; **59:** 349
mimetic rivalry **60:** 172
moral corruption **3:** 578, 589, 599, 604, 609; **18:** 332, 406, 412, 423; **27:** 366; **43:** 298; **54:** 84; **59:** 261, 265
morality **52:** 5; **59:** 251, 257
mythic or mythological elements **60:** 172
Neoclassical rules **3:** 537, 538; **18:** 276, 278, 281
nihilistic elements **27:** 354
Pandarus **59:** 245
patriarchy **22:** 58; **59:** 272, 337, 349
politics **3:** 536, 560, 606; **16:** 84; **59:** 225, 318
as "problem play" **3:** 555, 566
lack of resolution **43:** 277; **59:** 278
psychoanalytical criticism **43:** 287; **59:** 349
rape **43:** 357
satirical elements **3:** 539, 543, 544, 555, 558, 574; **27:** 341
sexuality **22:** 58, 339; **25:** 56; **27:** 362; **43:** 365; **59:** 323, 337, 349
sources **3:** 537, 539, 540, 541, 544, 549, 558, 566, 574, 587; **27:** 376, 381, 391, 400
staging issues **16:** 70; **18:** 289, 332, 371, 395, 403, 406, 412, 419, 423, 442, 447, 451; **59:** 225, 323
structure **3:** 536, 538, 549, 568, 569, 578, 583, 589, 611, 613; **27:** 341, 347, 354, 391
Thersites **13:** 53; **25:** 56; **27:** 381; **59:** 265
time **3:** 561, 571, 583, 584, 613, 621, 626, 634
Troilus
contradictory behavior **3:** 596, 602, 635; **27:** 362
Cressida, relationship with **3:** 594, 596, 606; **22:** 58; **59:** 245, 261
integrity **3:** 617

opposition to Ulysses **3:** 561, 584, 590
as a Trojan **59:** 257
as unsympathetic figure **18:** 423; **22:** 58, 339; **43:** 317; **59:** 261
as warrior **3:** 596; **22:** 339
Troilus and Cressida, or Truth Found too late (John Dryden adaptation) **18:** 276, 277, 278, 280, 281, 283
Trojan versus Greek values **3:** 541, 561, 574, 584, 590, 596, 621, 638; **27:** 370
Trojan War
as myth **43:** 293
Troy **43:** 287
Ulysses **59:** 245
Ulysses's speech on degree (Act I, scene iii) **3:** 549, 599, 609, 642; **27:** 396
value systems **3:** 578, 583, 589, 602, 613, 617; **13:** 53; **27:** 370, 396, 400; **59:** 234, 245, 287, 295, 318
violence **43:** 329, 351, 357, 365, 377
through satire **43:** 293

Twelfth Night **(Volumes 1, 26, 34, 46, 62)**

androgyny **60:** 129
ambiguity **1:** 554, 639; **34:** 287, 316
Antonio **22:** 69; **60:** 115
appetite **1:** 563, 596, 609, 615; **52:** 57
autobiographical elements **1:** 557, 561, 599; **34:** 338
bear-baiting **19:** 42
beginning **54:** 19
characterization **1:** 539, 540, 543, 545, 550, 554, 581, 594; **26:** 257, 337, 342, 346, 364, 366, 371, 374; **34:** 281, 293, 311, 338; **46:** 286, 324
Christian elements **46:** 338
comic elements **26:** 233, 257, 337, 342, 371; **51:** 1; **52:** 57
composition date **37:** 78
credibility **1:** 540, 542, 543, 554, 562, 581, 587
cross-dressing **62:** 297, 319
dark or tragic elements **46:** 310
desire **60:** 115, 129
Elizabethan culture, relation to **1:** 549, 553, 555, 563, 581, 587, 620; **16:** 53; **19:** 42, 78; **26:** 357; **28:** 1; **34:** 323, 330; **46:** 291; **51:** 15 **62:** 319, 348
ending **62:** 308
ethical or moral issues **52:** 57
fancy **1:** 543, 546
Feste
characterization **1:** 558, 655, 658; **26:** 233, 364; **46:** 1, 14, 18, 33, 52, 60, 303, 310
role in play **1:** 546, 551, 553, 566, 570, 571, 579, 635, 658; **46:** 297, 303, 310
song **1:** 543, 548, 561, 563, 566, 570, 572, 603, 620, 642; **46:** 297
festive or folklore elements **46:** 338; **51:** 15
gender issues **19:** 78; **34:** 344; **37:** 59; **42:** 32; **46:** 347, 362, 369; **60:** 129; **62:** 297, 319, 325
homosexuality **22:** 69; **42:** 32; **46:** 362; **60:** 115, 129
language and imagery **1:** 570, 650, 664; **22:** 12; **28:** 9; **34:** 293; **37:** 59; **62:** 343
love **1:** 543, 546, 573, 580, 587, 595, 600, 603, 610, 660; **19:** 78; **26:** 257, 364; **34:** 270, 293, 323; **46:** 291, 333, 347, 362; **51:** 30; **52:** 57; **62:** 297,
madness **1:** 554, 639, 656; **26:** 371
Malvolio
characterization **1:** 540, 544, 545, 548, 550, 554, 558, 567, 575, 577, 615; **26:** 207, 233, 273; **46:** 286; **62:** 339, 348
forged letter **16:** 372; **28:** 1
punishment **1:** 539, 544, 548, 549, 554, 555, 558, 563, 577, 590, 632, 645; **46:** 291, 297, 338
as Puritan **1:** 549, 551, 555, 558, 561, 563; **25:** 47
role in play **1:** 545, 548, 549, 553, 555, 563, 567, 575, 577, 588, 610, 615, 632, 645; **26:** 337, 374; **46:** 347; **62:** 339
music **1:** 543, 566, 596
mythic or mythological elements **60:** 265, 270, 287
Olivia **1:** 540, 543, 545; **46:** 286, 333, 369; **47:** 45; **62:** 325, 343
order **1:** 563, 596; **34:** 330; **46:** 291, 347
Orsino **46:** 286, 333; **47:** 45; **62:** 343
Ovid's Metamorphoses, relation to **60:** 265, 270, 287
philosophical elements **1:** 560, 563, 596; **34:** 301, 316; **46:** 297
plot **62:** 297, 339, 343, 348
Puritanism **1:** 549, 553, 555, 632; **16:** 53; **25:** 47; **46:** 338
psychoanalytic criticism **46:** 333; **62:** 348
Saturnalian elements **1:** 554, 571, 603, 620, 642; **16:** 53
Sebastian and Antonio, relations between **60:** 129
self-deception **1:** 554, 561, 591, 625; **47:** 45
self-indulgence **1:** 563, 615, 635
self-love or narcissism **60:** 265, 270, 287
sexual ambiguity and sexual deception **1:** 540, 562, 620, 621, 639, 645; **22:** 69; **34:** 311, 344; **37:** 59; **42:** 32; **62:** 319, 325
Shakespeare's canon, place in **1:** 543, 548, 557, 569, 575, 580, 621, 635, 638
Shakespeare's other plays, relation to **34:** 270; **46:** 303; **62:** 297, 308
sources **1:** 539, 540, 603; **34:** 301, 323, 344; **46:** 291 **60:** 265, 270, 287; **62:** 308
staging issues **26:** 219, 233, 257, 337, 342, 346, 357, 359, 360, 364, 366, 371, 374; **46:** 310, 369; **54:** 19
structure **1:** 539, 542, 543, 546, 551, 553, 563, 570, 571, 590, 600, 660; **26:** 374; **34:** 281, 287; **46:** 286; **62:** 308
subplot **62:** 297, 339, 343, 348
time **37:** 78; **46:** 297
tragic elements **1:** 557, 569, 572, 575, 580, 599, 621, 635, 638, 639, 645, 654, 656; **26:** 342
Viola **26:** 308; **46:** 286, 324, 347, 369; **60:** 115, 129; **62:** 308, 319, 325

The Two Gentlemen of Verona **(Volumes 6, 12, 40, 54, 63)**

absurdities, inconsistencies, and shortcomings **6:** 435, 436, 437, 439, 464, 507, 541, 560; **54:** 295, 311
appearance versus reality **6:** 494, 502, 511, 519, 529, 532, 549, 560
audience versus character perceptions **6:** 499, 519, 524
authorship controversy **6:** 435, 436, 437, 438, 439, 449, 466, 476; **63:** 361
characterization **6:** 438, 442, 445, 447, 449, 458, 462, 560; **12:** 458; **40:** 312, 327, 330, 365; **54:** 338; **63:** 336
Christian elements **6:** 438, 494, 514, 532, 555, 564; **63:** 357
education **6:** 490, 494, 504, 526, 532, 555, 568; **63:** 336
Elizabethan setting **12:** 463, 485
forest **6:** 450, 456, 492, 514, 547, 555, 564, 568
genre **6:** 460, 468, 472, 516; **40:** 320
identity **6:** 494, 511, 529, 532, 547, 560, 564, 568; **19:** 34
ironic or parodic elements **6:** 447, 472, 478, 484, 502, 504, 509, 516, 529, 549; **13:** 12; **54:** 295, 307; **63:** 336
Julia or Silvia **6:** 450, 453, 458, 476, 494, 499, 516, 519, 549, 564; **40:** 312, 327, 374; **54:** 325, 332; **63:** 336
language and imagery **6:** 437, 438, 439, 445, 449, 490, 504, 519, 529, 541; **28:** 9; **40:** 343
Launce and Speed, comic function of **6:** 438, 439, 442, 456, 458, 460, 462, 472, 476, 478, 484, 502, 504, 507, 509, 516, 519, 549; **40:** 312, 320; **63:** 336
letters, role of **63:** 341
letters, as theatrical device **63:** 341
love **6:** 442, 445, 456, 479, 488, 492, 494, 502, 509, 516, 519, 549; **13:** 12; **40:** 327, 335, 343, 354, 365; **51:** 30, 44; **63:** 336, 350
love versus friendship **6:** 439, 449, 450, 458, 460, 465, 468, 471, 476, 480; **40:** 354, 359, 365; **54:** 295, 307, 325, 344; **63:** 350
male-female relationships **63:** 357
marriage **48:** 32
mimetic rivalry **13:** 12; **40:** 335; **54:** 332
morality **6:** 438, 492, 494, 514, 532, 555, 564; **63:** 336
Proteus **6:** 439, 450, 458, 480, 490, 511; **40:** 312, 327, 330, 335, 359; **42:** 18; **54:** 325, 332
repentance and forgiveness **6:** 450, 514, 516, 555, 564
resolution **6:** 435, 436, 439, 445, 449, 453, 458, 460, 462, 465, 466, 468, 471, 476, 480, 486, 494, 509, 514, 516, 519, 529, 532, 541, 549; **19:** 34; **54:** 307, 311, 338
reversals **54:** 338
romantic and courtly conventions **6:** 438, 460, 472, 478, 484, 486, 488, 502, 507, 509, 529, 541, 549, 560, 568; **12:** 460, 462; **40:** 354, 374; **54:** 344; **63:** 341, 350
setting **12:** 463, 465, 485; **63:** 361
social order **63:** 357
sources **6:** 436, 460, 462, 468, 476, 480, 490, 511, 547; **19:** 34; **40:** 320; **54:** 295
staging issues **12:** 457, 464; **42:** 18; **63:** 361
structure **6:** 445, 450, 460, 462, 504, 526; **63:** 361
youth **6:** 439, 450, 464, 514, 568; **63:** 336
Valentine **54:** 325, 332

The Two Noble Kinsmen **(Volumes 9, 41, 50, 58)**

amorality, question of **9:** 447, 460, 492
audience response **58:** 330
authorship controversy **58:** 330

Shakespeare not a co-author **9:** 445, 447, 455, 461
Shakespearean portions of the text **9:** 446, 447, 448, 455, 456, 457, 460, 462, 463, 471, 479, 486; **41:** 308, 317, 355; **58:** 330
Shakespeare's part in the overall conception or design **9:** 444, 446, 448, 456, 457, 460, 480, 481, 486, 490; **37:** 313; **41:** 326; **50:** 326
ceremonies, rites, and rituals, importance of **9:** 492, 498
characterization **9:** 457, 461, 471, 474; **41:** 340, 385; **50:** 305, 326
chivalry **50:** 305, 348
class distinctions, conflict and relations **50:** 295, 305, 310
Emilia **9:** 460, 470, 471, 479, 481; **19:** 394; **41:** 372, 385; **42:** 368; **58:** 322, 338, 345, 356, 361
free will versus fate **9:** 474, 481, 486, 492, 498
friendship **9:** 448, 463, 470, 474, 479, 481, 486, 490; **19:** 394; **41:** 355, 363, 372; **42:** 368; **58:** 345, 356, 371
gender issues **42:** 368; **50:** 310
innocence to experience **9:** 481, 502; **19:** 394
irony or satire **9:** 463, 481, 486; **41:** 301; **50:** 348
the jailer's daughter **9:** 457, 460, 479, 481, 486, 502; **41:** 340; **50:** 295, 305, 310, 348, 361; **58:** 338, 371
language and imagery **9:** 445, 446, 447, 448, 456, 461, 462, 463, 469, 471, 498, 502; **41:** 289, 301, 308, 317, 326; **50:** 310; **58:** 322, 330
love **9:** 479, 481, 490, 498; **41:** 289, 355, 301, 363, 372, 385; **50:** 295, 361; **58:** 345, 356, 371
marriage **58:** 338, 345, 356
masque elements **9:** 490
Palamon and Arcite **9:** 474, 481, 490, 492, 502; **50:** 295, 305, 348, 361; **58:** 322, 338, 345, 356, 361
Prologue **54:** 35
relation to Shakespeare's other romances **54:** 35
sexuality **50:** 361; **58:** 338, 345, 356
sources **19:** 394; **41:** 289, 301, 363, 385; **50:** 326, 348; **58:** 361, 371
structure **37:** 313; **50:** 326, 361; **58:** 322

***Venus and Adonis* (Volumes 10, 33, 51)**

Adonis **10:** 411, 420, 424, 427, 429, 434, 439, 442, 451, 454, 459, 466, 473, 489; **25:** 305, 328; **28:** 355; **33:** 309, 321, 330, 347, 352, 357, 363, 370, 377; **51:** 345, 377
allegorical elements **10:** 427, 434, 439, 449, 454, 462, 480; **28:** 355; **33:** 309, 330
ambiguity **10:** 434, 454, 459, 462, 466, 473, 480, 486, 489; **33:** 352; **51:** 368, 377, 388
beauty **10:** 420, 423, 427, 434, 454, 480; **33:** 330, 352
the boar **10:** 416, 451, 454, 466, 473; **33:** 339, 347, 370; **51:** 359, 368
comic elements **51:** 377
the courser and the jennet **10:** 418, 439, 466; **33:** 309, 339, 347, 352
death, decay, and nature's destructiveness **10:** 419, 427, 434, 451, 454, 462, 466, 473, 480, 489; **25:** 305; **33:** 309, 321, 347, 352, 363, 370
dramatic elements **10:** 459, 462, 486
domesticity **51:** 359
eroticism or sensuality **10:** 410, 411, 418, 419, 427, 428, 429, 442, 448, 454, 459, 466, 473; **25:** 305, 328; **28:** 355; **33:** 321, 339, 347, 352, 363, 370; **51:** 345, 352, 359, 368
Faerie Queene (Edmund Spenser), compared with **33:** 339
forgiveness **51:** 377
Hero and Leander (Christopher Marlowe), compared with **10:** 419, 424, 429; **33:** 309, 357; **51:** 345, 377
comic elements **10:** 429, 434, 439, 442, 459, 462, 489; **33:** 352
hunt motif **10:** 434, 451, 466, 473; **33:** 357, 370
imagery **10:** 414, 415, 416, 420, 429, 434, 449, 459, 466, 473, 480; **25:** 328; **28:** 355; **33:** 321, 339, 352, 363, 370, 377; **42:** 348; **51:** 335, 388
love versus lust **10:** 418, 420, 427, 434, 439, 448, 449, 454, 462, 466, 473, 480, 489; **25:** 305; **28:** 355; **33:** 309, 330, 339, 347, 357, 363, 370; **51:** 359
morality **10:** 411, 412, 414, 416, 418, 419, 420, 423, 427, 428, 439, 442, 448, 449, 454, 459, 466; **33:** 330
negative appraisals **10:** 410, 411, 415, 418, 419, 424, 429
Ovid, compared with **32:** 352; **42:** 348; **51:** 335, 352
pictorial elements **10:** 414, 415, 419, 420, 423, 480; **33:** 339
popularity **10:** 410, 412, 418, 427; **25:** 328
procreation **10:** 439, 449, 466; **33:** 321, 377
reason **10:** 427, 439, 449, 459, 462, 466; **28:** 355; **33:** 309, 330
rhetoric **33:** 377; **51:** 335, 345, 352
Shakespeare's plays, compared with **10:** 412, 414, 415, 434, 459, 462
Shakespeare's sonnets, compared with **33:** 377
sources **10:** 410, 412, 420, 424, 429, 434, 439, 451, 454, 466, 473, 480, 486, 489; **16:** 452; **25:** 305; **28:** 355; **33:** 309, 321, 330, 339, 347, 352, 357, 370, 377; **42:** 348; **51:** 335
structure **10:** 434, 442, 480, 486, 489; **33:** 357, 377
style **10:** 411, 412, 414, 415, 416, 418, 419, 420, 423, 424, 428, 429, 439, 442, 480, 486, 489; **16:** 452
Venus **10:** 427, 429, 434, 439, 442, 448, 449, 451, 454, 466, 473, 480, 486, 489; **16:** 452; **25:** 305, 328; **28:** 355; **33:** 309, 321, 330, 347, 352, 357, 363, 370, 377; **51:** 335, 352, 377, 388
Wat the hare **10:** 424, 451

***The Winter's Tale* (Volumes 7, 15, 36, 45, 57)**

Antigonus
characterization **7:** 394, 451, 464
death scene (Act III, scene iii) **7:** 377, 414, 464, 483; **15:** 518, 532; **19:** 366
appearance versus reality **7:** 429, 446, 479; **57:** 336
art versus nature **7:** 377, 381, 397, 419, 452; **36:** 289, 318; **45:** 329; **57:** 278
audience perception, Shakespeare's manipulation of **7:** 394, 429, 456, 483, 501; **13:** 417; **19:** 401, 431, 441; **25:** 339; **45:** 374
autobiographical elements **7:** 395, 397, 410, 419
Autolycus **7:** 375, 380, 382, 387, 389, 395, 396, 414; **15:** 524; **22:** 302; **37:** 31; **45:** 333; **46:** 14, 33; **50:** 45
Christian elements **7:** 381, 387, 402, 410, 417, 419, 425, 429, 436, 452, 460, 501; **36:** 318; **60:** 40
counsel **19:** 401
court society **16:** 410; **57:** 305, 336
dramatic structure **7:** 382, 390, 396, 399, 402, 407, 414, 429, 432, 473, 479, 493, 497, 501; **15:** 528; **25:** 339; **36:** 289, 295, 362, 380; **45:** 297, 344, 358, 366; **57:** 278, 285, 347
ethnicity **37:** 306
folk drama, relation to **7:** 420, 451; **57:** 356
forgiveness or redemption **7:** 381, 389, 395, 402, 407, 436, 456, 460, 483; **36:** 318
fusion of comic, tragic, and romantic elements **7:** 390, 394, 396, 399, 410, 412, 414, 429, 436, 479, 483, 490, 501; **13:** 417; **15:** 514, 524, 532; **25:** 339; **36:** 295, 380; **45:** 295, 329; **57:** 347
grace **7:** 420, 425, 460, 493; **36:** 328
Hermione
characterization **7:** 385, 395, 402, 412, 414, 506; **15:** 495, 532; **22:** 302, 324; **25:** 347; **32:** 388; **36:** 311; **47:** 25; **49:** 18; **57:** 319
restoration (Act V, scene iii) **7:** 377, 379, 384, 385, 387, 389, 394, 396, 412, 425, 436, 451, 452, 456, 464, 483, 501; **15:** 411, 412, 413, 518, 528, 532; **49:** 18; **57:** 294, 367; **60:** 2, 40
supposed death **25:** 339; **47:** 25
trial of **49:** 18
as historical allegory **7:** 381; **15:** 528
homosexuality **48:** 309
hospitality **19:** 366
irony **7:** 419, 420
Jacobean culture, relation to **19:** 366, 401, 431; **25:** 347; **32:** 388; **37:** 306; **57:** 305, 336, 356
language and imagery **7:** 382, 384, 417, 418, 420, 425, 460, 506; **13:** 409; **19:** 431; **22:** 324; **25:** 347; **36:** 295; **42:** 308; **45:** 297, 333, 344; **50:** 45; **57:** 278, 285, 319, 347
Leontes
characterization **19:** 431; **45:** 366
jealousy **7:** 377, 379, 382, 383, 384, 387, 389, 394, 395, 402, 407, 412, 414, 425, 429, 432, 436, 464, 480, 483, 497; **15:** 514, 518, 532; **22:** 324; **25:** 339; **36:** 334, 344, 349; **44:** 66; **45:** 295, 297, 344, 358; **47:** 25; **57:** 294
Othello, compared with **7:** 383, 390, 412; **15:** 514; **36:** 334; **44:** 66; **47:** 25
repentance **7:** 381, 389, 394, 396, 402, 414, 497; **36:** 318, 362; **44:** 66; **57:** 294
love **7:** 417, 425, 469, 490; **51:** 30, 33, 44
Mamillius **7:** 394, 396, 451; **22:** 324
metadramatic elements **16:** 410
myth of Demeter and Persephone, relation to **7:** 397, 436

mythic or mythological elements **60:** 254, 281
nationalism and patriotism **32:** 388
nature **7:** 397, 418, 419, 420, 425, 432, 436, 451, 452, 473, 479; **19:** 366; **45:** 329
Neoclassical rules **7:** 376, 377, 379, 380, 383, 410; **15:** 397
Ovid's Metamorphoses, relation to **42:** 308; **57:** 319, 367 **60:** 281
Pandosto, compared with **7:** 376, 377, 390, 412, 446; **13:** 409; **25:** 347; **36:** 344, 374
Paulina **7:** 385, 412, 506; **15:** 528; **22:** 324; **25:** 339; **36:** 311; **57:** 319
Perdita
  characterization **7:** 395, 412, 414, 419, 429, 432, 452, 506; **22:** 324; **25:** 339; **36:** 328
  reunion with Leontes (Act V, scene ii) **7:** 377, 379, 381, 390, 432, 464, 480
plot **7:** 376, 377, 379, 382, 387, 390, 396, 452; **13:** 417; **15:** 518; **45:** 374; **57:** 285
rebirth, regeneration, resurrection, or immortality **7:** 397, 414, 417, 419, 429, 436, 451, 452, 456, 480, 490, 497, 506; **25:** 339 452, 480, 490, 497, 506; **45:** 366; **60:** 40
sheep-shearing scene (Act IV, scene iv) **7:** 379, 387, 395, 396, 407, 410, 412, 419, 420, 429, 432, 436, 451, 479, 490; **16:** 410; **19:** 366; **25:** 339; **36:** 362, 374; **45:** 374
sources **60:** 254, 281
staging issues **7:** 414, 425, 429, 446, 464, 480, 483, 497; **13:** 409; **15:** 518; **48:** 309
statue scene (Act V, scene iii) **7:** 377, 379, 384, 385, 387, 389, 394, 396, 412, 425, 436, 451, 456, 464, 483, 501; **15:** 411, 412, 518, 528, 532; **25:** 339, 347; **36:** 301; **57:** 294, 367; **60:** 40
subversiveness **22:** 302
symbolism **7:** 425, 429, 436, 452, 456, 469, 490, 493
textual issues **19:** 441; **45:** 333; **57:** 278, 285, 356
Time-Chorus **7:** 377, 380, 412, 464, 476, 501; **15:** 518
time **7:** 397, 425, 436, 476, 490; **19:** 366; **36:** 301, 349; **45:** 297, 329, 366, 374
trickster, motif of **22:** 302; **45:** 333
Union debate, relation to **25:** 347
violence **43:** 39
witchcraft **22:** 324
women, role of **22:** 324; **36:** 311; **42:** 308; **51:** 30; **57:** 294, 305, 319, 356; **60:** 254

ISBN 0-7876-5238-5
9780787652388
90000